Configuring Sales in SAP S/4HANA®

SAP PRESS

Christian van Helfteren

Configuring Sales in SAP S/4HANA®

Rheinwerk
Publishing

Editor Meagan White
Acquisitions Editor Emily Nicholls
Copyeditor Yvette Chin
Cover Design Graham Geary
Photo Credit Shutterstock.com/386811070/© Evgeny Karandaev
Layout Design Vera Brauner
Production Hannah Lane
Typesetting III-satz, Husby (Germany)
Printed and bound in the United States of America, on paper from sustainable sources

ISBN 978-1-4932-1851-6

1st edition 2020

Library of Congress Cataloging-in-Publication Data
Names: Helfteren, Christian van, author.
Title: Configuring Sales in SAP S/4HANA / Christian van Helfteren.
Description: 1st Edition. | Boston : Rheinwerk Publishing, 2020. | Includes index.
Identifiers: LCCN 2019043740 (print) | LCCN 2019043741 (ebook) | ISBN 9781493218516 (hardcover) | ISBN 9781493218523 (ebook)
Subjects: LCSH: SAP HANA (Electronic resource) | Selling. | Customer relations--Data processing.
Classification: LCC HF5438.25 .H454 2020 (print) | LCC HF5438.25 (ebook) | DDC 658.850285/53--dc23
LC record available at https://lccn.loc.gov/2019043740
LC ebook record available at https://lccn.loc.gov/2019043741

Contents at a Glance

Dear Reader,

Every year on the day before Christmas, my father and I go Christmas shopping.

While it's mostly an excuse to spend time together and watch the merry panic of other last-minute shoppers, there are a few items we pick up every year. A new version of Norton Antivirus from Staples (my father is a big believer in collecting the rebate from buying a physical copy of the software). A few bottles of wine for Christmas Day and New Year's Eve (one red, one white). Some stocking stuffers for my mom (discount fabric rolls always go over well).

But as I've edited this book while approaching the holiday season, it's been fascinating to see how all of the deals and sales we shop as consumers are engineered in vendors' ERP systems. Rebates require special conditions and settlement control. Setting discounts can be as easy as changing a price or can be enabled using validity dates, customer criteria, or volume. "Buy one, get one free" sales have their own special functionality using the condition technique. Even something as simple as buying two bottles of wine required a sales order to be set up before they even make it to the store. Suffice it to say, I have a newfound appreciation for the complexities of sales processes and the ERP system configuration that underpins them.

What did you think about *Configuring Sales in SAP S/4HANA*? Your comments and suggestions are the most useful tools to help us make our books the best they can be. Please feel free to contact me and share any praise or criticism you may have.

Thank you for purchasing a book from SAP PRESS!

Meagan White
Editor, SAP PRESS

meaganw@rheinwerk-publishing.com
www.sap-press.com
Rheinwerk Publishing · Boston, MA

Contents

Preface

SAP S/4HANA is the latest release of SAP's ERP suite. Every year, SAP releases a new SAP S/4HANA version referred to by the year and month of release, i.e., 1511 (November 2015), 1610 (October 2016), 1709 (September 2017), and 1809 (September 2018). These version numbers are the on-premise versions. SAP S/4HANA Cloud versions are also released on a quarterly release schedule (such as 1805). This book is written on-premise SAP S/4HANA 1809.

Although many users and consultants refer to the system simply as SAP (or just "S/4"), in this book, we'll use "SAP S/4HANA" when referring to system features regardless of whether these features are new. Thus, we'll allude to the fact that these features are all available in SAP S/4HANA 1809, so features described in this book may or may not be available on previous versions.

SAP HANA is the name of the in-memory database on which SAP S/4HANA is based and the source of the greatest improvements to the sales functionality over previous versions in terms of performance (i.e., response time). Many functionality improvements delivered in the earliest versions of SAP S/4HANA were made possible by the performance improvements brought about by the SAP HANA database.

In terms of deployment options, SAP S/4HANA is in line with previous versions where your company can take advantage of the complete configuration and enhancement capability of SAP. SAP S/4HANA Cloud, on the other hand, has limited configuration capability and almost no enhancement opportunity. SAP S/4HANA Cloud is suited for companies willing to adapt to the out-of-the-box configuration and willing to wait for some requirements to be incorporated into a future release by the SAP Support Marketplace (formerly known as the On-Line Service System [OSS]).

In this book, we'll use the on-premise version of SAP S/4HANA as our baseline. In other words, we'll refer to configuration and enhancements that can be made on the on-premise version. We'll make occasional reference to SAP S/4HANA Cloud's self-service configuration user interface (SSCUI) and the SAP Fiori Manage Your Solution app where you can choose the **Configure Your Solution** option (mainly organizational structure configuration). This option is the SAP S/4HANA Cloud version of Transaction SPRO. So, if you're implementing SAP S/4HANA Cloud, this book can still be helpful, although our focus is on SAP S/4HANA.

Objective of This Book

The objective of this book is to describe how you can set up and run SAP S/4HANA functionalities related to the sales and distribution of goods and services, also known as the *order-to-cash process*.

We'll provide a typical business process description where applicable, describe system configuration steps, and explore what is typically done by companies that use SAP.

This information is important when implementing SAP for the first time (known as a greenfield implementation) or when reimplementing/upgrading an SAP system (known as a brownfield implementation).

The process for system upgrades is not a focus of this book. Companies going through an upgrade effort to upgrade their SAP solution from a previous version into SAP S/4HANA have access to a robust suite of tools to identify opportunities for process improvements using new system features (the precheck report) as well as to identify issues with existing enhancements and custom developments that may require remediation (simplification database).

If you're looking for specific system upgrade information, search for training materials on how to use the available tools. These materials are the best sources for feature and improvement lists. You'll also find system integrators to partner with as well as consultants that specialize in system upgrades.

Many companies opt to reimplement a system instead of upgrading a system to eliminate the workflow, report, interface, conversion, enhancement, and forms (WRICEF) implemented so far instead of upgrading them all. In some instances, SAP S/4HANA will offer features that replace the customization put in place in SAP ERP, in particular, if your company is using a much older version.

Reimplementations are great opportunities for redesigning business processes using the knowledge gained over years of using SAP solutions. Be sure you bring in experienced consultants on this type of project to ensure that existing functionalities are not simply replicated in the new system. If replication is the goal, an upgrade project is usually faster and more cost effective.

Scope of This Book

This book covers topics related to capturing and fulfilling customer requirements, commonly referred to as sales, sales and distribution, or order-to-cash. We'll follow a logical sequence, covering set up first to fulfill the prerequisites of the following chapters. You can also use this sequence to set up blueprint workshops.

SAP S/4HANA is a fully integrated system since most functionalities have impact across several functional areas. However, business areas and project team resources should have their own areas of specialization. We'll approach issues from an area's perspective, even though the functionality is not necessarily compartmentalized.

In SAP ERP, these areas of specialization were commonly referred to as *modules*. Over the years, modules names have changed to reflect changes in the functionality made available in newer versions. However, not all consulting companies and companies that use SAP ERP solution have adapted to the new module names because the internal organization of resources don't necessarily have to change.

Although this book is focused on SAP S/4HANA Sales, you'll find companies referring to this solution as sales and distribution (SD) or order-to-cash (OTC). From an implementation project perspective, all these names are valid and interchangeable even though plenty of arguments can be made that they are not identical. We won't get caught up on this debate since we're focusing on business processes and functionalities using language that is accessible to all.

Companies also tend to create their own definitions of what this bundle of functionalities is called. You'll find names such as quote-to-cash (QTC), order-to-invoice (OTI), contract-to-cash (CTC), etc. Your company will own the implementation project and make decisions based on your specific business needs.

To qualify what we're referring to when we say, "SAP S/4HANA Sales," the functionalities described in this book are summarized in the diagram shown in Figure 1.

The diagram shown in Figure 1 depicts the main components of SAP S/4HANA Sales. The foundation is the master data; all subsequent transactions are created referring to master data.

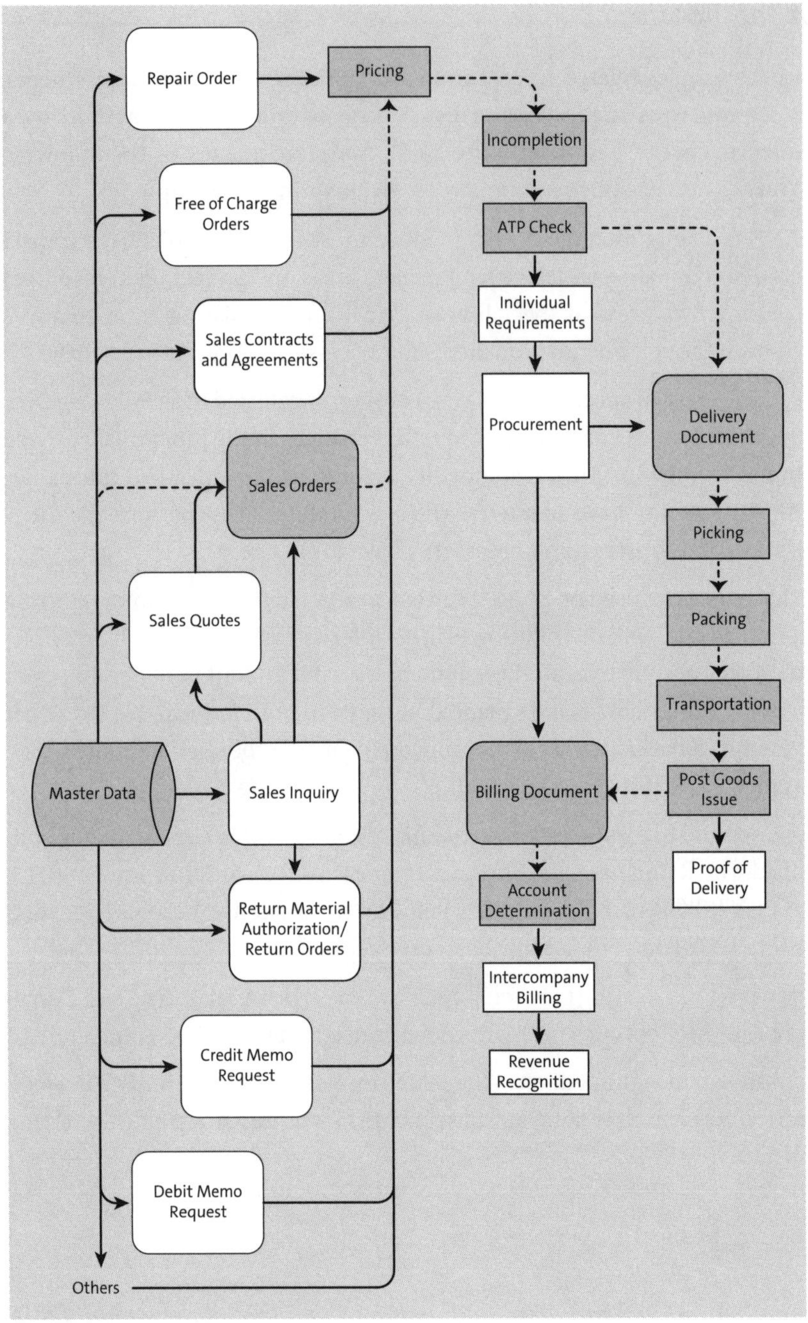

Figure 1 Sales and Distribution Overview

Usually, the core business of a company is conducted via sales orders, and the order entry process include several important subprocesses. In this book, we'll highlight the following four subprocesses:

- **Pricing**
  All required value-related calculations are included, such as sales prices, discounts, freight, taxes, rebates, profitability, etc.
- **Incompletion checks**
  Checks to ensure all the necessary information is in place before the order is considered complete, blocking the order at different levels otherwise.
- **Available to promise check**
  Checks available stock, including future procurement and manufacturing. The available to promise (ATP) check doesn't just check for stock on hand but also accounts for theoretical future availability.
- **Individual requirements**
  Process option that triggers subsequent procurement or manufacturing based on individual sales order demands/stock requirements. This subprocess is used for drop shipment requests sent to vendors, for special orders, for make-to-order processing, etc.

If you're selling physical products (not services), the stock allocated (confirmed) to the sales order during an ATP check makes the sales order relevant for logistics. The process starts by creating a delivery document, which is a controlled copy of the sales order with logistics information.

This delivery document is then used by the warehouse (logistics operations) to find and fetch the products necessary to fulfill the customer's order. Once this step is completed, we'll record the picking of the product(s).

The logistics operation team then packs the product and prepares the order for shipping. You can document which products are packed in which boxes using the packing operation (which is largely based on handling units).

Transportation management in SAP S/4HANA (TM in SAP S/4HANA) can then be used to negotiate and arrange shipping for the packed products.

When the shipment departs the facility, you'll need to immediately perform an operation called the *post goods issue operation*.

You can then control the receipt of the product by offering your customer the proof of delivery functionality.

As soon as the post goods issue operation is performed, the delivery document is ready for billing. Once executed, an invoice or billing document will be created.

The billing document will use account determination to create accounting and controlling documents. These documents will drive functionalities such as accounts receivables, revenue accounting, costing, profitability analysis, etc. For cross-company scenarios, you can also resolve intercompany billing at this time.

If you had any deferred revenue at the time of billing, you'll need to recognize that revenue over time or based on events using revenue recognition functionality.

Sales orders can also be used to sell services instead of or in addition to products. In this case, you wouldn't need to go through the delivery step since logistics would not be needed, so you may skip straight to billing.

In this brief description, we've covered the core business for most companies capturing orders, delivering, and invoicing customers. This description may represent 80% of what your company does, but these tasks typically represent only 20% of the functionality your company needs to operate.

Most of the functionality typically represents only a small portion of what the company actually does. Unfortunately, that smaller proportion of work often requires more time and effort from the project team on the core business versus the other processes.

These other processes, which are not shown in Figure 1, include the following:

- **Sales quotes**
  You may need to issue sales quotes to your customers you commit to price and commit availability. These quotes can be converted into orders or closed with the addition of a rejection reason documenting why the business fell through.
- **Sales contracts and agreements**
  These documents represent the formal deals you'll make with your customers and can be used as references when creating orders or billing directly.
- **Free of charge orders**
  Free of charge orders and free of charge deliveries are generally issued to resolve some form of dispute or to stimulate new business. These documents may still be

subject to freight and will be charged internally to a cost center or other financial element.

- **Repair orders**
  A repair order allows you to receive product back from a customer to perform service on the item and then ship the repaired item back to the customer using the same document. This process is used, for example, for billable subcontracting jobs to fulfill warranties to our customers.
- **Sales inquiries**
  To track customer complaints, you'll use sales inquiry documents. These documents can be converted into returns, quotes, or sales orders. Alternatively, companies with these types of requirements can use a customer relations management (CRM) tool, such as SAP C/4HANA, Salesforce, or others.
- **Return merchandise authorizations or order returns**
  If a customer wants to return a product, you can authorize that return via a return material authorization or return order, which would create an inbound delivery document. The warehouse (logistics operation) would record a post goods receipt when the items arrive. Using advance returns as described in this book, you can control what should happen with a return and specify the proper time to issue credit back to the customer.
- **Credit memo and debit memo requests**
  These documents start the process of crediting or debiting a customer for various reasons (other than a process already defined in the system).

SAP GUI and SAP Fiori

SAP S/4HANA allows you to use a desktop application called SAP GUI (graphic user interface) or applications on the web-based SAP Fiori launchpad as the UI. We'll discuss both options in the following sections.

SAP GUI

Using the SAP GUI, you can continue using the same screen layouts and overall look-and-feel as SAP ERP, or you can use the new SAP Fiori visual theme.

To toggle between these two formats, the SAP GUI Configuration app (desktop application installed along with SAP GUI) is available on your desktop. On the screen shown in Figure 2, to change to the SAP Fiori theme, select the **Activate SAP Fiori features** checkbox and then click **OK**.

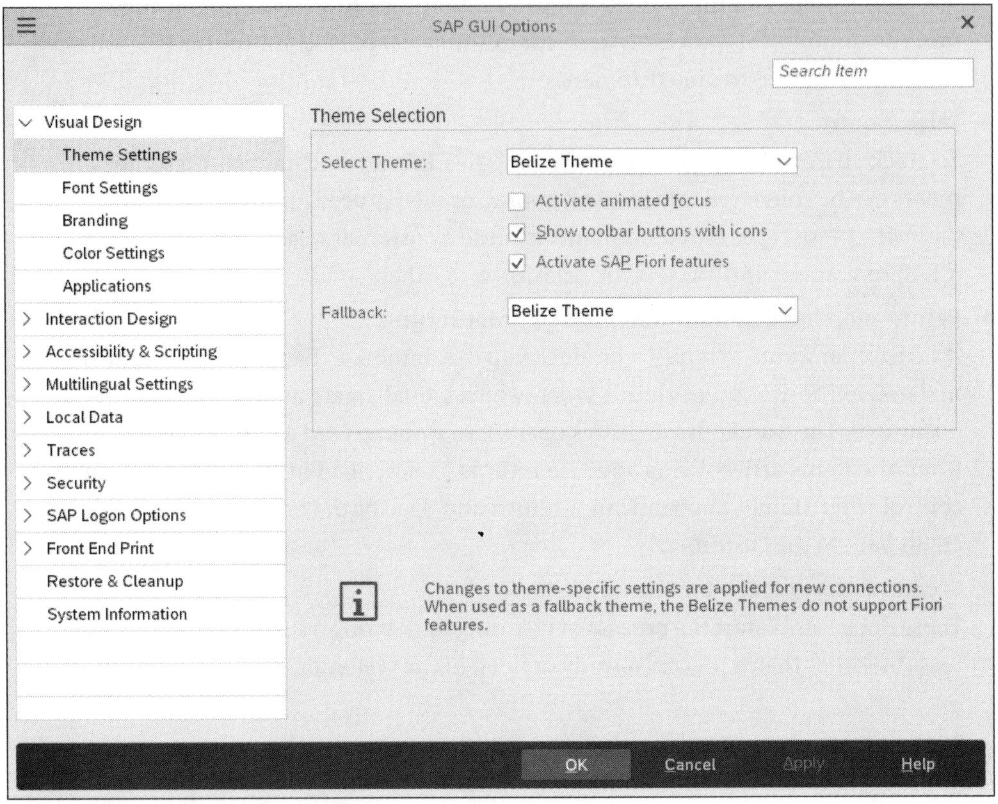

Figure 2 Switching SAP Fiori Visual Themes On/Off

In this book, we'll provide screenshots and instructions that use the SAP Fiori visual theme in SAP GUI. Note that, like any other desktop application, the SAP GUI has its own versioning (upgrades, patches, etc.). In this book, we'll use the SAP GUI version 7.5 and 7.6; in version 7.6, the SAP Fiori visual theme was upgraded.

To check the version of your SAP GUI, select the **System Information** option, as shown in Figure 2, or select **About SAP Logon...** menu option, as shown in Figure 3.

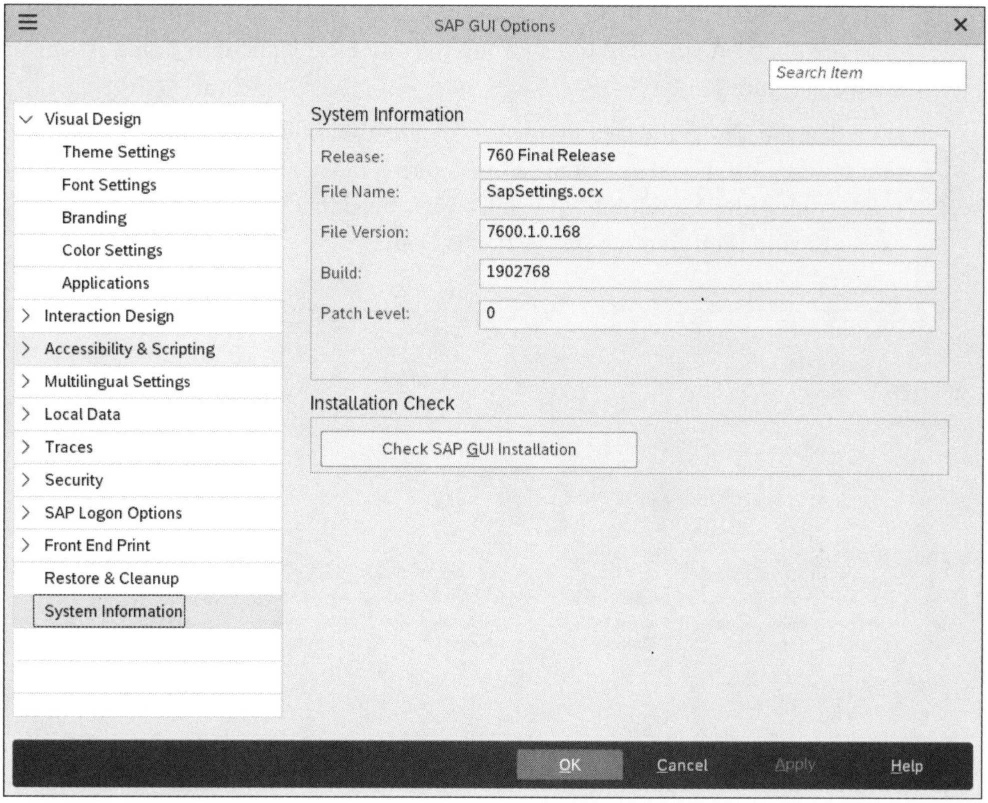

Figure 3 SAP GUI Version

SAP Fiori Launchpad

The web-based frontend is called SAP Fiori. The SAP Fiori launchpad is your home screen where your assigned apps and preliminary business information will be available as soon as the SAP Fiori launchpad is opened.

The best way to access the SAP Fiori launchpad is to use the link provided by the SAP Basis administrator containing the SAP Fiori launchpad URL. You can add that URL that your favorites to access the SAP Fiori launchpad directly on the web. This bookmark needs to be enabled but is a commonsense requirement for all companies using SAP Fiori.

Alternatively, you can access SAP Fiori launchpad using Transaction /UI2/FLP. But, first, you'll need to install and access SAP S/4HANA via the SAP GUI desktop app and then enter "/n/UI2/FLP" in the command box. Once you press (Enter), a browser window will open on your desktop showing the SAP Fiori launchpad home screen, as shown in Figure 4.

Note that the "/n" at the beginning of command typically controls whether the current transaction should be exited before entering the next transaction. However, for transaction codes containing "/," you'll always need to add "/n" to the beginning of the command even no other transaction is open.

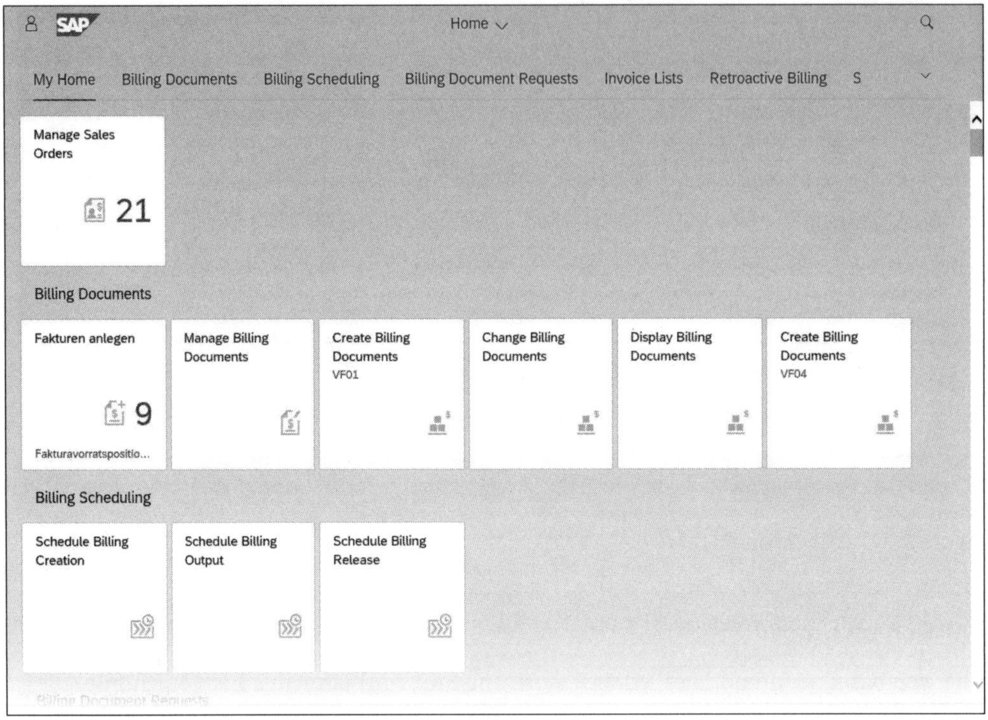

Figure 4 Sample SAP Fiori Launchpad Home Screen

Each tile shown on SAP Fiori launchpad home screen is an SAP Fiori app. Simply click on the tile, and the corresponding transaction will open. Alternatively, you can click on the magnifying glass icon in the upper-right corner of the screen to search for apps not shown as tiles on the home screen.

To modify the home screen, click on the person icon in upper-left corner of the screen and then drag and drop new apps onto the home screen.

Setting up SAP Fiori can be a significant effort and expense. Enabling your users to transact in SAP Fiori is an ongoing task and potentially a full-time job for one or more people.

SAP Fiori requires detailed definition of the apps each user will access. Without this information, the SAP Fiori launchpad would display nothing. Similar to the definition and management of security roles and profiles, with SAP Fiori, user attempting to execute a transaction won't see a message clearly stating they don't have access to it. The unauthorized apps simply won't exist to the user.

Your SAP Fiori support team must know the apps users can possibly ever need to execute and then do a careful, detailed, time consuming, elaborate work of activating them and then assigning them to the appropriate business roles. If done properly, business roles simplify the user experience and make the user experience more intuitive. When done poorly, your users will feel a level of frustration rarely seen in previous versions. Let's look at this conundrum more closely:

- If SAP Fiori apps are implemented and trained along with the core functionality, you'll need to define business roles while the business processes are defined to ensure accuracy. Failure to identify all the necessary tasks spoils the user experience, often causing them to revert back to using the SAP GUI.
- On the other hand, if you don't implement and train SAP Fiori along with the core functionality, leaving this step to a future phase, your users will need to be trained on the SAP GUI and then would need change management to transition to SAP Fiori.

Companies using SAP S/4HANA Cloud tend to use SAP Fiori and often have SAP define the business roles defined on their behalf. These roles are defined based on standardized business processes. SAP S/4HANA Cloud only allows limited customization to help ensure consistent business roles.

So, why would you go through the effort of setting up SAP Fiori apps? Some reasons include the following:

- Some apps are only available in SAP Fiori, mostly reports and graphs, but also functionalities like customer rebates, ATP with product allocation, etc. Going forward, more functionalities will be available only as an SAP Fiori app. To take advantage of these functionalities, you would need to use SAP Fiori.
- Web navigation/cloud-based services are considered the next steps in the natural evolution of computing.

- You can link SAP Fiori apps to other web-based software solutions, such as Salesforce. Note that, to connect data between the two system, more effort will be involved. However, you can link an order entry screen to business partner master data, then call the link to enable your users to use the web-based app to accomplish the task.
- Some users may prefer, be more productive, and be more willing to use the system with a tablet-like design in contrast to the tradition transaction code- and menu-based design of the SAP GUI. These users are often upper management. If willing and able, these users can perform some system tasks on their own with SAP Fiori's simple and intuitive UI instead of relying on team members to perform system tasks, for example, electronic approvals with proper audit trails.

Some companies decide to solely use the SAP GUI for the following reasons:

- No menu exists on SAP Fiori; instead, you'll need to browse for specific app names that can be long and sentence-like, often with no transaction codes assigned. Some examples of SAP Fiori app names are shown in Figure 4, (i.e., Manage Sales Orders, Manage Billing Documents, Schedule Billing Release, etc.).
- When searching for a specific app, you'll need to enter exact phrases to find what you're looking for. The system sometimes proposes transaction names as you type, but the autocompletion can be slow and incomplete.
- In terms of cost savings, SAP Fiori is an added cost that is easy to shrug off.

The most common approach is to use the SAP GUI and the primary systems access mechanism and enable SAP Fiori for users that have limited and easy-to-define business roles.

Target Audience

This book is intended for SAP implementation project team members and companies looking to reimplement their existing SAP ERP solutions. Although helpful for upgrade projects, we won't only be focused on functionality changes or specific upgrade instructions.

When assessing an implementation or an upgrade, team members from different business areas, usually without specific IT backgrounds, should be assigned to the project as key users. Your key users are a crucial success factor for implementations and upgrades. In this book, we hope to provide key users with guidance throughout the implementation or upgrade endeavor and provide the knowledge necessary for key users to actively participate in key design decisions. We'll also discuss the role of the consultant, what to expect, and what is required of them, in several instances.

Consultants interested in SAP S/4HANA Sales will also find valuable information in this book, especially consultants at the beginning of their careers or transitioning from other modules. Experienced sales and distribution (SD) and order-to-cash (OTC) consultants will benefit from learning about the new functionalities.

Finally, although this book features configuration instructions that anyone can understand, note that not all possible configurations are featured in detail in this book.

How to Read This Book

If you're want to learn all about SAP S/4HANA Sales, you can read this book from cover to cover. The configuration information provided in early chapters is important to subsequent chapters.

If you're troubleshooting specific issues, first check out the table of contents. The index also contains a comprehensive list of the topics found in the book, along with page references. The organization of this book was designed to match the most commonly-used activities in SAP S/4HANA Sales projects.

The business process related to a functionality is documented using examples based on our experience with companies that use SAP, but we'll also provide guidance on the flexibility to implement company-specific requirements.

You'll also find how often functionality is used and typical issues that arise. This information may help you design the solution during the implementation project and define its scope. The goal is to ultimately improve the quality of the solution.

For easy reference, let's summarize each of the chapters in this book:

- **Chapter 1: Organizational Structure and General Settings**
  In this chapter, we'll describe how to represent sales-relevant components of you company in the system.
- **Chapter 2: Business Partner Master Data**
  In this chapter, we'll describe how to identify the people and corporations we interact with within the system while conducting sales-related activity.
- **Chapter 3: Material Master Data Elements**
  In this chapter, we'll describe how to identify the goods and services (and related information) within the system relevant to supporting sales-related activities.

- **Chapter 4: Pricing and Condition Technique**
  In this chapter, we'll explain the basic concepts behind the condition technique using pricing and discuss many other system functions that use this feature.
- **Chapter 5: Sales Contract and Agreement Management**
  In this chapter, we'll talk about the mix of master data and transactional data that represent customer contracts and agreements.
- **Chapter 6: Sales Order Management**
  In this chapter, we'll cover how to capture the sales order and the many features available to ensure sales orders are complete and consistent.
- **Chapter 7: Available to Promise and Transfer of Requirements**
  In this chapter, we'll explain how the system checks and allocates available inventory to sales documents.
- **Chapter 8: Drop Shipments and Special Orders**
  In this chapter, we'll describe process alternatives for fulfilling sales orders using your vendors' logistics operations rather than your own.
- **Chapter 9: Shipping and Delivery**
  In this chapter, we'll describe system features used to process sales orders at the warehouse (picking, packing, shipping, and transportation).
- **Chapter 10: Billing and Invoicing**
  In this chapter, we'll describe how create invoices linking sales to accounts receivable, including different billing options you offer your customers.
- **Chapter 11: Stock Transfer Orders and Intercompany Sales**
  In this chapter, we'll describe the process of transferring stock between facilities within the same system representing either an intracompany or intercompany transfer.
- **Chapter 12: Customer Consignment**
  In this chapter, we'll describe how to store products at a customer's location and bill them only upon consumption.
- **Chapter 13: Customer Complaint Management**
  In this chapter, we'll describe how to handle different customer complaints post-sales and the related action required (returns, credit, debit, etc.).
- **Chapter 14: Reporting and Analytics**
  In this chapter, we'll briefly describe some of the most relevant sales reports available with SAP Fiori and SAP GUI.

Implementation Notes

For implementation, SAP S/4HANA uses a methodology called SAP Activate. The goal is to leverage SAP Best Practices embedded in preconfigured business processes, which are provided out of the box and were designed to allow your company to perform most of its own core business functions.

In this book, we won't go into this methodology in detail; however, you should understand its basic concepts to follow some of the information provided later. Figure 5 shows the six phases of SAP Activate.

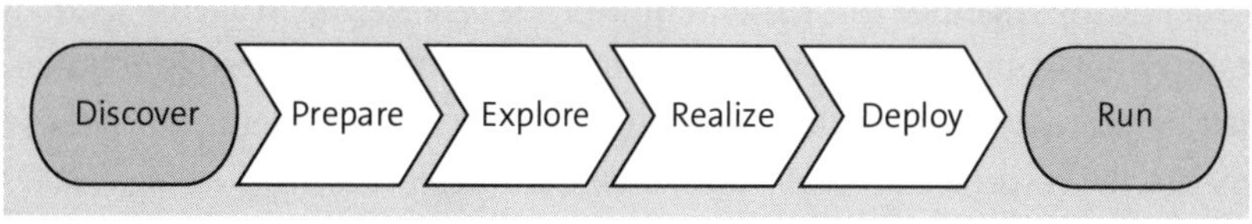

Figure 5 SAP Activate Phases

SAP Activate is recommended if the out-of-the-box, preconfigured business processes can support most of core business functions as they were designed to do.

If you're familiar with implementation methodologies, you may notice that we don't have a phase called the blueprint phase. We're not expected to produce a blueprint document with SAP Activate because the basic premise is that we'll adhere to the standardized business processes that come preconfigured with SAP S/4HANA. These business processes are also documented, thus replacing the need for project-specific blueprint documentation.

Your company will still need the exercise of conducting the requirements gathering we used to refer to as the blueprint phase. We'll refer to blueprints as the effort of gathering these requirements, not the effort of writing the document. Blueprinting effort happens during the explore phase.

The phases in SAP Activate are as follows:

- **Discover phase**
  In this phase, your company will select their implementation partners, define scope, choose the desired version, set up the necessary infrastructure, etc. all in preparation of project kick-off.
- **Prepare phase**
  In this phase, we'll gather initial requirements and select the applicable business processes from the SAP Best Practices list. At this time, an implementation partner

may prepare your system for use in creating demos and running prototyping sessions, which will take place in the next phase.

- **Explore phase**
  During this phase, your implementation partners will demonstrate preconfigured SAP business processes and document every concern raised by your company. This information will go through review sessions, resulting in a list of requirements. The outcome of this phase is a prioritized and approved list of requirements with estimates and the onboarding of all additional resources needed to realize these requirements.

  The work of putting together this list of requirements is referred to as fit-gap analysis. "Fit" requirements are addressed by out of the box, preconfigured functionality. Value can be created by documenting these requirements in detail since these requirements will resurface several times during the project.
- **Realize phase**
  At this point, you'll take the requirements list, assign requirements to the team, undertake the necessary configuration and development, and the test business functions individually. You'll then perform one or more cycles of integration tests to ensure all processes work with each other and with the data converted from your legacy systems.

  The outcome of this phase is a user acceptance test. At this time, you should have business approval that all processes are supported/work as needed and that the data is accurate/complete.
- **Deploy phase**
  The deploy phase includes go-live preparation, training, go-live itself, hypercare support, and the transition to the ongoing support team.
- **Run phase**
  In this phase, your company running SAP S/4HANA is assisted by the ongoing support team.

If little to no changes are required, SAP S/4HANA Cloud may be sufficient. If many changes are required, you'll need SAP S/4HANA. If you cannot adapt and if several complex changes are crucial, you may need to use a different methodology, such as the SAP ASAP methodology, which was used before SAP Activate.

Chapter 1
Organizational Structure and General Settings

An organizational structure consists of configuration entries that represent your company's management hierarchy. These entries are used across all sales functionalities to segregate data and transactions under their corresponding management branch. An organizational structure is also commonly used to restrict user access.

Before you can start loading data and performing transactions in SAP S/4HANA, you'll need to define your company's entities and sales areas in the system. This step involves identifying all legal entities that deliver goods and/or services to other entities (third parties or internal), regardless of profitability.

For sales, the organizational structure elements you'll need to define include sales areas (i.e., sales organizations, distribution channels, divisions, distribution chains, etc.); the sales office and sales groups; shipping and loading points; and the transportation planning point. Before we begin, however, let's briefly cover the prerequisite for all of these elements: the company code.

1.1 Company Codes

Generally, the work of identifying the relevant legal entities in your company is done by the finance department, resulting in a list of *company codes*. Each legal entity will be linked to a company code, which will be used for key financial functionalities, often regulatory and country specific.

For SAP S/4HANA Sales, you'll need to review financial inputs and identify which company codes correspond to subsidiaries that manage customer relationships and/or ship goods/services to business partners (third party or internal subsidiaries). We'll refer to these company codes as *sales-relevant company codes*.

Note

Sales-relevant company codes will bring in revenue but not necessarily make profits. You can manage this process in SAP S/4HANA Sales.

The most common sales-relevant company codes are your subsidiaries that manage your customer service operations. These entities are the first responders to customer requests and inquiries, such as sales orders, returns, debits/credits, etc. These entities are the most obvious sales-relevant company codes because they typically capture sales orders.

However, you'll also need to consider entities that transfer inventory to other subsidiaries as sales-relevant company codes. This scenario is often the case, for instance, if you have a separate legal entity focused solely on manufacturing that transfers finished goods to a different entity that is focused solely on sales.

In a large multinational corporation, the global blueprint phase during the implementation project will need to be comprehensive, since the sales work stream (for order-to-cash [OTC]) often lacks company codes that are still important to core business processes.

Often, the finance team needs time to research and ensure the design is complete and consistent. The company code is just one of many aspects that need to be addressed.

In a perfect world, these definitions (for company codes and sales organizations) would be created sequentially, but to make the best use of project resources, finance and sales blueprint workshops can be scheduled in parallel. Often, discussions about financial reporting structures occur at the same time as discussions about the sales organizational structure.

Ultimately, the finance and sales team leads must talk during the project preparation phase (prior to blueprint or as soon as possible). Defining most of the input needed from finance can be completed early on, even if unknown variables still exist.

This stage offers great opportunities for solution architects or integration mangers to step in. If these resources are not available, your project manager may need to play those roles even if only to clear cross-functional definitions before blueprinting.

Note

Several subjects may require cross-functional definitions, such as plants (defined by materials management) and sales employees (defined by human resources).

Next, entities will be assigned four-digit company codes. The naming convention for company codes is company specific, but SAP allows any combination of 4 alphanumeric characters. The longstanding recommendation of using Z or Y as the first character for your company codes is still valid but not as critical as it is for order types and other transactional codes.

The Z/Y first-character recommendation helped avoid conflicts with new codes that may be provided by SAP when deploying upgrades and new versions. These conflicts are easily resolved, but we recommend using the allowable namespace for your codes because this issue potentially arises every time new company codes are released by SAP. The likelihood that SAP issues new company codes that match the ones you've already defined is generally low, and therefore, the recommendation is often disregarded.

Instead, global corporations tend to define the first one or two characters as the country, followed by a code representing the legal entity. If your company doesn't yet have a global presence, we still recommend following similar guidelines in case your company goes global in the future.

In this chapter, we'll use a fictitious corporation called the American Automotive Parts Manufacturer (AAPM) in our examples. AAPM has a presence in United States and Canada with two distinct legal entities. These sales-relevant company codes were defined by finance with the company codes US01 and CA01, respectively, following a commonly used naming convention.

Figure 1.1 shows our example sales-relevant company codes we'll input when simulating finance.

Figure 1.1 Sample Sales-Relevant Company Codes

1.2 Sales Areas

You'll need at least one *sales area* defined for each sales-relevant company code. When implementing SAP S/4HANA, the definition of the sales area should be mostly natural/intuitive; the decision originates from the business team who has historical and strategic knowledge of the company. You may need to break sales areas down into multiple sales areas. However, first approaching the sales area as an element of its own to define before breaking it down is advisable.

In the following sections, we'll first provide an overview of sales areas and discuss how to design a sales area hierarchy using an example company. Then, we'll get into the technical details of all the elements that make up a sales area: sales organizations, distribution channels, and divisions. Then, we'll discuss how to set up the sales area itself, how to assign plants to your distribution chain, and how to assign a credit control area.

1.2.1 Designing the Sales Hierarchy

Sales areas represent groups within your organization that are responsible for managing distinct portions of the market, often with an upper management sales leader responsible for each sales, with assigned sales targets and key performance indicators (KPIs). We don't advise changing how these teams are structured for your implementation project.

For each sales transaction, you'll specify which sales area owns the resulting credit. Users will always need to specify or select a sales order at the time of order entry.

For customer master data, a sales area represents a separate set of sales data under the control and ownership of that particular sales team. You may, for instance, consider a customer as a distributor for one sales area and as a consumer for another sale area.

The sales area is comprised of three hierarchical levels (sales organization, distribution channel, and division). To decide how to divide a sales area across these levels, you'll need to consider implications on master data maintenance, security/authorizations, reporting, pricing, and other sales functionalities. Having an experienced SAP consultant recommend the best structure for each company code might be advisable.

Figure 1.2 shows the three hierarchical levels (sales organization, distribution channel, and division) that make up a sales area.

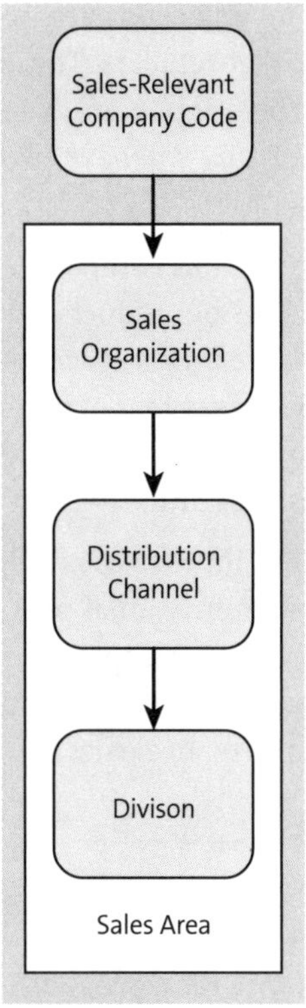

Figure 1.2 Sales Area Components (Sales Organization, Distribution Channel, and Division)

Organizational structure workshops can be confusing and hard to understand if you start the discussion by talking about individual *sales areas components*. Instead, we recommend organizing these discussions around how sales areas are configured, a more intuitive approach during workshops. During configuration, you'll first need to define the components before setting up the sales area. (During blueprinting, however, we recommend using the opposite approach—setting up the sales area then defining its components.)

Mistakes at this stage may lead to problems that are never addressed because of all the master data implications. Going through this exercise using the approach we recommended and spending time discussing the pros and cons are highly recommended. Again, changing these configurations after go-live, once all the master data and transactions exist in the system, is too disruptive and should be avoided. Determining sales area components are long-lasting decisions with far-reaching implications.

Let's use our example company AAPM as an example. This company sells parts to original equipment manufacturers (OEMs) as well as to aftermarket retailers. These two business models are completely different, with little overlap between them, even though the product might be the same. In our example, this company will have two sales areas: one for OEM sales and another for aftermarket sales.

AAPM also sells parts that are neither sold as original equipment nor as compatible replacements, but instead as add-on performance parts. These types of products follow a distinct sales approach and are managed by a dedicated sales team via specialty shops; however, these sales are still considered aftermarket sales. These types of parts have their own distinct brand and pricing strategy and require strong marketing campaign. These products are only sold by the United States business unit.

In this example, we have one legal entity for the United States, but three sales areas: OEM, aftermarket, and performance. The same corporation has international presence in another country (Canada) with a different legal entity and a corresponding sales-relevant company code. We'll need another two sales areas for this entity, also called OEM and aftermarket (since AAPM Canada doesn't sell performance parts).

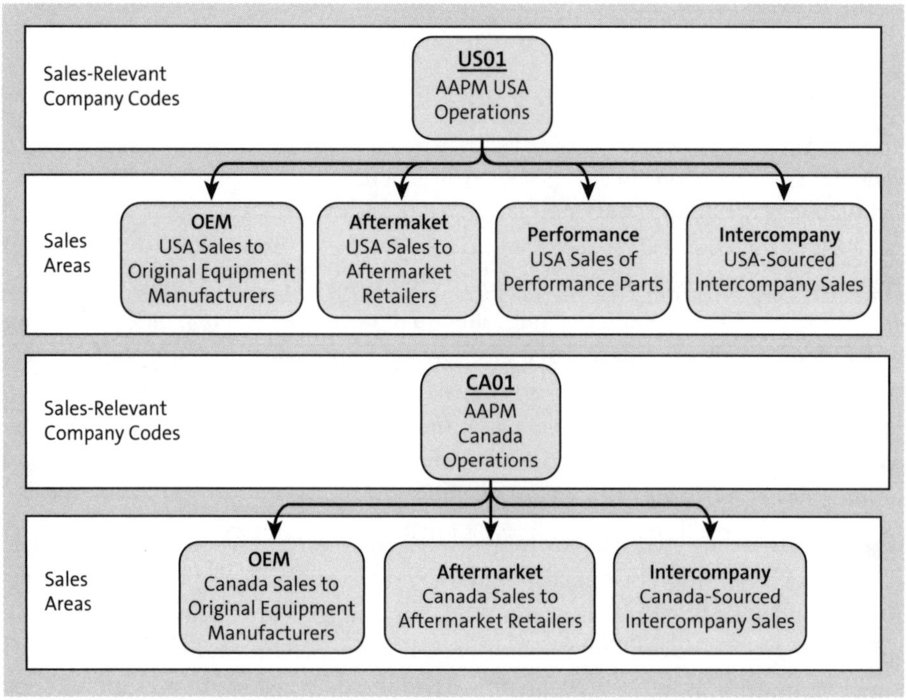

Figure 1.3 Proposed Sales Areas for Our AAPM Sample Company

Since we have two subsidiaries (USA and Canada), we can also transfer inventory between them (bidirectionally). The incoming revenue from the stock transfer isn't part of the OEM sales area or the aftermarket sales area, so we'll need a new sales area, which we'll call the *intercompany sales area*.

Figure 1.3 shows a graphical representation of the sales areas we've identified for AAPM.

1.2.2 Sales Organizations

Using the sales areas identified from our existing business information, we can start breaking down our sales areas into sales organizations, distribution channels, and divisions.

The most generic level of a sales area is the sales organization, which represents the sales-relevant company code in the system for sales-related functionality. This level is mandatory, and you must define at least one sales organization for each sales-relevant company code. Ideally, you'll only have one sales organization or as few sales areas as possible to make the best use of the system's features.

If you're considering defining more than one sales organization, keep in mind that you'll cannot define master data that will be valid across them. In other words, you'll maintain multiple sets of all sales master data, including business partners, material master data, pricing condition records, listings/exclusions, material determinations, output determinations, etc. System-level sales configuration would also require more entries once sales organizations are used as keys in determination tables.

Since sales organizations are available to most SAP S/4HANA Sales transactions, this level is commonly used to restrict access. Users from one sales organization should not maintain data that belongs to another sales organization, and sometimes, even display and reporting functionalities are restricted. You also have the option of granting users access without restricting them to a sales organization.

In our AAPM example, we'll define one sales organization for each sales-relevant company code. We'll use the same code for the sales organization as the company code. Many companies use the same value for both company codes and sales organization codes, but this approach isn't required; some companies adopt different naming conventions to distinguish between finance and sales entities, which is equally acceptable.

Figure 1.4 indicates how the *sales organizations* identified so far relate to the *sales-relevant company codes* for our AAPM sample company.

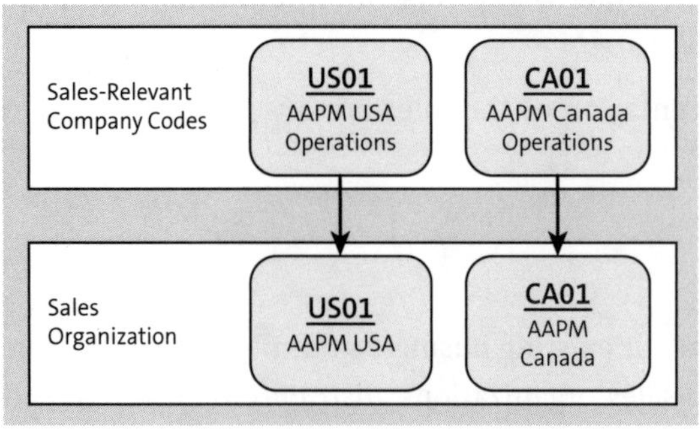

Figure 1.4 AAPM Sample Sales Organizations

In the following sections, we'll first create a sales organization and then assign it to a company code.

Creating Sales Organizations

In the SAP GUI, sales organizations can be configured in Transaction SPRO by following the menu path **SAP Customizing Implementation Guide • Enterprise Structure • Definition • Sales and Distribution • Define, copy, delete, check sales organization • Define Sales Organization.** On the screen that opens, click on the **New Entries** button or press F5.

> **Note**
> This transaction is also available for SAP S/4HANA Cloud under **Create Sales Organization (SOR)** in the self-service configuration user interface (SSCUI).

As shown in Figure 1.5, we'll focus on the US subsidiary for our AAPM sample company.

On this screen, maintain the **Sales Organization** code and description fields. You must also choose the **Statistics Currency** that should be used for reporting. However, once you select a currency, the system will issue a warning message, as shown in Figure 1.6.

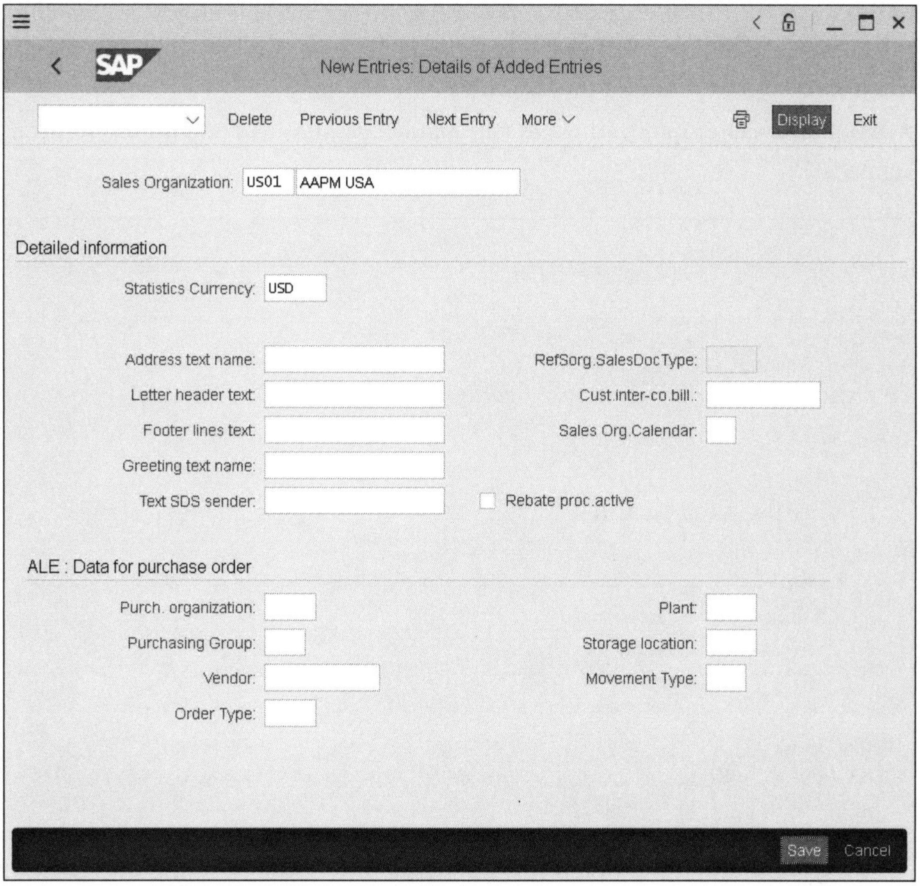

Figure 1.5 Creating New Sales Organizations

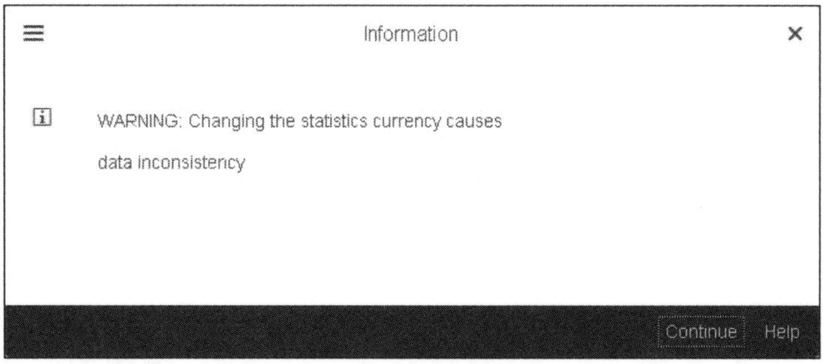

Figure 1.6 Statistics Currency Warning Message

At this stage, you can disregard this message, which is applicable only when changing the **Currency** of an existing **Sales Organization**; however the message does appear when entering a currency for the first time.

For each new sales organization, an **Edit Address** window will pop up, as shown in Figure 1.7.

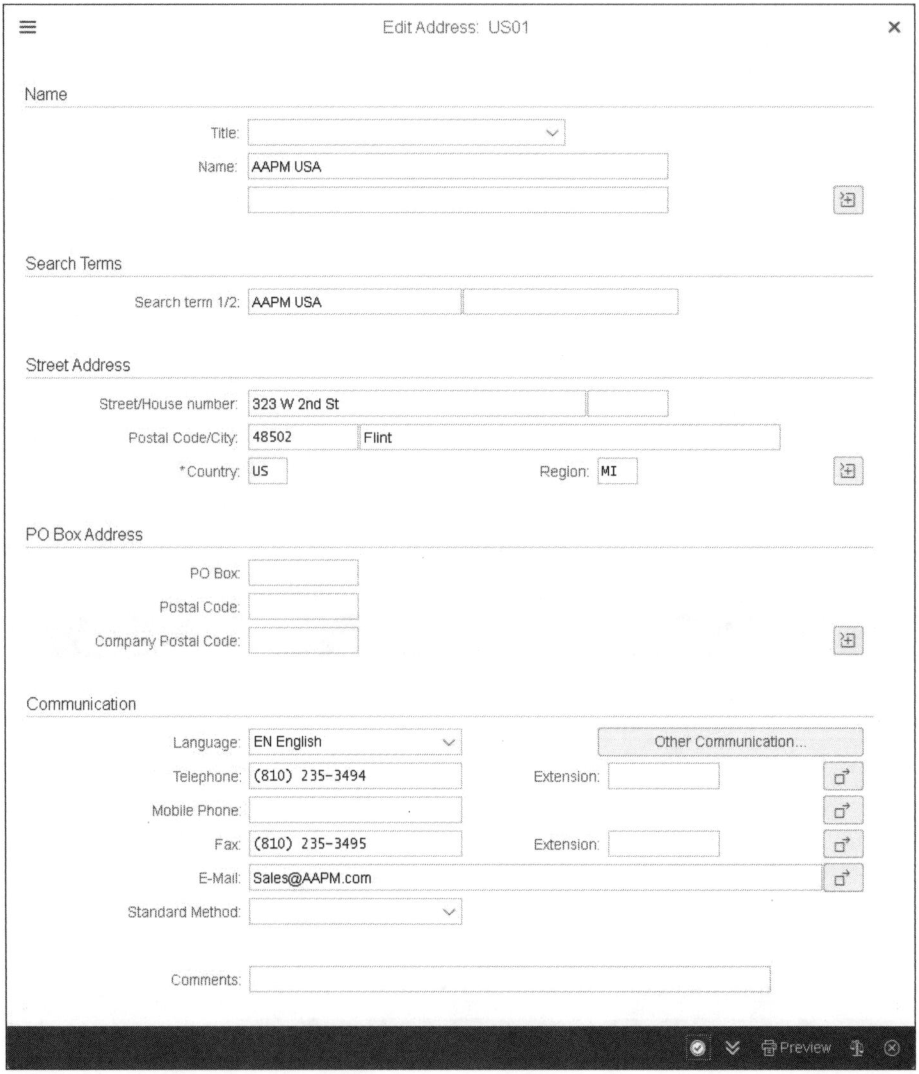

Figure 1.7 Sales Organization Address

The address information entered on this screen will be displayed in the header of related output forms (print, email, fax, etc.).

Assigning Sales Organizations to Company Codes

Now, you'll need to assign the sales organization to a sales-relevant company code by following the menu path **SAP Customizing Implementation Guide • Enterprise Structure • Assignment • Sales and Distribution • Assign Sales Organization to Company Code**.

Note

This transaction is also available for SAP S/4HANA Cloud under **Assign Company Code (CCD) to Company (CMP)** in the self-service configuration user interface (SSCUI).

As shown in Figure 1.8, using our sample company information, this screen shows all sales organizations configured in the system with a field (**CoCd**) available for indicating the company code they belong to. You'll need to enter a valid company code for each sales organization to use that company code for finance-relevant transitions such as sales of goods and services. Sales organizations are almost always assigned to a company code.

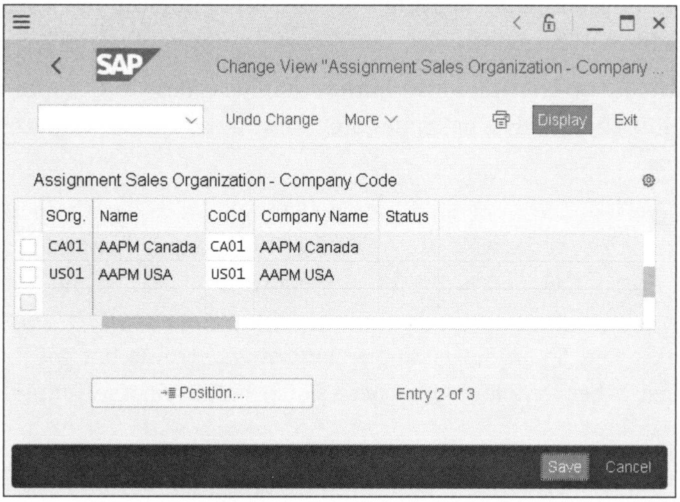

Figure 1.8 Assigning Sales Organizations to Sales-Relevant Company Codes

1.2.3 Distribution Channels and Distribution Chains

The next level of the sales area, called the *distribution channel*, represents the channels used by your company to distribute goods and services to your customers (third-party or internal subsidiaries). The distribution channel is where you'll specify your company's market approach and represents how your corporation is organized internally to manage your customers' expectations/satisfaction.

The distribution channel is attached to the sales organization. No standard SAP S/4HANA functionality makes use of the distribution channel on its own. Commonly, distribution channel codes are defined that belong to multiple sales organizations. However, data isn't necessarily grouped by these codes because you are always required to select a sales organization first.

Distribution channels allow you to maintain both customer and material master sales data specific to each channel as well as to maintain pricing condition records. However, you have the option of defining rules to allow distribution channels to share the same data. This feature is called a *common distribution channel*.

A combination of a sales organization and a distribution channel is called a *distribution chain*, a term that has existed since the earliest versions of the system, in particular when working with material master sales data statuses. However, this term was not often used in workshops or in the documentation, although the term is becoming more popular as newer versions are delivered. In SAP S/4HANA 1809, you'll see the term "distribution channel" frequently.

The naming convention for two-character distribution channel codes varies a great deal. With sales, the most commonly used codes are alphanumeric codes that are meaningful as acronyms.

In our AAPM example, we'll define three distribution channels and assign them to our two sales organizations. The codes we'll use are OE for original equipment manufacturer sales, AM for aftermarket, and IC for intercompany. Note that we did not include performance as a distribution channel because, in our example, performance is considered aftermarket sale. So, in our example, performance would not get its own distribution channel. Other companies may need a distribution channel for performance.

Figure 1.9 and Figure 1.10 show the distribution channels we'll define for our AAPM sample companies (US and Canada). The combinations of these distribution channels and sales organizations make up the distribution chains for AAPM.

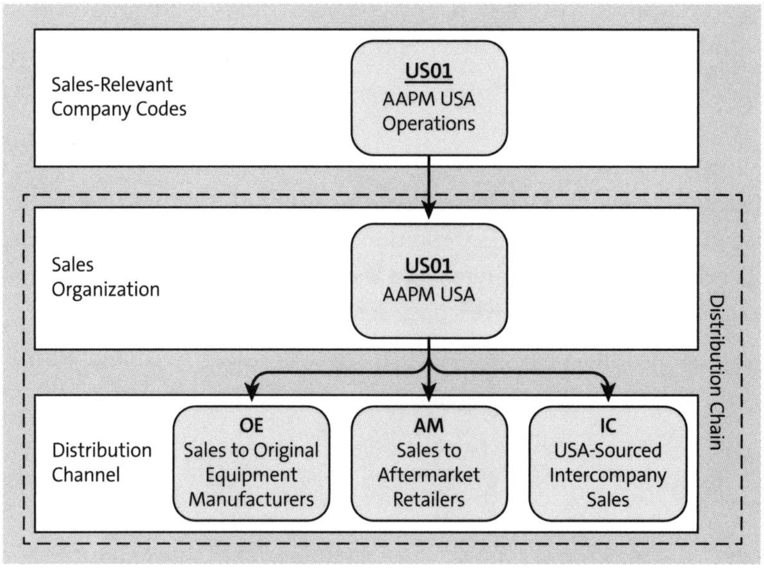

Figure 1.9 Sample Distribution Channel and Chain Definition for AAPM USA

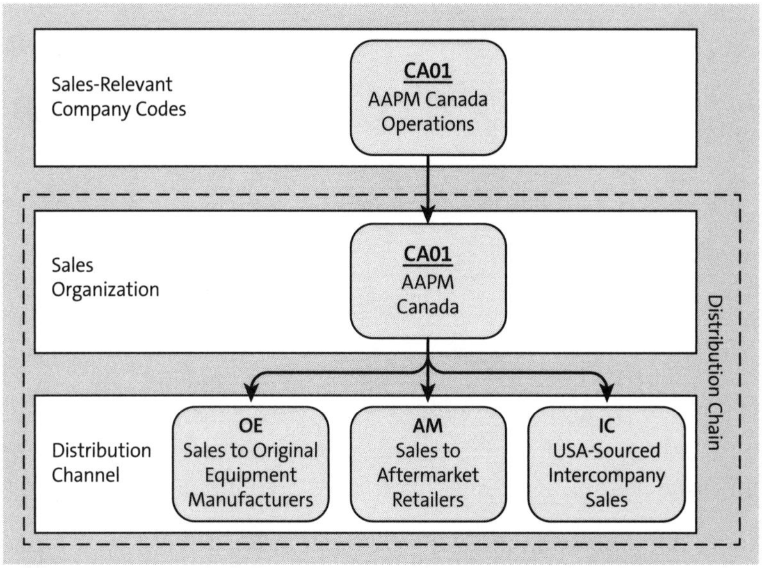

Figure 1.10 Sample Distribution Channel and Chain Definition for AAPM Canada

In the following sections, you'll learn how to create a distribution channel, how to create a distribution chain, and how to use the common distribution channels feature.

Creating Distribution Channels

To configure distribution channels, follow the menu path **SAP Customizing Implementation Guide • Enterprise Structure • Definition • Sales and Distribution • Define, Copy, Delete, Check Distribution Channel • Define Distribution Channel.** On the screen that opens, click on the **New Entries** button or press F5.

> **Note**
>
> This transaction is also available for SAP S/4HANA Cloud under **Create Distribution Channel (DCH)** in the self-service configuration user interface (SSCUI).

As shown in Figure 1.11, a screen will open displaying sample distribution channels for company code AAPM. Maintain the **Distr. Channel** and **Name** fields and then click **Save**.

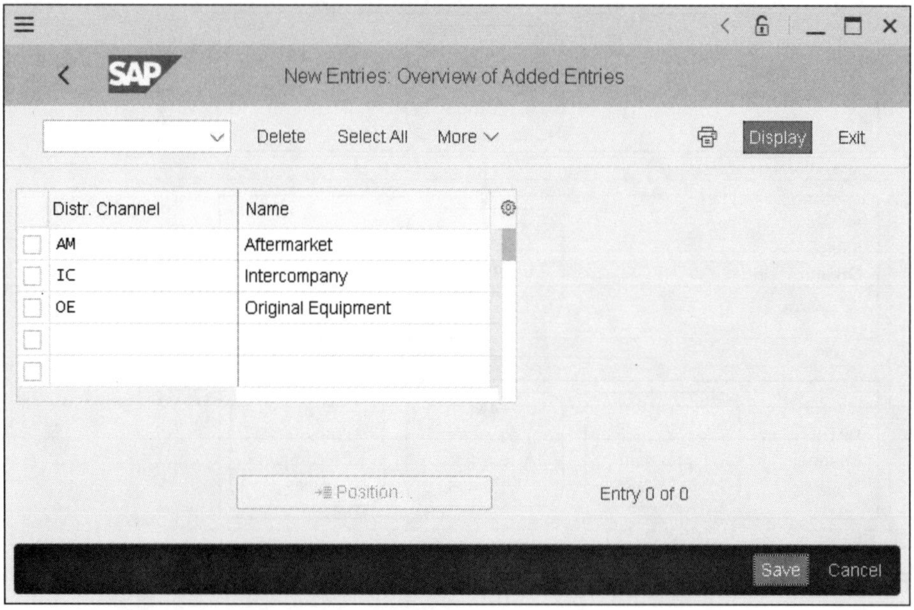

Figure 1.11 Creating New Distribution Channels

Creating Distribution Chains

Now, you'll need to assign the distribution channel to a sales organization to create a distribution chain by following the menu path **SAP Customizing Implementation Guide • Enterprise Structure • Assignment • Sales and Distribution • Assign Distribution Channel to Sales Organization.** On the screen that opens, click on the **New Entries** button or press F5.

> **Note**
>
> This transaction is also available for SAP S/4HANA Cloud under **Create Distribution Chain (SLC)** in the self-service configuration user interface (SSCUI).

As shown in Figure 1.12, a screen will open containing sample distribution chains for company code AAPM. On this screen, enter the sales organization (**SOrg.**) and distribution channel (**DChl**) in the corresponding fields.

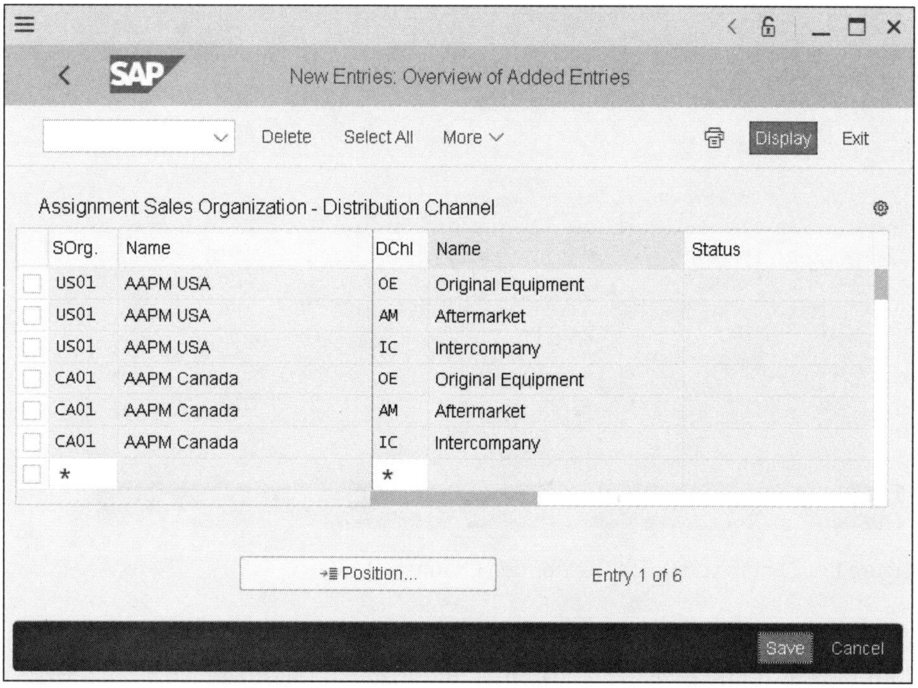

Figure 1.12 Creating Distribution Chains by Assigning Distribution Channels to Sales Organizations

Defining Common Distribution Channels

In some instances, you might need a separate distribution channel but don't need or want to maintain master data. For example, you might have separate distribution channels for reporting or security purposes but only want to maintain sales data on customers/materials and/or pricing condition records once. These initial values should then be considered as automatically valid for other distribution channels.

This linking of data is possible with a feature called a *common distribution channel*, which you can define by following the menu path **SAP Customizing Implementation Guide • Sales and Distribution • Master Data • Define Common Distribution Channels**.

As shown in Figure 1.13, a screen will appear showing all available common distribution channels we could define as a common distribution channel for our sample company code AAPM.

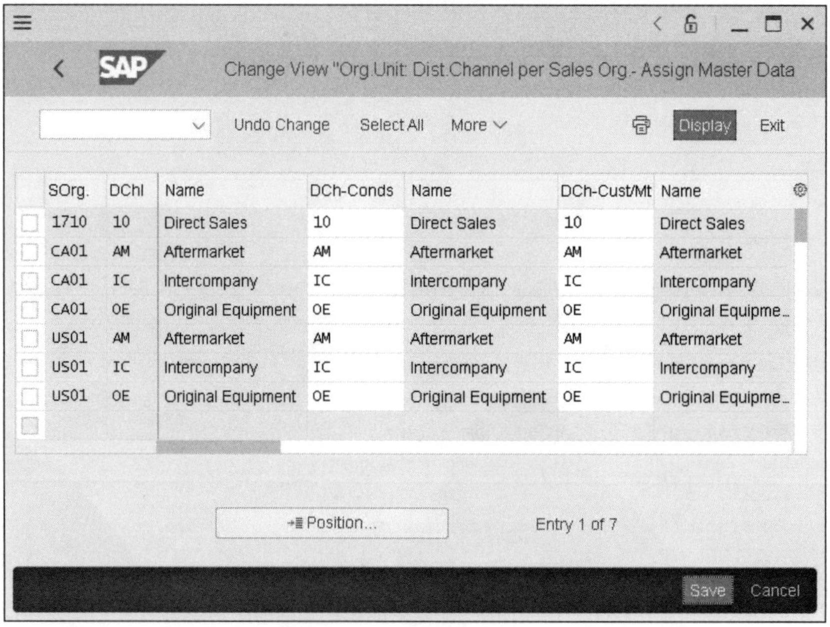

Figure 1.13 Defining Common Distribution Channels

On this screen, change the distribution channel used for maintaining pricing condition records (**DCh-Conds**) and customer and material sales data (**DCh-Cust/Mt**) by assigning a value in the corresponding column that is different from the value in the **DChl** column. By default, the system will use the same distribution channel, but you can then modify these values to use a different distribution channel if needed.

For instance, let's say we wanted intercompany distribution channels to use the customer and material master data defined for original equipment. In this case, we would perform the changes shown in Figure 1.14.

SOrg.	DChl	Name	DCh-Conds	Name	DCh-Cust/Mt	Name
CA01	IC	Intercompany	IC	Intercompany	OE	Original Equipment
US01	IC	Intercompany	IC	Intercompany	OE	Original Equipment

Figure 1.14 Sample Common Distribution Channels

1.2.4 Divisions

The last level of the sales area, called the *division*, represents a segment of the company motivated by special market requirements to commercialize certain types of products. A division should ideally identify a product category with its own dedicated sales team and corporate structure to support it. You'll need to define at least one division for each sales area. Often, a generic, nondescriptive division is assigned when no specific product line falls under this category.

A division is usually attached to a sales organization and a distribution chain. However, the functionality also allows you to use divisions on their own with their own product categories.

Divisions allow you to maintain business partner (customer) information that is classified as sales data and is specific to the division. However, you also have the option of defining rules to allow divisions to share the same data. This feature is called a *common division*. Once divisions are defined, you'll have all the necessary components required to create sales areas.

As with distribution channels, the naming convention for divisions involves a two-character code that varies quite a bit. The most commonly used codes are alphanumeric codes that are meaningful.

In our AAPM example, we'll define two divisions: a common division across all product lines and a division specific to performance parts. The codes will be 00 for common (already provided out of the box) and PP for performance parts. Note that, in our example, AAPM Canada does not sell performance parts.

Figure 1.15 and Figure 1.16 show the divisions we'll define for our example AAPM companies (US and Canada). The combination of these divisions and distribution chains will become the sales areas for our AAPM example companies (US and Canada).

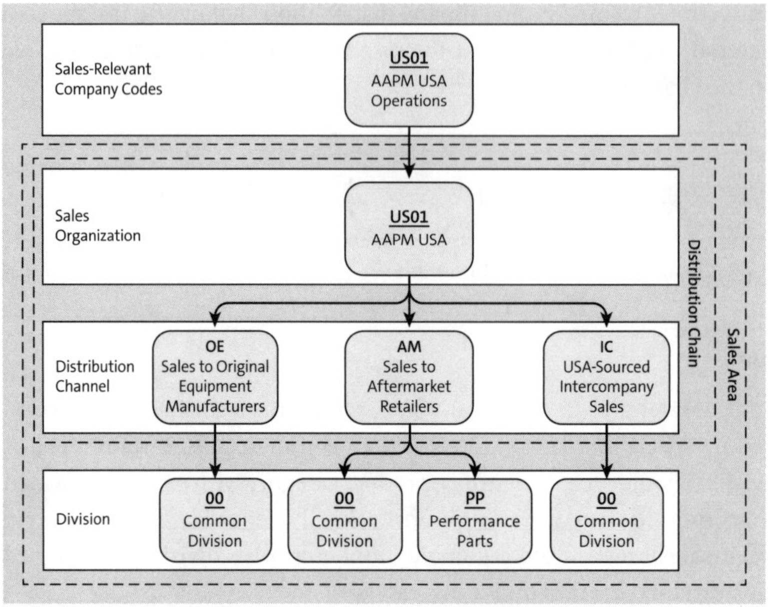

Figure 1.15 Sample Division Definition for AAPM USA

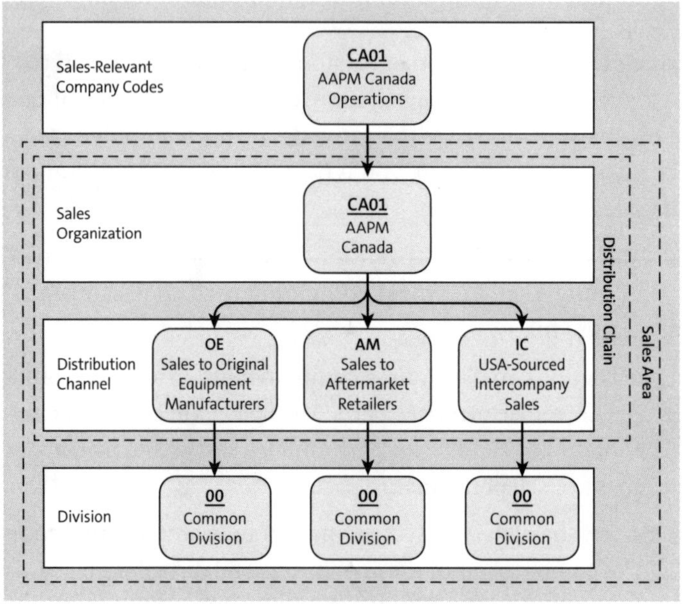

Figure 1.16 Sample Division Definition for AAPM Canada

In the following sections, we'll look at how to create divisions, how to assign divisions to sales organizations, and how to use the common division feature.

Creating Divisions

To configure distribution channels, follow the menu path **SAP Customizing Implementation Guide • Enterprise Structure • Definition • Logistics – General • Define, Copy, Delete, Check Division • Define Division**. On the screen that opens, click on the **New Entries** button or press F5.

> **Note**
> This transaction is also available for SAP S/4HANA Cloud under **Create Division (DIV)** in the self-service configuration user interface (SSCUI).

As shown in Figure 1.17, specify a two-character division code (**Division**) and add a description (**Name**). We'll create division **PP** for our sample company.

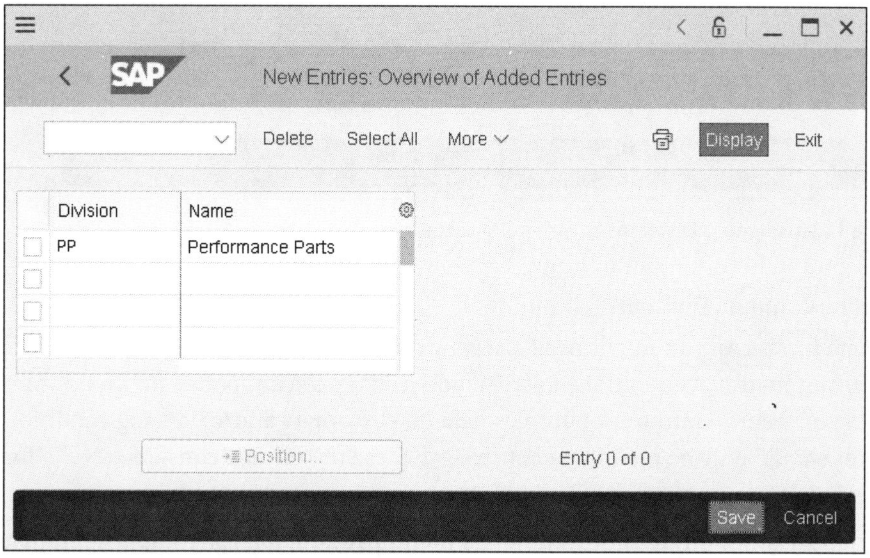

Figure 1.17 Creating New Divisions

Assigning Divisions to Sales Organizations

To assign divisions to sales organizations, follow the menu path **SAP Customizing Implementation Guide • Enterprise Structure • Assignment • Sales and Distribution •**

Assign Division to Sales Organization. On the screen that opens, click on the **New Entries** button or press F5.

As shown in Figure 1.18, enter the sales organization (**SOrg.**) and the division (**Dv.**). Notice the assignment of the **Dv 00** and **PP** to the AAPM sample sales organizations **US01** and **CA01**.

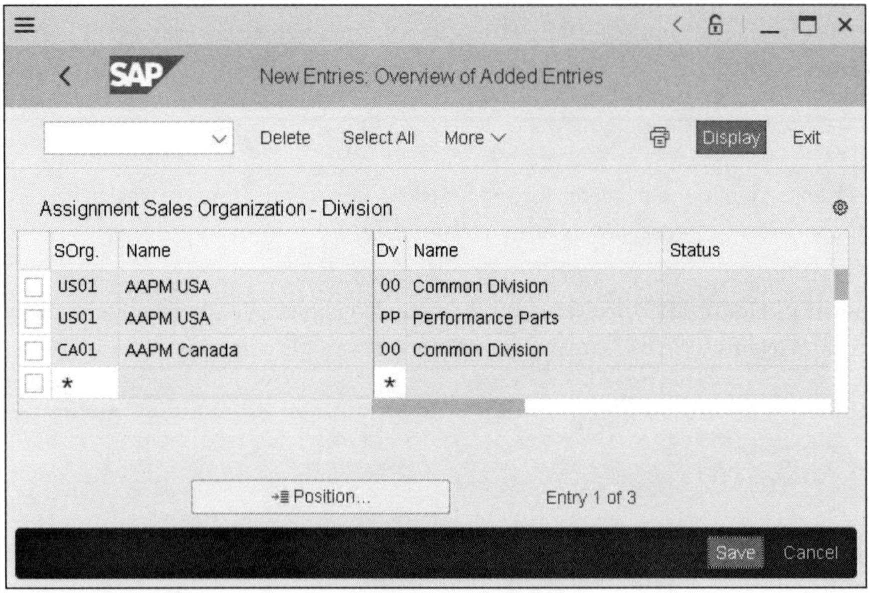

Figure 1.18 Assigning Divisions to Sales Organizations

Defining Common Divisions

In some instances, you might need a separate division without reference to master data maintenance. As mentioned earlier, you might need a separate division for reporting or security purposes, but sales data on customers and/or pricing condition records should only be maintained once since these records are considered valid for other divisions automatically.

To define a common division, follow the menu path **Customizing Implementation Guide • Sales and Distribution • Master Data • Define Common Divisions.**

As shown in Figure 1.19, a screen will appear showing all available options for defining a common division for our example company.

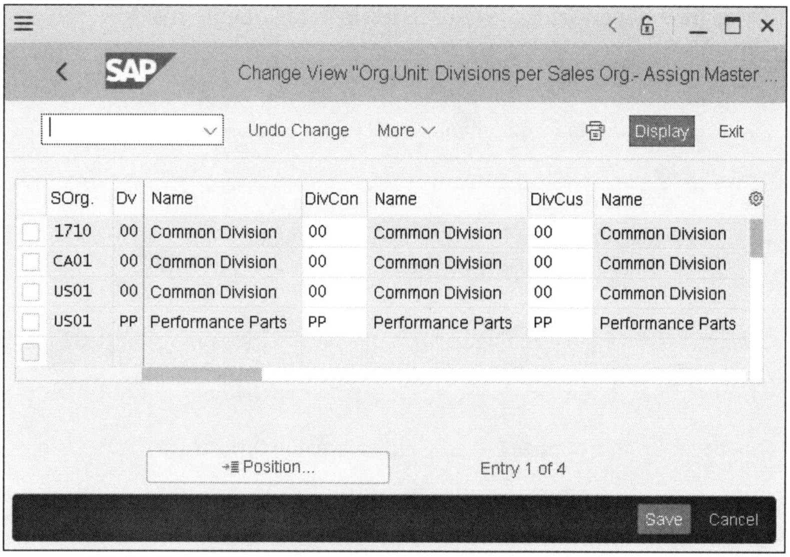

Figure 1.19 Defining a Common Division

On this screen, you can change the division you use for maintaining pricing condition records (**DCh-Conds**) and for customer data (**DCh-Cust**) by assigning a different value to these fields than the value indicated in the **Dv** column. By default, the system will assign the same divisions, but you can then modify these values use to a different division if needed.

For instance, to make the **Performance Parts** division use the customer master data defined for **Common Division**, change the value in the **DivCus** column to "00," as shown in Figure 1.20.

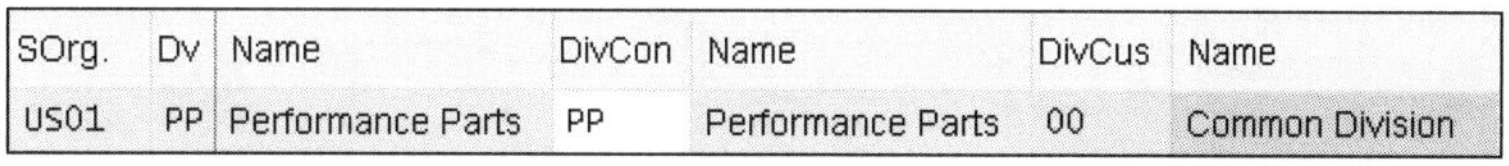

SOrg.	Dv	Name	DivCon	Name	DivCus	Name
US01	PP	Performance Parts	PP	Performance Parts	00	Common Division

Figure 1.20 Sample Common Division

1.2.5 Sales Areas

With all three components (sales organization, distribution channel, and division) defined and configured, now we're ready to set up the sales area. In this step, we'll assign the codes to each other, but no new code or description will be defined for the sales area itself.

In our example, we have seven sales areas, as listed in Table 1.1.

Sales Organization	Distribution Channel	Division	Sales Area
US01: AAPM USA	OE: Original Equipment	00: Common Division	US01-OE-00
US01: AAPM USA	AM: Aftermarket	00: Common Division	US01-AM-00
US01: AAPM USA	AM: Aftermarket	PP: Performance Parts	US01-AM-PP
US01: AAPM USA	IC: Intercompany	00: Common Division	US01-IC-00
CA01: AAPM Canada	OE: Original Equipment	00: Common Division	CA01-OE-00
CA01: AAPM Canada	AM: Aftermarket	00: Common Division	CA01-AM-00
CA01: AAPM Canada	IC: Intercompany	00: Common Division	CA01-IC-00

Table 1.1 Seven Sales Areas for AAPM

Figure 1.21 and Figure 1.22 show the sales areas we'll define for our AAPM sample companies (US and Canada).

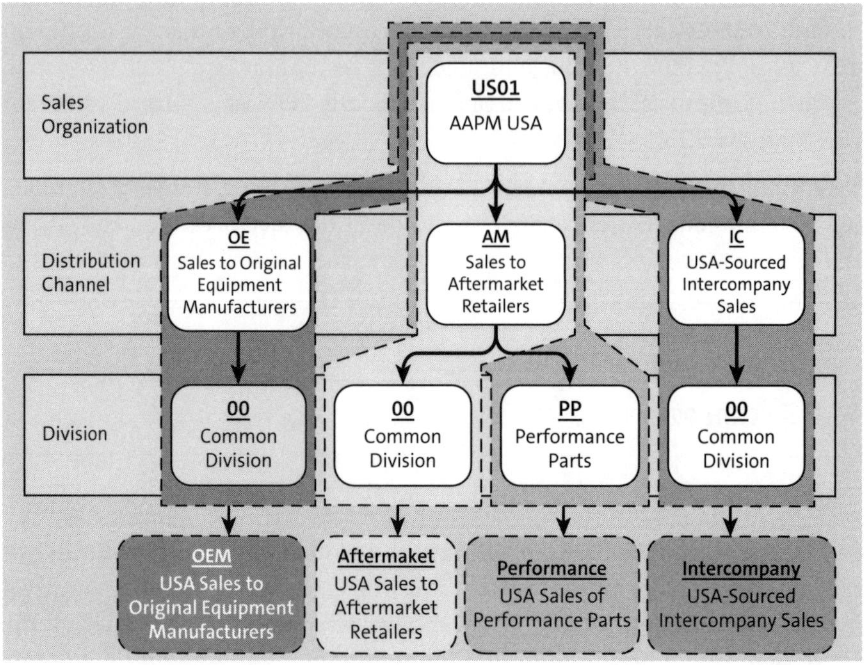

Figure 1.21 Sample Sales Areas for AAPM USA

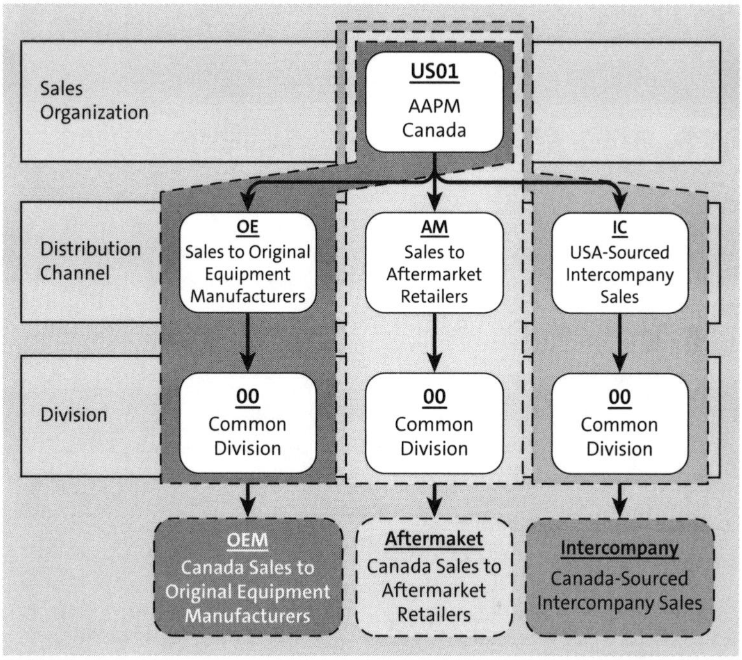

Figure 1.22 Sample Sales Areas for AAPM Canada

To configure a sales area, follow the menu path **SAP Customizing Implementation Guide • Enterprise Structure • Assignment • Sales and Distribution • Set Up Sales Area**. On the screen that opens, click on the **New Entries** button or press F5.

> **Note**
>
> This transaction is also available for SAP S/4HANA Cloud under **Create Sales Area (SLA)** in the self-service configuration user interface (SSCUI).

As shown in Figure 1.23, enter the sales organization (**SOrg.**), the distribution channel (**DChl**), and the division (**Dv**). The combination of these three fields creates the sales area. Our example contains the assignment of the sales organization, distribution channel, and division for our sample company AAPM, resulting in its seven sales areas.

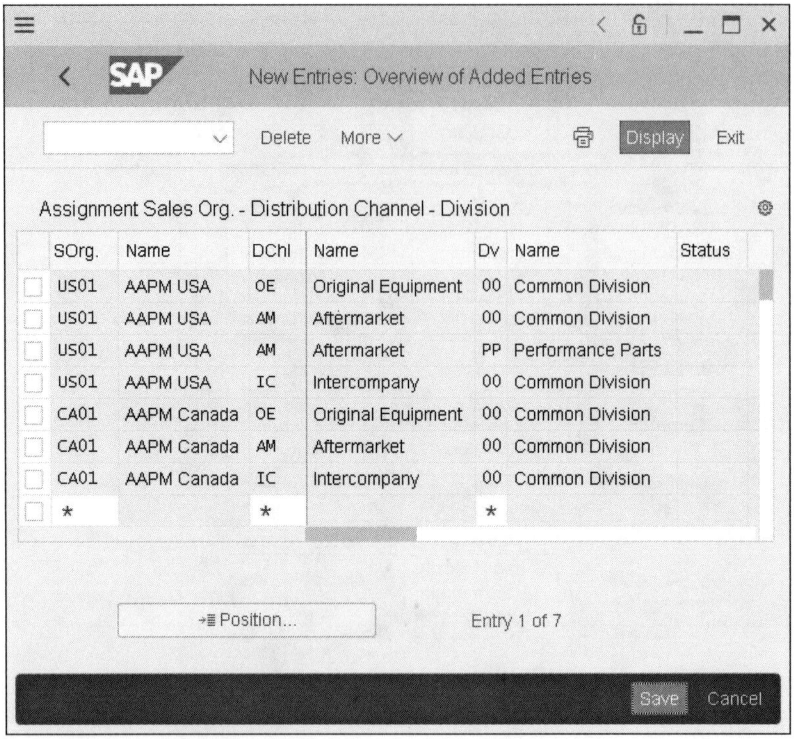

Figure 1.23 Setup Sample Sales Areas

1.2.6 Plant Assignment

From a sales standpoint, corporate facilities that hold inventory or serve as base for field service operations must be represented in the system as plants. Plants are used to control costs and inventory.

The work of defining plants in SAP S/4HANA calls under materials management (MM) and controlling. A plant must be assigned to a company code. Sales needs to identify which plants deliver goods and services to customers (third-party and internal subsidiaries) for each of the distribution chains configured in the system.

The plant is the link between the corporate entities responsible for inventory/service workforce costs and the corporate entities that generate revenue. This link is represented by the assignment of a distribution chain and plants. Note that plants and distribution chains may be assigned to different company codes, for example, in intercompany sales scenarios.

In our example, we'll consider the two sales organizations as plants. We'll also define a third-party logistics warehouse located centrally in the United States called "3PL Operations."

Figure 1.24 shows the plants we'll assign to our distribution chains for our sample company.

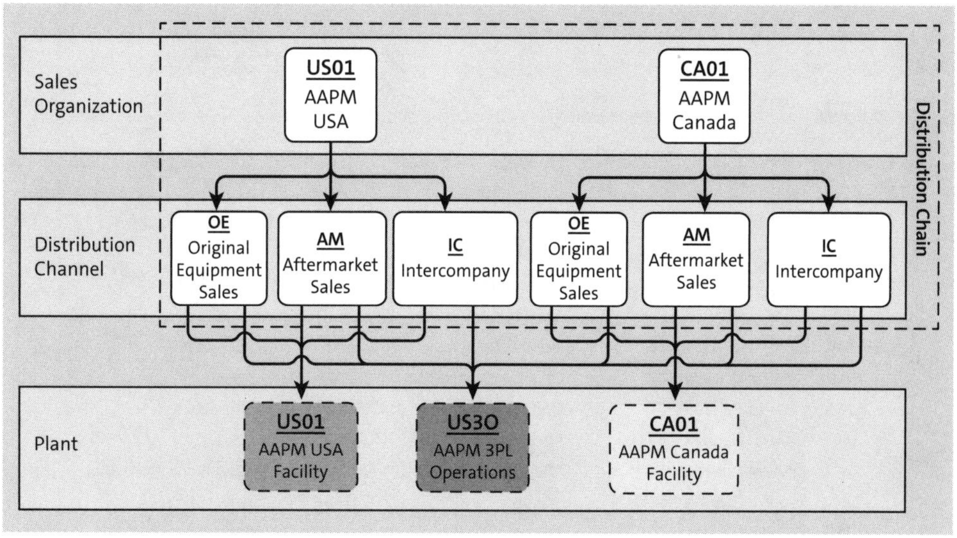

Figure 1.24 Sample Plant Assignment

To assign plants to distribution chains, follow the menu path **SAP Customizing Implementation Guide • Enterprise Structure • Assignment • Sales and Distribution • Assign Sales Organization – Distribution Channel – Plant.** On the screen that opens, click on the **New Entries** button or press F5.

Note

This transaction is also available for SAP S/4HANA Cloud under **Assign Plant (PLT) to Distribution Chain (SLC)** in the self-service configuration user interface (SSCUI).

In our example, the materials management team defined the plant codes as **US01** (**AAPM USA**), **US3O** (**AAPM 3PL Operations**), and **CA01** (**AAPM Canada**).

Figure 1.25 shows the assignment of a distribution chain to the appropriate plants. This assignment is achieved by entering the sales organization in the **SOrg.** column, entering the distribution channel in the **DChCust/Mt** column, and entering the plant in the **Plnt** column. These values would have been defined during blueprint workshops.

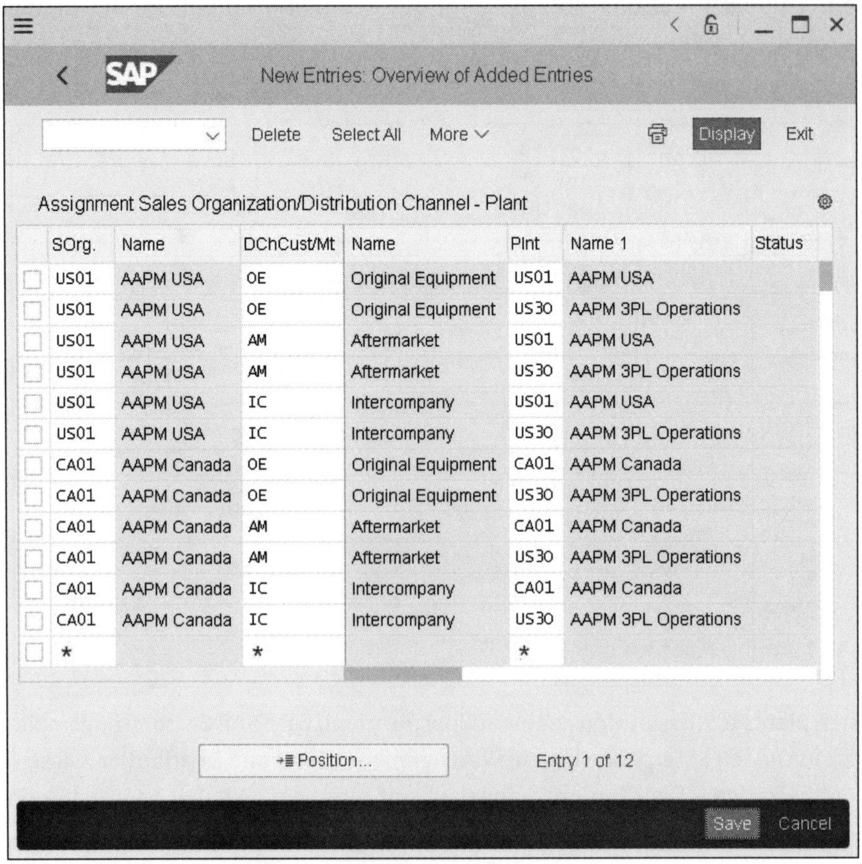

Figure 1.25 Assigning Plants to Distribution Chains

1.2.7 Credit Control Area Assignment

For each corporation, a team is responsible for making risk decisions related to customers' ability and willingness to fulfill their financial obligations. This decision-making may or may not be part of your accounts receivable department. In SAP S/4HANA, this team is represented in the system by the credit control area (**CCAr**).

The finance workstream manages decisions related to credit control areas. The sales department must provide input related to which sales areas should be assigned to which credit control areas. This assignment will be used by default when determining the credit worthiness of a given payer. You may also maintain a different credit control area on the customer master under the **Billing** tab on the **Sales Area Data** screen.

In our example, we have only one team managing credit risk for all subsidiaries. In other words, we'll only assign one default credit control area for all sales areas.

To assign credit control areas to sales areas, follow the menu path **SAP Customizing Implementation Guide • Financial Supply Chain Management • Credit Management • Integration with Accounts Receivable Accounting and Sales and Distribution • Integration with Sales and Distribution • Assign Sales Area to Credit Control Area.**

Once your sales areas are defined, enter the credit control area into the **CCAr** field to ensure that the right credit area can be identified even if the corresponding field is left blank on the customer master data.

As shown in Figure 1.26, all our sales areas have been assigned to the same default credit control area.

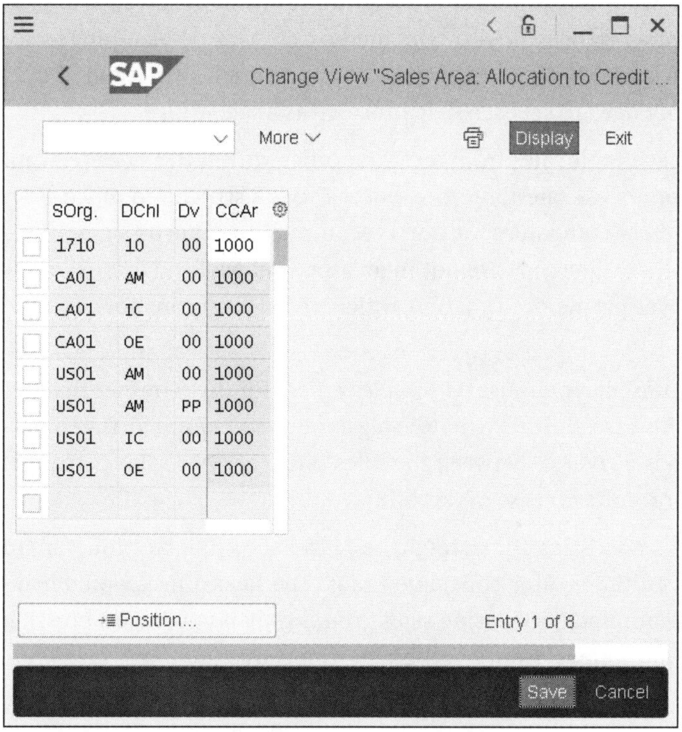

Figure 1.26 Assigning Sales Areas to Credit Control Areas

1.3 Sales Offices and Sales Groups

Companies with a salesforce organized in multiple offices, independent or affiliated, may need to control which offices own the sales credit from transactions. To manage this requirement, SAP S/4HANA offers sales offices and sales groups to help you manage your salesforce.

While discussing company codes and sales areas, the offices dedicated to field sales usually surface as possible relevant entities. Whether these field offices should have separate company codes is driven by whether these offices are legal entities under the responsibility of the corporation. The finance team will make this decision because, as legal entities, field offices may need to provide financial reporting to stakeholders and, in some countries, to the government tax agencies.

During workshops on organizational structure, you'll need to gather all the offices dedicated to field sales that are not separate legal entities (as determined by the finance team). Questions related to the business model and market approach must be asked to determine what functionalities are relevant for field offices, such as pricing, sales targets, customer returns, credit/debit memos, etc. One determining factor on this design decision is whether each field office has its own sales goals and KPIs. In this case, you'll probably need to set each field office up as a sales office.

Some companies manage their sales from a central office within the sales-relevant company code with some field sales presence, but without a structured office overseeing their work. For these companies, we don't recommend setting up sales offices or sales groups, since these elements are not mandatory. All we need in this case is individual sales employee partner information, which we'll describe in more detail in Chapter 2.

If the field offices are present, you must set up *sales offices* for them (rather than for each salesperson). In this case, the office may be big enough to require further breakdown. The sales group is a layer in between the sales office and the sales personnel used to group together results for ease of reporting.

Managing sales groups under sales offices might be a level of complexity you want to avoid. Managing sales groups is often considered a task the sales offices would manage themselves. We recommend only using sales groups only if you have a pressing need to monitor sales at this level from a corporate perspective.

In our example, we have sales offices in the United States focused on selling performance parts to competitive racing teams across the country (NASCAR, road racing, rallying, and drag racing). Other sales areas don't work with sales offices.

One of these sales offices (road racing) has three departments (touring, formula, and B-spec). They each have specific sales targets that are important to them and the compnay. The racing division is quite profitable, and AAPM needs to maintain a certain level of sales in these divisions. In this case, configuring the system with sales groups enables the road racing sales office to make reports and monitor sales for this division.

Figure 1.27 shows the proposed sales offices and sales groups, and the sales areas they'll be assigned to, for our sample company.

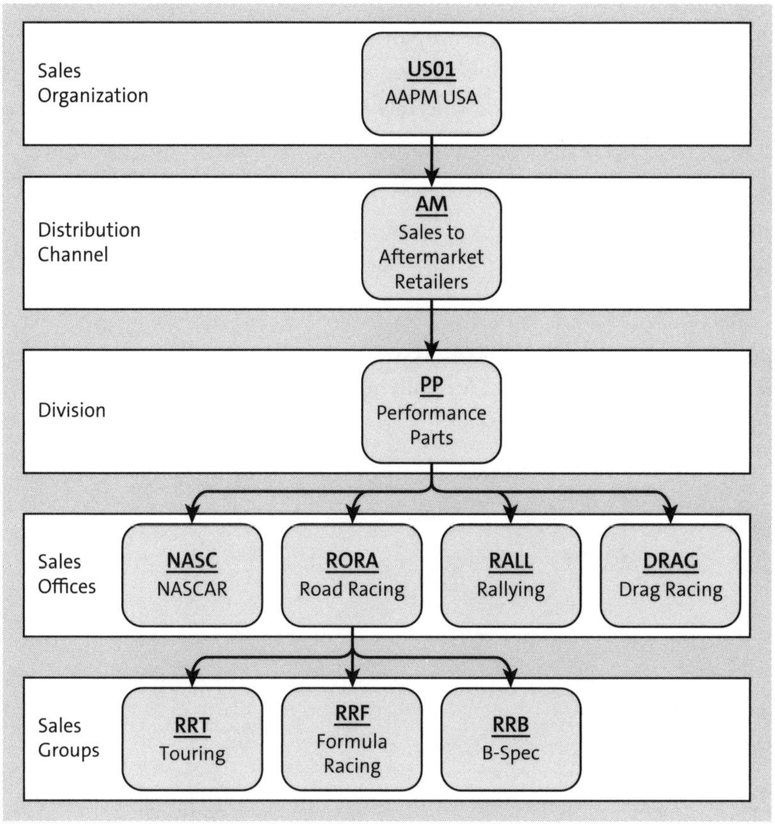

Figure 1.27 Sample Sales Offices and Sales Groups

In the following sections, we'll cover the steps for creating and assigning both sales offices and sales groups.

1.3.1 Sales Offices

Sales offices are organizational structure elements that represent an organized group of collaborators, based out of a single physical location, dedicated and assigned to the task of gathering customer requests and inquiries and ensuring their fulfillment. Sales offices, which are represented in the system by 4-digit codes, are assigned to the sales area under which they perform their duties. In the following sections, we'll cover how to create sales offices and assign them to sales areas.

Creating Sales Offices

To configure a sales office, follow the menu path **SAP Customizing Implementation Guide • Enterprise Structure • Definition • Sales and Distribution • Maintain Sales Office.** On the screen that opens, click on the **New Entries** button or press F5.

> **Note**
>
> This transaction is also available for SAP S/4HANA Cloud under **Create Sales Office (SOF)** in the self-service configuration user interface (SSCUI).

From our sample company AAPM, we created the following sales office codes: **NASC** for **NASCAR**, **RORA** for **Road Racing**, **RALL** for **Rallying**, and **DRAG** for **Drag Racing**. Each sales office will use its main office address.

As shown in Figure 1.28, we've created sales offices for our sample company.

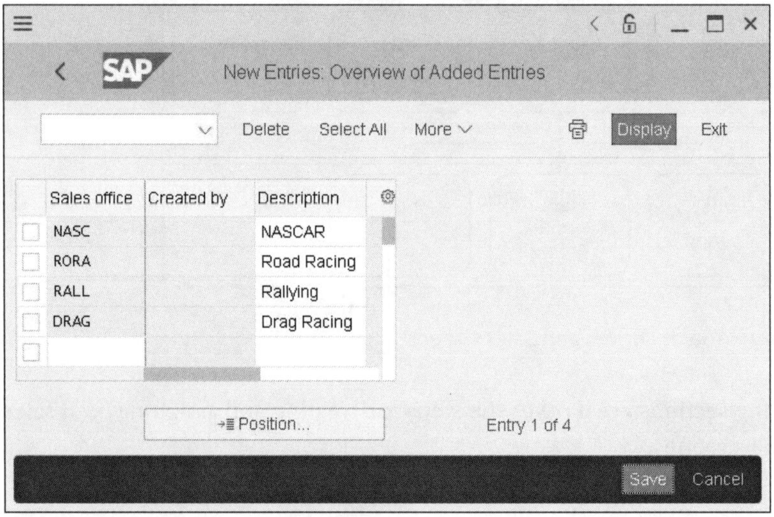

Figure 1.28 Creating New Sales Offices

For every new code entered in the **Sales Office** field, the **Edit Address** window will pop up, as shown in Figure 1.29. Since the fields in this window are relatively self-explanatory, we won't cover them in detail.

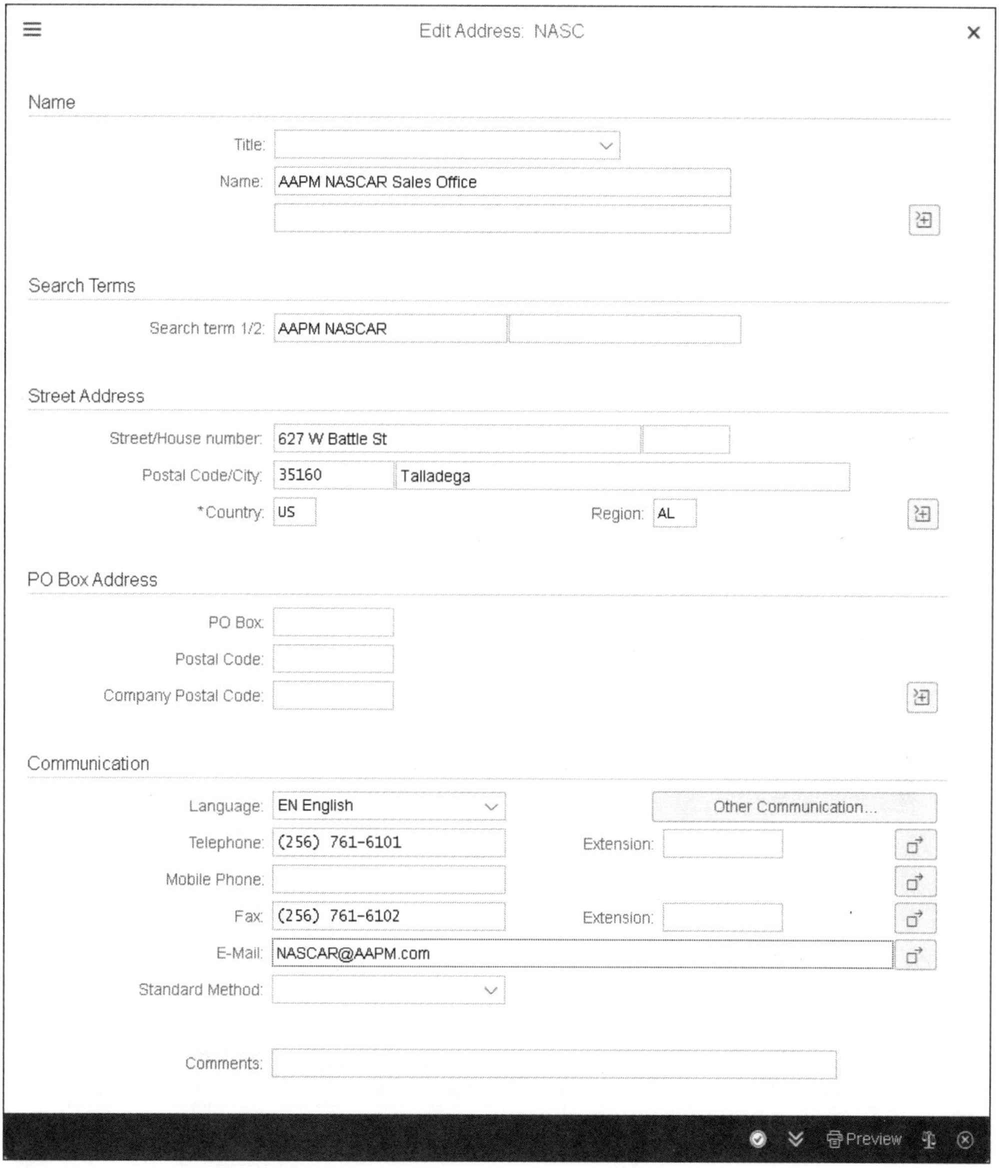

Figure 1.29 Sales Office Address Popup Window

Assigning Sales Offices to Sales Area

To assign a sales office to a sales area, follow the menu path **SAP Customizing Implementation Guide • Enterprise Structure • Assignment • Sales and Distribution • Assign Sales Office to Sales Area.** On the screen that opens, click on the **New Entries** button or press F5.

> **Note**
>
> This transaction is also available for SAP S/4HANA Cloud under **Assign Sales Office (SOF) to Sales Area (SLA)** in the self-service configuration user interface (SSCUI).

In our example, the sales offices identified belong to the performance parts sales area in the United States entity.

As shown in Figure 1.30, enter the sales organization (**SOrg.**), the distribution channel (**DChl**), the division (**Dv**), and the sales office (**SOff.**). Our example contains the assignment of sales offices to the appropriate sales areas in our AAPM sample company.

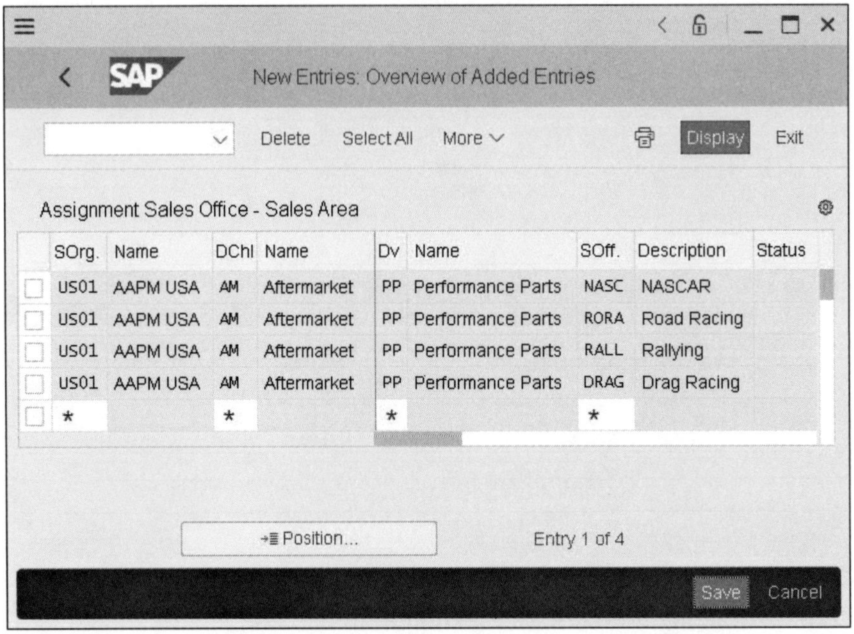

Figure 1.30 Assigning Sales Offices to Sales Area

1.3.2 Sales Groups

Sales groups represent departments within sales offices. Sales groups are represented in the system by three-digit codes and assigned to the sales office under which they perform their duties. In the following sections, we'll cover how to create sales groups and assign them to a sales office.

Creating Sales Groups

To configure a sales groups, follow the menu path **SAP Customizing Implementation Guide • Enterprise Structure • Definition • Sales and Distribution • Maintain Sales Group.** On the screen that opens, click on the **New Entries** button or press [F5].

> **Note**
>
> This transaction is also available for SAP S/4HANA Cloud under **Create Sales Group (SGR)** in the self-service configuration user interface (SSCUI).

As shown in Figure 1.31, specify a three-character sales group code (**Sales group**) and add a description (**Description**). Our example contains the sales groups created for our AAPM sample company.

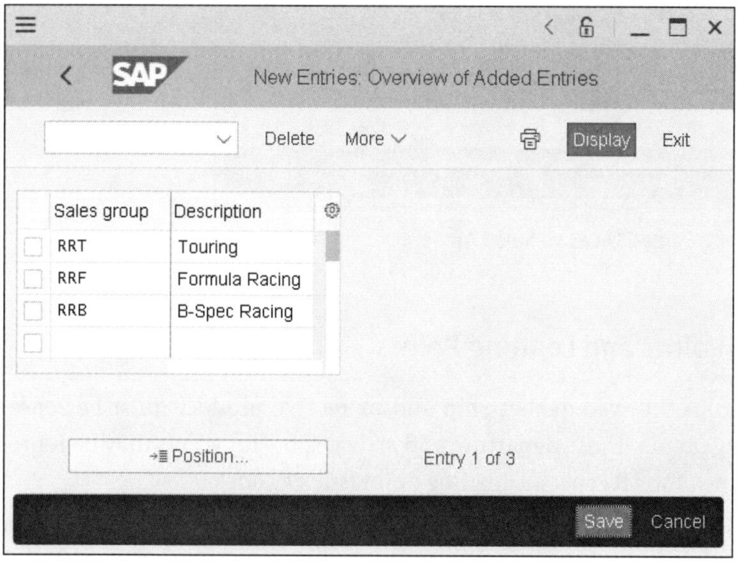

Figure 1.31 Creating New Sales Offices

Assigning Sales Groups to Sales Offices

To assign a sales group to a sales office, follow the menu path **SAP Customizing Implementation Guide • Enterprise Structure • Assignment • Sales and Distribution • Assign Sales Group to Sales Office.** On the screen that opens, click on the **New Entries** button or press F5.

As shown in Figure 1.32, enter the sales office (**SOff.**) and the sales group (**SGrp**). Now, the sales group has been assigned to a sales office. In our example, our sales groups all belong to the **Road Racing** sales office.

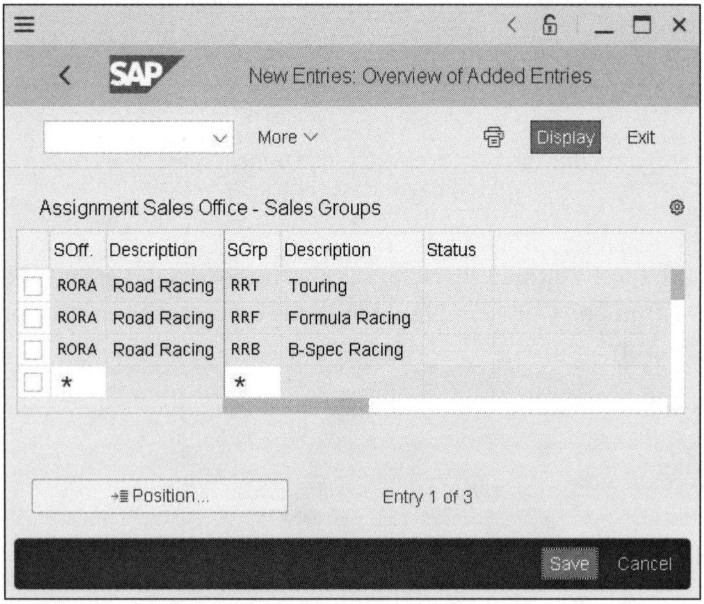

Figure 1.32 Assigning Sales Offices to Sales Areas

1.4 Shipping Points and Loading Points

All plants defined in the system that ship and/or receive product must be represented as shipping points. These departure and arrival spots for goods may be represented in detail, including its specific loading point (such as docks).

As mentioned earlier in Section 1.2.6, from a sales standpoint, corporate facilities that hold inventory must be represented in the system as plants, which are used to control cost and inventory.

The logistics component of SAP S/4HANA Sales is usually implemented as part of supply chain management (SCM), since warehouse operations are a natural part of supply chain management. However, the configuration for the outbound delivery document and related requirements remains under the control of sales.

This portion of system set up, referred to as *logistics execution*, does not refer to any specific execution of functionality but rather the execution of warehouse operations (including system functions) to move inventory.

The organizational structure for logistics execution uses a plant as a starting point and then identifies areas within the plant that are dedicated to shipping and/or receiving goods from customers (third-party and internal subsidiaries). You need at least one shipping point defined per plant to use the logistics execution functionality.

Shipping points are used to define the warehouse lead times, this is used when promising expected delivery dates to customers. They are also used to represent certain warehouse demands and requirements concerning service level agreements (SLAs), special picking procedures, special packing requirements, etc. So, you may have more than one shipping point defined per plant in case the plant has distinct areas that handle distinct types of warehouse operations.

Loading points could be used to represent the docks of a shipping point, and the system would be responsible for selecting which of the shipping docks to use based on master data criteria. At the time of picking, the warehouse operations would use the dock selected by the system to stage the product for packing and shipping.

Loading points are recommended for companies with large logistics warehouse operations that use inventory management (IM) in SAP S/4HANA as their warehouse management system (WMS), but loading points are not mandatory. Loading points are rarely configured because, if your logistics operation is relatively small, loading points are not necessary. If the logistics operation is large, companies tend to either use a third-party logistics provider or invest in embedded Extended Warehouse Management in SAP S/4HANA (embedded EWM in SAP S/4HANA) instead of using IM or a third-party WMS.

In our example, we'll define one shipping point for the plants US01 and CA01. For 3PL's operations (plant US3O), the warehouse has a special area to handle heavy items such as crate motors and full suspension assemblies. Thus, we'll define both a main shipping point (US3O) and a heavy item shipping point (USHI).

Loading points are not applicable for our example company because the US01 and CA01 warehouses are small and because the 3PL operation is a third-party company with its own warehouse management system.

Figure 1.33 shows a graphical representation of the proposed shipping points we'll set up for our sample company and the plants these shipping points will be assigned to.

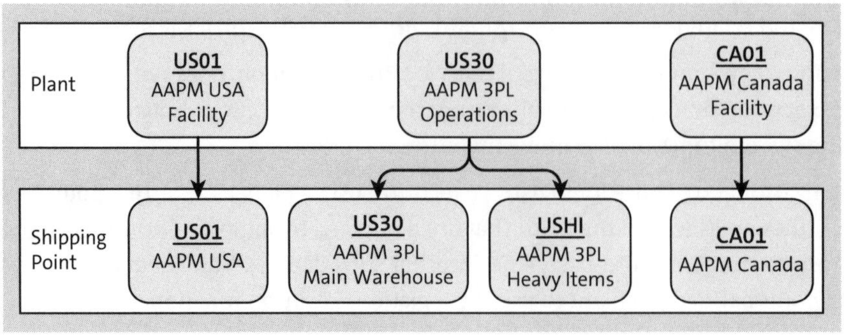

Figure 1.33 Sample Shipping Points

In the following sections, we'll show you how to set up both shipping points and loading points.

1.4.1 Shipping Points

A shipping point is the logistics execution organizational structure element that represents facilities dedicated to shipping and receiving goods from customers. Shipping points are represented in the system by a four-digit code and assigned to the plant under which they perform their duties.

In the following sections, we'll show you how to create and assign shipping points.

Creating Shipping Points

To configure shipping points, follow the menu path **SAP Customizing Implementation Guide • Enterprise Structure • Definition • Logistics Execution • Define, Copy, Delete, Check Shipping Point.** In the dialog box that appears, choose **Define Shipping Point.** On the screen that opens, click on the **New Entries** button or press F5.

Note

This transaction is also available for SAP S/4HANA Cloud under **Create Shipping Point (SPT)** in the self-service configuration user interface (SSCUI).

From our example company, we'll create the following shipping point codes:

- US01: AAPM USA
- CA01: AAPM Canada
- US3O: 3PL Main Warehouse
- USHI: 3PL Heavy Items

Each of these shipping points will be created using the main office address, as shown in Figure 1.34, which shows shipping point **US01**. The process is the same for the other shipping points.

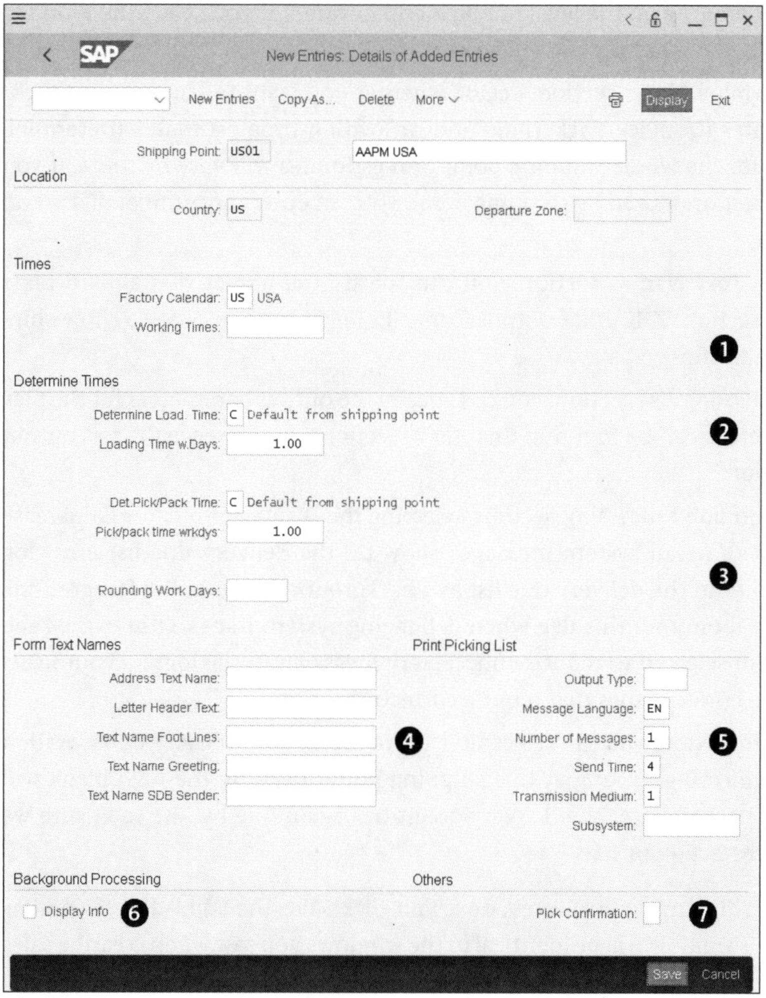

Figure 1.34 Creating New Shipping Points

Let's look more closely at some of the fields in the screen shown in Figure 1.34:

❶ In the **Location** section, the **Country** and **Departure Zones** must be assigned during route determination configuration, which we'll discuss in Chapter 9, Section 9.8. We can't assign these fields now because the transportation zones need to be defined first.

❷ In the **Times** section, specify the **Factory Calendar**, which will dictate work schedules and holidays applicable for this location.

You can also select **Working Times** (work shifts) at the warehouse. This option will allow for scheduling on the level of hours and minutes. If you select the **Working Times** option, the schedule will only use days.

❸ In the **Determine Times** section, decide whether you want to use constant pick/pack estimates (**Det.Pick/Pack Time**) and/or loading time estimates (**Determine Load Time**) for the whole shipping point or if estimates will vary by route. If you want estimates organized by shipping point, you can enter the number of days on this screen.

❹ In the **Form Text Names** section, you can specify the names of standard texts (using Transaction SO10) that output forms (i.e., pick lists) will use to show shipping point-specific messages.

❺ In the **Print Picking List** section, you can specify the output parameters for the pick list. More details can be found in Chapter 4, Section 4.7, where we discuss output determination.

❻ In the **Background Processing** section, selecting the **Display Info** flag will increase the amount of detail system messages show on the delivery due list error log (whether you run the delivery due list as a background job or in the foreground). Usually, you'd only set this flag when debugging system issues. Otherwise, keep this option unselected to reduce unnecessary messages in the logs so your users can focus on critical issues that require corrective action.

❼ In the **Others** section, you can select alternative methods in the **Pick Confirmation** field for confirming picking at this shipping point. Keeping the field blank will require the user to enter the delivery quantities again line by line to ensure we picked the correct quantities.

For every new shipping code entered, once you click **Save**, the **Edit Address** window will pop up. This window will be identical to the windows you saw when creating sales offices and sales organizations. Note that the shipping point address is used to determine taxes and thus must be complete and consistent.

Assigning Shipping Points to Plants

To assign shipping points to plants, follow the menu path **SAP Customizing Implementation Guide • Enterprise Structure • Assignment • Logistics Execution • Assign Shipping Point to Plant • Assign**.

> **Note**
>
> This transaction is also available for SAP S/4HANA Cloud under **Assign Shipping Point (SPT) to Plant (PLT)** in the self-service configuration user interface (SSCUI).

In our example, we'll have one shipping point for US, one for Canada, and two for the 3PL operations. We're using the same code as the plant except for the heavy items shipping point, since we created code USHI for this shipping point.

As shown in Figure 1.35, select the desired plant code and then click the **Assign** button. Then, choose the shipping point you wish to assign and press [Enter].

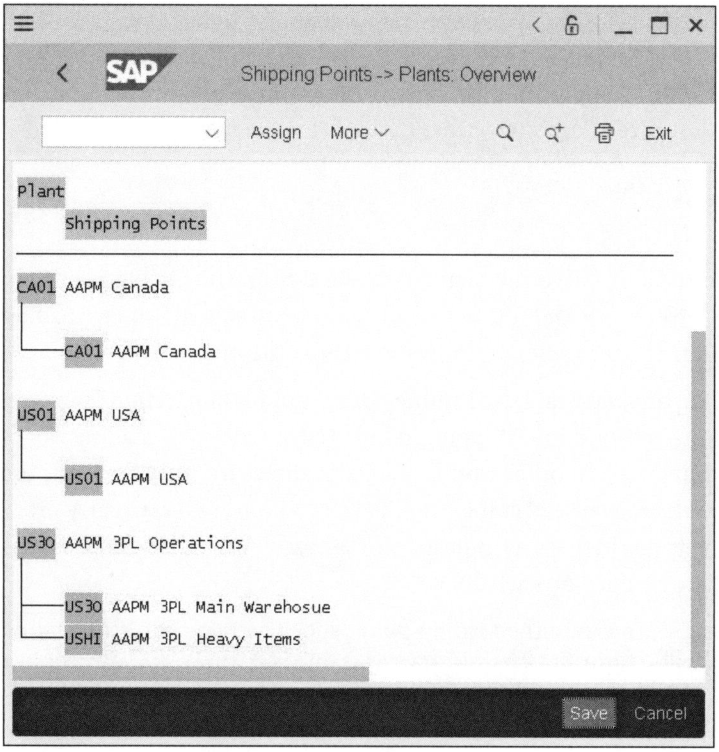

Figure 1.35 Assigning Shipping Points to Plants

1.4.2 Loading Points

Loading points are subdivisions of shipping points and can represent bays/docks at a warehouse.

Loading points are not commonly used since most companies don't need them, but this feature may be relevant if you need to identify specific docks/bays during delivery processing. A user can select the desired loading point in the delivery document header (Transaction VL01N/VL02N), as described in Chapter 9.

> **Note**
>
> You can implement a Business Application Programming Interface (BAPI) enhancement to determine the correct loading point when a delivery document is created. This functionality could be used to direct the picking/packing crew to stage the cargo on a specific dock. This scenario, however, conflicts with the need for flexibility in changing docks once docks are full. More information related to this BAPI can be found in Transaction SPRO by following the menu path **SAP Customizing Implementation Guide • SCM Extended Warehouse Management • Extended Warehouse Management • Business Add-Ins (BAdIs) for Extended Warehouse Management • Cross-Process Settings • Shipping and Receiving • Dock Appointment Scheduling • BAdI: Determination of Loading Point**. Please note this scenario requires coding and is considered an enhancement of workflow, report, interface, conversion, enhancement, and forms (WRICEF).

To configure loading points, follow the menu path **SAP Customizing Implementation Guide • Enterprise Structure • Definition • Logistics Execution • Maintain Loading Point**. On the screen that opens, click on the **New Entries** button or press [F5].

For our example company, we won't use loading points, but for illustration purposes, let's suppose that the heavy items shipping point (**USHI**) has three loading docks (forklift, crane, and manual). In other words, one dock allows for forklift access, the other is equipped with an overhead crane, and the third requires crew to carry products manually to the truck. In this way, our sample company AAPM can monitor how many heavy items are shipped on each dock.

As shown in Figure 1.36, to create the loading point, specify a two-character loading point code (**Loading Point**) and add a description (**Description**). Our example contains loading points that could be created for our sample company.

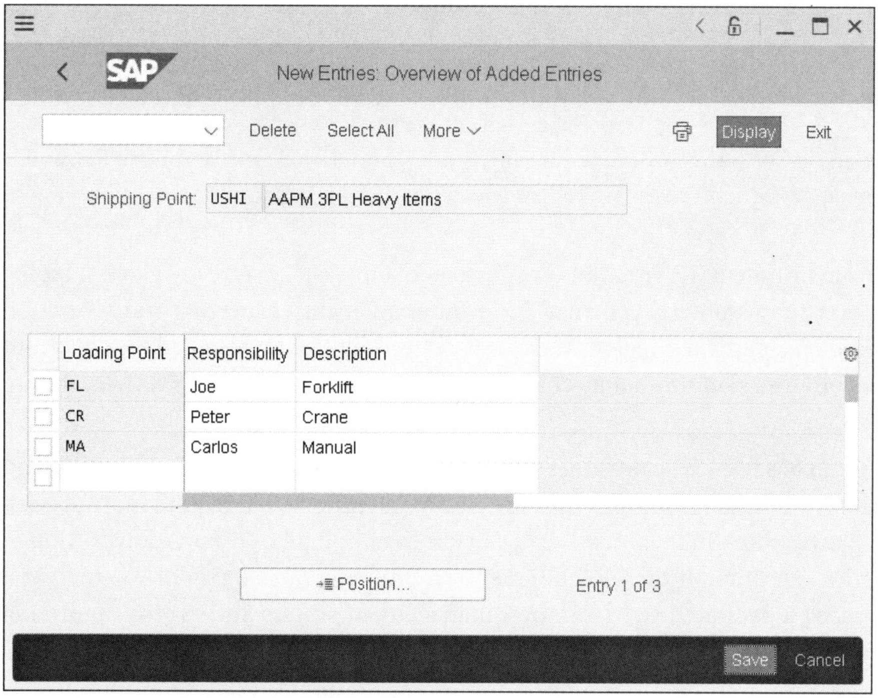

Figure 1.36 Creating New Loading Points

1.5 Transportation Planning Points

Some organizations have specific people responsible for planning, negotiating, hiring, and controlling transportation. In these cases, you can leverage the transportation functionality that's part of logistics execution. A transportation planning point is an organizational structure component that represents the people dedicated to the task of managing transportation.

Companies that hire third-party transportation partners (such as parcel carriers) may not manage transportation themselves. The driving criteria for this decision is usually freight costs.

If freight is a significant cost component, your company could benefit from dedicating resources to negotiating and controlling shipping cost on a shipment-by-shipment basis. In this case, you'll need to define at least one transportation planning point, which will enable you to use shipment documents, which we'll describe in more detail in Chapter 9.

Note

Transportation planning points are only used in shipment documents (as covered in Chapter 9, Section 9.8). Shipping points, on the other hand, are widely used in sales orders and deliveries. They are two different organizational structure elements, and should not be confused.

In an environment with multiple warehouses in different areas of the globe shipping products to customers, you may have different teams managing transportation focused on a particular region. Thus, each team would be represented by a different transportation planning point, which will enable freight negotiations with local companies.

The trend has been for companies to have global contracts with large transportation partners, but some businesses have specific requirements that require more specialized partnerships. In these cases, you can use the minimal transportation portion of logistics execution. If these requirements are more complex/significant, then you may need a dedicated transportation management system such as transportation management in SAP S/4HANA (TM in SAP S/4HANA).

TM in SAP S/4HANA is also a good option for companies that own and operate their own trucks, as owning and managing a fleet involves fulfilling more transportation requirements than using third-party transportation services.

Often, companies with complex transportation requirements may consider a third-party transportation management system, some with out-of-the-box integration with SAP S/4HANA. However, keep in mind that this usually restricts the functionality you can use on SAP S/4HANA and requires coordination and implementation effort. These variables can't be overlooked when selecting a third-party transportation management system.

In some instances, a company doesn't fit the complex requirements model in TM in SAP S/4HANA but still needs to implement shipment documents for consolidation or documentation reasons. Although not recommended due to the added complexity, commonly at least one transportation planning point might be needed.

The transportation planning point is assigned to a company code so that shipping costs can be managed by a different legal entity than the one shipping the goods without necessarily considering this activity an intercompany transaction.

If avoidable, refrain from using shipment documents and creating transportation planning points. Many companies that use SAP S/4HANA don't have complex transportation requirements. Your consultants can explain pros and cons suited to your particular needs and assist on this design decision.

For our example company, we'll create one transportation planning point for each country currently in scope. Each subsidiary will have their own group of people managing transportation for AAPM US (including 3PL operations) and AAPM Canada.

Figure 1.37 shows a graphical representation of proposed transportation planning points for our AAPM sample company and the company codes they will be assigned to.

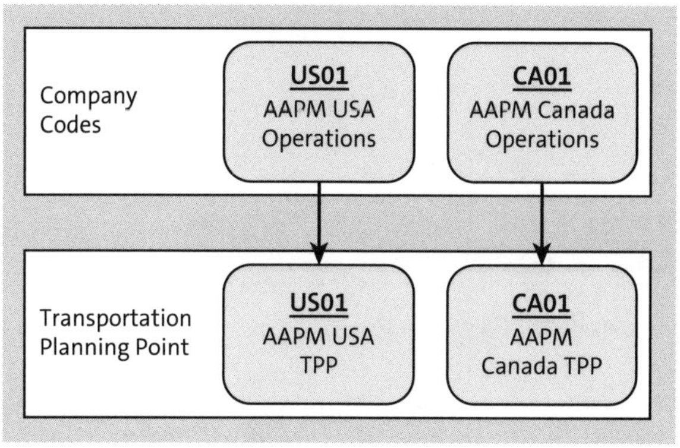

Figure 1.37 Sample Transportation Planning Point

To configure transportation planning points, follow the menu path **SAP Customizing Implementation Guide • Enterprise Structure • Definition • Logistics Execution • Maintain Transportation Planning Point.** On the screen that opens, click on the **New Entries** button or press F5.

For our example, we'll the same code (US01) that we used earlier to create the company code, the sales organization, the plant, and the transportation planning point. In other words, a one-to-one relationship exists between all these elements. Companies with the potential to expand may consider different/more complex naming conventions.

Even though each organizational structure element we mentioned earlier shares the same code in our example, elements can be assigned with completely different office addresses.

As shown in Figure 1.38, specify a four-character transportation planning code (**TPPt**) and enter the company code the transportation planning point belongs (**CoCd**). Our example contains the transportation planning points created for our example company codes.

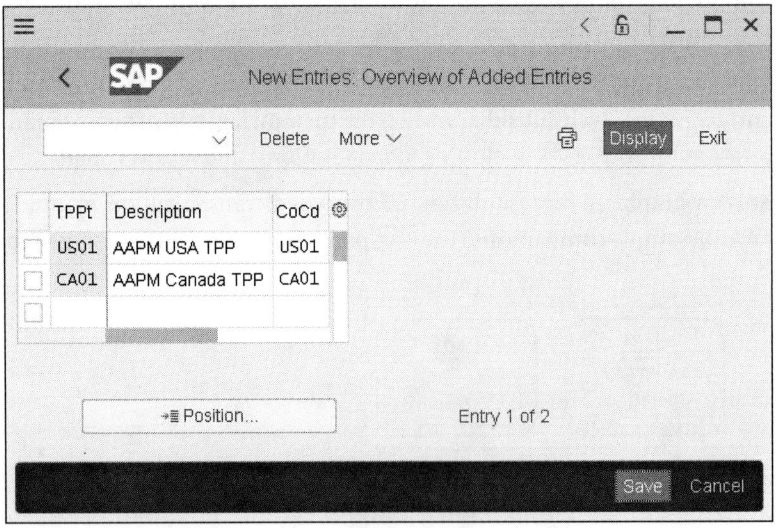

Figure 1.38 Creating New Transportation Planning Points

For every new code entered, the **Edit Address** window will pop up. This window will be identical to the windows you saw earlier when creating sales offices, sales organizations, and shipping points.

1.6 Summary

In this chapter, we defined the sales organizational structure by defining the following sales organization elements: sales organizations, distribution channels, divisions, sales areas, plant assignment, credit control area assignment, sales offices, sales groups, shipping points, loading points, and transportation planning points.

The organizational structure created in this chapter will be the starting point for further functionalities discussed throughout this book. Referring to these elements in every workshop conducted can be valuable. Some elements may motivate breakout sessions. In our sample company, for instance, we'll need breakout sessions to discuss how to assign sales offices and sales groups to customer master data.

In the next chapter, we'll start talking about the master data components of the SAP S/4HANA Sales, starting with business partners (customers).

Chapter 2
Business Partner Master Data

The companies and people that interact with your company are considered business partners. SAP S/4HANA has a centralized master data repository to organize these individuals and organizations, which you'll learn all about in this chapter.

To understand the concept behind business partner master data, think of customers and vendors from the standpoint of a physical location. If we establish a rule where each physical location will be considered a single business partner entry, we can then qualify that location with specific characteristics to make that entity play the role of a customer, a vendor, etc. If we define more than one business partner entry for the same physical location, SAP S/4HANA would consider these entries as data duplication.

Multiple business partner entries can exist at the same physical location. While some of these reasons are valid, most reasons are legacy concepts that are a struggle to move away from when converting data. Your master data consultant must be trusted to provide the information and project leadership required to ensure a clean break from legacy paradigms. However, business partner master data is significantly different in SAP S/4HANA when compared to business partner master data in SAP R/3 and SAP ERP. In this book, we'll outline the key design decisions to help you leverage new functionalities without undue influence from legacy concepts.

If business partner duplication is still required, SAP allows for this data duplication, even though SAP S/4HANA was designed allow little to no duplication of data. SAP S/4HANA even provides the ability to de-duplicate data entries in the future (through data archiving, a complex endeavor that may have undesirable side effects).

Duplication should be avoided because other data elements can be affected, especially customer-specific condition records, customer-material information records, etc., and reports and analysis results would require being combined across different entries. Your order entry team would need to be mindful of choosing the right customer entry. Errors can happen, and the consequences could be significant. The reduction/elimination of business partner duplication is a risk mitigation effort worth enduring.

At the time of data conversion, de-duplication takes place by analyzing source data from the legacy system in an intermediate repository. For example, you can standardize addresses using tools and third-party partner services available in the market. You can automate the identification of duplicates once an address is standardized. Users are often required to review all the data and choose the data to keep. You may need to keep track of legacy customer numbers that were combined for the conversion of other data elements and for day-to-day operations during the stabilization period.

With a de-duplicated list of business partners, you can start classifying and qualifying business partners based on the roles/functions they perform during business transactions with your company.

In this chapter, we'll cover the following topics:

- The basic business partner master data necessary to identify the type of partner we're maintaining
- The portion of business partner master data that is unique and relevant regardless of which organizational unit is transacting with the business partner
- The portion of business partner master data that represents how each sales organizational unit (sales areas) classifies the business partner
- The customer hierarchy feature for combining multiple business partners in a hierarchical fashion to represent larger conglomerates

2.1 Creating New Business Partners

In the following sections, we'll show you how to create a new business partner in SAP S/4HANA. First, we'll provide a quick overview of the business partner creation process in both the SAP GUI and SAP Fiori, without going into detail about the fields you'll fill in (which we'll cover in detail in Section 2.2). Next, we'll look at the three main attributes of a business partner record: the business partner number, the business partner role, and the business partner groupings.

2.1.1 Business Partner Creation Overview

To create new business partners, open Transaction BP and follow the menu path **More • Business Partner • Create • Organization**. On the screen shown in Figure 2.1, enter information about your new business partner.

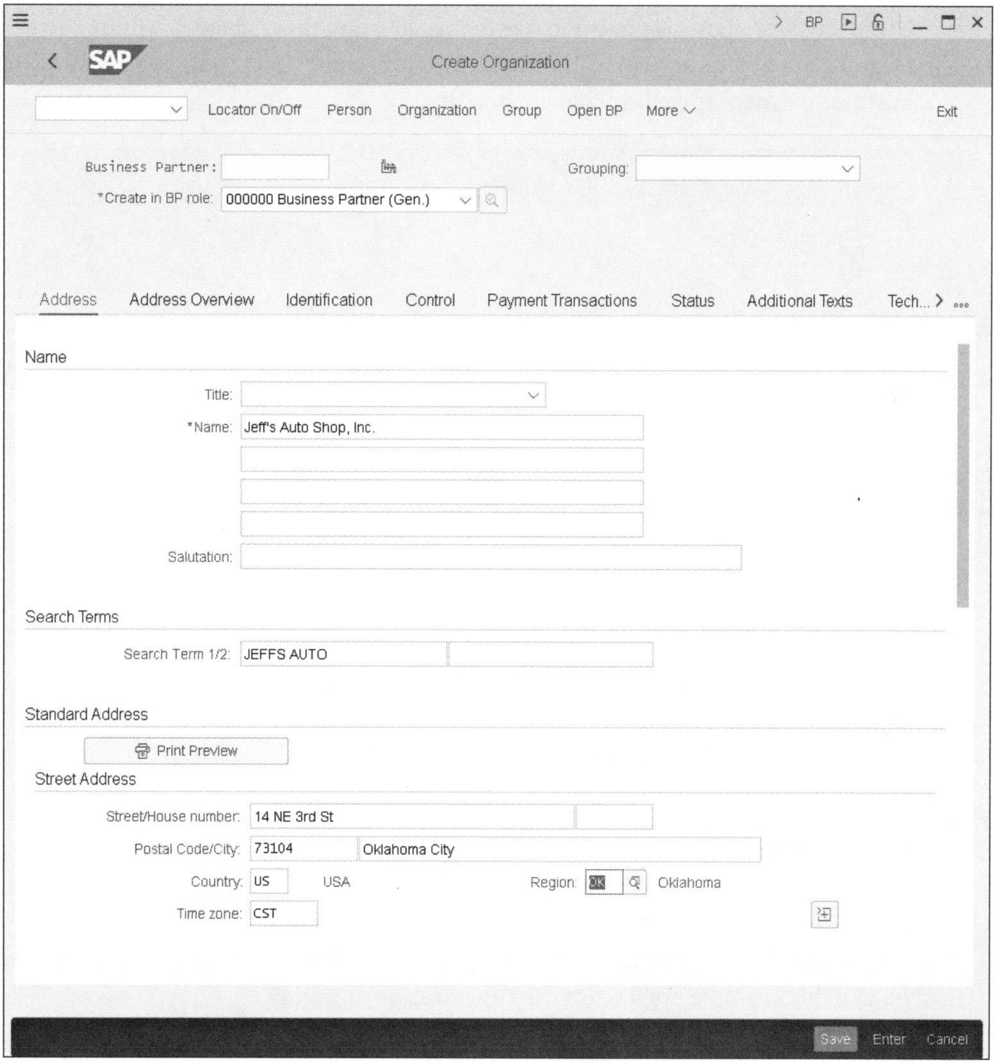

Figure 2.1 Entering a New Partner Organization in Transaction BP

In this book, we'll focus on the master data fields that are applicable to and affect sales-related functionalities. These fields are divided into several major groups organized under tabs and in sections for ease of reference. Each implementation project will require attention to different portions of this screen, so not all the information we'll cover in this chapter may be applicable.

Using SAP Fiori, business partners are managed using the Manage Business Partner Master Data app, as shown in Figure 2.2. This app allows you to search for existing business partners as well as to create new ones.

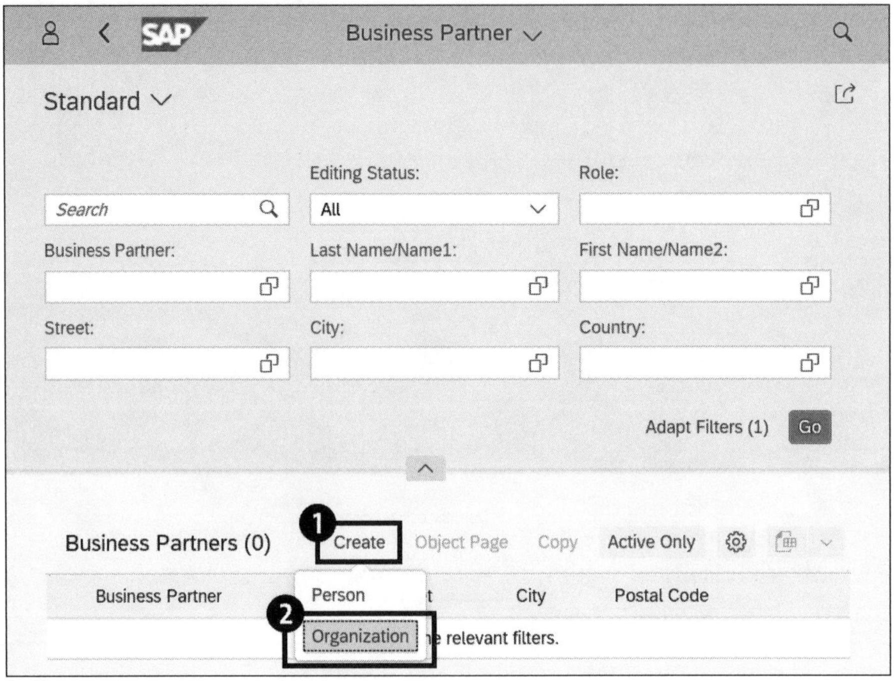

Figure 2.2 Managing Business Partner Master Data

As shown in Figure 2.2, the **Create** option ❶ allows you to create new business partners in SAP Fiori. You'll need to decide if the new partner is a **Person** or an **Organization**. In this example, we'll select the **Organization** option ❷.

The Manage Business Partner Master Data app will then open up a window where you'll enter the main business partner attributes and address information, as shown in Figure 2.3.

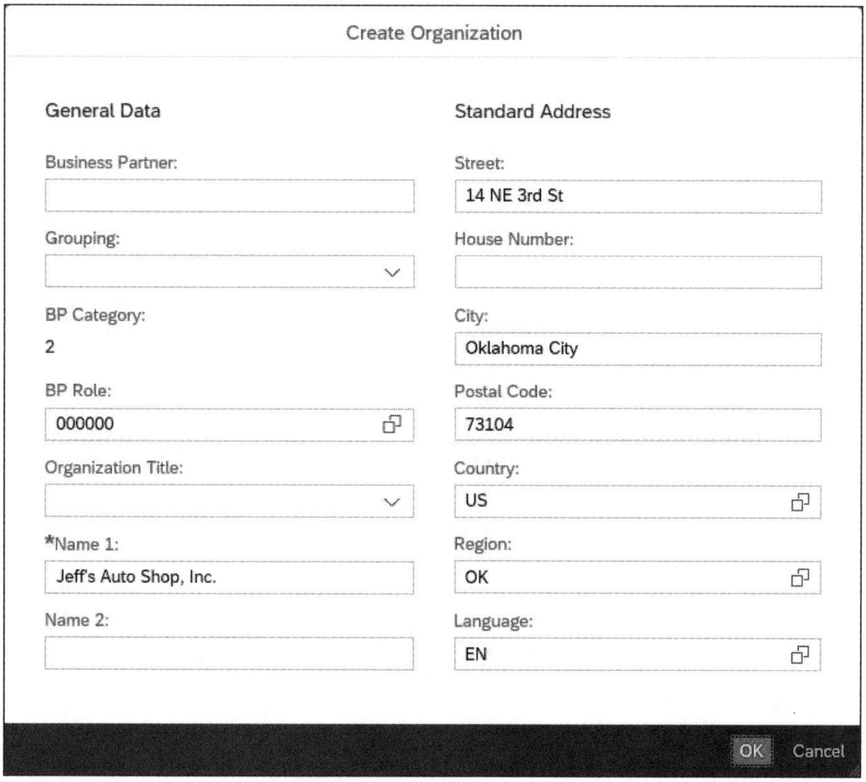

Figure 2.3 Create Organization Popup Window in SAP Fiori

Once you've populated the main business partner attributes and clicked **OK**, your business partner will be created. This app will also allow you to maintain other master data in a web-friendly layout, as shown in Figure 2.4.

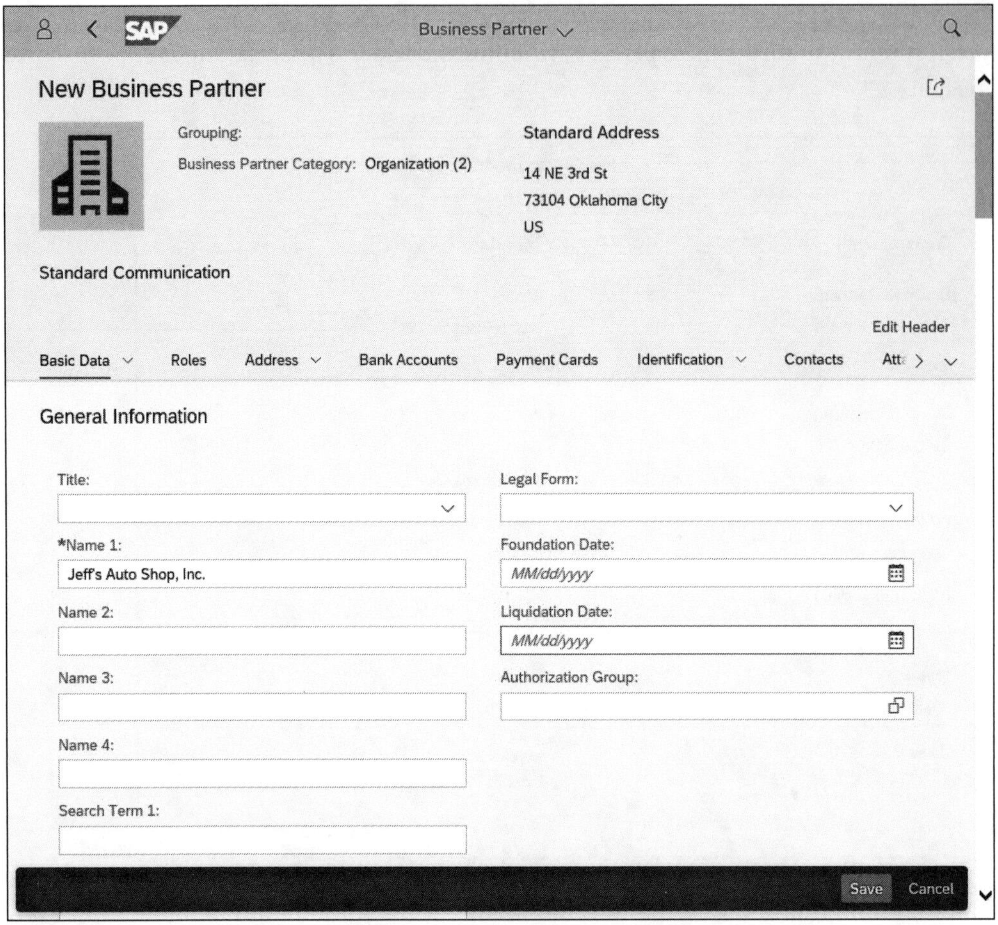

Figure 2.4 SAP Fiori Business Partner Master Data Screen

2.1.2 Main Business Partner Attributes

The three main fields in business partner master data are the **Business Partner** number, the **Grouping**, and the **Create in BP role/BP Role** fields (the label will depend on whether you're using SAP Fiori or the SAP GUI). Figure 2.5 shows these fields in both the SAP GUI ❶ and in SAP Fiori ❷.

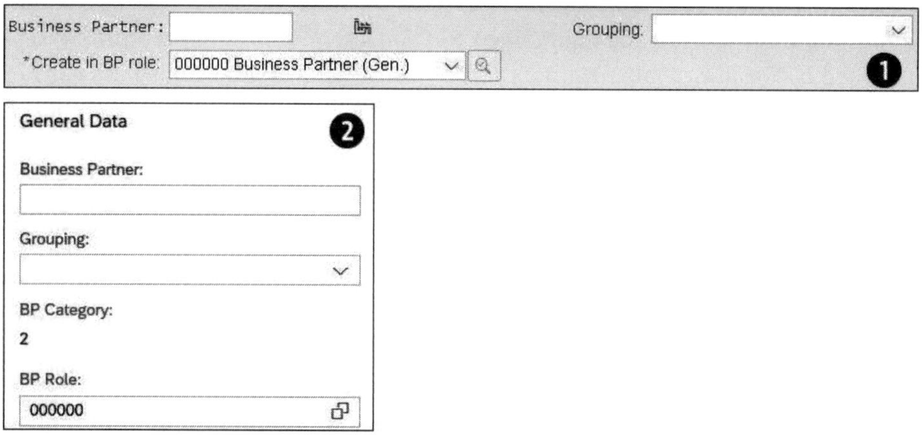

Figure 2.5 Main Business Partner Attributes (SAP GUI and SAP Fiori)

The **Business Partner** number only needs to be maintained if you're using external number ranges. Generally, companies use internal number ranges for most business partner master data entries, which we strongly recommend. If using internal number ranges, this field must be left blank when creating new business partners.

The **Grouping** controls which business partner roles are applicable and the number range settings. The business partner group allows you to define common characteristics applicable certain types of business partners.

The **BP Role** describes whether a business partner is a customer or a vendor.

We'll describe each of these fields in the following sections.

Business Partner Role

The specific set of attributes that transform a given business partner into a customer or a vendor in the system is called a business partner role (**BP Role** in the system). A business partner role is a key component of business partner master data. Not only is business partner role an attribute of the business partner but also a way to group relevant fields that are applicable for a certain purpose.

In the following sections, we'll look at the roles already provided by SAP and then move on to defining our own business partner roles and their categories.

Predefined Roles

Figure 2.6 shows how data is stored and how the business partner roles control what information can be seen and maintained. SAP S/4HANA has a single repository (represented by the gray oval in Figure 2.6) that will store all possible business partner data. Depending on the business partner role, certain repository fields will be considered relevant, hidden, mandatory, etc.

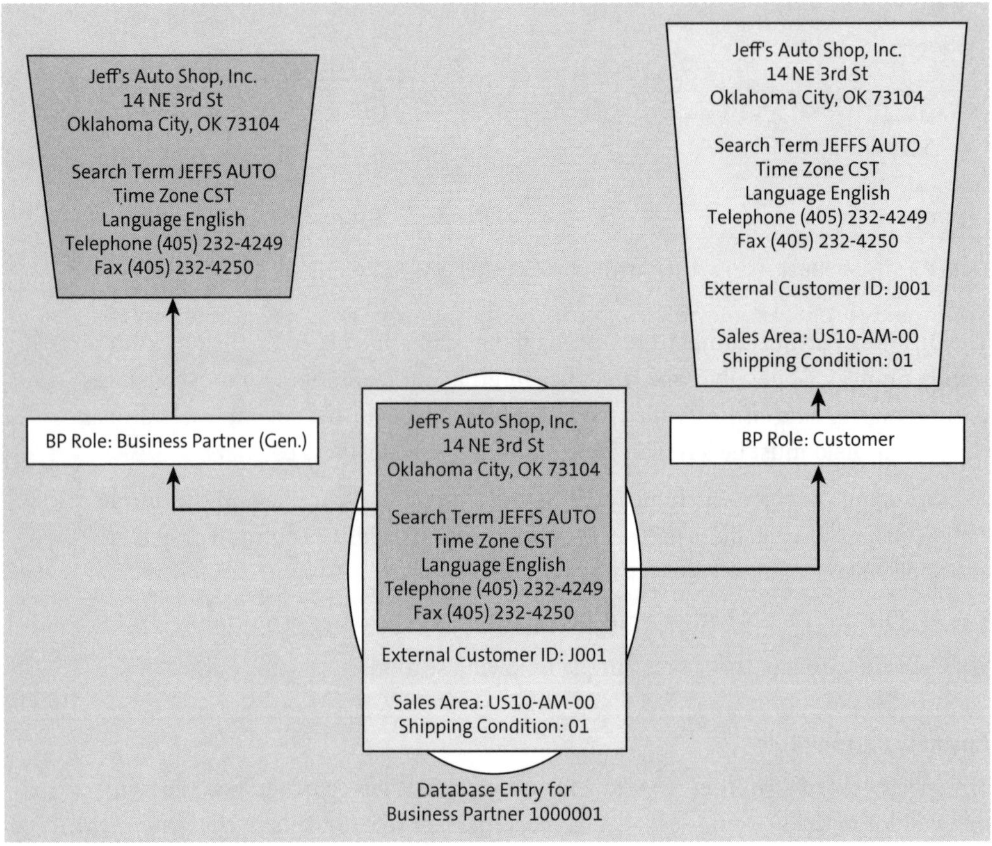

Figure 2.6 Business Partner Role Concept

The following business partner roles are provided by SAP out of the box:

- **Business partner (general)**
  The default business partner role assigned whenever you create any new business partner entry.

- **Service performer**
  Partner that performs services on your company's behalf.
- **Freelancer**
  Partner that is not an employee but performs similar functions on a part-time or full-time basis as a contractor.
- **Contact person**
  Partner that works for a different company but is someone you have (or want to have) direct contact with.
- **Employee**
  Company employees.
- **Customer (financial accounting)**
  Customers that can perform the function of a sold-to customer, a payer, and/or a bill-to customer.
- **Customer**
  Customers that can perform the function of a ship-to customer and/or other nonfinancial functions.
- **Supplier (financial accounting)**
  Vendors that will receive payments from your company.
- **Supplier**
  Vendors that will ship goods, provide services, or perform any other nonfinancial activity with your company.
- **Financial services business partner**
  Partners that do not transact directly with your company's commercial/supply chain departments (sales and/or procurement) but are required to fulfill financial functions.
- **Customs office**
  Government agencies responsible for import/export compliance inspection, certification, and control.
- **Bank**
  Financial institutions.
- **Collections management**
  Partner that performs collection services.
- **Credit management**
  Partner's credit profile information.

To transform a business partner entry into a customer, you would add the customer business partner role. If that business partner entry also acts as a vendor, you would add the vendor business partner role.

Needing to maintain more than one business partner role on a business partner occurs often. Once a field is maintained for a given business role, this field will be available for others. In other words, information for that field won't need to be entered multiple times, but you may still need to maintain multiple business partner roles if the applicable fields for each business partner role vary a great deal.

You can assign business partner roles to specific user profiles to restrict access, which is a main reason for defining business partner roles. For instance, the SAP Credit Management business partner role is usually restricted to the credit department only. Thus, the credit master data tabs and fields are only part of this business partner role. Conceptually, credit data could be assigned to the customer (financial accounting) business partner role since customers that pay bills usually require credit information. However, these fields are segregated into their own business partner role so that access restrictions can be implemented.

In previous versions of SAP, customer master entries were controlled using the *account group* as the major key field. In these versions, you had different *account groups* for sold-to customers, ship-to customers, payers, etc. While replicating this concept in newer versions may be tempting, account groups and business partner roles are not the same. Account groups still exist as an attribute of business partner master data. The business partner role is a function-oriented attribute of customer master data. Therefore, assigning the right business partner should come first, before you start adding various business partner role-based master data sets to it.

Defining Business Partner Roles

To configure business partner roles, follow the menu path **SAP Customizing Implementation Guide • Cross-Application Components • SAP Business Partner • Business Partner • Basic Settings • Business Partner Roles • Define BP Roles.** On the screen that opens, click on the **New Entries** button or press F5.

Figure 2.7 shows a typical new business partner role that may need to be created for customers that order online. Companies often decide to have different master data requirements for customers that only make orders via the web. This type of customer only pays via payment cards, so they usually don't require the complex master data set up for other types of customers.

On this screen, specify a six-character business partner role code (**BP Role**); we advise following the SAP customer namespace and using either "Z" or "Y" as the first character. You should not have an extensive list of business partner roles, so the naming convention for the remaining characters don't need to be strict.

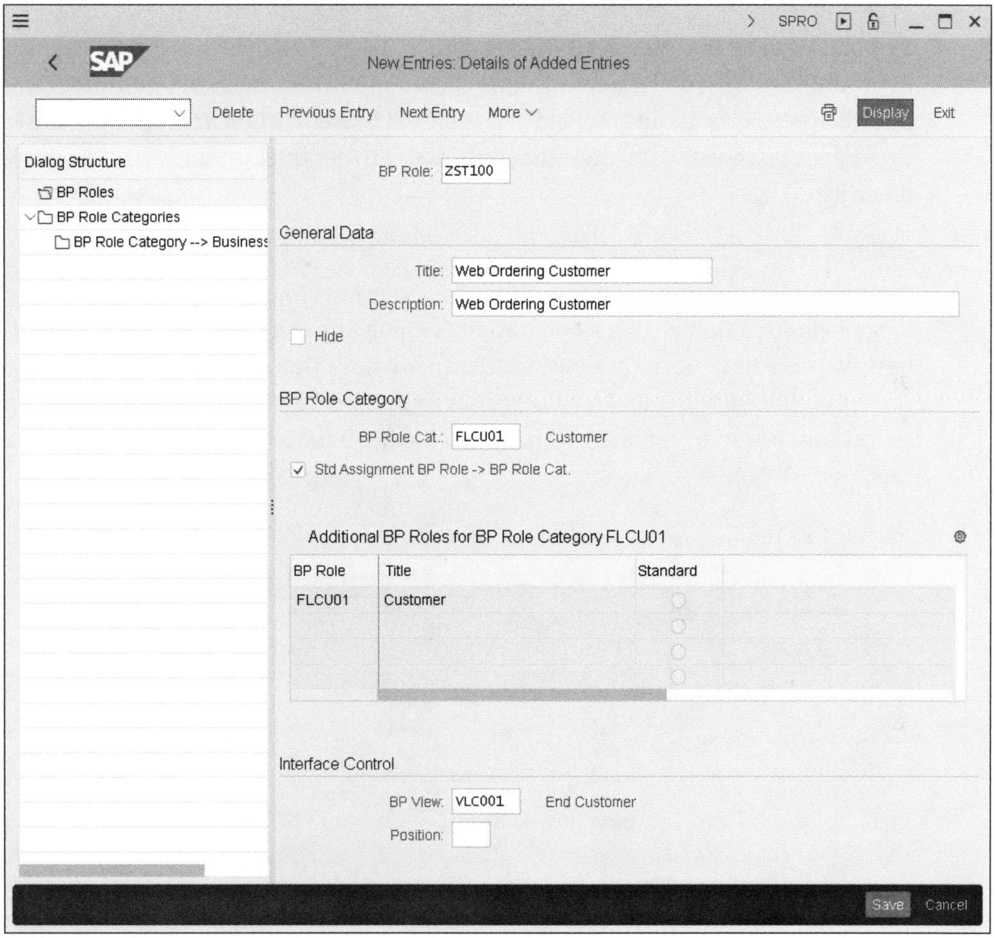

Figure 2.7 Defining New Business Partner Roles

You must also define a short name (**Title**) and a longer description (**Description**) for any new business partner role.

In the **BP Role Category** section, you'll classify the type of partner expected to use this new business partner role. In this case, we're defining a new business partner role for customers (FLCU01). We'll cover this business partner role in more detail in the next section.

In the **BP View** field, indicate the screen sequence and master data requirements for this business partner role. In this example, the web customer will be considered a consumer and will use the corresponding standard **BP View**.

You may want to control the **Position** in which this business partner role will appear in the dropdown list when creating new customers with Transaction BP. In our example, we won't worry about this field. But this field is useful when fine-tuning the user experience by showing the most used business partner roles on the top of the dropdown list.

Defining Business Partner Role Categories

To configure business partner role categories, follow the menu path **SAP Customizing Implementation Guide • Cross-Application Components • SAP Business Partner • Business Partner • Basic Settings • Business Partner Roles • Define BP Roles.** Once on the screen, double-click the **BP Role Categories** option in the **Dialog Structure** menu on the left, as shown in Figure 2.8. In this example, we'll focus on business partner role category VLC001.

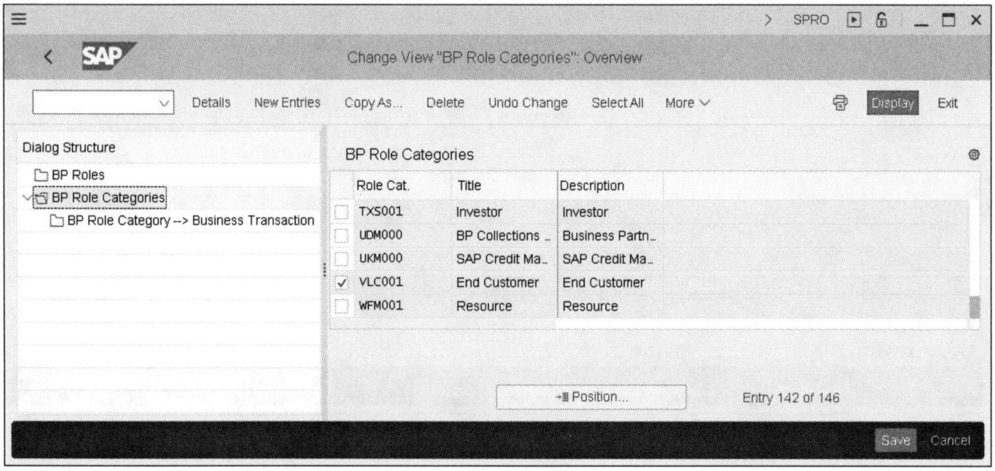

Figure 2.8 Business Partner Role Categories

Once you find the business partner role category you want to maintain, select it and then double-click **BP Role Category** and then on the **Business Transaction** option in the **Dialog Structure** menu on the left. We're going to use business partner role category VLC001, as shown in Figure 2.9.

On this screen, you can also modify the standard behavior by adding new entries by clicking on the **New Entries** button or by pressing F5. Select the business transaction you want to modify and then select the desired **Modf. Indicator** (modification indicator), as shown in Figure 2.9.

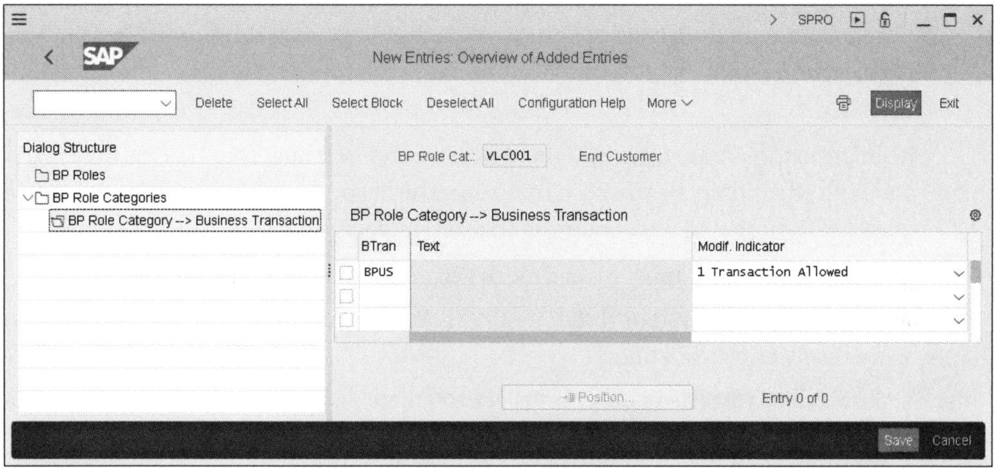

Figure 2.9 Sample Assignment of a Business Transaction to Business Partner Role Category

Business Partner Number, Grouping, and Number Ranges

A business partner number is a unique identifier in SAP S/4HANA that represents a business partner entity for all intents and purposes. The number can be up to 10 alphanumeric characters (letters and numbers) long. A business partner number may be assigned automatically by the system (from an internal number range) or manually entered by the user (from an external number range).

In this section, we'll focus our discussion on customers as business partners, since this book is about sales. Our discussion does take into account the fact that vendors are also business partners, but when we say, "business partner," we're referring specifically to customers. Thus, master data maintenance will specifically apply to business partners that purchase/receive goods and services from your organization.

Let's start by reviewing with some key considerations when designing your number ranges. Then, we'll go into detail about the technical steps for setting up number range intervals and statuses.

Number Range Considerations

External number ranges are recommended for special types of customers, such as one-time and intercompany customers, since you'll have only a few of those. For these business partners, number ranges should have a mnemonic value for them rather than be concerned with the data volume and ease of maintenance.

We do not recommend using this external number range for your regular customers and vendors when your business partner are maintained directly in SAP S/4HANA. Doing so adds an unnecessary layer of complexity and risk because future business partner numbers assigned from this number range would have to be entered manually.

Regular customers are usually defined with a numeric value. You'll decide how many and with what intervals when defining an external or internal number range. Some questions you should answer during this design decision include the following:

- How many entries must we be able to accommodate?
- Do we want the system to define the numbers automatically or do we want to manually enter the values?
- How many customers do you expect to create as business partner master data entries?
- For how many years must the number range interval last?
- Do you need to reserve intervals for future usage due to reasons unknown at this time?
- Should customer numbers be meaningful or not?

Previous versions of SAP and other systems have traditionally assigned meaning to customer numbers. Some reports may break down a customer number to extract classification information.

SAP S/4HANA has a unified repository for sold-to customer, ship-to customers, vendors, employees, competitors, bidders, etc. Any given business partner can transition from one type to the other. For example, a vendor may become a customer, a ship-to customer may become a sold-to customer, and a sold-to address may be used as a ship-to address. An employee may purchase products (thus becoming a customer), an employee may serve as a delivery address for products shipped to customers, and more.

Assigning meaning to your customer number might lead to duplication in master data entries, which should be avoided, as mentioned at the start of this chapter. In our earlier examples, you could end up with sold-to customer, ship-to customer, vendor, and employee entries for the same person or company, a situation common in master data in previous versions of SAP and other systems.

In SAP S/4HANA, we recommend removing all meaning from business partner numbers, the most impactful decision a company can make to avoid de-duplication and ensure consistency in business partner master data. In implementation projects, avoiding meaningful number ranges can be challenging since people find it difficult to believe something so basic to the current understanding of their data can be completely eliminated. One fear is that you would lose reporting capability.

Master data consultant must explain the new and expanded options for storing customer classification information among standard fields, reserved fields, and custom fields. Using these fields to store criteria previously assigned to a customer number itself intuitively seems more complex. You must accept that the price of the perceived "simplicity" is master data quality (resulting in duplication), and once customer records are in the system, going back will be impossible.

Business partner number ranges are controlled by the **Business Partner Group** or the **BP Group** field, not to be confused with **Business Partner Role Group** or **Business Partner Role Category Group**. Note that these latter fields are not covered in this book.

The standard business partner groups SAP provides reference the number ranges they represent. While considering these standard business partner groups as substitutes for account groups (used in previous versions to determine the number range), in SAP S/4HANA, the business partner group no longer carries significance as to which functions the business partner may perform. Therefore, configuring new business partner groups for sold-to customers, ship-to customers, payers, etc., as previously for account groups, is not conceptually accurate.

The definition of business partner groups must be focused on the number range they represent. Then, you can assign system user roles and profiles to specific business partner groups. You can also hide some groups altogether via configuration, which allows you to use different number ranges for groups of users rather than according to business partner function, as mentioned earlier, a significant paradigm shift from former versions of SAP ERP solutions.

Table 2.1 shows some standard out-of-the box business partner groups and their assigned number ranges.

BP Group	Short Name	Lower Limit	Upper Limit	Internal or External	Default Internal	Default External
BP01	Ext. Numeric Lo	0000000001	0000999999	External		
BP02	Int. Numeric	0001000000	0009999999	Internal	X	
BP03	Ext. Numeric Hi	0010000000	0999999999	External		
BP04	Ext. AlphaNum	0A	8Z	External		
BPAB	Ext. Alpha	A	ZZZZZZZZZZ	External		X
BPEE	Int. Numeric EE	9980000000	9999999999	Internal		
CPD2	CPD Sample Data	0A	8Z	External		
CPDA	CPD Ext.Alph.	A	ZZZZZZZZZZ	External		
CPDN	CPD Int.Num.	0001000000	0009999999	Internal		
CPDS	CPD Ext.Num. Hi	0010000000	0999999999	External		

Table 2.1 Business Partner Group Number Range Assignment

The business partner groups flagged as default will be used by default if a user leaves the **Business Partner Group** field blank when entering a new customer master record. If a user also leaves the **Business Partner Number** field blank, the default internal business partner group will be used (**BP02**). If a user enters a business partner number but leaves the **Business Partner Group** blank, the default external business partner group will be used (**BPAB**).

The standard out-of-the-box business partner groups and number ranges consume around 10% of the available customer numbers. The remaining 90% are available for you to use to create new types of partners in the future.

Figure 2.10 graphically shows the business partner numbers you can create on each interval and how much of a range is still available for you to use. Let's say that you win approximately 1,000 new customers per week in a particular business partner group: The shortest interval (number range 01) would still give you 20 years' worth of entries.

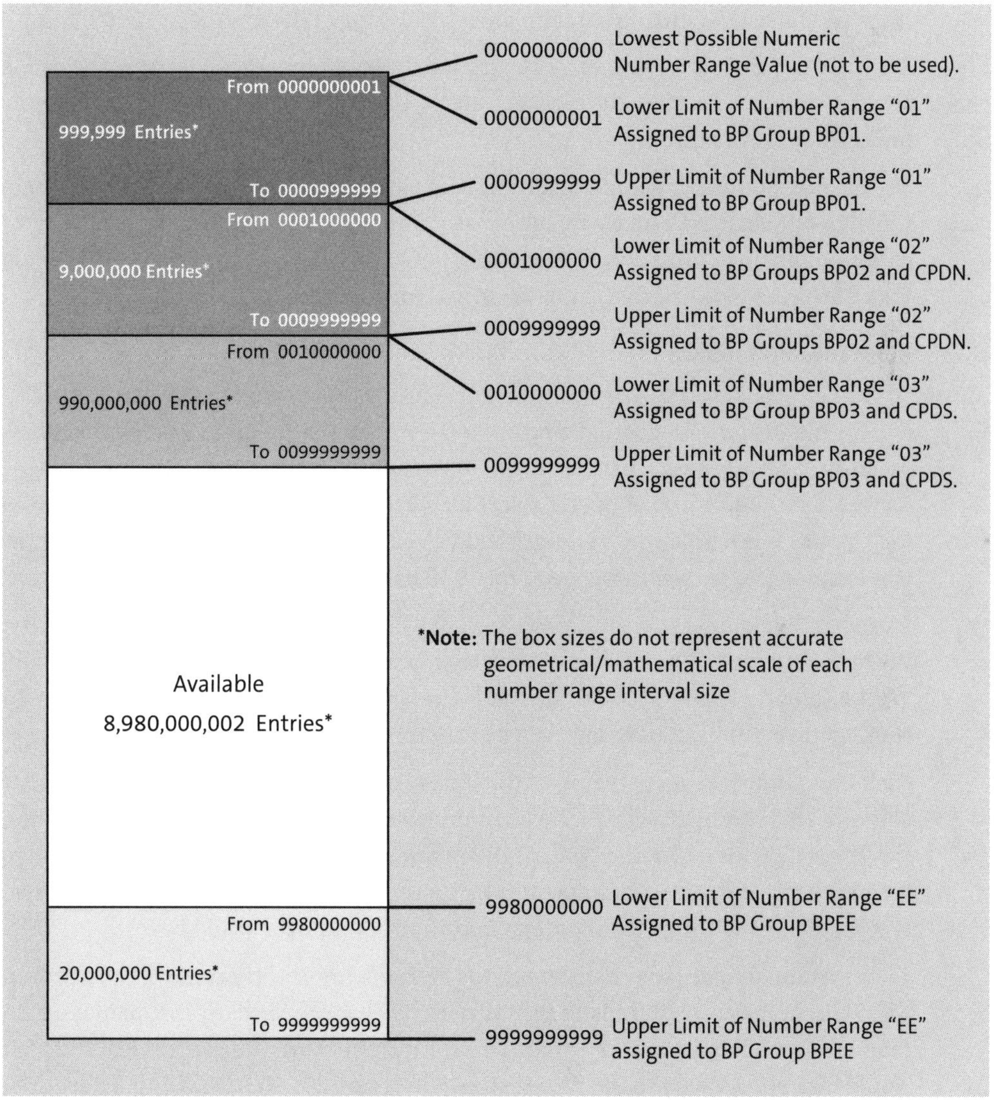

Figure 2.10 Out-of-the-Box Numeric Number Range Intervals and Business Partner Groups

Another important consideration with standard number range intervals is that different types of master data entries and transactions are reserved different ranges. Several key fields are 10 characters in length, such as sales orders (0000000000), delivery documents (0080000000), billing documents (0090000000), and inventory movements (4100000000). The system will function properly if overlap exists on these ranges across functionalities; the distinction is really to help you identify the type of master data or transaction just by looking at the number.

For instance, when a customer calls with a delivery number, you'll know the call is about a delivery because the number starts with 8. Customers would not notice unless they also use SAP solutions.

Segregating numbers by functionality still has merits, but the business partner functionality has changed, and we no longer recommend using number ranges to segregate components of this specific functionality because of the way business partners may transition between roles or have several roles at once.

Number Range Intervals

To configure business partner number range intervals, open Transaction BUCF or follow the menu path **SAP Customizing Implementation Guide • Cross-Application Components • SAP Business Partner • Business Partner • Basic Settings • Define Number Ranges**. On the screen that opens, select **Intervals** and then click **Insert Line** or press [F6]. A new line with a white background will be created at the top of this screen. In this example, we're creating a new interval to be used for web customers.

As shown in Figure 2.11, we entered the code "ZZ" in the **No** field for the new entry. We're using code "ZZ" for our new entry to stay within the SAP customer namespace. We'll also enter "9960000000" in the **From No.** field and "9969999999" in the **To Number** field. Our number range will be easy to spot, beginning with "996."

Note that number ranges are not automatically transported because of the **NR Status** column. This column contains the last number used within a number range. When creating a new customer, the system will increment this number and attempt to save the new entry. If an entry for the same value already exists in the system, a severe system failure (short dump) would occur, and all your new data would be lost.

Each system should have a different **NR Status** because otherwise a short dump would occur if you try to transfer the number range. Instead, many companies opt to manually set up new number ranges on each system using Transaction BUCF, which would take you directly to the screen shown in Figure 2.11. Note that you'll need special access to perform this action, including the ability to open the destination client for configuration, a task that can only be performed with SAP Basis/system administration access.

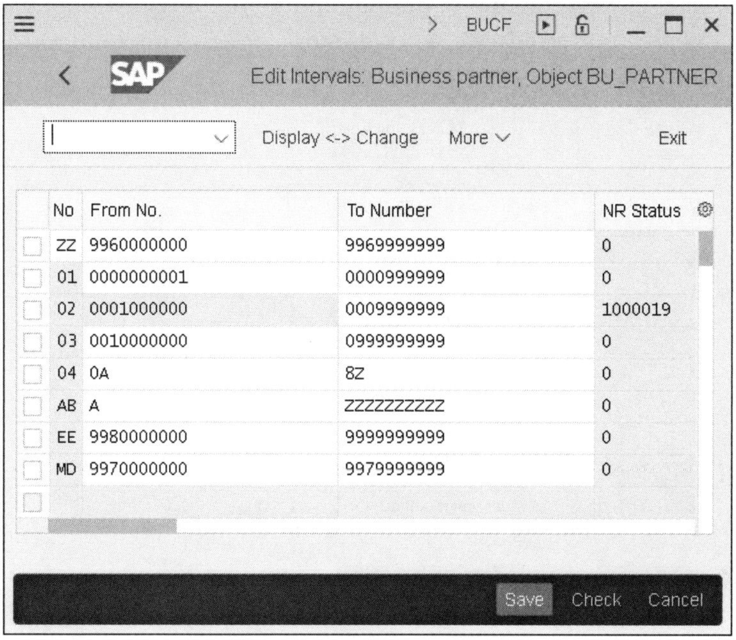

Figure 2.11 Business Partner Number Range Intervals

The system will notify you of this situation with a warning message, as shown in Figure 2.12.

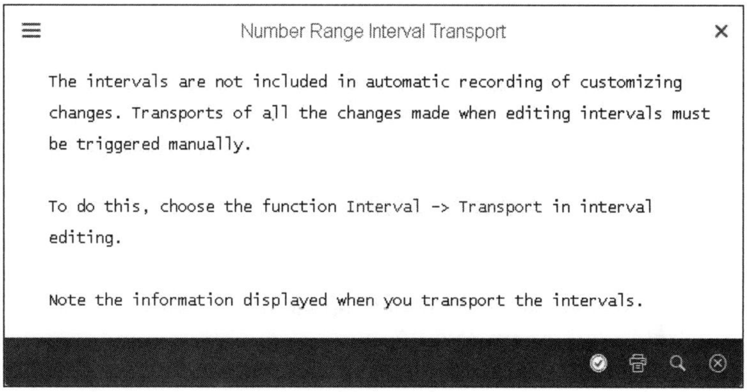

Figure 2.12 Number Range Transport Warning

You can manually add number range entries to a transport request and move the number range. Simply select the checkbox next to the number range you want to transport and then select **More • Interval • Transport**, as shown in Figure 2.13.

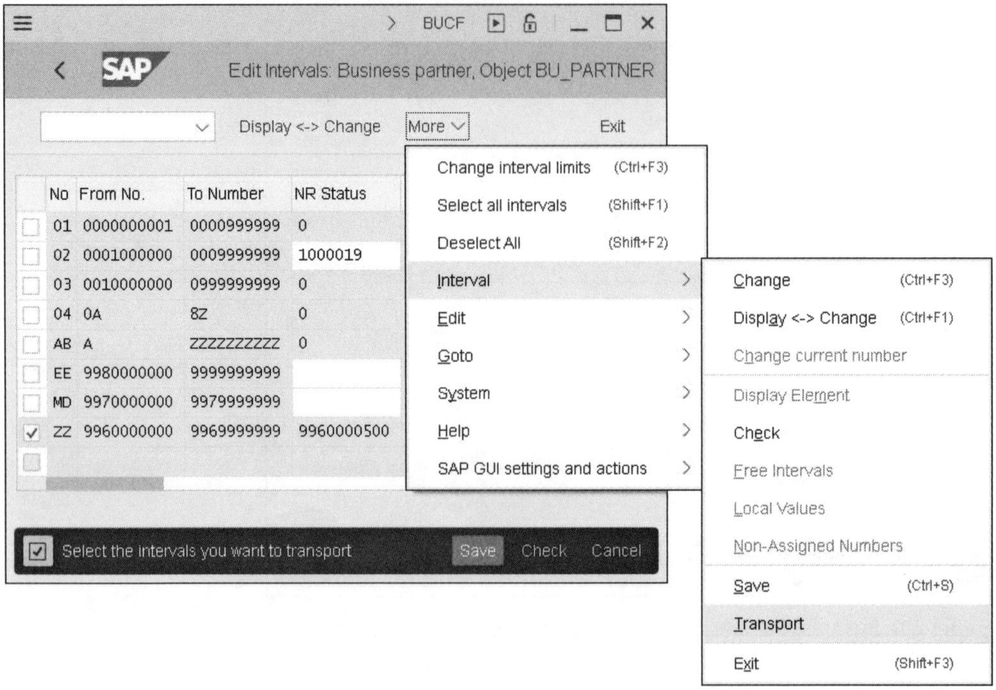

Figure 2.13 Manual Transport of Business Partner Number Ranges

> **Warning!**
> If this transport request is ever reimported to a destination system, a short dump will occur. In this case, you can use Transaction BUCF to update the **NR Status** to the latest value found, which will resolve the short dump. See the next section for how to do this.

You can also use Transaction SNUM or Transaction SNRO to maintain number ranges. But first, you'll need to know the **Number Range Object**. For **Business Partner Number Ranges**, the object is **BU_PARTNER** (central business partner).

Number Range Status

To configure business partner number range statuses, open Transaction BUCF or follow the menu path **SAP Customizing Implementation Guide • Cross-Application Components • SAP Business Partner • Business Partner • Basic Settings • Define Number Ranges • NR Status**.

In the example shown earlier in Figure 2.11, we skipped the first 500 numbers in the new number range just for illustration by entering the value "9960000500" in the **NR Status** column, as shown in Figure 2.14.

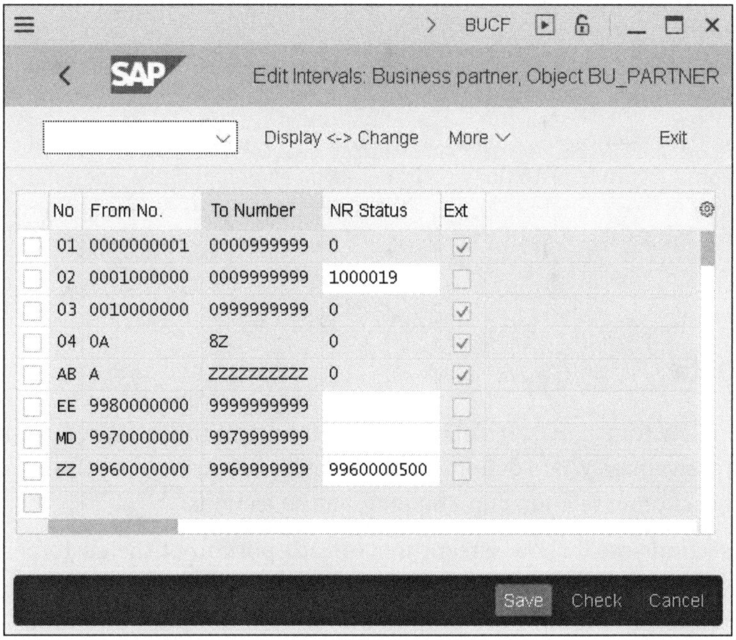

Figure 2.14 Changing the NR Status

One-Time Customers

Companies that deal directly with customers may end up with a vast amount of customer master entries if each customer is maintained as a business partner. Customer information is important for reports and market analysis, and no functionality can replace the ability to access this information.

However, if a consumer is not expected to become a repeat customer, managing their information via individual customer master entries is counterproductive. Instead, you can store their information at the transaction level instead of as master data. SAP S/4HANA refers to this functionality as a *one-time customer*. This data can still be used on reports and analytical tools, but only in the context of a transaction. For example, when looking at sales orders, deliveries, and billing documents, you would see all customer information, but when looking at a list of your company's customers, these entries would not appear.

To make use of this functionality, you must create a shell customer master entry using one of the business partner groups that begin with "CPD." Different types of one-time customers provided out of the box.

Once a user adds a shell customer number on a sales order, that user will also be required to enter other customer information, such as a name, address, etc. This data is saved and linked to the sales order. Once the order is processed, this link is copied to the other documents down the stream.

Many companies use one-time customers as ship-to addresses, which is natural when delivering products to a customer's customer (drop shipping). But a one-time customer could also be used as sold-to address, bill-to address, and even a payer. This approach is not commonly used due to concerns with credit and collections.

2.2 General Data

The general data in customer master data is mostly intuitive and is shared with finance (account receivables). When defining general data, you must ensure the data supports ordering, customer relationship, shipping, and collections.

In the following sections, we'll show screenshots of each portion of the customer master general data and refer to common questions raised by companies implementing SAP S/4HANA.

2.2.1 Address

As shown in Figure 2.15, four 40-character fields are used to store a customer's name (**Name**). The **Address** tab is rather extensive, so we'll go through multiple screenshots of the same screen. You can navigate from one portion of the tab to the other simply by scrolling down.

Search terms are portions of a customer's name that a user might intuitively search for. You can enter up to two search terms in the **Search Term 1/2** fields. You can also flag a customer as an **Undesirable Customer** and include a rationale classification code (**Reason Undes.**) and a comment (**Comment**) to justify this categorization.

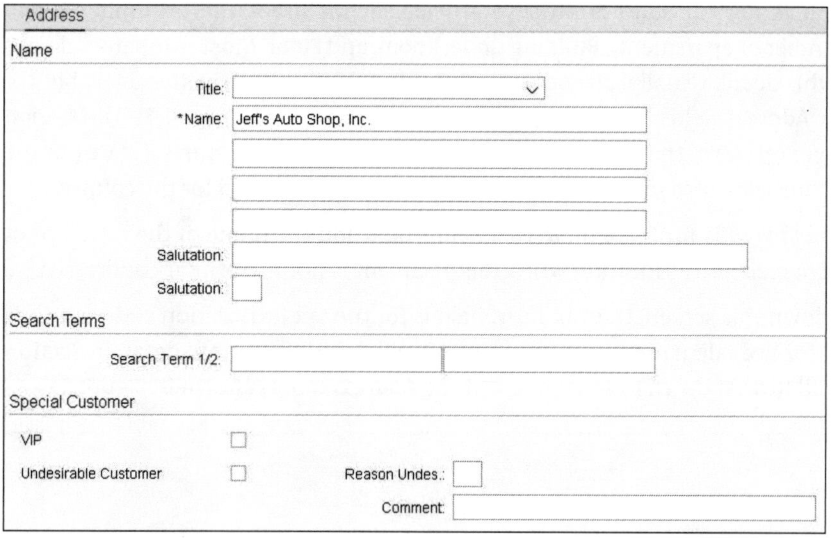

Figure 2.15 Business Partner Name Fields

Scroll down and you'll see the rest of the **Address** tab, as shown in Figure 2.16.

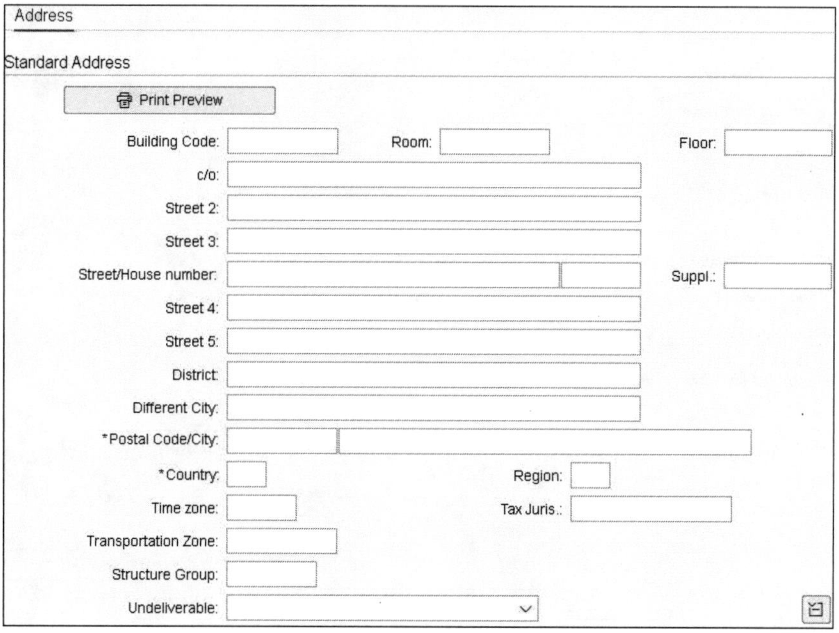

Figure 2.16 Business Partner Address Fields (1/2)

You can break down an address into several fields, such as **Street/House number**, **Suppl.** (suite number or apartment), **Building Code**, **Room**, and **Floor**. Most companies do not need all this detail. Usually, all address information is stored in the five available 40-character **Address** fields (**Street**, **Street 2**, **Street 3**, **Street 4**, and **Street 5**). The **Region** field is a generic term that can be used as a label for the field that stores a state (for the United States) or a province (for Canada). **District** is the label used for the county.

The **c/o** field stands for "care of. In this field, you'll add the name of the recipient of mail and parcels at this location when that recipient is not the primary addressee.

Further down this screen, the **Tax Juris.** field is for the tax jurisdiction code, which is the used for tax calculation purposes, which we'll describe in more detail in Section 2.2.9. Scroll further down to see the rest of the **Address** tab, as shown in Figure 2.17.

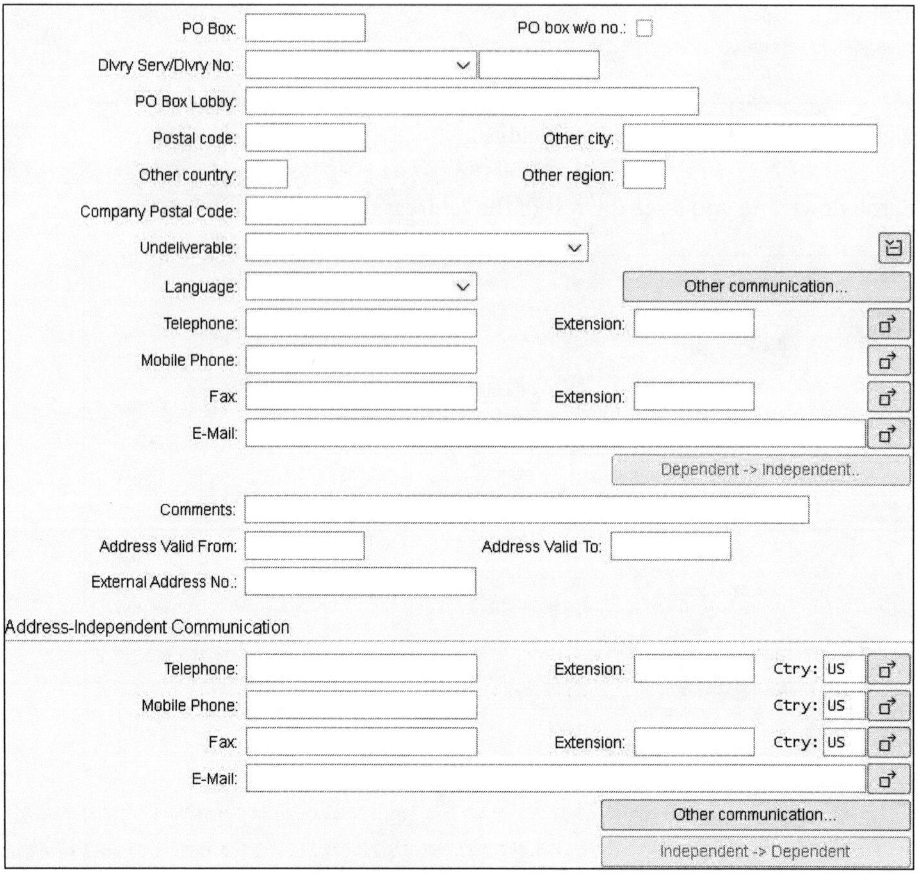

Figure 2.17 Business Partner Address Fields (2/2)

You can maintain several different phone numbers, including fax numbers and mobile numbers, and email address by clicking the icon to the right of each of these fields.

Clicking the **Other communication...** button on the bottom right of the screen enables you to specify other means of communication. The **Transportation Zone** field assigned here will also be used.

To configure transportation zones, follow the menu path **SAP Customizing Implementation Guide • Logistics Execution • Transportation • Basic Transportation Functions • Routes • Route Determination • Define Transportation Zones.**

As shown in Figure 2.18, specify a country code (**Ctry**) and a 10-character transportation zone code (**TranspZone**). You can also add a description (**Description**) that would allow your users to make the correct selections when maintaining business partner master data.

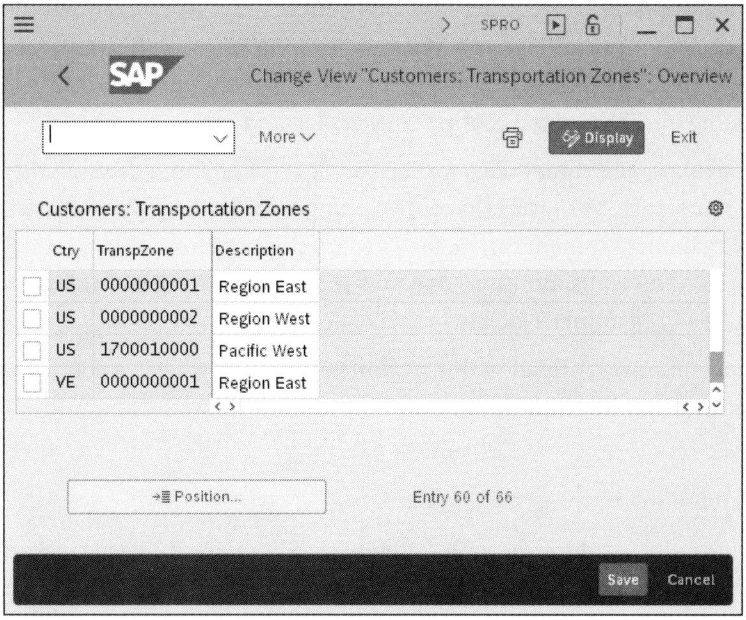

Figure 2.18 Transportation Zone Configuration

Each country must be split into as many transportation zone codes as necessary, depending on the common characteristics they share, i.e., which carriers service that zone, how long delivery requires, etc.

How you split a country depends on your business transportation requirements and is not the same for every company. If you use parcel carriers for your shipments, you can use the zones that your carriers use as their transportation zones.

A major factor in how you define your transportation zones should be based on shipping time while considering the multiple shipping conditions/service levels your company offers to customers. Focus on how your customers vary geographically and then create transportation zones for the most common variations and for exceptions.

For instance, for some shipping conditions/service levels, such as next-day parcel carrier delivery, you don't need to create a transportation zone for the country to represent this service level if all ship-to locations fit into the 1-day zone; you would only need difference levels to account for the exceptions to that service level (more than 1 day).

Some of the entries shown in Figure 2.18 are provided out of the box; for example, the United States is divided into east and west regions, allowing you to define different transportation lead times when shipping from your company's shipping points if the customer depending on which of the country they are located.

In our example, an extra entry was added for the Pacific West region, a decision that was motivated, for instance, by the fact that our shipping point is on the Pacific Coast, and we observed that our shipments arrive faster when shipping from that location. Thus, we could assign this transportation zone for a more accurate estimate of when products will arrive at a customer's facility in this region.

The transportation zones we defined in this section will be used when we configure route determinations later in Chapter 6, Section 6.4.3.

2.2.2 Address Overview

You can maintain multiple addresses with different validity dates to keep track of changes of address under the **Address Overview** tab, as shown in Figure 2.19. To add a new address with a validity period, click on the blank page icon at the bottom of the screen.

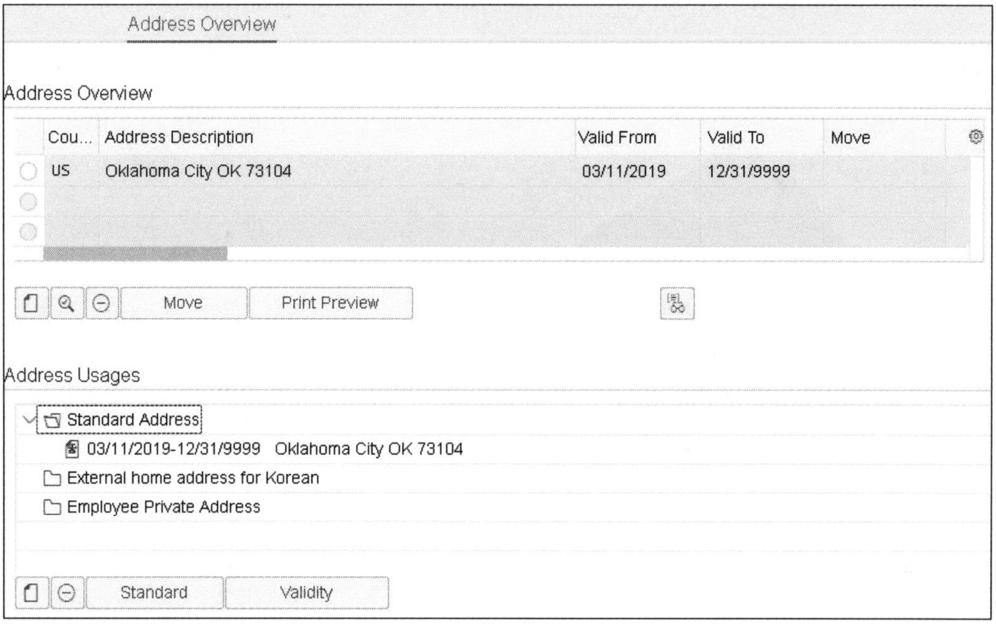

Figure 2.19 Address Overview Tab

2.2.3 Identification

As shown in Figure 2.20, different types of identification codes can be maintained for different kinds of business partners.

The **Legal form** field specifies the type of corporation registered with the government (LLC, corporation, etc.) Some countries have specific requirements regarding legal form. You may also want to use the **Legal entity** field to identify different types of third-party companies that partner with your clients.

The **Int. location no. 1**, **Int. location no. 2**, and **Check digit** fields store International Location Numbers (ILNs) for European customers. If registered to generate their own European Article Numbers (EANs), you would use **Int. location no. 2**; otherwise, use **Int. location no. 1**.

From a sales perspective, you would use the **Industries** section to classify a customer with the specific market they operate in. This information is shared across all of SAP S/4HANA for grouping customers by industry. You can add multiple industry values for companies that participate in several industries.

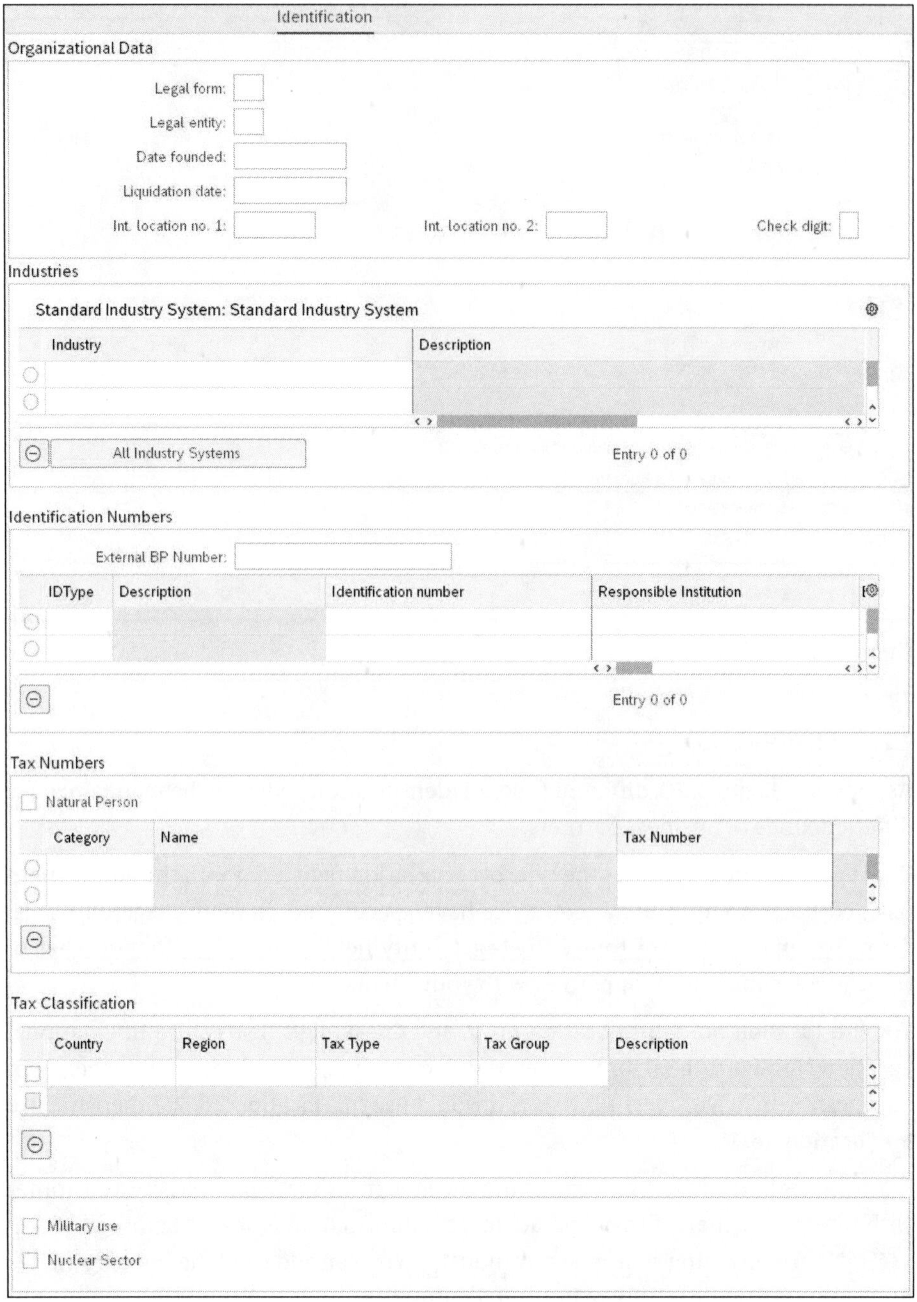

Figure 2.20 Identification

To create an industry sector for this field, follow the menu path **SAP Customizing Implementation Guide • Cross-Application Components • SAP Business Partner • Business Partner • Organizations • Maintain Industry Systems and Industries.**

Then, as shown in Figure 2.21, follow these steps:

1. Enter "0001" for the **Industry System** field and "Standard Industry System" for the **Description** field.
2. Double-click the **Industry Number System --> Industries** option in the **Dialog Structure** menu on the left.
3. Select the **Standard Industry Systems** line.
4. Click on the create industry (blank page) icon in the upper part of the screen.

Returning to the **Identification** tab, under the **Identification Numbers** section, the **External BP Number**. field can be used to maintain a legacy customer number, which is vitally important during a data conversion where you'll need to store existing legacy customer IDs in SAP S/4HANA.

You can also use this screen to add a customer's legal tax ID under the **Identification Number** section. This information is mandatory in some countries. For example, you would use an EIN for the US, a VAT registration number for European countries, a CNPJ number for Brazil, etc.

In the **Tax Classification** control window, you can make customer-level **Tax Group** assignment, which is country specific and depends on how your tax systems are implemented. (Many companies use external/third-party tax calculation systems such as Vertex, Taxware, Avalara, etc. The decision to use third-party tax calculation systems is usually driven by the need to outsource the maintenance of complex tax information.) Out of the box, SAP provides two tax groups indicating either customers where all taxes are applicable (**FULL**) or customers that are tax exempt (**NONE**).

The **Military Use** and **Nuclear Sector** flags apply to foreign trade compliance checks. You must maintain these flags accurately to avoid compliance issues.

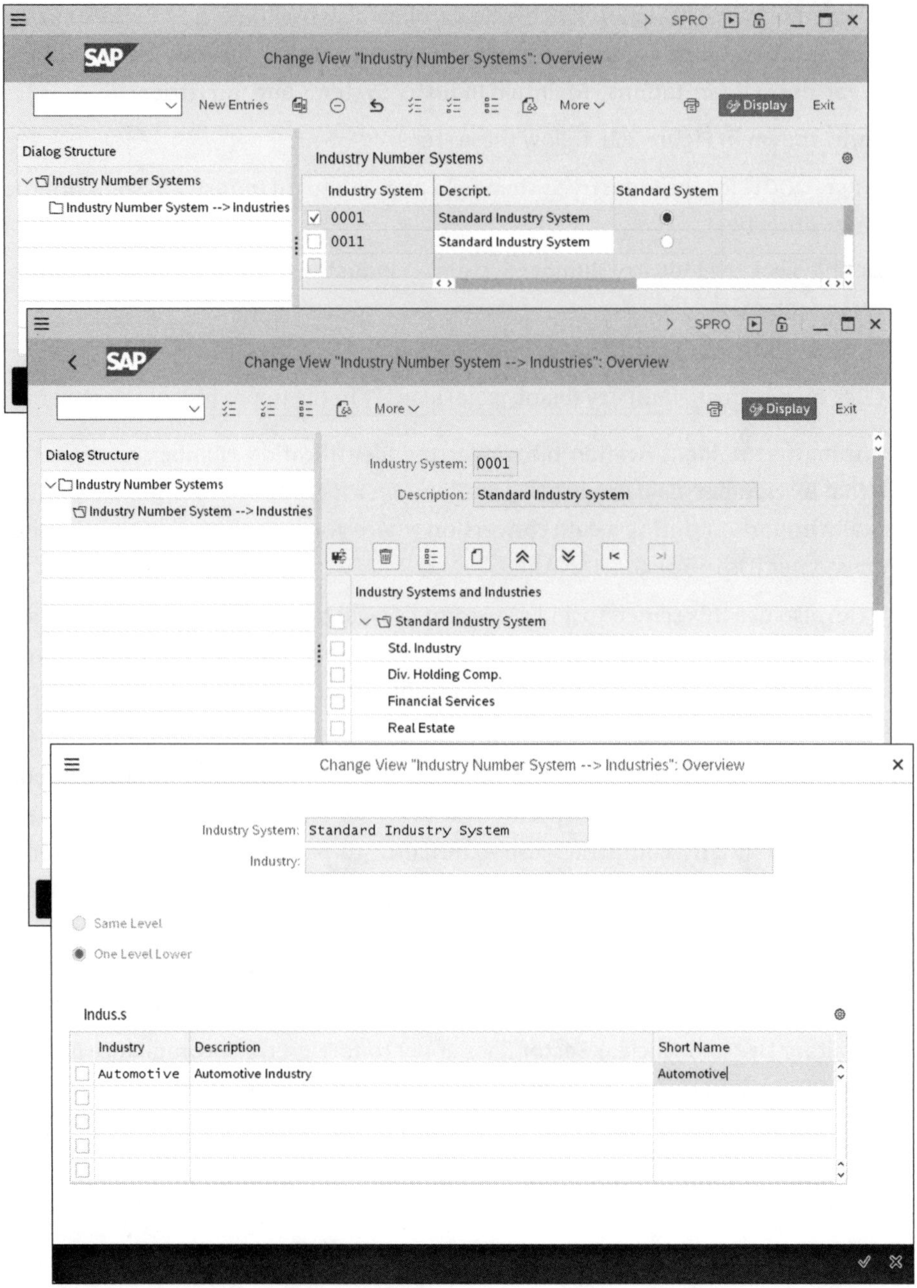

Figure 2.21 Creating New Industry Sectors

2

2.2.4 Control

Under the **Control** tab, shown in Figure 2.22, you can define a business partner type (**BP Type**), which qualifies the nature of this business partner entry. Some companies use these fields to classify customers as sold-to customers, ship-to customers, etc. Other companies use these fields to identify business partners that are primarily vendors versus primarily customers.

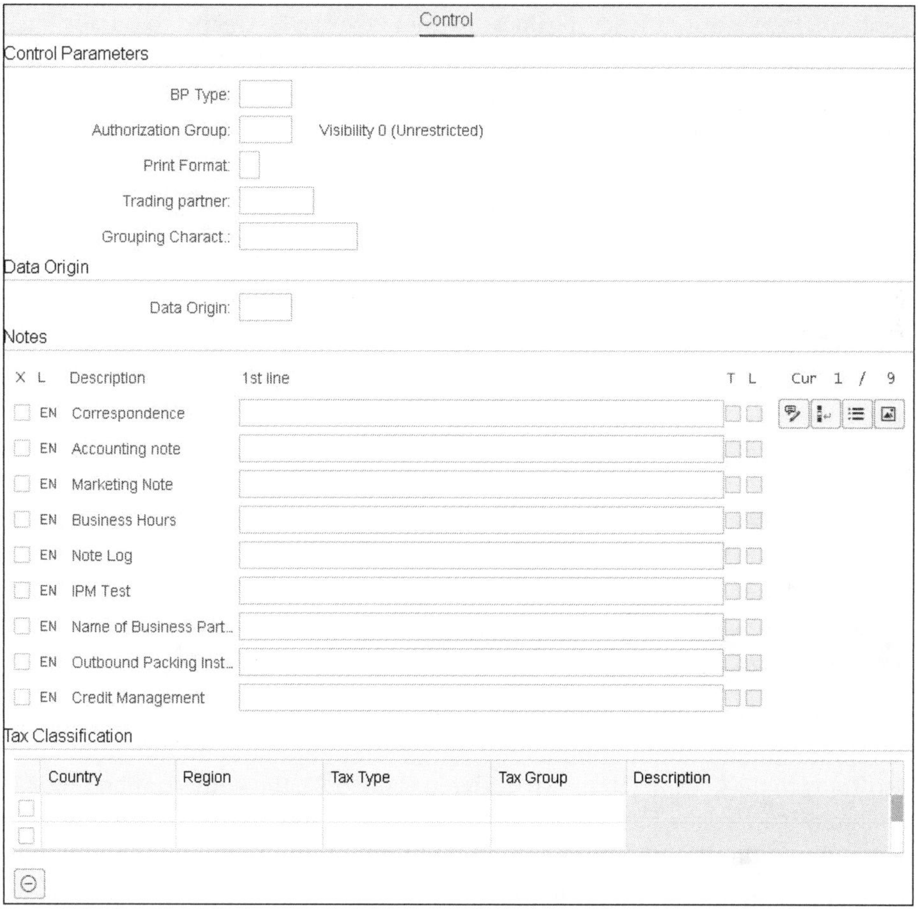

Figure 2.22 Control Tab

None of these approaches are defined as out of the box because conceptually a business partner can be any of these things by the addition of the corresponding business partner roles.

Make sure you have serious discussions about how your company will use these fields, perhaps with an experienced consultant to separate what is really needed versus what is a legacy paradigm from other systems or previous versions of SAP. Once defined, you can add new values by following the menu path **SAP Customizing Implementation Guide • Cross-Application Components • SAP Business Partner • Business Partner • Basic Settings • Business Partner Types • Define Business Partner Types**. On the screen that opens, click on the **New Entries** button or press F5.

As shown in Figure 2.23, a new business partner type can be created to classify business partners that are primarily vendors, a common request from the procurement team. On this screen, specify a four-character partner type code (**Partner Type**) and add a description (**Description**).

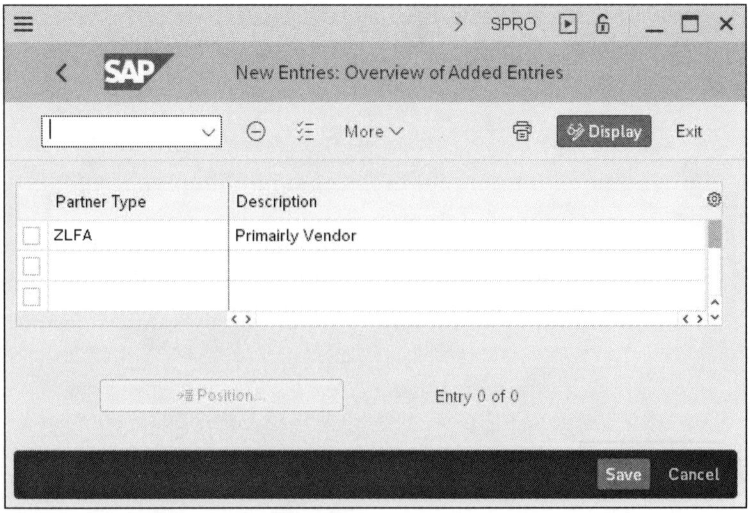

Figure 2.23 Business Partner Types

Returning to the **Control** tab shown earlier in Figure 2.22, the **Authorization Group** is used to restrict access to customer master data to users of a specific group. These groups are defined by the security team at SAP. Few companies require this field, although its use is common in large multinational corporations.

The **Print Format** field allows you to identify special needs customers, such as the visually impaired. Note that the forms for communications developed for your company should take visual impairment into account, but this field is typically not used.

The **Trading partner** field is used on customer master entries that represent companies belonging to another corporation (i.e., system companies, intercompany customers).

In these cases, you must select an existing company code that corresponds to this partner. With this mechanism, your financial systems will know that sales made to and by this partner may be cleared by processing company code-based postings instead of regular account receivables.

The **Grouping Charact.** field can be used to restrict access to subgroups of customers. This field is not commonly used.

The **Data Origin** field is important for identifying how a customer was created. For business partners created via automated data conversion, you must enter code "0001" (Legacy Data Transfer). You may need to add new entries if using external customer relations management (CRM) tools such as Salesforce for prospect qualification. When left blank, this field will require manual maintenance in SAP S/4HANA.

On this screen, you can also enter several types of freeform texts or notes. For example, perhaps you need to add an accounting note: Select this text type from the dropdown list and then click on the editor icon, as shown in Figure 2.24.

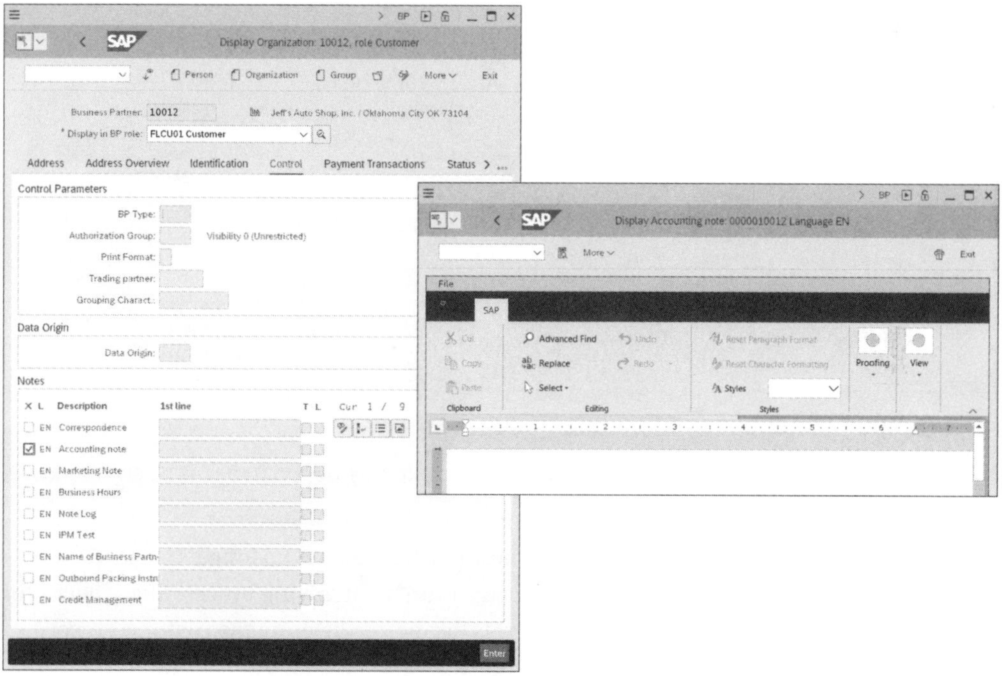

Figure 2.24 Customer General Text Editor

Under the **Control** tab, you can also enter a **Tax Classification** as described earlier in Section 2.2.3. You'll often see the same field on other screens.

2.2.5 Payment Transactions

The **Payment Transactions** tab, shown in Figure 2.25, is for maintaining a customer's **Bank Details** and/or **Payment Card** (credit card) information. This information is controlled by the finance team and can used to pay for ("clear") open account receivables entries.

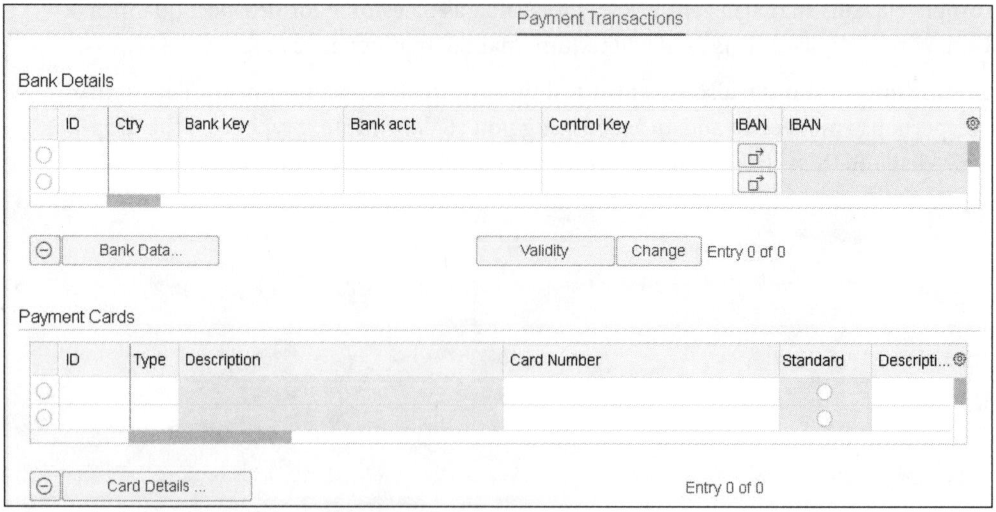

Figure 2.25 Payment Transactions Tab

2.2.6 Status

As shown in Figure 2.26, a number of allowable business partner statuses are available under the **Status** tab.

The **Archiving Flag** is used if this business partner entry is no longer in use. The entry is not immediately deleted; you'll need to run an archiving process that checks for open documents for customers with this flag before deleting the customer record.

The **Central Block** flag is a hard block that will prevent all users from interacting with this business partner. You should only use this block if the decision is final; that is, no open documents exist for the customer, and the customer will not be used in the future. The **Not Released** flag is used if a new business partner requires review and approval before users can interact with this business partner for transactions. The **Contact** field is used to control whether a user can contact this business partner.

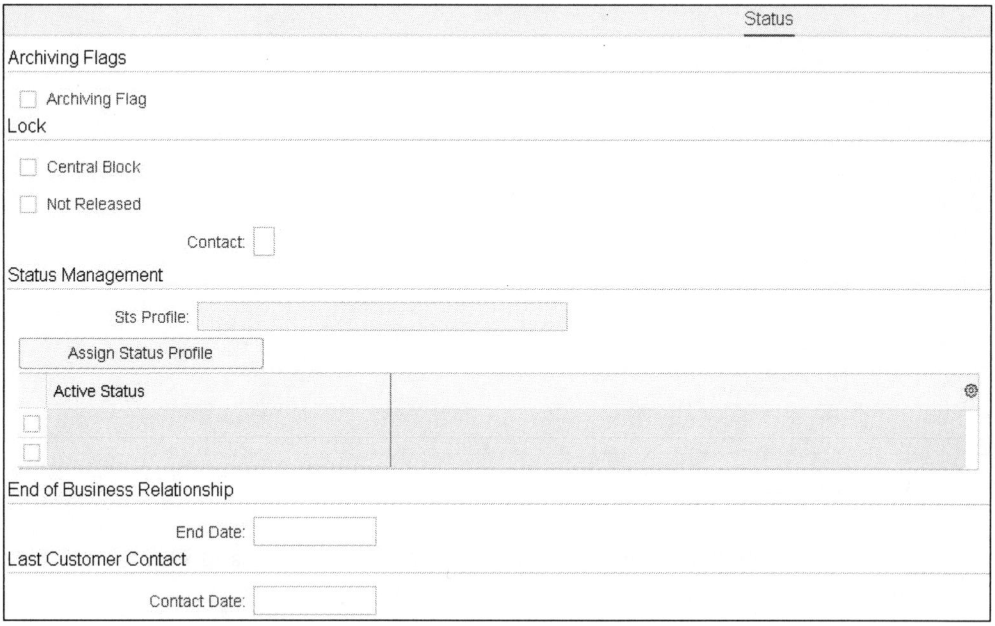

Figure 2.26 Customer Status

The **Status Management** section includes several controls to limit business partners to certain transactions. The status profile field (**Sts Profile**) drives which transaction are controlled. No status profiles are provided out of the box for business partners, and the configuration of this control should be considered part of service management, not part of sales.

The **End Date** indicates when business stops being conducted with this customer and when that decision was made. The **Contact Date** indicates the last time you interacted with the customer.

2.2.7 Legal Data

As shown in Figure 2.27, legal data for business partners is maintained under the **Legal Data** tab.

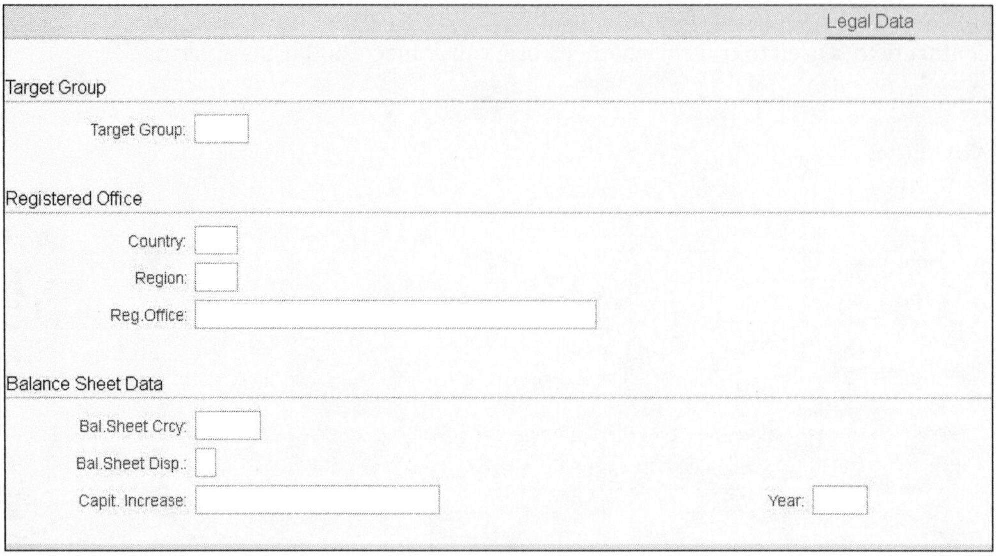

Figure 2.27 Legal Data

The fields in the **Registered Office** section (**Country**, **Region**, and **Reg. Office**) store information about the court of law we would petition if we ever needed to file suit against a business partner. This information may be used to represent any legal jurisdiction identification when the government needs to be involved as a mediator for our relationship with this customer.

The **Balance Sheet Data** fields belong to the finance team. This field is used to control information that affects balance sheet reports issued and shared with investors.

The **Target Group** field is used to classify business partners, but no values are provided out of the box. To configure target groups, follow the menu path **SAP Customizing Implementation Guide • SAP Banking • Settings for Financial Services • General Settings • Basic Settings • Define Target Group.** On the screen that opens, click on the **New Entries** button or press [F5].

As shown in Figure 2.28, on this screen, specify a four-character target group code (**Targ...**) and add a description (**Description**) The **BP Category** field must indicate whether this target group should be used when the business partner is an organization, a person, or a group.

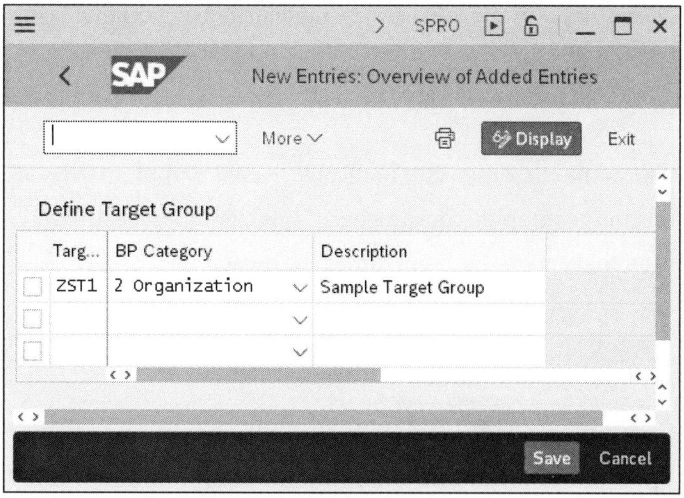

Figure 2.28 Creating New Target Groups

2.2.8 Customer: General Data

Next, we have the **Customer: General Data** tab, shown in Figure 2.29. Here, you'll see that the **Customer Number** shows as **<External>** because we are still creating the business partner. The **Customer Number** is used to keep backward compatibility with previous versions of the system. When using this business partner as a customer (like during sales order entry), we will use this number rather than the **Business Partner** number we saw in Figure 2.1. When using customer match code searches, the number shown on the search windows will be the **Customer Number**.

Here, we find the following fields:

- The **Account group** field used to control customer master data in previous versions of the system and is still present to assist with backward compatibility. This field is populated automatically based on configuration and cannot be changed here.
- The **Vendor** field allows you to link a vendor to a customer if they have different entries. In SAP S/4HANA, a business partner can be both a customer and a vendor, but in previous versions, distinct entries were required, and this field was necessary to link them.
- The **Authorization** field is similar to the **Authorization Group** field under the **Control** tab. However, this field applies to customers only.

- The **Group** field is a freeform text field you can use to identify conglomerates (i.e., business partner groups) that a given customer or vendor belongs to.
- The **Express station** field contains the station the customer uses to receive express shipments via rail.
- **Train station** is the station the customer uses to receive normal shipments via rail.
- **Location code** contains the geographic coordinates of this customer location.
- The **Plant** is the location that services this customer the most.

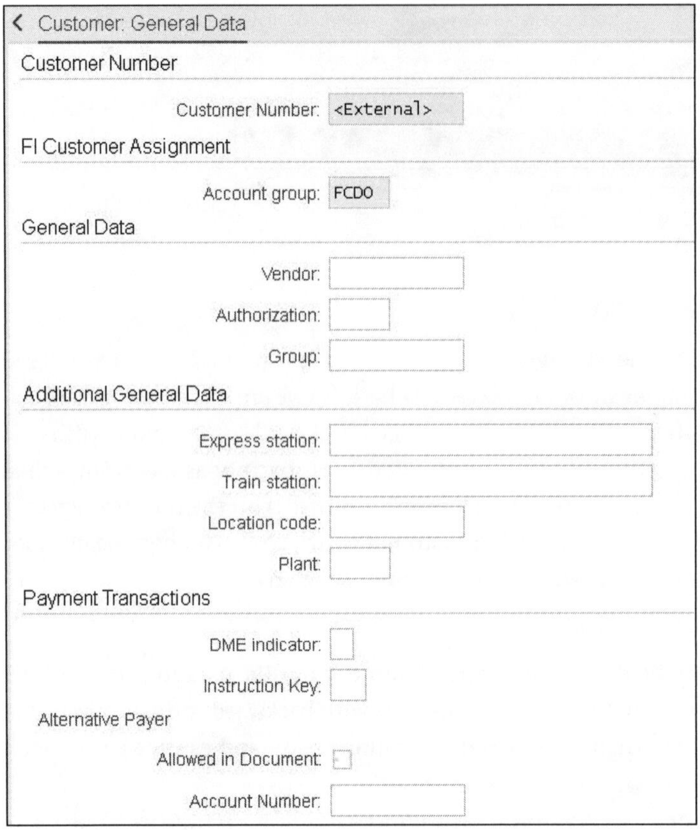

Figure 2.29 General Data (1/2)

The **Payment Transactions** section, shown in Figure 2.29, and **Additional Payment Transaction Data** section, shown in Figure 2.30, contain numerous fields such as **DME indicator**, **Instruction Key**, **Allowed in Document**, **Account Number**, **Alt. payer (Account Number)**, and **Fi.Year Variant** as well as the **Permitted Payee** button, which all belong to the finance functionality and won't be covered in this book.

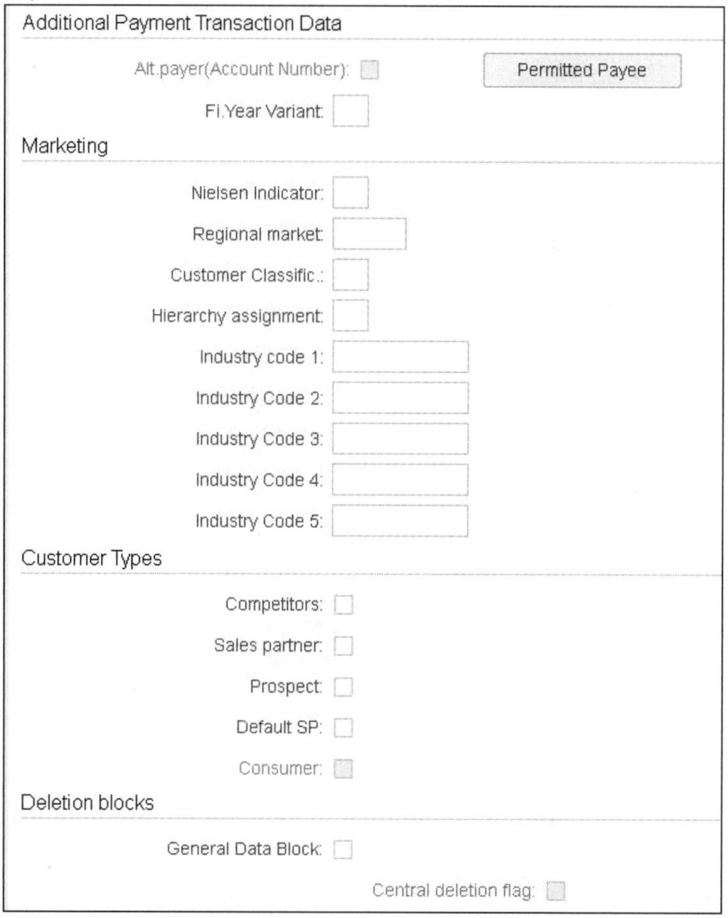

Figure 2.30 General Data (2/2)

The **Marketing** area of the **General Data** tab allows you to record marketing information about this customer, such as the following information:

- **Nielsen Indicator**
  Customer classification according to the A.C. Nielsen company, a global measurement and data analytics company. If this information is maintained correctly, you can use Nielsen ratings on your reports. Usually your marketing team will maintain their own data, and using this field would make their tasks more efficient,

although few companies configure these indicators. To configure Nielsen indicators, follow the menu path **SAP Customizing Implementation Guide • Sales and Distribution • Master Data • Business Partners • Customers • Marketing • Define Nielsen ID.** On the screen that opens, click on the **New Entries** button or press F5.

As shown in Figure 2.31, on this screen, specify a two-character Nielsen indicator code (**Nielsen indicator**) and add a description (**Description**).

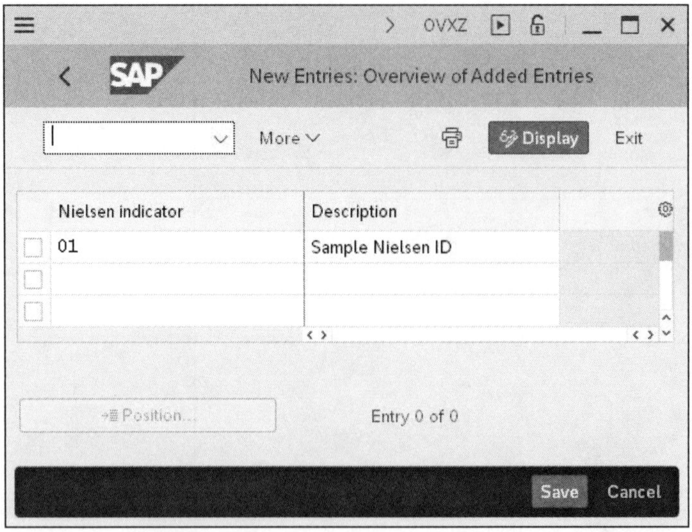

Figure 2.31 Defining Nielsen IDs

- **Regional market**
  No longer in use, this field is used for backward compatibility with previous versions.
- **Customer Classific.**
  Generic classification for this customer regardless of the sales area that serves them. Out of the box, SAP uses an A/B/C classification, which is typically based on their buying volume. But this field can be used for other purposes. To change these values, follow the menu path **SAP Customizing Implementation Guide • Sales and Distribution • Master Data • Business Partners • Customers • Marketing • Define Customer Classifications.** On the screen that opens, click on the **New Entries** button or press F5.

  As shown in Figure 2.32, on this screen, specify a two-character customer classification code (**Customer Classification**) and add a description (**Description**).

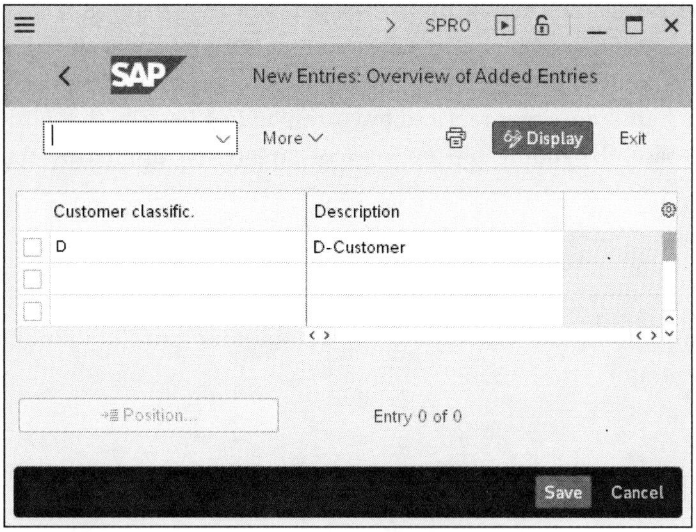

Figure 2.32 Creating New Customer Classification Codes

- **Hierarchy assignment**
  Qualifies the version of the customer hierarchy this customer belongs to. See Section 2.4 for details.
- **Industry Code 1**, **2**, **3**, **4**, and **5**
  Previously used instead of the **Industries** field discussed earlier in Section 2.2.3. Now, these fields are used only for backward compatibility with previous versions.

The **Customer Types** section has several flags to specify a customer master entry as **Competitors**, **Sales Partner**, **Prospect**, **Default SP** (sold-to party, used as the default when the field is left blank on sales orders), and **Consumer**.

2.2.9 Customer: Tax Data

Typically, companies in the US use third-party tax calculation software such as Vertex, Taxware, Avalara, etc. Many other countries have the option of using third-party software as well.

The motivation is that third-party tax solutions can take care of the master data maintenance required to calculate local taxes correctly. For standard tax calculations, responsibility for determining liability falls on the department that maintains the relevant data. Although complex and labor intensive, failing in this responsibility may cause litigation with local governments.

If using a standard tax calculation, the **Customer: Tax Data** tab, shown in Figure 2.33, may contain some important fields, but other sales area data/sales information fields need to be considered (Section 2.3.3). Using a third-party tax solution, these fields should still be used but are sometimes replaced by corresponding fields in the third-party solution's database, depending on the level of integration offered by the selected tool.

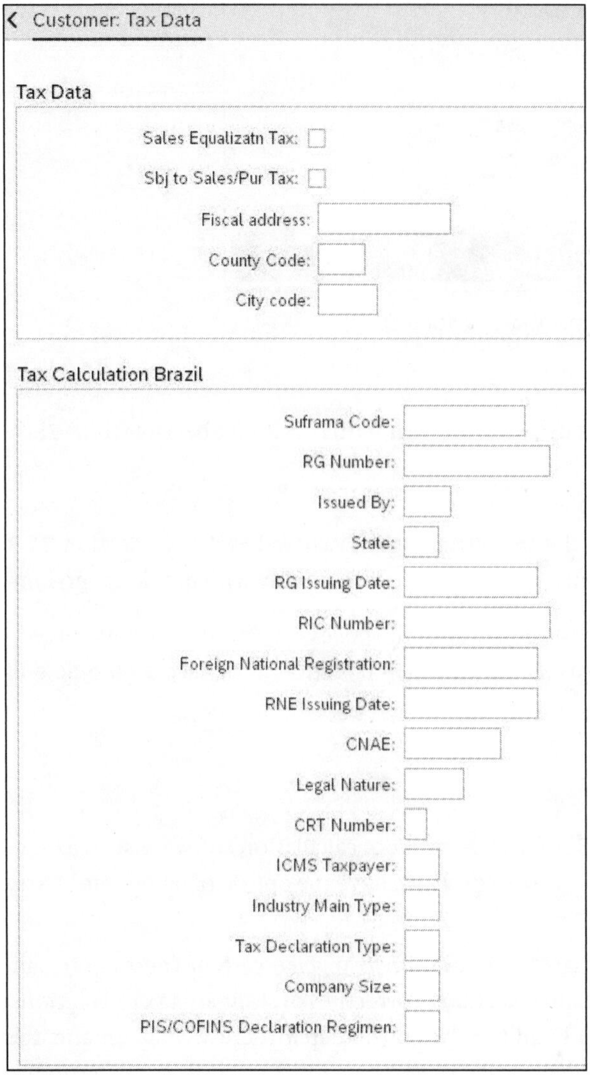

Figure 2.33 Customer Tax Data

We recommend maintaining this master data in SAP S/4HANA and then creating an interface to the third-party tax solution, so that SAP can serve as the single source of truth—the only system that can be integrated with all other solutions and that can be all encompassing. The tax software can't serve as the single source of truth because it only does taxes.

Companies that don't use these fields must contact the specific authorized users with access to and knowledge of the third-party tax solution whenever a customer's status changes, which may take time and delay sales.

Tests and simulations also require the participation of these tax resources, which are not commonly available for this type of assignment, thus delaying the deployment of new systems, changes, and bug fixes.

Some third-party tax solutions simply don't have the ability to integrate and maintain standard tax fields, which is often reflected in licensing costs. In other words, the cheapest third-party tax solution will probably have the worst integration with SAP.

Thus, a company using these solutions may spend a lot more time and potentially expensive resources to make the third-party solution work in the long term. If your company perceives this requirement as an additional cost, the cheapest option quickly becomes the most expensive.

The decision to adopt a third-party tax solution usually lies within the finance department and is geared towards the reporting capability of the tool, but be sure to consider integration as factor as well.

This tab contains a number of notable fields, such as the following:

- The **Sales Equalizatn Tax** relevancy flag is used in Spain. If required for your company, maintaining information in your master data is advisable.
- The **Sbj to Sales/Pur Tax** field is used to indicate when Value-Added Tax (VAT) is required. This scenario is common in Europe. If required for your company, maintaining information in your master data is advisable.
- The **Fiscal address** field allows you to indicate a separate customer as the address for tax purposes. This scenario is common in Italy. If required for you company, maintaining this information in your master data is advisable.
- The **County Code** and **City code** fields are used to calculate local taxes and are useful when determining the tax jurisdiction code. In the US, the tax jurisdiction code is determined by the postal code (zip code), so these fields are not required and are

typically not maintained in SAP, even when required. Companies that don't use third-party tax solutions would need to maintain these fields.

- The **Tax Calculation Brazil** section is only applicable for the country of Brazil, and the fields contained in this section will not be covered in this book.

2.2.10 Customer: Additional Data

The **Customer: Additional Data** tab, shown in Figure 2.43, contains the reserved fields for customer master data; these database fields are designed so that companies using SAP can define business-specific usage for them.

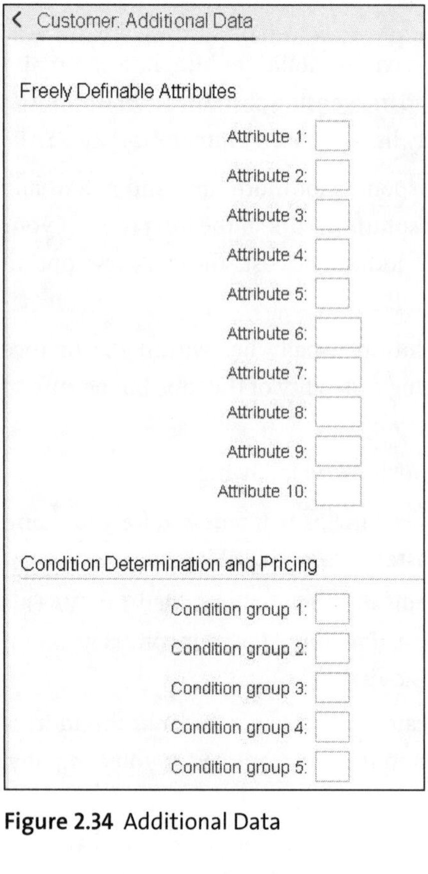

Figure 2.34 Additional Data

One important characteristic about the **Condition group** fields is that, even though they appear five times on this screen, only one list of valid values is configured. You'll set up all five values with that configured list and assign these values to your customers, which enables you to define condition records that are applicable when a customer fulfills any specific condition group.

For example, let's say that one of your customers can be considered both a distributor and a repair shop. You'll assign the value of "Distributor" to **Condition group 1** and the value of "Retail Shop" to **Condition group 2**. In this way, you'll know the business partner is most often a distribution but also a retail shop.

You can then define a discount program for repair shops where these customers would be eligible even though their primary classification is something else; for condition determination purposes, these business partner become eligible. If this type of requirement exists, condition groups may be used. Most companies do not use these field and consider their maintenance a complex endeavor.

To define customer condition groups, follow the menu path **SAP Customizing Implementation Guide • Logistics – General • Business Partner • Customers • Control • Define Condition Groups**. On the screen that opens, click on the **New Entries** button or press F5.

On this screen, shown in Figure 2.35, define the values for **Distributor** and **Retail Shop** as in our previous example by specifying a two-character customer condition group code (**CustomerCondGrp**) and adding a description (**Description)** for each condition.

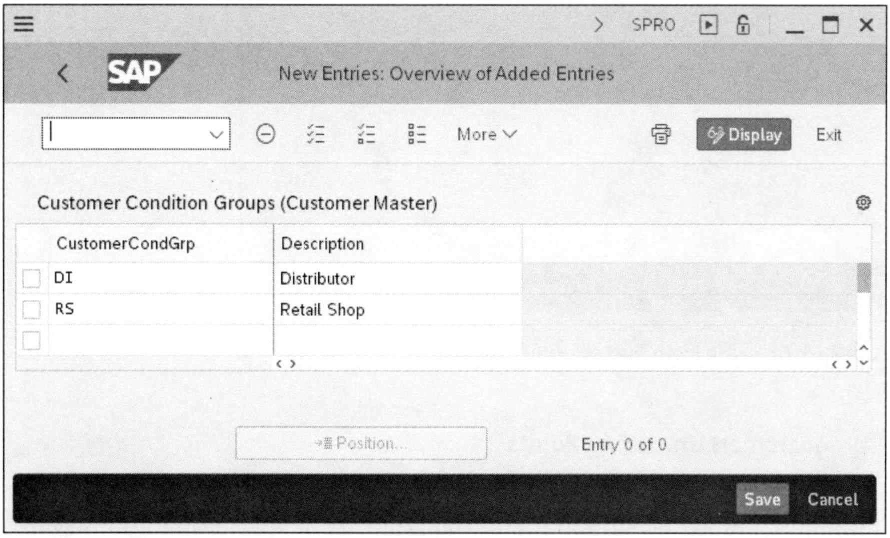

Figure 2.35 Defining New Customer Condition Groups

To configure and use customer attributes, follow the menu path **SAP Customizing Implementation Guide • Logistics – General • Business Partner • Customers • Control • Define Attributes**.

Select the attribute you wish to maintain (**Attribute 01** through **10**) from the list by double-clicking on the desired option and then clicking on the **New Entries** button or pressing F5. For our example, we'll select customer **Attribute 01**. You'll see the screen shown in Figure 2.36.

On this screen, specify a two-digit customer attribute code (**A1**) code and add a description (**Description**). **Customer Attribute 1** through **5** are 2 characters long, and **Customer Attribute 6** through **10** are 3 characters long. When choosing where to store these codes, you must consider how many entries you expect to need in the future and the consumption of these codes. Ideally, you shouldn't run out of codes to use, since not many values are configured in this context, but still, meaningful codes are often in short supply.

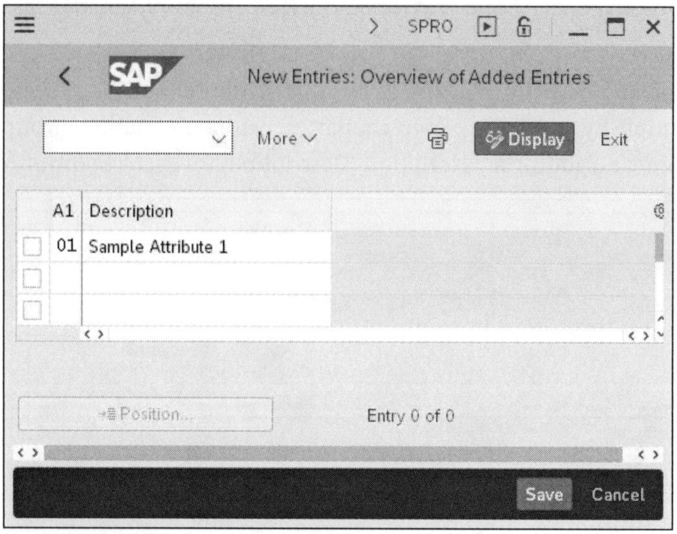

Figure 2.36 Creating New Customer Attribute 1

2.2.11 Customer: Unloading Points

Under the **Customer: Unloading Points** tab, shown in Figure 2.37, you'll maintain each **Unloading Point**, **Receiving Point**, and **Departments** at that customer's location. Maintaining receiving loading dock IDs and gate numbers are typical uses for these fields. If your customer requires the carrier to deliver a product to a specific dock and/ or get into the customer's facility through specific gates, you can maintain this information in these fields. For some customers, these fields could be mandatory. Once this information is stored, this information can be displayed on your shipping documents.

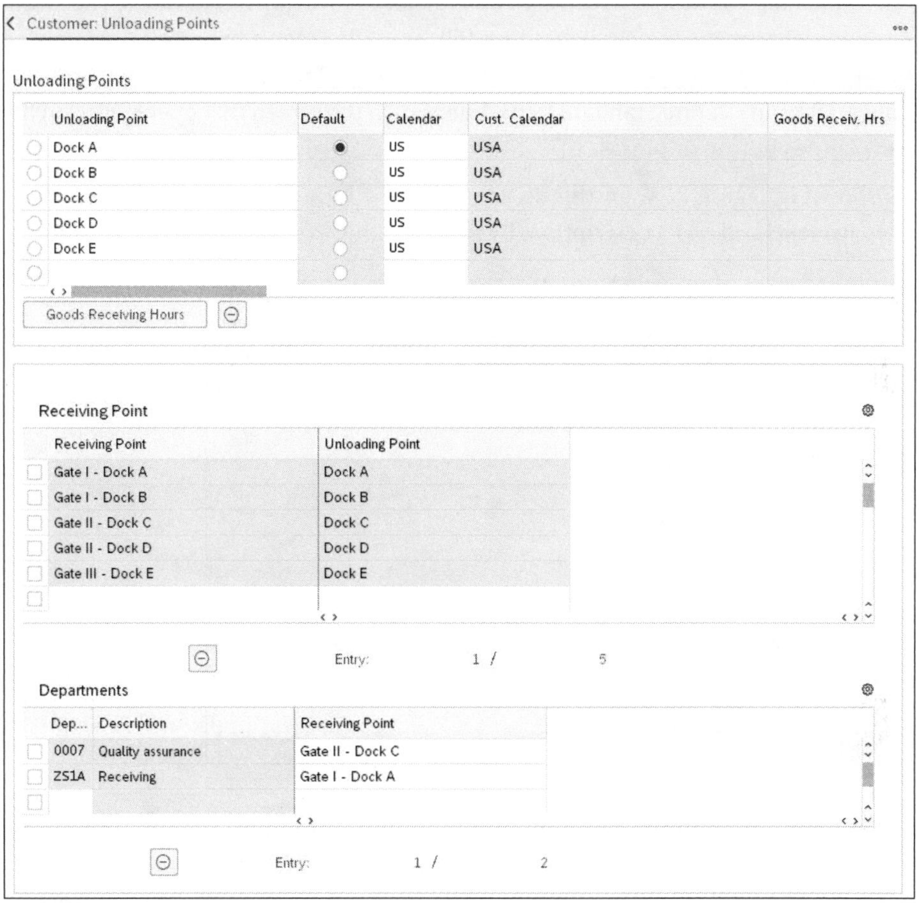

Figure 2.37 Unloading Points

When an order is entered, you'll be prompted to select the unloading points to deliver your products. During the available to promise (ATP) check, the expected delivery date will observe the restrictions set on this screen under the selected unloading point.

You can also assign a calendar to an unloading point, which allows you to restrict deliveries to certain days of the week, define the holidays this customer's warehouse observes, and define work shifts by clicking the **Goods Receiving Hours** button. With this information, you can guarantee delivery dates to your customers (see Chapter 7, Section 7.1 and Section 7.2, for more details).

The **Unloading Points** and **Receiving Points** fields are freeform text fields. The calendar and department are configured by following the menu path **SAP Customizing Implementation Guide • Sales and Distribution • Master Data • Business Partners • Contact Person • Define Standard Departments.** On the screen that opens, click on the **New Entries** button or press F5.

As shown in Figure 2.38, on this screen, specify a four-character department code (**Department**) and add a description (**Description**).

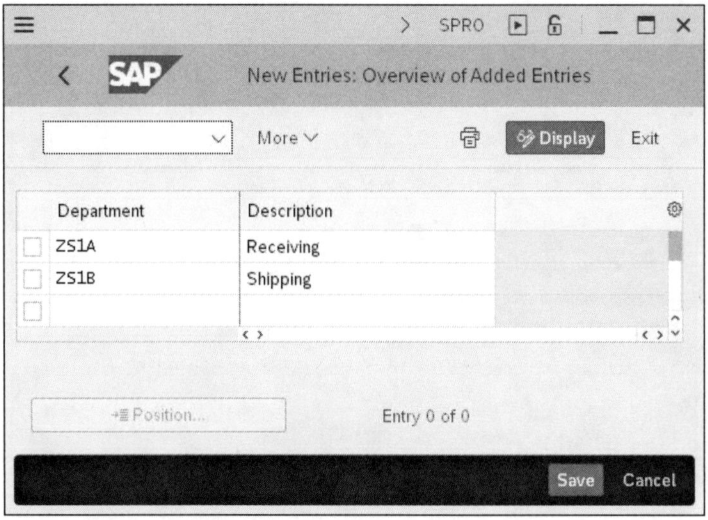

Figure 2.38 Creating New Departments

Returning to the **Customer: Unloading Points** tab, you can now assign unloading points to receiving points and assign receiving points to departments.

Your customer's work shifts can be maintained by clicking the **Goods Receiving Hours** button below the **Unloading Point** area. You can configure shifts as a group or enter shifts individually in the popup window shown in Figure 2.39.

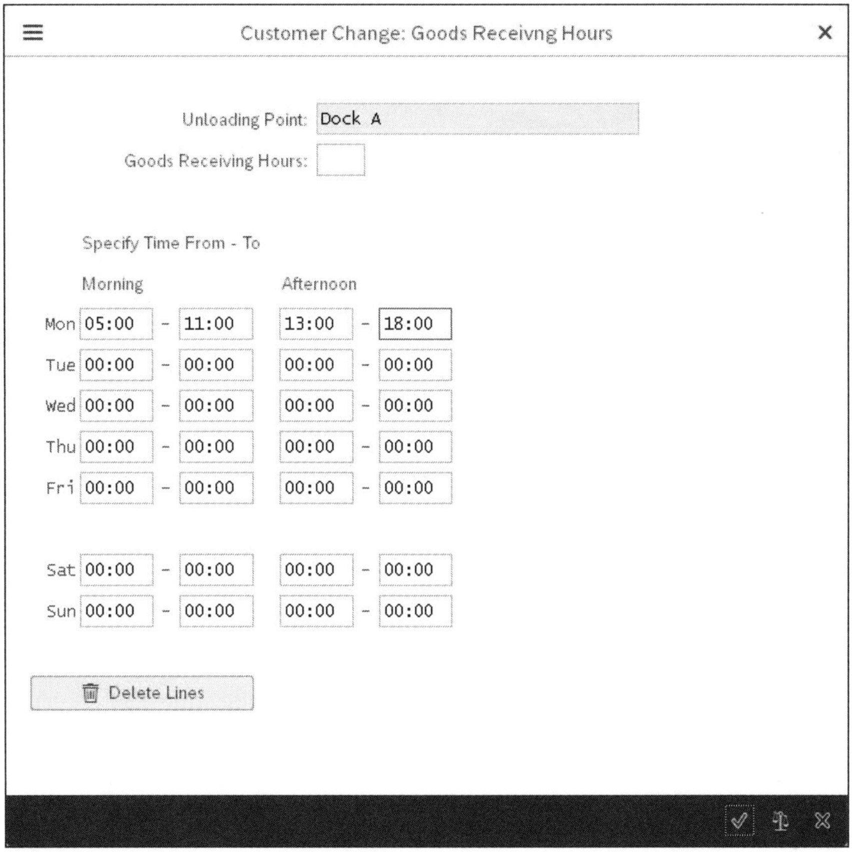

Figure 2.39 Goods Receiving Hours Popup Window

2.2.12 Customer: Texts

Under the **Customer: Texts** tab, shown in Figure 2.40, you can maintain freeform text that can be duplicated in various transactions. These texts are defined as defaults that are copied into documents but can be changed on an order-to-order basis if necessary.

To maintain texts, select the desired text type and language and click on the **Edit Text** button. A text editor will appear similar to the one described earlier in Section 2.2.4 and shown in Figure 2.24.

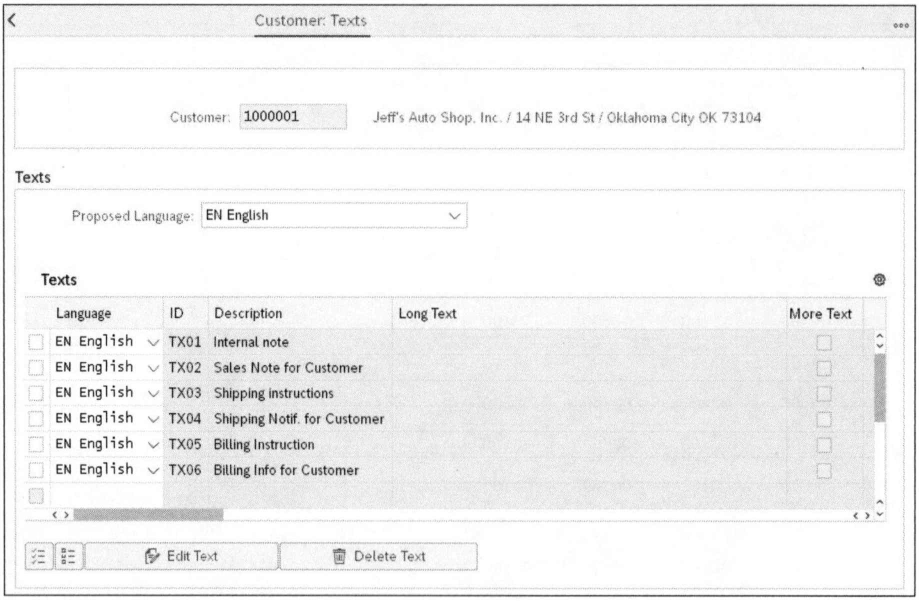

Figure 2.40 Customer General Data Texts

More details about configuration will be provided in Chapter 6, Section 6.3.10 because sales texts are most commonly copied over to sales documents than the ones on this screen.

2.3 Sales Information

When a business partner is assigned the **Customer** business partner role, the **Sales and Distribution** button will appear on the command bar, as shown in Figure 2.41. Clicking this button allows you to add sales information.

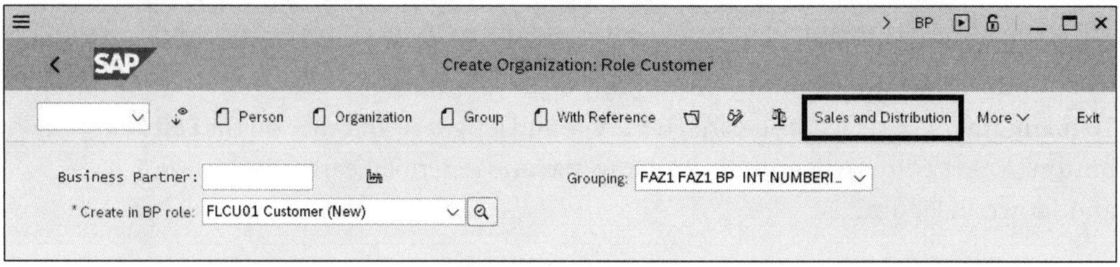

Figure 2.41 Sales and Distribution Button

Once you click the **Sales and Distribution** button, you'll need to choose the **Sales Area** under which sales information will be entered. To create the first sales area for a customer, simply enter the sales organization, distribution channel, and division directly into the corresponding fields, as shown in Figure 2.42.

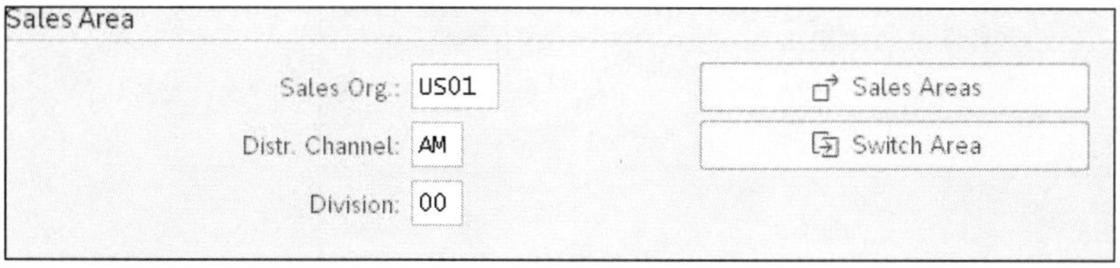

Figure 2.42 Sales Area Selection

If you're using Transaction BP to modify an existing customer's sales data, you can manually enter an existing sales area by clicking on the **Switch Area** button to switch between sales areas, which opens sales area-relevant fields for editing. Clicking the **Sales Areas** button will display all sales areas currently created for this customer. You can select an existing sales area or add new sales areas to this list by clicking the button at the bottom of the window.

In the following sections, we'll walk through the fields contained under each tab and describe how to configure their values.

2.3.1 Orders

The **Orders** tab, shown in Figure 2.43, can be divided into two main sections: **Order** information and **Pricing/Statistics**. We'll discuss these two areas in the following sections.

> **Note**
>
> In the **Account Management** section at the bottom, the **Relevant for Settlement Management** flag indicates whether this customer needs to be considered when calculating settlements of certain programs, such as rebates. This field is important if your company runs these kinds of programs. In the rebate settlement context, sales to customers without this checkbox activated would be ignored when calculating the total amount of sales during a period to determine when a customer is eligible for a rebate.

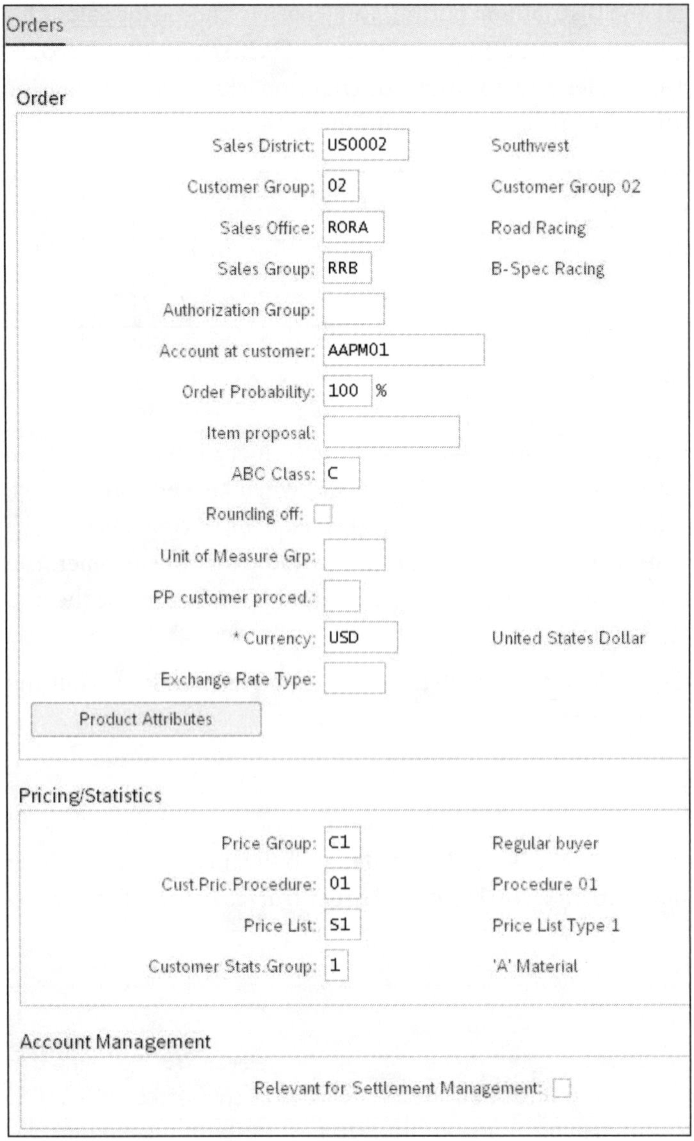

Figure 2.43 Customer Orders Information

Orders

The **Sales District** field represents the portion of a marketplace this customer belongs to. Companies usually use a geographical definition for these districts, but you don't have to. The **Sales District** field is an important field used in sales reporting.

To configure sales districts, follow menu path **SAP Customizing Implementation Guide • Sales and Distribution • Master Data • Business Partners • Customers • Sales • Define Sales Districts.** On the screen that opens, click on the **New Entries** button or press F5.

As shown in Figure 2.44, specify a six-character sales district code (**Sales District**) and add a description (**Description**) for each sales district.

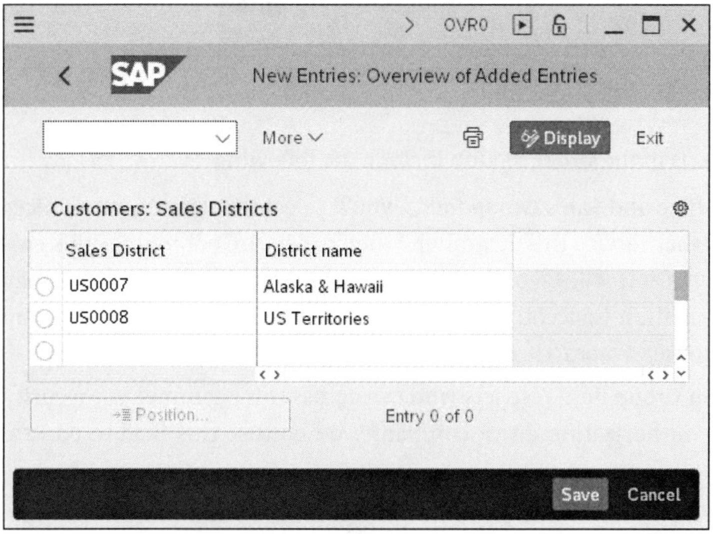

Figure 2.44 Defining New Sales Districts

To configure customer groups, follow the menu path **SAP Customizing Implementation Guide • Sales and Distribution • Master Data • Business Partners • Customers • Sales • Define Customer Groups.** On the screen that opens, click on the **New Entries** button or press F5.

As shown in Figure 2.45, specify a two-character customer group code (**Customer Group**) and add a description (**Description**) for each customer group.

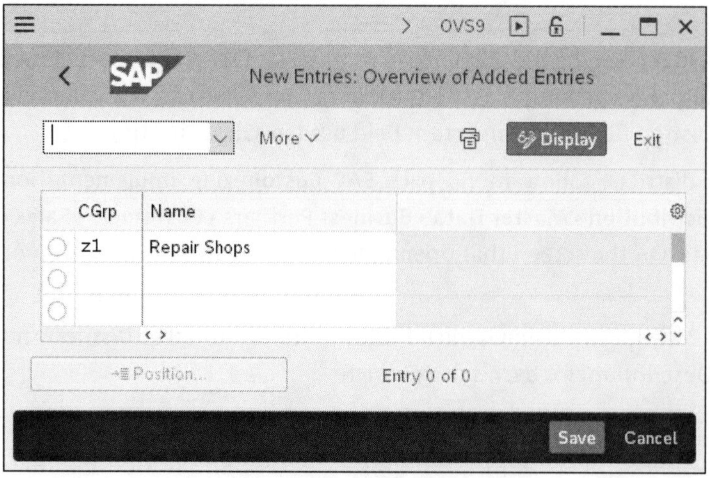

Figure 2.45 Defining New Customer Groups

Other important fields in the **Order** section include the following:

- With the **Sales Office** and **Sales Group** fields, you'll select the default sales offices and sales groups that service this customer. When orders are entered for this customer, this information will be assigned to the order by default. You can may change this information to account for exceptions. If no specific office or group services this customer, you can leave these fields blank.
- The **Authorization Group** field restricts who can access this customer via security roles and profile authorization. Most companies do not use this field to control customer access.
- The **Account at Customer** field represents your company's number in this customer's system, which can improve customer communications.
- If your company creates quotes, you can use the **Order Probability** field to indicate how likely this customer's quotes will turn into sales orders.
- If this customer regularly orders the same set of materials on their orders, you can use the **Item proposal** field to prepopulate the most common materials during sales order entry.
- The **ABC Class** indicator qualifies this customer according to their buying volume with "A" being the customer with the higher volume, "B" the next tier down, and so on. You can use this indicator to sort and filter report data.

- The **Unit of Measure Grp** field is used if your company allows orders with different units of measurement (UoMs). This group would restrict which UoMs this customer can choose from when entering orders for this sales area.
- The **PP customer proced.** field allows you to use more complex selection criteria to propose items on sales orders. This functionality is called *cross-selling* and uses the condition technique to define the criteria for assigning the appropriate product proposal. In Chapter 4, Section 4.4, we'll describe the configuration steps to enable this functionality, as well as the related *dynamic product proposal* functionality in Chapter 4, Section 4.5.
- Out of the box, **Currency** is a mandatory field. This currency will be used by default when entering sales orders and issuing invoices. This currency is not necessarily the same currency you maintain your prices in and is not the official financial reporting currency. This field will be prepopulated with the currency configured in the sales organization.
- When the sales order currency is different than the price in the master data, you'll need to perform a conversion. In some countries, you'll have several exchange rates to choose from. The **Exchange Rate Type** field specifies which of multiple exchange rates this customer uses by default. This exchange rate may also be changed during sales order entry.

Finally, the **Product Attributes** button indicates whether this customer rejects materials flagged with one of these attributes. No out-of-the-box meaning is given to any of these fields; meaning will be assigned when implementing SAP during the project. You can change the description of this field to represent the assigned meaning as with all reserved fields.

The material master data has the same list of product attributes. If a material has one of these attributes set, and the customer master has the same attribute set, then you'll encounter an exception if you ever attempt to enter an order for this customer and material combination.

This scenario is applicable only for sales order types configured to check for product attributes (either warning dialog message or error). Flagging one of these attributes on the material master will not stop any customer from purchasing products, only the products with a matching flagged product attribute.

Many companies find this functionality confusing, and few use this functionality as designed. Instead, many companies use material master product attributes as reserved fields for Boolean informational master data.

Pricing/Statistics

Moving on the **Pricing/Statistics** area, the customer **Price Group** controls which types of discounts are applicable. To configure customer price groups, follow the menu path **SAP Customizing Implementation Guide • Sales and Distribution • Basic Functions • Pricing • Set Price-Relevant Master Data Fields • Set Pricing Groups for Customers.** On the screen that opens, click on the **New Entries** button or press F5.

As shown in Figure 2.46, specify a two-character customer price group code (**Customer Price Group**) and add a description (**Description**). More details about the **Price Group** field can be found in Chapter 4.

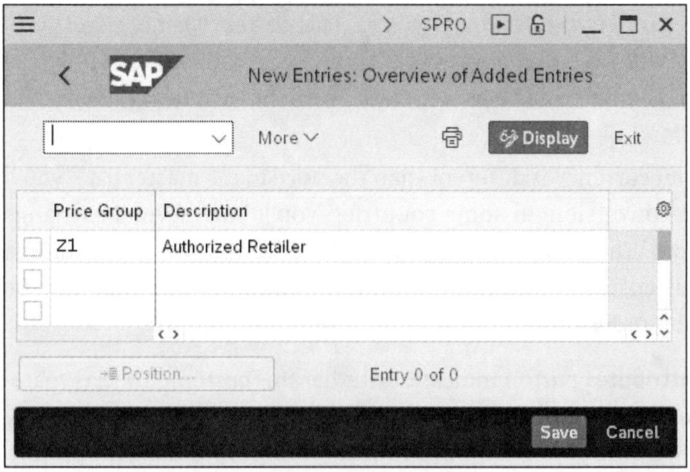

Figure 2.46 Defining New Customer Price Groups

The **Cust.Pric.Procedure** field (from Figure 2.43) is used to qualify major differences in how sales prices, freight, and taxes are calculated in what are called *pricing procedures*.

We recommend using as few pricing procedures as possible. Usually, companies have one value for this field for all customers. However, if significant differences in how prices are calculated exist, such as *cost plus* versus *list minus* approaches depending on the type of customer, having different values for this field would be appropriate.

Of course, for simplicity, you could use only one pricing procedure, but this approach is not always recommended. Complexity must factor into the decision to use a single pricing procedure versus multiple pricing procedure. More details about this field are found in Chapter 4, Section 4.1.5.

The price list is used when multiple prices are used in the marketplace for the same material. In these instances, each price must be represented by a price list type. You don't have to use price lists if your goal is ease of maintenance; instead, you can maintain base prices by material number and manage differences via discount and surcharge percentages. To configure customer price lists, follow the menu path **SAP Customizing Implementation Guide • Sales and Distribution • Basic Functions • Pricing • Set Price-Relevant Master Data Fields • Set Price List Types for Customers.** On the screen that opens, click on the **New Entries** button or press F5.

As shown in Figure 2.47, specify a two-character price list type code (**Price List Type**) and add a description (**Description**).

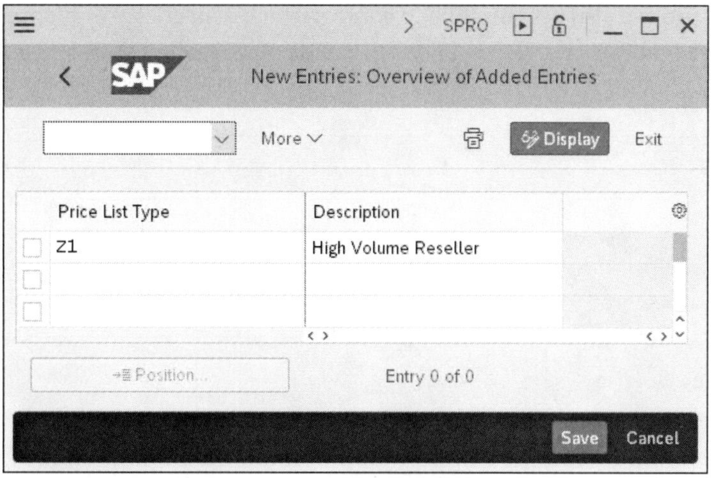

Figure 2.47 Defining New Customer Price List Types

The **Customer Stats.Group** field dictates the level of detail you want to track for reporting on this customer's information. Companies that use this field generally classify customer data for daily, weekly, monthly, and quarterly reporting.

In SAP ERP, you would accumulate sales volume information based on this period information to increase reporting performance as part of the Logistics Information System (LIS)/Sales Information Systems (SIS) definition.

Companies tend to define the same rules across all customers and thus use the same value for this field for all materials. This approach enables you to drill down to the same level of detail for any customer in the system; the downside to this approach is largely technical, related to performance and storage consumption.

In SAP S/4HANA, one main advantage is improved performance when retrieving transactional data that affects reporting performance. But storage space is costly and complex to manage, so you may still want a separate reporting database for historical data. As a result, you can archive data from your transactional systems to maintain peak performance.

2.3.2 Shipping

Under the **Shipping** tab, shown in Figure 2.48, the first field is the **Delivery Priority** field, which resolves conflicts in stock allocation (see Chapter 7 for more details). Customers with a lower delivery priority value will take available stock before customers with higher values. You can also use this field to control which deliveries are shipped first if the warehouse is at capacity and you need to decide of which orders should go out first.

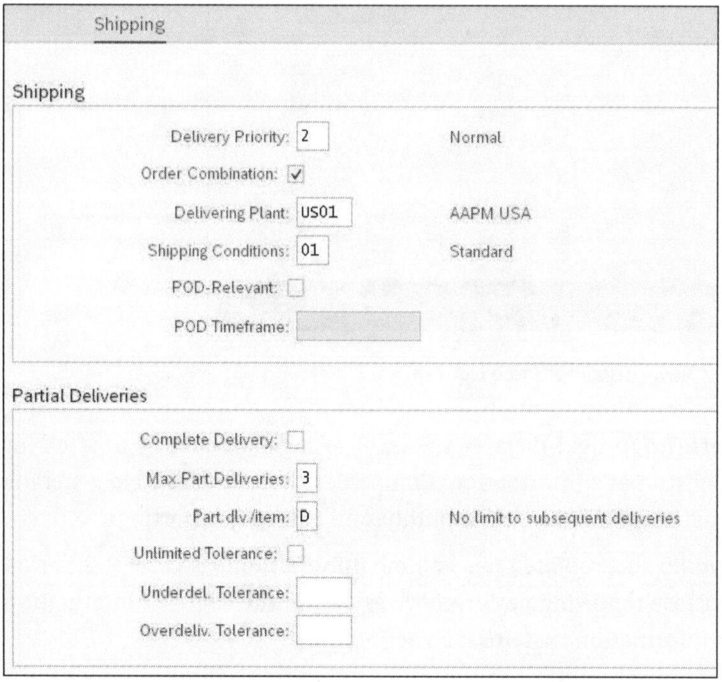

Figure 2.48 Shipping Information

Using the **Delivery Priority** field is not mandatory, and most companies use the same value for all customers. Many companies feel that the decision which customer order take stock or ship first should be made on a case-by-case basis and can't be mandated as a rule at the customer master level. You can still change the delivery priority at the sales order level. You can also use this functionality even if the ultimate decision is made at the individual order level, but you must remember to review this field. If you forget, the default value for the customer master will be used.

Some companies have used this field successfully for the major customers (such as large retailers and manufacturers) to avoid the penalties that these customers may impose for noncompliance with agreed-upon delivery windows.

To configure delivery priorities, follow the menu path **SAP Customizing Implementation Guide • Sales and Distribution • Master Data • Business Partners • Customers • Shipping • Define Delivery Priorities.** On the screen that opens, click on the **New Entries** button or press F5.

As shown in Figure 2.49, specify a two-character delivery priority code (**Delivery priority**), maintain a production priority value (**Production priority**), and add a description (**Description**).

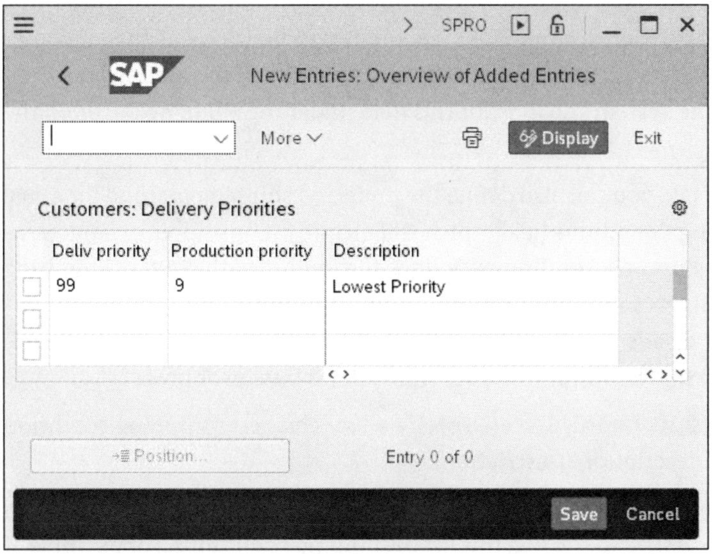

Figure 2.49 Defining New Delivery Priorities

The **Production Priority** field is used when the demand generated by a sales order factors into material requirements planning (MRP) to create planned production orders. Demands with a lower value in the **Production Priority** field will be scheduled to be produced first. However, this functionality is part of production planning (PP) and will not be covered in this book.

Return to the **Shipping** tab, the **Order Combination** flag controls whether this customer can combine separate orders into the same shipment. This field affects how a customer receives information electronically, for instance, via an advanced shipping notification (ASN). The customer recipients of the ASN need to be ready to identify their customer purchase order number at the line level and not at the header.

When printing packing slips, you may have different customer purchase orders (POs) at the line level. If your customer can handle customer POs at the item level, typically, you can allow order combinations by activating this flag. Otherwise, you must leave this flag blank.

The **Delivering Plant** indicates the preferred sourcing facility when entering orders using this customer and the ship-to address. This field is contingent on the material being maintained for this plant (see Chapter 3, Section 3.1.4, for details). If this field is blank, the default delivery plant found on the material master sales view will be used.

You can overwrite this default delivery plant for specific materials using the customer-material information record. The sales order will first look at the customer material information record; if the plant is not maintained or if the material does not exist at that plant, the system will look for this field under the **Shipping** tab or on the material master.

Under the **Shipping** tab, you can also define the preferred shipping method for a customer in the **Shipping Conditions** field, which will dictate other shipping characteristics. To configure shipping conditions, follow the menu path **SAP Customizing Implementation Guide • Logistics Execution • Shipping • Basic Shipping Functions • Shipping Point and Goods Receiving Point Determination • Define Shipping Conditions.** On the screen that opens, click on the **New Entries** button or press F5.

As shown in Figure 2.50, on this screen, specify a two-character shipping condition code (**SC**) and add a description (**Description**).

We recommend keeping the list of shipping conditions as short as possible. You can remove redundant carriers to shorten this list of shipping conditions. For example, if next-day air service is offered both by FedEx and UPS, you could have a "Next Day Air" shipping condition instead of both "FedEx Next Day Air" and "UPS Next Day Air" shipping conditions. The carrier is then specified by the partner function **SP** (carrier), which we'll describe in detail in Section 2.3.5.

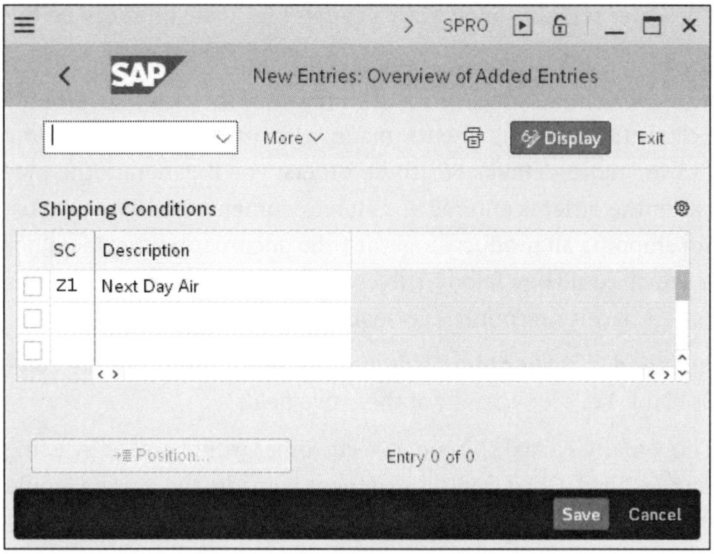

Figure 2.50 Defining New Shipping Conditions

The **POD-Relevant** and **POD Timeframe** fields indicate that, whenever a product is shipped to this customer, you'll need to wait to confirm whether the delivery was really delivered or not. This proof of delivery may be done manually or electronically via an interface from the carrier. Most carriers offer this service, but you'll need to set it up. Some countries (such as China) require proof of delivery on all shipments. Some customers may also require proof of delivery before processing your invoices, so you may want to avoid sending invoices when you lack proof of delivery.

Another functionality called valuated stock-in-transit (VSIT) uses the proof of delivery functionality to defer the cost of goods sold (COGS) accounting for revenue recognition purposes, which we'll describe in more detail in Chapter 9. If shipments to this customer require proof of delivery by default, you must select the **POD-Relevant** flag.

Your company may want to define a default amount (in days) after which proof of delivery will be automatically marked. You can use this option by entering a default number of days in the **POD Timeframe** field. This value can still be changed at the order level.

The **Complete Delivery** flag controls whether a customer accepts partial shipments. For example, if you don't have the full quantity available for the products they ordered, these customers have agreed that products can be shipped as they become available. If the customer does not accept partial shipment, this flag must be left blank; in this case, the order remains open until all quantities in all lines can be fulfilled.

Some countries require the **Complete Delivery** flag be activated for export shipments because of the strict customs arrangements made with order-based pro-forma invoices (Section 2.3.3 for more details). For these orders, you'll generate the pro-forma invoice right after the order is entered and start documentation with the customs office. Thus, not shipping all products together, the documentation would not reflect the shipment, which could be a felony, subject to penalties. Thus, marking this flag for export customers in certain countries is required.

The **Max.Part.Deliveries** and **Part.dlv./item** fields are only applicable when the **Complete Delivery** field is blank. Let's look briefly at these two fields:

- You may control how many partial shipments a customer would accept by using the **Max.Part.Deliveries** field. Once the last shipment is made, the system would not perform further shipments.
- You can also control whether each line may be shipped partially by using the **Part.dlv./item** field. For instance, a customer may allow you to ship partial orders as long as each line is shipped in full.

After picking products and preparing for shipping, you may realize that you have more or less quantity than what the customer originally ordered. Some customers may allow you to ship and charge for the actual quantity being shipped. If so, you can either specify an **Unlimited Tolerance** of quantity differences by marking this flag or indicate an **Underdel. Tolerance** percentage for short shipments or **Overdeliv. Tolerance** percentage when we ship more than what they ordered.

In case of short shipments, the order may be considered completely shipped even if the shipped quantity is less than the ordered quantity. This functionality is common for companies that use volumes or any physically measurable unit of measurement. The precision of shipping quantity depends on logistics variables that are often hard to control.

2.3.3 Billing

Under the **Billing** tab, shown in Figure 2.51, the first field is the **Subs. Invoice Proc.** flag, which indicates whether a customer requires manual maintenance of a billing document after it is created and printed. This field will prevent an order from being transferred to accounting immediately (see Chapter 10 for additional details). This field is not commonly used since most companies strive to eliminate manual intervention at the time of billing. Making changes to the billing document is often considered risky since the price may not match the sales order. That difference may cause issues with the customer as well as cause reporting inconsistencies between order and invoice data.

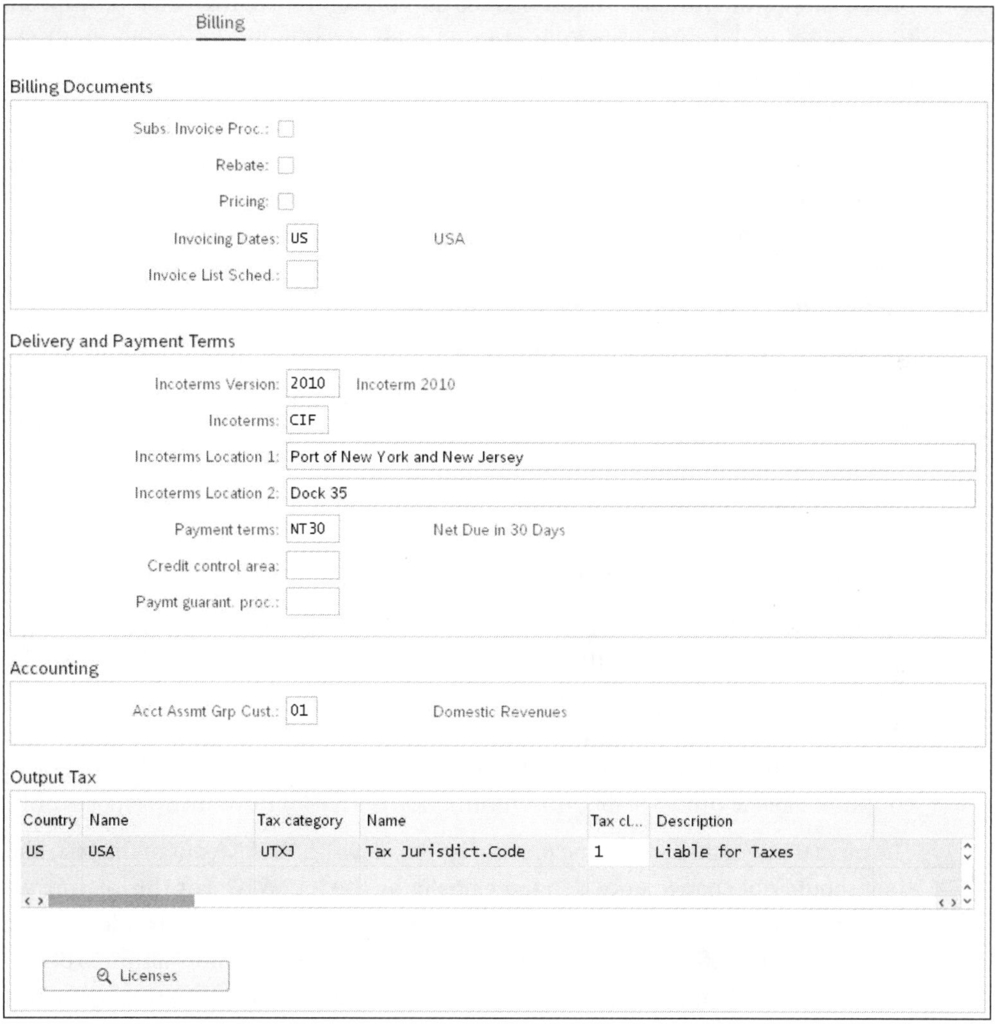

Figure 2.51 Billing Information

The **Rebate** flag indicates whether a customer is eligible for rebate programs. The **Pricing** flag is used in conjunction with the customer hierarchy set up. If a customer has this flag, price calculations will be affected; otherwise, the hierarchy assignment is used only for reporting purposes, and pricing will be unaffected.

If you specify a calendar in the **Invoicing Dates** field, the system will define scheduled billing dates, which are only dates marked as working days. Thus, you'll only create invoices on working days according to that calendar, skipping weekends and holidays, depending on how the billing background job and variants are set up.

Some companies use these fields to create calendars for customers that only accept billing on a few days of the week or month. You can define a calendar with only those days defined as working days, and the billing date will only be assigned the next available date according to this calendar. Billing dates are defined at the time of order entry. When the billing background job is scheduled, the billing date can be used as the main selection criteria. For more details, see Chapter 10.

The **Invoice List Sched.** calendar control when the invoice list is created. This field is used if your company needs to create an invoice right away due to an accounting requirement, but this invoice won't necessarily be sent immediately to customers. On a later date (according to this calendar), invoices are combined into an invoice list and sent to the customer as a single document. This feature is often used by large online retailers but also some brick-and-mortar companies because this approach reduces the accounts payable complexity for our customers.

The International Commercial Terms (Incoterms) fields (**Incoterms Version**, **Incoterms**, **Incoterms Location 1**, and **Incoterms Location 2**) refer to the terms defined by the International Chamber of Commerce (ICC) and World Trade Organization (WTO). The goal of these fields is to represent the transfer of ownership of goods when they are shipped. In many countries, this information also dictates who pays for freight. In countries like the United States, this information is used for insurance purposes only.

The official Incoterm codes come preconfigured on SAP S/4HANA out of the box, and they should not change once defined globally by the ICC/WTO. For this reason, we won't describe the configuration steps available to create new fields. Ideally, you would adapt the definition of Incoterms in the US (i.e., use this information to define who pays for freight), but most companies end up using one of the reserved fields instead (**Customer Groups 1** through **5**, described in more detail in Section 2.3.6).

ICC released a new version of Incoterms in 2010, and a new version may come in the future. SAP S/4HANA allows for new versions via the **Incoterms Version** field, which specifies which preconfigured **Incoterms** codes are valid for the selected version. For some Incoterms, you'll need to indicate the place where the transfer of ownership takes place in the **Incoterms Location 1** and **2** fields, for instance, a port, a warehouse, an origin, a destination, etc.

On this tab, you'll also specify the **Payment terms** you use with this customer. This information may be changed on the sales order, but depending on your credit check settings, an order may be put hold for manual review by the credit department. Most companies use the same **Payment terms** on the sales order unchanged, as defined on this customer master data field. The configuration of payments terms is performed by the finance team.

The credit check policy is defined by the **Credit control area**, which has a default value, configured by the company code assigned to the sales organization. This field allows you to assign the customer to a **Credit control area** different than the default setting from the company code. If not specified, you'll use the default. Companies tend to use only one credit control area to keep credit check rules simple. The configuration of credit control area is performed by the finance team.

The **Paymt guarant. proc.** field is part of the accounts receivable collections functionality. A typical use is for letters of credit, which are used to ensure customers pay their invoices. Typically, letters of credit are also used for customers with which you don't have a relationship, that are unwilling to pay upfront, or that are from countries that you don't usually do business in. The configuration of the credit control area is performed by the finance team.

The **Acct Assmt Grp Cust.** field is used for revenue account determination. You can have different revenue accounts for different types of customer. If required by the finance team, you can create new revenue accounts by creating new values for this field associated with the account determination configuration, which we'll describe in Chapter 10.

To configure account assignment groups, open Transaction OVK8 or follow the menu path **SAP Customizing Implementation Guide • Sales and Distribution • Basic Functions • Account Assignment/Costing • Revenue Account Determination • Check Master Data Relevant For Account Assignment • Customers: Account Assignment Groups.** On the screen that opens, click on the **New Entries** button or press F5.

In the screen shown in Figure 2.52, specify a two-character customer account assignment group code (**Acct Assmt Grp Cust.**) and add a description (**Description**).

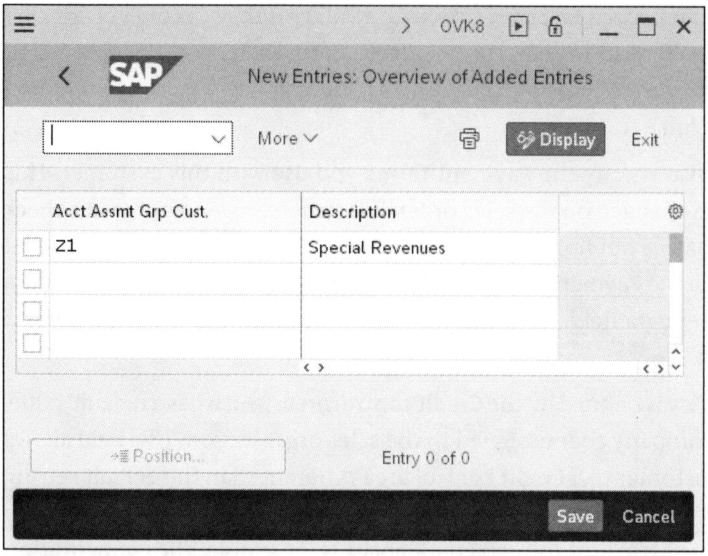

Figure 2.52 Defining New Customer Account Assignment Groups

Returning to the **Billing** tab, the **Output Tax** section of this screen will display the **Tax Category** defined for the countries where you have plants that can fulfill orders entered by this distribution chain. The country-based configuration for these tax categories are standard and are unlikely to change, so we won't describe their configuration in this book.

For each **Tax Category** that appears in this section, you'll need to select the **Tax Classification** that this customer is eligible for. This code typically indicates if the customer is taxable or tax exempt for that type of tax. Some countries may have other classifications to choose from that will affect the tax rate that is applicable to this customer.

This information should ideally be interfaced to the external tax calculation tools your company utilizes, a situation we described in detail in Section 2.2.9.

2.3.4 Documents

The **Documents** tab, shown in Figure 2.53, allows you to monitor and maintain the condition technique-based output message determination. Using SAP GUI, customer condition technique-based output types and determination procedures are configured by following the menu path **SAP Customizing Implementation Guide • Cross-Application Components • Output Control**. Further configuration details will be provided in Chapter 4, Section 4.7.

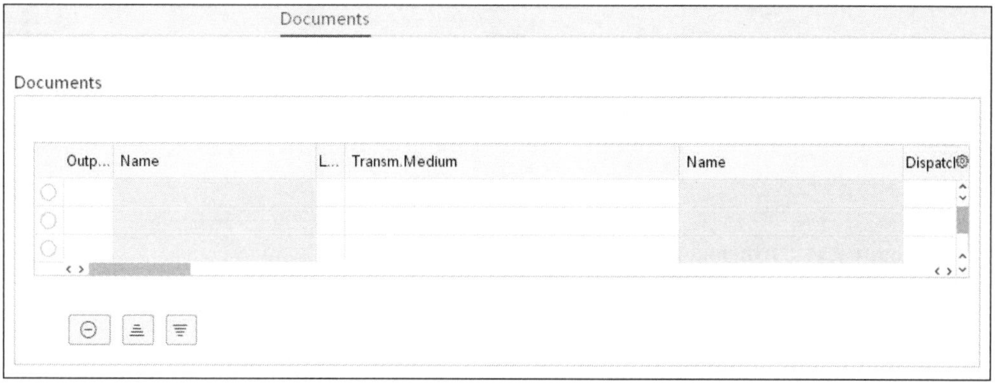

Figure 2.53 Documents (Output Control)

For business partners, outputs are mostly used to interface data to external systems. For instance, if you're using a third-party CRM tool such a Salesforce or Siebel, you'll need to send these tools information about your customers created in SAP S/4HANA to ensure their business partner number, as well as the relevant master data, are up to date.

This master data transfer takes place via IDocs (Intermediate Documents) with message type DEBMAS also referred to as Application Link Enabling (ALE) or Electronic Data Interchange (EDI). We won't go into the full details of this functionality, which is technical in nature and outside the scope of this book.

You can also define outputs for customers that allow you to print their master data out using a predefined format. This requirement is rather uncommon but still achievable.

2.3.5 Partner Functions

The partner function and partner determination functionality, available under the **Partner Functions** tab, shown in Figure 2.54, is the mechanism for defining relationships between customer master entries according to the role they play in sales transactions.

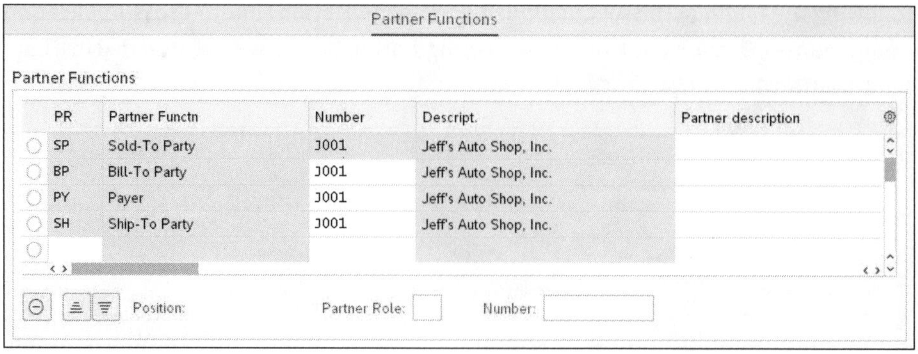

Figure 2.54 Partner Functions

Once a customer is created, you'll need to assign partner functions on this screen using the **PR** field to qualify the roles they may play. Four basic partner functions are defined to process sales orders:

- **Sold-to Party (SP)**
  The customer will send you purchase orders that will become sales orders in SAP S/4HANA. This value represents a customer location, where the buyer is based.
- **Bill-to Party (BP)**
  Customer that will receive your invoices for processing. This value represents a customer location that manages vendor invoices. In some countries, this value dictates important fiscal characteristics.
- **Payer (PY)**
  Entity that will pay for the product you sell to this customer. This value represents the location where the customer's accounts payable department performs its duties.
- **Ship-to (SH)**
  Entity that will receive the product you sell to this customer. This entity may be part of your customer's organization or not. Commonly, shipments to the address of your customer's customers are called *drop shipment locations*. You only need to enter these entities in the master data if you expect to use them multiple times. Otherwise, we recommend using the one-time customer functionality for one-off drop ship orders.

On this screen, you can only enter the sold-to party partner function (**SP**) once, but you can enter multiple values for the other partner functions.

When an order is entered for a sold-to party, you'll be prompted to review any multiple entries maintained on the other three partner functions. You can select from the list. At the order level, you can have one (and only one) of each of these four partner functions on each line. If these functions are the same across all lines, you'll only need to make the selection once, in the header.

Some other noteworthy partner functions you can select on this screen include the following:

- **Contact Person (CP)**
  Individual people that may play a role in this sold-to customer's sales orders. These people must be created as business partners in this same transaction but using the **Person** option instead of **Organization** on the initial screen of Transaction BP.
- **External Sales Agent (ES)**
  Entities that assist your company in selling product/services to this customer.
- **Special Stock Partner (SB)**
  Entities that may house products intended for this sold-to customer under consignment. More details can be found in Chapter 12, Section 12.1.
- **Forwarding Agent (CR)**
  The carrier that this customer prefers you use when you ship products to them.
- **Sales Employee (SE)**
  The employee at your company that services this customer.
- **Employee Responsible (ER)**
  The employee at your company that acts as the account manager for this customer.

Companies often find adding new partner functions for various business-specific purposes necessary. To configure partner functions, open Transaction VOPAN or follow the menu path **SAP Customizing Implementation Guide • Sales and Distribution • Basic Functions • Partner Determination • Set Up Partner Determination**. On the screen that opens, select the **Partner Functions** option in the **Dialog Structure** menu on the left by double-clicking on it and then clicking on the **New Entries** button or press [F5].

Figure 2.55 shows Transaction VOPAN. If you follow the menu path instead, you'll be taken straight to the customer master configuration screen for partner functions.

As shown in Figure 2.55, we're creating a new partner function so we can maintain all the mechanics that work at this customer's location. This fictitious requirement for our example AAPM company requires that we share technical information related our product directly to the customer's mechanics. This type of requirement requires the configuration of new partner functions on the customer master.

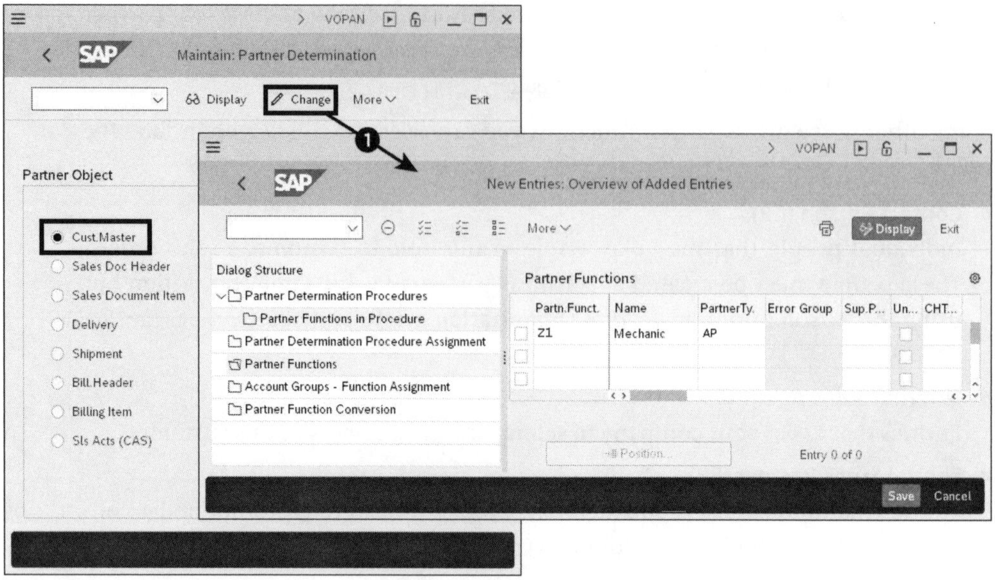

Figure 2.55 Creating New Partner Functions for the Customer Master

On this screen, specify a two-character partner function code (**Partn.Funct.**) and add a description (**Name**). You'll also need to maintain the partner type (**PartnerTy...**) used to populate the partner numbers for this new partner function. You can use the customers (KU), vendors (LI), and contact person (AP) partner types and more. In our example, the mechanics must be created as people (**AP**).

The **Error Group** appears automatically once you select a partner type. This field controls the kind of validation that must be made to the partner number selected for this partner function when a user maintains it on the master data screen.

The **Sup.Partn.Func** column (**Higher Level Partner Function**) is used when a sales order is entered. If this field is blank, this partner function will be copied from the sold-to field (SP). You can change this behavior by selecting the partner function SH. Thus, all mechanics would be copied from the ship-to party instead. In our example, we'll use the default information (from the sold-to pary) because these customers usually drop ship materials to their customers, and thus keeping the mechanics under the sold-to master data makes the most sense.

The **Unique** flag controls whether you can enter multiple partners on the customer master data partner function screen or only one partner can be entered. The sold-to partner function comes out of the box with this flag activated, which is why you can only enter one partner.

Note that creating new partner functions on this screen is not sufficient to make them available for data entry on the customer master. You must also assign the new partner function to a determination procedure either by opening Transaction VOPAN or by following the menu path **SAP Customizing Implementation Guide • Sales and Distribution • Basic Functions • Partner Determination • Set Up Partner Determination**. Select the **CUST** partner determination procedure by clicking on the selection box. Then, select the **Partner Functions in Procedure** option in the **Dialog Structure** menu on the left by double-clicking on it and then clicking the **New Entries** button or press [F5]. As shown in Figure 2.56, which shows Transaction VOPAN, select the **CUST** option and click on the **Change** button as we did earlier when configuring the partner function.

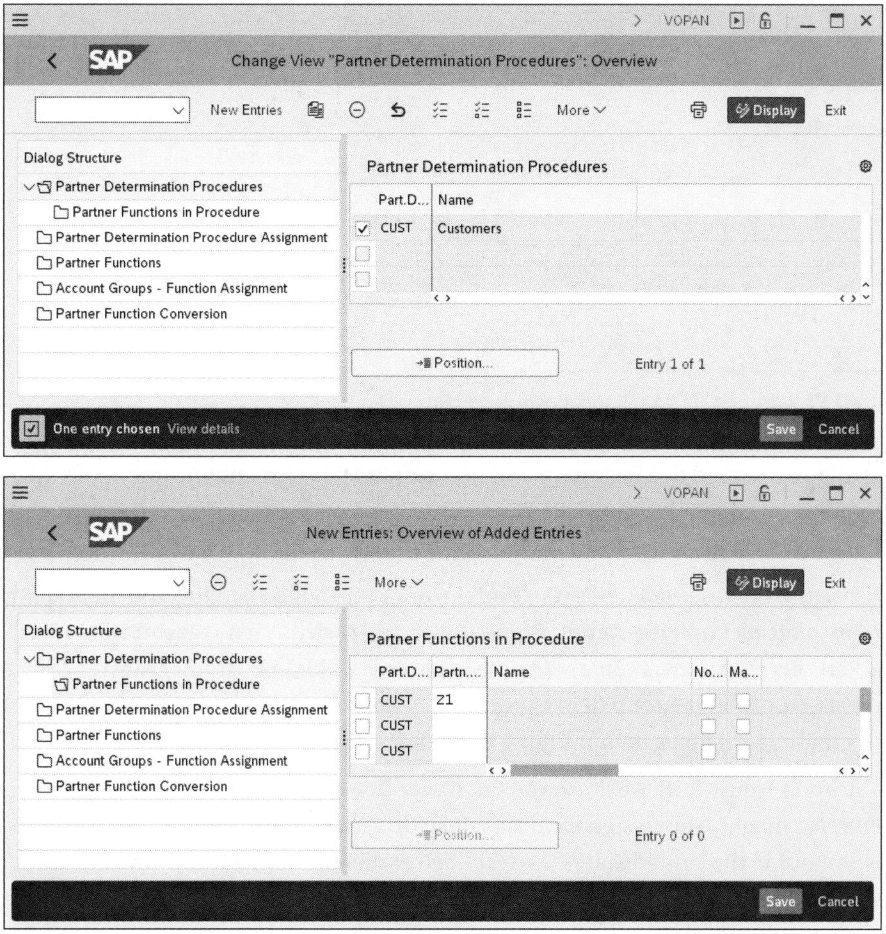

Figure 2.56 Adding New Partner Functions to Determination Procedures

On this screen, enter the new partner function to be added to the procedure under the partner function column (**Partn...**). You can also indicate whether the partner associated with this partner function can be changed after being entered on a sales order by flagging the not modifiable column (**No...**). You can also flag the new partner function as mandatory by selecting the mandatory check box (**Ma...**).

2.3.6 Additional Data

Similar to the reserved general data fields described in Section 2.2.10, the **Additional Data** tab has five fields, as shown in Figure 2.57, which are provided by SAP but reserved for your company's specific applications. These fields do not have any predefined meaning, and you can configure and use them freely.

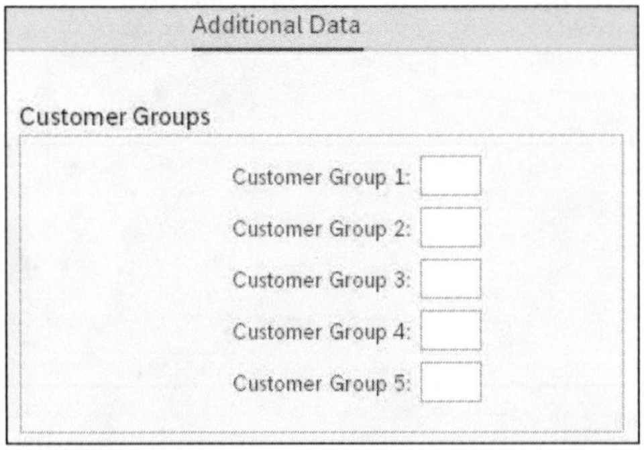

Figure 2.57 Additional Data (Sales Reserved Fields)

To change a reserved field's description, you would use a text enhancement in Transaction CMOD. This task is typically considered development, and so will not be covered in this book.

To configure the reserved fields (**Customer Group 1** through **5**), follow the menu path **SAP Customizing Implementation Guide • Sales and Distribution • Master Data • Business Partners • Customers • Sales • Maintain Reserve Fields In Customer Master.** Select the desired **Customer Group** field to configure and click **New Entries** or press [F5]. In our example, we'll focus on modifying **Customer Group 1**.

As shown in Figure 2.58, we'll use the **Customer Group 1** field as an indicator of who will pay for freight. This designation is usually driven by the Incoterms in most countries, but not in the United States (as described earlier in Section 2.3.3). On this screen, specify a three-character customer group code (**Customer Group 1**) and enter a description (**Description**).

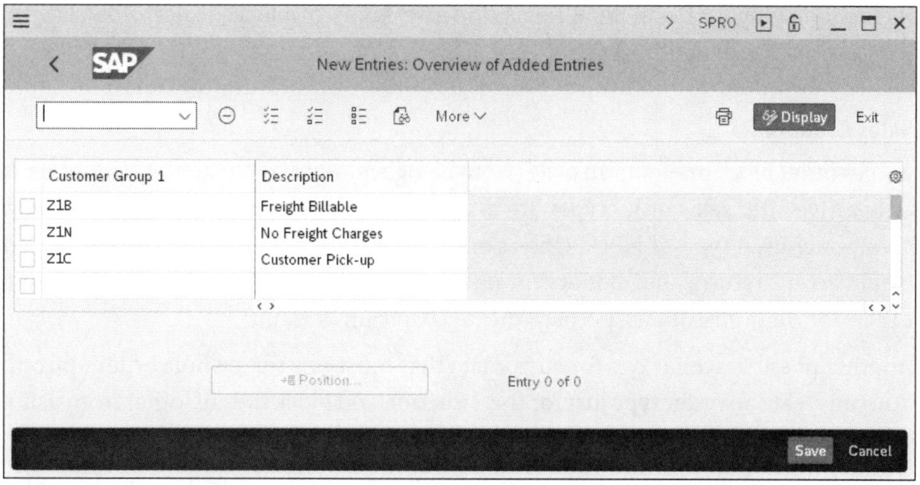

Figure 2.58 Creating New Customer Group 1 Entries

2.3.7 Status

Under the **Status** tab, shown in Figure 2.59, you can manage the blocks/holds that are assigned by default to this customer. Each block/hold may be applicable to **All Sales Areas** or to a **Selected Sales Area**.

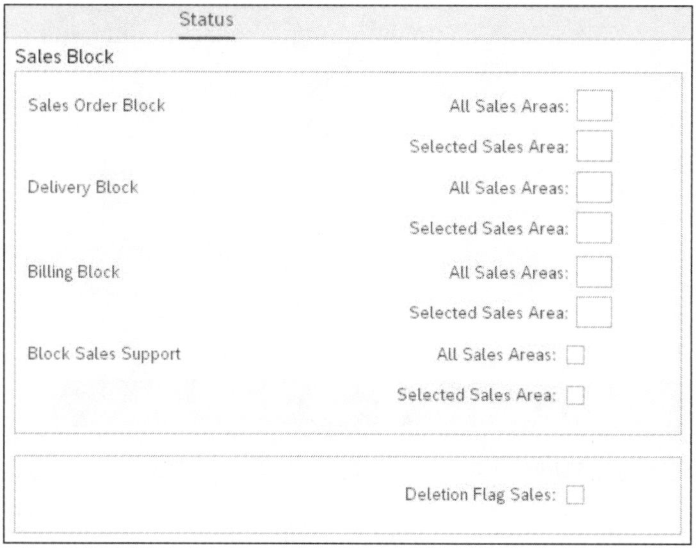

Figure 2.59 Customer Sales Status

In the following sections, we'll focus on three kinds of blocks: sales order blocks, delivery blocks, and billing blocks.

Sales Order Block

A sales order block prevents an order from being entered for a customer. This block is only active after sales order types are assigned to it. This block is probably the least commonly used type of block. One common use is for customers from which you would accept returns, but not accept new orders. You can also block free of charge orders for these customers, perhaps due to suspicion of fraud.

Another possible scenario is for customers that must pay for a whole order upfront. You can create an order type just for this situation and block the customer from using the regular terms in more traditional sales order types.

To configure sales order blocks, follow the menu path **SAP Customizing Implementation Guide • Sales and Distribution • Sales • Sales Documents • Define And Assign Reasons For Blocking • Define Blocking Reasons for Sales Documents.** On the screen that opens, click on the **New Entries** button or press F5.

As shown in Figure 2.60, select a language (**Language**) for the new sales order block, specify a two-character sales document block code (**Sales Document Block**) and add a description (**Description**).

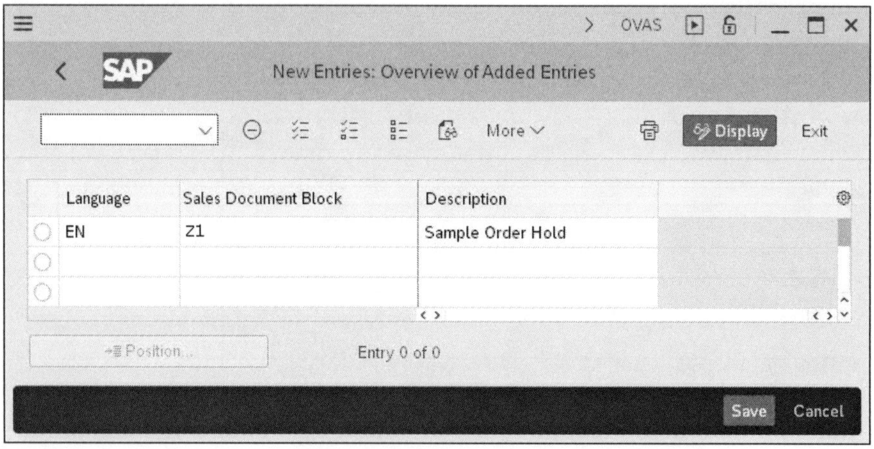

Figure 2.60 Defining a New Sales Order Block

Next, assign a sales order block to a sales order type by following the menu path **SAP Customizing Implementation Guide • Sales and Distribution • Sales • Sales Documents •**

Define And Assign Reasons For Blocking • Assign Blocking Reasons to Sales Document Types. On the screen that opens, click on the **New Entries** button or press F5.

As shown in Figure 2.61, select the **Sales Document Block** and a **Sales Document Type**. In our example, customers with the sales order block Z1 will be blocked from having orders entered of sales order type OR.

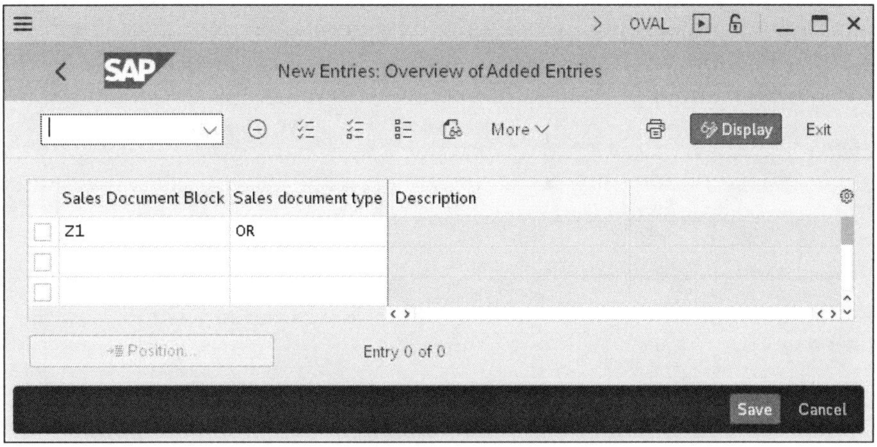

Figure 2.61 Assigning Sales Order Blocks to Sales Order Types

Note that the terms "sales order" and "sales documents" are being used interchangeably because "documents" can also refer to order types that are not customer orders, but instead a free of charge delivery, a return material authorization (RMA), or a credit/debit order. However, in the United States, companies that use SAP S/4HANA solutions generally refer to all of these documents as "orders."

Delivery Block

A delivery block is used to prevent specific logistics activities, such as the following:

- Allocation of stock to a sales order
- Printing/issuing of order confirmation forms
- Creation of delivery documents
- Picking
- Shipping/post goods issue operation
- Drop shipment purchase requisition creation

These activities can take place across all customer orders or on an order-by-order basis.

Depending on the delivery block code you select, one or more of these logistic activities could be blocked for the customer. Note that a delivery block may also be assigned at the order level by default to the sales order based on order type configuration. In this case, the delivery block is not controlled by these customer master fields.

To configure delivery blocks, follow the menu path **SAP Customizing Implementation Guide • Logistics Execution • Shipping • Deliveries • Define Reasons for Blocking in Shipping.** On the screen that opens, click on the **New Entries** button or press [F5].

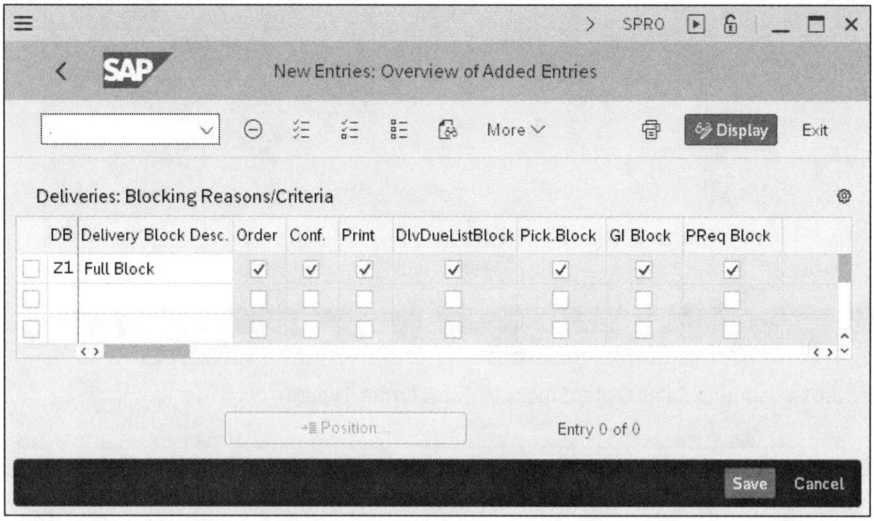

Figure 2.62 Defining New Delivery Blocks

As shown in Figure 2.62, specify a new two-character delivery block code (**DB**) and add a description (**Delivery Block Desc.**). Next, select the following checkboxes:

- **Order**

  When checked/assigned on the customer master, this flag indicates that this block is applicable on an order-by-order basis. In other words, each order entered for this customer will, by default, be assigned with this delivery block. To process the sales order, you would need to remove this block on the order.

  When the **Order** field is blank, this delivery block, when assigned to the customer, will block all sales orders entered for this customer. To process any of these orders, you would need to remove the delivery block from the customer master.

Until you remove this block from the customer master, even though each order will not have a delivery block assigned to them, the orders will continue to be blocked as if did.

Once removed from the customer master, all orders would be immediately unblocked.

- **Conf.**
  This flag controls whether confirmed stock on this order schedule line should be saved or the confirmed quantity is just displayed (see Chapter 7 for more details). When marked, this flag will cause the confirmed quantity to be ignored when saving the order. You'll see a confirmed quantity of zero when displaying the order, but when creating or changing the order, the actual confirmed quantity information will be displayed.

  Thus, even though the ATP check is telling us that stock is available on a given date, we won't commit or allocate that stock to this order due to this delivery block.

  As a result, the stock will be kept available for other sales orders to use/allocate. Depending on how you set up your ATP check rules, this functionality may be already the case for all orders, in which case this flag is not relevant.

  When the **Conf.** field is blank, the order could still allocate stock even though the delivery block is assigned.

- **Print**
  This flag controls the printing/issuing of order confirmations and other order-based forms. When selected, this delivery block will prevent output messages from the sales order. If left blank, message behavior is not affected.

  This option is commonly used when you need to review an order received via EDI 865 before sending an EDI 866 order confirmation response back to the customer.

- **DlvDueListBlock**
  This flag controls whether delivery documents can be created as part of batch processing for a sales order when this block is assigned. In general, you'll use Transaction VL10 (Delivery Due List) to create delivery documents for several orders at once, often as a background job, but also for online transactions. The delivery block affects this behavior when the **DlvDueListBlock** checkbox is selected. The behavior is not affected when this field is blank.

  Note that users can overwrite the standard behavior of these blocks as described in this list rather easily. Therefore, you should not use these blocks to hold orders as a security measure, but instead to manage what may happen automatically and what requires manual review.

- **Pick.Block**
  This flag controls whether picking operations can be performed for an existing delivery document. When selected, this delivery block will stop stock picking operations. When blank, picking will be allowed even if the delivery block is present.
- **GI Block**
  This flag controls whether shipments can be completed for a delivery document via the post goods issue operation or not. When selected, documents with this delivery block will stop post goods issue operations from occurring.

  However, this block may cause problems because the warehouse usually ships products first before performing the post goods issue operation on the SAP S/4HANA transaction. If this block is present, you'll be blocked from registering the shipment in the system even though the product has already left the warehouse.

  If you activate this flag for the delivery block, you'll need to ensure the warehouse has a way to check for this flag before shipping the product out the door.
- **PReq Block**
  This flag controls where a purchase requisition should be created for a sales order with this delivery block. This flag is applicable for individual purchase requirement scenarios such as drop shipping and special orders. When active, purchase requisitions cannot be created for orders with this delivery block. When blank, you can create purchase requisitions even though the delivery block is active.

Billing Block

A billing block stops the issuing of invoices for this customer. This block does not affect order entry or logistics, just the creation of the billing document. This block is commonly used with credit and debit memos to allow for a review of the memo request before awarding credit or issuing additional debit to customers.

At the customer master level, a billing block can allow you to review shipments and orders before issuing invoices. Companies may use this functionality if unsure about pricing policies, payment terms, and other financial information on the sales order. Using a billing block allows you time to perform a final review before any invoice is issued, which is not common since this step adds significant additional manual effort and may cause delays that could result in accounting problems. Ideally, the shipment and invoice should happen on the same date to make reconciliation easier, but a billing block may add an undesirable gap between these events.

Commonly, billing blocks are configured during projects that are not assigned to all the necessary billing document types, which is ineffective because invoices are issued when they're not supposed to. In other words, unless the billing block is assigned to all the billing document types it is intended to block, the block won't hold, and an invoice could be created even if the document is blocked.

To configure billing blocks, follow the menu path **SAP Customizing Implementation Guide • Sales and Distribution • Billing • Billing Documents • Define Blocking Reasons for Billing • Define Blocking Reasons for Billing.** On the screen that opens, click on the **New Entries** button or press F5.

As shown in Figure 2.63, specify a two-character billing block code (**Billing Block**) and add a description (**Billing Block Desc.**).

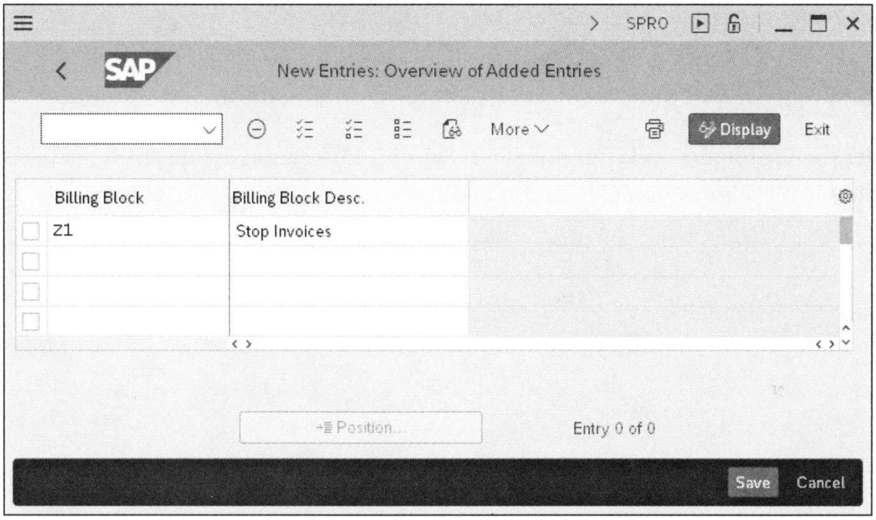

Figure 2.63 Defining New Billing Blocks

To assign billing blocks to sales order types, follow the menu path **SAP Customizing Implementation Guide • Sales and Distribution • Billing • Billing Documents • Define Blocking Reasons for Billing • Assign Blocking Reasons to Billing Types.** On the screen that opens, click on the **New Entries** button or press F5.

As shown in Figure 2.64, select the **Sales Document Block** and a **Sales Document Type**. In our example, we specified that customers with the sales order block Z1 will not be allowed to have orders of sales order type OR entered.

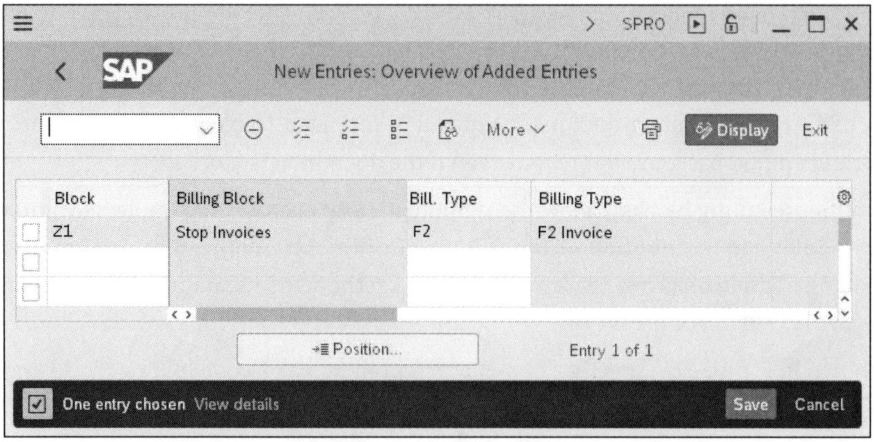

Figure 2.64 Assigning Billing Document Types to Billing Blocks

2.3.8 Customer: Texts

Under the **Customer: Texts** tab, shown in Figure 2.65, you can assign freeform texts applicable for this customer when conducting business under this sales area.

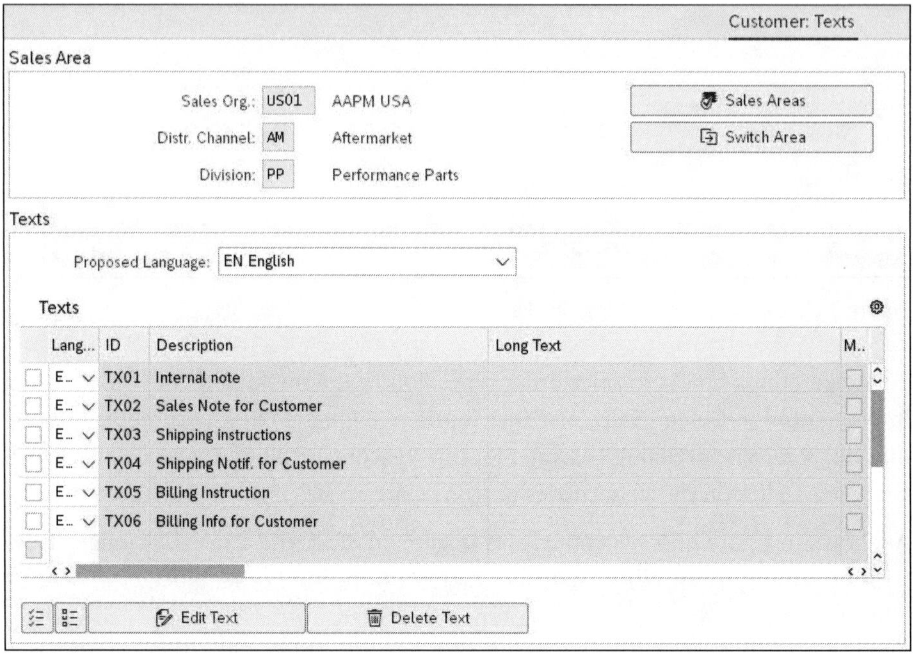

Figure 2.65 Customer Sales Texts

Select the desired type of text (text **ID**) and then click the **Edit Text** button on the bottom of the screen. An editor window opens where you can enter text (as discussed earlier in Section 2.2.4).

To configure text control, open Transaction VOTXN or follow the menu path **SAP Customizing Implementation Guide • Sales and Distribution • Basic Functions • Text Control • Define and Assign Text Determination Procedures • Configuration: Texts**. Select **Sales & Distribution** under **Customer** and click on the **Text Type** button. On the screen that opens, click on the **New Entries** button or press F5.

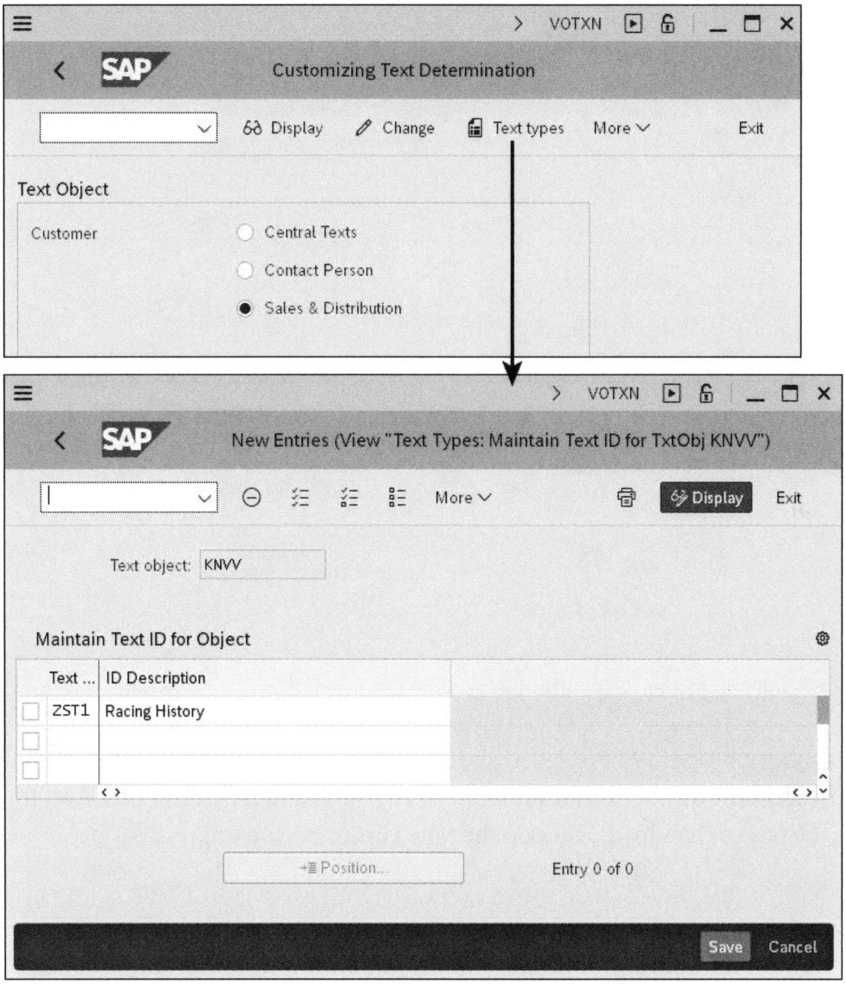

Figure 2.66 Defining New Text Types of Customer Sales Information

On the next screen, shown in Figure 2.66, specify a four-character text type code (**Text...**) and add a description (**ID Description**). This action won't make the new text type available immediately on the customer master. You still need to assign the text to the text determination procedure via Transaction VOTXN or by following the menu path **SAP Customizing Implementation Guide • Sales and Distribution • Basic Functions • Text Control • Define and Assign Text Determination Procedures • Configuration: Texts.** As earlier, select **Sales & Distribution** under **Customer** and then click on the **Change** button, as shown in Figure 2.67.

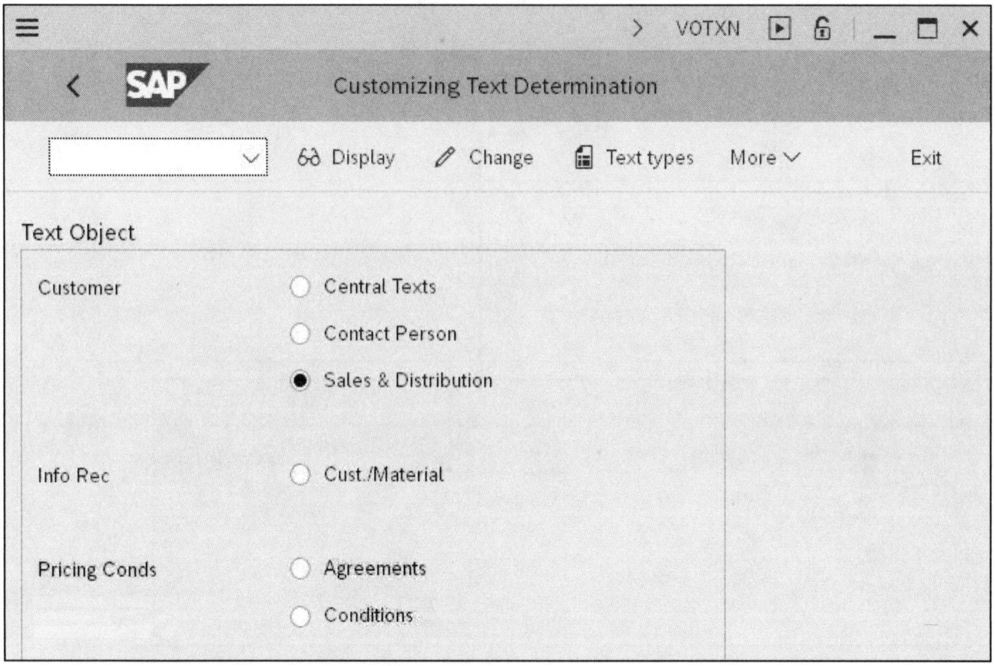

Figure 2.67 Selecting Sales & Distribution and the Change Button

Next, as shown in Figure 2.68, select text determination procedure **TO** and then double-click the **Text ID's in Textprocedure** option in the **Dialog Structure** menu on the left. On the screen that opens, click on the **New Entries** button or press F5.

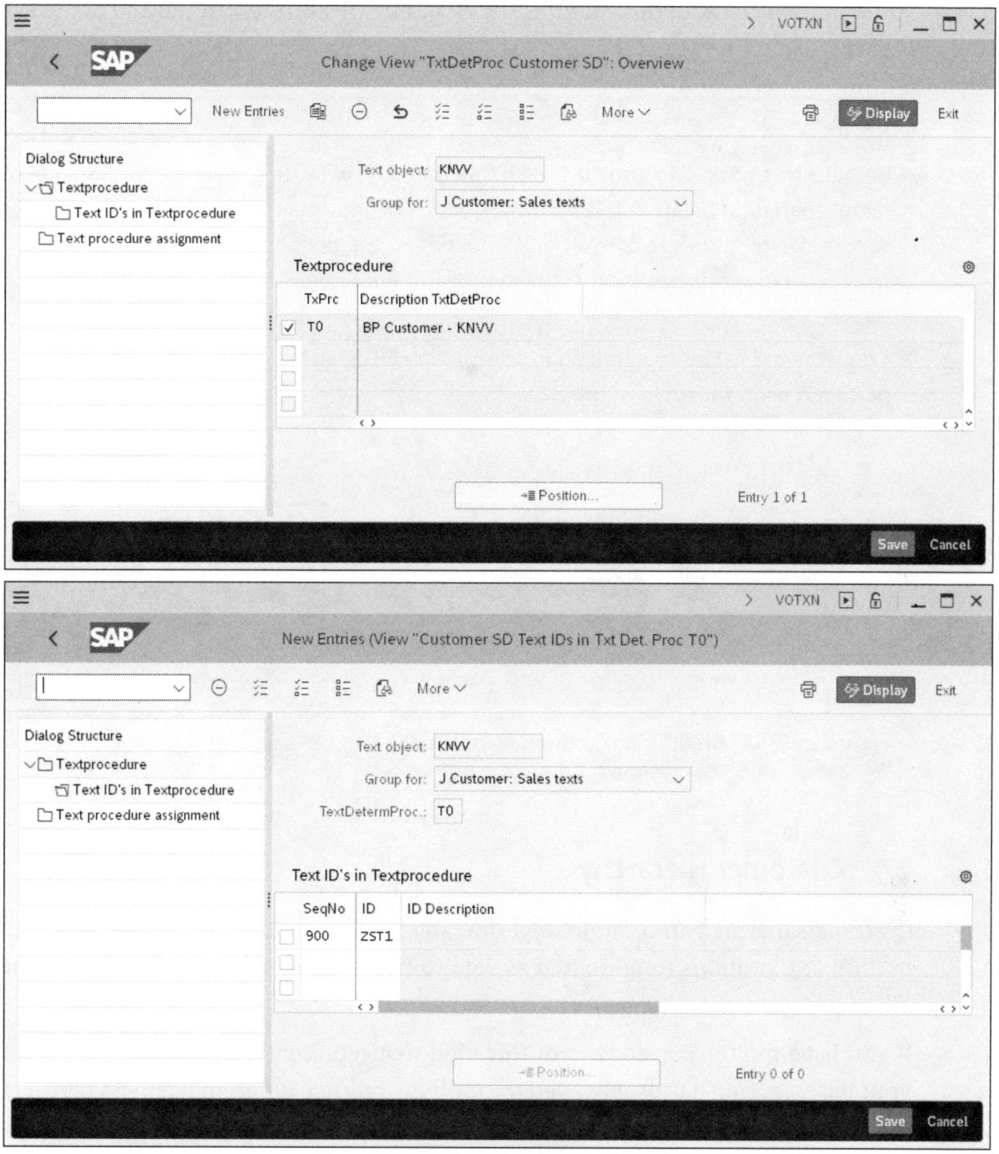

Figure 2.68 Assigning Text Types to Text Determination Procedures

On this screen, specify a three-digit sequence step number (**SeqNo**) indicating where within the procedure this text type should appear and define the text type code (**ID**)

you want to include. In this example, we're adding the next text at the end of the list of text types.

Note

Because this book is focused on sales functionality, we won't cover credit management configuration in detail. However, this configuration may be important for some sales resources to consult and understand the policies currently in place and thus to manage orders with credit holds and know what to do to remedy these issues.

Credit master data is maintained in Transaction BP using the corresponding business partner role, as shown in Figure 2.69.

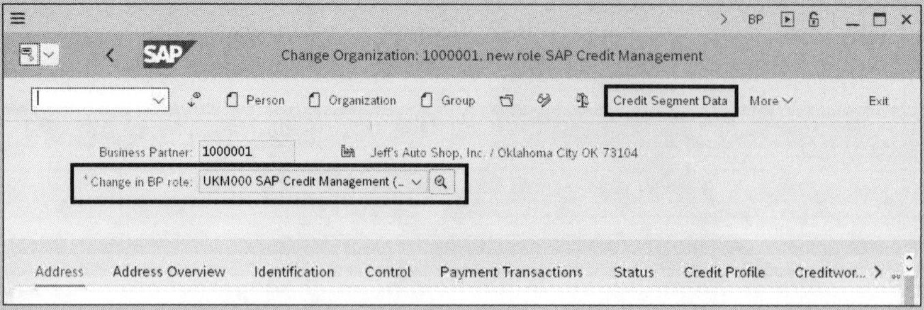

Figure 2.69 SAP Credit Management Master Data

2.4 Customer Hierarchy

Customers that are part of large conglomerates may have different purchasing teams in different locations (represented as sold-to parties), different payers, or different bill-to parties.

If you have multiple customers of this kind that represent a significant portion of your business, you'll probably need to combine multiple different business partners into a structure that represents how they are related to each other. In SAP S/4HANA, you can describe these business partners using a customer hierarchy definition.

Before you can define or assign customer hierarchies, you must define customer hierarchy types. Currently, no customer hierarchy types are provided out of the box because this functionality is expected to be modified in future versions of SAP S/4HANA.

Be sure you keep this caveat in mind if you implement this functionality for your company. If you can postpone the adoption of this functionality, you can avoid rework when the new version is available. You must also assign account groups for the customer hierarchy and assign a sales area for the customer hierarchy to implement and define restrictions for these custom hierarchies.

2.4.1 Define Customer Hierarchy Types

To configure customer hierarchy types, follow the menu path **SAP Customizing Implementation Guide • Sales and Distribution • Master Data • Business Partners • Customers • Customer Hierarchy • Define Hierarchy Types.** On the screen that opens, click on the **New Entries** button or press F5.

As shown in Figure 2.70, specify a one-character customer hierarchy type code (**CustHType**), give this customer hierarchy type a name (**Name**), and specify the partner function (**PartFun...**) that will be used as the starting point when searching for a hierarchy structure.

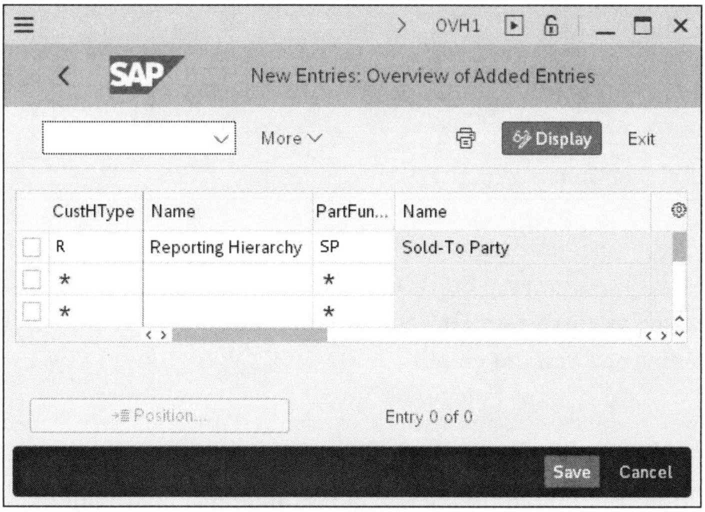

Figure 2.70 Defining New Customer Hierarchy Types

2.4.2 Assign Account Groups for Customer Hierarchy

To assign account groups to each other in the context of a customer hierarchy definition, follow the menu path **SAP Customizing Implementation Guide • Sales and**

Distribution • Master Data • Business Partners • Customers • Customer Hierarchy • Assign Account Groups. On the screen that opens, click on the **New Entries** button or press F5.

As shown in Figure 2.71. you can indicate, for a given customer hierarchy type (**CustH-Type**), which account groups (**Acct Group**) should be assigned to which higher-level account group (**HgLvAcctGr**).

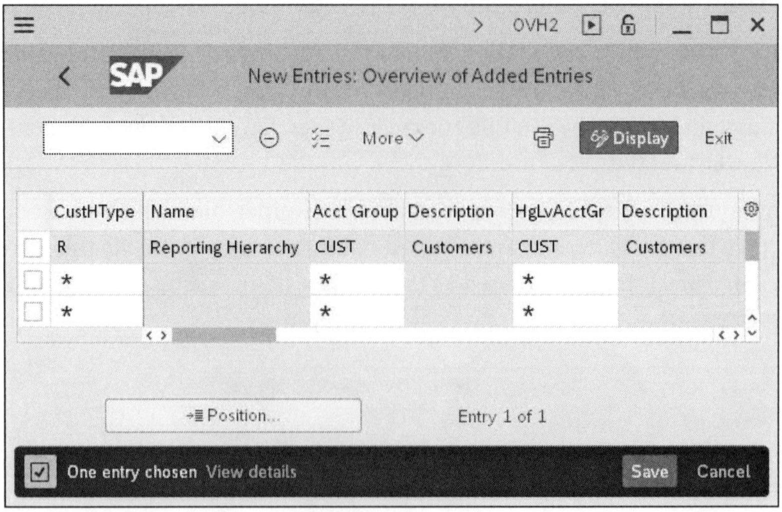

Figure 2.71 Assigning Account Groups

Account groups used to be an important key field definition of the customer master; in SAP S/4HANA, we have the account group **CUST** defined by default for all business partners that are created as customers. So, account group **CUST** is likely sufficient unless you need to define new account groups.

2.4.3 Assign Sales Areas for Customer Hierarchy

To assign sales areas to each other in the context of customer hierarchy definition, follow the menu path **SAP Customizing Implementation Guide • Sales and Distribution • Master Data • Business Partners • Customers • Customer Hierarchy • Assign Sales Areas.** On the screen that opens, click on the **New Entries** button or press F5.

As shown in Figure 2.72 on this screen, indicate, for a given customer hierarchy type (**CustHType**), which sales areas (**Sales Org.**, **Distr. Chl**, and **Division**) may be assigned to which higher-level sales area (**HgLvSlsOrg**, **HLDstrCh**, and **HgLvDivis.**).

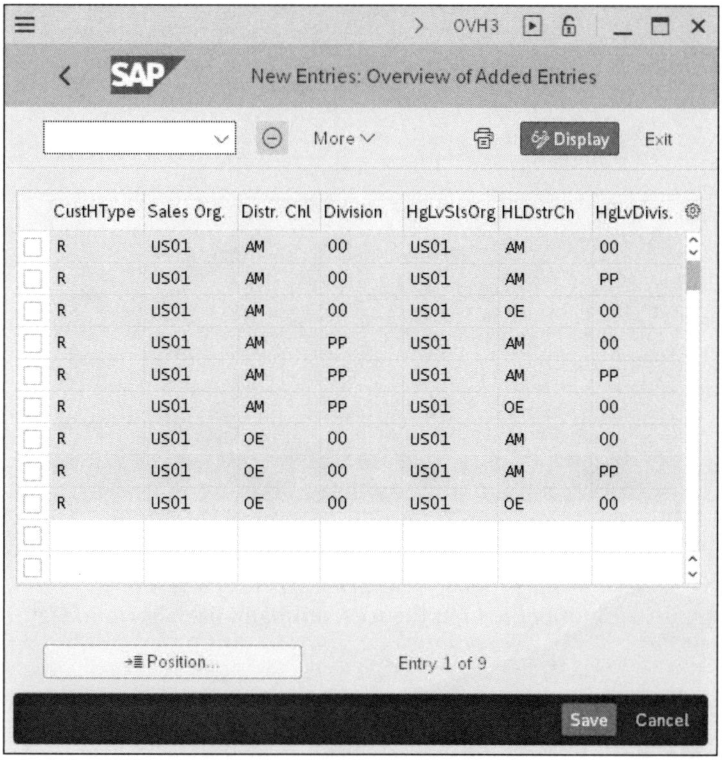

Figure 2.72 Assigning Sales Areas to Be Used for Customer Hierarchies

2.4.4 Assign Customer Hierarchy

Once configuration is completed, you can use Transaction VDH1N to define a customer hierarchy assignment. On the screen shown in Figure 2.73, select the desired **Customer hierarchy type** and the starting customer number (**Customer**). You may want to change the **Validity date** field if this assignment is not valid immediately.

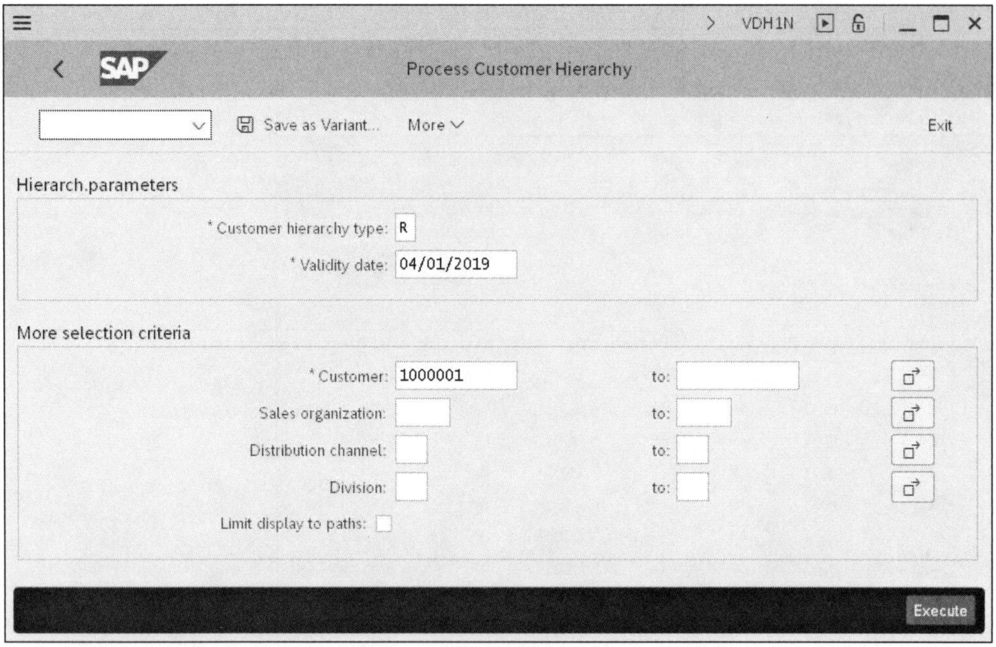

Figure 2.73 Transaction VDH1N: Customer Hierarchy Definition

Next, click on the create assignment icon in the top command bar, shown in Figure 2.74.

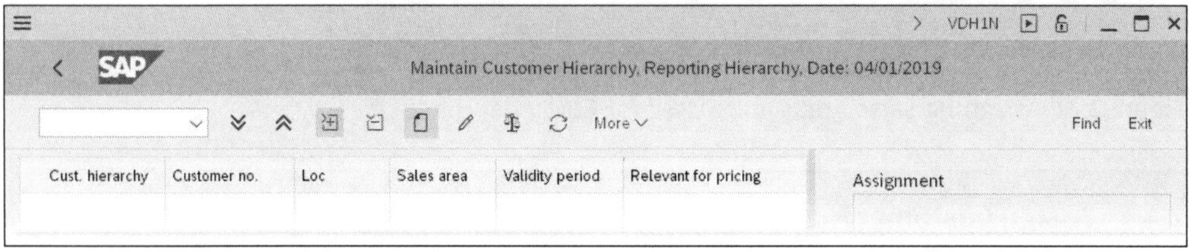

Figure 2.74 Create Assignment Button

Now, you can select an upper-level customer and a lower-level customer, as shown in Figure 2.75.

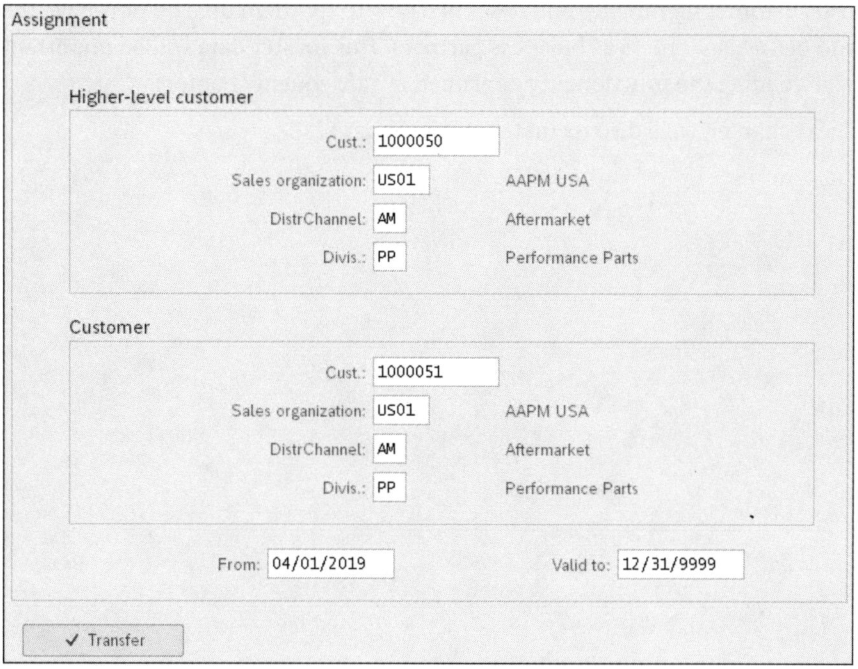

Figure 2.75 Assigning Customers for Customer Hierarchy Definition Purposes

Once the assignment is made, the structure will be displayed on the left side of the screen, as shown in Figure 2.76.

Cust. hierarchy	Customer no.	Loc	Sales area	Validity period	Relevant for pricing	Rel.f.rebate	Hierarchy assignment	Acct group
Peterson independent Auto Shops	1000050	US-76111 Haltom City	US01/AM/PP	04/01/2019 - 12/31/9999			00	CUST
Jeff's Auto Shop, Inc.	J001	US-73104 Oklahoma City	US01/AM/PP	04/01/2019 - 12/31/9999			00	CUST
Macaronis Automotive	1000051	US-75103 Canton	US01/AM/PP	04/01/2019 - 12/31/9999			00	CUST

Figure 2.76 Defined Customer Hierarchies

Once satisfied with the assignment, click **Save**, and the customer hierarchy will be defined and available for use in reporting, pricing, rebates, etc.

2.5 Summary

In this chapter, we covered the process of creating new customer and business partners in an SAP S/4HANA system. We discussed some general data required to configure business partners and then moved on to sales-specific information. We also looked at customer hierarchies and described how to set them up. You now have the ability to define customers as business partners. This master data will be important for understanding the functionality explained in subsequent chapters.

In the next chapter, we'll discuss material master data.

Chapter 3
Material Master Data Elements

Goods and services are represented in SAP S/4HANA as materials. In this chapter, we'll describe the sales master data elements you'll use to enable the order-to-cash (OTC) functionality.

Several master data elements are consider part of sales. In this chapter, we'll cover most sales-related master data elements. We'll walk through the steps for creating new material master entries in Transaction MM01, for modifying materials in Transaction MM02, and for display materials in Transaction MM03. The material master is organized in several views. In this chapter, we'll only discuss views related to sales, namely, the following:

- **Sales: sales org. 1**
- **Sales: sales org. 2**
- **Sales: General/Plant**
- **Intl Trade: Export**
- **Sales text**

The layout of the material master views is organized by theme and is not restricted by database tables, which is often a source of great confusion. Note that fields in any given view may be replicated from other views. We'll mention fields inherited from other views when applicable for clarification and to avoid confusion.

Other views may be added to the material master when the material starts being used. These views will display inventory and costing information, serving as queries specific to this material.

The material master is usually responsibility of the materials management (MM) team. In manufacturing organizations, this responsibility may have been transferred to the production planning (PP) team. In addition to defining the utilization of views belonging to them by functionality, the PP team may also be responsible for defining the fields on the **Basic data 1** and **Basic data 2** tabs, which contain information shared across all lines of business.

However, a portion of the material master is dedicated to sales and thus must remain the responsibility of the sales team. While the sales portion is much less complex than other part, the other teams won't have the information necessary for making decisions on the sales team's behalf.

Note that a material cannot be created with just sales views, and you'll need several of the other material master views to obtain the correct results out of the sales process. Therefore, we recommend learning as much as you can about the other views.

In the following sections, we'll focus on the sales views on the material master and walk you through the related configuration steps. We'll also discuss the customer-material information record, a repository that allows you to define customer-specific attributes from your materials.

3.1 Sales Organization Data: Sales View 1

Figure 3.1 shows the **Sales: sales org. 1** view of the material master. We'll use this screen as a reference when discussing the fields contained in this view throughout this section.

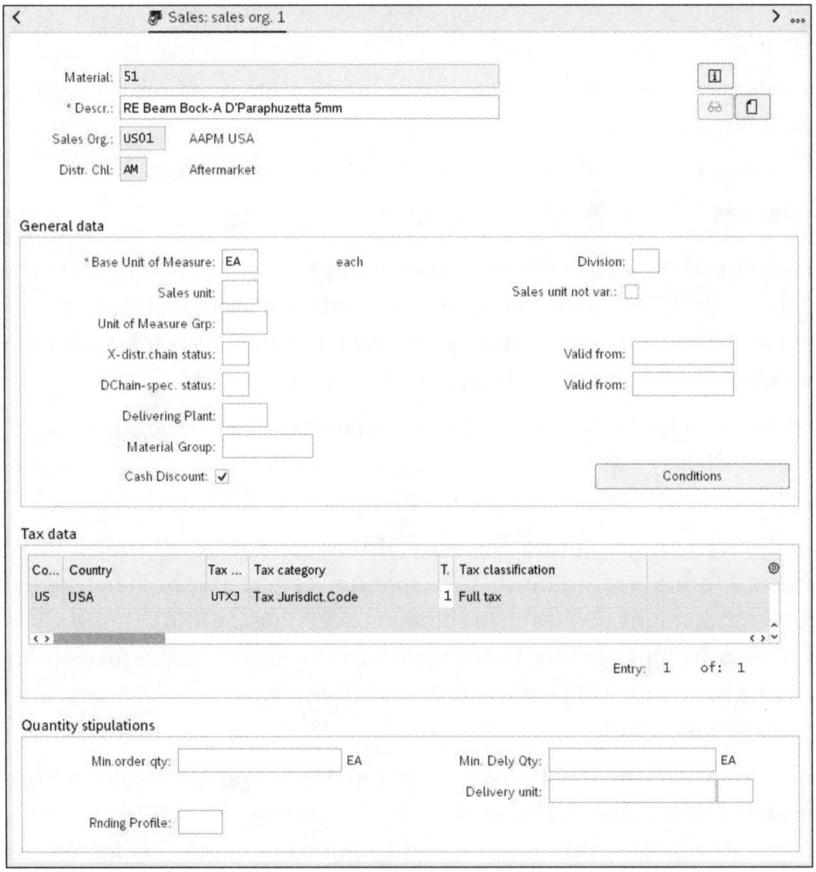

Figure 3.1 Sales Organization Data 1 View of the Material Master

The description (**Descr.**), **Base Unit of Measure**, **Division**, and **Material Group** fields are defined in the **Basic data** views. You're not expected to change these fields on the sales views; this information is displayed for reference.

In the following sections, we'll walk you through the most important fields and sections under this tab.

3.1.1 Base Unit of Measure

The **Base Unit of Measure** reference field indicates the stock-keeping unit of measurement (UoM). Orders can be entered in any UoM that can be converted back into this stock-keeping unit, so you may need to maintain unit of measurement conversions.

In the **Sales unit** field, you can specify a default UoM to be used when entering sales orders. If a user doesn't specify a UoM when ordering this material, the value in the **Sales unit** field is used by default. In the **Sales: sales org. 1** view, if you leave this field blank, the system will use the **Base Unit of Measurem**. This approach should only be followed if most of your customer orders use a UoM different than the stock-keeping unit. If you don't enter a unit of measurement conversion before assigning a value in the **Sales unit** field, a popup window will appear to prompt you to add a conversion.

By clicking on the **Additional Data** button, you can maintain unit of measurement conversions specific to the material under the **Units of measure** tab, as shown in Figure 3.2.

Under the **Units of measure** tab, you can specify alternative units of measurement (**AUn** column) and indicate a numerator (**Y** column) to calculate the conversion to the stock-keeping/base unit of measurement.

You can also enter an alternate unit of measurement CV (case) and indicate that 1 case (CV) corresponds to 12 units. Thus, if a sales order for a case of material is created, this quantity will be converted into the stock-keeping unit (each) to the tune of 12 to 1. For example, if a customer orders 2 cases, they will receive 24 units.

You may also enter a European Article Number (EAN)/Universal Product Code (UPC) for this material when sold in the alternative unit of measurement (in this example, CV/case). An EAN/UPC is important, for instance, if cases are packaged and labeled for retail. In these scenarios, most companies will want to maintain the dimensions, volume, and weight of each case.

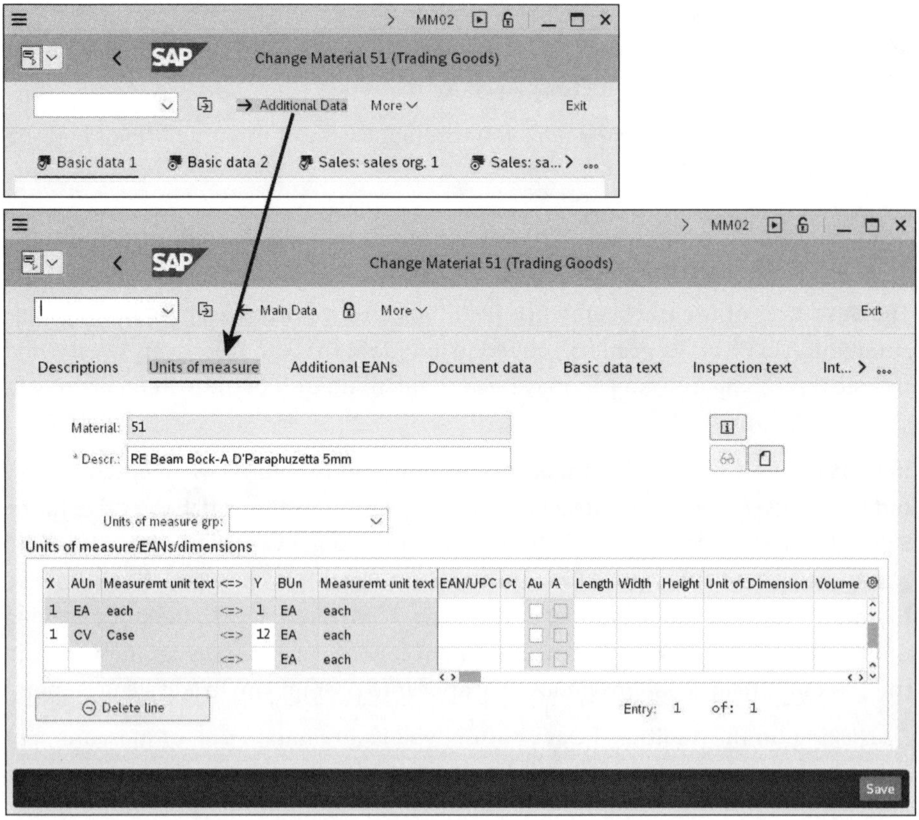

Figure 3.2 Unit of Measurement Conversion

3.1.2 Unit of Measure Group

You can also restrict which UoMs can be selected when sales orders are entered by maintaining the **Unit of Measure Grp** field. Note that this field configuration (as well as the help and documentation) is primarily designed for use by the purchasing team, but sales functionalities are associated with this field. The sales functionality only allows the selection of sales UoMs assigned to this UoM group at the time of sales order entry.

To configure unit of measurement groups, follow the menu path **SAP Customizing Implementation Guide • Materials Management • Purchasing • Order Optimizing • Quantity Optimizing and Allowed Logistics Units of Measure • Unit of Measure Groups • Edit.** On the screen that opens, click on the **New Entries** button or press F5.

On the screen shown in Figure 3.3, specify a four-character unit of measurement group code (**Unit of measure group**) and maintain all the alternative units of measurement (**Alt. unit of measure**) that should be included in this new group.

Our example contains a new UoM group called **ZST1** that includes three UoMs: **CV** (case), **CRT** (crate), and **PAL** (pallet).

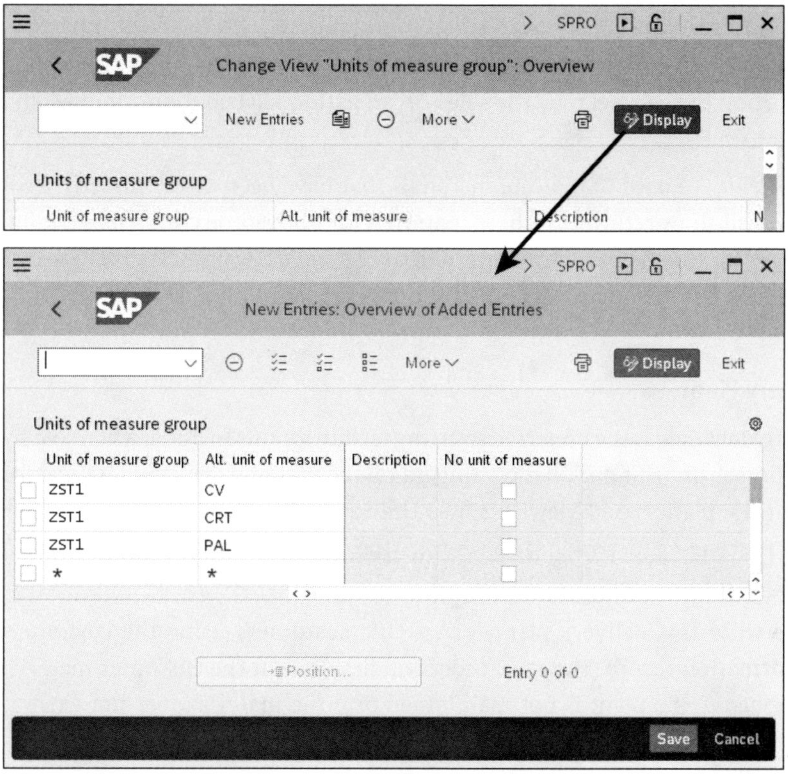

Figure 3.3 Unit of Measurement Group Definition

3.1.3 Material Status

Several master data material statuses are available for you to restrict business activity. Using materials management (MM) configuration, each status may restrict goods receipts, sales orders, returns, etc. A material status may also restrict all of these documents at once.

The material status fields in the master data are always maintained with a **Valid From** date so you can plan status changes ahead of time.

One example of a material status field is the **X-distr.chain status/Valid from** field, which stand for "cross-distribution chain status." The value defined in this field is valid across all the distribution chains that you may extend this material to. So, if you make a change in this field on this view, all other sales organization and distribution channel combinations that make up a distribution chain will be affected.

Another material status field is the **DChain-spec. status/Valid from** field, which stand for "distribution chain-specific status." The status defined in this field will *only* affect the distribution chain currently being maintained in this sales view and indicate on the upper portion of the screen by the sales organization, distribution channel, and distribution chain.

Often, these fields are used to indicate materials that have been discontinued (obsolete). You can still allow returns for these materials (or not). Some companies configure new values for this field, such as "pre-release" to indicate materials that are not yet available for sales but are ready for planning and procurement.

3.1.4 Delivery Plant

The **Delivering Plant** field is the preferred sourcing facility for this material when sold by this distribution chain. This option is contingent on the material being maintained for this plant on the plant-based views such as the **Sales: General/Plant** (Section 3.3), **MRP**, and/or **Purchasing** (depending on whether the material is to be purchased from a vendor or is manufactured).

You can overwrite this delivery plant for specific customers using the customer-material information record. The sales order will first look at the customer-material information record; if a plant is not maintained or if the material does not exist at that plant, the system will look at the delivery plant in the shipping view of the customer master. If the plant is not maintained on the customer or if the material does not exist at that plant, the system will look at the **Delivering Plant** field on this screen.

3.1.5 Material Group

Material groups are defined by the procurement team but are used in sales-related functionalities as an internal grouping number, i.e., for classification criteria used by your company that may or may match how the market (sales department) classifies them.

To configure material groups, open Transaction OMSF or follow the menu path **SAP Customizing Implementation Guide • Logistics – General • Material Master • Settings for Key Fields • Define Material Groups.** On the screen that opens, click on the **New Entries** button or press F5.

As shown in Figure 3.4, specify a four-character material group code (**Matl Group**) and add a description (**Material Group Desc.**). You can control which group may use this code by assigning an authorization group (**AGrp**). You can also assign a default unit of measurement for material weight figures (**DUW**).

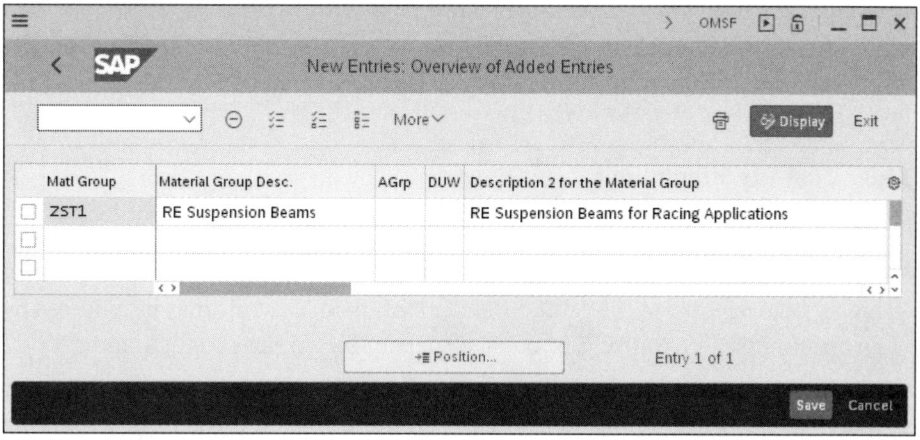

Figure 3.4 Defining Material Groups

3.1.6 Cash Discount and Conditions

The **Cash Discount** field can be a source of concern in some companies. The system will flag this field by default, which will make this material relevant for a specific type of accounts receivable discount at the time of collections. This type of discount depends on when the payment is made and not on the material. The ID field is flagged by default by the SAP program code and not controlled by configuration. This field is often ignored. The default flag setting can only be changed by SAP on their standard code.

Clicking the **Conditions** button will take you to the pricing condition records maintenance screen (for more details, see Chapter 4, Section 4.1) and is a shortcut for maintaining sales prices.

3.1.7 Tax Data

The **Tax Data** section of this screen displays the **Tax Category** defined for the countries where you have plants that can fulfill the orders entered by this distribution chain. The country-based configuration for these tax categories is standard and unlikely to change, so we won't describe this configuration in this book. In the rare case that it is required, the finance team will usually be the ones to take care of this configuration.

For each **Tax Category** in this section, you'll need to select the **Tax Classification** that applies to this material. This code typically indicates whether the material is taxable or exempt for that type of tax. Some countries may have other classifications that will affect the tax rate applicable for this customer. This information should ideally be interfaced to the external tax calculation tools your company utilizes.

3.1.8 Quantity Stipulations

In the **Quality Stipulations** section, the following four fields are important:

- The **Min.order qty** field indicates that your customers may only order a quantity higher than or equal to the value entered in this field. This rule may be enforced by an error message, a warning, or not at all depending on sales configuration.
- The **Min. Dely Qty** field affects the creation of a delivery document after the sales order is ready for shipping. Deliveries will only be created if you have at least the value entered in this field available to ship. This rule may be enforced by an error message, a warning, or not at all depending on sales configuration.
- The **Delivery unit** field indicates whether you can only order and ship multiples of the value entered in this field. For instance, if a material can only be sold in pairs, you would enter "2ea" in this field. This rule may be enforced by an error message, a warning, or not at all depending on sales configuration.
- The **Rnding Profile** field indicates that the system can automatically round the quantity up or down to the nearest allowed multiple (depending on the chosen profile). If a customer orders 1 unit but the delivery unit is 2 units, the system would automatically round the ordered quantity to 2 units.

3.2 Sales Organization Data: Sales View 2

Figure 3.5 shows the **Sales: sales org. 2** view of the material master. We'll use this screen as a reference when discussing the fields contained in this view throughout this section.

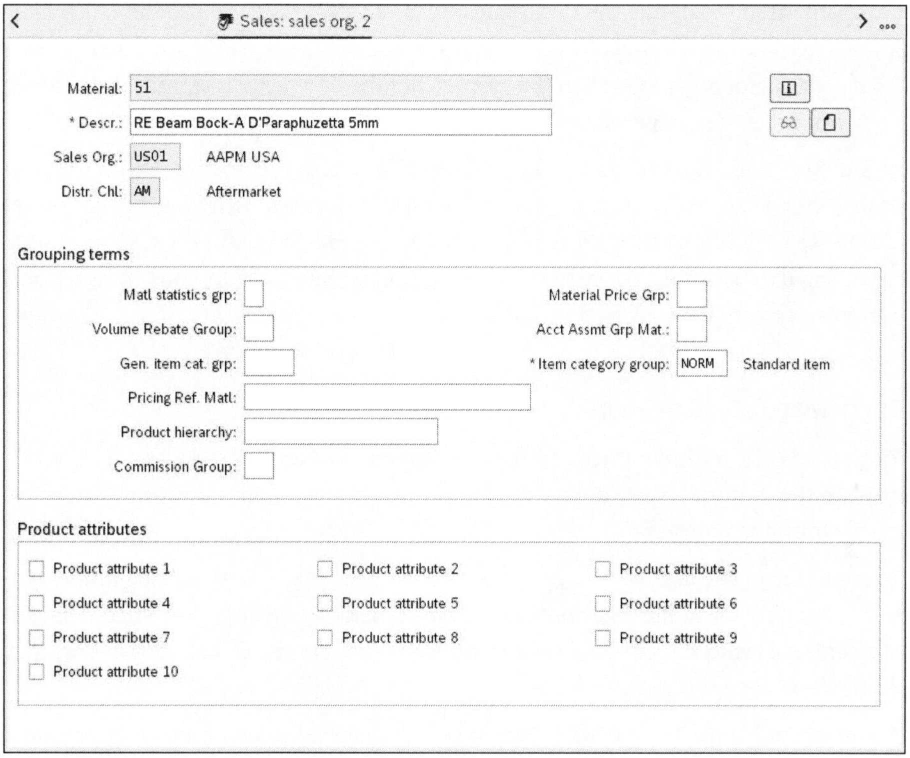

Figure 3.5 Sales Organization Data 2 View of the Material Master

The description (**Descr.**), item category group (**Gen. item cat. grp**), and **Division** fields are defined in the **Basic data** views. You're not expected to change these fields in the sales views, and this information is displayed for reference.

In the following sections, we'll walk through the fields available under this tab.

3.2.1 Material Statistics Group

The **Matl statistics grp** field dictates the level of detail you want when tracking and reporting on this material's information. Companies that use this functionality generally classify material data according to daily, weekly, monthly, and quarterly reporting.

Previously in SAP ERP, you would accumulate sales volume information based on period-based information to increase reporting performance as part of the Logistics Information System (LIS)/Sales Information Systems (SIS) definition.

Companies tend to define the same rules across all materials and use the same value for this field for all materials. This consistency enables users to drill down to the same level of detail for any material in the system, but the downside is technical, related to performance and storage space consumption.

In SAP S/4HANA, the main advantage to use this field is the positive impact performance when retrieving transaction data, which affects reporting performance. But storage space is often costly and complex to manage, so you may still want a separate reporting database for historical data so you can archive data in your transactional systems to maintain peak performance.

3.2.2 Material Price Group

You can use the **Material Price Grp** field to control different types of discounts applicable to the material. More details how to set up pricing based on this field or others can be found in Chapter 4.

To configure material price groups, follow the menu path **SAP Customizing Implementation Guide • Sales and Distribution • Basic Functions • Pricing • Set Price-Relevant Master Data Fields • Set Pricing Groups for Materials**. On the screen that opens, click on the **New Entries** button or press F5.

As shown in Figure 3.6, specify a two-character material price group code (**Material Price Grp**) and add a description (**Description**).

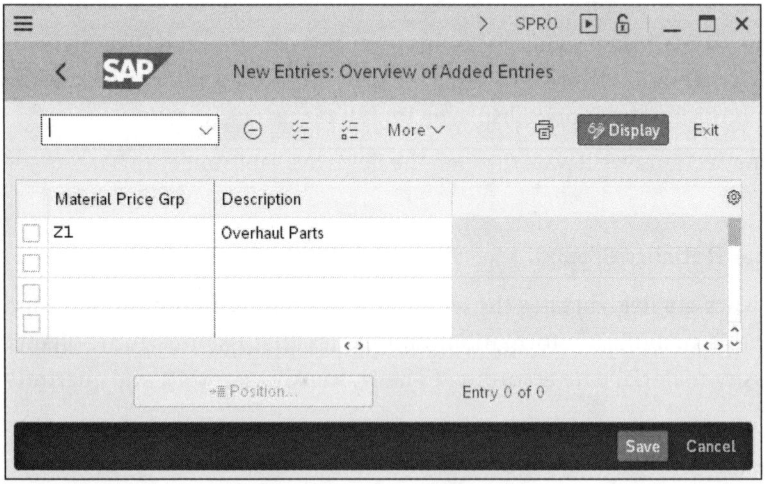

Figure 3.6 Defining New Material Price Groups

3.2.3 Material Volume Rebate Group

The **Volume Rebate Group** field can be used to group materials that are eligible for rebate programs. You'll then define rebate settlement rules that apply to the group, thus allowing customers to purchase any of the materials assigned to that group and to be eligible for the same rebate. More details about this field can be found in Chapter 5, Section 5.2.

To configure material volume rebate groups, follow the menu path **SAP Customizing Implementation Guide • Sales and Distribution • Billing • Rebate Processing • Define Material Rebate Group**. On the screen that opens, click on the **New Entries** button or press F5.

As shown in Figure 3.7, specify a two-character volume rebate group code (**VRG**) code and add a description (**Description**).

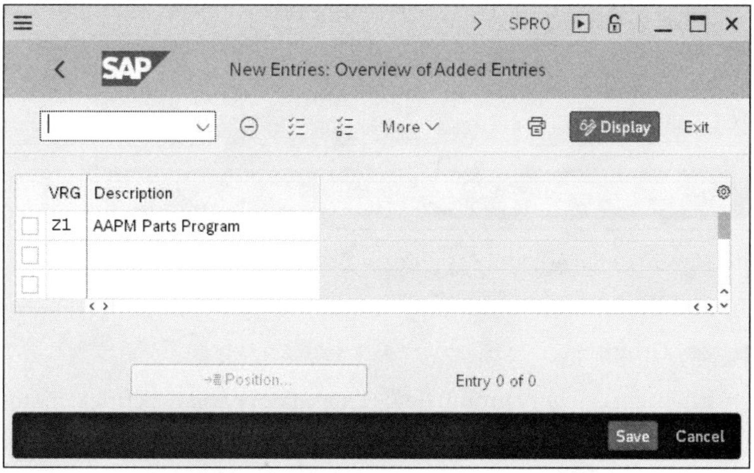

Figure 3.7 Defining New Material Volume Rebate Groups

3.2.4 Material Account Assignment Group

The **Acct Assmt Grp Mat.** field is used for revenue account determination. You can specify different revenue accounts depending on the type of material. If a requirement from the finance team, we recommend creating new values for this field associated with the account determination configuration, which we'll describe in Chapter 10.

To configure material account assignment groups, follow the menu path **SAP Customizing Implementation Guide • Sales and Distribution • Basic Functions • Account**

Assignment/Costing • Revenue Account Determination • Check Master Data Relevant For Account Assignment • Materials: Account Assignment Groups. On the screen that opens, click on the **New Entries** button or press F5.

As shown in Figure 3.8, specify a two-character material account assignment group code (**Acct Assmt Grp Mat.**) and add a description (**Description**).

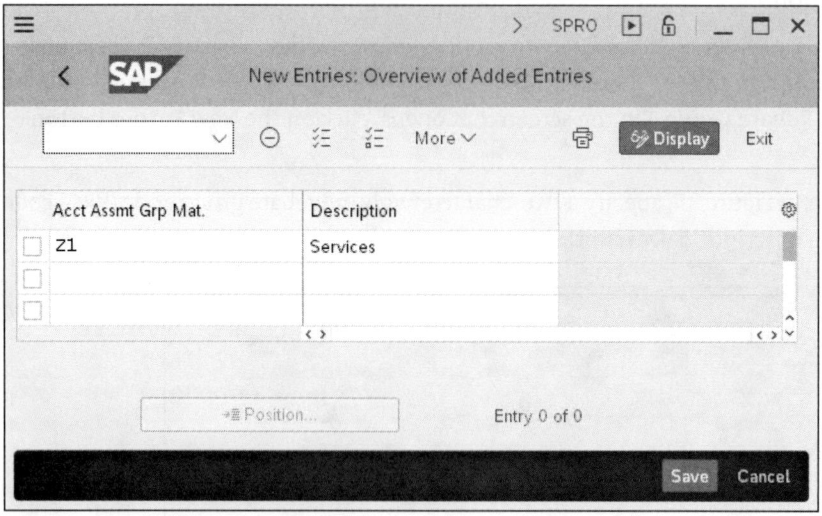

Figure 3.8 Defining New Material Account Assignment Groups

3.2.5 Item Category Group

The **Gen. item cat. grp** (item category group) field is mandatory and is a critical material master field for sales. This field determines the item category on a sales order. The item category is a type of line in a sales order and specifies whether the line item is billable or not, shippable or not, costed or not, etc. We'll go into more detail about configuring this functionality in Chapter 6.

To configure item category groups, follow the menu path **SAP Customizing Implementation Guide • Sales and Distribution • Sales • Sales Documents • Sales Document Item • Define Item Category Groups**. On the screen that opens, click on the **New Entries** button or press F5.

As shown in Figure 3.9, specify a four-character item category group code (**ItCGr**) and add a description (**Description**).

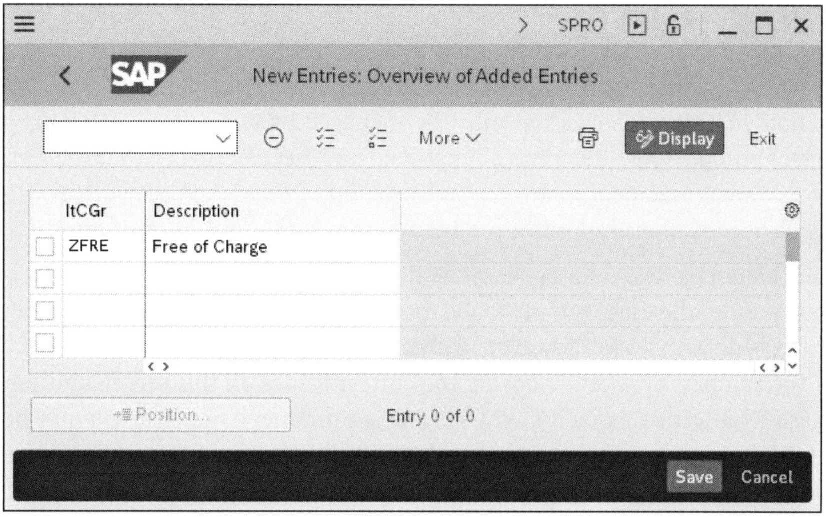

Figure 3.9 Defining New Item Category Groups

In Chapter 6, we'll use the information defined in this field to determine item categories.

3.2.6 Pricing Reference Material

The **Pricing Ref. Matl** field is used when this material will follow prices defined at the material number level of another material number. This approach is used for companies that have discrete materials created for variants of the same products, such as different colors. You can take one of the colors of product, such as white, and use its information as the pricing reference material. When creating multiple materials for different color options, you would enter the white material number in the **Pricing Ref. Matl** field. Thus, you'll only need to enter a price for the white material, and all other colors of products will automatically be defined with its price. More details regarding pricing calculation and condition records will be covered in Chapter 4, Section 4.1.

3.2.7 Product Hierarchy

The **Product hierarchy** field is the most often used grouping criteria in reporting. Its definition is complex and frequently a source of conflict. One of the sales pitches for SAP S/4HANA is that the whole company could speak the same language, look at the same numbers, track the same targets, and get the same results. This consistency cannot be achieved by the system's programming but instead is achieved through the sharing of the same master data fields across different disciplines. The **Product hierarchy** field embodies this universality and is used for finance, controlling, sales, and planning, which also brings challenges. One department may require more granularity than another. This specialization must be managed by employees with a deep knowledge of product lines and a cross-functional mindset (the ability to take input from multiple areas and incorporate this information as necessary). Executive decisions may be needed to dismiss some requirements, but must not be the norm.

The **Product hierarchy** field is an 18-character field that is subdivided into three hierarchical codes, from the most generic to the most specific. Technically, you can modify this structure with ease; however, increasing the number of levels directly increases the complexity when choosing the correct values on this screen and can often negatively affect data quality. When creating a product hierarchy, you may be tempted to include everything you need in this field, but doing so is counterproductive and must be avoided. Other fields are available for use in grouping, and you must leverage those fields instead of overburdening a product hierarchy with meaning.

A good practice is to keep the standard structure. Figure 3.10 shows the three-level standard structure for product hierarchy. Changes to this structure can be common, but adding more levels can lead to difficulty when entering products.

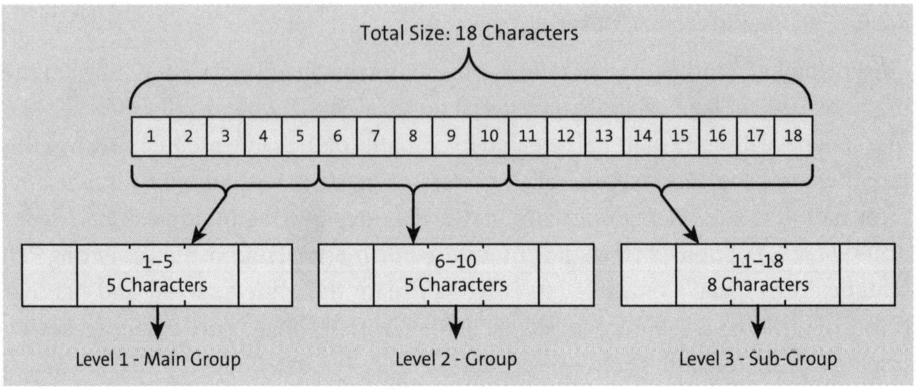

Figure 3.10 SAP Standard Product Hierarchy Structure

When configuring values for each level, you should keep the number of options in each level to a minimum. Your end users will need to select one level at a time, and only a few features are available for sorting or filtering the options available within each level. Obsolete entries tend to pile up over the years, making choosing the correct values harder. Obsolete options should have descriptions that clearly indicate they are no longer valid.

To configure product hierarchies, open Transaction V/76 or follow the menu path **SAP Customizing Implementation Guide • Logistics – General • Material Master • Settings for Key Fields • Data Relevant to Sales and Distribution • Define Product Hierarchies.** On the screen that opens, select the **Maintenance: Prod. Hier.** button and then click on the **New Entries** button or press F5.

As shown in Figure 3.11, in our example, we're creating three levels for our example company AAPM's suspension components, specifically beams.

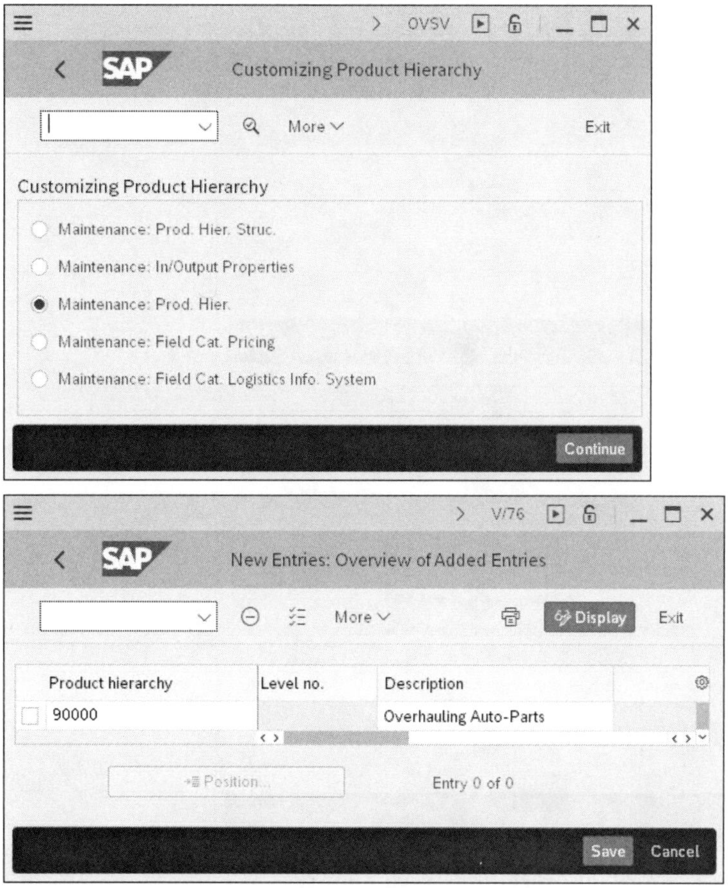

Figure 3.11 Defining a New Product Hierarchy (Level 1)

Note that you must create the most generic level first and save the entry before you can enter the next more granular level because lower-level data entry features recursive validation for the higher levels built into this transaction.

On the second screen shown in Figure 3.11, specify a five-character product hierarchy level 1 code (**Product hierarchy**) and add a description (**Description**). Save your changes.

Next, as shown in Figure 3.12, enter the same level 1 code created by the previous step, followed by a new five-character code to define level 2. The combination of the level 1 code and the new level 2 code will be the new **Product hierarchy**. Add a description (**Description**) for the product hierarchy and save your changes.

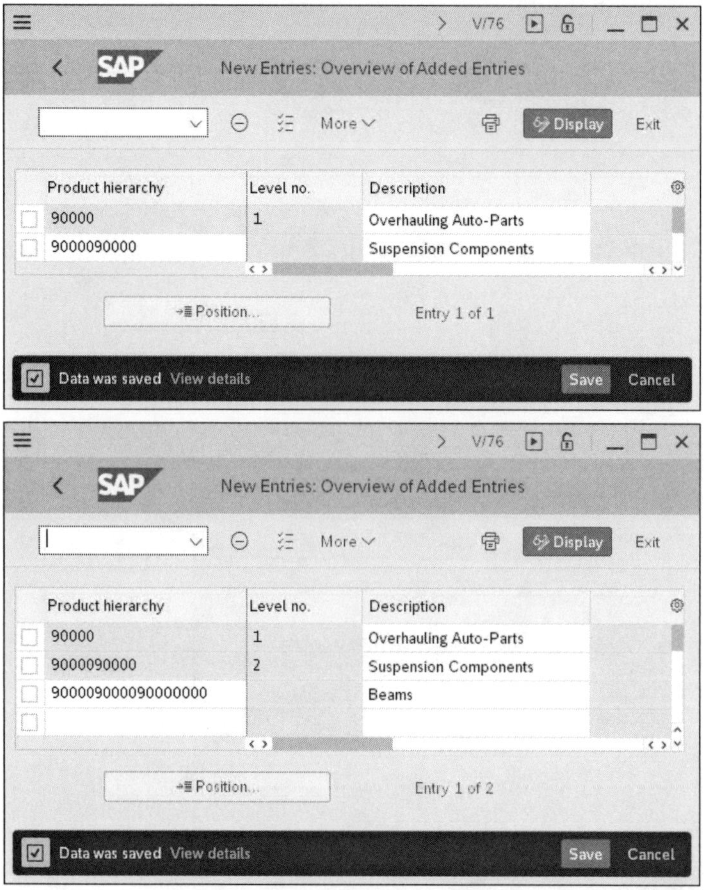

Figure 3.12 Defining a New Product Hierarchy (Levels 2 and 3)

Then, enter the same level 1 and 2 codes created by in the previous step and add a new eight-character code defined for Level 3. The combination of the level 1 and 2 codes with the new level 3 code will be the new number in the **Product hierarchy** field. Add a description (**Description**) for the product hierarchy and save your changes.

Level 1 codes must be unique. Level 2 codes can only exist under level 1, so level 2 codes can repeat across level 1 codes. Similarly, since level 3 codes only exist under both level 1 and level 2, level 3 codes can repeat across combinations of level 1 and level 2.

Some companies may be tempted to break a product hierarchy down into three independent codes (one for each level). We do not recommend this approach because, if a code repeats across Level 1, you'll end up with inconsistent reporting. So, whenever you assign any values to lower levels of the product hierarchy, you must ensure to include all upper levels to avoid inconsistencies.

Product hierarchies are used in several standard functionalities and reports as well as in custom features built for your company.

3.2.8 Commission Group

The **Commission Group** field groups materials that share the same commission policy. Sales reps may earn different commission rates from different commission groups.

To configure commission groups, follow the menu path **SAP Customizing Implementation Guide • Logistics – General • Material Master • Settings for Key Fields • Data Relevant to Sales and Distribution • Define Commission Groups**. On the screen that opens, click on the **New Entries** button or press [F5].

As shown in Figure 3.13, specify a two-character commission group code (**Com**) and add a description (**Description**).

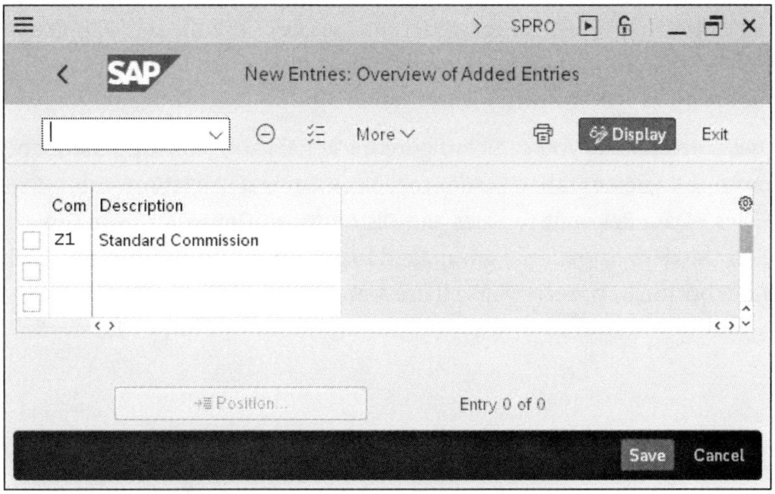

Figure 3.13 Defining New Commission Groups

3.2.9 Material Groups 1 through 5

The **Sales: Sales Org. 2** tab is also where we'll find the material master reserved fields (similar to the reserved fields in the customer master described in Chapter 2, Section 2.2.10). These fields are called **Material Group 1** through **Material Group 5**, as shown in Figure 3.14. Although used by many companies, in this version of SAP S/4HANA, these fields are hidden out of the box.

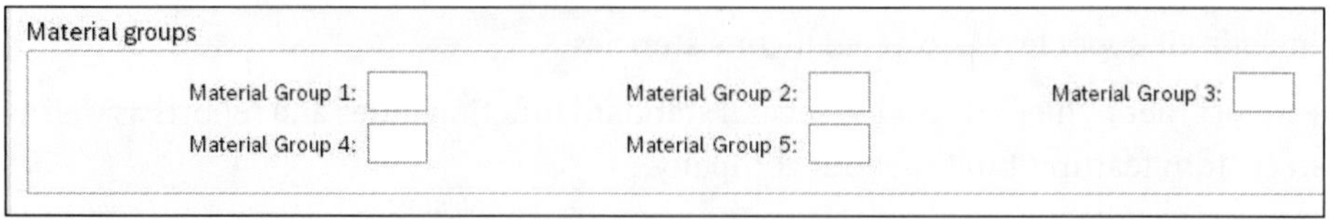

Figure 3.14 Material Groups 1 through 5 on the Sales View 2

To make these fields appear, you must modify the fields available on the various material master screens by opening Transaction OMS9 or by following the menu path **SAP Customizing Implementation Guide • Logistics – General • Material Master • Field Selection • Maintain Field Selection for Data Screens.**

As shown in Figure 3.15, select the desired field selection group (**Field sel. group**) ❶. For the material master reserved fields, the field selection group is **54**. Press [Enter].

The fields included in the selected field selection group will be displayed right underneath it in the **Fields** section. You can modify the behavior of these fields for specific field references (**Field ref.**), such as specific material types. In our example, we're modifying these fields to be optional for material types **FERT** (Manufactured) ❷ and **HAWA** (Sourced) ❸. This configuration is usually owned by the MM team, and configuration must be set up in synchronicity with them.

Now that the fields are visible, you can configure these fields by following the menu path **SAP Customizing Implementation Guide • Logistics – General • Material Master • Settings for Key Fields • Data Relevant to Sales and Distribution • Define Material Groups.** Once there, select the desired material group field to configure (1 through 5) and click on the **New Entries** button or press [F5]. We'll use **Material Group 1** in our example.

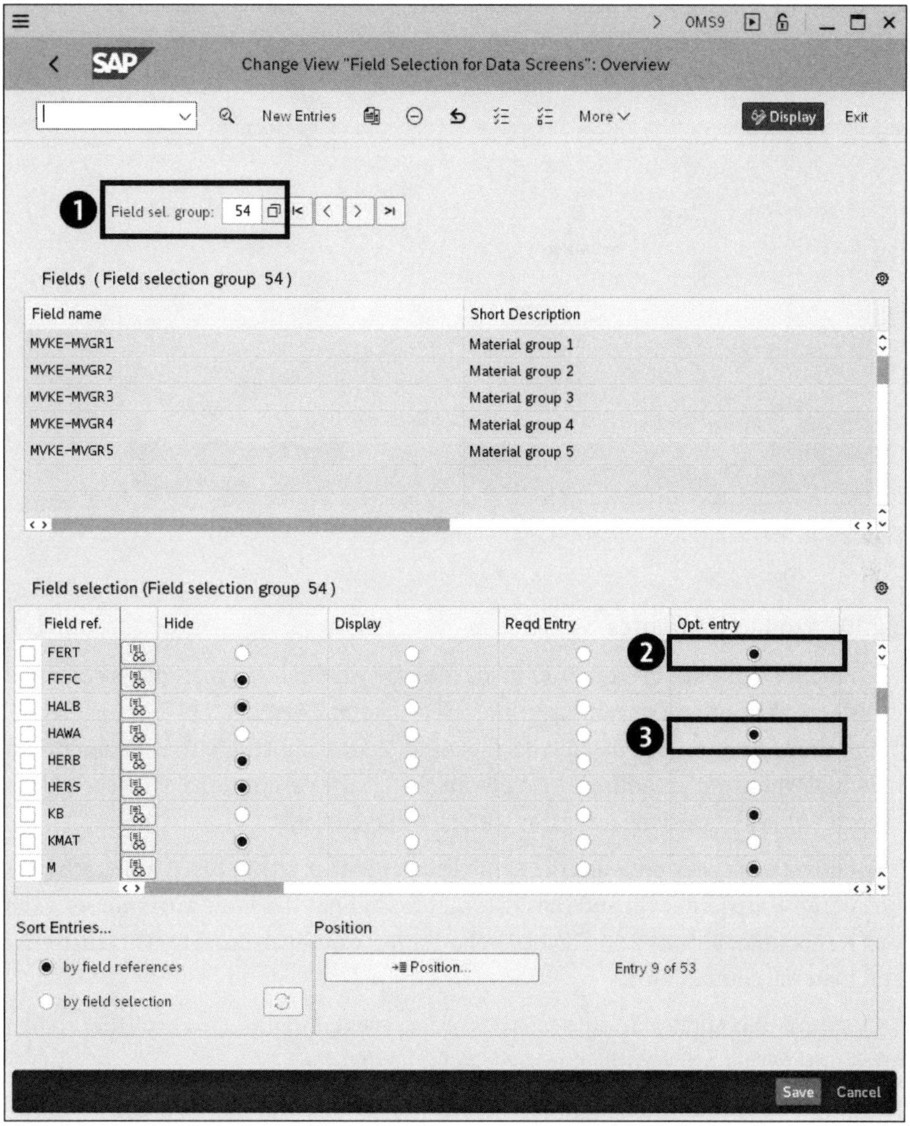

Figure 3.15 Changing the Field Status for the Material Reserved Fields

After selecting **Material Group 1**, the screen shown in Figure 3.16 will appear. On this screen, specify a three-character material group code (**Material Group 1**) and add a description (**Description**).

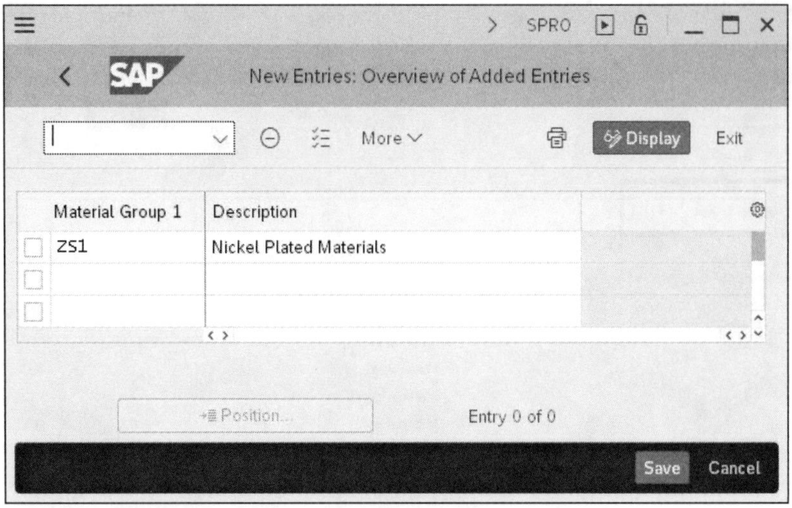

Figure 3.16 Defining New Material Group 1 Entries

3.2.10 Product Attributes

The **Product Attribute 1** through **10** fields indicate whether this material is governed by sales restrictions on certain customers (see Chapter 2, Section 2.3.1 for more detail). These fields have no out-of-the-box meaning. Your company will determine their meaning when implementing SAP. You can change the descriptions of these fields to represent the assigned meanings, as with all reserved fields.

The customer master data has the same list of product attributes. If a material has one of these attributes set and the customer master has the same attribute set, then you'll encounter an exception if you ever attempt to enter an order for this customer and material combination.

This approach is applicable only for sales order types configured to check for product attributes (either for warning messages or for errors).

Flagging one of these attributes on the material master will not stop any customer from purchasing material, only the customers with matching flagged product attributes. Many companies use material master product attributes as reserved fields for informational Boolean master data, such as if a material has particular characteristics that makes it relevant for sales activities like on-site advertisement or if the material is part of a year-end promotions to collaborators. Custom use of this field is often redundant with existing SAP S/4HANA features, and should ideally be avoided.

3.3 Sales: General/Plant Data

Figure 3.17 shows the **Sales: General/Plant** view of the material master. We'll use this screen as a reference when discussing the fields contained in this view throughout this section.

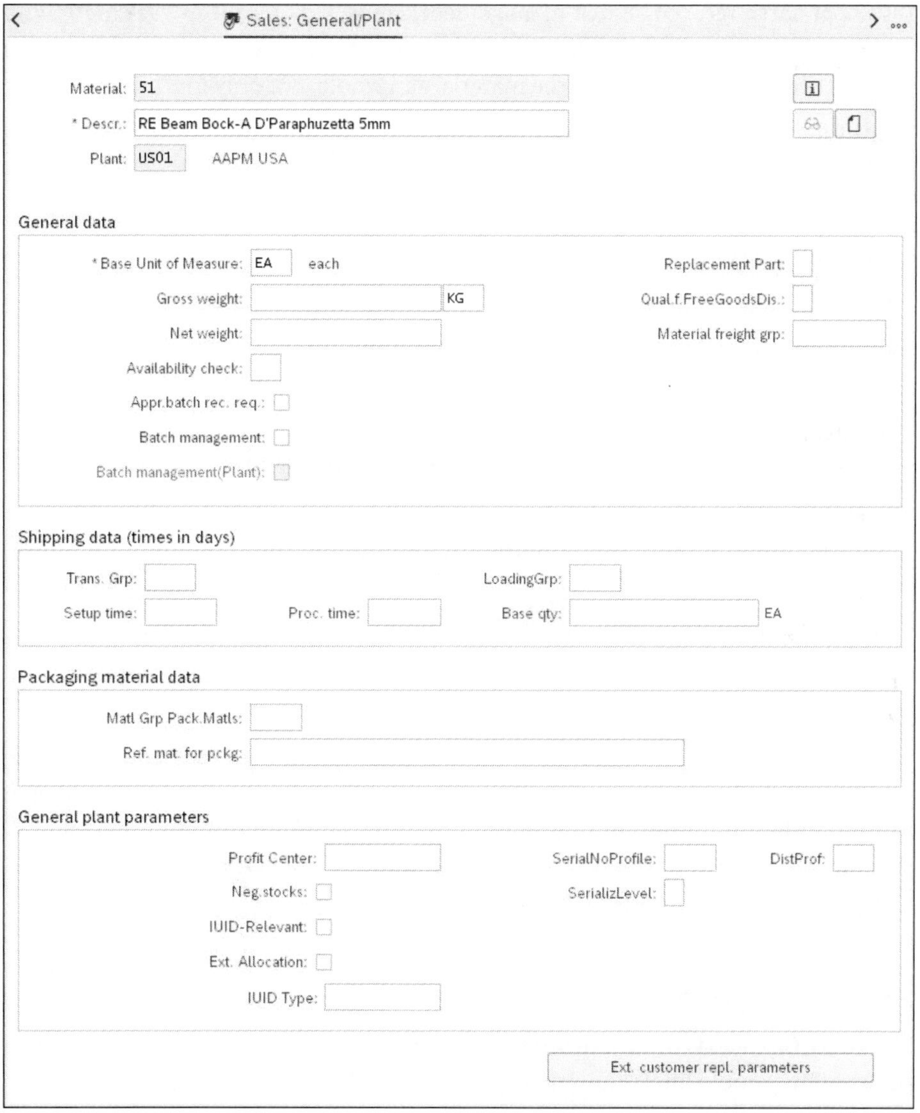

Figure 3.17 General/Plant Data View of the Material Master

Note that, even though a sales view, the data on this screen is mostly tied to the plant, not to the distribution chain, as can be seen by the **Plant** displayed under the **Material** number and **Description** (instead of the distribution chain that appears under the **Sales: sales org. 1** and **Sales: sales org. 2** tabs).

The **Description, Base Unit of Measure, Gross weight, Net weight, Qual.f.FreeGoods-Dis., Appr.batch rec. req., Batch management, Trans. Grp, Matl Grp Pack.Matls,** and **Ref. mat. for pckg** fields are considered basic data. If you modify these fields on this screen, these changes will affect the material as a whole, not only for this plant.

In the following sections, we'll look at the most important fields on this tab, broken out by section.

3.3.1 General Data

The **Replacement Part** field allows you to indicate whether this material a replacement part or a finished good for Value-Added Tax (VAT) calculation purposes. This field is not typically used by US-based companies.

The **Qual.f.FreeGoodsDis.** field controls whether a material may be received from a vendor free of charge. Currently, this field serves as information only for sales.

The **Material freight grp** field classifies materials by their freight requirements. For instance, you can use this field to indicate that a flatbed truck is required for shipping. This field is not used often.

The **Availability check** field controls the rules that apply when calculating promised delivery dates and when allocating stock to sales documents for this material. We'll cover how to configure this functionality in Chapter 7.

You can control whether the stock of this material requires batches (lots) at the material basic data level (**Batch management**) or at the plant level (**Batch management(Plant)**). Simply selecting the relevant checkboxes will change the behavior of all stock movement transactions that do not require/feature batch numbers. The decision whether to flag this field lies with the MM team.

3.3.2 Shipping Data

The **Trans. Grp** field is used to determine special transportation requirements for this material that would affect the delivery route. Most companies use third-party carriers, and this field is used only for materials that require special transportation arrangements. If your company owns delivery trucks, this field becomes an important part of route determination and transportation planning, which we'll discuss in more detail in Chapter 9, Section 9.8.

To configure transportation groups, follow the menu path **SAP Customizing Implementation Guide • Logistics Execution • Shipping • Basic Shipping Functions • Routes • Route Determination • Define Transportation Groups**. On the screen that opens, click on the **New Entries** button or press F5.

As shown in Figure 3.18, specify a four-character transportation group (**Trans. Grp**) code and add a description (**Description**).

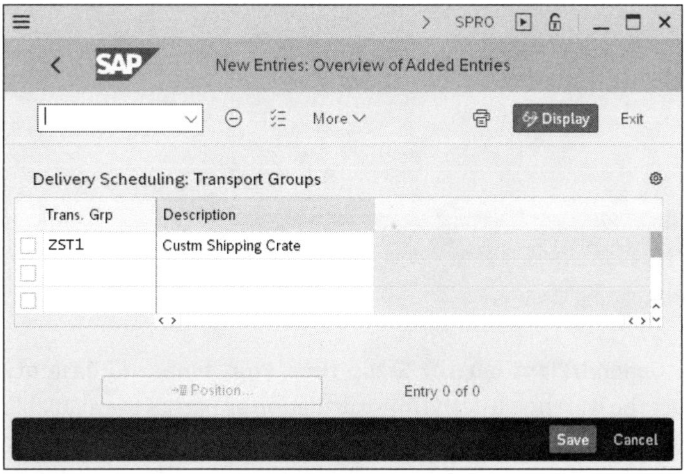

Figure 3.18 Defining New Transportation Groups

Back under the **Sales: General/Plant** tab, the **Loading Grp** field indicates special requirements for picking, packing, and/or loading products at the logistics warehouse. This field is commonly used if a material is particularly large, heavy, small, or delicate; requires refrigeration; is sensitive to dust; is liquid; requires measurement, etc.—anything that would differentiate the material from the other materials from a logistics standpoint. This field is also used to determine the shipping point and thus is an importation organizational structure element for logistics. This field can also cause an order to be split into multiple delivery documents. In Chapter 9, we'll get into this functionality and its impact in more detail.

To configure loading groups, follow the menu path **SAP Customizing Implementation Guide • Logistics Execution • Shipping • Basic Shipping Functions • Shipping Point and Goods Receiving Point Determination • Define Loading Groups**. On the screen that opens, click on the **New Entries** button or press F5.

As shown in Figure 3.19, specify a four-character loading group code (**LGrp**) and add a description (**Description**). Chapter 9 contains other related configuration items for loading groups.

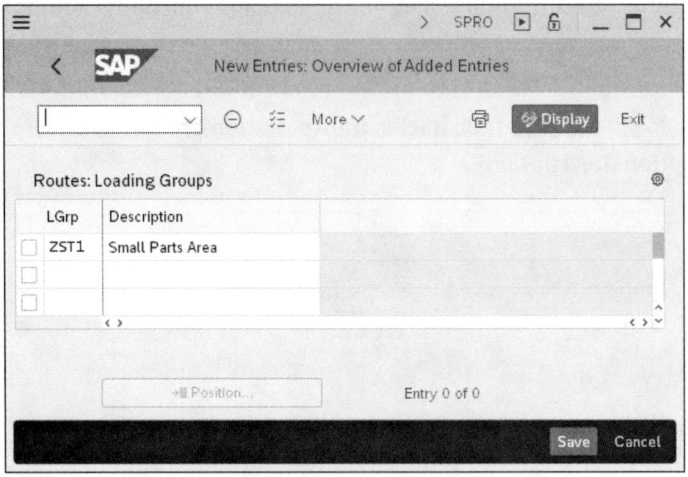

Figure 3.19 Defining New Loading Groups

Back under the **Sales: General/Plant** tab, the **Setup time**, **Proc. time**, and **Base qty** fields allow you to affect the warehouse lead time calculation as part of the available to promise (ATP) check functionality (see Chapter 7, Section 7.2, for more details). The **Setup time** field represents a flat number of days required regardless of quantity. The **Proc. time** field represents the number of days required to process each base quantity (**Base qty**).

3.3.3 Packaging Material Data

The **Matl Grp Pack.Matls** and **Ref. mat. for pckg** fields relate to packing. **Matl Grp Pack.Matls** indicates the type of packaging material that must be used (cardboard box, wood/metal crate) to orient the warehouse at the time of packing. **Ref. mat. for pckg** is the material number that represents the box, crate, etc. that must be used with specific dimensions, tare weights, etc. Some companies control inventory for these boxes and reorder inventory automatically once depleted, which is MM functionality.

For more details about this functionality, refer to Chapter 9. Most companies ignore these fields because they aren't necessary for packing. You only need these fields if the packing operation has complex requirements and is driven by the system. Most companies simply record packing in the system after the packing process has been completed physically, based on operator decisions.

To configure material packaging groups, follow the menu path **SAP Customizing Implementation Guide • Logistics Execution • Shipping • Packing • Define Material Group for Packaging Materials**. On the screen that opens, click on the **New Entries** button or press F5.

As shown in Figure 3.20, specify a four-character material packaging group code (**GrPM**) and add a description (**Description**).

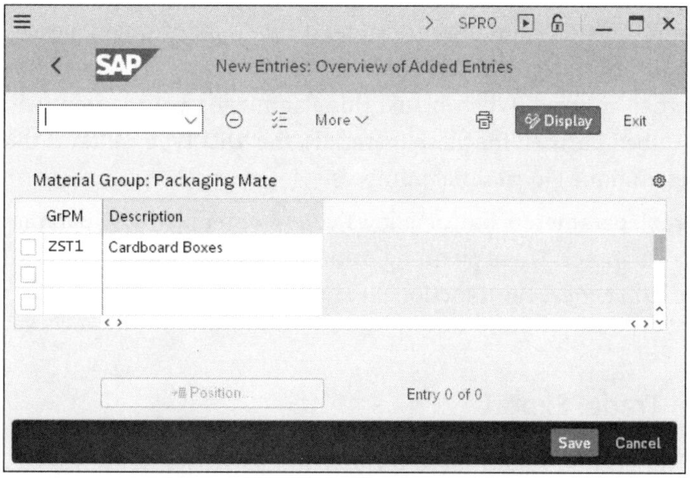

Figure 3.20 Defining New Material Packaging Groups

3.3.4 General Plant Parameters

Finally, in the **General plant parameters** section, you'll maintain the following fields:

- The **Profit Center** field is used for critical costing functionalities managed by the controlling area. This field is not part of sales configuration but is typically defined as a mandatory field for setting up the material master data.
- The **SerialNoProfile** field indicates how a material is serialized. The code chosen will dictate several aspects of the serial number and is defined by the MM team. You won't change the value in this field before moving inventory because the system won't allow changes.

- The **SerializLevel** field indicates whether, for serialized materials, the serial number must be unique for this material number only or across different material numbers.
- The **DistProf** field is used for cross-docking at the time of goods receipt. This MM functionality is an expedited way to move goods straight from the receiving dock to the outbound area.
- The **Neg.stocks** flag indicates whether this material can accept negative stock at this plant.
- The **IUID Type** flag controls whether a unique item identifier (UII) must be used for this material. This number is required if serial numbers cannot repeat across different companies and must be unique worldwide. If this level of uniqueness is required, the **Ext. Allocation** flag indicates that the serial number is defined outside your system when marked. When blank, this flag means your system will define the serial number. Further, for these materials, the **IUID Type** contains the format used for these unique global serial numbers.
- The **Ext. customer repl. parameters** button allows you to enter planning parameters specific for this customer. These planning parameters are part of MM and PP functionality, so we won't cover this functionality in this book.

3.4 International Trade: Export

Figure 3.21 shows the **Intl Trade: Export** view of the material master. We'll use this screen as a reference when discussing the fields contained in this view throughout this section.

The **Intrastat Group** involves the Intrastat regulatory reporting system used by the European Union (EU). This field classifies materials when reporting data and transaction to various governmental agencies.

The **CAS number (pharm.)** is a registration code for the World Health Organization (WHO) that allows for customs-free foreign trade transactions.

The **PRODCOM no.** is a registration used for production statistics in the European Union (EU). (PRODCOM stands for Production Communautaire.)

You'll use the **Control code** field to store the official customs material codes, such as from the Harmonized Tariff Schedule (HTS) codes, commodity codes, and Nomenclatura Comum do Mercosul (NCM) codes used in Latin America. These codes can be used for tax calculations in some countries and for regulatory reporting in other countries but are generally used to communicate with the customs offices for foreign trade purposes. You'll typically display this code on your commercial and pro-forma invoices.

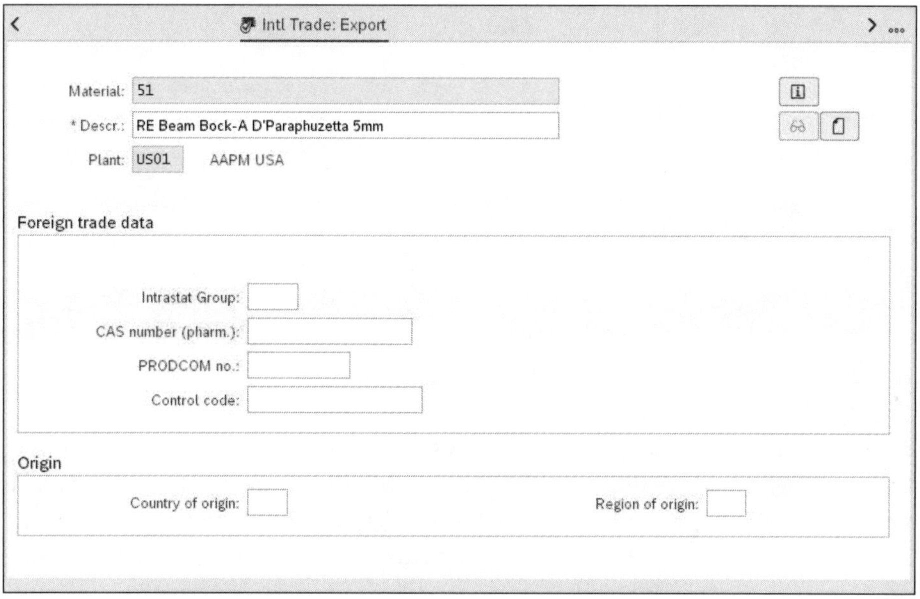

Figure 3.21 International Trade (Export) View of the Material Master

To configure control codes, follow the menu path **SAP Customizing Implementation Guide • Financial Accounting • Financial Accounting Global Settings • Tax on Sales/ Purchases • Basic Settings • India • Goods and Services Tax • General Settings • Maintain HSN and SAC**. On the screen that opens, click on the **New Entries** button or press [F5]. Note that, even though the configuration menu path and the example shown in Figure 3.22 are for India, you can enter codes valid for any other country.

As shown in Figure 3.22, specify the **Country** for which this code is valid, enter the official up-to 16-character control code issued by the country in question (**Control Code**), and specify up to five 60-character lines' worth of **Description**.

Back under the **Intl Trade: Export** tab, the **Country of origin** is the country where this product was manufactured. This information is required by custom offices of several countries to receive product into the country and is thus usually shown on a commercial invoice.

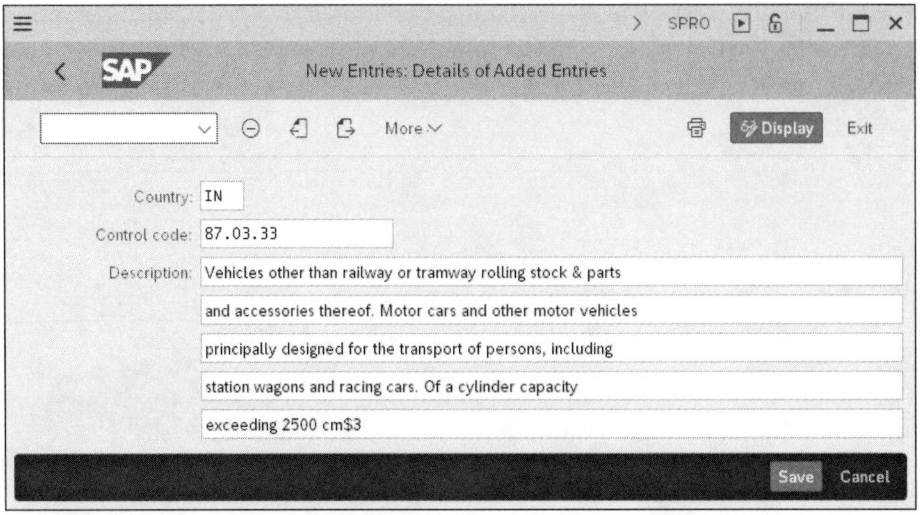

Figure 3.22 Defining New Control Codes

Some companies with large export business segments may manufacture some of their products in more than one country. In this situation, the natural approach would be to have separate material master entries, one for each country where the product is manufactured. However, this approach creates complexity when entering products. This complexity can be addressed using material substitution/determination (which we'll cover in Chapter 4, Section 4.3), but a common alternative is to assign the country of origin at the batch master data level using batch characteristics. This option eliminates the need to have multiple material numbers for the same product and allows for more flexibility during picking.

The **Region of origin** is the state or province where the product was manufactured originally. Only a few countries require this information to be included in a commercial invoice, so this field is usually left blank.

3.5 Sales Text

Under the **Sales text** tab, shown in Figure 3.23, you can enter a long freeform text description of the material from a sales perspective. This text can be later displayed on forms and sent to other systems (internal and external). However, few companies use this text because of the effort required to maintain this information for all materials.

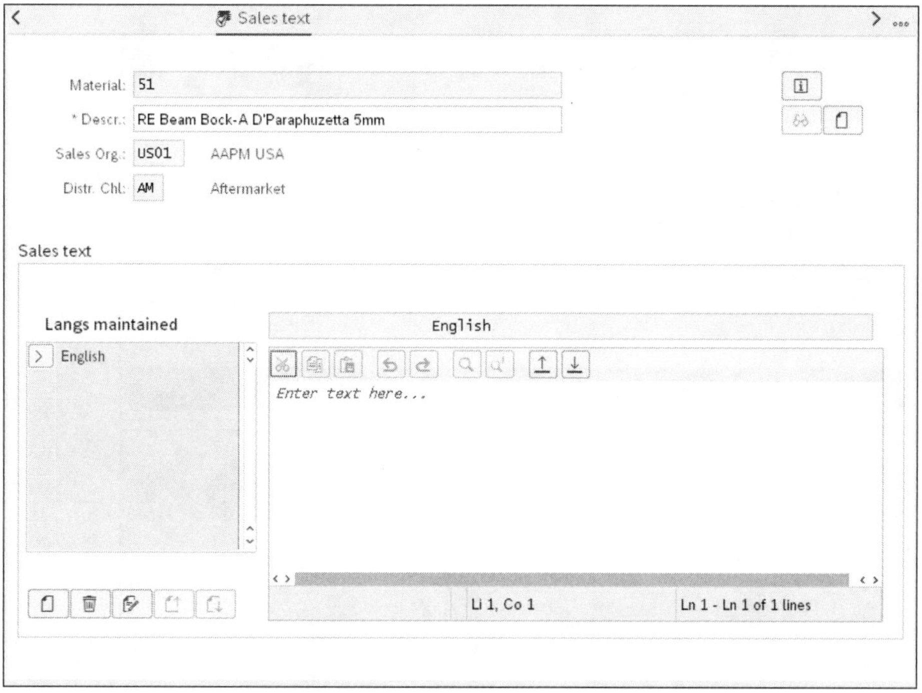

Figure 3.23 Sales Text View of the Material Master

3.6 Customer-Material Information Records

A customer-material information record is a repository that allows you to define customer-specific attributes from your materials.

This approach is commonly used for large customers with enough leverage to require vendors to supply with the customer's material number on all print and electronic communications. This approach may also be used when you want to enter orders using the customer's material number.

Several other attributes can be use on the customer-material information record. Let's look at each of them.

The customer-material information record is created in the SAP GUI by opening Transaction VD51, is modified by opening Transaction VD52, and is displayed by opening Transaction VD53. Using Transaction VD51, Figure 3.24 shows what the customer-material information record maintenance screen looks like.

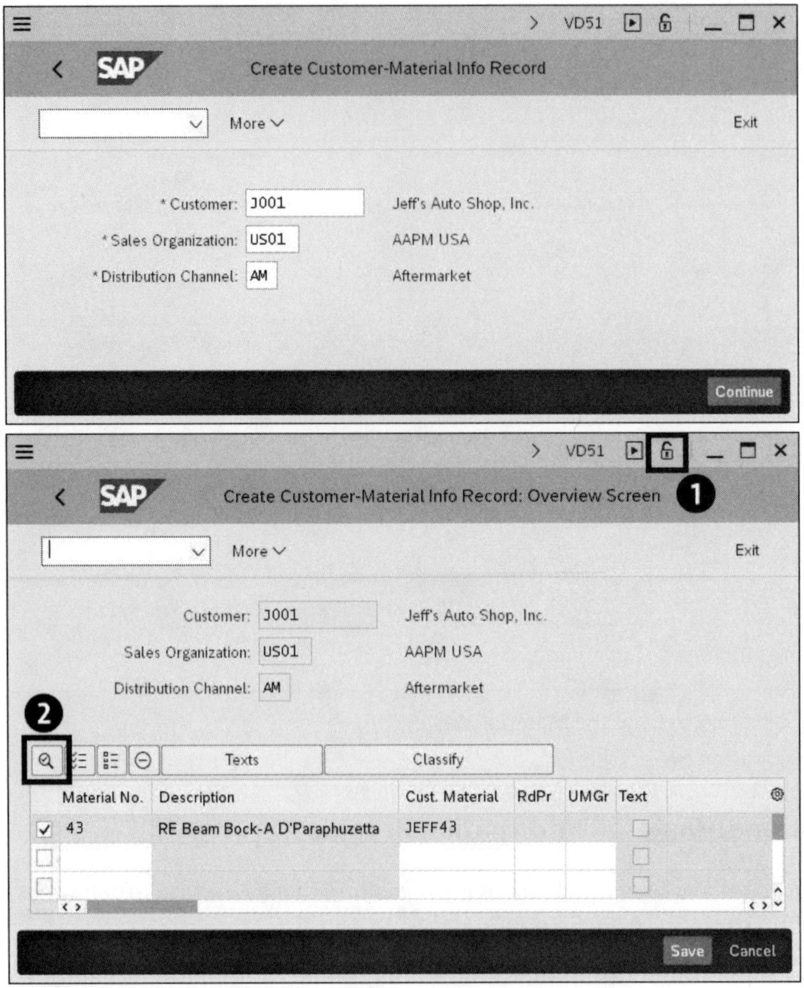

Figure 3.24 Transaction VD51: Customer-Material Information Record

Start by specifying the customer for which this customer-material information record is being entered in the **Customer** field. Note that the customer-material information record is entered for the ship-to customer, not for the sold-to customer. To change the customer for this customer-material information record, no configuration is available, and you'll need to implement a user exit. You'll also select the distribution chain (**Sales Organization** and **Distribution Channel**) for which this customer-material information record is valid.

After you click the unlock icon ❶, the next screen will allow you to maintain a list of material numbers (**Material No.**) and the customer's number corresponding to each customer material record (**Cust. Material**). Once this information is entered, select the line and then click on the **Details** button ❷, which will open the details screen shown in Figure 3.25.

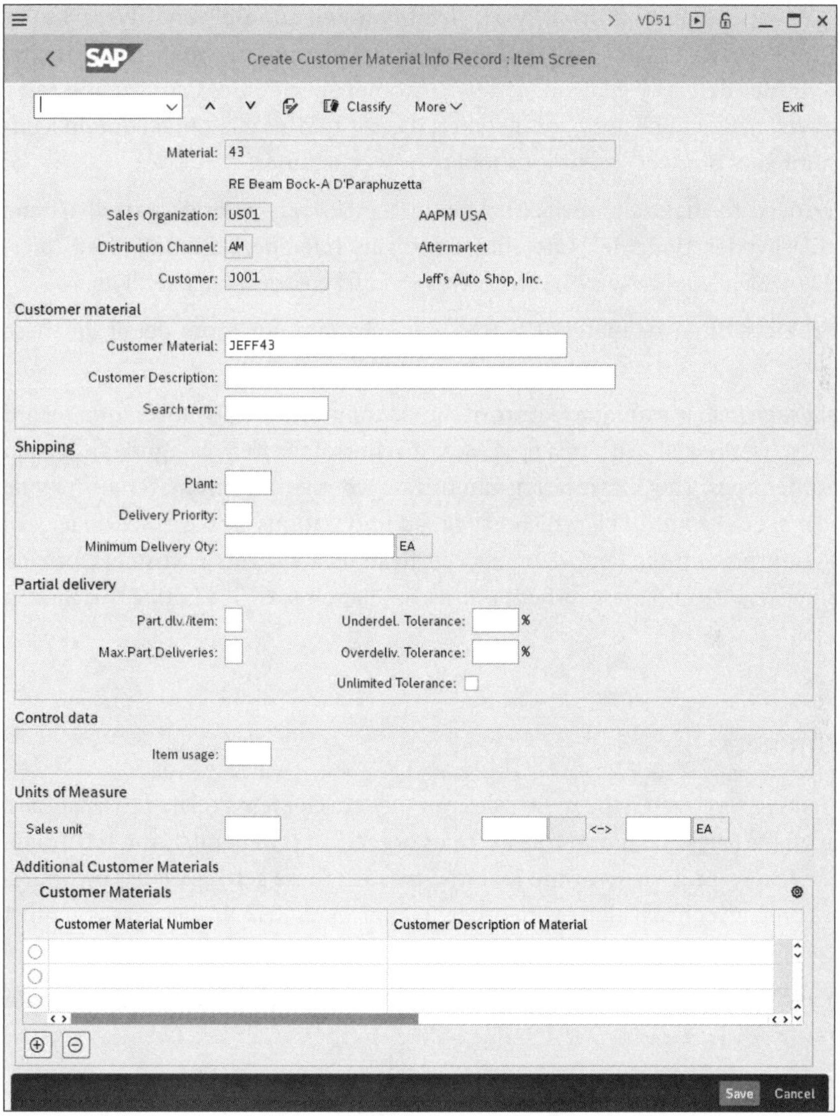

Figure 3.25 Customer-Material Information Record Details

On this screen, you can enter a customer-specific description (**Customer Description**) for this material and a search term (**Search term**).

You can also indicate your preferred sourcing **Plant** to be used by default on sales orders whenever this customer purchases this material. This approach is often used when a specific warehouse is located near this customer.

You may use special minimum delivery quantity (**Minimum Delivery Qty**) and sales unit of measurement (**Sales unit**) values that would overwrite the corresponding material master data as well as indicate a customer-specific UoM conversion (**<->**). This conversion would be used, for instance, if cases for this customer contain a different number of products than cases sold to other customers.

You may need to maintain special values in the **Delivery Priority**, **Part.dlv./item**, **Max.Part.Deliveries**, **Underdel. Tolerance**, **Overdeliv. Tolerance**, and **Unlimited Tolerance** fields, which would overwrite the corresponding customer master data.

Consult the customer or material master data chapters for more detail on these fields.

The **Item usage** field is a unique feature of the customer-material information record that is often overlooked. With this field, you can control the item categories assigned to sales order lines. This information can dictate whether certain materials may be sent under special conditions, which has broad implications. You can set up special incompletion procedures (enforcing special fields just for this customer), pricing (such as free goods), and many other options. In Chapter 6, we'll describe this field in more detail.

3.7 Summary

In this chapter, we covered the main sales master data elements related to materials, focusing on the **Sales: sales org. 1**, **Sales: sales org. 2**, **Sales: General/Plant**, **Intl Trade: Export**, and **Sales Text** views of the material master. These settings must be understood in a broader context along with other areas of SAP S/4HANA, because you must have a complete set of data to operate normally.

In the next chapter, we'll discuss pricing and the condition techniques in SAP S/4HANA Sales.

Chapter 4
Pricing and the Condition Technique

The term "condition technique" describes a system feature that allows you to define data repositories and define corresponding rules to retrieve and utilize the information. In this chapter, we'll show you how to use the condition technique for numerous pricing and sales scenarios.

The condition technique is present in multiple system features. In this chapter, we'll highlight the most common uses of the condition technique. Pricing is the first feature that comes to mind that utilizes the technique, so we'll use start with pricing as a benchmark.

In this chapter, we'll also cover the following condition technique-based functionalities:

- Free goods
- Material determination
- Cross-selling
- Dynamic product proposals
- Listing/exclusion
- Output determination
- Bonus buys

Note

Most of the screenshots in this chapter use the classic theme in the SAP GUI. The configuration and master data screens look better using this theme.

4.1 Pricing

Figure 4.1 shows the basic concepts behind the condition technique in pricing, starting with the operational pricing procedure and moving down to the master data condition records.

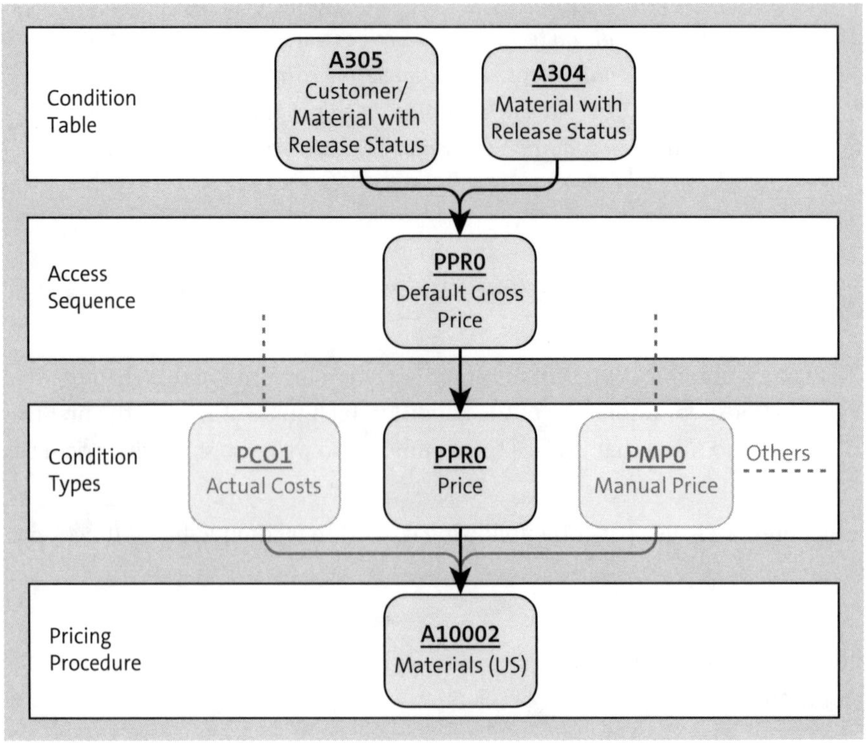

Figure 4.1 Pricing Condition Technique Overview

When a sales order is entered, a *pricing procedure* is assigned to the order using the configuration described in Section 4.1.5. A pricing procedure contains a list of *condition types*, which we'll describe in more detail Section 4.1.4. A pricing procedure also contains subtotals represented by *steps*, which interact mathematically with each other following rules you configure to calculate key sales order figures, such as net value, taxes, freight, etc.

Any given condition type, as assigned to a pricing procedure step, may be sourced from pricing *condition records* (master data) stored in *condition tables*, which we'll cover in Section 4.1.2. If the condition type is configured with an access sequence, described in Section 4.1.3, that access sequence dictates which condition table key is used, how many condition records will be used, and the order in which you must prepare relevant condition records (master data) out of condition tables. The result becomes the pricing procedure step value.

Before we get into these processes in too much detail, let's first look at the master data related to pricing condition records.

4.1.1 Pricing Condition Records: Master Data

Pricing master data is called a *pricing condition record* to keep the description generic and to indicate that this record is used for a wide variety of elements within pricing. You'll use condition records to describe all condition technique-based master data.

You can maintain pricing condition records using the condition technique by opening Transaction VK11. A similar transaction is also enabled in the SAP Fiori app Create Condition Records (Sales).

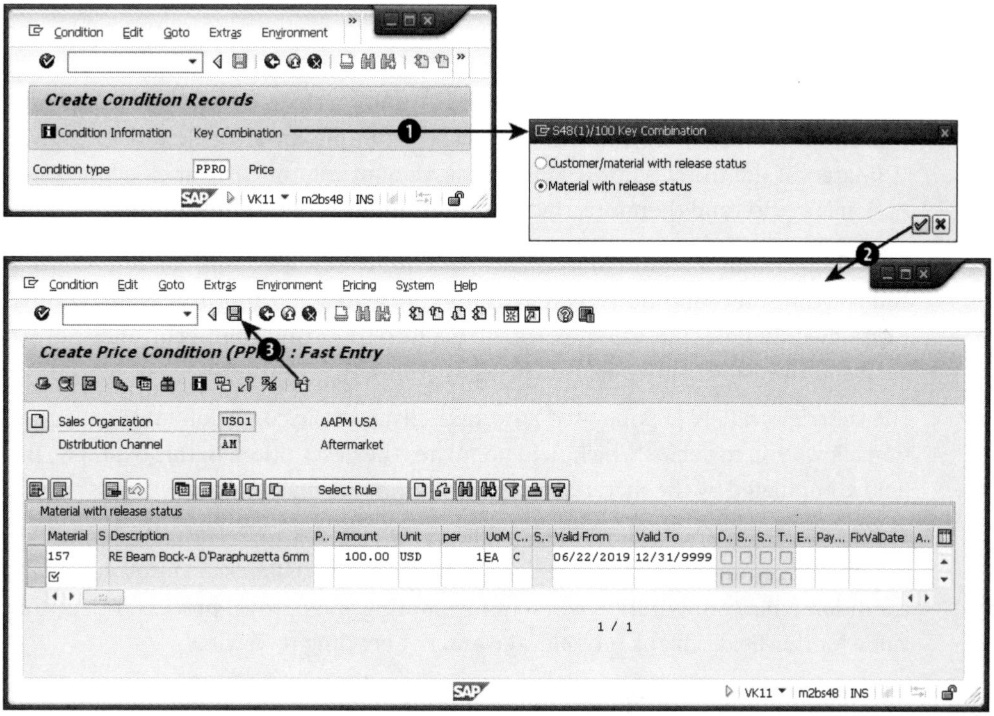

Figure 4.2 Creating Pricing Condition Records via Transaction VK11

As shown in Figure 4.2, you'll take the following actions to maintain the condition record:

❶ First, you'll need to select the condition type (**Condition type**) for which you want to maintain condition records. You can use the match code search to browse through all condition types configured for sales pricing, but the condition types don't indicate which pricing procedures they are used in. You can find this information by looking at the pricing analysis under the **Condition** tab of the sales order.

❷ Then, click on the **Key Combination** command button. The system will find the *access sequence* assigned to the selected *condition type* and all the different condition tables assigned to it. You'll see a list of the relevant *condition tables* with their descriptions to allow you to make selections.

If you simply press [Enter], instead of clicking the **Key Combination** button, the system would respond the same way if more than one condition table is available to choose from. If only one condition table exists on the access sequence, this popup window would not be displayed.

❸ This next screen is generated by the system from the selected condition tables and is affected by the configuration of the condition type. For our example, you'll need to enter the header information for the distribution chain (**Sales Organization** and **Distribution Channel**). You can then enter multiple lines for material numbers (**Material**) and the condition value in the **Amount** column. (In our case, the condition is a price, and therefore, the value is an amount, not a percentage.)

The release status (column **S**) indicates the current status of this condition record, and you can enter condition records that require review and approval. This column is a display-only field; if a value exists in this field, the condition record has not yet been approved and cannot be used on sales orders.

The **Description** field is populated automatically, and the condition table configuration allows you to decide which field populates the description. In this example, this field is populated by the material description from the master data.

The processing status column (**P..**) allows you to block or release this condition record. The column is only visible if you selected the **with Release Status** flag on the condition table configuration when implementing an approval process. The default value for this field is blank (not blocked and not pending review).

The **Unit** column is a unit of measurement (UoM) for the condition amount or a percentage in the **Amount** field. Since we are creating a price condition type, the unit will be a currency code (USD = US dollars). For discount percentage condition types, you would use a percent value. The default value for this field comes from the company code of the sales organization as specified in the header of this screen.

The condition pricing unit (**per**) allows you to use prices for multiple units of a quantity. This approach is commonly used when you need more decimal places. The condition amount or percentage (**Amount**) only allows for two decimal places; so if you need, for example, three decimal places, you would define a two-decimal price for groups of 10 (**10** in the **per** field and **EA** in the **UoM** field). The default value is for groups of 1 if not otherwise specified.

The unit of measurement column (**UoM**) is used in conjunction with **per** to specify the quantity that the condition amount or percentage is valid for. The default value comes from the unit of measurement we defined earlier in Chapter 3, Section 3.1.1. If that field is also blank, the system will use the **Base Unit of Measurement** in the **Sales Org. 1** view, also known as the stock-keeping unit of measurement.

The calculation type (**C..**) controls how the pricing procedure on the sales order calculates the *condition value* using this condition amount or percentage (**Amount**). The default code comes from the condition type configuration.

The scale basis column (**S..**) is a display-only field from the condition type configuration that indicates whether you can enter scale base values for this condition record. If a value is displayed in this field, you can click the **Scale** button on the command bar or press F2 to enter the scale data.

The **Valid to** and **Valid From** columns control the period during which this price will be valid. The default values for these fields are controlled by the condition type configuration. Not that, if you select a validity period that overlaps with an existing price, this screen would automatically adjust the validity period on the existing condition record to eliminate overlap.

The selection indicator (**D..**), when checked, indicates that this condition record is for display only and is never used by any functionality. The condition type configuration controls whether condition records with this flag checked are deleted from the database or are kept for future reference.

The condition supplement column (first **S..**) indicates whether more information has been entered for this condition record. The scales column (second **S..**) indicates that scales have been entered for this condition record, while the texts column (**T..**) indicates that texts have been maintained for this condition record.

The condition exclusion indicator (**E..**) excludes other condition types when this condition type is present. The default is set up on the condition type.

The payment term column (**Pay...**) allows you to choose a payment term applicable whenever this condition record is assigned to an order. This feature is intended for special prices valid only for certain terms (usually due net). This field will overwrite the payment term entered on the header of the order. Most companies do not use this field because users often fail to realize this value is assigned. Your sales reps could end up promising a customer payment terms found in the header. Then, when the actual invoice is issued, the line item payment term is used, leading to customer complaints.

The fixed value date column (**FixValDate**) is used when you want the payment to start counting on a specific fixed date. The additional value days column (**A..**) is used to add extra days to the payment terms.

4.1.2 Pricing Condition Tables

Condition tables are the master data repositories where pricing-relevant information is stored. These tables are actual database repositories created by a configuration activity that we'll walk you through later in this section. To maintain entries in the condition tables, you must first define an access sequence (Section 4.1.3) and then define a condition type (Section 4.1.4).

Often, SAP implementation projects involve adding new condition tables. Pricing is often one of the business-specific strategic requirements that must be addressed and configured during implementation. SAP provides several condition tables out of the box that do cover most common requirements, so you should use these predelivered condition tables as much as possible.

To create condition tables, open Transaction V/03 or follow the menu path **SAP Customizing Implementation Guide • Sales and Distribution • Basic Functions • Pricing • Pricing Control • Define Condition Tables • Create Condition Tables**. Alternatively, you can open Transaction VOKO (Pricing Configuration) and navigate to **Environment • Condition Table • Create**.

In the example shown in Figure 4.3, we're creating condition table 902, which uses the **Sales Organization** and the **Payer** as keywords.

To create a condition table, follow these steps:

❶ First, specify a three-digit condition number (**Table**); this number must begin with "9" to indicate that is not provided by SAP (allowable namespace). You can use an existing table (**Copy from Condition Table**), which speeds up this step, when a table with some of the same fields you need for the new table exists. In this case, we don't have an existing condition table to use as reference, but this approach is quite common. When your entries are complete, press [Enter].

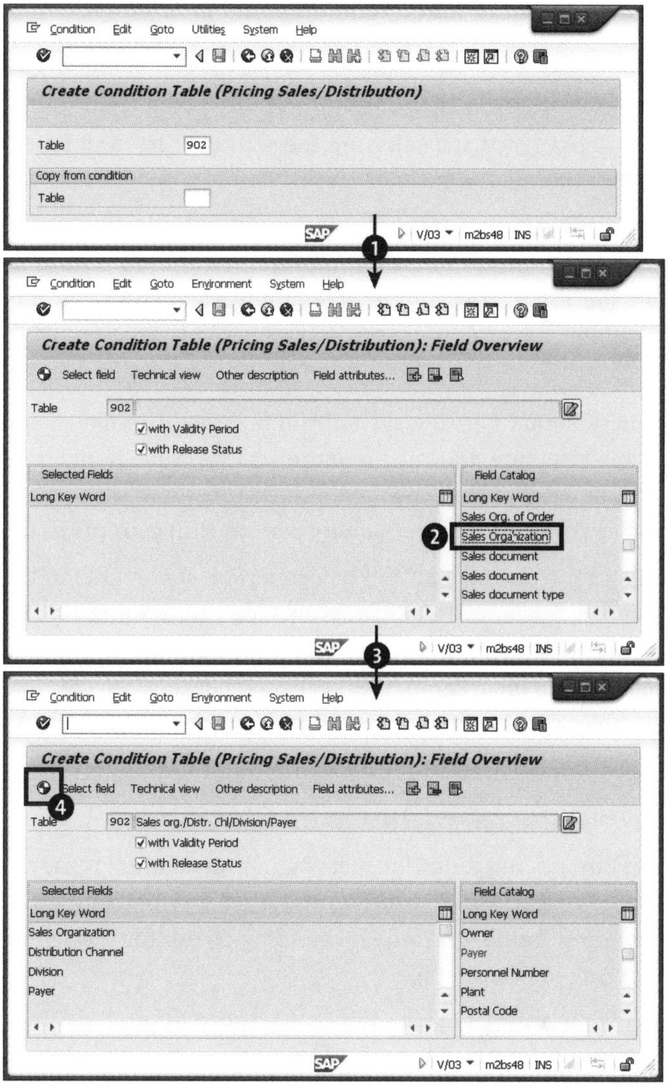

Figure 4.3 Creating Condition Tables

❷ The **Create Condition Table (Pricing Sales/Distribution): Field Overview** screen will open. On the right, you'll find the **Field Catalog** with a list of fields currently available to choose from. You can add new fields to this screen by configuring and changing ABAP Dictionary. You'll need to scroll up/down in the **Field Catalog** window to find the field you want; the entries are not sorted alphabetically by field description, but by technical field name. Once you find the first field, double-click the field to copy the field to the left side of the screen in the **Selected Fields** window. The sequence in which fields are added greatly affects the functionality and usability of the new condition table.

❸ Now, repeat this process, looking for and selecting the second, third, and fourth fields until the list of fields is complete and consistent.

❹ Once you've selected all the fields you want in the new condition table, click on the generate icon, as indicated. The system will create a database table called "AXXX," where "A" indicates that this is a pricing condition table and XXX is the condition table number. In our example, table A902 is generated along with the maintenance screens.

If you select the **with Validity Period** flag, the system will incorporate valid-to and valid-from dates to the table structure and maintenance screens. You should only unselect this flag for control tables that have the same values; for actual pricing data, you'll probably select this flag so you can define validity periods with your prices.

The **with Release Status** flag controls the addition of a condition status field to the table structure and maintenance screen. This feature enables you to enter pricing condition records but flag them as inactive pending later review and release. Only a few companies use this feature, and most companies keep this checkbox selected just to keep custom condition tables consistent with out-of-the-box condition tables.

4.1.3 Pricing Access Sequences

An access sequence defines how pricing condition records (master data) are retrieved from the database. You'll indicate the order in which to access tables, whether the system stops searching once one is found, and which key value to use for the search (either from the sales order data or elsewhere).

The maintenance of access sequences is a common step in implementation projects. To maintain access sequences, follow the menu path **SAP Customizing Implementation Guide • Sales and Distribution • Basic Functions • Pricing • Pricing Control • Define Access Sequences • Maintain Access Sequences.** Alternatively, you can open Transaction VOKO (Pricing Configuration) and navigate to **Environment • Condition Type • Access Sequences.** For either option, on the screen that opens, click on the **New Entries** button or press [F5].

In our example, we'll a new access sequence using the new condition table 902 created in Section 4.1.2. To begin, follow these steps:

1. On the screen shown in Figure 4.4, you'll first need to define and enter a four-character access sequence code (**Acc...**) and add a description (**Description**). The code needs to begin with "Z" to indicate that the access sequence is not provided by SAP (allowable namespace). For pricing access sequences, the **Access Category** field must be left blank; for rebates, you must use access category 1. constipated

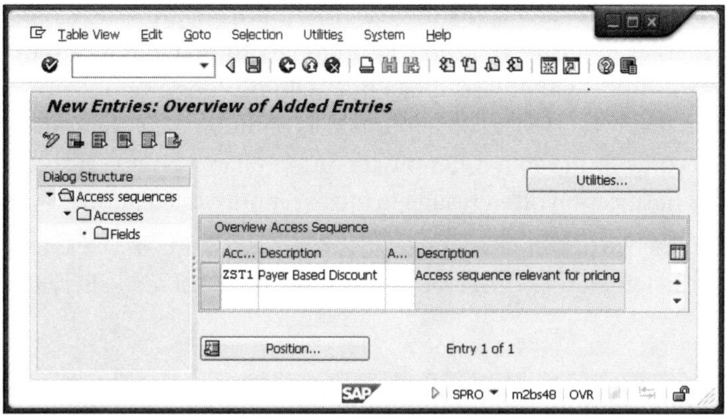

Figure 4.4 Creating a New Access Sequence

2. Now, select the entry you just created and double-click on **Accesses** in the **Dialog Structure** menu on the left side of the screen, which will open the screens shown in Figure 4.5.

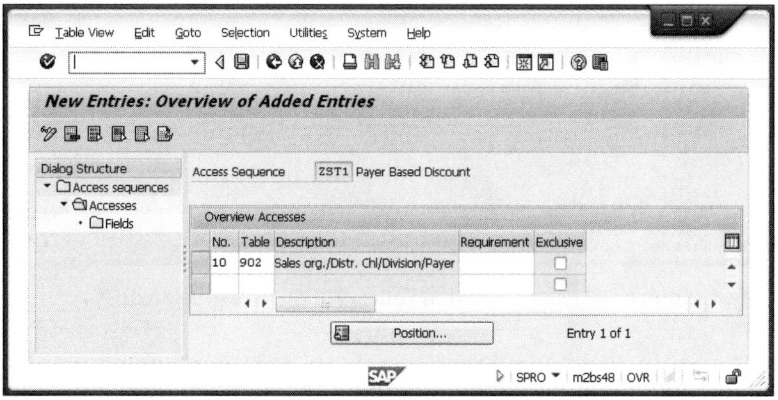

Figure 4.5 Adding Condition Tables to an Access Sequence

3. Next, enter each table on the lines available on this screen. You assign each line with a number (**No.** column; we recommend using increments of 10) and the table number you want. You can also use a VOFM routine, which is ABAP code written using the forms in Transaction VOFM, in the **Requirement** column. This approach allows for greater flexibility when determining whether this data is applicable. The **Exclusive** flag is also an important option when multiple tables are specified: When selected, this flag indicates that the system should stop searching for further tables once data is found in one table. Without this flag, the system will retrieve all entries found in all the tables and apply them all to the pricing procedure. Most companies flag all lines as **Exclusive** to keep condition record maintenance more intuitive and less error prone. Otherwise, while maintaining condition records, a user has no indication that condition records found in a condition table were added to other condition records found in a different condition table within this access sequence. This lack of notification often results in incorrect price calculations.
4. Then, select the new line we just created and double-click on **Fields** in the **Dialog Structure** menu on the left side of the screen, which opens the screen shown in Figure 4.6.

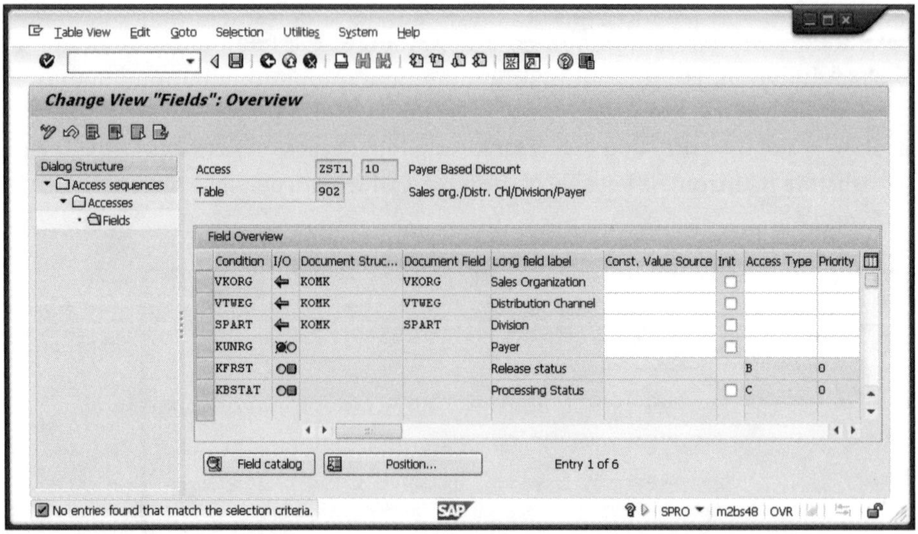

Figure 4.6 Specifying Source Fields for Condition Tables within Access Sequences

5. On this screen, confirm the source fields you want to use keys when searching for condition records (master data) on this condition table. In our example, the system automatically chooses the source for most fields except for the payment, as

indicated by the red traffic light. Alternatively, you can define a fixed value to use as a source when searching for condition records on the **Cont. Value Source** column.

6. To resolve the issue indicated by the red traffic light, you'll need to select the corresponding line and then click on the **Field catalog** button on the bottom of the screen, which opens the screen shown in Figure 4.7.

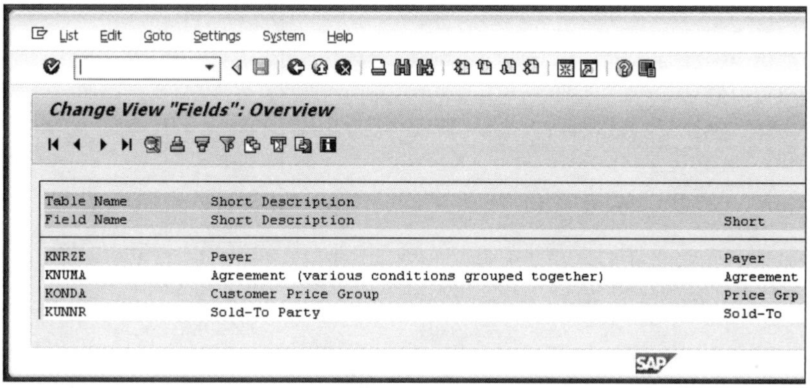

Figure 4.7 List of Available Fields to Use as Sources to Find Entries on the Condition Table

7. The system will show a list of all allowable fields you can choose from. Locate the desired field (**Payer**) and double-click on that entry.
8. With all field sources correctly identified, you can now save the new access sequence.

4.1.4 Pricing Condition Types

A pricing condition type represents a value that may be involved in the calculation of certain sales order key figures (such as sales price, freight, taxes, etc.). A pricing condition type also dictates how to obtain the input master data necessary and how to calculate the output amount. Condition types are processed at the time of sales order entry as part of a pricing procedure. At that time, each condition type may use a *condition amount or percentage* retrieved from the condition records (master data).For example this could be from the **Amount** field we maintained in Section 4.1.1.

The pricing procedure (Section 4.1.5) indicates the *condition base value* to be used by the condition type. Using the calculation type as configured, the condition type will calculate the *condition value*. The result (*condition value*) of one condition type may be used as the input for another. Figure 4.8 shows this entire process.

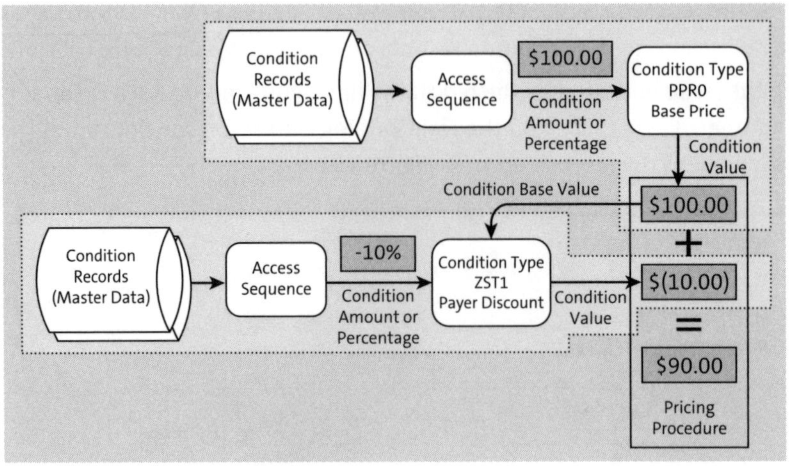

Figure 4.8 Condition Type Interaction

The standard condition type PPRO is configured out of the box as a price condition dependent on the order quantity. As shown in Figure 4.8, the condition records are obtained according to the access sequence, and its condition value is calculated as $100.00 (considering order quantity of 1 unit).

In our example, we created the new condition type ZST1 and configured this condition type to be a discount percentage calculation based on the payer. In the ZST1 condition record, we entered "-10%," as the *condition amount or percentage*. When using condition type PPRO's *condition value* of $100.00 as the *condition base value*, ZST1's condition value will be calculated as $(10.00) or negative 10 dollars. The pricing procedure configuration will add these values together, thus arriving at a net value of $90.00.

To configure condition types, follow the menu path **SAP Customizing Implementation Guide • Sales and Distribution • Basic Functions • Pricing • Pricing Control • Define Condition Types • Set Condition Types for Pricing.** Alternatively, you can open Transaction VOKO (Pricing Configuration) and navigate to **Condition Type • Condition Types • Definition.** For either option, on the screen that opens, click on the **New Entries** button or press F5.

In the example shown in Figure 4.9, we're creating a condition type that is a discount percentage applied over the net price, depending on who is the payer on the sales order header. This condition type could be used when multiple sold-to customers place orders using the same payer customer. Using this discount, you would only need to maintain condition records for the payer, rather than for each of the sold-to customers. You can clearly indicate why the sold-to customer is getting this discount by maintaining the condition type description.

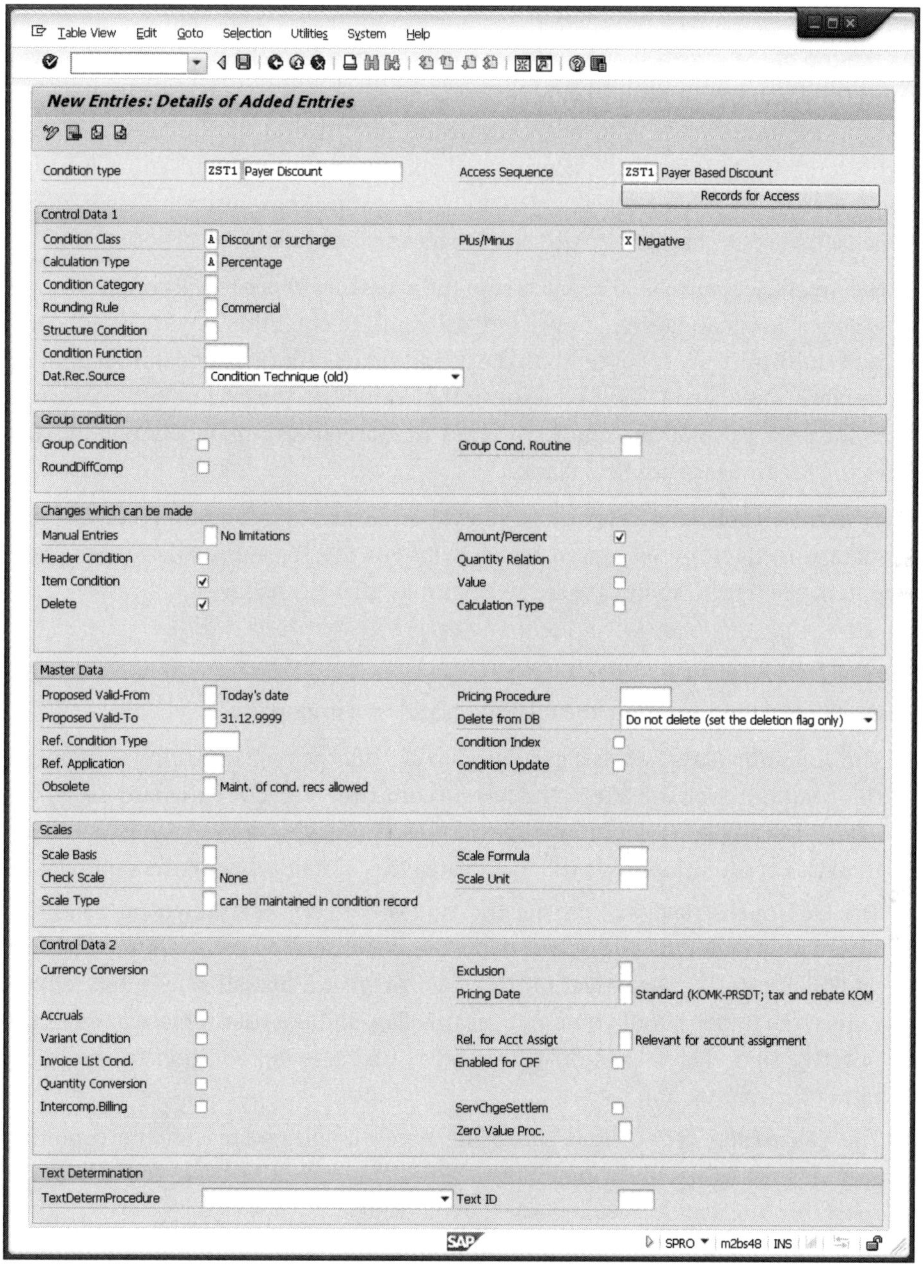

Figure 4.9 Creating New Condition Types for Pricing

In the following sections, we'll look at each section on this screen.

General Condition Type Information

At the top of the screen shown in Figure 4.9, specify a four-character condition type code (**Condition type**) and add a description. The description must be user friendly, not just for your internal users, but also because this information may be customer facing if this condition type becomes incorporated into customer communications (which is configured in the pricing procedure). Often, companies show discounts on invoices, which enhances transparency with customers and facilitates price negotiations.

In the **Access Sequence** field, you'll assign the access sequence to the condition type. This step is not mandatory; in our case, we want the condition type to calculate its input value from a source other than the condition records (master data). A common example is when a condition type uses other values on the pricing procedure as a base for price calculation. Condition types that are always manually entered also have the **Access Sequence** field blank.

Clicking on **Records for Access** button allows you to maintain condition records (master data) directly from this screen, which helps you test the automatically generated maintenance screen. Some of these settings may affect its behavior.

Control Data 1

In the **Control Data 1** section, the following fields are important:

- The **Condition Class** field is a code used to classify the type of pricing component this condition type will affect. The system compares this code with hard-coded values. One example is a condition type of class "B" (**Prices**). On the pricing procedure, this class of condition types will inactivate other conditions with the same class.
- The **Plus/Minus** field will restrict the values that can be entered on condition records and under the **Condition** tab of the sales order. For discounts, for example, you'll indicate "X" (**Negative**) for this field to ensure that all values entered will reduce the total price. If you don't set this flag, and the user forgets to enter the negative sign, this value would become a surcharge (an addition to the price), rather than a discount.
- The **Calculation Type** field dictates the type of value stored on the condition records (master data) and how these values are used in pricing procedures. The most common values used include the following:
  - **A: Percentage**
    Condition records are stored as percentages and applied over the condition base value to calculate the condition value.

- **B: Fixed amount**
  Condition records are stored as currency values and used unchanged in the pricing procedure calculation.
- **C: Quantity**
  Condition records are stored as currency values and multiplied by the order quantity before being used in the pricing procedure calculation.
- **D: Gross weight**
  Condition records are stored as currency values and multiplied by the gross weight before being used in the pricing procedure calculation. Note that, when selling a product by weight, the order quantity should be used instead of its weight, which is used mostly for freight calculation.
- **F: Volume**
  Condition records are stored as currency values and multiplied by the volume before being used in the pricing procedure calculation. Note that, when selling product by dimensional units of measurement, the order quantity should be used instead of its volume, which is mostly used for freight calculation.
- **G: Formula**
  Condition records are stored as currency values and used by a VOFM formula to determine the condition value used in the pricing procedure.
- **S: Number of shipping units**
  Condition records are stored as currency values and multiplied by the number of packages shipped out of the warehouse before being used on the pricing procedure calculation. This value is mostly used for freight calculation.

- The **Condition Category** field is another way to classify a condition type by referring to the pricing element they affect. This approach is not used often with SAP S/4HANA at the order level but may be relevant for specific scenarios and for more flexible pricing rules.
- The **Rounding Rule** field indicates how the condition value should be rounded if more the calculation results in more than the allowed number of decimal places. You may want to always round values up or down. The default is for *commercial rounding* (i.e., for two decimal places, we add 0.005 and truncate all decimal places starting with the third decimal place).
- The **Structure Condition** field indicates if a condition should appear multiple times or just once with the total of all values.
- The **Condition Function** field (CRM) classifies certain conditions to control whether they are displayed individually or as a total.

- The **Dat.Rec.Source** field (CRM) controls whether you want to use the condition records defined using condition tables or other sources. With this field, you can also control whether condition records should be stored using the new SAP S/4HANA table structures or using table structures available in older versions of the system. This choice affects the degree of older functionality you can use in lieu of performance and database usage.

Group Condition

In the **Group Condition** section, the following fields are important:

- The **Group Condition** flag indicates to the system that you want to summarize the values across all sales order lines before using this sum as the *scale base value* for the **Scale Basis** configured on this screen. The resulting condition value is considered applicable to all relevant lines as per **Group Cond. Routine** (is present), and the value is pro-rated to each sales order line according to each line value.
- The **Group Cond. Routine** field is a VOFM routine ID you can use to select only the lines on a sales order that match the criteria you specify (in routine ABAP code). Only the sales order lines that match this criterion will be considered when calculating the *scale base value* for **Group Conditions**. If no formula is used, all lines will be considered.
- The **RoundDiffComp** flag, when selected, indicates that any rounding differences resulting from pro-rating the condition value should be equalized on the final sales order line.

Changes Which Can Be Made

In the **Changes which can be made** section, the following fields are important:

- The **Manual Entries** field controls whether you allow users to manually modify the condition information at the time of order entry. The system keeps track of manual changes; however, we recommend only allowing manual changes on the conditions designed specifically for manual changes. The values the system determines should be kept as reporting references.
- The **Amount/Percent** flag indicates that you want to allow users to modify the *condition amount or percentage* obtained from the condition records or other sources.
- The **Header Condition** flag indicates that this condition type is a header condition type. A user would need to interact with to the header of the sales order to maintain values for this condition type. Note that header conditions cannot use condition

records to determine their *condition amount or percentage*; these values can only be manually entered by the user.

- The **Quantity Relation** flag indicates that you want to allow users to modify the quantity conversion used to calculate quantity-relevant condition types.
- The **Item Condition** flag indicates that this item condition is relevant to each line of a sales order.
- The **Value** flag indicates that you want to allow users to manually modify the condition value calculated by the system for this condition type on the sales order pricing procedure.
- The **Delete** flag indicates that you want to allow users to manually delete a condition type from a sales order pricing procedure.
- The **Calculation Type** flag indicates that you want to allow users to manually modify the calculation type configured for a condition type on the sales order pricing procedure.

Master Data

The following fields control the behavior of the condition records maintenance screen that is automatically generated based on this configuration and the condition table configuration:

- The **Proposed Valid-From** field controls the default valid-from date that should be proposed if a user leaves the **Valid-From** field blank when creating a new condition record.
- The **Proposed Valid-To** field controls the default valid-to date that should be proposed if a user leaves the **Valid-To** field blank when creating a new condition record.
- The **Pricing Procedure** field indicates where this condition type may be used as a condition supplement to other condition types in the pricing procedure.
- The **Delete from DB** field controls whether a deleted condition record should be removed from the database (when selected) or simply saved with a deletion flag (when blank). The effect is largely the same; however, deleted condition records would continue to be displayed, but with the deletion flag. Users often struggle at first with how deletion flags work because they consider the deletion flag too inconspicuous. For this reason, many companies configure all their condition types with this field selected.

- The **Ref. Condition Type** field shares the same condition records across different condition types. If you enter a value in this field, all condition records must be maintained for the condition type indicated here. If you attempt to enter a condition record for a condition type we're configuring, the system will issue a message saying we must use the reference condition type instead.
- The **Ref. Application** field is used in conjunction with the **Ref. Condition Type** to identify the condition records that this condition type will use. This feature allows you to use condition records defined for other functionalities to valuate sales documents.
- The **Condition Index** field controls the automatic creation of a table (classified as an index table) along with the condition records, thus allowing this data to be fetched without specifying the condition type and condition table number. This option is used for service pricing.
- The **Condition Update** field specifies whether maximum or maximum values should control possible values when maintaining fields on condition records. This option limits the manual changes your users can make on the pricing procedure at the time of sales order entry.
- The **Obsolete** field is no longer to be used in SAP S/4HANA.

Scales

The **Scales** section allows you to define variable *condition amount or percentages* for your condition records depending on certain sales order key figures, as follows:

- The **Scale Basis** field identifies which sales order key figures you want to use as a basis for scale. The codes B (**Value**) and C (**Quantity**) are the most commonly used options, but you can also use weight or volume. For instance, if you use C (**Quantity**), you can define a sales price of $10 valid when the customer purchases up to 10 units; if they order between 11 and 20 units, the price would be $9.50 per unit, and over 20 units, the price would be $8.75 per unit. This bulk pricing approach is common in many industries.
- The **Scale Formula** field is a VOFM routine that allows you to interfere with how the *scale base value* is calculated before it is used to retrieve condition records.
- The **Check Scale** field dictates the order in which the scales are maintained (ascending versus descending); ascending order is the most common.
- The **Scale Unit** field is the unit of measurement in which the sales condition records are maintained.

- The **Scale Type** field controls the type of scale master data (and the restrictions they represent) to be used for this condition type.

Control Data 2

In the **Control Data 2** section, the following fields are important:

- The **Currency Conversion** flag, when checked, indicates that you want to convert the condition records maintained into the chosen currency of the sales order before multiplying the unit price by the order quantity, which affects rounding.
- The **Exclusion** field is a code you can configure to indicate condition types that are mutually exclusive. The code is made available on the sales order pricing procedure and may be used to deactivate other conditions.
- The **Pricing Date** field controls which sales order dates will be used to search for condition records by comparing this date against the validity dates.
- The **Accruals** flag indicates that the condition value calculated for this condition type may be relevant for accounting accruals. At the time of billing, accrual documents are posted using the accrual account determined by the account determination configuration (see Chapter 10 for more details).
- The **Variant Condition** flag indicates that this condition type may use variant configuration characteristics to determine its relevance.
- The **Rel. for Acct Assigt** flag controls whether the condition value of this condition type is relevant for regular account determination or if you'll use the **Accounting** indicator defined in controlling instead. The FI/CO team will notify the sales team when to use the accounting indicator after setting it up in SAP S/4HANA Finance.
- The **Invoice List Cond.** flag identifies condition types that should only appear on the invoice list billing document. The invoice list is a feature that allow you to summarize all invoices issued to a customer over a period of time and issue a single document. Large customers prefer (and sometimes require) you only send one summarized billing document per month (or other periods).
- The **Enabled for CPF** flag controls the utilization of a pricing feature called *configurable parameters and formulas (CPF)*. Flagged condition types would use CPF method to calculation the condition value.
- The **Quantity Conversion** flag is applicable when the sales unit of measurement used on the sales order line is different than the stock keeping unit. If this field is flagged, the conversion is order specific; otherwise, the system performs the

conversion at the time the price is calculated and ignores any changes made during the sales document conversion.

- The **Intercomp.Billing** flag indicates that this condition type is applicable only for intercompany billing documents (see Chapter 10 for more details).
- The **ServChgeSettlem** flag indicates that this condition type is only relevant for service charge settlement billing documents created for trading contracts.
- The **Zero Value Proc.** field allows you to choose how condition exclusions behave when the condition value of this condition type is zero. By default, when the condition value is zero, the system will act the same way as if that condition type was missing. If zero represents a valid value, you'll need to change this code to "A."
- The **TextDetermProcedure** field allows you to define condition type-specific texts to help users and customers understand certain condition types. This feature is not often used but may be helpful for condition types that don't appear very often.
- The **Text ID** field is the code used to store the default freeform description for this condition type. The freeform text is displayed under the **Condition** tab after clicking the **Analysis** button.

4.1.5 Pricing Procedures

A pricing procedure combines condition types and defines the interaction among them. When you enter a sales order, you'll use the configuration described in the following sections to assign a pricing procedure to the sales order.

Setting Pricing Procedures

To configure pricing procedures, follow the menu path **SAP Customizing Implementation Guide • Sales and Distribution • Basic Functions • Pricing • Pricing Control • Define And Assign Pricing Procedures • Set Pricing Procedures.** Alternatively, you can use Transaction VOKO (Pricing Configuration) and the menu options **Condition Type • Pricing Procedure • Pricing Procedures**.

You'll then find the desired pricing procedure on the list, select it, and then double-click on **Procedures – Control Data** in the **Dialog Structure**.

In our example shown in Figure 4.10, we'll start by modifying **Procedure A17J02**. You'll usually start with a standard SAP pricing procedure even when creating a new one.

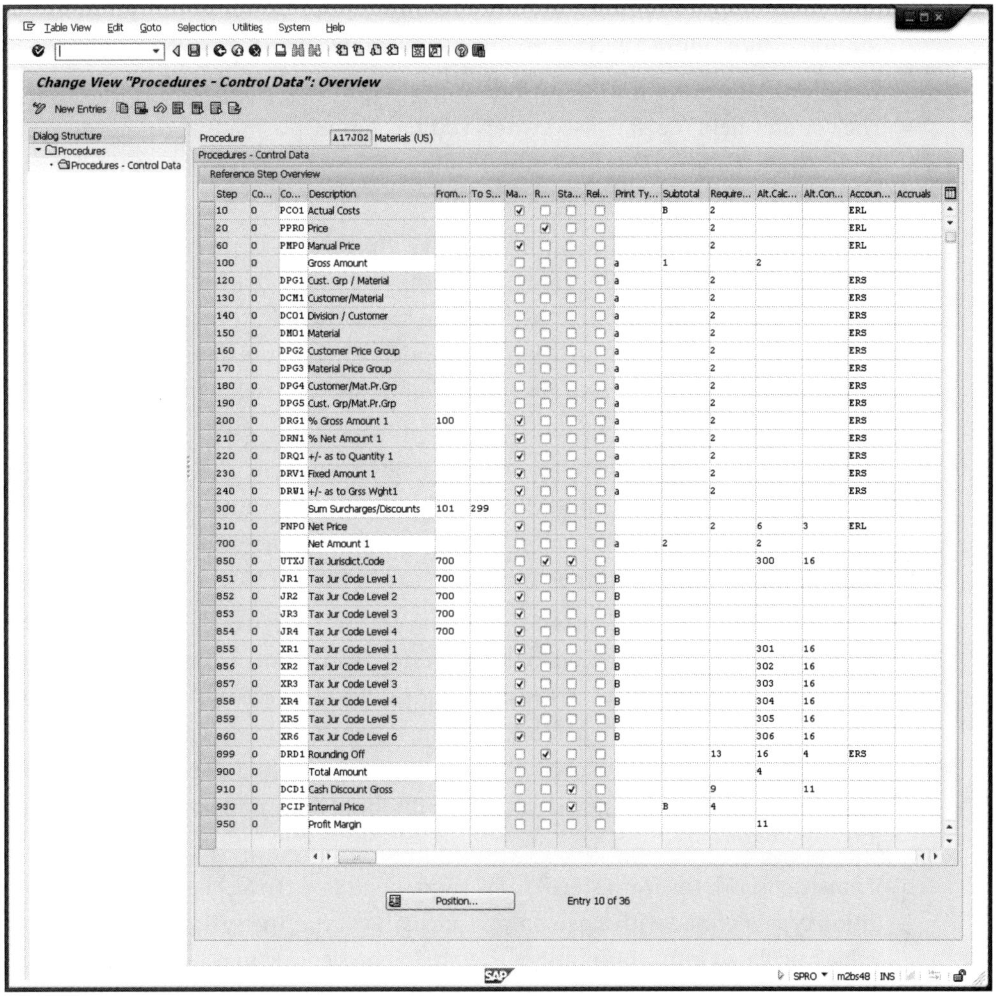

Step	Co...	Co...	Description	From...	To S...	Ma...	R...	Sta...	Rel...	Print Ty...	Subtotal	Require...	Alt.Calc...	Alt.Con...	Accoun...	Accruals
10	0	PCO1	Actual Costs			☑	☐	☐	☐		B	2			ERL	
20	0	PPR0	Price			☐	☑	☐	☐			2			ERL	
60	0	PMP0	Manual Price			☑	☐	☐	☐			2			ERL	
100	0		Gross Amount			☐	☐	☐	☐	a	1		2			
120	0	DPG1	Cust. Grp / Material			☐	☐	☐	☐	a		2			ERS	
130	0	DCM1	Customer/Material			☐	☐	☐	☐	a		2			ERS	
140	0	DCO1	Division / Customer			☐	☐	☐	☐	a		2			ERS	
150	0	DMO1	Material			☐	☐	☐	☐	a		2			ERS	
160	0	DPG2	Customer Price Group			☐	☐	☐	☐	a		2			ERS	
170	0	DPG3	Material Price Group			☐	☐	☐	☐	a		2			ERS	
180	0	DPG4	Customer/Mat.Pr.Grp			☐	☐	☐	☐	a		2			ERS	
190	0	DPG5	Cust. Grp/Mat.Pr.Grp			☐	☐	☐	☐	a		2			ERS	
200	0	DRG1	% Gross Amount 1	100		☑	☐	☐	☐	a		2			ERS	
210	0	DRN1	% Net Amount 1			☑	☐	☐	☐	a		2			ERS	
220	0	DRQ1	+/- as to Quantity 1			☑	☐	☐	☐	a		2			ERS	
230	0	DRV1	Fixed Amount 1			☑	☐	☐	☐	a		2			ERS	
240	0	DRW1	+/- as to Grss Wght1			☑	☐	☐	☐	a		2			ERS	
300	0		Sum Surcharges/Discounts	101	299	☐	☐	☐	☐							
310	0	PNP0	Net Price			☑	☐	☐	☐			2	6	3	ERL	
700	0		Net Amount 1			☐	☐	☐	☐	a	2		2			
850	0	UTXJ	Tax Jurisdict.Code	700		☐	☑	☑	☐				300	16		
851	0	JR1	Tax Jur Code Level 1	700		☑	☐	☐	☐	B						
852	0	JR2	Tax Jur Code Level 2	700		☑	☐	☐	☐	B						
853	0	JR3	Tax Jur Code Level 3	700		☑	☐	☐	☐	B						
854	0	JR4	Tax Jur Code Level 4	700		☑	☐	☐	☐	B						
855	0	XR1	Tax Jur Code Level 1			☑	☐	☐	☐	B			301	16		
856	0	XR2	Tax Jur Code Level 2			☑	☐	☐	☐	B			302	16		
857	0	XR3	Tax Jur Code Level 3			☑	☐	☐	☐	B			303	16		
858	0	XR4	Tax Jur Code Level 4			☑	☐	☐	☐	B			304	16		
859	0	XR5	Tax Jur Code Level 5			☑	☐	☐	☐	B			305	16		
860	0	XR6	Tax Jur Code Level 6			☑	☐	☐	☐	B			306	16		
899	0	DRD1	Rounding Off			☐	☑	☐	☐			13	16	4	ERS	
900	0		Total Amount			☐	☐	☐	☐				4			
910	0	DCD1	Cash Discount Gross			☐	☐	☑	☐			9		11		
930	0	PCIP	Internal Price			☐	☐	☑	☐		B	4				
950	0		Profit Margin			☐	☐	☐	☐				11			

Figure 4.10 Defining Pricing Procedures

On this screen, you'll maintain all of the following fields:

- The **Step** field is a sequential number that specifies the order in which pricing procedure lines should be displayed for maintenance under the **Condition** tab of the sales order. This value is also used for cross-referencing the from step (**From...**) and to step (**To S...**) fields.

  Usually, you'll want to skip numbers from one line to another (10, 20, 30...) to allow for space to add new lines in between existing numbers in the future. You can also reserve more space between lines for calculating pricing elements, for instance, the pricing procedure A17J02 skips lines 60 to 100 to allow for more information to be added in these lines for gross/base price calculations.

- The counter field (**Co...**) is used when you have multiple manual condition types under the same **Step**. This field is not commonly used, so most companies have all lines in this field filled with zeros.
- The condition type field (**Co...**) is where you'll link the condition type to this pricing procedure line. The system will automatically populate the **Description** field and block it from changes. If you leave this field blank, then this pricing procedure line will be a *subtotal*, i.e., a summation of the pricing procedure lines indicated by the from step (**From...**) and to step (**To S...**) fields. The subtotal name must be entered in the **Description** field; this field is kept open for changes on subtotal lines.
- The from step (**From...**) and to step (**To S...**) fields are used by the pricing procedure to calculate the *condition base value*. For instance, on line 300, we have a subtotal called **Sum Surcharges/Discounts**: The *condition base value* will calculate all pricing procedures lines with **Step** numbers between 101 and 299.

  If you leave the to step field (**To S...**) blank, the system will use only the value from the line with the **Step** specified in the from step field (**From...**). For instance, on line 200 (condition type **DRG1 – % Gross Amount 1**), we have **100** in the from step field (**From...**), and the to step field (**To S...**) is blank. If the **Condition Amount or Percentage** for DRG1 is entered as "-10%," this percentage will be applied to the other gross value on line 100, ignoring any other discount indicated on lines 101 through 199.

  If you leave both the from step (**From...**) and the to step (**To S...**) fields blank on condition types defined with a percentage calculation type, the system will use the *net value* calculated until this point of the pricing procedure. In other words, the system will sum all active pricing procedure lines (prices, discount, freight, etc.) with a **Step** lower than the one we're in.
- The manual flag (**Ma...**) indicates that this pricing procedure line should only be added to the sales order **Conditions** tab if the user manually selects it. Adding these lines can also be achieved via an interface, but the system will not populate pricing procedure lines automatically, even if condition records found are found for them.
- The required flag (**R...**) indicates that this pricing procedure will be considered incomplete unless a value is defined for this line.
- The statistical flag (**Sta...**) indicates that this line should not affect the sales order value; this line will later be used on statistical reports and analysis.

- The relevant for account determination flag (**Rel...**) indicates that the value on this line must be posted to accounting at the time of billing.
- The print type field (**Print Ty...**) is a code used by standard output forms, such as the order acknowledgment and the invoice. These forms will print sales document information, and you can use this flag to control whether this pricing procedure line must show on the form. Companies that build their own forms may or may not choose to observe this field's functionality.
- The **Subtotal** field controls whether this pricing procedure line value must be stored for future usage on reports as a sales order line and header fields (KZWI1, KZWI2, KZWI3, KZWI4, KZWI5, and KZWI6).

  If you don't assign a pricing procedure line to one of these subtotals, you can still consult its value once this value is saved with the sales order. However, the subtotal fields are available on all standard order-based reports, and the pricing procedure lines are only available of select pricing analysis reports.

  Standard subtotals exist related to other system functionalities (not just reporting) that you can interface with by assigning a value in this field. Fields such as BONBA (rebate basis 1), PREVA (preference value), BRTWR (gross value), CMPRE (credit price), WAVWR (cost), and GKWRT (statistical value).

  You can also store values for later use in VOFM formulas (XWORKD, XWORKE, XWORKF, XWORKG, XWORKH, XWORKI, XWORKJ, XWORKK, XWORKL, and XWORKM).
- The requirement field (**Require...**) is a VOFM routine number that allows you to define whether a pricing procedure line is relevant depending on flexible criteria. If this routine indicates the line is not relevant, this line won't be shown even if matching condition records are found.
- The alternative calculation type field (**Alt.Calc...**) is a VOFM routine number that allows you to define a different way to calculate the *condition value*. The standard method is to use the *condition amount or percentage* and apply this value over the *condition base value* (as controlled by the configured condition type).
- The alternative *condition base value* calculation field (**Alt.Con...**) is a VOFM routine number that allows you to define a different way to calculate the *condition base value*. The standard method was described earlier in this list: Use either the from step (**From...**) and to step (**To S...**) or use the *net value*.
- The account key (**Accoun...**) determines which financial account to use and to which to post this value at the time of billing. For more details on account determination, see Chapter 10.

- The accruals key (**Accruals**) is similar to the account key but is used to determine the accrual account instead of the revenue account, if applicable.

Setting Pricing Procedure Determination

To configure a pricing procedure determination, follow the menu path **SAP Customizing Implementation Guide • Sales and Distribution • Basic Functions • Pricing • Pricing Control • Define And Assign Pricing Procedures • Set Pricing Procedure Determination.** On the screen that opens, click on the **New Entries** button or press F5.

On the screen shown in Figure 4.11, for all sales areas (**Sales Organization**, **Distribution Channel**, and **Division**) defined on the organization structure configuration, you should consider all possible entries configured for **Doc. Pricing Proc.** (assigned to the sales order type) and **Cust.Pric.Procedure** (assigned to the customer in the sales area data on the business partner master data).

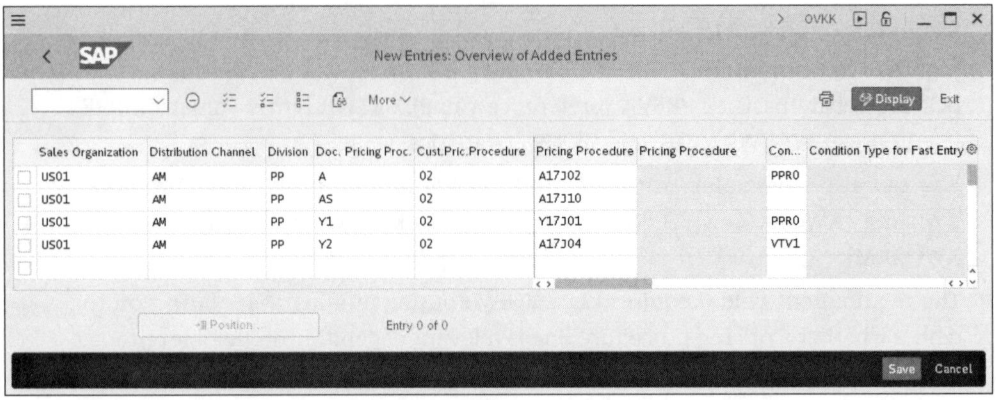

Figure 4.11 Assigning Pricing Procedures

The combinations of these fields that we'll use in our configuration and master data must be entered on this screen and assigned a **Pricing Procedure**. For combinations that aren't expected to be used often, you must also enter their assignments on this screen; otherwise, neither end users nor interfaces will be able to enter sales orders, instead throwing a hard error message that should be avoided.

If there is configuration missing for a given combination of sales area, customer pricing procedure code, and document pricing procedure code, the systems would issue a hard error message preventing the order from being entered. So, we must only omit configuration combinations that we specifically don't want the system to allow.

4.2 Free Goods

Free goods is a system functionality that allows you to define promotions where you'll award free product when customers that fulfill certain purchasing requirements. Many retailers advertise this type of promotion as "buy one, get one free."

Using this feature, you can select the products eligible for promotion and the quantity a customer must order to get free product. You can also award a different material from the one they order.

Similar to what we've done for the pricing condition technique, the following sections will cover the master data (Section 4.2.1), condition tables (Section 4.2.2), access sequences (Section 4.2.3), condition types (Section 4.2.4), and procedures (Section 4.2.5) for free goods.

4.2.1 Free Goods Condition Records: Master Data

Maintaining free goods condition records using the condition technique is achieved by opening Transaction VBN1. As shown in Figure 4.12, you'll need to select the **Discount Type** for which you want to maintain condition records. Out of the box, SAP provides condition type YAOO for handing discounts.

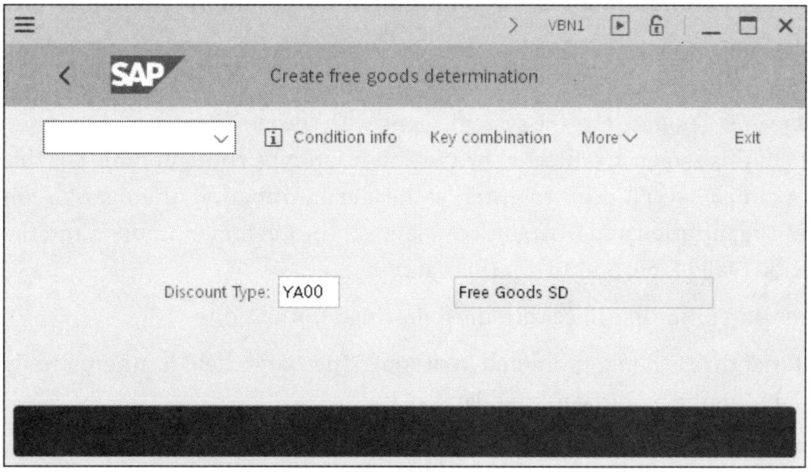

Figure 4.12 Creating Free Goods Condition Records

You can then click on the **Key combination** command button or simply press `Enter` to reach the screen shown in Figure 4.13. The system will open a popup window if more than one condition table exists, the same way that Transaction VK11 does. If only one condition table exists (as in condition type YA00), no popup window will appear.

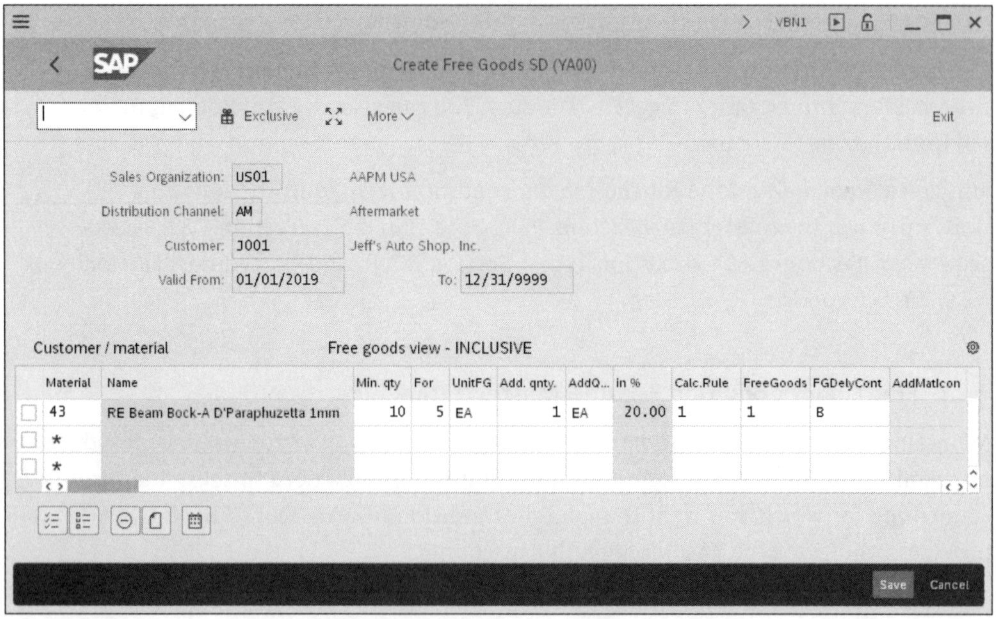

Figure 4.13 Creating Free Goods Condition Records (Master Data)

The next screen is generated by the system, along with the condition tables, and several aspects of this screen are affected by the condition type configuration. For this particular example, you'll need to enter, as header information, the distribution chain (**Sales Organization** and **Distribution Channel**), the **Customer** number, and the validity period (**Valid From** and **To**) for this data.

You can then enter multiple lines with the following information:

- The material that is being promoted (**Material**). The **Name** field is automatically populated from the material master data.
- The minimum quantity (**Min. qty**) that would make sales of this product relevant for free goods.
- The amount of product the customer shall receive free when ordering (**For**), for example, 25 units or more.
- The unit of measurement (**UnitFG**) for the two previous quantity fields.

- The additional quantity (**Add. qnty.**) and its unit of measurement (**AddQ...**) fields are used in conjunction with the calculation rule (**Calc. Rule**) VOFM routine. For the standard **Calc. Rule**, the **Add. qnty.** is a multiplier of the **For** quantity. For example, if **Min. qty** = 25 ea, **For** = 5 ea, and **Add. qnty.** = 2 ea, 10 units will be free, and 15 units will be billable.
- The **in %** field is a display-only field that shows the discount that this promotion corresponds to. In this example, if we're awarding 5 units free out of each 25 units we sell, we're ultimately giving the customer a 20% discount off their purchase.
- The **FreeGoods** category indicates if the free good quantity (**For**) is to be awarded in addition to the ordered quantity (**2 – Exclusive**) or as part of the ordered quantity (**1 – Inclusive**). With either option, the sales order is incremented with a new automatically generated line for the free of charge portion of the quantity. If you use category **3 – Inclusive** rebate (without item generation; only for sales), no additional line is created.
- The **FGDelyCont** field controls how the free-of-charge material is delivered. Typically, you would want to deliver these free goods along with the billable products (using code E, but A, B, and C are also options), but you also have the option of sending free goods regardless (blank).

If you use **FreeGoods Category 2 (Exclusive)** and/or want to enter different levels at which a customer would receive different levels of free products, you would use scales by clicking the scale icon, which opens the screen shown in Figure 4.14. You can encourage customers to order more product by awarding more free goods.

If you change the **FreeGoods Category** to **2 (Exclusive)**, the additional material for free goods field (**AddMat FrGd**) will be enabled. In this field, you'll indicate a different material than the one ordered. The material's description will be displayed.

You can award different materials for each quantity level we're defining; for instance, a customer purchasing 5 units of a product might get a key ring; 10 units, a hat; and 20 units, a shirt.

The main difference between a discount and inclusive free goods is how the customer perceives the transaction. A discount makes the price known and clear and unmistakably indicates that the free items are a temporary promotion. Exclusive free goods are a unique method of awarding different part numbers as prizes. Few companies use this feature. A discount is considered the simpler approach.

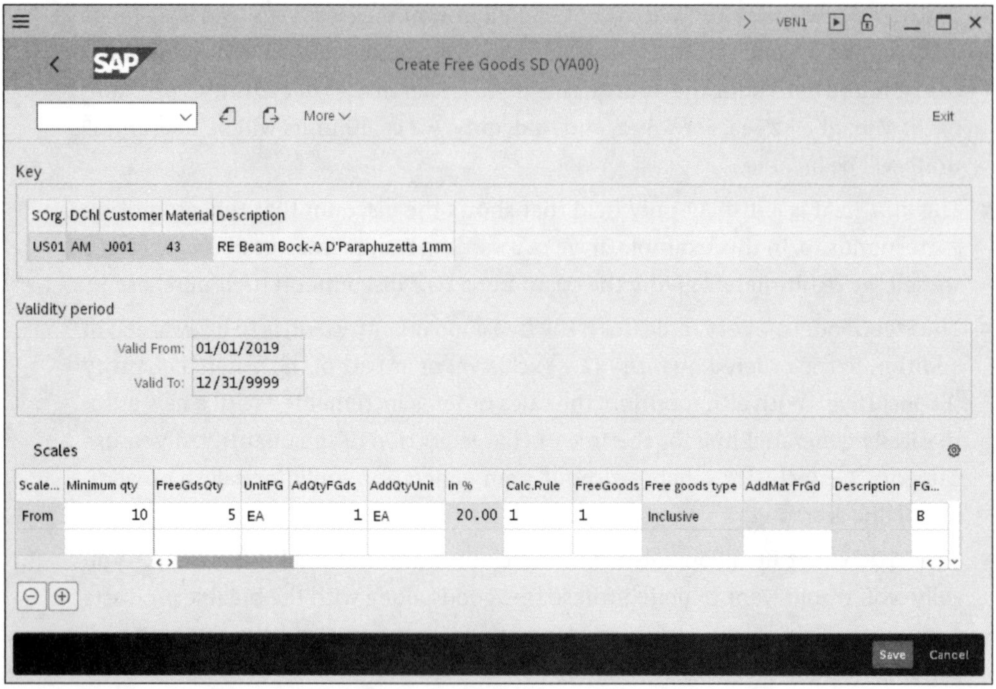

Figure 4.14 Entering Free Goods Scales Using the Scaled Button

4.2.2 Free Goods Condition Table

Condition tables are master data repositories where information relevant to free goods is stored. These tables are actual database repositories created by opening Transaction V/N2 or by following the menu path **SAP Customizing Implementation Guide • Sales and Distribution • Basic Functions • Free Goods • Condition Technique for Free Goods • Maintain Condition Tables.**

In our example, shown in Figure 4.15, we're creating a free goods condition table with only a customer number for illustration purposes. Note that we're using the same table 902 used for the pricing example in Section 4.1.2. This selection is allowed because each condition technique functionality has a different application code ("N" for free goods, "A" for pricing), so this code makes the configuration unique with its functionality even though they both use the condition technique.

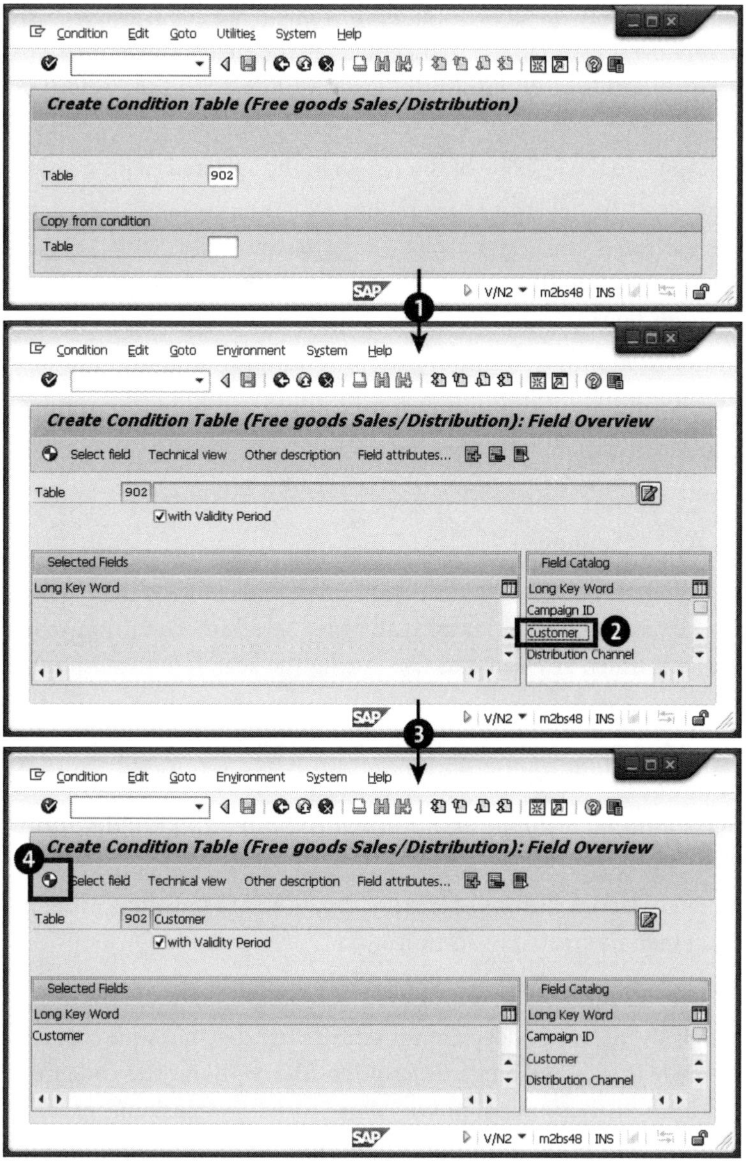

Figure 4.15 Creating Free Goods Condition Tables

To create the free goods condition table, follow these steps:

❶ On this screen, first specify a three-digit condition table number (**Table**). This number must begin with "9" to indicate that it is not provided by SAP. Press [Enter].

❷ The system will then display the **Create Condition Table (Free goods Sales/Distribution): Field Overview** screen. On the right, you'll see the **Field Catalog** with a list of fields currently available to choose from. Once you find the first field (**Customer**), double-click it.

❸ The field will be copied to the left side of the screen in the **Selected Fields** window.

❹ Once you've selected all the fields you want in the new condition table, click on the generate icon, as indicated. The system will create a database table with the name "KOTNXXX," where "KOTN" indicates that this condition table is for free goods and XXX is the condition table number. In our example, table KOTN902 is generated along with the maintenance screens.

The **with Validity Period** flag, when checked, will incorporate valid-to and valid-from dates to the table structure and maintenance screens.

4.2.3 Free Goods Access Sequence

The access sequence defines how free goods condition records (master data) will be retrieved from the database. You'll indicate the order in which condition tables should be accessed and which key value to use during the search (either from the sales order data or other data).

To maintain free goods access sequences, follow the menu path **SAP Customizing Implementation Guide • Sales and Distribution • Basic Functions • Free Goods • Condition Technique for Free Goods • Maintain Access Sequences.** On the screen that opens, click on the **New Entries** button or press F5.

In the example shown in Figure 4.16, we're creating a new access sequence using the condition table 902, which we created in Section 4.1.2.

To maintain the free goods access sequences, follow these steps:

❶ On the **New Entries: Overview of Added Entries** screen, first specify a four character access sequence code (**Acc...**) and add a description (**Description**). The code must begin with "Z" to indicate that it is not provided by SAP (allowable namespace).

❷ Then, select the new entry you created and double-click the **Accesses** option in the **Dialog Structure** menu on the left side of the screen.

❸ Next, enter each table on the lines available on this screen. Assign each line with a number (**No.** column; we recommend using increments of 10) and the table number you want. You can also use a VOFM routine on the **Requirement** column, which will allow for great flexibility when determining whether or not this data is applicable.

❹ Then, select the new line we just created and double-click on the **Fields** option on the **Dialog Structure** menu on the left side of the screen.

❺ With all field sources correctly identified, you can now save the new access sequence.

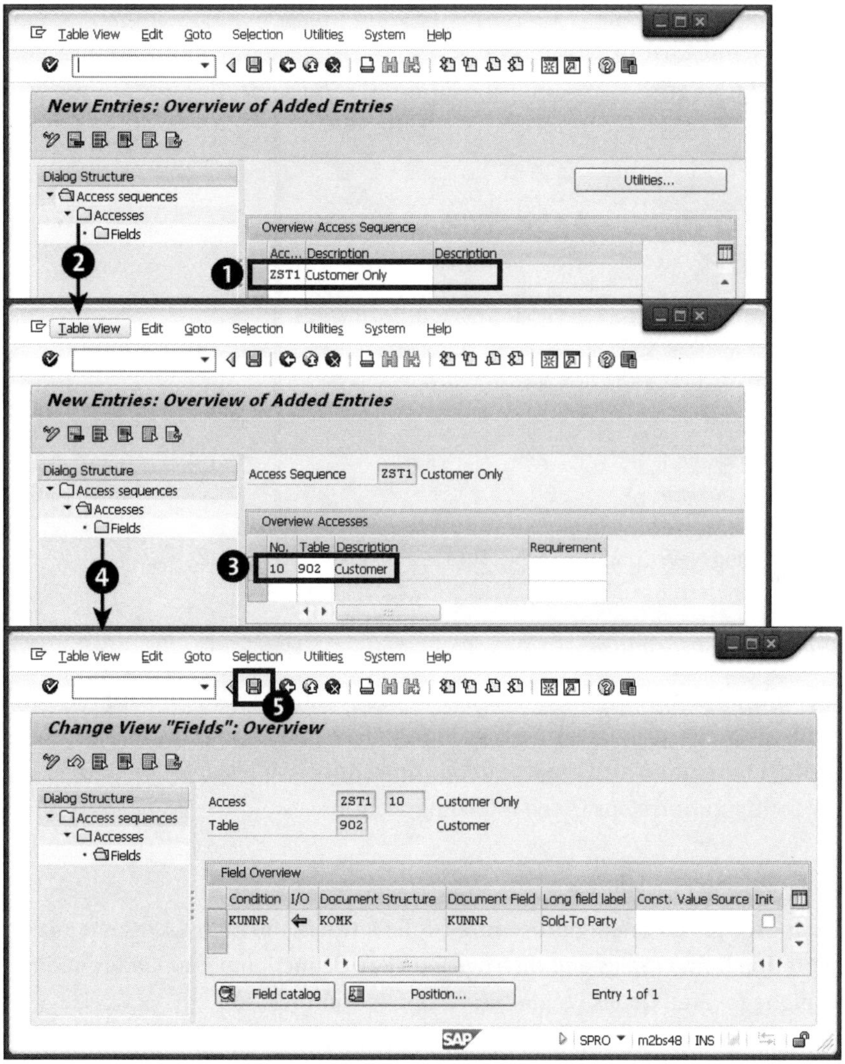

Figure 4.16 Maintaining Free Goods Access Sequences

4.2.4 Free Goods Condition Type

By creating condition types for free goods, you'll make new tables and access sequences available for usage.

To maintain free goods condition types, follow the menu path **SAP Customizing Implementation Guide • Sales and Distribution • Basic Functions • Free Goods • Condition Technique for Free Goods • Maintain Condition Types**.

As shown in Figure 4.17, select the desired condition type (**CTyp**) and the access sequence (**AS**) it must use (when applicable).

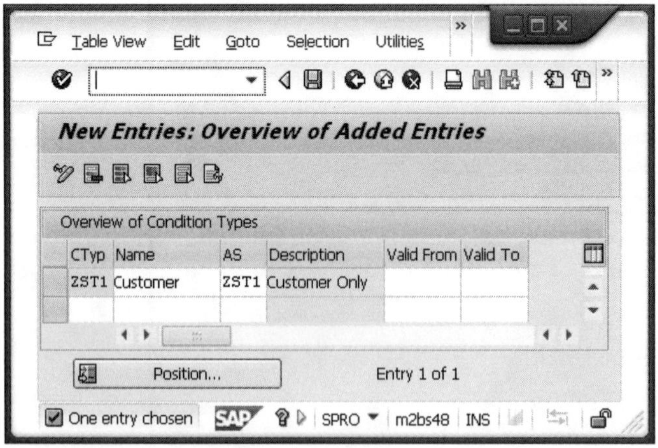

Figure 4.17 Creating New Condition Types for Free Goods

4.2.5 Free Goods Procedure

The free goods procedure is where you'll list the condition types that are relevant. Then, you'll activate free goods by assigning the free goods procedure to the sales area and order types for which the free goods procedure is applicable. We'll cover the necessary configuration steps in the following sections.

Maintaining Pricing Procedures

To maintain free goods pricing procedures, follow the menu path **SAP Customizing Implementation Guide • Sales and Distribution • Basic Functions • Free Goods • Condition Technique for Free Goods • Maintain Pricing Procedures**.

In the example shown in Figure 4.18, we're modifying the standard free goods **Procedure YA0001** by adding a new step using the new free goods condition type ZST1.

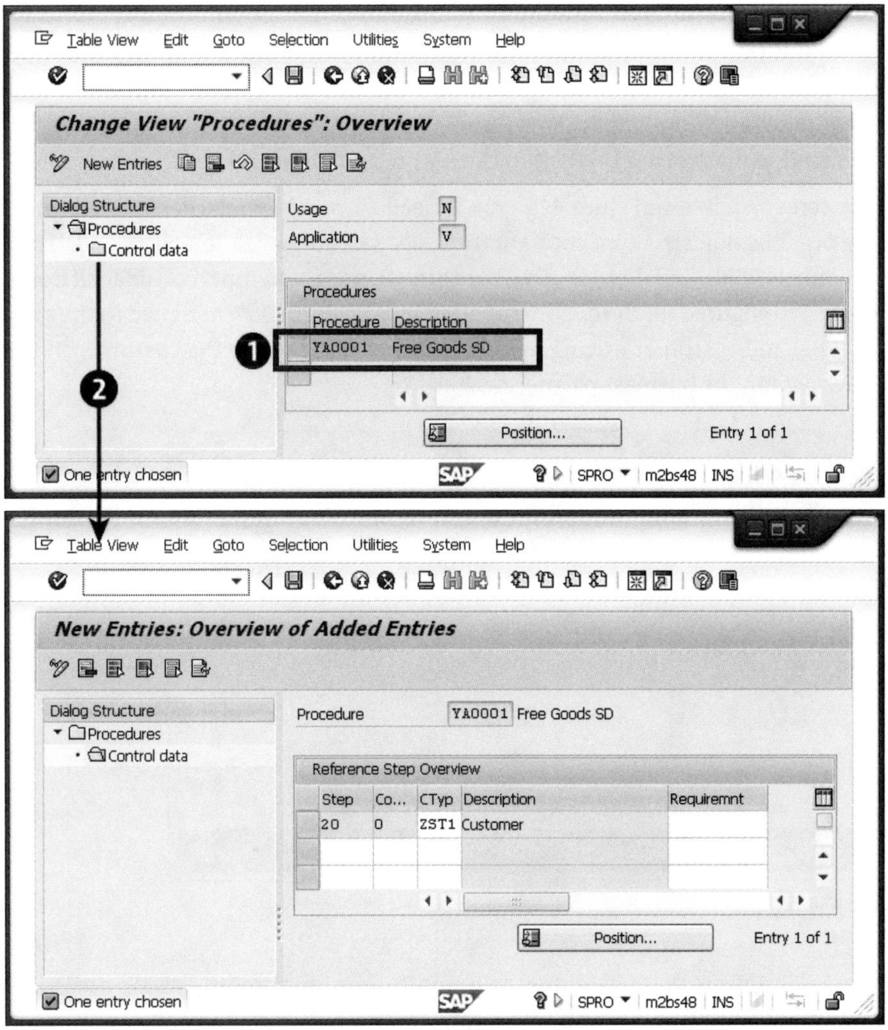

Figure 4.18 Maintaining Pricing Procedures for Free Goods

To set up a pricing procedure for free goods, follow these steps:

❶ Select the pricing procedure you want to change and then double-click on **Control Data** under the **Dialog Structure**.

❷ Click on the **New entries** button, or press F5, and enter the new step number (**Step**) and free goods condition type (**CTyp**).

Activating Free Goods Determination

To configure free goods procedure determination, follow the menu path **SAP Customizing Implementation Guide • Sales and Distribution • Basic Functions • Free Goods • Condition Technique for Free Goods • Activate Free Goods Determination.** On the screen that opens, click on the **New Entries** button or press F5.

On the screen shown in Figure 4.19, you'll need to consider all sales areas defined during organization structure configuration, i.e., sales organization (**SOrg.**), distribution channel (**DChl**), and division (**Dv**). For each element, you must consider all possible entries configured for the document pricing procedure (**DoPr** assigned to the sales order type) and customer pricing procedure (**CuPP** assigned to the customer in the sale area data in the business partner master).

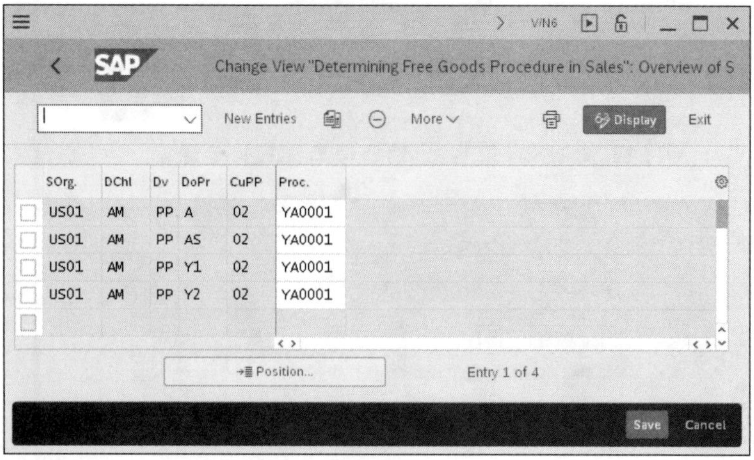

Figure 4.19 Activating Free Goods Determination

The combinations of these fields that you want to use issue free goods for, according to your configuration and master data, must be entered on this screen and assigned to a free goods pricing procedure (**Proc.**).

4.3 Material Determination

Material determination (also referred to as material substitution) is a system functionality that allows you to replace an ordered material with another. A typical use for this feature are obsolete materials. When a customer orders an obsolete material, the system will replace that material with the newer version.

Although a common requirement, many companies don't make use of this feature, instead having customer service contact the customer and manually replace the material when appropriate. This approach avoids issues where a customer may have concerns about the specs of the newer material.

The determination/substitution of a material can also be implemented before the complete stock consumption of the obsolete material. This qualified product selection is also part of the material determination feature and can be quite beneficial for companies, although not widely known.

Some companies also use this feature when implementing SAP and define an internally assigned material number. The market may perceive legacy part numbers (from a previous system) as intuitive and want to keep on ordering using them. In any case, you can substitute the old part number with a new one.

You can also use this feature to maintain the material number that our customers use in their systems. This approach is somewhat redundant because you can maintain customer material numbers on the customer-material information record (Transaction VD51). The difference is that, if you maintain this data on the customer-material information record, you'll need to enter the customer's material number in the **Customer Material Number** field. In contrast, using material determination, you can enter this number directly in the **Material Number** field at the time of sales order entry.

Note, however, that the out-of-the-box condition type Y001 does not include the customer as part of the substitution key, so one customer material number would affect all other customers' orders. Most companies do not use material determination to store customer material numbers and use the customer-material information record instead.

Similar to what we've done for pricing and free goods, the following sections will cover the master data (Section 4.3.1), condition tables (Section 4.3.2), access sequences (Section 4.3.3), condition types (Section 4.3.4), and procedures (Section 4.3.5) for material determination.

4.3.1 Material Determination Condition Records: Master Data

The maintenance of material determination condition records using the condition technique is achieved by opening Transaction VB11, as shown in Figure 4.20. First, you'll need to select the material determination type (**Material determ.type**) for which want to maintain condition records. Out of the box, SAP provides condition type Y001.

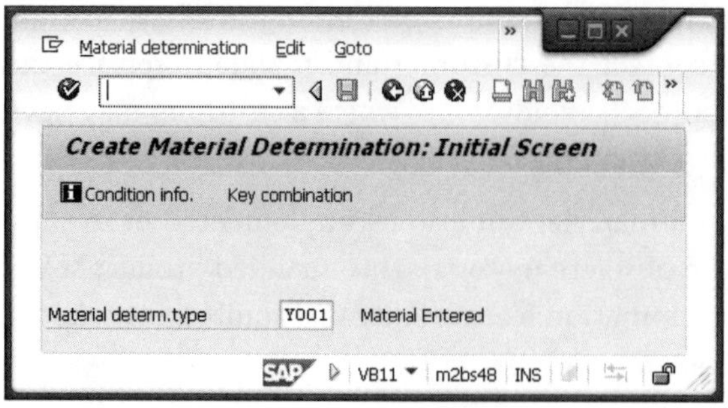

Figure 4.20 Creating New Material Determination Condition Records

Now, click on the **Key Combination** command button or press Enter. The system will open a popup window if more than one condition table exists. If only one condition table exists (as in condition type Y001), no popup window will appear.

The next screen, shown in Figure 4.21, is generated by the system along with the condition tables based on the condition type configuration.

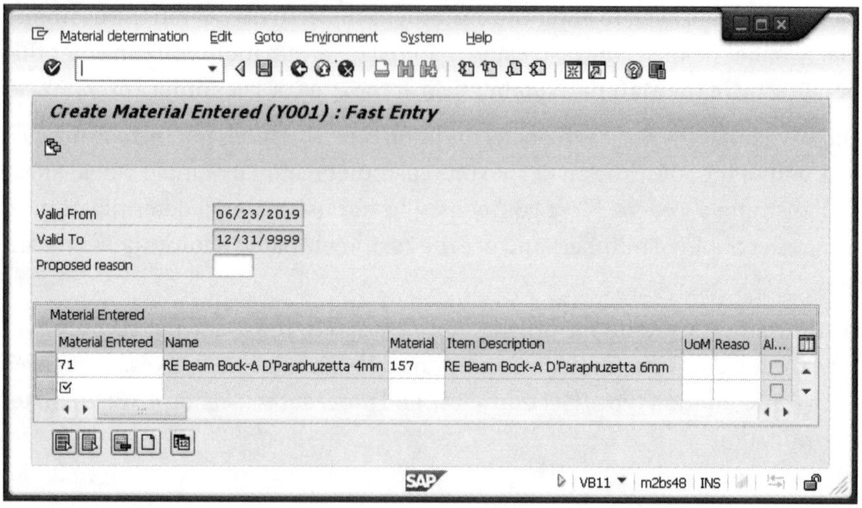

Figure 4.21 Fast Entry Screen for Material Determination Condition Records

For this particular example, you can directly enter multiple lines with the following information:

- The **Material Entered** field indicates the material that should be replaced. The **Name** is automatically populated from the material master data if a valid material number, with material master data maintained in this system, is entered. You can enter any other material number in this field, which covers both your own legacy material numbers and also customer material numbers.

- A valid material number (**Material**) that you'll use to replace the **Material Entered** at the time of sales order entry. The **Item Description** field is automatically populated from the material master data.
- You can select a unit of measurement (**UoM**) to be used on orders for the **Material**. This value may be used, for instance, if the obsolete product had been sold in cases but the substitute material is usually sold in individual units. For the substitution, you'll want to ensure you're using the same units of measurement to match customer expectations.
- If you're using material substitution for multiple purposes, you add a reason (**Reaso**) to identify the specific purpose of this substitution. We'll show you how to define new values for this field shortly.

As shown in Figure 4.22, you can add multiple alternatives for the material when a user selects an obsolete material on the **Item Overview** tab of the sales order (Chapter 6, Section 6.2.2).

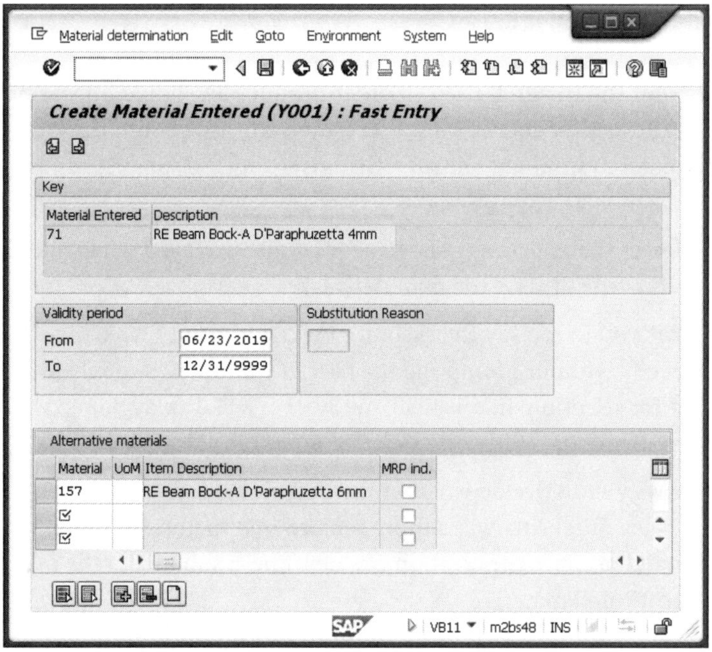

Figure 4.22 Material Determination: Multiple Alternatives

Substitution reasons are maintained by opening Transaction OVRQ or by following the menu path **SAP Customizing Implementation Guide • Sales and Distribution • Basic Functions • Material Determination • Define Substitution Reasons**. On the screen that opens, click on the **New Entries** button or press F5.

On the screen shown in Figure 4.23, specify a four-character material determination/ substitution reason code (**SbstReason**) and add a description (**Description**).

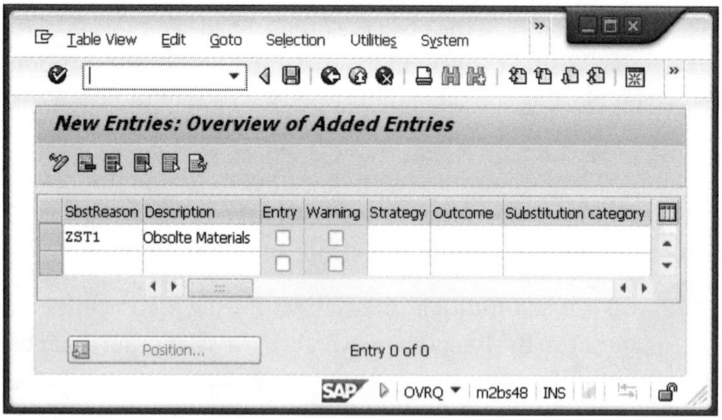

Figure 4.23 Defining New Substitution Reasons

You can indicate whether the material used to order production should appear on forms such as order acknowledgments and invoices by selecting the **Entry** flag. When checked, the material entered would be shown; otherwise, only the substitute material will be shown.

The **Warning** flag indicates that a warning message must be displayed when a user enters a sales order before substituting the material.

The **Strategy** field allows you to modify the system's behavior. If left blank, the substitution will occur directly without prompting the user. If you enter "A" (Substitute products are displayed for selection) in this field, the system will display popup window requesting user confirmation before the substitution takes place.

The **Outcome** field allows you to decide whether the default behavior is affected (if left blank). The same sales order line will simply replace one material by another. Other codes (A or B) would result in the creation of a new line, a subitem of the main line, containing the substituted material.

The **Substitution Category** field is used on repair orders. If a user enters a material that corresponds to a piece of equipment to be repaired, a service material that better represents the service activity will be substituted for the equipment itself.

4.3.2 Material Determination Condition Tables

Condition tables are master data repositories where material determination-relevant information is stored. These tables are actual database repositories created by opening Transaction OV16 or by following the menu path **SAP Customizing Implementation Guide • Sales and Distribution • Basic Functions • Material Determination • Maintain Prerequisites for Material Determination • Create Condition Tables**.

In our example shown in Figure 4.24, we're creating a material determination condition table with a customer number and a material numbered entered for illustration purposes. Note that we're using the same table 902 that we used in our pricing example in Section 4.1.2, which is allowed because each condition technique functionality has a different application code ("D" for material determination, "A" for pricing). This code makes the configuration unique with its functionality even though they share the condition technique.

To create material determination condition, follow these steps:

❶ On this screen, first specify a three-digit condition table number (**Table**). This number must begin with "9" to indicate that this number is not provided by SAP (allowable namespace). Press [Enter].

❷ The system will then display the condition table generator **Field Overview** screen. On the right, you'll find the **Field Catalog** with a list of fields currently available to choose from. Once you find the first field (**Customer**), double-click it.

❸ This field will be copied to the left side of the screen on the **Selected Fields** window.

❹ Once you've selected all fields you want on the new condition table, on the generate icon, as indicated. The system will create a database table with the name "KOTDXXX," where "KOTD" indicates that this table is a material determination condition table and XXX is the condition table number. In this example, the table KOTD902 would be generated along with the maintenance screens.

The **with Validity Period** flag, when checked, will incorporate valid-to and valid-from dates to the table structure and maintenance screens.

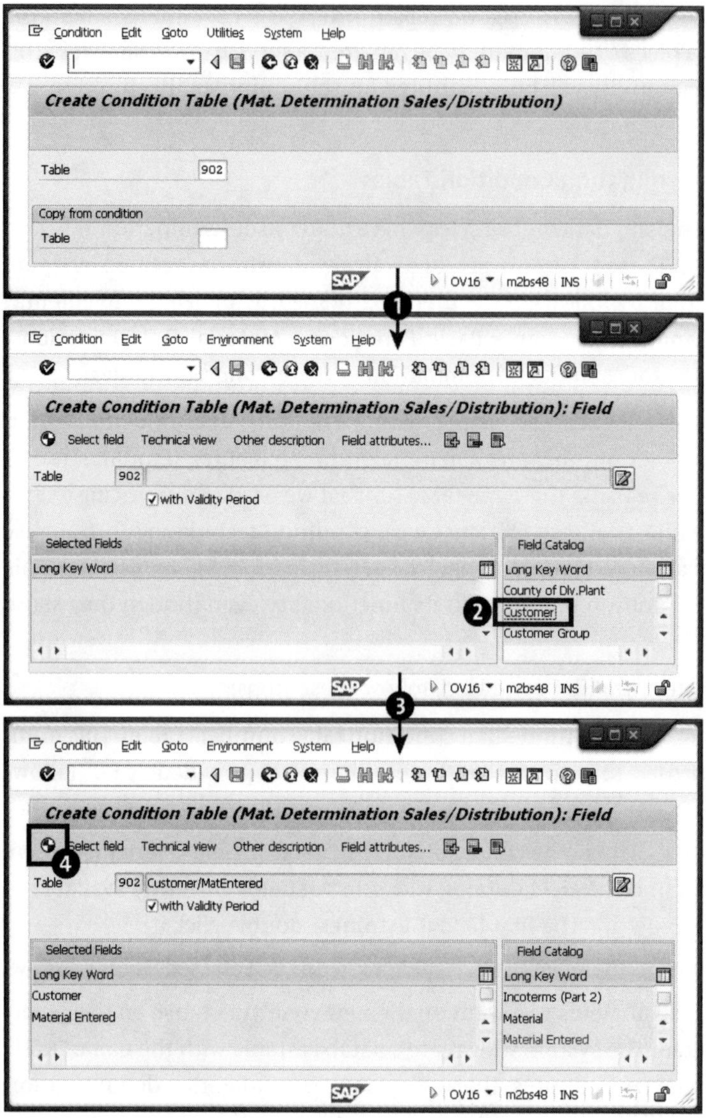

Figure 4.24 Creating Material Determination Condition Tables

4.3.3 Material Determination Access Sequences

An access sequence defines how the material determination condition records (master data) will be retrieved from the database. You'll indicate the order in which condition tables should be accessed and which key value to use during search (either sales order data or other data). To maintain material determination access sequences, follow the menu path **SAP Customizing Implementation Guide • Sales and Distribution • Basic Functions • Material Determination • Maintain Prerequisites for Material Determination • Maintain Access Sequences.** On the screen that opens, click on the **New Entries** button or press F5.

In our example shown in Figure 4.25, we're creating a new access sequence using the new condition table 902 created in the previous section.

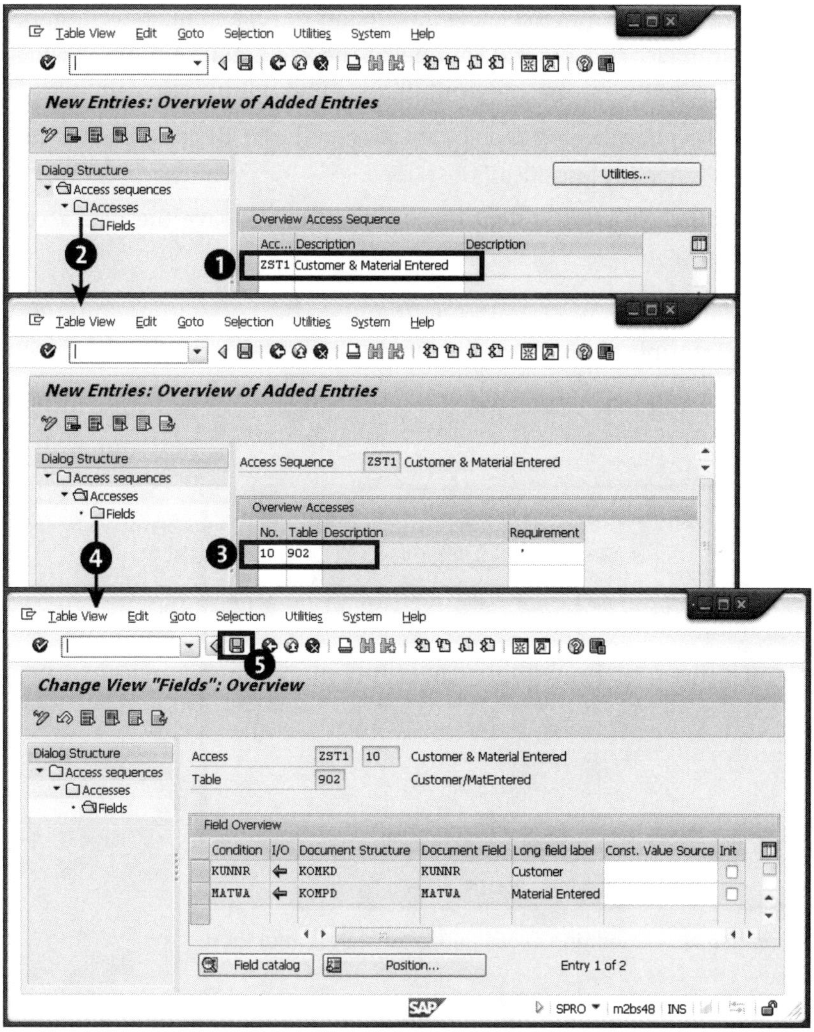

Figure 4.25 Maintaining Material Determination Access Sequences

To create the material determination access sequence, follow these steps:

❶ On this screen, first specify a four-character access sequence code (**Acc...**) and add a description (**Description**). The code must begin with "Z" to indicate that it is not provided by SAP (allowable namespace).

❷ Then, select the new entry we just created and double-click on the **Accesses** option on the **Dialog Structure** menu on the left side of the screen.

❸ Next, enter each table on the lines available on this screen. Assign each line a number (**No.** column—we recommend using increments of 10) and the table number you want. You can also use a VOFM routine on the **Requirement** column, which allows for greater flexibility when determining whether this data is applicable.

❹ Then, select the new line created and double-click on the **Fields** option on the **Dialog Structure** menu on the left side of the screen.

❺ With all field sources correctly identified, you can finally save the new access sequence.

4.3.4 Material Determination Condition Types

Condition types for material determination make the new tables and access sequences available for usage.

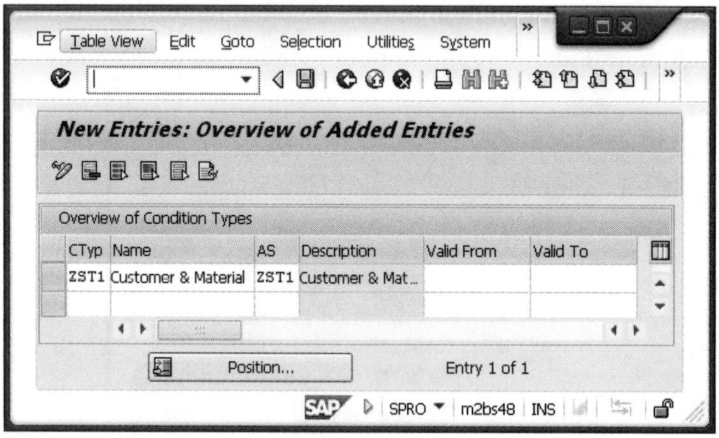

Figure 4.26 Creating New Condition Types for Material Determination

To maintain material determination condition types, follow the menu path **SAP Customizing Implementation Guide • Sales and Distribution • Basic Functions • Material Determination • Maintain Prerequisites for Material Determination • Define Condition Types.** On the screen that opens, click on the **New Entries** button or press F5.

On the screen shown in Figure 4.26, specify a four-character material determination condition type (**Ctyp**) and provide a name (**Name**), indicating the access sequence (**AS**) that it utilizes. You can define validity dates if desired.

4.3.5 Material Determination Procedures

The material determination procedure is where you'll list the condition types to be checked by a sales order whenever a new material number is entered as well as list the sequence in which they must be checked.

You'll then activate material determination by assigning the material determination procedure to the desired sales areas and order types. We'll cover the necessary configuration steps for both sales areas and order types in the following sections.

Maintaining Material Determination Procedures

To maintain material determination procedures, follow the menu path **SAP Customizing Implementation Guide • Sales and Distribution • Basic Functions • Material Determination • Maintain Prerequisites for Material Determination • Maintain Procedure.** On the screen that opens, click on the **New Entries** button or press F5.

❶ On the screen shown in Figure 4.27, specify a six-character material determination procedure code (**Procedure**) and add a description (**Description**). Press Enter. Then select the line.

❷ Next, double-click on the **Control Data** option under the **Dialog Structure**.

❸ Click on the **New Entries** button or press F5 and then enter the new **Step** number and material determination condition type (**CTyp**).

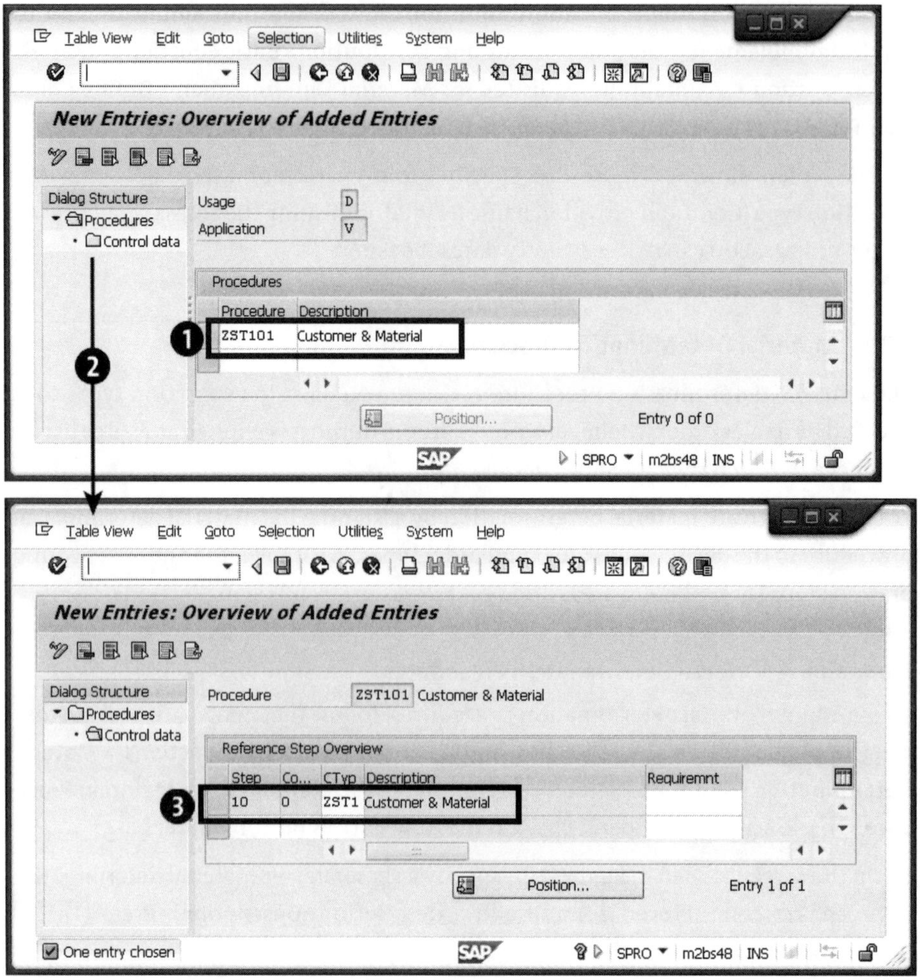

Figure 4.27 Maintaining Procedures for Material Determination

Assigning Procedures to Sales Document Types

To configure material determination procedure, follow the menu path **SAP Customizing Implementation Guide • Sales and Distribution • Basic Functions • Material Determination • Assign Procedures To Sales Document Types**.

On the screen shown in Figure 4.28, find the sales order type to which you want to assign your new procedure and then enter the material determination procedure code in the **MatDeterm** column.

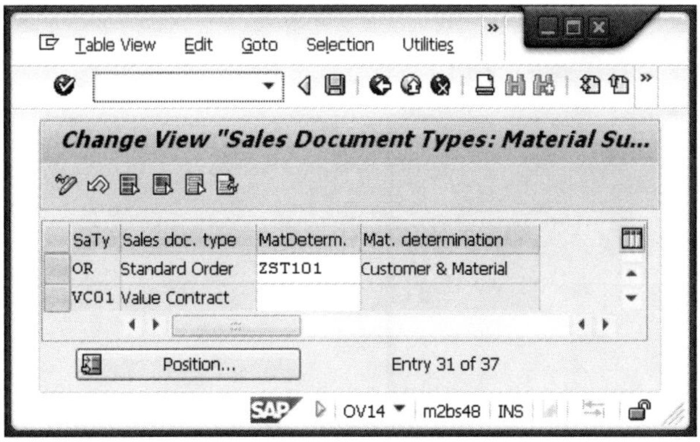

Figure 4.28 Assigning Procedures to Sales Document Types for Material Determination

4.4 Cross-Selling

Cross-selling is a system functionality that allows you to offer additional products to customers when they make orders. This concept is prevalent in fast-food restaurants, where "Would you like fries with that?" is ubiquitous. Another retail example would be being offered extended warranty policies when buying expensive consumer electronics.

Companies that use this feature usually offer accessories with more expensive equipment sales, commonly known as *add-on products*. This feature is not widely used even though often documented as a requirement during implementation but later removed from the scope. This requirement is a prime candidate for rationalization and cost-savings because legacy systems rarely have a similar feature.

As we've done for pricing, free goods, and material determination, the following sections will cover the master data (Section 4.4.1), condition tables (Section 4.4.2), access sequences (Section 4.4.3), condition types (Section 4.4.4), and procedures (Section 4.4.5) for cross-selling. We'll also discuss two configuration components specific to cross-selling in Section 4.4.6 and Section 4.4.7.

4.4.1 Cross-Selling Condition Records: Master Data

Maintaining cross-selling condition records using the condition technique is achieved by opening Transaction VB41, as shown in Figure 4.29. First, you'll need to select the cross-selling **Material determ.type** for which want to maintain condition records. SAP doesn't provide a condition type for cross-selling, so we'll show you how to configure condition type ZST1 in our example in Section 4.4.4.

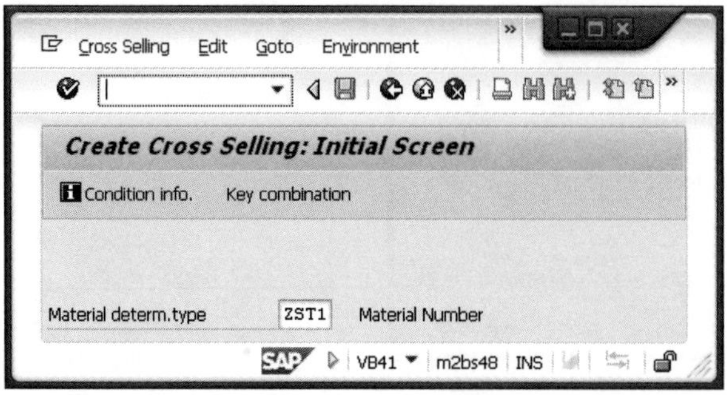

Figure 4.29 Creating New Cross-Selling Condition Records

Now, click on the **Key Combination** command button or press Enter. The system will open a popup window if more than one condition table exists. If only one condition table exists (as in condition type ZST1), no popup window will appear.

The next screen, shown in Figure 4.30, is generated by the system along with the condition tables. Several aspects of the screen are affected by the condition type configuration.

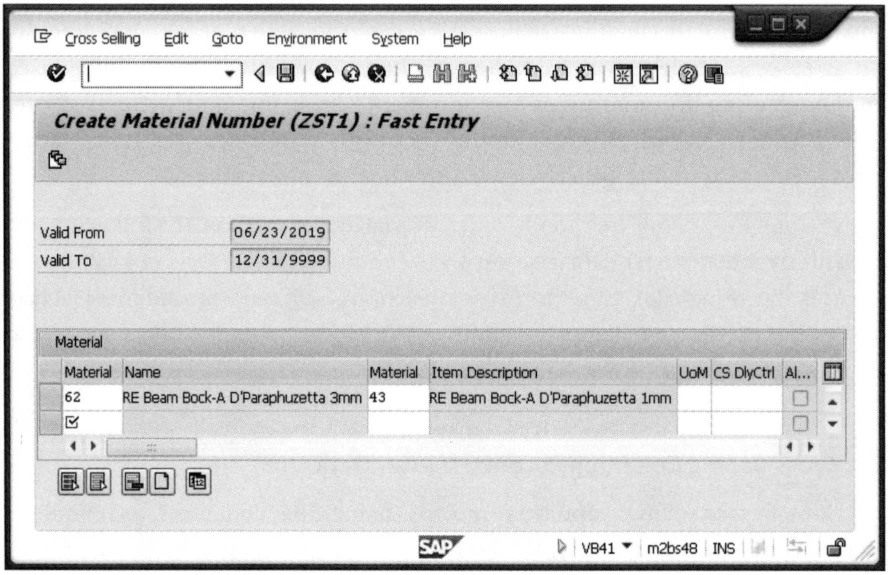

Figure 4.30 Creating Cross-Selling Master Data

For this particular example, you can modify the default values for **Valid To** and **Valid From** dates on the header and then directly enter multiple lines with the following information:

- In the **Material** column (first column from the left), the specified material, when ordered, should trigger the cross-selling procedure. The **Name** field is automatically populated from the material master data.
- The first of the material numbers (**Material**, third column from the left) that we'll offer to the customer as an add-on to the order.
- A unit of measurement (**UoM**) to be used on the order for the **Material** (third column). Specifying a unit of measurement may be useful, for instance, if this product is usually sold in cases, but when offering as an add-on, we're sending individual units.
- The cross-selling delivery control field **(CS DlyCtrl)** allows you to decide whether to ship the product and the add-on together or if shipping them separately is acceptable.

Once the line information is entered, you can enter additional materials to be offered. Select the line and click on the button, or press F2, which will open the screen shown in Figure 4.31.

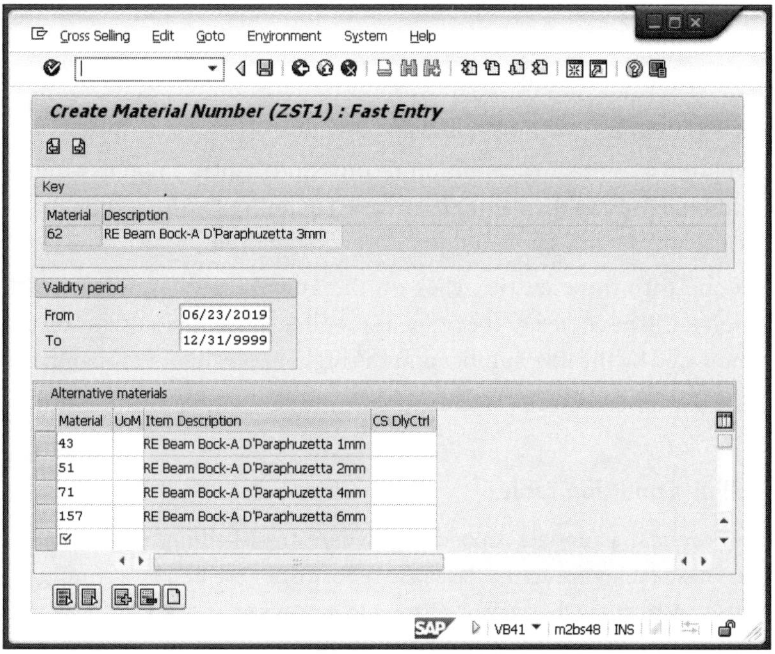

Figure 4.31 Entering Multiple Add-On Products for Cross-Selling

On this screen, you can add multiple materials to be offered as add-ons on the sales order entry screen. Using the data shown in Figure 4.31, when a sales order is entered, you would see a system response, as shown in Figure 4.32.

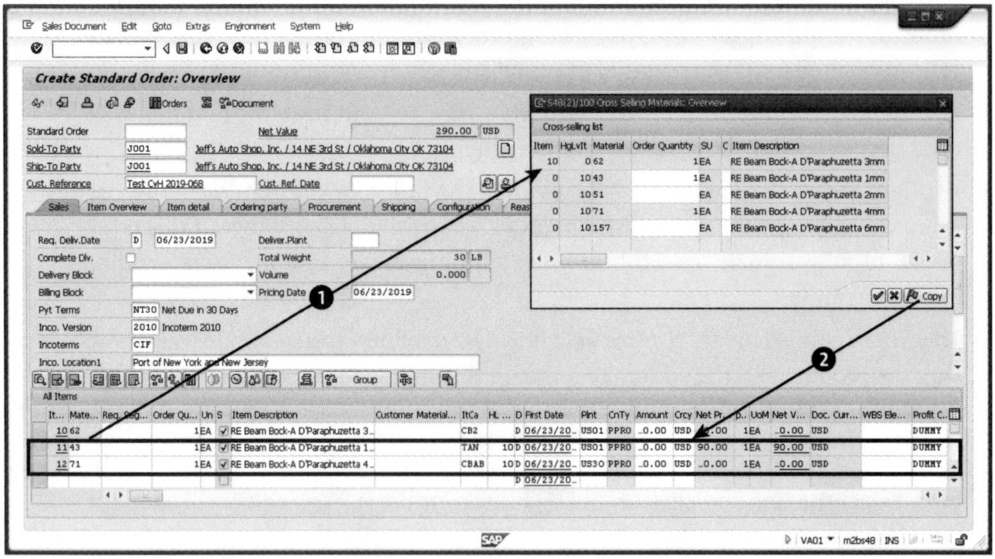

Figure 4.32 Sales Order Entry with Cross-Selling

To specify the add-ons on offer, follow these steps:

1. Enter the material number "62" on the first line and press Enter.
2. The system will find cross-selling condition records and display a popup window with all the add-ons. You can then enter the desired quantity for the add-on material for the customer. Materials without quantities are ignored.
3. Once you're done with these entries, click on the **Copy** button. The items with quantities entered will be copied to the order as new lines that are subitems on the first line (as indicated by the line number and the higher-level item number in the **HL...** column).

4.4.2 Cross-Selling Condition Tables

Condition tables are the master data repositories where cross-selling-relevant information is stored. These tables are actual database repositories created by a configuration activity. In this section, we'll use a condition table provided by SAP.

To display cross-selling condition tables, open Transaction OV48 or follow the menu path **SAP Customizing Implementation Guide • Sales and Distribution • Basic Functions • Cross-Selling • Define Determination Procedure for Cross-Selling • Display Condition Tables.** Cross-selling condition tables can also be created by opening Transaction OV46 or be modified by opening Transaction OV47. On the screen shown in Figure 4.33, enter **Table** "011" for display and then press [Enter].

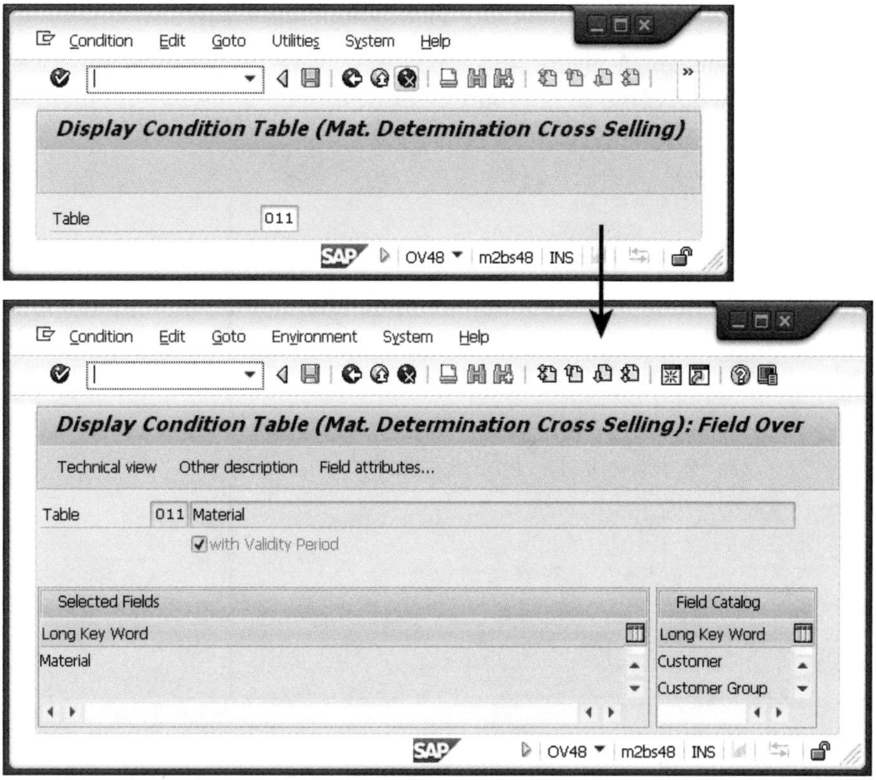

Figure 4.33 Displaying Cross-Selling Condition Tables

The system will display the **Display Condition Table (Mat. Determination Cross Selling): Field Over** screen with the fields it currently has under the **Selected Fields** window. This corresponds to a database table with the name "KOTDXXX," where "KOTD" indicates that this condition table is for cross-selling and XXX is the condition table number. In our example, we're looking at table KOTD011.

The **with Validity Period** flag, when checked, incorporates valid-to and valid-from dates to the table structure and maintenance screens.

4.4.3 Cross-Selling Access Sequences

The access sequence defines how the cross-selling condition records (master data) will be retrieved from the database and the order in which condition tables should be accessed.

To maintain cross-selling access sequences, follow the menu path **SAP Customizing Implementation Guide • Sales and Distribution • Basic Functions • Cross-Selling • Define Determination Procedure for Cross-Selling • Maintain Access Sequences.**

In our example shown in Figure 4.34, we're displaying the cross-selling access sequence provided out of the box by SAP called C001.

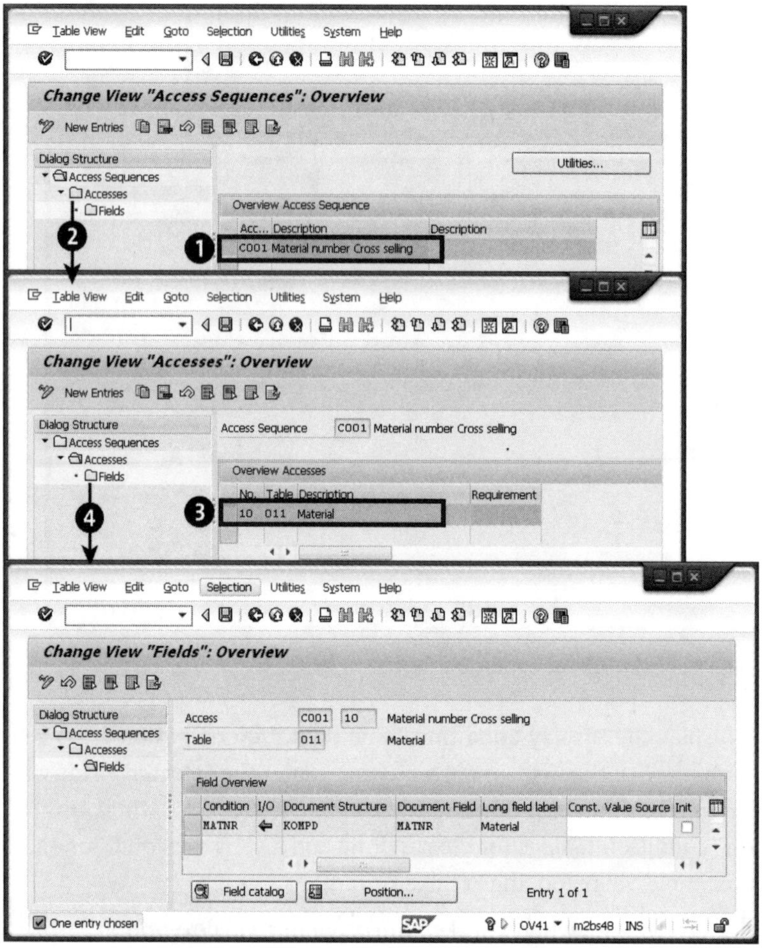

Figure 4.34 Maintaining Cross-Selling Access Sequences

To maintain the cross-selling access sequence follow these steps:

1. On this screen, select cross-selling access sequence C001.
2. Then, double-click on the **Accesses** option in the **Dialog Structure** menu on the left side of the screen.
3. Next, select the step containing the condition table 011.
4. Double-click on the **Fields** option on the **Dialog Structure** menu on the left side of the screen.

4.4.4 Cross-Selling Condition Types

Condition types for cross-selling make the new tables and access sequences available for usage. To maintain cross-selling condition types, follow the menu path **SAP Customizing Implementation Guide • Sales and Distribution • Basic Functions • Cross-Selling • Define Determination Procedure for Cross-Selling • Define Condition Types.** On the screen that opens, click on the **New Entries** button or press [F5].

As shown in Figure 4.35, specify a four-character cross-selling condition type (**Ctyp**) and add a name (**Name**), indicating the access sequence (**AS**) that it utilizes. You can define validity dates if desired.

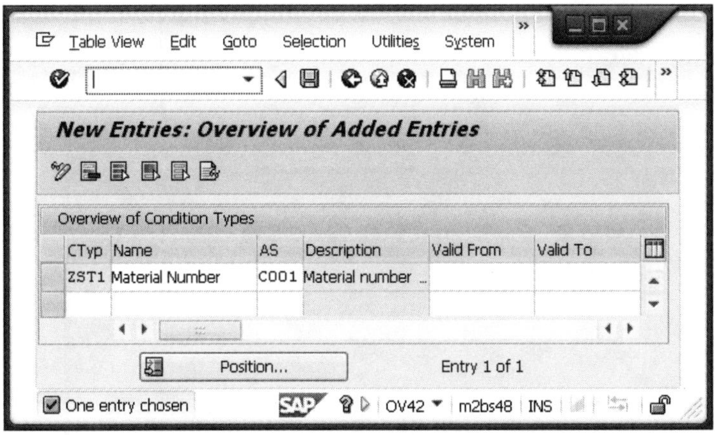

Figure 4.35 Creating New Condition Types for Cross-Selling

4.4.5 Cross-Selling Procedures

The cross-selling procedure is where you'll list the relevant condition types. Then, you'll activate cross-selling by assigning the cross-selling procedure to the desired sales areas and order types. To assign a cross-selling procedure to sales documents, you'll need to define values for the customer cross selling procedure codes and sales document type cross selling procedure codes, which we'll discuss in the following sections.

Maintaining Cross-Selling Procedures

To maintain cross-selling procedures, follow the menu path **SAP Customizing Implementation Guide • Sales and Distribution • Basic Functions • Cross-Selling • Define Determination Procedure for Cross-Selling • Maintain Procedure**. On the screen that opens, click on the **New Entries** button or press F5.

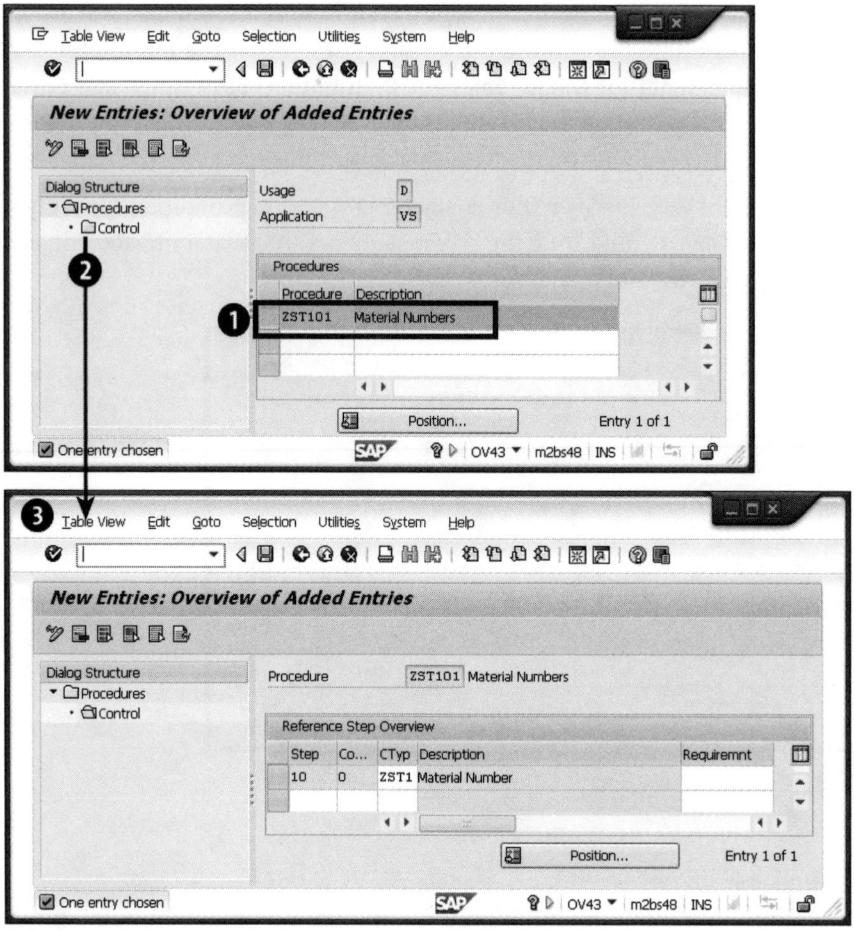

Figure 4.36 Maintaining Procedures for Cross-Selling

To maintain cross-selling procedures, on the screen shown in Figure 4.36, follow these steps:

❶ Specify a six-character cross-selling procedure code (**Procedure**) and add a description (**Description**). Press [Enter] and then select the line.

❷ Next, double-click on the **Control** option under the **Dialog Structure**.

❸ On the new screen that appears, click on the **New entries** button or press [F5] and enter the new **Step** number and cross-selling condition type (**CTyp**).

Defining Customer Procedures for Cross-Selling

To define customer cross-selling/product proposal procedures, follow the menu path **SAP Customizing Implementation Guide • Sales and Distribution • Basic Functions • Cross-Selling • Maintain Customer/Document Procedures For Cross-Selling • Define Customer Procedure for Cross-Selling.** This configuration can also be accessed for dynamic product proposals, which we'll discuss in more detail in Section 4.5, by following the menu path **SAP Customizing Implementation Guide • Sales and Distribution • Basic Functions • Dynamic Product Proposal • Define Customer Procedure for Product Proposal**. For either menu path, on the screen that opens, click on the **New Entries** button or press [F5].

As shown in Figure 4.37, specify a two-character customer cross-selling/product proposal procedure code (**PPCustProc**) and add a description (**Description**). This code is assigned to the customers on the business partner master data as discussed in Chapter 2, Section 2.3.1.

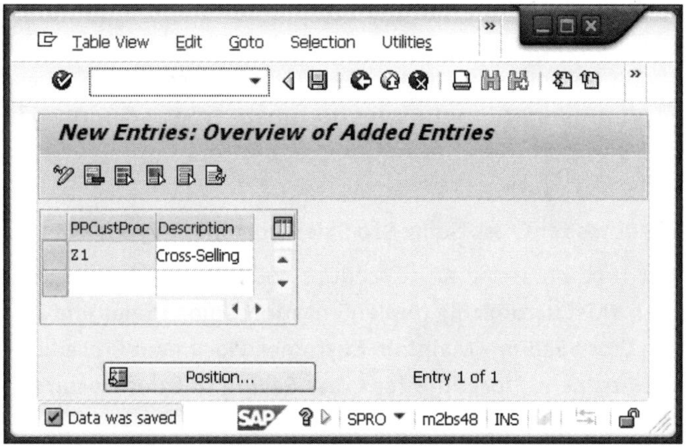

Figure 4.37 Creating New Customer Cross-Selling Procedures

Defining Document Procedures for Cross-Selling

To configure sales document type cross-selling procedure codes, follow the menu path **SAP Customizing Implementation Guide • Sales and Distribution • Basic Functions • Cross-Selling • Maintain Customer/Document Procedures For Cross-Selling • Define Document Procedure for Cross-Selling.** This configuration may also be accessed for dynamic product proposal by following the menu path **SAP Customizing Implementation Guide • Sales and Distribution • Basic Functions • Dynamic Product Proposal • Define Document Procedure for Product Proposal**.

For either menu path, on the screen that opens, click on the **New Entries** button or press F5. The screen shown in Figure 4.38 will open.

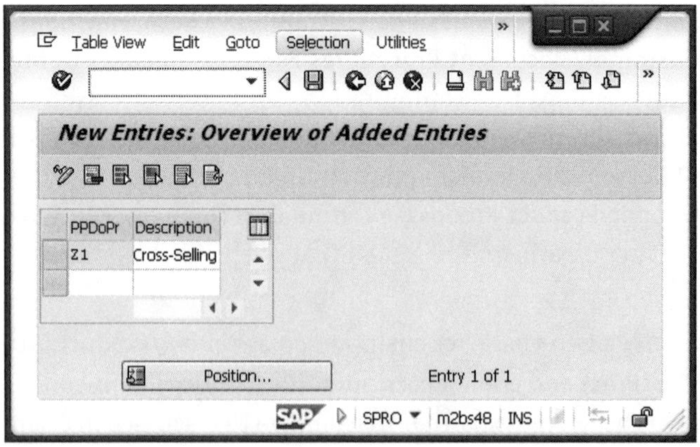

Figure 4.38 Creating a New Sales Document Type Cross-Selling Procedure

On this screen shown in Figure 4.38, specify a two-character sales document type cross-selling procedure code (**PPDoPr**) and add a description (**Description**). These order type procedure codes are assigned to the sales document type as described in the next section.

Assigning Document Procedures for Cross-Selling to Sales Document Types

To assign sales document type cross-selling procedure codes to sales document types, follow the menu path **SAP Customizing Implementation Guide • Sales and Distribution • Basic Functions • Cross-Selling • Maintain Customer/Document Procedures For Cross-Selling • Assign Document Procedure for Cross-Selling to Sales Document Types**.

This configuration may also be accessed for dynamic product proposals by following the menu path **SAP Customizing Implementation Guide • Sales and Distribution •**

Basic Functions • Dynamic Product Proposal • Assign Document Procedure for Product Proposal to Sales Document Types.

For either menu path, on the screen that opens, click on the **New Entries** button or press [F5]. Figure 4.39 shows what you'll see following the menu path and screen commands as specified.

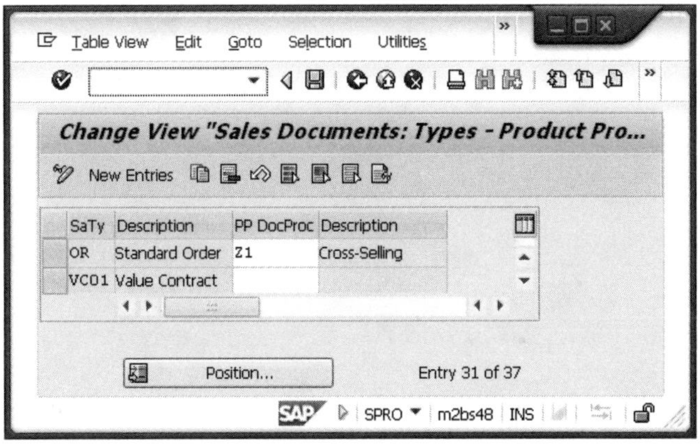

Figure 4.39 Assigning Cross-Selling Order Type Procedures Codes to Sales Document Types

On this screen, find the sales order type to which you want to assign your procedure and then enter the cross-selling procedure code in the **PP DocProc** column.

4.4.6 Cross-Selling/Dynamic Product Proposal Profiles

Note that, for cross-selling, unlike other condition technique-based functionalities, procedure determinations are not used. Instead, we'll specify a cross-selling profile that also includes dynamic product proposal procedures (Section 4.5) and a pricing procedure determination (Section 4.1).

The goal of a cross-selling profile is to implement the ability to define different combinations of features depending on the sales area, customer, and order type. In this section, we'll cover both defining and assigning cross-selling profiles.

Defining Cross-Selling Profiles

To configure cross-selling profiles, follow the menu path **SAP Customizing Implementation Guide • Sales and Distribution • Basic Functions • Cross-Selling • Define And Assign Cross-Selling Profile • Define Cross-Selling Profile**. On the screen that opens, click on the **New Entries** button or press [F5].

On the screen shown in Figure 4.40, specify a six-character cross-selling profile (**Cross-selling prof.**) and add a description.

You can then indicate a dynamic **Product proposal proc.** that is applicable for this cross-selling profile. If you activate this feature, you would get cross-selling proposal popup windows for the materials in the product proposal.

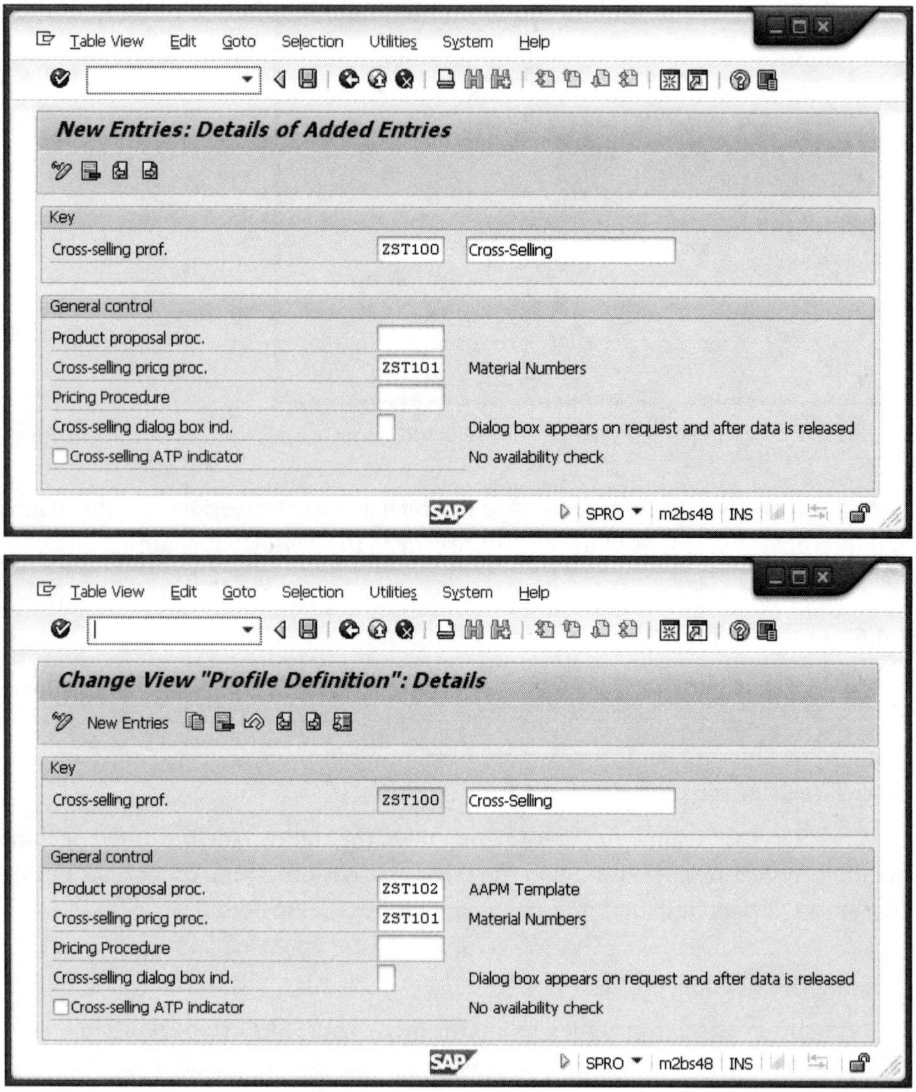

Figure 4.40 Defining a New Cross-Selling Profile

Next, indicate the cross-selling pricing procedure ZST101 (**Cross-selling prof.**) we defined when we maintained cross-selling procedures in Section 4.4.5. You can also overwrite the configuration maintained when setting the pricing procedure determination in Section 4.1.5 by assigning a **Pricing Procedure** on this screen.

You can suppress the default behavior of the popup window for add-on materials, as shown in Figure 4.32, by changing the value on **Cross-selling dialog box ind.** to "A" (which means the dialog box will appear only on request). With this approach, the cross-selling popup window will only appear if a user clicks on the corresponding button on the order entry screen; otherwise, the popup window would not interfere with sales order entry.

The **Cross-selling ATP indicator**, when checked, only proposes add-on materials when these materials are available in stock.

Assigning Cross-Selling Profiles

To assign cross-selling profiles, follow the menu path **SAP Customizing Implementation Guide • Sales and Distribution • Basic Functions • Cross-Selling • Define And Assign Cross-Selling Profile • Assign Cross-Selling Profile.** On the screen that opens, click on the **New Entries** button or press F5.

On the screen shown in Figure 4.41, you'll need to consider all the possible values for the following fields and decide which fields are applicable:

- Sales areas (**SOrg**, **DCh**, and **Division**) defined in the organization structure configuration
- Cross-selling customer procedure code (**CS cust. Proc.**) maintained when we defined customer procedures for cross-selling, which we also assigned to the business partner/customer master data, in Section 4.4.5
- Cross-selling sales order type procedure code (**CS doc. Proced.**) maintained when we defined customer procedures for cross-selling in Section 4.4.5

For each combination, you'll need to decide whether a relevant cross-selling profile exists and, if so, assign its code in the **CS profile** column. The **Description** field will be populated by the systems based on the selected **CS Profile** (cross-selling procedure) and its corresponding configuration. No difference exists between maintaining a key combination without a value in the **CS profile** column or not maintaining a combination at all.

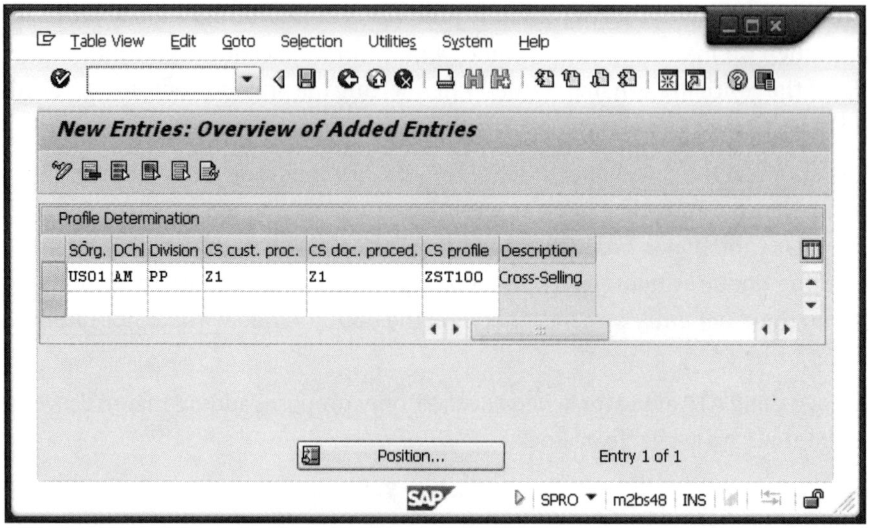

Figure 4.41 Assigning Cross-Selling Profiles

4.4.7 Special Item Category Determination

When a user makes a selection in the cross-selling popup window, shown earlier in Figure 4.32, the system will create subitems for the add-ons on the sales order. To enable the creation of this subitem, you'll need to perform an additional configuration step entitled **Assign Item Categories**. Figure 4.42 shows how special item category determination works.

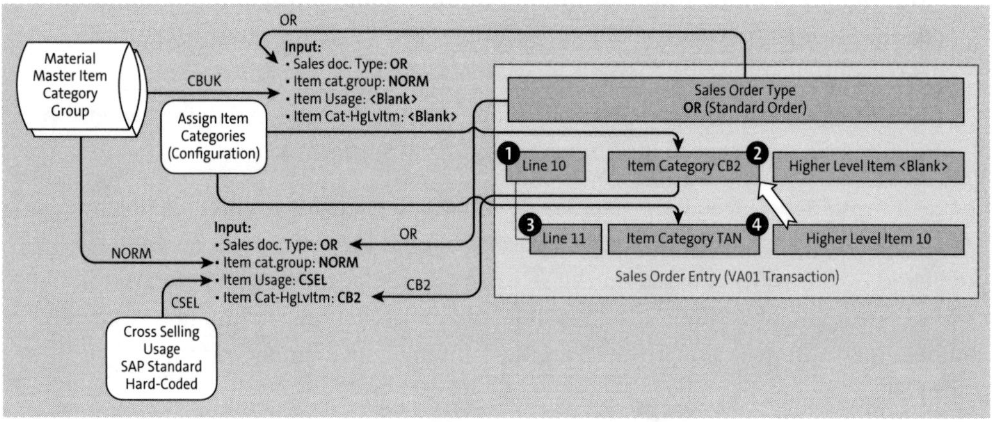

Figure 4.42 Assigning Item Categories

Let's walk through each step next:

❶ As you enter lines on a sales order, the first line is assigned the line number 10. The item category is determined using the following input parameters:

- For the **Sales Order Type** field, enter "OR" (from the header of the sales order)
- For the **Item Category Group** field, enter "CBUK" (from the material master sales view)
- Leave **Item Usage** blank (hard-coded in SAP S/4HANA)
- The **Item Category** of the line is indicated by the higher-level item number. For the main item (first line you entered), this will be blank because the higher-level item number field is also blank.

❷ The standard SAP configuration will determine the default item category CB2 to be assigned to line 10.

❸ The system will find the cross-selling configuration and master data, and a popup window will show the available add-on items. The user enters a quantity for one of the materials and then clicks the **Copy** button. At this time, the system will add a new line with the higher-level item number defined as 10. The line number will be assigned as 11 to ensure this subitem appears under line 10 (as per the order type configuration). The item category on the new line 11 is determined using the following input parameters:

- For the **Sales Order Type** field, enter "OR" (from the header of the sales order)
- For the **Item Category Group** field, enter "CBUK" (from the material master sales view)
- For the **Item Usage** field, enter "CSEL" (cross-selling; hard-coded in SAP S/4HANA)
- The **Item Category** of the line is indicated by the higher-level item number CB2

❹ The configuration described in this section specifies that the default item category TAN should be assigned to line 11.

In the following sections, we'll show you how to define item category usage and then assign item categories.

Defining Item Category Usage

To configure item category usage, follow the menu path **SAP Customizing Implementation Guide • Sales and Distribution • Sales • Sales Documents • Sales Document Item • Define Item Category Usage.** On the screen that opens, click on the **New Entries** button or press F5.

Cross-selling item category usage CSEL is not provided out of the box, and before you can perform an item category assignment, you'll need to configure it. On the screen shown in Figure 4.43, specify a four-character item category usage code (**Usg.**) and add a description (**Description**).

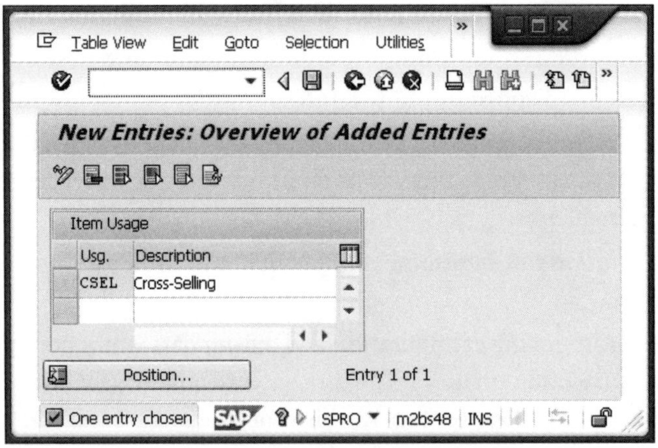

Figure 4.43 Defining a New Item Category Usage

Assigning Item Categories

To configure item category determination (assignment), follow the menu path **SAP Customizing Implementation Guide • Sales and Distribution • Sales • Sales Documents • Sales Document Item • Assign Item Categories**. On the screen that opens, click on the **New Entries** button or press [F5].

The cross-selling item category usage CSEL is not provided out of the box, and before you can perform the item category assignment, you'll need to configure the item category usage.

On the screen shown in Figure 4.44, enter the item category assignment key by maintaining the following information:

- Sales order type (**Sales doc. type**)
- Item category group (**Item cat.group**)
- item category usage (**Item Usage**)
- Item category of the line indicated by the higher-level item number (**ItemCat-HgL-vItm**)

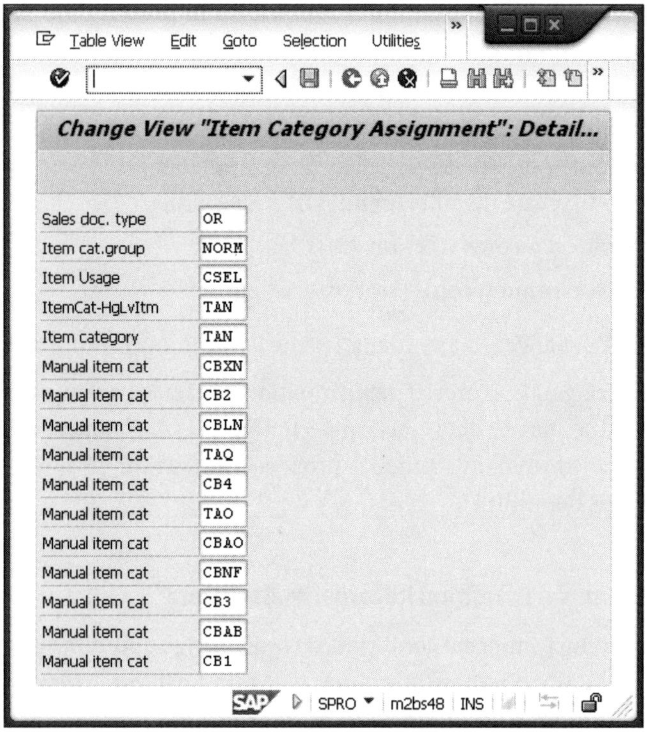

Figure 4.44 Assigning Item Categories

Next, select what the default/proposed **Item Category** should be. You can also specify up to 11 other possible manual item categories (**Manual item cat**) that a user can manually choose from when manually modifying the item category on a sales order. Users are only allowed to choose from the list of options specified on this screen.

4.5 Dynamic Product Proposals

A dynamic product proposal is a system functionality that allows you to use several data sources to default as materials on a sales order. The goal is to expedite order entry time, in particular for customers that tend to order the same products repeatedly.

A product proposal condition records (master data) transaction is available that you can use to maintain with the specific purpose of defaulting materials on customer orders (Section 4.5.1). But with dynamic product proposals, you can also set up the following defaults:

- Material from sales order history, i.e., using previous orders to prepopulate the materials on a new order.
- Material from customer-material information record, as described in Chapter 3. The customer-material information record is where you'll maintain the part numbers your customer uses for the products you sell (among other data), and you can use this record as a source to create defaults for lines of a sales order.
- Material from listing condition records (Section 4.5.3).
- Materials from exclusion condition records (Section 4.5.3).

Note that a user can still make changes to an order after the list of items is proposed.

As we've done for pricing, free goods, material determination, and cross-selling, the following section will cover the master data (Section 4.5.1), the access sequence, and the procedures (Section 4.5.2) for dynamic product proposal. In Section 4.5.3, we'll focus on how the procedure is determined.

4.5.1 Dynamic Product Proposal Condition Records: Master Data

Maintenance of dynamic product proposal condition records using condition technique is achieved using Transaction VB41, as shown in Figure 4.45. First, you'll need to select the dynamic product proposal (**Item Proposal Type**), which is configured as a sales order type. In our case, we're using the document type PV, provided by SAP out of the box.

We'll also select the sales area (**Sales Organization**, **Distribution Channel** and **Division**), **Sales Office** and **Sales Group** this product proposal is applicable for.

The next screen (**Create Item Proposal: Overview**) is a subset of the sales order entry screen showing only the fields applicable for product proposal. Although not mandatory, we recommend you add a description (**Description**) for this product proposal to make it easier to find it later. You can also define values for the **Valid-From Date** and **Valid-To Date** fields on the header if applicable. You'll then enter one or more lines with the following information:

- The material (**Material**) that should be proposed for sales orders that use this template. The **Item Description** field is automatically populated from the material master data.
- The target quantity (**Target Quantity**) that should be proposed, which is optional. Even if you specify a valid quantity, a user may copy the proposal without quantities at the time of sales order entry.

- You can change the unit of measurement (**UoM**); otherwise, the system will default to the corresponding value from the material master.

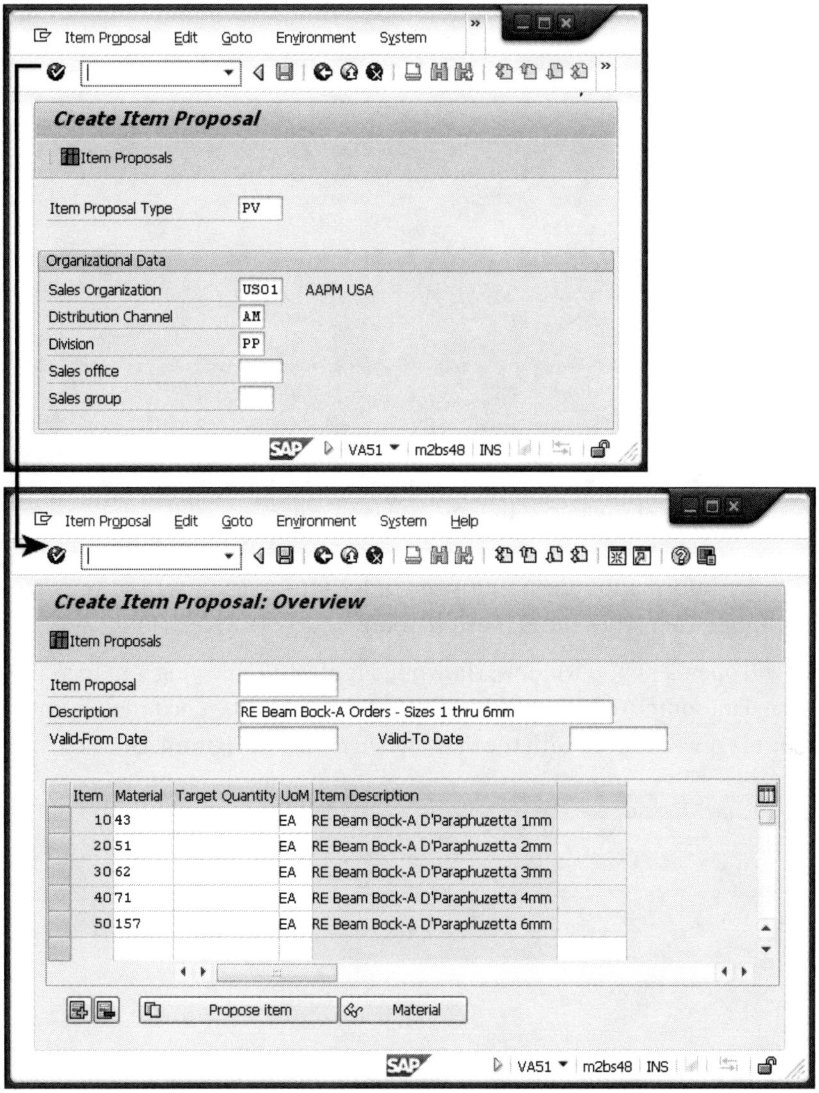

Figure 4.45 Creating New Dynamic Product Proposal Master Data

Using the data shown in Figure 4.45, when a sales order is entered, lines will be proposed, as shown in Figure 4.46.

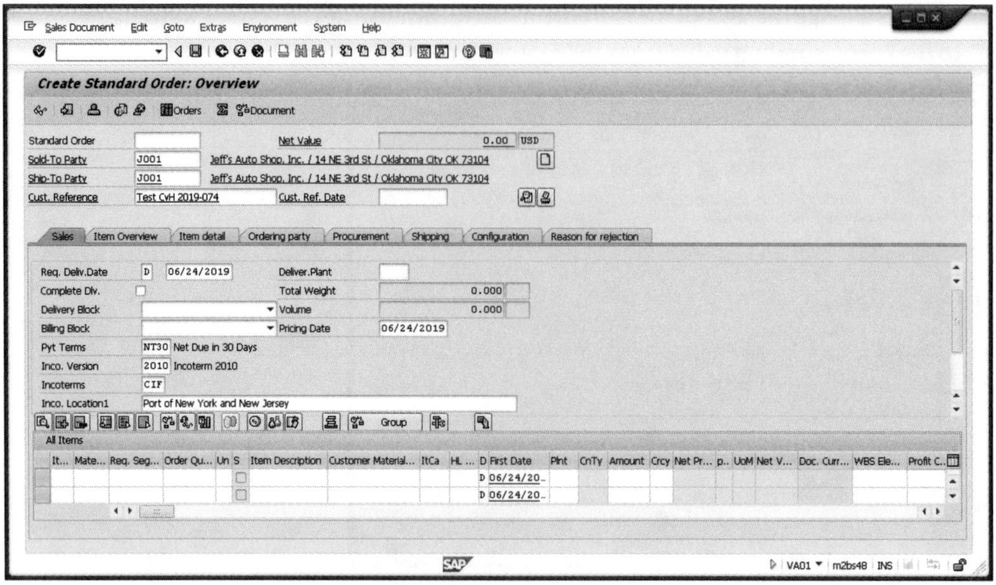

Figure 4.46 Sales Order Entry with Dynamic Product Proposal

Enter the header information including sales order type, customer, and purchase order (PO) number. Then, click the [button] button or press Ctrl+F11.

The system will open a popup window, shown in Figure 4.47, allowing you to search and select the data source to be used when proposing items. The document number 50000000 is the one we saved with the data shown earlier in Figure 4.45.

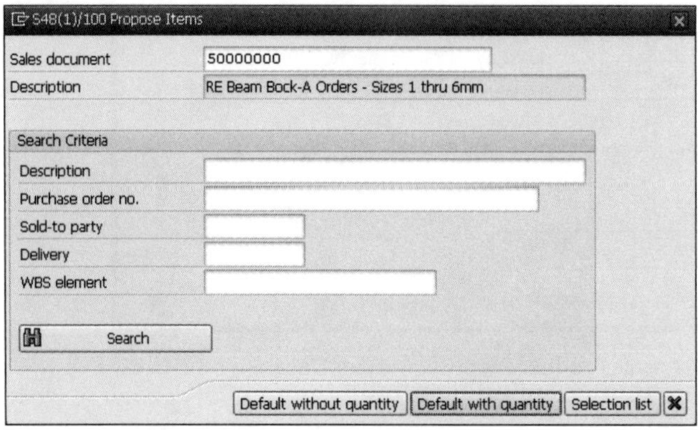

Figure 4.47 Sales Order Popup Window Prompting the User to Select the Source Data for the Product Proposal

Note that you can assign the product proposal document number to the business partner master data on the **Orders** tab, discussed in Chapter 2, Section 2.3.1, which would become the default item proposal document number in this popup window.

Once you click the **Default with Quantity** button, the items on the product proposal will be copied into the new order being created, as shown in Figure 4.48.

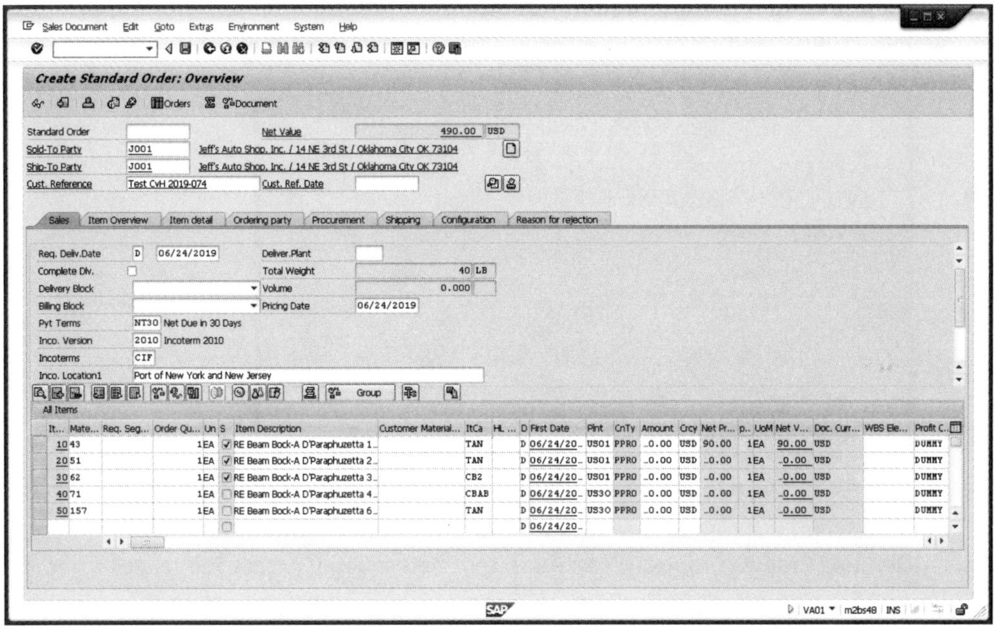

Figure 4.48 Sales Order with Lines Containing Items Proposed Dynamically by the System

4.5.2 Dynamic Product Proposal Procedures and Access Sequences

A dynamic product proposal is unique among other condition technique-based system functionalities because no condition types or condition tables are involved. Instead, you'll define a dynamic product proposal procedure and its access sequences in a single step and use function modules instead of tables to retrieve and apply the source data to the sales order at the time of proposal.

Three configuration activities for dynamic product proposals are shared with cross-selling, which we discussed earlier in Section 4.4.5. In the following sections, we'll describe the configuration steps necessary to define valid sources for dynamic product proposals for your company and discuss their behavior.

Maintaining Tables of Origin for Product Proposals

To configure dynamic product proposal sources/tables of origin, follow the menu path **SAP Customizing Implementation Guide • Sales and Distribution • Basic Functions • Dynamic Product Proposal • Maintain Table of Origin for Product Proposal.** On the screen that opens, click on the **New Entries** button or press [F5].

On the screen shown in Figure 4.49, specify a one-character dynamic product proposal source code (**Srce**) code and add a description (**Description**).

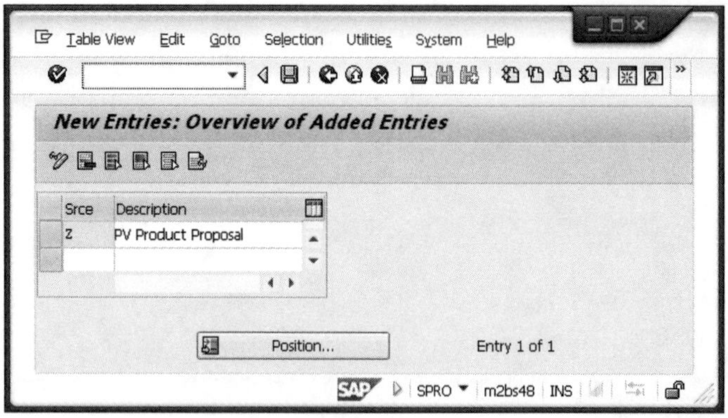

Figure 4.49 Maintaining Dynamic Product Proposal Source/Table of Origin

Defining Product Proposal Procedures and Determining Access Sequences

To maintain dynamic product proposal procedures, follow the menu path **SAP Customizing Implementation Guide • Sales and Distribution • Basic Functions • Dynamic Product Proposal • Define Product Proposal Procedure and Determine Access Sequences.** On the screen that opens, click on the **New Entries** button or press [F5].

As shown in Figure 4.50, two steps are needed to maintain the procedures for dynamic product proposals, as follows:

❶ On this screen, enter a six-character dynamic product proposal procedure code (**PP Proced.**) and add a description (**Description**). You can also define parameters for background updates of the product proposal order history, including the number of periods in the order history (**N..**), the period type (**PeriodType**), and the column headings (**Column Hdg**). Press [Enter] and select the line we just created.

❷ Next, double-click on the **Access Sequence** option under the **Dialog Structure**. On the screen that opens, click on the **New Entries** button or press [F5] and enter the new level number (**Level**) and the dynamic product proposal function module (**Function Module**). Some of the function modules you can use include the following:

- SD_DPP_CUSTOMER_MATERIAL_INFO: Materials from customer-material information record
- SD_DPP_EXCLUSION: Material from exclusion
- SD_DPP_HISTORY: Material from order history
- SD_DPP_LISTING: Material from listing
- SD_DPP_PRODUCT_PROPOSAL: Material from product proposal
- SD_DPP_CROSS_SELLING: Cross-selling condition records
- SD_DPP_READ: The consolidated data generated by program SDPVGEN as per the configuration described in Section 4.5.3

You can also specify attributes specific to the selected function module (**FM Attributes**), define what to do with the results of the function module (**FM acty**), assign a data source code (**Srce** as configured in the previous section), and specify how results should be sorted (**Sorting**).

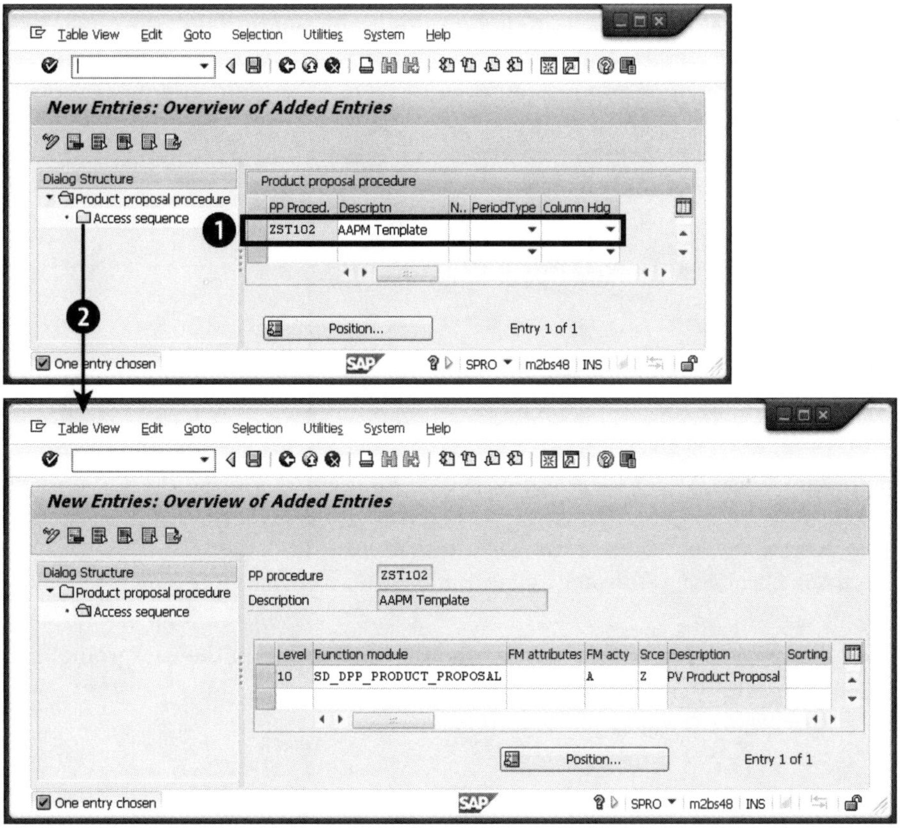

Figure 4.50 Maintaining Procedures for Dynamic Product Proposal

4.5.3 Procedure Determination for Product Proposals

If the volume of data you want to use for product proposal causes performance concerns, the system makes several tools available to optimize the source data. In the following sections, we'll describe the configuration steps necessary to assign and activate product proposal for selected sales areas.

Maintaining Procedure Determinations (in the Background) for Product Proposals

To configure the product proposal procedure determination for background processing, follow the menu path **SAP Customizing Implementation Guide • Sales and Distribution • Basic Functions • Dynamic Product Proposal • Maintain Procedure Determination (in Background) for Product Proposal.** On the screen that opens, click on the **New Entries** button or press F5.

As shown in Figure 4.51, assign the sales area (sales organization **SOrg.**, distribution channel **DChl**, and division **Dv**) and the product proposal customer procedure code (**PPCustProc** as defined in the Defining Customer Procedures for Cross-Selling section). For each relevant combination, assign a product proposal procedure (**PPPr** as defined in earlier in Figure 4.54).

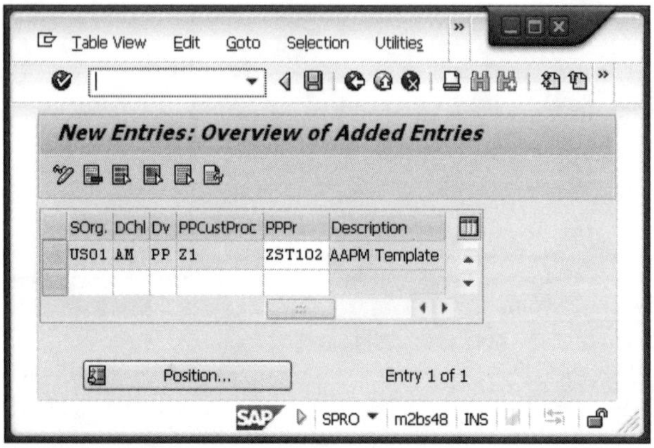

Figure 4.51 Maintaining Procedure Determination for Background Processing

Once defined, you can schedule program SDPVGEN to run in the background and update a repository that can be used to propose materials.

Maintaining Procedure Determinations (Online) for Product Proposals

To configure the product proposal procedure determination for online processing, follow the menu path **SAP Customizing Implementation Guide • Sales and Distribution • Basic Functions • Dynamic Product Proposal • Maintain Procedure Determination (Online) for Product Proposal.** On the screen that opens, click on the **New Entries** button or press F5.

As shown in Figure 4.52, assign the sales area (sales organization **SOrg.**, distribution channel **DChl**, and division **Dv**); sales office (**SOff.**); sales group (**SGrp**); the product proposal customer procedure code (**PPCustProc**); and the product proposal document type procedure code (**PPDoPr**). For each relevant combination, assign a product proposal procedure (**PPPr**).

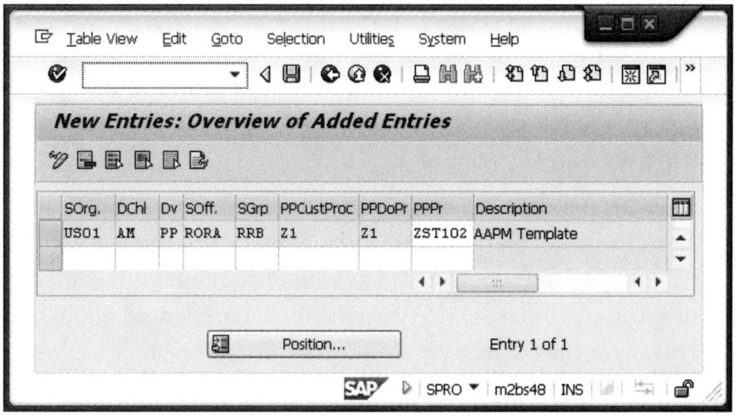

Figure 4.52 Maintaining Procedure Determination for Online Processing

4.6 Listing/Exclusion

Listing/exclusion is a system functionality that allows you to restrict the material that a customer may order. The reasons why a company might use this feature vary from industry to industry, but some of the most common reasons relate to customer qualifications. Let's say only some customers should be allowed to purchase certain specialty materials through agreements made with them. Your company needs this customer's buying power, but they'll agree to a special agreement only if you can ensure they have some type of exclusivity.

The term "listing/exclusion" indicates that two features have the same objective. You'll use a listing when the customer is only allowed to order materials maintained on the condition records, and you'll use an exclusion when the customer can order any material except for the ones maintained on the condition records.

Requirements like this are quite common and is usually part of the scope of implementation projects. Due to the risk of violating agreements with important customers, this feature is often considered medium to high priority.

Companies often don't like the way master data has been traditionally maintained in this repository. The out-of-the-box configuration uses combinations of customer and material, which requires a lot of recurring maintenance. For example, every time a new material or a new customer is created, you'll need to come back to this master data and add the corresponding entries. Instead, you can define new key combinations, which we'll walk you through in this chapter using the customer group from the business partner master data and the material group from the material master data.

One complaint about this feature is the vague nature of its error messages. If a user tries to enter an order for an unauthorized key combination, a generic message will appear that doesn't specify the reason. Unfortunately, you can't modify these messages without complex/risky ABAP development.

So, if you define multiple master data key combinations, your users will find it hard to understand why they can't enter an order and could only consult the master data to find out the cause. This limitation is not enough reason to dissuade your company from using this feature. The customer service team is often experienced enough to be able to intuit the reason for the error.

Similar to what we've done previously, the following section will cover the master data (Section 4.6.1), condition tables (Section 4.6.2), access sequences (Section 4.6.3), condition types (Section 4.6.4), and procedures (Section 4.6.5) for the listing/exclusion functionality.

4.6.1 Listing/Exclusion Condition Records: Master Data

The maintenance of listing/exclusion condition records using the condition technique is achieved by opening Transaction VB01. Because the processes are so similar for both listings and exclusions, we'll just walk you through the process for listings, noting where differences for exclusions exist.

First, you'll need to select the condition type (**List/excl.type**) for which want to maintain condition records. In our example, we're creating a condition type for listing "ZSTL" and a condition type for exclusion "ZSTE" (Figure 4.53). We'll cover the creation of condition types in more detail in Section 4.6.4.

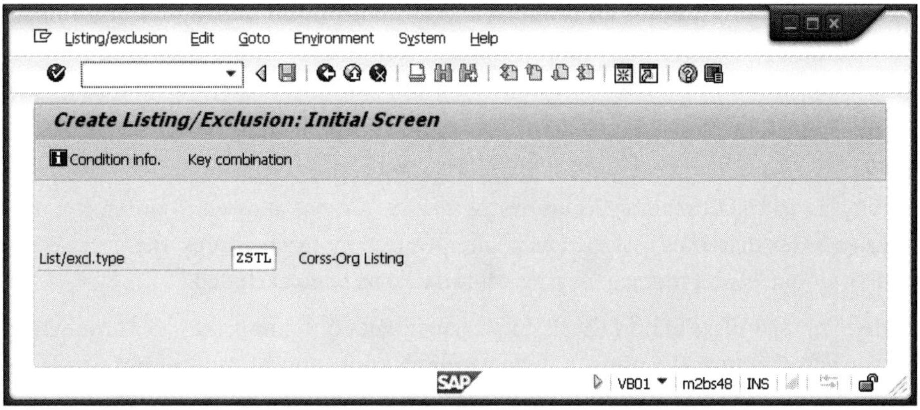

Figure 4.53 Creating a New Listing Condition Record

Now, click on the **Key Combination** command button or press Enter. The system will open a popup window if more than one condition table exists. If only one condition table exists (as in condition types ZSTL and ZSTE), no popup window will appear. The next screen, shown in Figure 4.54 is generated by the system along with the condition tables.

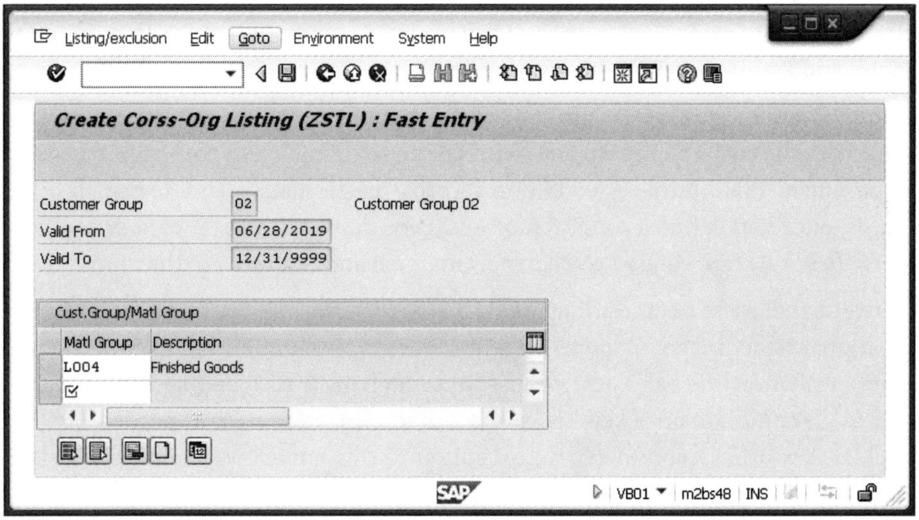

Figure 4.54 Creating Listing/Exclusion Condition Records

First, in the header, select the customer group (**Customer Group**) for which you want to define restrictions.

For a listing (ZSTL), enter all material group codes (**Matl Group**) that customers belonging to the **Customer Group** on the header can order. If a user tries to order materials assigned with any other material group, the order entry screen would issue a message saying, **Material * is not listed and therefore not allowed.**

For an exclusion (ZSTE), enter the material group code (**Matl Group**) that customers belonging to the **Customer Group** on the header are *not* allowed to order. If a user tries to order materials assigned with one of these material groups, the order entry screen would issue a message saying, **Material * has been excluded.**

Note that, regardless of how the listing/exclusion is configured, the sales order entry screen will simply notify users that the material is not allowed but does not notify the user whether the listing/exclusion is based on the customer group or on the material group.

4.6.2 Listing/Exclusion Condition Tables

Condition tables are master data repositories where listing/exclusion relevant information is stored. These tables are actual database repositories created by opening Transaction OV05 or by following the menu path **SAP Customizing Implementation Guide • Sales and Distribution • Basic Functions • Listing/Exclusion • Maintain Condition Tables for Listing/Exclusion.** You can also use Transaction OV06 to modify the tables and Transaction OV07 to display them.

In our example shown in Figure 4.55, we're creating a listing/exclusion condition table with the customer group and material group to fulfill a hypothetical customer requirement that optimizes condition records/master data maintenance. In other words, once you define a condition or exclusion rule with master data using these keys, these rules are valid as you add new material and customer to the master data.

Note also that we're not including the sales area as part of the key nor any other organizational structure component; we're considering these rules are valid across the company. Often, the sales area or distribution chain is included on the condition technique condition table keys to leave room for new sales areas as needed. Listing/exclusion is usually considered an exception to this guideline because the restrictions are usually hard set and the chance of creating an organizational structure element in the future that that is an exception is small.

Note that we're using the same table 902, which we used for our pricing example in Section 4.1.2. This choice is allowed because each condition technique functionality has a different application code ("G" for listing/exclusion; "A" for pricing). This code makes the configuration unique with its functionality even though they use the condition technique.

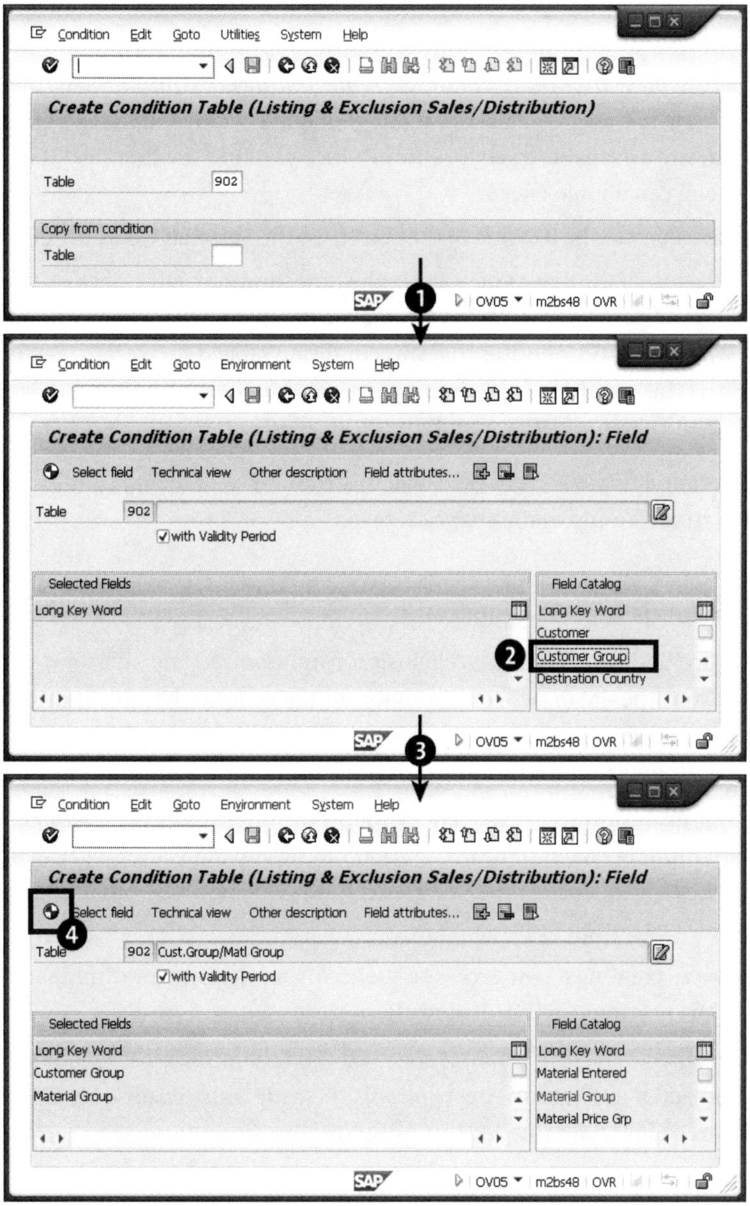

Figure 4.55 Creating Listing/Exclusion Condition Tables

To create listing/exclusion condition tables, follow these steps:

❶ On this screen, you'll first need to choose a three-digit condition table number (**Table**). This number must begin with "9" to indicate that is not provided by SAP (allowable namespace). Press [Enter].

❷ The screen then displays the **Create Condition Table (Listing & Exclusion Sales/Distribution): Field Overview** screen. On the right, you'll find the **Field Catalog** with a list of fields currently available to choose from. Once you find the first field (**Customer Group**), you can double-click it.

❸ The field will be copied to the left side of the screen on the **Selected Fields** window.

❹ Once you've selected all the fields you want in the new condition table, click on the generate icon, as indicated. The system will create a database table with the name "KOTGXXX," where "KOTG" indicates that this condition table is for listings/exclusions and XXX is the condition table number. In this example, the table KOTG902 would be generated along with the maintenance screens.

The **with Validity Period** flag, when checked, will incorporate valid-to and valid-from dates to the table structure and maintenance screens.

4.6.3 Listing/Exclusion Access Sequences

The access sequence defines how listing/exclusion condition records (master data) will be retrieved from the database. You can indicate the order in which condition tables are accessed and specify the key value to use during the search (either from sales order data or other data).

To maintain listing/exclusion access sequences, follow the menu path **SAP Customizing Implementation Guide • Sales and Distribution • Basic Functions • Listing/Exclusion • Maintain Access Sequences for Listing/Exclusion.** On the screen that opens, click on the **New Entries** button or press [F5].

In our example, we're creating a new access sequence using the new condition table 902 we created in the previous section. Follow these steps:

1. On the screen shown in Figure 4.56, first specify a four-character access sequence code (**Acc...**) and add a description (**Description**). The code must begin with "Z" to indicate that this code is not provided by SAP (allowable namespace).

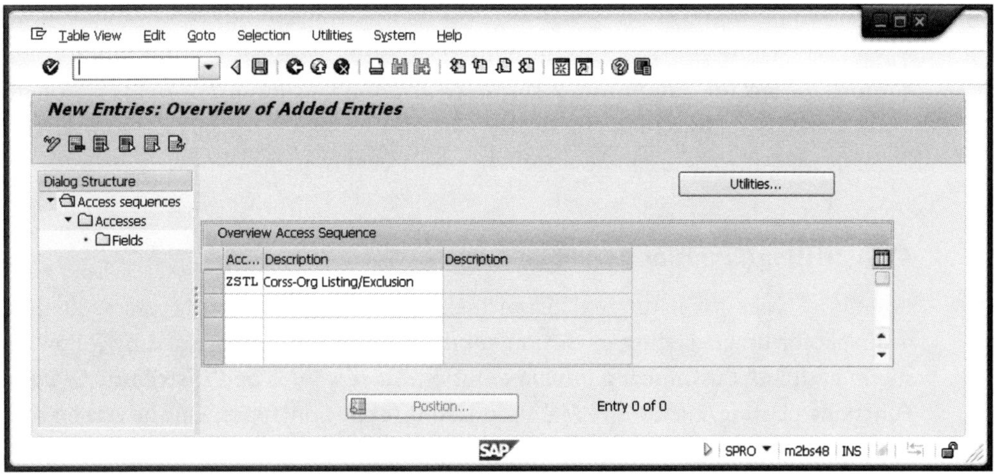

Figure 4.56 Maintaining Listing/Exclusion Access Sequences

2. Then, select the new entry created and double-click on the **Accesses** option on the **Dialog Structure** menu on the left side of the screen, leading to the screen shown in Figure 4.57.

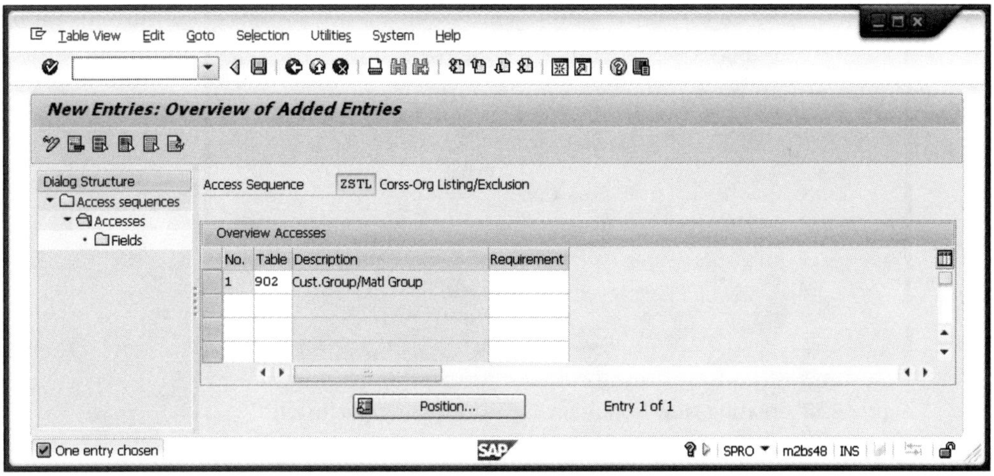

Figure 4.57 Assigning Condition Tables to the Access Sequence

3. Next, enter each table on the lines available on this screen. Assign each line with a number (**No.** column; we recommend using increments of 10) and the table number

you want. You can also use a VOFM routine in the **Requirement** column to allow for great flexibility when determining whether this data is applicable or not.

4. Finally, select the new line we just created and double-click on the **Fields** option on the **Dialog Structure** menu on the left side of the screen. With all field sources correctly identified, you can now save the new access sequence.

4.6.4 Listing/Exclusion Condition Types

Condition types for listing/exclusion make the new tables and access sequences available for usage. Listing/exclusion condition types are maintained by following menu path **SAP Customizing Implementation Guide • Sales and Distribution • Basic Functions • Listing/Exclusion • Maintain Listing/Exclusion Types.** On the screen that opens, click on the **New Entries** button or press [F5].

As shown in Figure 4.58, specify a four-character listing/exclusion condition type (**Ctyp**) and add a name (**Name**), indicating the access sequence (**AS**) that it utilizes. You can define validity dates if desired.

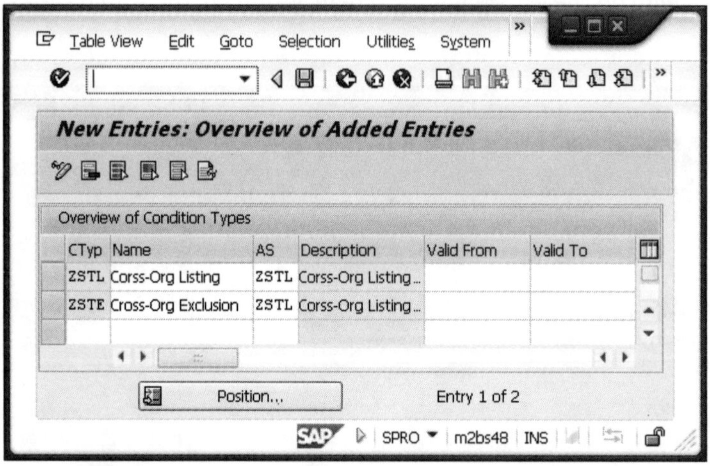

Figure 4.58 Creating New Condition Types for Listing/Exclusion

4.6.5 Listing/Exclusion Procedures

The listing/exclusion procedure is where you'll list the relevant condition types. Then, you'll activate the listing/exclusion by assigning the listing/exclusion procedure to the desired sales order types. In the following sections, we'll show you how to maintain procedures for listings/exclusions and then how to assign them.

Procedures for Maintaining Listing/Exclusion Procedures

To maintain listing/exclusion procedures, follow the menu path **SAP Customizing Implementation Guide • Sales and Distribution • Basic Functions • Listing/Exclusion • Procedures for Maintaining Listing/Exclusion.** On the screen that opens, click on the **New Entries** button or press F5.

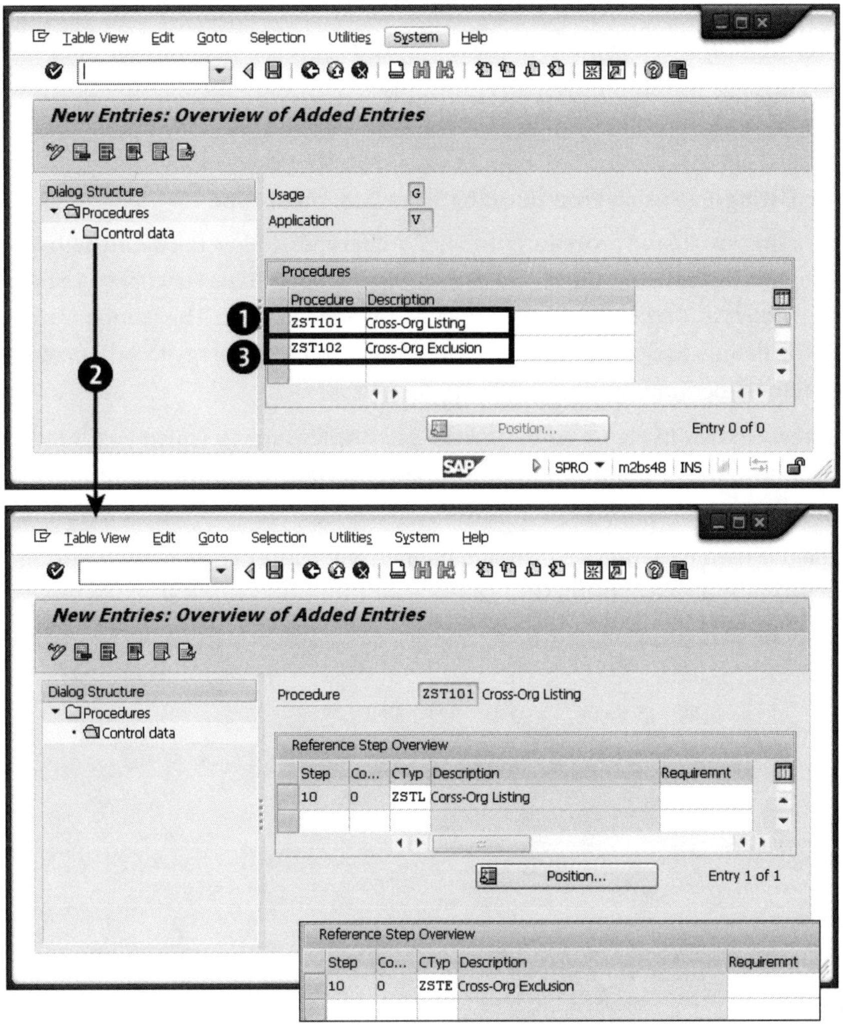

Figure 4.59 Maintaining Procedures for Listing/Exclusion

To maintain the procedure for listings/exclusions, on the screen shown in Figure 4.59, follow these steps:

❶ On this screen, specify a six-character listing and exclusion procedure code (**Procedure**) and add a description (**Description**). Press [Enter] and then select the line we just created.

❷ Next, double-click on the **Control Data** option under the **Dialog Structure**.

❸ Click on the **New entries** button or press [F5] and enter the new **Step** number and listing/exclusion condition type (**CTyp**). Repeat steps 2 and 3 for the exclusion procedure.

Activating Listing/Exclusion Procedures by Sales Document Type

To assign listing/exclusion procedures to sales order types, follow the menu path **SAP Customizing Implementation Guide • Sales And Distribution • Basic Functions • Listing/ Exclusion • Activate Listing/Exclusion By Sales Document Type**. This configuration serves as the listing/exclusion procedure determination (in analogy to other condition technique functionality).

On the screen shown in Figure 4.60, find the sales order type to which you want to assign your procedures and then enter the listing and exclusion procedure codes in the **Listing** and **Exclusion** fields.

The **Pro** field is used to define what should happen when a key combination is found in both a listing and an exclusion.

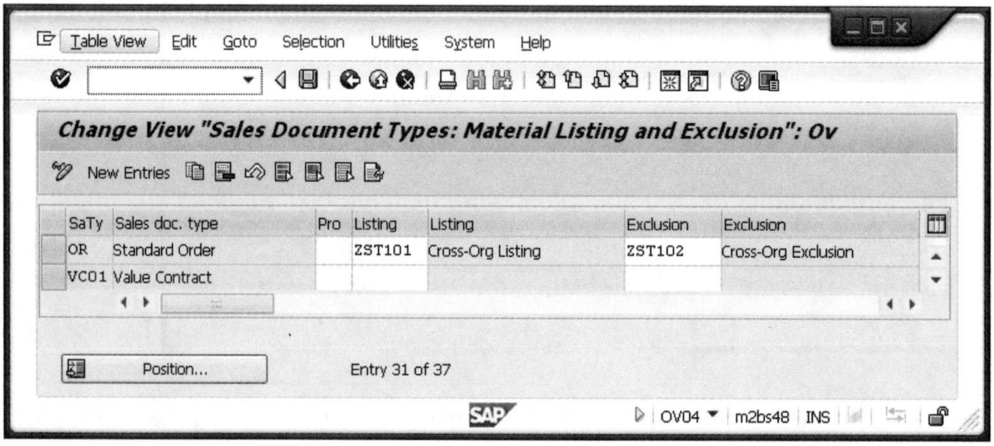

Figure 4.60 Assigning Listing/Exclusion Procedures to Sales Document Types

4.7 Output Determination and Management

Output determination is a system functionality that allows you to control outgoing communications to people and other systems. SAP S/4HANA allows you to manage communication with third-party personnel using a rule-based framework called BRFplus. When communicating with other systems within your company or elsewhere (commonly referred to as Electronic Data Interchange [EDI]), you'll need to use the condition technique-based output determination feature described in this section.

Condition technique-based output determination is also the method used in SAP ERP and is enabled across the system for different system transactions as identified by application code. For sales, the most common application codes are listed in Table 4.1.

App	Description	Meaning
V	Sales/Distribution	Generic code for sales, this code is valid across all sales applications
V1	Sales	Sales documents such as orders, returns, credit/debit memos, inquiries, etc.
V2	Shipping	Delivery documents, part of the logistics execution functionality
V3	Billing	Invoices, credit memos, intercompany billing, and other billing documents

Table 4.1 Most Common Sales Application Codes

The functionality and configuration steps are similar. We'll use the V1 (sales) application to describe this feature and refer to other applications as appropriate.

As we've done previously, the following section will cover the master data (Section 4.7.1), condition tables (Section 4.7.2), access sequences (Section 4.7.3), condition types (Section 4.7.4), and procedures (Section 4.7.5) for output determination.

4.7.1 Output Determination Condition Records: Master Data

Maintaining output determination condition records using the condition technique for the V1 (sales) application is achieved by opening Transaction VV11. For the V2 (shipping) application, you would open Transaction VV22; for V3 (billing), Transaction VV31.

First, as shown in Figure 4.61, you'll need to select the **Output Type** for which you want to maintain condition records. In our example, we're using the **Order Confirmation** (acknowledgment) form provided by SAP out of the box, output type **BA00**.

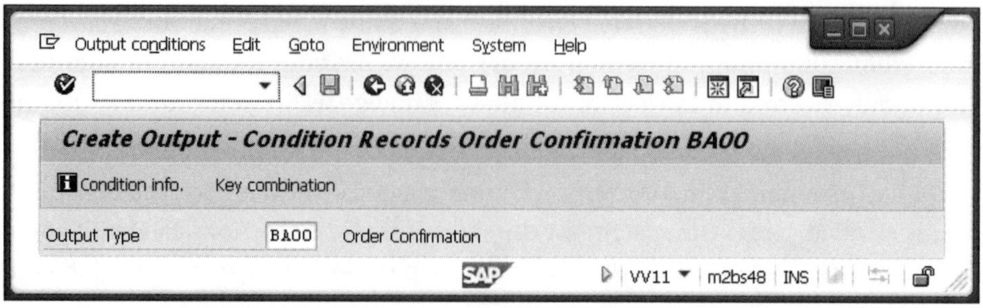

Figure 4.61 Creating a New Output Determination Condition Record

Next, click on the **Key combination** command button or press Enter; the system will open a popup window if more than one condition table exists. If only one condition table exists (as in condition type BA00), no popup window will appear. The next screen, shown in Figure 4.62, is generated by the system along with the condition tables.

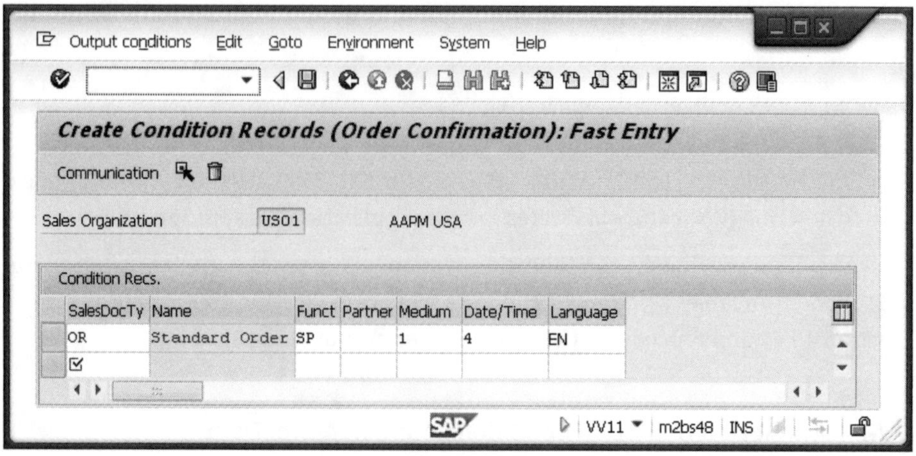

Figure 4.62 Creating Output Determination Condition Records

Next, select the **Sales Organization** for which you want to define order acknowledgment output parameters on the header portion of this screen. Then, you can select multiple entries with the following information:

- The sales order type (**SalesDocTyp**) that this output should be relevant for. In our example, we entered "OR" (**Standard Order**) so that, whenever an order with this type is created and conditions are fulfilled, the system would automatically issue an order acknowledgment message to the customer. The **Name** is the order type description populated automatically based on the selected order type. In our case, you can press `Enter` so that the system will fetch the default values for the other fields on this line, as defined in the output condition type configuration.
- Enter a partner function (**Funct**) that this message will be addressed to. We selected **SP** (or **AG**; both refer to the sold-to party), which is the business partner (customer) that sent us their purchase order.
- You can enter a fixed business **Partner** number that shall receive this message or leave the field blank so that the system takes the **AG** partner (sold-to-party) from the sales order.
- Now, specify the **Medium** in which this message must be sent. In our example, we're using **1** (**Print**) because this output will be printed and manually sent to the customer (mailed, fax, scan/email). Many companies still use this method to allow for review before sending. You can also use **5** (**External Sent**) to email the output directly to the customer, but this approach requires some setup by the SAP Basis team even though commonly adopted by companies that use SAP. Some companies still use the **2** (**Fax**) output.
- Then, select the dispatch **Date/Time**, which specify when a message will be issued. In our example, we selected **4** (**Immediately**) to print this output as soon as the order is entered. Many companies prefer to use **1** (**Batch Job**) so that all outputs are triggered together, which allows for extra time to make changes to an order before sending the order out, which can save you the trouble of reissuing an order after changes are made. Batch jobs are also sometimes required due to technical reasons, such as allowing an order to finish its postprocessing activities before sending a confirmation.

  You can also use **3** (**Transaction**) that makes this output ready and available to be sent but only if/when the user decides to. This option is often used for print outputs to save on paper.
- Next, indicate the **Language** you want to use when issuing the output. The forms contain texts, such as field labels and column heading tags, that can be implemented in multiple languages. This field is how you'll select the output language among the available languages. US companies usually issue all their output in English, but some include French for Canada due to their regulations.

Finally, select the line you just entered by clicking on the gray box at the beginning of the line as indicated. Click the **Communication** button on the command bar, which leads to the screen shown in Figure 4.63. Depending on the output medium you selected (**Medium**), the communication parameters will vary. For print outputs, the communication parameters are necessary to indicate the printer (**Output Device**) you want to use.

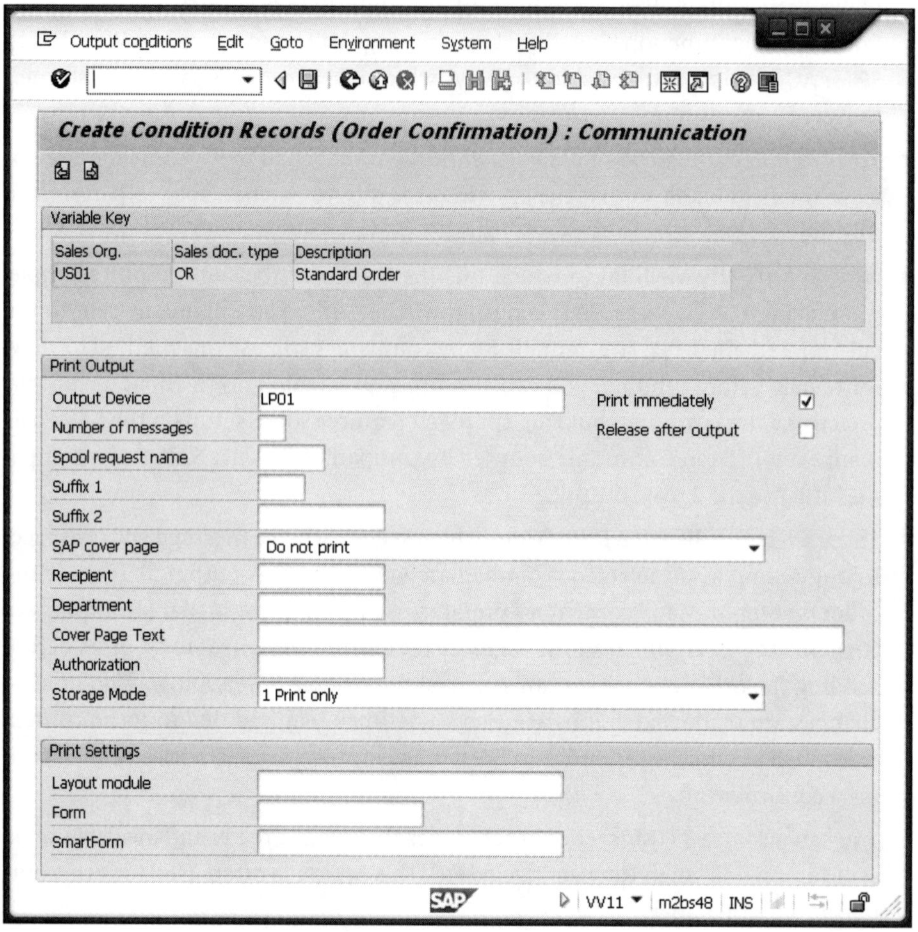

Figure 4.63 Output Condition Records Communication Data Details

Usually, the **Print Immediately** flag is activated, which would send the output to the print as soon as the output is generated. Otherwise, the output is queued and must later be released using Transactions SP01 and SP02.

The other fields on this screen identify this output on the printer queue so that separating an order acknowledgment from other documents sent to this printer is easier. If you leave these fields blank as indicated, the print output would look like all others.

You also have option of printing a cover page, which is common when sending faxes. At the bottom of the screen, some form options allow for variation of the form (when programmed as such) for each output condition record.

Note that the out-of-the-box configuration allows for maintenance based only on sales organization and order type. A common need is to change the output parameters for different customers. Companies often set up automated email outputs for a select group of sold-to customers and keep print output as the default for all others. To fulfill this requirement, you'll need to include a condition table on the access sequence that features the sold-to customer as part of its key. Let's walk through the configuration steps step by step.

Note, however, that as soon as you perform a configuration change, depending on the extent of output condition records, you may need to undertake an automated data conversion effort instead of a simple manual cut-over activity. The long-term maintenance of condition records also requires training and special attention by your business.

4.7.2 Output Determination Condition Tables

Condition tables can serve as master data repositories where output determination-relevant information can be stored. These tables are actual database repositories created by opening Transaction V/56 or by following the menu path **SAP Customizing Implementation Guide • Sales and Distribution • Basic Functions • Output Determination • Output Determination • Output Determination Using the Condition Technique • Maintain Output Determination for Sales Documents • Maintain Condition Tables • Maintain Output Condition Table for Sales Documents.** Transaction V/57 can also be used to modify condition tables, and Transaction V/58 can be used to display them.

As shown in Figure 4.64, note that we're using the same table 902 we used for our earlier pricing example in Section 4.1.2. This overlap is allowed because each condition technique functionality has a different application code ("B" for output determination and "A" for pricing). This code makes a configuration unique in its functionality even though the condition technique may be shared.

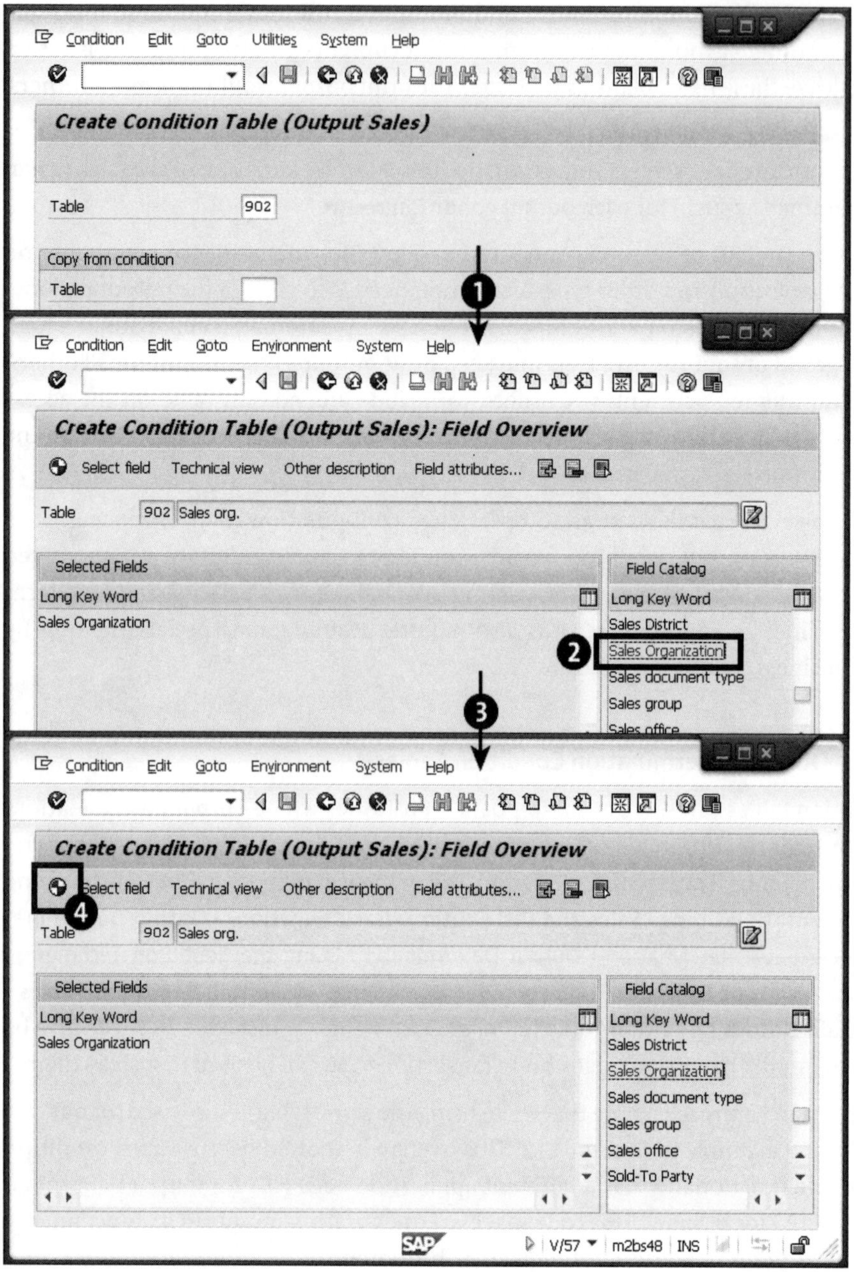

Figure 4.64 Creating Output Determination Condition Tables

To create output determination condition tables, follow these steps:

❶ On this screen, first specify a three-digit condition table number (**Table**). This number must begin with "9" to indicate that it is not provided by SAP (allowable namespace). Press `Enter`.

❷ The system then displays the **Create Condition Table (Output Sales): Field Overview** screen with a **Field Overview**. On the right, you'll find the **Field Catalog** with a list of fields currently available to choose from. Find the first field (**Sales Organization**) and double-click on it.

❸ The field will be copied to the left side of the screen, in the **Selected Fields** window.

❹ Once you've selected all the fields you want in the new condition table, click on the generate icon, as indicated. The system will create a database table with the name "BXXX," where "B" indicates that this condition table is for output determination and XXX is the condition table number. In our example, table B902 would be generated along with the maintenance screens.

4.7.3 Output Determination Access Sequences

The access sequence defines how output determination condition records (master data) will be retrieved from the database. You'll indicate the order in which condition tables should be accessed and specify which key values to use during the search (from sales order data or other data).

To maintain output determination access sequences, follow the menu path **SAP Customizing Implementation Guide • Sales and Distribution • Basic Functions • Output Determination • Output Determination • Output Determination Using the Condition Technique • Maintain Output Determination for Sales Documents • Maintain Access Sequences.** On the screen that opens, click on the **New Entries** button or press `F5`.

In our example shown in Figure 4.65, we're creating a new access sequence using the new condition table 902, which we created in the previous section. We're also including the same table used by the out-of-the-box configuration of the order acknowledgment output (BA00).

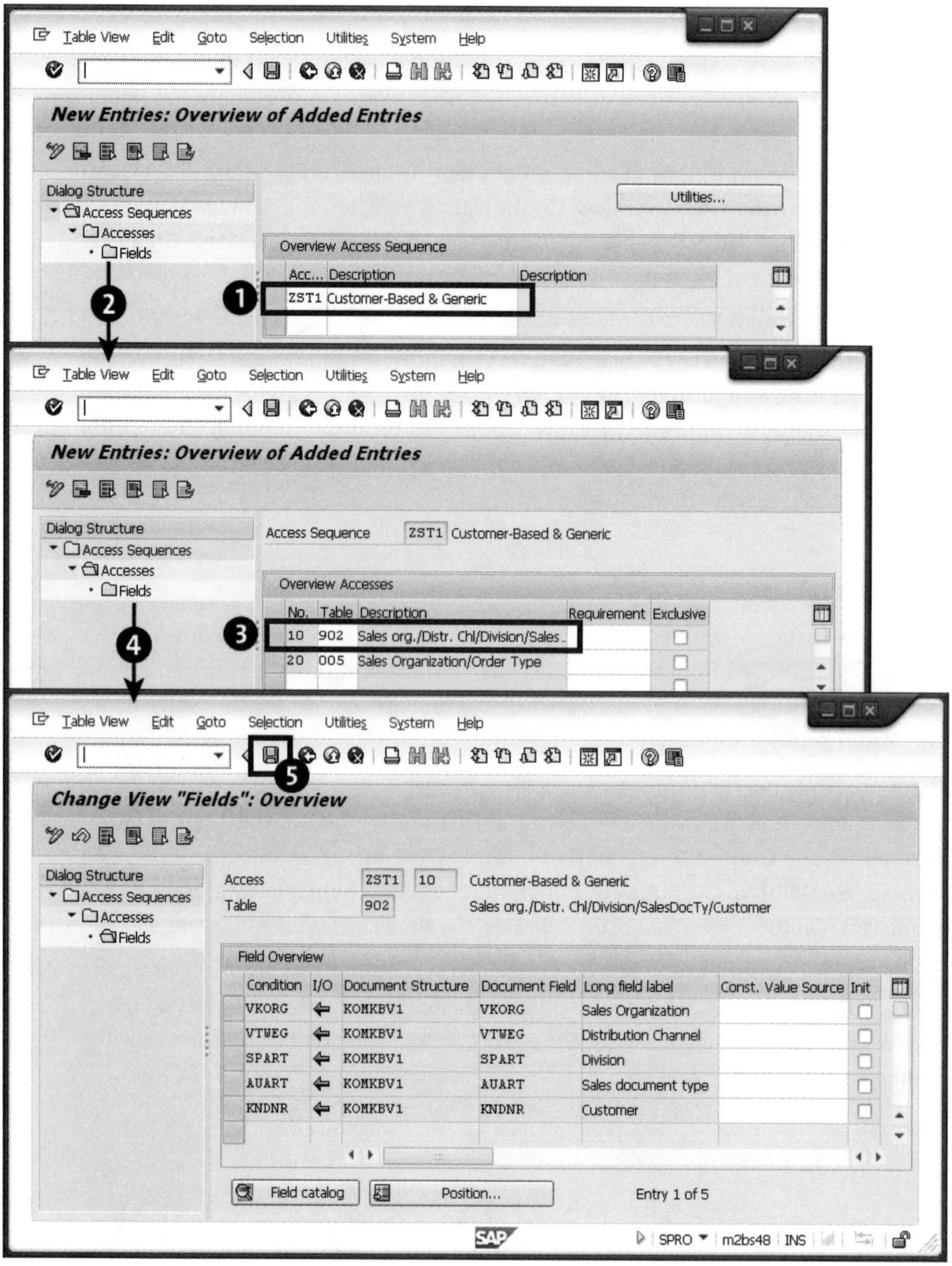

Figure 4.65 Maintaining Output Determination Access Sequences

To maintain the output determination access sequence, follow these steps:

❶ On this screen, first specify a four-character access sequence code (**Acc...**) and add a description (**Description**). The code must begin with "Z" indicating that is not provided by SAP (allowable namespace).

❷ Then, select the new entry created and double-click the **Accesses** option in the **Dialog Structure** menu on the left side of the screen.

❸ Next, enter each table on the lines available on this screen. You'll assign a number (**No.** column) to each line and enter the table number you want. You can also use a VOFM routine in the **Requirement** column, which allows for great flexibility when determining if data is applicable or not.

❹ Then, select the new line we just created and double-click on the **Fields** option on the **Dialog Structure** menu on the left side of the screen.

❺ With all field sources correctly identified, you can finally save the new access sequence.

4.7.4 Output Determination Condition Types

Condition types for output determination make new condition tables and access sequences available for usage. To maintain output determination condition types, follow the menu path **SAP Customizing Implementation Guide • Sales and Distribution • Basic Functions • Output Determination • Output Determination • Output Determination Using the Condition Technique • Maintain Output Determination for Sales Documents • Maintain Output Types**. On the screen that opens, click on the the **New Entries** button or press [F5].

At the top of the screen shown in Figure 4.66, enter the output type (**Output Type**) and add a description. In each of the tabs, maintain the following fields:

- **General Data**
  - The **Access Sequence** field indicates the access sequence that the condition type utilizes.
  - The **Access to Conditions** flag indicates that the output type should be automatically populated when a matching condition record is found based on the selected access sequence. If unchecked, users need to manually add this output type to sales orders.
  - The **Cannot be Changed** flag indicates that this output type must only be determined automatically based on condition records and cannot be modified manually.

- The **Multiple Issuing** flag indicates that this output type must be determined every time the sales order is modified. For customer-facing outputs, this flag can cause serious issues.
- The **Partner-Independent Output** flag indicates that this output type does not require the identification of a partner function.
- The **Do not Write Processing Log** flag indicates that the system is not required to generate an output log.
- The **Change Output/Replacement of Text Symbol** sections are relevant for forms developed using SAPScript, which is much older technology replaced by SmartForms. Some companies still use SAPScript; if yours does, indicate the program and form name on these fields.

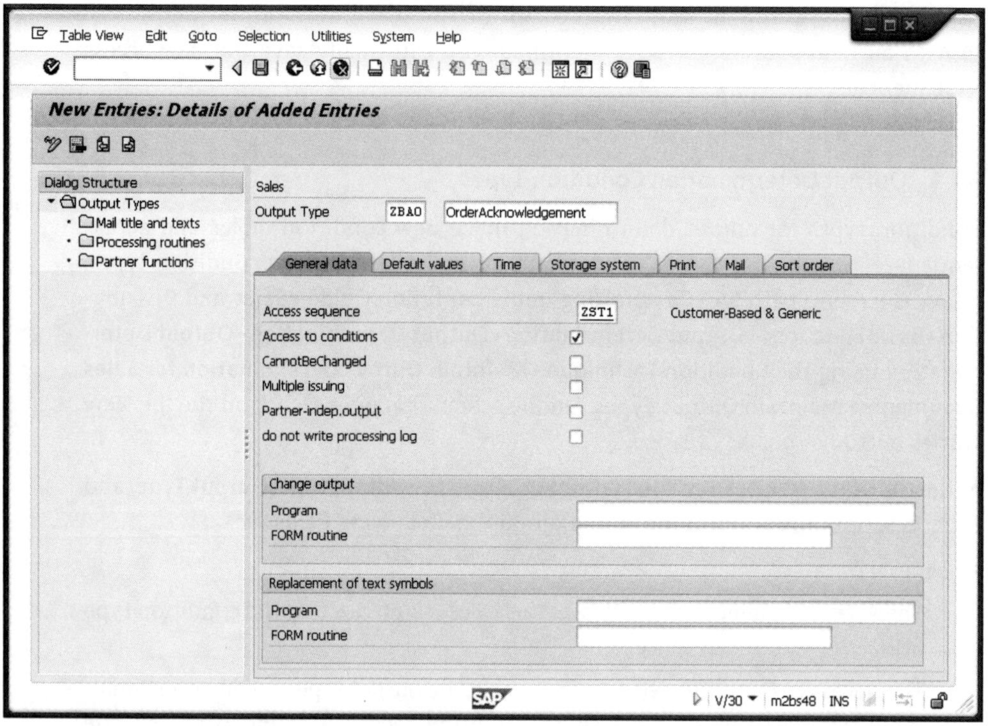

Figure 4.66 Output Type Configuration: General Data

- **Default values**

  Under this tab, you can indicate the values that the system must propose when a user is maintaining condition records.

- **Time**
  Under this tab, you can restrict certain values from being used in the dispatch **Date/Time** field on condition records.
- **Storage system**
  Under this tab, you can indicate what should happen with the output once issued.
- **Print parameters**
  Under this tab, you can control which fields you want to use to release printing jobs.
- **Mail**
  Under this tab, you can define parameters that allow for the automated mailing of print outputs.
- **Sort Order**
  Under this tab, shown in Figure 4.67, is used when we're issuing outputs using the dispatch **Date/Time** option 1 (Background Job); you can define how the printouts must be sorted, which affects efficiency by avoiding the need to browse a potentially large pile of paper to find a specific document you want. You can also use this tab to determine the order in which emails must be sent out.

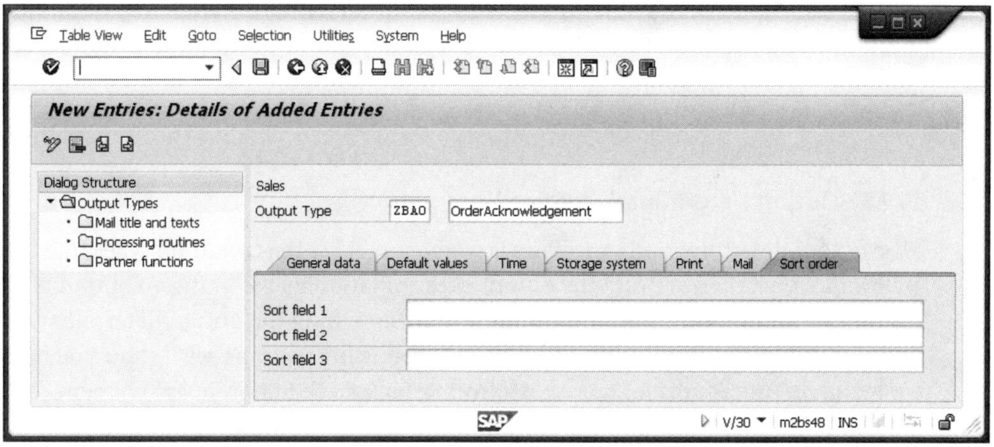

Figure 4.67 Output Type Configuration: Sort Order

Clicking the **Mail title and texts** option in the **Dialog Structure** menu, you can specify language-specific texts used to identify the output, as shown in Figure 4.68. This option typically is used as the email subject line.

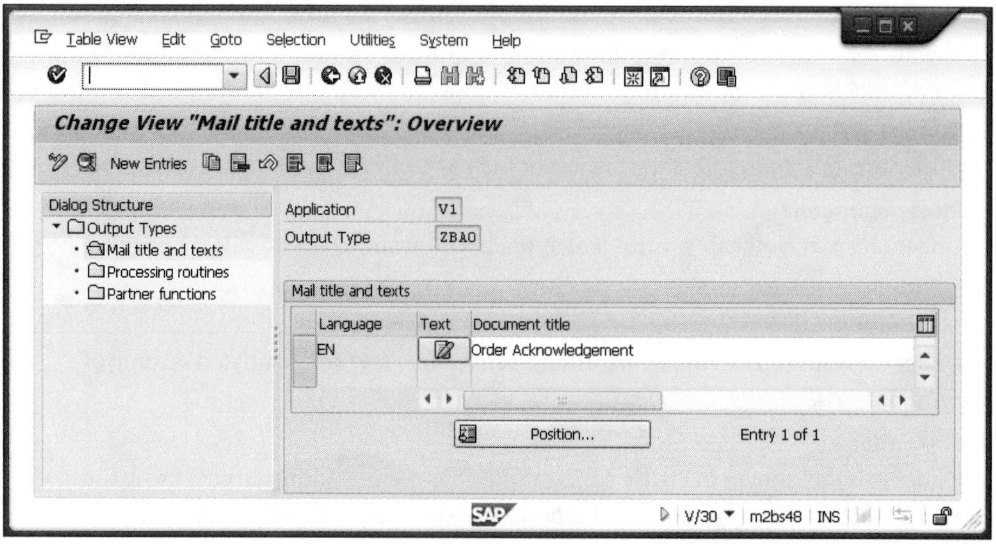

Figure 4.68 Output Type Configuration: Mail Title and Texts

Click **Processing Routines** in the **Dialog Structure** and indicate the name of the PDF/SmartForm routines you want to use. You can further define different definitions for each dispatch medium. By clicking the **Partner Function** option in the **Dialog Structure** menu, you can define the partner functions that are allowed for each dispatch medium.

4.7.5 Output Determination Procedures

The output determination procedure is where you'll list the condition types that are relevant. You'll then activate the output determination by assigning an output type to the output determination procedure and by assigning the output determination procedure to desired sales order types. In the following sections, we'll show you how to maintain procedures for output determination and then how to assign them.

Maintaining Procedure

To maintain output determination procedures, follow the menu path **SAP Customizing Implementation Guide • Sales and Distribution • Basic Functions • Output Determination • Output Determination • Output Determination Using the Condition Technique • Maintain Output Determination for Sales Documents • Maintain Output Determination Procedure.** On the screen that opens, click on the **New Entries** button or press [F5].

On the first screen, shown in Figure 4.69, specify a six-character output determination procedure code (**Procedure**) and add a description (**Description**). Press Enter. Then select the line.

Next, double-click the **Control Data** option under the **Dialog Structure**. On the screen that opens, click on the **New Entries** button or press F5 and enter the new step number (**Step**) and output determination condition type (**CTyp**). In this example, we're also setting up requirement routine 002 (**Requirement**) so that the output is only issued when the order is complete.

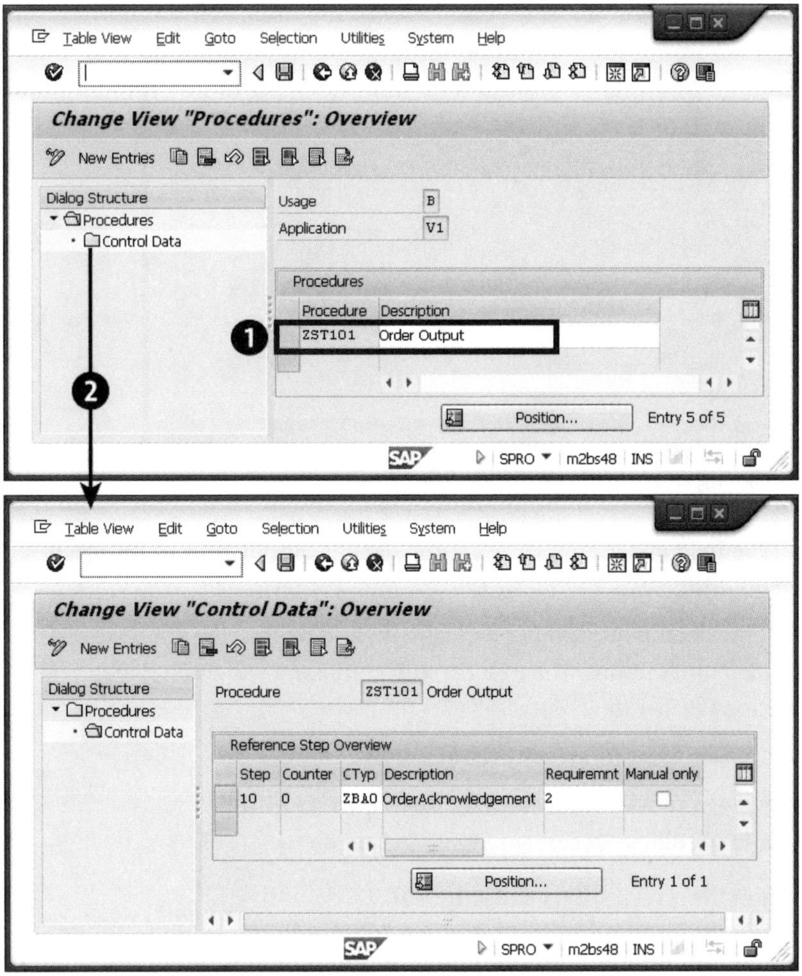

Figure 4.69 Maintaining Procedures for Output Determination

Assigning Procedures to Sales Document Types

To configure output determination procedures, follow the menu path **SAP Customizing Implementation Guide • Sales and Distribution • Basic Functions • Output Determination • Output Determination • Output Determination Using the Condition Technique • Maintain Output Determination for Sales Documents • Assign Output Determination Procedures • Allocate sales document header.**

On the screen shown in Figure 4.70, you'll need to find the sales order type (**SaTy**) to which you want to assign your procedure and then enter the output determination procedure (**Out.pr**).

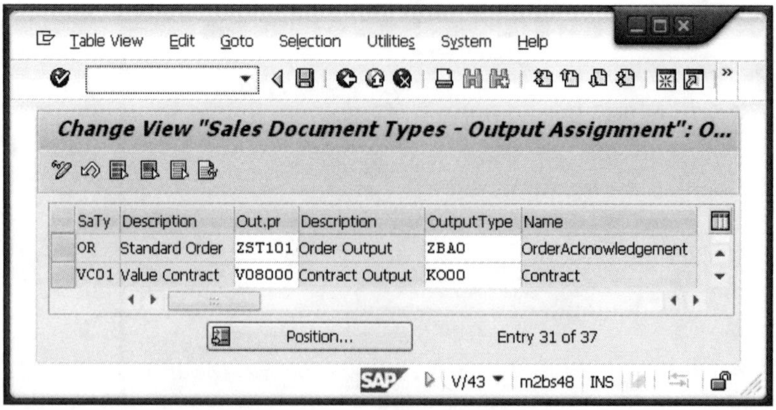

Figure 4.70 Assigning Output Determination Procedures to Sales Document Types

The **Output Type** field allows you to select the default output type to be processed when a user entering an order requests the document to be issued.

After we select the document number we want, instead of pressing enter we use one of the following menu options. The exact screen command will differ depending on which transaction you are in:

- Transaction VA02: **Sales Document • Issue Output To**
- Transaction VL02N: **Outbound Delivery • Issue Delivery Output**
- Transaction VF02: **Billing Document • Issue Output To**

This will result in the screen shown in Figure 4.71.

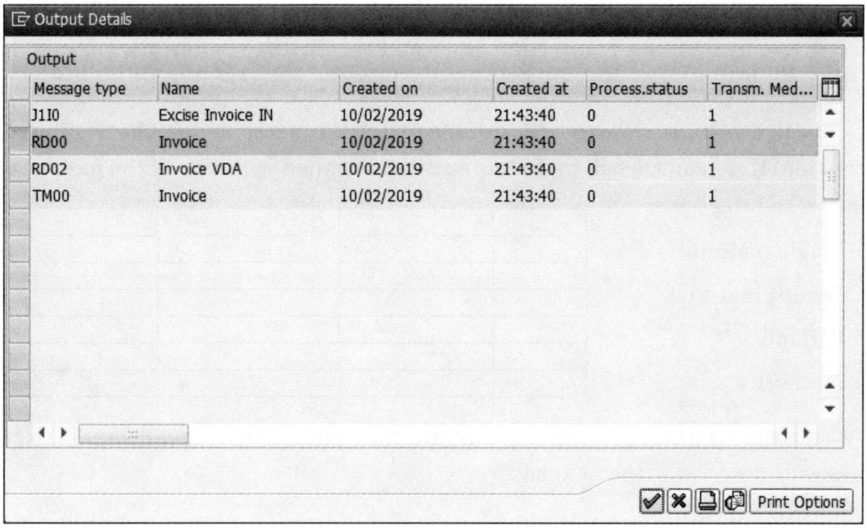

Figure 4.71 Output Type Details

4.8 Bonus Buy

Bonus buy is a feature that conditions discounts upon the purchase of a combination of materials or material groups. Bonus buy is only applicable for an SAP S/4HANA Retail (often called IS-Retail) environment; this requirement is enforced by the need to maintain material categories. We won't cover all aspects of bonus buys since this book is not specific for SAP S/4HANA Retail.

In this section, we'll highlight how to set up bonus buys, from material categories and master data to bonus buy profiles, number ranges, condition types, access sequences, condition tables, and pricing schemas.

4.8.1 Bonus Buy Material Categories

To use materials in a transaction, the material must be maintained with a material category on the basic data or sales views of the material master.

The **Material Category** field is not available on the material master data maintenance screen. A separate master data maintenance transaction contains the material category MM41, which does not allow any changes unless you activate SAP S/4HANA Retail (or the `ISR_Retail` Business Function Set). This decision is an action performed by the SAP Basis/infrastructure team. You can determine whether or not SAP S/4HANA Retail is active by opening Transaction SFW5 and the **Switch Framework Browser**. If not active, you'll first need to request activation before proceeding.

By default, all materials are assigned with the material category blank. Once material category MM41 is available, all materials must be assigned with one of the four relevant material categories:

- **00: Single material**
- **01: Generic material**
- **02: Variant**
- **10: Sales set**

Only with a material category set can you use the material with bonus buy master data, we we'll describe in the next section.

4.8.2 Bonus Buy Master Data

You can maintain bonus buy master data by opening Transaction RDMBBY01. Note that a global setting to allow the use of this transaction. Unless this change is made, the system only allows the maintenance of bonus buys using Transaction VBK1.

First, as shown in Figure 4.72, you'll need to enter the **Bonus Buy Profile**, which we'll configure in Section 4.8.4. Then, click **Continue** or press [Enter].

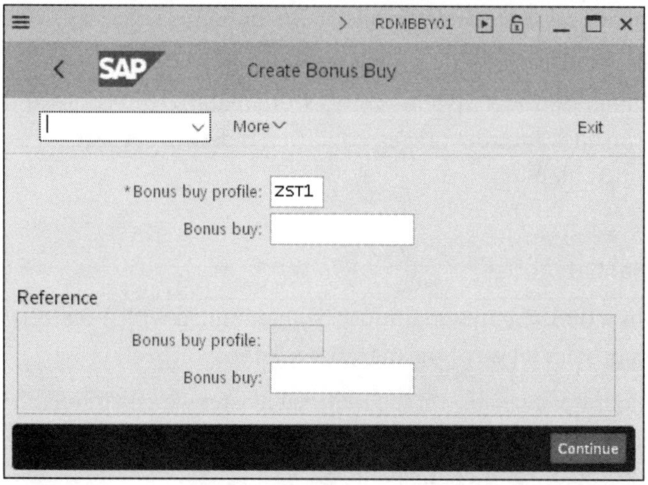

Figure 4.72 Creating Bonus Buy Master Data: Initial Screen

On the next screen, shown in Figure 4.73, maintain the following header data fields:

- **Bonus Buy** and its description
- **Valid From** and **To**
- **Bonus Buy Currency**

We then maximize the **Organizational Data**.

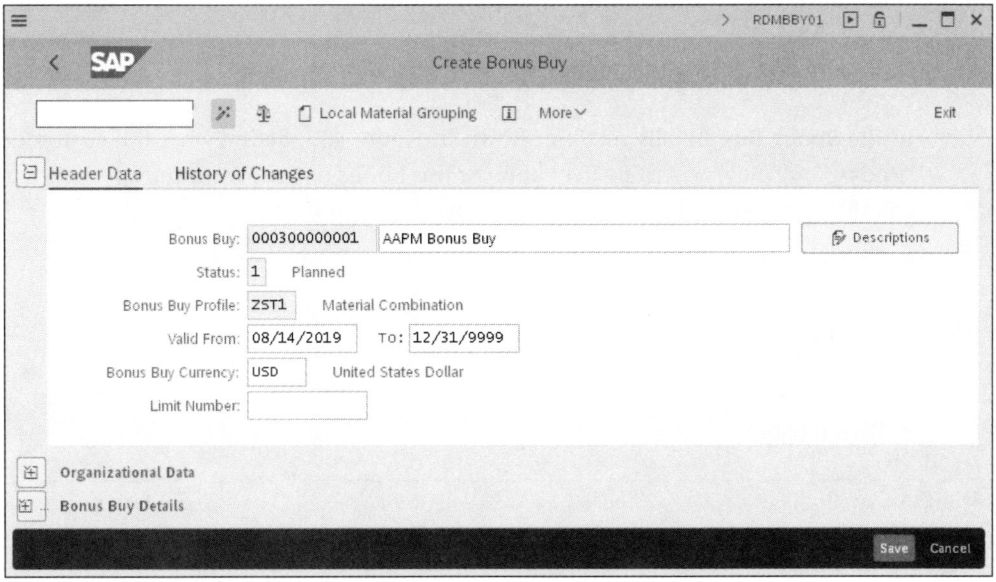

Figure 4.73 Creating Bonus Buy Master Data: Header Data

Then, click the **Insert Row** icon under **Organizational Data**, as shown in Figure 4.74, and populate the following fields:

- Sales organization (**SOrg.**)
- Distribution channel (**DChl**)
- Price list type (**PL**)
- **Valid From** and **Valid To** dates for this organizational data

If applicable, you can also indicate the plant. We then maximize the **Bonus Buy Details**.

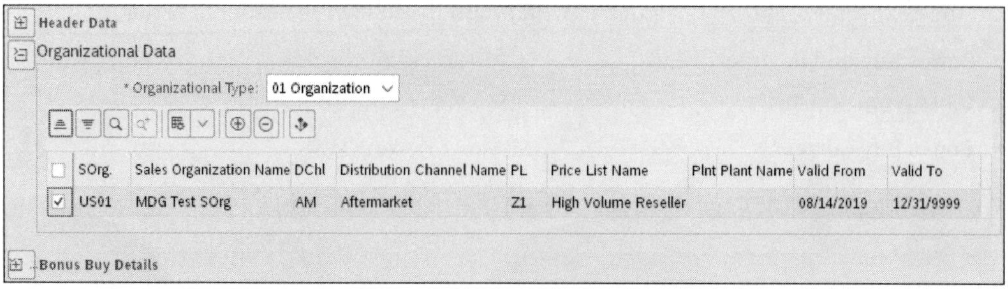

Figure 4.74 Creating Bonus Buy Master Data: Organizational Data

In the **Bonus Buy Details** section, shown in Figure 4.75, define what the customer needs to buy (**Buy**) according to qualify for this bonus buy program and specify what will they get (**Get**) using the following fields:

- **Line Item Type**
- Line item **Id**
- **Quantity**
- **Sales Unit**
- **Discount Type**

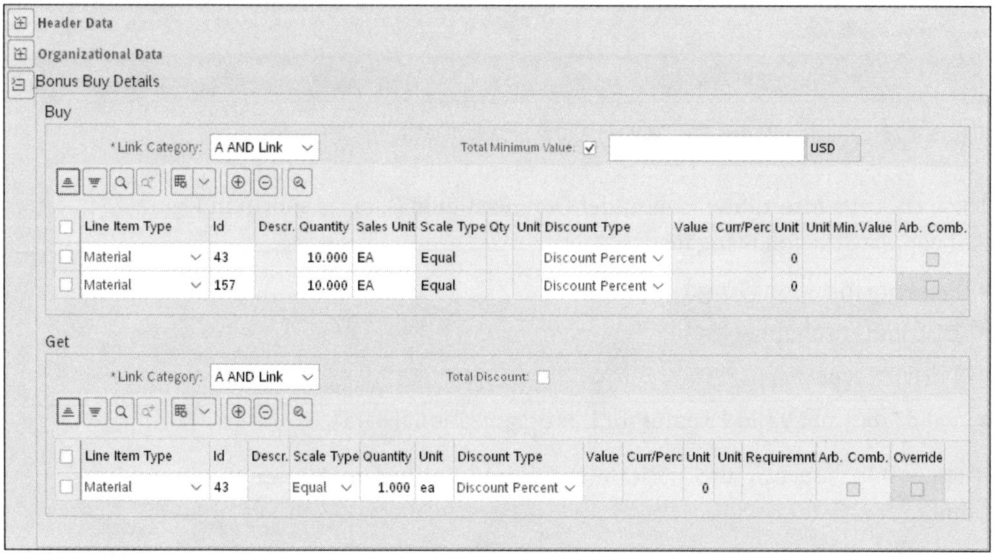

Figure 4.75 Creating Bonus Buy Master Data: Bonus Buy Details

4.8.3 Maintaining the Bonus Buy Application

To maintain bonus buy condition records (master data), follow the menu path **SAP Customizing Implementation Guide • Sales and Distribution • Basic Functions • Bonus Buy • Maintain Application**.

As shown in Figure 4.76, select the new **Bonus Buy Application** code **N** for Transaction RDMBBY01 (Maintenance of Condition Records/Master Data) instead of the transaction used in previous versions of the system (Transaction VBK1).

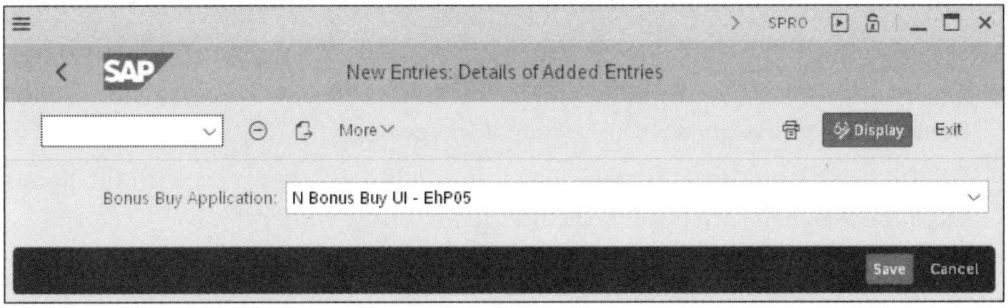

Figure 4.76 Maintaining Bonus Buy Maintenance Application

4.8.4 Bonus Buy Profiles

To configure bonus buy profiles, follow the menu path **SAP Customizing Implementation Guide • Sales and Distribution • Basic Functions • Bonus Buy • Maintain Bonus Buy Profiles.** On the screen that opens, click on the **New Entries** button or press F5.

As shown in Figure 4.77, specify a four-character bonus buy profile code (**BB Profile**) and add a description (**Profile Description**).

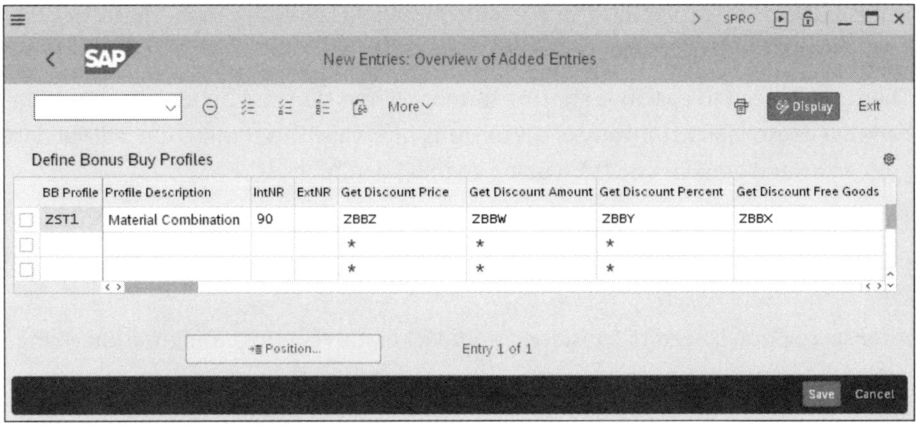

Figure 4.77 Defining a New Bonus Buy Profile

You'll need to specify the internally assigned number range interval number (**IntNR**) and an externally assigned number range interval number (**ExtNR**), if applicable. These values will define the bonus buy document number when created in Transaction RDMBBY01, as described in Section 4.8.1.

You can then indicate the bonus buy condition types used in this profile, as follows:

- **Get Discount Price** represents a discounted price condition type, as defined Section 4.8.6, with the **Bonus Buy Type** assigned with the code **P** (price).
- **Get Discount Amount** represents a currency-based discount amount condition type, with the **Bonus Buy Type** assigned with the code **R** (fixed discount).
- **Get Discount Percent** represents a discounted percentage condition type, with the **Bonus Buy Type** assigned with the code **%** (percentage).
- **Get Discount Free Goods** represents a free goods condition type, with the **Bonus Buy Type** assigned with the code **N** (free goods).

4.8.5 Bonus Buy Number Ranges

To configure bonus buy number range intervals, open Transaction RDMBBYNR01 or follow the menu path **SAP Customizing Implementation Guide • Sales and Distribution • Basic Functions • Bonus Buy • Maintain Number Ranges**.

In our Transaction RDMBBYNR01 example shown in Figure 4.78, we're creating a new internally assigned number range called **90** to be used in bonus buy master data. To start, click on the **Intervals** button and then click the **Insert Line** button or press F6 to create a new number range interval.

Next, specify a two-character number range interval number (**No**). We recommend using entries that start with a 9 or a Z, which are in the allowable namespace, to avoid conflict with future upgrades.

Then, you'll need to specify a starting number (**From No.**) and upper limit (**To Number**) that doesn't fall within any of the existing intervals. This transaction will validate your entry and prevent you from using an invalid number.

The **Ext** column, if left blank, indicates whether this range should be used for internally assigned number ranges. For externally assigned number ranges, you would select this flag.

After saving, you'll need to consider the impact of moving this configuration change across different systems.

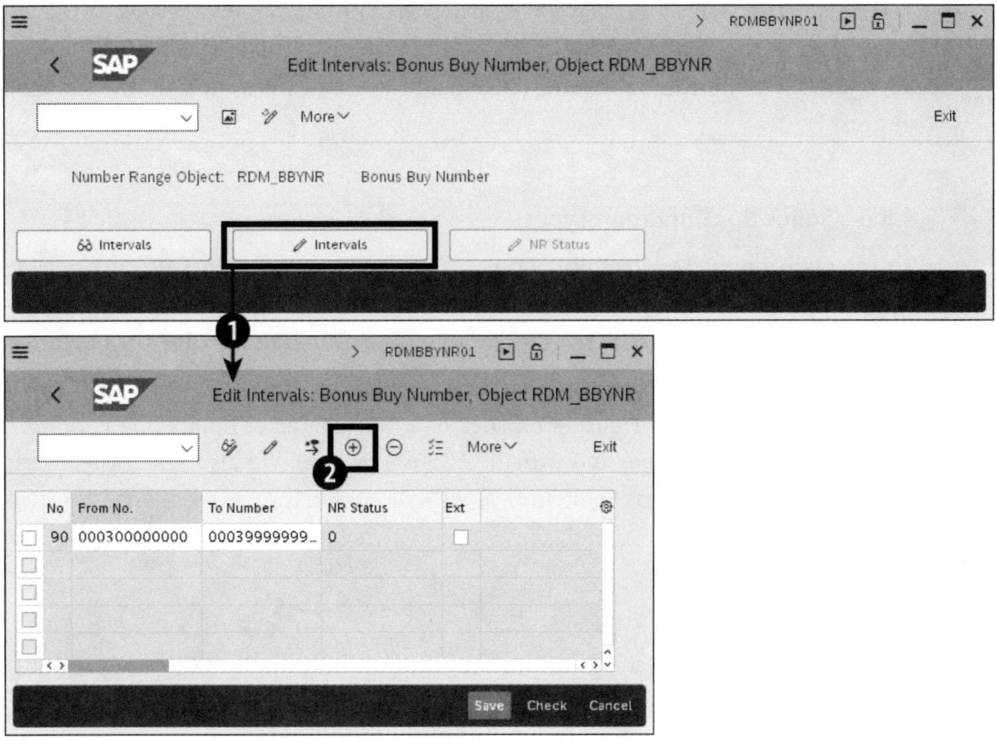

Figure 4.78 Defining a New Bonus Buy Number Range Interval

Number ranges are not automatically transported because of the **NR Status** column. This column contains the last number used within this number range. Each system would have a different NR status. Thus, when transporting number ranges from one system to another, copying the status value would cause a short dump. Thus, instead of transporting number ranges, companies often opt to manually set up new number ranges on each system.

When saving a new number range, the system will warn you if number ranges may overlap.

Transaction RDMBBYNR01 would take you directly to this screen. Note also that you'll need special access to perform this action, including open the destination client for configuration, a task that can only be perform with SAP Basis/system admin access.

You can also use Transaction SNUM or SNRO to maintain number ranges. But you'll need to know the number range object: For bonus buy number ranges, the object is **RDM_BBYNR** (bonus buy number). You would then click the **Interval Editing** button or press F7.

4.8.6 Bonus Buy Condition Types

To maintain bonus buy condition types, follow the menu path **SAP Customizing Implementation Guide • Sales and Distribution • Basic Functions • Bonus Buy • Maintain Condition Types.** On the screen that opens, click on the **New Entries** button or press F5.

On the screen shown in Figure 4.79, specify a four-character bonus buy condition type code (**Condition type**) and provide a name (**Name**). We also select the access sequence it will use (**Access Sequence**), as we'll discuss in the next section.

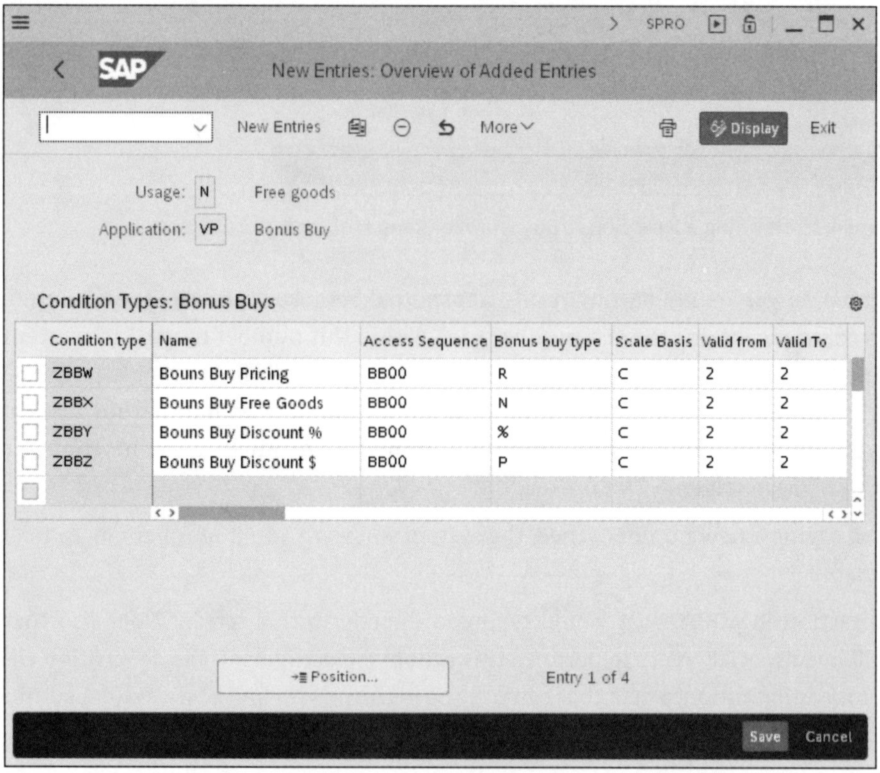

Figure 4.79 Creating New Condition Types for Bonus Buy

The **Bonus Buy Type** indicates the calculation type, whether percentage (**%**), fixed discount (**R**), free goods (**N**), or price (**P**). This selection will affect the layout of the bonus buy condition record (master data) maintenance screen and ultimately affect the way bonus buy discounts are calculated.

You must define at least one bonus buy condition type for **Bonus Buy Types %** (percentage), **R** (fixed discount), and **P** (price) to create a bonus buy profile, as described in Section 4.8.4. **Bonus Buy Type N** (free goods) is optional.

Scale Basis allows you to define different discount amounts depending on the total relevant quantity, value, weight, etc., that a customer must purchase to be eligible. This value also affects the layout of the bonus buy condition records (master data) maintenance screen and ultimately affect the way bonus buy discounts are calculated.

The **Valid From** and **Valid To** fields are indicators that allow you to select the default validity dates the system will propose on the maintenance screen for bonus buy condition records (master data), whenever an end user leaves these fields blank.

4.8.7 Bonus Buy Access Sequences

To maintain bonus buy access sequences, follow the menu path **SAP Customizing Implementation Guide • Sales and Distribution • Basic Functions • Bonus Buy • Maintain Access Sequence.**

In our example shown in Figure 4.80, we're displaying the existing access sequence **BB00** and focusing on the condition table **201** (displayed in the following section) for illustrative purposes.

To maintain bonus buy access sequences, follow these steps:

❶ Find and select the desired **Access Sequence** (**BB00**) to be displayed.

❷ Then, double-click on the **Accesses** option on the **Dialog Structure** menu on the left side of the screen.

❸ Next, select the access sequence step number (**No.**) containing the desired condition table **201**.

❹ Finally, double-click on **Fields** in the **Dialog Structure** menu on the left side of the screen.

Now, review the field sources and exit the transaction.

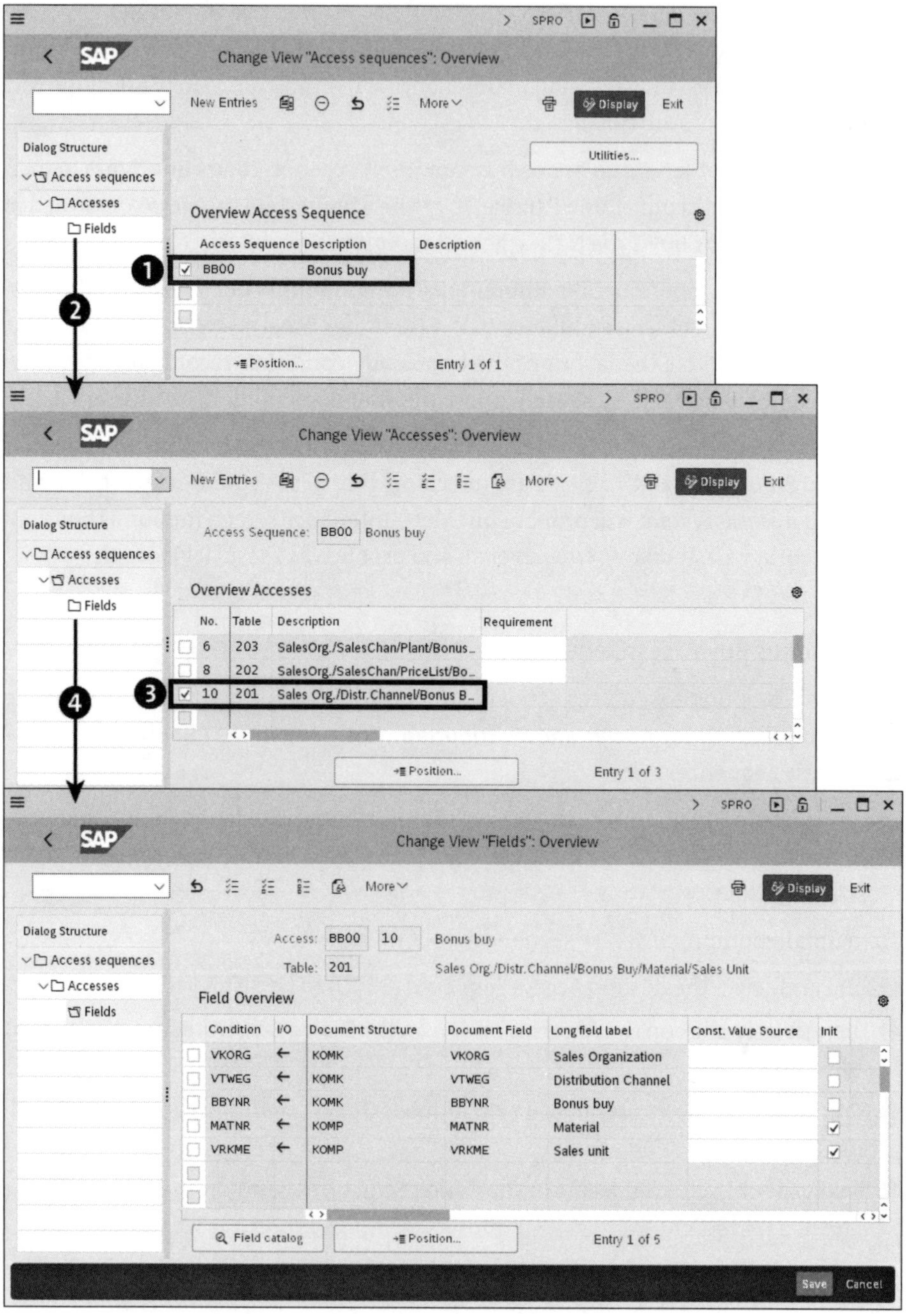

Figure 4.80 Displaying Bonus Buy Access Sequences

4.8.8 Bonus Buy Condition Tables

To maintain bonus buy condition tables, open Transaction VBKB or follow the menu path **SAP Customizing Implementation Guide • Sales and Distribution • Basic Functions • Bonus Buy • Maintain Condition Table**.

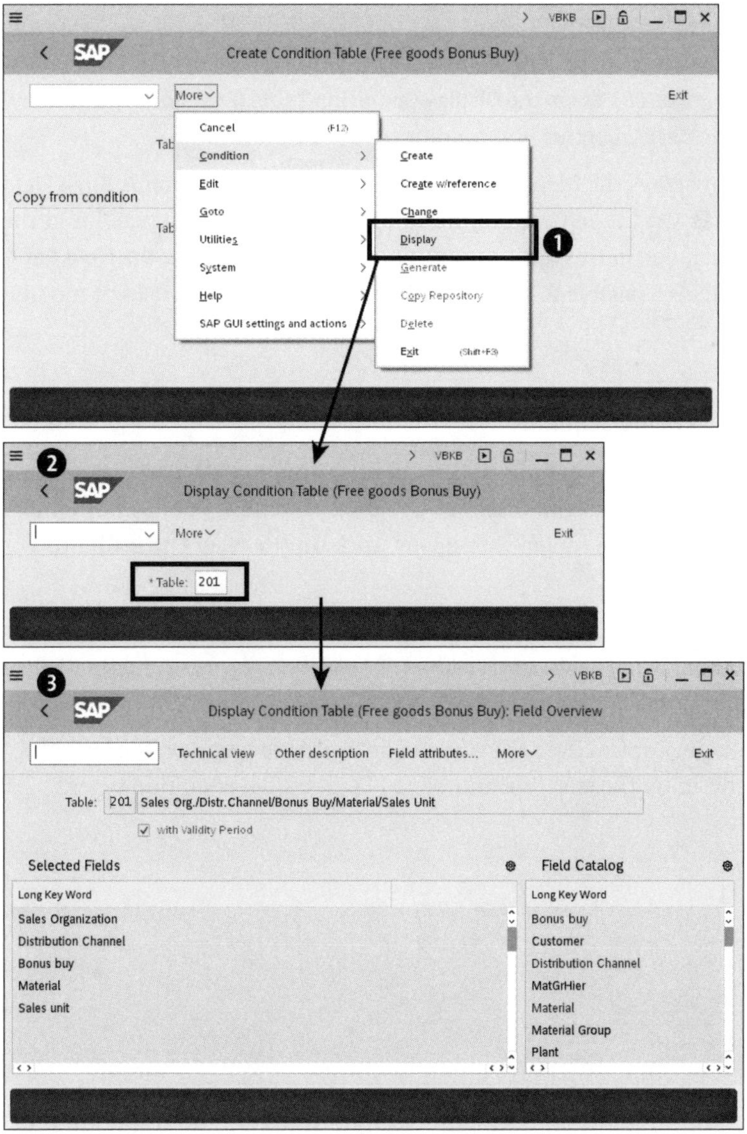

Figure 4.81 Displaying Bonus Buy Condition Tables

In our example shown in Figure 4.81, we're displaying the existing bonus buy condition table 201. Each condition technique functionality has a different application code and a corresponding table prefix. "KOTN" is the prefix for bonus buys. Therefore, condition table 201 is the representation of database table KOTN201, which was generated by the system when table 201 was first configured.

By default, Transaction VBKB will allow you to create condition tables. Open the transaction and switch to display mode by using the menu options **Condition • Display** as shown in Figure 4.81 ❶. On the **Display Condition Table (Free goods Bonus Buy)** screen ❷, enter the desired bonus buy condition table and press Enter.

The system then displays the **Display Condition Table (Free goods Bonus Buy): Field Overview** screen ❸. On the left side of the **Selected Fields** window, you'll find the fields currently included in this table as keys. On the right, you'll find the **Field Catalog** with a list of fields available to choose from when creating new tables or modifying existing ones.

4.8.9 Bonus Buy Pricing Schemas

To configure bonus buy pricing procedures, follow the menu path **SAP Customizing Implementation Guide • Sales and Distribution • Basic Functions • Bonus Buy • Maintain Pricing Schema**. On the screen that opens, click on the **New Entries** button or press F5.

On the first screen shown in Figure 4.82, specify a six-character bonus buy procedure code (**Procedure**) ❶ and add a description (**Description**). Press Enter and then select the line you just created.

Next, double-click on **Control Data** ❷ in the **Dialog Structure** menu on the left side of the screen. Finally, enter the step line number and the desired condition types.

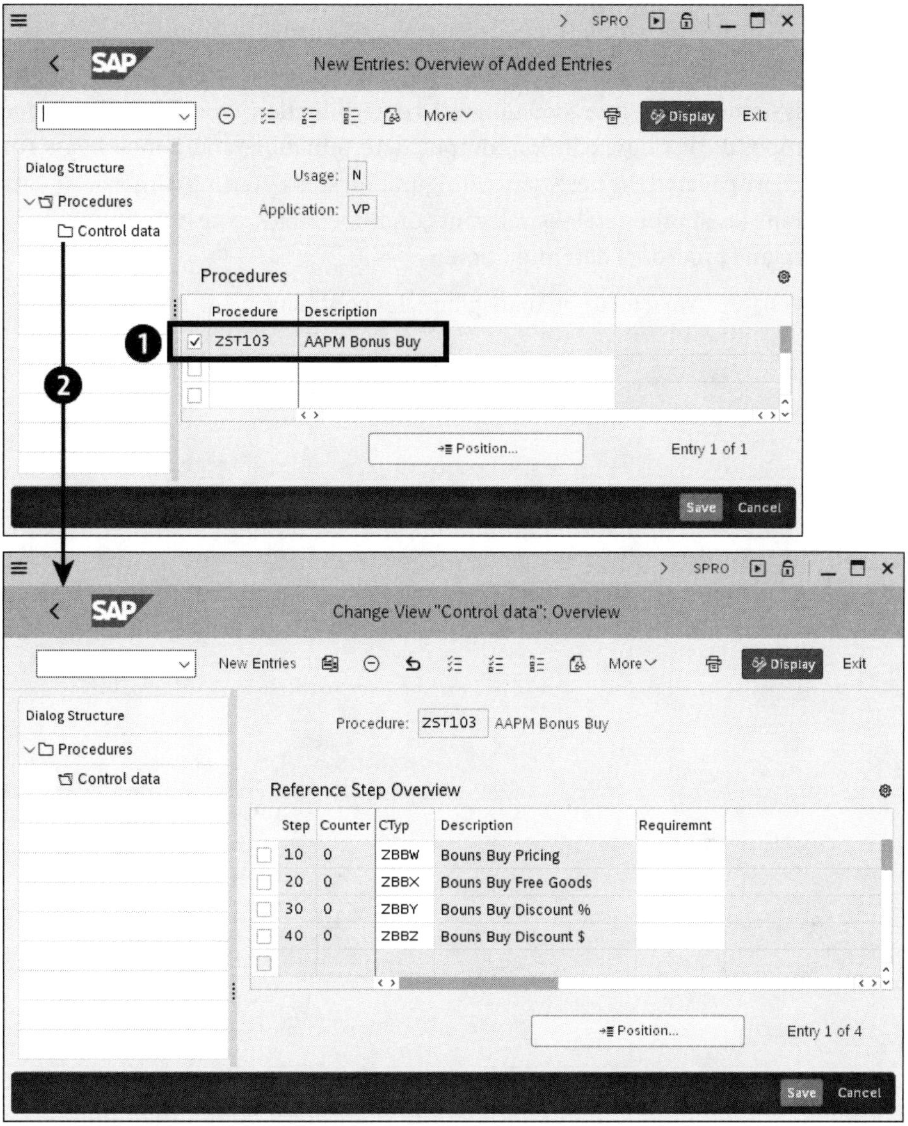

Figure 4.82 Defining a New Bonus Buy Pricing Procedure

4.9 Summary

In this chapter, we covered the main condition technique-based features of the SAP S/4HANA system: pricing, free goods, material determination, cross-selling, dynamic product proposals, listing/exclusion, output determination, and bonus buys. For each feature, we covered the necessary configuration steps, starting with master data and describing (as appropriate) the relevant condition tables, access sequences, condition types, and procedure determination.

In the next chapter, we'll focus on managing sales contracts in SAP S/4HANA Sales.

Chapter 5
Sales Contract and Agreement Management

Sales contracts are used to represent binding agreements between your company and its customers. Sales contracts could serve as a legal contract or a commercial agreement or both. By representing these contracts in the system, you can automate their processing and trace their evolution.

Companies that have contracts with their customers usually need to control how those contracts affect the sales prices, availability, and other transactional data, and SAP S/4HANA Sales' contract and agreement functionality helps you with all those tasks.

Note that, for contract authoring, a different tool is provided by SAP called SAP Contract Lifecycle Management. If a significant enough portion of your business requires contracts, and the contracts are written by your company implementing SAP, this tool is worth evaluating.

In SAP S/4HANA Sales, contracts and agreements are sales document that are maintained before transactions can start happening. Note, however, that a contract is also a transactional element of its own. In this chapter, we'll focus on both sales contracts (Section 5.1) and sales rebate agreements (Section 5.2).

5.1 Master, Value, and Quantity Contracts

In SAP S/4HANA, you can limit sales conditions by quantity or value in quantity contracts and value contracts, respectively. In other words, you can define a special price for a customer up to a certain quantity or a total dollar value. Once they purchase the agreed limit, that customer can no longer take advantage of the special contract price. This type of contract is not used to define the minimum quantity they need to purchase before being eligible for a discount, which is handled by rebate contracts (Section 5.2).

Quantity contracts (Section 5.1.2) and value contracts (Section 5.1.3) define upper limits that prevent a customer from depleting the whole inventory available at deeply discounted prices. These contracts are commonly used as negotiation tools; the prices offered often have a low profit margin and are awarded in exchange for other businesses or to launch a new product line.

If your company uses sales order stock, such as in a make-to-order manufacturing scenario, quantity and value contracts allow you to share inventory manufactured for one document with another based on the contract number. The stock would be assigned to the contract and not to the specific document that generated the demand.

In some scenarios, you may have several contracts that are part of the same business deal. In this case, you may benefit from having a master contract (Section 5.1.1) with which you can create other transactions. This approach allows you to control functionality across all documents and tie them all together for reporting and profitability analysis.

In SAP S/4HANA 1809, the master contract document type is not provided out of the box, but you can configure it if necessary. Few companies use master contracts.

Figure 5.1 shows how the types of contracts interact with each other and with sales orders. The master contract, when needed, is created first. Next, you'll create other quantity and/or value contracts with reference to the master contract.

A subsequent sales order can be created with reference to either the quantity or the value contract. If you don't create the sales order with reference to the contract, the sales order won't take advantage of any of the data defined for in the quantity or value contract. In the following sections, we'll walk you through this process.

Contracts can also be used in conjunction with the billing plan functionality to allow for periodic billing (monthly, quarterly, etc.) on a membership basis through subscription-based agreements. These types of agreements can be implemented in other types of sales documents, but with contracts, you are able to create other sales documents that reference the contract and limit the quantity and value of those sales document. For example, if your company offers monthly subscription packages to customers that, amongst other benefits, allow them to place sales order at a very low price during the subscription period, you can limit them to only purchasing five of select materials during that time. You can create a quantity contract with a billing plan and specify the materials and maximum quantities that a customer can order as part of this subscription contract.

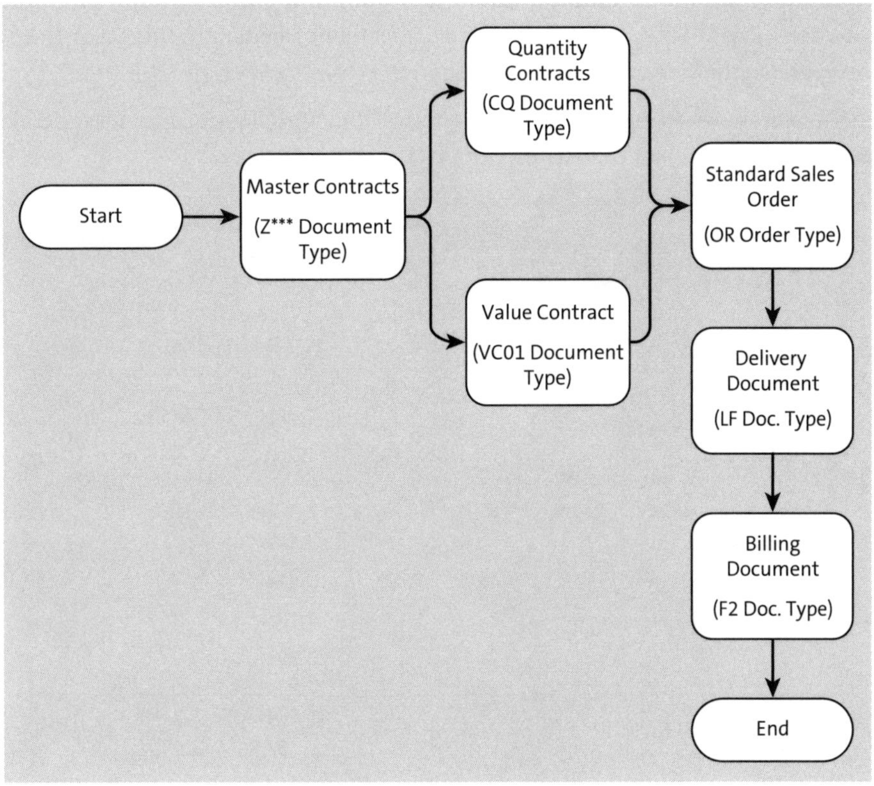

Figure 5.1 Quantity, Value, and Master Contract Processing

More details about billing plans can be found in Chapter 10.

5.1.1 Master Contracts

Master contracts can serve the quantity and value contracts in the same way they can serve to sales orders—as a source of the contract-relevant data and a way to group relevant document together.

Since no master contract types are defined out of the box, you must first define master contract types. Before you can enter a master contract with this new document type, you'll also need to define reference sales document types and define referencing procedures. We'll walk you through all of these steps in the following sections.

Defining Master Contract Document Types

To configure sales document types, such as master contracts types, open Transaction VOV8 or follow the menu path **SAP Customizing Implementation Guide • Sales and Distribution • Sales • Sales Documents • Sales Document Header • Define Sales Document Types**. On the screen that opens, click on the **New Entries** button or press [F5].

On the screen shown in Figure 5.2, specify a four-character sales document type code (**Sales Document Type**) and add a description (**Description**).

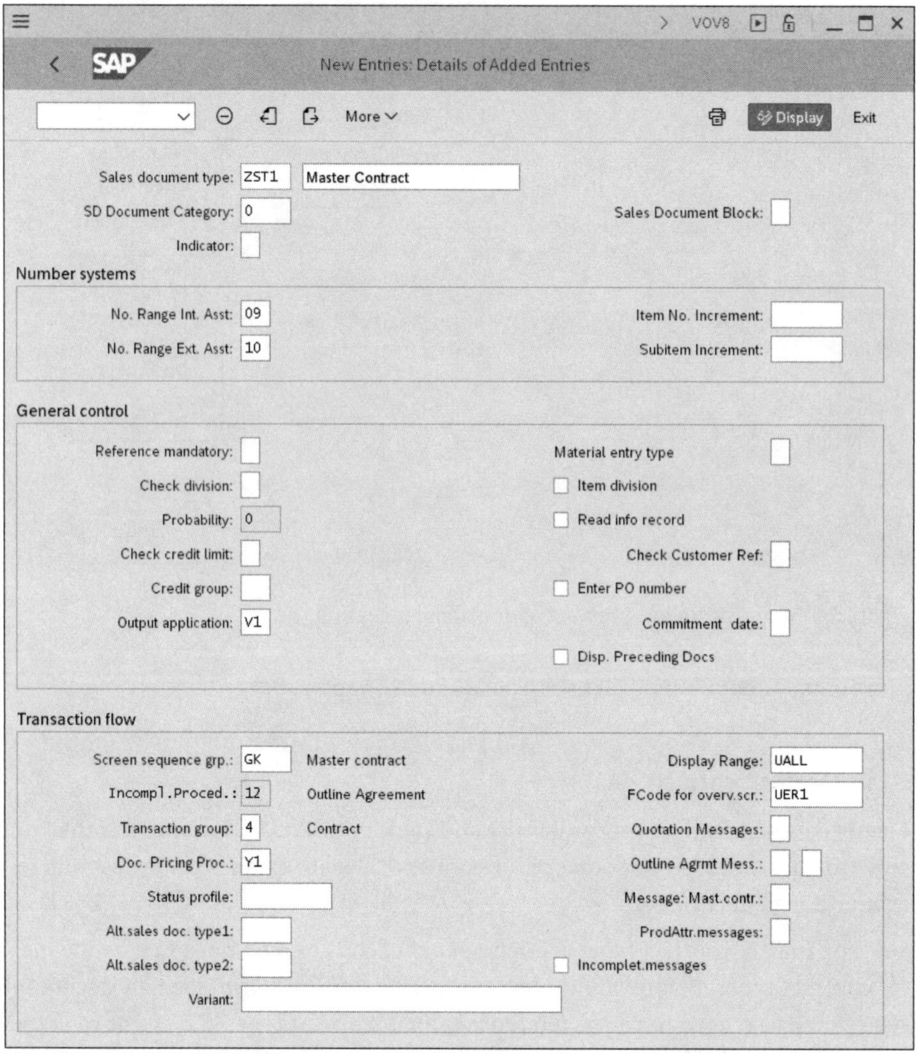

Figure 5.2 Defining Master Contract Document Types

This screen includes the data you'll need to maintain to successfully define a master contract. Chapter 6, Section 6.1.1 has more details about other configuration fields on this screen.

For now, we're only highlighting the field that are mandatory for master contracts, as follows:

- The **SD Document Category** must be "0" (**Master Contract**).
- The **Screen Sequence Grp.** must be "GK" (**Master Contract**).
- The **Transaction Group** must be "4" (**Contract**).

The other fields may be modified according to your company's requirements.

Defining Reference Sales Document Types

To configure reference sales document types for master contracts, open Transaction VORB or follow the menu path **SAP Customizing Implementation Guide • Sales and Distribution • Sales • Sales Documents • Contracts • Master Contract • Define Referencing Requirements • Define Reference Sales Document Types**. On the screen that opens, click on the **New Entries** button or press F5.

First, select the target sales document type (**TarDoc**) and source document type (**Source**). In the screenshot shown in Figure 5.3, we're specifying that, for master contract ZST1, which we created, we'll be allowed to create both quantity and value contracts.

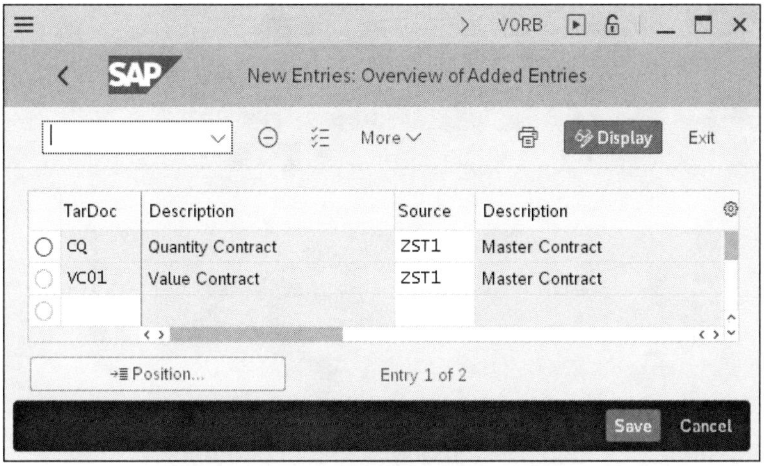

Figure 5.3 Defining Reference Sales Document Types

Defining Referencing Procedures

To configure referencing procedures, open Transaction VORB or follow the menu path **SAP Customizing Implementation Guide • Sales and Distribution • Sales • Sales Documents • Contracts • Master Contract • Define Referencing Requirements • Define Referencing Procedures**. On the screen that opens, click on the **New Entries** button or press F5.

As shown in Figure 5.4, you must first specify a four-character reference procedure code (**Ref.Proc.**) and add a description (**Description**). Then, press Enter and select the entry you just created. Next, double-click on the **Fields** option under **Dialog Structure** menu tree on the left side of the screen. Now, you can enter the fields that you want to copy from the master contract onto the contracts that refer to it.

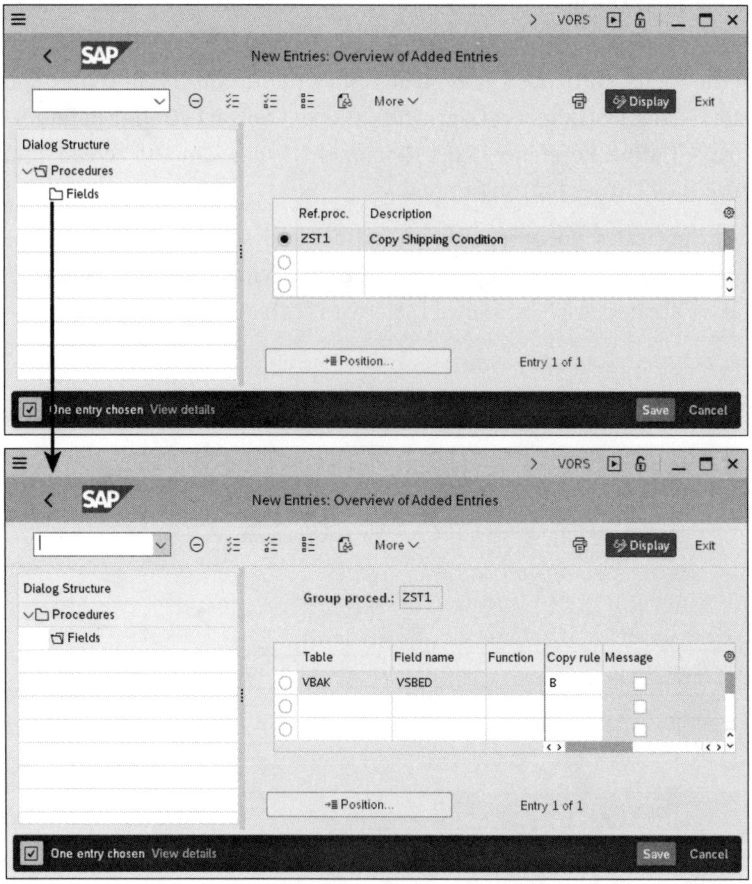

Figure 5.4 Defining Referencing Procedures

In our example, we're including the **Shipping Condition** field (field VSBED in table VBAK) and indicating the **Copy Rule** B (always copy).

These settings replace the copy control configuration and is unique for master contracts. With this approach, you won't enter a copy control configuration for a master contract, and doing so is actually discouraged. In Section 5.1.2 and Section 5.1.3, we'll describe how to assign quantity and values contracts to master contracts without creating them with reference.

Creating Master Contract

Once this configuration is in place, open Transaction VA41 to create a master contract. Select the contract types you want configure and enter the data shown in Figure 5.5 and Figure 5.6. In this particular master contract, we're defining a special shipping condition, **03 (Immediately)**, for this master contract. All contracts linked to this master contract will be eligible for the special shipping condition.

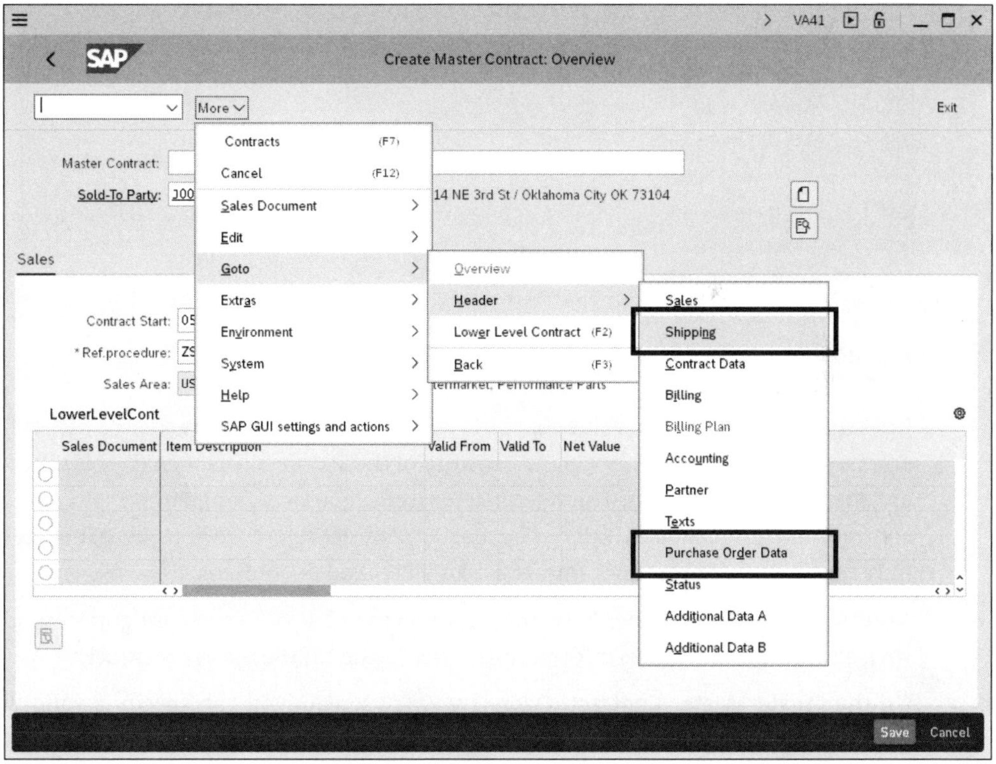

Figure 5.5 Create Master Contract Overview Screen

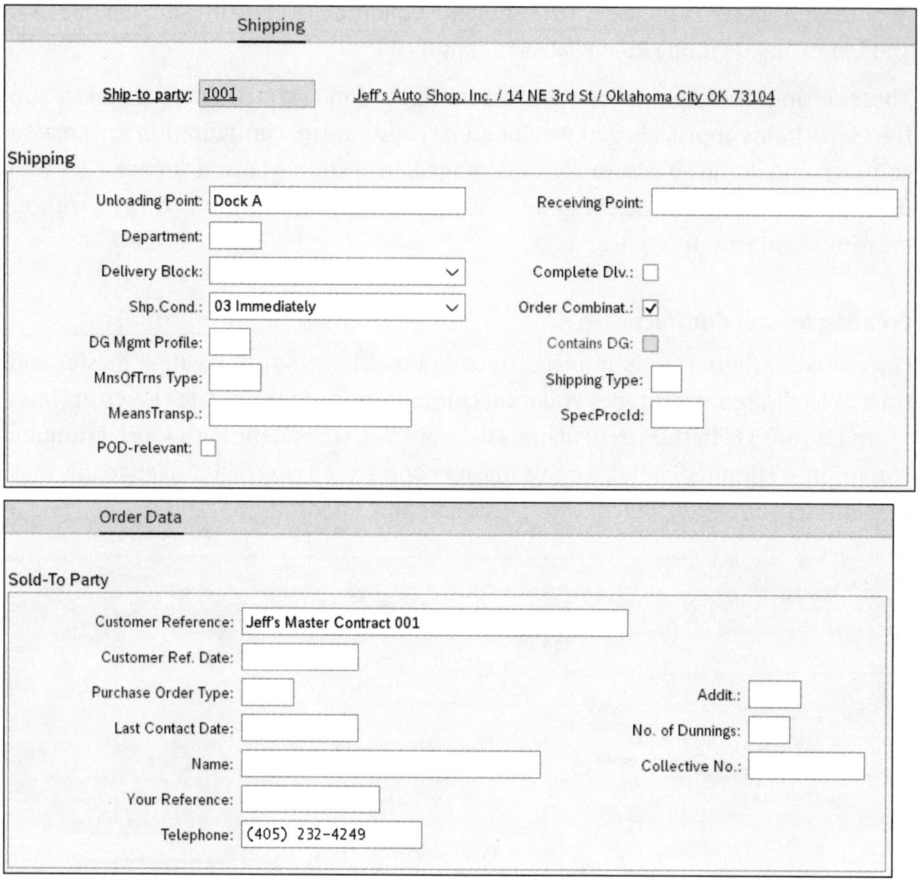

Figure 5.6 Shipping and (Purchase) Order Data Tabs

Note that the quantity and value contracts will affect the sales orders created with reference to them, limiting the value or quantity of these orders. That behavior is different than master contracts. The reference procedure affects the quantity and value contract and thus the sales orders. The master contract reference procedure includes only the fields that must be common across all related documents.

Note also that the **Customer Reference** is set as mandatory in our configuration, so we'll also need to enter this information in the header of the master contract.

On the **Create Master Contract: Overview** entry screen, you can specify a validity period (**Contract Start** and **Contract End** dates), which indicates that the interval of time during which this contract can be used to create sales orders.

You're required to enter the **Reference Procedure** configured in the previous section.

Now, you can go to the header of the master contract and enter the **Customer Reference** on the **Order Data** tab and the **Shipping Conditions** on the **Shipping** tab.

5.1.2 Quantity Contracts

Quantity contracts are created using Transaction VA41. Figure 5.7 shows the item overview screen you'll use to enter contract data after selecting the **CQ** document type on the initial screen and clicking the **Continue** button. Do not click the **Create with Reference** button, even if you have a master contract to use as reference.

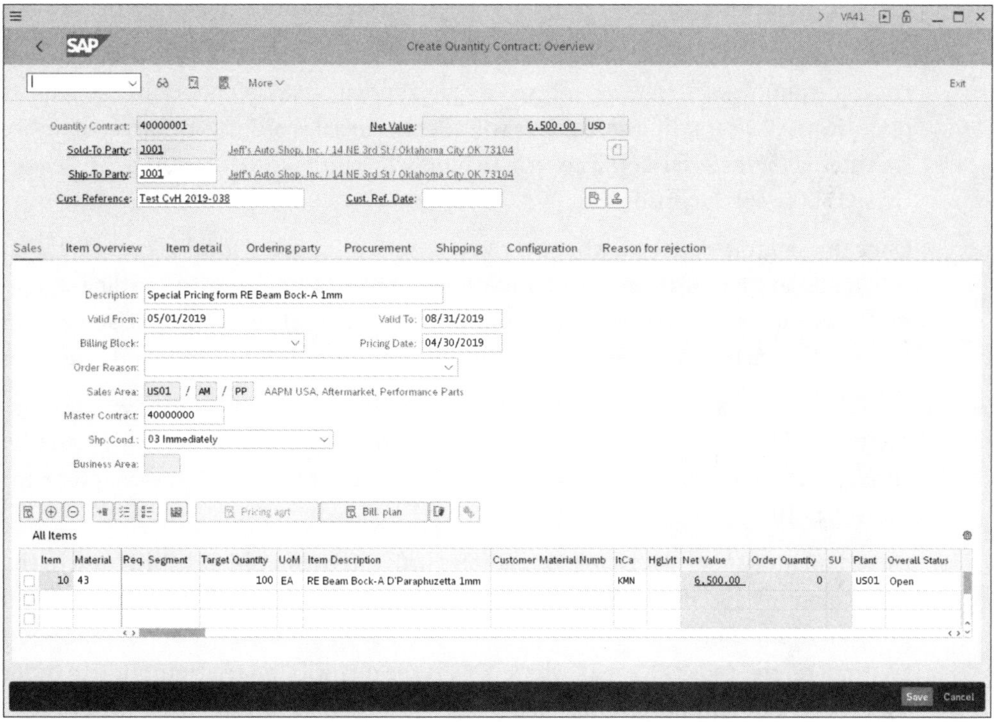

Figure 5.7 Creating a Quantity Contract

Let's highlight the fields that are different on this screen when compared to the standard sales order described in Chapter 6.

For contracts, you'll need to enter a description (**Description**) to help when browsing for the correct document at the time of sales order entry. you'll also need to enter a validity period (**Valid From** and **Valid To** dates), which indicates that the interval of time during which this contract can be used to create sales orders.

You can also select a master contract (**Master Contract**) to link to this quantity contract. This approach will trigger the reference procedure, which will copy all relevant fields from the master contract into this quantity contract. Note, however, that because we're not using the copy control, the document flow is not updated with the master contract reference. To see all quantity and value contracts created with this type of reference, you can display the master contract in Transaction VA43.

Other fields, when populated, can be copied over to sales orders created with reference to this contract (according to the copy control configuration and routines defined). Make sure you only populate the fields you want to copy over to the sales order—the main reason you're setting up a master contract in the first place.

For our example contract, we entered a special price of $65.00 per unit; the regular price is $100.00 per unit. These prices will affect your sales orders. The target quantity we entered for material 43 will control that only 100 units of this material can be purchased at the special price.

Once this contract is saved, whenever you enter a sales order for this customer and this material, the message **For this material <XXX> there are open outline agreements** will appear with options to **Continue**, **List**, or **Cancel**. By selecting **List**, you can browse the existing contracts relevant to this customer and material and select the relevant one.

Alternatively, you can create sales orders with reference to a quantity contract by clicking the corresponding button on the initial sales order screen (see Chapter 6 for more details).

Once a quantity contract is linked to a sales order line, you can only order up to the target quantity specified on the quantity contract (in this example, 100 units). If you order anything more, you'll get an error message saying, **Target qty of reference: 100 EA (total referenced: <XXX>ea)**, where XXX is the quantity we're attempting to order over the 100-unit limit. You'll need to correct this field before being allowed to continue.

You can add another line to the sales order without reference to the contract to represent the delta quantity above the target quantity on the contract, as shown in Figure 5.8. The special pricing conditions on the contract would not affect this new line, so you'll need to ensure the customer understands that some units don't fall under the special price.

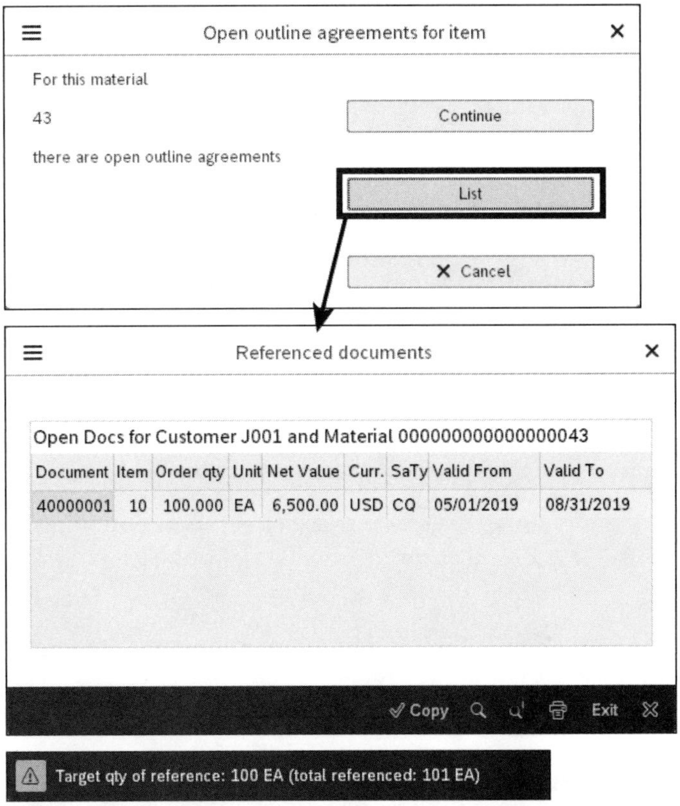

Figure 5.8 Sales Order Messages for Quantity Contracts

For orders created electronically via interfaces such as Electronic Data Interchange (EDI) and web sales interfaces, problems may arise. If you receive orders via these channels, you'll need to automate contract selection via custom development; otherwise, these sales orders would fail.

5.1.3 Value Contracts

Value contracts are created using Transaction VA41. Figure 5.9 shows the **Create Value Contract: Overview** screen where you'll enter contract data after selecting document type VC01 on the initial screen and clicking the **Continue** button. Do not click the **Create with Reference** button, even if you have a master contract to use as reference.

As before, we'll highlight the fields that are different on this screen when compared to the standard sales order described in Chapter 6.

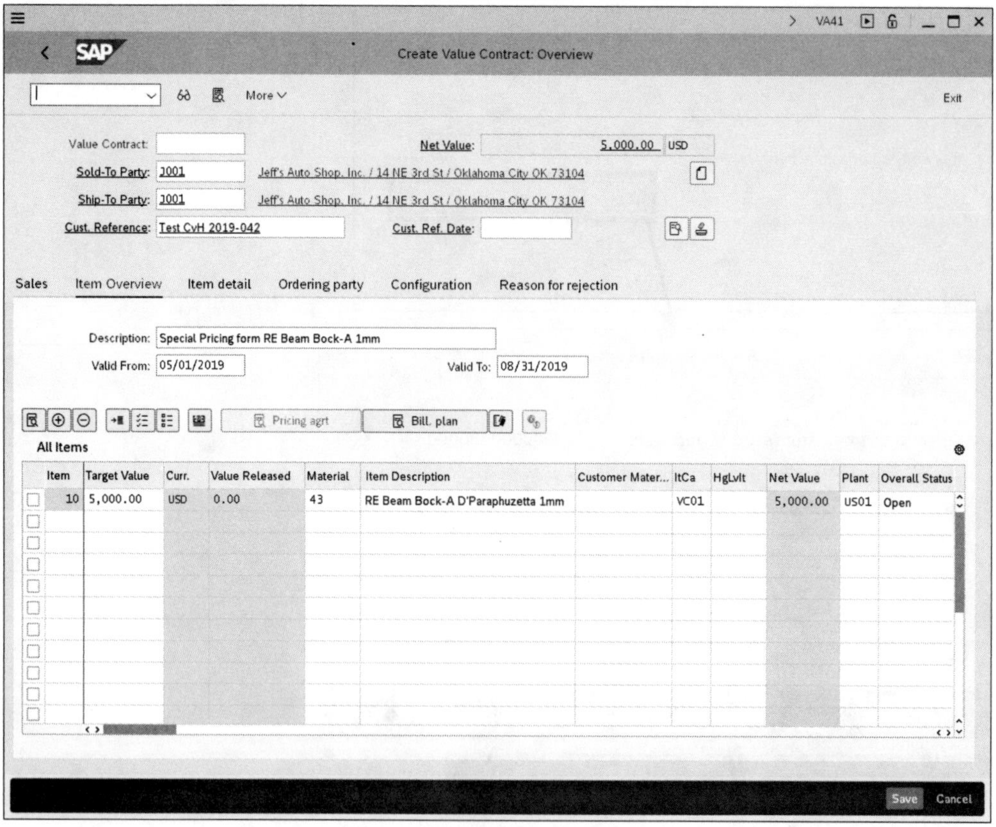

Figure 5.9 Create Value Contract: Overview Screen

For contracts, we'll need to enter a description (**Description**) to help when browsing for the correct document at the time of sales order entry. You'll also need to enter a validity period (**Valid From** and **Valid To** dates), which indicates the interval of time during which this contract can be used to create sales orders.

At the line level, notice that no quantity field exists. Instead, you'll enter a **Target Value** for this line and specify the material. This contract will be valid for orders created up to the dollar amount specified.

You can also select a **Master Contract** to link to this value contract under the **Sales** tab of the **Create Value Contract: Overview** screen, as shown in Figure 5.10. This approach will trigger the reference procedure, which will copy all relevant fields from the master contract into this value contract. Note, however, that because we're not using copy control, the document flow is not updated with the master contract reference.

To see all value and quantity contracts created with this type of reference, you can display the master contract in Transaction VA43.

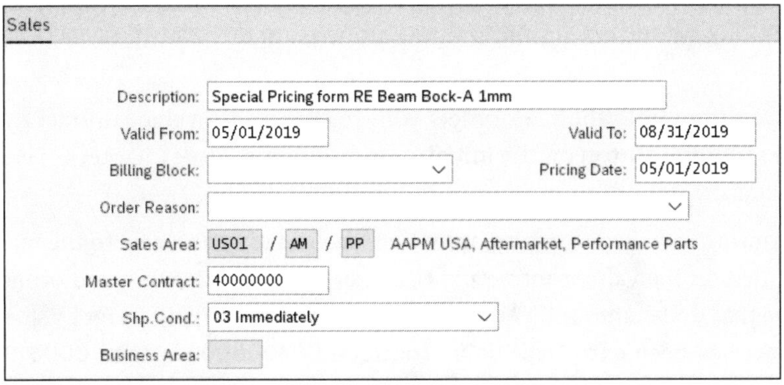

Figure 5.10 Sales Tab

Other fields, when populated, can be copied over to the sales orders created with reference to this contract (according to the copy control configuration and routines defined). Make sure you only populate the fields you want to copy over to the sales order—the main reason you're setting up a master contract in the first place.

For this contract, we entered a special net 60 days (**NT60**) payment term (as opposed to the regular net 30 payment term this customer is usually eligible for). This information is entered in the header details under the **Billing Document** tab, as shown in Figure 5.11.

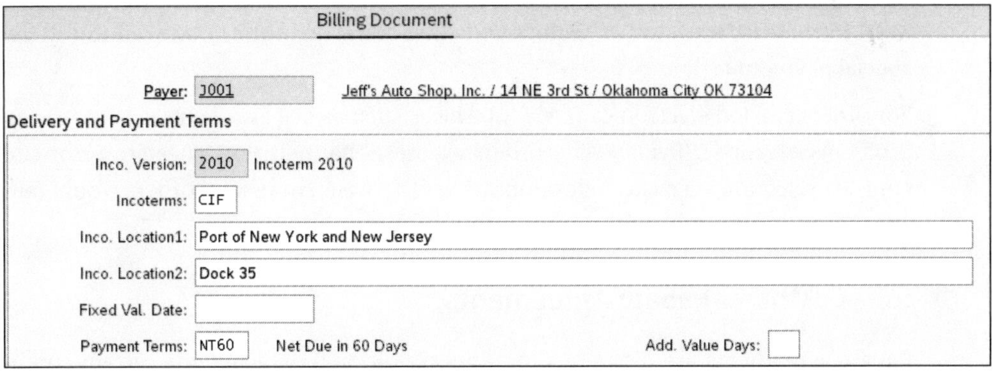

Figure 5.11 Header Details: Billing Document Tab

Once this contract is saved, whenever you enter a sales order for this customer and this material, the message **For this material XXX there are open outline agreements** will appear with options to **Continue**, **List**, or **Cancel**. By selecting **List**, you can browse through the existing contracts relevant to this customer and material and select the relevant one.

Alternatively, you can create the sales orders with reference to a value contract by using the corresponding button on the initial sales order screen (see Chapter 6, Section 6.1.1, for details).

Once a value contract is linked to a sales order line, you can only order up to the target value specified on the value contract (in this example, $5,000.00). If you order anything above that dollar amount, you'll get an error message saying, **Target value of value contract has been exceeded! Value contract: 0040000002, Item: 000010 Difference rate: 100.00 USD Document cannot be saved.** You'll need to correct this order before being allowed to continue, typically by lowering the quantity to keep the order within the value limit.

Note that this message only appears when you attempt to save the order because the pricing calculation may not be complete until you save.

In our example, payment terms are updated to **NT60** (net 60 days) for this line only because value contract is linked to the sales order line. The header payment term still uses the default from the customer master.

So, you can add more lines to the sales order that don't reference the value contract to represent the delta quantity that pushes the line value above the target value on the contract. The special payment terms NT60 would not affect this new line. You'll need to ensure the customer understands that some quantities don't fall under the special payment terms.

For orders created electronically via interfaces such as EDI and web sales interfaces, problems may arise. If you receive orders via these channels, you'll need to automate contract selection via custom development; otherwise, these sales orders would fail.

5.2 Customer Rebate Agreements

Rebate agreements are discount programs conditional on achieving certain conditions. Consumers are often familiar with rebates when purchasing products from retailers and getting cash back after submitting receipts to the manufacturers. Usually, companies implementing SAP are on the paying side of these rebate programs.

Rebates are often handled via a clearing partner that takes care of the paperwork and sends us data via EDI. This scenario is common in consumer electronics industry.

For corporate customers, the most common rebates are based on sales volume targets. A customer is eligible for the discount only if they purchase over a given dollar amount within a predefined period; otherwise, the discount is forfeited.

Note that significant differences exist between how SAP S/4HANA handles rebates versus SAP ERP. SAP S/4HANA will account for the conditional discount based on regular sales invoices. The amount corresponding to the discount is posted to a separate account to indicate that this amount will not likely become revenue. This accounting feature is called *rebate accruals*: Rebates are accrued on the relevant customer invoices.

As shown in Figure 5.12, at the end of the rebate program period, if a customer meets the sales volume targets, you would credit their account with the corresponding amount accrued based on their invoices.

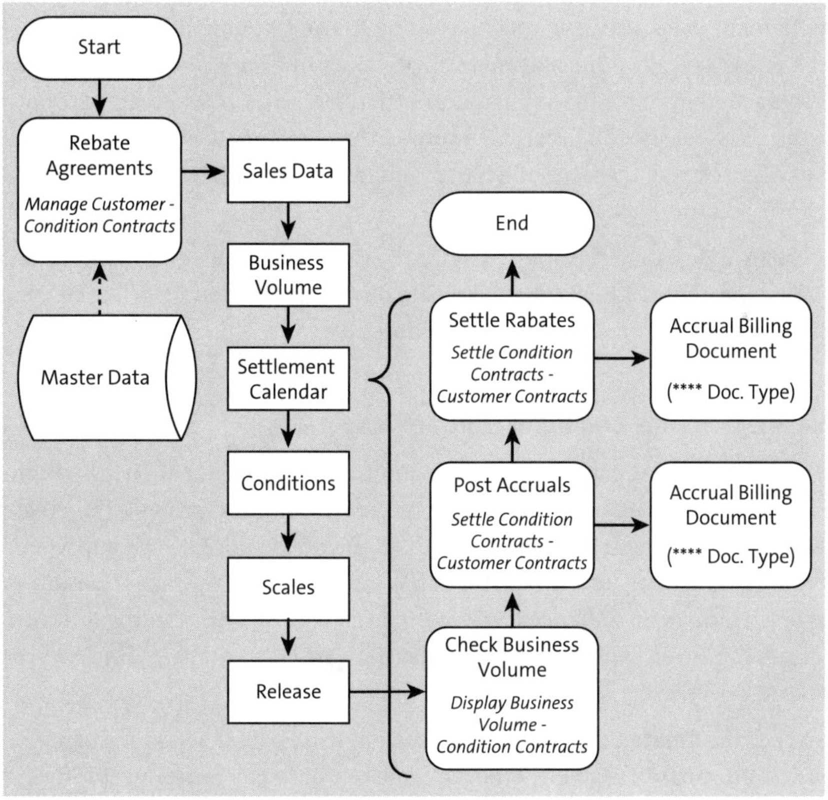

Figure 5.12 SAP S/4HANA Sales Rebate Processing

This process is referred to as *rebate settlement*. Sales rebate agreements in SAP S/4HANA are called *customer condition contracts*. This difference in name is to highlight that SAP is designed to allow this functionality to fulfill business requirements other than sales rebates.

In Section 5.2.1, we'll create customer condition contracts (rebate agreements). Then, we'll start monitoring transactions that are considered relevant for the rebate agreement; the total amount of these transactions compose the *business volume*. Monitoring the business volume is a recurring task. The main goal of the rebate program is to motivate customers to purchase more goods and services, so enabling you to monitor sales and follow up with customers can bring in more sales.

On the accrual date, planned according to the *settlement calendar*, you'll need to *post accruals*, typically done automatically by a background job. This activity signals to finance to "set money aside" to pay for rebates depending on how likely a customer is to achieve the goals set to receive the rebate.

On the settlement date, again planned according to the settlement calendar, you'll *settle the rebates*, typically done automatically by the same background job used for accruals. This activity will credit the customer with the rebates to which they are entitled. You can also "release" the accrual amounts the customer was not able to take advantage of, converting these amounts to revenue or to other financial accounts as defined by the accounting team.

Several accruals and settlements may exist for the same rebate agreement, culminating in a *final settlement* at which time the rebate program would end. We'll cover customer rebate settlement in more detail in Section 5.2.2.

5.2.1 Manage Customer Condition Contracts App

The SAP Fiori app Manage Customer Condition Contracts provides an overview of your existing rebate agreements, and by clicking the **Create Contract** link, you can create new ones, as shown in Figure 5.13. You can also call the Create Sales Rebate app, which skips this initial overview screen. Another app, the Maintain Contract – Condition Contracts app, features an enhanced SAP Fiori-based user interface. Using SAP GUI, you can create condition contracts using Transaction WCOCO with the same steps as described in this section.

When you click the **Create Contract** link, the system will ask you what type of agreement you want to create. Decide whether the rebate will be customer specific or will include multiple customers and whether corresponding rebate settlements should be issued immediately. Alternatively, you could set up a two-step process that allows for review before a settlement is processed. The goods-related rebate agreements options are used when taxes must be calculated following the invoice in which the rebate was accrued.

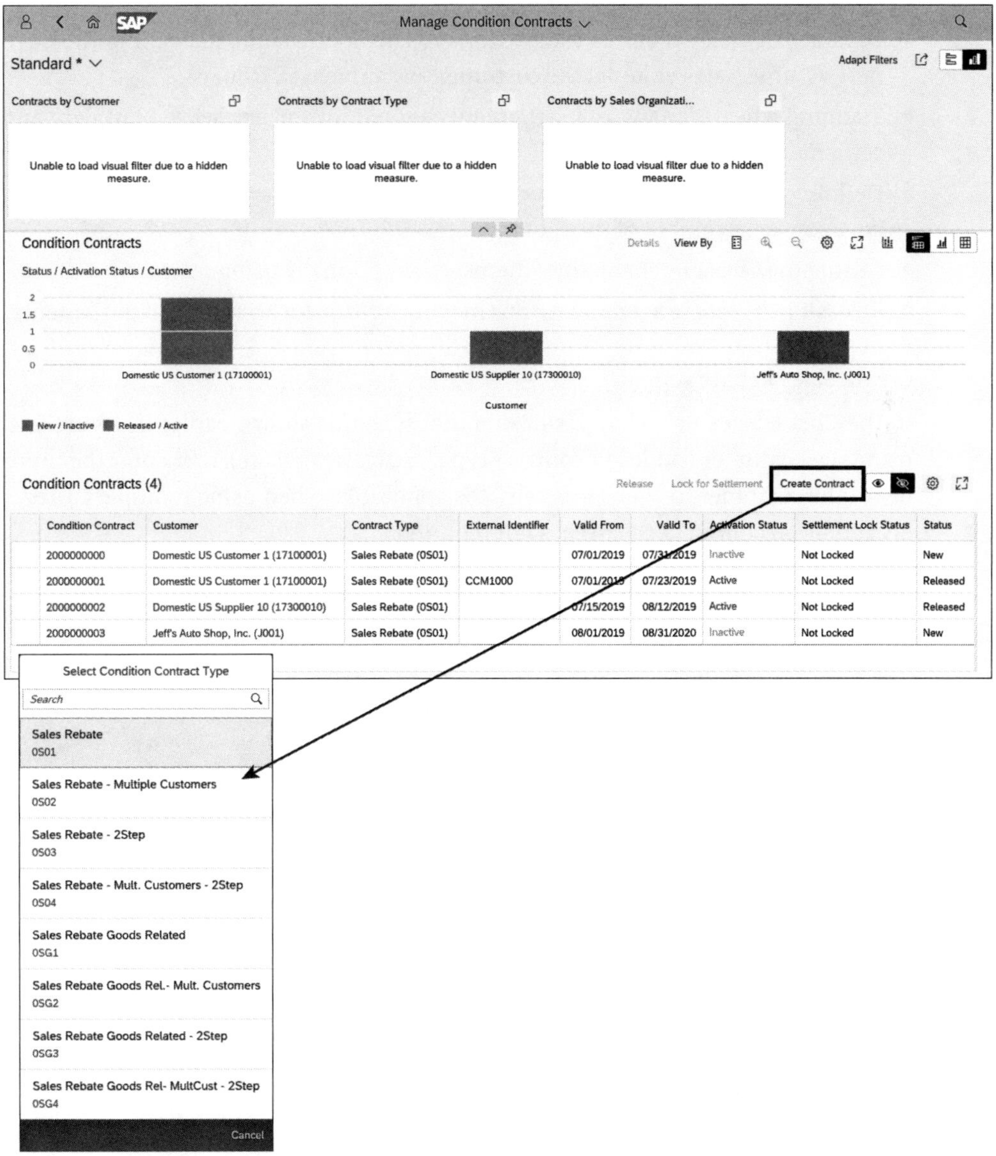

Figure 5.13 Creating a New Customer Condition Contract for Sales Rebates

In the following sections, we'll cover the following steps for managing condition contracts:

- Specifying relevant sales data, used to identify the organization structure elements responsible for the corresponding credit memos/billing documents, specifically data on the **Basic Data**, **Sales**, **Administration**, and **Status Header** tabs.
- Defining the relevant sales transactions to consider when determining the business volume (sales volume) the customer has purchased from us.
- Planning when accruals and settlements should take place (settlement data and settlement calendar).
- Defining conditions, i.e., how much to accrue and how to award rebates to customers upon achievement of the set target.
- Setting the sales target amounts themselves, optionally using scales.
- Releasing the rebate agreement, thus making it ready for accruals and settlements.

Create Sales Rebate App

In the Create Sales Rebate app, whose initial screen is shown earlier in Figure 5.14, using the customer condition contract type OS01 (sales rebate), first enter the number of the customer to which this rebate is applicable; when using multiple customers condition contracts, this step is not required.

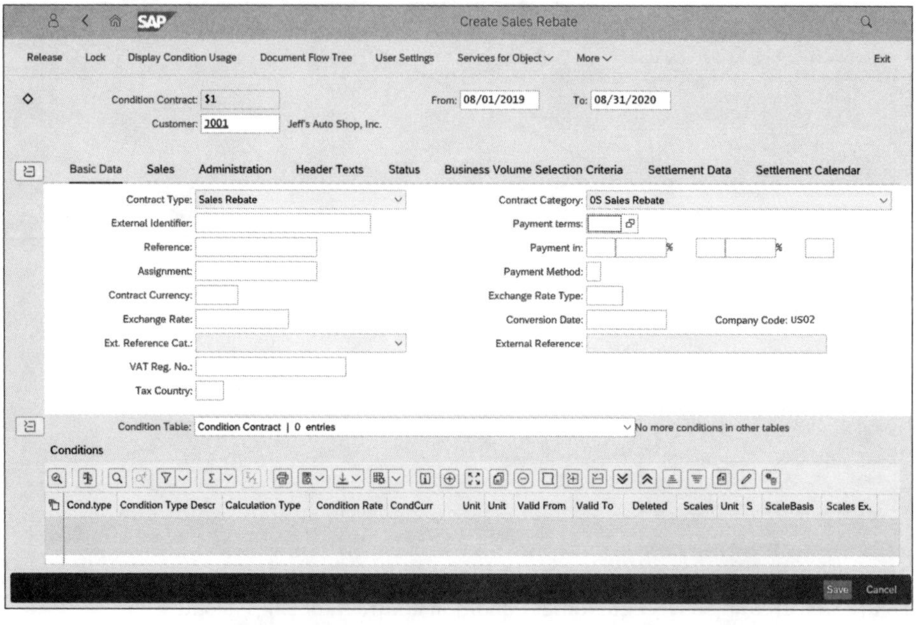

Figure 5.14 Sales Rebate Agreement (Condition Contracts): Basic Data Tab

Now, define the contract validity period using the **From** and **To** date fields. The **To** date must match the date on which you'll perform the final settlement generating the last credit to the customer under this agreement. Upon saving the rebate agreement, the document number will be assigned by the system, using an internally assigned number rage, which is then displayed in the **Condition Contract** field.

In the following sections, we'll walk you through each tab in this app.

Command Bar

In the Create Sales Rebate app, the following command bar buttons are available:

- The **Release** button is used to activate this document. The condition contract is initially created with an inactive status and will remain inactive until you press this button to release/activate it.
- The **Lock** button puts this condition contract on hold; no further accruals or settlements can be created until you release it by clicking the **Release** button.
- The **Display Condition Usage** button shows other contracts that use the condition types included on this contract, as shown in detail in Figure 5.22.
- The **Document Flow Tree** button shows all documents created with reference to this condition contract.
- The **User Settings** button allows you to set user defaults and preferences.
- The **Services for Object** button controls interfaces related to the contract.

Basic Data

The **Basic Data** tab, shown in Figure 5.14, has the following fields:

- The **Contract Type** field is the description of the selected contract type.
- The **Contract Category** field is configured based on the contract type and display in this field as reference. (See the Defining Condition Contract Types section for additional details.)
- The **External Identifier** field is a reference that the customer uses for this sales rebate (when applicable).
- The **Payment terms**, **Payment in**, and **Payment Method** fields describe how to make payments to customers, based on the rebate credits generated from this contract. Usually, companies credit a customer account to use on future purchases and only issue direct payments upon request.
- The **Assignment** and **Reference** fields are identification numbers that allow the accounting team to communicate with the customer and with the sales department.

This information will be copied to the account postings and will be available for accounts receivable functionality. Using copy control configuration, you can define the rules for populating this field automatically with the sales order number, with the invoice number, or with other fields.

- The **Contract Currency** field is the currency in which the amounts contained in this contract are expressed.
- The **Exchange Rate Type** field is used in multicurrency environments, when more than one exchange rate is maintained, to identify which rate must be used in this document.
- The **Exchange Rate** field defaults from the exchange rate repository, but you can make changes when applicable.
- The **Ext. Reference Cat.** and **External Reference** fields are used for integrated environments where contracts are created electronically from these data sources. These fields are then populated and used when sending data back.
- The **VAT Reg. No.** field is a tax registration number used in Europe and other countries for Value-Added Tax (VAT) purposes.
- The **Tax Country** field is the country in which the customer is registered for VAT purposes.

Sales

Under the **Sales** tab, shown in Figure 5.15, you'll see the following fields: **Sales Organization**, **Distribution Channel**, **Division**, **Sales office**, and **Sales group**. These fields are sales organizational structure elements responsible for this rebate agreement.

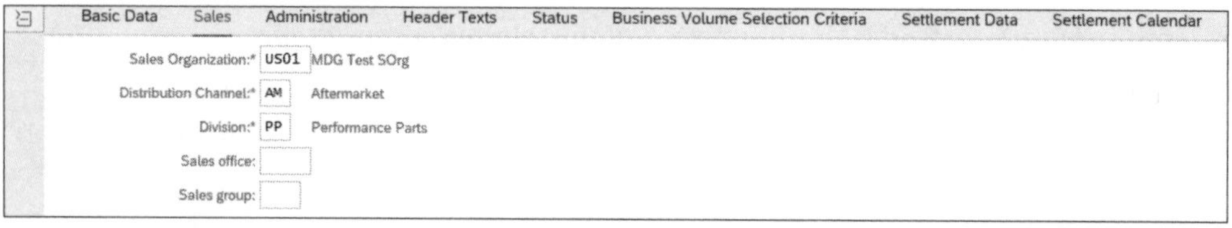

Figure 5.15 Sales Rebate Agreement (Condition Contracts): Sales Tab

Administration

The **Administration** tab, shown in Figure 5.16, has the following fields:

- **Created By**, **Created On**, **Created At**, and **Time Zone** fields identify the user ID that created this contract and when the contract was created.
- **Last Changed By**, **Last Changed On**, and **Last Changed At** fields identify the last user ID that modified this contract and when the contract was last modified.

- **External Partner** is used with EDI to identify the partner that sent you contract data electronically (when applicable).

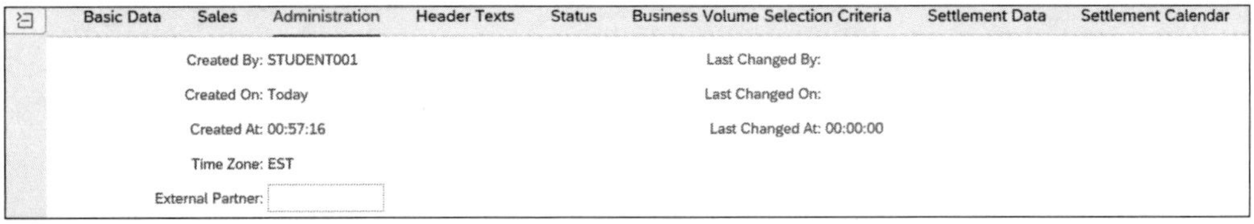

Figure 5.16 Sales Rebate Agreement (Condition Contracts): Administration Tab

Header Texts

Under the **Header Texts** tab, shown in Figure 5.17, you can maintain freeform texts as configured on the header text procedure assigned to the contract type.

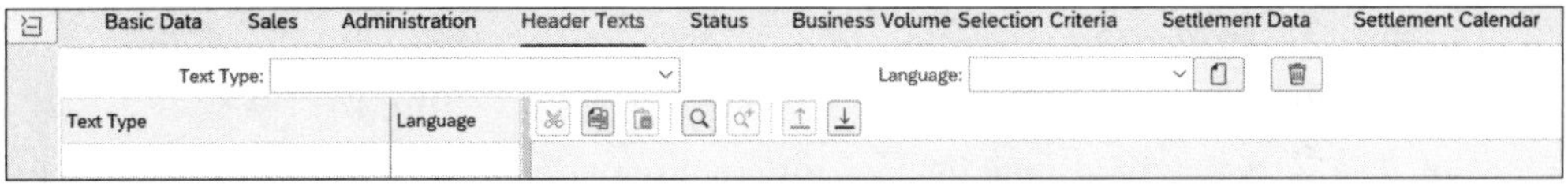

Figure 5.17 Sales Rebate Agreement (Condition Contracts): Header Texts Tab

Out of the box, the configuration has two text IDs: one for internal notes and another for external notes (to be shown to the customer).

Status

The **Status** tab, shown in Figure 5.18, is used to define the status profile assigned to the contract type configuration. Depending on the selected profile, the fields will be populated differently and serve different purposes.

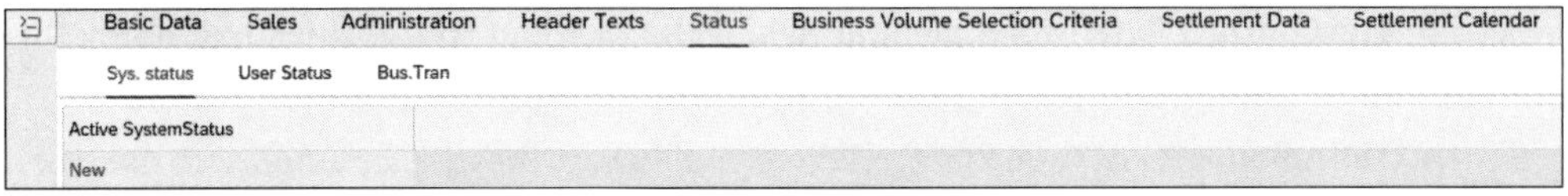

Figure 5.18 Sales Rebate Agreement (Condition Contracts): Status Tab

Business Volume Selection Criteria

The **Business Volume Selection Criteria** tab, shown in Figure 5.19, is an important tab where you'll make selections to filter the relevant invoices and credit memos that should be considered when calculating the sales/business volume this customer has purchased from your company.

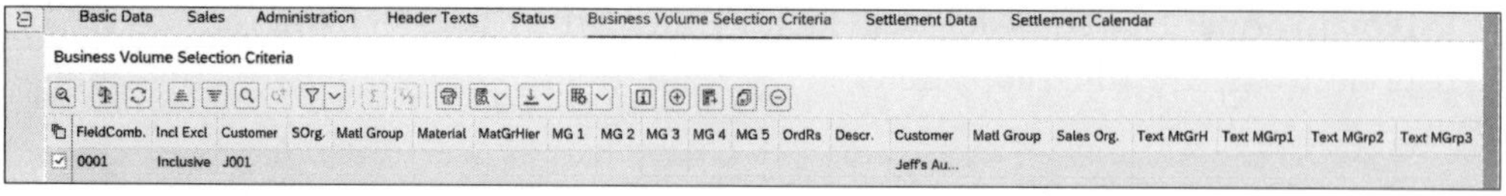

Figure 5.19 Sales Rebate Agreement (Condition Contracts): Business Volume Selection Criteria Tab

First, select the **FieldComb.**; this code will control which other columns will be used. After selecting the desired code and pressing [Enter], the necessary fields will be made available. In our example, we're using the field combination **0001**, and the **Customer** column will be made available for entry.

You can also control where this condition should be used to include or exclude invoices, based on business volume, by making selections in the **Incl Excl** column.

Settlement Data

The **Settlement Data** tab, shown in Figure 5.20, has the following fields:

- The **Settlement Material** field is a different material number to be used when issuing credits to the customer under this rebate agreement. If you leave this field blank, the same material used on the original sales invoice will be used. Select a different settlement material if you don't want the rebate credit to appear in material-based reporting and also to reduce the number of lines on the rebate credit billing document, which may potentially be quite long. This field also affects material-dependent tax calculations.
- The **Settlement Type Customer** field defines whether and how to credit the customers on settlement credit memo billing documents that are created based on this rebate agreement.
- The **Contract Extension Calendar** field is the calendar to use when extending this rebate agreement after its validity period has expired.
- The **Amount Fields Group** field is where you'll select the invoice amount to use when calculating the sales/business volume. This field is used to determine whether and how much rebate the customer is eligible for.
- The **Settlement Unit of Measure** field is the unit of measurement (UoM) to be used when calculating the sales/business volume. If selling products using multiple UoMs, you can use this field to convert multiple UoMs into a uniform UoM to make your reports easier to read.

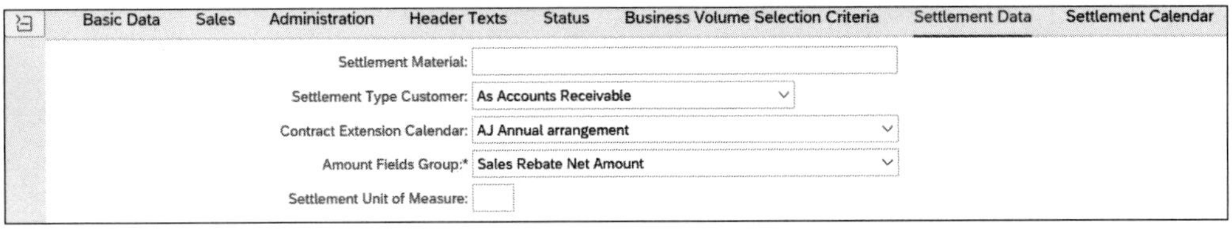

Figure 5.20 Sales Rebate Agreement (Condition Contracts): Settlement Data Tab

Settlement Calendar

The **Settlement Calendar** tab, shown in Figure 5.21, is another important tab for condition contracts. Under this tab, you'll plan the dates during which the sales/business volume the customer achieved should be assessed before issuing an accrual or a settlement credit.

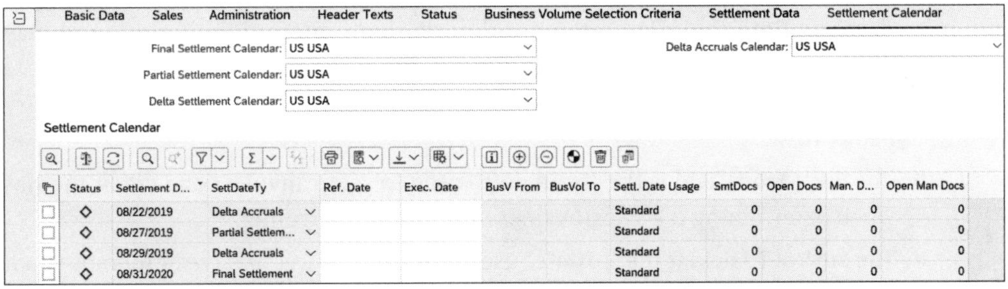

Figure 5.21 Sales Rebate Agreement (Condition Contracts): Settlement Calendar Tab

This tab can also be used after a rebate agreement is created to monitor its progress. The **Final Settlement Calendar**, **Partial Settlement Calendar**, **Settlement Calendar**, **Settlement Calendar**, and **Delta Accruals Calendar** fields identify different factory calendars to use for each rebate activity. You can use these fields to avoid non-working days when planning dates.

The elements of a calendar include the following fields:

- The **Status** icon indicates whether this settlement calendar entry is due to be processed, late, etc.
- The **Settlement D...** field is the date of this settlement calendar entry.
- The **SettDateTy** field represents the settlement calendar entry type:
  - **<Blank> Final Settlement** is the date on which we'll issue the final settlement credit to the customer under this rebate agreement.

  - **1 Partial Settlement** is for issuing partial settlement credits to the customer under this rebate agreement.
  - **2 Delta Settlement** is used for adjusting a previous settlement made to the customer under this rebate agreement. The delta settlement option considers settlements already made when determining a new settlement amount.
  - **3 Delta Accruals** is used the date on which business volume should be checked and for "setting money aside" to pay for a rebate that will likely be credited to the customer. This credit is achieved by creating an accrual billing document.
- The **Ref. Date** field is the date when a partial settlement should take place, according to this settlement calendar, to be used as a reference when calculating delta settlements. The delta is the difference, incremental or decremental, from the partial settlement issued, adjusting the remaining settlement due to changes. This date may must be before the **Settlement D...** and is mandatory for delta settlements.
- The **Exec. Date** field is the date when the settlement should be processed. You may want to allow for a few days of buffer between the **Settlement D...** and the date when the settlement creates credits, for review and for making any necessary adjustments.
- The **BusV From** field is the "from date" used to select invoices and credit memos when determining the sales/business volume of a customer.
- The **BusVol To** field is the "to date" used to select invoices and credit memos when determining the sales/business volume of a customer.
- The **Settl. Date Usage** field indicates whether you'll need to process retroactive accruals on this date or not. The system determines this retroactive accruals based on the sequence of events you're maintaining and then displays this status to notify your users to confirm that this activity is on purpose and not accidental.
- The **SmtDocs** field is the amount of the settlement billing document created on this date so far.
- The **Open Docs** field is the amount of the open settlement billing document being processed on this date.
- The **Man. D...** field is the amount of the manual settlement billing document created on this date so far.
- The **Open Man Does** field is the amount of the open manual settlement billing document being processed on this date.

Figure 5.22 shows the **Conditions** section of the sales rebate agreement (condition contracts), where you'll define the targets for the rebate to be relevant as well as define the applicable awards.

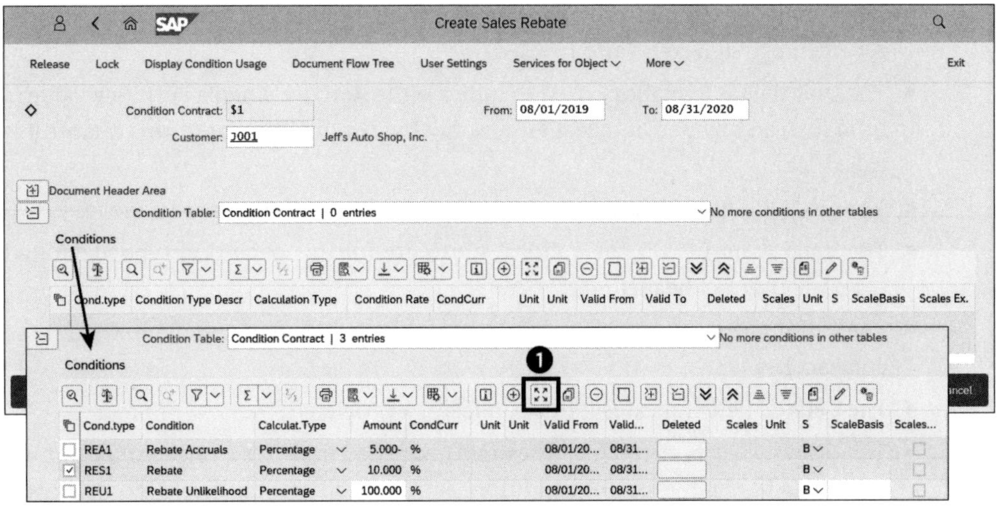

Figure 5.22 Adding Condition Types to Sales Rebate Contract

The **Condition Table** field represents the pricing condition table in use on this condition contract. You'll find the following columns on this screen:

- The condition type you select (**Cond.type**) indicates the purpose of the condition record being maintained. The main condition types provided out of the box for sales rebates include the following:
  - **REA1Rebate Accruals** indicates the percentage of the sales invoice amount that should be accrued (money "set aside"). This amount will be used later when awarding rebate credits upon fulfillment of the established sales targets.
  - **RES1Rebate** indicates the percentage of the sales invoice amount that will be awarded to the customer under the titles of rebate credits upon fulfillment of the established sales targets, which are maintained under **Scales**.
  - **REU1Rebate Unlikelihood** indicates the percentage of the accrued amount that must be released back into revenue if the customer fails to achieve the established sales targets.
- The **Condition** field is the condition type description.
- The **Calculat.Type** field is where you'll select a percentage or a fixed amount to take off the invoice.
- The **Amount** field is the percentage or fixed value corresponding to the condition type.

- The **CondCurr** field is the currency in which the value in the **Amount** is expressed. A percentage sign could also be used.
- The **Unit** field is a quantity used to indicate the **Amount** when a currency value is used instead of a percentage. On sales pricing condition records, this quantity is called "per."
- The next **Unit** field is the unit of measurement for the **Unit** quantity above.
- The **Valid From** field is the validity start date for this condition type, defaulted from the contract header.
- The **Valid...** field is the validity end date for this condition type, defaulted from the contract header.
- The **Deleted** field indicates if this condition was deleted.
- The **Scales** field is the value threshold that the customer's sales volume must achieve to be eligible for this condition. You may add new threshold by clicking on the scales icon ❶.
- The third **Unit** field is the currency for the **Scales** field.
- The **S** field is the scale type, by default, the base scale, but you can use a **To-Scale** (found via match code search) for descending scales or other scenarios.
- The **Scale Basis** field qualifies the contents of the **Scales** field. Other than the invoice amount, you also base this condition type on quantities, weights, etc.
- The **Scales...** flag indicates that scales have been maintained for this condition type.

Defining Condition Contract Types

To configure customer condition contract types, follow the menu path **SAP Customizing Implementation Guide • Logistics – General • Settlement Management • Condition Contract Management • Condition Contract Maintenance • Define Condition Contract Types**.

Figure 5.23 shows what you'll see following the menu path and screen commands as specified. This configuration is shared with materials management (MM) for vendor rebates, so many fields on this screen are intended for vendor rebates for which your company, as the customer of these vendors, is eligible.

After creating the contract type, you must enter further contract type details by selecting the line you just created and clicking on the details icon 🔍 or pressing [F2].

When creating new entries, as shown in Figure 5.24, you must specify a four-character condition contract type code (**Condition Contract Type**) and add a description.

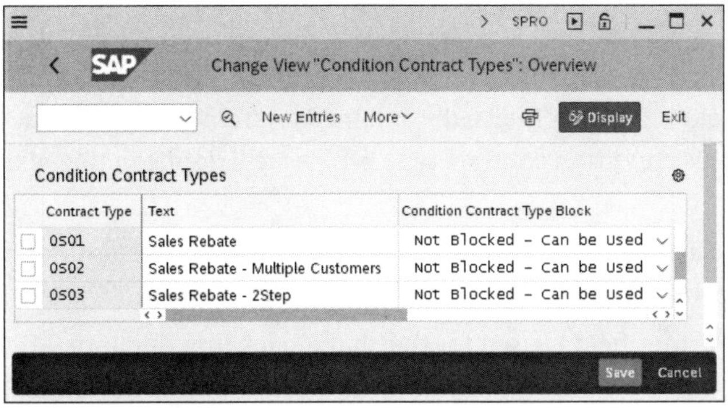

Figure 5.23 Defining Condition Contract Types

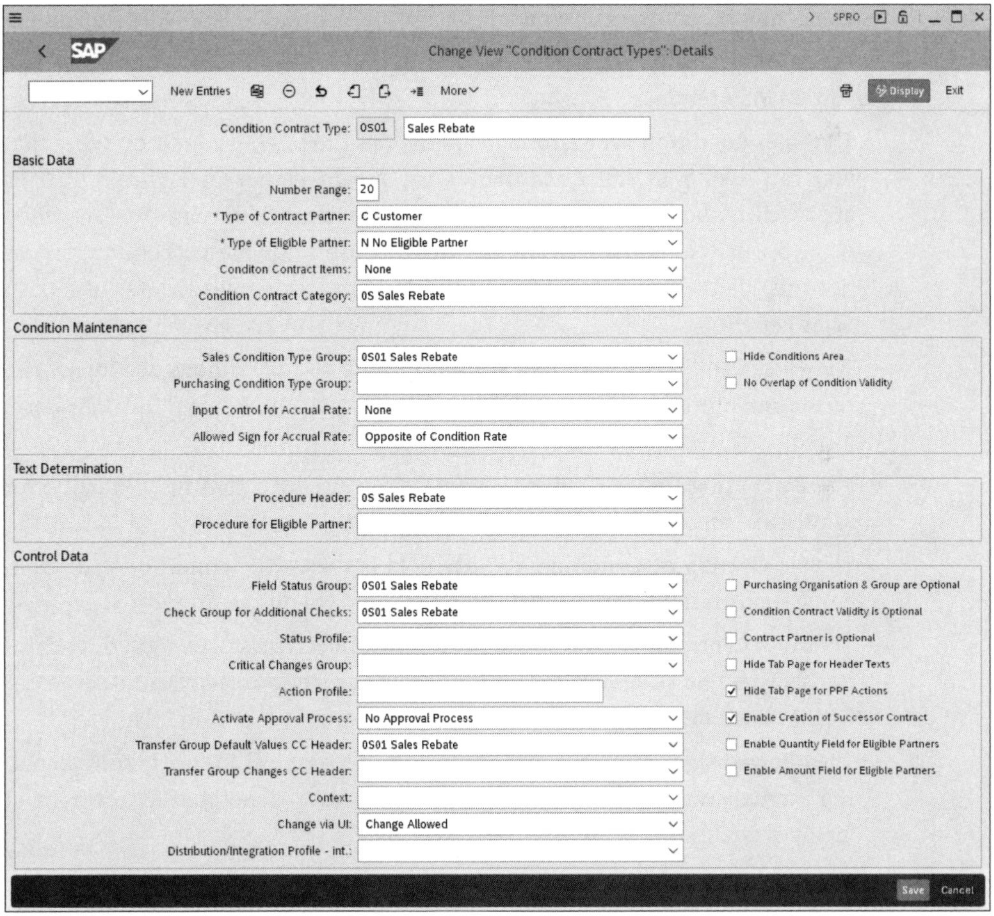

Figure 5.24 Condition Contract Type Details

Let's look at each area on this screen as follows:

- **Basic Data**
  - The **Number Range** field is used for internally assigned (system generated) document numbers for this condition contract type, which we'll define in the next section.
  - The **Type of Contract Partner** field is where you'll qualify this contract type as a customer condition contract used on sales rebates.
  - The **Type of Eligible Partner** field is used for the chargeback functionality (MM scope). For sales, assign code **N**.
  - The **Condition Contract Items** field is used for MM functionality; for sales, assign code **None**.
  - The **Condition Contract Category** field controls contract-related functionality in SAP standard code; for sales, assign code **0S Sales Rebate**.
- **Condition Maintenance**
  - The **Sales Condition Type Group** field qualifies the pricing condition types that you can assign in the **Conditions** area, shown earlier in Figure 5.22. This approach reduces the list of conditions from which a user may select when using the match code search and ensures that users don't select condition types not intended for this type of condition contract. For sales rebates, use **0S01 Sales Rebate**.
  - The **Hide Conditions Area** flag is used to hide the **Conditions** section of the rebate maintenance screen. For sales rebates, you must leave this flag unselected.
  - The **Purchasing Condition Type Group** field is used for MM functionality; for sales, leave this field blank.
  - The **No Overlap of Condition Validity** field prevents the condition type from being used on multiple contracts with the same validity period.
  - The **Input Control for Accrual Rate** field allows for accruals to be settled synchronously when no scales are maintained. Scales are used to accrue and settle different rebate rates according to the volume of purchase thresholds.
  - The **Allowed Sign for Accrual Rate** field is used to control the arithmetic sign of the accrual condition, which affect the accounting generated by the accrual (debit or credit).

- **Text Determination**
  - The **Procedure Header** field refers to text determination procedure for the condition contract header, which we'll describe in the Defining Text Determination Procedures section, using the table `WCOCOH` text object. Note that this field is not related to sales text determination (Transaction VOTXN), which we'll describe in Chapter 6, Section 6.3.10.
  - The **Procedure for Eligible Partner** field is the eligible partner text determination procedure using the table `WCOCOH` text object. Note that this field is also related to sales text determination.
- **Control Data**
  - The **Field Status Group** field is a code representing the screen layout used for this transaction. For sales rebates, use **0S01 Sales Rebate**.
  - The **Purchasing Organization & Group are Optional** flag, when selected, indicates that the **Purchasing Organization** and **Purchasing Group** fields do not need to be populated for a condition contract to be considered complete. Note that condition contracts do not use the same incompletion procedure functionality used in SAP S/4HANA Sales.
  - The **Check Group for Additional Checks** field is a code representing the checks built into the transaction that are not applicable to all condition contracts. You must maintain a code here to activate the condition contract. For sales rebates, use **0S01 Sales Rebate**.
  - The **Condition Contract Validity is Optional** flag indicates that, for this type of condition contract, no validity period must be set up. For sales rebates, you'll need validity periods, so you must keep this field blank.
  - The **Status Profile** field controls the statuses that can be applied to the condition contract. This option is used for managing more complex portions of the contract lifecycle using the system. In other words, to enter prospect contracts and put them through a qualification process, perhaps step by step by several applicable teams, you can define statuses that represent multiple states of progress. This process could be understood as an approval workflow, but note that this process doesn't manage the sequence of steps it must go through like an approval workflow.

    Most companies do not enter a contract until it is ready to be released. A release function allow for an approval step that should be sufficient for most companies.

- The **Contract Partner is Optional** flag controls whether you must specify a business partner number in the header of the condition contract; when selected, this flag makes the field optional.
- The **Critical Changes Group** field is a code representing a group of condition contract fields that, when changed, would trigger the recalculation of a contract accrual and/or a settlement.
- The **Hide Tab Page for Header Texts** flag, when selected, eliminates the ability to enter text on the condition contract.
- The **Action Profile** field is part of the post-processing framework (PPF). Depending on the code you select, the PPF functionality controls and allows for automated follow-up.
- The **Hide Tab Page for PPF Actions** flag, when selected, eliminates PPF data on the condition contract maintenance screen. If you're not using PPF, we recommend hiding these fields.
- The **Activate Approval Process** field controls an out-of-the-box approval process for rebate agreements.
- The **Enable Creation of Successor Contract** flag indicates whether users can create condition contracts with reference to this contract type.
- The **Transfer Group Default Values CC Header** field is a code representing default values to be automatically populated on the condition contract tables for the type. For sales rebates, use **0S01 Sales Rebate**.
- The **Enable Quantity Field for Eligible Partners** flag indicates whether to allow the maintenance of quantity and unit of measurement data for eligible partners.
- The **Transfer Group Changes CC Header** field is a code representing whether and how default values must be updated on condition contract tables after a document has been saved, if the default values are modified.
- The **Enable Amount Field for Eligible Partners** flag indicates whether to allow the maintenance of amount data for eligible partners.
- The **Context** field is a code representing this condition contract type in a feature called the transformation application.
- The **Change via UI** field indicates the type of condition contract that may be maintained using Transaction WCOCO.
- The **Distribution/Integration Profile - Int.** field controls distribution of this condition contract information to external modules.

Defining Condition Contract Number Ranges

To configure condition contract number range intervals, open Transaction OWCB_CC10 or follow the menu path **SAP Customizing Implementation Guide • Logistics – General • Settlement Management • Condition Contract Management • Condition Contract Maintenance • Define Number Ranges**.

In the example shown in Figure 5.25, using the **Intervals** button, you can browse the multiple number ranges available for use on condition contracts. In our example, we're displaying number range 20 (**No**) used on the condition contract type 0S01. For more information on modifying number ranges, see Chapter 6, Section 6.1.3.

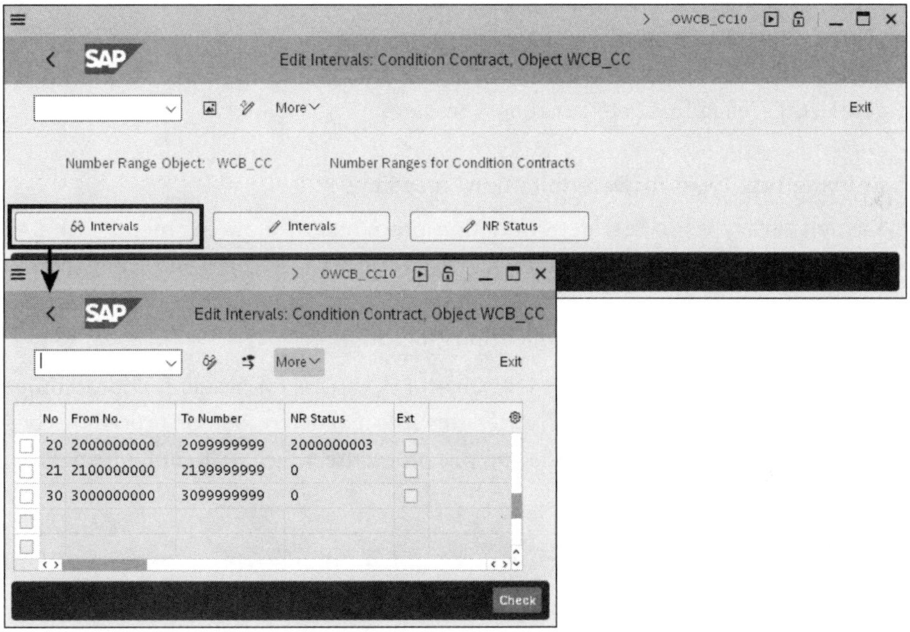

Figure 5.25 Displaying Condition Contract Number Range Intervals

Defining Text Determination Procedures

To configure text determination procedures, follow the menu path **SAP Customizing Implementation Guide • Logistics – General • Settlement Management • Condition Contract Management • Condition Contract Maintenance • Text Control • Define Text Determination Procedures**.

As shown in Figure 5.26, specify the **Text Object** (**ZCOCOH** for header text procedures and **WCOCOI** for eligible partners procedures). Then, specify a two-character text determination procedure code (**TxPrc**) and add a description (**Text**).

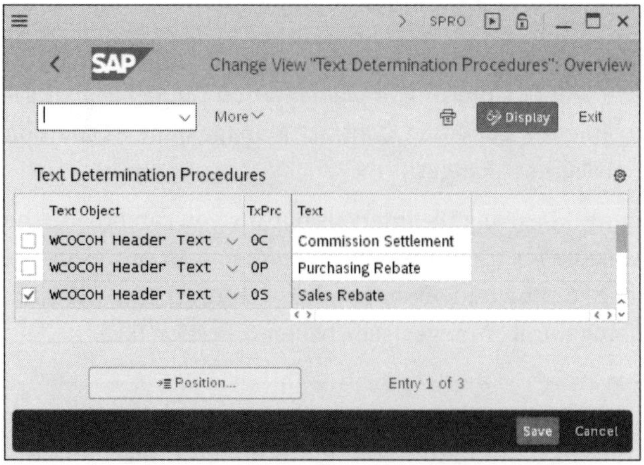

Figure 5.26 Defining Text Determination Procedures

Specifying Text Types for Determination Procedures

To assign text types to text determination procedures, follow the menu path **SAP Customizing Implementation Guide • Logistics – General • Settlement Management • Condition Contract Management • Condition Contract Maintenance • Text Control • Specify Text Types for Text Determination Procedure**.

As shown in Figure 5.27, enter the **Text Object** ("ZCOCOH" for header text procedures and "WCOCOI" for eligible partner procedures), the text determination procedure code (**TxPrc**), and the **Text ID** to be included on this procedure, which we'll configure next.

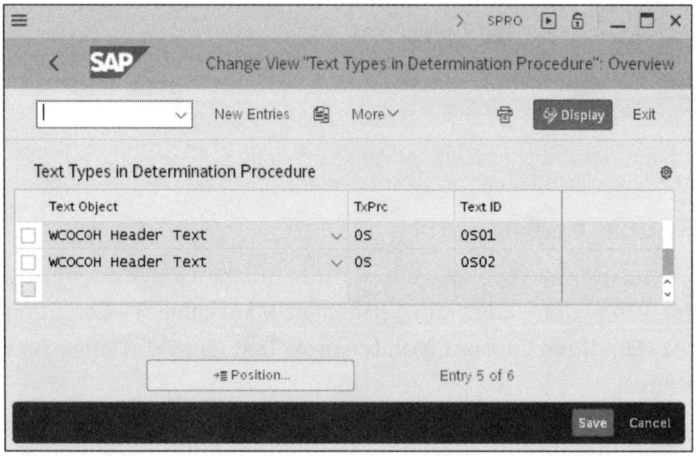

Figure 5.27 Specifying Text Types for the Text Determination Procedure

Defining Text Types for Header Texts

To configure condition contract header text types, follow the menu path **SAP Customizing Implementation Guide • Logistics – General • Settlement Management • Condition Contract Management • Condition Contract Maintenance • Text Control • Define Text Types for Header Texts.**

As shown in Figure 5.28, specify a four-character text ID code (**Text ID**) to be used in the headers of your condition contract and add a description (**Description**).

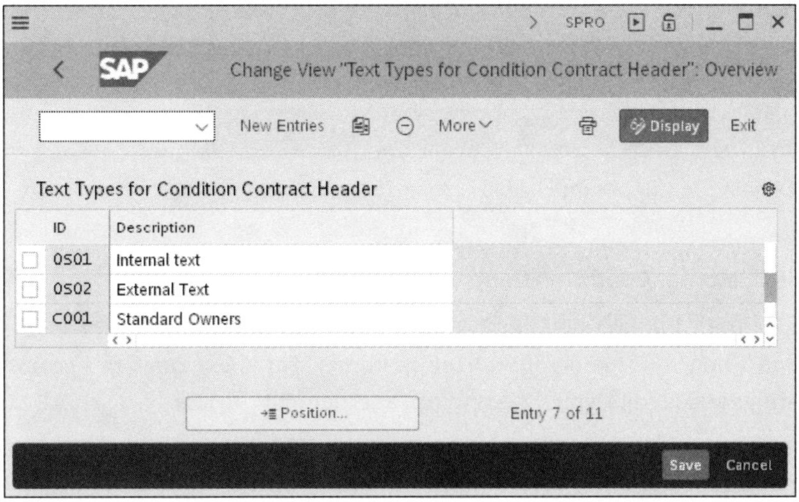

Figure 5.28 Defining Text Types for Condition Contract Header Texts

Defining Text Types for Eligible Partner Texts

To configure eligible partner header text types, follow the menu path **SAP Customizing Implementation Guide • Logistics – General • Settlement Management • Condition Contract Management • Condition Contract Maintenance • Text Control • Define Text Types for Eligible Partner Texts.**

As shown in Figure 5.29, specify a four-character text ID code (**Text ID**) to be used on eligible partners and add a description (**Description**).

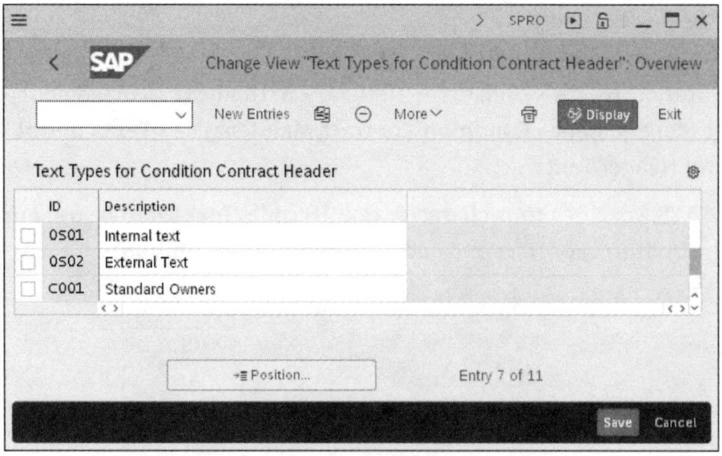

Figure 5.29 Defining Text Types for Eligible Partner Texts

5.2.2 Settle Customer Condition Contracts App

A condition contract defines rules about when to accrue a portion of sales for rebate payments and when to issue credits to the customer. For these rules to become account postings and credits, you'll need to run a settlement process.

For this process, you can use the SAP Fiori app Settle Condition Contracts – Customer Contracts or open Transaction WB2R_SC in the SAP GUI. This process is usually scheduled to run as a background job, which avoids having to remember to do this activity periodically.

Some companies struggle with the concept of automatic settlement, which reduces flexibility while saving time and effort. For these companies, rebates credits are often considered an important business tool. If rules are set and automatically processed, you can no longer use these rebates as leverage to bring in more business. You can manually manage settlements with no impact to system functionality other than the time you team spends on manual settlements.

In any case, you can run the settlement manually, in simulation mode, to test the background job and take any corrective action necessary.

When you start using rebates in SAP S/4HANA, settlement is particularly important. Understanding condition contract data and its impacts is important for anyone managing rebates even if only a few employees are involved in the implementation effort.

In the following sections, we'll show you how to set up the criteria for the settlement of condition contracts and then discuss how to define activity reasons for this process.

Condition Contract Settlement Selection Criteria

In the following sections, we'll discuss the main areas of the **Settlement of Customer Condition Contracts** screen.

Settlement Control

As shown in Figure 5.30, on the settlement selection screen, in the **Settlement Control** section, you'll control which settlement dates of the condition contract should be process in this execution of the settlement run.

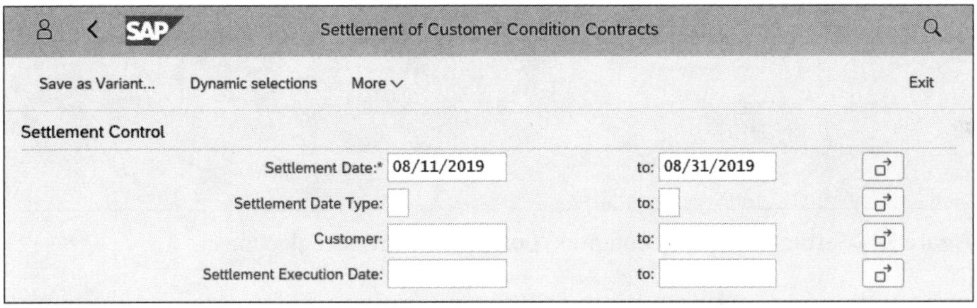

Figure 5.30 Settling Customer Condition Contracts: Selection Screen

The four fields in the **Settlement Control** area are as follows:

- The **Settlement Date** field is a mandatory field that filters the dates on the settlement calendar of the condition contracts selected for processing.
- The **Settlement Date Type** field allows you to process only certain types of dates on the settlement calendar of the selected condition contracts. This field is used when you want to schedule accrual-only jobs, settlement-only jobs, etc.
- The **Customer** field allows you to restrict, by customer, which condition contracts to process.
- The **Settlement Execution Date** field is a mandatory selection that filters the execution dates on the settlement calendar of the condition contracts selected for processing. Note that the execution date is optional on the settlement calendar entries. If you filter data using this field and the corresponding field is not populated on the settlement calendar, that field will not be selected for processing.

Contract Selection

The next part of the **Settlement of Customer Condition Contracts** screen, **Contract Selection** section, is shown in Figure 5.31. In this section, you can filter condition contracts that are should be processed. By restricting the number of contracts, you can increase performance.

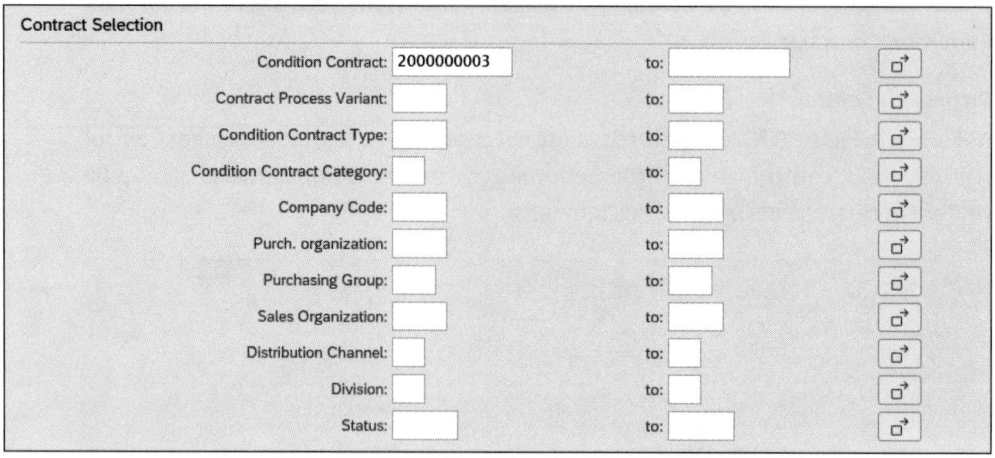

Figure 5.31 Settling Customer Condition Contracts: Contract Selection

The important fields in this section include the following:

- The **Condition Contract** field allows you to restrict settlement processing, by condition contract number, to limit the condition contracts to process. This field is often used when running settlement in the foreground.
- The **Condition Contract Type** field allows you to restrict, by condition contract type, the condition contracts to process. For instance, you can indicate that only sales rebates, type 0S01, should be settled.
- The **Condition Contract Category** field allows you to restrict, by condition contract category, the condition contracts to process. For instance, you can indicate that the settlement should only involve sales customer contracts.
- The **Company Code** field allows you to restrict, by company code, the condition contracts to process. This field is important for access control in environments with multiple company codes. Users often are only authorized to process documents belonging to the company code for which they work.
- The **Purch. organization** field allows you to restrict, by purchasing organization, the condition contracts to process. This field is used for vendor rebates, not sales.

- The **Purchasing Group** field allows you to restrict, by purchasing group, the condition contracts to process. This field is used for vendor rebates, not sales.
- The **Sales Organization**, **Distribution Channel**, and **Division** (the sales area) fields allow you to restrict, by sales area, the condition contracts to process. This field is important for access control in more complex environments. Users often are only authorized to process documents belonging to the sales areas under which they work.
- The **Status** field allows you to restrict, by specific status codes, the condition contracts to process. This field ensures only document of a specific status are processed. This field requires the utilization of a status profile in contract type configuration.

Default Data

The **Default Data** section, shown in Figure 5.32, allows you to modify the default data used by this process to create the settlement documents.

Figure 5.32 Settling Customer Condition Contracts: Default Data

The fields in this section are as follows:

- The **Posting Date** field is the date you want to use on the billing document created by this execution, which is used by accounting to identify which period the document belongs to. Note, however, that you can't use a posting date from closed accounting periods. You can only backdate a posting into a period that hasn't been closed yet.
- The **Document Date** field is the billing document date you want to use on the document created by this execution; this date is also used in sales reports.
- The **Activity Reason** field may be used to qualify special circumstances in which we're adjusting customer rebates. The steps for defining new reason codes is described in the Defining Activity Reasons section.

Program Run Control

The **Programm Run Control** section, shown in Figure 5.33, controls the actions executed during the settlement run and the desired quantity/quality of traceability messages the system should generate.

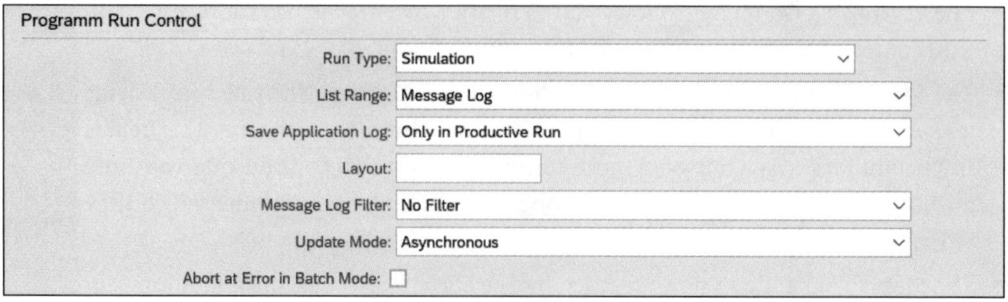

Figure 5.33 Settling Customer Condition Contracts: Program Run Control

The fields and checkboxes in this section are as follows:

- The **Run Type** field indicates whether only active (released) contracts should be included on the run or whether inactive contracts should be simulated as well.
- The **List Range** field indicates what should be displayed after the settlement run has concluded.
- The **Save Application Log** field indicates whether the resulting report/log should be saved for future consultation. If you're running several simulations, you may not want to include the resulting logs, which consume system resources and make it harder to find the actual execution logs.
- The **Layout** field is the customized report layout saved using the ABAP List Viewer list display, which allows you to manipulate, save, and duplicate layouts of your preference.
- The **Message Log Filter** field allows you to remove some messages that you may consider unnecessary, thus making the log easier to read.
- The **Update Mode** field allows you to make the settlement process run more quickly and start several work processes (potentially running in parallel) to create the resulting billing document asynchronously. If you don't expect many documents, you can run the settlement job synchronously, and once the job finishes running, all documents would already be created, and any messages issued would be included in the log.
- The **Abort at Error in Batch Mode** flag indicates a serious error message will abort the execution of a given condition contract; processing will stop on other condition contracts as well. This option avoids having the same error message issued several times for different documents.

Parallel Processing

The **Parallel Processing** section, shown in Figure 5.34, contains technical settings that allow you to create settlement documents in parallel, thus optimizing system resources (such as CPU and memory). This option will be important depending on the volume of contracts your company expects.

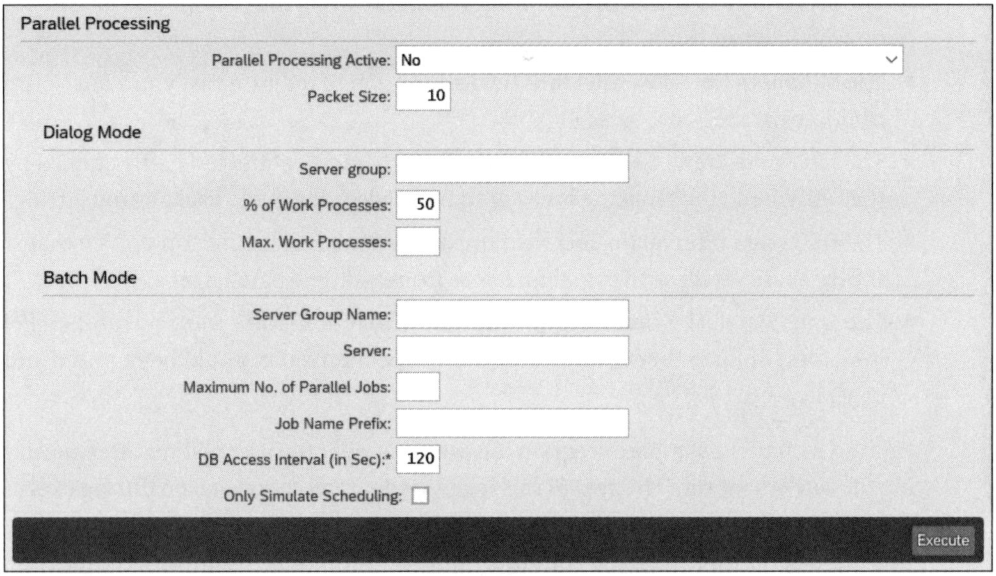

Figure 5.34 Settling Customer Condition Contracts: Parallel Processing

The important fields and checkboxes in this area include the following:

- The **Parallel Processing Active** field allows you to request the execution of asynchronous work processes to take place in parallel. This option optimizes processing time but can put a toll on hardware resources. The next setting ensure that your hardware can handle the load generated by this execution.
- The **Packet Size** field is the number of condition contracts processed on each parallel process. A large number reduces the benefit of parallel processing; a small number consumes more hardware resources.
- The **Server group** field identifies a group of application servers to handle the load of creating billing documents when running the settlement in the foreground.
- The **% of Work Processes** field indicates the percentage of available work processes that should be dedicated to parallel processing.

- The **Max. Work Processes** field identifies the maximum total number to parallel work processes that can be run at any time.
- The **Server Group Name** field identifies a group of application servers to handle the load of creating billing documents when running the settlement in the background (as batch jobs).
- The **Server** field identifies a specific server name where the background job should be scheduled and should run.
- The **Minimum No. Of Parallel Jobs** field allows you to indicate that you want to run multiple parallel jobs.
- The **Job Name Prefix** field identifies the first character of the job name created by the settlement, thus making is easier to find these jobs in the background job log.
- The **DB Access Interval (in Sec)** field must be defined to ensure you don't exhaust the database server with constant access from multiple parallel jobs.
- The **Only Simulate Scheduling** flag indicates that you don't want to run parallel jobs, just simulate their creation to assess how many jobs would be required and other aspects.

Figure 5.35 shows a sample execution log, which is what the user will see after executing the settlement run. The goal of this log is to report all actions taken during execution. If any settlement documents were created, you'll see the document numbers in this log. If certain dates on the condition contract settlement calendar were ignored, you'll see the reason documented as well (but not for dates excluded via selection criteria).

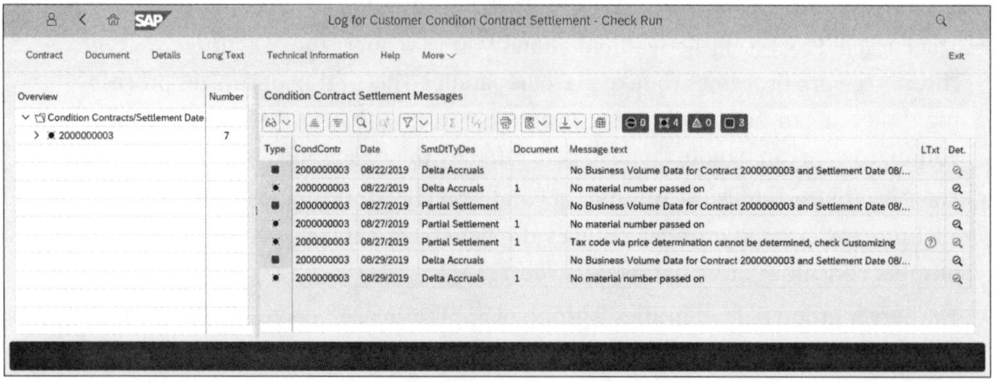

Figure 5.35 Execution Log of Condition Contract Settlement

Defining Activity Reasons

To configure activity reasons, follow the menu path **SAP Customizing Implementation Guide • Logistics – General • Settlement Management • Basic Settings • Define Activity Reasons**.

As shown in Figure 5.36, when creating new entries, specify a three-character activity reason code (**Activity Reason**), add a description (**Description**), and indicate a movement category (**Movement Category**), which indicates whether this settlement run is related to goods movement or value posting.

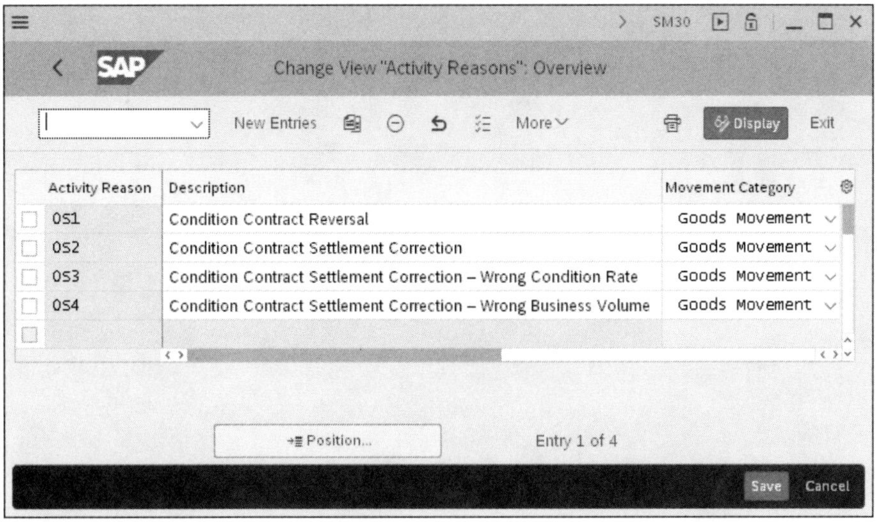

Figure 5.36 Defining Activity Reasons

5.3 Summary

In this chapter, we covered the benefits of creating contracts and rebate agreements in SAP S/4HANA Sales and walked you through the necessary configuration steps. In particular, we covered master, value, and quantity contracts. We also covered custom rebate agreements, including their management and settlement. Maintaining contracts in the system enables you to have long-term transactions to manage all related business conducted over time, thus making your contracts easier to track and follow up on.

In the next chapter, we'll cover sales order management in SAP S/4HANA Sales.

Chapter 6
Sales Order Management

The main component of SAP S/4HANA Sales is the sales order functionality. This feature allows your company to capture customer requests so that the system can assist you in fulfilling them.

The standard sales order process handles the core business of most companies that use SAP S/4HANA. Figure 6.1 shows the process of selling tangible goods to external customers.

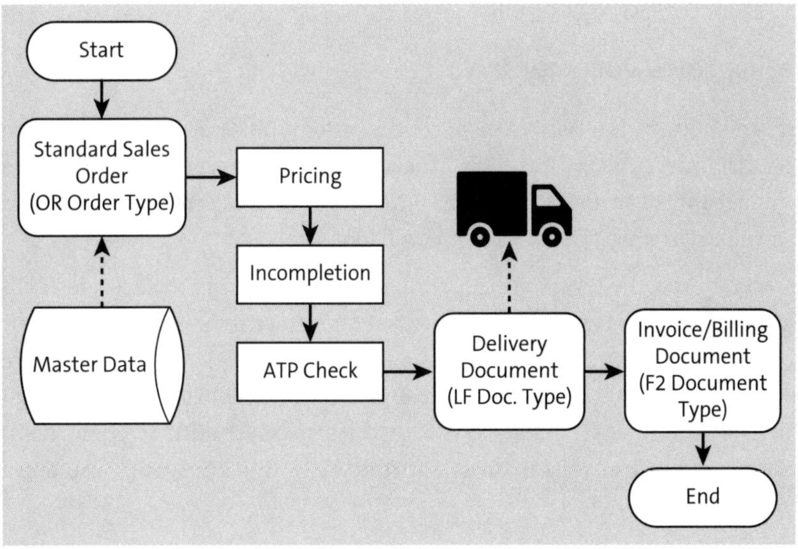

Figure 6.1 Basic Standard Sales Order Process When Selling Tangible Goods

The process starts with the sales order, which may be created manually using Transaction VA01 or the SAP Fiori app Create Sales Order. Commonly, sales orders are created via interfaces such as Electronic Data Interchange (EDI) directly from customers or from sales channels such as web sales, mobile apps, third-party customer relations management (CRM) tools such as Salesforce and others.

In this chapter, we'll use Transaction VA01 to create a sales document type, walking you through the necessary configuration settings step by step. We'll then describe the usage of each tab used for creating a standard sales order, first starting with the overview tabs, then moving on to the header and item data tabs.

Within the sales order entry screen, we'll highlight a few noteworthy processes from other chapters, especially pricing (discussed in Chapter 4) and the available to promise (ATP) check (discussed in Chapter 7) as well as the incompletion procedure, which is a log of incomplete items, in Section 6.5. We'll also mention the corresponding tabs for order-relevant functionalities.

After a sales order is created and all its processes completed successfully, it will become relevant for shipping and then billing. Chapter 9 and Chapter 10 will delve into details on these functions. In this chapter, we'll focus on the activities that occur when a sale is registered in the system. We'll also describe commonly used variations of standard orders, such as rush orders (Section 6.6) and cash sales (Section 6.7).

6.1 Creating Sales Documents

On the first screen in Transaction VA01, enter the order type (**Order Type**), as shown on Figure 6.2. An order type is often called the *sales document type*; these terms are used interchangeably. You must select an order type on this screen because this information will drive what the next screens will look like.

To be precise, you'll use the term "sales document" when referring to multiple document categories (free of charge orders, returns, credit/debit memo requests, deliveries, billing, quotes, inquiries, and contracts as well as regular sales orders). Orders are intended only for sales orders, but this is not always the case. For example, although on this screen the field is labeled **Order Type**, you can also create returns, credit/debit memo requests, and other types of sales documents. In this book, we'll use these terms interchangeably.

The order type will also affect number ranges, pricing, reporting, delivery blocks, mandatory reference, order data validation criteria, ATP check rules, partner determination, texts, output messages, incompletion, credit checks, shipping, and billing. In Section 6.1.1, we'll describe the control settings for some of these functionalities, while other functionalities are described in other chapters in this book.

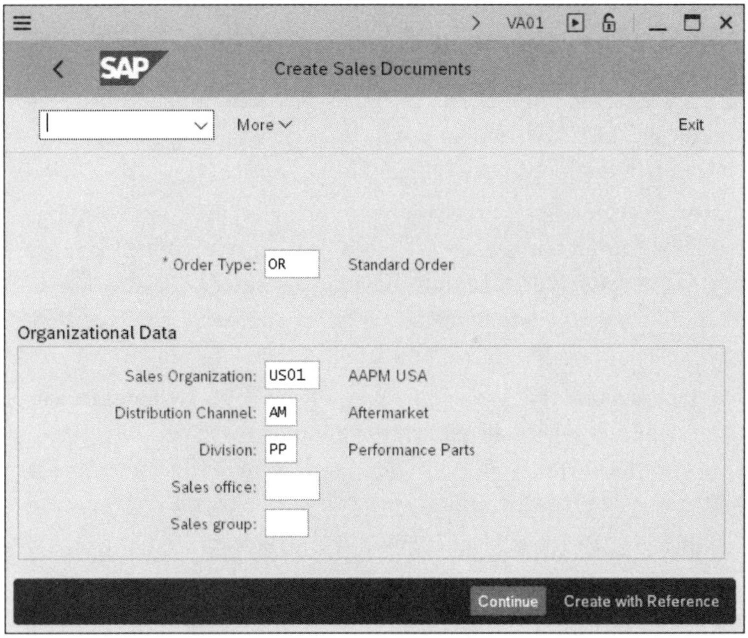

Figure 6.2 Creating a Sales Order in Transaction VA01: Initial Screen

Change Existing Configuration or Create New Types?

A common debate is whether you should change the existing configuration that SAP has provided out of the box for order types (such as OR), or if you should create new document types from copies of those standard order types (for example, ZOR) to keep the SAP-provided configuration (OR) pristine for reference. SAP may change the OR configuration in future support packages (new version releases and upgrades), and thus, you may need to rework your configuration changes. When using your own custom order type ZOR, no problems will arise when SAP updates the system since SAP never changes or creates new document types beginning with the letter "Z," which is referred to as the "SAP allowable namespace".

Companies that are risk-oriented often set a rule to always create a new document type whenever changes are required, but invariably, some of the standard order types may be changed along the way. Thus, the rule has so many exceptions that the rule ends up becoming merely a suggestion.

From experience, by eliminating the substantial effort required to replicate document types, changing the standard document types might be more efficient, cost effective, and higher quality. You must only create new order types if you're changing the intended nature of the order type. For instance, you must never make OR free of charge; you must use CBFD for free of charge orders or create a new order type because OR is specifically for billable orders. But if you're only turning product attribute messages on or off, the effort is not justified.

When you duplicate (copy) an existing order type, SAP copies its copy control settings automatically, which is helpful but is never all encompassing. Many functionalities may stop working in the new order, type thus requiring a greater understanding of all business processes scenarios/exceptions and a lot of additional configuration, testing, and rework.

Changing an order type is a task that should take only a few minutes, whereas creating a new document type and setting all related configuration may take several days. The risk of making new document types fully operational is harder to convey but is quantitatively higher than the risk of eventually being impacted by a system upgrade that affects a change you've made on standard document types.

SAP provides numerous order types with SAP S/4HANA, of which you'll usually want to restrict some order types from being enabled, tested, or ready to use for your company. This control is accomplished by the configuration steps described in Section 6.1.2.

As shown in Figure 6.2, you'll maintain the fields in the **Organizational Data** section to specify which part of your organization should take credit for the sale. If you leave the fields in this section blank, this information will be taken from the customer master. If this customer has been extended to more than one sales area (as defined by the **Sales Organization**, **Distribution Channel**, and **Division** fields), this transaction will prompt you to choose from the available options.

You can also maintain the **Sales office** and **Sales group** fields, which is important if you have dedicated personnel that must ensure that all the orders they enter always use their sales office and sales group when applicable. The values entered on this screen will be used on this sales order regardless of the customer master data settings. These fields are commonly left blank to accommodate all sales departments that process sales orders.

In the following sections, we'll describe the configuration steps related to this screen, but for now, let's focus on the sales order type configuration (Section 6.1.1), the assignment of sales order types to sales areas (Section 6.1.2), and the specification of the number ranges the sales order type should use (Section 6.1.3).

6.1.1 Sales Order Types

To configure sales document types, open Transaction VOV8 or follow the menu path **SAP Customizing Implementation Guide • Sales and Distribution • Sales • Sales Documents • Sales Document Header • Define Sales Document Types**. On the screen that opens, select the order type OR and then click the **Details** button or press [F2].

As shown in Figure 6.3, when creating a new code, on the **Change View "Maintain Sales Order Types": Details** screen, specify a four-character sales document type (**Sales document type**) and add a description. The **SD Document Category** field is a code used in several transactions and functions by SAP S/4HANA code to drive critical functionalities. This field can be understood as "the type of order type." For instance, if you use "H," the system will treat the pricing on the order as a credit.

The **Indicator** field also drives order functionality and is used for invoice correction documents only; other document types will have this field blank. The **Sales Document Block** field prevents a user from using this order type, either temporarily or permanently.

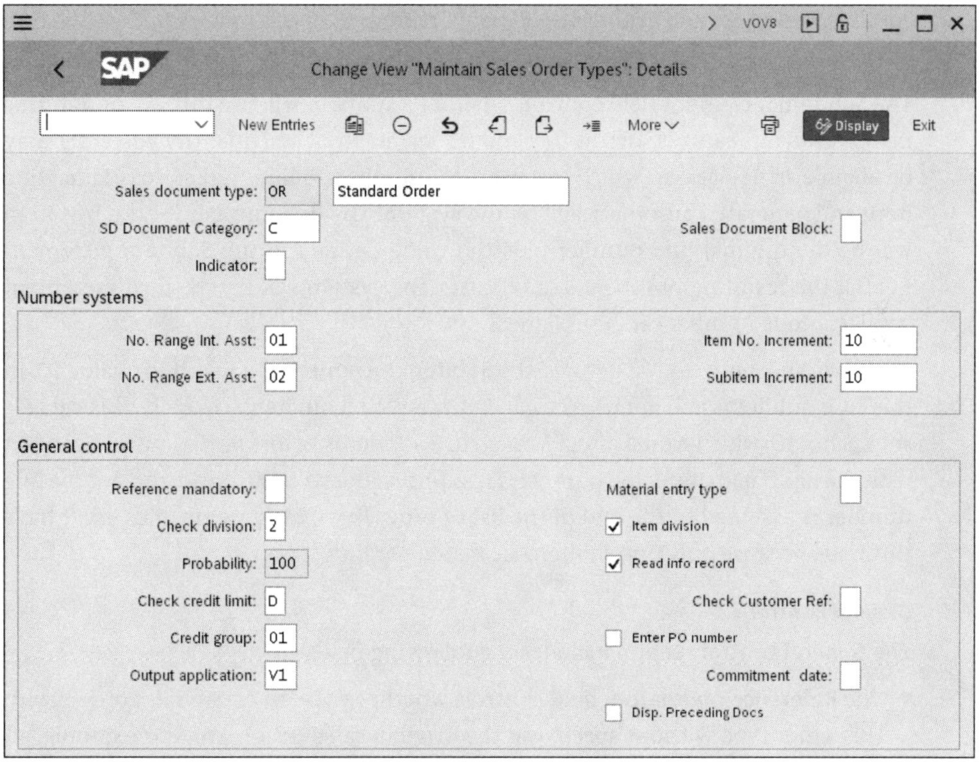

Figure 6.3 OR Sales Order/Document Type Configuration

Let's now look at each of the areas available on this screen.

Number Systems

The number range used for this order type can be defined by maintaining the fields in the **Number systems** section. The **No. Range Int. Asst** field is for internally assigned number ranges and is used when the system should determine what the next order number should be (calculated from the last order number it generated plus 1). **No. Range Ext. Asst** is for externally assigned number ranges, where the user will enter what the sales order number should be.

In Section 6.1.3, we'll describe in detail how to set up number ranges for sales orders, but we recommend using the standard whenever possible. Companies with high sales volumes could run out of numbers and thus must increase the size of the intervals for number ranges; during implementation, you should be able to foresee this eventual probability and increase number range intervals from the beginning.

The **Item No. Increment** field is a numeric value used when the system assigns line numbers at the time of sales order entry. The first line will be 0 plus the number you specify in this field, and every line will be an increment of this initial number. The out-of-the box configuration uses increments of 10 to allow for subitems to be created.

The **Subitem Increment** field controls whether a subitem will use this gap or not. This field is used for features such as free goods: The material and quantity you enter may be eligible as free goods, which are awarded on separate lines linked to original line item and generated automatically by the system. The line number for the free item will be the original line number plus the value defined in the **Subitem Increment** field: If the resulting number already exists, the system will try the next increment until a unique number can be assigned.

As shown in Figure 6.3, we defined the **Subitem Increment** field with the value 10. In this case, subitems will not use the gap between the main items. Usually, this value is set as 1 not 10, which would afford you up to 9 subitems before you come into conflict with the next main item line number. This conflict doesn't cause an error, but the line number is assigned to the end of the list of order lines. Most companies don't have this issue because only one subitem is created per line, if ever.

General Control

The **General control** section includes the following fields:

- The **Reference mandatory** field controls whether you can create sales orders with this order type without specifying the original sales document. For example, an invoice correction (order type CBII) should only be created with reference to an existing invoice. Therefore, order type CBII is defined with the **Reference mandatory** field maintained with "M" (with reference to a billing document).

- The **Material entry type** field enables the utilization of product catalogs, which is typically used when setting up web ordering. This functionality won't be covered in this book.
- The **Check division** field controls whether the division (organizational structure component) maintained on the material master needs to be validated against the division selected on the header of the sales order. You can issue a warning or restrict this mismatch using an error message. Note that you can only maintain one division per material number. If you activate this check, you must make sure that each material always belongs to a single division and that only that division is authorized to sell this material. This approach is rare, so few companies use this validation. Be careful since using this validation may require the duplication of material master entries or the creation of new divisions when not appropriate.
- The **Item division** flag, when selected, means that the order line field will copy the value from the material master; if unselected, the field will be populated with the same value as defined on the order header.
- The **Probability** field is only applicable for quotations and represents the likelihood of this quote becoming a sales order. This field is used when allocating stock to the quote. If the quote is likely to become a sales order, you can save stock to ensure fulfillment on the promised date.
- The **Read info record** flag indicates that the system should read customer-material information records (see Chapter 3, Section 3.6, for more information) and use their values to populate the corresponding sales order line fields. If unchecked, values from the customer-material information records won't be used in the sales order.
- The **Check credit limit** field is the type of credit check for which this order type is relevant. For a free of charge order, you won't want to do a credit check or a less restrictive type of check. On returns, you won't want a check credit at all.
- The **Credit group** field classifies this order type from a credit check perspective. Each credit group may have its own settings.
- The **Check Customer Ref** field controls whether the system should check if the customer purchase order number field (called the *customer reference*) must be checked for duplication. This check may avoid the duplication of data, for instance, when different customer service representatives (CSRs) enter the same order, the

second CSR would get an error message indicating a repeated order. When receiving orders via EDI, this field would also help prevent the duplication of orders when reprocessing EDI messages.

- The **Enter PO number** flag, when selected, will populate the customer purchase order number (customer reference) field with the sales order number when the sales order number field is left blank by a user or by an interface. This option can be used on return orders, but most companies leave the field blank instead (whenever possible).
- The **Output application** field is the main key for output determination using condition techniques (see Chapter 4, Section 4.7, for more details). The V1 (sales) application is assigned to sales orders, and you'll rarely use anything else.
- The **Commitment date** field is used to document the expected delivery date promised to the customer. The date calculated by the ATP check may change when you reschedule the order, but the commitment date would remain unchanged so that you can run reports and identify late deliveries. If you use the ATP check promised date, you would not include all late orders on the report (if the order was rescheduled).
- The **Disp. Preceding Docs** flag, when selected, would mean that some details from the reference document will appear on this document's order entry screen.

Transaction Flow

Figure 6.4 shows the next set of sections on the **Change View "Maintain Sales Order Types": Details** screen, accessed by scrolling down from the screen shown in Figure 6.3.

The **Transaction flow** section includes the following fields:

- The **Screen sequence grp.** field is the code that corresponds to variations of the order screen you can choose from. This code will make certain tabs appear (or not) and affects the order in which the tabs appear.
- The **Display Range** field controls which lines of an order will be displayed. You can hide subitems by default and only show subitems if a user selects them. Most documents show all items (UALL).
- The **Incompl.Proced.** code controls the list of fields that must be populated and determines which functions must be stopped when fields are empty. This field is display-only on this screen; to change this value, you'll need to follow the configuration activities documented in Section 6.5.

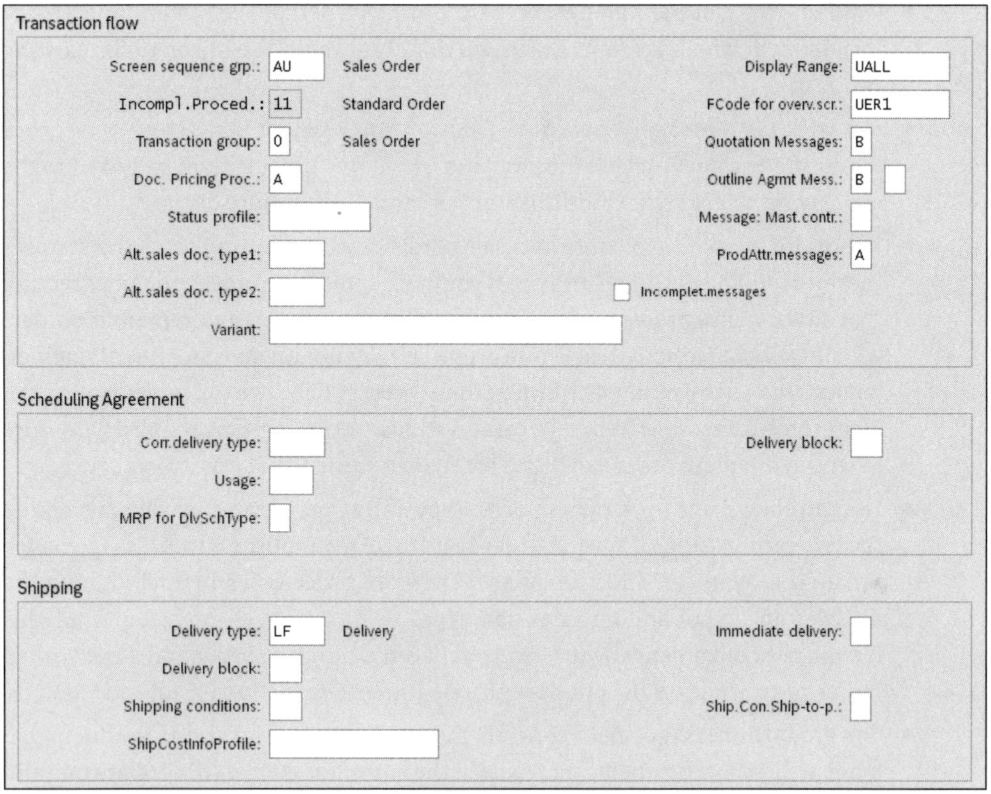

Figure 6.4 Transaction Flow, Scheduling Agreement, and Shipping for OR Sales Order Type Configuration

- The **FCode for overv.scr.** field controls the default tab the screen will show right after the initial screen.
- The **Transaction group** field controls which transaction is used to maintain documents of this type. For example, **Transaction group** 0 is maintained using Transaction VA01; **Transaction group** 3 is maintained using Transaction VA31, etc.
- The **Doc. Pricing Proc.** field is used by pricing to determine the pricing procedure on these sales orders (see Chapter 4, Section 4.1, for more details). This field is assigned in other configuration transactions as well.
- If your company uses quotations, you can use the **Quotation Messages** field to control whether the system should check for existing quotes when an order is entered, which prompts the user if this order should be linked to the existing quotation.

- Similarly, the **Outline Agmt Mess.** field controls whether the system must check for contracts, which prompts the user if this order should be linked to the existing contract.
- Similarly, the **Message: Mast.contr.** field controls whether the system must check for master contracts, which prompts the user if this order should be linked to the existing master contract. (See Chapter 5, Section 5.2, for more details.)
- The **Status profile** field controls a sales order feature that indicates the statuses that an order may be in regardless of shipping or billing. Some companies require that orders follow processes that are controlled, a common requirement for orders with linked service activities. These activities may not involve SAP functionalities, but a status can be maintained when these process have been completed. You can block some users from flagging a certain status and define copy requirement rules to stop subsequent order functions based on a particular status.
- You can allow users to change an order type during processing, which may require the redetermination of several order features. If you must allow users to change order types, you can allow up to two alternate order types by maintaining the **Alt.sales doc. type1** and **Alt.sales doc. type2** fields. Although not often used, this feature is a convenient way to toggle between a standard order and a rush order, for instance, while on the phone with a customer. See Section 6.6 for more details.
- The **ProdAttr.messages** field controls the product attribute check. Product attributes are 10 checkbox fields that exist in the customer master (**Order Data** tab) and on the material master (**Sales View 2**). The **ProdAttr.messages** field specifies the desired behavior when materials with a selected product attribute are ordered by customers with the same product attribute selected. You can issue a warning only or issue an error message that stops further processing of the sales order.
- The **Incomplet. messages** flag, when selected, will suppress the popup message telling the user that the document has been found to be incomplete during the incompletion check. The user will be directed to the list of missing fields that must be fixed to make the document complete. Although not often used, some companies may find this option more efficient, in particular, for rush orders. Note that this flag prevents users from saving an order that is incomplete; they must make the document complete before saving it.
- The transaction **Variant** field allows you to hide fields on the screen for this order type. You can also define these variants using Transaction SHDO, but this setup is rather complex.

Scheduling Agreement

The **Scheduling Agreement** section includes the following fields:

- The **Corr.delivery type** field is the type of delivery document for correcting shortages or overages on agreed delivery quantities.
- The **Delivery block** field is the code assigned to scheduling agreements when tolerance checks are unsuccessful. The user will later need to perform a corrective action and remove the block to allow the document to be processed.
- You can specify the default **Usage** code for this type of document.
- The **MRP for DlvSchType** field allows you to control just-in-time (JIT) material requirements planning (MRP). JIT settings are part of the production planning (PP) functionality, so this field is usually set for and by the production planning team.

Shipping

The **Shipping** section includes the following fields:

- The **Delivery type** field is the default delivery type when creating a delivery document for this order type. You can use a different delivery type, but this default will be used when the user doesn't specify a different type.
- The **Immediate delivery** flag controls whether delivery documents should be created immediately along with the sales order. Some companies may activate this flag for most document types, which doesn't allow any time for users to correct order entry errors. Note also that subsequent delivery processing and backorder management are processes that must take place after the order is entered regardless of this flag. For rush orders, activating this flag is recommended.
- You can assign a default **Delivery block** to be assigned to all sales orders entered with this order type. Users must remove the block before the order can be processed by logistics.
- You can define the **Shipping conditions** that an order of this type must use, which would override the customer master value. This option is commonly used for returns and rush orders.
- If you don't specify the shipping conditions in the **Shipping conditions** field, this information would be copied from the sold-to customer master data. You can change this information with the **Ship.Con.Ship-to-p.** field, which would allow you to copy the address from the ship-to customer master data instead.
- The **ShipCostInfoProfile** field indicates the costing process to use for freight. This functionality requires setting up many details regarding freight, and most companies

in the US either use precontracted third-party carriers and/or use their own trucks; in these cases, the freight calculation is simple, and this field is not applicable. If you need to determine freight charges based on more complex criteria, setting up a freight cost profile and assigning it to this field is recommended.

Billing

Figure 6.5 shows the final sections of the **Change View "Maintain Sales Order Types": Details** screen, accessed by scrolling down from the screen shown in Figure 6.4.

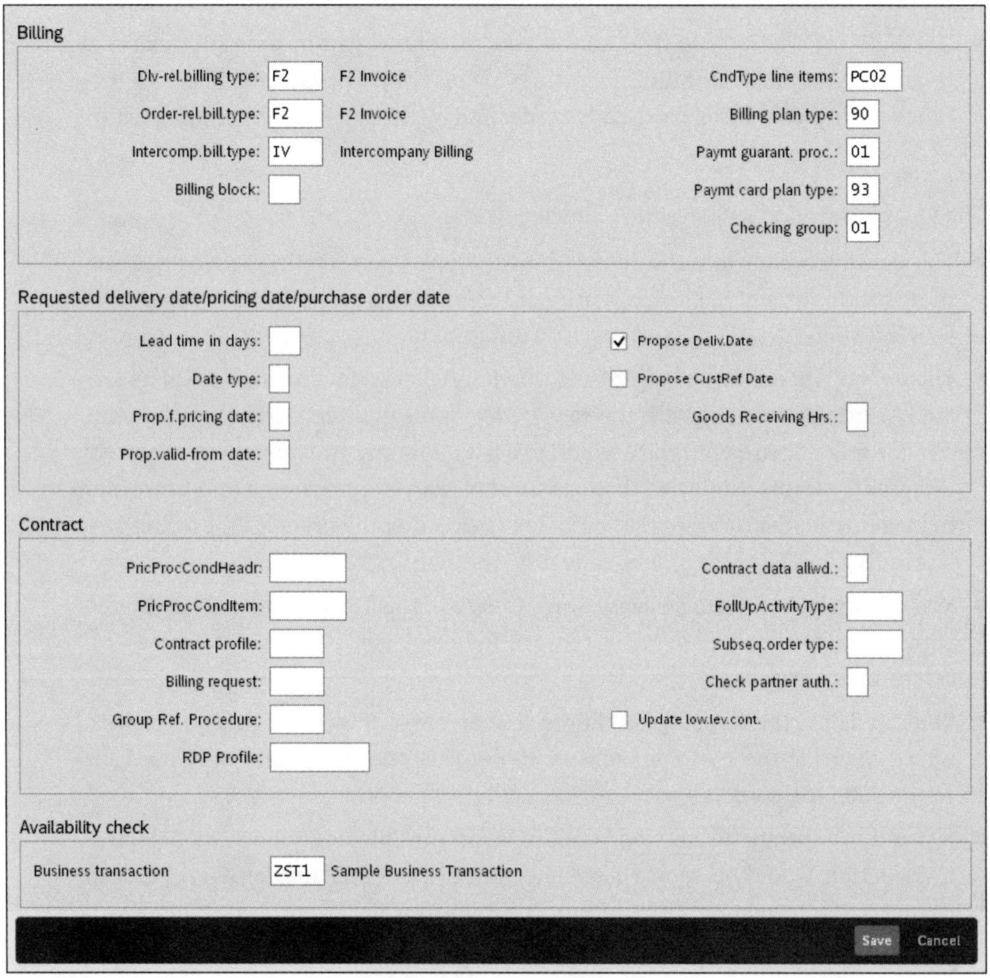

Figure 6.5 Billing, Order Dates, Contract, and Availability Check for OR Sales Order Type Configuration

The **Billing** section includes the following fields:

- You can specify the default billing type to be used when invoices are created with reference to a delivery document number in the **Dlv-rel.billing type** field and/or with reference to the sales order itself in the **Order-rel.bill.type** field.
- The **CndType line items** field is a useful feature for sales order entry, enabling a column or list of order lines on the **Item Overview** tab where you can enter a dollar value. This amount will be copied into the pricing procedure with the pricing condition type specified in the **CndType line items** field.
- When you assign a **Billing plan type** to this order type, you can activate this functionality as described Chapter 10, Section 10.3.
- If intercompany sales are configured for this organizational structure, you'll need to create intercompany billing documents to transfer revenue between company codes, which is achieved by creating a billing document with the document type specified by the **Intercomp.bill.type** field.
- The payment guarantee procedure key (**Paymt guarant. proc.**) is used when you need to use letters of credit or other means of ensuring the customer will pay for the goods or services delivered. This functionality is set up by finance when appropriate, and this field allows you to differentiate the type of transaction. Out of the box, SAP has only one valid value for this field (01).
- You can assign a default **Billing block** to the order type that will be present on all orders created with this type. A user will need to remove the billing block before being able to create an invoice. This block is used for credit/memos and simple return orders.
- The **Paymt card plan type** field is used to activate the credit card functionality. This field can also be used for PayPal and other web-based payment methods. When used, you'll also need to define the **Checking group** to which this order type belongs. The payment card processing is configured based on the checking group, not the order type, which allows you to share the same settings across different order types.

Requested Delivery Date/Pricing Date/Purchase Order Date

The **Requested delivery date/pricing date/purchase order date** section includes the following fields:

- When creating a sales order, the system may propose a requested delivery date (**Propose Deliv.Date**) that represents when the customer wishes to receive the products they are ordering. You can define a default number of days that to use as a rule in the **Lead time in days** field; this number of days will be added to today's date to propose the default requested delivery date. If you specify zero days, today's date will be used. If you don't want the system to propose any default requested delivery date, uncheck the **Propose Deliv.Date** flag. Note, however, that you'll need to always manually enter a date on this field. Most companies use a default requested delivery date with 1 or 2 days as the default lead time for sales from stock. This field is important for ATP checks, where the requested delivery date is the baseline upon which ATP decides whether you can fulfill the customer request (backward scheduling) or not (forward scheduling); see Chapter 7, Section 7.1, for more details.

- The **Date type** field allows you to use different types of requested delivery dates; most companies use a full date, but you can also use week, month, etc.
- The **Propose CustRef Date** flag controls whether the system should populate the customer purchase order date with today's date by default. This field should contain the date on which the customer created their purchase order, which may not be the date on which you received the purchase order (called the sales order date). The customer purchase order date informs you whether the customer had a delay in sending you the request or if you took too long to enter their request in the system. This field is not mandatory, and most companies don't spend a lot of effort on this field nor propose to use today's date as the default for this field.
- The **Prop.f.pricing date** fields indicates how the pricing date should be populated on the sales order. The pricing date is mandatory and will always be populated by the system, but you can use different default values other than today's date. The pricing date is used to find pricing condition records and may affect the final price to the customer, for instance, when running temporary promotions/discounts. If you backdate the pricing date, you can still award an expired discount on a given sales order. This approach is useful if the purchase order wasn't entered into your SAP S/4HANA system immediately upon receipt.
- The **Prop.valid-from date** field allows you to define a default value for the valid-from date used on contracts, quotes, inquiries, scheduling agreements, etc. No validity date is used on sales orders. When appropriate, you can prepopulate the valid-from date with today's date or the first date of next month by default, thus eliminating the need for manual entry.
- The **Goods Receiving Hrs.** field controls whether the system will perform scheduling down to the time of day when each logistics task is to be completed. Few companies schedule at this level, but when organizing warehouse shift workloads and

planning transportation, this feature could be beneficial even though many details can be time consuming to define and maintain. Companies that do use this feature may find it unreliable after go-live due to business changes, even though the system feature itself is not an issue.

Contract

The **Contract** section includes the following fields:

- You can specify a pricing procedure to be used in the header of contracts in the **PricProcCondHeadr** field. This value would overwrite the pricing procedure determination described in Chapter 4, Section 4.1.4. This feature may be used, for instance, on fixed price contracts with periodic billing (billing plans).
- The **Contract data allwd.** field controls whether this order type needs contract information to be defined. This decision will also make contract fields, such as validity date and description, appear on the sales order entry screen.
- You can also specify a different pricing procedure to be used at the line level in the **PricProcCondItem** field.
- The **FollUpActivityType** field is a way to document what should be done after this contract is entered. No values come configured out of the box, and this field is not often used.
- The **Contract profile** field allows for the definition of template contract dates to speed up order entry.
- The **Subseq.order type** field is the sales order type you'll create with reference to this contract by default. You can specify other document types, but if you use the **Subsequent Function** menu option in Transactions VA41, VA42, and VA43, the document type indicated in this field will be used by default.
- When you need to submit a request to create a billing document, the **Billing request** field is where you'll specify the document type for that billing request sales order. Some common examples of billing requests are credit/debit memos and invoice corrections. For contracts, you can also use billing request documents instead of performing billing based on the contract itself.
- The **Check partner auth.** field is used when you want to allow different customers to share the same contract, but only a select group of customers, not any customer on the master data.
- The **Group Ref. Procedure** field is used on master contracts to control which fields should be copied into contracts that refer to it (see Chapter 5).

- The **Update low.lev.cont.** flag controls whether relevant changes made to the master contract must be replicated into the contracts that refer to it.
- The risk distribution plan profile (**RDP Profile**) is usually maintained by request of the finance team.

Availability Check

The **Business transaction** field is used by rule-based ATP checks to control the type of transaction an order type represents. Rules may include the type of transaction when deciding which orders take priority in stock shortage scenarios.

6.1.2 Assigning Sales Area to Sales Document Types

In this example, we'll assign a sales document type for sales orders across all sales areas of our example company, American Automotive Parts Manufacturer (AAPM). No differences should exist between the order that one sales area may use versus that of another. However, before you assign a sales order type to a sales area, you'll need to complete a few prerequisites first.

As shown in Figure 6.6, to define reference sales organizations, follow the menu path **SAP Customizing Implementation Guide • Sales And Distribution • Sales • Sales Documents • Sales Document Header • Assign Sales Area To Sales Document Types • Combine Sales Organizations**. On the screen that opens, click on the **New Entries** button or press F5 and then enter the reference sales organization in the **Ref. SOrg** field.

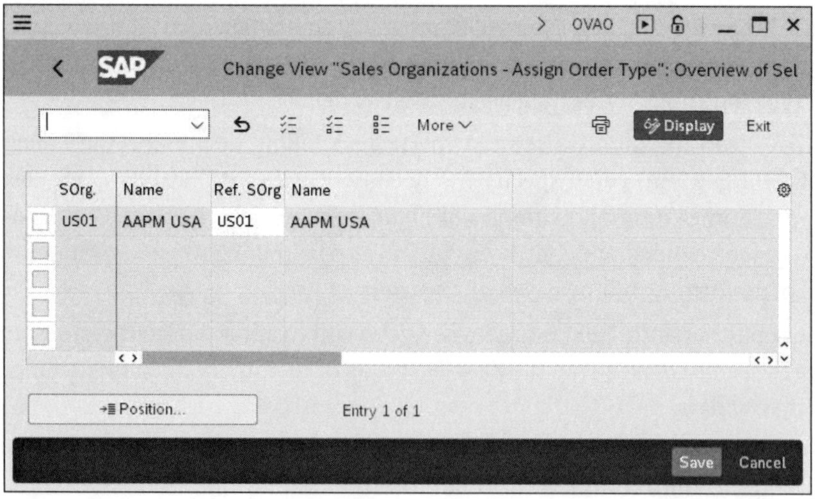

Figure 6.6 Combine Sales Organizations

As shown in Figure 6.7, to define reference distribution channels, follow the menu path **SAP Customizing Implementation Guide • Sales And Distribution • Sales • Sales Documents • Sales Document Header • Assign Sales Area To Sales Document Types • Combine Distribution Channels**. On the screen that opens, click on the **New Entries** button or press F5 and then enter the reference distribution channel in the **RefDistCh** field.

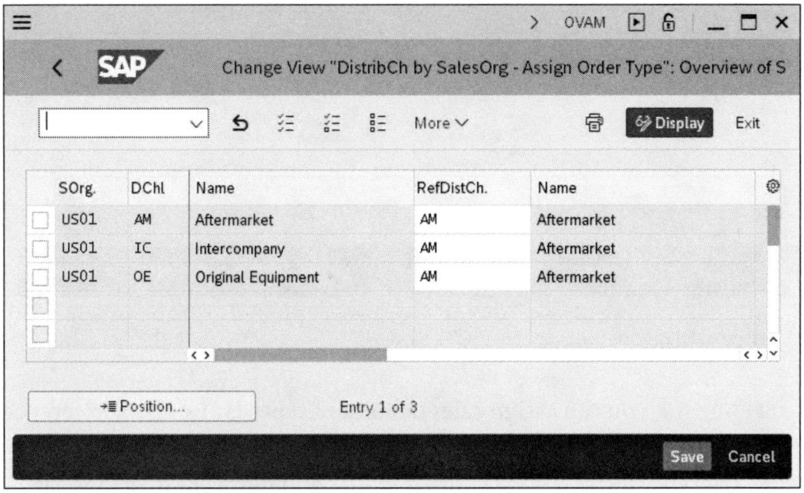

Figure 6.7 Combine Distribution Channels

As shown in Figure 6.8, define a reference division for sales documents by following the menu path **SAP Customizing Implementation Guide • Sales And Distribution • Sales • Sales Documents • Sales Document Header • Assign Sales Area To Sales Document Types • Combine Divisions**. On the screen that opens, click on the **New Entries** button or press F5 and enter the reference division in the **RefDivDoc** field.

Now, having completed these prerequisites, to assign sales order types to sales areas, follow the menu path **SAP Customizing Implementation Guide • Sales and Distribution • Sales • Sales Documents • Sales Document Header • Assign Sales Area to Sales Document Types • Assign Sales Document Types Permitted for Sales Areas**. On the screen that opens, click on the **New Entries** button or press F5.

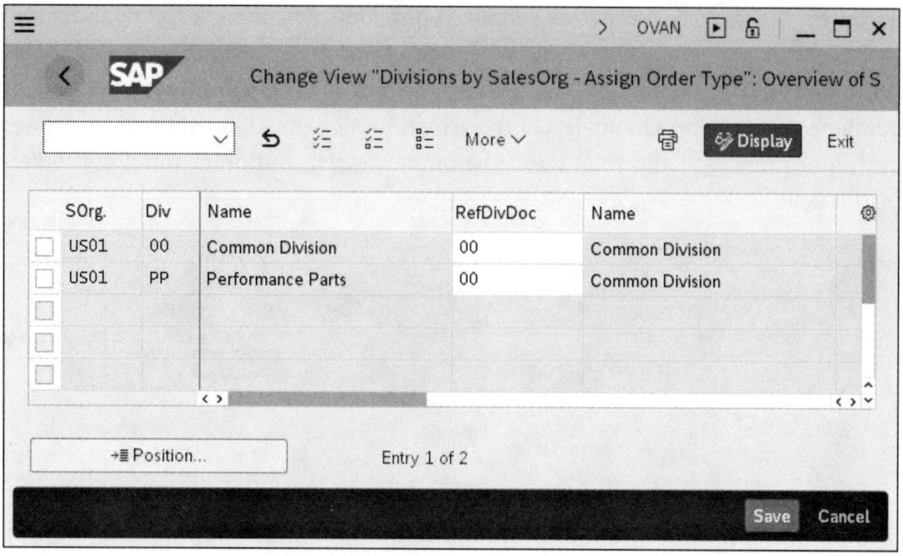

Figure 6.8 Combine Divisions

As shown in Figure 6.9, you can assign sales document types (**SaTy**) to the reference organizational structure elements defined previously, that is, reference sales organizations (**Ref.S**), reference distribution channels (**RefD**), and reference divisions (**Div**).

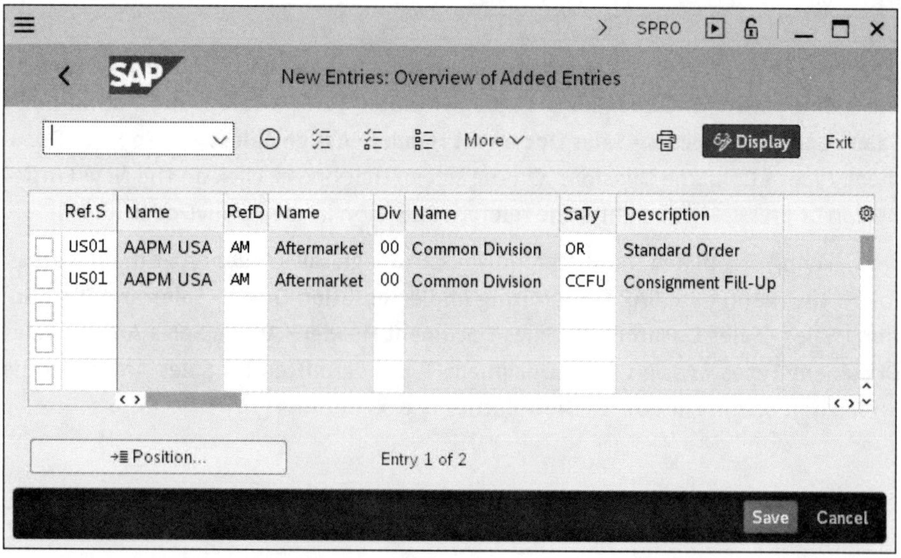

Figure 6.9 Assign Sales Document Types Permitted for Sales Areas

6.1.3 Sales Orders Number Ranges

To configure sales order number range intervals, open Transaction VN01 or follow the menu path **SAP Customizing Implementation Guide • Sales and Distribution • Sales • Sales Documents • Sales Document Header • Define Number Ranges For Sales Documents**.

In our example shown in Figure 6.10, we're creating a new internally assigned called "ZZ" for illustration purposes only. Clicking the **Edit Intervals** button will take you to a new screen ❶ where you'll click the **Insert Line** button or press F6 to create a new number range interval.

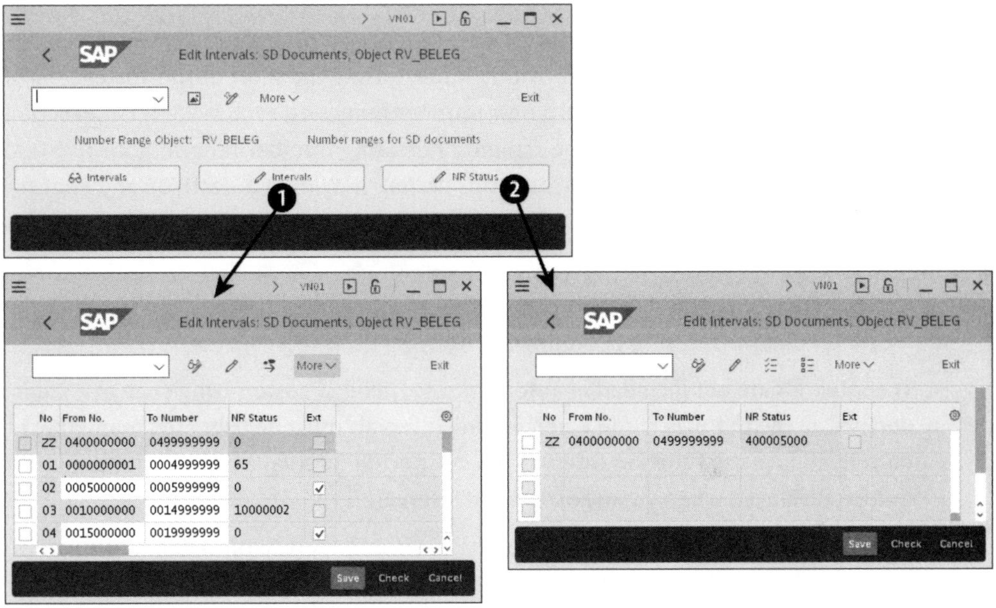

Figure 6.10 Defining Sales Order Number Range Intervals and Status

You'll need to specify a staring number (**From No.**) and an upper limit (**To Number**) that does not overlap any existing intervals. This transaction will validate your entry and prevent you from using an invalid number.

The **Ext** column indicates if this range is to be used for internally assigned number ranges or for externally assigned ones. If you select this field by clicking the checkbox on the left, the number range ZZ can be used in the **No. Range Ext. Asst** field when configuring the sales order type in Transaction VOV8. If the **Ext** field is blank, then ZZ can only be used in the **No. Range Int. Asst** field.

Using number ranges for externally assigned document numbers implements a validation check that prevents users from selecting numbers that could conflict with internally assigned number ranges, which would cause a short dump.

Once you save your number range, you'll need to consider the impact of moving this configuration change across different systems.

Number ranges are not automatically transported because of the **NR Status** column. This column contains the last number used within this number range. When you create a new customer, the system will increment this number and attempt to save the new entry. If an entry already exists in the system for the same value, you would get a severe system failure (short dump), and all your new data would be lost.

Each system has a different **NR Status**, and if you transport a number range from one system to the other, you would copy this value causing the short dump. Instead, most companies opt to manually set up new number ranges on each system. Transaction VN01 will take you directly to the screen for creating number ranges. Note also that you'll need special access to perform this action, including a destination client for configuration, a task that can only be performed with SAP Basis/system admin access.

The system will notify you of this potential short-dump situation when saving the new interval by displaying the following warning message:

The intervals are not included in automatic recording of customizing changes. Transports of all the changes made when editing intervals must be triggered manually. To do this, choose the function Interval -> Transport in interval editing. Note the information displayed when you transport the intervals.

You can manually add number range entries to a transport request and move a number range, by selecting the number range you want to transport and then using the **Interval • Transport** menu options.

Warning

If this transport request is ever reimported into the destination system, a short dump would occur. In this case, you can use Transaction VN01 to update the **NR Status** field to the latest value found.

You can also use Transaction SNUM or SNRO to maintain number ranges. But you'll need to know the number range object. For sales order number ranges, the object is **RV_BELEG** (number ranges for SD documents).

If you click on the **NR Status** button (Figure 6.10 ❷), you can modify the last number internally assigned by the system. Note that changing this number may cause severe damage to the system. You cannot use a number lower than the latest number found on sales documents within this range. Clicking the **NR Status** button is typically only done to prevent potential short dumps.

As shown in Figure 6.10, in our example, we're skipping the first 500 numbers in the new number range by entering the value "400005000" in the **NR Status** column.

6.2 Creating Standard Orders: Overview

The overview tabs contain a mix of header and line information that allows you to enter most of the required sales order information without having to navigate through multiple screens and tabs. Often, you'll need to navigate to header or line details, but the goal is to handle most orders without always having to navigate to multiple tabs.

In the following sections, we'll walk you through each of tabs on the **Create Standard Order: Overview** screen. In the final two sections, we'll walk you through the **All Items** area, which is present on several tabs. Next, we'll walk through the process of defining item categories, a configuration task you'll need to complete to be able to fully fill out these tabs.

6.2.1 Sales

As shown in Figure 6.11, the **Sales** tab will appear when you select a standard sales order (**Document Type OR**) on the initial **Create Sales Documents** screen (i.e., after clicking on the **Continue** button shown in Figure 6.2). This tab is intended to cover the typical needs of your customer service team by combining the most commonly used fields in a concise layout.

You'll use this screen to maintain fields that appear on several other screens, which will refer to this screen for these values.

At the top of the screen, for each of the tabs, you'll see the following fields:

- The **Standard Order** field is where you'll enter the order number, following the external number range configured for this sales order type. Usually you'll leave this field blank and let the system assign the next number according to the internal number range you configured for this sales order type. However, in some instances, you'll want to assign the number yourself, such as in some data conversion scenarios, but this approach is also uncommon. Note that this field name changes according to the configured description of the sales order type selected on the **Create Sales Documents** screen, shown earlier in Figure 6.2.

- The **Net Value** field is a display-only field that will show the total net value of the order as you're entering its lines.

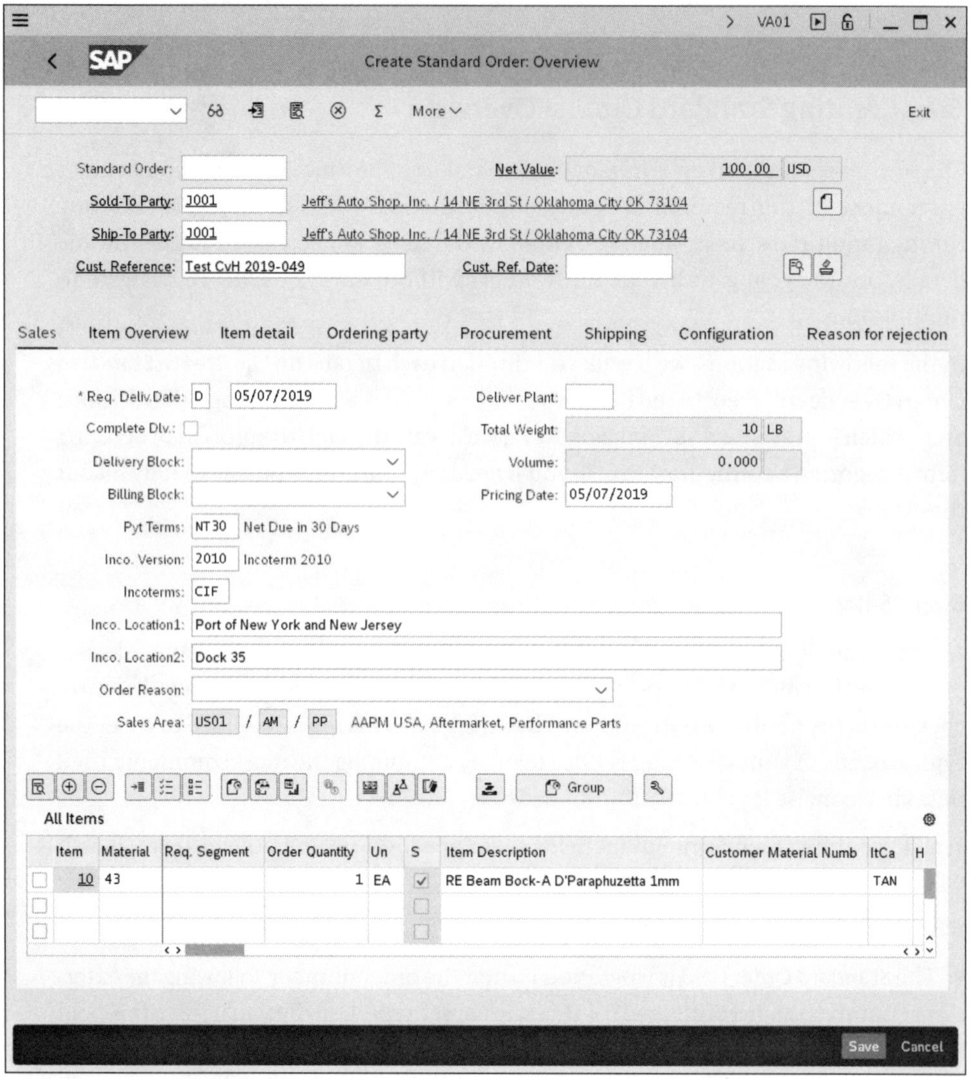

Figure 6.11 Overview: Sales

- You must select the **Sold-To Party** representing the customer/business partner that sent you this purchase order (i.e., company under which the buyers perform their work).
- You can select a **Ship-To Party** representing the customer/business partner that will receive the shipment of products or take delivery of services. If you leave this field blank, the value configured on the business partner master data (partner function) will be used; if more than one ship-to party is found in the master data, a popup window will present the possible options for this field. Note that you can also enter a business partner that is not currently maintained on the master data.
- The **Cust. Reference** field is the customer's purchase order number, which is often mandatory.
- The **Cust. Ref. Date** field is the purchase order date, i.e., the date on which the customer created their purchase order. Note that this date is not the date on which you received the purchase order (which is the sales order date). The customer purchase order date informs you whether the customer had a delay in sending you the request or if you took too long to enter their request in the system. This field is not mandatory, and most companies don't spend a lot of effort on this field.

Moving on to the **Sales** tab itself, we find the following fields:

- The **Req. Deliv.Date** field (requested delivery date) is the date on which the customer wishes to receive the products they are ordering. The requested delivery date is the baseline upon which ATP decides whether you can fulfill the customer request (backward scheduling) or not (forward scheduling); see Chapter 7, Section 7.1, for more details.
- You can select a default delivery plant (**Deliver.Plant**) to be used on all lines. Often, you won't make a selection in this field (**Deliver.Plant**) instead use the master data defaults you've already set up.

Note

If a material was not extended to the plant specified in the **Deliver.Plant** field, the order won't be valid, the system will then look for a plant defined in the customer-master information record. If no customer-master information record exists, or if a plant hasn't been defined or is not valid, the system will look for a plant defined on the customer master data. In this case, if no plant has been defined or is valid, the system will search for a plant on the material master. If no plant is defined or is valid, the **Deliver.Plant** field will be left blank, and you'll need to select a plant for the line, as shown in Figure 6.12.

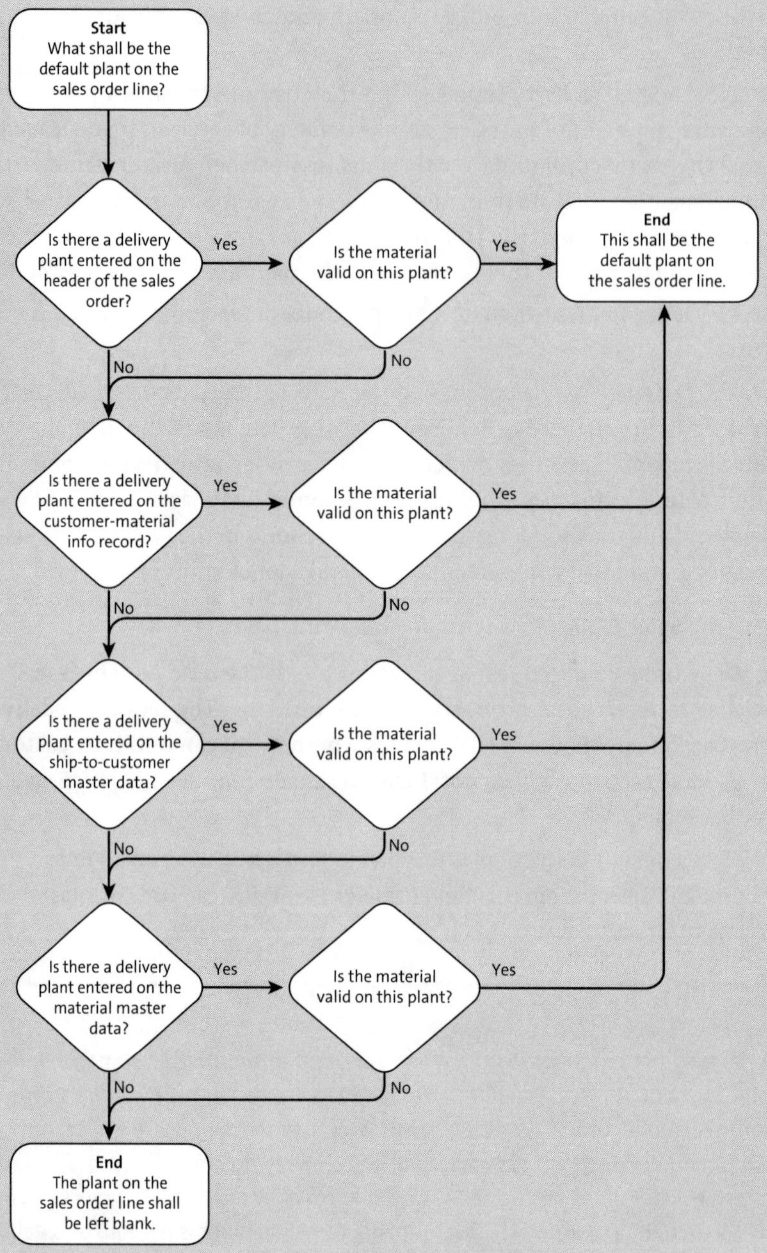

Figure 6.12 Default Delivery

- The **Complete Dlv.** flag controls whether you can make partial shipments to this customer on this order if not enough stock is available to ship. When selected, delivery documents won't be created automatically and will keep all available stock allocated to the order until the pending inventory becomes available and is allocated to the order. If you create a delivery document manually, this flag will cause a warning message, but the delivery document will be allowed for creation.
- The **Total Weight** field is a display-only field showing the total gross weight of the order as you're entering its lines.
- The **Volume** field is a display-only field showing the total volume of the order as you're entering its lines.
- The **Delivery Block** field is a code that controls whether you can perform delivery document-related functions for this order. Depending on the code you choose, different operations will be forbidden. In some rare instances, a delivery may not block any function. Consult Chapter 2, Section 2.3.7, for more details.
- The **Billing Block** field, when assigned, will stop invoices from being create based on this sales order or any of its delivery documents. This block is commonly used on credit/debit memos and simple returns.
- The **Pricing Date** field is mandatory and will always be populated by the system according to the order type configuration. This field is used to find pricing condition records and may affect the final price to the customer, for instance, when running temporary promotions/discounts. If you backdate the pricing date, you can still award an expired discount on a given sales order. This approach is useful if the purchase order wasn't entered into your SAP S/4HANA system immediately upon receipt.
- The **Pyt Terms** (payment terms) field is a key, defined by finance, representing the number of payments and how many days after invoicing the customer must pay for the products/services.
- The **Inco. Version**, **Incoterms**, **Inco. Location1**, and **Inco. Location2** fields refer to the International Commercial Terms defined by the International Chamber of Commerce (ICC) and the World Trade Organization (WTO). These fields are populated from values on the customer master, but you can change these values on the order. The goal is to represent the transfer of ownership of goods when they are shipped. In many countries, this field also dictates who pays for freight. In countries like the United States, this field does not affect freight and is used for insurance purposes only.

The official Incoterm codes are preconfigured in SAP S/4HANA and should not change once defined globally by the ICC/WTO. Ideally, the ICC definitions will be adapted in US companies (i.e., to define who pays for freight), but most companies end up using one of the reserved fields instead (**Customer Group 1** through **Customer Group 5**).

ICC released a new version of the Incoterms in 2010, and another new version may come in the future. SAP S/4HANA allows for new versions via the **Incoterms Version** field, which controls which preconfigured **Incoterms** codes are valid for the selected version.

For some Incoterms, you're required to indicate the place where the transfer of ownership takes place in the **Inco. Location1** and **Inco. Location2** fields, which could be a port, warehouse, origin, destination, etc.

- The **Order Reason** field is mandatory for free of charge deliveries, credit/debit memos, returns, etc. but is commonly left blank for standard orders. You can use this field for standard orders to indicate why a customer is purchasing an item, for instance, the price, a television commercial, etc. but this scenario is uncommon. See Chapter 13, Section 13.2.1, for more information about the configuration of this field.
- The **Sales Area** field (sales organization, distribution channel, and division) shows the organizational structure elements you selected on the initial screen. If you left these fields blank on the initial screen, the system will use values from the customer master data of the selected sold-to customer. If the customer was extended for more than one sales area, the system will open a popup window with possible options for you to select. These display-only fields are for reference only.

Under the **All Items** section of this screen, you can maintain lines of the sales order. You'll see the most important fields of the sales order lines and some fields that simplify data entry. Section 6.2.9 has details for each column in this section of the screen.

6.2.2 Item Overview

The **Item Overview** tab, shown in Figure 6.13, has fewer header details so you can focus on entering multiple lines on the same screen before having to page up and down. We already discussed some fields under this tab (**Requested Deliv.Date** and **Delivering Plant**) in Section 6.2.1, and we'll discuss the line fields (**All Items**) in Section 6.2.9.

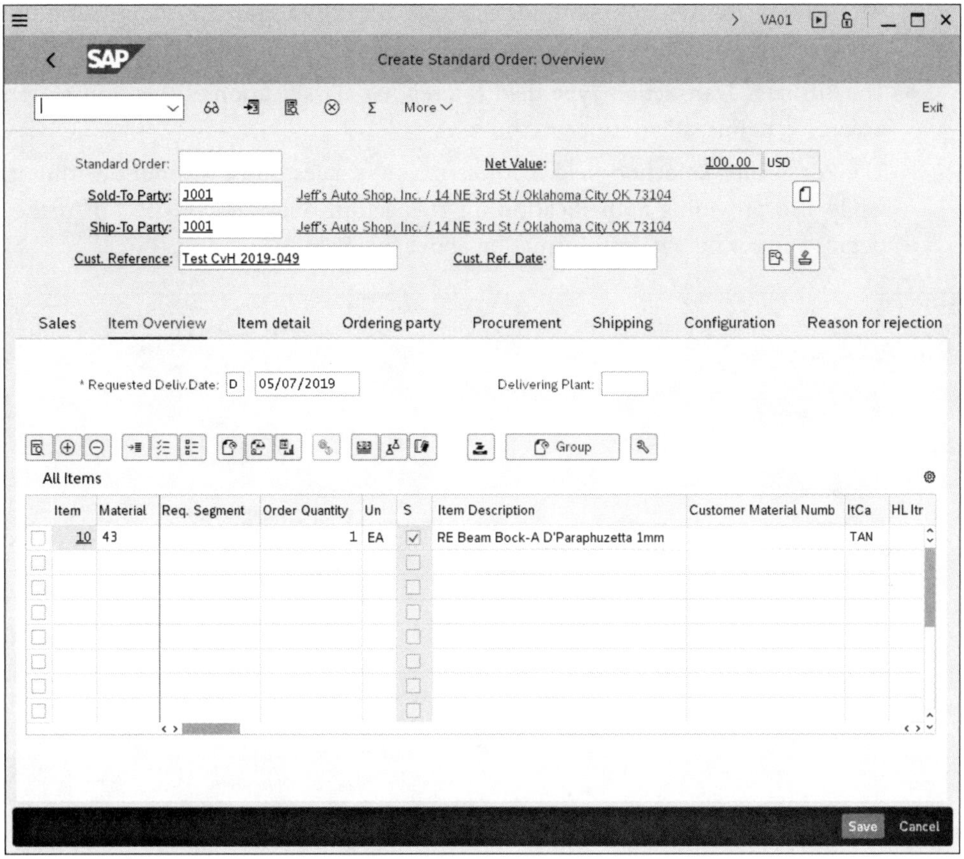

Figure 6.13 Overview: Item Overview (Summary)

6.2.3 Item Detail

The **Item Detail** tab, shown in Figure 6.14, has contains several detailed fields for the selected line. You can navigate from line to line using the arrow icon on the top of the tab; another icon allows you to create new lines. This tab is used to review and make changes to the detail fields shown but is not often used.

Most of the fields on this tab were detailed in Section 6.2.1, and the **All Items** fields will be discussed in Section 6.2.9. However, this tab does introduce a few new fields, such as the following:

- The **Unit Conversion** field is a display-only set of fields that derive from the material master by default. These fields show the material-specific conversion between various units of measurement, for example, for boxes, crates, bags, etc., and the stock-keeping UoM (usually "ea" for "each").

- The **Business Transaction Type** field is a regular classification of this transaction according to Intrastat (European Union).
- The **Reason for Rejection** field is for canceling a sales order without deleting it, while also providing a justification for this action. See Section 6.2.5 for further details and configuration information about this field.

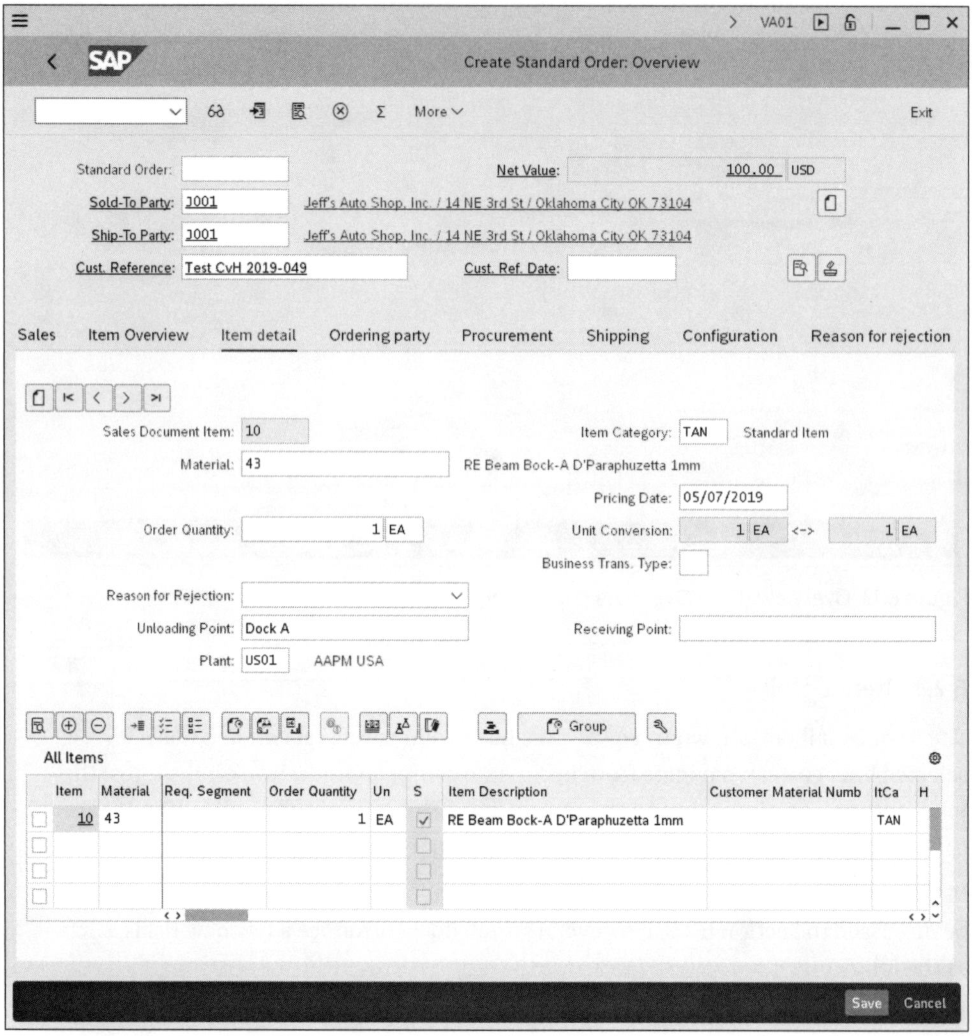

Figure 6.14 Overview: Item Detail

- The **Unloading Point** field is a specific location within the ship-to customer facility where the goods should be delivered. For more details, see Chapter 2, Section 2.2.11.
- The **Receiving Point** field is a sublocation from the unloading point as defined for the ship-to customer (when applicable).

6.2.4 Ordering Party

The **Ordering party** tab, shown in Figure 6.15, focuses on the customer purchase order information and is used when you need to capture all details from a customer purchase order. This information is usually required when sending data electronically back to the customer via EDI.

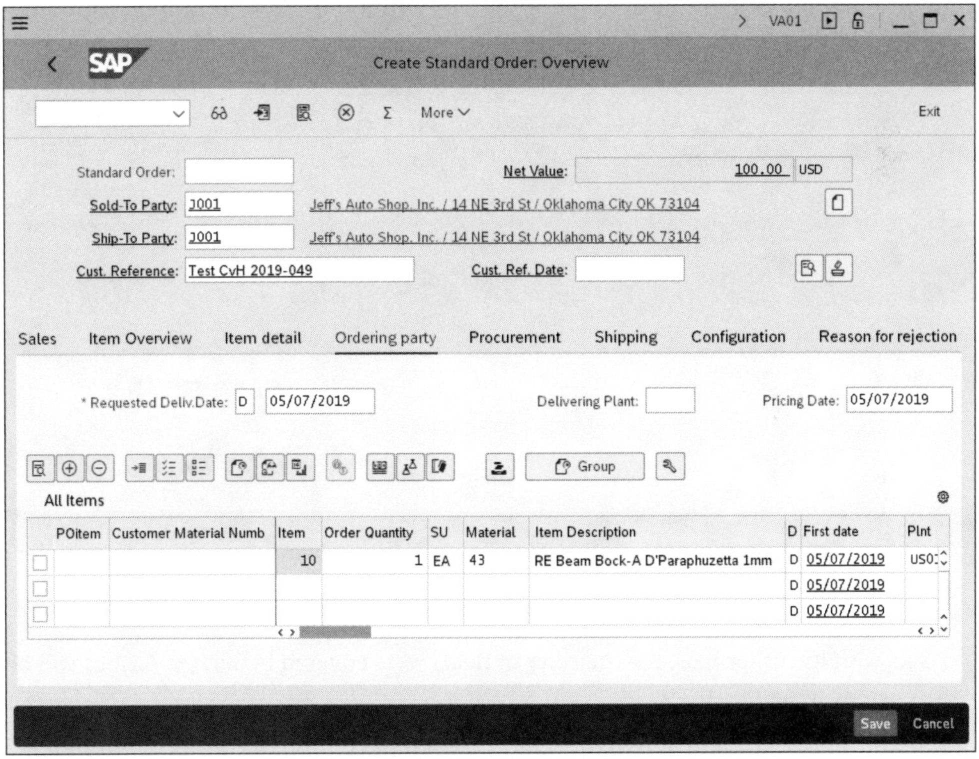

Figure 6.15 Overview: Ordering Party

Most fields on this tab were detailed in Section 6.2.1 and Section 6.2.9. However, we must mention one new line-level field: The **POitem** field is the line number on the customer purchase order we received. SAP S/4HANA will still assign the line number as specified in the order type configuration; this field is for information and customer reference only.

6.2.5 Procurement

The **Procurement** tab, shown in Figure 6.16, focuses on how you'll source and obtain the necessary inventory to fulfill this sales order. This tab introduces the concept of schedule lines, which we'll define in Section 6.4.7.

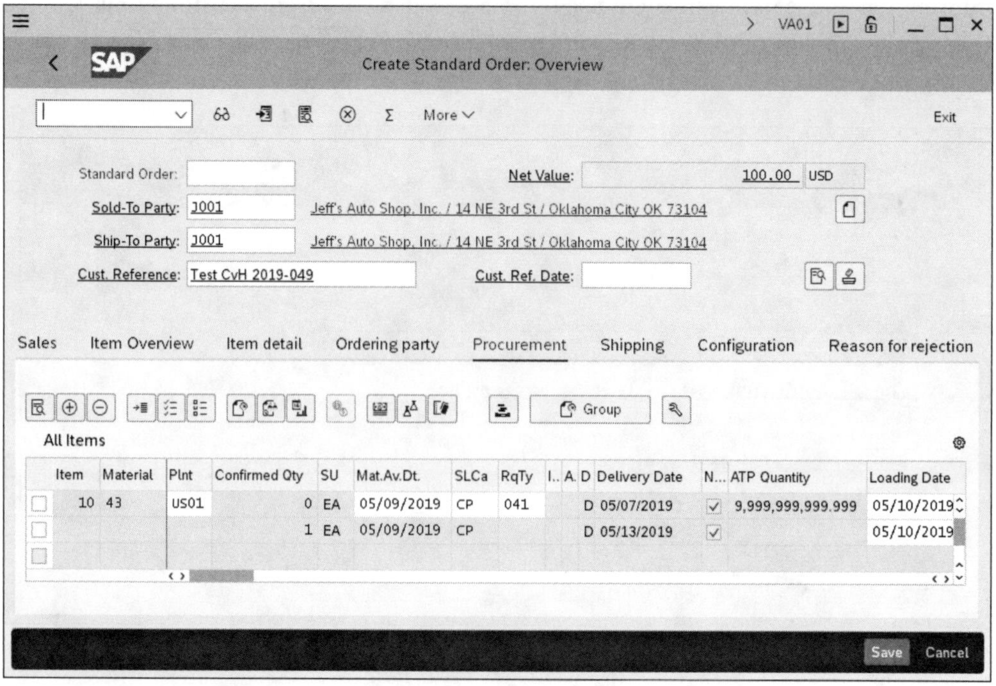

Figure 6.16 Overview: Procurement

As with the other tabs, the majority of fields were covered in Section 6.2.1 or will be covered in Section 6.2.9.

However, one field to note is the requirement type column (**RqTy**), which is often the reason you'll use this tab. This code classifies the need for inventory that this sales order represents from a material requirements planning (MRP) perspective. The configuration of this field is owned by the production planning team, and you should not to attempt to fulfill sales requirements using the functionality involved with this field. We'll provide more details about requirement types in Chapter 7, Section 7.3.

This field is commonly used to toggle between make-to-order versus make-to-stock situations. Thus, sales should be aware of this field, its purpose, and what to do when you want to make new product to fulfill this order and when to use existing inventory. If you're a distribution company rather than a manufacturer, sales would probably not use this field.

You can still use the **Procurement** tab for an overview of all lines and their corresponding schedule lines. Using the **Schedule lines** tab described in Section 6.4.7, you would need to maintain each line individually, but under this tab, you can scroll down through all of them in a single list.

6.2.6 Shipping

The **Shipping** tab, shown in Figure 6.17, focuses on how you'll get product to the customer, summarizing fields available on the header and lines related to creation of the delivery document, picking, packing, shipping, and transportation. This tab introduces you to the *delivery group* concept.

Delivery groups ensure that items are shipped only when all its components are available. The **Delivery Group** field is a freeform numeric value. SAP S/4HANA will check for lines with matching delivery group values to form sets of order lines that must be shipped together.

In scenarios such as structural items (kits/phantom items), material is not inventoried; instead, the components of a material are sellable on their own. As a kit, these components may involve special pricing. The item category can be configured to automatically assign delivery groups to lines belonging to the same structure, thus ensuring these items ship together and giving the receiving customer the impression that these items are a single product. This functionality enables you to combine highly profitable items with high-volume but low-profitability items. The final outcome is better profitability and higher customer satisfaction.

The **Shipping** tab is where you'll modify delivery groups in the case of backorders or special customer requirements. You can also modify delivery groups to optimize freight.

By assigning lines to groups, you can also reduce the number of partial shipments and ensure a significant amount of product is sent on each shipment. For example, let's consider an order with a few high-priced devices with several attachments/accessories for each, as ordered by the customer on the same order.

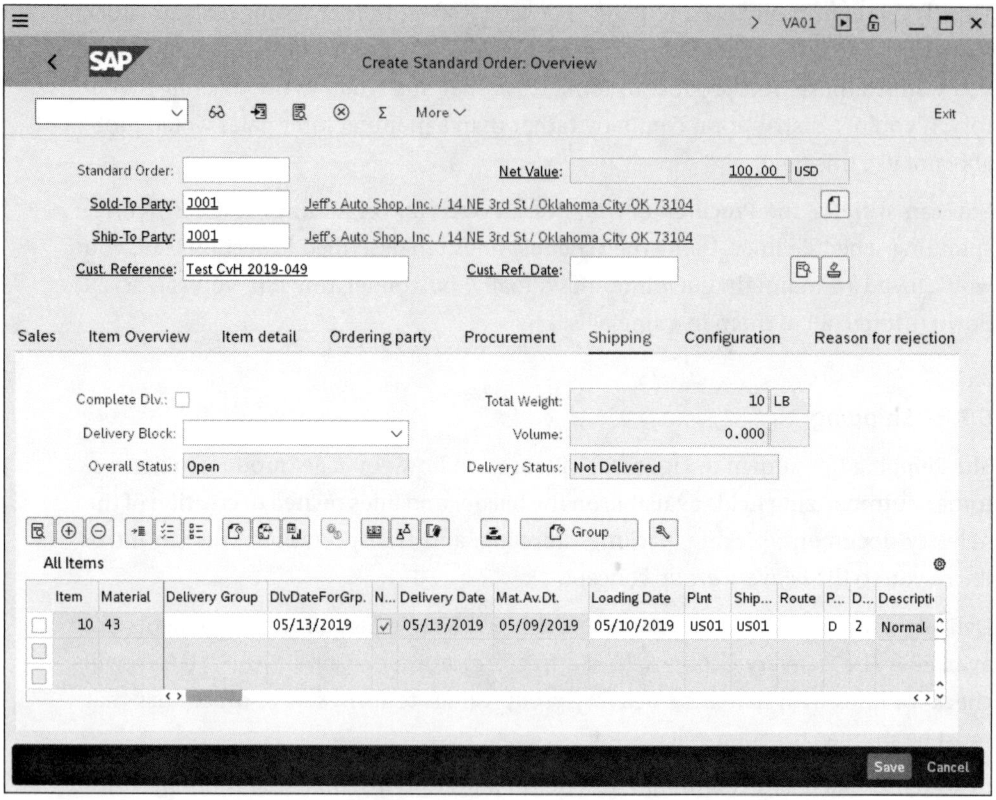

Figure 6.17 Overview: Shipping

You may have all the relevant attachments/accessories in stock but not the equipment/devices themselves, which need to be assembled and prepared for shipping, thus consuming more warehouse lead time than the smaller parts. Without specifying delivery groups, you would ship all the attachments/accessories to the customer, who will then have to wait for the actual devices to arrive later.

From a profitability standpoint, you can bill the customer for faster shipping product this way; however, from the customer point of view, this situation is frustrating. You would achieve higher levels of customer satisfaction by shipping each piece of equipment with its corresponding accessories, so assigning delivery groups to these lines using this tab is worth the effort.

You can also maintain the requirement type field (**RqTy**) on this tab, as defined in Section 6.2.5, by scrolling to the right.

6.2.7 Configuration

The **Configuration** tab, shown in Figure 6.18, focuses on selecting the correct configuration of a material in a variant configuration environment, for example, to use the same material number while selecting specific values for certain predefined characteristics as requested by the customer on this specific sales order line.

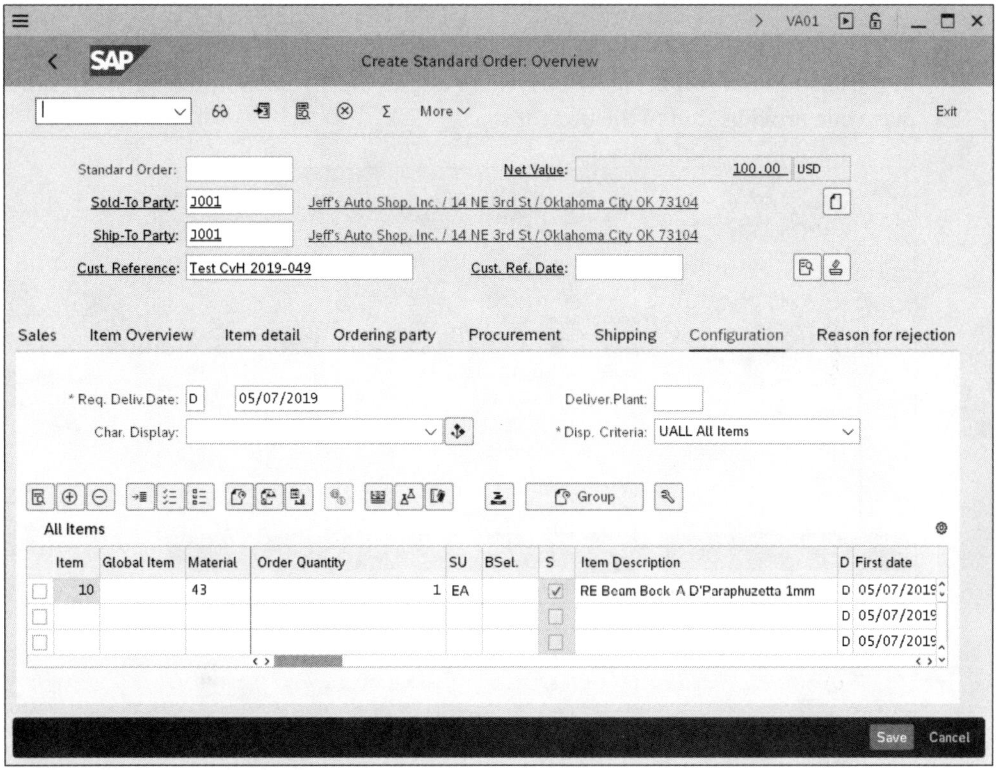

Figure 6.18 Overview: Configuration

This tab includes the following fields:

- The **Char. Display** field is a predefined layout in which the configurable material characteristics are made available for maintenance, which we'll show you how to configure shortly. Once you select a value for **Char. Display**, the configured characteristics will be added to the order lines window as if they were line fields to make viewing and maintaining values across all lines easier. You can define a default value for this field in your user profile parameters with the parameter ID VAM.

- The **Disp. Criteria** field is defined in the order type configuration and made available on this screen so you can change this value when necessary. This value affects how many and what types of sales order lines are shown on this screen.

To configure the display values of characteristics display, follow the menu path **SAP Customizing Implementation Guide • Sales and Distribution • Sales • Sales Documents • Fast Entry of Characteristic Values in Sales Documents • Define Characteristics Display for Overview Screen**.

In the example shown in Figure 6.19, we're displaying an existing characteristics display code provided out of the box for sales.

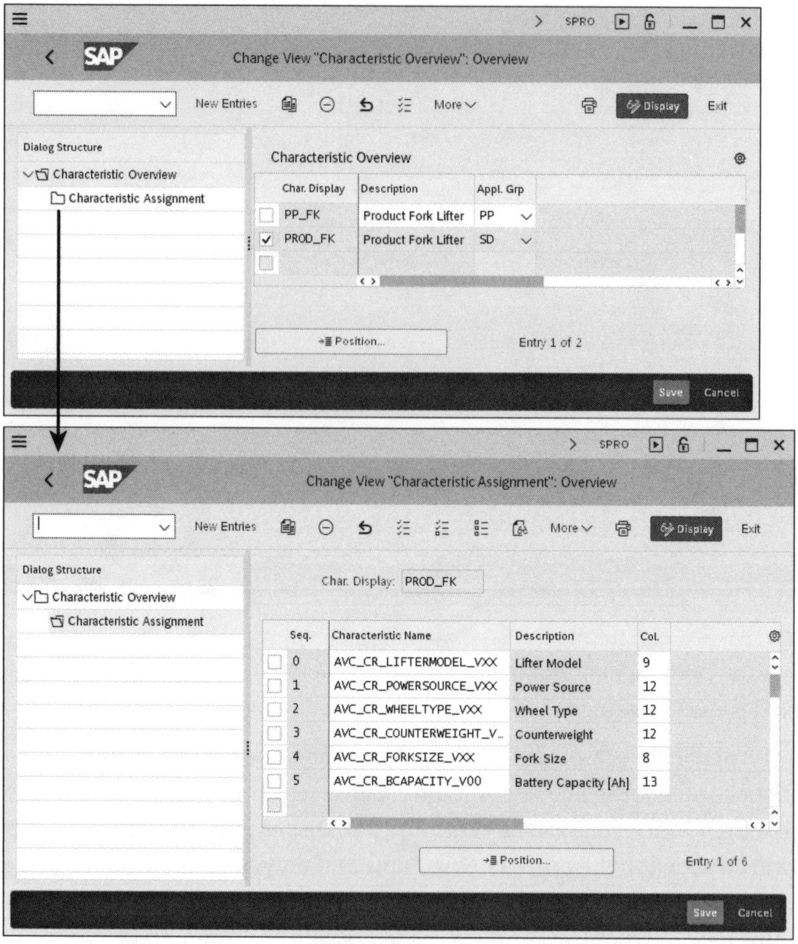

Figure 6.19 Defining Characteristics Display for Overview Screen

This configuration activity relies heavily on the variant configuration characteristics set up in Transaction CT04, which outside of the scope of sales. Typically, the production planning team or a team tasked with variant configuration will be responsible for this feature, so we won't discuss variant configuration further in this book.

The **Char. Display** field is for an eight-character code for a valid characteristic code created in Transaction CT04 (Classification System Characteristics). For each **Char. Display**, you'll also enter a description (**Description**) to help users select the right entry. You must also identify the intended purpose of this characteristic in the **Appl. Grp** field, by selecting **PP** or **SD**. Only **Char. Display** codes defined with **SD** codes can be used under the **Configuration** tab on the **Create Standard Order: Overview** screen. The characteristics defined with **PP** are used for production orders.

Once you define the **Char. Display**, select the entry and double-click on the **Characteristic Assignment** option in the **Dialog Structure** on the left, as shown in Figure 6.19.

A screen will open where you'll enter the list of relevant **Characteristics Name** entries (as defined by the variant configuration team in Transaction CT04) that you want added to the **Configuration** tab of the sales order.

You can also specify the order in which these characteristics appear using the **Seq.** field and also use the **Col.** field to define the default width of the column, measured in number of characters.

6.2.8 Reason for Rejection

The **Reason for rejection** tab, shown in Figure 6.20, focuses on the rejection/cancellation of sales order lines. Once the reason for rejection is assigned, the line is no longer relevant for delivery, billing, or any other functions. Using a reason for rejecting is better than deleting the line so you can keep track of the reason why the line was deleted.

To define reasons for rejection, follow the menu path **SAP Customizing Implementation Guide • Sales and Distribution • Sales • Sales Documents • Sales Document Item • Define Reasons For Rejection**. On the screen that opens, click on the **New Entries** button or press F5.

On the screen shown in Figure 6.21, specify a two-character rejection reason (**Rejection Reason**) and add a description (**Description**). The code itself, when assigned to the sales order line, will prevent an order line from being shipped and billed to the customer.

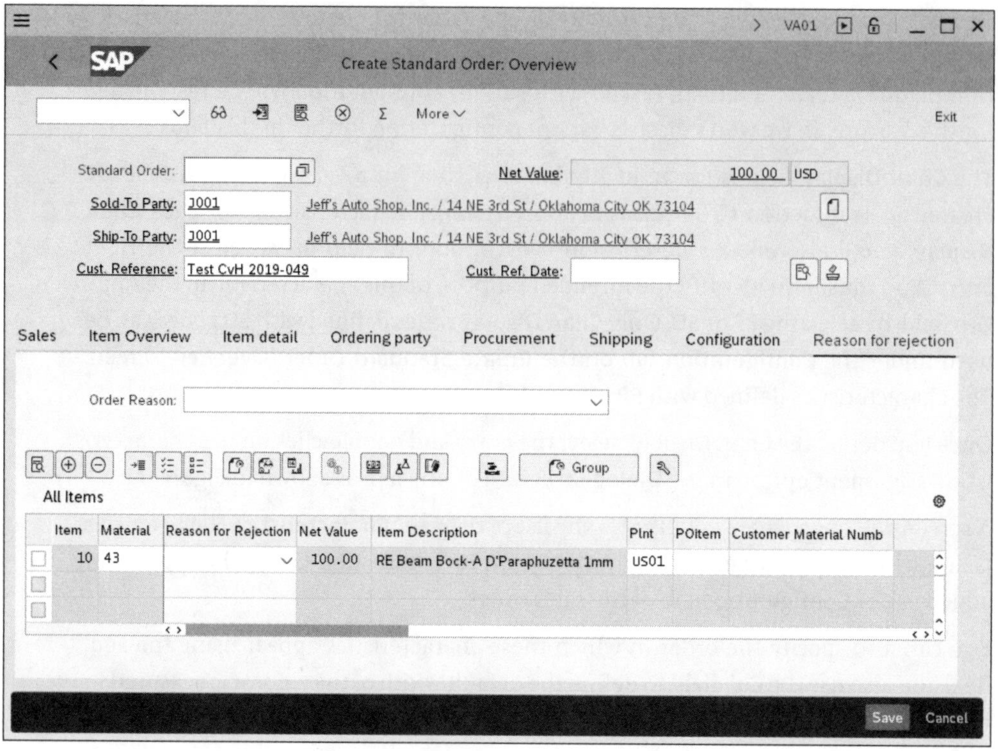

Figure 6.20 Overview: Reason for Rejection

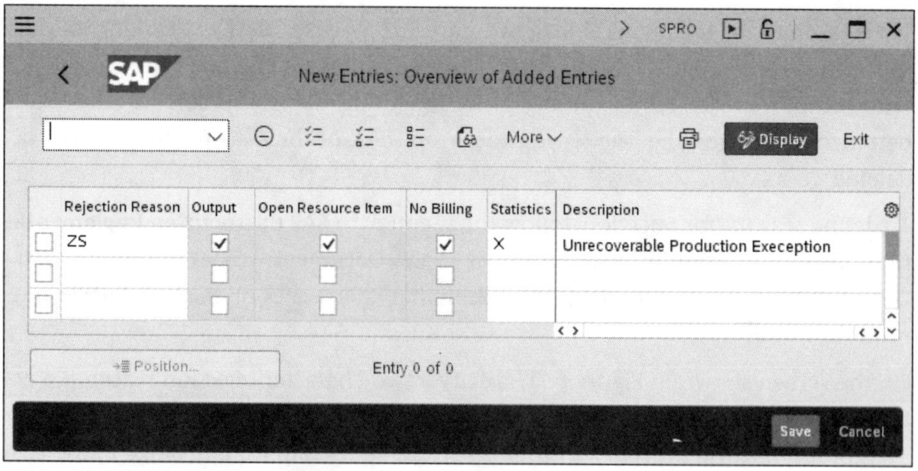

Figure 6.21 Defining New Reason for Rejection Codes

You can still show rejected lines on order-based forms and other electronic output message by using the **Output** flag. Codes with this flag selected will now be shown on interfaces.

In service scenarios with resource-related billing, the **Open Resource Item** flag, when selected, indicates that the rejected line should make the order relevant for an additional debit memo request. The **No Billing** flag, when selected, prevents a rejected line from being copied into the billing document and, as a consequence, from being shown in invoice forms and interfaces.

6.2.9 All Items

On the tabs of the **Standard Order: Overview** screen, the **All Items** section allows for the entry of order lines, as shown in Figure 6.22. Because there are so many possible columns for this area, we have split this figure in half, enabling you to see more of the columns. To access additional columns in the system, just scroll right. Note that you can see different columns on different order types. You can also add new columns using the configuration (gear) icon on the top right corner right above the **All Items** grid.

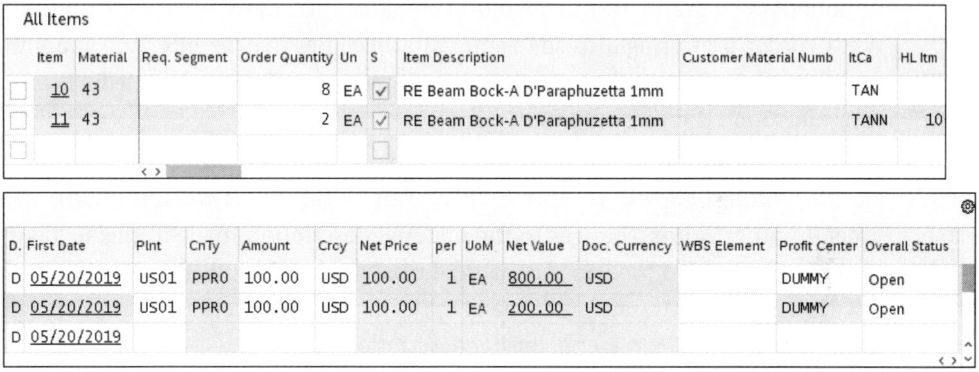

Figure 6.22 All Items Window

By default, the columns included in this window include the following fields:

- The **Item** field is the number of the sales order line as assigned by the system according to the order type configuration, typically it starts with 10 and is incremented by 10 (10, 20, 30, etc.). You can manually select the desired line, but it is not necessary.
- The **Material** field is your material number from the material master data. If you're using the material determination feature (see Chapter 4, Section 4.3), you can enter the value to be translated into your official material number in this field.

- The **Req. Segment** field corresponds to a new technique called *stock segmentation*, which divides your inventory into logical "buckets" called *requirement segments* from which you can pick and fulfill sales orders. This feature allows for the allocation of on-hand inventory to specific purposes. The order will only pick from their assigned requirement segment, leaving remaining on-hand inventory available for other orders. Once the selected requirement segment is exhausted, you can decide on an alternative or keep the order in backorder status until new inventory is added. Many companies use storage locations for this purpose; on this version, using storage locations is no longer necessary, and you should use inventory segmentation instead, which is a materials management (MM) configuration.
- The **Order Quantity** field is the quantity the customer is purchasing, expressed in the unit of measurement indicated in the **Un** column.
- The **S** field is a display-only indicator that tells you if more than one schedule line has been assigned to this sales order line. This situation often means this line is part of a backorder scenario, i.e., the requested delivery date can't be fulfilled as requested. The **S** indicator may also mean that you entered multiple requested delivery dates and quantities for the same line on the schedule line screen. Although possible and easy to do, most companies do not use this feature on this type of order, preferring instead to enter multiple lines than to enter one line with multiple schedule lines. For scheduling agreements, multiple schedule lines on a single line item is rather common.
- The **Item Description** field is populated by default from the material master data, and the column allows you to manually change this value to suit a particular order. In other words, changes to the material description made in this field are not reflected (copied back) to the material master data. If you had defined a material description on the customer-master information record, that description will be used instead of the material master description.
- The **Customer Material Numb** field is the material number your customer used for your material number in their system. When entering a sales order, you can type in this field instead of into the **Material** field. If a matching customer-master information record entry is found, the system takes care of assigning your internal material number.
- The **ItCa** field is the item category or type of sales order line. This key field drives major order-related functionalities. We'll discuss, in Section 6.2.10, how to configure item categories using the standard item category TAN as an example.

- The **HL Itm** field represents a higher-level item number that this line is a component of, which is used for structured items such as sales bills of materials (BOMs) like kits/phantom items and in some configurable materials-related applications.
- The **Deliv.Date** field is the type of date you are using for the requested delivery. This value is copied from the corresponding header field.
- The **First Date** field is the first requested delivery date copied from the **Req. Deliv.Date** field from the header that is applicable to this line. The customer may request this date, or you can use the default lead time configured on the order type as a default.
- The **Plnt** field is the plant to which you want to ship product or from which to deliver services.
- The **Batch** field is the material lot you want to use to fulfill this order. Usually, you would select the batch at the order line level for standard orders. On a return, this field is only sometimes used.
- The **CnTy** field is the pricing condition type to use if you enter a value in the next column (**Amount**).
- The **Amount** field is the price for this line if you decide to enter the price manually, thus overwriting the condition records found for this key combination. See Chapter 4 for more details.
- The **Crcy** field is the currency in which the **Amount** is expressed in.
- The **Net Price** field is a display-only field that shows this line's net price as calculated by the pricing procedure. Often this net price is the unit price.
- The **per** field indicates a quantity for which the **Net Price** is valid for.
- The **UoM** field is the unit of measurement for the **per** field.
- The **Net Value** field is a display-only field that shows this line's total net price (**Net Price** multiplied by the quantity) as calculated by the pricing procedure.
- The **Doc. Currency** field is a display-only field copied from the header document currency in which **Net Price** and **Net Value** are displayed.
- The **WBS Element** field stands for work breakdown structure (WBS) element, which is an element of a costing structure, referred to as a *project*, that this line is part of/ assigned to. This functionality is handled by the project systems (PS) functionality. Assigning a WBS element to the line will cause the cost of this line to roll up into the total of the project.
- The **Profit Center** field is a costing element assigned to the material master used to control costs. This field is part of controlling.
- The **Overall Status** field indicates if this line is still in process or has already been processed.

6.2.10 Defining Item Categories

To define item categories, open Transaction VOV7 or follow the menu path **SAP Customizing Implementation Guide • Sales and Distribution • Sales • Sales Documents • Sales Document Item • Define Item Categories.** Enter the item category "TAN" and then click the **Details button** or press F2.

As shown in Figure 6.23, to create a new item category code, on this screen, specify a four-character item category (**Item category**) and add a description.

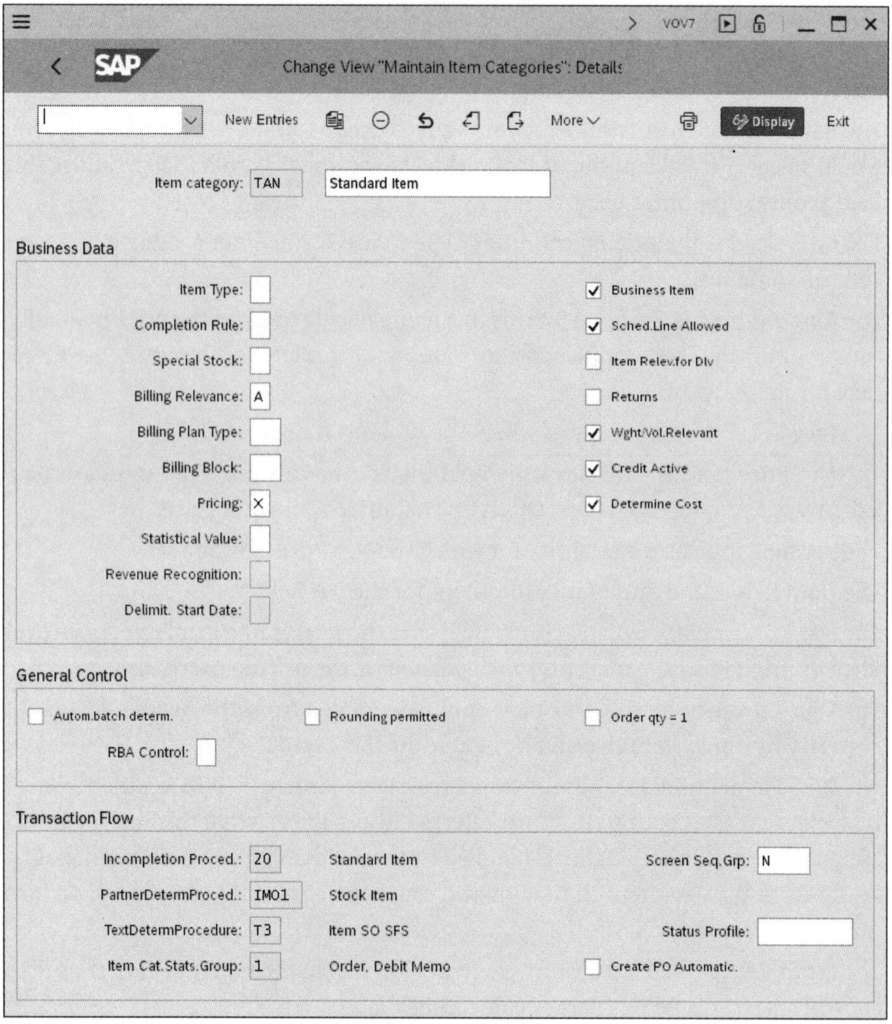

Figure 6.23 TAN Item Category Configuration, Part 1

In the following sections, we'll talk about the major areas on this screen.

Business Data

The **Business Data** section includes the following fields:

- The **Item Type** field is a code used in several transactions and functions by SAP Standard code to drive important functionalities. This value can be understood as the "type of item category." By default, the value is blank, which represents that the line is shippable and billable. Another commonly used value is "A" for *value items*, which are billable lines that do not correspond to items that need to be shipped. Some companies prefer to use value items to represent fees and additional charges instead of using condition types.
- The **Business Item** flag controls whether you can modify financial data fields. These fields are stored on table VBKD. If this flag is unselected, these fields would not be modifiable at the line level, only on the header.
- The **Completion Rule** field is used to control when non-shippable lines should be considered complete. For instance, contract lines are considered complete when you have created orders for all quantities. For completed contracts, you would use **Completion Rule** "C" (item is completed after the target quantity is fully referenced).
- The **Sched.Line Allowed** field is used when you have non-shippable items, but you want schedule lines to be created.
- The **Special Stock** field allows the line to consume special stock types, such as customer stock (consignment) or sales order stock. If this field is blank, the ATP check only looks at normal stock.
- The **Item Relev.for Delivery** field is used when you have non-shippable items, but you want to include them in the delivery anyway. This feature can be used, for instance, for value items to ensure they appear on the same invoice as shippable items.
- The **Billing Relevance** field is where you'll indicate if the line is relevant for billing based on the sales order, delivery document, not relevant at all, relevant only for pro-forma invoices, etc.
- The **Returns** flag is required for lines that represent goods coming back from customers instead of going to customers.
- The **Billing Plan Type** field is how you can activate the **Billing Plan** tab and related functionality at the line level. See Chapter 10, Section 10.3, for more details. Even if the billing plan is maintained at the header, you'll need to assign the billing plan to indicate that this line is part of the plan. If you don't, it would be billed separately.

- The **Wght/Vol.Relevant** field is used when you have non-shippable items, but you want to maintain weight and volume for it. This feature is commonly used for items you don't track in inventory (such as marketing material), but you do ship this material to customers.
- You can assign a default **Billing Block** to the line that will be present on all orders created with this type. A user will need to remove this block before invoices can be created. This block is not often used.
- The **Credit Active** flag allows you to exclude lines from the credit exposure calculation. When unselected, the value corresponding to line will not be included on the total sales order value when checking if the customer's credit limit is high enough to approve this order.
- The **Pricing** field controls if this line is relevant for pricing calculations or if no pricing is involved. Pricing for free goods is when you have price calculated, but you've applied a 100% discount, which would still allow you to charge for freight and freight taxes, even if no charge is being applied for products.
- The **Determine Cost** flag will make the cost condition type (VPRS, EK01, etc.) appear in the pricing procedure. If the material is not costed, the line that sells it to customer should have this flag selected.
- The **Statistical Value** field controls whether the value of this line should be included in the total sales order value or whether this information is just for statistical purposes or for information only.
- The **Revenue Recognition** and **Delimit. Start Date** fields are part of the revenue recognition process. When a sales order is billed, the account document is created without posting to a revenue account, instead becoming deferred revenue. Then, over time, you'll gradually recognize this revenue. This feature is common for intellectual property/royalty billing environments.

  Many companies may be concerned with the recognition of revenue for shippable items at the time of goods receipt instead of at the time of shipping. The fields are not required for that functionality, and the valuated stock-in-transit (VSIT) is an alternative. Most companies reclass the revenue of undelivered items manually via a journal entry before month end using the expected transportation lead times.

  The configuration of these fields is blocked out of the box and requires a special access key from SAP to use, which can be obtained via SAP Note 820417. This functionality is inherited from older versions of the system. SAP also offers SAP Revenue Accounting and Recognition for companies with complex revenue recognition requirements.

General Control

The **General Control** section includes the following fields:

- The **Autom.batch determ.** flag indicates that, for this line, the system should assign the batch to the sales document (usually the delivery document) based on specified rules. The warehouse would pick product off the shelf while observing the batch the system specifies. This feature eliminates the need for the warehouse to enter the batch when registering the picking operation, thus ensuring the rules are followed and the right batch is picked.

  Most companies leave this field blank. When the delivery document is created, the warehouse decides which batch to pick from. The batch is then entered at the time of registering picking operation.
- The **Rounding permitted** flag controls whether the rounding profile on the material master can be used to modify the quantity on sales document lines with this item category. Without this flag, the rounding profile would not be observed. This configuration is industry specific: Companies that sell product by length, weight, or volume commonly use this feature, while companies that transact in countable units of measurement tend to not use rounding.
- The **Order qty = 1** flag will automatically assign the quantity of one on this item category. This flag is applicable, for instance, on value items that represent a fee.
- The **RBA Control** field controls what kind of action may be taken by the rule-based ATP check. You can allow plants and/or materials to be substituted under certain conditions as defined by rules.

Transaction Flow

The **Transaction Flow** section includes the following fields:

- The **Incompletion Proced.** code controls the list of fields that should be populated and which functions must be stopped when not for lines with this item category. This field is display-only on this screen; to change this value, you would need to perform other configuration activities, as documented in Section 6.5.
- The **Screen Seq.Grp** code corresponds to variations of the order line screens from which you can choose. This code will make certain tabs appear or not and affect the order in which they do appear.
- The **PartnerDetermProced.** code defines the partner functions that may be assigned at the line level (if any). This field is display-only on this screen; to change this

value, you would need to perform other configuration activities, as documented in Section 6.4.8.

- The **TextDetermProcedure** code defines the text types that may be assigned at the line level (if any). This field is display-only on this screen; to change this value, you would need to perform other configuration activities, as documented in Section 6.4.9.
- The **Status Profile** field controls a sales order line feature that indicates the statuses that the order line may be in, regardless of shipping or billing. Some companies need order lines to follow processes that are controlled, which is common on order lines with linked service activities. These activities may not use SAP functionality to be completed, so the status represents when the activities have been completed. You can restrict who can flag certain statuses and define copy requirement rules to stop subsequent order functions based on status.
- The **Item Cat.Stats.Group** field is a code used by the logistics information system (LIS) to determine the type of transaction from a reporting perspective. The LIS is a reporting functionality that uses summarized data updated with transactional data. The summarized data may then be used for reporting with better performance. This field is display-only on this screen.

  This feature was more important in SAP ERP; in SAP S/4HANA, the database has much better performance, and in most cases, reports can read transactional data directly. This book will not include full details about the LIS.
- The **Create PO Automatic.** flag controls the creation of purchase orders as well as of purchase requisitions in sales order-driven individual requirement scenarios (see further details in Chapter 8).

Bill of Material/Configuration

Scrolling down from the screen shown earlier in Figure 6.23, you'll see the rest of the fields on this screen, as shown in Figure 6.24.

The **Bill of Material/Configuration** section includes the following fields:

- The **Config. Strategy** field controls behavior of configurable materials.
- The **Mat. Variant Action** field controls whether a configurable material should be replaced with its specific material variant. A *configurable material* uses the same material number for multiple variations of its configuration whereas a *material variant* is a material master entry with a material number that represents a specific configuration of a material. Material variants are used when you need to keep inventory for a given configuration and not make the product to order as originally intended in a configurable material scenario.

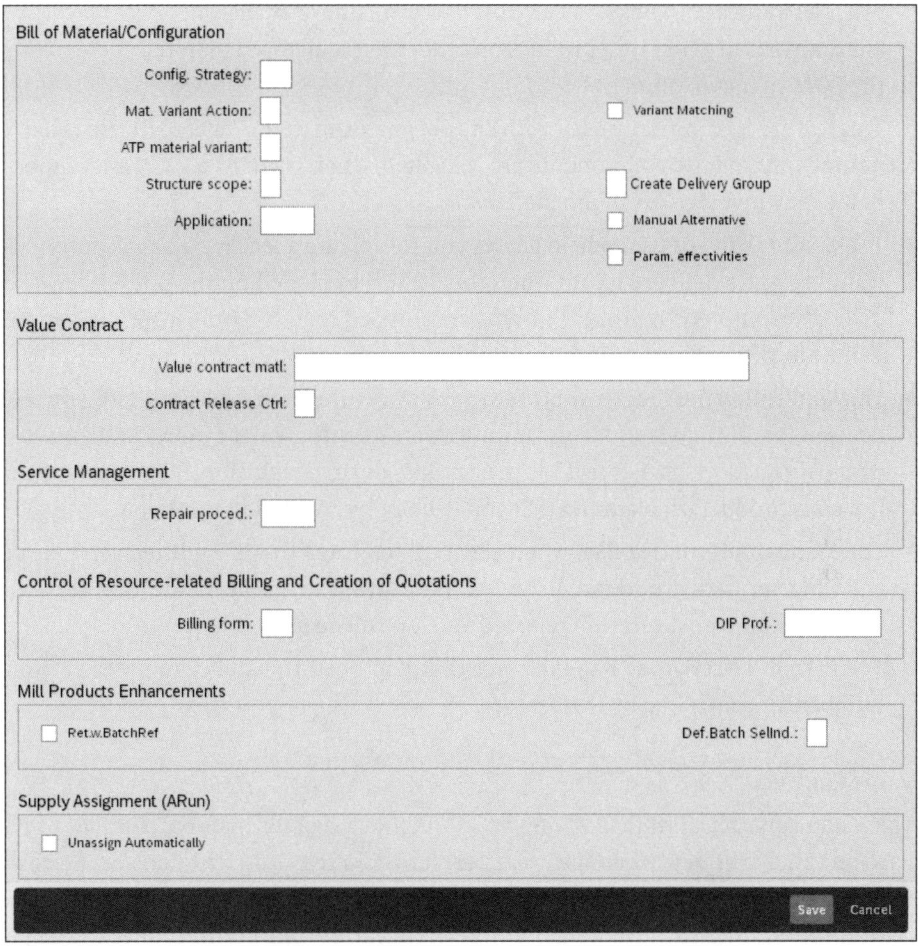

Figure 6.24 TAN Item Category Configuration, Part 2

- The **Variant Matching** flag activates an order feature that will search for a material variant for the selected configuration.
- The **ATP material variant** field conditions the substitution of a configurable material by a material variant based on the available stock allocated to the order by the ATP check. If no stock is available, you can use the configurable material and follow the normal process.
- The **Structure scope** field is where you'll activate bill of materials (BOM) explosion at the sales order level. If the components of a structured material are shippable on their own, you can benefit from having the BOM explosion appear on the sales

order as individual lines and control their availability at the sales order level. An alternative is to generate a production order for a structured material and explode the BOM in that document.

This feature is commonly used with kits or "phantom items," where the material is not inventoried; its components are sellable on their own. As a kit, these components may involve special pricing.

- The **Create Delivery Group** field allows you to activate a feature that will automatically assigns a delivery group when the BOM is exploded on the sales order. The delivery groups ensure that the items are shipped together only when all components are available.
- The **Application** field represents the type of structured item this item category will be used for. This code controls, among other features, what type of BOM master data (Transaction CS01) is used as master data during explosion. BOM master data is part of production planning (PP) and will not be covered in this book.
- The **Manual Alternative** flag, when checked, indicates that if multiple versions of BOM master data are found, users will be allowed to select the desired version. Otherwise, the most recently released version will be used.
- The **Param. effectivities** flag indicates that you need the ability to enter version numbers as controlled by this feature.

Value Contract

The **Value contract matl** field allows you to define a default material number to be used on value contracts when the user doesn't make a selection. The **Contract Release Ctrl** field is where you'll indicate the desired system response when attempting to create orders with this type of line, with reference to a value contract after the value on the contract has been exhausted.

Service Management

The **Repair proced.** field represents the steps to be followed to repair a product, which is defined as part of service management.

Control of Resource-Related Billing and Creation of Quotations

The **Billing form** field indicates the method of billing for services. Options include 01 (fixed rate/list price) or 02 (costs/time and material). The **DIP Prof.** (dynamic item processor profile) field is a code that summarizes service data based on predefined criteria into dynamic items that can be used for sales price calculation, resource-related billing, etc.

Mill Products Enhancements

The **Ret.w.BatchRef** flag indicates that, when batch-managed products are returned, the batch characteristics must be copied from the original sales order onto the return order. The **Def.Batch SelInd.** flag controls how much leeway users have to modify the batch selection.

Supply Assignment (ARun)

The **Unassign Automatically** flag is part of the supply assignment functionality. When checked, supply assignment will not occur automatically when you change, delete, or reject this sales order line.

6.3 Creating Standard Orders: Header Data

The sales order header data contains information applicable to all lines on the sales order. You can navigate to the header detail tabs by clicking on the header details icon, as shown in Figure 6.25.

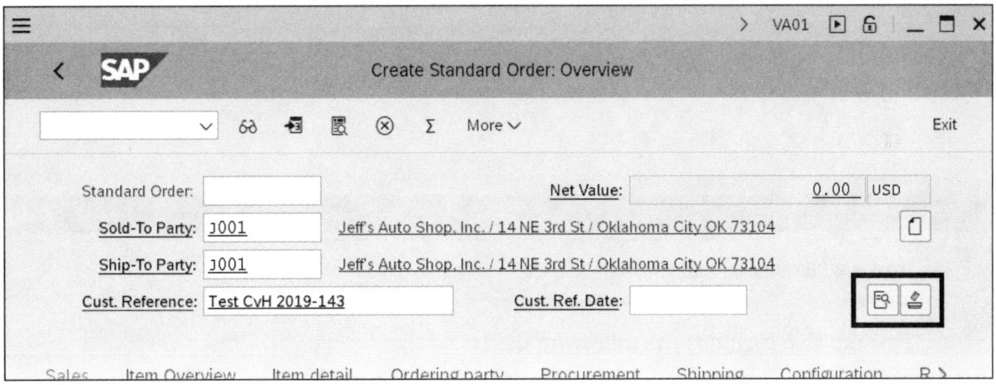

Figure 6.25 Header Details Icon

In the following sections, we'll walk you through each of the tabs available on the **Create Standard Order: Header Data** screen.

6.3.1 Sales

The first tab of the header details is the **Sales** tab, shown in Figure 6.26, which contains two fields (**Order Reason** and **Pricing Date**), which we described earlier in Section 6.2.1.

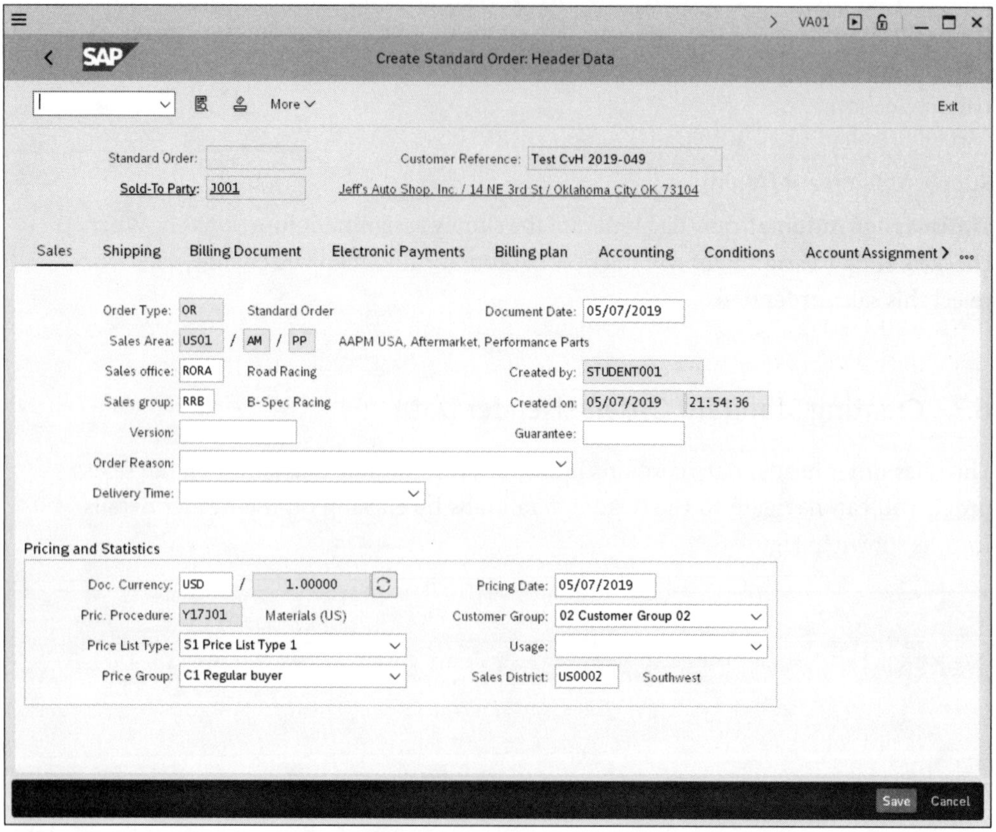

Figure 6.26 Header Details: Sales

This tab also includes the following fields:

- The **Order Type** field is a display-only field copied from the initial **Create Sales Documents** screen shown earlier in Figure 6.2. You can use the order type description found on the title of the window (**Create Standard Order: Header Data**) or on the sales order number field.
- The **Document Date** field is the date when the sales order was entered in the system; this date may be modified manually.

- The **Sales Area** field (sales organization, distribution channel, and division) is a display-only field copied from the initial **Create Sales Documents** screen.
- The **Sales office** and **Sales group** fields, along with the organizational structure elements (sales area), represent the organizational element responsible for this order. This information is prepopulated either from the initial **Create Sales Documents** screen or from customer master data. You can make changes to these values.
- The **Created by** field is the ID of the user that entered this order. For orders entered electronically (via EDI), the system user ID assigned by your security department would appear in this field.
- The **Created on** field is a system-assigned date and time indicating when this order was created. This information cannot be modified manually and is often used instead of **Document Date** because the created-on date is more precise and accurate/reliable.
- The **Version** field is a change control number for this sales order based on input in other areas of the company, such as production planning or engineering. You can use this field to keep track of necessary changes the order requires, but this field is not often used.
- The **Guarantee** field represents the beginning of the warranty period (when defined at the order level).
- The **Delivery Time** field is the agreed or contractual timeframe that must be used as the target date to fully deliver/fulfill this order. This field may also be used later in reporting. We'll briefly describe the configuration steps to define values for this field soon. This field is rarely used but can be convenient for companies that have different targets on an order. Most companies have a single target set as a guideline across all orders.
- The **Doc. Currency** field is the currency in which this order value must be expressed. SAP S/4HANA allows you to maintain master data in different currencies and perform conversion based on this code. (The exchange rate is a display-only field to the right of the currency code.) This field defaults from the customer master data but may also be changed.
- The **Pric. Procedure** field is a display-only field assigned according to configuration described in Chapter 4, Section 4.1.5.
- The **Customer Group** field is a major grouping criterion used in reporting as defined in Chapter 2, Section 2.3.
- The **Price List Type** field is a price qualifier as defined in Chapter 2, Section 2.3.1, and Chapter 4, Section 4.8.

- The **Usage** code represents what your customers will do with the product or services being sold on this order. If you enter a value in this field, this information will be valid for all lines of an order, unless otherwise specified at the item level. In some countries, knowing the purpose for the material being purchased is important. In the US, companies use this field in ways often diverging from its original intended purpose, and the actual usage of the product is inferred by other fields that qualify the customer as a distributor, retailer, manufacturer, etc. Many companies use the **Customer Group** fields to implement this classification.
- The **Price Group** field is a grouping criterion used for discounts and pricing policies as defined in Chapter 2, Section 2.3.1.
- The **Sales District** field is a geographically oriented grouping criterion used for reporting as defined in Chapter 2, Section 2.3.1.

To configure agreed delivery times, follow the menu path **SAP Customizing Implementation Guide • Sales and Distribution • Sales • Sales Documents • Define Agreed Delivery Times**. On the screen that opens, click on the **New Entries** button or press [F5].

As shown in Figure 6.27, specify a three-character delivery time code (**Del**); indicate an amount of time (**Pe**, for time period); the unit of time for that amount (**TU**, for delivery time unit) as "1" day; and add a description (**Description**).

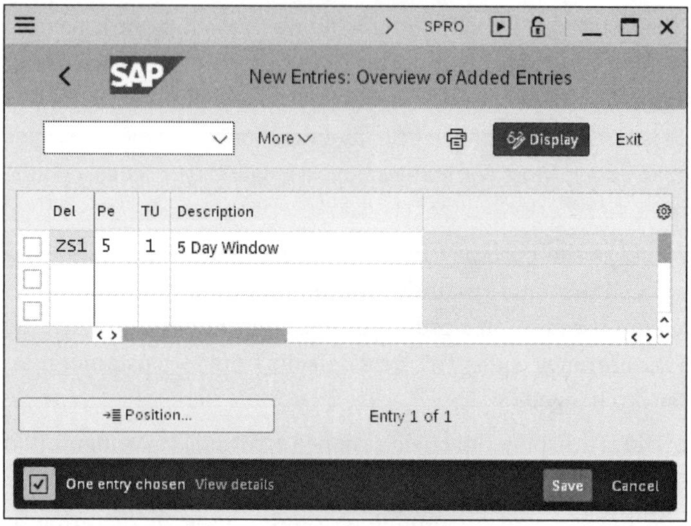

Figure 6.27 Defining Agreed Delivery Times

6.3.2 Shipping

The first tab of the header details is the **Shipping** tab, as shown in Figure 6.28. This tab contains some fields already described earlier: The **Ship-to Party**, **Delivery Block**, **Complete Dlv.**, **Total Weight**, and **Volume** fields were covered in Section 6.2.1, and the **Unloading Point** and **Receiving Point** fields were covered in Section 6.2.3.

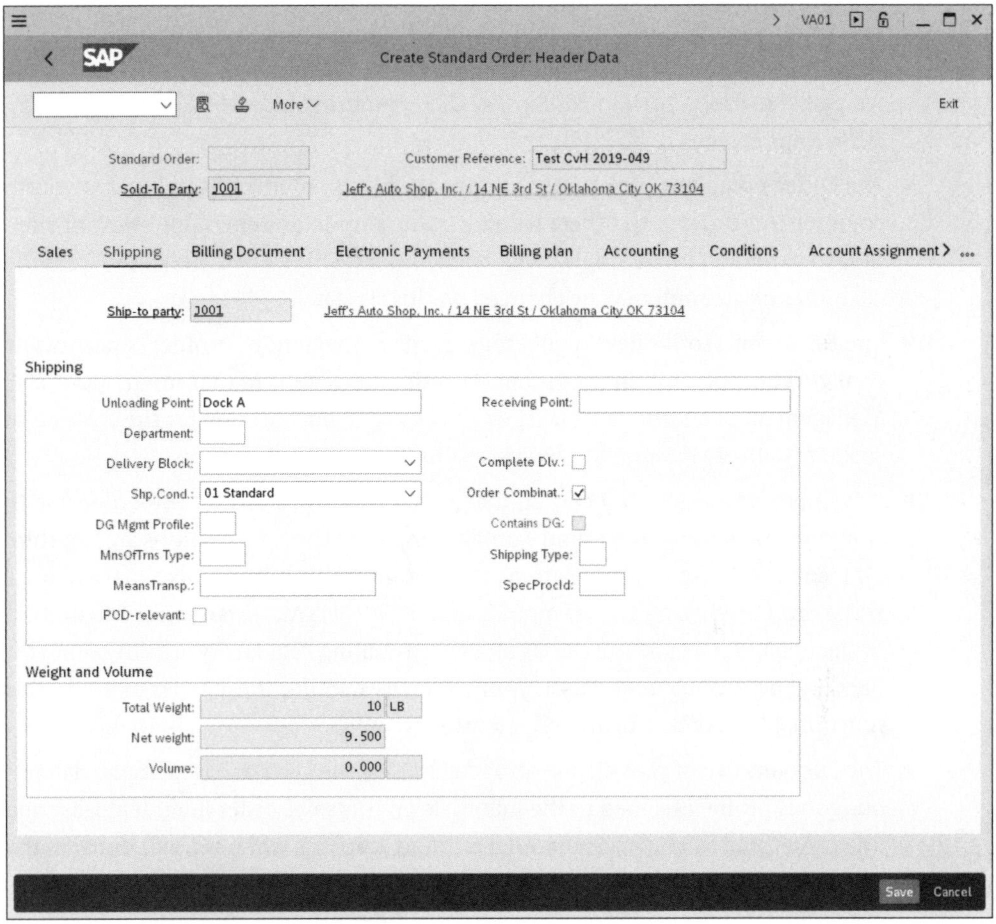

Figure 6.28 Header Details: Shipping

The **Shipping** tab also includes the following fields:

- The **Department** field is a code that represents the area within the ship-to customer's receiving location that will responsible for goods receipt. This information is defaulted from the customer master data (see Chapter 2, Section 2.2.11, for more details on configuration).

- The **Shp.Cond.** field (shipping conditions) is a code that indicates logistics and transportation requirements from the customer and/or company policy applicable for all lines in this sales order. This information is defaulted from the customer master data (see Chapter 2, Section 2.2.1 and Section 2.3.2, for more details on configuration). At a minimum, you must indicate shipping conditions for the carrier services you allow the customer to choose from. For instance, if you're shipping via parcel carriers, such as FedEx and UPS, you must indicate **Ground**, **Next Day**, **3-Day Ship**, etc.
- The **Order Combinat.** flag (order combination), when checked, will allow you to combine this order with others with the same ship-to and the same relevant shipping information into a single delivery document. This value is defaulted from the customer master and may be changed on this screen.
- The **DG Mgmt Profile** field (dangerous goods management profile) is part of the configuration of SAP Environment, Health, and Safety Management (SAP EHS Management), and this value will be used as a splitting criterion for the creation of separate delivery documents, which results in separate shipments.
- It is important to identify certain dangerous goods profiles on the order due to shipping restrictions they entail. Some examples of these restrictions are not shipping corrosive and explosive items in the same shipment, no explosives on air shipment, etc. We won't cover more complex SAP EHS Management configuration in the book, but this feature does allow for fulfilling regulatory requirements for handling hazardous materials. If your company handles these types of items, this functionality may be worth implementing.
- The **Contains DG** flag is a display-only field set by the system based on the dangerous goods profile assigned to the materials on this sales order lines. If at least one line containing a dangerous material is found, this flag, when set, will signal to the order entry person that special shipping arrangements will be needed and perhaps other regulatory requirements need to be fulfilled.
- The **MnsOfTrns Type** field (means of transportation type) is a packaging material type that represents how you'll pack, stack, and prepare products for shipping. This information may be entered on the order to capture customer requirements

and then used by the warehouse to drive how the shipment is prepared. See Chapter 9, Section 9.7, for more information on packaging material type configuration.

- The **MeansTransp.** field (means of transportation) is the specific packaging material number corresponding to the box, crate, pallet, etc. that you'll use to ship materials contained on this order. This information will be used to perform the packing operation. More details on the corresponding chapter.
- The **Shipping Type** field is a code that represents how product will make its way from your warehouse to the customer (truck/road, ship/sea, airplane/air, etc.). This information may be relevant if you're setting up certain restrictions. One example is for dangerous goods: If a material is explosive, air transportation should never be used. The shipping type is where you'll indicate that the selected shipping condition should never be by air. We'll discuss how to configure shipping types shortly.
- The **SpecProcId** field represents company-specific processes that the warehouse should use to drive special logistics requirements.
- The **POD-relevant** flag, when checked, indicates that, whenever you ship product to this customer, whether the delivery was really delivered or not must be controlled. This confirmation may be performed manually or electronically via an interface from the carrier. Most carriers offer this service, but you'll need to set up the integration. Consult Chapter 9, Section 9.10, for more details.
- The **Net weight** field is a display-only field that calculates the sum of the net weights of all lines on a sales order. This value is automatically calculated and displayed in this field.

To configure shipping types, follow the menu path **SAP Customizing Implementation Guide • Logistics Execution • Transportation • Basic Transportation Functions • Routes • Define Routes • Define Shipping Types.**

As shown in Figure 6.29, specify a two-character shipping type code (**PT**) and add a description (**Description**). Then, define the mode of transportation (**MdTr**) and shipping type procedure group (**STPG**) to be used in the shipping cost calculation. Chapter 9, Section 9.8, has more details about this process, but we won't go too deeply into transportation in this book.

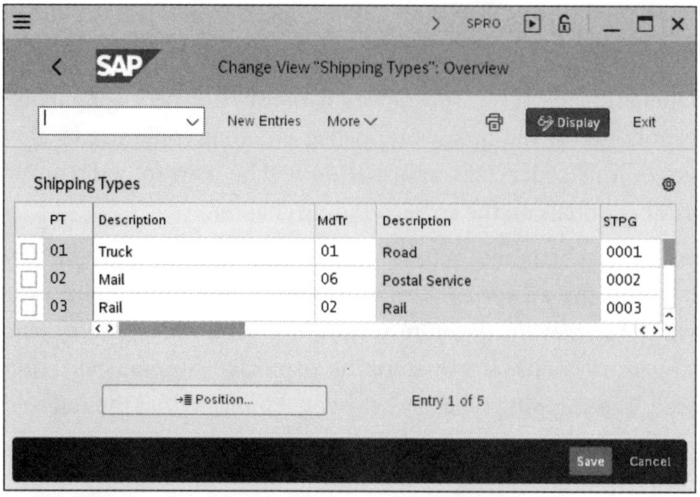

Figure 6.29 Define Shipping Types

6.3.3 Billing Document

The third tab of the header details is the **Billing Document** tab, as shown in Figure 6.30. This tab contains some fields described earlier: The **Incoterms Version**, **Incoterms**, **Incoterms Location1**, **Incoterms Location2**, **Payment terms**, and **Billing block** fields were discussed in Section 6.2.1. The **Unloading Point** and **Receiving Point** fields were previously discussed in Section 6.2.3.

The **Billing Document** tab includes the following fields:

- The **Payer** field is a display-only field containing the customer number responsible for paying for this order. This value is assigned as soon as a sold-to party is chosen in Chapter 2. This value may be changed under the **Partner** tab (Section 6.4.8).
- The **Fixed Value Date** field is the date from which you'll start counting the payment term period. Usually, this field is blank so that the invoice date and the payment terms reference date are used, but you can negotiate specific deals and enter a value in this field, although rare.
- The **Add. Value Days** field allows you to grant the customer a few extra days as a grace period. Both the **Fixed Value Date** and **Add. Value Days** fields should only be set up after approval from finance.
- The **Man.Inv.Maint.** (manual invoice maintenance) flag, when checked, places a hold on the billing documents created for this order, allowing for review and modification before creating the subsequent accounting documents and the corresponding

invoice output (print, email, EDI, interface, etc.). This flag is not often activated, but you can keep it in mind as a resource to cover exceptions and highly demanding customers.

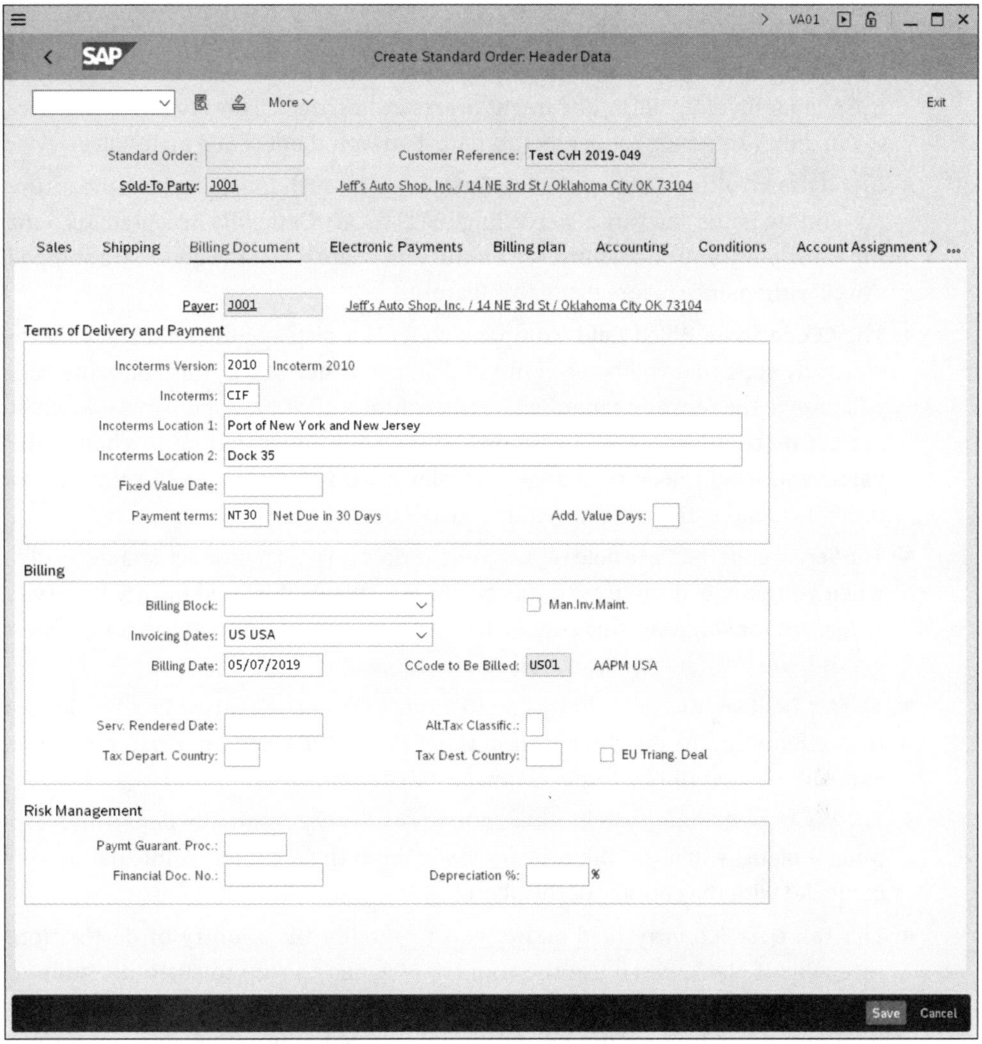

Figure 6.30 Header Details: Billing

- The **Invoicing Dates** field is a factory calendar where the "working days" are used as opportunities to issue invoices to this customer. This field is commonly used for big retailers and automakers. Often, these types of customers only receive invoices on certain days of the month or the week. You'll need to define factory calendars with non-working days for all days when invoices should not be issued and have working days only for those days when the customer receives invoices. In this way, even after you ship the product and create the invoice, the system will hold the invoice until the next working day and only then issue the invoice.

- The **Billing Date** field is the date on which you want to create an invoice. Note that the regular invoice/billing document prerequisites are still observed. For instance, if you didn't ship the product by this date, you would not create an invoice.
- If you use **Invoicing Dates** or **Billing Date** fields to push invoicing into the future, accounting issues may arise. According to US GAAP (Generally Accepted Accounting Principles), you should invoice on the same date when the goods are shipped. Check with finance before using this feature.
- The **CCode to Be Billed** field (company code) is a display-only field showing the company code that will be used in invoicing. In other words, this company code will receive the revenue generated by this sale as well as be responsible for related taxes. The company code is assigned to the sales organization; to change this value, you would need to change the sales organization, so you'll create a new order if changing the company code is necessary.
- The **Serv. Rendered Date** field represents the date on which product was shipped or when you provided services to this customer. This field is used mostly in service scenarios; for shipping, this date is determined by the system at the time of post goods issue (see Chapter 9, Section 9.9, for more details).
- The **Alt.Tax Classific.** field allows you to modify the customer tax classification for this order only. The tax classification is defined at the customer master level and controls whether the customer is taxable or exempt.
- The **Tax Depart. Country** field allows you to modify the country of departure/shipping. If blank, you'll use the country assigned to the shipping point that usually coincides with the country of the plant.
- The **Tax Dest. Country** field allows you to modify the country of destination/receiving. If blank, you'll use the country assigned to ship-to customer address. This feature is useful for export scenarios where the customer takes care of the final legs of freight. Even though delivery is thus not fully under your control, you still have a legal duty to record the final destination to ensure you are not shipping to an embargoed country.
- The **Paymt Guarant. Proc.**, **Financial Doc. No.**, and **Depreciation %** fields are used in some instances by finance to ensure payments are collected, usually, through a letter of credit. Most companies do not require letters of credit on a significant

enough number of transactions to justify implementing this feature instead preferring orders to be blocked for credit and then released only when the letter of credit is received/verified. Finance is responsible for implementing this feature, so the corresponding configuration is not included in this book.

6.3.4 Electronic Payments

The fourth tab of the header details is the **Electronic Payments** tab, as shown in Figure 6.31. This tab allows you to enter credit card details or online payment systems, such as PayPal, Google Pay, Amazon Payments, etc. Due to Payment Card Industry Data Security Standards (PCI DSS) concerns, companies that transact using credit cards or other online payment systems do not enter the actual unencrypted payment information on this screen; instead, third-party solutions like Paymetric are used. Thus, companies don't generally use this functionality, so we won't cover it in this book.

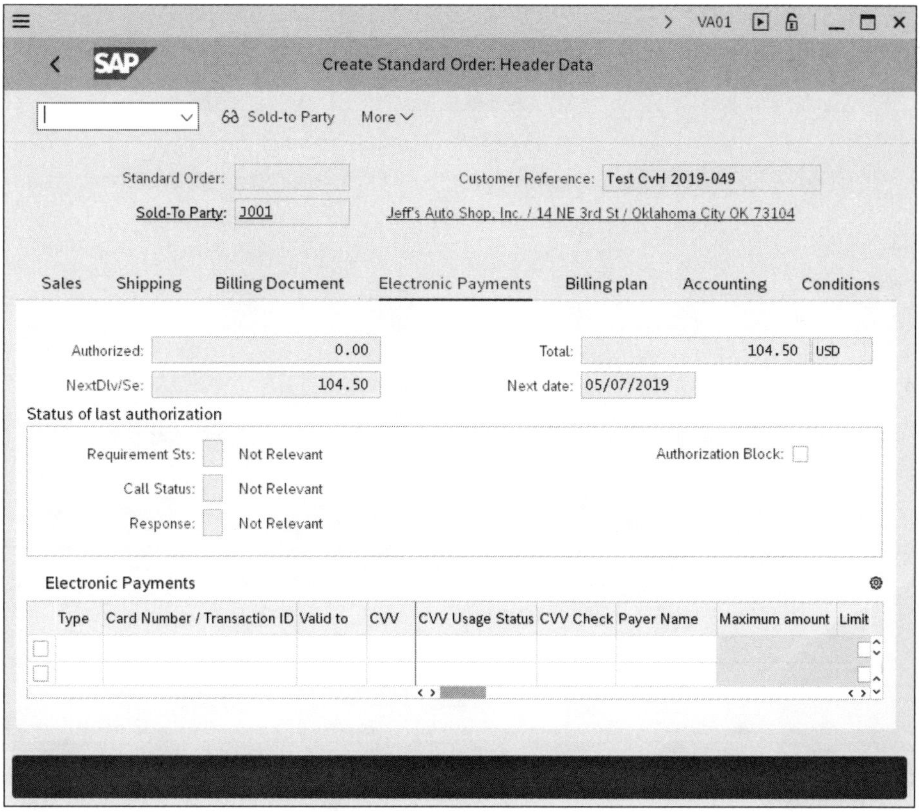

Figure 6.31 Header Details: Electronic Payments

6.3.5 Billing Plan

In the sales order header, under the **Billing Plan** tab, shown in Figure 6.32, you can define dates and amounts when invoices will be issued. This feature is used when you don't want to create an invoice for the full amount of sales after the shipment of product. Certain businesses require billing before shipment, such as engineered-to-order products, common in government defense contracts. This feature enables customers to finance the research and development of products according to their specific applications/requirements, which is referred to as *milestone billing*. Each phase of the development of the product is considered a milestone, and you can issue invoices at each milestone.

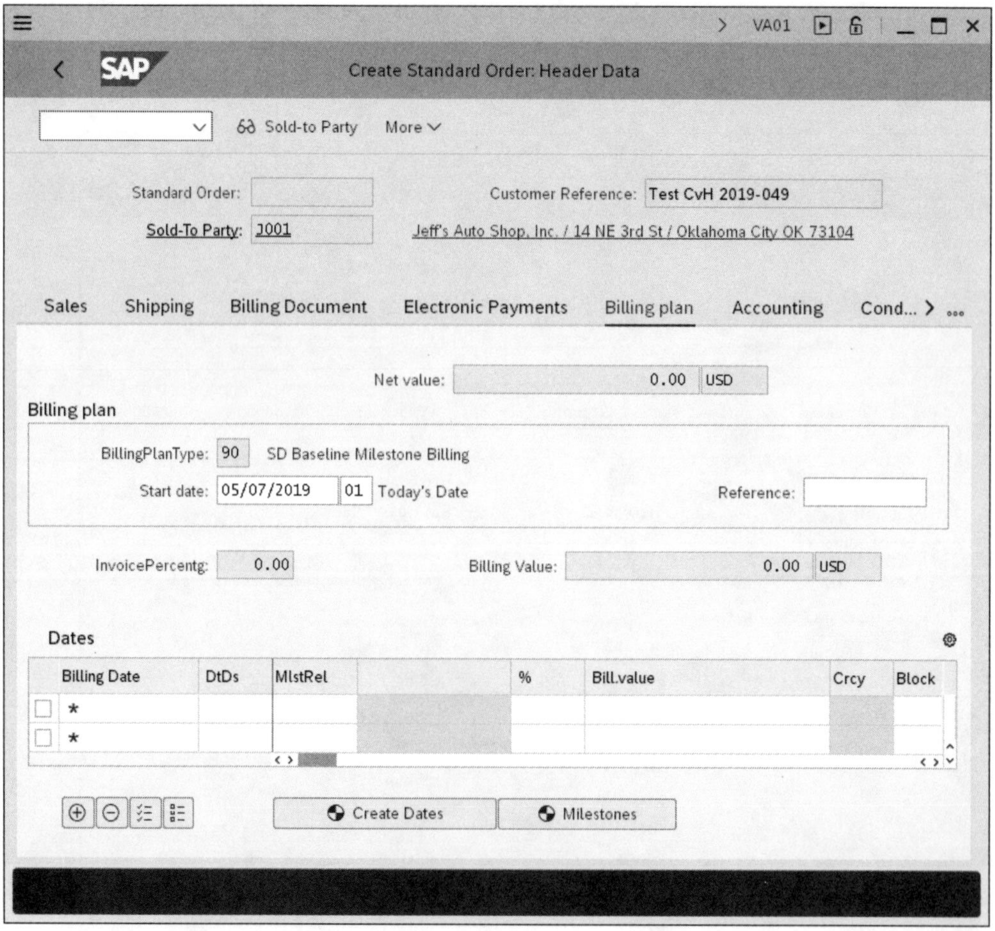

Figure 6.32 Header Details: Billing Plan

If product development driven by customer sales orders is a significant part of your company's business, you probably would need functionalities from project systems (PS). These functionalities can manage the budgeting and costs of all product development project activities, with many features to control and manage project execution. When using PS, you can trigger milestone billing based on the completion of specific project activities (network or WBS elements).

Using SAP S/4HANA Sales, you can manage milestone billing activity with dates and billing blocks. This functionality relies on a manual, cross-departmental process to decide the right time to issue an invoice. In other words, a user must check if the time to bill the customer (based on the planned date and only upon confirmation) has come and would remove the billing block from the corresponding billing plan line to issue an invoice.

Billing plans can also be used for periodic billing. This feature issues invoices based purely on dates. These dates may be assigned automatically based on predefine schedules. This approach is commonly used with rental or lease contracts.

Companies can also use billing plans to manage down payments. You can issue invoices upfront and collect payments before releasing sales orders for shipping, production, third-party ordering, or any other features. Alternatively, a customer may be blocked during a credit check and must wait for down payments to be collected by finance independently from the sales order. Many companies see this approach as a simpler option, but you can't control order features based on payment in this case.

The additional fields available on this tab include the following:

- The **Net value** field shows the total order value that will be used as a base for calculating billing plan amounts.
- The **BillingPlanType** field is assigned to the sales order type via configuration (Transaction VOV8) and displayed on this screen for reference.
- The **Start date** field is defaulted based on the date rules configured in the billing plant type. See Chapter 10, Section 10.3.2, for configuration details.
- The **Reference** field is a billing plan number that you can use as a template to create dates and amounts on this billing plan. This field may also be configured by the billing plant type.
- The **InvoicePercentg** and **Billing Value** fields keep track of the billing amount you've already planned for and monitor how much is still remaining. You don't need to plan for the entire billing amount; in some instances, you can leave the reminder of the billing for later processing after shipping.

- The **Billing Date** field is the date on which you want to issue an invoice.
- The **DtDs** field (date description) is a code qualifying what the date in the **Billing Date** field represents.
- The **MlstRel** field (milestone relevance) is a code qualifying the type of project milestone completion this date represents.
- The **%** field (percentage of value to be invoiced) is used when you've negotiated a percentage of payment on this date rather than a fixed amount.
- The **Bill.value** field is when you've negotiated a fixed amount to be billed on this date.
- The **Crcy** field (currency) will be used in invoices and is copied from the sales order currency and displayed in this field for reference.
- The billing block field (**Block**) is usually assigned by default and allows users to check if the billing should really happen on this date as planned. Unless removed, the billing/invoicing will not take place.
- The **Mstn** flag indicates that you have a PS milestone assigned to this date. This field can be accessed by scrolling to the right in the **Dates** section, as shown in Figure 6.33.
- The **BR** field (billing rule) controls how the amount is calculated on this line.
- The **BillSt** field (billing status) is displayed on this screen to track the dates that were already processed, i.e., the ones that already created invoices. This information is useful when displaying a document after it has been created.
- The **PayT** (payment terms) field is used on the invoice that will be created on this date. You can allow a few days for the customer to pay before this invoice is considered overdue.
- The **DCat** field (date category) is a configured type of billing date for this line.
- The **BillingType** field (billing document type) is the sales document type to used when the invoice/billing document ID is created for this line.
- The **Exch.Rt.Act** field (exchange rate for accounting)is used in multicurrency environments to define the exchange rate to be used.
- The **Milestone No.** field (milestone number) is the PS milestone reference number (network or WBS element).
- The **Fixed Date** indicator controls the origin management of this date over time. This date may be fixed or controlled by PS milestones automatically.

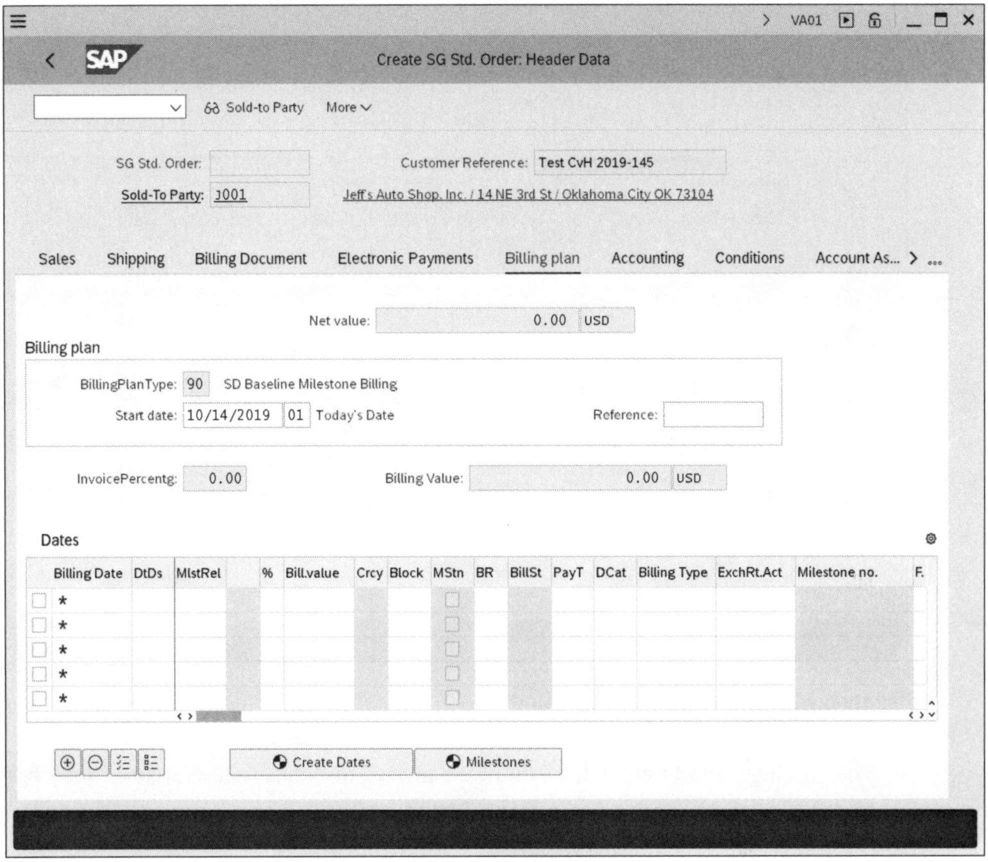

Figure 6.33 Header Details: Billing Plan Additional Fields

6.3.6 Accounting

The **Accounting** tab, shown in Figure 6.34, includes details related to how the accounting department will classify this transaction after billing.

This tab includes the following fields:

- The **AccAssmtGrpCust** field is the account assignment group defined on the customer master and copied to this field. This information is used for account determination at the time of billing.
- The **Payment Method** field is how the customer is expected to send payment for the invoice created, with direct or indirect reference to this sales order.

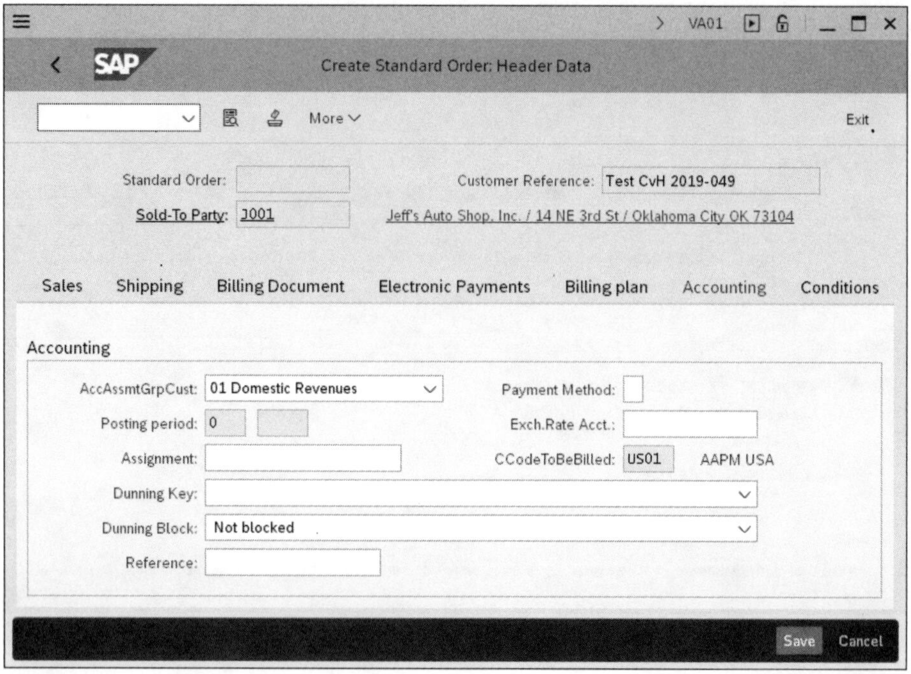

Figure 6.34 Header Details: Accounting

- The **Posting period** field is the inventory month and date, which may or may not match the calendar period as defined during controlling configuration. This information is displayed on this screen for reference.
- The **Exch.Rate Acct.** field is the exchange rate used in multicurrency scenarios to convert the invoice value (used in the customer's currency) into the accounting currency used for financial reporting, such as revenue reporting.
- The **Assignment** and **Reference** fields are identification numbers that allow the account team to communicate with the customer and with the sales department. This information will be copied to the account postings and will be available in the accounts receivable functionality. Using copy control configuration, you can define rules to populate this field automatically with the sales order number, with the invoice number, or with other fields.
- The **CCodeToBeBilled** field is the identification of the finance organizational structure element (the company code) that will be used on the billing document and will be responsible for receiving payment from the customer.
- The **Dunning Key** and **Dunning Block** fields are used by the accounts receivable functionality to manage the amount and frequency of contact with the customer

to collect payment. This information is set by the financial portion of the customer master data and the SAP S/4HANA Finance functionality and configuration.

6.3.7 Conditions

The **Conditions** tab for the header data, shown in Figure 6.35, includes summarized pricing information from all document lines. This tab is also used to maintain header conditions. Chapter 4, Section 4.1, covers all the necessary configuration details for this screen.

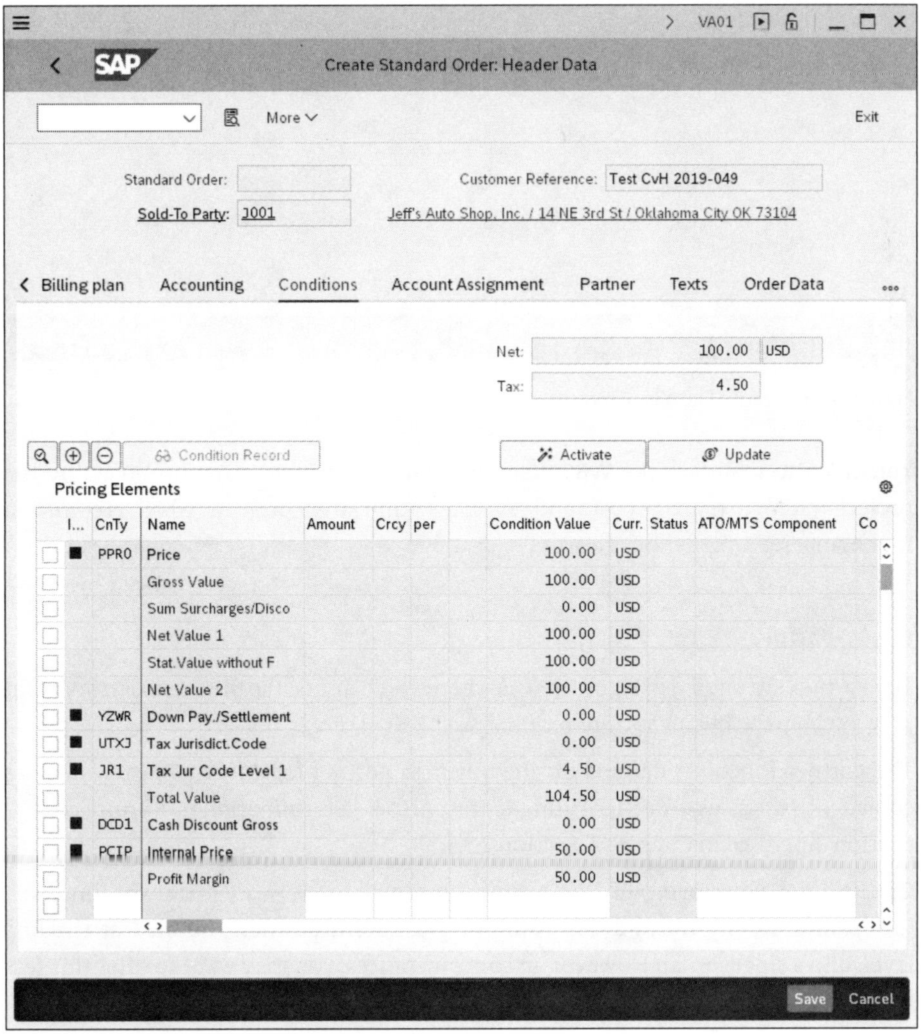

Figure 6.35 Header Details: Conditions

6.3.8 Account Assignment

Under the **Account Assignment** tab, shown in Figure 6.36, you can consult the **Business Area** (when applicable) as defined by the finance organizational structure. This field is used by SAP S/4HANA Finance, but is not a very popular feature in the US.

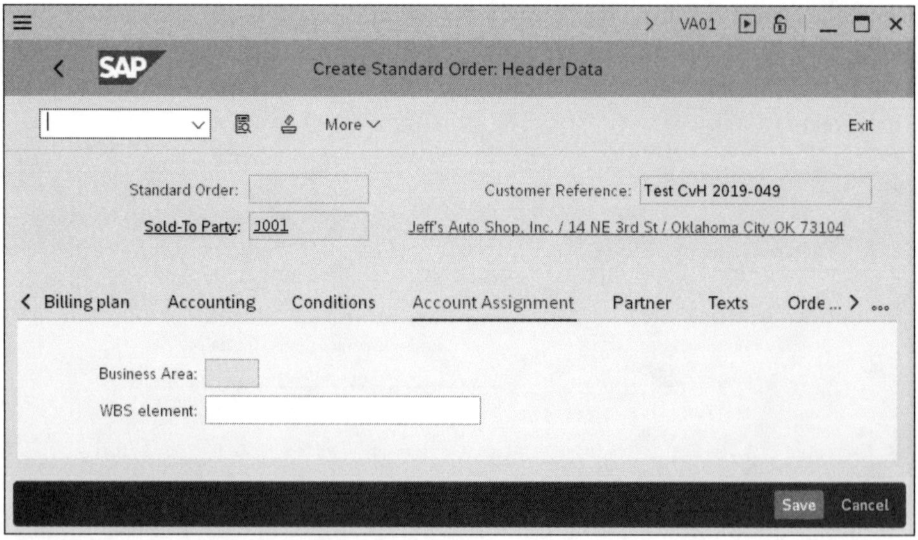

Figure 6.36 Header Details: Account Assignment

You can also maintain the **WBS element** (work breakdown structure) used by the project system to manage costs and revenue within larger projects, which is common for engineered to order businesses.

6.3.9 Partner

The **Partner** tab, shown in Figure 6.37, is where you'll define the business partners that play a role in the business transaction.

The partner functions defined on the business partner (customer) master data are copied into the sales order according to the partner determination procedure configuration described in Chapter 2, Section 2.3.5.

On the order, you can modify the business partners in the header or at the line level. Companies usually try to avoid combining different partners, defined at the line level, into a single order. However, in some instances, you may want to offer this feature as an added service to your customers.

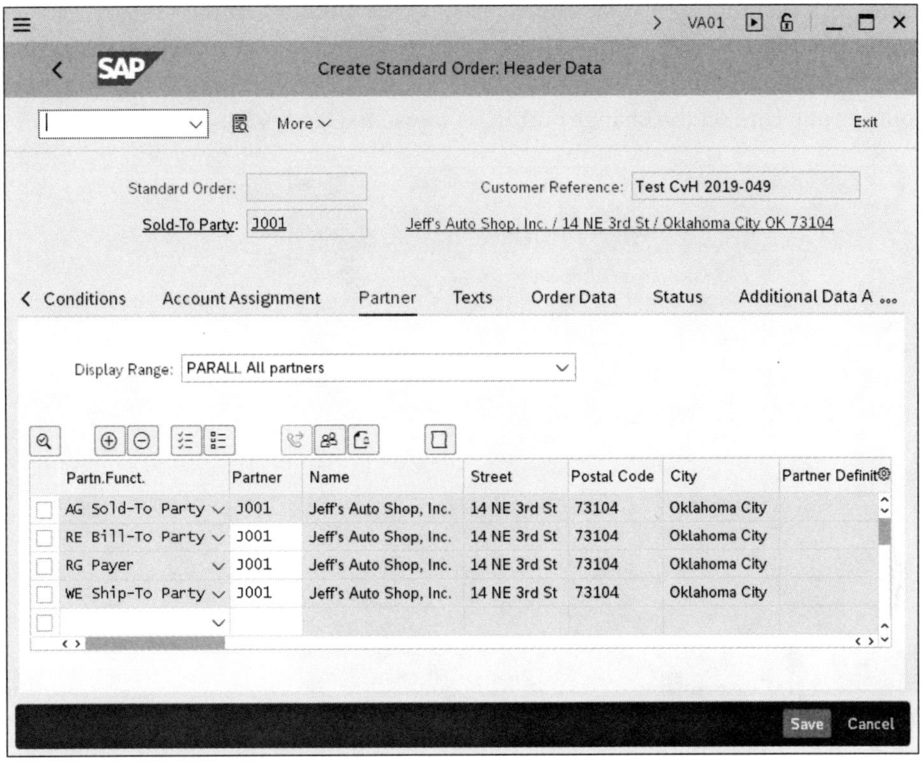

Figure 6.37 Header Details: Partner

For instance, a customer may be ordering a significant amount of product to be delivered to their employees at the end of the year as a bonus. In that case, you can offer to deliver product directly to employee addresses. You would need to represent each employee as a ship-to party on each line. This situation would require a lot of data entry if the order is entered manually. Thus, typically, you would receive the order electronically to ensure that data is consistent.

Ship-to partners are part of the header **Partner** tab of the delivery document so the order would be split, but ship-to partners are not part of the header of the invoice. Therefore, you'll have a single order and a single invoice but many shipments.

A common requirement is to add a custom partner function representing third-party sales activity by partners that are not employees. After the sale, this partner would not be responsible for this customer.

To add partner functions to partner function determination procedures, open Transaction VOPAN or follow the menu path **SAP Customizing Implementation Guide •**

Sales and Distribution • Basic Functions • Partner Determination • Set Up Partner Determination. In Transaction VOPAN, you must select the **Sales Doc Header** option (when assigning the partner function to the line, select the **Sales Document Item** option) and click on the **Change** button, as shown in Figure 6.38.

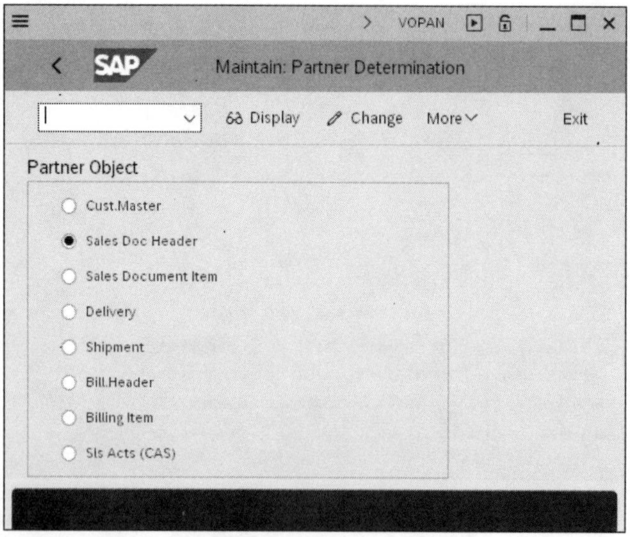

Figure 6.38 Choosing the Partner Object Type for Configuration

On the screen that opens, select the **S002 Partner Determination Procedure** by clicking on the selection box and then double-click on the **Partner Functions in Procedure** option in the **Dialog Structure** on the left, as shown in Figure 6.39.

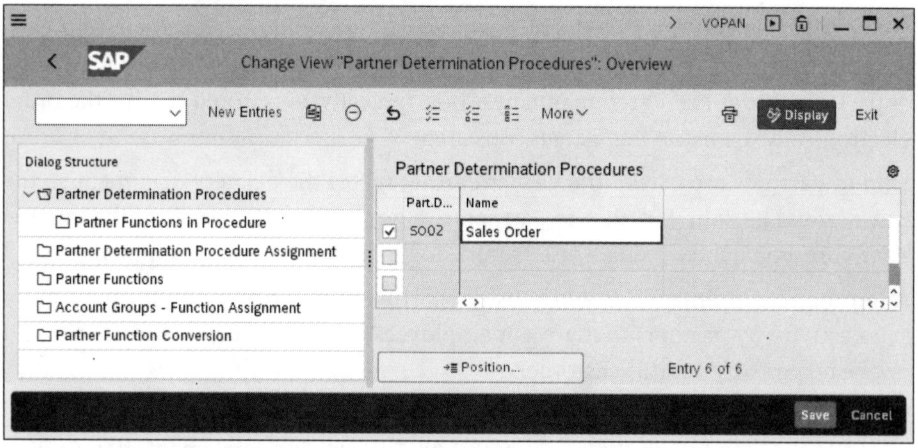

Figure 6.39 Selecting the Partner Determination Procedure

As shown in Figure 6.40, browse for the partner function currently assigned and click on the **New Entries** button or press [F5] to add a new one.

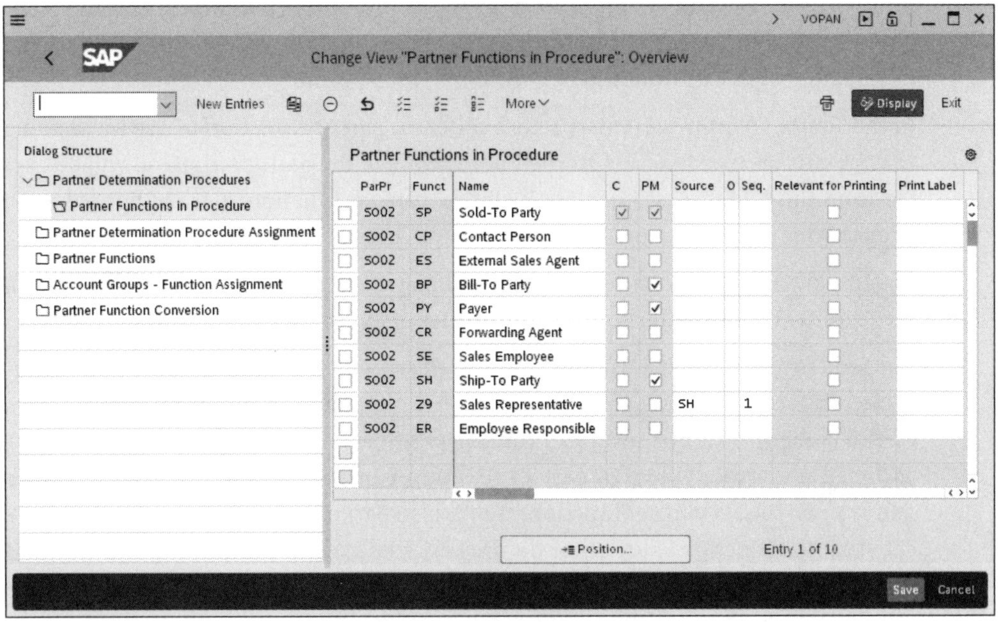

Figure 6.40 Browsing the Partner Function in the Procedure

On next screen, shown in Figure 6.41, enter the new partner function we want add to the procedure under the partner function (**Funct**) column.

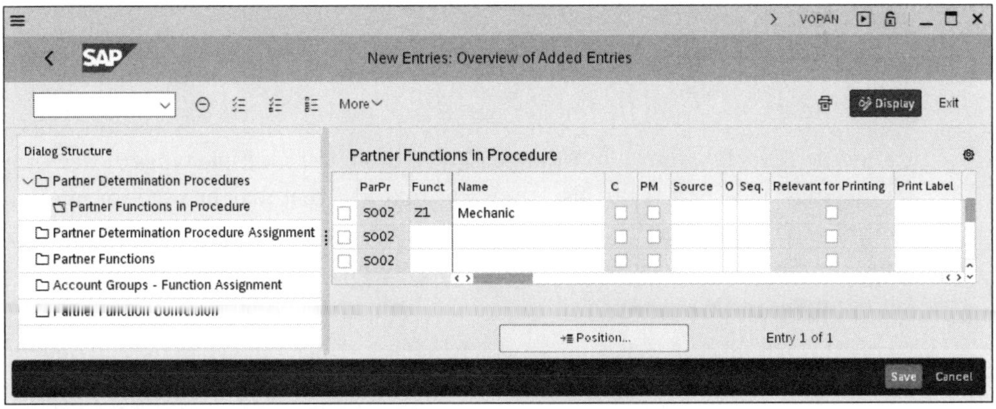

Figure 6.41 Adding a New Partner Function to the Determination Procedure

The not modifiable (**C**) column ensures the partner is copied from the specified source and that users may not change this information.

You can select the partner mandatory (**PM**) column, which indicates that, even if the partner is not copied form the customer, a partner must be entered manually on the order; otherwise, the order will be considered incomplete.

In the **Source** column, you can specify a different partner function where we're going to copy this partner function from. If not specified, the partner function will be copied from the sold-to customer. For instance, partner function Z9 is configured to be copied from the ship-to (partner function source **SH**).

The origin (**O**) allows you to extend the **Source** selection to other system tables such as customer credit master data, customer hierarchy, etc.

The sequence column (**Seq**) allows you to control which partner functions are determined first, second, third, etc. This sequence is necessary due to the recursive nature of this assignment. For instance, the SH partner source (in the **Source** column), assigned as a source on the Z9 partner function, can only be determined after you've determined the SH partner function itself is also part of the procedure, so you'll indicate that the function must occur on the first step after the initial determination. If you have another partner function sourced from the Z9 partner function, that function must be assigned as the second sequence (**Seq**).

You can also indicate if a partner function is **Relevant for Printing** or for electronic output (email, fax, etc.) on the corresponding forms created based on the sales order header, such as an order acknowledgment form. You can also specify the label to be used to describe this partner on the form in the **Label** field. If not specified, the description of the partner function will be used.

6.3.10 Texts

Under the **Texts** tab, shown in Figure 6.42, you can enter multiple types of freeform textual messages (text types, also known as text IDs) that may be used for internal controls/documentation as well as for customer communication (when printed/issued on forms such as order acknowledgments, picking lists, packing slips, bills of lading, invoices, etc.).

Under this tab, no clear indication of which text type will be shown to the customer is available. You'll need to create documentation and train your users to be aware of which texts are customer-facing. Internal notes should not be printed on forms; accidents do happen, but taking precautionary change management steps can mitigate this risk. Alternatively, consider changing the text type description to indicate whether these texts will print.

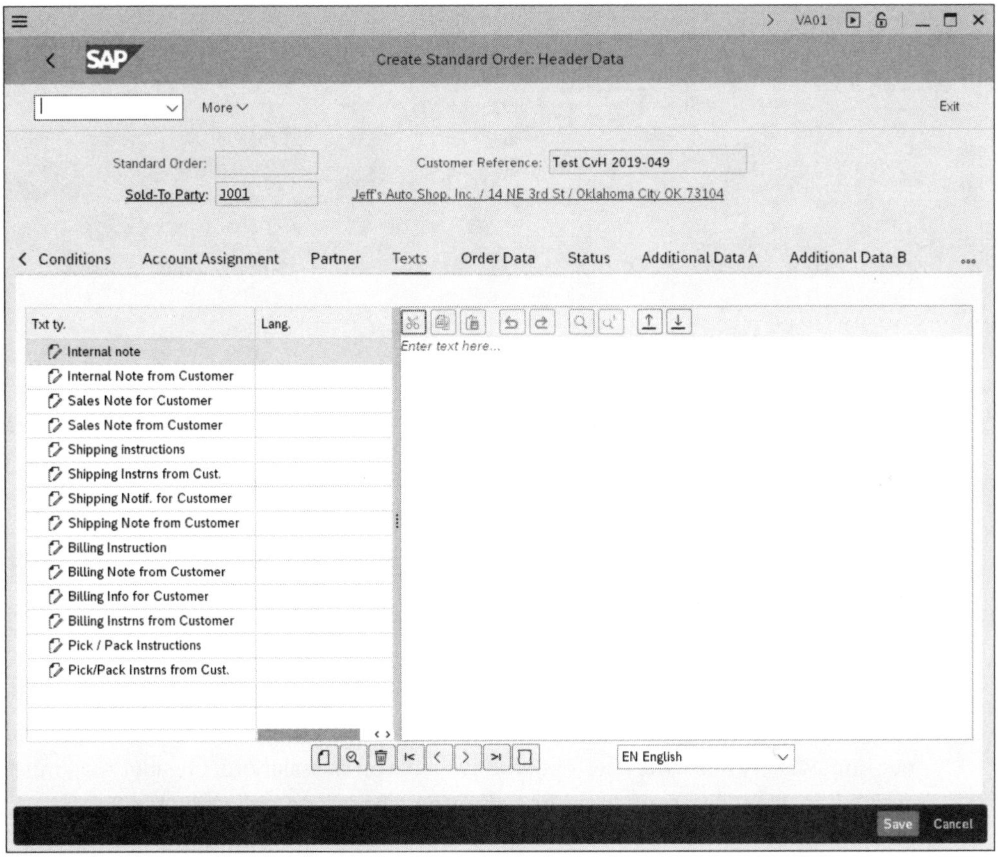

Figure 6.42 Header Detail: Texts

In the following sections, we'll look at how to create a new text type, assign text types to sales order text determination procedures, and walk through the text determination access sequence.

Creating a New Text Type

To create new text types (text IDs) using the sales order text control configuration, open Transaction VOTXN or follow the menu path **SAP Customizing Implementation Guide • Sales and Distribution • Basic Functions • Text Control • Define and Assign Text Determination Procedures • Configuration: Texts.**

As shown in Figure 6.43, select **Header** under **Sales Document** and click on the **Text Types** button. Then, click on the **New Entries** button or press F5.

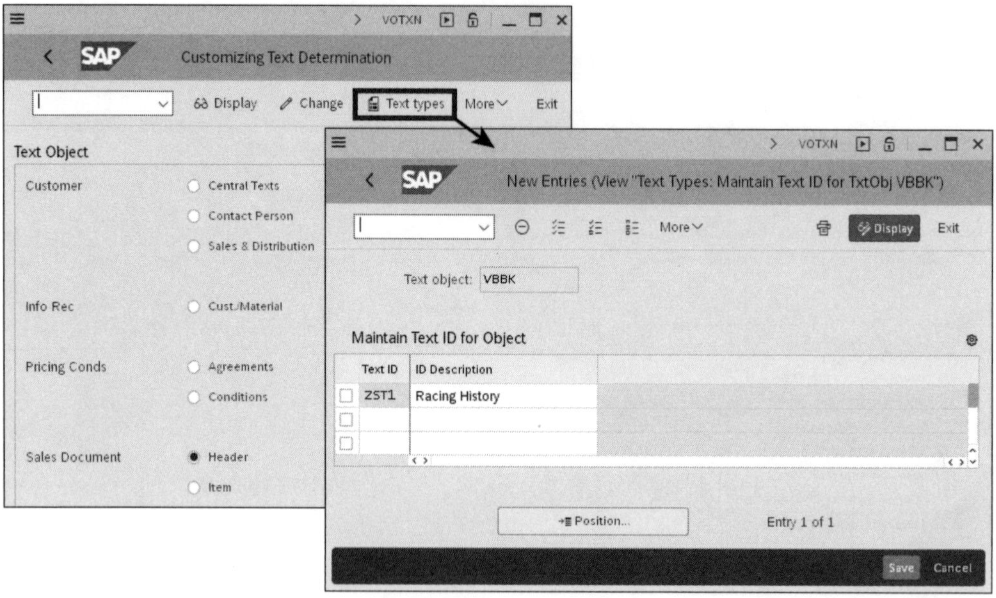

Figure 6.43 Defining New Text Types for Sales Orders

On the **New Entries (View "Text Types: Maintain Text ID for TxtObj VBBK")** screen, specify a four-character text type (**Text ID**) and add a description (**Description**). This action will not immediately make the new text type available on the sales order header; you must assign it to a text determination procedure, which we'll describe next.

Assigning Text Types to Sales Order Text Determination Procedures

To configure text control, open Transaction VOTXN or follow the menu path **SAP Customizing Implementation Guide • Sales and Distribution • Basic Functions • Text Control • Define and Assign Text Determination Procedures • Configuration: Texts**. Then, select **Header** under **Sales Document** and click on the **Change** button, as shown earlier in Figure 6.43.

As shown in Figure 6.44, select text determination procedure **T3** and double-click on the **Text ID's in Textprocedure** menu option in the **Dialog Structure** on the left.

As shown in Figure 6.45, browse the text IDs currently assigned or click on the **New Entries** button or press F5 to add a new one.

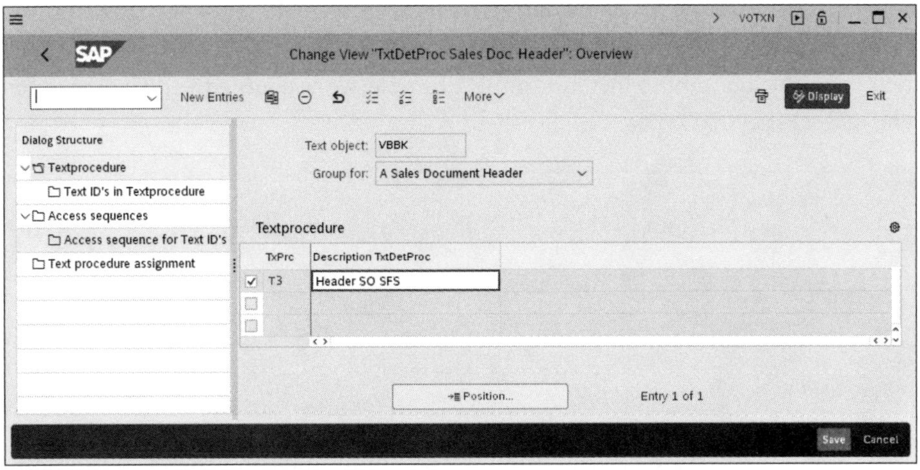

Figure 6.44 Selecting the Text Determination Procedure

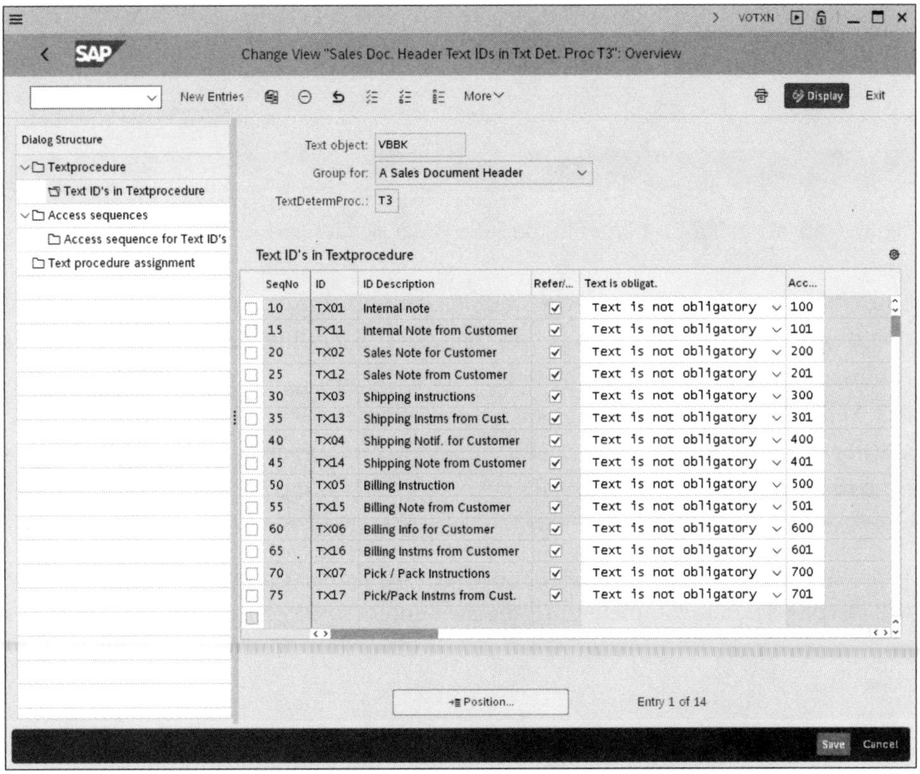

Figure 6.45 Browsing the Text IDs Currently Assigned to the Selected Procedure

On the screen shown in Figure 6.46, specify a three-digit sequence step number (**SeqNo**) indicating where within the procedure this text type should appear and the text type (**ID**) you want to include. In this example, we're adding the next text at the end of the list of text types.

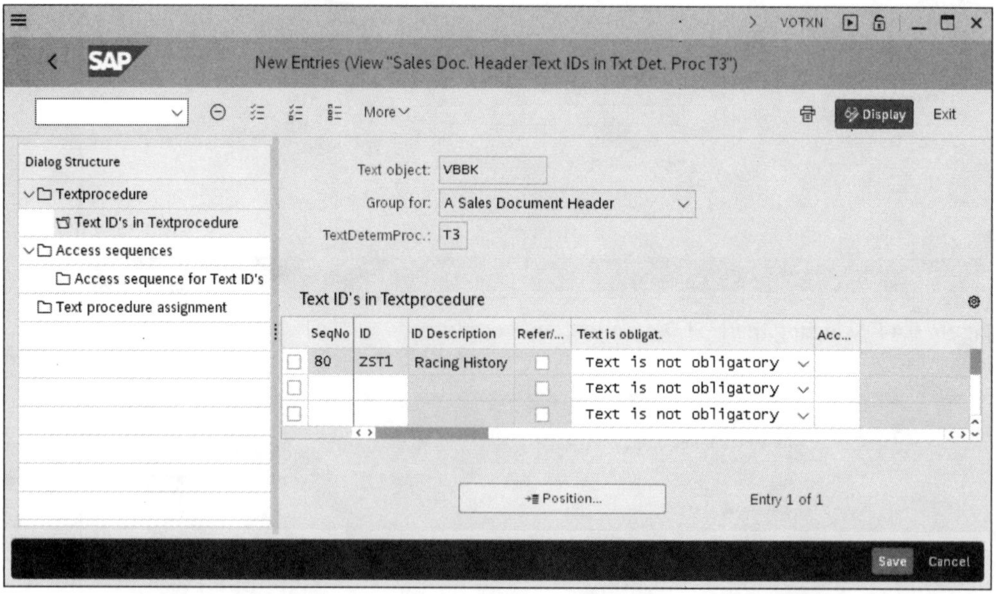

Figure 6.46 Assigning Text Types to the Sales Order Header Text Procedure

You can also indicate whether a text should be modifiable or only display the original text from the master data, copied into the sales order. When selected, the **Reference** flag indicates that, by default, the text is not duplicated, unless a user modifies this flag. For instance, any changes made to the customer master data text will immediately be reflected in all existing sales documents configured to copy text as **Reference** from that customer master entry. If unchecked, the text is copied at the time of order entry, and any changes made to the master data text will not be reflected.

You can define whether a text is mandatory with the **Text is obligat.** flag. The order will be considered incomplete until the user enters some content into this text ID's freeform text field.

Note that, in Chapter 2, we created text ID ZST1. Even though the codes are the same, these text IDs are different because they belong to different text objects (i.e., sales order header VBBK and customer master sales data KNVV). To define that the KNVV ZST1 text must be copied into the VBBK ZST1 text ID, you'll need to define an access sequence as described next. You'll also need to assign the access sequence in the **Acc...** column.

Text Determination Access Sequences

To configure access sequences for text control, open Transaction VOTXN or follow the menu path **SAP Customizing Implementation Guide • Sales and Distribution • Basic Functions • Text Control • Define and Assign Text Determination Procedures • Configuration: Texts.** Then, select **Header** under **Sales Document** and click on the **Change** button, as shown earlier in Figure 6.43.

Next, double-click on the **Access Sequence** option in the **Dialog Structure** menu on the left, as shown in Figure 6.47. Then, click on the **New Entries** button or press F5.

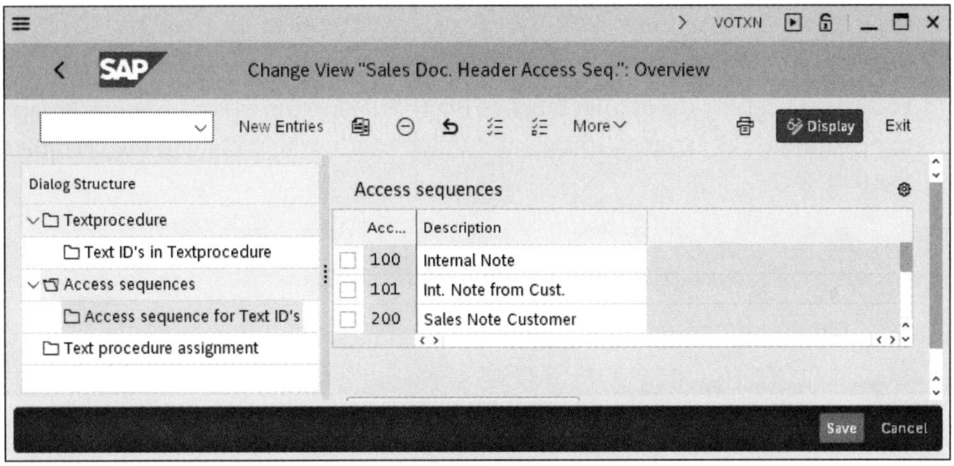

Figure 6.47 Browsing through Existing Access Sequences

As shown in Figure 6.48, specify a four-digit access sequence number (**Access sequence**) and add a description (**Description**). Then, select the entry you just created and double-click on the **Access Sequence for Text ID's** option in the **Dialog Structure** menu on the left.

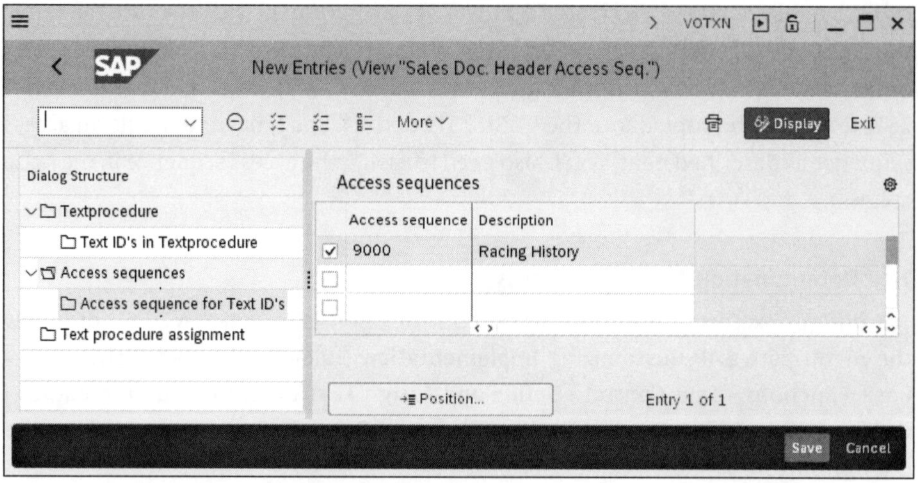

Figure 6.48 Adding a New Access Sequence

Next, as shown in Figure 6.49, select a step sequence number (**SeqNo**) and define the origin (**Text object**, in this case **KNVV**, customer master sales data) and text ID (**ID**, in this case **ZST1**, racing history).

You can also specify the partner function (**Partn.Funct.**) from which to derive the customer number, as assigned to the sales order, to use when fetching the customer master text.

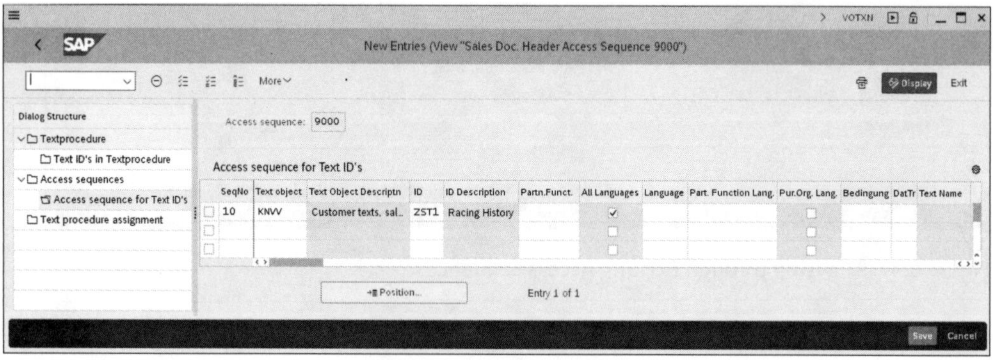

Figure 6.49 Adding Text ID Sources to Access Sequence

You can maintain texts in multiple languages on the customer master and on the sales order. Thus, when defining the access sequence, make sure you specify whether the system should copy texts in **All Languages**, specify a **Language** to use when copying texts, define a partner function from which to fetch the language (**Part. Function Lang.**) or specify that the language to be used is configured on the purchasing organization (**Pur. Org. Lang.**). You must select one of these four language selection fields for the text to be copied; otherwise, the access sequence will not copy any text.

The requirement (**Bedingung**) and data transfer (**DatTr**) fields are VOFM routines that you can implement whether or not this text type should be copied depending on criteria that you can define freely, thus allowing for great flexibility.

Finally, you must assign the access sequence you just created to the text ID in the sales order text determination procedure, shown earlier in Figure 6.46. Now, you can populate the **Access Seq.** column with the new code we created (**9000**), as shown in Figure 6.50.

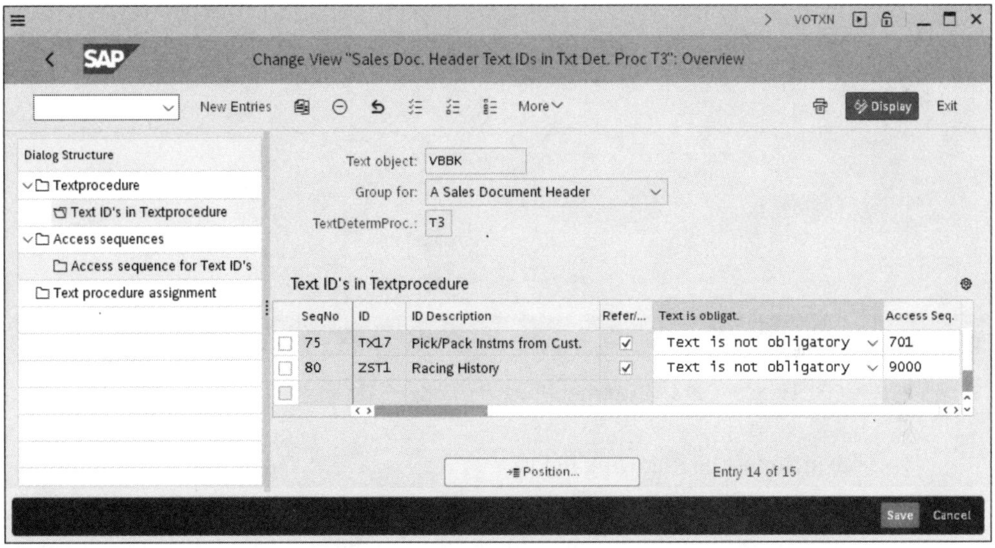

Figure 6.50 Assigning a New Access Sequence to Text Determination Procedure Steps

6.3.11 Order Data

The **Order Data** tab, shown in Figure 6.51, contains detailed information regarding customer purchase orders you receive, allowing you to efficiently communicate with customers both verbally and electronically.

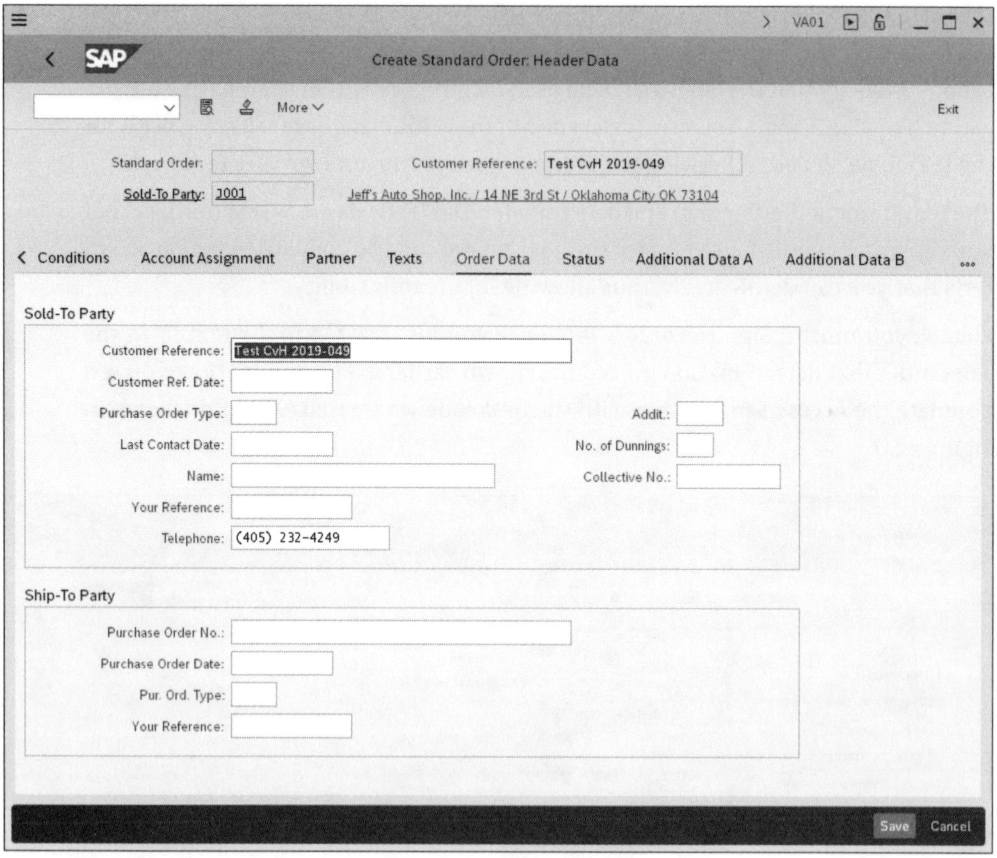

Figure 6.51 Header Data: Customer Purchase Order Data

This tab includes the following fields:

- The **Customer Reference** field contains the purchase order number as defined in the customer's system. This value may be assigned at the line level if you're combining multiple purchase orders in a single sales order. This practice is not common but is possible if business needs arise.
- The **Customer Ref. Date** field contains the purchase order date as understood by the customer. Note that the customer may send the purchase order on a later date. The date in this field is intended to represent when the purchase order was created in the customer's system, not in yours. This date may be assigned at the line level, although doing so is not common.

- The customer **Purchase Order Type** field is a code you can configure to classify the customer purchase order, often used to identify the order source (i.e., fax, email, EDI, phone, etc.). This code is ideal for identifying orders created from e-commerce platforms such as websites and mobile apps. This value may be assigned at the line level, although doing so is uncommon.

  To configure customer purchase order types, follow the menu path **SAP Customizing Implementation Guide • Sales and Distribution • Sales • Sales Documents • Sales Document Header • Define Purchase Order Types**. On the screen that opens, click on the **New Entries** button or press F5.

  As shown in Figure 6.52, specify a four-character purchase order type (**Pur. Ord. Type**) and add a description (**Description**).

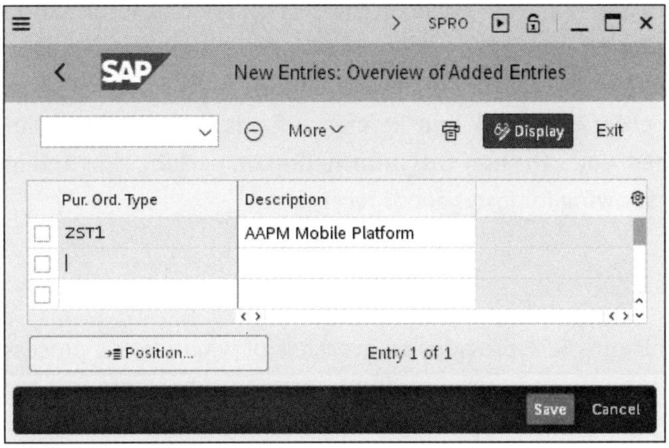

Figure 6.52 Defining New Customer Purchase Order Types

- The **Addit.** field can be used as a suffix for the customer purchase order number (**Customer Reference** field).
- The **Last Contact Date** and **No. of Dunning** fields are related to accounts receivable collections activities that control the amount and frequency of follow-up contact with a customer when attempting to collect a debt.
- You can specify the **Name** of your point of contact at the customer's organization who is responsible for this sales order. This information may be shown on forms and communications, thus improving the chance that the communication finds its way to the right person more quickly.
- The **Collective No.** field may be freely assigned and is an alphanumeric code controlled manually by user to create groups of documents that belong together (by

using matching values). This number may be used later in reporting and order processing (logistics and billing).

- The **Your Reference** field is another number that your customer gives to this sales order. When contacting them, you can use this number to expedite and help them find the right document more quickly. The customer purchase order (PO) usually serves this purpose well, and most companies end up using this field for other purposes. For instance, when an order is created in an external system (Salesforce or SAP C/4HANA), you can enter the cart ID in this field for reference. Reference values may be assigned at the line level.
- The **Telephone** field is the phone number to use when contacting the person identified in the **Name** field.

The purchase order information we've described in this section refers to information from the purchase order sent by your customer's buyer, that is, the sold-to customer. You can also define different values for the **Purchase Order No.**, **Purchase Order Date**, **Pur. Ord. Type**, **Purchase order item**, and **Your Reference** fields as defined by your ship-to customer. If defined, you can show this information on packing slips and in logistics paperwork, thus allowing for faster goods receipt.

6.3.12 Status

The **Status** tab, shown in Figure 6.53, provides an overview of where in the process this sales document is. These statuses may represent complex subprocess that are sequential or may run in parallel. This tab includes the following fields:

- The **Overall Status** field indicates if this order has been fully processed or if any transaction is still required to complete it. To find details, including related document numbers, you can consult the document flow.
- The **Rejection Status** field on the header indicates if any lines have been canceled (rejected) for any reason.
- The **Reason for Rejection** field on the line indicates that this line was canceled and provides the reason why.
- The **Delivery Status** field on the line indicates if you've created a delivery for the full quantity of this line, a partial quantity, or none at all. On the header, this field refers to the total delivery-relevant quantity of the order as a whole.

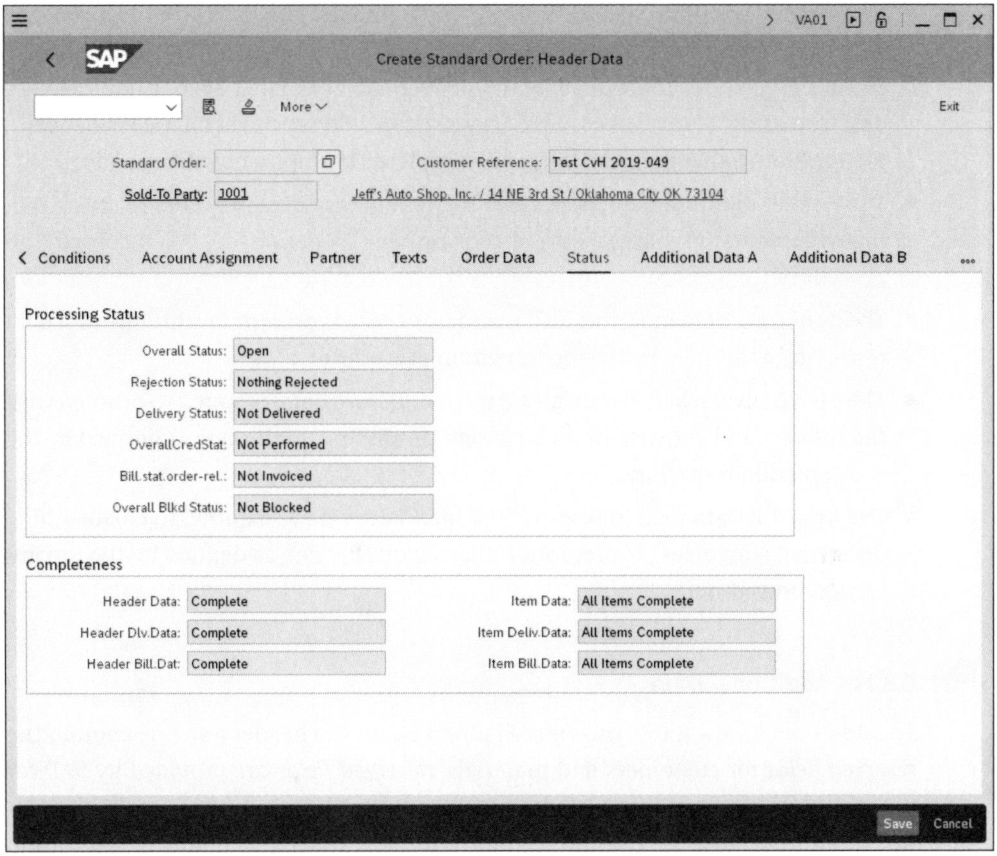

Figure 6.53 Header Details: Status

- The **OverallCredStat** field (overall credit status) indicates if the order has been approved, not relevant, rejected, or manually released from a credit standpoint.
- The **Bill.stat.order-rel.** field (billing status for order related billing), for orders that are relevant for billing without deliveries, indicates if the billing document has already been created or not. This check is used on credit/debit memos, service sales, etc.
- The **Overall Blkd Status** field indicates if a block has been assigned to this order at any level.
- The **Header Data** field indicates if the mandatory header data is present or if data is missing as defined by the incompletion procedure.

- The **Header Dlv.Data** field indicates if the mandatory data, required to proceed with the delivery and logistics steps, is present or missing as defined by the incompletion procedure. You can allow the delivery to be created even if non-delivery data is missing. Many companies decide to stop delivery based on the header completion status; that is, if anything is incomplete, no shipment will be made.
- The **Header Bill.Data** field indicates if the mandatory data, required to create billing documents (invoices), is present or missing as defined by the incompletion procedure.
- The **Item Data** field indicates if all mandatory data is present for this line or if data is missing as defined by the incompletion procedure.
- The **Item Deliv.Data** field indicates if the mandatory data, required to proceed with the delivery and logistics steps, is present or missing on this line as defined by the incompletion procedure.
- The **Item Bill.Data** field indicates if the mandatory data, required to create billing documents (invoices), is present or missing on this line as defined by the incompletion procedure.

6.3.13 Additional Data

The **Additional Data A** tab, shown in Figure 6.54, on the header and line contain the *reserved fields* for customers and materials. *Reserved fields* are provided by SAP for you to use for your specific business needs and don't have specific uses defined out of the box. Consult Chapter 2 and Chapter 3 for more details, including configuration instructions.

The **Additional Data B** tab, shown in Figure 6.55, is provided without any fields out of the box to allow you to add new fields to sales orders and make these fields available for maintenance on these tabs. Companies implementing SAP often add new fields to the sales order. However, adding new fields would require development and can be expensive, not only during the implementation project itself but also after go-live in terms of maintenance and support for these fields during the lifetime of the system.

Often, companies start from a position against implementing any development with SAP S/4HANA and control closely when requirements surface. This control is important and necessary, but stakeholders need to understand the business cost of not implementing these requirements. Successful controls are conducted by committee that include multiple parties and meet regularly.

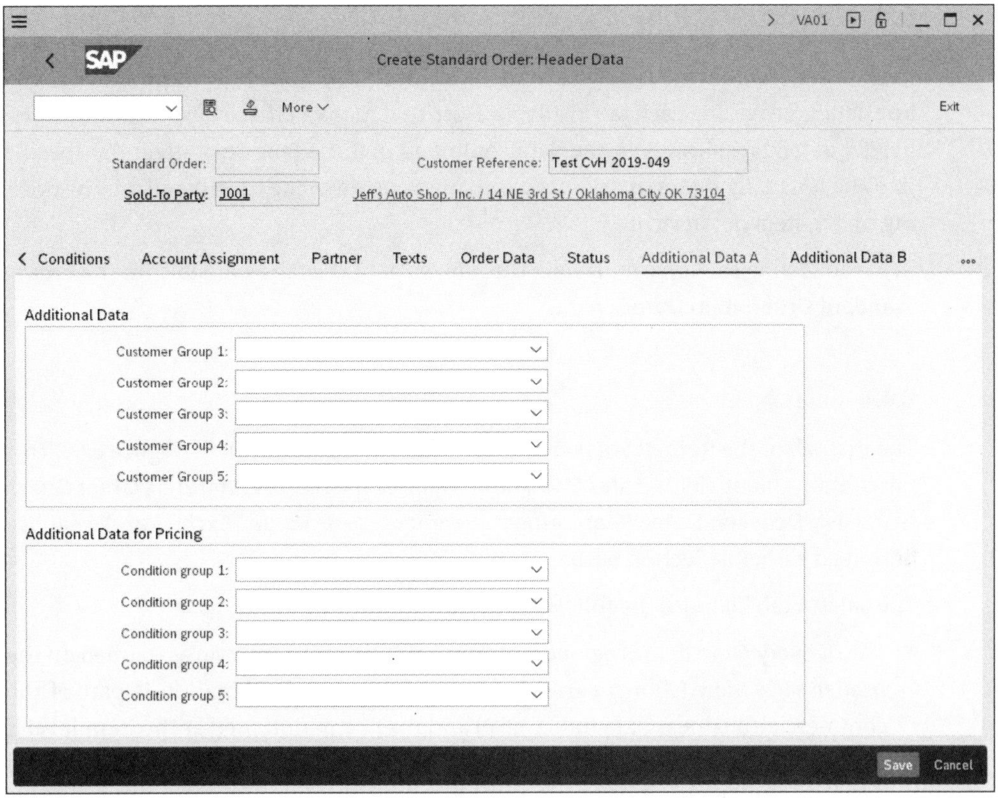

Figure 6.54 Header Data: Additional Data A Tab

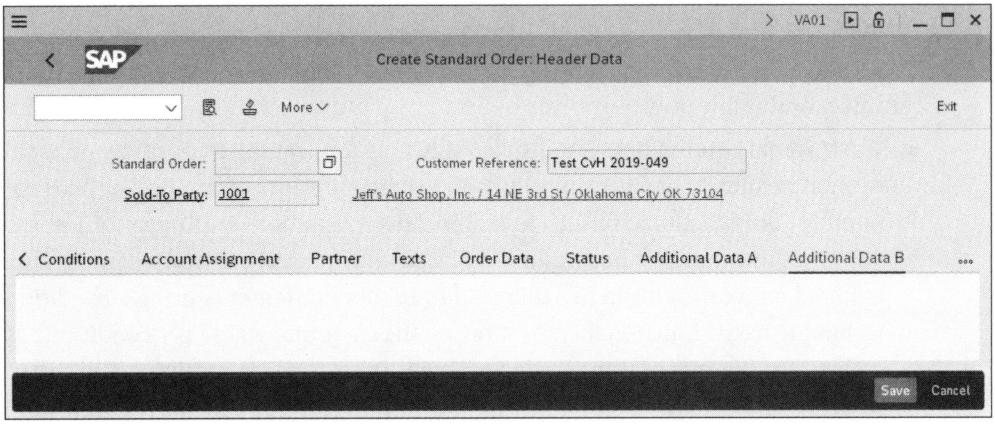

Figure 6.55 Header Data: Additional Data B Tab

6.4 Creating Standard Orders: Item Data

In this section, we'll focus on the item detail tabs (sometimes also referred to as the line details), covering each tab available. Note that many of these tab labels match the header detail tabs; however, the data contained in these tabs only affect the specific line and is usually material oriented. You can navigate to the item detail tabs by clicking on the item details icon.

In the following sections, we'll walk through each of the tabs available on the **Create Standard Order: Item Data** screen.

6.4.1 Sales A

The first tab of the item details screen is the **Sales A** tab, as shown in Figure 6.56. This tab contains many fields (**Sales Document Item**, **Item Category**, **Material**, **Order Quantity**, **First Delivery Date**, **Requirement Segment**, **Net Value**, **Exch. Rate**) that we described earlier in Section 6.2.9.

The **Sales A** tab includes the following fields:

- The **Delivery Time** field is agreed/contractual fulfillment interval as defined on the header sales view (shown earlier in Figure 6.26). This information is part of the commercial/business data (table VBKD) and may be maintained at the item level if the item category is configured to allow for modifications. If maintained, this field will overwrite the header value for this line only.
- The **Pricing Date** field is the key date used for pricing reference as defined on the header sales overview (Section 6.2.1). Part of the commercial/business data (table VBKD), this field may be maintained at the item level if the item category is configured to allow for modifications. If maintained, this field will overwrite the header value for this line only.
- The **Material Entered** field is a display-only field for keeping track of the material entered (manually or electronically) before being replaced by a different material number via a functionality such as material determination (see Chapter 4, Section 4.3). If the material number was not replaced, the material entered will match the material number. You can use this field to fulfill requirements using a condition technique-based functionality. As a result, the customer would get conditions as defined for the material they selected even if they end up receiving a different material number. Most companies simply use this field to consult/report in case of disputes.

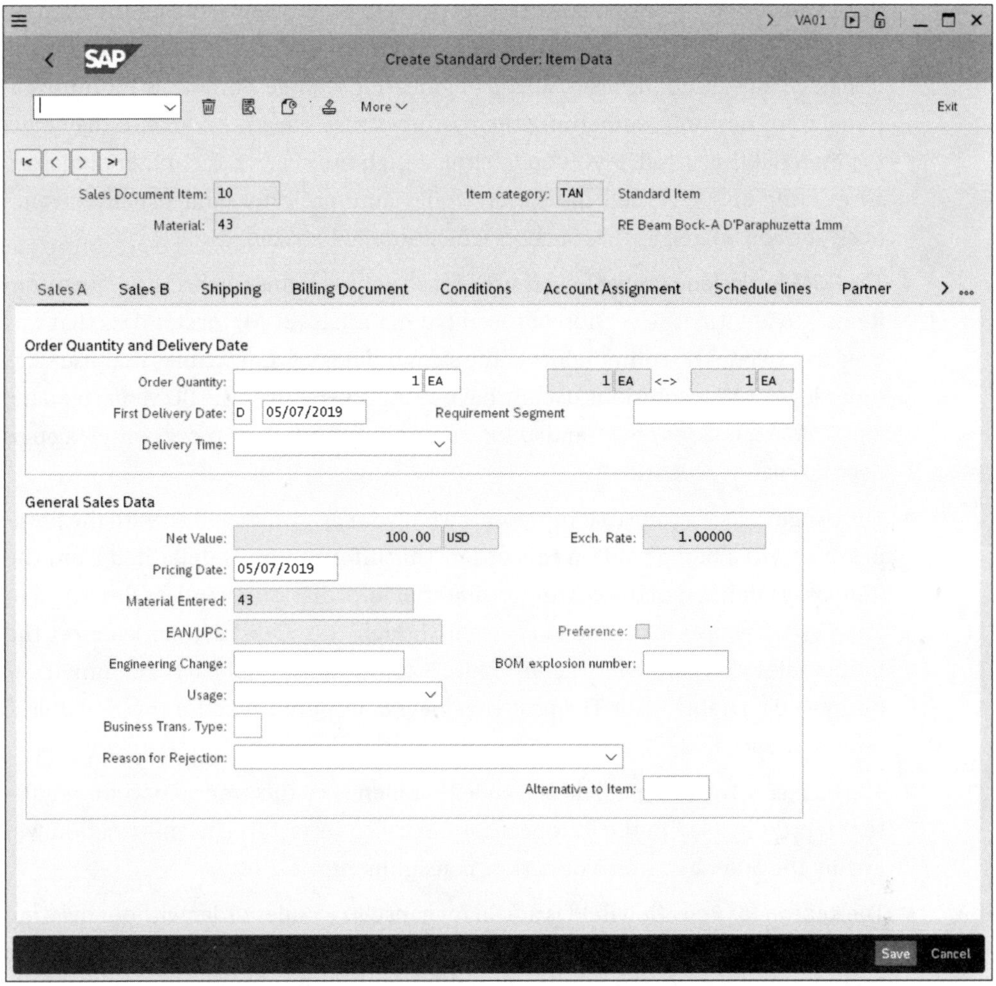

Figure 6.56 Item Details: Sales A

- The **EAN/UPC** field (European Article Number/Universal Product Code) is the product barcode usually shown on packaging, commonly used in live retail transactions. The code is usually registered with international regulatory agencies such as GS1 (Global Standards One). Some customers order with this number via EDI. The value is defaulted from the material master. You can maintain several entries with different formats, but you'll need to choose the appropriate one for an order on this screen. Few customers require this information to be provided by your company (as a vendor), but the ones that do are usually large and important customers.

- The **Engineering Change** field is the design version of the product as defined by engineering controls. Companies can create new material numbers when the design changes, and in this case, the engineering change number is for informational purposes only, something the customer may consult to ensure they have the material they need. If you update the design number on the material master, all existing and returned inventory would automatically (and usually erroneously) be considered as that version, which should be avoided.
- The **BOM explosion number** field is used for structural items (such as kits/"phantom items") to identify the version of the bill of materials (BOM) master data that was used to explode the components at the sales order level. Companies that use sales order-level BOM explosions usually have a single version of the BOM master data, and BOM explosions are intended for the implementation of more complex engineering change scenarios.
- The **Usage** field is a code that represents what your customer will do with the product or services being sold on this order. This information is defaulted from the item usage defined in the customer-material information record, as described in Chapter 3, Section 3.6. Note that, even though this field also appears on the header sales view, shown earlier in Figure 6.26, this data is not part of commercial/business data (table VBKD). The header value is considered valid for this line unless otherwise specified.
- The **Business Trans. Type** field is a code that identifies this transaction for regulatory reporting used in the European Union called Intrastat. This information will qualify the order as a sale, a donation, consignment, etc.
- The **Reason for Rejection** field is a field for canceling a sales order without deleting record of the sales order while also providing a justification for this action. See Section 6.2.5 for further details and configuration information so that controlling agencies can understand the information in this field.
- The **Alternative to Item** field is the line number that this line is an alternative to. You can enter this manually to indicate that you're selling this item as an alternative to another item. On quotes and inquiries, this information is useful to understand: Even though you provided quotes based on a different item, you'll deliver this alternative item due to special unforeseen conditions such as a backorder (stock shortage).

6.4.2 Sales B

Because many sales-related fields exist at the item level, you'll work in two tabs for better organization. The **Sales B** tab, shown in Figure 6.57, is a continuation of the **Sales A** tab.

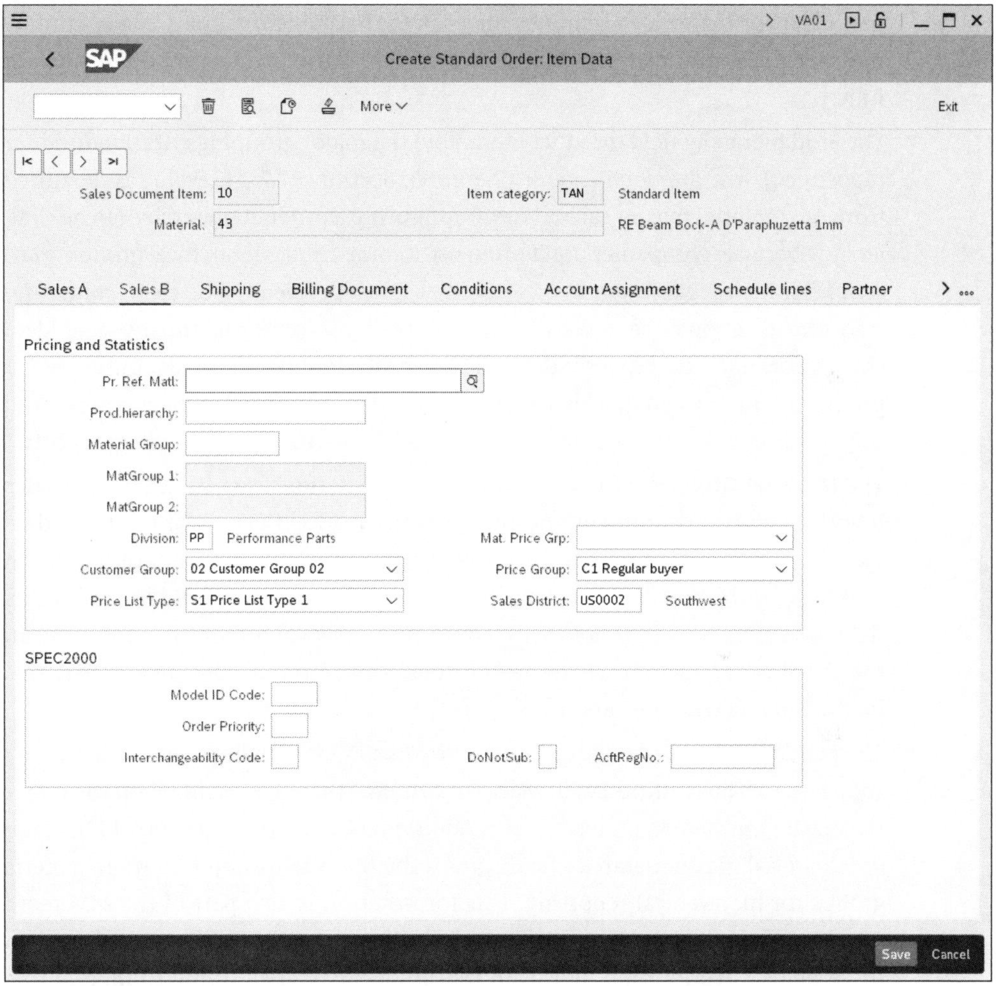

Figure 6.57 Item Details: Sales B

The **Sales B** tab includes the following fields:

- The pricing reference material (**Pr. Ref. Matl** field) is the material number you want to use for pricing purposes. This value is defaulted from the material master and reduces the amount of pricing master data (condition records) when mostly shared across different variations of the same products. If you have multiple material numbers representing different colors of the same product, you can enter the same material number as the pricing reference material. As a result, you won't need to maintain prices for each material number (color). This feature is useful in particular for material variants created for configurable materials. Many companies struggle with these concepts at first but later use this feature quite successfully.

- The **Prod.hierarchy** field (product hierarchy) is a major grouping criterion used for reporting. For more details, refer Chapter 3, Section 3.2.7. The value is defaulted from the material master sales views. Configuring a product hierarchy can be challenging because companies don't often use a compatible hierarchical grouping criterion on their legacy systems. So, the new concept needs to be clear, configuration entries should be reviewed by several areas of the company, and data conversion must be properly defined based different legacy fields. In the end, a product hierarchy can quickly become a common language for the company and can help implement compatibility among sales, finance, and controlling reports.
- The **Material Group** field is a major grouping criterion used to harmonize sales reporting with procurement and production. This field is part of the basic data view of the material master and also appears in the sales views. The configuration of values for this field is not driven by sales. For this reason, we did not cover this field in Chapter 3. Sales is not expected to create new values for this field; you can request the MM team to create new values. Thus, from a sales perspective, this field is only relevant for reporting.
- The **MatGroup 1** and **MatGroup 2** fields are display-only material group hierarchy values, not to be confused with **Material Groups 1** through **5** defined on the material master and shown under the **Item Additional Data A** tab (Section 6.4.14). These two material group hierarchy fields group the **Material Group** into more generic groups for hierarchical reporting. This information is also part of the MM team scope, and sales will use it for reporting only. You can build functionality based on these fields Keep in mind, however, that issues may arise trying to modify this structure to suit your needs; it belongs to other teams, and your requirements may affect them negatively.
- The **Division** field is the organizational structure element entered on the header of the sales order or the corresponding value defined on the basic data views of the

material master. The item category configuration will dictate when to default this value from the header, from the material master, or not at all. You can also activate validation to ensure you're only entering materials from the same division. Companies usually allow cross-division sales. Thus, enforcing this validation is usually considered bad for overall business and should only be implemented if strong reasons exist that would justify the loss of business.

- The **Mat. Price Grp** field (material price group) is a grouping criterion used for material-level pricing conditions (discounts and surcharges) as defined in Chapter 3, Section 3.2.2.
- The **Customer Group** field is a major reporting criterion as defined on the header sales overview (Section 6.3.1). This information is part of the commercial/business data (table VBKD) and may be maintained at the item level if the item category is configured to allow for modifications. If maintained, this value will overwrite the header value for this line only. Custom reports must consider that this field is populated on the line; otherwise, issues may arise.
- The **Price Group** field is the key date used for customer-level pricing conditions (discount/surcharges) as defined in the header sales overview (Section 6.3.1). This information is part of the commercial/business data (table VBKD), and may be maintained at the item level if the item category is configured to allow for modifications. If maintained, this value will overwrite the header value for this line only.
- The **Price List Type** field is the key data used for customer-based price determination (when applicable) as defined on the header sales overview (Section 6.3.1). This information is part of the commercial/business data (table VBKD) and may be maintained at the item level if the item category is configured to allow for modification. If maintained, this value will overwrite the header value for this line only.
- The **Sales District** field is a geographical reporting criterion as defined on the header sales overview (Section 6.3.1). This information is part of the commercial/business data (table VBKD) and may be maintained at the item level if the item category is configured to allow for modification. If maintained, this value will overwrite the header value for this line only.
- The **Model ID Code**, **Order Priority**, **Interchangeability Code**, **DoNotSub**, and **AcftRegNo.** fields are used by the aerospace industry as defined by the Air Transportation Association (ATA) e-Business Program called SPEC2OO. The field refer to parts sold to repair or overhaul aircrafts.

6.4.3 Shipping

The third tab of the item details is the **Shipping** tab, as shown in Figure 6.58. This tab contains a display-only field with the **Ship-to party** information as described earlier in Section 6.2.1.

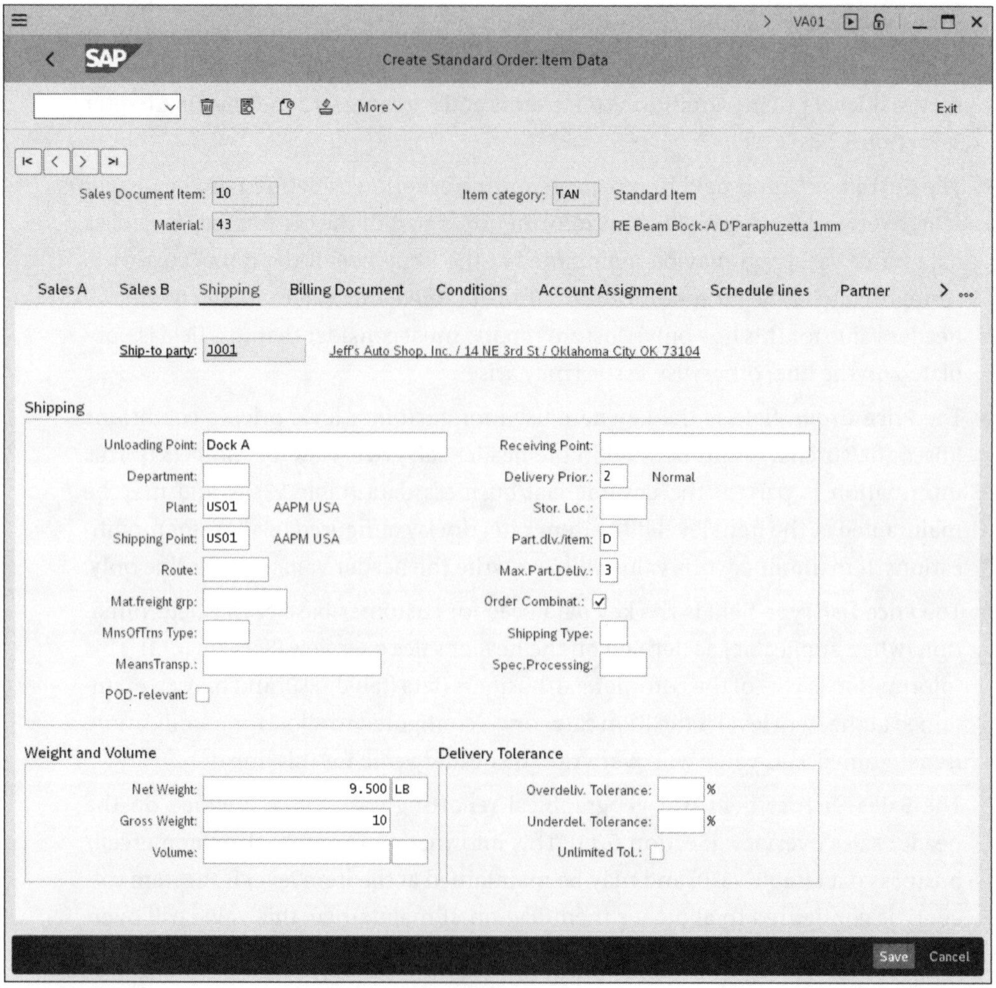

Figure 6.58 Item Details: Shipping

The **Shipping** tab includes the following fields:

- The **Unloading Point**, **Receiving Point**, and **Department** fields are defined on the header (Section 6.2.3 and Section 6.3.2), but may be changed at the line level using this screen to allow a single order to result in several deliveries to different locations (gates, unloading docks, etc.) within the ship-to customer's facility.

- The **Delivery Prior.** field represents the order in which backorders should be fulfilled once inventory is available. This priority value is defaulted from the customer master (consult Chapter 2, Section 2.3.3, for more details).
- The **Plant** field is the facility from which you'll deliver product to the customer. The plant may also be entered in several other views (Section 6.2.9). This value is defaulted from the customer-master information record, from the business partner master data, or from the material master data (in this order). See the note in Section 6.2.1 for more details.
- The **Stor. Loc.** field (storage location) represents the area within the plant where the stock is stored. Companies often define logical storage locations to segregate inventory, which is a somewhat controversial approach but quite common. Using logical storage locations would require a user to manually assign the storage location, which is a step to be avoided. Stock can be segregated in a number of other ways such as through product allocation, rule-based ATP, reservations, etc.
- The **Shipping Point** field represents the location within the warehouse where a team is focused on issuing the necessary paperwork for shipping, commonly located next to the departure docks. This key is used to create delivery documents (see Chapter 9 for more details) and control warehouse lead times. The value of this field is generally automatically selected based on the shipping conditions, loading group, and plant. We'll look at configuring shipping points later in this section.
- The **Part.dlv./item** field controls whether each line may be partially shipped. The value is defaulted from the customer master; see Chapter 2, Section 2.3.2, for more details.
- The **Route** field identifies the detailed transportation arrangements chosen to deliver this line to the customer. The route determines the expected transportation lead time (see the Defining Routes section for more details). In complex transportation scenarios, the route is used as a splitting criterion (see Chapter 9) at the time of dispatch. Routes are assigned automatically based on as defined via configuration (see the Route Determination section for more details).

  Companies that own their own delivery fleet would use this field as the actual delivery routes that their trucks will follow. Companies that use parcel carriers may enter routes simply to represent different amount of transportation lead time in days. Companies that use different, full truckload carriers tend to create routes for each carrier and make use of the **Service Agent** field configured when defining route codes.

- The **Max.Part.Deliv.** field (maximum partial deliveries) indicates how many partials deliveries this customer allows. This value is defined in the business partner/customer master data (see Chapter 2, Section 2.3.2, for more details).
- The **Mat.freight grp** field (material freight group) classifies materials by freight requirements. This value is defined in the material master data (see Chapter 3, Section 3.3.1, for more details).
- The **MnsOfTrns Type**, **MeansTransp.**, **Shipping Type**, **Spec.Processing**, and **POD-relevant** flags are defined on the header (Section 6.3.2) and may be changed at the line level, which would affect only this line. These fields are part of the commercial/business data (table VBKD) but may be maintained at the item level if the item category is configured to allow for modification.
- The **Net Weight**, **Gross Weight**, and **Volume** fields are defaulted from the material master basic data views. You can modify these values on this screen, but usually would only do so when these fields have been left blank in the material master by mistake and are set as mandatory on the order.
- The **Overdeliv. Tolerance**, **Underdel. Tolerance**, and **Unlimited Tol.** flags control whether this customer allows you to deliver a quantity different than the ordered quantity and how much variance the customer would tolerate. This value is defaulted from the customer master and may be changed on this screen.

Let's now walk through the three configuration activities you'll need to perform under this tab: shipping point determination, route definition, and route determination.

Shipping Point Determination

To define a shipping point determination, follow the menu path **SAP Customizing Implementation Guide • Logistics Execution • Shipping • Basic Shipping Functions • Shipping Point and Goods Receiving Point Determination • Assign Shipping Points.**

On the screen shown in Figure 6.59, you'll need to consider all possible combinations of shipping conditions (**SC**, defaulted on the order from the customer master); loading groups (**LGrp**, defaulted on the order from the material master); and plant (**Plnt**, defaulted on the order from either the customer-master information record, the customer master, or the material master).

For each combination, you must choose one default/proposed shipping point (**PrShp**) and then list up to 11 alternative shipping points that the user may select manually (**MShPt**). You can document the user ID responsible for each entry on the **Created by** column; the system does not automatically assign this value.

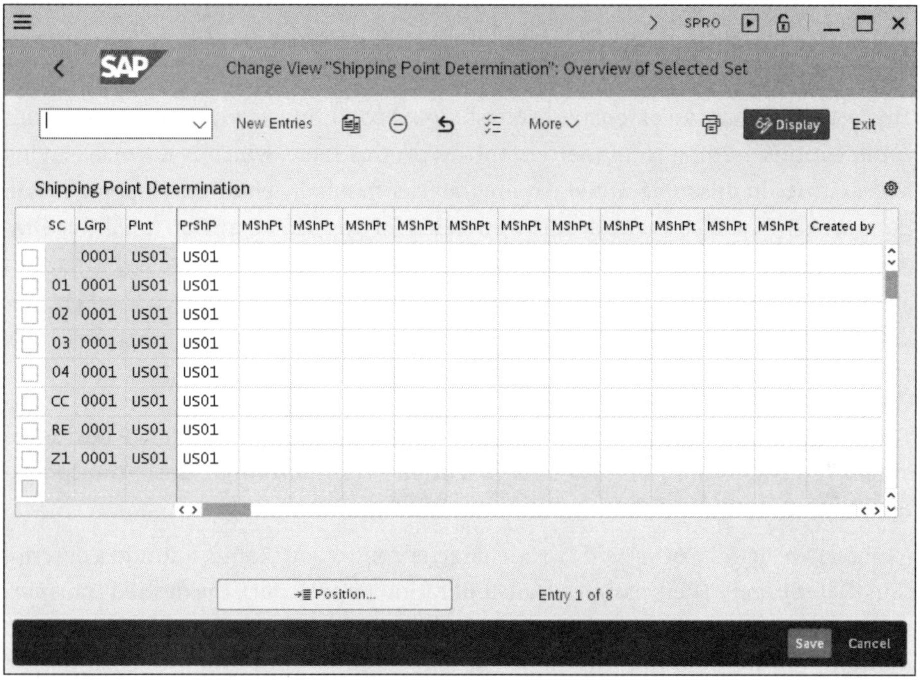

Figure 6.59 Shipping Point Determination

Note that you can only enter shipping points that are assigned to the selected plant in the organizational structure definition (see Chapter 1 for more details).

Note also that needing more than 12 shipping point for the same key combination is highly unlikely; needing more than 12 may be a sign of functional errors that should be addressed before going live.

One question that may arise is whether to enter assignments for blank **CS**, **LGrp**, and **Plnt** values, although the decision is usually at your discretion. Entries with blank keys can be used to determine shipping points when a sales order is entered even if you don't have a value for the key fields. In most scenarios, you'll have only one shipping point, and you can define values, as shown in the first line of Figure 6.59, with a blank shipping condition. Including blank values is advisable for a better, more complete user experience but won't cause issues either way.

You'll also need to consider returns when making these assignments. For returns, the conceptually correct name for this field is "receiving point" (once goods and coming back into the warehouse), even though most screens would still call it the "shipping point." Usually, you'll create special shipping conditions for returns and then assign these shipping conditions to the order type via configuration (Section 6.1.1).

The result is usually an extensive list of shipping condition, loading group, and plant combinations, leading to numerous entries on this table, which is normal. Having fewer entries in this table would require the user manually enter the shipping conditions, which should be avoided, unless intended for a legitimate reason (unlikely). Otherwise, you should strive to consider all possible scenarios, exceptions, and variations and represent all these possibilities as combinations. A simple approach would be utilizing a spreadsheet and then copying and pasting batches of entries into this screen.

Defining Routes

To configure a route, open Transaction OVTC or follow the menu path **SAP Customizing Implementation Guide • Logistics Execution • Transportation • Basic Transportation Functions • Routes • Define Routes • Define Routes and Stages.**

As shown in Figure 6.60, specify a six-character route code (**Route**) and add a description (**Description**). Then, assign a transit duration (**TransitDur**), the desired transportation lead time (**TransLdTm.**) expressed in days, and a factory calendar (**Cal**) used to indicate non-working days (if any) that should considered when calculating the expected delivery date. You can also express the desired transit duration and transportation lead time in hours (**Trav.Dur.** and **TrLeadTime Hr**).

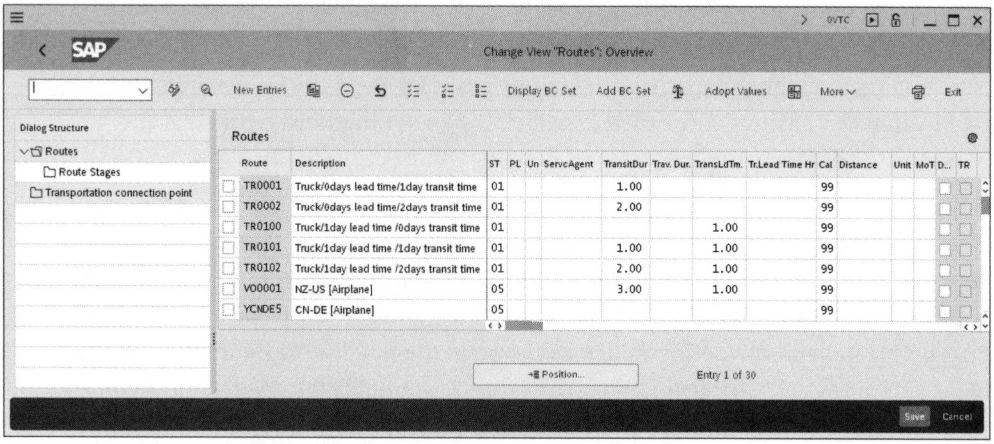

Figure 6.60 Defining Routes

The transportation lead time (**TransLdTm.**) is the amount of time required to prepare cargo for shipping, such as the preparation of special crates, pallets, and containers used for export. The transit duration (**TransitDur**) is the portion of time required for the carrier to take the product from your door to the customer's door. Companies often use a transportation lead time referring to the whole process, but splitting the time into appropriate fields can be useful. The ATP check creates specific expected dates for each step of the process, thus allowing for better planning. So, even if currently this feature is not important, configuring this level of detail will enable your company to better plan for future logistics activities.

Each route is also assigned to a main shipping type (**ST**, described earlier in Section 6.3.2), a preliminary leg shipping type (**PL**), and a subsequent leg shipping type (**Un**). For instance, sea freight typically involves a truck to take the product to the port, where the product is put on a boat to the next port. On arrival, the product is put on another truck to be moved from the port to the customer's location. In this case, **ST** would 04 (Sea), **PL** would be 01 (Truck), and **Un** would also be 01 (Truck).

The service agent (**ServcAgent**) is the freight forward vendor you're using on this route. In export scenarios, often companies use a partner that handles the whole export process, including customs requirements. Some companies use this field for full truckload carriers as well. You may also want to document the distance (**Distance**) in any unit of measurement (**Unit**).

Route Determination

To define a route determination, follow the menu path **SAP Customizing Implementation Guide • Logistics Execution • Transportation • Basic Transportation Functions • Routes • Route Determination • Maintain Route Determination**.

On the screen that opens, you must consider all possible combinations of departure/shipping countries (**CDep**) with transportation zones (**DepZ**) and of destination/receiving countries (**DstC**) with transportation zones (**RecZ**). The country (**Name**) and transportation zone description (**Description**) are displayed for reference.

The departure country and transportation zones are defined in the shipping point addresses, as described in Chapter 1, which includes detailed configuration steps. The destination country and transportation zones are defined in the ship-to business partner/customer master data and may be changed on the **Partner** tab of the sales order (Section 6.4.8). The configuration of transportation zones is described in Chapter 2, Section 2.2.1.

For each departure/destination combination, you must configure a route determination by double-clicking on the **Route Determination Without Weight Groups (Order)** option in the **Dialog Structure** on the left, as shown in Figure 6.61.

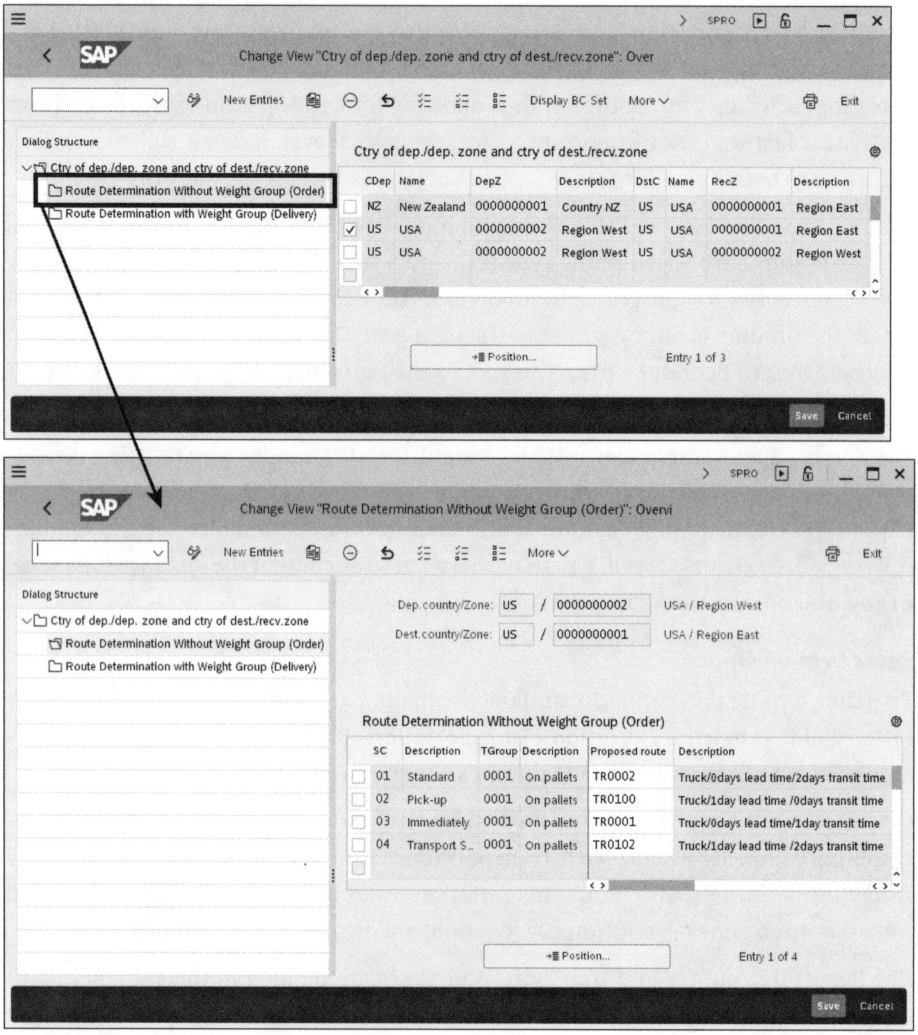

Figure 6.61 Route Determination

Next, select the shipping conditions (**SC**) representing the transportation service level you are offering your customers and the transportation group (**TGroup**) defined on the material master data (see Chapter 3, Section 3.3.2). For each combination, specify a proposed route in the **Proposed Route** field.

You can assign routes to blank values, similar to the shipping point determination, to enable a route even when the transportation group is not known.

You can end up with a long list of entries, and unfortunately, the spreadsheet copy-and-paste approach cannot help in this case because of the screen's layout. Instead, you'll need to build a Legacy System Migration Workbench (LSMW) or a batch input folder (Transaction SM35) to create numerous entries. Other third-party tools, such as WinShuttle or Quadrate, may be used.

6.4.4 Billing Document

The fourth tab of the item details is the **Billing Document** tab, as shown in Figure 6.62. The **Payer**, **Incoterms Version**, **Incoterms**, **Incoterms Location 1**, **Incoterms Location 2**, **Fixed Value Date**, **Payment terms**, **Add. Value Days**, **Billing Block**, **Invoicing Dates**, **Billing Date**, **Serv. Rendered Date**, **Man.Inv.Maint.**, **Paymt Guarant. Proc.**, **Financial Doc. No.**, and **Depreciation %** fields are defined on the header (Section 6.3.3), but may be changed at the line level using this screen.

This tab includes the following fields:

- The **AcctAssmtGrpMat** field (material account assignment group) is a grouping criterion used to differentiate material from an accounting standpoint. This field is typically used to differentiate between the sale/delivery of goods versus revenue generated from providing services. This code is assigned at the material master and is rarely change at the order level. This value is later used during revenue account determination (see Chapter 10, Section 10.4.1, for more details).
- The **Payment Method** field is a code identifies how payments are expected to be sent by the customer (check, direct debit, etc.).
- The **Posting period** field is a display-only field indicating the month and year that will be used to create the accounting postings generated by this sales order as it is being processed. This value affects month-end closing: After the month is closed by finance, you can no longer post in that period. This positing period is controlled internally and is usually updated based on the shipping date at the time of invoicing. This field may be used for reporting to project incoming revenue before month end.
- The **Exch.Rate Acct.** field allows you to specify the exchange rate to be used when creating accounting document. This value may be applicable when different currencies are used in different documents. If you don't modify the value in this field, the default rate maintained in the system is used.

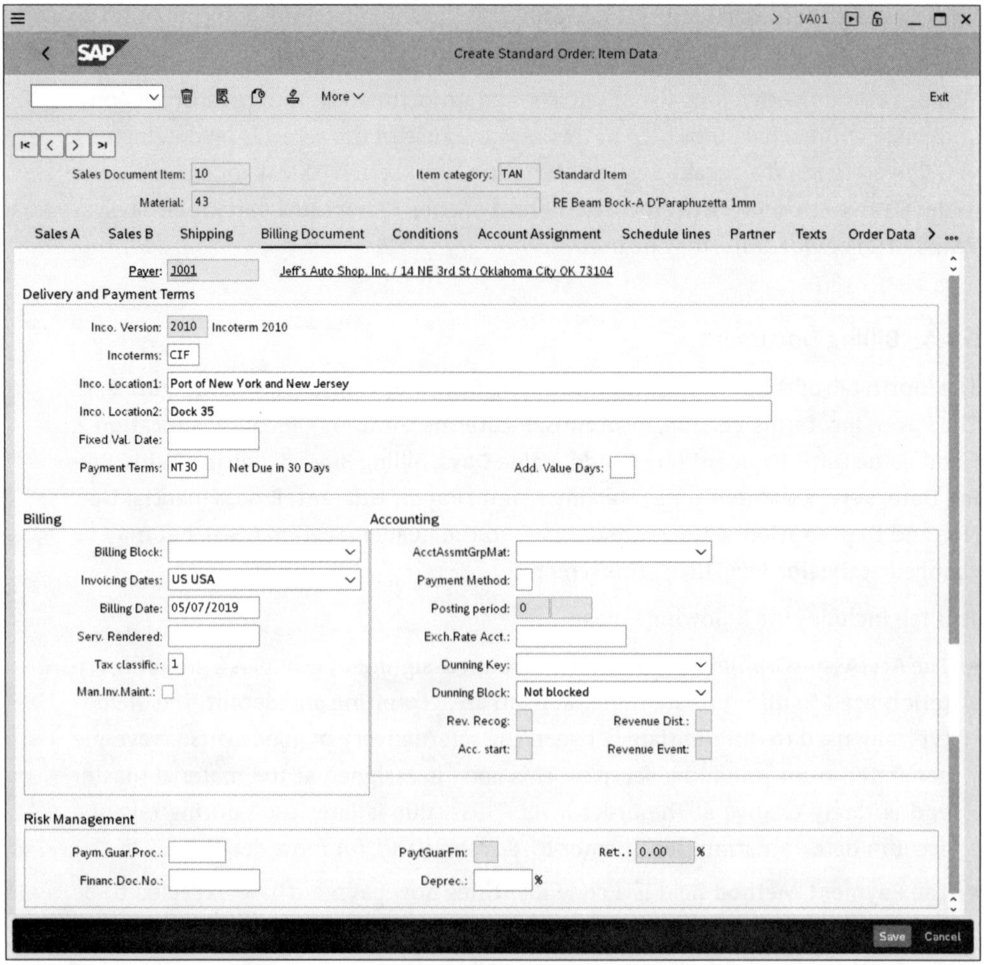

Figure 6.62 Item Details: Billing

- The **Dunning Key** and **Dunning Block** fields control the amount and frequency of contact between your accounts receivable department and the payer's accounts payable department. Dunning is part of SAP S/4HANA Finance functionality.
- The **Rev. Recog** code is a display-only field indicating special modes of revenue recognition, which are defined at the item category level (Section 6.2.10 for more details). This value is used for special scenarios such as billing schedules, milestone-based billing, intellectual property billing, and variable warranty period scenarios. See Chapter 9, Section 9.10, for more details on revenue recognition for shipping-based sales.

- The **Acc. start** code is a display-only field used on time-based revenue recognition (as specified in the **Rev. Recog** field). This value is also defined at the item category level.
- The **Revenue Dist.** field qualifies the amount and frequency of revenue recognition postings and how postings should be determined.
- The **Revenue Event** field indicates what event will trigger revenue recognition.
- The **PaytGuarFm** (form of payment guarantee) and **Ret.** (percent rate of guaranteed value) fields are part of SAP S/4HANA Finance and are used to ensure payment will be collected (usually via a letter of credit). These fields indicate the type and amount of this line's value will be collected as a payment guarantee.

6.4.5 Conditions

The **Conditions** tab, shown in Figure 6.63, shows detailed pricing information executed based on the pricing procedure we configured in Chapter 4, Section 4.1.5.

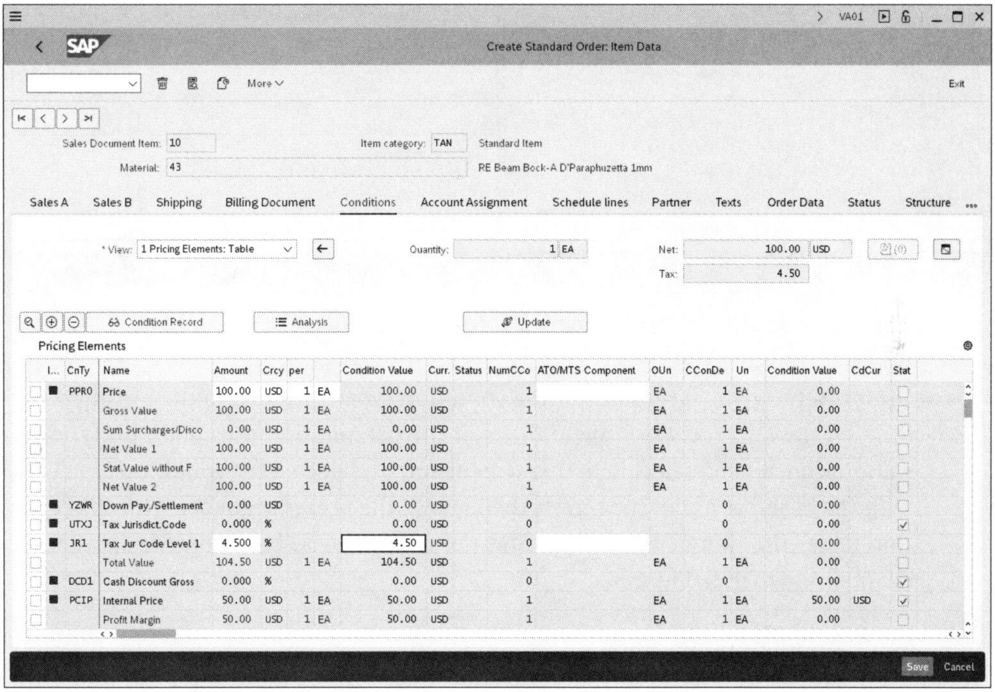

I...	CnTy	Name	Amount	Crcy	per		Condition Value	Curr.	Status	NumCCo	ATO/MTS Component	OUn	CConDe	Un	Condition Value	CdCur	Stat
	PPR0	Price	100.00	USD	1	EA	100.00	USD		1		EA	1	EA	0.00		
		Gross Value	100.00	USD	1	EA	100.00	USD		1		EA	1	EA	0.00		
		Sum Surcharges/Disco	0.00	USD	1	EA	0.00	USD		1		EA	1	EA	0.00		
		Net Value 1	100.00	USD	1	EA	100.00	USD		1		EA	1	EA	0.00		
		Stat.Value without F	100.00	USD	1	EA	100.00	USD		1		EA	1	EA	0.00		
		Net Value 2	100.00	USD	1	EA	100.00	USD		1		EA	1	EA	0.00		
	YZWR	Down Pay./Settlement	0.00	USD			0.00	USD		0			0		0.00		
	UTXJ	Tax Jurisdict.Code	0.000	%			0.00	USD		0			0		0.00		✓
	JR1	Tax Jur Code Level 1	4.500	%			4.50	USD		0			0		0.00		
		Total Value	104.50	USD	1	EA	104.50	USD		1		EA	1	EA	0.00		
	DCD1	Cash Discount Gross	0.000	%			0.00	USD		0			0		0.00		✓
	PCIP	Internal Price	50.00	USD	1	EA	50.00	USD		1		EA	1	EA	50.00	USD	✓
		Profit Margin	50.00	USD	1	EA	50.00	USD		1		EA	1	EA	0.00		

Figure 6.63 Item Details: Conditions

Under this tab, you'll find the base/list price, discounts/surcharges, freight, handling, other fees/charges, taxes, cost, profitability information, etc.

If you don't see the price you're expecting or have other questions related to the presence/absence of condition types on this tab, you can click the **Analysis** button, as shown in Figure 6.64.

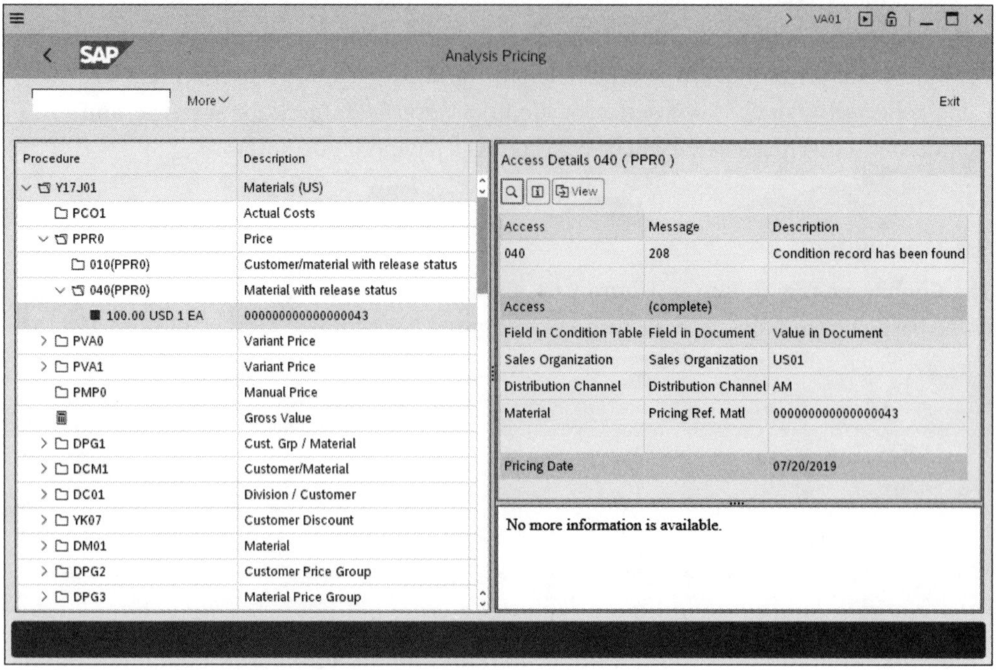

Figure 6.64 Analysis of Item Conditions

On this screen, you'll see a list of the condition types included in the pricing procedure on the left. You can browse through the list and find the condition type you want to consult and select it. In this screenshot, we selected the condition type PPR0 with the base/list price. The screen then shows the access sequence with the condition tables that were consulted to find the price of $100 based on the distribution channel and material number.

6.4.6 Account Assignment

Under the **Account Assignment** tab, shown in Figure 6.65, you'll see the business area and WBS element for scenarios where each line may use a different account.

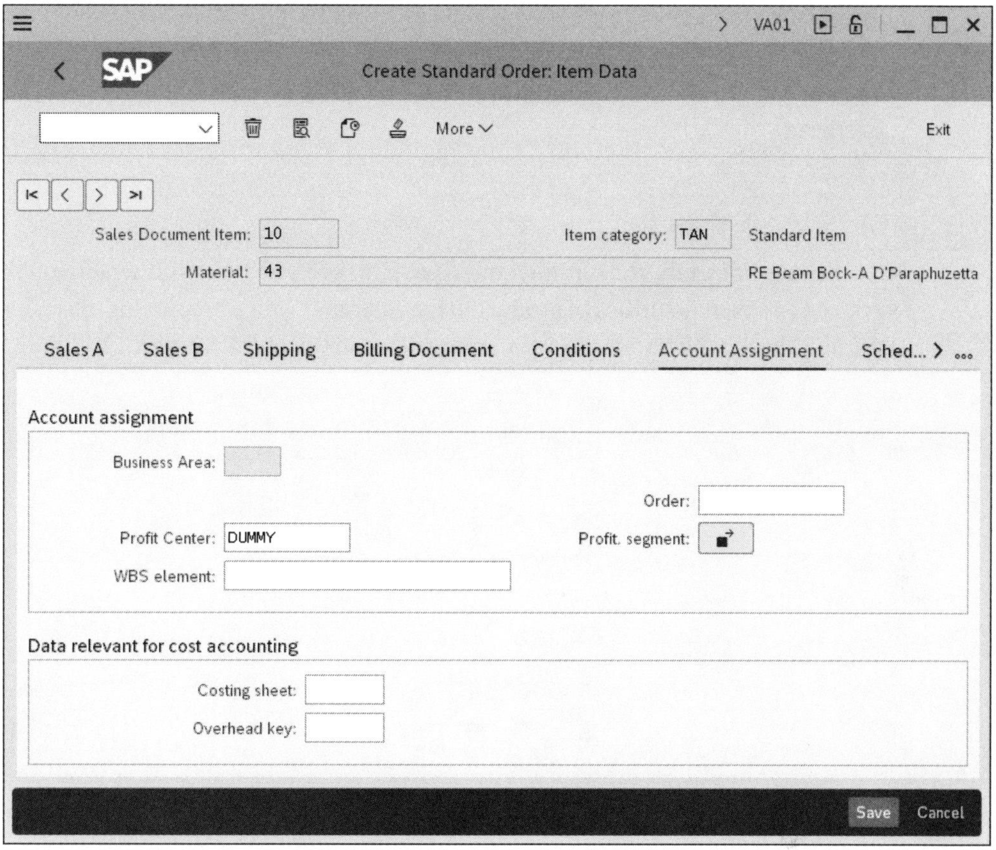

Figure 6.65 Item Details: Account Assignment

This tab includes the following fields:

- The internal **Order** field is also used by controlling to capture and group costs belonging to the same initiative.
- The **Profit Center** field is copied from the material master and represents portion of the company's revenue-producing business. This field is not used as a material grouping criteria by sales but is a major component of controlling.
- The **Profit. segment** button opens the window where a list of fields may be maintained. These fields are configured and defined by profitability analysis). You don't usually need to maintain values in this window; they should be derived from sales order fields based on rules. When the derivation rules fail, an incompletion message will appear requiring you to click this button and manually populate the

fields. However, you must also contact the controlling/profitability analysis team to report the issue so that the rules may be fixed.

- The **Costing sheet** and **Overhead key** fields are used by controlling to calculate overhead.

6.4.7 Schedule Lines

The **Schedule Lines** tab, shown in Figure 6.66, is where you'll consult when you're expected to deliver quantities of product to the customer. This tab contains the result of the ATP check, which we'll discuss in more detail in Chapter 7, Section 7.2.

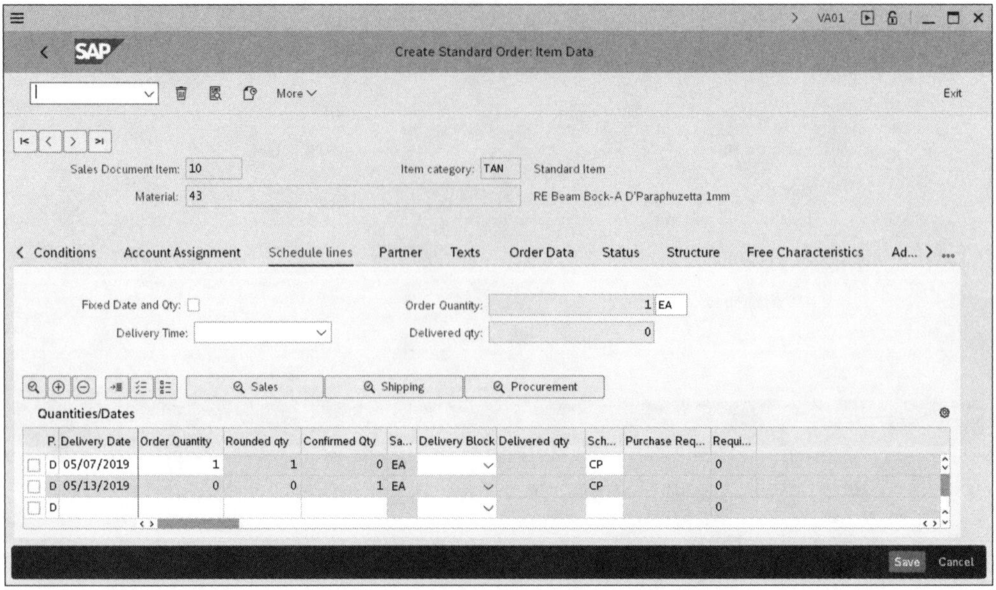

Figure 6.66 Item Details: Schedule Lines

From a sales order entry standpoint, this tab is used to maintain one or more requested **Delivery Dates** from the customer and corresponding **Order Quantities**. After the ATP check runs, these fields/columns also display the promised date with a gray background (second line on the screenshot).

The schedule line category (**Sch...**) column controls several aspects of the schedule line functionality. In the following sections, we'll look at how to configure and assign these categories.

Schedule Line Categories

To configure schedule line categories, open Transaction VOV6 or follow the menu path **SAP Customizing Implementation Guide • Sales and Distribution • Sales • Sales Documents • Schedule Lines • Define Schedule Line Categories.** On the screen that opens, select the item category CP and then click the **Details** button or press F2.

When creating a new code, as shown in Figure 6.67, specify a two-character schedule line category (**Sched.line cat.**) and add a description.

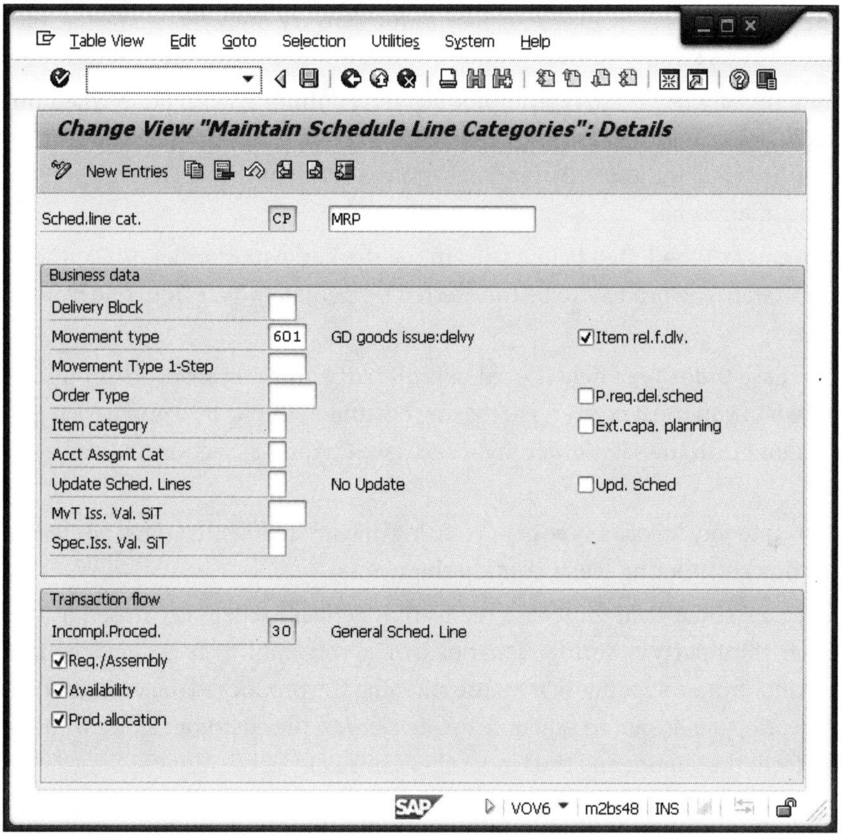

Figure 6.67 Displaying Schedule Line Category CP

This tab includes the following fields:

- The **Delivery Block** field is default block you can assign to this schedule line. The order will not be processed by logistics until a user manually removes this block.

Depending on the block chosen, different functions will be blocked. Companies do not generally use this block because it is only visible on the schedule line tab of the sales order. You can use reports to monitor and release these blocks, but unless this process is done every day, users may forget to check the schedule line tab of the sales order lines. An order may be left blocked and forgotten until the customer complains. Thus, most companies would rather use the delivery block on the header of the sales order.

- The **Movement type** field is the inventory movement type performed when the processing the post goods issue operation for delivery documents created with reference to this schedule line (see Chapter 9, Section 9.4.10, for more details).
- The **Item rel.f.dlv** flag (item relevant for delivery) defines an exception when this schedule line category is assigned to a sales document that is not relevant for delivery. This flag indicates that this schedule is relevant for delivery even if the sales document is not.
- The **Movement Type 1-Step** field is used in the stock transport order (STO) process when you want the product to be transferred immediately over from one plant to the order.
- The purchase **Order Type** field is used in third-party ordering solution (drop shipments) when you must create a purchasing document (typically a purchase requisition) along with the sales order upon save (see Chapter 8, Section 8.1.1, for more details).
- The **Item category** field is a type of purchasing document line that must be created in a third-party ordering scenario (drop shipments).
- The **P.req.del.sched** field (purchase requisition delivery schedule) is used in special-order third-party ordering scenarios (when you want to receive goods into your facility from a supplier first before shipping the product to the customer). In this scenario, you'll want to schedule the delivery to the customer along with the receipt from the vendor and thus must check this flag.
- The **Ext.capa. planning** flag (external capacity planning) indicates that you want the system to plan for the supplier's capability in a third-party ordering scenario. This flag is used when you have a certain contracted vendor performance that you can count on and when demand is expected to be higher than the agreed capability. Usually, in this case, you would start stocking your own warehouse instead.
- The **Acct Assgmt Cat** field (account assignment category) allows you to indicate that this schedule line will require an additional costing element to be used (such

as cost center) when consuming stock at the time of the post goods issue operation. This field is used for free of charge orders since the cost of product shipped for free is often charged internally. In a simpler costing environment, finance often wants to avoid using cost centers and would rather create different accounts instead. In more sophisticated costing environments, you may want to use projects, internal orders, etc.

- The **Update Sched. Lines** field is used in third-party ordering scenarios to controls if/how the sales order schedule line should be updated with purchase order delivery information. Suppliers may provide you with an advanced shipping notification (ASN) before you receive a product, and you can reflect this information on the schedule line or wait until product is fully received at our warehouse. The value in the **Update Schedule Lines** field from the purchase order controls whether schedule lines should be updated at all.
- The **MvT Iss. Val. SIT** field (movement type for issuing valuated stock in transit) is the movement type to be used after you record proof of delivery (POD) for valuated stock in-transit (VSIT) scenarios (as described in Chapter 9, Section 9.10).

  For VSIT scenarios, you'll configure a **Movement Type** that places the product in an in-transit status at the time of shipping, when the post goods issue operation is performed on the delivery (such as 687 used for customer VSIT scenarios). Then, in the **MvT Iss. Val. SIT** field, you'll use movement type 601 (COGS) to consume inventory after you've received proof of delivery. For stock transfer VSIT scenarios (used on stock transfer orders), you wouldn't consume inventory; instead, you would transfer inventory to the destination plant.
- You can qualify specific consumption or stock transfer movements using the **Spec.Iss. Val. SIT** indicator (specification for issuing valuated stock in transit). For stock transfer VSIT scenarios, you can indicate that you're transferring the stock to the destination plant. For customer VSIT scenarios, use code 3 to consume stock.
- The **Incompl.Proced.** code controls the list of fields that must be populated in sales order schedule lines of this type and which functions must be stopped when not populated. This field is display-only on this screen; to change this value, you'll perform other configuration activities documented in Section 6.5.
- The **Req./Assembly** field (transfer of requirements/begin assembly order from sales) controls whether quantities on this sales order schedule line should be transferred to material requirements planning (MRP) as a requirement. MRP may use sales order requirements as demand to drive production or purchasing. The usage of this check needs to be aligned with the PP team.

- The **Availability** field indicates that you want to run ATP checks for this schedule line category. If unchecked, the system will confirm the quantity even if no stock on-hand exists or incoming procurement expected.
- The **Prod.allocation** field controls whether this schedule line must follow product allocation rules (part of ATP check). The product allocation feature allows you to set limits for customer order on controlled materials. Consult Chapter 7, Section 7.5, for more details.

Assigning Schedule Line Categories

To assign schedule line categories to item categories, follow the menu path **SAP Customizing Implementation Guide • Sales and Distribution • Sales • Sales Documents • Schedule Lines • Assign Schedule Line Categories.** On the screen that opens, click on the **New Entries** button or press F5.

As shown in Figure 6.68, indicate the **Item category**, the **MRP Type**, and the default/proposed schedule line category (**PropSchdLineCat.**) to be used. You can also allow manual changes to the default schedule line category by listing up to 9 possible alternatives using the manual schedule line category (**ManSchedLin Cat.**) fields.

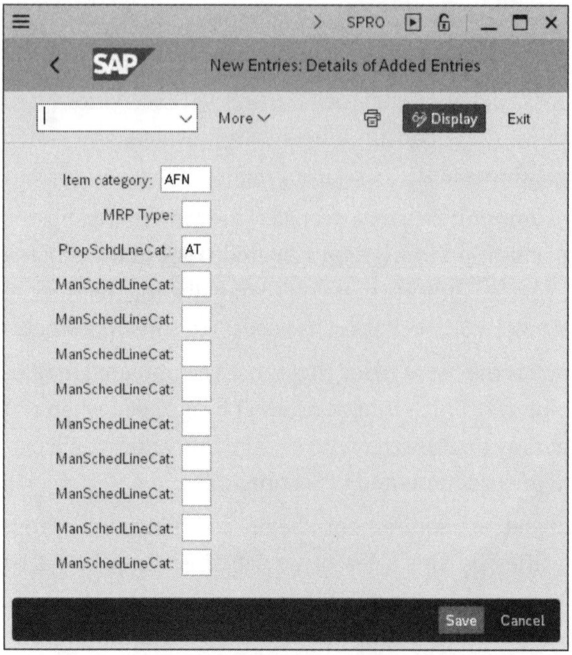

Figure 6.68 Assigning Schedule Line Categories to Item Categories

Note that, if you leave the **MRP Type** field blank, this blank will be default setting for all MRP types. If you have a different record in this configuration table for the MRP type maintained on the material master, that configuration will be used; otherwise, the system will search for an entry with a blank **MRP Type** field.

6.4.8 Partner

The **Partner** tab, shown in Figure 6.69, allows you to modify the business partners involved in this business transaction at the item level. If no changes are made, the partners specified in the header are valid for all lines.

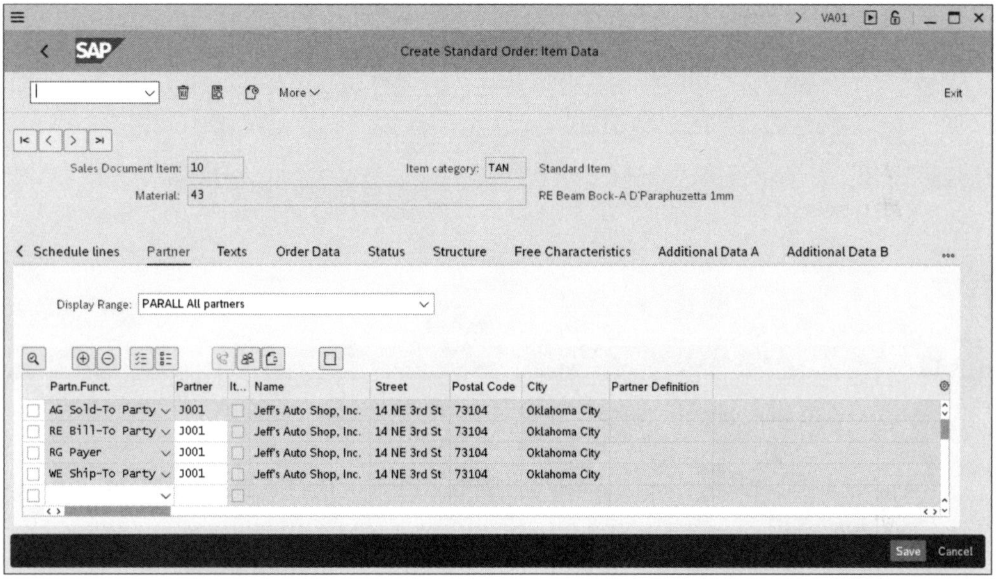

Figure 6.69 Item Details: Partner

This screen behaves the same way as the header **Partner** tab described earlier in Section 6.3.9.

6.4.9 Texts

The **Texts** tab, shown in Figure 6.70, allows you to maintain item-specific notes (freeform texts).

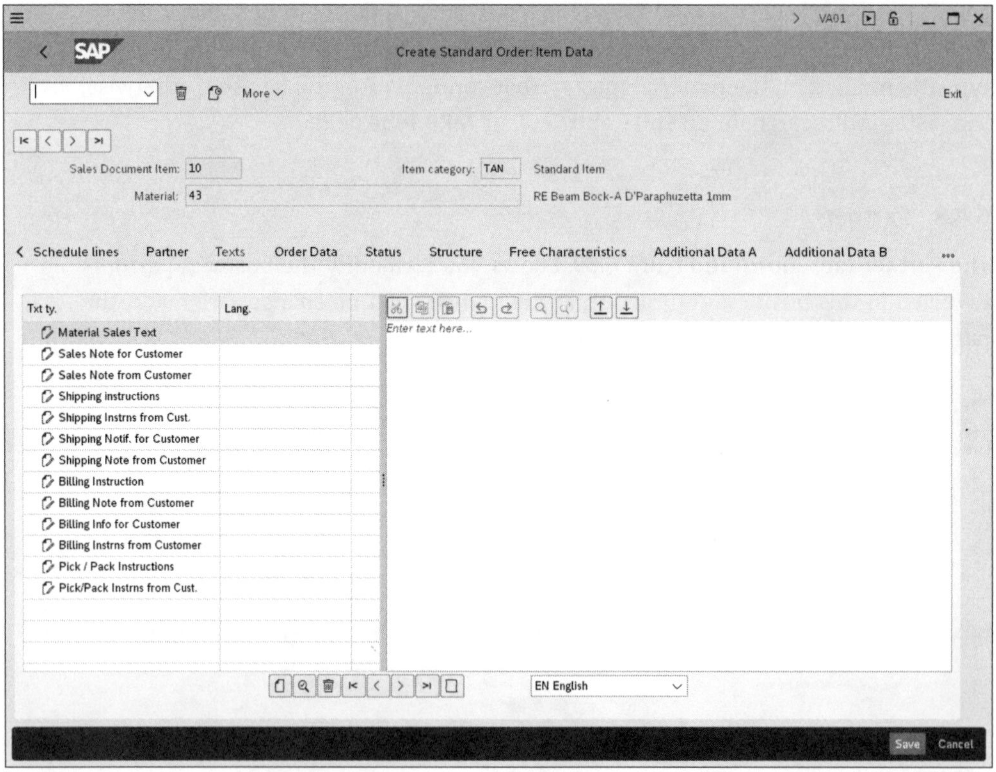

Figure 6.70 Item Details: Texts

This screen behaves the same way as the **Texts** tab in the header, described earlier in Section 6.3.10.

6.4.10 Order Data

The **Order Data** tab, shown in Figure 6.71, allows you to maintain item-specific information regarding the customer purchase order.

This tab includes the following fields:

- The **Purchase order item** field (line number) represents the line on your customer's purchase order. This field helps communicate data to customers electronically, who can easily match you sales order line to their purchase order line.

- The **Customer Material** field is the material number of your product in the customer's system. This value may be maintained in the customer-master information record database (as described in Chapter 3, Section 3.6) or entered directly on this screen.

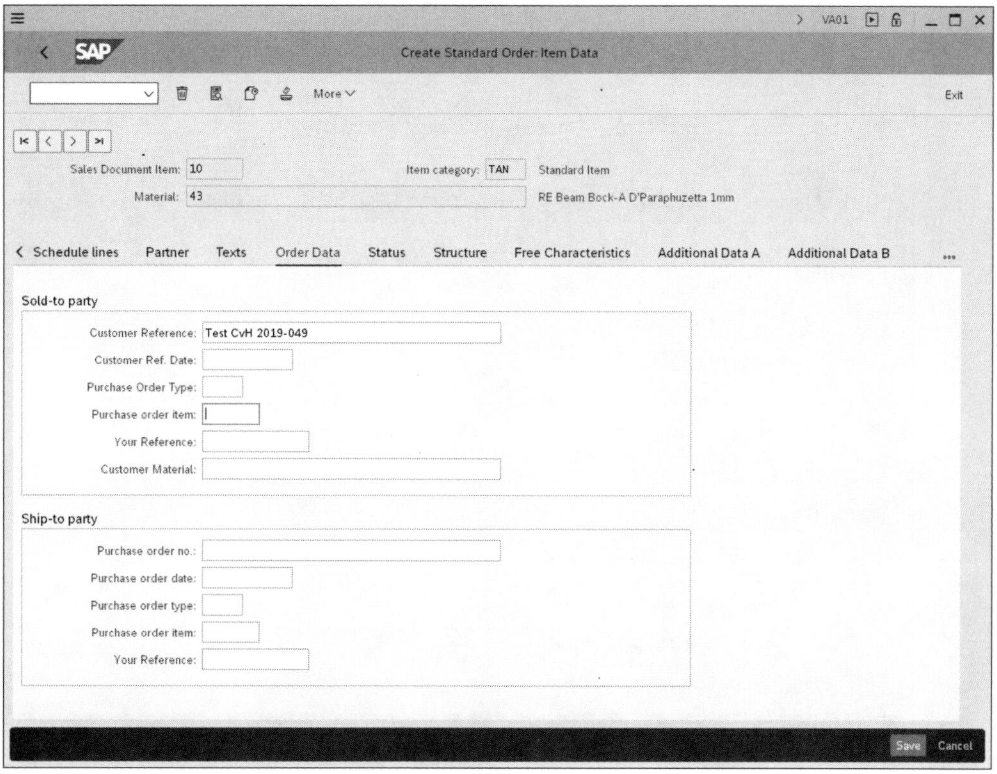

Figure 6.71 Item Details: Customer Purchase Order Data

6.4.11 Status

The **Status** tab, shown in Figure 6.72, allows you to monitor line-specific statuses, which is useful for tracking fulfillment issues.

These field match the ones in the header (Section 6.3.12), but these values are specific to this line only.

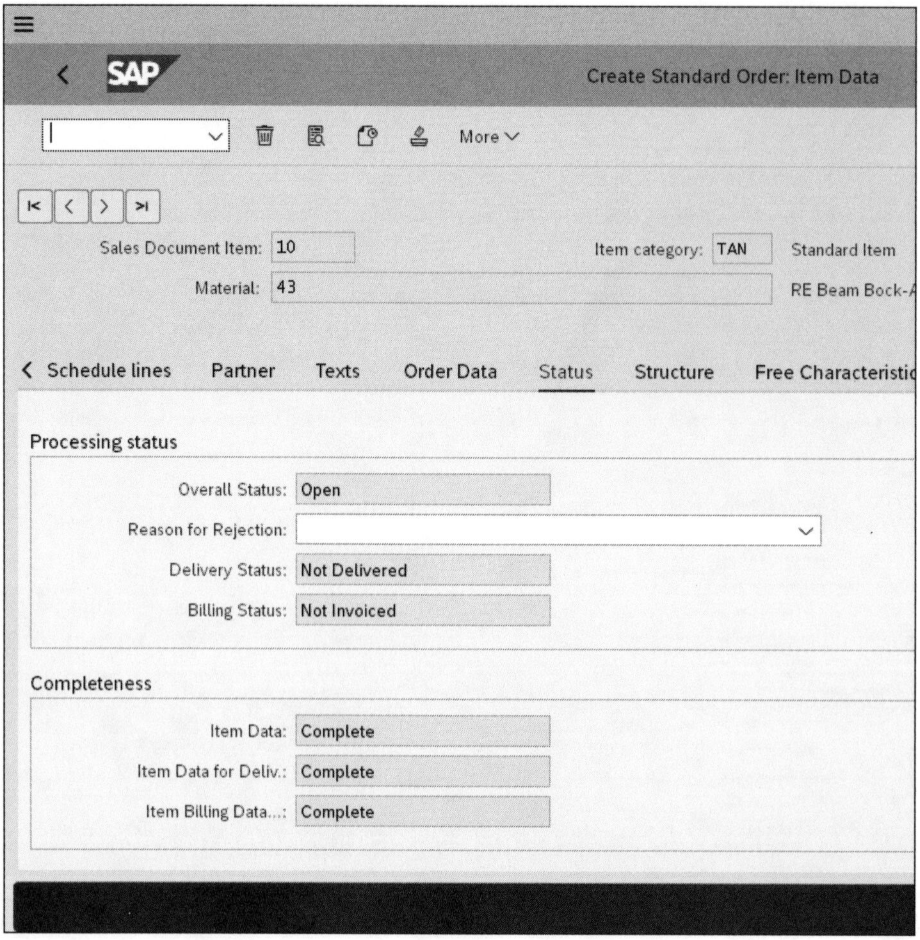

Figure 6.72 Item Details: Status

6.4.12 Structure

The **Structure** tab, shown in Figure 6.73, illustrates the relationship between the sales order lines. This tab useful for variant configuration scenarios with sales BOM explosions.

Under this tab, you'll see the items that refer to this item via the higher-level item number field (**HgLvlt**).

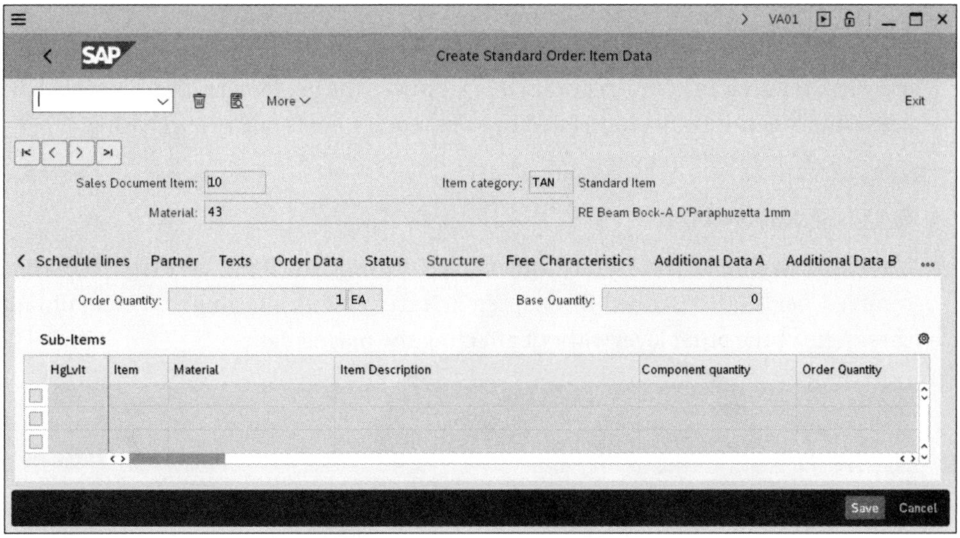

Figure 6.73 Item Details: Structure

6.4.13 Free Characteristics

The **Free Characteristics** tab is part of the commodity management functionality. This tab, shown in Figure 6.74, enables the flexible classification of material master data on analytical reports.

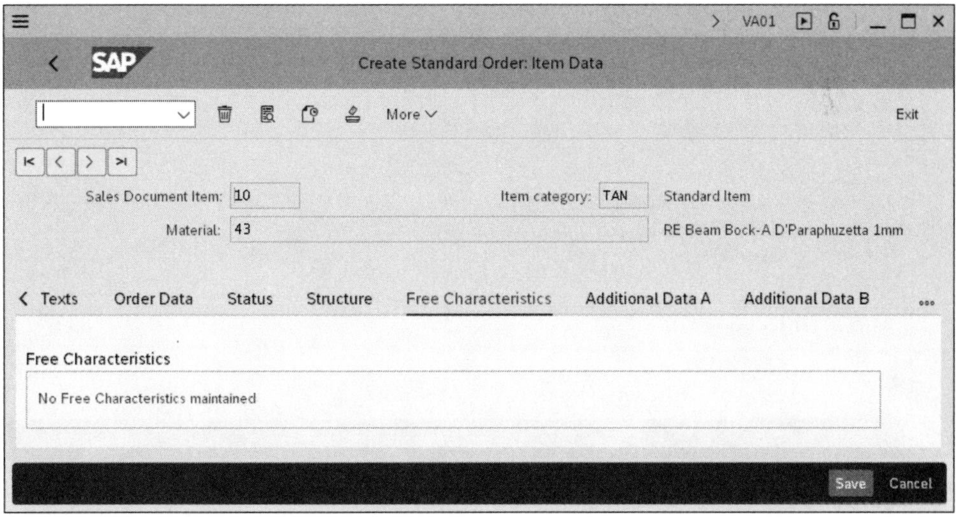

Figure 6.74 Item Details: Free Characteristics

The definition of these characteristics is typically part of the MM scope. On this screen, you can query the free characteristics defined by the MM team, which may be important when tracking analytical report issues. However, the implementation of these characteristics is generally not motivated by sales requirements but by purchasing.

6.4.14 Additional Data

Under the **Additional Data A** tab, shown in Figure 6.75, you'll see the material master reserved fields (as described in Chapter 3, Section 3.2.9), allowing you to maintain these field at the order level without affecting the master data.

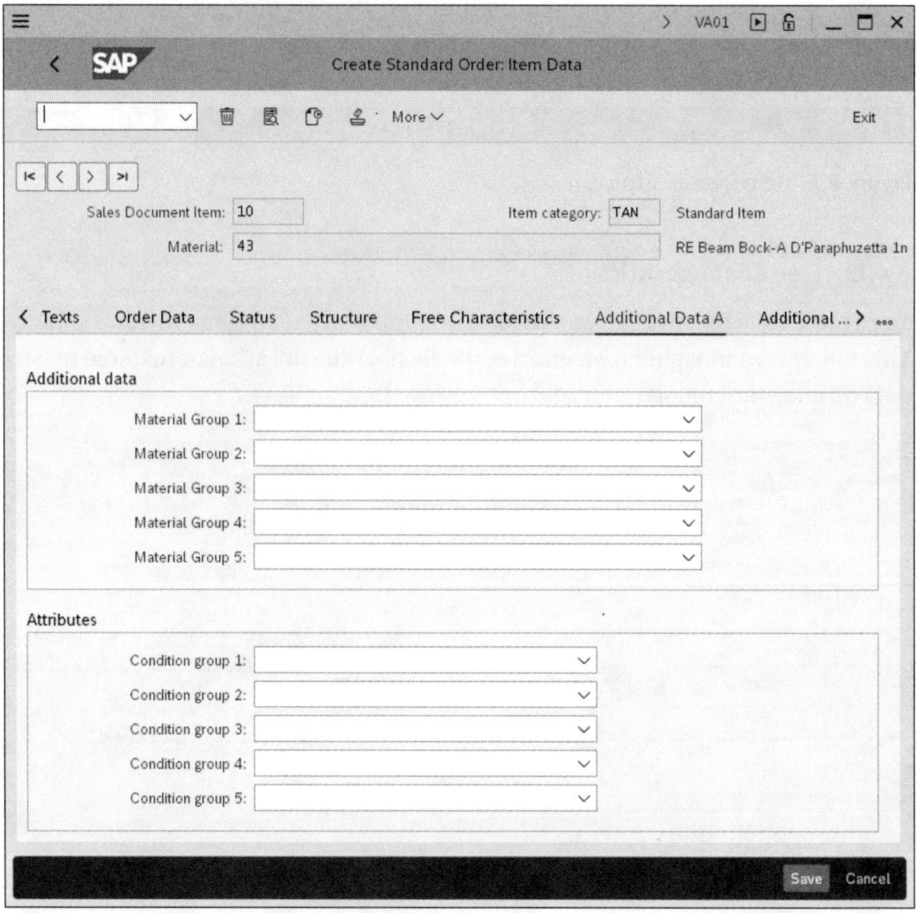

Figure 6.75 Item Details: Additional Data A

On this screen, you can also modify the header condition group affecting this line, which would be used instead of the header values.

For details of the **Material Group 1** through **5** fields, refer to Chapter 3, Section 3.2.9. For details about the condition group, refer to the **Additional Data A** tab discussed in Section 6.3.13.

The **Additional Data B** tab, shown in Figure 6.76, serves the same purpose as the **Additional Data B** tab on the header, for defining new fields. However, on this tab, you'll implement fields that affect this line only.

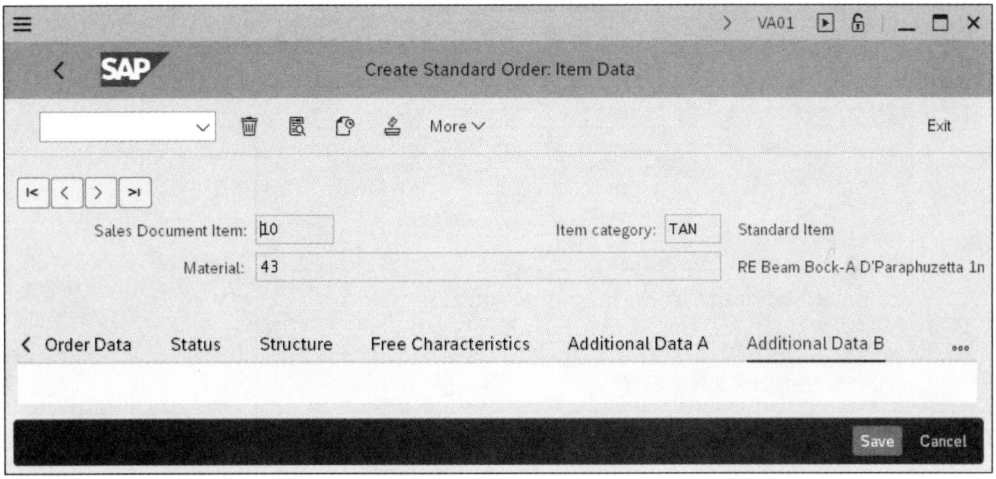

Figure 6.76 Item Details: Additional Data B

6.5 Incompletion Procedure: Log of Incomplete Items

Sales documents often require a variable list of fields to be populated/maintained to be considered complete. This list varies a great deal from company to company depending on the system features utilized and how these features were implemented. Fields used for reporting may also be considered critical enough to be enforced during order entry.

SAP S/4HANA allows you to define which sales order fields are mandatory using a feature called the *log of incomplete items*, the *incompletion log*, or the *incompletion procedure*.

During sales order entry, the incompletion check is executed after data is entered and saved. The system performs a final check and issues a warning if any information is missing, as shown in Figure 6.77.

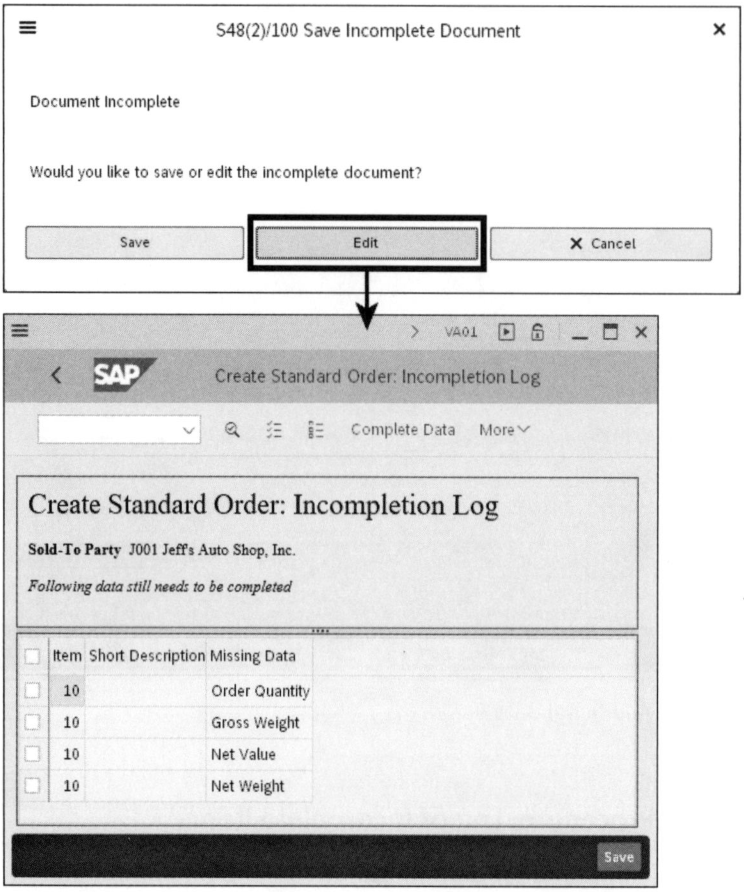

Figure 6.77 Incompletion Message and Log When Saving Incomplete Orders

When you save an incomplete sales document, you'll be prompted with a window reporting its status. At this time, you can proceed and **Save** the order with an incomplete status or **Edit** and complete the order. Often, users opt to click on the **Edit** button to see exactly what is missing.

Once you click **Edit**, you'll access the incompletion log with a list of fields that are missing. On this screen, you can select one or more of the fields and click on the **Complete Data** button.

The system will navigate the screen with the missing field where you'll be allowed to maintain the field efficiently.

You can consult the incompletion log at any time using the sales order maintenance Transactions VA01 (Create), VA02 (Change), and VA03 (Display). Alternatively, you can use the menu options **Edit • Incompletion Log** or press Ctrl+F8.

To configure the incompletion log, open Transaction OVA2 or follow the menu path **SAP Customizing Implementation Guide • Sales and Distribution • Basic Functions • Log of Incomplete Items • Define Incompleteness Procedures.** On the screen that opens, click on the **New Entries** button or press F5.

Select the sales documents for which you want to maintain incompletion procedures, as represented by the **Incompleteness Groups**. As shown in Figure 6.78, we selected sales order header group **A**, but we can also use this configuration to check sales order lines, schedule lines, partners, delivery documents, etc.

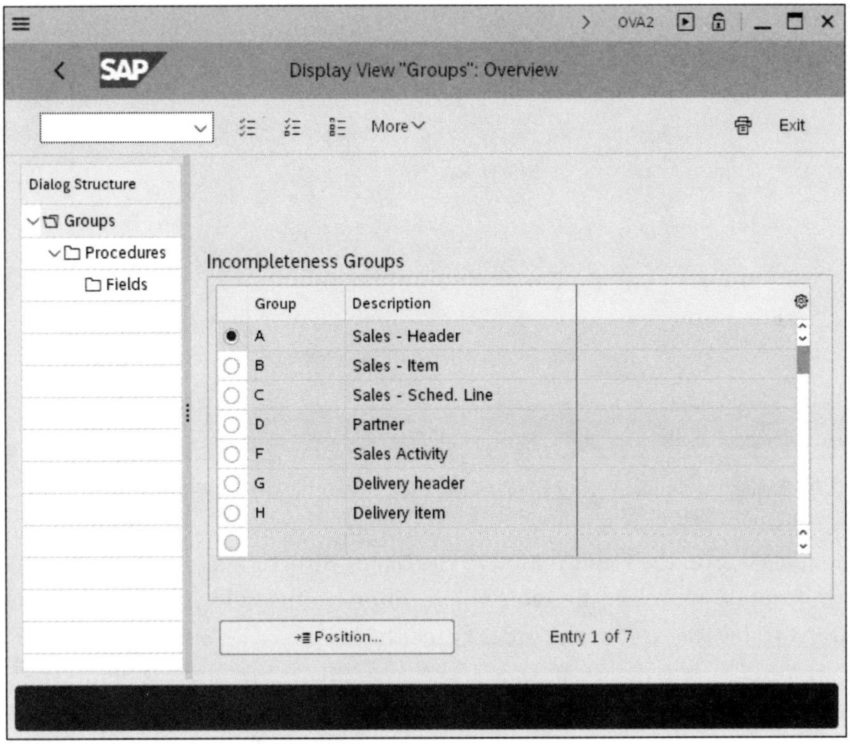

Figure 6.78 Browsing and Selecting a Incompleteness Group

After making a selection, double-click on the **Procedures** option in the **Dialog Structure** menu on the left.

Then, browse through multiple incompletion procedure codes (**Procedure**) and select the desired incompletion procedure, as shown in Figure 6.79. This code appears in the sales document type configuration. In our example, **11** is the incompletion procedure assigned to the standard order type OR.

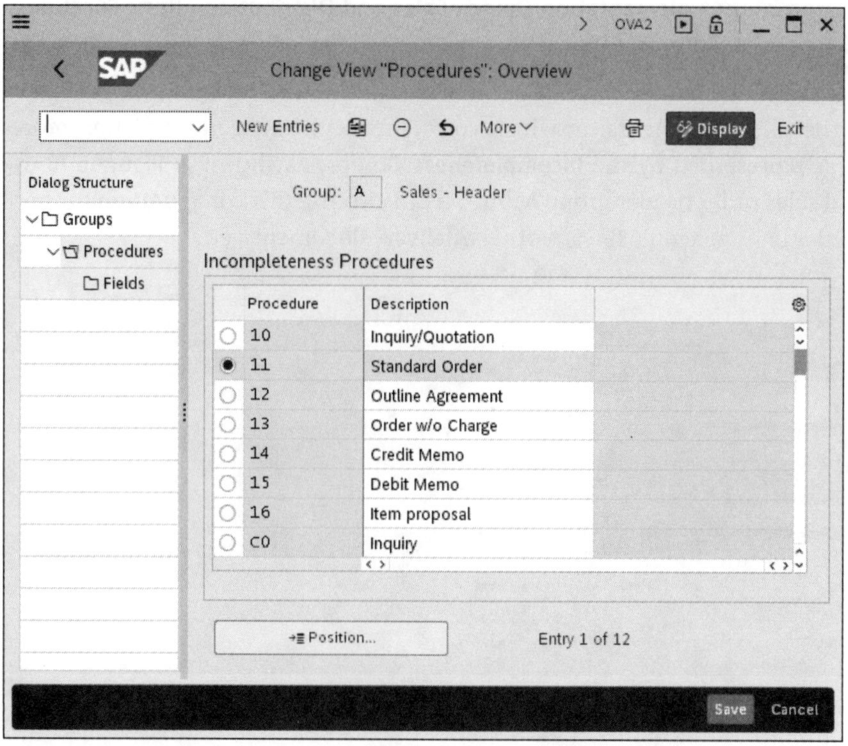

Figure 6.79 Browsing and Selecting the Desired Incompleteness Procedure

Next, double-click on the **Fields** option in the **Dialog Structure** menu on the left. As shown in Figure 6.80, select the **Table** where you have the field you want to make mandatory. (Table VBAK is the sales order header table.)

Then, select the **Field Name** you want to make mandatory, in our case, **AUGRU** for requiring order reasons.

You must indicate the sales order screen (**Screen**) where this field is found. Now, users can click on the **Complete Data** button on the **Create Standard Order: Incompletion**

Log screen, and the system will know which screen to open for the user. **KKAU** is the code for the **Create Standard Order: Header Data** screen shown earlier in Figure 6.26.

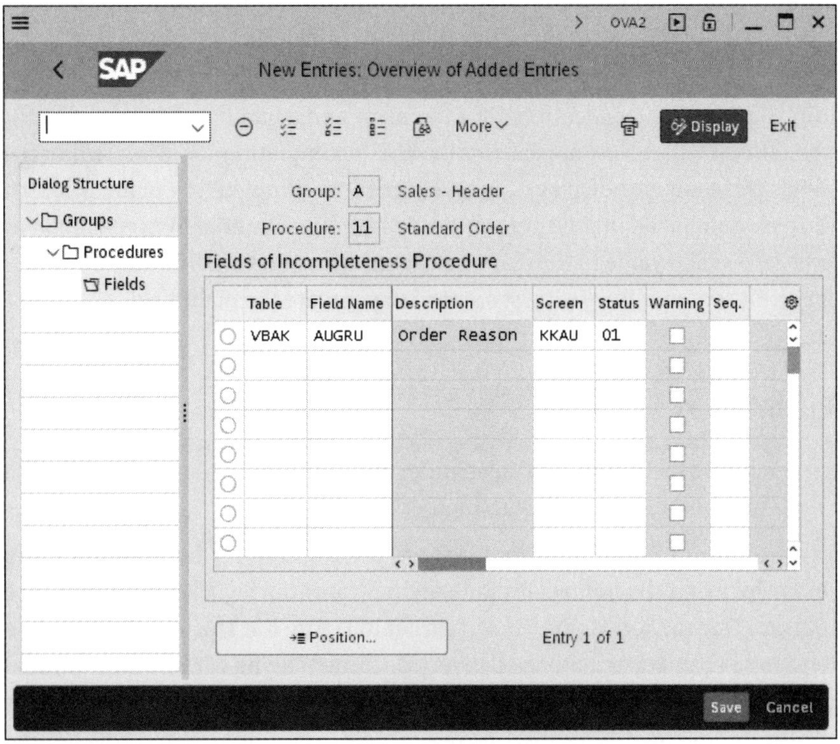

Figure 6.80 Adding New Fields to the Selected Incompleteness Procedure

The **Status** column indicates which system functions must be stopped when this field is not populated. The code **01** means this field is part of the general data of the sales order, which doesn't affect delivery or billing, but needs to be present for the order to be considered complete. You can adjust the copy control configuration to allow delivery even if this field is not present, but the order would still appear as incomplete on reports and due lists.

If you select the **Warning** flag, the system will issue a warning message to inform the user that a field is mandatory immediately upon detecting that the field is not populated. You should avoid flagging too many fields with this warning; otherwise, the user would need to click through many messages whenever a line is entered.

The sequence (**Seq**) field controls the order in which fields are checked, for instance, if on the sales order line, you define both the plant (VBAP-WERKS) and profit center (VBAP-PRCTR) fields as mandatory. The profit center is defaulted from the material master using the plan as the key. So, if you don't have the plant identified on the sales order, you won't have the default profit center either.

By defining a lower sequence number for the plant and a higher value for the profit center, you'll make the plant appear first on the incompletion log. Thus, when the user follows the sequence displayed on the screen to complete the plant field, the profit center would be populated automatically from the material master as soon as the user enters a valid value in the plant field. Otherwise, they may struggle to determine the profit center before being prompted to populate the plant field.

6.6 Rush Orders

Previous versions of SAP provided sales order type SO (rush order) to capture the delivery of a product immediately with high priority.

If order type SO is not available on your system, you can convert any order type into a rush order by using the **Immediate Delivery** indicator during the sales order type configuration (Transaction VOV8), shown earlier in Figure 6.4. This change will cause the system to save and distribute the delivery document along with the sales order.

You can also define special transportation service levels, such as Next Day Air, for the **Shipping Condition** field in Transaction VOV8.

Companies use this type of order when remediating issues cause by mistakes. This order type is also common in the aerospace industry for airplane on ground (AOG) scenarios.

Notifying the warehouse of rush orders is vitally important and can achieved with special picking list titles, issued either by SAP S/4HANA or by a third-party warehouse management system (WMS).

6.7 Cash Sales (Retail)

Previous versions of SAP provided sales order type BV (cash sales) to capture the delivery of a product immediately upon payment in a retail environment.

If order type BV is not available on your system, you can convert any order type into cash sales by changing the **Billing Relevance** indicator during the sales order type configuration (Transaction VOV8) to order-based billing, as shown earlier in Figure 6.5.

Figure 6.81 shows the cash sales process. Note that other methods of payment, such as checks or credit cards, are also accepted. Cash sales refers to the fact that the customer is at the counter ready to pick up the product.

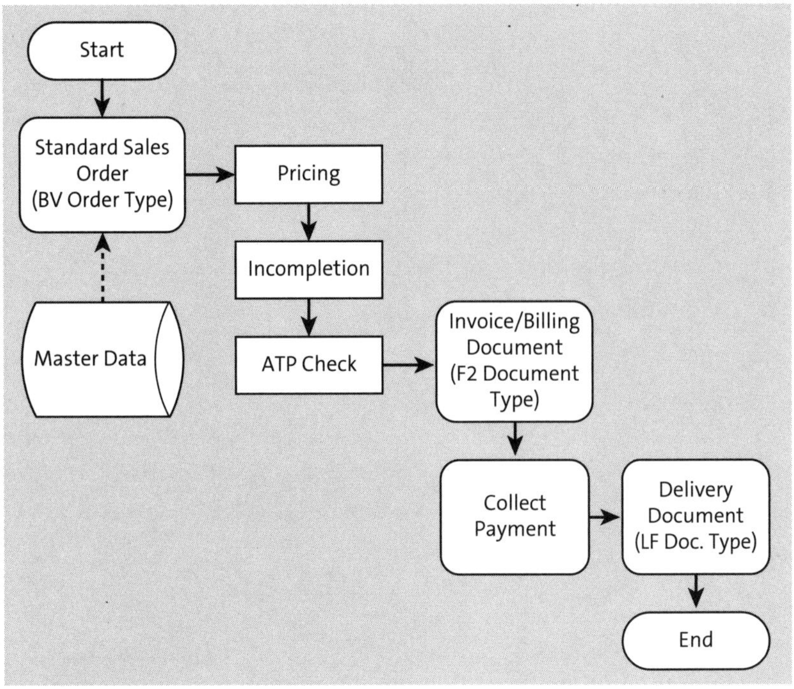

Figure 6.81 Cash Sales Process

The first step for a cash sales order is billing. Once an invoice is issued, you'll collect and clear payment immediate and only then create a delivery document.

A delivery may be sent to the warehouse with special hand-delivery shipping conditions or sold off-the-shelf directly from the store inventory. In either case, you'll still need the delivery to perform the post goods issue operation and consume inventory.

Companies use this type of order when they have storefront operations at the factory that fulfills customer orders over the counter.

6.8 Summary

Sales document processing is a core functionality of SAP S/4HANA Sales and where you'll spend most of your time during implementation. By the end of this chapter, you should understand the various tabs of the sales order entry screen and should be able to perform the necessary configuration for fields related to entering sales orders. This knowledge should enable you to venture into the configuration of other order types type by adapting out-of-the-box capabilities to meet your company's needs.

Chapter 7
Available to Promise and Transfer of Requirements

When processing sales documents that involve the physical movement of tangible goods, you'll need to verify their availability. This verification takes place using a system functionality called the available to promise (ATP) check.

An ATP check is not a simple stock check; the functionality verifies several other system variables (in addition to on-hand inventory) to determine when you should expect inventory to be ready for logistics operations, including picking, packing, shipping, and transportation steps until the product is ultimately delivered to the customer's ship-to address.

An ATP check includes incoming purchase orders (POs) from vendors, stock transfer orders from other plants, production orders from manufacturing, and more. You can control competing demands and other backorder scenarios based on theoretical availability with an ATP check.

Since SAP S/4HANA 1809, advanced ATP has been available. This functionality encompasses the legacy ATP check that was part of SAP ERP, now referred to as the "product availability check." SAP S/4HANA for advanced ATP refers to four components:

- The product availability check
- Product allocation
- Backorder processing
- Supply assignment

In this chapter, we'll provide a lot of details about the product availability check functionality, also known as ATP check, in Sections Section 7.1 through Section 7.4. We'll also cover product allocation in Section 7.5 and rule-based ATP checks in Section 7.6.

7.1 Product Availability Check

Backward and forward scheduling are important to understand ATP check results and to avoid misinterpretation and operational mistakes that may impact your customers. We'll look at the role of scheduling in product availability checks in the following sections.

7.1.1 Backward Scheduling

Backward scheduling is used when a customer requests a delivery date that is achievable. You would schedule what must happen before that date in order for the product to be delivered on that date, by subtracting lead times from the requested delivery date to determine when each logistics task (picking, packing, shipping, and transportation) must be completed and ultimately when material needs to be available for each stage.

In the diagram shown in Figure 7.1, a sales order has a requested delivery date far enough in the future to successfully perform backward scheduling and to define the dates on which each logistic tasks must be completed.

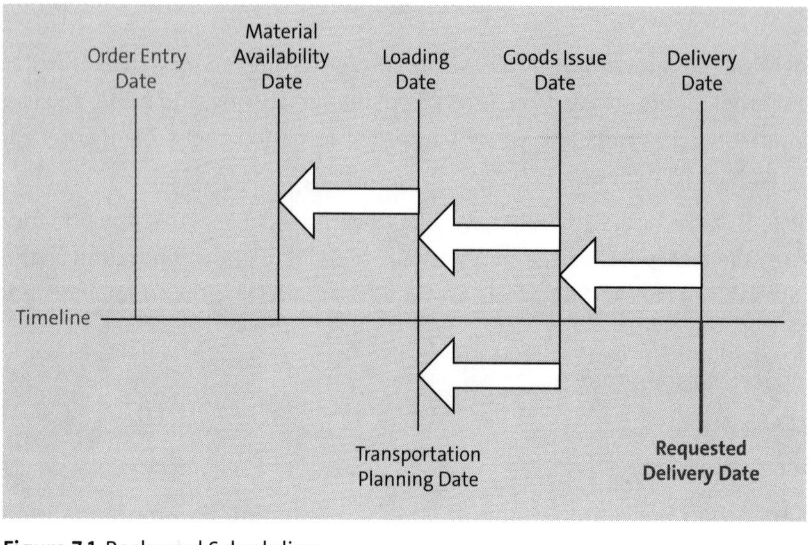

Figure 7.1 Backward Scheduling

In this scenario, the requested delivery date and the expected delivery date are the same, so we'll measure on-time delivery by comparing the requested delivery date with the actual delivery date.

The product availability check always performs backward scheduling and assign its results to the sales. We'll review this functionality in more detail in Section 7.2.2.

7.1.2 Forward Scheduling

Forward scheduling is used when a customer requests a delivery date you cannot achieve. In these circumstances, you'll use already configured input parameters to determine when the earliest date on which you can commit to delivery of this product.

In the diagram shown in Figure 7.2, a sales order has a requested delivery date that is too near, and we don't afford have enough time for all the estimated logistics tasks to be completed before that requested delivery date. This scenario also arises if you don't have enough inventory and still want to make commitments based on theoretical availability, i.e., incoming procurement (purchase, production, transfers, etc.).

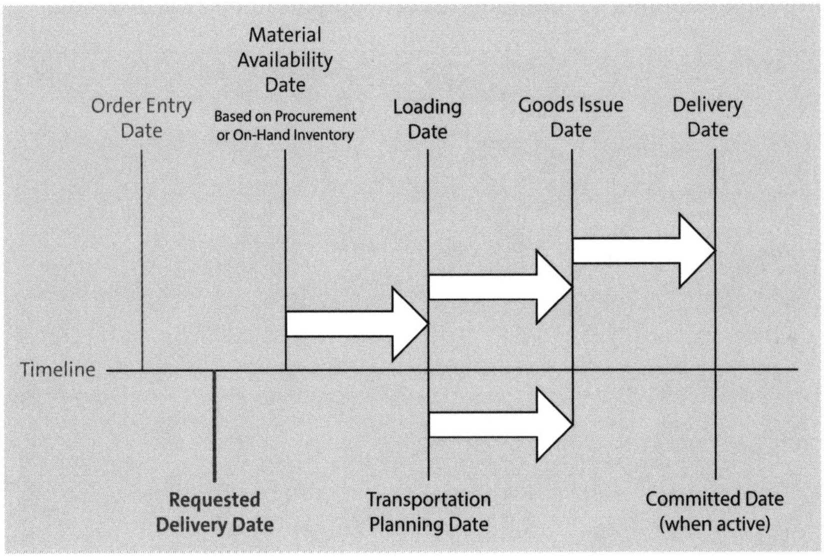

Figure 7.2 Forward Scheduling

In this scenario, you could use the commitment date to control on-time delivery, as configured on the sales order type (Transaction VOV8, see Chapter 6 for more details). All three dates (the requested delivery date, the commitment date, and the actual delivery date) are considered when evaluating on-time delivery key performance indicators (KPIs) to allow for the analysis of warehouse speed as well as of customer experience.

7.2 Available to Promise Checks

An ATP check runs whenever you need to check for inventory availability; in this section, we'll focus on using ATP checks for sales orders. An ATP check can also affect delivery documents, stock transfer orders, production orders, etc.

In the following sections, we'll highlight the moments during the sales order entry process when the ATP check will run and describe the related configuration steps in detail.

7.2.1 Process Overview

When a sales order is entered, as shown in Figure 7.3, your first experience with the ATP check will be the **Availability Control** window, shown in Figure 7.4, which appears right after you enter a new line. This window will appear whenever you can't deliver the product to the customer by the requested delivery date (forward scheduling).

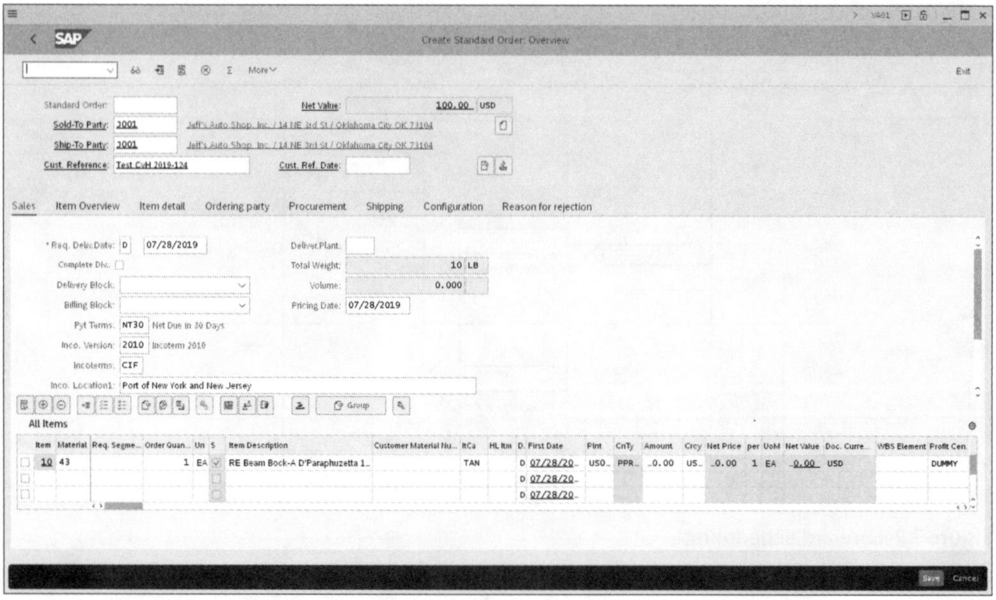

Figure 7.3 Sample Sales Order Entry Screen

The **Availability Control** window may offer several options for delivery, such as partial delivery, complete delivery, and system-proposed delivery. Even if these options are the same, this window would still appear to inform the user that the requested delivery cannot be fulfilled, and the customer needs to be informed of the situation.

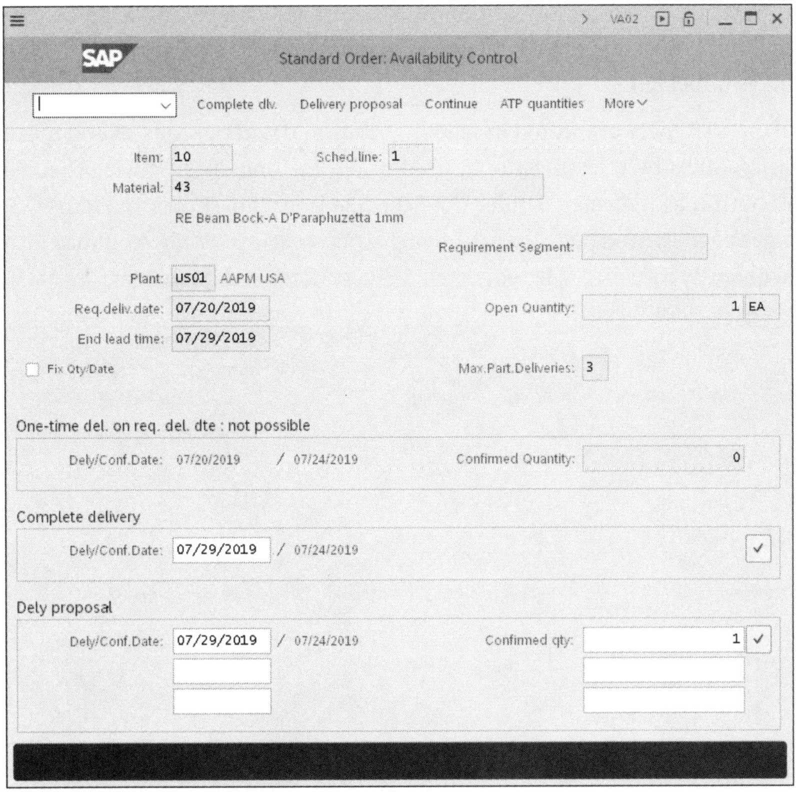

Figure 7.4 Availability Control Window

Once you select the customer-selected forward scheduling delivery mode (**Complete dlv.**, **Delivery proposal**, **Continue**, **ATP quantities**, etc.) in the **Availability Control** window, the system will return to the screen shown earlier in Figure 7.3.

You can suppress the **Availability Control** window via configuration as described in the Configuring Default Settings by Sales Area section in Section 7.2.3. Note, however, that this configuration is defined at the sales area level and will affect all order types.

Some companies don't validate requested delivery dates and find this notification inconvenient every time they perform forward scheduling. We do not recommend turning this notification off for any reason; a more appropriate approach would be to define a default number of days to push the default requested delivery date forward when configuring the sales order type (Transaction VOV8). With this method, you could always perform backward scheduling, and the **Availability Control** window will not appear unless an exception arises. During forward scheduling, your customer service reps must notify customers of potential issues to achieve any level of customer satisfaction. You can run ATP checks as many times as necessary by clicking the button as indicated.

The results of the ATP check are stored in schedule lines, and you can consult and make changes on these lines by selecting the desired order line and clicking the **Schedule Lines for Item** button as indicated. Under the **Schedule Lines** tab, shown in Figure 7.5, you can change the requested delivery date, which affects each line only. You may also split the total quantity into multiple requested delivery dates and quantities.

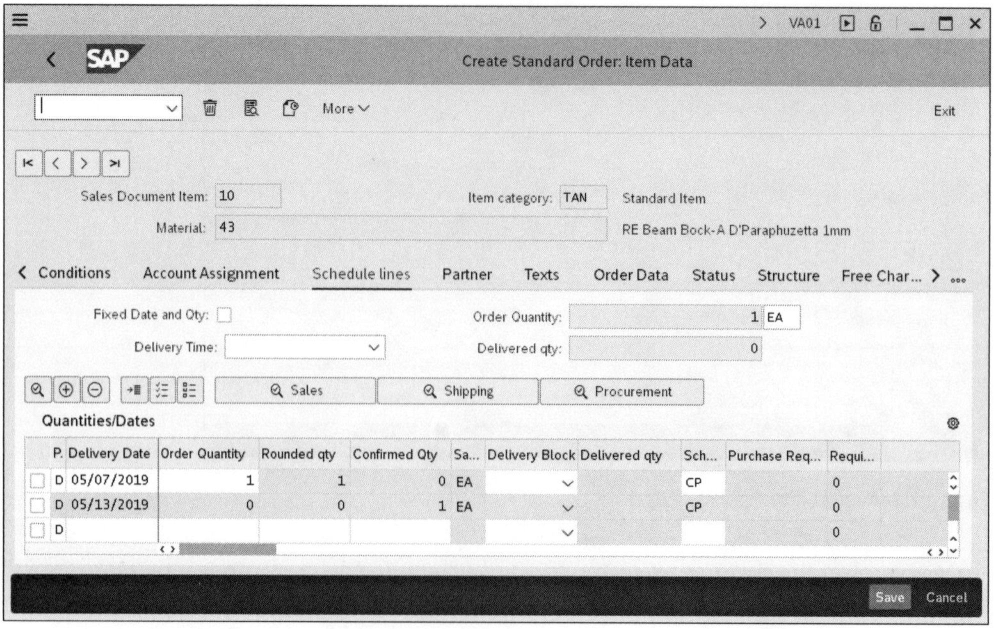

Figure 7.5 Sales Order Line: Schedule Line Tab

The lines with a gray background are generated by the ATP check after forward scheduling to indicate when the expected delivery date does not match the requested delivery date. In backward scheduling scenarios, confirmed quantities are displayed on the same line as ordered quantities because the expected delivery date matches the requested delivery date.

You can identify whether a schedule is using forward scheduling when the corresponding line with a gray background appears. Note also that the confirmed quantity is zero for backward planning schedule lines but populated for forward planning schedule lines.

7.2.2 Schedule Line Details

After the ATP check runs, schedule lines are created that contain a lot more detail you can consult, which we'll describe in this section.

You can consult the **Scheduling Line Details** (as shown earlier in Figure 7.5) by selecting a schedule line and clicking the details icon on the left or clicking on the one of the detail buttons (**Shipping**, **Sales**, and **Procurement**), which will take you straight to the corresponding tab.

Each schedule line is assigned a delivery date (also known as a *schedule line date*). All the details we're going to describe refer to events taking place on that date, in the **Delivery Date** field. For our first task, select the **05/07/2019** date.

By clicking on **Sales**, as shown in Figure 7.5, you'll be taken to the **Sales** tab, shown in Figure 7.6.

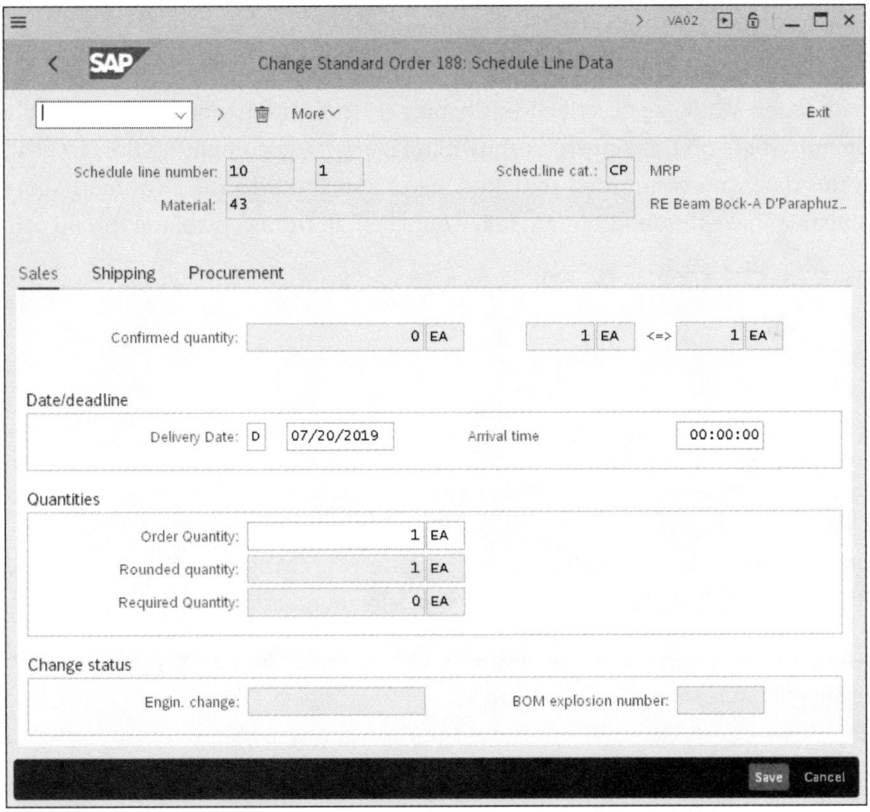

Figure 7.6 Sales Details Tab for the Schedule Line

This tab has the following important fields:

- The **Confirmed quantity** field and the quantity conversion details indicate the available stock earmarked for consumption by this sales order once delivered on the delivery date for this schedule line. Note this depends on the ATP check rules that we'll configure under Configuring the Scope of the Availability Check in this section.
- When a schedule line for which we're displaying sales details has a white background, that line contains an **Order Quantity** requested to be delivered on the requested **Delivery Date.** You may specify a date type (week, month, etc.) and an **Arrival Time**.
- Based on rounding rules, the system calculates and displays a **Rounded quantity**.
- Based on the transfer of requirements configuration, which we'll discuss in detail in Section 7.3, you may consult the **Required Quantity** that is transferred to material requirements planning (MRP) as demand.
- If you set the **Commitment Date** indicator during sales order type configuration (Transaction VOV8, as described in Chapter 6), the system would also display a **Committed qty** on this screen, as shown in Figure 7.7, documenting the fact that, on this date, you committed to delivering this quantity to the customer. Many companies have this requirement and would benefit from controlling this option.

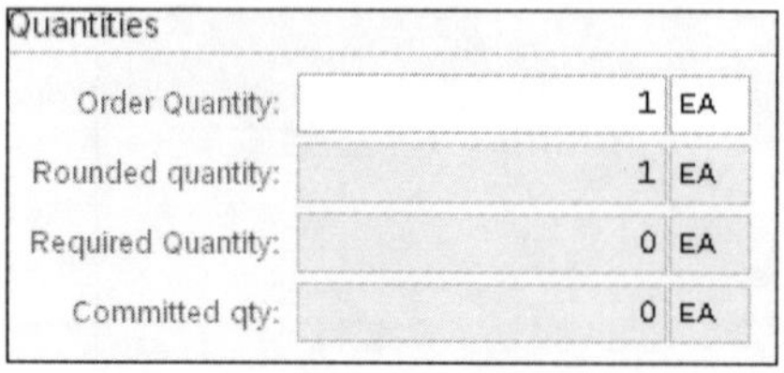

Figure 7.7 Committed Quantity Field (When Enabled)

- You'll also see material details regarding engineering changes (**Engin. change**) and bill of materials (BOM) explosion (**BOM explosion number**), when applicable.

Returning to the screen shown in Figure 7.5, by clicking on **Shipping**, you'll be taken to the **Shipping** tab, shown in Figure 7.8.

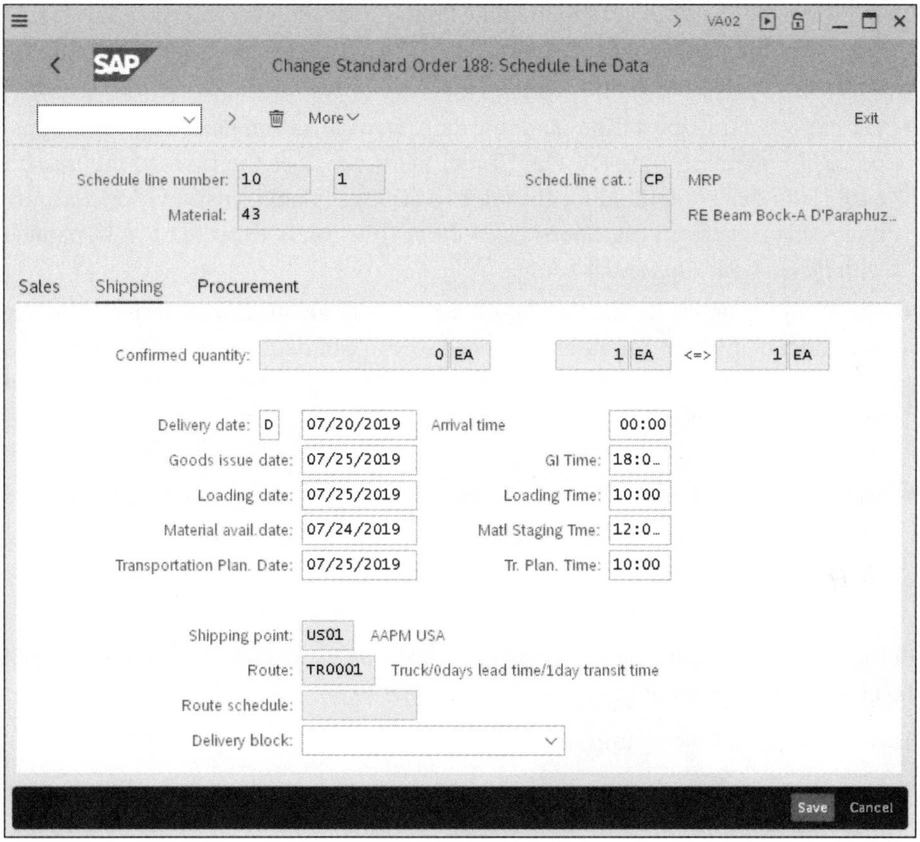

Figure 7.8 Schedule Line Data: Shipping Tab

This tab has the following important fields:

- You'll again see the **Confirmed quantity** field and quantity conversion details, as shown earlier under the **Sales** tab.
- The date type, **Delivery date,** and **Arrival time** fields are also shown under the **Sales** tab. Schedule lines with white backgrounds involve *backward planning*, and this date represents both the requested and the expected **Delivery date**.
- The expected **Goods issue date** and **GI Time** fields are calculated based on the requested/expected **Delivery date** minus the total transportation time assigned to the route.
- The expected **Loading date** and **Loading Time** fields are calculated based on the **Goods issue date** minus the packing and loading time assigned to the shipping point and/or route.

- The expected material availability date (**Material avail date**) and material staging time (**Matl Staging Tme**) fields are calculated based on the **Loading Date** minus the picking time assigned to the shipping point.
- The expected transportation planning date (**Transportation Plan. Date**) and transportation planning time (**Tr. Plan. Time**) fields consider the time configured on each route that is required for the team to arrange (plan) transportation and subtracts this time from the **Goods issue date**. This task is expected run in parallel with picking, packing, and loading.
- The **Shipping point**, **Route**, and **Route schedule** fields displayed derive from the sales document item for quick reference so you can determine the source of the lead times used in the ATP calculation. Note that, if you only use days instead of hours when you configure shipping points and routes, time-related fields would be suppressed on these screens.
- The **Delivery block** field affects this schedule line only. Note that, when you have this block assigned, a delivery date will not be fulfilled unless the block is removed before the logistics tasks restricted by it (as detailed in the configuration) are about to be executed.

Returning to the screen shown in Figure 7.5 again, by clicking on **Procurement**, you'll taken to the **Procurement** tab, as shown in Figure 7.9.

This tab has the following important fields:

- The **Schedule line date** field is the expected and/or requested delivery date (depending on whether this schedule line is for forward or backward scheduling, as indicated by the gray or white background). This date is also shown and described under the **Sales** and **Shipping** tabs. The term schedule line date is often used on other transactions and reports.
- The **Order Quantity** and **Rounded quantity** fields are shown under the **Sales** tab.
- The plant/storage location fields (**Plant/Stge. Loc.**) on this screen are copied from the sales document item, and displayed here for quick reference.
- The value in the **Movement type** field on this screen derives from the schedule line category configuration. This movement type will be used during the post goods issue operation to consume or transfer inventory.
- If this order is a third-party order, such as a drop shipment order from your vendor direct to you customer, the system creates and assigns a **Purchase Requisition** document and line number to this schedule line. You can click the **Edit** button to modify this purchase requisition.

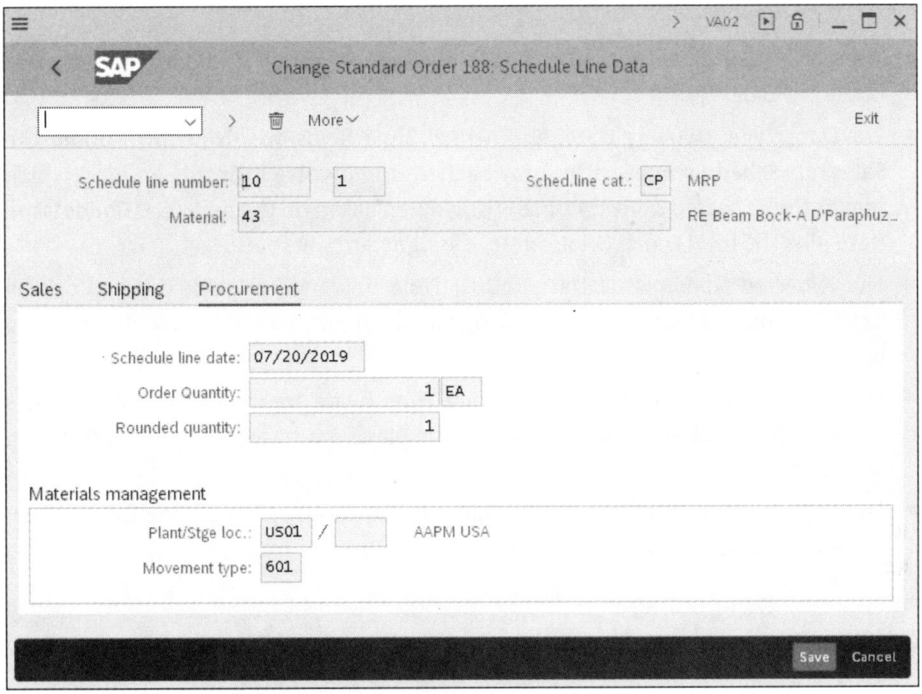

Figure 7.9 Schedule Line Data: Procurement Tab

For our next task, again consult the **Scheduling Line Details** by selecting it and clicking the details icon on the left or clicking one of the detail buttons (**Shipping**, **Sales**, and **Procurement**), which takes you straight to the corresponding tab. This time, select the checkbox next to **05/11/2019**.

Under the **Sales** tab, you'll see the same fields shown earlier in Figure 7.6. Let's look at how these fields differ with a forward scheduling line:

- Once **Confirmed Quantity** contains the quantity expected on forward schedule lines. If no confirmed quantities exist, the system would not add the forward schedule line and leave the order unconfirmed.
- Once a schedule line has a gray background (indicating forward planning), the **Order Quantity** fields should be empty.
- On this screen, the **Committed Quantity** field indicates that what we promised to the customer by the date in the **Delivery date** field. This information can be used later to measure performance.

Under the **Shipping** tab, note the following fields:

- The **Confirmed Quantity** and quantity conversion details fields are the same as under the **Sales** tab.
- The **Date Type**, **Delivery Date,** and **Arrival Time** fields are also shown under the **Sales** tab. Schedule lines with a gray background involve *forward planning*, which means the expected **Delivery Date** is calculated based on the expected **Goods Issue Date** plus the total transportation time assigned to the route.
- The expected **Goods Issue Date** and **GI Time** fields are calculated based on the expected **Loading Date** plus the packing and loading time assigned to the shipping point and/or route.
- The expected **Loading Date** and **Loading Time** fields are calculated based on the expected **Material Availability Date** plus the picking time assigned to the shipping point.
- The expected **Material Availability Date** and **Material Staging Time** fields determine when you can expect the material to be available in stock.

Note

If you have on-hand inventory available, you may still need to perform forward planning if the total warehouse and transportation lead time prevents you from meeting the requested delivery date.

If you don't have inventory available, the ATP check uses the expected delivery date from incoming purchase orders/stock transfer orders, expected confirmed dates from production order, fixed lead times from the material master, and other dimensions as configured under Configuring the Scope of the Availability Check in Section 7.2.3.

If the scope of check configuration and relevant incoming documents do not allow for the ATP check to determine when the stock will be available, there no confirmed quantity will be determined, and no forward scheduling line will be created. Orders in this state require you to run the ATP check again before the order can be processed by logistics (starting with delivery document creation) using a transaction that we'll describe in Section 7.2.4. Note that orders with forward planning are also considered backorders.

- The expected transportation planning date (**Transportation Plan. Date**) and transportation planning time (**Tr. Plan. Time**) fields consider the time each route requires for the team to arrange (plan) transportation and subtracts this time from the **Goods issue date**. This task is expected run in parallel with picking, packing and loading.

- The **Shipping Point**, **Route**, **Route Schedule**, and **Delivery Block** Fields on this screen have the same values as shown earlier in Figure 7.8.

The fields under the **Procurement** tab have the same values, as shown in Figure 7.9.

7.2.3 Availability Overview and Scope of ATP Check

Depending on the material master availability check group (discussed under Defining the Availability Check Group in this section), you can determine the behavior of the ATP check and specify which system components should be considered and which should be ignored (as defined under Configuring the Scope of the Availability Check in this section). In this section, we'll describe how you can view the scope of the check and the parameters that the ATP check considers.

Navigation

Under the **Sales Order Schedule Line** tab, you'll see the ATP check in action by following the menu options **More • Environment • Availability**. You can also consult the scope of the check being used by clicking on the corresponding button on the command bar, as shown in Figure 7.10.

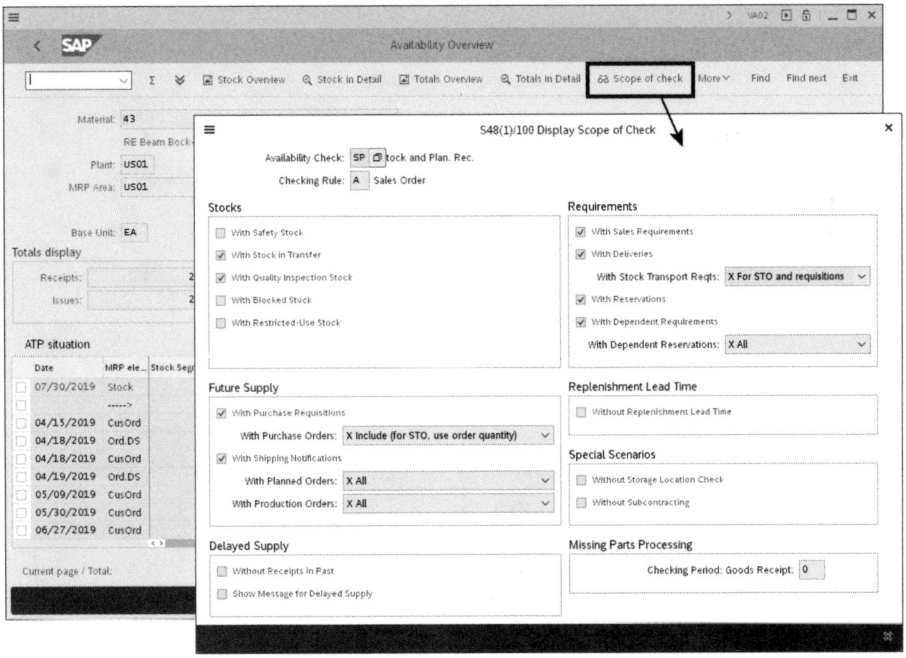

Figure 7.10 Availability Overview and Scope of Check

On the **Availability Overview** screen, you'll see the on-hand inventory on the first line indicated by the **MRP Element** column value **Stock**.

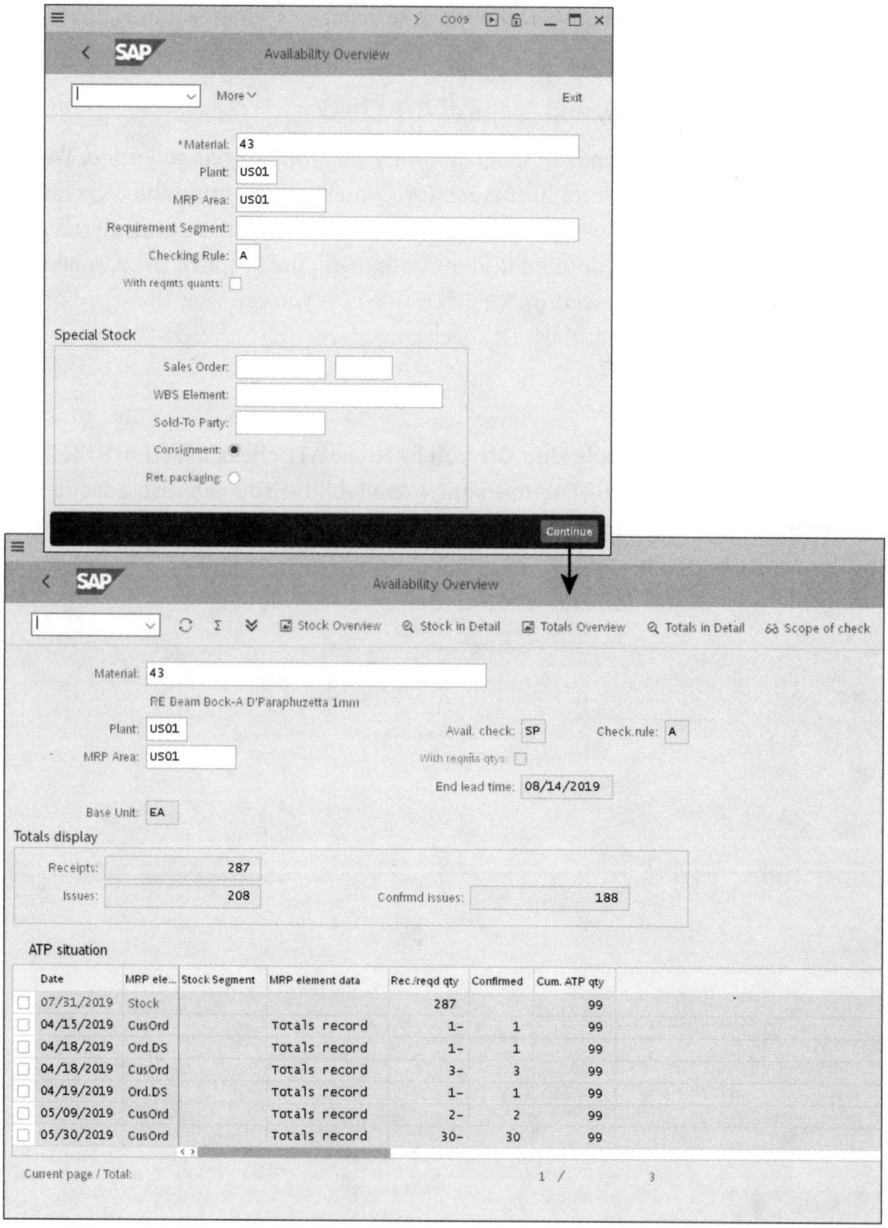

Figure 7.11 Accessing Availability Overview via Transaction CO09

The subsequent lines show the consumption of stock by sales orders (**MRP Element** column value **CusOrd**).

If you have incoming purchase orders, requisitions, planned production orders, production orders, reservation, etc., and these elements are included in the scope of the check, these values would also appear as lines on this screen.

You may also see an indication of the material master replenishment lead time here. If replenishment lead time is being used, you will find the value **----->** in the **MRP Element** column.

Using the **Stock Overview**, **Stock in Detail**, **Totals Overview**, and **Totals in Detail** command bar buttons, you can control how much detail is displayed, thus allowing you to more quickly understand the ATP check results.

You can also access the **Availability Overview** screen by opening Transaction CO09, as shown in Figure 7.11.

Configuring the Scope of the Availability Check

To configure the scope of the ATP check, open Transaction OVZ9 or follow the menu path **SAP Customizing Implementation Guide • Sales and Distribution • Basic Functions • Availability Check and Transfer of Requirements • Availability Check • Availability Check with ATP Logic or Against Planning • Configure Scope of Availability Check**.

As shown in Figure 7.12, two important fields appear at the top of the screen:

- The **Availability Check** group is a material master attribute, which we'll configure under Defining the Availability Check Group in this section. This group allows you to use different rules depending on the material ordered. Most companies use the same group for all materials to reduce complexity. One exception is for make-to-order materials; for those materials, you'll need to use a different group. Out of the box, you also have access to availability check group ST, which is configured to use only on-hand inventory, ignoring any other incoming stock.
- The **Checking Rule** field is a code that represents the type of document/functionality to which these ATP check rules apply. In our example, enter "A" in the **Checking Rule** field to specify the rules that govern the scope of the sales order ATP check scope. For delivery documents, enter "B" in the **Checking Rule** field.

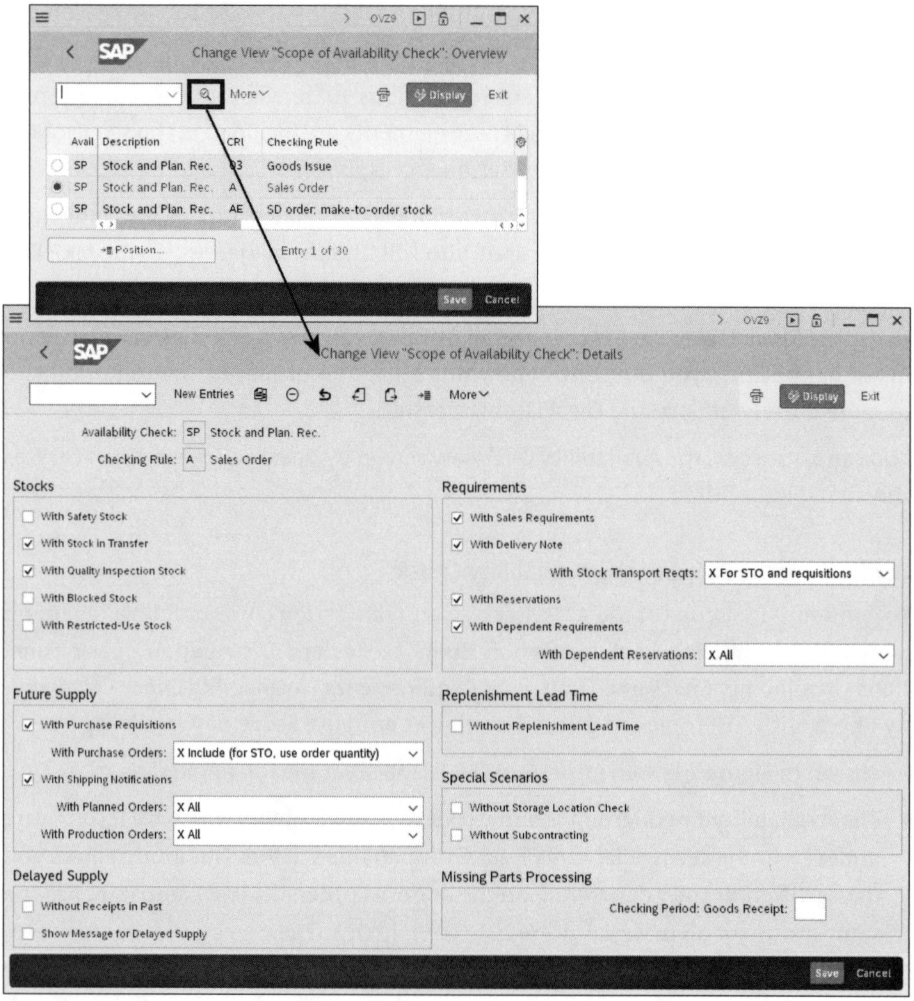

Figure 7.12 Configuring Scope of Availability Check

In the following sections, we'll discuss each section of this screen in more detail.

Stock

The **With Safety Stock** flag indicates that you want to allocate stock even if the material master indicates that several units of an item should be reserved as safety stock. If you select this flag, you'll consume all inventory to the last available item, ignoring safety stock.

The **With Stock in Transfer** flag indicates that you want to allocate stock that is in the process of being transferred from other plants. Once the transfer is complete, this stock would already be allocated and ready for shipment to customers.

The **With Quality Inspection Stock** flag indicates that you want to allocate stock currently flagged for quality inspection. Note, however, that usually you would not allow shipments of this type of stock, but by selecting this flag, you can allocate this stock and ship this stock once available. Note also that, if inspection takes a long time, the ATP check dates could be missed. If your company has a time-consuming inspection process, you may not want to consider this type of stock for ATP purposes on sales orders.

The **With Blocked Stock** flag indicates that you want to allocate stock even if this stock is blocked by inventory management. We do not recommend selecting this flag, which could invalidate ATP check results. Blocked stock may not be released for several days after an order is entered, and by selecting this flag, you're saying that the ATP check should simply consider this stock as available right now.

The **With Restricted-Use Stock** flag indicates that you want to allocate stock belonging to batches (lots) that are flagged as **Restricted**. We do not recommend selecting this flag because the stock may not be available until several days after the order is entered, and by selecting this flag, you're saying that the ATP check should simply consider this stock as available right now.

Requirements

The **With Sales Requirements** flag indicates that stock already allocated to other sales orders must no longer be considered available for other orders. Selecting this flag is important; otherwise, you could end up allocating the same stock on multiple orders, but only one order will be delivered. The others would result in customer experience problems.

The **With Delivery Note** flag indicates that stock already allocated to a delivery document must no longer be considered available for new sales orders. Once you create a delivery document, the allocation is transferred from the order and is allocated to the delivery. This flag is very important; deliveries are usually processed quickly by the warehouse, and the stock will be reduced at the end of the process (at the time of the post goods issue operation). If you remove this flag, you could end up allocating to new orders product that is already in process at the warehouse, meaning these orders would never be delivered, resulting in customer experience issues.

The **With Stock Transport Reqts** flag indicates that stock already is allocated to stock transfer orders and/or requisitions must no longer be considered available on other orders. This flag is important to keep selected; otherwise, you could end up allocating products that are already in the process of being transferred to other plants, and the sales order would not be delivered as promised, resulting in customer experience issues. If the order is processed before the pending stock transfer orders are received, a short pick (i.e., an order shipped with less than the requested quantity) could occur when processing the stock transfer orders, which should be avoided.

The **With Reservations** flag indicates that stock reserved using an MM functionality called the *material reservation functionality* must no longer be considered available for sales orders. Removing this flag indicates that material reservation must not affect sales orders. With other checking rules, you can still keep this controlling the material reservation functionality. Unless the inventory management team is answerable for high levels of on-hand inventory, it doesn't make sense for them to control whether sales orders can use available inventory.

The **With Dependent Requirements** flag indicates that stock that being used as a component, a subassembly, or a raw material in in-process production orders must no longer be considered available for sales orders. Removing this flag indicates that you can "steal" stock from production, which is not advisable in particular in complex production scenarios with multiple components. You could cause serious problems for the production team.

The **With Dependent Reservations** flag indicates that stock reserved by the production team for use in the future as a component, a subassembly, or a raw material on a production orders must no longer be considered available for sales orders. You'll need to collaborate with the production team to ensure these reservations are used in a responsible manner. Ideally, production stock included on reservations should impact their bottom line and not sales, which is not often the case. Sometimes, production makes large stock reservations without realizing the impact on the sales side. Often, companies resolve this conflict by using separate storage locations for production stock versus sellable stock, but then transferring stock is like "stealing" stock from storage locations with no control because inventory management lacks an ATP check for transfer posting stock movements.

Future Supply

The **With Purchase Requisitions** flag indicates that, for purchase requisitions created to procure more stock, the system can consider that product as available for allocations on sales orders. Be aware, however, that often the expected delivery date on the purchase requisition is not reliable at all. When activated, this flag would in turn make the ATP check promise unreliable dates to your customers, thus causing customer experience issues. Thus, many companies remove purchase requisitions from the scope of the ATP check.

The **With Purchase Orders** indicator controls whether, for incoming purchase orders procuring more stock (including stock transfer orders), that product should be considered available for allocation to sales order. Be aware, however, that often the expected delivery date on the purchase requisition is not very reliable. When this flag is activated, the ATP check may promise somewhat unreliable dates to your customers, thus causing customer experience issues. Thus, many companies remove purchase orders from the scope of the ATP check. However, doing so will also exclude stock transfer orders from the ATP check, which is a problem. The expected delivery dates for stock transfer orders are often more reliable than delivery dates from external vendors.

The **With Shipping Notifications** flag controls whether advanced shipping notifications (ASNs), represented as inbound deliveries in the system, should be considered available stock for allocation to sales orders. ASNs are sent by the external vendors after products leave their warehouse and usually can be trusted more than the expected delivery dates found on purchase orders or purchase requisitions. For stock transfer orders, inbound deliveries can be created automatically by a background job. This flag is commonly used.

The **With Planned Orders** indicator controls whether planned production orders created automatically by the MRP background job (part of production planning [PP]) should be considered available stock for allocation to sales orders. This approach is sometimes used, but you should only use firmed planned production orders, which are often manually modified and rescheduled after MRP creates them. Once production "firms" these production orders, the planned confirmation date can usually be trusted, but the reliability of these dates depends on the definition of the production process and how realistic planning has been observed to be historically.

The **With Production Orders** indicator controls whether production orders created from planned production orders should be considered available stock for allocation to sales orders. This option is often used especially released production orders, which are usually quite accurate and are rarely missed.

Replenishment Lead Time

The **Without Replenishment Lead Time** flag controls whether the lead time maintained in the material master (a volume-independent fixed amount of days required to replenish inventory once fully allocated) is ignored. Companies that are serious about promising dates usually activate this flag to ignore the lead time entered on sales orders. The main reason is the fact that we would commit to delivering any quantity after this amount of days. Other companies that don't promise delivery dates tend to like this information to get a ballpark idea of when stock may be available and generally don't suffer negative consequences when these dates are missed.

Another serious issue with using a fixed lead time is that the system will attempt to fulfill the promise date as this date is the rule. If product is received before the promised date, the system would prevent immediate shipment to avoid premature, early delivery. To bypass this issue, you can schedule background jobs to create delivery documents with a date interval far enough in the future. The system will then perform a delivery ATP check (rule "B") and only create the delivery document if stock is available. Note that we don't advise considering the promise dates as important in some orders but not in others, which is just too complex to manage. You could gain this flexibility, however, by adding different shipping points, one for planned shipping and the other for shipping "whenever."

Special Scenarios

The **Without Storage Location Check** flag indicates that you want to ignore the storage location field on the sales order line when performing an ATP check. If not selected, the ATP check will check all storage locations when the field on the sales order line is left blank; when populated, the ATP check will only look for stock at the selected storage location level. If selected, we would always perform the ATP check at the plant level. Doing so means that stock available across all MRP-relevant storage locations would be considered available to be allocated this sales order. This would be the case even if the **Storage Location** field on the sales order line is populated with a valid storage location code.

If this flag is not checked, we would check all MRP-relevant storage locations only if the **Storage Location** field in the sales order line is left blank. If the user makes a selection than only stock under the selected storage location would be considered.

When a delivery is created, the storage location is copied from the order, and when you perform the post goods operation, you'll need to reduce inventory at the storage location level and may need to manually change the storage location on the delivery by indicating the storage location where stock is available.

The **Without Subcontracting** flag indicates that you want to ignore stock that is being processed by a third-party vendor who is contracted to work on our products. If you don't select this flag, the subcontracting stock would be considered as available for allocation to sales orders. The decision about whether to ignore this stock depends on the nature of the work that your vendors perform for you.

Delayed Supply

The **Without Receipts in Past** flag indicates that incoming stock with an expected delivery date in the past should be considered as a missed receipt and is not expected to be received anymore. This situation is rather unusual since, unlike a simply delayed delivery, you're not expecting a delivery at all.

The **Show Message for Delayed Supply** flag indicates that you want the system to inform you of delayed receipts.

Missing Parts Processing

The **Checking Period: Goods Receipt** flag is used for scenarios where the replenishment lead time should be used when planning the components of a production order. This flag allows you to proceed with processing production orders and notifies the MRP controller (as defined on the material master) about the missing parts, for remediation. This functionality is part of production planning and does not affect sales.

Defining the Availability Check Group

To configure ATP check groups, open Transaction OVZ2 or follow the menu path **SAP Customizing Implementation Guide • Sales and Distribution • Basic Functions • Availability Check and Transfer of Requirements • Availability Check • Availability Check with ATP Logic or Against Planning • Define Availability Check Group**.

When creating new entries, as shown in Figure 7.13, click the **New Entries** button to add new lines, and then specify a two-character availability check group code (**Av**) and add a description (**Description**).

The important indicators on this screen are as follows:

- Displayed for reference, the **TotalSales** field controls how sales order demand (i.e., requirements) are transferred to MRP (which is part of PP). The PP team will need to be involved in this configuration.
- Displayed for reference, the **TotDlvReqs** field controls how delivery document demand (i.e., requirements) are transferred to MRP (which is part of PP). The PP team will need to be involved in this configuration.
- Displayed for reference, the **Block QtRq** flag indicates that the material must be blocked while the ATP check runs to avoid competing ATP checks considering available quantities and running in parallel. Companies that use the same material in several orders, stock transfer orders, production orders, MRP, etc., may have issues with this flag activated. When a competing ATP check finds a blocked material, the check returns no result, and the order is not processed until you run the

ATP check again when the material is no longer blocked. If your company has a large list of materials, you can keep this flag activated to ensure consistency and to manage exceptions as they occur.

- The **No PAC** flag indicates that you want to turn off the regular ATP check when running advanced ATP check.
- The **Accumul.** field controls whether planned incoming inventory (from production, purchasing, transfer, etc.) should be considered, along with order demands, to determine the available stock on future orders. This flag controls the behavior of committed quantities, when configured on the sales order type (using Transaction VOV8, as described in Chapter 6).
- The **RelChkPlan** field affects the ATP check on components of production orders, rather than the planned date that defined when the product should be available. You can specify that the ATP check uses the planned dates as truth without further checks. This decision is made by the PP team.
- The **Advanced ATP** is where you'll indicate whether to make use of the advanced ATP check functionality (also called *rule-based ATP*, which we'll cover in Section 7.6).

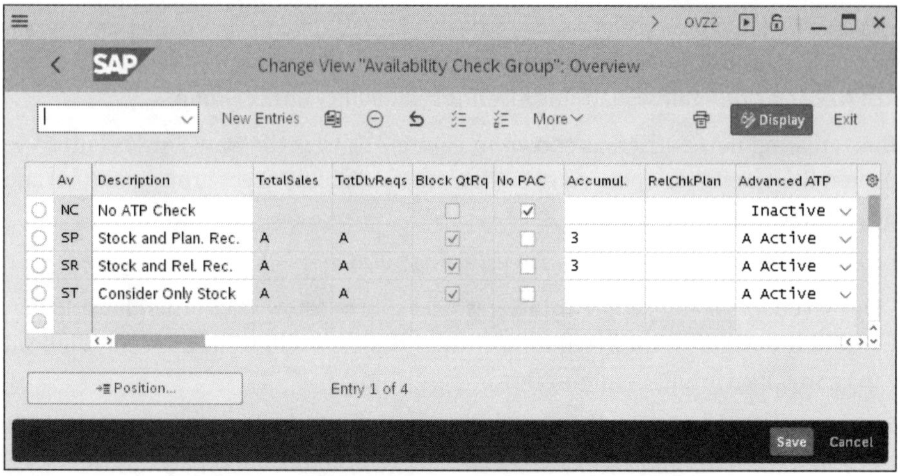

Figure 7.13 Defining Availability Check Groups

Configuring Default Settings by Sales Area

To configure the default settings for sales area ATP checks, follow the menu path **SAP Customizing Implementation Guide • Sales and Distribution • Basic Functions • Availability Check and Transfer of Requirements • Availability Check • Availability Check with ATP Logic or Against Planning • Configure Default Settings by Sales Area**.

As shown in Figure 7.14, find the desired sales area (**Sales Org.**, **Distr. Chl**, and **Division**) and assign the default **Fixed Date and Qty** flag (checked or unchecked) and the availability check rule (**Avail.check rule**), which controls the behavior of the **Availability Control** window that appears whenever you're performing forward scheduling.

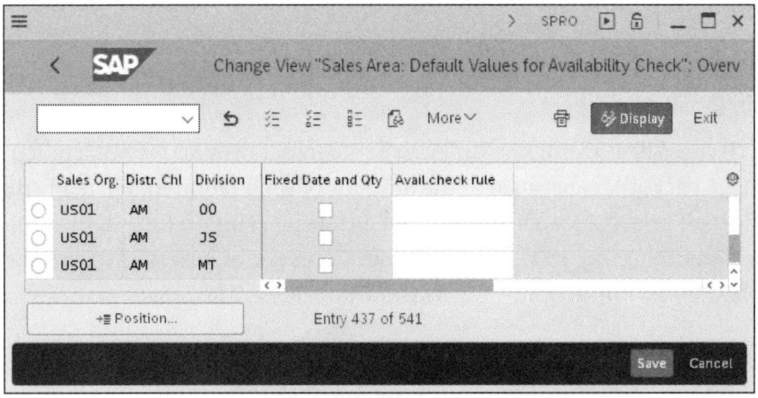

Figure 7.14 Configuring Default ATP Check Settings by Sales Area

7.2.4 Backorder Rescheduling

In SAP S/4HANA, the term "backorder" describes a sales order in which you're unable to deliver the ordered products by the requested delivery date. In other words, backorders are sales orders containing lines where you cannot successfully perform backward planning ATP checks. The resulting material availability date would be in the past, causing the system to perform forward planning.

When forward planning cannot determine a material availability date, the resulting schedule lines will contain no confirmed quantity. This scenario is most obvious type of backorder, which we'll refer to as *unconfirmed orders*.

Every company sells products will encounter backorder situations, and sales orders in this state may require ATP checks to be executed again before they can be delivered.

Forward planning can reduce the amount of rework required to process backorders. A confirmed backorder is a sales order with a confirmed quantity on a future date based on the theoretical availability of the product based on incoming procurement and/or lead times considered during forward planning. The system, by default, expects forward planning to be true. Deviations need to be monitored and handled as exceptions.

Unconfirmed orders always require further action before they can be processed. Unconfirmed orders are not considered relevant for further processing until a new ATP check is executed and confirmed quantities are assigned.

In other words, unconfirmed backorders don't have enough stock allocated to them—that's what made them backorders. Once new stock is received from purchasing, production, stock transfers, etc., the backorders would not automatically allocate the newly available stock. For backorders to allocate new stock, we need to run the ATP check again for all backorders.

Running the ATP check again, order by order, using Transaction VA02 is not a practical way to manage backorders because of the amount of time required. We may still do it for specific high priority orders, but it is not a scalable solution for a higher volume of transactions. One way to run an ATP check on several orders is to use the backorder rescheduling Transaction V_V2, as shown in Figure 7.15.

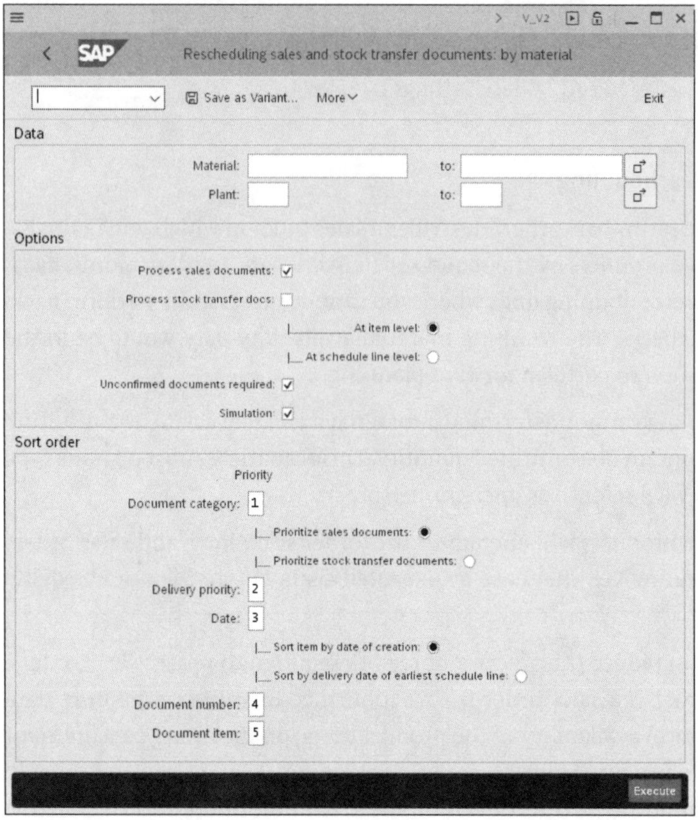

Figure 7.15 Backorder Rescheduling Transaction V_V2

Note that running an ATP check against a large number of orders is time consuming. SAP S/4HANA has better performance than SAP ERP, but the process is still a significant drain to system resources and relatively slow due to the amount of processing and database updating that must be performed. So, companies tend to schedule this task to run in the background and keep the number of orders to be processed to the necessary minimum.

The important fields on this screen are as follows:

- When running in the foreground, we recommend restricting which orders should be rescheduled by **Material** and **Plant** whenever possible. Background job variants usually run without selections in these fields.
- The **Process sales documents** flag indicates that you want to process sales orders in this execution.
- The **Process stock transfer docs** flag indicates that you want to process stock transfer orders in this execution.
- The **At item level** and **At schedule line level** radio buttons control whether you want to reschedule the order line as a whole based on the order quantity or if you want to respect multiple order dates and quantities as requested at the schedule line level. This approach may be considered important when processing scheduling agreements; however, once you're processing backorders, you're already not fulfilling the requested quantities on the selected dates. If you consider this process to be a remediation on a "as soon as possible" basis, you can use the **At item level** selection.
- The **Unconfirmed Documents Required** flag indicates that you only want to process backorders that are unconfirmed sales orders. Orders with confirmed quantities based on forward planning dates are also considered backorder but would not be included because they have confirmed quantities.

  Once this process finds a record matching the selection made on this screen, the system looks at all pending orders with a material and reschedules them all following the priority described further down on this screen to allocate stock.
- The **Simulation** flag indicates you don't want to update any sales documents. Instead, this transaction will issue a report detailing what changes would be made. If you aren't sure how this behaves, we recommend run the check on simulation mode, reviewing the reports, and then running the check again without this flag activated to update the orders.

- The **Sort Order** section is where you'll set the criteria you must use when not enough stock is available for all orders. Documents that are on the top of the sorted list of orders according to the **Priority** number assigned to each criteria:
  - The **Document Category** allows you to **Prioritize Sales Documents** or **Prioritize Stock Transfer Documents**. By default, the priority is 1, with the sales order first, meaning that you would assign available stock to all open sales orders before checking the first stock transfer order.
  - The **Delivery Priority** is a sales order header field defaulted from the customer master. By default, the priority is 2, meaning that the sales order with the smallest value in the **Delivery Priority** field would be allocated available stock first. Then, if any stock is left, you would then start assigning stock to orders with higher delivery priority values.
  - The **Date** field has two options: **Sort item by date of creation** or **Sort by Delivery Date of earliest schedule line**. By default, the priority is 3 and uses creation date, meaning the sales orders entered first would be fully allocated before attempting to allocate stock to other orders. If you select the earliest schedule line date, you would allocate stock to orders that are due first even if these orders were entered after other orders (scheduled to be delivered in the future). This approach would avoid having inventory sitting in the warehouse allocated on planned sales order that would only ship on a future date.
  - The **Document number** is the sales order or stock transfer order number and is usually the second to last criteria.
  - The **Document item** is the last criteria and only affects stock allocation when the same material appears more than once on the same sales order.

Note

SAP S/4HANA also allow you to define more complex rules to automatically resolve backorders using the SAP HANA rules framework.

7.3 Transfer of Requirements

Sales orders are one of many ways in which you can allocate inventory. The need for product represents a *demand* or *requirement* that must be fulfilled. Stock *requirements* are transferred into material requirements planning (MRP), which considers demand/requirements from various sources (including sales) and compare against available inventory and incoming procurement sources. When identifying shortages, MRP creates purchase requisitions, planned production orders, etc., based on its configuration, to start the stock replenishment process.

MRP need details about the kind of requirements it is receiving to define whether and how the existing inventory availability will be consumed (consumption strategy) and the appropriate replenishment action to be taken. MRP is controlled by a code called the *requirement class*, which we'll cover in Section 7.3.1.

Next, for sales, the *requirement class* is based on a different code called the *requirement type*, which assigned to the sales order line (as shown on the **Procurement Overview** tab of the sales order). The requirement type is assigned automatically and is determined from on the item category and a material master data field called **MRP Type**.

You can also turn off the transfer of requirements, by schedule line category, as described in Section 7.3.4. This decision is relevant to sales, to logistics, and to customer, but not important to MRP and the areas responsible for procurement.

You could make changes to the requirement type and class after discussions with your production planning team, who are responsible to setting up MRP. The configuration activities described in this section are often conducted by the PP team, not the sales team.

7.3.1 Configuring Requirement Classes

To configure requirement classes, open Transaction OVZG or follow the menu path **SAP Customizing Implementation Guide • Sales and Distribution • Basic Functions • Availability Check and Transfer of Requirements • Transfer of Requirements • Configure Requirement Classes.**

Figure 7.16 shows what you'll see following the menu path and screen commands as specified. On this screen, when creating new codes, the production planning team can specify a three-character requirements class code (**Reqmts Class**) and add a description (**Description**).

This configuration is often a cross-functional, time-consuming activity for companies that follow make-to-order scenarios, when the manufacture or assemble products only occurs after a customer makes an order.

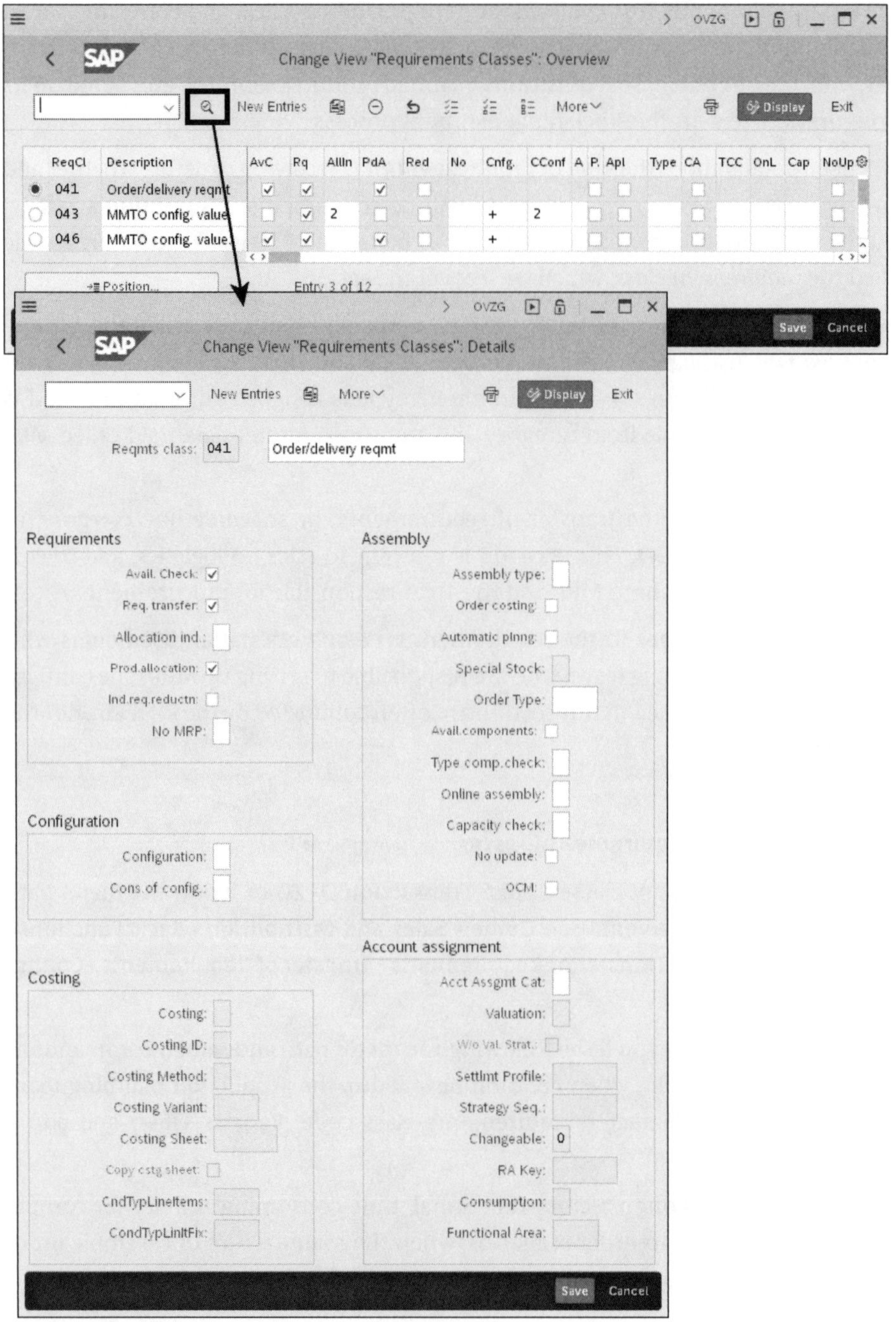

Figure 7.16 Configuring Requirement Classes

The following areas on this screen are important:

- **Requirements**
  - The **Avail. Check** flag indicates that this requirement class requires an ATP check run.
  - The **Req. transfer** flag indicates that this requirement class is relevant for the transfer of requirements.
  - The **Allocation ind.** indicator is part of the consumption strategy of independent requirements.
  - The **Prod.allocation** flag indicates that this requirement class is relevant for production allocation (which we'll discuss in more detail in Section 7.5).
  - The **Ind.req.reductn** flag indicates that, in a make-to-stock scenario, this order must be considered part of independent requirements planning. This type of planning is called *independent requirements planning*, because in make-to-stock scenarios, you plan to replenish stock without specifying a sales document that will be used to consume it.
  - The **No MRP** indicator is used by MRP to identify whether this requirement class is part of a plan or an unplanned requirement. You would usually start an ad hoc procurement process for unplanned requirements, not for planned ones.
- **Assembly**
  - The **Assembly type** indicator indicates the type of assembly to be used for requirements of this class.
  - The **Order costing** flag indicates that costs are calculated at the order level.
  - The **Automatic Plnng** flag indicates that, in make-to-order scenarios, the production planning process must start automatically once the sales document is saved.
  - The **Special Stock** indicator is a stock qualifier that allows you to use customer stock, order stock, etc. instead of the unrestricted use stock and indicates the storage location level for planning purposes.
  - The production **Order Type** is the type of document to be used on make-to-order scenarios.
  - The **Avail.components** is used on make-to-order scenarios with assembly requirements to indicate that you want to perform an availability check on the component level of the production order. This method is relevant because, if any components are missing, you cannot fulfill the requirement by the planned completion date.

- The **Type comp.check** field is used to dictate the type of ATP check to be conducted on the component level.
- The **Online assembly** field is used when creating the assembly order and encountering a component shortage. This indicator determines whether messages are issued or not in this case.
- The **Capacity check** field indicates whether you want, in make-to-order scenarios, to consider production capacity when planning for estimated production times or whether you want to use lead times regardless of capacity for planning.
- The **No update** field indicates, in make-to-order scenarios, whether changes made to the assembly production order must be replicated to the sales order, which may result in changes to the expected dates. If you activate this flag, you want to manually manage assembly order updates on sales orders.
- The **OCM** field, standing for "order change management," indicates that you want to control order changes.

- **Configuration**
  - The **Configuration** indicator is used for materials that are configurable (have multiple variant configurations). In this field, you'll indicate whether configuration is allowed, mandatory, not relevant, etc.
  - The **Cons.of config** indicator controls whether you want to consume components based on the selected configuration.
- **Costing**
  The **Costing**, **Costing ID**, **Costing Method**, **Costing Variant**, **Costing Sheet**, **Copy cstg sheet**, **CndTypLineItems**, and **CondTypLinItFix** fields are used by controlling and affect how costs are calculated for this requirement class.
- **Account assignment**
  - The **Acct Assgmt Cat** indicator controls the usage of auxiliary accounting elements such as cost centers, work breakdown structure (WBS) elements, etc.
  - The **Valuation**, **W/o Val. Strat.**, **Settlmt Profile**, **Strategy Seq.**, **Changeable**, **RA Key**, **Consumption** and **Functional Area**. fields used by SAP S/4HANA Finance to control how activities under this requirement class are accounted.

7.3.2 Configuring Requirement Types

To configure requirement types, open Transaction OVZH or follow the menu path **SAP Customizing Implementation Guide • Sales and Distribution • Basic Functions •**

Availability Check and Transfer of Requirements • Transfer of Requirements • Configure Requirement Types.

As shown in Figure 7.17, specify a three-character requirement type code (**RqTy**) and add a description (**Requirements Type**). Then, enter the requirement class (**ReqCl**) that corresponds to this requirement type (**RqTy**).

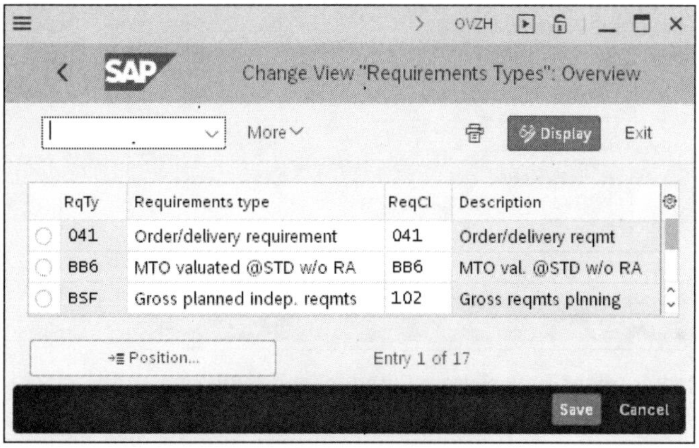

Figure 7.17 Configuring Requirement Types

7.3.3 Determining Requirement Type by Item Category and MRP Type

To assign requirements types to item categories and MRP types, follow the menu path **SAP Customizing Implementation Guide • Sales and Distribution • Basic Functions • Availability Check and Transfer of Requirements • Transfer of Requirements • Determine Requirement Type by Item Category and MRP Type**.

Figure 7.18 shows what you'll see following the menu path and screen commands as specified.

When adding entries to this configuration, you'll need to take the desired item categories (**ITCA**) and then consider all material master data that you want to allow for these entries, focusing on the MRP type (**TYP**) assigned to them (MRP types are defined by the production planning [PP] team).

You may want a different requirement type (**RQTY**) for each possible MRP type (**TYP**) or always use the same value for all types. This decision can only be made after analyzing the material master.

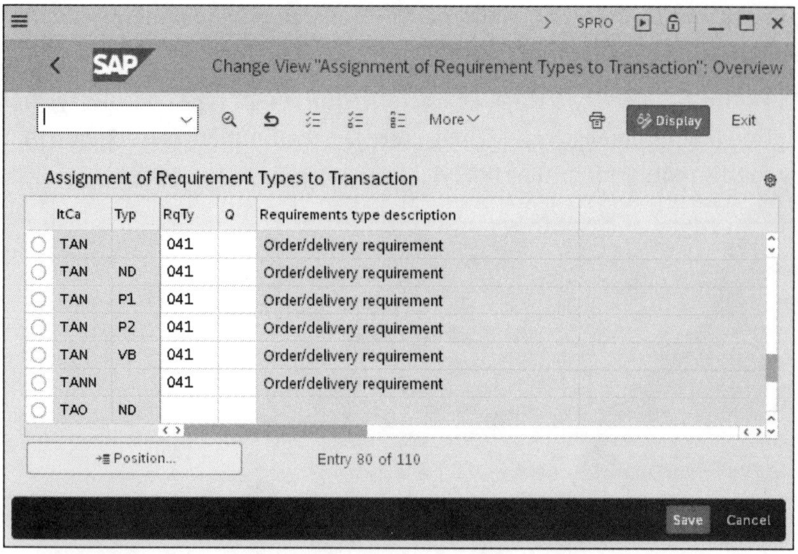

Figure 7.18 Determining Requirement Type by Item Category and MRP Type

Alternatively, you can also indicate the origin of the requirement type in a requirement type determination (**Q**) to modify the method used to determine the requirement type.

If you use **Q** code **0**, then the assignment made on this screen would not be used. Instead, the system would use the MRP strategy group maintained on the material master and the corresponding PP configuration to define which requirement type is appropriate to use.

The entries defined on this screen with a blank MRP type (**Typ**) are the default assignments to be used when the specific MRP type on the material master can't be found in this configuration table.

7.3.4 Defining Procedure for Each Schedule Line Category

To define the applicable procedures (ATP check, transfer of requirements, product allocation) for each schedule line category, follow the menu path **SAP Customizing Implementation Guide • Sales and Distribution • Basic Functions • Availability Check and Transfer of Requirements • Transfer of Requirements • Define Procedure For Each Schedule Line Category**.

On the screen shown in Figure 7.19, you'll see the desired schedule line category (**SLCa**). Select the corresponding flags to activate the ATP check (**AvC**), the transfer of requirements (**Rq**), and the product allocation (**All.**).

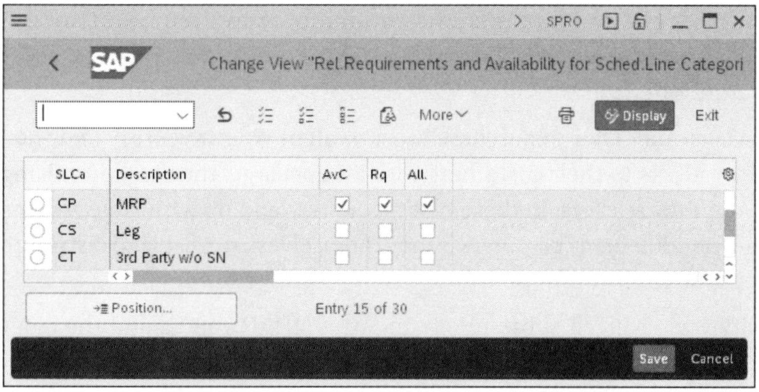

Figure 7.19 Defining Procedure for Each Schedule Line Category

7.4 Segmentation Strategy

Materials management (MM) uses an inventory segmentation feature to segregate inventory quantities for specific purposes. This feature is usually implemented to assist with procurement planning.

Companies often debate over how best to implement this common requirement, in particular, if materials are sourced from multiple vendors using the same material number. To implement this feature, the MM team must define the relevant segments on the material master.

On the sales order, you can then choose a *requirement segment* at the line level (as described in Chapter 6, Section 6.2.2), which would restrict the inventory that may be allocated to an order during ATP check.

One way to populate the requirement segment automatically would be to implement ABAP code in a BADI (Business Add-In) called `BADI_SD_SPEC_SEG`, enhancement spot `ES_SGT_APPL_SPEC_SEGMENT`.

Using the SAP HANA rules framework, you can also define rules to automate the choice of requirement segment to used based on flexible rules that may be maintained by the user. The SAP HANA rules framework evolved from BRF (Business Rule Framework) and BRFplus, which had been available in previous versions.

7.5 Product Allocation

Product allocation allows you to set buying limits on customers or groups of customers, which is sometimes required by companies that have new releases in high demand in the market. The goal is usually to allow for proportional supply across different regions, thus enabling a broad, but solid, market presence and high customer satisfaction regardless of region.

In some cases, a customer tries to purchase most or all of your inventory and then distribute these products to their customers with an upcharge, thus compromising the success of your new releases. In these cases, you may end up with large returns coming from these middleman customers if they themselves are unable to distribute all the stock they took from you.

This functionality was changed substantially in SAP S/4HANA 1809, and the older functionality that shares the same name and purpose still appears on the configuration menu. In this book, we'll focus on the new functionality, which is available using SAP Fiori apps. The following sections contain the applicable configuration steps for product allocation.

7.5.1 Activate Product Allocation

To activate the product allocation functionality, follow the menu path **SAP Customizing Implementation Guide • Cross-Application Components • Advanced Available-to-Promise (aATP) • Product Allocation (PAL) • Activate Product Allocation**.

As shown in Figure 7.20, you can activate the product allocation functionality by changing the value of the **Activate** column to **1 Yes**.

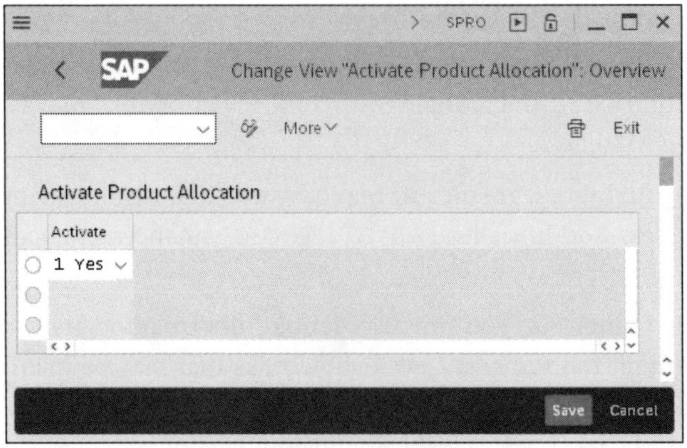

Figure 7.20 Activating Product Allocation

7.5.2 Configure Product Allocation Object

The product allocation functionality in SAP S/4HANA is available through the SAP Fiori app Configure Product Allocation, as shown in Figure 7.21.

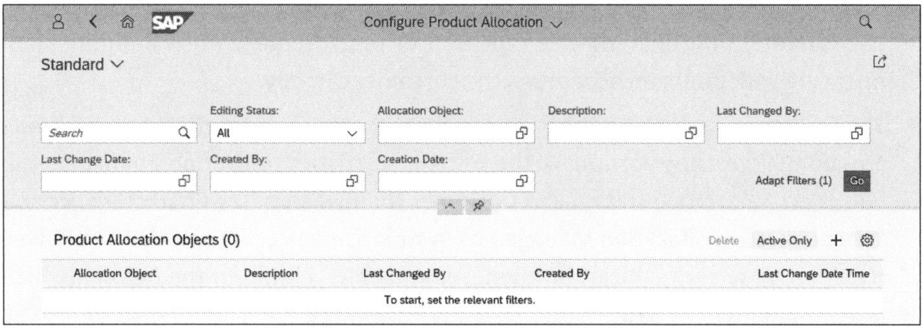

Figure 7.21 Configuring Product Allocation Parameters

Upon opening this SAP Fiori app, you can search for existing product allocation objects. To create a new entry, click the plus (+) icon, which will open the screen shown in Figure 7.22.

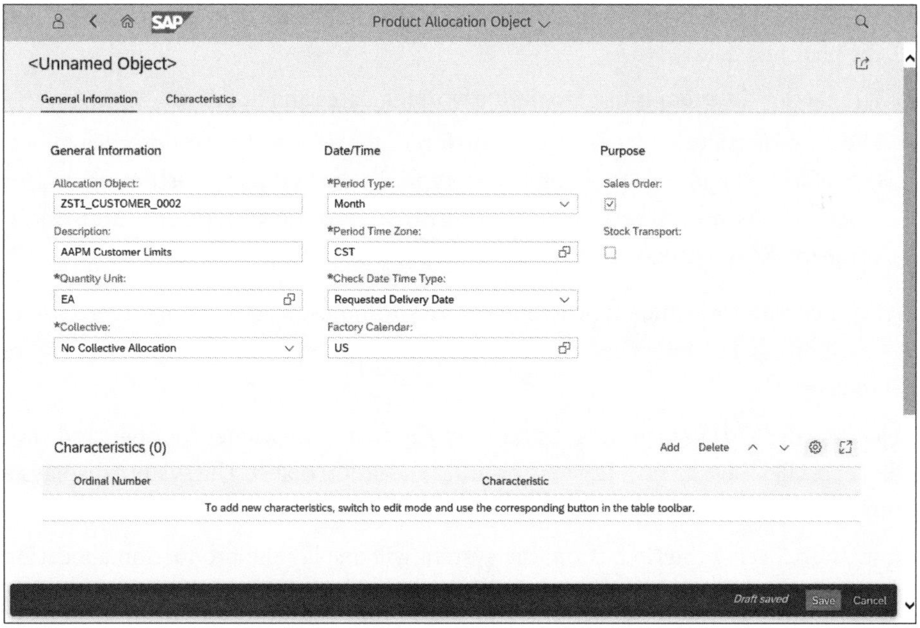

Figure 7.22 Creating Product Allocation Objects

Next, specify an 18-character product allocation object code (**Allocation Object**) and add a description (**Description**).

On this screen, you'll maintain the following fields under the **General Information** tab:

- The **Quantity Unit** field indicates the unit of measurement when defining planning data with limits on how much the customer can buy.
- The **Collective** control indicator determines whether a customer's buying limits are cumulative using portions of the key characteristics you define. For instance, if you select **Sales Organization** and **Customer Number** from the **Characteristics** and select **Collective Allocation Managed by System**, the system would define a collective limit by sales organization whenever you enter a limit for the full key (which is a combination of sales organization and customer).
- The **Period Type** field is the unit of time during which a customer accumulates buying volume to compare against the planning data limit control (monthly, weekly, etc.)
- The **Period Time Zone** is the time zone used to control the period, which will affect when one day ends and the next begins.
- The **Check Date Time Type** specifies which sales order date field is compare against the planning data.
- The **Factory Calendar** is used to define working dates and holidays.
- The **Purpose** (**Sales Order** or **Stock Transfer**) indicates whether this product allocation object is applicable for sales orders (typically to third-party customers) and/or stock transfer orders between plants configured in the system, i.e., inter-/intra-company sales within the same global corporation.

Next, click **Add** to include new characteristics to be used as planning data keys to define limits and to determine allocation success/failure. The screen shown in Figure 7.23 will open.

Select the desired characteristic, in our case the sold-to **Customer Number**, and click **Ok**. Then, click **Save** to save the new product allocation object. The system displays a confirmation page, shown in Figure 7.24. Click the back arrow icon.

Now, after clicking the **Go** button, the system will display the production allocation object we just created.

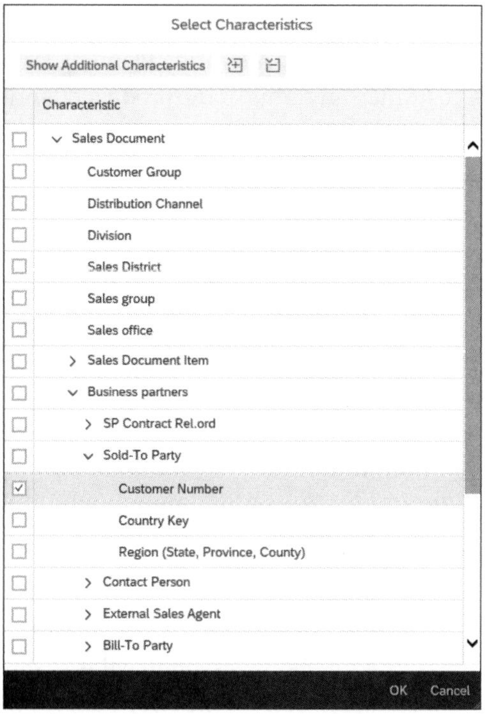

Figure 7.23 Selecting Characteristics

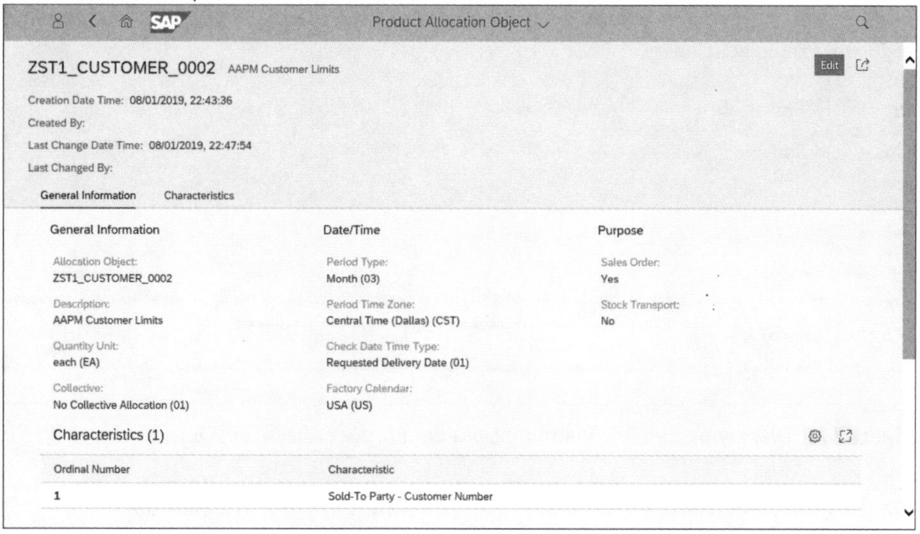

Figure 7.24 Reviewing Product Allocation Object

7.5.3 Manage Product Allocation Planning Data

The next SAP Fiori app we'll explore is the Manage Product Allocation Planning Data app, shown in Figure 7.25. This app limits customers in terms of the product quantities they may purchase over time, as defined during configuration.

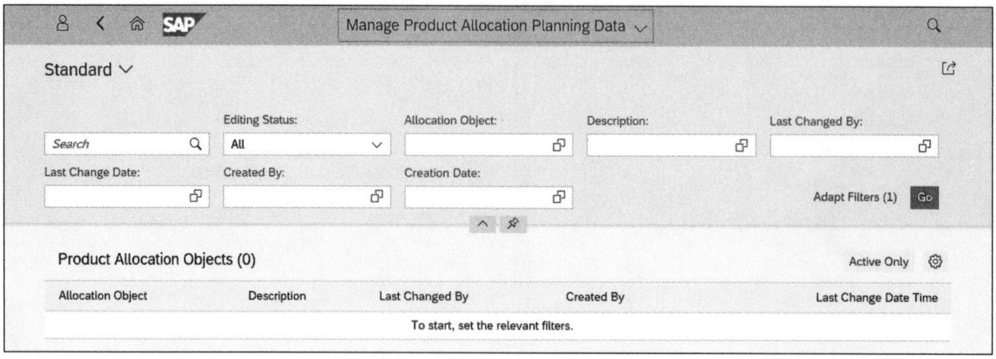

Figure 7.25 Maintaining Product Allocation Planning Data

In this app, you'll use the filters and click **Go** to find the desired product allocation object. Then, you'll click on the forward arrow icon on the corresponding line to display the current planning data. To make changes, click **Edit** on the screen shown in Figure 7.26.

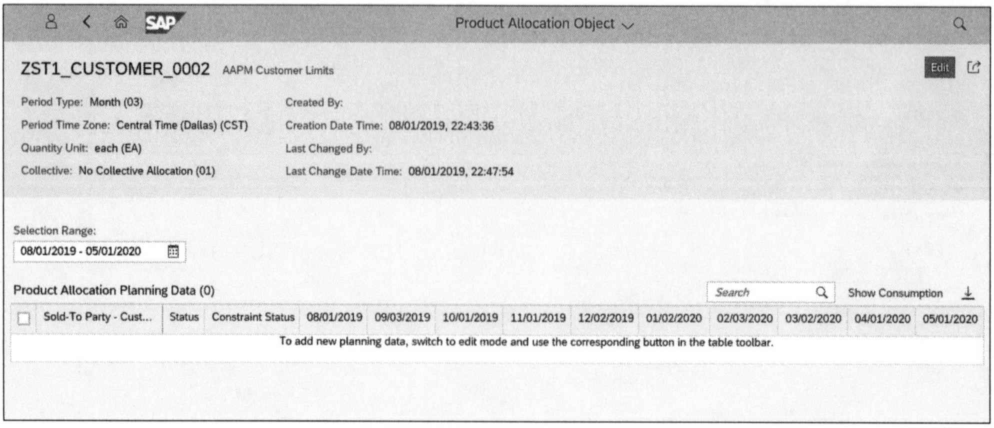

Figure 7.26 Displaying Existing Planning Data per Product Allocation Object

On the next screen, shown in Figure 7.27, click **Add** to include the new data.

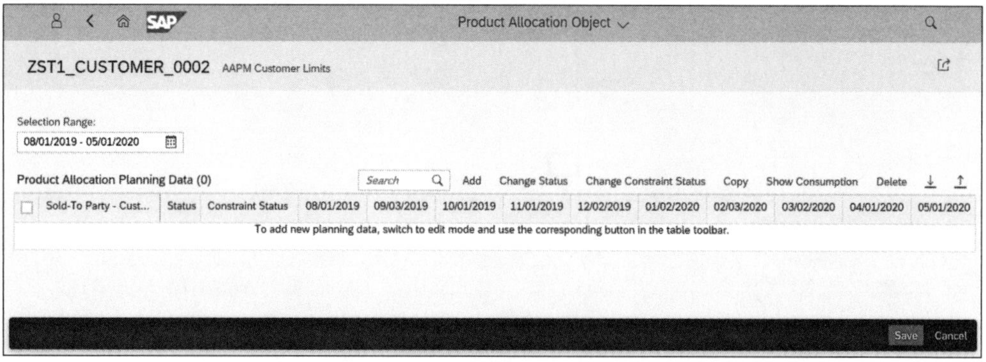

Figure 7.27 Adding Planning Data per Product Allocation Object, Part 1

On the line that appears, shown in Figure 7.28, enter the sold-to customer number (**Sold-to Party Cust**) and the quantity they are allowed to buy in each period (in this case, months as defined on this product allocation object) and click **Save**.

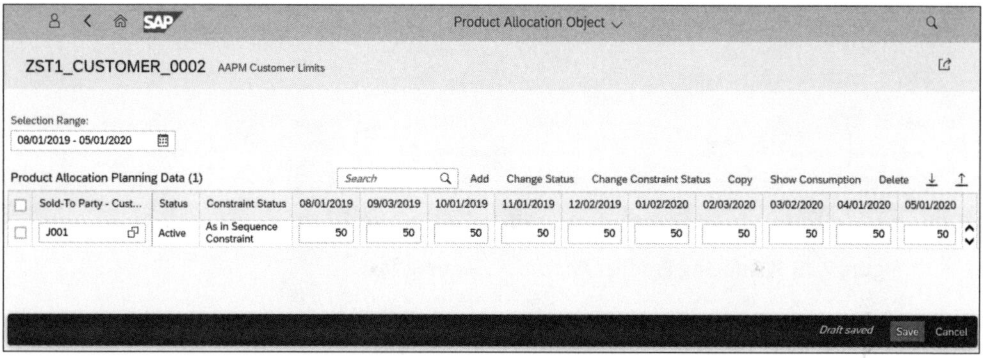

Figure 7.28 Adding Planning Data per Product Allocation Object, Part 2

7.5.4 Manage Product Allocation Sequences

The Manage Product Allocation Sequences app, shown in Figure 7.29, allows you to indicate the relevant object that must be verified and the sequence in which objects must be checked.

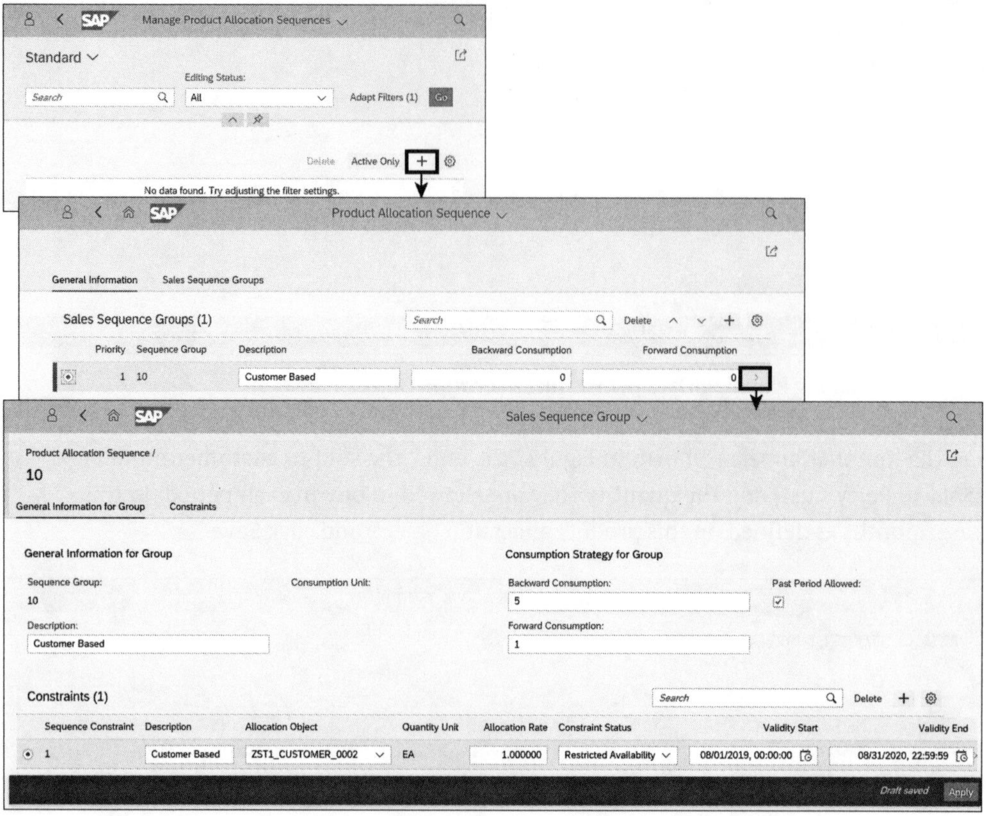

Figure 7.29 Managing Product Allocation Sequences

In the Manage Product Allocation Sequences app, follow these steps:

1. Click the plus (**+**) icon to add new sequence.
2. Click on the forward arrow icon on the first sequence generated by the system.
3. Enter sales sequence group general information:
   - Add a description (**Description**) for this sequence group.
   - Assign a **Backward** and **Forward Consumption** number of periods to check when authorizing sales order quantities.
   - Decide whether unused quantities from past periods are allowed (roll-over quantities) with the **Past Period Allowed** flag.

- Define constraints by adding a description (**Description**); specifying the product (**Allocation Object**); maintaining the **Allocation Rate**, **Constraints Status**, **Validity Start**, and **Validity End** fields.
- Click **Apply**.

7.5.5 Assign Product to Product Allocation

The Assign Product to Production Allocation app, shown in Figure 7.30, is where you'll assign the product allocation to a material to indicate that the material is a restricted product as per configured rules.

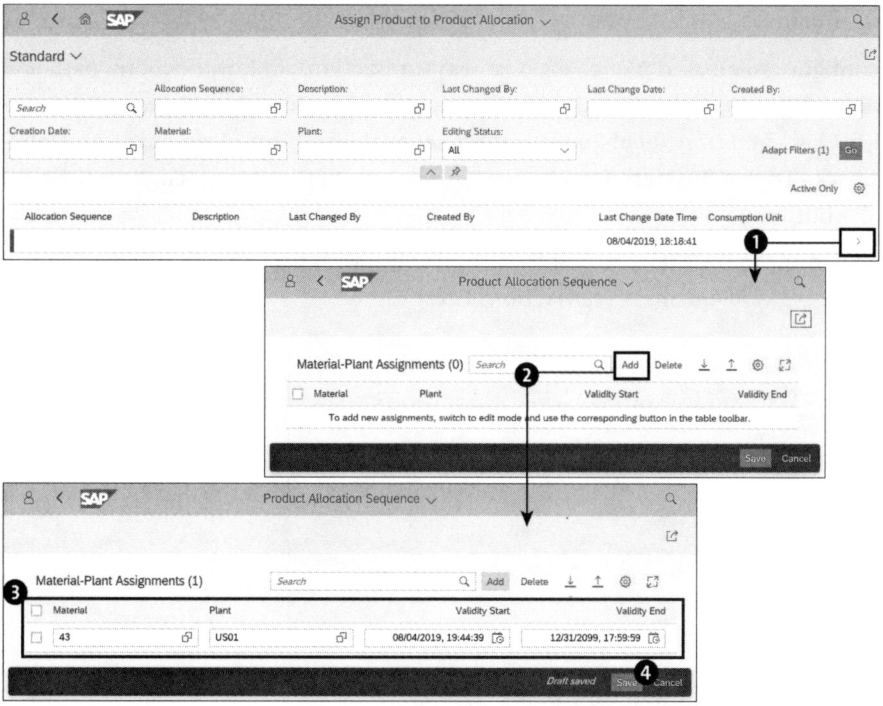

Figure 7.30 Assigning a Product to Product Allocation

In the Assign Product to Production Allocation app, follow these steps:

❶ Click the forward arrow icon on the desired allocation sequence.

❷ Click **Add**.

❸ Enter the desired **Material**, **Plant**, **Validity Start** date, and **Validity End** date.

❹ Click **Save**.

7.6 Rule-Based ATP

A rule-based ATP check is an SAP Advanced Planning and Optimization (SAP APO) feature that is now part of SAP S/4HANA. The sales team participates in setting up these rules by defining different business transactions that generate different types of demand. In this way, demand can be classified so that SAP S/4HANA can handle different kinds of demand in different ways.

The following section contain the sales configuration steps required to enable rule-based ATP checks.

7.6.1 Business Transactions

To configure rule-based ATP check business transactions, follow the menu path **SAP Customizing Implementation Guide • Sales and Distribution • Basic Functions • Availability Check and Transfer of Requirements • Availability Check • Rule-based Availability Check • Define Business Transaction**. On the screen that opens, click on the **New Entries** button or press F5.

As shown in Figure 7.31, specify a four-character business transaction code (**BT**) and add a description (**Business Transaction: Text**).

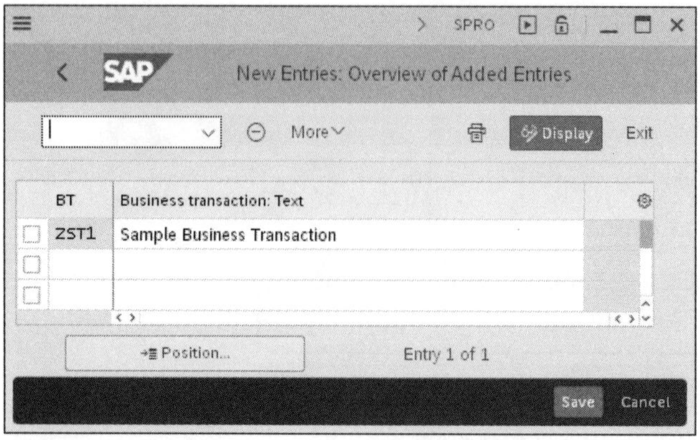

Figure 7.31 Defining New Business Transaction

Note

Rule-based ATP check business transactions are assigned at the sales order level in Transaction VOV8, as described in Chapter 6.

7.6.2 Sales Order Level

In addition to assigning rule-based ATP check business transactions to sales order types, you can also assign business transactions to sales order types by following the menu path **SAP Customizing Implementation Guide • Sales and Distribution • Basic Functions • Availability Check and Transfer of Requirements • Availability Check • Rule-based Availability Check • Assign Business Transaction to Sales Order Type**.

This configuration menu path leads to the same transaction described in Chapter 6 for configuring order types (Transaction VOV8). The rules-based ATP check business transaction can be maintained at the bottom of the detail screen when configuring sales order types.

7.6.3 Item Level Rules

You also need to allow the rule-based ATP check to make changes to the sales orders by setting the **RBA Control** indicator when configuring item categories, as described in Chapter 6, using Transaction VOV7.

The following options are available:

- **<Blank>: Subitems Allowed, Plant Substitution in Item Not Allowed**
  The default setting for item categories, the rule-based ATP check is not allowed to change the plant on the sales order line itself. Instead, the rule-based ATP check process will create a new subitem for that line with the new plant, keeping the original line for future reference.
- **C: Subitems and Plant Substitution in Item Not Allowed**
  The rule-based ATP check is neither allowed to change the plant on the sales order line nor to create new subitems. The rule-based ATP check is only allowed to change the confirmed quantity, the ATP check outcome.
- **D: Subitems Not Allowed, Plant Substitution in Item Allowed**
  The rule-based ATP check can change the plant on the sales order line but is not allowed to create new subitems.
- **E: Subitems and Plant Substitution in Item Allowed**
  The rule-based ATP check can change the plant on the sales order line and also allowed to create new subitems.
- **N: Rules-Based ATP Check Not Allowed**
  The rule-based ATP check is not allowed to make any changes to the ATP check (product allocation) outcome.

7.7 Summary

An ATP check is a mandatory component of SAP S/4HANA, and you can set it up as to be simple or as complex as needed, using different features to fulfill automation requirements. In this chapter, we covered several elements of SAP S/4HANA for advanced ATP, including product availability checks, ATP checks, transfer of requirements, and segmentation strategies. We also covered product allocation and rule-based ATP.

In the next chapter, we'll discuss drop shipments and special orders.

Chapter 8
Drop Shipments and Special Orders

Sales processes drive procurement for unforecasted demand and/or products you don't carry in inventory, thus requiring intermediate transactions between vendors and customers. These processes can be implemented using sales functionalities designed for third-party ordering, also known as drop shipments, and for individual purchase orders (POs), also known as special orders.

From a sales perspective, individual requirements are a type of setting on a material that defines how you procure inventory to fulfill sales orders with that material on an order by order basis. Planning and procurement use the term "individual requirements" for other types of demand, not only sales orders. In this chapter, we'll focus on individual requirements related to sales, which is commonly used for materials that you don't want to maintain stock for. Instead, you'll start procurement only after the sales orders are entered. Companies often refer to this process as "make-to-order" or "procure-to-order."

With *collective requirements*, you would still wait for sales orders to be entered before procuring inventory. You would accumulate multiple orders over a set period of time or set quantity and only then start the procurement process. You may use individual requirements in a material requirements planning (MRP) setting, which would not affect sales order functionality and is often the preferred method in manufacturing organizations for whom MRP is a central part of the system and is relied upon heavily.

In distribution-focused companies, the sales order plays the central role, and procurement occurs based on reorder points/safety stock. These companies can have the sales order configured in such a way that customer service has control over the individual requirements and triggers the procurement process as soon as the sales order is created. This process is easy to track.

This chapter covers sales order features that allow you to create purchase requisitions along with the sales orders. Keep in mind other options exist for achieving this approach using MRP, but this chapter is focused on the sales functionality designed for these special procurement scenarios.

In the following sections, we'll explain the difference between third-party ordering/ drop shipments (Section 8.1) and individual purchase order/special orders (Section 8.2). We'll then walk through the steps after a sales order has been entered that you'll need to understand in a complete an end-to-end process: converting purchase requisitions to purchase orders (Section 8.3), interfacing purchase orders to vendors (Section 8.4), registering goods receipts (statistical or otherwise in Section 8.5), vendor invoice receipts (Section 8.6), and finally customer billing (Section 8.7).

We won't go into details about planned production orders created along with sales orders as this approach is rarely used. Manufacturing organizations tend to use MRP for this type of requirement.

8.1 Drop Shipments

The most common type of sales order-driven individual requirement is what companies in the United States refer to as "drop shipments." In the following sections, we'll first look at an overview of the drop shipment process, before discussing some drop shipment-specific configuration necessary when defining schedule line categories.

8.1.1 Process Overview

Drop shipment is the language used in day-to-day operations to refer to the process shown in Figure 8.1.

Material master data can be set up with item category group CBNA (as described in Chapter 3, Section 3.1.2). Item category group CBNA is used when the vendor doesn't provide you with a shipping notification known as an advanced shipping notification (ASN). In other words, you'll wait for the vendor invoice before issuing your own invoice to the customer.

Using item category group CBOR (third-party sales order with shipping notification), you expect the vendor to provide the ASN, and then you'll issue your own invoice to the customer based on the quantities specified in the ASN. Item category CBOR is used because the invoice will be issued sooner than normal and is also compatible with other delivery-based customer billing scenarios such as standard orders.

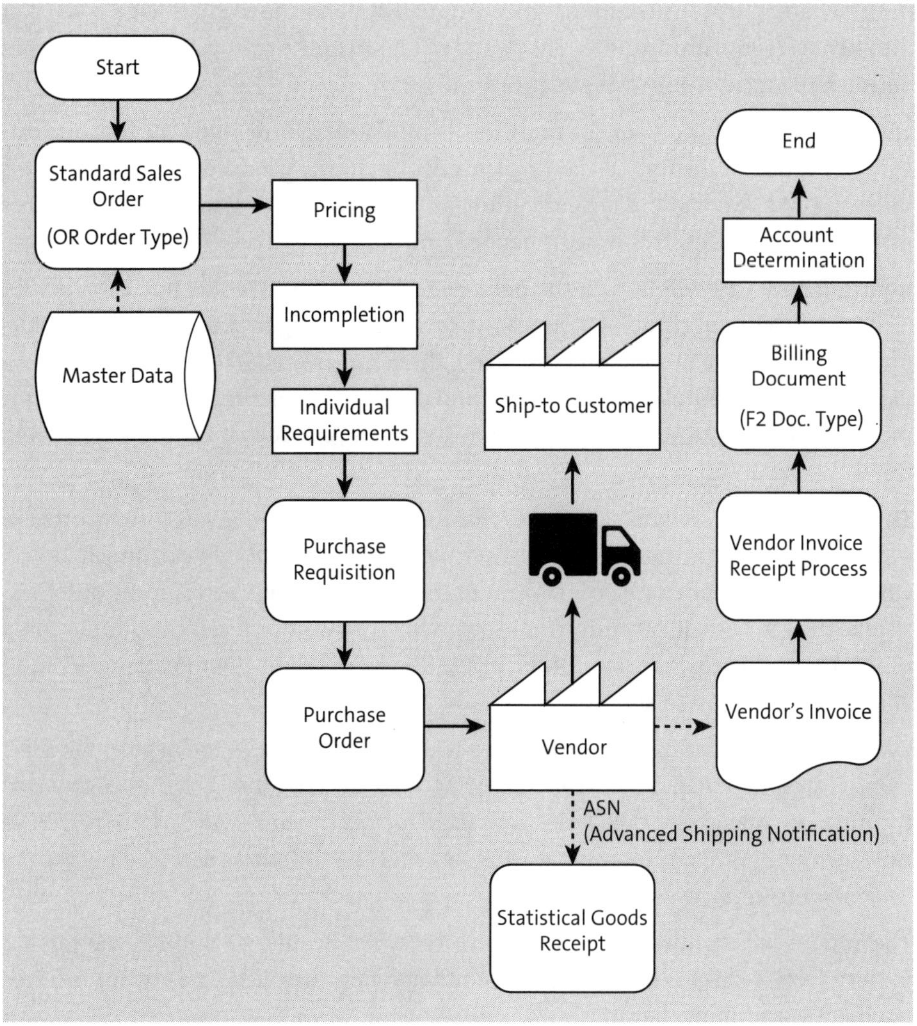

Figure 8.1 Sales Drop Shipping Scenario

The decision to use item category group CBNA or CBOR depends on how reliable you consider your vendor to be in notifying you of shipments. When you receive goods receipt notification electronically, for instance, via Electronic Data Interchange (EDI) message 856, using item category group CBOR is common, but if you rely on manual email notifications, you may consider using item category group CBNA.

In this chapter, we'll use item category group CBNA and show you how to convert it into item category group CBOR. The goal is to highlight the configuration differences between the related item categories CB1 and CB2.

Once you enter a sales order, for example, using standard order type OR, the item category assigned to the line containing the CBNA material will be defined as CB2. This line will only be complete once the purchase requisition is created and its number assigned to the order. This process happens automatically when you save the order.

Item category CB2 will lead to the determination of the schedule line category CT (third-party without shipping notification), which is configured with a purchase document type. After the sales order is saved, the purchase requisition number can be viewed on the **Schedule Line** tab of the line details (see Chapter 6, Section 6.4.7, for more details). On the purchase requisition document, the delivery address will match the ship-to address.

The purchasing team will take the purchase requisition and convert into a purchase order. This process is usually performed by a background job that can be scheduled. Once created, the purchase order is sent to the vendor either electronically (EDI message 850) or via email, fax, print/mail, etc. When the vendor receives your purchase order, they will create a sales order in their system using your customer ship-to address as their ship-to address.

Once the vendor fulfills your order, they will send you an ASN message either electronically or via email, phone call, fax, print/mail, etc. You'll record the ASN by performing an operation called the *statistical goods receipt*, which is a materials management (MM) operation that indicates that the order was received but inventory won't be created.

The vendor will then send you their invoice, which would go through the regular invoice receipt process that MM uses for other vendor invoices. The vendor receives payment via accounts payable.

Once the vendor invoice is received, a sales order containing the CB2 line will become relevant for billing, which is usually processed by a background job. The invoice is created, sent to your customer, and payment is collected by accounts receivable. This process is now concluded.

The statistical goods receipt could make the CB2 sales order line relevant for billing right away, but the out-of-the-box configuration waits for the vendor invoice to be received before you issue your invoice to the customer. This scenario is controlled by the **Billing Relevance** flag on the item category configuration: If you leave the value as

"F" (Order-Related Billing Doc. - Status according to Invoice Qty), the system will wait for the vendor invoice to be received. If you enter "G" (Order-Related Billing of the Delivery Quantity), the invoice would be issued after the statistical goods receipt. Most companies in the US enter "G," a common business practice to issue an invoice at the time of shipping. However, you must be mindful that, once you perform this change, if you don't perform the statistical goods receipt, this invoice will not be issued even if the vendor sends you an invoice.

8.1.2 Schedule Line Category

In Chapter 6, we showed you how to configure schedule line categories, which is where you'll activate the drop shipping functionality. Let's now look at the portion of configuration relevant for drop shipments.

To configure sales document scheduling line categories, open Transaction VOV6 or follow the menu path **SAP Customizing Implementation Guide • Sales and Distribution • Sales • Sales Documents • Schedule Lines • Define Schedule Line Categories**. On the screen that opens, select the item category CB and then click the **Details** button or press F2.

As shown in Figure 8.2, the purchase **Order Type** is used for a third-party ordering solution (drop shipment). You must create a purchasing document (typically a purchase requisition) along with the sales order upon save.

The **Item Category** field is a type of purchasing document line that must be created for third-party ordering scenarios (drop shipment). The **Purchase Requisition Delivery Schedule** field is used in special order, third-party ordering scenarios (for instance, when you want to receive goods from the supplier into your facility first before shipping to the customer). In this scenario, you'll schedule the delivery to the customer along with the receipt from the vendor. Thus, you must select this flag.

The **Account Assignment Category** field allows you to indicate that the purchasing document created by this schedule line will require an additional costing element (such as a cost center). The **Update Schedule Lines** field is used in third-party ordering scenarios to control if/how you want to update the sales order schedule line with purchase order delivery information. Suppliers may provide you with an ASN before you receive product. You may want to reflect this scenario on the schedule line or wait until product is fully received at your warehouse. The **Update Sched. Lines** (from the purchase order) flag controls whether you want to update schedule lines at all.

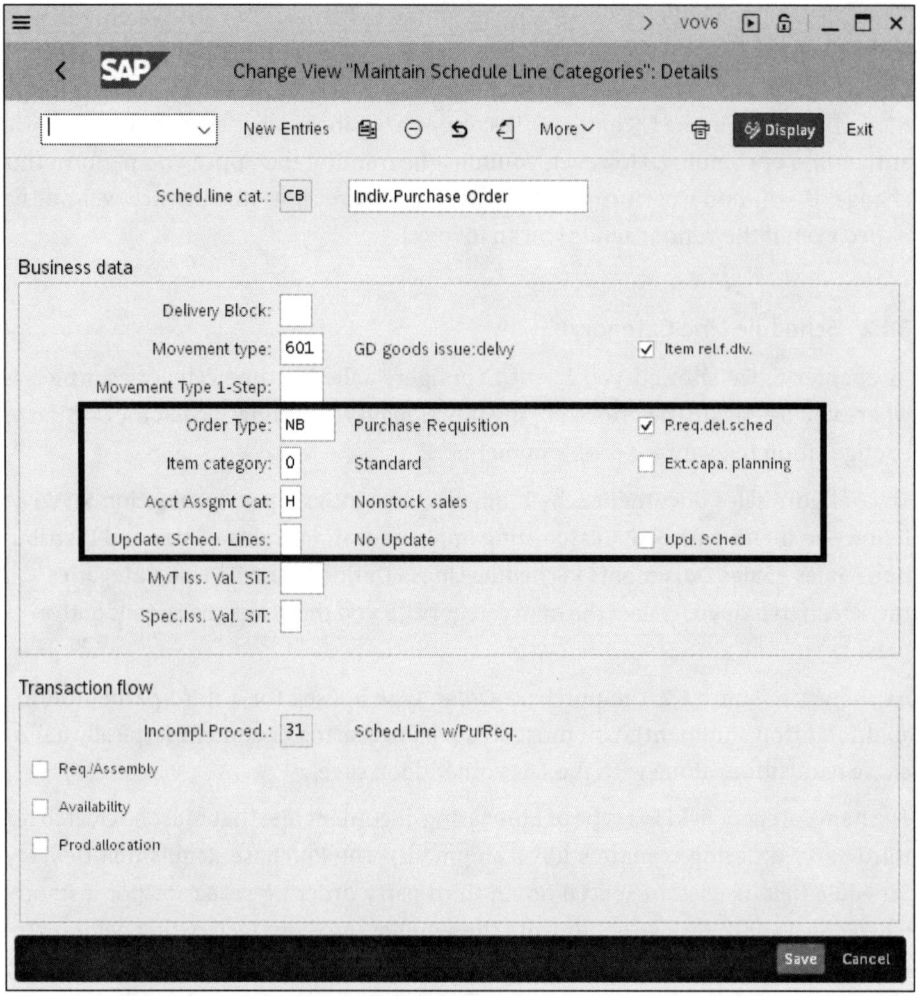

Figure 8.2 Displaying the CB Schedule Line Category

8.2 Special Orders

Another case of sales order-driven individual requirements is what companies in the United States refer to as "special orders." This language is used in day-to-day operations to refer to the process shown in Figure 8.3.

The material master data can be set up with the item category group CBUK (bought-in). Once you enter a sales order, such as a standard order of type OR, the item category assigned to the line containing the CBUK material will be defined as field CBAB. This line will only be complete once the purchase requisition is created and its number assigned to the order, which happens automatically when you save the order.

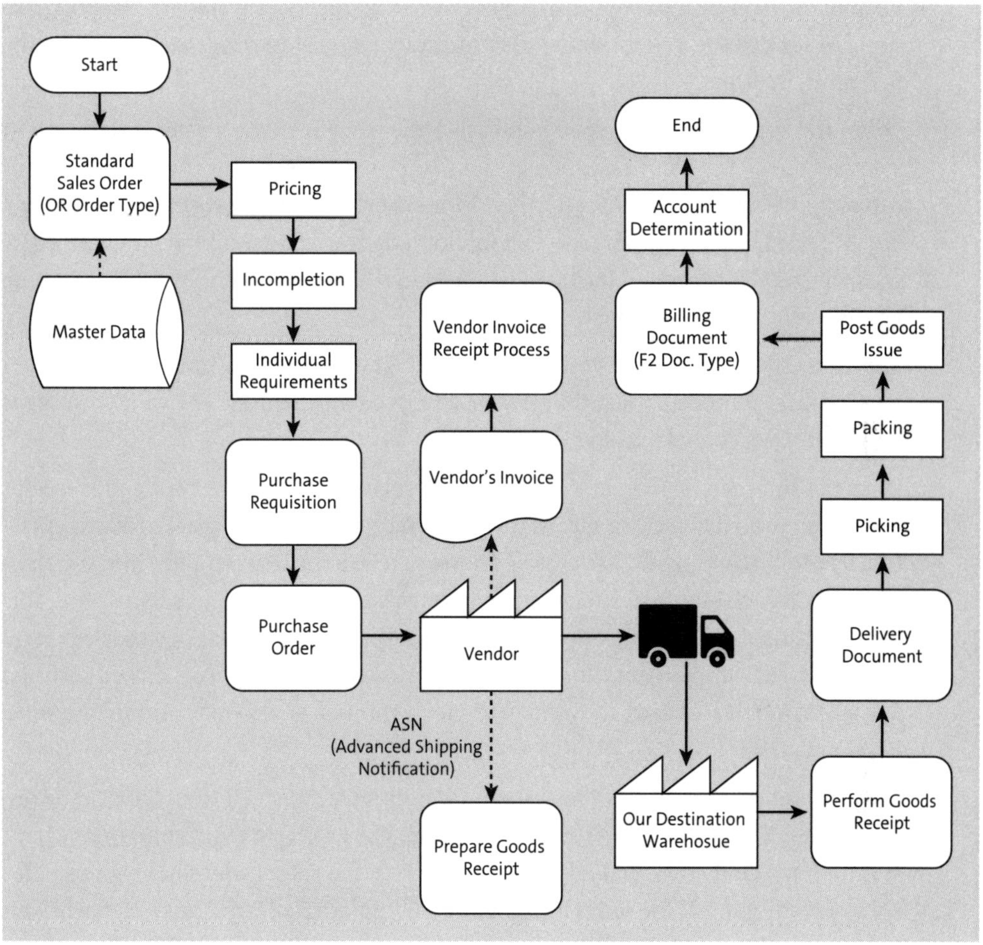

Figure 8.3 Sales Special Order Scenario

Item category CBAB will lead to the determination of the schedule line category CB (individual purchase order), which is configured with a purchase document type. After the sales order is saved, the purchase requisition number can be viewed on the **Schedule Line** tab of the line details. On the purchase requisition document created along with the sales order, the delivery address will match the plant's address, which is the plant you assigned to the sales order line.

The purchasing team will convert the purchase requisition into a purchase order, usually through by a background job they've scheduled. Once created, the purchase order is sent to the vendor either electronically (via EDI message 850) or via email, fax, print/mail, etc.

When the vendor receives your purchase order, they'll create a sales order in their system using your plant's address as their ship-to address. Once they've fulfill your order, they'll send you an ASN message either electronically or via email, phone call, fax, print/mail, etc. You can create an inbound delivery based on the purchase order with the ASN information included to speed up the goods receipt process when the goods arrive at the warehouse.

The vendor will then send you their invoice, which would go through the regular invoice receipt process that MM uses for other vendor invoices. The vendor receives payment via accounts payable.

Once the shipment arrives at the warehouse, you would issue the post goods receipt on the inbound delivery (or record the goods receipt on the purchase order, as specified by MM). You can also use cross-docking to move the item straight into the shipping area, which eliminates the need for putaway and picking, thus saving time. This MM functionality can be set up, but you must discuss this scenario with them early during system implementation so that this functionality is incorporated into the scope. Although standard and simple to process, this scenario may require the work of several teams.

Once goods are available at the shipping warehouse, the stock would appear as on-hand in the storage location used for shipping. The available to promise (ATP) check will find on-hand stock and allocate this stock to the sales order, making the order ready for shipping. If the order is flagged as a **Complete Delivery**, the system will wait for stock availability before stock is completely allocated and ready for delivery.

The delivery document is then created (either manually or via s background job) and sent to warehouse (electronically or a printed pick list). The warehouse team will pick product off the shelf (whenever necessary) and bring this product to the packing team. Once packed and ready to ship, you'll perform the post goods issue operation, where inventory is consumed into the cost of goods sold (COGS) inventory account.

After the post goods issue operation, the delivery becomes relevant for billing (usually via a background job), accounts receivable collects payment, and the process is complete.

8.3 Purchase Requisitions and Purchase Orders

The purchasing documents created for the drop shipments and special orders scenarios are within the scope for the MM team. For the sales team, you may need to find and view these documents.

The link between the sales order and the purchase requisitions is managed at the schedule line level. This process is fully detailed in Chapter 6, but in this section, we'll walk you through a sales order with a special order line.

The purchase requisition number (**Purchase Req...**) and line number (**Requi..**) are available under the **Schedule lines** tab of the sales order, as shown in Figure 8.4. You can also select the desired schedule line and click on the details icon.

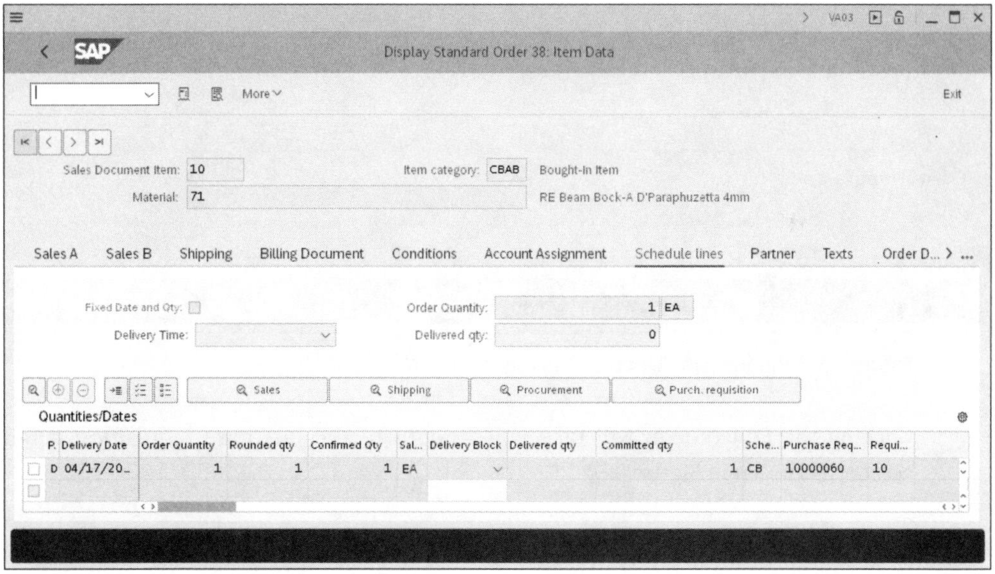

Figure 8.4 Sales Order Line Details: Schedule Lines Tab

The screen shown in Figure 8.5 will open where, under the **Procurement** tab, you'll also find the purchase requisition number (**Purchase Requisition**) and the line number next to it.

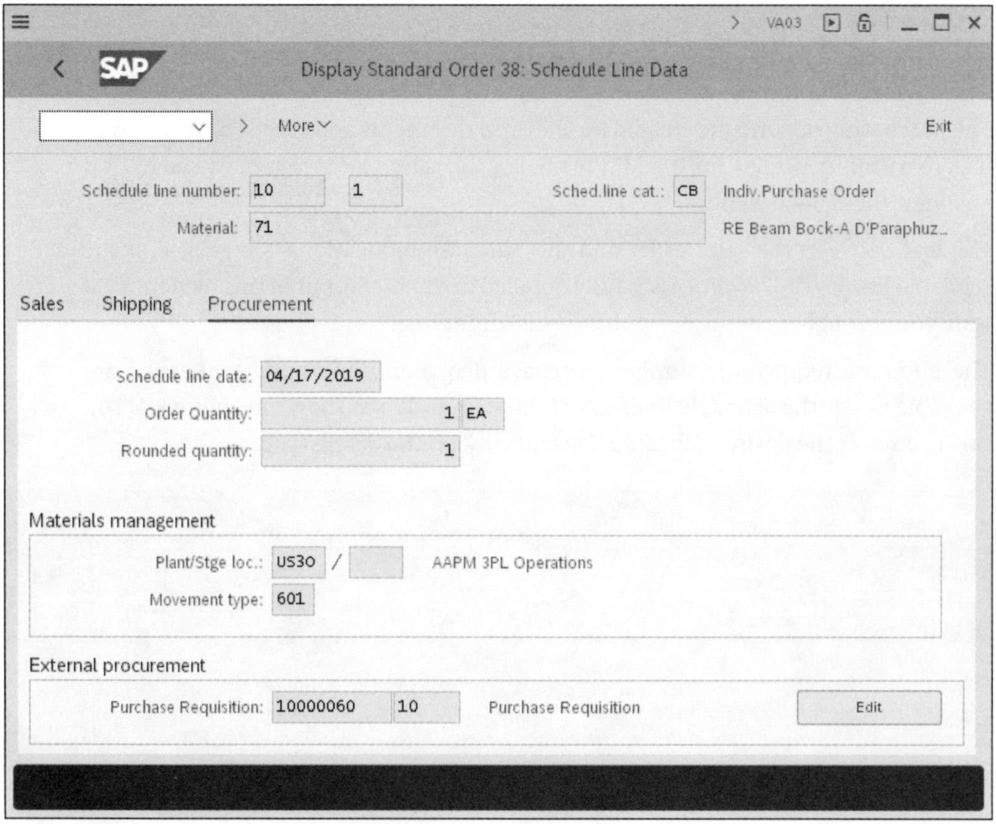

Figure 8.5 Schedule Line Details: Procurement Tab

Clicking the **Edit** button will take you straight to the purchase requisition detail screen, as shown in Figure 8.6.

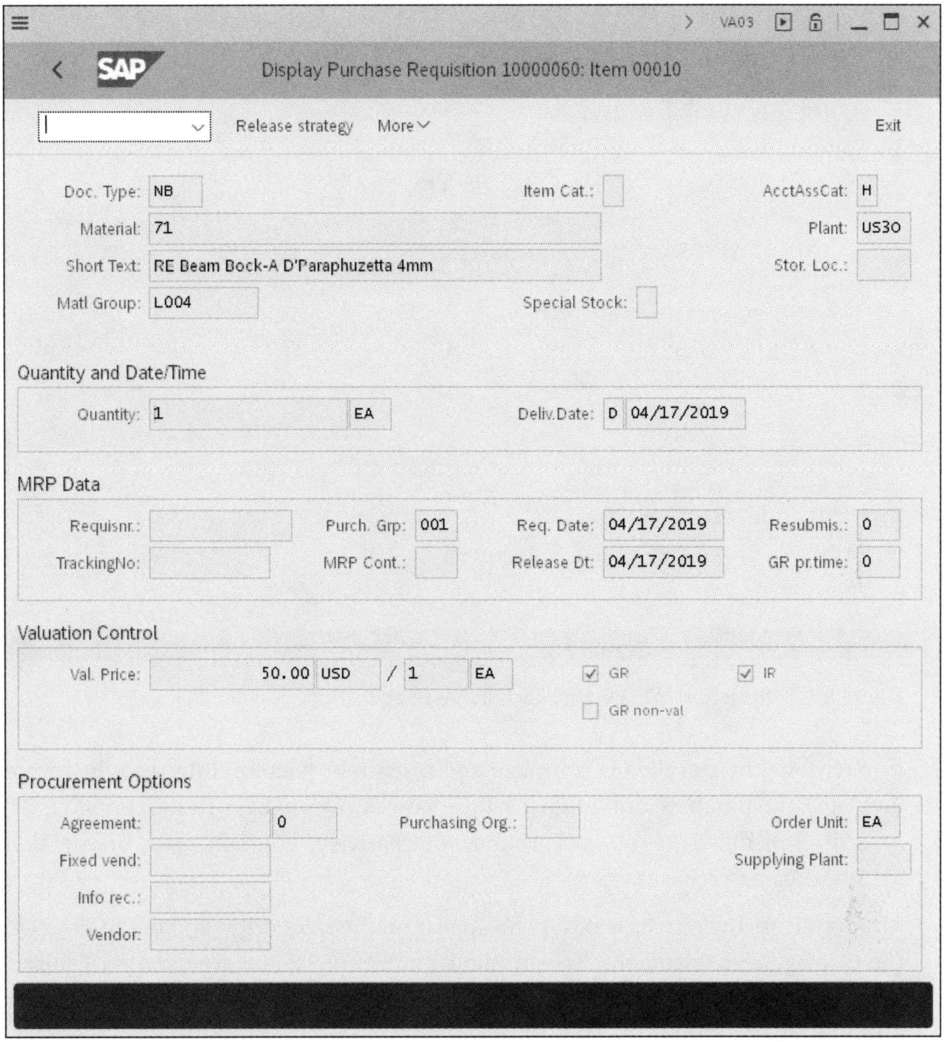

Figure 8.6 Purchase Requisition Details

Alternatively, you can take the purchase requisition number found on these screens and use Transaction ME53N to display details about the purchase requisition, as shown in Figure 8.7.

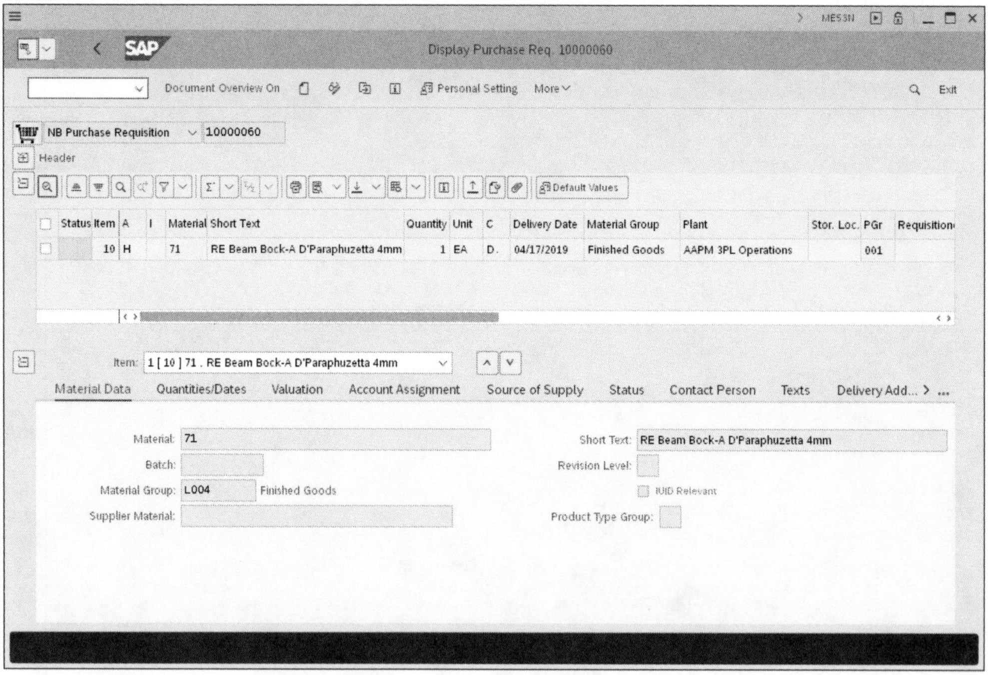

Figure 8.7 Transaction ME53N: Display Purchase Requisition

If purchasing master data is complete and consistent (vendor, info records, source lists, etc.), the purchase order may be automatically created via Transaction ME59N, typically scheduled in the background. Alternatively, you can open Transaction ME21N (Create Purchase Order).

After creation, the purchase order will appear on the sales order document flow. On the **Display Sales Documents** screen, shown in Figure 8.8 and accessed via Transaction VA03, you'll enter the desired sales order number and click on the document flow icon .

As shown in Figure 8.9, browse for the right purchase order number. If you click on the purchase order number and then click on the **Display Document** button, Transaction ME23N will open, as shown in Figure 8.10, with the selected purchase order opened for querying.

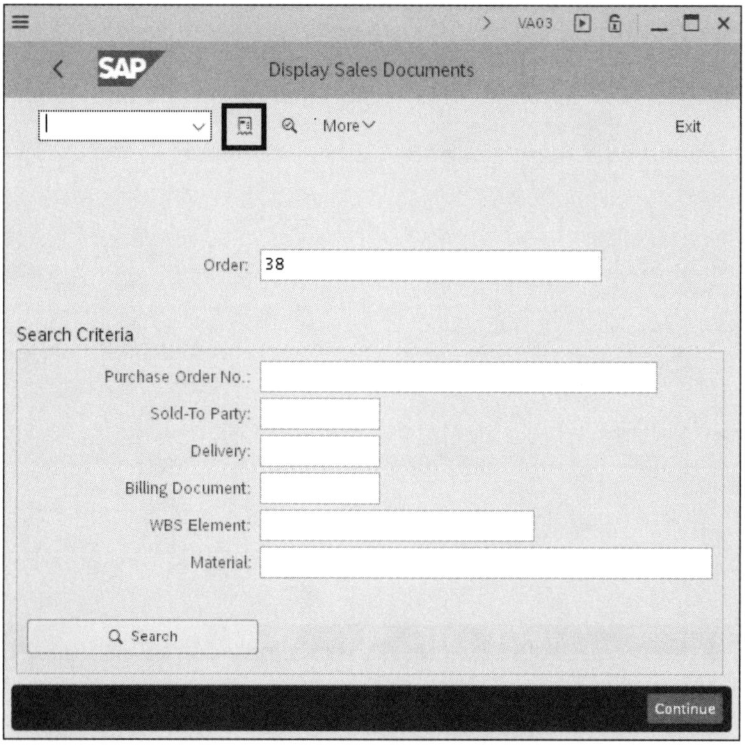

Figure 8.8 Display Sales Order Transaction VA03: Main Screen

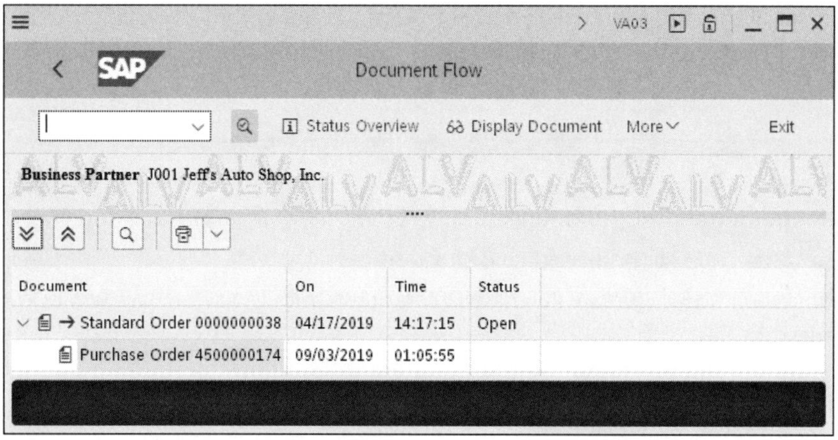

Figure 8.9 Sales Order Document Flow

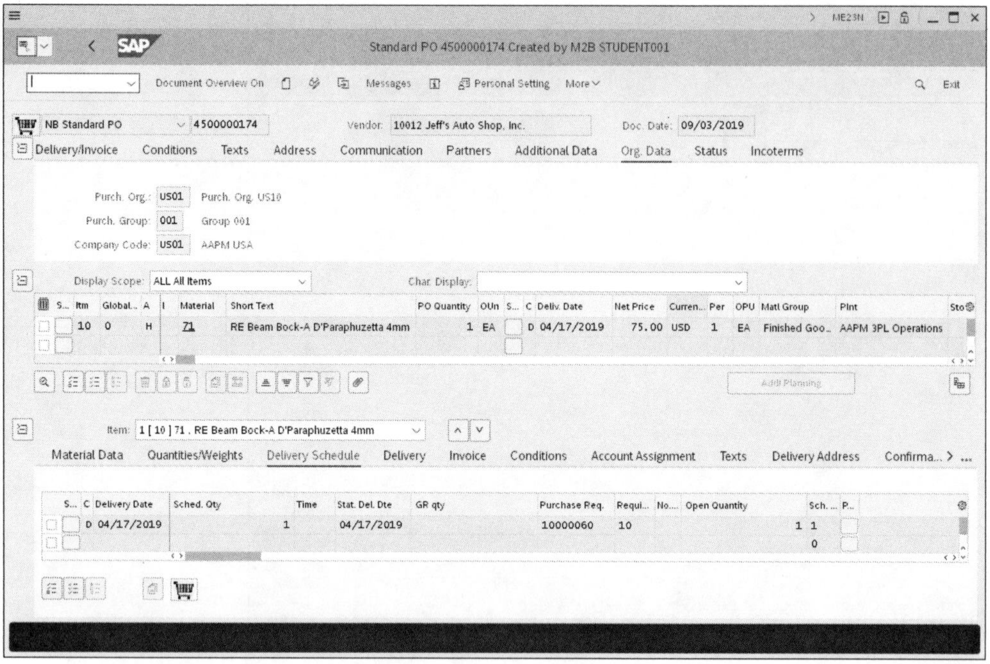

Figure 8.10 Purchase Order Display

You can also open Transaction ME23N to display the purchase order using the number from the document flow.

You can set automatic purchase orders for certain vendors; however, all purchase requisitions from this vendor would be affected, not just drop shipments and special orders.

Note

The MM transactions we've mentioned so far in this chapter include the following:

- Transaction ME53N (Display Purchase Requisitions)
- Transaction ME59N (Create Purchase Orders automatically via Purchase Requisitions)
- Transaction ME21N (Create Purchase Orders)
- Transaction ME23N (Display Purchase Orders)

8.4 Vendor Interfaces

Purchase orders is usually transferred to your suppliers/vendors electronically. Once they ship product to the requested delivery address, you'll also receive a an ASN.

Vendor interfaces are within the scope of the MM team and, while implemented for standard purchase orders, can be leveraged for drop shipping and special order scenarios. You'll work in the following interfaces for these scenarios:

- **Purchase order interfaces**
  Purchase order interfaces, commonly known by the X.12 name EDI 850, are sent from your company to the vendor. Once received, the vendor creates a sales order and starts processing the order.
- **Advanced shipping notifications**
  Once the vendor ships product to the requested delivery address, they'll put together an ASN interface to send to you, which is known by the X.12 name EDI 856. Once you receive the ASN, normally, you would create an inbound delivery document containing all the details from the ASN. This approach is implemented to facilitate the receipt of product once the product reaches the warehouse.

8.5 Statistical Goods Receipt

In drop shipping scenarios, the product won't be received at your warehouse, so you'll take the ASN and perform an operation called the *statistical goods receipt*. This operation won't affect your own inventory but does signal to the system that the PO has been "received."

The statistical goods receipt may also be performed manually once you receive notification that the vendor shipped the requested product.

The system operation required to register a statistical goods receipt is the same as a regular goods receipt. The line type of the purchase order controls whether inventory must be incremented or not.

This option is useful because a common practice is to issue invoices to the customer as soon as product is shipped. In drop shipping scenarios, this approach may only be achieved using a statistical goods receipt.

8.6 Vendor Invoice Receipt

In both drop shipping and special order scenarios, the vendor will send you an invoice after they ship product.

You would follow the same process to receive and pay for these types of invoices as you would for other purchasing scenarios, via Transaction MIRO.

Some companies prefer to issue their invoices to the customer in drop shipping scenarios after receiving the invoice from the customer. This approach eliminates the need for performing a statistical goods receipt. Depending on vendor performance in sending you notifications and invoices, this decision should be made during the blueprint phase of the implementation project.

8.7 Drop Shipment Billing

The lines on the sales order that correspond to drop shipping transactions are relevant to order-related billing. No outbound delivery documents are required, unlike standard orders and special orders. To enable order-based billing, you'll need to assign a billing document type to the sales order types (Section 6.1.1), which will be used to sell items through drop shipping.

You'll then need to configure the billing copy control for drop shipment billing (Section 8.7.2). This billing copy control is necessary to help you decide when to issue the invoice to the customer.

Finally, you'll also need to change the **Billing Relevance** indicator during the configuration of item categories (Section 6.2.10) to indicate you want to use the goods receipt quantity.

8.7.1 Sales Order Types

To configure sales document types, open Transaction VOV8 or follow the menu path **SAP Customizing Implementation Guide • Sales and Distribution • Sales • Sales Documents • Sales Document Header • Define Sales Document Types**. On the screen that opens, select the order type OR and then click the **Details** button or press [F2].

As shown in Figure 8.11, specify the default billing type to be used when creating invoices with reference to a sales order itself, as specified in the **Order-rel.bill.type** field.

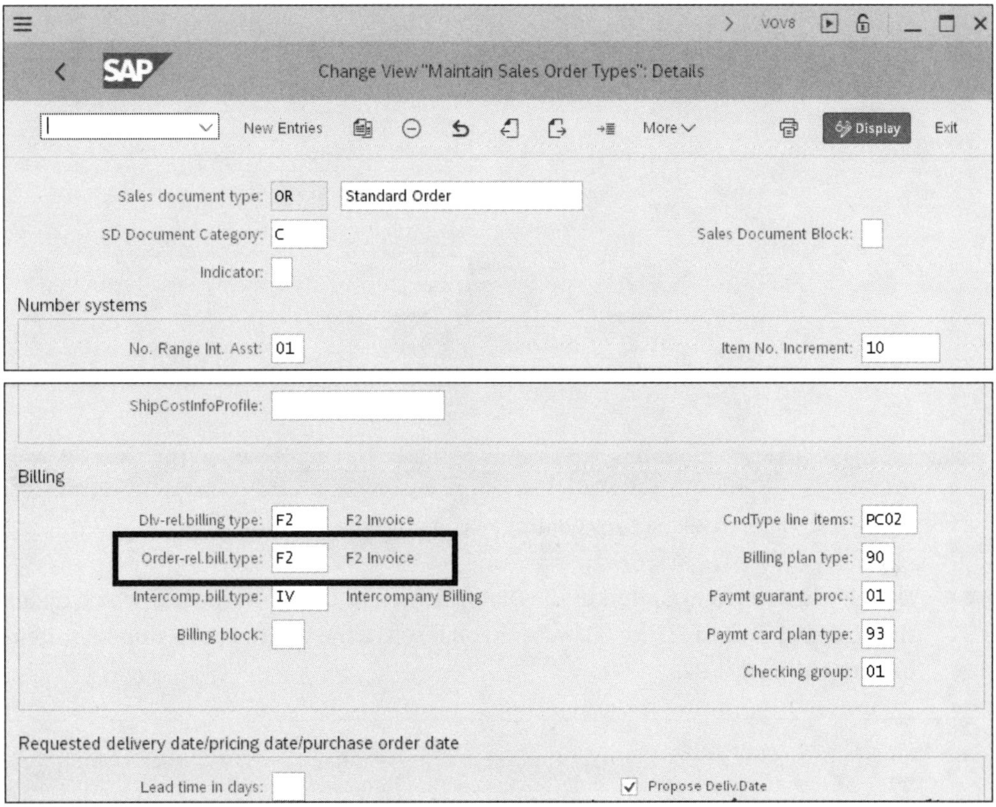

Figure 8.11 OR Sales Order/Document Type Configuration

8.7.2 Billing Copy Control for Drop Shipment Billing

To configure the sales order-to-billing document copy control, open Transaction VFTA or follow the menu path **SAP Customizing Implementation Guide • Sales and Distribution • Billing • Billing Documents • Maintain Copying Control for Billing Documents • Copying Control: Sales Document to Billing Document**.

First, as shown in Figure 8.12, select the copy control for **Source** order type **OR** (**Standard Order**) to target (**Tgt**) **Billing Type F2** (invoice).

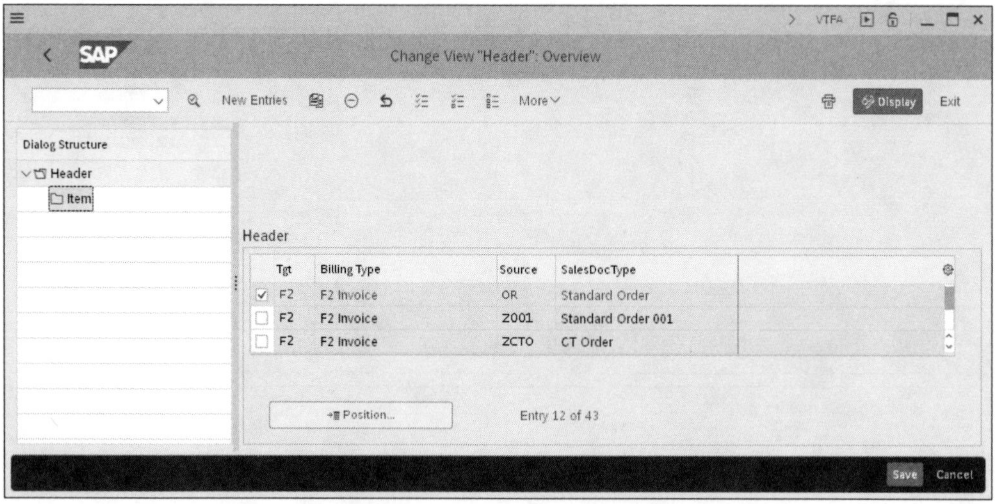

Figure 8.12 Order to Billing Copy Control: Document Type Selection

Double-click the **Item** option in the **Dialog Structure** menu on the left, which opens the screen shown in Figure 8.13 where you'll select the desired drop shipment item category (**ItmCtg**) **CB2**.

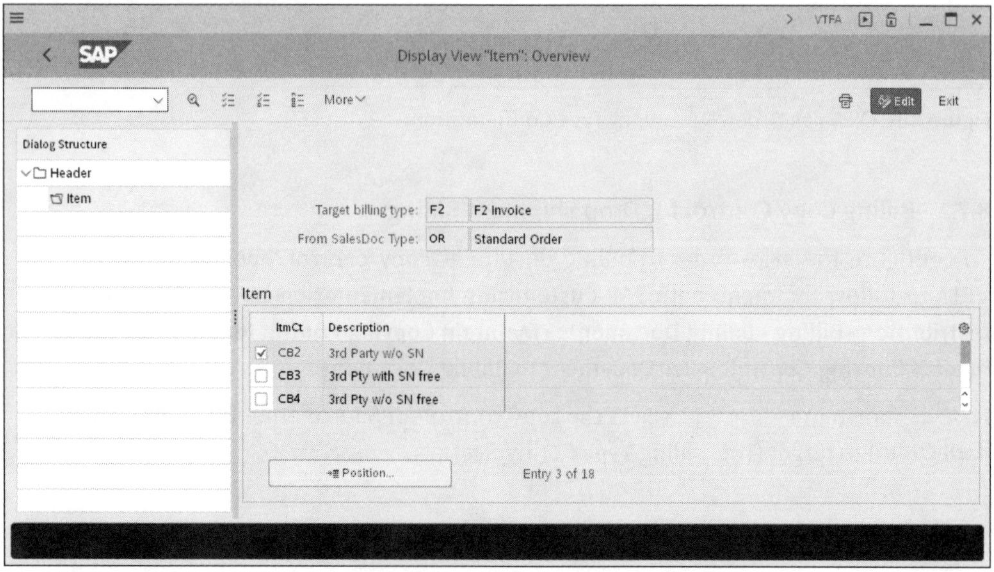

Figure 8.13 Order to Billing Copy Control: Item Category Selection

Click on the details icon, and you'll be taken to the screen shown in Figure 8.14. On this screen, you may modify when the drop shipment invoice from your company to the customer should be created by maintaining the **Billing Quantity** field.

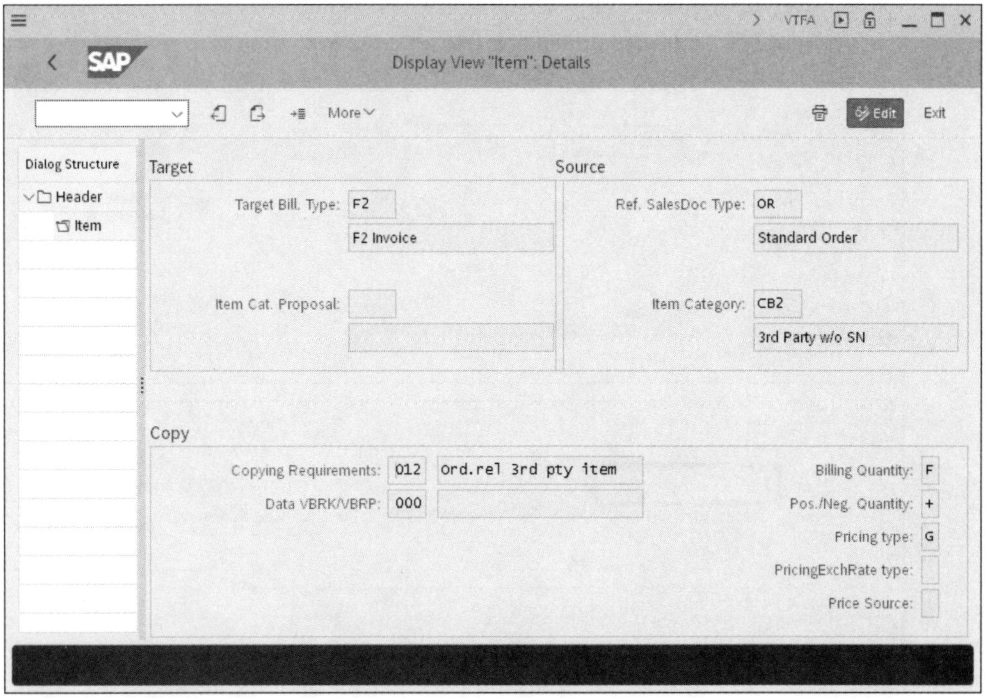

Figure 8.14 Order to Billing Copy Control: Item Category Details

By default, this field is set as **F** (invoice receipt quantity minus invoiced quantity), which requires you to receive a vendor invoice before issuing your own invoice to your customer.

Most companies prefer to issue an invoice as soon as the vendor notifies you that product has been shipped. In this case, change the **Billing Quantity** field to **E** (goods receipt quantity minus invoiced quantity).

8.7.3 Item Categories

To configure sales item categories, open Transaction VOV7 or follow the menu path **SAP Customizing Implementation Guide • Sales and Distribution • Sales • Sales**

Documents • Sales Document Item • Define Item Categories. On the screen that opens, select the item category CB2 and then click the **Details** button or press F2.

As shown in Figure 8.15, the **Billing Relevance** field indicates if a line is relevant for billing based on the vendor invoice quantity. This field comes configured out of the box using code **F** (**Order-Related Billing Doc. - Status According to Invoice Qty**).

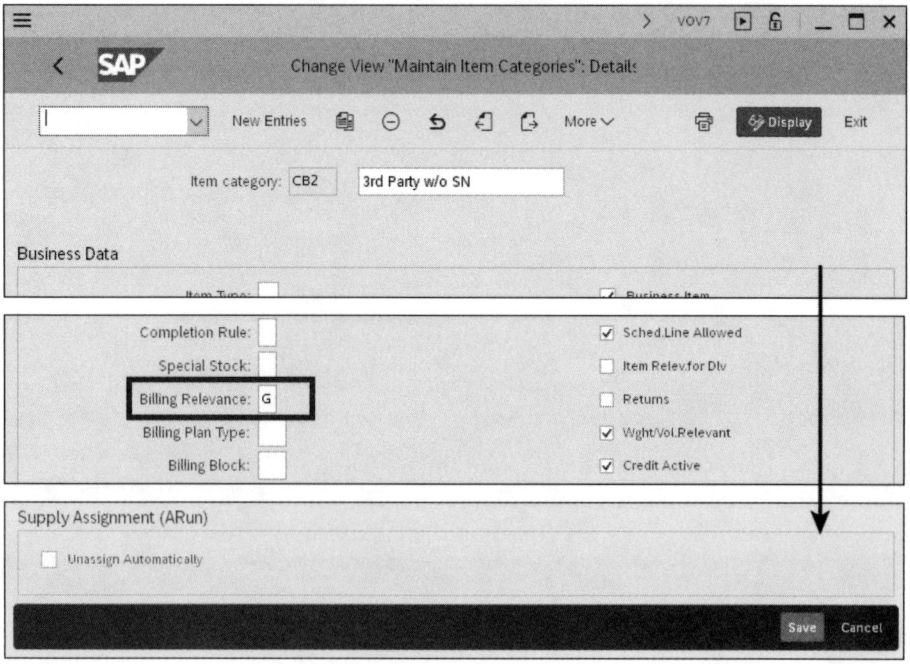

Figure 8.15 CB2 Item Category Configuration

To create a customer invoice based on a statistical goods receipt, you'll need to change the **Billing Relevance** field to **G** (**Order-Related Billing of the Delivery Quantity**), as shown in Figure 8.15.

8.8 Summary

Drop shipments are common for high-volume, low-price (low-margin) items, and special orders are common for low-volume, high-price materials as well as for custom made items. In this chapter, we covered drop shipment and special order scenarios in detail, including the related configuration steps so that you can recommend and implement these scenarios when applicable.

Chapter 9
Shipping and Delivery

In SAP ERP, sales functionalities were bundled with distribution. In SAP S/4HANA Sales, distribution functionalities are still present and still important even when using enhanced warehouse management systems (WMS). This chapter discusses distribution from a sales perspective and describes the interfaces with other functionalities necessary for delivering tangible goods to customers.

Once you're ready to process a sales order that requires the shipping of physical product, the next step is to create a delivery document. A *delivery document* contains a subset of data that is relevant for logistics. This document is created with reference to the order and is completed once product is shipped. These types of delivery documents are referred to as *outbound deliveries*, which will be the focus of this chapter.

You can also create delivery documents with reference to purchase orders (POs) and returns. These delivery documents are used to receive and put away products rather than ship products. These types of delivery documents are referred to as *inbound deliveries* (Section 9.10). For stock transfer orders (STOs), you may need both outbound and inbound deliveries created with reference to the same document (see Chapter 11 for more details).

Figure 9.1 shows a simple conceptualization of logistics processing. You may combine multiple orders into a single delivery, split a single order into multiple deliveries, interface deliveries to warehouses outside your organization, use warehouse management functionalities, etc.

After a delivery document is created, picking, packing, and shipping (post goods issue operation) will be performed. The following sections will detail each stage, including optional steps, starting with basic settings (Section 9.1); delivery documents (Section 9.2, Section 9.3, and Section 9.4); and decentralized warehouse management (Section 9.5). Then, we'll look more closely at picking (Section 9.6), packing (Section 9.7), transportation planning (Section 9.8), the post goods issue operation (Section 9.9), proof of delivery (Section 9.10), document flow (Section 9.11), and inbound deliveries (Section 9.12).

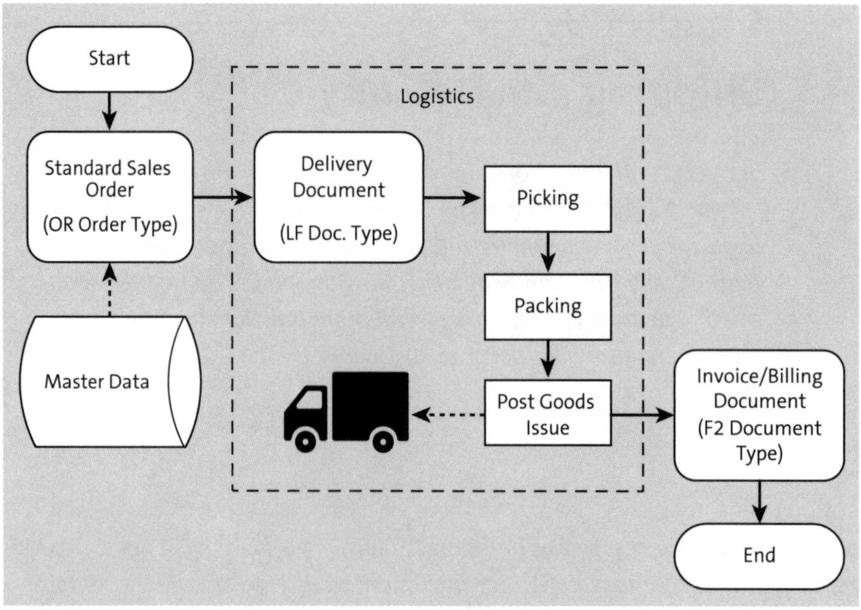

Figure 9.1 Basic Logistics Processing for Outbound Deliveries

9.1 Shipping Points

Some preliminary configuration steps are necessary to enable logistics functionalities in the system.

Logistics uses a different organizational structure element called the *shipping point*. You create shipping points when configuring the organizational structure, which we covered in Chapter 1. Before you can use shipping points, you'll need to define which shipping points are allowed for a given combination of factors (shipping conditions, loading groups, and plants).

A shipping point is assigned when a sales order is entered (either via this configuration or manually using one of the 11 manual options we'll configure later). Shipping points are also used for tax determination purposes when representing the departure point for shipments to customers. Shipping points also drive the configuration of transportation.

To assign shipping points to the shipping condition, loading group, and plant, follow the menu path **SAP Customizing Implementation Guide • Logistics Execution • Shipping • Basic Shipping Functions • Shipping Point and Goods Receiving Point**

Determination • Assign Shipping Points. On the screen that opens, click on the **New Entries** button or press F5.

On the screen shown in Figure 9.2, maintain the **SC** (shipping condition), **LGrp** (loading group), and **Plnt** (plant) fields. These details are necessary to define which shipping point should be assigned by default, also known as the *proposed shipping point* (**PrShp**) to the sales order and which shipping points may be manually selected by users (**MShPt**) also known as a *manual shipping point* (11 possible options are available). We recommend that you always think about all possible combinations and only leave out combinations that are genuinely not allowed.

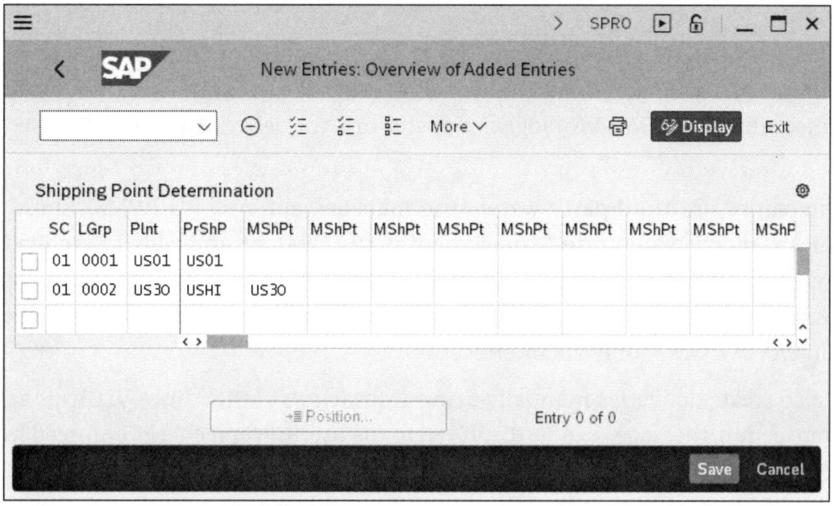

Figure 9.2 Assigning Shipping Points

A common practice is to only create assignments for wellZS-documented scenarios. This approach speeds up the configuration activity but is often the source of urgent issues after go-live. Once your users assume full ownership of the system, they may start processing new variants of the processes defined during the implementation project, which is normal and should be expected.

If certain combinations lack configured shipping points, your users won't be able to process orders. If you configure entries and include all possible shipping points as manual alternatives, you would allow for these exceptions without the need for urgent configuration.

Another recommended practice is to enter configurations for blank values in the loading group field (**LGrp**). This field is not mandatory and if no value is entered, you can still consider this scenario valid. Alternatively, you can make the field mandatory on the material master.

You can configure entries for a blank shipping condition (**SC**), but this field is mandatory both in the customer master and in the sales order. So, a blank **SC** field would only be helpful if an order is incomplete. If you have configuration set up for the blank shipping conditions, the shipping point would still be determined even when the order is incomplete (without a shipping condition).

9.2 Delivery Documents

The delivery document is typically created in the background. This system-create document is not often maintained by the sales user. If the warehouse uses inventory management in SAP S/4HANA for logistics operations, the delivery document is used daily.

Many companies use third-party warehouse management systems (WMS), standalone SAP Extended Warehouse Management (SAP EWM), or embedded Extended Warehouse Management in SAP S/4HANA (embedded EWM). The delivery document is still necessary, but even the warehouse team would not maintain this document directly in SAP S/4HANA, only via interfaces.

You can also create deliveries manually using Transaction VL01N. Since VL01N is an online transaction, messages can be displayed to the user. Several checks enforced in the background, and warning messages are displayed in Transaction VL01N so that the user has the opportunity to read these messages and take the necessary action or ignore the warning, as applicable. For example, if an order is flagged as an incomplete delivery, Transaction VL01N would allow the creation of partial deliveries and issue a message informing the user that the document is not complete.

In the following sections, we'll use Transaction VL01N to guide you through the information contained in delivery documents. The following sections are organized to match the tabs found on delivery documents, and we'll provide detailed information about each tab and walk you through the related configuration steps.

9.2.1 Create Delivery: Overview

When creating deliveries using Transaction VL01N with reference to a sales order, you must select the shipping point (**Shipping Point**), selection date (**Selection Date**), and order number (**Order**), as shown in Figure 9.3.

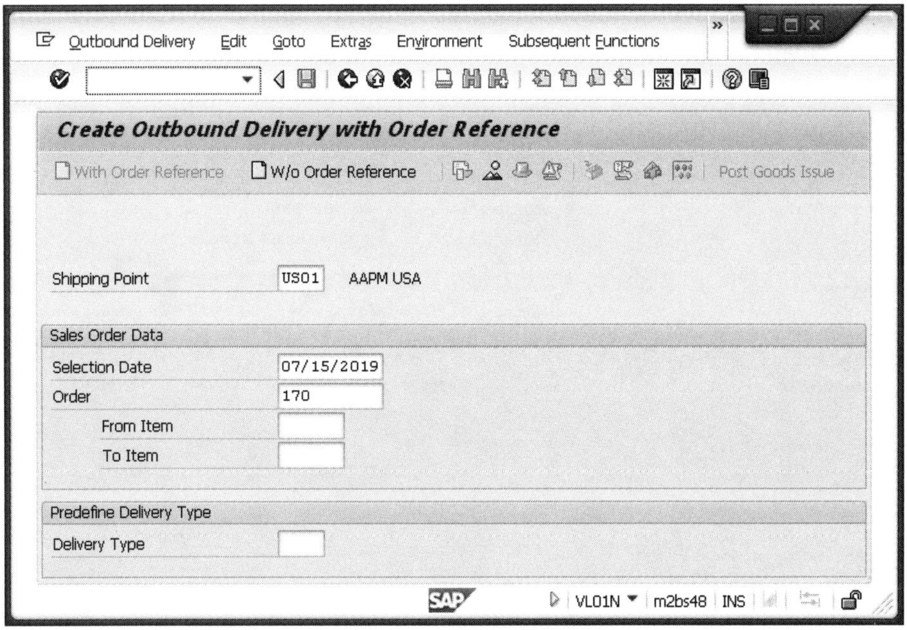

Figure 9.3 Create Delivery: Main Screen

The shipping point must be assigned to at least one of the sales lines (**Order**). You also must have at least one sales order line's (**Order**) schedule lines relevant for delivery on a date on or before the **Selection Date**; otherwise, you'll get a message saying no schedule lines are due for delivery up until that date.

You can also select a line number (**From Item** and **To Item**) interval to consider for this delivery document as well as add or delete lines before saving the delivery. The sales order type from the selected sales order is assigned with a default delivery document type using Transaction VOV8; you may select a different one using the **Delivery Type** field (Section 9.2.2 for configuration instructions).

Next, you'll use the menu options **Outbound Delivery • Delivery Sales Order** to open the **Item Overview** tab, the first of the tabs made available by default on the **Delivery Create: Overview** screen, as shown in Figure 9.4. This tab is typically used delete lines, modify quantities, and add more lines from the same or other sales orders.

The second tab (**Picking**), shown in Figure 9.5, is used by the warehouse when working with inventory management (IM) to populate the picking quantities (**Picked Qty** column). A storage location (**SLoc**) must be entered on each line, which is usually done automatically via the configuration described in Section 9.2.4. If a material is flagged for batch management on the material master data, you must also select or confirm the automatic determination of the **Batch** (lot) numbers.

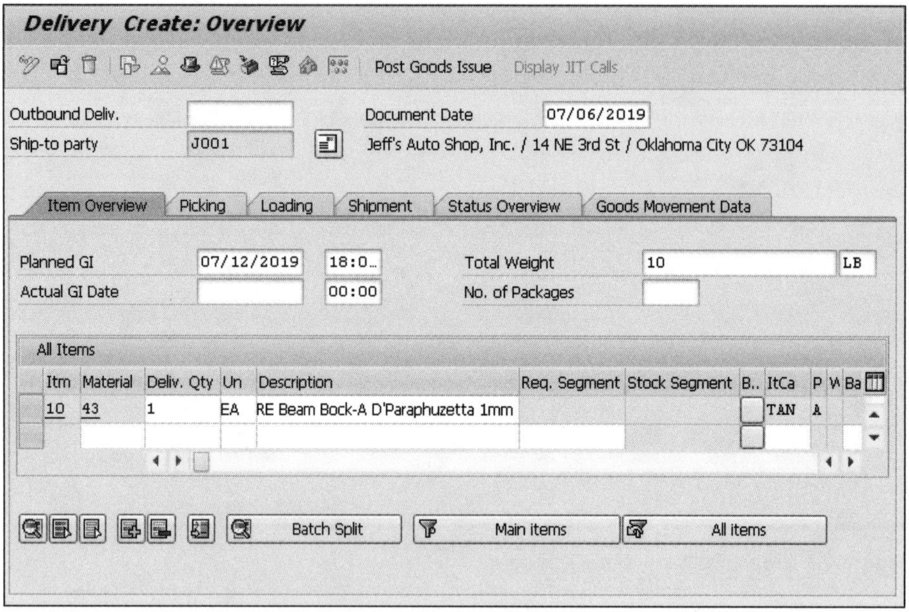

Figure 9.4 Delivery Overview Screen: Item Overview Tab

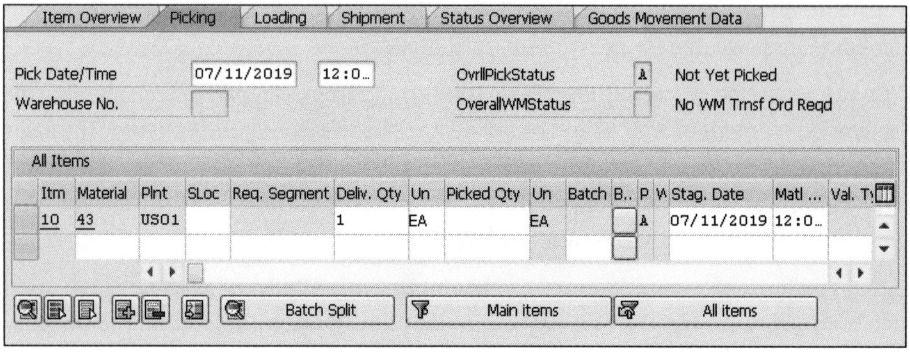

Figure 9.5 Delivery Overview: Picking Tab

For serialized materials, the serial number profile assigned to the material master may also dictate whether a serial number is assigned on the delivery document. If so, you'll need to indicate the picked serial number by selecting the lines with serialized materials one by one and using the menu options **Extras • Serial Numbers**. This step is often considered an issue by many high-volume businesses. Using WM, embedded EWM, SAP EWM, and third-party WMS, many features are available for this task to be accomplished; however many small and medium-sized businesses with few serialized materials can still opt to handle serial numbers manually.

Under the **Loading** tab, shown in Figure 9.6, you can change the gross weight and volume of each line (defaulted from the sales order and from the material master). This tab is rarely used, since most companies do not update these fields at the line level, only the total weight of the whole delivery or of each *handling unit*, which is a generic term for any kind of packing medium, during packing.

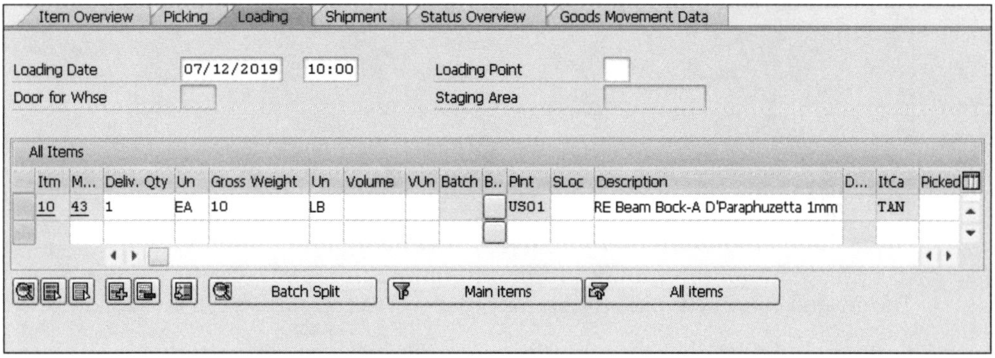

Figure 9.6 Delivery Overview: Loading Tab

The **Shipment** tab, shown in Figure 9.7, controls initial transportation planning requirements (when applicable) such as **Route** assignment at the header level.

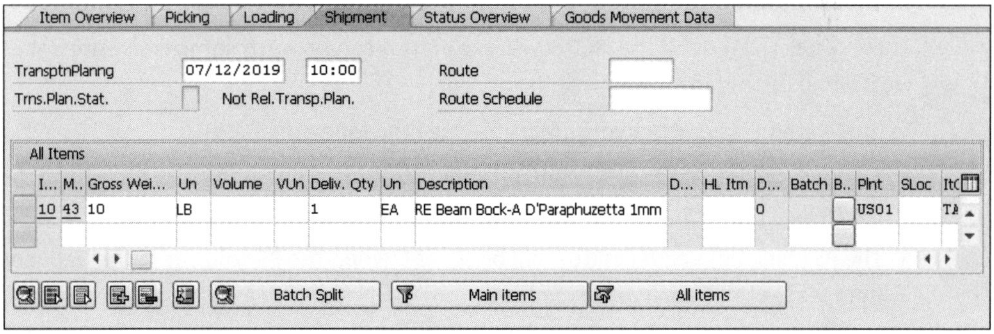

Figure 9.7 Delivery Overview: Shipment Tab

Under the **Status Overview** tab, shown in Figure 9.8, you can view the status for all subsequent activities this delivery may be subject to. Once you learn to interpret these status codes and understand what each column represents, you can tell which steps still need to take place and which have already been completed.

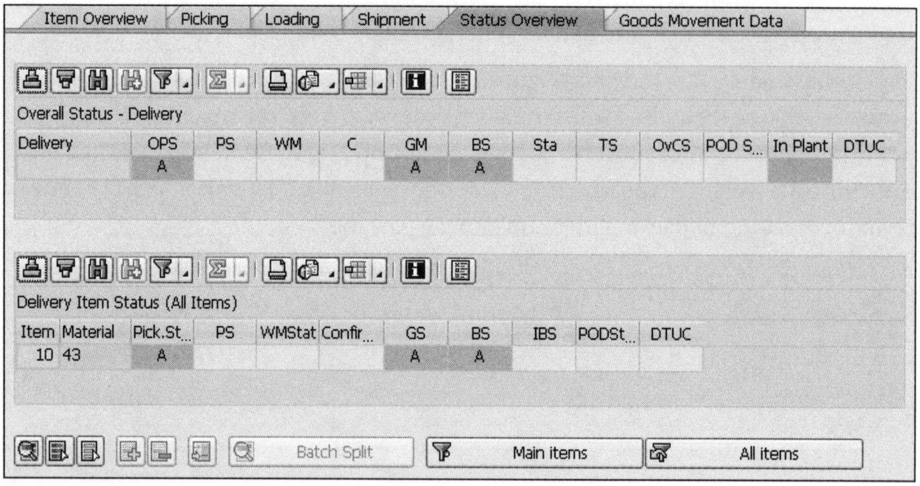

Figure 9.8 Delivery Overview: Status Overview Tab

The general concept behind the status codes you see on this screen is as follows:

- Blank: Indicates that the status is not applicable; whenever a status is blank, the activity is not relevant and cannot be executed for this delivery.
- **A**: indicates the status is applicable but the activity has not yet been completed.
- **B**: indicates that the activity has been partially executed but not yet completed.
- **C**: indicates the activity has been completed.

These codes apply to all the status you see on this screen, with some exceptions that we'll detail further in subsequent lists.

In the **Overall Status – Delivery** area, you'll see the following fields:

- The **OPS** (overall picking) header status will be set as **C** when the **Pick.St.** column in the **Delivery Item Status (All Items)** area is set as **C** (complete).
- The **PS** (packing) header status will be set as **C** when the **PS** column in the **Delivery Item Status (All Items)** area is set as **C**.
- The **WM** (warehouse management) header status will be set as **C** when the **WMStat** column in the **Delivery Item Status (All Items)** area is set as **C**.
- The **C** (pick confirmation) header status will be set as **C** when the **Confir** column in the **Delivery Item Status (All Items)** area is set as **C**.

- The **GM** (goods movement) header status will be set as **C** when the **GS** column in the **Delivery Item Status (All Items)** area is set as **C**.
- The **BS** (billing) header status will be set as **C** when the **BS** column in the **Delivery Item Status (All Items)** area is set as **C**.
- The **Sta** (total status): When no more statuses are pending completion, i.e., when header statuses **OPS**, **PS**, **WM**, **C**, **GM**, and **BS** are set as either blank or **C**, this header status will be set as **C**.
- The **TS** (transportation planning) header status will be set as **C** when you create a shipment document for this delivery.
- The **OvCS** (overall credit) header status will be set as **C** if credit checks are active on this delivery document and the document has been approved for credit. If the delivery has been manually released, this header status will be set as **D**.
- The **POD** (proof of delivery) status will be set as **C** when the **PODst** column in the **Delivery Item Status (All Items)** area is set as **C**.
- The **In Plant** field relates to vendor processes as defined by the MM team. This field will affect the behavior of the inbound shipment document "registration" status.
- The **DTUC** (delivery-related trading unit change) header status will be set as **C** when the **DTUC** column in the **Delivery Item Status (All Items)** area is set as **C**.

In the **Delivery Item Status (All Items)** area, you'll see the following fields:

- **Item** (delivery document line number)
- **Material** (material number)
- The **Pick** (picking) status will be set as **C** once you enter a picked quantity on the delivery line.
- The **PS** (packing) status will be set as **C** once a line was been packed by a handling unit.
- The **WM** (warehouse management) status will be set as **C** once a transfer order is created and confirmed, following all the steps defined by the WMS or embedded EWM configuration.
- The **Confir** (WM or embedded EWM configuration picking/putaway confirmation) status will be set as **C** once the WMS or embedded EWM configuration transfer order is confirmed.
- The **GS** (goods movement) status will be set as **C** after the post goods issue operation for this delivery line has been completed.

- The **BS** (billing) status will be set as **C** once an invoice is created with reference to this delivery line.
- The **IBS** (intercompany billing) status will be set as **C** once an intercompany billing document is created with reference to this delivery line.
- The **POD** (proof of delivery) status will be set as **C** once you register that a product has been delivered at the customer's ship-to location.
- The **DTUC** (delivery-related trading unit change) status relates to a feature that allows for a change of ownership of batches; once completed, this status will be set as **C**.

The **Goods Movement Data** tab, shown Figure 9.9, contains details regarding the stock movement document that is/was created at the time of the post goods issue operation. The movement type (**M...**) is attached to the schedule line category (601 is the default out-of-the box movement type for sales/cost of goods sold).

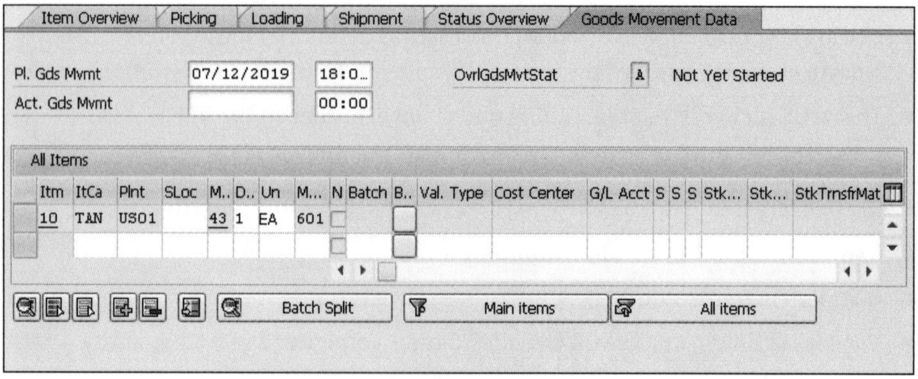

Figure 9.9 Delivery Overview: Goods Movement Data Tab

In the delivery document, you'll find an item category, similar to what we described for sales orders in Chapter 6, Section 6.2.10. We'll discuss how the item category controls the behavior of delivery document in Section 9.2.5.

9.2.2 Defining Delivery Document Types

To configure delivery document types, open Transaction EC23 or Transaction OVLK or follow the menu path **SAP Customizing Implementation Guide • Logistics Execution • Shipping • Deliveries • Define Delivery Types**.

Using Transaction OVLK, once you locate the delivery document type LF, you would select the corresponding line. Then, click on the details icon to display the configuration. Using Transaction EC23, all fields will be available on the initial screen; you can still select a line and display its details, but the same fields would be displayed only in a different format.

In our example shown in Figure 9.10, we're displaying a delivery document of type LF, which is the most commonly used delivery document type for product sales. Commonly, companies create new delivery types, but doing so is usually not required.

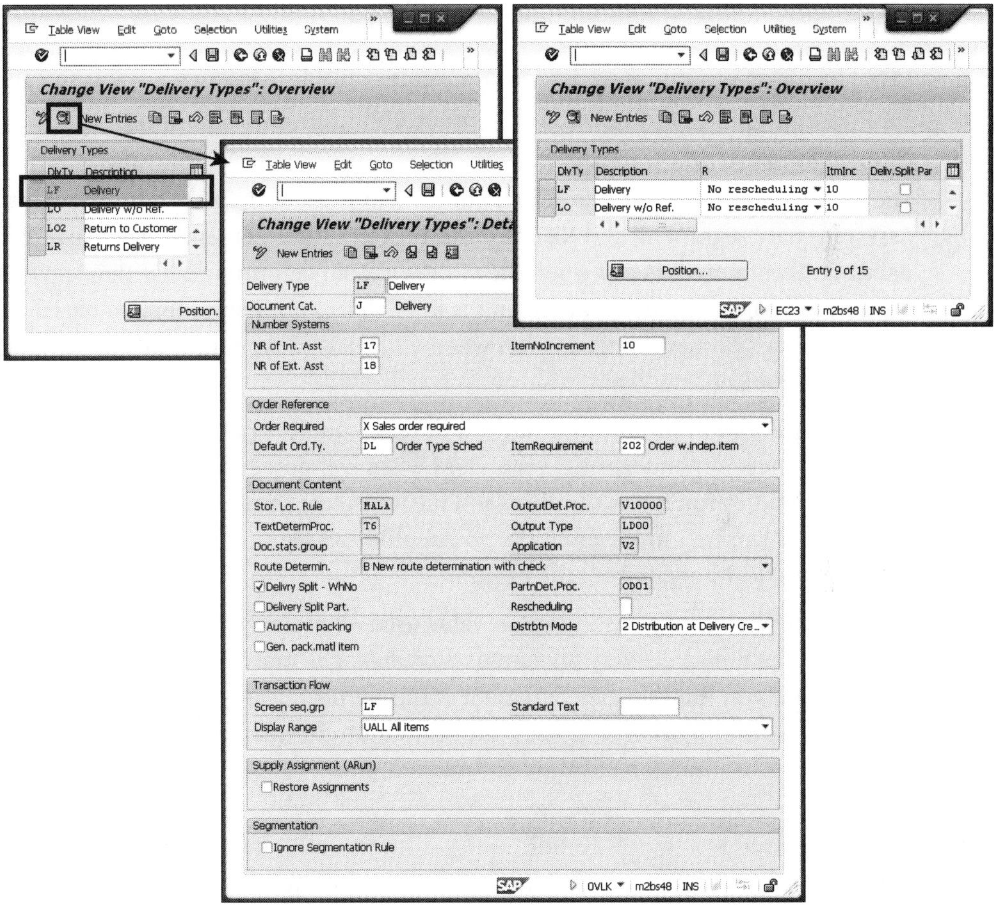

Figure 9.10 Displaying Delivery Document Type LF

Using either Transaction OVLK or EC23, specify a four-character delivery document type (**DlvTy**) and a description (**Description**). In the example shown in Figure 9.10, we aren't creating a new delivery document type, but instead displaying delivery document type LF, which is provided by SAP out of the box.

The document category code (**Document Cat.**) is used in several SAP Standard transactions and functions to drive critical functionalities. This value can be understood as a "type of document type." For instance, if you use "J," the system will know that this document type is for outbound deliveries that can be modified using Transaction VL02N. If you use "T" or "7," the system will know this document type is for inbound deliveries.

In the following sections, we'll describe the fields available in each area of this screen.

Number Systems

The number range used for this delivery document must be defined in the **NR of Int. Asst** (internal assignment) and **NR of Ext. Asst** (external assignment) fields. An internal assignment range is used when the system should determine what the delivery document number should be, based on the last delivery number generated plus one. An external assignment range is used when you want to type in what the delivery document number should be.

In Section 9.2.3, we'll describe in detail how to set up number ranges for delivery documents. We recommend using the standard whenever possible. High-volume companies commonly run out of numbers and must increase the size of the intervals for their ranges. During implementation, you should foresee this problem happening and increase the intervals from the beginning.

The **ItemNoIncrement** field is a numeric value used when the system assigns the item number at the time a delivery document is created. The first line will be 0 plus this number and every line takes an increment of this number. The out-of-the box configuration uses increments of 10 to allow for subitems to be created. This field may also be maintained Transaction EC23, in the **ItmInc** column.

Order Reference

You'll use the **Order Required** flag to control whether you can create delivery documents with this type without specifying the original sales document.

If you allow delivery documents to be created without reference to a sales document, the system will create a dummy entry on the sales order tables along with the delivery document. That entry will have the sales order type as specified in the **Default Ord. Ty**. field and will obey the requirement conditions defined by the **Item-Requirement** field in Transaction VOFM (ABAP code written using the forms found in Transaction VOFM).

Document Content

In the **Document Content** area of this screen, you'll see the following fields:

- The **Stor. Loc. Rule** field is a code that represents the method of determining the storage location on the delivery document lines. MALA is the default for outbound deliveries; it uses the configuration described in Section 9.6.
- The **OutputDet.Proc.** field is the output determination procedure assigned to this delivery document type. The **Output Type** is the default output format for this delivery type to be used if the user requests a printout without specifying the output type. Along with the **Application** code, it identifies the relevant forms used to print/email/fax/EDI this delivery document to users, customer, or other systems. See the Chapter 4, Section 4.7, for details.
- The **TextDetermProc.** field is the text determination procedure assigned to this delivery document type. See Chapter 6, Section 6.3.10, for details.
- The **Doc.stats.group** field controls when you consider this delivery type complete from a statistical analysis (reporting) perspective whenever you want to overwrite the default transactional status settings. This field is used by the logistics information systems (LIS) reporting.
- The **Route Determin.** field indicates the type of route determination approach to be used for this delivery type; you may either use the route as assigned to the sales order or determine a new one using the delivery information to find the most appropriate one (for instance, utilizing weight groups, which tends to be more accurate).
- The **Delivry Split - WhNo** field, whether using SAP EWM, embedded EWM, or a third-party WMS, must be defined with an organization structure element called a *warehouse number*. When required, you will often define multiple warehouse numbers per shipping point. By checking this flag, you're indicating that the warehouse number must be used as a split criterion. In other words, you would now create a single delivery document with lines belonging to different warehouse numbers. This feature allows you to use the delivery number to perform more warehouse management functionality; otherwise, you must use a transfer order

that represents a subset of the delivery document. These deliveries are likely to be only partially processed when using transfer orders.

- The **PartnDet.Proc.** field is the partner determination procedure assigned to this delivery document type. The business partner/customer describes partner function and procedure configuration.
- The **Delivery Split Part.** flag indicates that the partner functions included on the partner determination procedure assigned to this delivery must be used as a split criterion. In other words, if the orders used to create a delivery have different partners, these orders won't be combined, and you would create multiple delivery documents with matching partners.
- The **Rescheduling** field controls whether the delivery documents pending processing are relevant for backorder rescheduling. This feature is useful when you configure the system to create deliveries based on expected availability (ATP check). The rescheduling process will confirm or adjust availability based on actual stock quantities. This field may also be maintained with Transaction EC23 under column **R**.
- The **Automatic Packing** field activates a system feature that proposes packaging. Companies that use this feature invest in material master data set up. The proposed packaging is made available to the warehouse team, who are expected to follow this direction. Most companies that perform packing in the system tend to leave this field open and manually indicate how the product was packed, leaving this flag unchecked.
- The **Gen. Pack. Matl. Item** field is used when you bill the customer for packaging materials. After packing, the packaging material (cardboard box, metal crates, pallets, containers, etc.) is added to the delivery document as a new line and is later copied into the billing document (invoice).
- The **Distrbtn Mode** field is used to control when the delivery documents should be sent to a decentralized warehouse system.

Transaction Flow

In the **Transaction Flow** area of this screen, you'll see the following fields:

- The **Screen seq.grp** field is a code that represents the screen layout used in the delivery document maintenance transactions: Transaction VL01N (Create), Transaction VL02N (Modify), and Transaction VL03N (Display).

- The **Standard Text** field is maintained in Transaction SO10. Once assigned in this field, you can program output forms to print its contents. Different text can be defined for each delivery document type.
- The **Display Range** field indicates which of the delivery document lines are to be displayed by default. For structure items (sales BOM, configurable materials, etc.), this field may be used to hide components by default (UHAU). They user would have to use the **Select All Lines** button to switch this to display all the lines (UALL). Most companies use UALL for delivery like the image above because the components are relevant for picking other warehouse operations.

Supply Assignment

The **Restore Assignment** field is part of the allocation run functionality, traditionally part of the SAP Apparel and Footwear industry solution. When checked, the changes may to the delivery are updated back to the sales order with the corresponding supply assignment code.

Segmentation

The **Ignore Segmentation Rule** field is part of the segmentation strategy maintenance functionality within advanced available to promise (ATP). When checked the delivery will ignore the segmentation. This approach is used for special types of delivery documents that are exempt from the ATP rules for segmentation of inventory and availability. See Chapter 7 for details.

9.2.3 Number Ranges for Delivery Documents

To configure number ranges for delivery documents types, open Transaction VN01 or follow the menu path **SAP Customizing Implementation Guide • Logistics Execution • Shipping • Deliveries • Define Number Ranges for Deliveries.** On the screen that opens, click on the display **Intervals** button.

Note this menu path leads you to the same configuration transaction used for sales orders number ranges; the number range object (**RV_BELEG**) is used for all types of sales documents (orders, deliveries, billing documents, etc.)

In our example, on the Transaction VN01 screen, shown in Figure 9.11, we're displaying the internal (**17**) and external (**18**) number range assigned to the delivery document type LF.

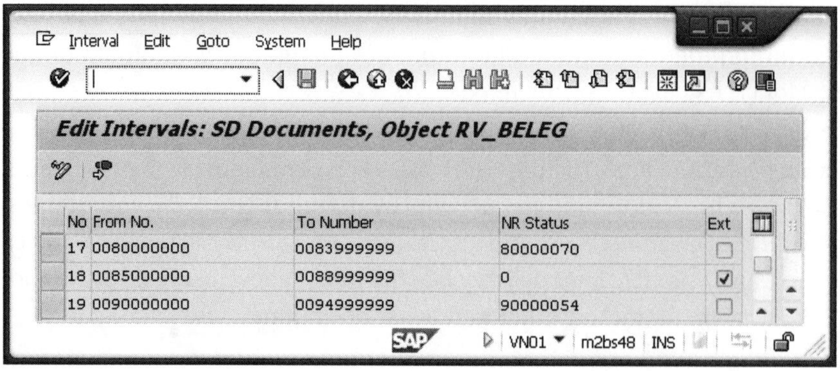

Figure 9.11 Displaying Delivery Documents Number Range Intervals

On this screen, browse for the desired number range code (**No**). Document numbers start with (**From No.**) and are incremented by one until the upper limit (**To Number**) is reached. The **NR Status** field shows the last number used for this number range; in our example, the last document number created was 80000070, so the next document you create will be 80000071.

The **Ext** column indicates if this range should be used for internally assigned number ranges (the system controls what the next document number should be) or externally assigned number ranges (entered by the user).

Having number ranges for externally assigned document numbers implements a validation check that prevents users from selecting a number that could conflict with an internally assigned range, which would cause a short dump.

9.2.4 Assigning Picking Locations

To assign storage locations for picking, follow the menu path **SAP Customizing Implementation Guide • Logistics Execution • Shipping • Picking • Determine Picking Location • Assign Picking Locations.**

As shown in Figure 9.12, identify the storage location (**SLoc**) to be used for picking (also known as the picking location) to the shipping point (**ShPt**), plant (**Plnt**), and storage conditions (**SC**). During configuration, often, the **SC** field is confused with the shipping condition, which is incorrect. Storage conditions are in the material master under the plant data and classify a material according to special storage requirements, such as refrigeration, special dimensions, weights, etc.

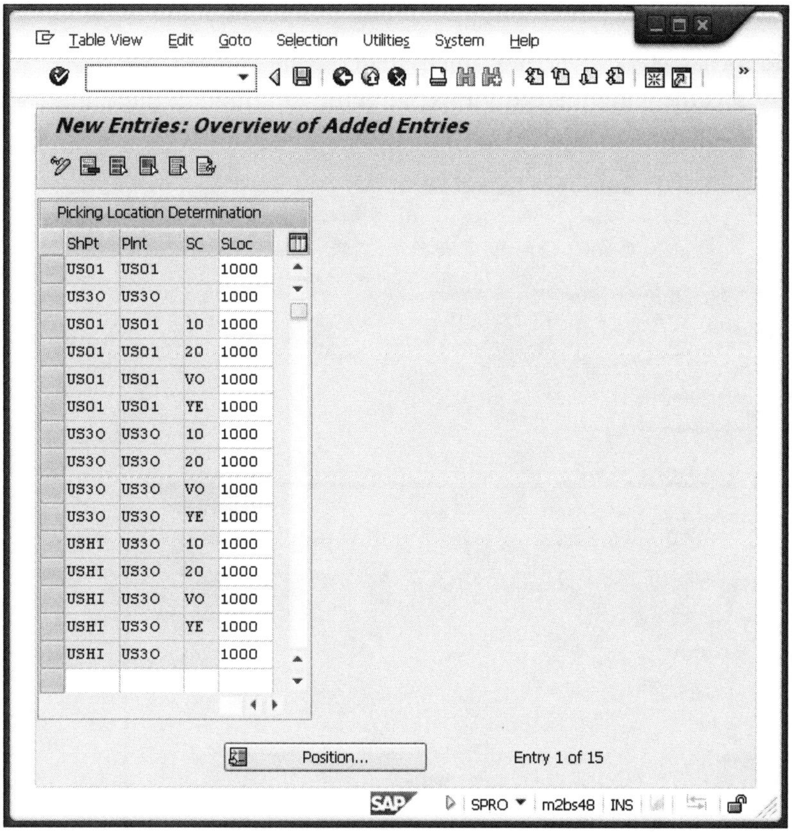

Figure 9.12 Assigning a Picking Location

You should assign values to blank storage conditions (**SC**) since this field is not mandatory on the material master.

9.2.5 Item Categories for Deliveries

To configure item categories for delivery documents, open Transaction OVLP or follow the menu path **SAP Customizing Implementation Guide • Logistics Execution • Shipping • Deliveries • Define Item Categories for Deliveries**.

In our example shown in Figure 9.13, we're displaying the delivery document item category TAN, which is the most commonly used item category for product sales. You'll regularly use item category TAN for deliveries as for sales orders, and this screen contains the details for that item category affecting logistics.

On the initial screen, follow these steps:

❶ Specify a four-character delivery document item category (**ItCa**). Once you locate the delivery document item category TAN, select the corresponding line.

❷ Click on the details icon to display the configuration details.

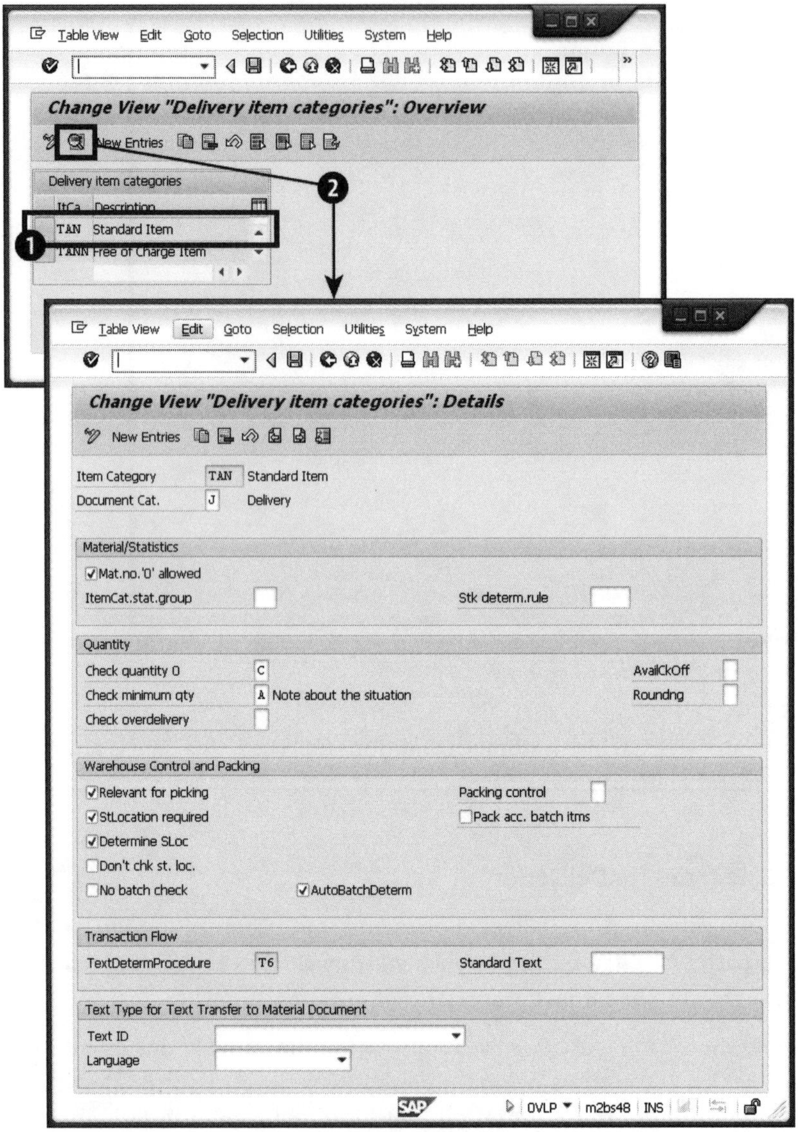

Figure 9.13 Displaying Delivery Document Item Category TAN

The document category (**Document Cat.**) is a code used in several transactions and functions by SAP S/4HANA to drive critical functionalities. This category tends to always match the category assigned to the header. In other words, inbound delivery item categories (T) are assigned to inbound delivery types (T) and outbound items (J) to outbound types (J).

In the following sections, we'll describe the fields available in each area of this screen.

Material/Statistics

In the **Material/Statistics** area of this screen, you'll see the following fields:

- The **Mat. No. '0' Allowed** flag indicates that users may leave the material number blank on a delivery document line with this item category.
- The **ItemCat.stat.group** indicates the type of transaction for statistical analysis reporting. You have two possible values (order or returns), which simplifies the understanding of delivery documents.
- The **Stk determ.rule** field allows you to use stock determination rules when allocating stock to this delivery document line; if not in use, you would use a standard ATP check allocation.

Quantity

In the **Quantity** area of this screen, you'll see the following fields:

- The **Check quantity 0** flag controls whether you want to create delivery lines without quantity. This approach is used by companies that want all sales order lines to appear on the delivery regardless of whether any quantity will be delivered. This approach would allow you to print an invoice reflecting all sales order lines, and the quantity of zero would take care of calculating the corresponding sales order value. The customer should be aware that you have other lines on their purchase order that you're still processing. Companies that adopt this approach also show quantities that were already delivered for these lines and backorder quantities that will be delivered in the future.

  Most companies enter "C" in this field, which avoids delivery lines without quantities.
- The **AvailCkOff** field allows you to turn off the ATP check for this item category, so even if no stock is available, you would still allow the order line with full quantity to appear on the delivery. This approach is used for lines corresponding to services, fees, or other financial charges that you want copies to the delivery document for inclusion along with the product on the customer invoice.

- The **Check minimum qty** field indicates whether you want to enforce the minimum order quantity maintained on the material master data on this delivery document. If not enough stock is available to fulfill the minimum order quantity requirement, the delivery line would not be created with that quantity.
- The **Roundng** field indicates whether you want to round the delivery quantity up or down. Rounding is used when delivering products based on dimensions or volumetric units of measurement and depends on customer approval as documented in the customer master data.
- The **Check overdelivery** field indicates how you want the system to behave when the delivery quantity is greater than the ordered quantity.

Warehouse Control and Packing

In the **Warehouse Control and Packing** area of this screen, you'll see the following fields:

- The **Relevant for picking** flag indicates if picking is required or not. Some companies do not recognize the value of the picked quantity line by line on the delivery and remove this flag. However, the downside is inaccurate delivery quantities.

  Ideally, you must only remove this flag when taking other reliable measures to ensure the picked quantity is accurate before product can be shipped.
- The **Packing control** field controls whether the packing operation must be performed, may or may not be performed, or if you don't allow packing at all. Packing in SAP is a time-consuming step, and some warehouses opt to not execute packing to improve cycle times. These businesses, however, have lower customer satisfaction and may encounter difficulties in providing accurate tracking information electronically, leading to a subpar customer experience.
- The **Pack acc. batch items** flag, when checked, indicates that you may pack the delivery quantity for a given line into handling unit regardless of the batch numbers they use. Using batch split functionality, you may split a single delivery line across multiple batches. If the flag is checked, when you perform packing, you would not need to worry which batch is in which box, thus speeding up the packing operation by the warehouse while maintaining acceptable parcel traceability from the customer standpoint.
- The **StLocation required** flag indicates that you need to indicate the storage location (**Sloc**) on delivery lines with this item category. If you remove flag, the **Sloc** field can be blank.

- The **Determine Sloc** flag indicates that you want the system to propose a picking storage location according to the configuration described in Section 9.2.4.
- The **Don't chk st. loc.** flag turns off a master data check that takes place once the storage location is entered, designed to ensure that the material has been extended to the selected storage location. This option is used for inbound deliveries when the movement type is configured to create the master data automatically when the goods receipt is processed.
- The **No batch check** flag turns off the batch master data check for the batch number entered in the delivery line.
- The **AutoBatchDeterm** flag enables an automated batch determination based on rules. This approach is used when the system picks the batch that the warehouse must ship. Logistics often dislikes this method because they would not only have pick the correct product from the shelf but also browse through the various batches to find the correct batch. Most companies leave the batch field blank on the delivery document and register the batch picked on the delivery using radio frequency (RF) guns and other automation features.

Transaction Flow

In the **Transaction Flow** area of this screen, you'll see the following fields:

- The **TextDetermProcedure** field is the text determination procedure assigned to this delivery document item category. See Chapter 6, Section 6.3.10, for more details.
- The **Standard Text** field is maintained in Transaction SO10. Once assigned, you can program output forms to print contents out. This feature allows for different texts to be defined for each delivery document item category.

Text Type for Text Transfer to Material Document

In the **Text Type for Text Transfer to Material Document** area of this screen, you'll see the following fields:

- The **Text ID** field is the text ID within the assigned text determination procedure that will contain freeform text that must be copied over to the post goods issue stock movement document.
- The **Language** field specifies the language in which the **Text ID** field is maintained for use when copying the freeform text to the post goods issue stock movement document.

9.3 Create Delivery: Header Details

The delivery header detail tabs contain more information in addition to the overview tabs we've covered so far. You'll often use these header detail tabs to maintain data on the delivery. We'll call out some common uses for each tab in the following sections.

9.3.1 Processing

Companies use the **Processing** tab of the delivery, shown in Figure 9.14, after identifying issues, such as delays, to determine where in the process the problem occurred and to define who should be contacted to resolve the issue.

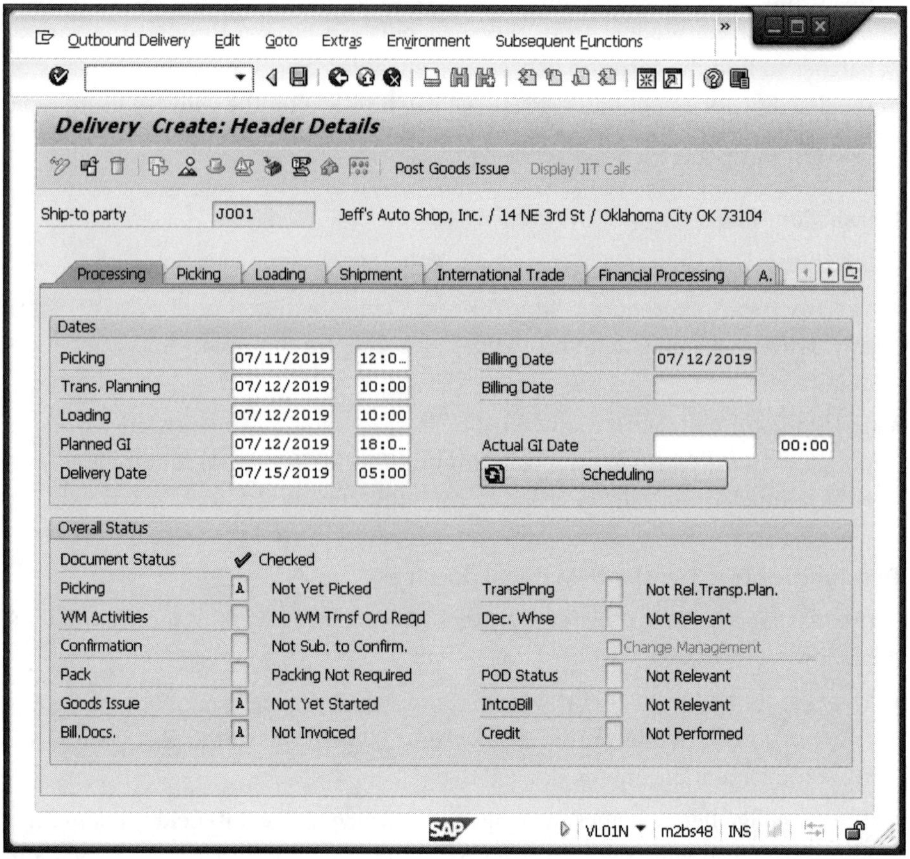

Figure 9.14 Delivery Document Header Processing Tab

The **Processing** tab displays status information regarding the delivery document as a whole, including the following fields:

- The dates in the **Dates** section are determined based on lead time configuration of the shipping point and routes. These dates may be used as a guideline to manage warehouse and transportation activity. These fields can also be used in reports as key performance indicators (KPIs):
  - The **Picking** field is the date and time when you forecast picking to be completed by the warehouse crew and registered in the system. By this date/time, the product must be off the shelves and ready for packing.
  - The **Trans. Planning** field is the date and time when you forecast transportation planning activities to be completed. This date may start right after picking and run in parallel with packing and loading.
  - The **Loading** field is the date and time when you forecast packing and loading to be completed by the warehouse crew and registered in the system. By this date/time, the product must be packed, labeled, and inside the vessel that will later transport the product out of the warehouse.
  - The **Planned GI** field is the date and time when you forecast the shipment to depart your warehouse shipping docks and registered in the system during the post goods issue operation (commonly referred to as the "planned PGI date"). By this date/time, the product must be moving towards the ship-to customer address.
  - The **Actual GI Date** field is the date and time when you actually register the shipment of product (also known as the "PGI date").
  - The **Delivery Date** field is the date and time when you forecast the customer will receive the product at the ship-to address location. By this date/time, the product must be physically located at the customer's facility.
  - The **Scheduling** button recalculates dates and times. When you have delays, this button may be useful for providing customer service with an updated forecast.
  - The **Billing Date** field is typically determined based on the planned PGI date. This date is when you should be able to create an invoice (as soon as product is shipped). Depending on system configuration and master data, you can change this behavior, such as using invoicing dates on the customer master.
  - Note that two **Billing Date** fields exist; the second field is used for intercompany billing and is populated for intercompany transactions (when the company code from the sales organization is different than the company code from the plant).

- Most fields in the **Overall Status** section can also be consulted on the **Status Overview** tab. The status codes share the same convention as discussed in Section 1.2.1. The fields found in this section include the following:
  - The **Document Status** field indicates, in an icon format, that this delivery document was validated by the system and may be used to guide logistics operations. You can deactivate this check if logistics takes place in external systems.
  - The **Picking** header status will be set as **C** when all delivery lines **Picking** status are set as **C**.
  - The **TransPlnng** (transportation planning) header status will be set as **C** when you create a shipment document for this delivery.
  - The **WM Activities** (warehouse management) header status will be set as **C** when all delivery lines **WM Activities** are set as **C**.
  - The **Dec. Whse** header status will be set as **A** when this delivery is to be sent to a different system, outside this SAP environment, using the decentralized warehouse functionality. After the product is sent, this status will be set as **B**. After you receive confirmation that product was shipped, this status will be set as **C**.
  - The **Confirmation** header status will be set as **C** when all delivery lines of **Confirmation** status are set as **C**.
  - The **Pack** (packing) header status will be set as **C** when all delivery lines of **Pack** status are set as **C**.
  - The **POD Status** (proof of delivery) header status will be set as **C** when all delivery lines of **POD** status are set as **C**.
  - The **Goods Issue** (goods movement) header status will be set as **C** when all delivery lines of **Goods Issue** status are set as **C**.
  - The **IntcoBill** (intercompany billing) header status will be set as **C** when all delivery lines of **Interco.BS** status are set as **C**.
  - The **Bill.Docs.** (billing) header status will be set as **C** when all delivery lines **Billing Doc.** of status are set as **C**.
  - The **Credit** (overall credit) header status will be set as **C** if credit checks are active on this delivery document and the document has been approved for credit. If the delivery has been manually released, this header status will be set as **D**.

9.3.2 Picking

The header **Picking** tab, shown in Figure 9.15, shows summarized information about the picking process for the delivery.

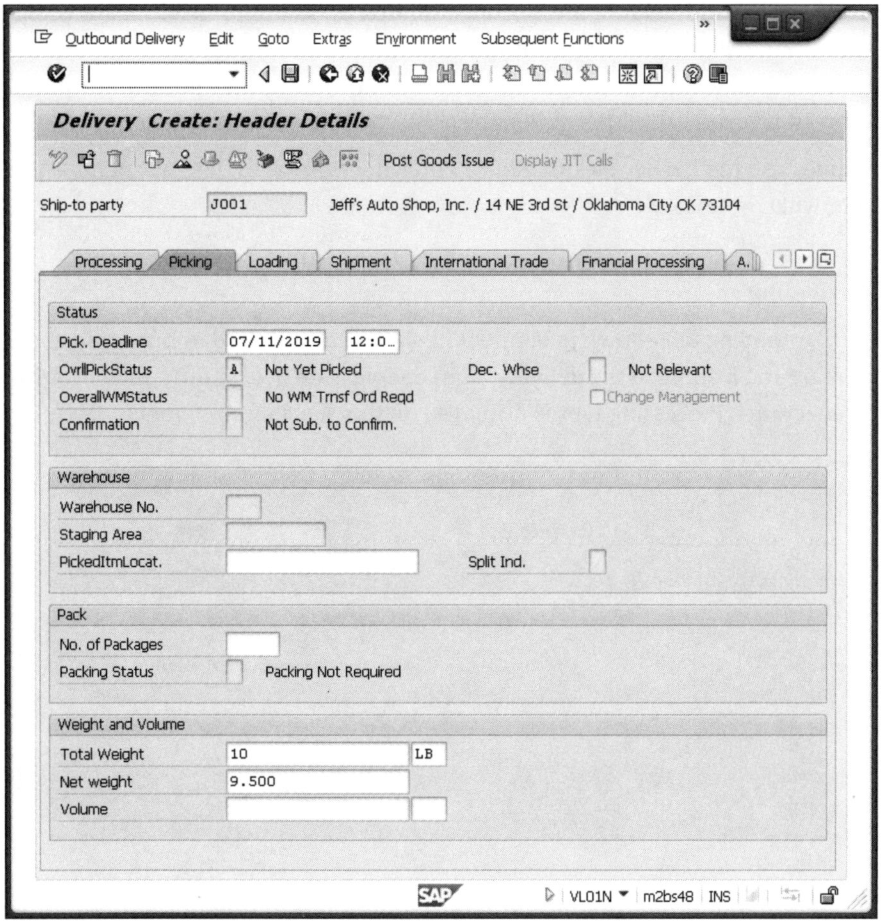

Figure 9.15 Delivery Picking Header Tab

Picking-related statuses shown under the **Status Overview** and **Processing** tabs are displayed on this screen for reference. You can consult the warehouse number (**Warehouse No.**), staging area (**Staging Area**), and picked item location (**PickedItm.Locat**) fields as assigned/determined by the WMS or embedded EWM configuration. The split indicator flag (**Split Ind.**) flag controls whether the delivery will be fulfilled from more than one warehouse number. The **No. of Packages** field contains the number of handling units used to pack products contained in this delivery. This value may be entered manually even if the packing operation is not performed using the corresponding system function. The packing status shown under the **Status Overview** and **Processing** tabs are displayed again in this screen for reference.

The total weight and volume are calculated based on material master data copied into the order and from the order into the delivery. You may change these values to reflect the actual values for weight and volume. In some industries, the customers and/or carrier require this information be accurate, with some tolerance.

Companies use the header **Picking** tab to enter the number of packages and actual weights, when necessary.

9.3.3 Loading

The header **Loading** tab, shown in Figure 9.16, shows summarized information about the packing and loading of the delivery. The **Loading Date** field shown under the **Status Overview** and **Processing** tabs is displayed on this screen for reference.

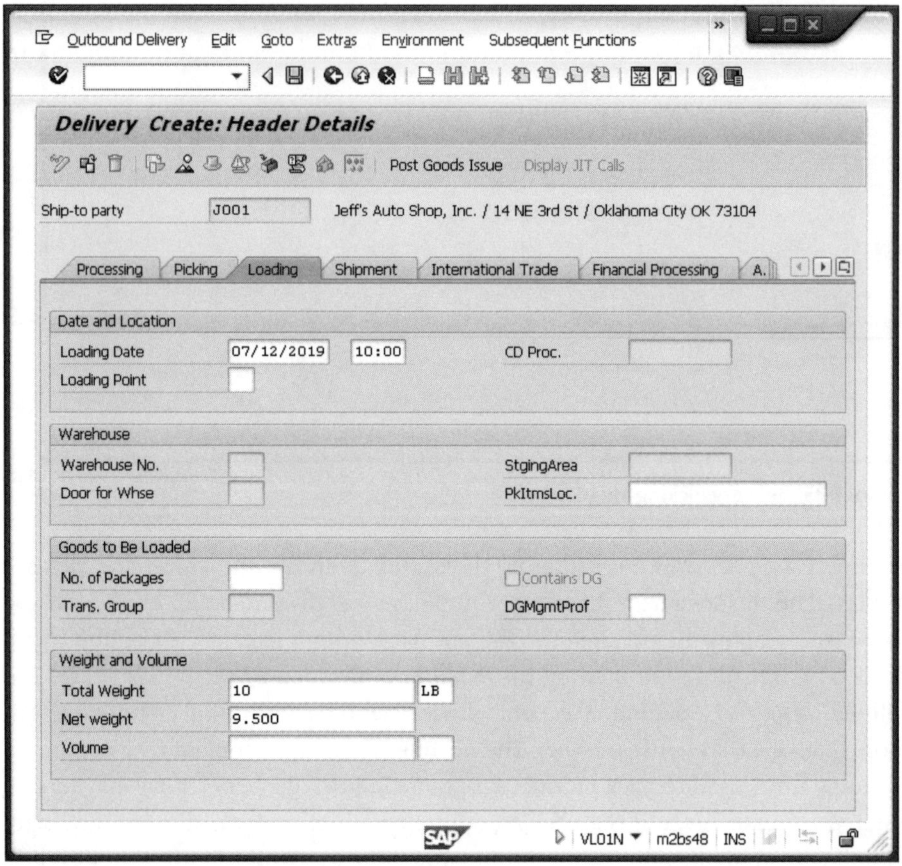

Figure 9.16 Delivery Loading Header Tab

The **CD Proc.** field is a number that identifies a cross-docking operation, which is when an incoming product from a vendor or manufacturer comes packaged into the receiving docks of the warehouse and goes directly to the outbound docks without ever being put away on your warehouse shelves. This option eliminates a great deal of processing time and expedites the fulfillment of customer orders from external sources. We recommended cross-docking when you can't use drop shipping and when the purchase from the external source is made specifically to fulfill a customer order (such as in a special order scenario). The **CD Proc.** number is defined during the configuration of the purchase order and receiving, which is part of the MM scope.

On this screen, you may consult the warehouse number (**Warehouse No.**), staging area (**Staging Area**), warehouse door (**Door for Whse**), and picked item location (**PlItmSLocat.**) fields as assigned and determined by the WMS or embedded EWM configuration.

The **No. of Packages** field, defined during packing and/or on the **Picking** tab, is also available under this tab. The **Trans. Group** field is shown from the material master data for informational purposes.

The **Contains DG** (dangerous goods) flag is checked whenever materials have been defined on the material master with a dangerous goods profile (shown under the item **Loading and Shipment** tab). The dangerous goods management profile (**DGMgmtProf**) represents the process of handling deliveries containing specific types of dangerous goods.

Handling dangerous goods is part of SAP Environment, Health, and Safety Management (SAP EHS Management), which enables compliance with special regulatory requirements when handling/transporting materials with toxic, corrosive, explosive, or other characteristics. Companies avoid using SAP EHS Management if dangerous goods are not the core business, but if you don't have a large volume and/or great variety of dangerous goods, the configuration is not too complex, and data maintenance is not an unreasonable burden considering the value of ensuring compliance.

The total weights and volumes shown under the **Picking** tab are also available on this screen for reference. Companies use the header **Loading** tab to enter the number of packages and their actual weights interchangeably with the **Picking** tab, when necessary.

The **Picking** tab is also one of the few places where you can assign a loading point and dangerous goods management profile to a delivery if configured in the organizational structure, although these fields are not often used on this screen.

9.3.4 Shipment

The header **Shipment** tab, shown in Figure 9.17, summarizes information about the departure of a product from your facility. The **TransptnPlanning** (transportation planning), **Loading**, **Planned GI** (planned goods issue date), and **Delivery Date** fields, as well as the **TrnsPlnSta** (transportation planning status) field shown under the **Status Overview** and **Processing** tabs, are available on this screen for reference.

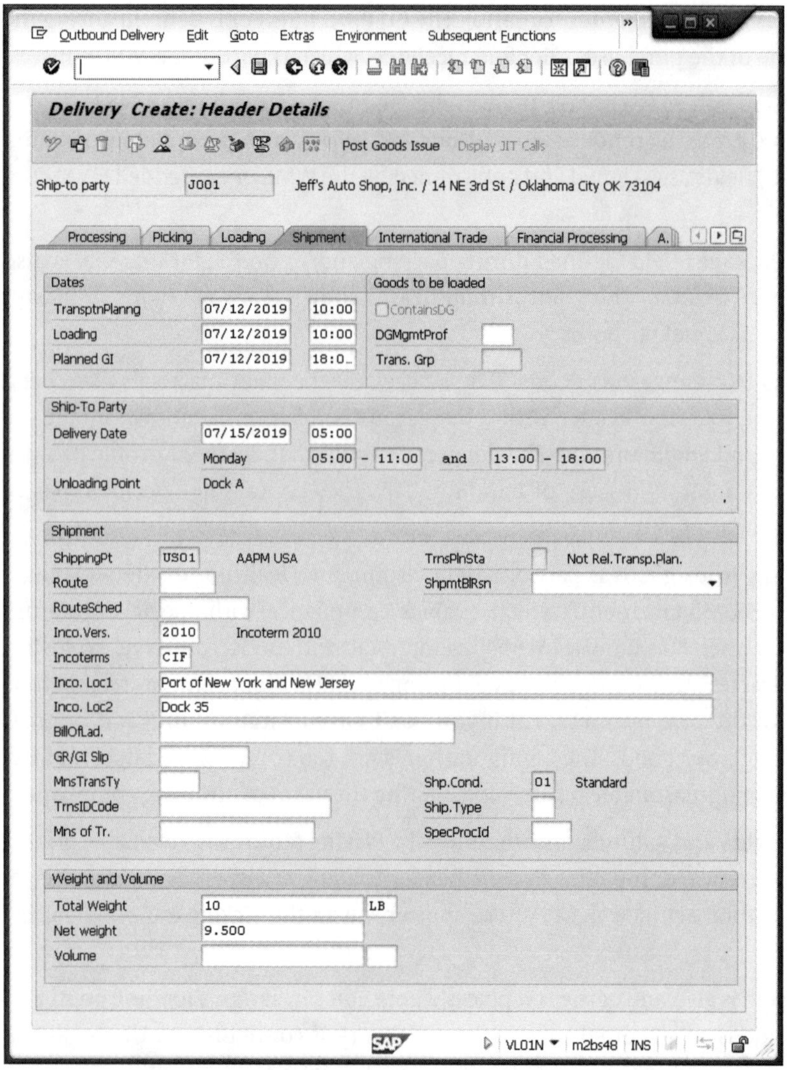

Figure 9.17 Delivery Shipment Tab (Header)

Other fields under the **Shipment** tab include the following:

- The **ContainsDG** (dangerous goods) flag and the **DGMgmtProf** (dangerous goods management profile) field, maintained under the **Loading** tab, are available on this screen for reference.
- The **Trans. Grp** field is shown from the material master data for informational purposes.
- The selected ship-to party **Unloading Point** field and corresponding delivery window are displayed.
- You may also consult the shipping point (**ShippingPt**) field for the shipping point originally specified when the delivery was first created.
- The **Route** and **RouteSched** fields are assigned by the sales order and may be redetermined based on weight groups via configuration. You may also change the assignment manually on this tab. These fields are important for the next step (transportation); relevance is determined at the route level.
- The **ShpmtBlRsn** field allows you to block transportation until the block is manually removed under this tab.
- The **Inco.Vers.**, **Incoterms**, **Inco. Loc1**, and **Inco. Loc2** fields are defaulted from the business partner master data on the sales order and copied to the delivery. You may change these under this tab.
- The **BillOfLad.** field is the number of the document used by the carrier to identify this shipment. Thus, the number may be a collective tracking number representing all handling units included in this delivery document. This information is important for all carrier communications (electronic or otherwise) and is usually required.
- The **GR/GI Slip** field is the number of the material movement used to decrement (for outbound deliveries) or increment (for inbound deliveries) inventory quantities during the post goods issue operation. This value is may be used when integrating with external systems to allow for traceability. This value may also be entered manually, although doing so is rare.
- The **MnsTransTy** field qualifies the type of packaging material used required for this delivery. This value is defaulted based on the order type to the sales order and then copied over to this field. This value may be modified and will be used when arranging transportation.
- The **Shp.Cond.** field is the transportation service level defaulted on the order from the customer master and used for determining the shipping point and route. This value is displayed under this tab for reference only.

9

- The **TrnsIDCode** field is a freeform identification text for the truck or vessel that will ship the product. This value may be manually entered so that this information is shown on dispatch paperwork.
- The **Ship. Type** field qualifies the type of transportation required for this delivery. This value is copied from the sales order and will be used to arrange transportation.
- The **Mns of Tr.** field is a code configured in the system to identify the known semi-trucks, or other transportation equipment that will be used to ship this delivery document.
- The **SpecProcId** flag is a special processing indicator you can configure to qualify special conditions that affect freight calculation and arrangements. This flag is business specific and optional, depending on your requirements. To configure special processing indicators, follow the menu path **SAP Customizing Implementation Guide • Logistics Execution • Transportation • Basic Transportation Functions • Define Special Processing Indicator**.

  As shown in Figure 9.18, specify a four-character special processing indicator code (**SpPI**) and add a description (**Description**).

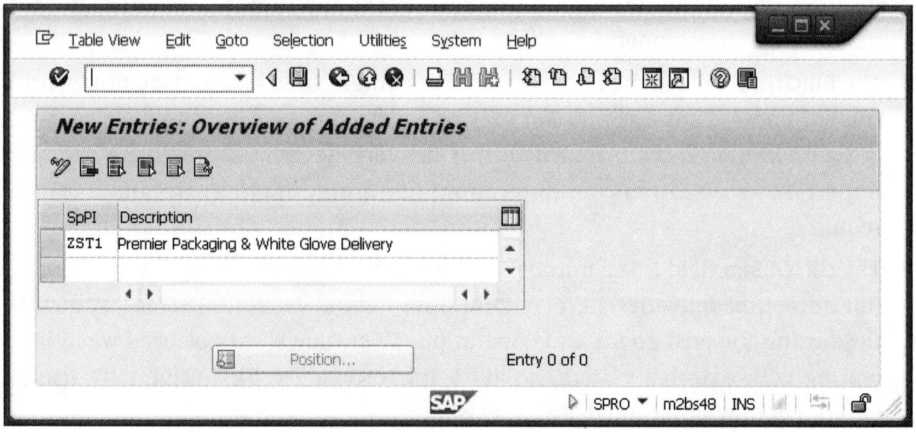

Figure 9.18 Defining New Special Processing Indicators

- The **Total Weight** and **Volume** fields from the **Picking** and **Loading** tabs are also available on this screen for reference.

The **Shipment** tab is often used by companies that perform the post goods issue operation manually to populate the bill of lading number.

9.3.5 International Trade

Foreign or international trade requirements can get quite complex depending on which government regulations you need to observe. SAP offers SAP Global Trade Services to ensure compliance with many regulations. Some information appears throughout SAP S/4HANA Sales and other areas of SAP S/4HANA, but if your company has complex trade compliance requirements, even if not related international trade, you should consider implementing SAP Global Trade Services.

The data under the **International Trade** tab, shown in Figure 9.19, allows you to view and modify the basic information used as input for trade compliance checks and other documentation.

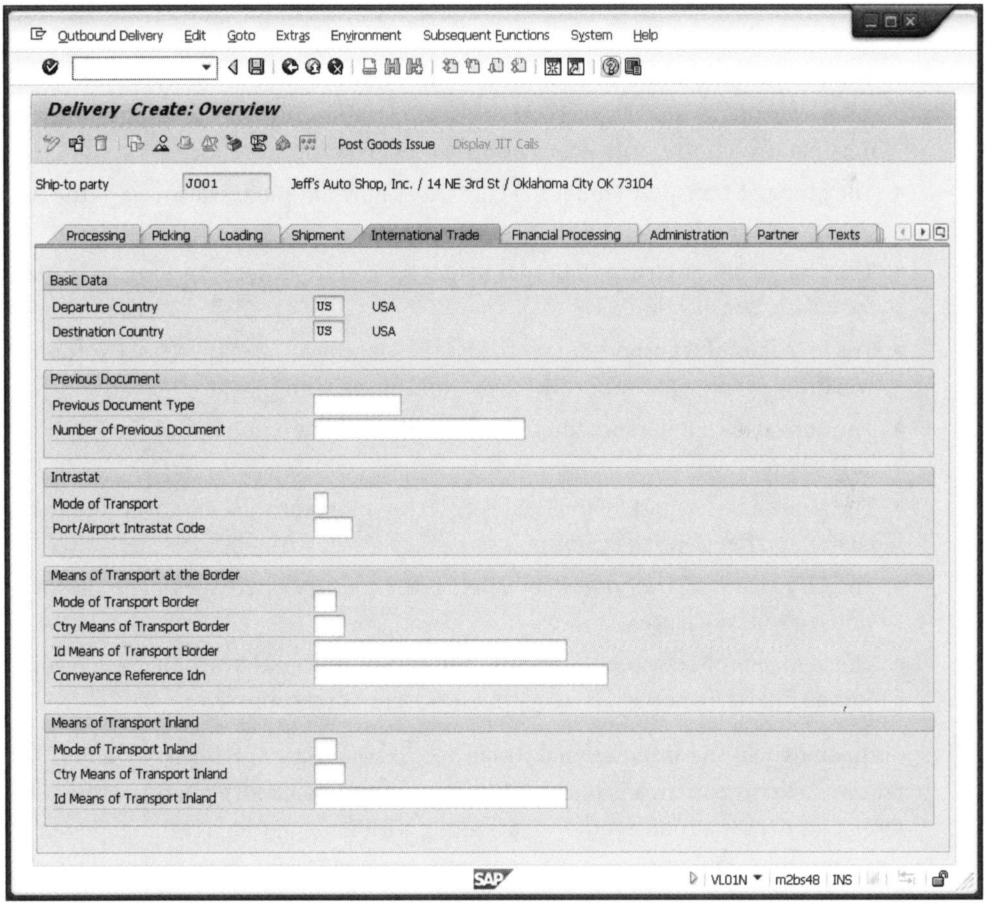

Figure 9.19 Delivery International Trade (Header)

Under the **International Trade** tab, you'll see the following fields:

- The **Departure Country** field is copied from the shipping point address and made available on this tab.
- The **Destination Country** field is copied from the ship-to customer address and made available on this tab.
- The **Previous Document Type** field is a qualifier that describes the type of export declaration you issue (when required). You may configure which types of documents that are applicable to your business. This information is used in Europe.
- The **Number of Previous Document** field is the export declaration document number. This information is common in Europe.
- The **Mode of Transport** field is an Intrastat code that describes how product will be transported to the customer. This information is used in Europe.
- The **Port/Airport Intrastat Code** field is an Intrastat code that describes the entry gateway (such as a port or airport) at which the product will be brought into the destination country. This information is used in Europe.
- The **Mode of Transport Border** field describes how the goods will arrive at the border for customs inspection.
- The **Ctry Means of Transport Border** field is the country where the goods will arrive for customs inspection.
- The **Id Means of Transport Border** field is the identification of the vessel/truck that will bring product to the border for customs inspection.
- The **Conveyance Reference Idn** field is the identification number of the shipment at the border.
- The **Mode of Transport Inland** field is how the shipment will be transported to the customer after clearing customs.
- The **Ctry Means of Transport Inland** field is the country where the final transportation leg will take place.
- The **Id Means of Transport Inland** field identifies the vessel/truck that will be used for the final transportation leg within the destination country.

Companies use the **International Trade** tab so that SAP S/4HANA generates the required export paperwork. In the US, many companies hire freight forwarding services that handle export requirements along with making freight arrangements. In this case, you would not utilize this screen, and the freight forwarder will already have these details. In Europe, this tab is used more frequently since Intrastat fields are regulatory and must be populated.

9.3.6 Financial Processing

Under the header **Financial Processing** tab, shown in Figure 9.20, the **Billing status**, **Billing Date**, intercompany **Billing Date**, and **Totals Status** dates shown on the **Status Overview** and **Processing** tabs are available on this screen for reference.

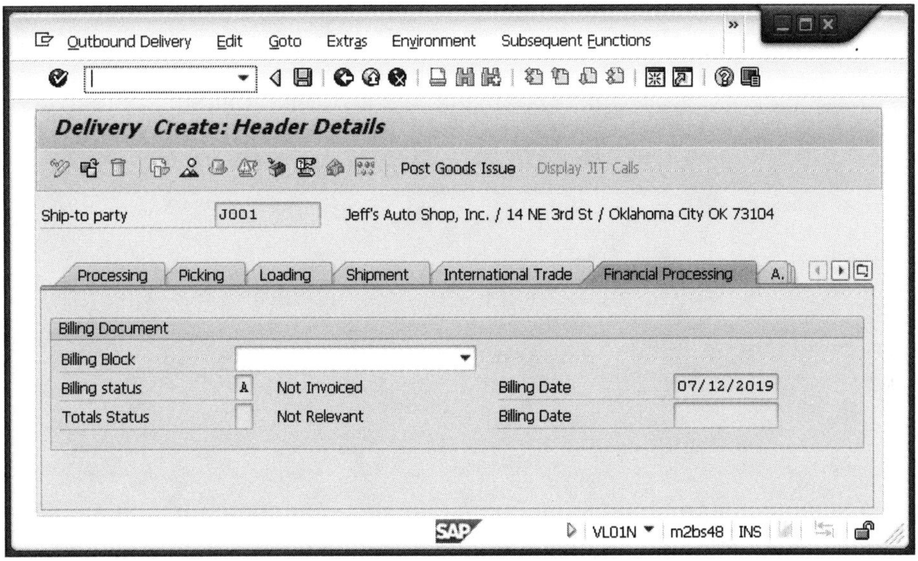

Figure 9.20 Delivery Financial Processing Header Tab

The **Billing Block** field is copied from the sales order and must be removed on this screen to allow billing to take place, even after the billing has been removed from the sales order. Neither the order nor the delivery can have a billing block for invoices to be created, which may cause confusion if you don't deal with billing blocks regularly.

9.3.7 Administration

The **Administration** tab, shown in Figure 9.21, contains header data that controls basic delivery processing behavior. Under the **Administration** tab, you'll see the following fields:

- The **Ext. Delivery** field records the document number from outside the system used to identify this delivery document. The qualifier code following this field describes the type external reference you're entering.

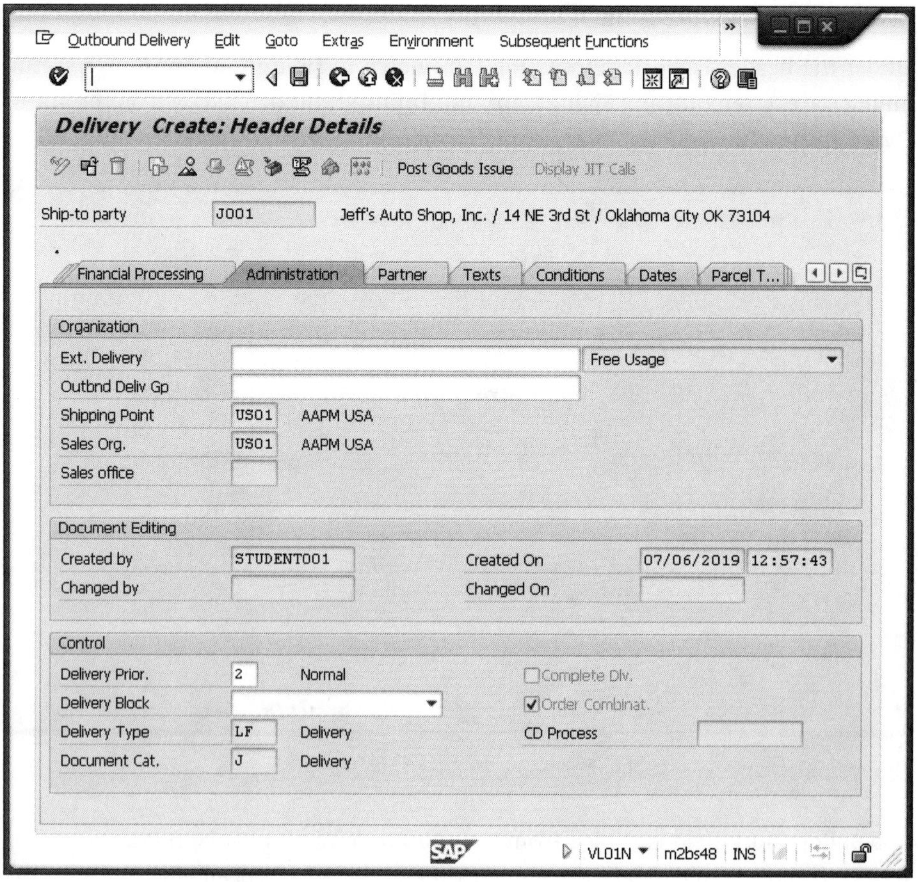

Figure 9.21 Delivery Administration Header Tab

- The **Outbnd Deliv Gp** field allows you to group delivery documents together by assigning a number in this field that can be matched across different documents.
- The **Shipping Point** and **Delivery Type** fields selected on the initial screen are displayed on this screen for reference.
- The **Sales Org.** and **Sales office** field are copied from the preceding document (sales order, purchase order, etc.).
- The **Created by**, **Created On**, **Changed by**, and **Changed On** fields are auditing fields that indicate the user that created the document, the date/time when it was created as well as the user that last modified the document and date when that changed occurred.

- The **Delivery Prior.**, **Complete Dlv.**, and **Order Combinat.** fields are defaulted from the business partner master data on the sales order and copied to the delivery. You may change these values under this tab.
- The **Delivery Block** field prevents orders from being processed by certain logistics tasks (see the configuration steps in Chapter 6). The block may allow the delivery document to be created but would stop picking, the post goods issue operation, etc. In this case, you would need to remove the delivery block on this screen before blocked tasks can be processed.
- The **CD Process** field is the cross-docking ID shown under the **Loading** tab, displayed on this screen for reference.
- The **Document Cat.** field is configured on the delivery document type.

9.3.8 Partner

Under the **Partner** tab, shown in Figure 9.22, you can consult the partner functions that were configured as relevant for the delivery document. These partner functions will cause a delivery split to ensure that orders from different partner are not shipped together.

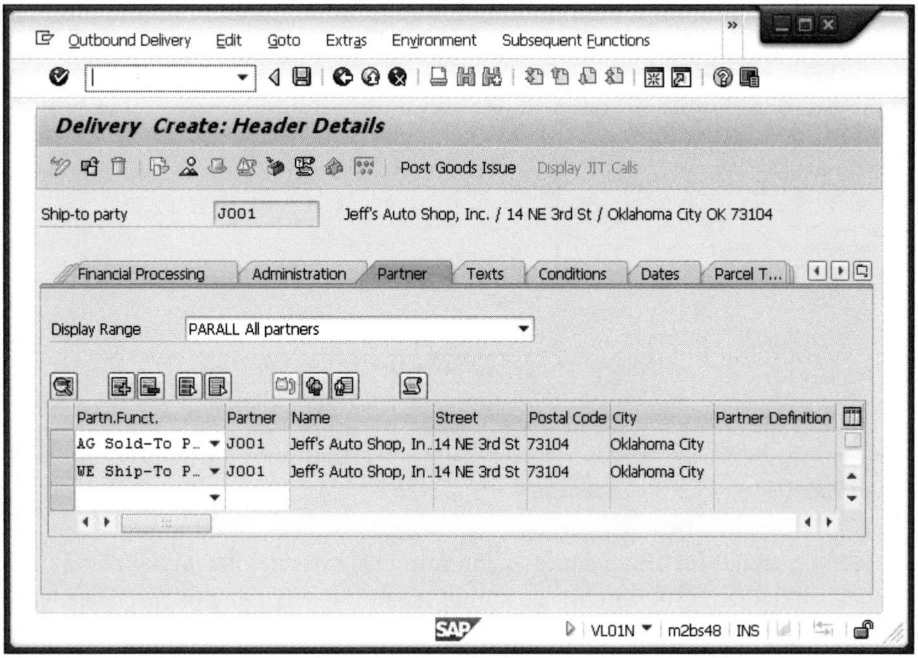

Figure 9.22 Delivery Partner Tab (Header)

Some companies use the forwarding agent partner function to document the carrier responsible for transporting a delivery to the customer. This value is often assigned on the customer master and/or sales order and copied into this tab. You would then use the **Partner** tab to modify value before shipment for exceptional cases.

9.3.9 Texts

Texts defined on the customer master and copied to the sales order may be copied to the delivery document as well. Texts can also be defined as delivery specific. Under the **Texts** tab, shown in Figure 9.23, you may modify the texts defaulted from the order, for instance, adding information to be printed out in logistics paperwork.

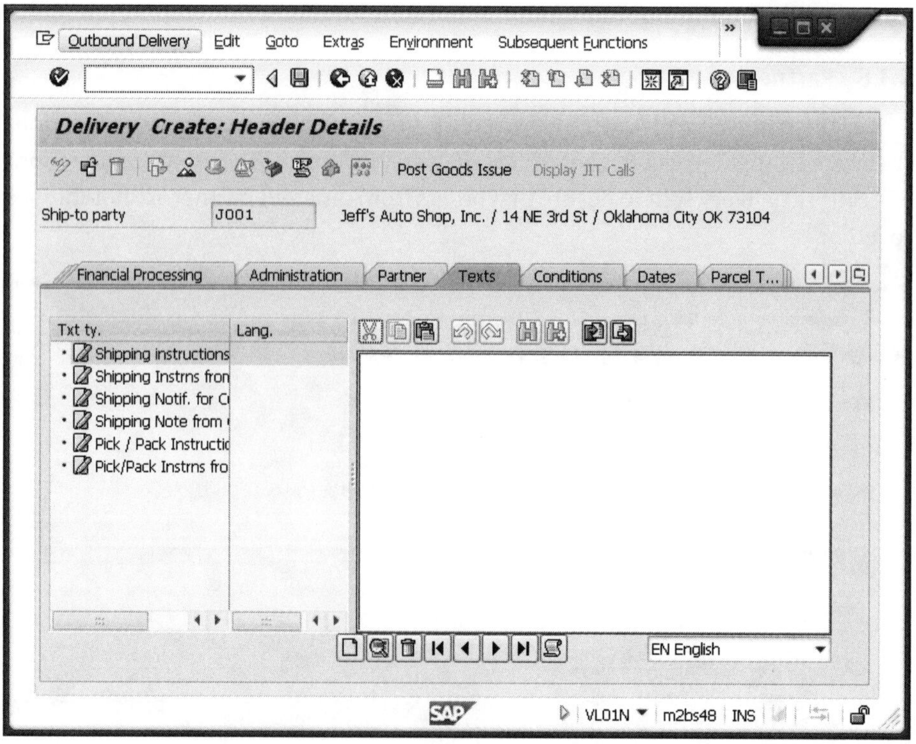

Figure 9.23 Delivery Texts Header Tab

A common usage for this feature is for shipping instructions. Many companies include special requests from the customer regarding packaging or special delivery procedures. Some companies avoid using text for this purpose because the warehouse can struggle implementing checks to enforce these requirements. But once a customer demands special handling, you'll need to address this issue.

Some companies define texts as data repositories for custom information that doesn't make sense elsewhere. However, we recommend you use the **Custom Fields** tab to add new fields, as intended.

9.3.10 Conditions

The **Condition** tab, shown in Figure 9.24, may contain delivery-related pricing components, such as freight, duties, fees, etc.

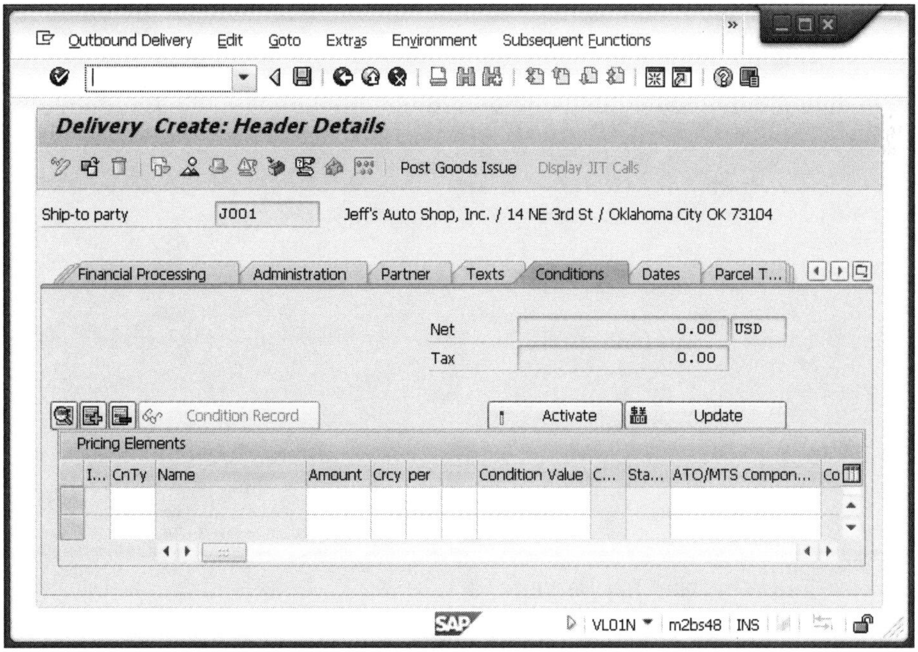

Figure 9.24 Delivery Conditions Header Tab

Delivery documents allow for pricing but are not intended for all sales order prices, only freight and warehouse fees and charges that apply to the delivery. Conditions entered under this tab are then copied into the invoice by combining the pricing procedure on the order with the values entered on this screen.

To ensure this combination works correctly, you must ensure that the step numbers you use to configure condition types on the delivery pricing procedure match exactly the step number on the sales order pricing procedure.

Copy control rules also must specify that the conditions on the invoice should originate from the order and delivery, not just the sales order.

9.3.11 Dates

The **Dates** tab, shown in Figure 9.25, allows you to define events that are expected for this delivery document. These events are freely defined and are used to track performance.

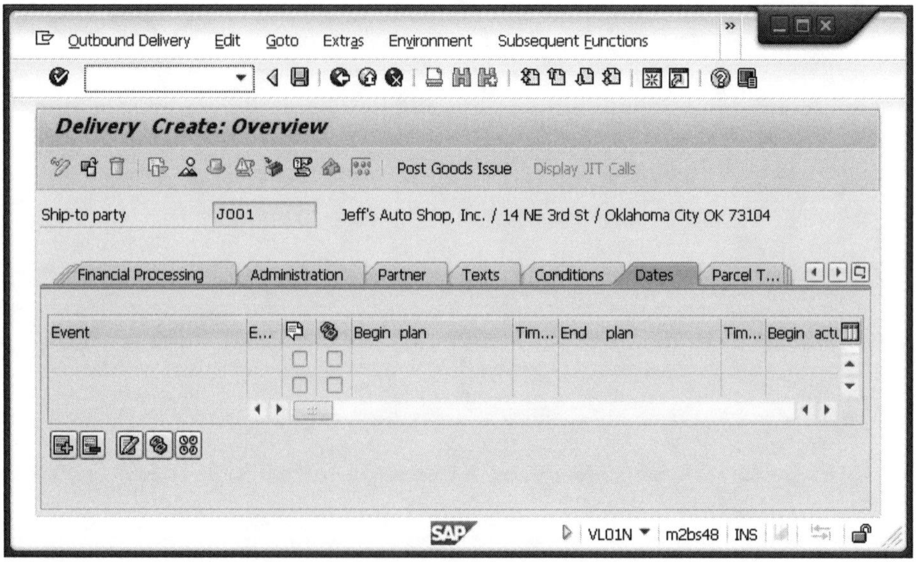

Figure 9.25 Delivery Dates Tab (Header)

These dates are not commonly used by many companies, and the companies that use these dates (previously part of SAP Event Management) typically implement these dates after the system goes live and the solution is mature. Some typical examples are:

- Warehouse lead time: You can define an event that starts when the warehouse receives the delivery (when it is created) and ends at the post goods issue operation. The interval can be measured and reported to assist on corrective measures, such as team sizing and work shift durations.

- Transportation lead time: Event that start at the post goods issue and ends upon the delivery of the product to the customer. You can define expectations and monitor execution. You can define actions to be taken when the delivery is running late, such as proactive customer communications.

9.3.12 Parcel Tracking

The **Parcel Tracking** tab, shown in Figure 9.26, summarizes shippable handling units for a quick overview of delivery progress.

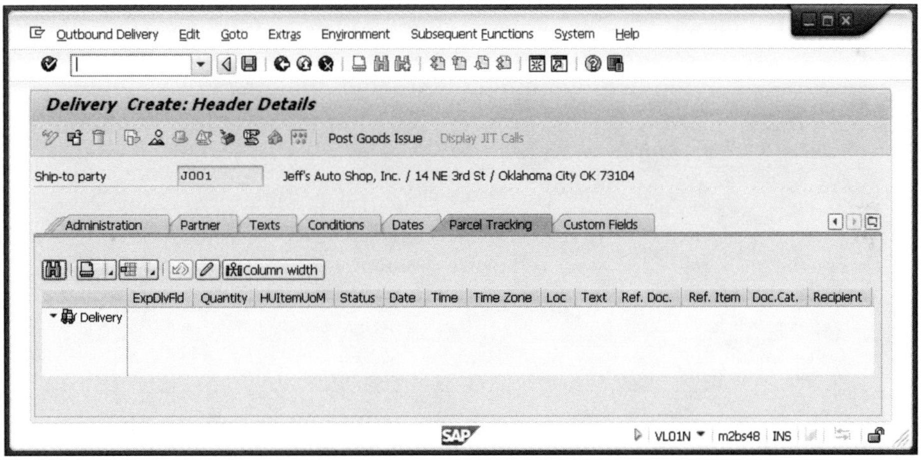

Figure 9.26 Delivery Parcel Tracking Tab (Header)

In instances when shipping product via parcel carriers, you'll define the handling units (during packing) and assign tracking numbers provided by the carrier.

You may then receive messages from the parcel carriers linked to these tracking numbers with updates regarding the transportation stages. If this integration with parcel carriers is implemented, the details of the transportation activity are shown under this tab.

> **Note**
>
> The **Custom Fields** tabs for both header and item details are similar to the **Sales Order Additional Data B** tabs. These customizable fields are provided with no content to allow you to define your own fields and make them available for your users to maintain.

9.4 Create Delivery: Item Details

The delivery item details tabs contain more information in addition to the overview tabs we've covered so far. You'll often use these header detail tabs to maintain data on the delivery. We'll call out some common uses for each tab in the following sections.

9.4.1 Processing

Statuses are displayed under the item **Processing** tab, as shown in Figure 9.27.

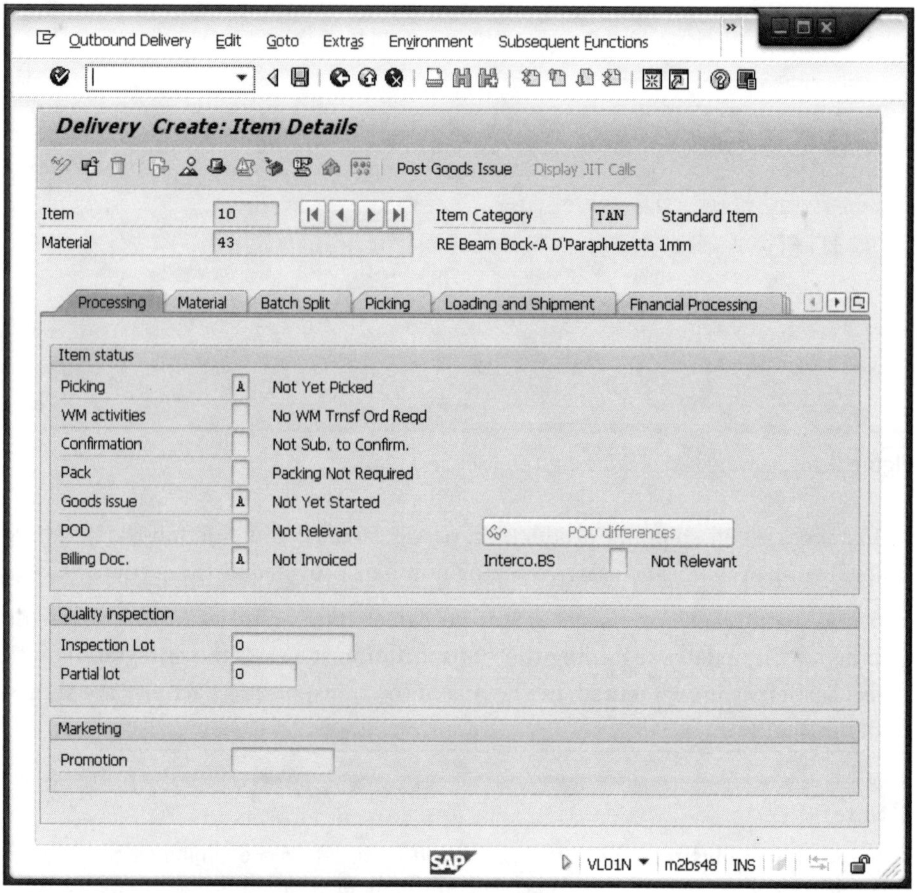

Figure 9.27 Delivery Document Processing Item Tab

The following statuses correspond to item statuses also displayed under the **Status Overview** tab:

- The **Picking** status will be set as **C** once you enter picked quantity on the delivery line.
- The **WM activities** (warehouse management) status will be set as **C** once a transfer order is created and all the steps defined by the WMS or embedded EWM configuration have been completed and confirmed.
- The **Confirmation** (WMS or embedded EWM picking/putaway) status will be set as **C** once the WMS or embedded EWM transfer order is confirmed.
- The **Change Management** flag indicates that you can make changes to this delivery, in a decentralized warehouse scenario, and the change will be replicated to the external system.
- The **Pack** (packing) status will be set as **C** once the line was been packed by a handling unit.
- The **Goods issue** (goods movement) status will be set as **C** after you process the post goods issue operation for this delivery line.
- The **POD** (proof of delivery) status will be set as **C** once you register that product has been delivered at the customer's ship-to location.
- The **Billing Doc.** (billing) status will be set as **C** once an invoice is created with reference to this delivery line.
- The **Interco.BS** (intercompany billing) status will be set as **C** once an intercompany billing document is created with reference to this delivery line.
- The **Inspection Lot** document number field controls activity performed by quality management (QM). In some instances, you may define inspections to be performed at the time of shipping, which is common in the aerospace and defense industries.
- The **Partial lot** field is a subset of the **Inspection Lot**.
- The **Promotion** field is used to identify inbound deliveries taking advantage of special promotional conditions; the value is copied from the purchase order when applicable.

9.4.2 Material

Most companies seldom use the **Material** tab, shown in Figure 9.28, whether to view data or make changes to the data. The **Item Descr.**, **Cust.material**, **Engin. Change**, **BOM expl.number**, and **Mat.freight grp** fields are copied from the sales order.

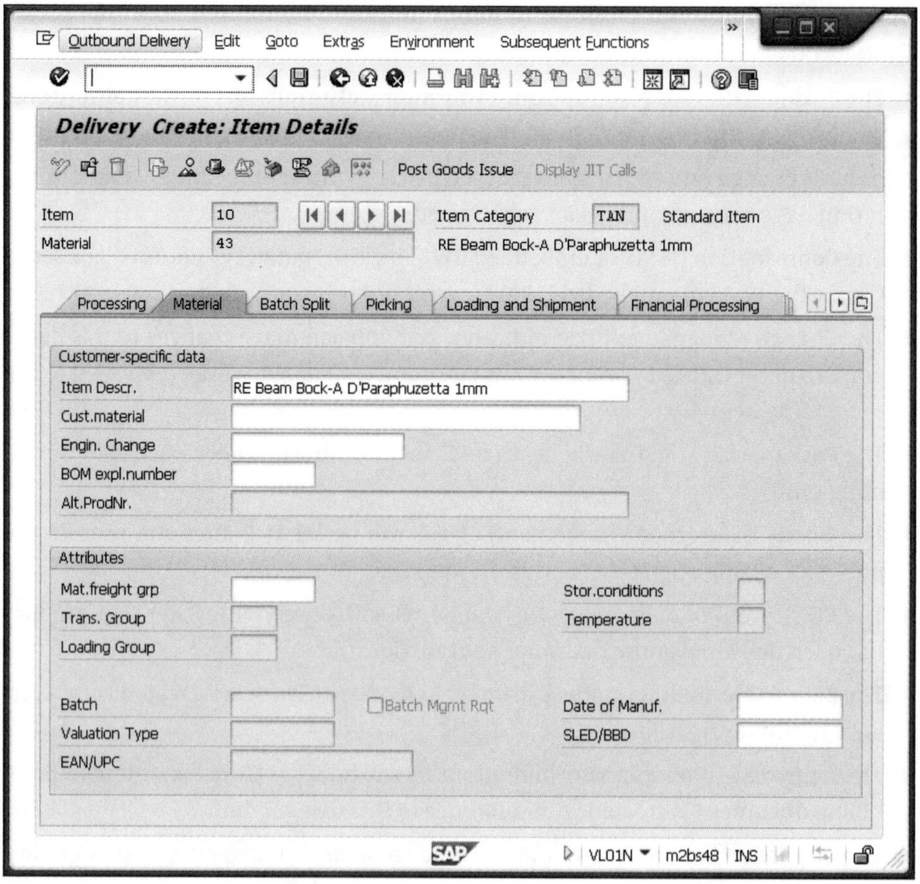

Figure 9.28 Delivery Item Material Tab

The **Alt.ProdNr.** field is defined by the decentralized warehouse for the material that they will ship on your behalf. The **Stor.conditions**, **Trans. Group**, **Temperature**, **Loading Group**, **Batch Mgmt Rqt**, **Valuation Type**, and **EAN/UPC** fields are populated from the material master data for informational purposes.

The batch number (**Batch**) is assigned to this delivery line during the picking operation; the **Date of Manuf.** (date when the product with this lot was produced) and **SLED/BBD** (shelf life expiration date/best before date) fields are copied from the batch master data and may be changed on this screen.

9.4.3 Batch Split

A *batch split process* takes place during picking, which is when the warehouse team has picked from more than one batch to fulfill one delivery line. When registering picking, you'll need to indicate that that line needs to be split into multiple lines to accommodate the batch numbers picked.

To access the batch split functionality under the **Picking** tab, select the desired line and click on the **Batch Split** button, as shown Figure 9.29.

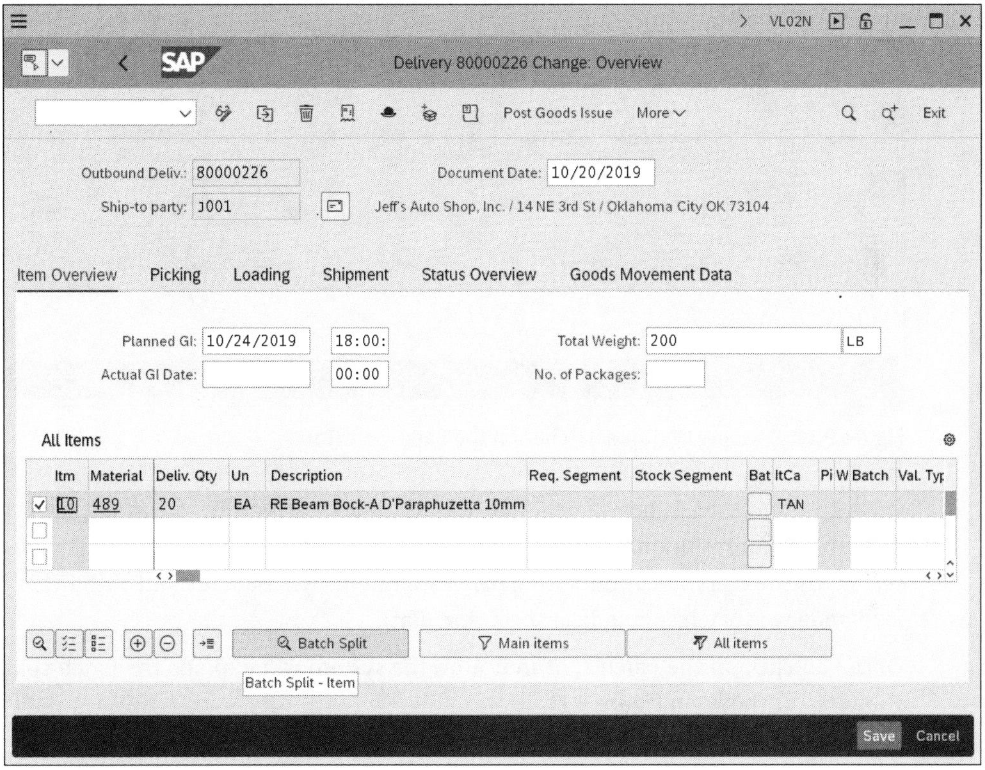

Figure 9.29 Calling Batch Split

The screen shown in Figure 9.30 will be displayed where you can enter multiple batch numbers and quantities.

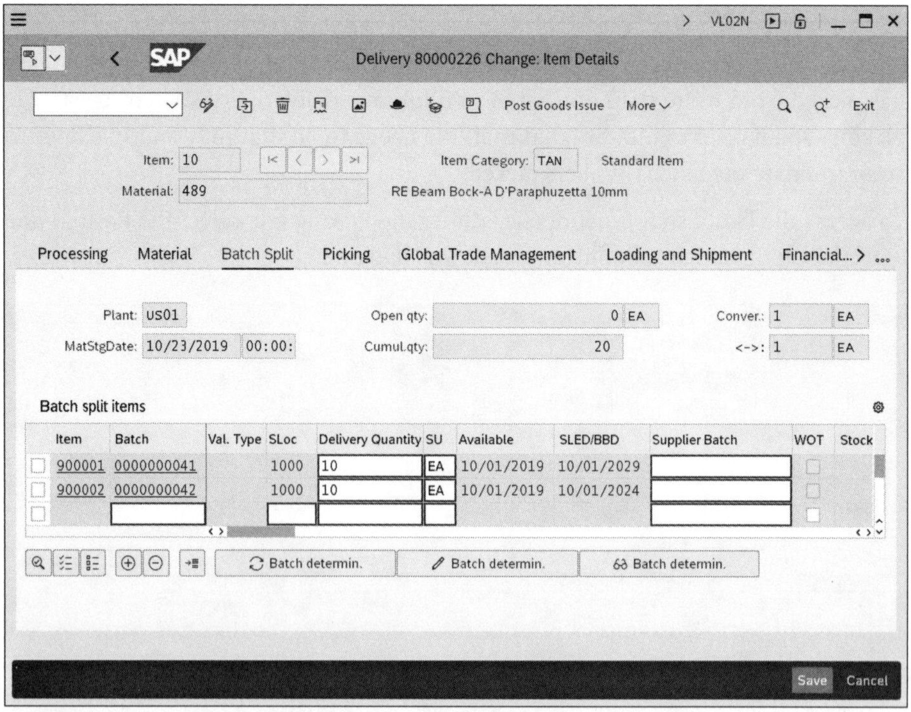

Figure 9.30 Entering Multiple Batches on the Batch Split Tab

Once the operation is completed, exit the batch split screen by pressing F3. As shown in Figure 9.31, only the main item that was split will be displayed. On this screen, the delivery lines containing batch split items will be indicated with the icon under the batch split indicator column (**Bat**).

Once you click on the batch split indicator, the system will explode the batch split subitems, as shown in Figure 9.32.

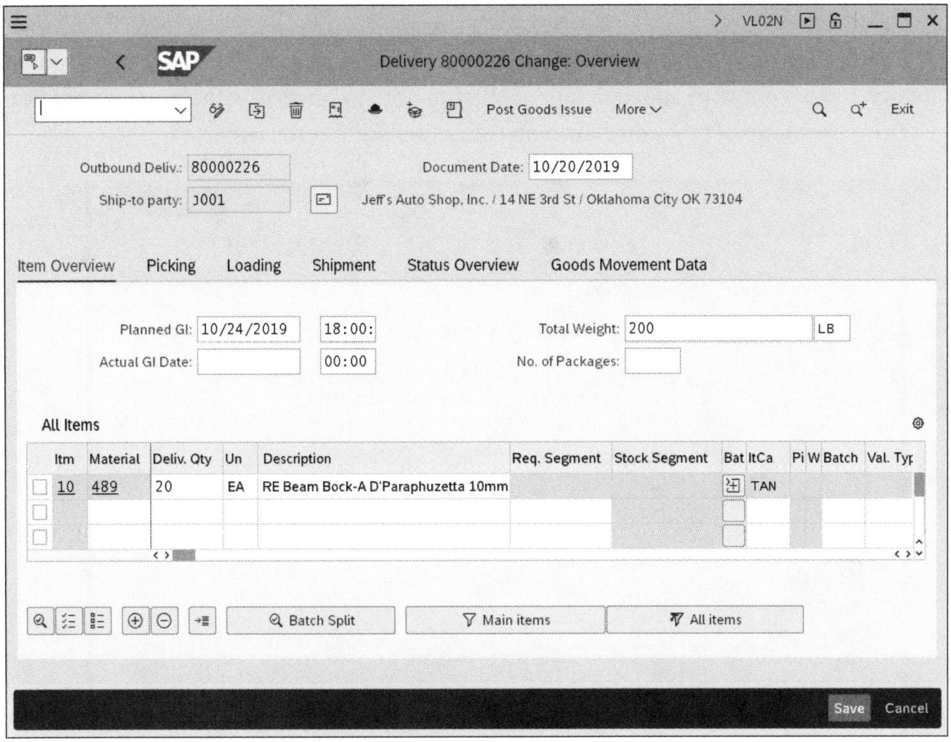

Figure 9.31 Picking Tab Showing the Batch Split Indicator

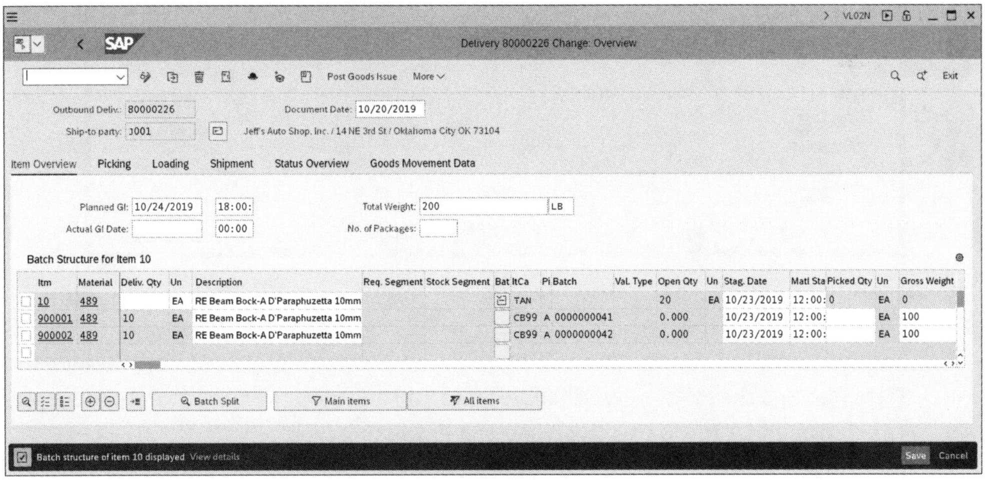

Figure 9.32 Picking Tab with Expanded Batch Split Lines

9.4.4 Picking

Under the item **Picking** tab, shown in Figure 9.33, you can maintain the delivery quantity and weight with added details such as quantity conversion factors. Information from the **Material** tab is displayed on this screen for reference.

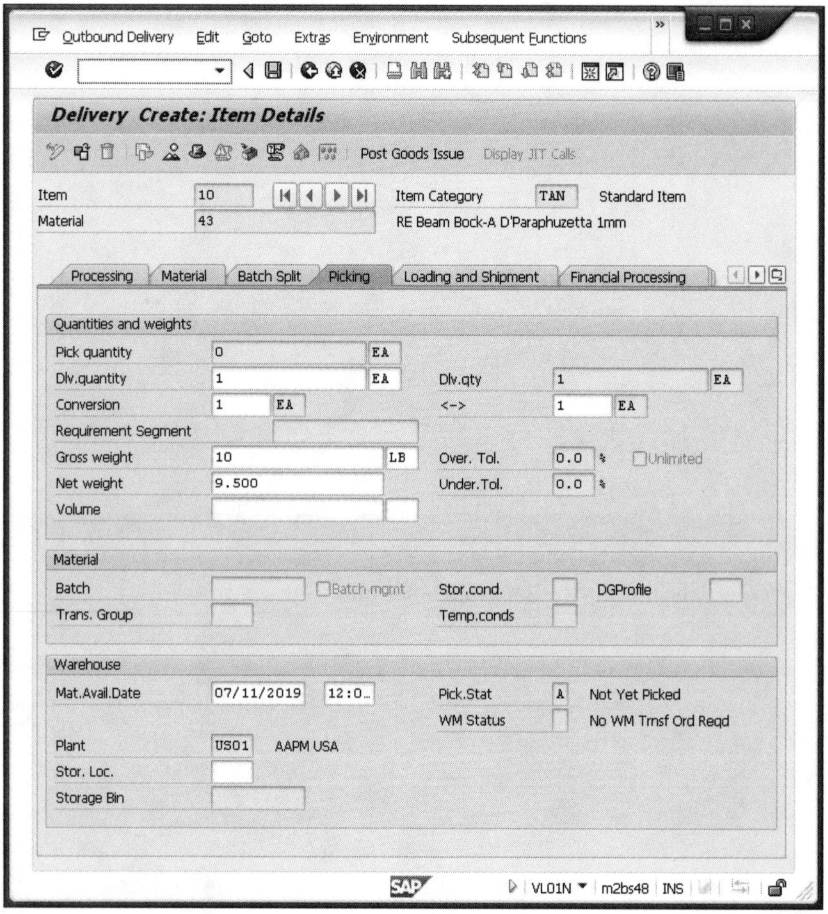

Figure 9.33 Delivery Picking Item Tab

You may also maintain expected material availability dates (as shown under the **Dates** tab and the sales order **Schedule Lines** tab) and view the current warehouse status shown under the **Status Overview** and **Processing** tabs.

The **Plant** is displayed, and you can maintain the storage location (**Stor. Loc.**) on this screen. If you aren't using WM or embedded EWM, inventory management (IM) allows for only the **Storage Bin** defined per storage location on the material master storage views. This freeform text field describes a location within the warehouse where the stock is kept, typically with an aisle and shelf address. Most companies find this data insufficient and either implement SAP EWM or embedded EWM, or use a third-party WMS. But this screen is a simple and quick solution for low-volume operations.

Companies seldom use the line **Picking** tab to manipulate quantity conversions. Other fields are maintained directly on the overview screen.

9.4.5 Loading and Shipment

Under the item **Loading and Shipment** tab, shown in Figure 9.34, the **Loading Group**, **Trans. Group**, **Door**, **Mat. Freight Group**, **Dangerous Goods Profile**, and **EAN/UPC** fields are populated from the material master data for informational purposes.

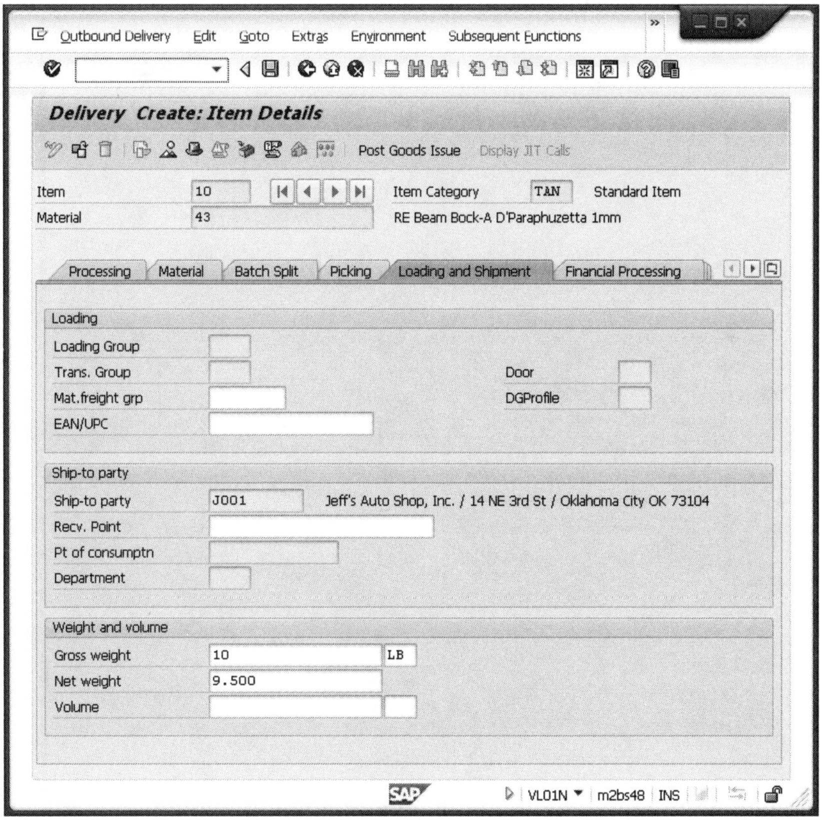

Figure 9.34 Delivery Loading and Shipment Item Tab

You can also consult ship-to customer-specific information (**Ship-to)** including the **Receiving Point** (as defined on the business partner address and assigned to the sales order). You can make changes under this tab.

The line-level **Weight and volume** (as shown under the **Picking** tab) are also available on this screen, but this information is rarely maintained at the line level.

Companies seldom use the line **Loading and Shipment** tab to manipulate receiving points. But for some of your customers, receiving points may be critical, and they may reject your shipment if not specified.

9.4.6 Financial Processing

Under the item **Financial Processing** tab, shown in Figure 9.35, the **Billing Status** and **Interco. BillSt** (intercompany billing status) fields, also shown on the **Status Overview** and **Processing** tabs, are available on this screen for reference.

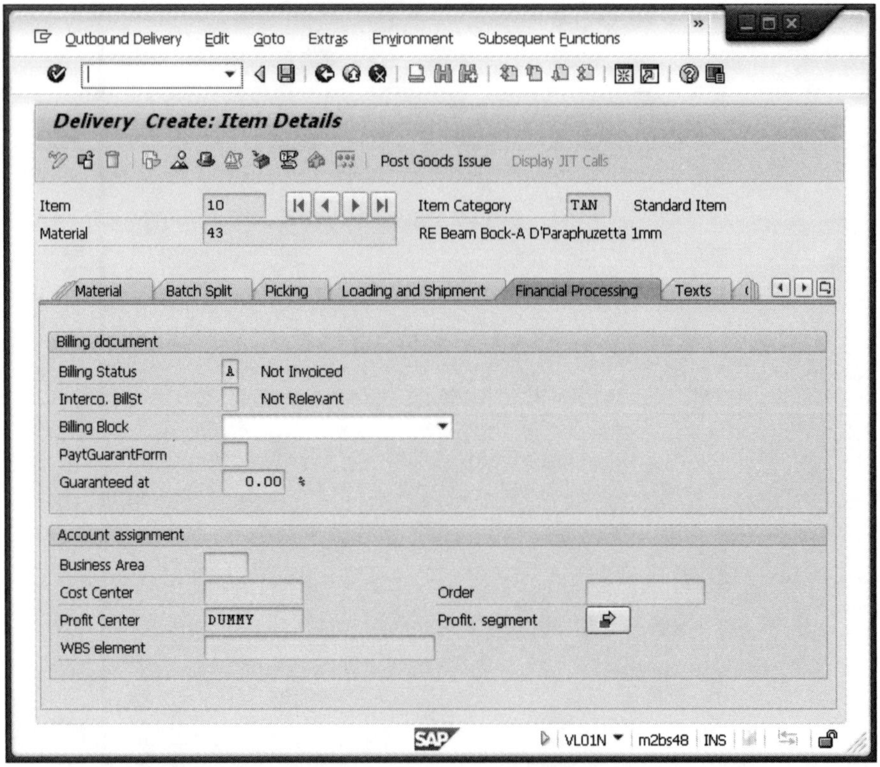

Figure 9.35 Delivery Financial Processing Item Tab

Other available fields include the following:

- The **Billing Block** field from the sales order can also be assigned at the line level. In this case, the block must be removed before the invoice can be created.
- The payment guarantee form (**PaytGuarantForm**) and the guaranteed percentage (**Guaranteed at**) fields, which relate to letters of credit, are shown on this screen for reference but are on the sales order. This information may be relevant if you're only allowed to ship after a letter of credit has been issued.
- The **Account assignment** section contains information about inventory accounting that is used by controlling. These fields are copied from the sales order and are used when decrementing inventory at the time of the post goods issue operation. This information also come into play for the invoice accounting; in particular, the profitability segment (**Profit. segment**) is used by profitability analysis.

Note

These fields are part of the controlling functionality and often are determined automatically. A typical warehouse user is not expected to maintain these fields.

- Most companies use the **Profit Center** as defined on the material master, copied to the sales order line and then copied to this delivery line. This information is used by accounting to group postings together and reduce the number of entries to review in reports.
- The **Cost Center** may be used for free of charge shipments as assigned to the order reason. This value represents the area within the company that is responsible for cost of the product given away for free. Some typical examples include capturing warranty costs, cost of sales, and marketing.
- A work breakdown structure (WBS) element (**WBS element**) is part of project systems (PS). WBS elements capture costs and profits within a larger initiative, for example, custom/engineered products.
- The internal **Order** field is another way to register cost/profit as part of a more encompassing activity without the need to define projects.

9.4.7 Texts

The item **Texts** tab, shown in Figure 9.36, is nearly identical to that of the header details, except that this tab contains text types assigned to the line rather than the header, and the line number is displayed on the item level text tab.

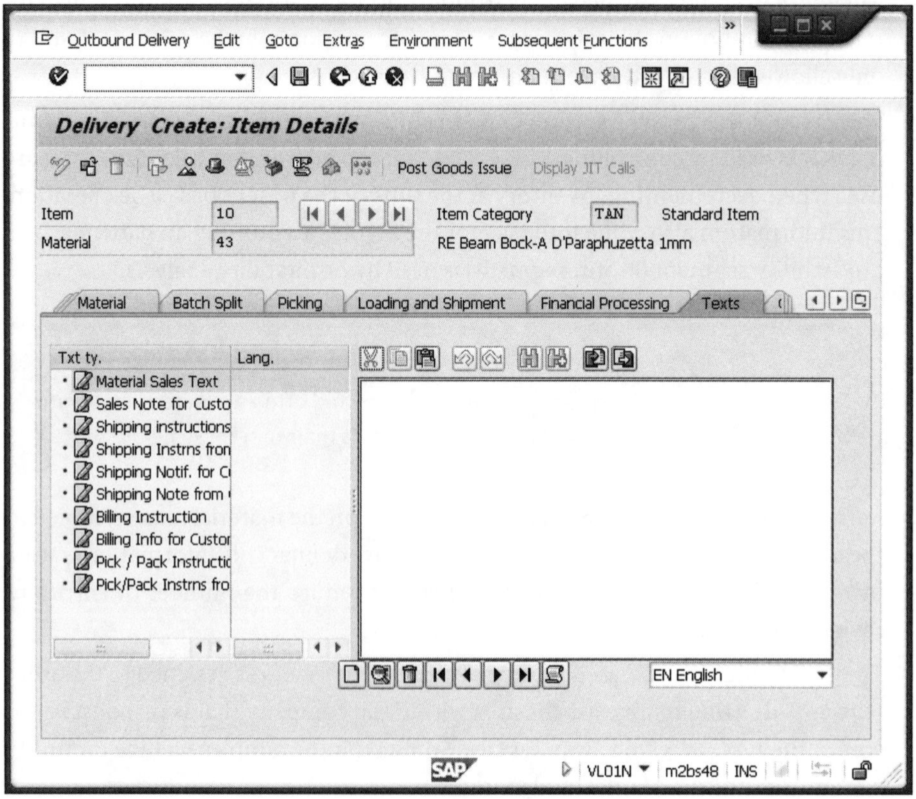

Figure 9.36 Delivery Texts Tab (Item Details)

9.4.8 Conditions

Under the item **Conditions** tab, shown in Figure 9.37, you'll see details about the delivery pricing calculation, when applicable. Most companies enter freight costs, duties, fees, and other-delivery related charges as header conditions, but when automated using the pricing functionality (as described in Chapter 4, Section 4.1), you would see the corresponding details at the line level.

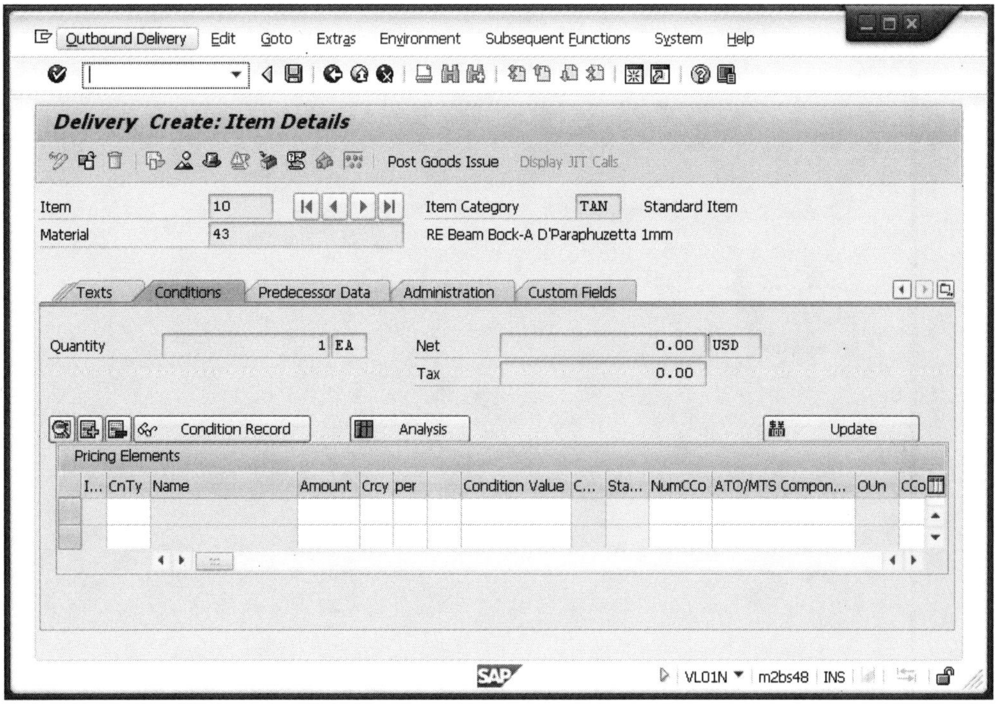

Figure 9.37 Delivery Conditions Tab (Item Details)

9.4.9 Predecessor Data Tab

The **Predecessor Data** tab, shown in Figure 9.38, shows information from the document used as the origin when creating this delivery document line. The document flow sometimes shows the document number from the preceding document to allow you to navigate to the corresponding display transaction, but when the preceding document is a purchase document, the document flow has some limitations. Using this tab, you can consult the preceding document information in any case.

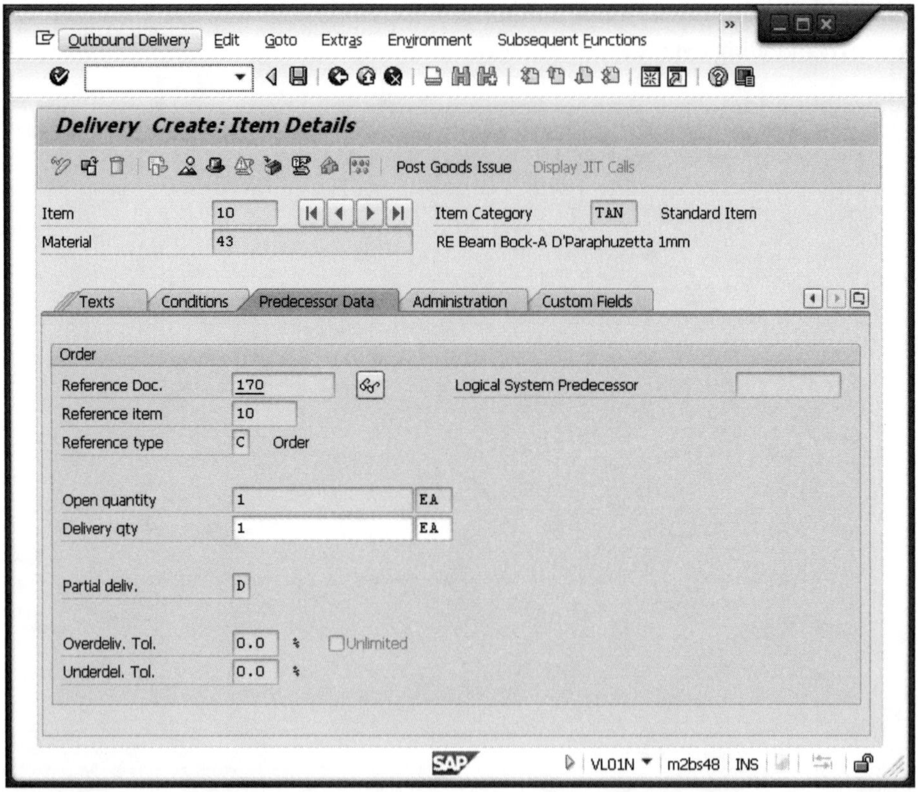

Figure 9.38 Delivery Predecessor Data Tab

9.4.10 Administration

Similar to the header **Administration** tab, the item **Administration** tab, shown in Figure 9.39, shows basic line processing details related to the operations that are applicable/required to this specific line, as controlled by the fields under this tab.

On this tab, you'll see the following fields:

- The **Distr. Channel** and **Division** fields are copied from the original sales order. This information is assigned at the line level on the delivery to allow for combinations of orders with different values in these fields. Note, however, that a copy control routine is configured out of the box that would cause a delivery split when these fields are different. This configuration may be modified to enable this combination.

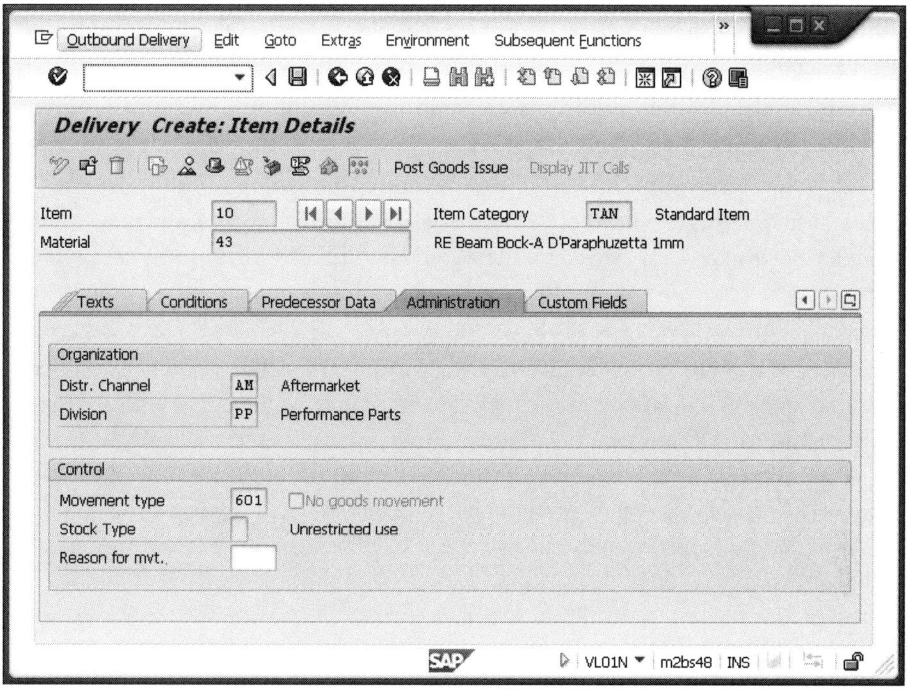

Figure 9.39 Delivery Administration Tab (Item Details)

- The **Movement type** and **Stock Type** fields are defined on the sales order schedule line level and copied on this screen. Once you perform the post goods issue operation, a movement of this type will be created to adjust stock levels to reflect the shipment of the product.
- The **Reason for mvt.** field is a movement type qualifier that you can configure to allow for the differentiation of different circumstances in which a shipment is made. For sales (movement type 601), this field is not usually applicable; for donations or other types of free of charge orders, this field can be used to allow for inventory movement-based reporting that filters postings by reason code.

Incompletion Procedure (Log of Incomplete Items)

Much like the sales order incompletion procedure, the delivery process also allows you to define mandatory fields that block a delivery from being processed. The incompletion procedure, accessed by following the menu path **More • Edit • Incompleteness**, is the tool for enforcing completeness and for requiring users to populate the fields you consider mandatory.

During implementation projects, a common requirement is for warehouse input before processing the post goods issue. Usually, an incompletion procedure is set up to ensure this requirement is observed by the warehouse.

Note also that this requirement can cause delays at the warehouse, and many companies avoid adding any activity for the warehouse to perform to ensure peak performance. The warehouse team often sees paperwork as an unnecessary burden and tend to reduce paperwork to a bare minimum.

You'll need to arbitrate the conflict between customer service and warehouse operations to guide this decision: On one hand, you must provide customers with accurate information and delivery; on the other, you must process orders as quickly as possible. One proven way to achieve consensus is to define warehouse KPIs not only based on picking, packing, shipping performance, and delivery accuracy but also on information accuracy and timeliness. With these KPIs defined, everyone can work towards the same goal.

9.5 Decentralized Warehouse Integration

SAP S/4HANA provides functionality to integrate with third-party warehouse management systems (WMS), which is a common requirement for medium-sized to large operations.

Embedded EWM in SAP S/4HANA is fully capable of handling high sales volumes efficiently. Companies often opt to implement and integrate third-party solutions because of out-of-the box features they provide such as enhanced automation (RF guns, robotics, etc.).

To integrate a third-party WMS, you'll need to perform some configuration steps and then work on defining the interface mapping. Mapping entails the effort of explaining to third-party specialists what each required field means and defining with them the best way to receive data from SAP S/4HANA and to send data back.

Figure 9.40 shows a diagram representing the common data exchange that takes place between SAP S/4HANA and a decentralized warehouse.

Once the decentralized warehouse functionality is activated, all relevant master data (customers, material, batches, vendors, etc.) would be replicated to the third-party warehouse.

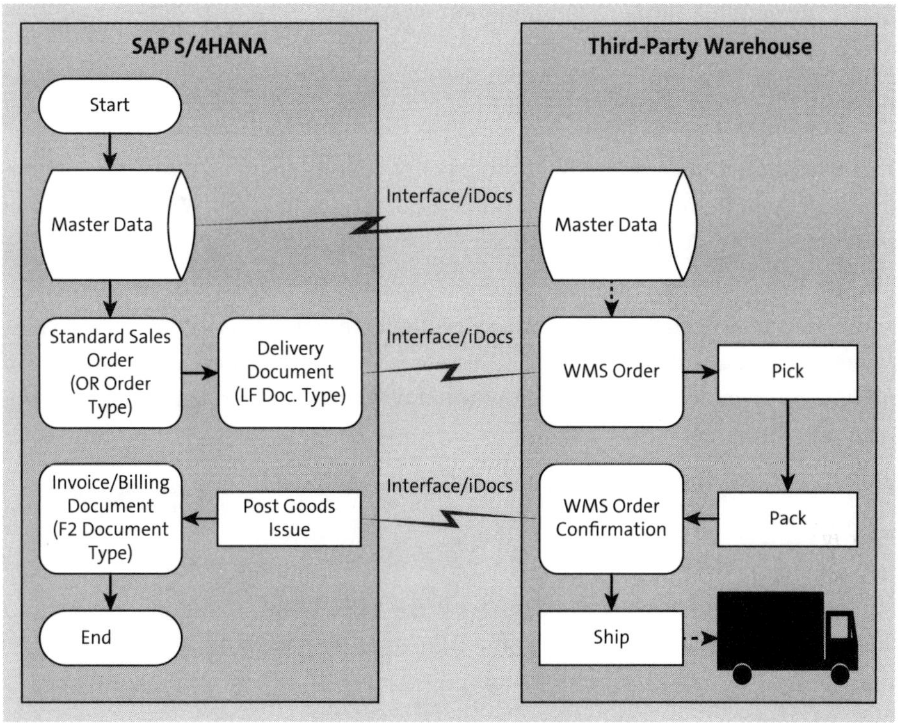

Figure 9.40 Decentralized Warehouse Integration

Once a relevant delivery document is created (such as a sales delivery), this document will be sent to the third-party warehouse and treated as a WMS order (different WMSs have different names for this document). This document is the base for the third-party WMS to manage operations (pick/pack/ship). Once the warehouse operator registers a shipment (commonly referred to as WMS order confirmation), the system must send a message back to SAP S/4HANA. This message will record packing information, and the post goods issue operation is performed. The delivery then becomes relevant for invoicing.

The following sections describe how you can set up the required elements to enable decentralized warehouse management.

9.5.1 Basic Decentralized WMS Integration Set Up

The third-party warehouse must be represented in the system with a warehouse number, which is part of the WM organizational structure configuration. You'll then activate the decentralized WMS integration and generate the distribution model, as we'll describe in the following sections.

Activating Decentralized WMS

To activate the decentralized WMS functionality, follow the menu path **SAP Customizing Implementation Guide • Logistics Execution • Decentralized WMS Integration • Central Processing • Application • Activate Decentralized WMS**.

As shown in Figure 9.41, search for the warehouse number (**Whse no.**) configured on the WMS organizational structure and select the **External WMS** flag. This flag signals to the system that transfer orders are not required for this warehouse; instead, a delivery document will be sent to the external WMS via the interface indicated in the **Dist. Mode** column.

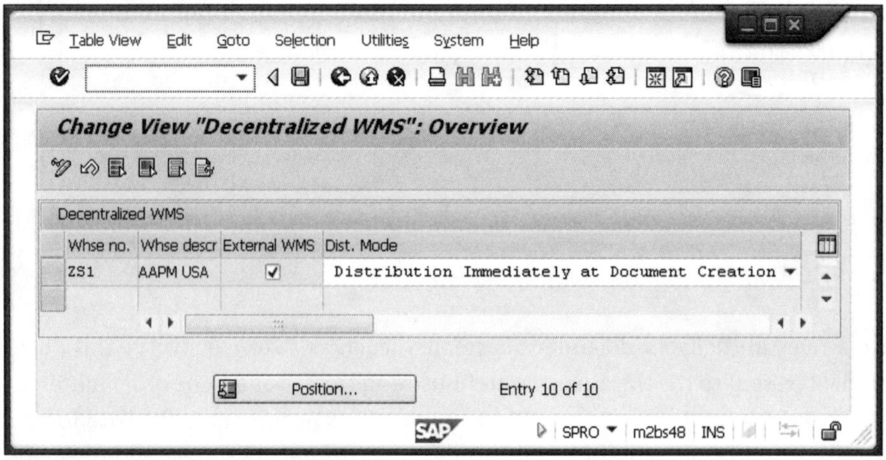

Figure 9.41 Activating Decentralized WMS

Generating a Distribution Model

To generate the decentralized WMS distribution model, open Transaction OL19 or follow the menu path **SAP Customizing Implementation Guide • Logistics Execution • Decentralized WMS Integration • Central Processing • Distribution • Distribution Model**.

As shown in Figure 9.42, you'll need to specify the interface iDoc type that is relevant for the decentralized warehouse number (**Whse Number for WMS Component**). The details on this screen depend on the interface development that will be defined with the third-party warehouse team.

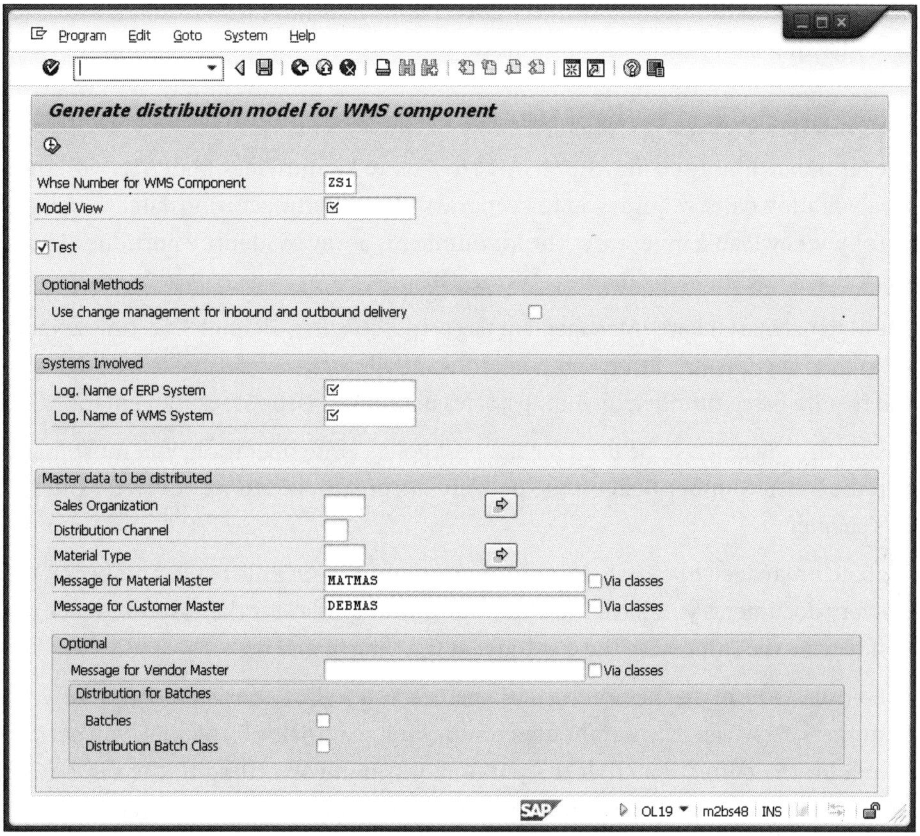

Figure 9.42 Generating Decentralized WMS Distribution Model

You must first identify the external systems with SAP S/4HANA, which is performed by either the SAP Basis team or your development leads. You must add the codes they define in the **Log. Name of ERP System** (identifying the SAP S/4HANA system) and **Log. Name of WMS System** (identifying the third-party WMS) fields.

You'll also specify the relevant distribution chains (**Sales Organization** and **Distribution Channel**) and **Material Type** for master data, which restricts which master data entries will be sent to the warehouse.

9.5.2 Batch Determination

In the following sections, we'll first provide you with an overview of the batch determination process in SAP S/4HANA. Then, we'll show you how to activate automatic batch determination for the delivery document. Finally, we'll describe how to allocate a batch search procedure to a sales area.

Process Overview

The term "batch" is used in SAP S/4HANA to refer to lot numbers. Materials with shelf life expiration dates require you to keep track of the manufacturing data when looking at your available inventory. The lot number is a way to identify portions of your stock that share the same manufacturing date.

The **Material Master Batch Management** flag (as described in Chapter 3, Section 3.3) activates this functionality. From that point forward, all stock movements for the material will require batch number, including a sales post goods issue stock movement.

To identify the batch to be used for the post goods issue operation, you must maintain the **Batch Number** field on the delivery document, which we covered earlier in this chapter.

For batch-managed materials, instead of manually entering the batch number on the delivery document, you have the option of defining rules for the system to pick the best batch to be shipped to the customer at the time of picking.

These rules automate the criteria and ensures you follow consistent rules for your customers. However, the warehouse crew picking materials off the shelf will need to search for the correct batch. If the putaway was done according to the same rules we're observing at the time of picking, batch picking is achievable with only minor impact on performance, but sometimes, this warehouse design characteristic can be a struggle for some logistics operators to fulfill. For those cases, the batch determination is not recommended.

If the putaway allows for automated batch assignment, note that the additional time required for the warehouse crew to pick the correct batch may be offset by the time the office required to record the picked batches in the system if performing batch picking manually and not using, for example, automated RF gun-enabled functions.

Activate Automatic Batch Determination for Delivery Item Categories

To activate batch determination for each delivery document item category, follow the menu path **SAP Customizing Implementation Guide • Logistics – General • Batch Management • Batch Determination and Batch Check • Activate Automatic Batch**

Determination in SD • Activate Automatic Batch Determination for Delivery Item Categories.

On the screen shown in Figure 9.43, browse through the existing entries for the item category (**ItCa**) and select the automatic batch determination (**Auto batch determin**) flag for the entries where you want the system to pick the batch.

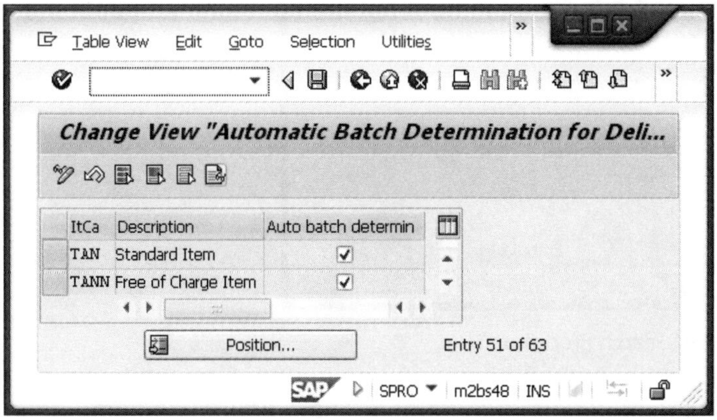

Figure 9.43 Activating Automatic Batch Determination for Item Categories

Allocating SD Search Procedure/Activate Check

To allocate batch search procedures to sales areas and sales order types, follow the menu path **SAP Customizing Implementation Guide • Logistics – General • Batch Management • Batch Determination and Batch Check • Batch Search Procedure Allocation and Check Activation • Allocate SD Search Procedure/Activate Check.**

On the screen shown in Figure 9.44, you'll need to consider all sales areas (**Sales Org**, **Distr Chl**, and **Division**) and all sales order types for which automatic batch determination is relevant and define the search procedure (**Search proced.**) they need to use. You may also indicate if the batch must be checked (**Check Batch**), which is often done to avoid shipping expired products or questionable-quality batches to customers. Note that, in some instances, free of charge shipments may use this otherwise rejected material.

The search procedure is part of MM configuration and uses the condition technique to define the criteria used to identify the correct batch. On this screen, you may also include batch characteristics as criteria.

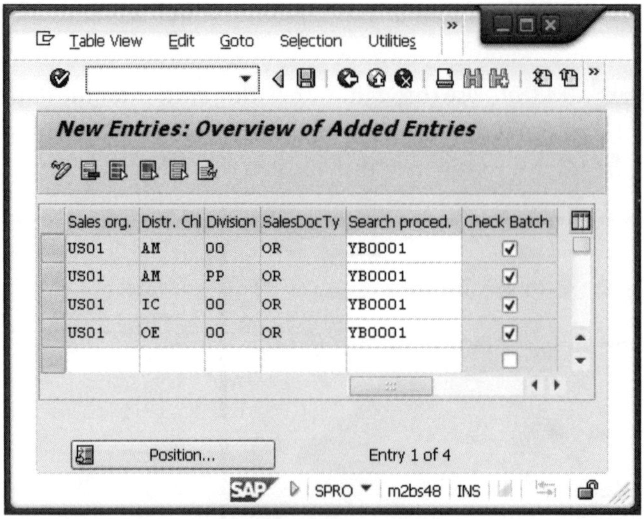

Figure 9.44 Allocating SD Search Procedure

9.6 Picking/Transfer Orders

The picking operation (see Figure 9.45) is executed to confirm the quantities that the warehouse collected from the warehouse shelves.

For warehouse operations without automation features (such as RF guns), the warehouse picks product according to printed document commonly referred to as a picking list, a pick ticket, or a delivery note. These forms are printed from the delivery document. SAP S/4HANA has a standard form and output condition type (LD00) to print out this document. Companies that decide to continue using paper picking lists usually customize this form and implement changes to support their own business requirements.

The picking team uses that paper picking list to locate the product within the warehouse. Once the product on the paper picking list is picked, they'll take notes on the paper itself indicating the actual quantity they picked. When exceptions occur such that the full quantity can't be picked, they would indicate so on the paper, usually highlighting the problem to the best of their ability.

After product is brought to the packing area, the picking lists, with crew notes, can be gathered and sent to the system operator who will review all quantities and make the necessary adjustments to delivery quantities to reflect any exceptions.

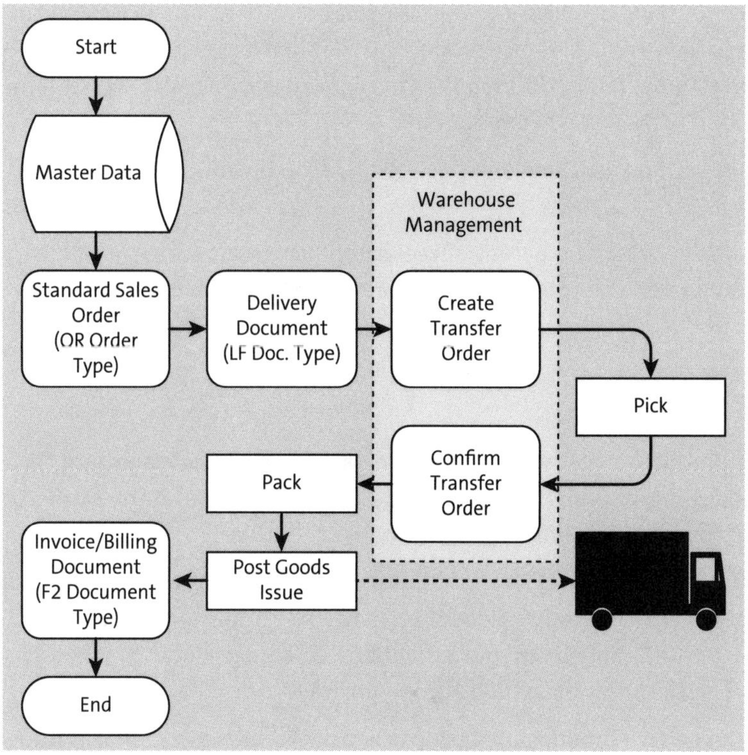

Figure 9.45 Using Warehouse Management for Picking

To assist the warehouse operator with these tasks and ensure the operator reviews manual notes on every line on a picking list, the system requires operators to type in the picked quantities on every line of the delivery under the **Picking** tab of Transaction VL02N (covered earlier in Section 9.4.4).

If any discrepancy is detected, the system will issue an error message. The operator must then change the delivery quantity to match the picked quantity. This updates the quantity that will be used to invoice the customer and is how you'll ensure that you aren't billing a customer for product you're not shipping.

Companies that use the embedded EWM do not need to perform this manual task. The picking step may be turned off when configuring the delivery item category (covered earlier in this chapter).

Instead of entering the picked quantity, the embedded EWM features a document called a *transfer order*. This document is created with reference to the delivery document using Transaction LT03.

A transfer order contains detailed location information where product should be picked. The warehouse would still pick product off the shelf and bring it to the packing area. The system operator confirms the transfer order using WM transactions such as Transaction LT12 or RF gun applications.

Other logistics operations (packing and post goods issue operation) may continue unchanged.

If you use third-party WMS and decentralized warehouse integration, picking happens automatically when you receive the WMS order confirmation interface.

9.7 Packing

When shipping product to customers, items are packed as needed to ensure their integrity while keeping consistent with standard package sizes from the carrier to optimize freight costs through efficient vessel space utilization.

Often, a customer order is packed into multiple shipping boxes. Each box is labeled individually and may end up shipping on different trucks. The customer may receive these shipments at different times, and exceptions could occur that would affect transportation; packages may even be lost along the way.

Therefore, knowing which products are inside which packages is relevant. This information allows you to provide accurate delivery tracking information to your customers and manage exceptions more efficiently. If the material is batch managed and/or serialized, traceability may be required at different levels.

With larger shipments, often you'll be required by your customer to provide detailed packaging information via an advanced shipping notification (ASN). That information is used by the customer to receive whole containers, and all products contained in those containers, simply by scanning the container ID, including information about batches and serialization information. To enable your customers to achieve this process, they may require you to perform a fully detailed packing operation to conduct business with them.

With export shipments, you may need to use expensive and time-consuming packaging operations and materials. Keeping track of the packing activity and materials utilized could be useful. Your inventory of packaging materials may be tracked and automatically replenish if you keep track of materials used during packing activities. This information is not necessarily a big concern when thinking of cardboard boxes, which are customarily ordered in large lots and managed visually. However, when using specialty packaging, tracking packing materials is an important concern.

If a company implementing SAP S/4HANA considers any packing requirement worth adding an additional managed step to the warehouse operations, you would use the packing functionality after picking is completed (when applicable).

To complete packing, in Transaction VL02N, typically, you would click the corresponding packing icon. You can also use Transaction HU02 to perform this operation, which allows for greater flexibility regarding what is included in each box. This approach is not commonly used for sales/shipping because using Transaction VL02N was designed for shipping and is considered the simplest approach.

To complete packing, follow these steps:

1. Call the packing screen from the Transaction VL02N screen by entering the **Outbound Delivery** number and clicking the packing icon (see Figure 9.46).

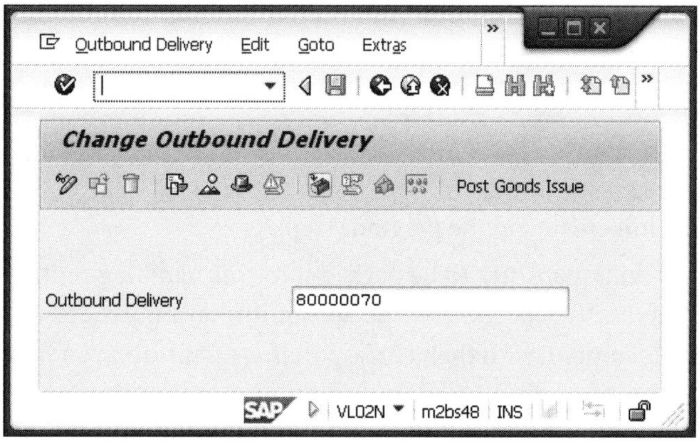

Figure 9.46 Packing a Delivery Document Using Transaction VL02N

2. On the **Processing of Handling Units for Outbound Delivery** screen, shown in Figure 9.47, first create a new packing medium (such as a box), known as a handling unit, which a generic term to describe any kind of packing medium. To create a new packing material, select the **Packaging Materials** number that represents the type of box that you're using to pack materials in, which will add the default dimensions for this box and allow you to control its inventory. Packing materials use a specific material type (VERP). Then, press Enter to create the handling unit.

   You can also select an existing **Handling Unit** number, which allows you to pack products for multiple delivery documents into the same box.

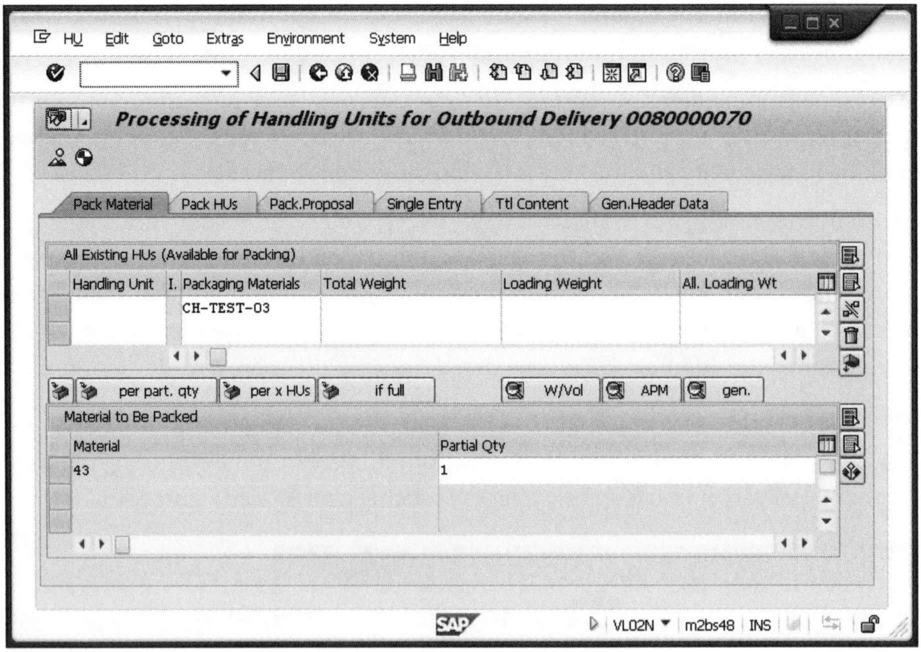

Figure 9.47 Delivery Packing Screen

3. Now, select the handling unit created in the previous step.
4. Next, select the materials and quantities to be packed into this handling unit, as shown in Figure 9.48. The bottom portion of the screen displays a list of lines included on the delivery document, with their corresponding quantities. You may change the **Partial Quantity,** indicating you packed only part of that line in this box, before proceeding to the next step.
5. Click on the **Pack** button. You may repeat these steps if there are other boxes or lines to be packed until all lines and quantities are packed.
6. Once all lines are fully packed, click **Save**, and the packing activity is completed.

You can configure the system to perform these actions automatically. You would then print the packaging information on the pick list and direct the warehouse to follow the instructions. For this approach, you must ensure the packing material dimensions on the material master are accurate and the packing rules are defined for all possible scenarios. This approach is not often used by companies in the US; instead, the warehouse is expected to visually optimize packing rather than follow hard automated rules.

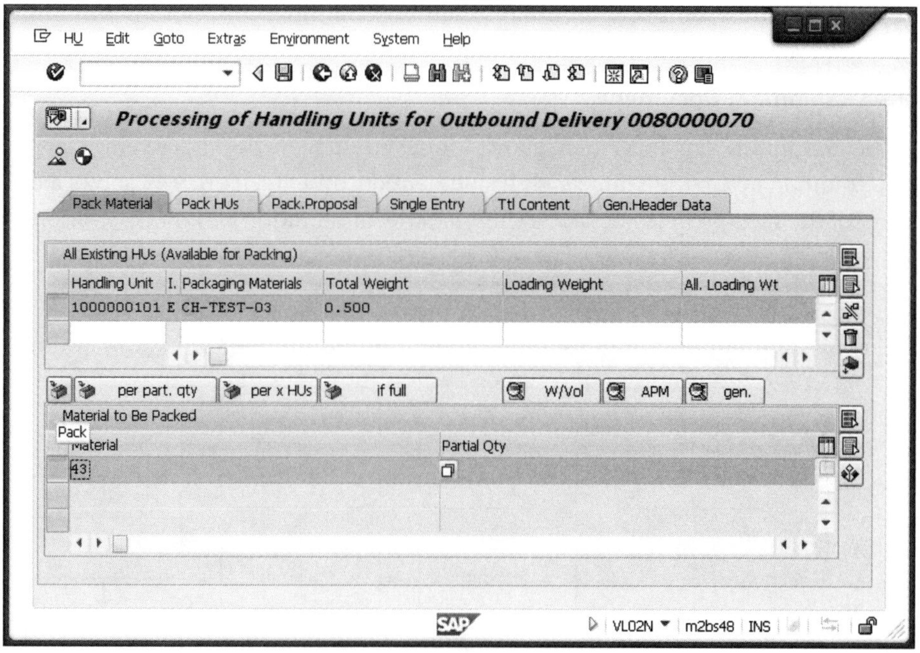

Figure 9.48 Packing Delivery Lines to Handling Units

9.8 Transportation Planning

SAP ERP featured the transportation management functionality as part of the sales and distribution (SD) module, which is still available in SAP S/4HANA. However, SAP also offers embedded transportation management in SAP S/4HANA (TM in SAP S/4HANA) with more features that should be considered. We'll won't cover embedded TM in SAP S/4HANA deeply in this book; rather, we'll rather focus on transportation features specific to SAP S/4HANA Sales.

Companies that use their own delivery trucks and companies that negotiate freight on a shipment-by-shipment basis both require this functionality. Companies that have exclusivity deals with specific carriers do not need to spend time on transportation planning because this work is performed by the contracted carrier on your behalf.

The following section describe the process and related configuration steps to utilize the transportation features of SAP S/4HANA Sales.

9.8.1 Shipment Document

Sales transportation management allows for the grouping of deliveries being shipped to a common destination into single a shipment document. Figure 9.49 shows a diagram of the sales process, including shipment documentation and transportation.

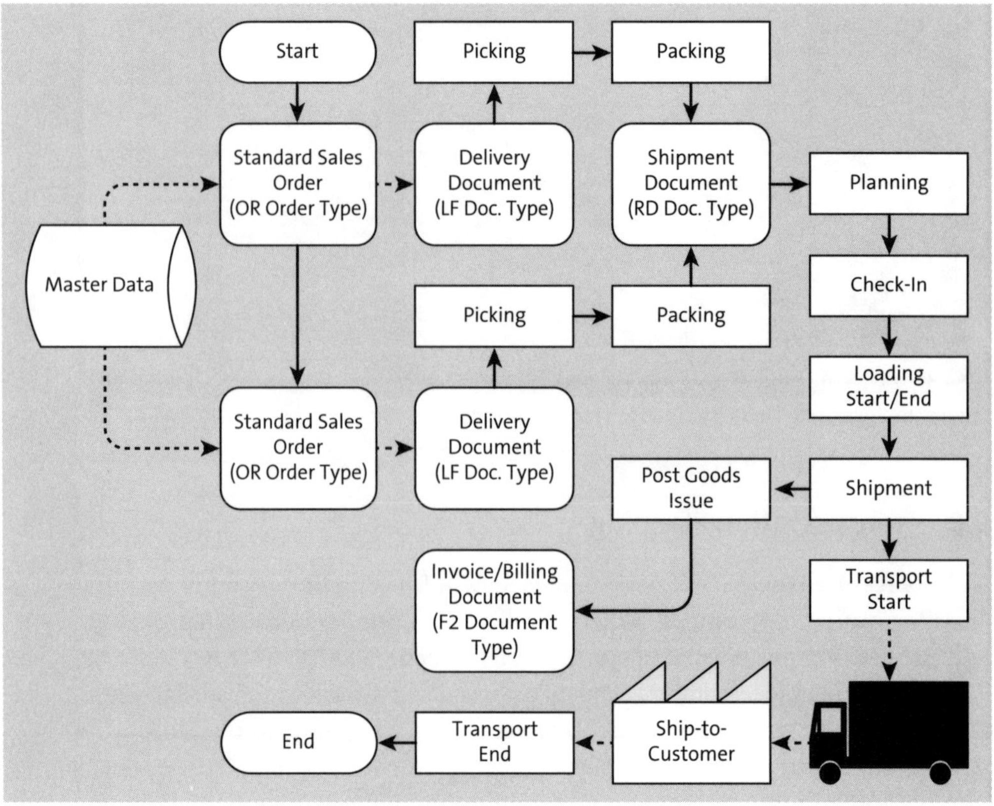

Figure 9.49 Shipment Document

After you create a sales order, based on master data, stock is allocated via an ATP check, and the order becomes relevant for delivery processing. The delivery documents are then created. At this time, you could create and assign deliveries to the shipment document, but usually, you'll wait until picking and packing operations are completed to confirm product quantities, the number of packages, theirs weights/volumes, etc.

After picking and packing operations are completed, you'll create a shipment document and assign the packed deliveries to it. You could also create a shipment document based on expected departure schedules and later assign deliveries, but using the process as illustrated, you'll know the size and content of the shipment (if this information is important to your company when arranging freight).

Using information from the shipment document, you can tender freight from multiple carriers and decide which carrier will win the contract for this cargo.

If your company owns delivery trucks, you can decide which truck and driver will deliver this shipment and which route they will follow. Once the route has been defined, you'll record the completion of the transportation planning phase.

Once the delivery truck is at the warehouse dock, you can register its check-in to indicate the truck is available for loading. You may then start loading the truck with your products. Once the truck is loaded, you'll record the completion of loading in the system as well. After all other necessary preparation steps are completed (if any), this shipment document is considered complete, and you'll record its status as well. The shipment completion operation must be configured with an activity profile to perform the post goods issue operation on all deliveries assigned to the shipment document (Section 9.8.6 for more details on this assignment).

The shipment document may be created manually using Transaction VT01N or automatically using Transaction VT04. We'll use Transaction VT01N to illustrate this process, through the following steps:

1. On the **Create Shipment: Initial Screen**, shown in Figure 9.50, select the transportation planning point (**TransportPlanningPt**, the organizational structure element responsible for transportation as described in Chapter 2) and the shipment document type (**Shipment Type**, Section 9.8.5 for configuration details).

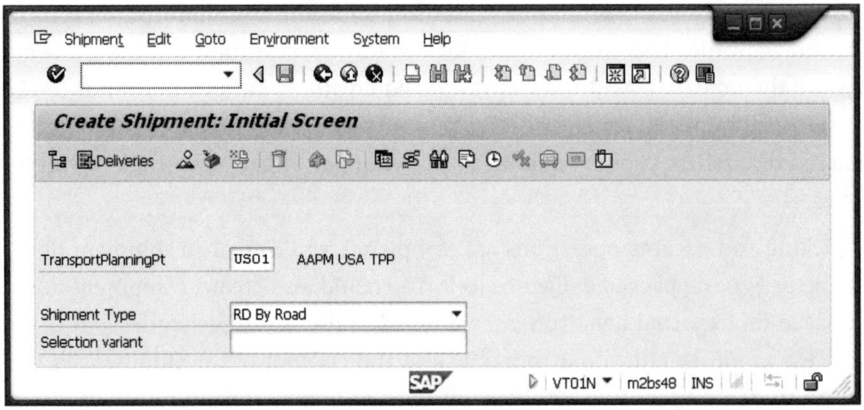

Figure 9.50 Create Shipment: Initial Screen

2. Next, you'll usually add the delivery document that is part of this shipment by clicking the **Deliveries** button, as shown in Figure 9.51, or pressing F6.

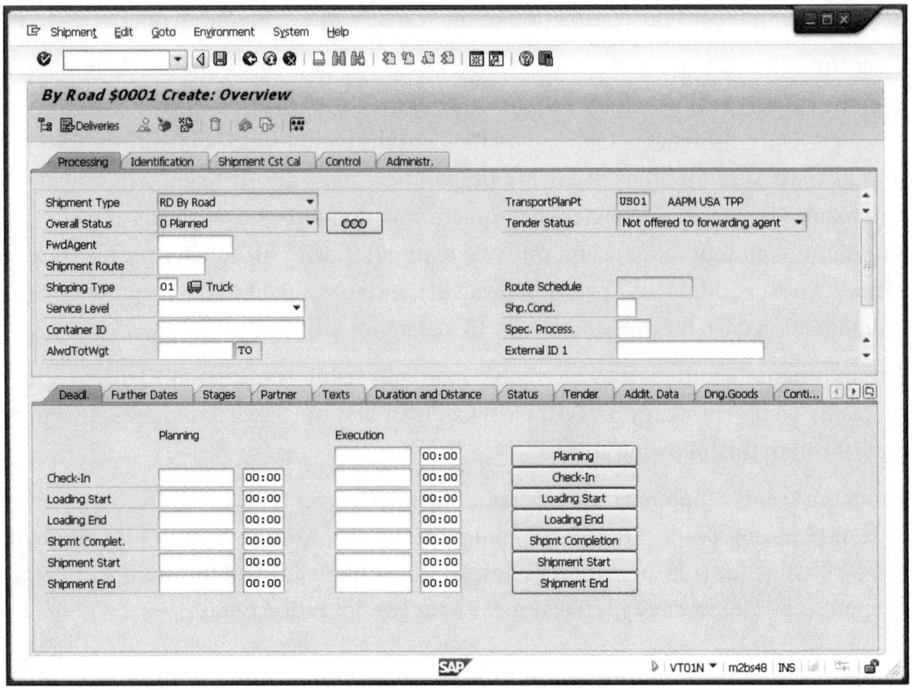

Figure 9.51 Create Shipment: Overview Screen

3. The popup window shown in Figure 9.52 and Figure 9.53, will appear where you can filter which deliveries will show up for selection in the next step. The default selection variant is configured in the shipment document type. Once you've finish adding the selection criteria, click on the **Execute** button or press F8.

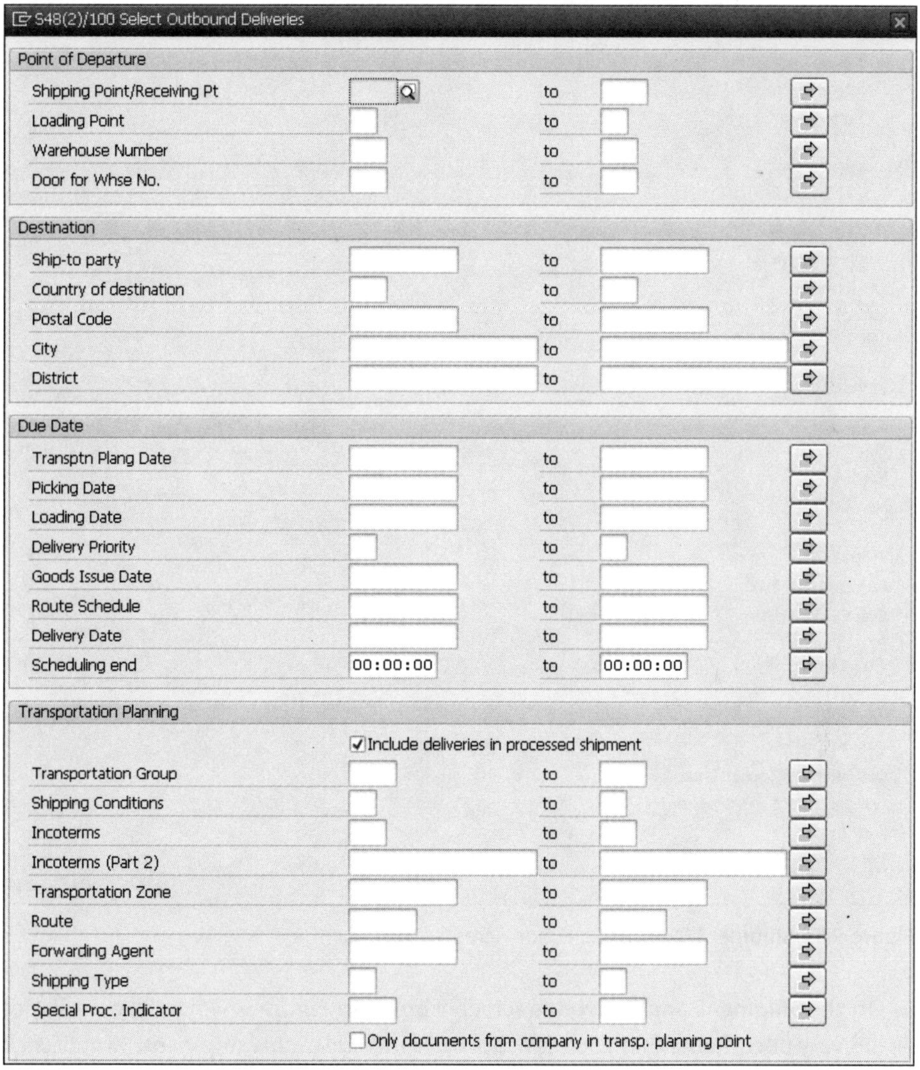

Figure 9.52 Shipment Due List Selection Screen (1/2)

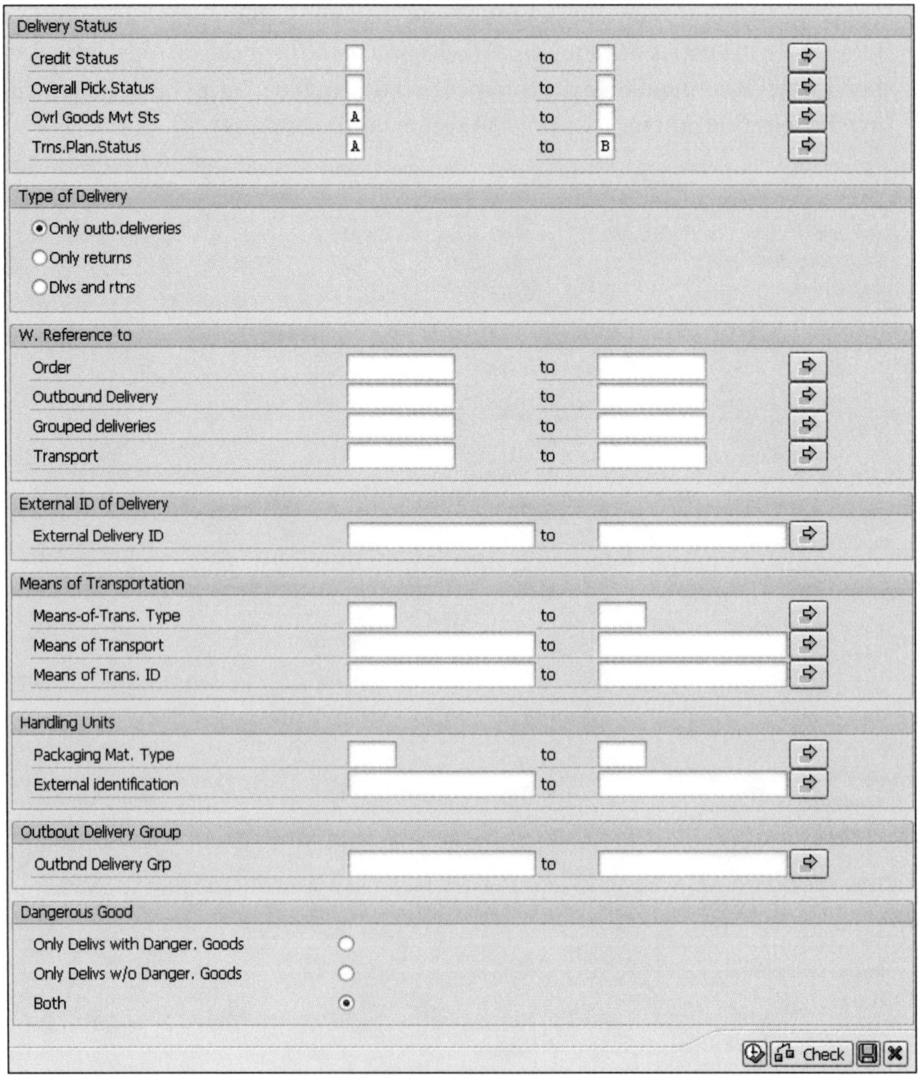

Figure 9.53 Shipment Due List Selection Screen (2/2)

4. On the **Shipment and Deliveries** screen, shown in Figure 9.54, you'll see a list of delivery documents that you may choose to include in this shipment. Simply click on the desired delivery document number.

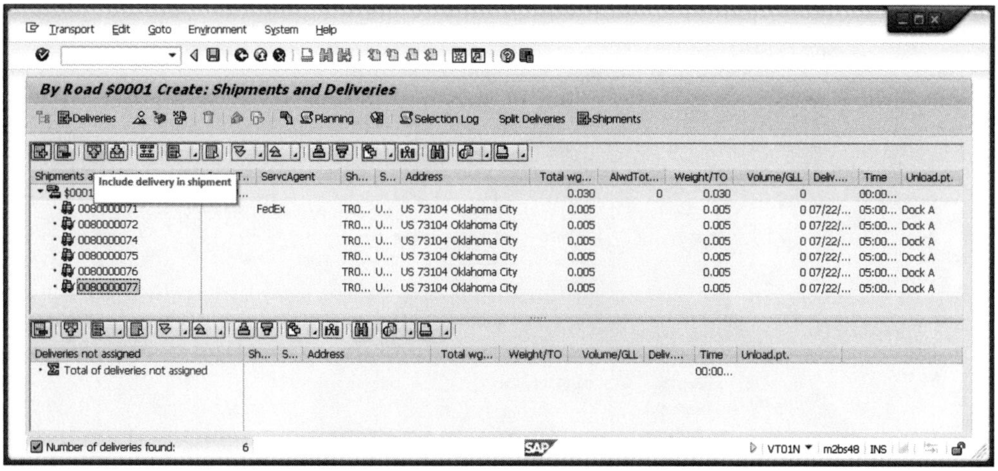

Figure 9.54 Browsing and Adding Delivery to Shipment Documents

5. Click on the **Include Deliveries in Shipment** button, and the delivery will be included. Repeat these steps for all deliveries that are part of this shipment.
6. Once all deliveries have been selected and included in this shipment, click on the **Overview of the Current Shipment** button to go back to the main screen.

From this point forward, you'll use the status button to control activities for this shipment: **Planning**, **Check-In**, **Loading Start**, **Loading End**, **Shipment Completion**, **Shipment Start**, and **Shipment End**. You'll describe each of the status earlier in this chapter when describing the process flow diagram, shown earlier in Figure 9.49.

9.8.2 Defining Routes

To configure routes, open Transaction OVTC or follow the via menu path **SAP Customizing Implementation Guide • Logistics Execution • Transportation • Basic Transportation Functions • Routes • Define Routes • Define Routes and Stages.** On the screen that opens, select the desired route and then click on the **Details** button or press F2.

In the screen shown in Figure 9.55, we'll focus on transportation requirements. Note that we already covered other aspects of this configuration in Chapter 6, Section 6.2.6.

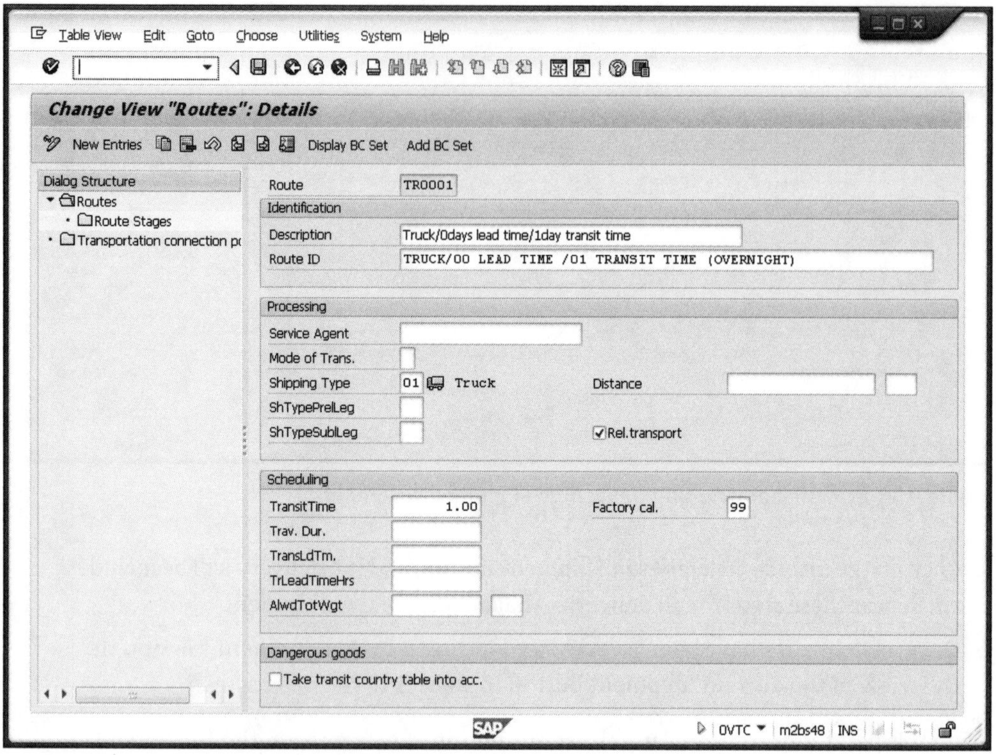

Figure 9.55 Defining Route Details

On this screen, maintain the details for a given route. To activate transportation, select the relevant for transportation (**Rel.transport**) flag. You may also assign a carrier (vendor) number on the **Service Agent** field, which is done if you are defining carrier-specific routes. Otherwise, the carrier will have to be selected on the shipment document.

The other **Processing** fields qualify the type of route you're using and will help define default values on the shipment document:

- In the **Mode of Trans.** field, you can use 1 for sea, 3 for road, 4 for air, etc.
- In the **Shipping Type** field (01 for truck), you can add new detailed types such as flatbed trucks for large items.
- The **ShTypePreLeg** (shipping type of preliminary leg) field is used, for instance, when using a truck to take product to the port before the product goes on a ship.

- The **ShTypeSubLeg** (shipping type of subsequent leg) field is used, for instance, if you use a truck to pick up product at the airport and take it to the customer.
- The **Distance** field allows you to define the distance that this route represents. You can use this value as input when calculating freight.

Using this configuration transaction, you can also add route schedule details and transportation connection points. This information is useful for complex transportation scenarios including consolidation warehouses, routes involving multiple vessels, etc.

9.8.3 Maintaining Transportation Relevance

You must activate transportation relevance for each delivery document type, item category, and route (which we covered earlier in Section 9.8.2).

To activate transportation, follow the menu path **SAP Customizing Implementation Guide • Logistics Execution • Transportation • Shipments • Maintain Transportation Relevance**. On the screen that opens, you'll see three options, as shown in Figure 9.56.

Name of Activity
Maintain transportation relevance for delivery types
Maintain transportation relevance for delivery item types
Maintain transportation relevance for routes

Figure 9.56 Maintain Transportation Relevance Menu

As shown in Figure 9.57, follow these steps:

❶ For the menu option **Maintain transportation relevance for delivery types**, you'll find the delivery document type and set the transportation relevance by selecting the relevant for transportation (**Rel.Transport**) flag.

❷ For the menu option **Maintain transportation relevance for delivery item types**, you'll find the delivery item category and set transportation relevance by selecting the relevant for transportation (**Rel.Transport**) flag.

❸ On the menu option **Maintain transportation relevance for routes**, you'll find the route and set transportation relevance by selecting the relevant for transportation (**Rel.Transport**) flag.

The shipment document can only be created if all three of these flags are assigned; otherwise, you won't be able to find deliveries to add to the shipping document.

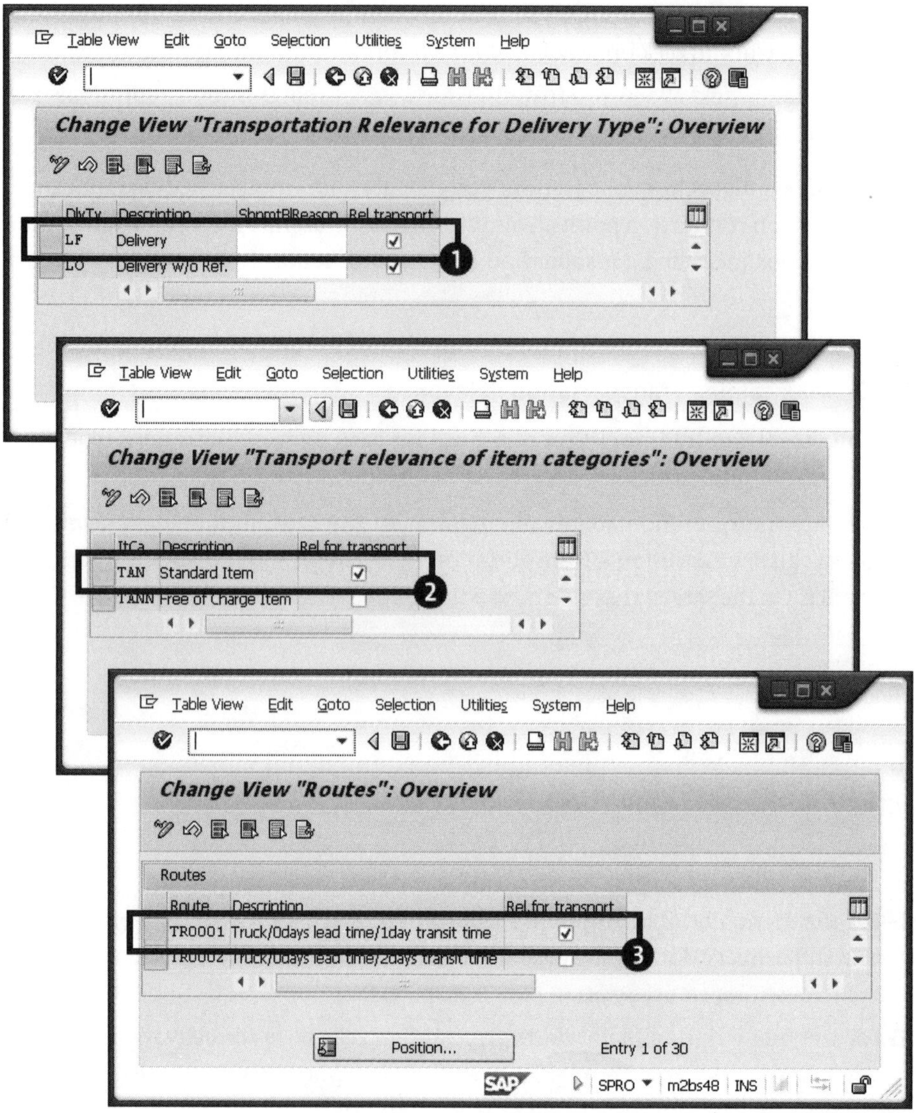

Figure 9.57 Maintaining Transportation Relevance

9.8.4 Number Ranges for Shipment Documents

To configure number ranges for delivery documents types, open Transaction VN07 or follow menu path **SAP Customizing Implementation Guide • Logistics Execution •**

Transportation • Shipments • Define Number Ranges for Shipments. On the screen that opens, click on the display **Intervals** button.

Note this menu path leads you to a configuration screen seen that is similar to the screen for sales orders and delivery document number ranges. However, on this screen, we're specifically maintaining entries for the number range object **RV_TRANSPO**.

Figure 9.58 shows the Transaction VN07 screen. See Chapter 6 for detailed instructions on how to change number ranges.

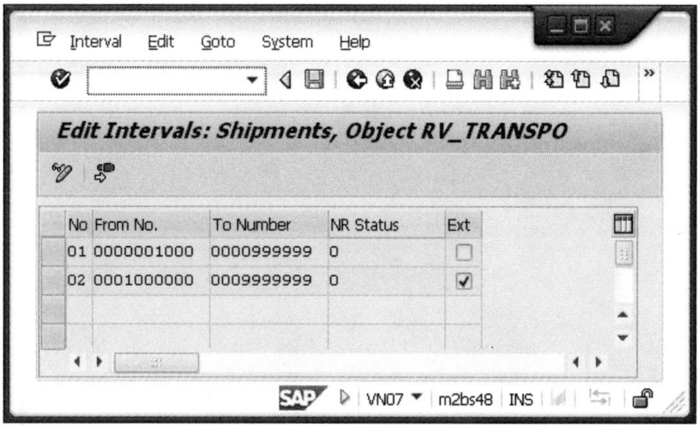

Figure 9.58 Displaying Shipment Documents Number Range Intervals

9.8.5 Defining Shipment Types

To configure shipment types, open Transaction VN07 or follow the menu path **SAP Customizing Implementation Guide • Logistics Execution • Transportation • Shipments • Define Shipment Types**.

Figure 9.59 shows the Transaction VN07 screen. Note that the detailed screen appears automatically when only one entry is found. If more than one entry exists, you'll need to select the desired entry and click the **Details** button. At the top of this screen, the document category (**Document Cat.**) is fixed, defined as "8," indicating this document type is used on shipment documents.

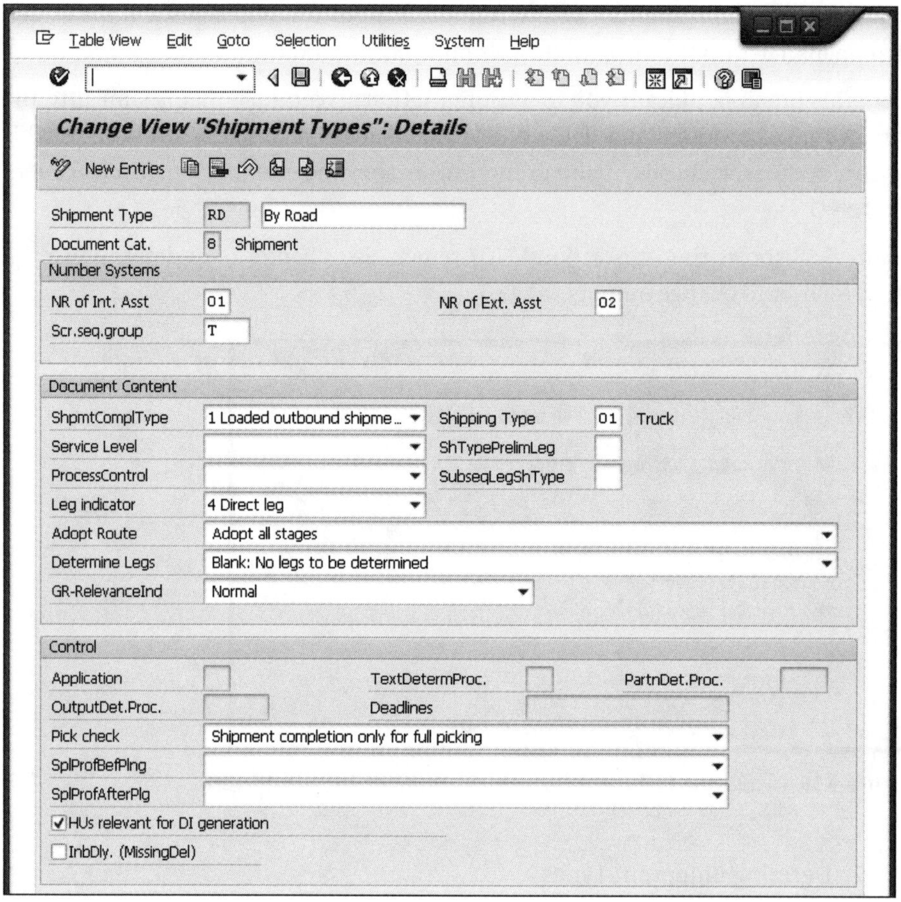

Figure 9.59 Defining Shipment Types (1/2)

In the following sections, we'll discuss the important fields in each area of this screen.

Number Systems

The number range used for this shipment document type must be defined in the **NR of Int. Asst** (internal assignment) and/or **NR of Ext. Asst** (external assignment) fields. The internal assignment range is used when the system determines what the shipment document number should be, based on the last document number generated plus one. The external assignment range is used when you want to enter the shipment document number. Section 9.2.3 shows the intervals for these number range codes.

The **Scr.seq.group** field is a code that corresponds to variations of the shipment document screen you may choose from. This field will make certain tabs appear (or not) and affect the order in which the tabs appear.

Document Content

In the **Document Content** area of this screen, you'll see the following fields:

- The **ShpmtComplType** field is used to identify the type of process this shipment document type is used for (inbound or outbound). This field is used by the system to determine what actions are necessary to determine when shipment is completed.
- The **Shipping Type** field is a code that represents how the product will make its way from your warehouse to the customer (truck/road, ship/sea, airplane/air, etc.). This information would be relevant if setting up certain restrictions and is used as a default value for this type of shipment.
- The **Service Level** field is how you execute this shipment (general express, etc.)
- The **ProcessControl** field describes how transportation takes place (individual or collective/single mode or multiple).
- The **ShTypePrelimLeg** (shipping type of preliminary leg) field is used, for instance, when using a truck to take a product to the port before the product goes on a ship.
- The **SubseqLegShType** (shipping type of subsequent leg) field used, for instance, if using a truck to pick a up product at the airport to take to a customer.
- The **Leg indicator** field describes how many legs will be needed to deliver the product. Code 4 is used for direct shipments from your warehouse to the customer.
- The **Adopt Route** field allows you to filter route stages before these stages are assigned to the shipment document (if any).
- The **Determine Legs** field controls whether the legs need to be identified and how much detail is required.
- The **GR-RelevanceInd** field allows for multilevel goods receipt (for use in purchasing).

Control

In the **Control** area of this screen, you'll see the following fields:

- The **Application**, **TextDetermProc.**, **PartnDet.Proc.**, and **OutputDet.Proc.** fields identify the output determination that is assigned to the shipment document type. The configuration of these values is done in a different Transaction SPRO menu option and uses condition techniques.

- The **Deadlines** field identifies the event that represents this shipment document type and is configured elsewhere. Once the shipment document is completed, this event will be considered complete.
- The **Pick check** field controls whether you can complete this shipment document type even if some of the delivery have not been fully picked.
- The **SplProfBefPlng** and **SplProfAfterPlg** fields control whether you can perform delivery split for document assigned to this shipment document type.
- The **HUs Relevant for DI Generation** field indicates that the handling units assigned to the deliveries items during packing are relevant for the shipment document type for output forms and interfaces.
- The **InbDly. (MissingDel)** field is used by purchasing and indicates that you allow shipment documents with this shipment document type to be create even is the inbound delivery is not yet available.

Proposal

In the **Proposal** area of this screen (shown in Figure 9.60), you'll see the following fields:

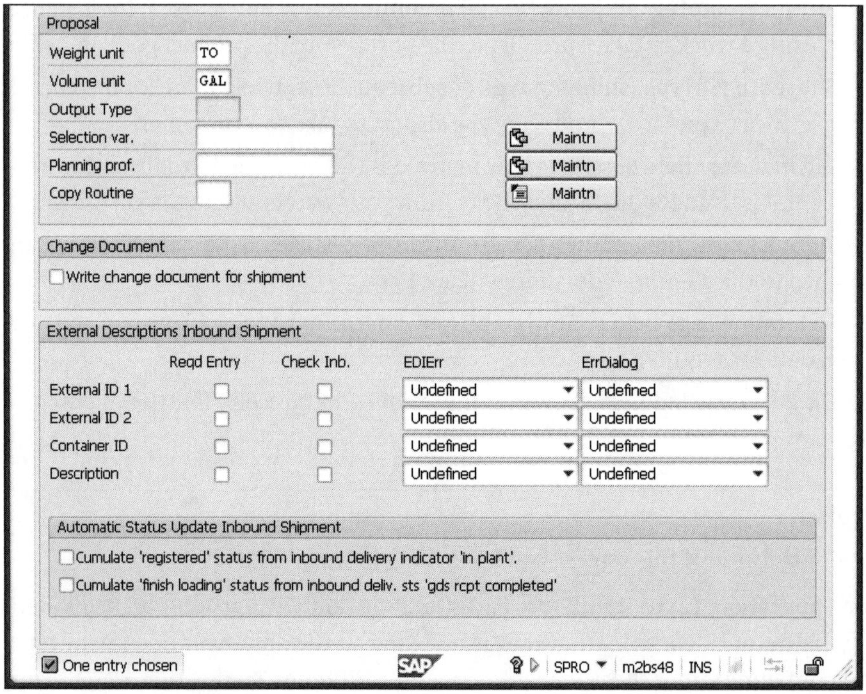

Figure 9.60 Defining Shipment Types (2/2)

- The **Weight unit** field is the default weight unit of measurement used by this shipment document type.
- The **Volume unit** field is the default volume unit of measurement used by this shipment document type.
- The **Output Type** field displays the default output type configured for this shipment document type; this is used when the user trigger output without specifying the output type.
- The **Selection var.** field is the default selection variant used by this shipment document type when adding deliveries to it. It allows you to prepopulate selection criteria fields (such as the organizational structure) eliminating the need for the user to enter the same values over and over.
- The **Planning prof.** field is the default selection variant used by this shipment document type when processing several deliveries using Transaction VT04 (Shipment Due List Report).
- The **Copy Routine** field uses a VOFM routine to control how delivery document fields are copied into the shipment document allowing for great flexibility.

Change Document

The **Write change document for shipment** field controls whether you want to automatically generate an audit trail for manual changes made to this shipment. By selecting this flag, we'll add a potentially large amount of records to the change documents table. Thus, this flag must only be activated if really necessary.

External Descriptions Inbound Shipment

In the **External Descriptions Inbound Shipment** area of this screen, you'll see the following fields:

- The **Reqd Entry** flag indicates that the corresponding field (**External ID 1**, **External ID 2**, **Container ID**, and **Description**) is mandatory for this shipment document type.
- The **Check Inb.** flag indicates that the value entered on the corresponding field (**External ID 1**, **External ID 2**, **Container ID**, and **Description**) is unique for this shipment document type and may not be used in more than one document. This flag is used to avoid duplication and is especially important when you receive shipment information electronically (via EDI).

- The **EDIErr** field controls the type of message (error, information, warning, or none/undefined) that must be issued when the corresponding field (**External ID 1**, **External ID 2**, **Container ID**, and **Description**) is not unique when you receive shipment information electronically (via EDI).
- The **ErrDialog** field controls the type of message (error, information, warning, or none/undefined) that must be issued when the corresponding field (**External ID 1**, **External ID 2**, **Container ID**, and **Description**) is not unique when entering shipment information manually via Transaction VT02N.

Automatic Status Update Inbound Shipment

In the **Automatic Status Update Inbound Shipment** area of this screen, you'll see the following fields:

- The **Cumulate 'registered' status for inbound delivery indicator 'in plant'** field will automatically set the status of the shipment document when all delivery documents contained therein are flagged with the **In Plant** status, as described in Section 9.3.1.
- The **Cumulate 'finish loading' status for inbound deliv. sts 'gds rcpt completed'** field indicates that the delivery document **Loading** status must be set as complete when the delivery is assigned to the shipment document.

9.8.6 Defining and Assigning Activity Profiles

To define activity profiles, you'll need to first create a variant for program RV56ABST using Transaction SE38 (also used to write ABAP code). This variant is what is referred to as an *activity profile*, and we'll describe how to create activity profiles in this section.

To assign activity profiles (program RV56ABST variants) to shipment document types and statuses, follow the menu path **SAP Customizing Implementation Guide • Logistics Execution • Transportation • Shipments • Define and Assign Activity Profiles**.

Let's now look at the steps necessary to create an *activity profile* via Transaction SE38:

1. In Transaction SE38, as shown in Figure 9.61, enter program name "RV56ABST".
2. Select the **Variants** radio button.
3. Click on the **Change** button.
4. On the **ABAP: Variants – Initial Screen** shown in Figure 9.62, define a 14-character variant name (**Variant**) for the activity profile.
5. Click on the **Create** button.

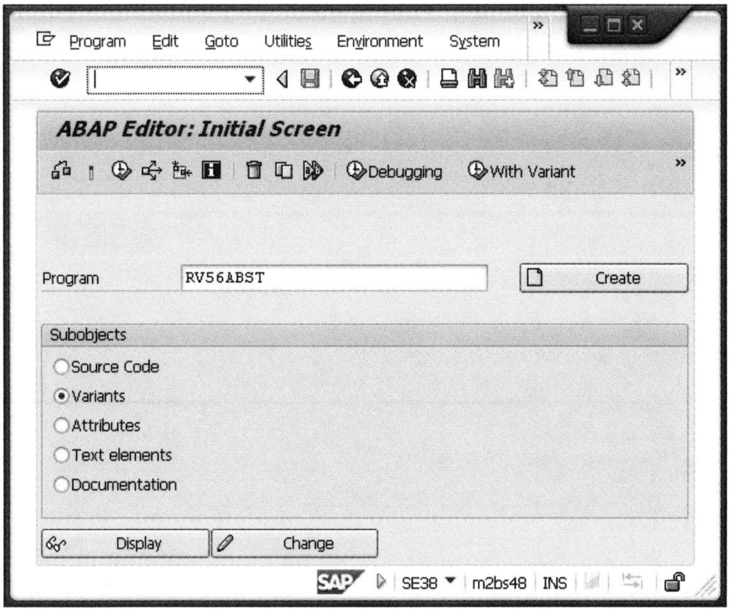

Figure 9.61 Creating Variants for Program RV56ABST

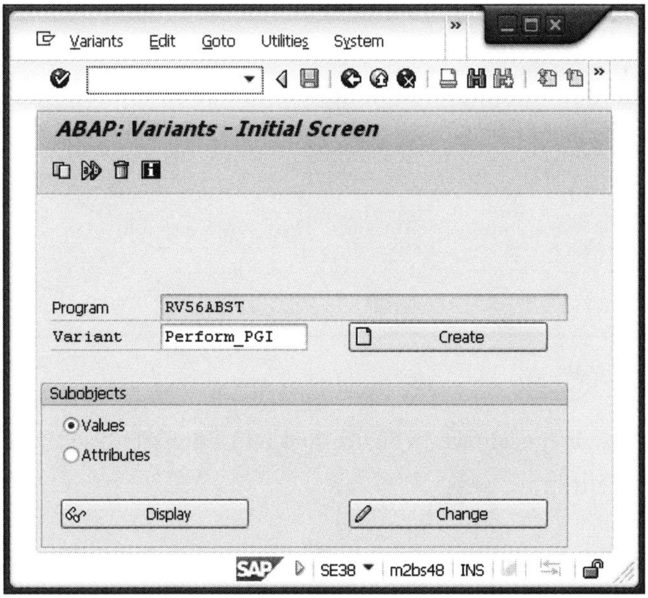

Figure 9.62 Defining the Variant Name

6. On the **Edit Variants: Report RV56ABST, Variant PERFORM_PGI** screen, shown in Figure 9.63, select the **Carry out goods issue posting during save** radio button. Several other functions can be enabled on this screen, but this function is the most commonly used.
7. Click on the **Attributes** button.

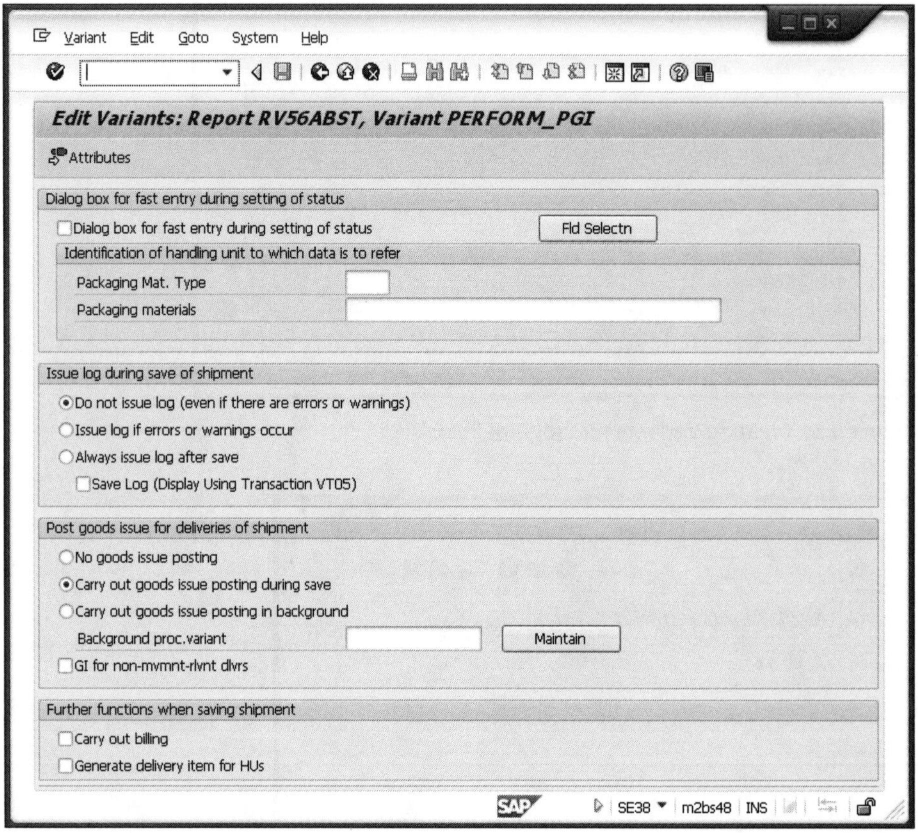

Figure 9.63 Selection Screen Details

8. On the **Variant Attributes** screen, shown in Figure 9.64, add a description for the activity profile (**Description**).
9. Click on the **Save** button.
10. On the **Change View "Activity Profiles for Shipment Types": Overview** screen shown in Figure 9.65, enter the *activity profile* defined earlier under the **At completion**

column. This column corresponds to the **Shipment Completion** column on the Transaction VT02N screen.

11. Click on the **Save** button.

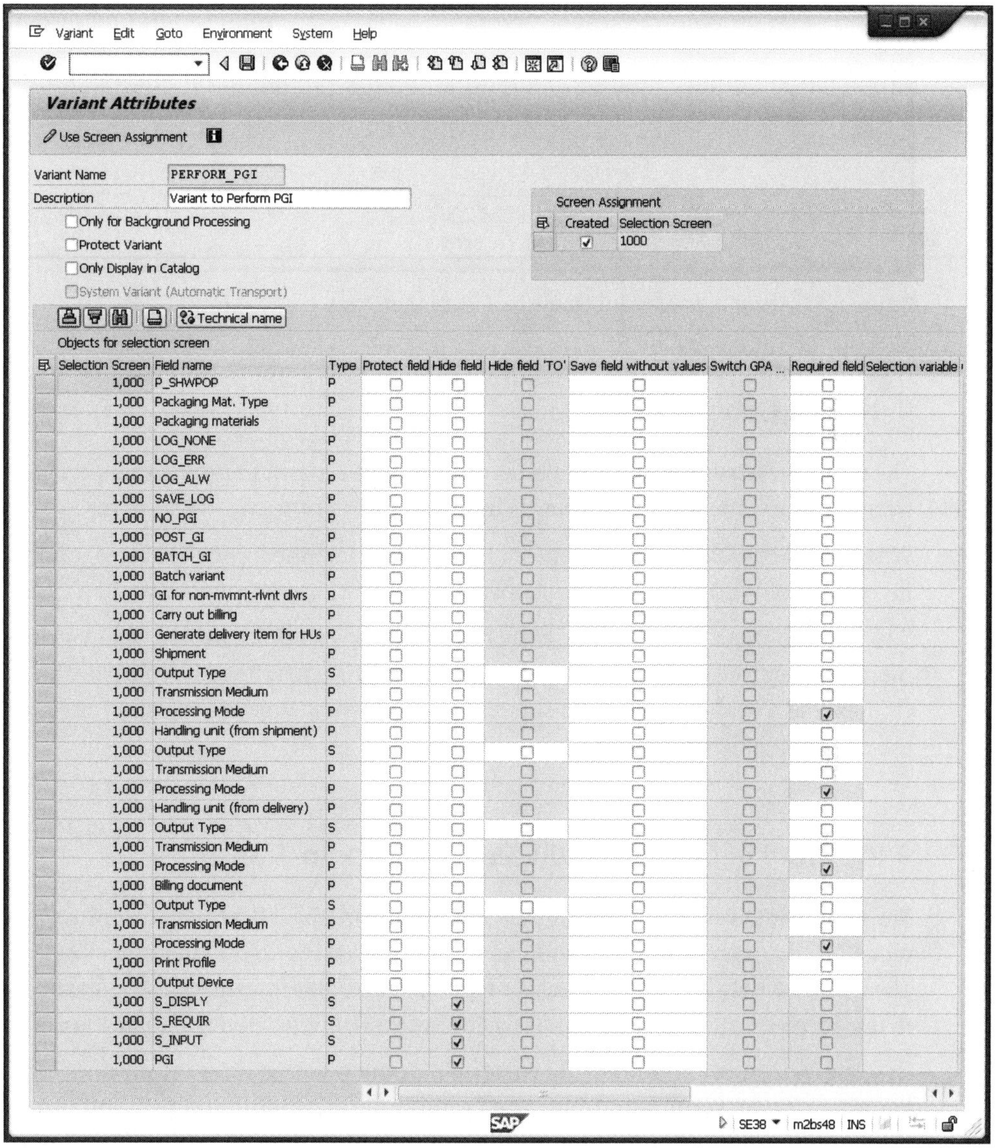

Selection Screen	Field name	Type	Protect field	Hide field	Hide field 'TO'	Save field without values	Switch GPA ...	Required field	Selection variable
1,000	P_SHWPOP	P							
1,000	Packaging Mat. Type	P							
1,000	Packaging materials	P							
1,000	LOG_NONE	P							
1,000	LOG_ERR	P							
1,000	LOG_ALW	P							
1,000	SAVE_LOG	P							
1,000	NO_PGI	P							
1,000	POST_GI	P							
1,000	BATCH_GI	P							
1,000	Batch variant	P							
1,000	GI for non-mvmnt-rlvnt dlvrs	P							
1,000	Carry out billing	P							
1,000	Generate delivery item for HUs	P							
1,000	Shipment	P							
1,000	Output Type	S							
1,000	Transmission Medium	P							
1,000	Processing Mode	P						X	
1,000	Handling unit (from shipment)	P							
1,000	Output Type	S							
1,000	Transmission Medium	P							
1,000	Processing Mode	P						X	
1,000	Handling unit (from delivery)	P							
1,000	Output Type	S							
1,000	Transmission Medium	P							
1,000	Processing Mode	P						X	
1,000	Billing document	P							
1,000	Output Type	S							
1,000	Transmission Medium	P							
1,000	Processing Mode	P						X	
1,000	Print Profile	P							
1,000	Output Device	P							
1,000	S_DISPLY	S		X					
1,000	S_REQUIR	S		X					
1,000	S_INPUT	S		X					
1,000	PGI	P		X					

Figure 9.64 Variant Attributes

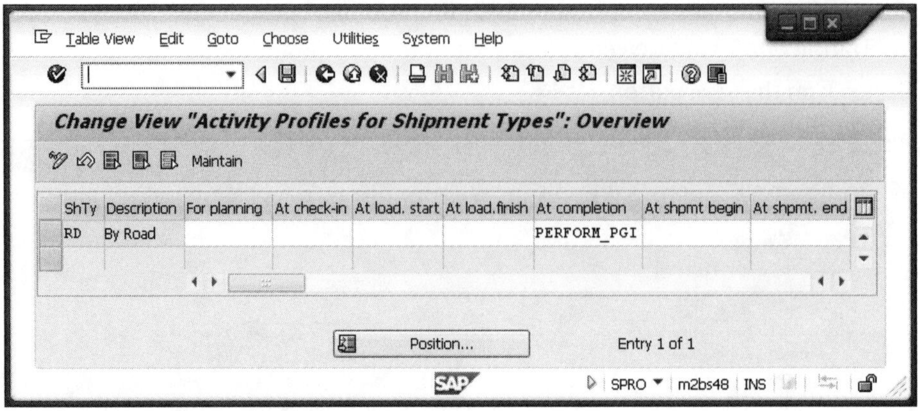

Figure 9.65 Assigning a Variant Name to a Shipment Type

9.9 Post Goods Issue

The *post goods issue operation* is a term describing the moment products depart your warehouse and start heading towards the customer, in other words, shipping.

When you record this event, inventory is typically consumed, and the corresponding inventory accounting entries are created to represent the cost of goods sold (COGS).

You can also use the post goods issue operation to record data about when a shipment has occurred and control warehouse performance to reflect the company's performance as a whole, which is considered one of the most important factors affecting the customer experience/customer satisfaction.

9.10 Proof of Delivery and Valuated Stock-in-Transit

The proof of delivery (POD) feature is a system feature that allows you to control and record the date and time when products are delivered at the ship-to customer location. The invoice is only created after delivery is confirmed. This information is relevant for many purposes, such as shipment traceability, confirming delivered quantities, etc.

In some countries, commonly the customer is only invoiced after the product is delivered. In the US, some companies don't want the post goods issue operation to post the COGS on a date than different the date for revenue postings from the invoice. To solve this problem, consider the valuated stock-in-transit (VSIT) functionality, which we covered in Section 9.10.2.

You must control which lines are relevant for POD via the configuration steps described in Section 9.10.1.

9.10.1 Proof of Delivery

Proof of delivery is recorded in Transaction VLPOD, as shown in Figure 9.66. To use Transaction VLPOD, you must flag the business partner (customer) data **POD-relevant** flag under the **Shipping** tab of the sales and distribution data for the customer business partner role. The customer must be flagged in this way before entering sales orders for this functionality to be available.

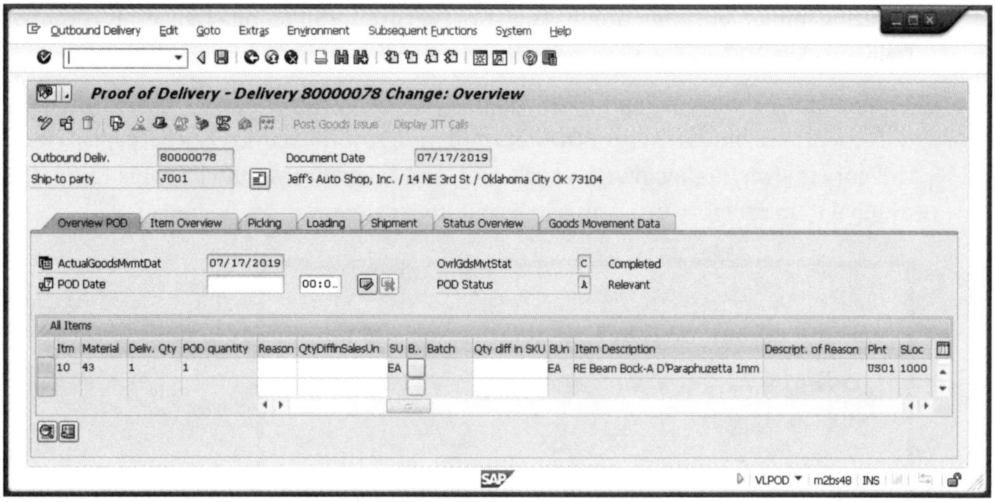

Figure 9.66 Transaction VLPOD to Record Proof of Delivery

In this transaction, enter the **POD Date** with the date and time when product was delivered at the ship-to customer address.

You can also use the **Qty Diff Sales Un** or **Qty Diff SKU** fields to indicate that the delivered quantity was different than the quantity specified on the delivery document. You can enter the delivery quantity using the sales unit of measurement (**Sales UN**) or base UoM/stock-keeping unit of measurement (**SKU**). You can use the **Reason** column to indicate why the quantity is different (typically items have been damaged or lost in transit).

Most companies do not use the proof of delivery functionality, and the ones that do are mostly concerned with the POD date and time.

This feature is often implemented along with an interface from the carrier or from the customer to capture this information without the need manual user input to register the POD date on all relevant deliveries. This fairly simple interface is available from most carriers and worth the effort to reduce and assist with customer complaints. If you have EDI interfaces with your customer, they may also be ready to send this interface.

You can also set the POD to be registered automatically based on a fixed number of days on the customer master. This approach may be considered if registering the delivery date and time is understood as a burden but still required.

To assign POD relevance to delivery item categories, follow the menu path **SAP Customizing Implementation Guide • Logistics Execution • Shipping • Deliveries • Proof of Delivery • Set POD-Relevance Depending on Delivery Item Category**.

On the screen shown in Figure 9.67 you find the item category (**Ite...**) used on delivery documents and maintain the **POD-Relevant** indicator that controls whether this item category is always relevant, never relevant, or if relevance should be copied from the original item category (used on batch split item categories, for instance).

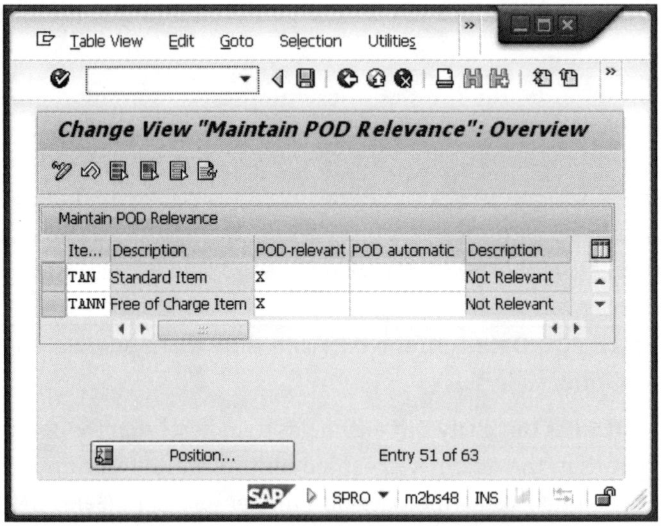

Figure 9.67 Maintaining POD-Relevance by Delivery Item Category

On this screen, you may also activate the **Automatic POD** using the fixed amount of days maintained on the customer master data.

9.10.2 Valuated Stock-in-Transit

Recently in the United States, many publicly traded companies are concerned about recognizing revenue on sales of product only when products are actually delivered to the customer. This concern is a result from International Financial Reporting Standards (IFRS) 15 and Accounting Standards Codification (ASC) 606, published in May 2014.

Revenue in this context refers to an account posting that represents sales of goods and services. This posting was traditionally done when the invoice is created, but since May 2014, many companies and their auditors see this practice as a regulatory compliance issue and now require revenue be accounted only when product is delivered.

The simplest way to achieve this change in accounting is to reclassify revenue, before month end, for invoices issued a given number of days before the end of the month into a *deferred revenue* account. The number of days considered for deferment represents the estimated amount of time that product will take to reach the customer. After month end, the deferred revenue is reclassified back into revenue. This approach is sufficient for many accounting departments and for auditors.

Revenue resulting from sales of goods also bring challenges regarding the cost of goods sold (COGS) required in inventory accounting, especially without matching revenue. COGS is often reclassified in the same way as revenue before the end of the month.

For other companies, in particular companies with longer and/or irregular transportation lead times, this approach to deferred revemie is consider inaccurate and therefore inadequate. This is common on companies that ship bulky products with freight arranged shipment by shipment.

For these companies, you can activate the SAP S/4HANA feature normally used for stock transfers for use with customer deliveries with the implementation of an enhancement pack and configuration. This approach is called *valuated stock-in-transit* (VSIT) and is also referred to as the *transfer of title at customer location*. This feature leverages the proof of delivery functionality described earlier in Section 9.10.1.

VSIT features special stock movement types assigned to the sales order schedule line via a configuration that places stock in an in-transit status upon the post goods issue operation, rather than consuming these quantities into a COGS account. You can query in-transit inventory quantities via Transaction MB5SIT, and these quantities remain valuated in your inventory books until the POD is registered.

Once you run Transaction VLPOD or receive a delivery notification EDI message from the carrier, the system will consume in-transit inventory into a COGS account. The delivery also becomes relevant for billing, which is typically processed by a background job on the same day.

Movement type 687 must be assigned to the schedule line category configuration as described in Chapter 6. Movement type 687 is only available after the implementation of the corresponding SAP enhancement pack.

The enhancement pack also includes out-of-the box configuration that allows you to use VSIT by providing you with the special sales order type ORNC, which uses different schedule line categories (N1 and N2) preassigned with the post goods issue operation movement type 687 and VSIT movement type 601.

9.11 Document Flow

The document flow feature is available on sales documents to show references between documents. With deliveries, you can quickly find the sales order used as a reference to create this document. Figure 9.67 shows the navigation between orders and deliveries using the document flow.

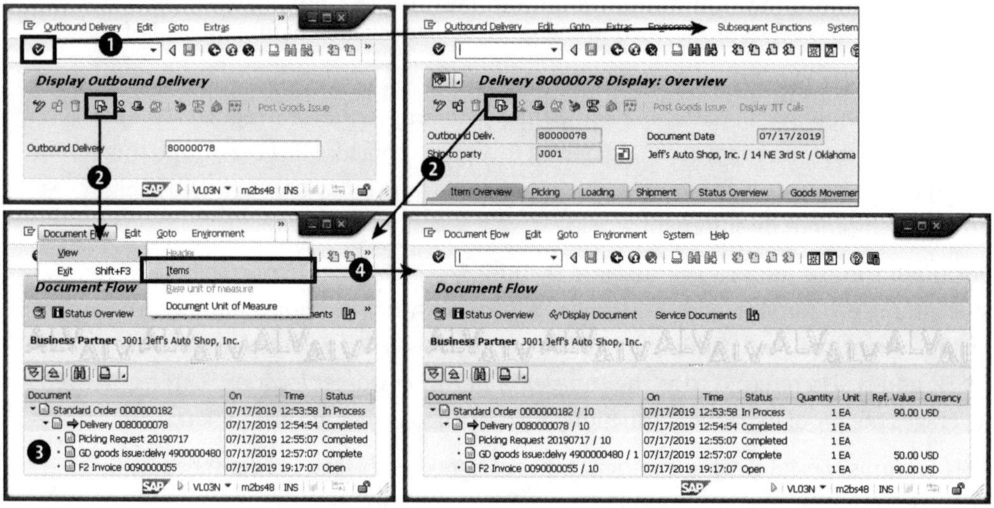

Figure 9.68 Delivery Document Flow

❶ In Transaction VL03N (Display) or VL02N (Change), you can select a delivery document number and press Enter to display/modify it.

❷ Clicking the document flow icon on either the initial screen or on the **Item Overview** tab will open the **Document Flow** screen.

❸ When you open the **Document Flow** screen from the initial screen or from the header of the Item Overview Screen, the document flow will be summarized at the header level. If you've highlighted a line on the Item Overview screen, when you click on the document flow icon, information pertaining to that specific line will be displayed.

❹ Follow the menu options **Document Flow • View • Items** to see document flow information for each delivery line in full detail. This information is useful for tracking issues.

9.12 Inbound Deliveries

Inbound deliveries are used to receive product and manage related logistics operations. Purchasers use inbound deliveries as part of MM configuration. Inbound deliveries related to sales are used for customer returns, services, and stock transfer order scenarios.

In Chapter 13, we'll cover authorizing and identifying returns in detail. In this section, we'll focus on the additional configuration steps required to process inbound deliveries.

To define the receiving point to be used in inbound deliveries, follow the menu path **SAP Customizing Implementation Guide • Logistics Execution • Shipping • Basic Shipping Functions • Shipping Point and Goods Receiving Point Determination • Assign Goods Receiving Points for Inbound Deliveries.** On the screen that opens, click on the **New Entries** button or press F5.

On the screen shown in Figure 9.69, enter the combination of **Plant**, **Storage Location**, and **Shipping Point** to be used as receiving point. You must consider all possible combinations that are relevant for goods receipt.

When more than one shipping point is assigned to the same plant and storage location combination, you can define a priority so the system can decide which of shipping point to use.

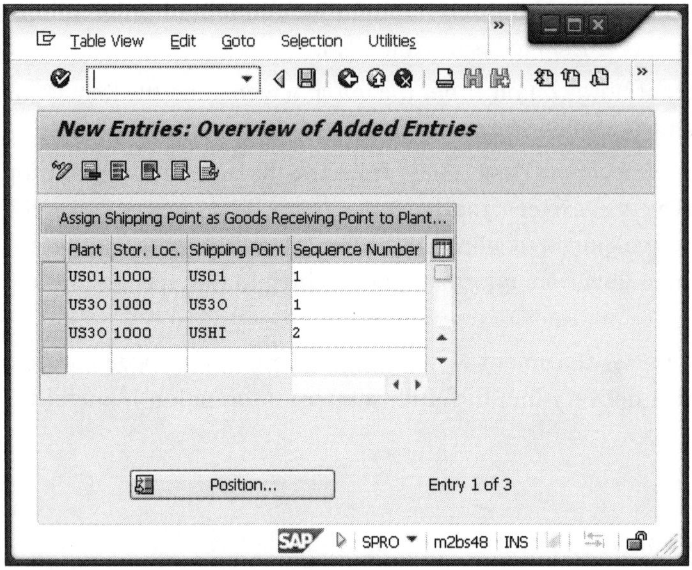

Figure 9.69 Assigning Shipping Points

This determination is used when the inbound delivery is created to ensure only valid combinations are used and to define default values when required.

9.13 Summary

Logistics functionalities are required for all companies with revenue streams that include delivering products, even if you use a warehouse management system such SAP EWM, embedded EWM, or a third-party solution. You should now understand the distribution portion of SAP S/4HANA Sales well enough that you can participate and assist in making decisions about the best logistics solution for your company. Once the design is defined, you should be comfortable enough to work on the required configuration during implementation.

Chapter 10
Billing and Invoicing

The term "billing document" is a generalization to represent invoices, credit memos, and other documents that serve as links between sales and finance. Billing documents will be required for many business transactions, and we'll walk you through some common scenarios requiring special billing documents in this chapter.

Most companies create billing documents automatically using background jobs. SAP S/4HANA was designed to resolve issues upfront (like pricing, payment terms, account determination, credit management, etc.), in the sales order, which in SAP ERP or even older ERP systems was managed and reworked at the time of billing. During implementation projects for billing, usually, requirements are handled with sales configuration, which enables you to treat billing as an automated system action.

In the following sections, we'll cover the steps and screens involved in creating billing documents (Section 10.1), invoice lists (Section 10.2), billing plans (Section 10.3), accounting and revenue recognition (Section 10.4), intercompany billing (Section 10.5), and proforma invoices (Section 10.6).

10.1 Creating Billing Documents

You can manually create billing documents in Transaction VF01, where you can closely control and affect how billing takes place and even make changes to some fields to affect the actual outcome of the billing process. This approach is not often used as the main billing mechanism, but for illustration, we'll manually create billing documents to guide you through the billing functionality. Companies generally prefer billing documents be created automatically via background jobs to ensure completeness without manual intervention.

In the following sections, we'll first look at the initial screen of Transaction VF01 and discuss some of the configuration activities necessary to fill out its fields. Next, we'll walk through the header and item detail screens to make changes before saving the new invoice. For ease, we've broken out the header details and items details into separate sections for their initial tabs but kept the header and item information combined for partners, conditions, and texts, since only a few differences exist between those screens. Purchase order (PO) information remains on its own, since that information is only relevant for item-level details.

10.1.1 Initial Document Selection and Document Overview

When creating a billing document using Transaction VF01, as shown in Figure 10.1, you can select several document numbers (**Document**) to process at once. The system will attempt to combine these documents whenever possible. It will split them when combination is not possible. If a split occurs, you will be given a list of billing documents that are about to be created. At that time, you can view the details of why the documents were split.

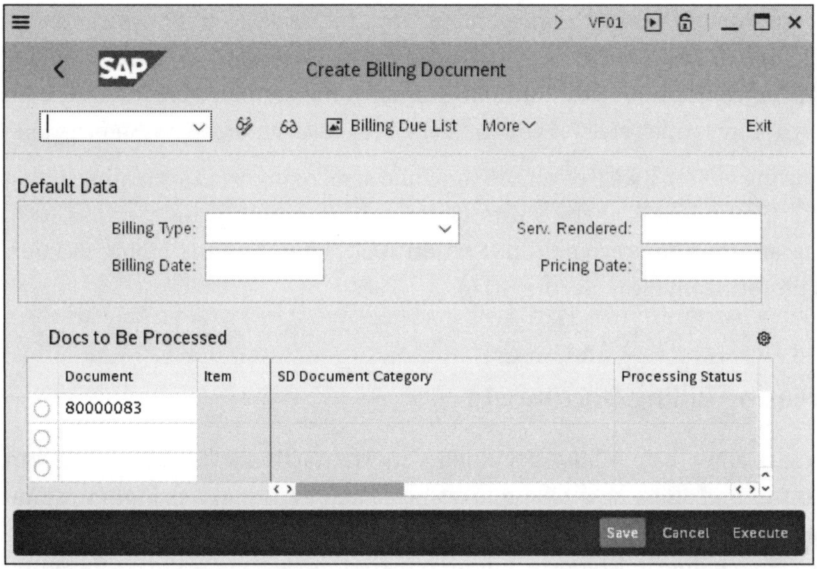

Figure 10.1 Transaction VF01: Document Selection

Figure 10.1 shows the initial Transaction VF01 screen where you'll choose the document to be processed. Press Enter or F8, which opens the screen shown in Figure 10.2.

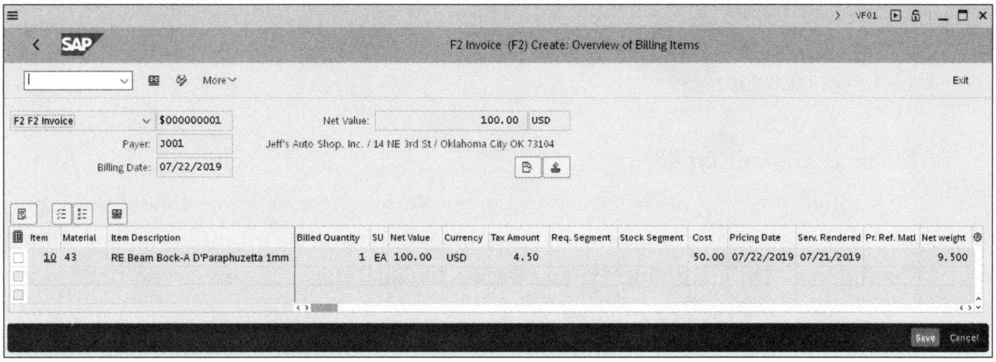

Figure 10.2 Transaction VF01: Overview

You also can change the default values assigned by the system, including the following fields:

- Underneath the search bar on the left, the billing type is assigned to the sales order type configuration. If you leave this field blank, the system will use the document number to find the sales order that originated the billing document and use the order type of the sales order document to configure the billing document type. If you select a document type, the system will attempt to use your selection regardless of the configuration issues that may arise. We'll discuss configuration details in the Billing Document Type section.
- The billing type is used when creating proforma invoices. Usually, you'll open Transaction VF01 and enter the billing document type "F5" for sales order-based proforma invoices or enter "F8" for delivery-based proforma invoices (Section 10.6 for more details).
- The **Billing Date** field allows you to affect the invoice date; unless specified, the system will match the billing date as defined on the delivery document (for delivery-related billing) or the sales order (for order-related billing).
- The **Pricing Date** field allows you to change the pricing date assigned to a sales order, causing a recalculation of the invoice price.
- You'll use the **Serv. Rendered** field to specify a date for creating invoices for services provided to a customer, on a date different than today

If you press [Enter], the system will display an overview of the billing document that is about to be created. Click the **Save** button or press [F11] to create the billing document without any further steps.

The following sections include configuration details for billing document types, shown earlier in Figure 10.1, as well as the billing number range associated with the billing document type.

Billing Document Type

To configure billing document types, open Transaction VOFA or follow the menu path **SAP Customizing Implementation Guide • Sales and Distribution • Billing • Billing Documents • Define Billing Types • Define Billing Types.** On the screen that opens, select the **Billing Type F2** and then click on the **Details** button or press F2, which will open the screen shown in Figure 10.3.

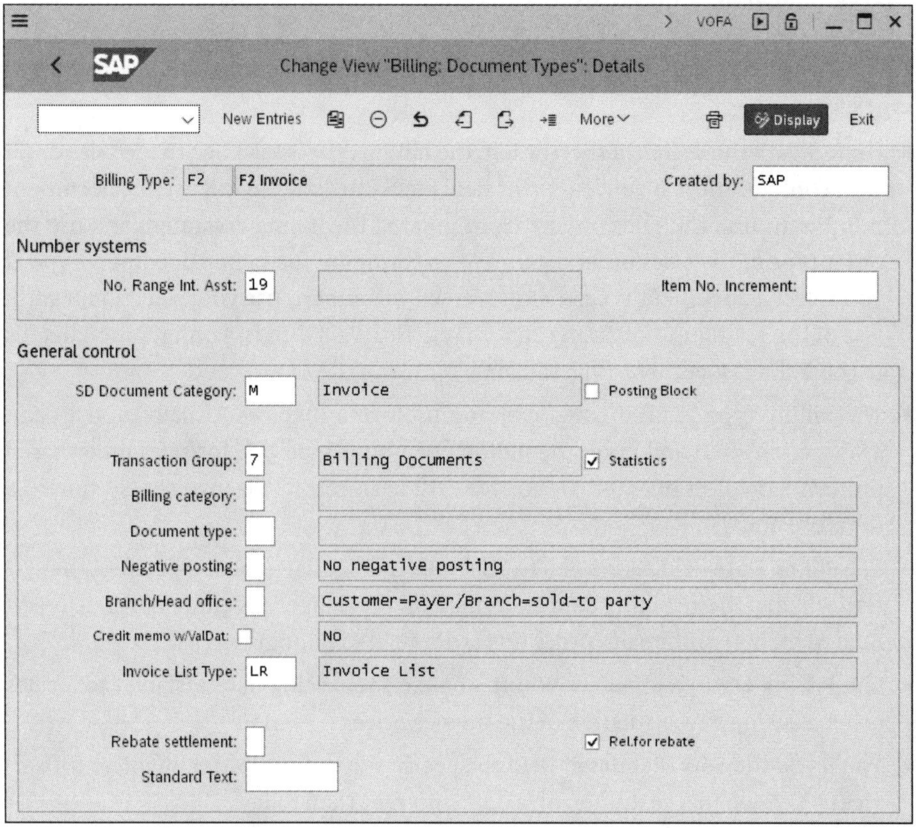

Figure 10.3 F2 Billing Document Type Configuration (1/2)

To create a new code, on this screen, specify a two-character billing document type code (**Billing Type**) and add a description. You can also specify the user ID responsible for creating this entry in the **Created by** field.

In the following sections, we'll go through each area on this screen in detail.

Number Systems

The number range used for this billing document type is defined in the **No. Range Int. Asst** (internal assignment) field; an internal assignment range is the only type of range available for use in billing documents. In the Defining Number Ranges for Billing Documents section, we'll provide details on how to set up number ranges for sales orders. We recommend using the standard whenever possible. Commonly, high-volume companies to run out of numbers and must increase the size of the intervals for the ranges. During implementation, you should foresee this need arising and increase intervals from the beginning.

The **Item No. Increment** field is a numeric value used when the system assigns line numbers at the time of sales order entry. The first line will be 0 plus this number, and every line will increment this number. The copy control configuration defines whether the line number from preceding documents should be copied or if you'll assign new numbers.

General Control

In the **General control** section, you'll find the following fields:

- The **SD Document Category** field is a code used in several transactions and functions by SAP S/4HANA to drive critical functionality. This information can be understood as a particular billing document type. For instance, if you enter "M," the system will understand that the pricing on the invoice corresponds to a debit (charge) to the customer (and thus the billing document is an invoice).
- The **Posting Block** flag, when checked, indicates that this billing document won't be posted to accounting automatically upon saving the document. Instead, you'll need to post the document using Transaction VFX3 online or via a background job.
- The **Transaction Group** field controls the flow within the billing document transaction and is used heavily by SAP S/4HANA to handle user input and navigation.
- The **Billing category** field is used by SAP S/4HANA to handle the billing document by grouping the document type into different types of billing and driving the corresponding functionality.

- The accounting **Document type** field is used on down payment documents to specify a different type of account posting. This information is required because pending accounts receivables and incoming down payments are processed differently than normal invoices. These items may not appear as revenue and will be used later to clear the actual invoice issue after goods are delivered or services are rendered. See Section 10.3 for more details.
- The **Negative posting** field reverses the sign (positive/negative) of accounting postings created by this billing document. Maintaining the field is not required for documents classified as cancellation billing documents or credit memos. This field will reverse the sign of the postings associated with the configured category, so for cancellations and credit memos, the positive sign (credit) will be flipped to reflect a negative balance (debit).
- The **Branch/Head office** field controls which partners are passed to accounting for the **Customer** and **Branch** fields. You can use the sold-to party as the customer instead of the default (payer). The branch field is populated by default with the sold-to customer.
- The **Credit memo w/ValDat** (credit memo with value date) flag is for credit memos created with reference to a billing document. When checked, the fixed value date will be automatically populated with the reference billing document baseline date, making it easier for finance to clear the document by applying a credit towards the pending account receivables entries from the reference billing document.
- The **Invoice List Type** field indicates the billing document type for invoice lists to be used (Section 10.2 for more details).
- The **Rebate settlement** field is used when this billing document type will be used in customer rebate agreements (as described in Chapter 5, Section 5.2).
- The **Rel.for rebate** (relevant for rebates) flag indicates that this billing document type is relevant for rebate calculation purposes.
- The **Standard Text** field is not currently in use and does nothing in SAP S/4HANA at the moment.

Cancellation

In the **Cancellation** section (see Figure 10.4), you'll find the following fields:

- The **Cancell.billing type** field is the billing document type that will be created automatically by Transaction VF11 when cancelling this billing document type. For instance, when you cancel an F2 invoice, the system will create an S1 cancellation document with same values but as credits so that the net result between the two documents is zero.

- The **Copying Requirements** field is a VOFM routine used to control the copying of information from document of this document type (F2) into the new cancellation document (S1).
- The **Reference number** field controls how the reference field on the cancellation account document should be populated. This information is copied into corresponding account postings and is used by finance for accounts receivable functionalities.
- The **Assignment Number** field controls how the assignment field on the cancellation account document should be populated. This information is copied into corresponding account postings and is used by finance for accounts receivable functionalities.

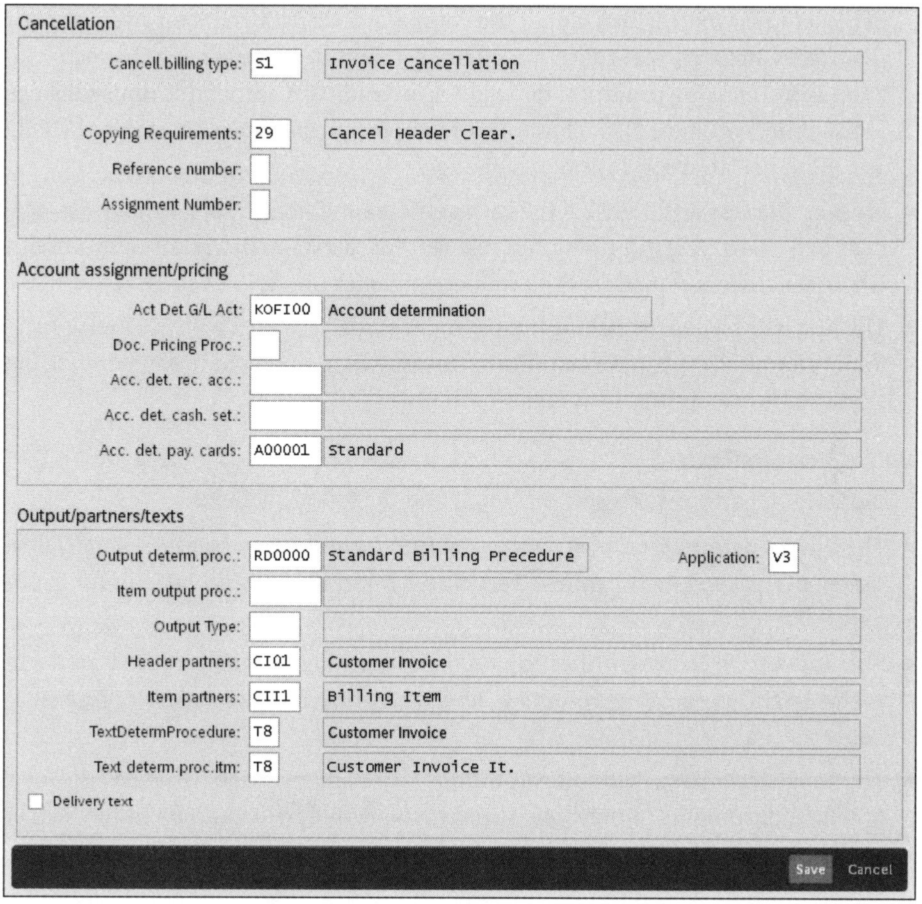

Figure 10.4 F2 Billing Document Type Configuration (2/2)

Account Assignment/Pricing

In the **Account assignment/pricing** section, you'll find the following fields:

- The **Act Det.G/L Act** field is the revenue account determination procedure to be used (Section 10.4 for more details).
- The **Doc. Pricing Proc.** field is used when determining the pricing procedure on the billing document. The pricing procedure is typically assigned in the sales order and copied to the billing document unchanged. However, in some rare cases, you may need to implement a different pricing procedure on the billing document by changing this field.
- The **Acc. det. rec. acc.** field is the reconciliation account determination procedure to be used. Most companies assign a reconciliation account to the business partner (customer) master data, under the company code data views for the customer finance business partner role. You can use this feature to determine the reconciliation account using condition techniques instead. This scenario is unusual since most companies have only a few (one or two) reconciliation accounts and usually assigning a customer is considered enough.
- The **Acc. det. cash. set.** field is the cash settlement account determination procedure to be used. This information is relevant for cash sales in a retail environment where the customer pays for the product upon pick up.
- The **Acc. det. pay. cards** field is the payment cards account determination procedure to be used. This information is relevant when you collect payments using credit cards or web-based payment methods.

Output/Partners/Texts

In the **Output/partner/texts** section, you'll find the following fields:

- The **Output determ.proc.** field controls output forms and messages issued by document of this type. See Chapter 4, Section 4.7, for more details about this functionality.
- The **Application** field identifies the type of output determination used on documents of this type: **V3** represents billing, **V1** represents sales order, **V2** represent deliveries, etc.
- The **Item output proc.** field controls output forms and messages issued by the lines of billing documents of this type. Usually, you would issue outputs to the header using procedure assigned in the **Output determ.proc** field.

- The **Output Type** field is the default output message to be issued when a user requests a printout using Transaction VF02 without specifying the output type.
- The **Header partners** field is configured using Transaction VOPAN as described in Chapter 6. This field may be set up to behave differently depending on whether the document is a billing document or a sales order. To access the billing document partner configuration, simply change the selection on the initial Transaction VOPAN menu screen.
- The **Item partners** field is for the determination procedure that defines the partner to be assigned on the billing document line.
- The **TextDetermProcedure** field is the text determination procedure used on the header of billing documents of this type, indicating the text IDs that are relevant and the access sequences that define where to copy text content from. See Chapter 6, for details about using Transaction VOTXN to configure text determination procedures.
- The **Text determ.proc.itm** field is the text determination procedure used on the lines of billing documents of this type, indicating the text IDs that are relevant and the access sequences that define where to copy text content from.
- The **Delivery text** flag indicates that you want to copy texts from the delivery document.

Defining Number Ranges for Billing Documents

To configure billing document number range intervals, open Transaction VN01 or follow the menu path **SAP Customizing Implementation Guide • Sales and Distribution • Billing • Billing Documents • Define Number Range for Billing Documents**. On the screen that opens, click on the display **Intervals** button.

> **Note**
>
> This menu path leads you to the same configuration transaction used for sales orders number ranges; the number range object **RV_BELEG** is used for all types sales documents (orders, deliveries, billing documents, etc.).

In our example shown in Figure 10.5, we're displaying the internal number range (**19**) assigned to the billing document type F2.

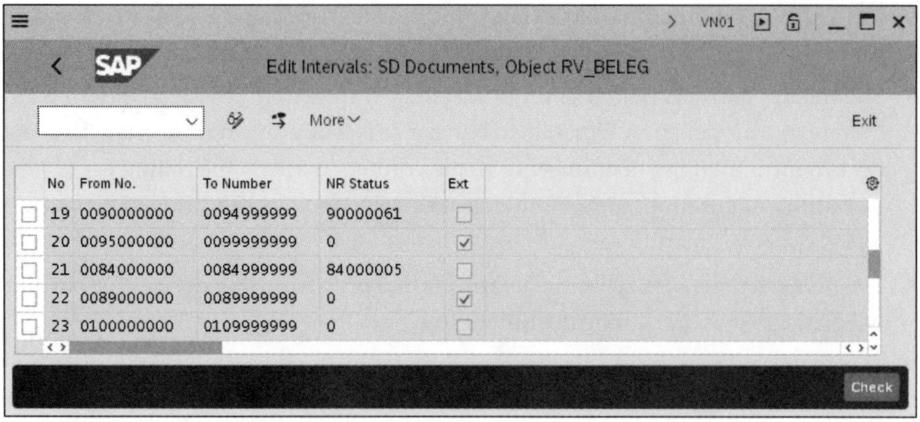

Figure 10.5 Defining Billing Document Number Range Intervals and Status

On this screen, browse for the desired number range code (**No**). The document numbers start with (**From No.**) and are incremented by 1 until they reach the upper limit (**To Number**). The **NR Status** field shows the last number used for this number range; in our example, the last document number created was 90000061, and the next document you'll create will be 90000062.

The **Ext** column indicates if this range is intended for internally assigned number ranges (the system controls what the next document number should be) or, when checked, externally assigned number ranges (entered by the user). Note that only internal number ranges may be used on billing documents.

10.1.2 Header Details

The **Header Detail** tab, shown in Figure 10.6, contains more fields than the overview screen. These tabs allow you to query and modify these fields, resulting in different invoice behavior. Typically, you are only allowed to perform changes while creating the billing document and before the accounting document is created.

Even so, making any changes is highly unusual. These tabs are normally used to view data while tracking business issues, disputes, or questions.

In the following sections, we'll look at each major area on this screen in detail.

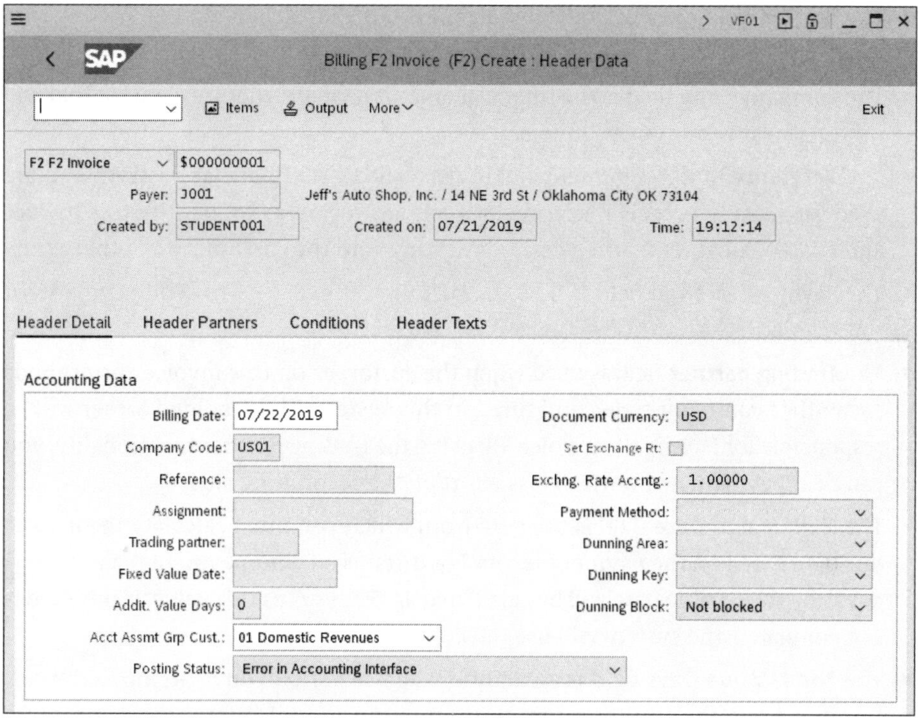

Figure 10.6 Billing Document Header Details (1/2)

Accounting Data

In the **Accounting Data** section, you'll find the following fields:

- The **Billing Date** field is used in reporting to indicate the date on which this invoice was created. Note, however, that this date may not match the current calendar date, and you can modify this field. Some companies implement changes to ensure this date always matches the goods issue date, which simplifies the reconciliation between the cost of goods sold (COGS) posted during post goods issue and the revenue posted by this invoice.
- The **Document Currency** field is copied from the sales order currency and is used to value this document and its corresponding outputs, such as the invoice form.
- The **Exchng. Rate Accntg.** field is used in multicurrency environments to define the exchange rate to be used when converting values expressed in this document's currency to the company code currency used for accounting and legal reporting.

- The **Set Exchange Rt** flag indicates that, even if the exchange rate changes, you must use the exchange rate specified in the **Exchng. Rate Accntg** field.
- The **Company Code** field is the financial organizational structure element that will capture the revenue of this invoice.
- The **Reference** and **Assignment** fields are copied into financial postings and are used for accounts receivable and other accounting areas to identify this invoice and related documents when communicating with the customer and other areas.
- The **Payment Method** field is how the customer is expected to send payment for this invoice.
- The **Trading partner** field is used when the customer on this invoice corresponds to another company code configured in this system. The **Trading Partner** will be responsible for paying the invoice. By using the trading partner functionality, you can clear payments with much less effort on the accounting side.
- The **Fixed Value Date** field is the date from which you must calculate the invoice due date based on the payment terms. For instance, if your payment term is net 15 days, the fixed value date will be calculated as 15 days plus this value. If this field is not populated, the system will use the **Billing Date** field.
- The **Addit. Value Days** field is an additional grace period you're giving to the customer in addition to the payment terms period when calculating the due date for payment.
- The **Dunning Area**, **Dunning Key**, and **Dunning Block** fields are used by an accounts receivable functionality that manages the amount and frequency of contact with the customer when collecting payment. This information is set by the financial portion of the customer master data and SAP S/4HANA Finance functionality and configuration.
- The **Acct Assmt Grp Cust.** field is the account assignment group defined on the customer master, which is copied to the order and then copied from the order to this billing document. This group is used for account determination at the time of billing. The configuration of this field was described in Chapter 2, Section 2.3.3.
- The **Posting Status** field is a status indicator describing whether the corresponding accounting document has been created. Companies typically do not print or issue invoices unless the accounting document has been created. Account determination errors may occur that prevent postings to accounting, and this status is one way to verify that.

Price Data

In the **Price Data** section (see Figure 10.7), you'll find the following fields:

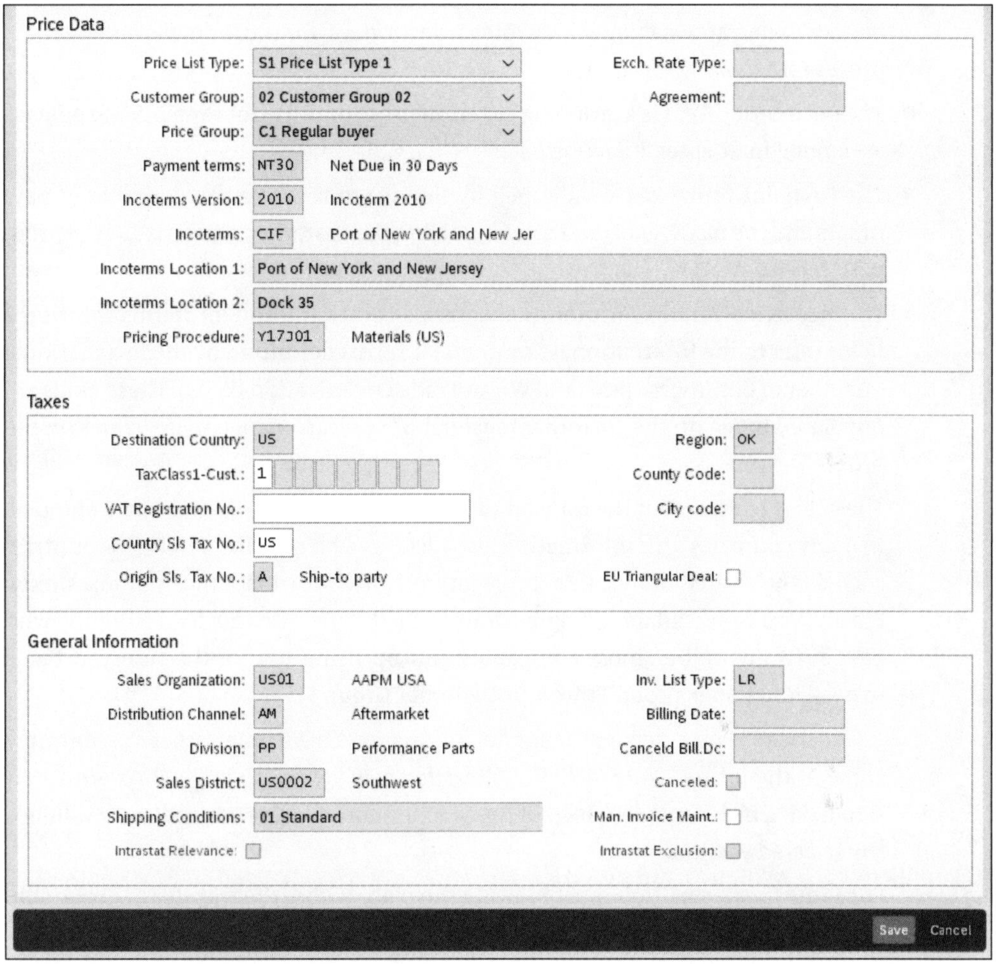

Figure 10.7 Billing Document Header Details (2/2)

- The **Price List Type** field is a price qualifier as defined in Chapter 2, Section 2.3.1, and Chapter 4, Section 4.8.2.
- The **Exch. Rate Type** field is a code that specifies which of multiple exchange rates should be used in this invoice. This information is applicable in multicurrency environments that also maintain multiple exchange rates.

- The **Customer Group** field is a major grouping criterion used for reporting as defined in Chapter 2, Section 2.3.1.
- The **Agreement** field identifies the rebate agreement responsible for creating this invoice (when applicable). See Chapter 5, Section 5.2, for more details about rebate processing.
- The **Price Group** field is a grouping criterion used for discounts and pricing policies as defined in Chapter 2, Section 2.3.1.
- The **Payment terms** is a key defined by finance to represent the number of payments and the number of days after invoicing the customer must pay for the products/services.
- The **Incoterms Version**, **Incoterms**, **Incoterms Location 1**, and **Incoterms Location 2** fields refer to the International Commercial Terms definition by the International Chamber of Commerce (ICC) and World Trade Organization (WTO). These fields are populated based on the customer master, but you can change these values on the order.

  The goal is to represent the transfer of ownership of goods when they are shipped. In many countries, this information also dictates who pays for freight. In countries such as the United States, this information is used for insurance purposes only. Ideally, you would adapt ICC definitions in the US (i.e., use this field to define who pays for freight), but most companies end up using one of the reserved fields instead (**Customer Group 1** through **Customer Group 5**).

  ICC released a new version of the Incoterms in 2010, and another version may come in the future. SAP S/4HANA allows for new versions via the **Incoterms Version** field, which controls which of the preconfigured **Incoterms** codes are valid for the selected version.

  For some Incoterms, you must indicate the place where the transfer of ownership takes place on the **Incoterms Location 1** and **2** fields, which represent ports, warehouses, origins, destinations, etc.
- The **Pricing Procedure** field is a display-only field based on the configuration described in Chapter 4, Section 4.1.

Taxes

In the **Taxes** section, you'll find the following fields:

- The **Destination Country** field is copied from the ship-to customer address and made available under this tab.
- The **Region** field is copied from the ship-to customer address and made available under this tab.
- The **TaxClass1-Cust.** field is a list of customer tax classifications that may be applicable to this document. For each departure plant address, the system will use the departure country to find the tax calculation configured. Sometimes, more than one tax category (represented by tax/pricing condition types) is maintained in the customer master data. This screen accommodates up to 9 fields. For each tax category, you can enter a tax classification to indicate whether the customer is taxable or exempt. Some countries such as Canada have more than one tax classification, but few countries use more than three. Most countries use only one.
- The **County Code** field is a code representing the county and is not required when using a jurisdiction code. Also, most companies do not control the county with a code; they define the county name as part of the customer address. Third-party tax software such as Vertex, Taxware, etc. may populate the county name on the address automatically when determining the jurisdiction code.
- The **City code** field is a code representing the city and acts similarly to the **County Code** field.
- The **VAT Registration No.** field is the legal identification registered with the government for your company for tax reporting purposes. This field is used in Europe and other countries.
- The **Country Sls Tax No.** field is the country code of the government that issued the **VAT Registration No.**
- The **Origin Sls. Tax No.** field indicates which partner function number, i.e., customer number, relates to the **VAT Registration No.**; typically, this partner is the ship-to customer (**A**).
- The **EU Triangular Deal** flag indicates that this invoice is being charged to the customer on behalf of another company that is part of the European Union (EU). Maintaining this flag is required for regulatory reporting.

General Information

In the **General Information** section, you'll find the following fields:

- The **Sales Organization**, **Distribution Channel**, and **Division** (the sales area information) fields are copied from preceding documents and represent the sales organizational structure that will capture the revenue generated by this invoice, which is the sales order that was selected in the header of the sales order.
- The **Inv. List Type** field indicates that this billing document is relevant for invoice lists, a feature that allows you to gather all invoices issued for a given customer over a period of time and consolidate them into a single document with this document type.
- The **Billing Date** field is the date of this invoice, which may not match the current calendar date. This date can be changed on the initial screen.
- The **Canceld Bill.Dc** field is used for cancellation billing documents to indicate the original billing document number that was cancelled by this cancellation document. Cancelling a billing document is accomplished by Transaction VF11.
- The **Cancelled** flag is activated by the system when a billing document is cancelled using Transaction VF11. Whenever you see a document with this flag, you'll also find a separate cancellation billing document, with this invoice number populating the **Canceld Bill.Dc** field.
- The **Sales District** field is copied from preceding documents and represents a geographical location where this sale was initiated for reporting purposes. The configuration of this field was described in Chapter 2, Section 2.3.1.
- The **Shipping Conditions** field is copied from preceding documents and represents the shipping service level your company offered to the customer. This information usually affects pricing.

10.1.3 Item Details

The **Item Detail** tab, shown in Figure 10.8, contain more fields than the overview screen. These tabs allow you to query and modify these fields, resulting in different invoice behaviors. Typically, you can only perform changes while creating the billing document, before the accounting document is created. Even so, making any changes is rather unusual, and these tabs are normally used to view data while tracking business issues, disputes, or questions.

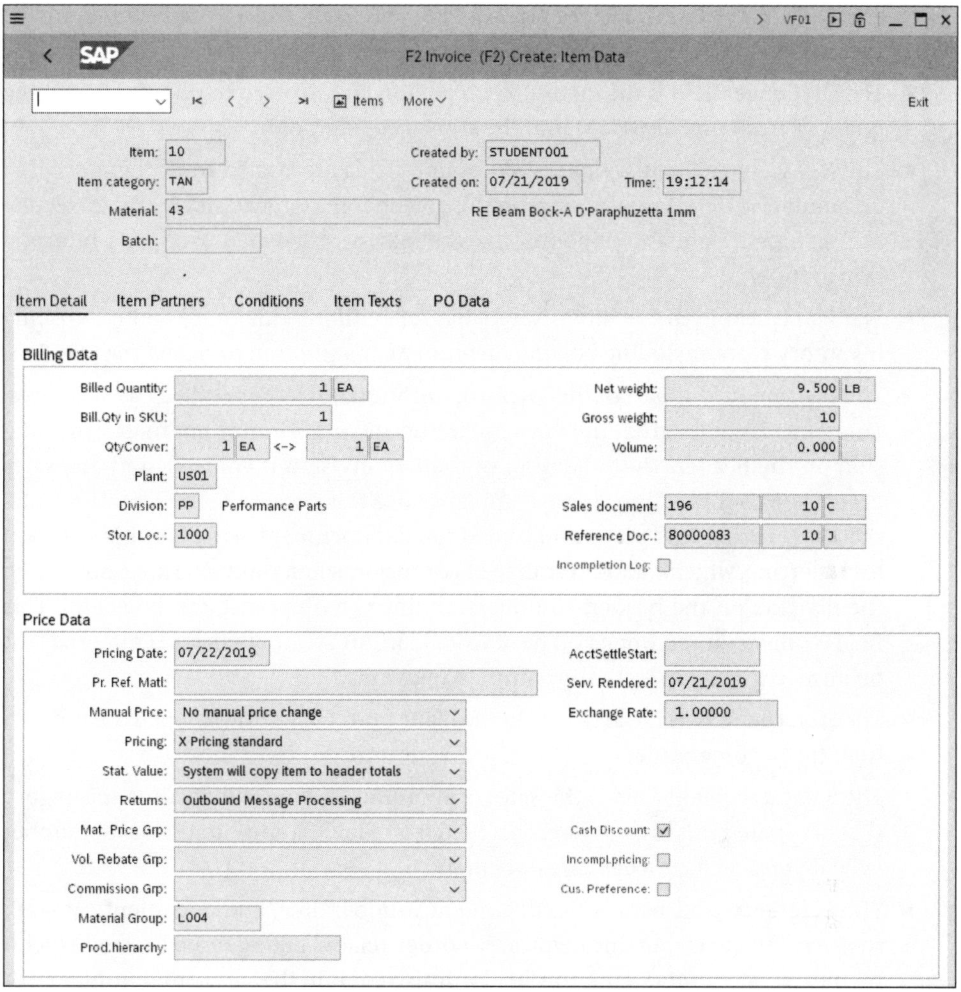

Figure 10.8 Billing Document Item Details (1/2)

In the following sections, we'll look at each major area on this screen in detail.

Billing Data

In the **Billing Data** section, you'll find the following fields:

- The **Billed Quantity** field is the quantity that will be shown on the invoice and used as the basis for price calculation, expressed in the sales unit of measurement (UoM), the small field to the right of the quantity.

- The **Bill.Qty in SKU** field is the quantity converted into the stock keeping unit of measurement for reference.
- The **QtyConver** field is the quantity conversion facture used to transfer the billing quantity from the sales UoM into the stock-keeping UoM.
- The **Net weight**, **Gross weight**, and **Volume** fields are copied from the preceding documents (delivery) and shown on this screen for reference and for price calculations. Some freight and handling charges may be calculated using this information as input.
- The **Plant** field is the facility responsible for fulfilling this order and controlling inventory costs, including posting inventory consumption to reflect the COGS.
- The **Division** field is part of the sales organizational structure called the sales area. This value is copied from the sales order line and may or may not match the division on the header. The validation of the line division is controlled by the sales order type configuration. Some companies use this field, as defined on the material master **Basic Data** views and copied to sales document, as a grouping criterion for reporting, which may be a source of confusion when this value does not match the division on the header, so understanding the difference can be useful. This field is only required when you need to validate and restrict sales of a material that belongs to a division by the appropriate sales area.
- The **Stor. Loc.** field is the area within the **Plant** from which you shipped the product to fulfill customer order.
- The **Sales document** field is the sales order number, line, and document category that originated this invoice line. This field is a reliable source for the order number even if you also have a delivery document.
- The **Reference Doc.** field is the document number, line, and document category that was used to create this invoice. For order-related billing (used for credit/debit memos, service orders, etc.), this field will also contain the sales order number. For delivery-related billing, this field will contain the delivery document number.
- The **Incompletion Log** flag indicates this invoice was created for a document considered incomplete. This situation is possible if the incompletion criteria and copy control rules are configured to allow for the billing of incomplete documents.

Price Data

In the **Price Data** section, you'll find the following fields:

- The **Pricing Date** field is used to find pricing condition records and may affect the final price to the customer when you're running promotions/discounts. This value is copied from the preceding document and may affect the invoice price if you recalculate price either via copy control configuration or manually using this dialog transaction. This field is important when allowing documents issued outside the promotional period to be eligible for expired promotions (discounts).

- The **AcctSettleStart** field is used when this invoice is the result of an accrual on a rebate agreement. The field will contain the start date of the accrual period, which is used to calculate the rebate basis.
- The **Pr. Ref. Matl** (pricing reference material) field is the material number used for pricing purposes. The value is copied from the preceding document.
- The **Serv. Rendered** field is used in service billing to indicate the date on which services were provided to the customer. You can select this value on the initial screen.
- The **Manual Price** field indicates that manual changes have been made to pricing. This field is used for auditing and control reporting.
- The **Exchange Rate** field allows you to specify the exchange rate to be used when the document currency is different than the condition records (pricing master data).
- The **Pricing** field is a code defined on the item category configuration that controls whether a line requires a price or if the item is free of charge.
- The **Stat. Value** field is also defined on the item category configuration. This value indicates if this line value should be considered in the calculation of the total value of the sales order.
- The **Returns** indicator represents the direction of this document. Sales and bills to the customer (where they will pay you and/or you ship product to them) have this field blank. Other codes correspond to incoming movements (where you pay them and/or you receive product from them).
- The **Mat. Price Grp**, **Vol. Rebate Grp**, **Commission Grp**, **Material Group**, and **Prod.hierarchy** fields and the **Cash Discount** flag are material master data fields set as defaults from the sales order (consult Chapter 3 for more details). These fields may be modified on the sales order, and after processing, these values are copied into this billing document. When issuing reports, you can decide to use values from the material master data fields, which will affect how historical data is displayed after you change the values configured for these fields.
- The **Incomplete.pricing** (incomplete pricing) flag indicates this invoice was created for a document with missing pricing components. This situation is possible if allowed by incompletion criteria and copy control rules.
- The **Cus. Preference** (customs preference) flag indicates this sale is eligible for preferential treatment at the customs office.

Accounting

In the **Accounting** section (see Figure 10.9), you'll find the following fields:

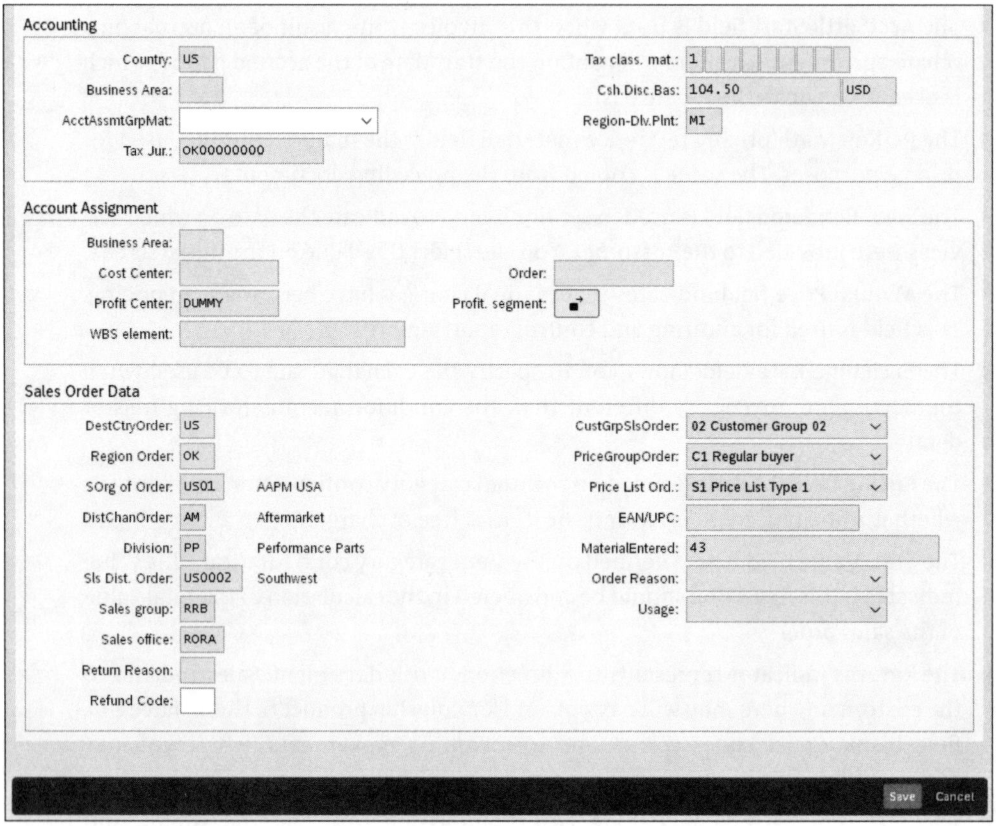

Figure 10.9 Billing Document Item Details (2/2)

- The **Country** (departure country) field is copied from the shipping point address as configured and made available on this tab.
- The **Tax class. mat.** field is a list of multiple material tax classifications that may be applicable to this document. For each departure plant address, the system will use the departure country to find the tax calculation configured. Sometimes, more than one tax category (represented by tax/pricing condition types) are maintained on the material master data. This screen accommodates up to 9 material tax classifications. For each tax category, you would enter a tax classification to indicate if the material is taxable or exempt. Some countries such as Canada have

more than one material tax classification, but few countries use more than three. Most countries use only one.

- The **Business Area** field is displayed as defined by the finance organizational structure. Its utilization greatly impacts SAP S/4HANA Finance and is not a popular feature among SAP users in the US.
- The **Csh.Disc.Bas** field is the amount, in the document currency, used to calculate a discount when the customer pays for their invoice in a manner preferred by your company. The discount is usually defined as percentage. This cash discount is an accounts receivable functionality.
- The **AcctAssmtGrpMat** (material account assignment group) field is a grouping criterion used to differentiate materials from an accounting standpoint. This field is typically used to differentiate between revenue from sales/delivery of goods versus revenue from providing services. This value is copied from the preceding document.
- The **Region-Dlv.Plnt** field represents the US state from which goods are shipped, which is used for tax calculation purposes.
- The **Tax Jur.** field is the tax jurisdiction code from the ship-to customer. This code represents the location of the ship-to customer for tax calculation purposes. In the US, using third-party tax software such as Vertex, Taxware, etc. is quite common, and these solutions automatically determine the correct jurisdiction code based on the zip code entered in master data or in sales documents.

Account Assignment

In the **Account Assignment** section, you'll find the following fields:

- The **Business Area** field is displayed as defined by the finance organizational structure. Its utilization greatly impacts SAP S/4HANA Finance and is not a popular feature among SAP users in the US.
- The **Cost Center** field may be used for free of charge shipments as assigned to the order reason (as discussed in Section 10.4.2). This value represents the area within the company that is responsible for cost of the product that is given away for free. Some typical examples include warranty, cost of sales, and marketing.
- The internal **Order** field is another way to register cost/profit as part of a more encompassing activity/initiative without the need to define projects.

- Most companies use the **Profit Center** field copied from the preceding document. This value is used by accounting to group postings together and reduce the number of entries to review in reporting.
- The **Profit. segment** button takes you to a window where a list of fields may be maintained. These fields are configured and defined by profitability analysis in SAP S/4HANA. You won't usually need to maintain values on this screen, since they are generally derived from sales order fields based on rules. When the derivation rules fail, you'll get an incompletion message that requires you to click this button and manually populate the field, but you must also contact the profitability analysis team to report the issue so that the rules can be fixed.
- The **WBS element** field stands for work breakdown structure (WBS), which is an element of a costing structure, referred to as a project, that this line is part of/assigned to. This functionality is handled by the project systems (PS) functionality. Assigning a WBS element to the line will cause the cost of this line to roll up into the total of the project.

Sales Order Data

In the **Sales Order Data** section, you'll find the following fields:

- The **DestCtryOrder** field is copied from the ship-to customer address and made available on this tab.
- The **CustGrpSlsOrder** (customer group) field is a major grouping criterion used on reporting as defined in Chapter 2, copied into the sales order, and displayed on this screen for reference.
- The **Region Order** field is the US state defined on the ship-to customer address displayed on this screen for reference. We're using the generic term "region" rather than "state" because some countries like Canada and China would call these "provinces."
- The **PriceGroupOrder** field is a grouping criterion used for discounts and pricing policies as defined in Chapter 2, Section 2.3.1.
- The **SOrg of Order** field is the sales organization. This value is a major component of the sales organization structure as defined on the sales order header and displayed on this screen for reference.
- The **DistChanOrder** field is the distribution channel. This value represents a component of the sales organization structure as defined on the sales order header and is displayed on this screen for reference.

- The **Division** field is a component of the sales organizational structure as defined on the sales order header and is displayed on this screen for reference.
- The **Price List Ord.** field is a key used for customer-based price determinations (when applicable). This value is defined on the sales order header and is displayed on this screen for reference.
- The **EAN/UPC** (European Article Number/Universal Product Code) field is a product barcode usually shown on packaging, commonly used in live retail transactions. This code is usually registered with international regulatory agencies such as GS1 (Global Standards One). The value is defaulted from the material master on the sales order line and displayed on this screen for reference.
- The **MaterialEntered** field is a display-only field to keep track of the material you entered (manually or electronically) before the material was replaced by a different material number via a functionality such as a material determination procedure (see Chapter 4, Section 4.3 for details). This value is defined on the sales order header and displayed on this screen for reference.
- The **Sls Dist. Order** field is a geographically oriented grouping criterion used for reporting. This value is defaulted from the customer master on the sales order line and is displayed on this screen for reference.
- The **Order Reason** field is defined on some sales orders headers but commonly mandatory on returns and credit/debit memos. This field is displayed on this screen for reference. See Chapter 13, Section 13.2, for more information on the configuration of this field, which may be used to determine the cost center, as described in Section 10.4.2.
- The **Sales office** and **Sales group** fields are part of the sales organizational structure defaulted from the customer master on the sales order line and is displayed on this screen for reference.
- The **Usage** field is a code that represents what your customer will do with the product or service sold on the order. This value is defaulted from customer-master information record into the sales order line and is displayed on this screen for reference.
- The **Return Reason** and **Refund Code** fields are applicable in advanced return scenarios. These values are entered when advanced return orders are created, and these fields are displayed on this screen for reference.

10.1.4 Partners

The **Partner** tab, shown in Figure 10.10, identifies the corporation and/or people (business partners) that are involved in the business transaction that this billing document represents.

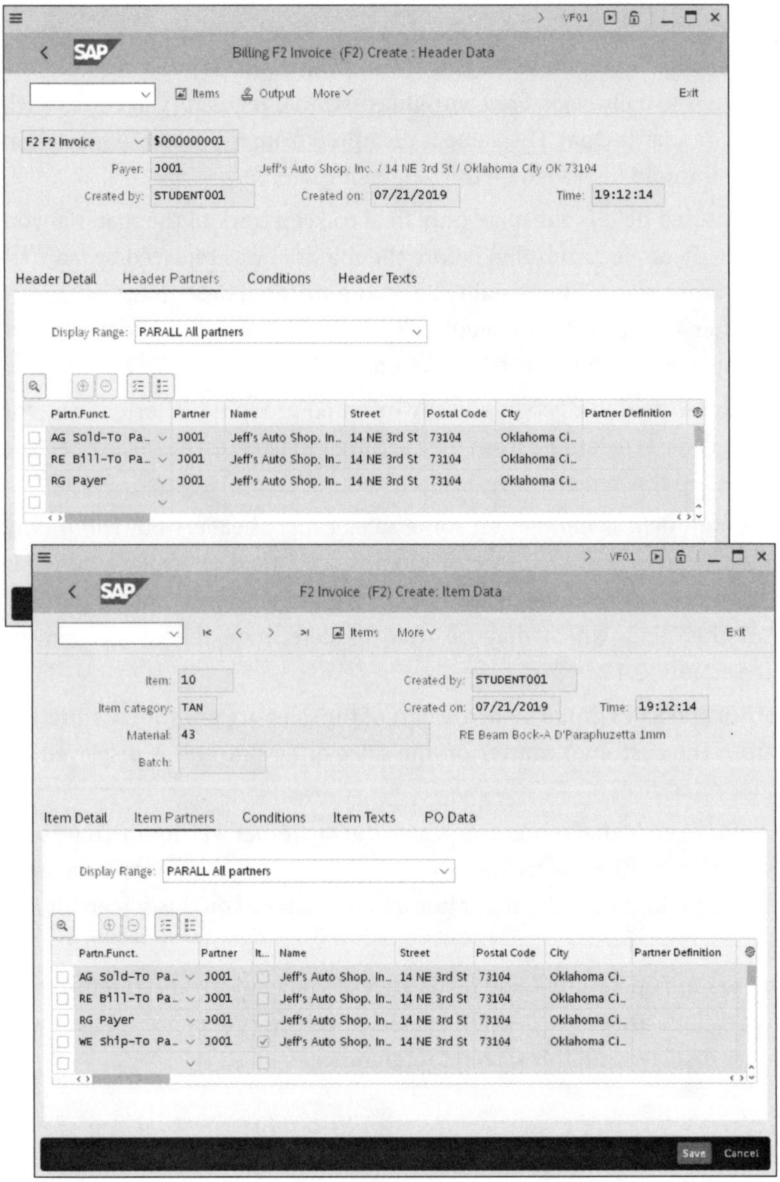

Figure 10.10 Billing Document Partners

We described how to configure partner functions using Transaction VOPAN in Chapter 6, Section 6.3.9.

In the billing document, the header **Partners** tab controls the split of invoices. Any new partner functions added on this screen will cause an invoice split. Note that you don't have a ship-to address in the header. The goal is to allow you to combine delivery documents with different ship-to addresses on the same invoice.

Under the item **Partners** tab, you'll see all four main partner functions, including the ship-to customer for reference and tax calculation purposes.

10.1.5 Conditions

The **Conditions** tabs, shown in Figure 10.11 and Figure 10.12, display the pricing components copied from the order and sometimes from the delivery as well. The resulting combination of conditions from preceding documents are what constitute the pricing of this billing document, the details of which can be found under this tab.

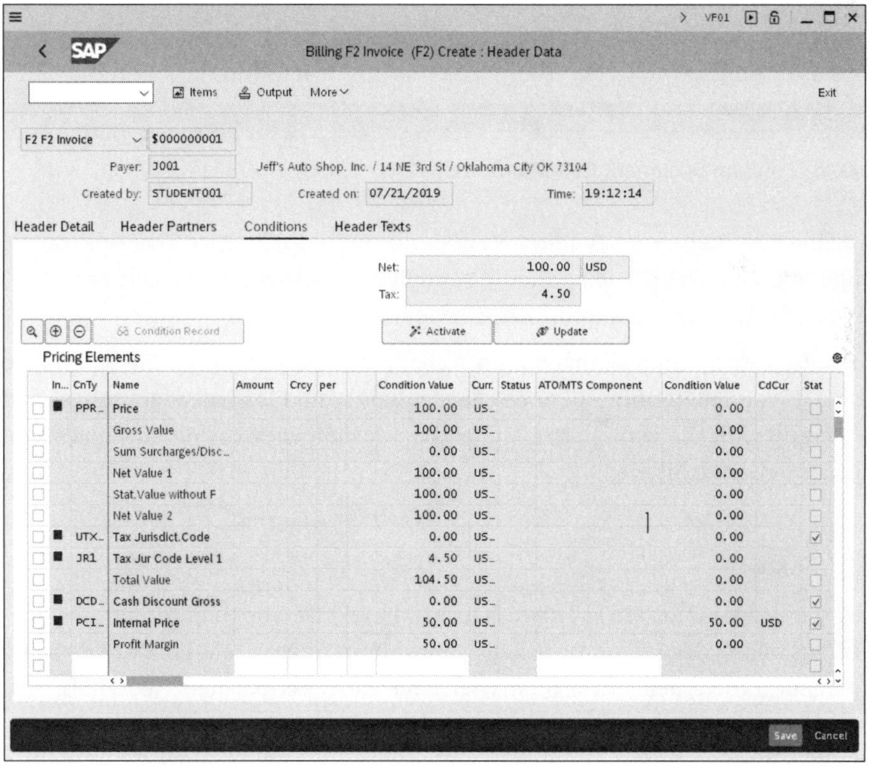

Figure 10.11 Billing Document Conditions: Header Data

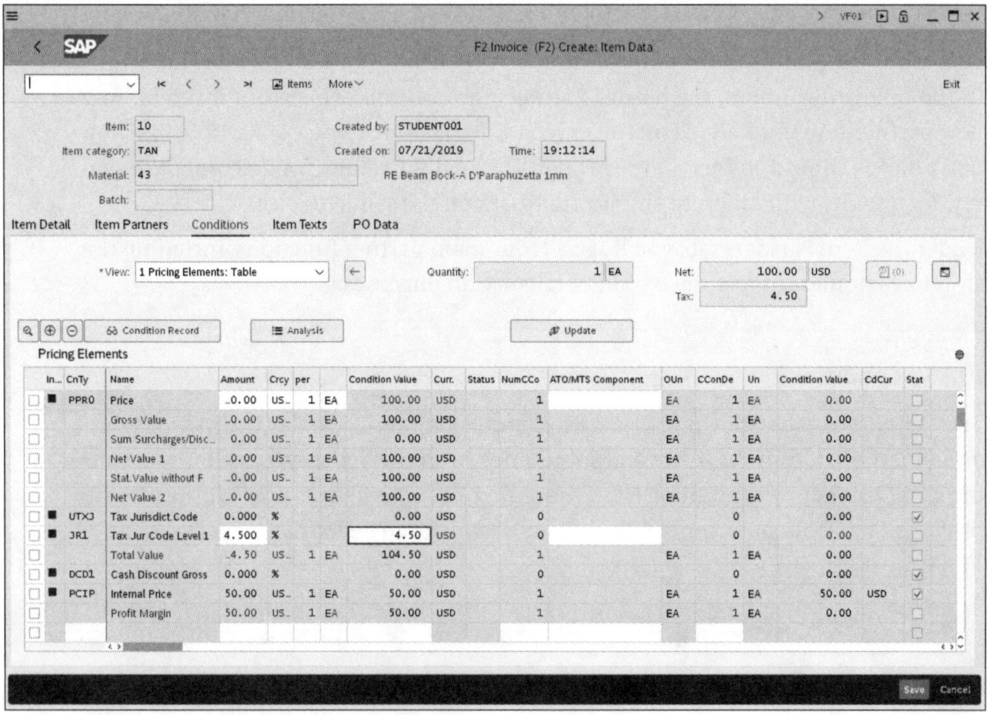

Figure 10.12 Billing Document Conditions: Item Data

The billing document has a **Conditions** tab similar to the sales order. The copy control configuration dictates if pricing should be copied (unchanged or partially refreshed) or if a totally new pricing determination should be run.

Companies usually copy all manual price changes and redetermine the other price changes. If you redetermine all price changes, you would lose manual changes and may end up with the wrong price and end up dealing with customer remediation measures (credit/debit memos).

10.1.6 Texts

Under the **Header Texts** tab shown in Figure 10.13, text IDs and their contents belonging to this billing document are usually copied from or with reference to preceding documents (orders/deliveries) or master data (business partners, materials, customer-material information record, etc.).

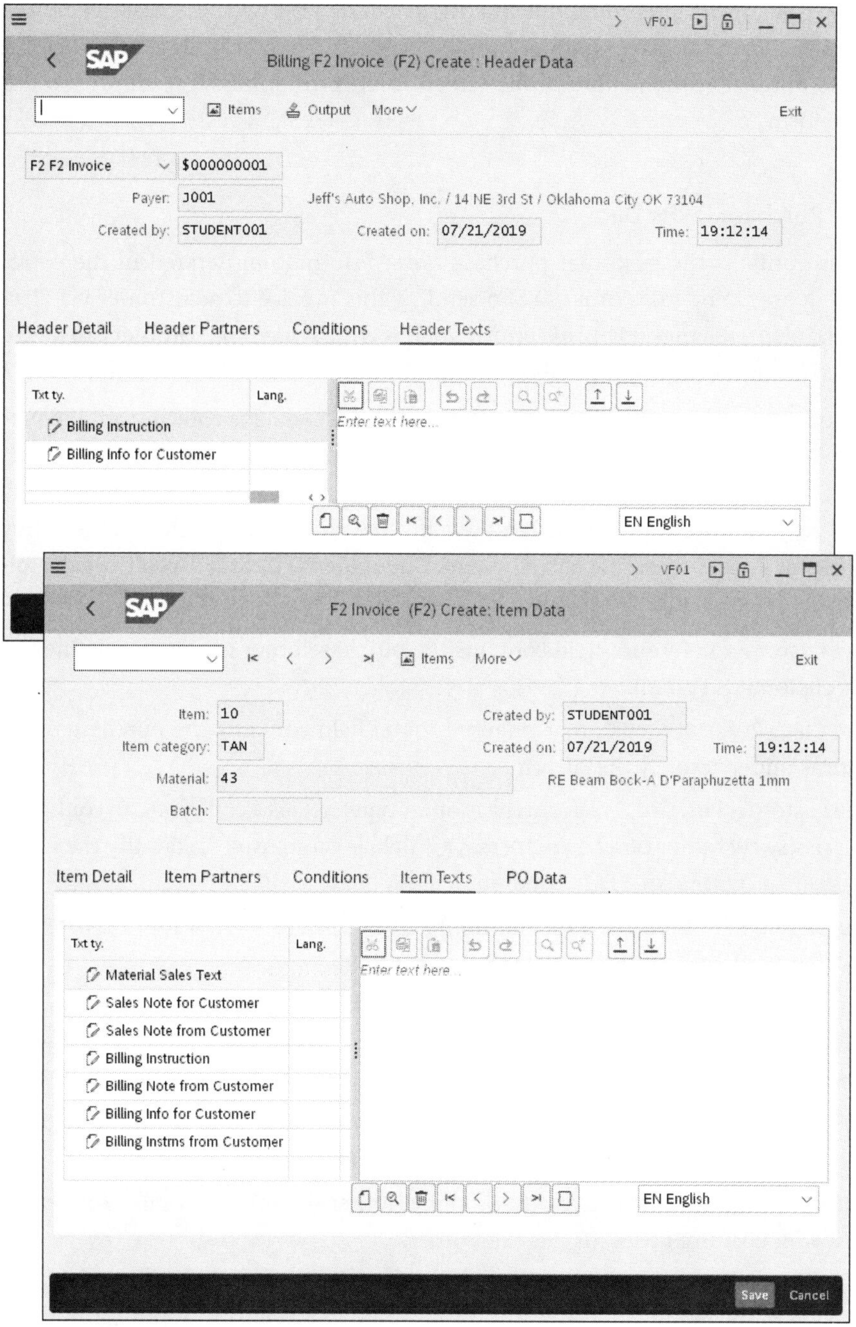

Figure 10.13 Billing Document Texts

Text is copied from preceding documents, as configured by the access sequences defined in the text control configuration described in Chapter 6, Section 6.3.10. You can also enter text manually on this screen to affect the messages shown on the invoice form.

10.1.7 Purchase Order Data

This tab contains the customer purchase order information entered in the corresponding preceding sales order. When sending this invoice to a customer via Electronic Data Interchange (EDI), this information is critical so your customer can locate the PO the sales order corresponds to.

When the billing document is created, the customer PO data is copied from the preceding sales order into this tab. This information must be part of the invoice, in particular when sending invoices electronically via EDI, email, etc. This information is critical so your customer can match your invoice with their purchase order, thus allowing for faster processing and payment. Under the **PO Data** tab, you'll see the following fields (see Figure 10.14):

- The **Customer Reference** field contains the purchase order number as defined in the customer's system.
- The **Cust. Ref. Date** (customer reference date) field contains the purchase order date as understood by the customer.
- The customer **Pur. Ord. Type** (purchase order type) field is a code you can configure to classify customer purchase orders. This field is often used to identify the order source, e.g., fax, email, EDI, phone, etc.
- The **Supplement** field (used for addition) may be used as a suffix for the customer purchase order number (**Customer Reference** field).
- The **Last Contact Date** and **Number of Contacts** fields, related to the accounts receivable collections activity, control the amount and frequency of follow-up contact with a customer when attempting to collect a debt.
- The **Name** field is your point of contact within your customer's organization who is responsible for the sales order that originated this invoice.
- The **Your Reference** field is another number (other than the **Customer Reference**) that your customer uses for this sales order.
- The **Telephone** field is the phone number to use when contacting the person identified in the **Name** field.

- The **Purchase order item** (line number) field is populated from the customer purchase order.
- The **Customer Material** field is the material number of your product in your customer's system.

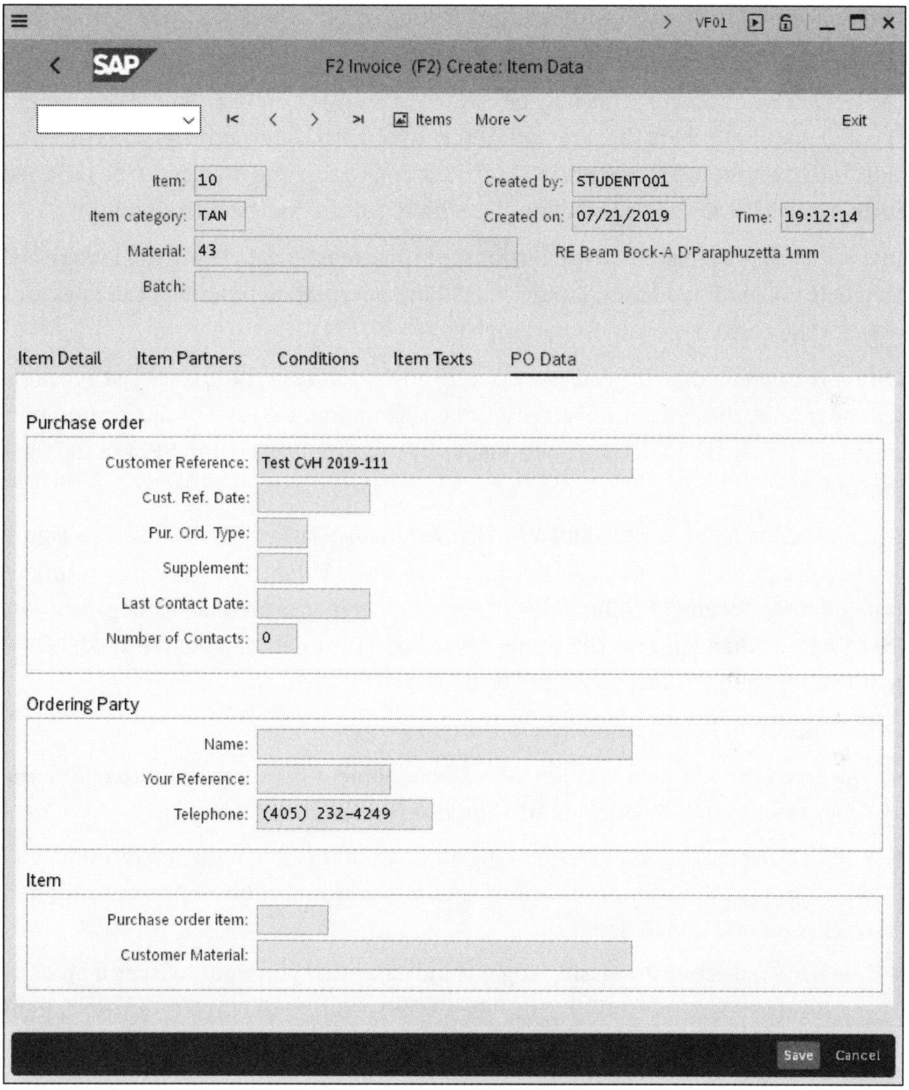

Figure 10.14 Billing Document Customer Purchase Order Data

10.2 Invoice Lists

An invoice list is a feature that allows you to gather all the invoices issued for a given customer over a period of time and consolidate these invoices into a single billing document. You can then communicate the invoice summary to the customer and perform accounts receivable functions using the consolidated document rather than using each individual document.

Invoice list billing documents may be created in Transaction VF21, where you'll input the document numbers that are part of the invoice list. Alternatively, you could use the due list report in Transaction VF24 to pick and choose the invoices to be included in an invoice list. Often, Transaction VF24 is a scheduled as a background job.

Invoice lists are activated on the business partner master data using the **Invoice List Schedule Calendar** field found under the **Billing Information** tab under the sales area data for the customer business partner role.

On every calendar date flagged as a working business day in the **Invoice List Schedule Calendar** field, the system will attempt to create an invoice list. For illustration purposes, we'll walk through this functionality by running Transaction VF24 in the foreground.

In Transaction VF24, on the **Edit Worklist for Invoice Lists** screen, shown in Figure 10.15, you can filter the invoices by the **Billing Date**; **Billing Type** (billing document type); **Billing Document** (billing document number); sales area (**Sales Organization**, **Distribution Channel**, and **Division**); **Payer**; and **Destination Country** fields. Only invoices matching these criteria will be displayed.

Other important fields include the following:

- The **Sort Criterion** field requires ABAP development but allows you to define the order in which billing documents should appear on the invoice list.
- The **List Display** flag indicates that, when you run this job in the background, you want the job to issue a list of documents, which would allow you to monitor and track the execution in detail.
- The **Issue Collective Processing Log** flag indicates that you want to issue a processing log describing system actions taken when creating the invoice list document as a background job.

You can select one of three possible ways to update invoice lists, which affect system performance, as follows:

- The **Asynchronous** option uses work processes that keep on running after the invoice is created.
- The **Synchronous via VB Log** option waits until all work processes are finished before the invoice is saved and issues a log describing the process.
- The **Synchronous without VB Log** option performs the sale without issuing a log.

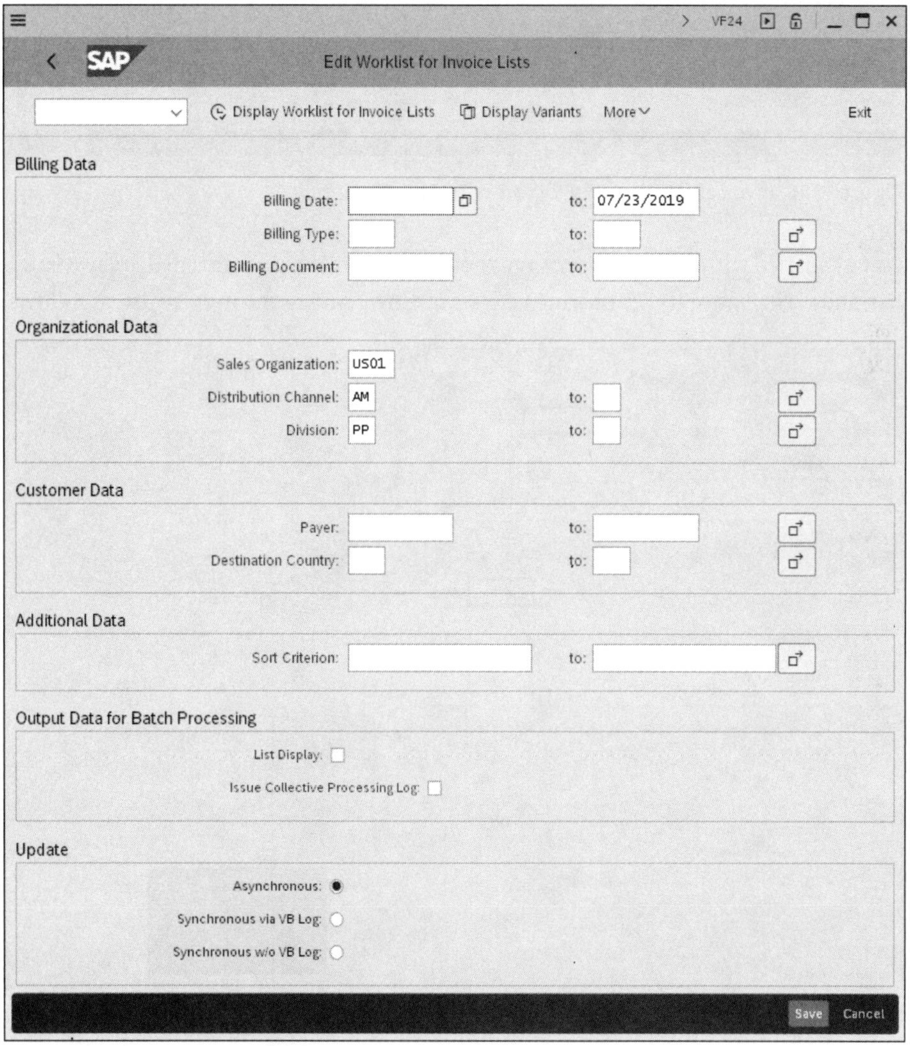

Figure 10.15 Transaction VF24: Invoice List Selection Screen

After you click **Execute**, the selection report appears, as shown in Figure 10.16, appears, showing all invoices that match the initial selection. You can deselect the ones you don't want to include in the invoice list. The columns on this report match the data we described earlier in Section 10.1.

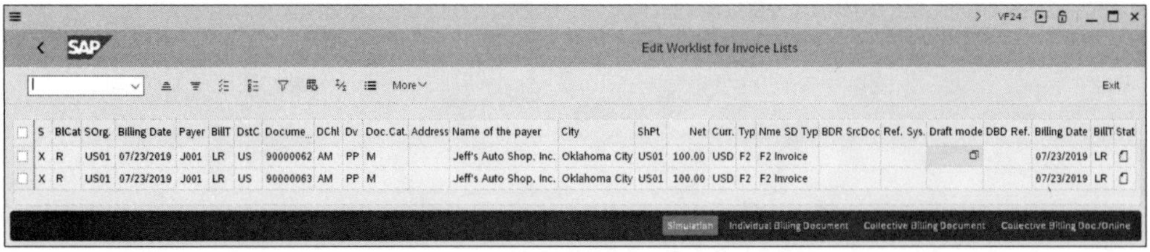

Figure 10.16 Invoice List Selection Report with Two Invoices

Once satisfied with the selection, save the invoice list. The system will display a worklist, shown in Figure 10.17, showing actions taken by saving the invoice list, as follows:

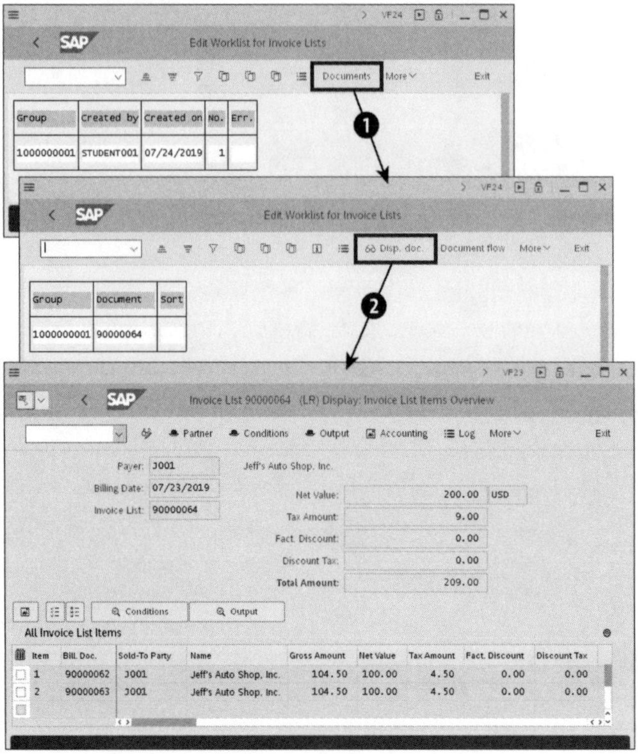

Figure 10.17 Invoice List Creation: Worklist

❶ On the first **Edit Worklist for Invoice Lists** screen, you'll find the number of invoice list billing documents created (**No.** column) and any errors encountered (**Err.** column). On this screen, you'll create one invoice list to ensure no errors have arisen. To see the invoice list billing document numbers that were created, you'll need to click on a worklist item and then click on the **Documents** button in the command bar.

❷ The system displays all document numbers created. You can view the contents of each document by clicking a document number and then clicking on the **Display Document** button in the command bar.

The system then takes you to Transaction VF23, showing the invoice list billing document content.

Note that the lines on the invoice list document are billing document numbers, with their values. Note also that the invoice list has total values calculated and displayed on the header.

10.3 Milestone Billing, Periodic Billing, and Down Payments

Some companies may need to collect payments before the contracted goods and/or services can be delivered. This scenario results in an accounting concern regarding how payments are registered and traced to ensure you link payments to the correct order process. The differences between each type of billing discussed in this section are as follows:

- Milestone billing is when you issue invoices upon achievement of set project completion tasks.
- Periodic billing is when you issue invoices based on agreed dates.
- Down payment is when you collect payment before the delivery of goods and services. This payment may be in full or partial, in a lump sum or installments.

In the following sections, we'll describe the functionality you'll use to fulfill these kinds of requirements, through billing plans.

10.3.1 Billing Plans

Billing plans allow you to define a strategy regarding when, how much, and how many times you'll invoice a customer before the delivery of goods/services. Figure

10.18 shows a diagram of how billing plans affect otherwise standard order processing.

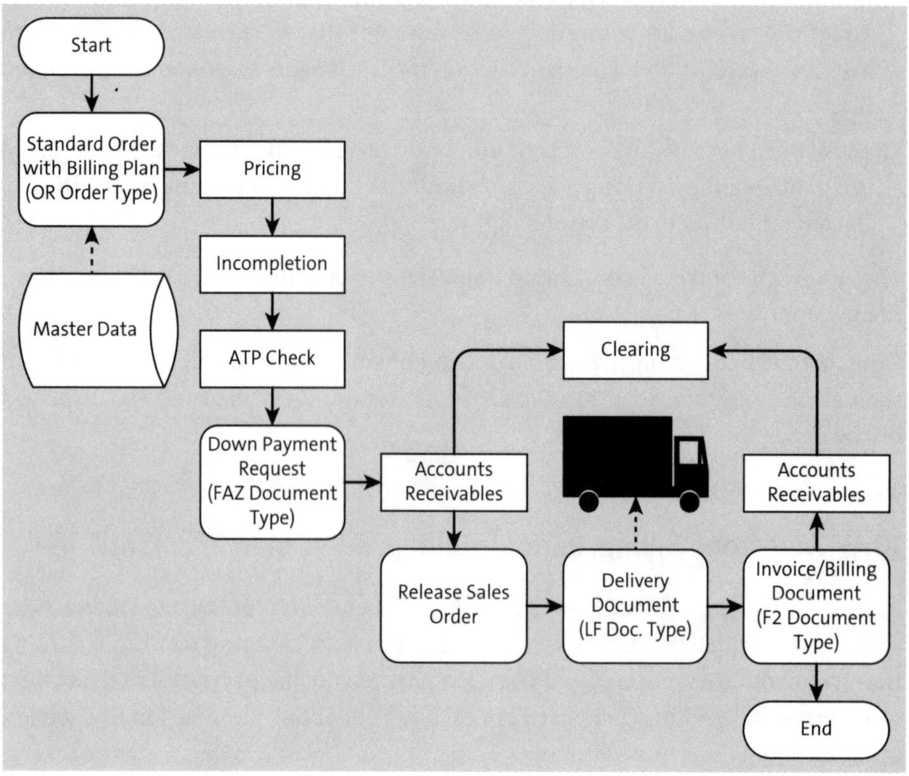

Figure 10.18 Billing Plan Functionality

When using a billing plan, the process starts by entering a sales order with an assigned billing plan type and ensuring you have the billing plan data defined. In Chapter 6, Section 6.3.5, we described the **Billing Plan** tab on the sales document header. We also explained how to assign a billing plant type to the sales order type in Transaction VOV8. In Section 10.3.2, we'll explain how you can create your own billing plan types.

An order with a billing plan is subject to pricing, incompletion procedures, and ATP checks just like regular orders; however, typically, you'll assign a delivery block to the order header to ensure orders are not be shipped until initial payments are collected, an easy, out-of-the-box way to control the impact of pending billing plans on shipping.

Usually, you'll have a separate order type for use with billing plans where you'll assign a default delivery block to it during the configuration of the order type. Using a default delivery block ensures users won't forget to block the order upon creation.

You can implement VOFM routines for copy requirements to check if billing plan-based invoices have been paid before allowing the delivery to be created.

Once an order with a billing plan is saved, if no billing block exists on the billing plan lines, the next step would be to create an invoice. Billing document type FAZ is provided out of the box as an invoice for this type of purpose. Although described as a down payment invoice, you can use this billing document type for other scenarios, such as milestone billing.

The FAZ invoice is sent to the customer using billing document output processing, and accounts receivable works with the customer to receive payment and apply that amount to the FAZ invoice number. This amount is not accounted as sales or revenue; instead, the **Special G/L Indicator** makes this amount relevant for the clearing procedure without affecting financial revenue reporting. The finance team must be involved to ensure you're using the appropriate type of accounts receivable entry; we'll call it a *note pay account* for reference, even though a different account is not necessarily being used.

Once the FAZ invoice is paid and cleared by accounts receivables using the note pay account, the customer service team needs to be notified, either proactively with accounts receivables notifying customer service or by customer service monitoring the status of all open FAZ invoices and keeping track as they clear. This step is often a source of delays; the process must be well defined and followed. If you implement automated checks, this step would no longer be necessary.

Once the customer service representative checks whether the necessary FAZ payments have been cleared, the delivery block assigned to the order can be removed to allow the order to proceed to logistics. When delivering a product, a delivery document will be created and processed by the warehouse.

Once goods are shipped and the post goods issue operation is registered, thus relieving inventory and feeding the COGS account, the delivery is relevant for billing, just like in a non-billing plan scenario.

The regular invoice type is created (F2), but the total invoice pricing is reduced by the amount already paid on the FAZ invoice via pricing condition type AZWR. This pricing condition type needs to exist on your pricing procedure whenever the billing plan is active. The system will calculate its value automatically and deduct the invoice price to reflect payment already made.

The AZWR amount is also sent to accounting to clear the corresponding value on the note pay account and convert the amount into revenue. Any remaining balance is charged to the customer at this time on the F2 invoice.

The F2 invoice is passed to accounting, and accounts receivable will collect any remaining payment. With clearing, the process is closed.

10.3.2 Defining Billing Plan Types

To configure billing plan types, open Transaction OVBO or follow the menu path **SAP Customizing Implementation Guide • Sales and Distribution • Billing • Billing Plan • Define Billing Types • Maintain Billing Plan Types for Milestone Billing.** On the screen that opens, select the **BillingPlanType 90** and then click on the **Details** button or press F2. The screen shown in Figure 10.19 will open.

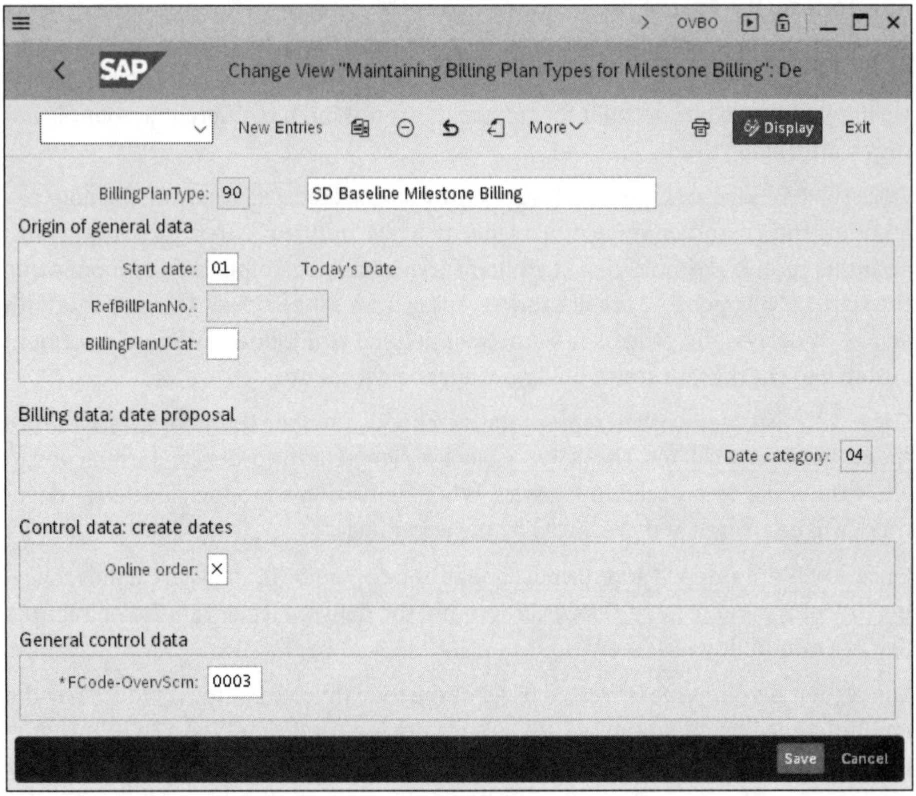

Figure 10.19 Billing Plan Type 90 Configuration

When creating a new code, on this screen, specify a two-character billing plan type code (**BillingPlanType**) and add a description. Other important fields on this screen include the following:

- The **Start date** field controls the default start date in billing plans.
- The reference billing plan number is the template billing plan you can create and assign in the **RefBillPlanNo**. This information is used to prepopulate the billing plan screen with fields copied from the billing plan number indicated here. Billing plans are saved on a separate set of tables, using their own internally assigned number range as primary keys. This primary key is the number you can use in this field to indicate a billing plan to use as reference.
- The **BillingPlanUCat** (billing plan usage category) field controls what you'll use the billing plan line for. Leaving the field blank will mean the basic functionality as described in this section will be used.
- The **Date category** field is used on the sales order billing plan tab when the billing plan line (also known as billing plan dates) are entered to qualify the event expected to take place on this date. This field is the equivalent of an item category for a billing plan line/date.
- The **Online order** indicator controls the automatic creation of billing deadlines when the order is entered online, and the plan dates are not populated by the interface.
- The **FCode-OvervScrn** (function code of overview screen) field controls the structure of the billing plan screen on the sales order. By changing this code, you would get different fields on this tab for different types of plan usage.

10

10.4 Accounting Documents and Revenue Recognition

When accounting-relevant billing documents are created, the system will use the account determination procedures assigned to the billing document type to determine the accounts that must be affected based on the condition types found in the pricing procedure.

The accounting relevance of billing documents is controlled by the **SD Document Category** assigned to the billing document type configuration. For instance, proforma invoices have the **SD Document Category** field defined as U, which indicates accounting documents should not be created.

Revenue recognition control can be driven by sales item category configuration, as we'll see later in Section 10.5.1.

10.4.1 Revenue Account Determination

General ledger account determination is also referred to as revenue account determination, but this process is not restricted to just revenue accounts. This feature uses the condition technique to assign the general ledger account to the values expressed on the pricing procedure and assigned to pricing condition types (see Chapter 4, Section 4.1, for more details).

In the pricing procedure, you'll assign three-character account keys to lines containing condition types that are relevant for accounting. The most commonly used account keys include the following:

- **ERL: Revenue: Assigned to Sales Price condition types such as PPRO**
- **ERS: Sales Discounts/Surcharges**
- **ERF: Freight Charges**
- **MWS: Sales/Output Tax**

Often, you'll create new account keys as described in the Defining Account Key section. Requirements fulfilled by this configuration typically start with finance, who may request you segregate a given amount calculated on the pricing procedure from the common account keys mentioned earlier. For example, let's say your company has many types of discounts and one of them is really aggressive. Finance may want you to post that specific aggressive discount into a different account, other than the account with the ERS account key.

The general ledger account determination procedure is typically assigned to the billing document type configuration. The Defining Account Determination Procedure section will describe the out-of-the-box configuration for the KOFI00 procedure. In the following sections, we'll describe the configuration related to revenue account determination.

You also must maintain condition records to define the correct general ledger account number to be used for each key combination (condition table), which requires the configuration activity described in the Assigning General Ledger Accounts (Condition Records) section.

Defining Account Key

To configure account keys, follow the menu path **SAP Customizing Implementation Guide • Sales and Distribution • Basic Functions • Account Assignment/Costing •**

Define and Assign Account Keys • Define Account Key. On the screen that opens, click on the **New Entries** button or press [F5].

Note that you can also use this menu path and the **Assign account keys** option to assign the account key to the pricing procedure, but this approach is not common. Instead, this assignment is typically done directly on the pricing procedure configuration screen.

On the screen shown in Figure 10.20, specify a three-character account key (**ActKy**) and add a name (**Name**).

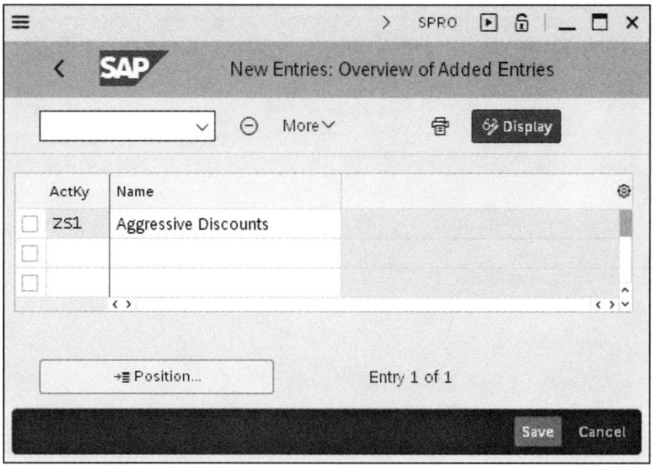

Figure 10.20 Creating New Account Keys

Defining Account Determination Procedure

To configure general ledger account determination procedures, follow the menu path **SAP Customizing Implementation Guide • Sales and Distribution • Basic Functions • Account Assignment/Costing • Revenue Account Determination • Define and Assign Account Determination Procedures • Define Account Determination Procedure**. As shown in Figure 10.21, perform the following steps:

❶ First, select the desired general ledger account determination procedure (**Procedure**).

❷ Then, double-click the **Control Data** option in the **Dialog Structure** menu on the left.

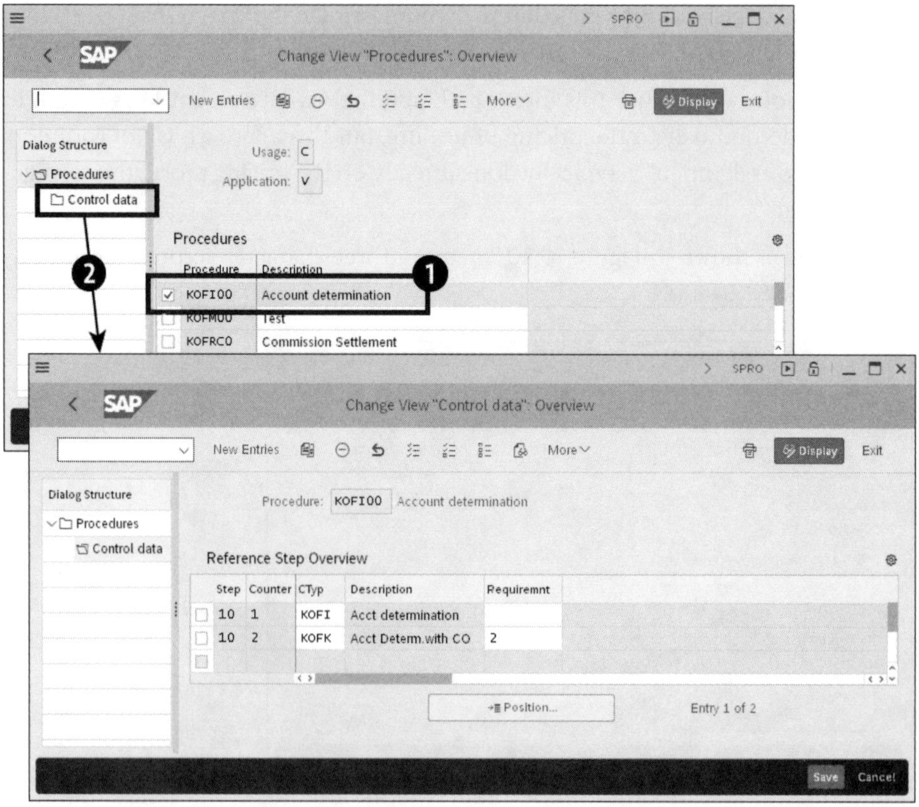

Figure 10.21 Displaying Account Determination Procedure KOFI00

On the **Change View "Control data": Overview** screen, you can verify that the KOFI00 account determination procedure will use the account determination condition types (**CTyp**) KOFI and KOFK, but only if the **Requirement** VOFM routine **2** is fulfilled. This information is important to understand how you get to the account numbers; for more details, check out the Defining Account Determination Condition Types section. For more details about access sequences, condition types, and procedures, consult Chapter 4.

Defining Account Determination Access Sequences

To configure general ledger account determination access sequences, follow the menu path **SAP Customizing Implementation Guide • Sales and Distribution • Basic Functions • Account Assignment/Costing • Revenue Account Determination • Define Access Sequences and Account Determination Types • Define Access Sequences**.

As shown in Figure 10.22, follow these steps:

❶ First, select the desired general ledger account determination **Access** sequence KOFI.

❷ Next, double-click the **Accesses** option in the **Dialog Structure** menu on the left.

❸ Then, browse through the condition tables assigned to the access sequence and select the condition table you want to check in terms of fields and technical settings.

❹ Double-click the **Fields** option in the **Dialog Structure** menu on the left.

❺ Once satisfied, click the **Exit** button.

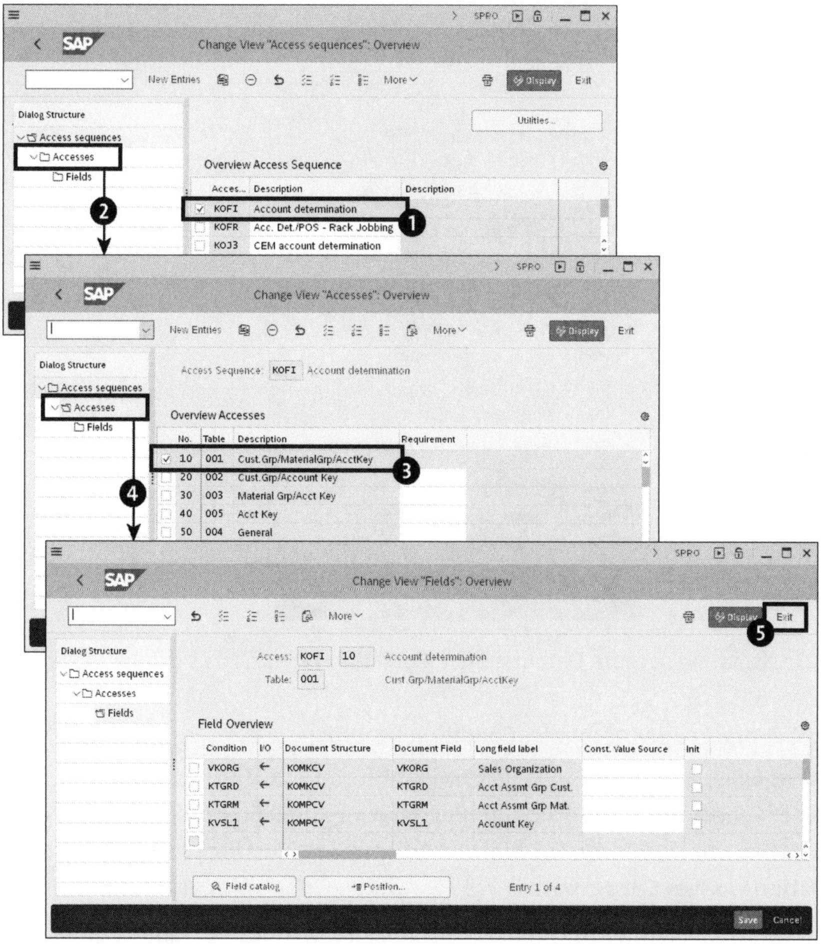

Figure 10.22 Displaying Account Determination Access Sequence KOFI

The access sequence is assigned to the condition type, which we'll describe in the following section.

Defining Account Determination Condition Types

To configure general ledger account determination condition types, follow the menu path **SAP Customizing Implementation Guide • Sales and Distribution • Basic Functions • Account Assignment/Costing • Revenue Account Determination • Define Access Sequences and Account Determination Types • Define Account Determination Types**.

On the screen shown in Figure 10.23, you find account determination condition type (**CTyp**) KOFI assigned to the access sequence (**AS**) KOFI.

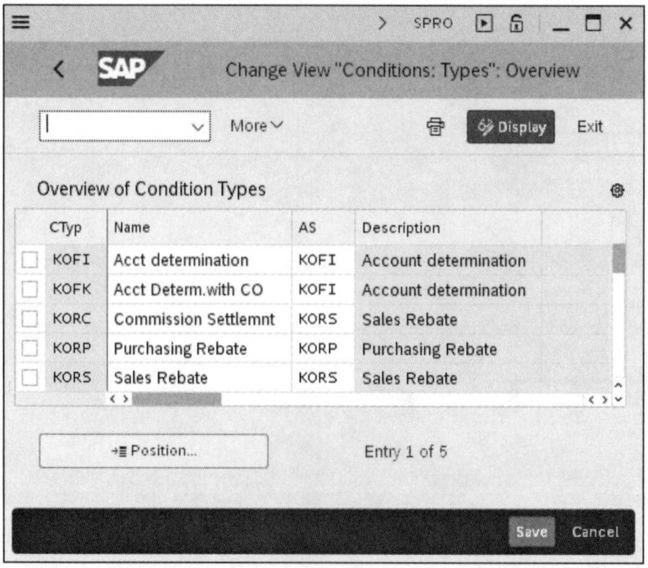

Figure 10.23 Displaying Account Determination Condition Type KOFI

Assigning General Ledger Accounts (Condition Records)

To maintain general ledger accounts determination condition records, open Transaction VKOA or follow the menu path **SAP Customizing Implementation Guide • Sales and Distribution • Basic Functions • Account Assignment/Costing • Revenue Account Determination • Assign G/L Accounts**.

The screen shown in Figure 10.24 contains a list of all the condition tables defined for account determination. We'll focus on the condition tables assigned to the KOFI access sequence. Double-click on the desired condition table, and the corresponding condition record maintenance screen will appear.

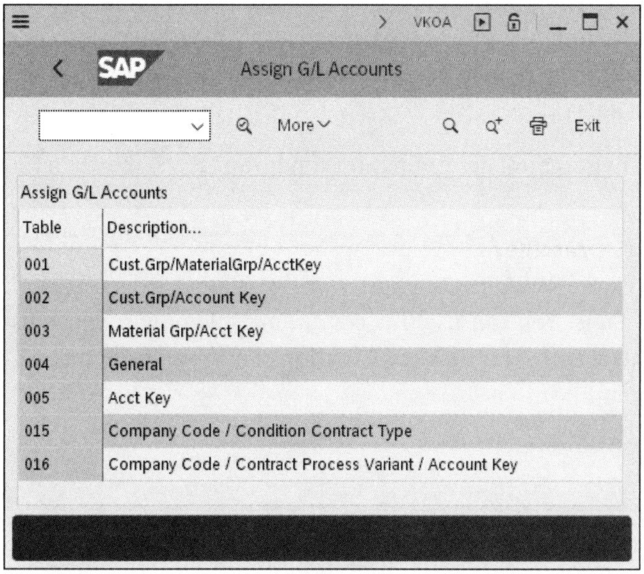

Figure 10.24 Account Determination Condition Records (VKOA)

In each record, as shown in Figure 10.25, the following fields are always present:

- The application (**App**) is always set as **V**, indicating this record is used for sales.
- The condition type (**CndTy**) indicates the condition type for which this entry is valid.
- The chart of accounts (**ChAc**) is the financial configuration element assigned to the company code and identifies the list of general ledger accounts that your company uses.
- The sales organization (**SOrg.**) is the sales organization structure element for which this entry is valid.
- The general ledger account number (**G/L Account**) is the general ledger account number to be used for this key combination.
- The accruals account number (**Accruals Acc.**) refers to a general ledger account used for special kinds of account postings, to the accruals account.

Two additional fields are only sometimes present:

- The customer account assignment group (**AAGC**) is a business partner (customer) master data attribute that allows you to use different general ledger accounts depending on this customer classification.
- The material account assignment group (**AAGM**) is a material master data attribute that allows you to use different general ledger accounts depending on this material classification.

Let's now look at the first five account determination condition tables, shown in Figure 10.24:

1. **001: Cust.Grp/MaterialGrp/AcctKey**
   This table, shown in Figure 10.25, is the most specific general ledger account assignment condition table. You can use this condition table only if you must maintain different general ledger for each combination of customer and material account assignment group.

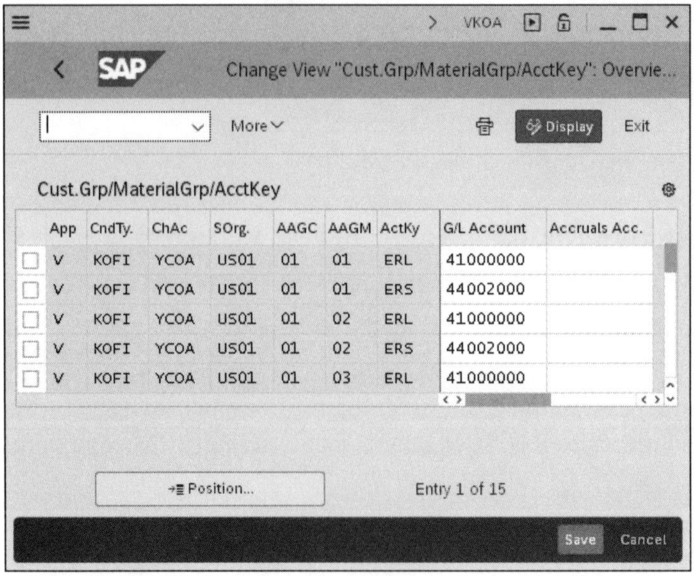

Figure 10.25 Cust.Grp/MaterialGrp/AcctKey

2. **002: Cust.Grp/Account Key**
   You can use this condition table, shown in Figure 10.26, only if you must maintain different general ledger accounts for each customer account assignment group.

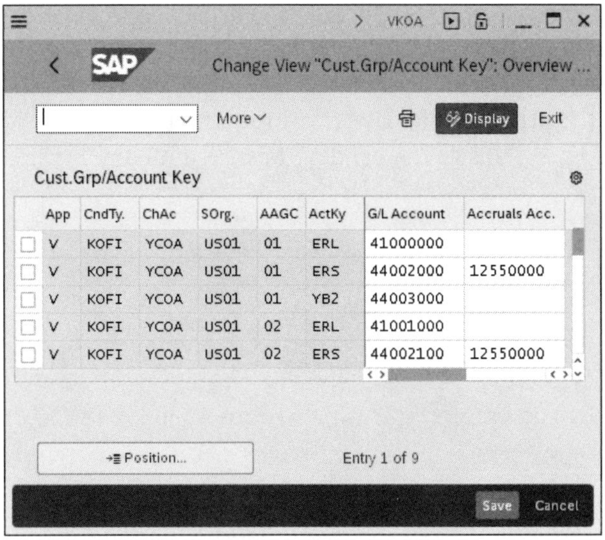

Figure 10.26 Cust.Grp/Account Key

3. **003: Material Grp/Acct Key**
   You can use this condition table, shown in Figure 10.27, only if you must maintain different general ledger accounts for different customer account assignment groups.

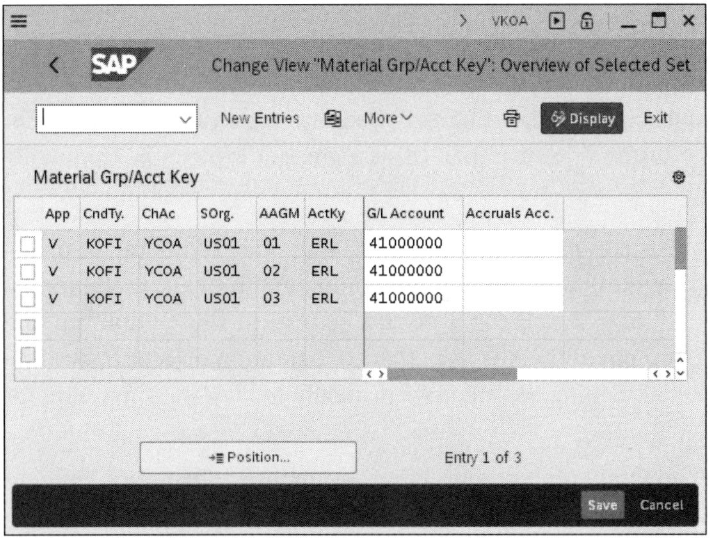

Figure 10.27 Material Grp/Acct Key

4. **004: General**
   This assignment is the most generic general ledger account assignment, shown in Figure 10.28, and is valid regardless of the account key. You must only use this key if the account is used to catch all postings for later investigation. Finance will need to decide to use this key or to transfer the pending invoice until any missing assignments are maintained.

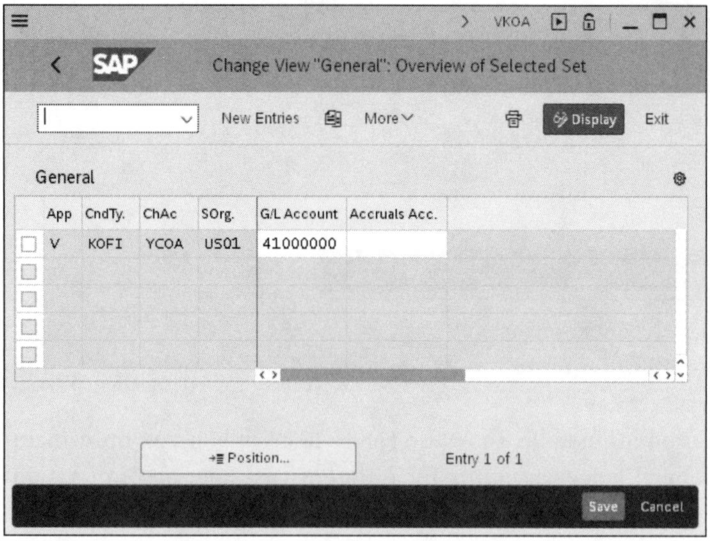

Figure 10.28 General

5. **005: Account Key**
   This condition table, shown in Figure 10.29, is used to assign an account by account keys regardless of customer or material. This assignment is the most commonly used assignment.

Condition records are usually considered master data for other condition technique features. For account determination, condition records are defined as a configuration activity. Therefore, you'll maintain the condition records in this transaction and transport them to other environments like other configuration objects, thus eliminating the need for maintaining these entries manually or via data conversion for every environment.

Thus, general ledger account numbers must be created in the configuration environment, typically by finance using Transaction FS00. Without the definition of the general ledger account, you won't be able to make the assignment.

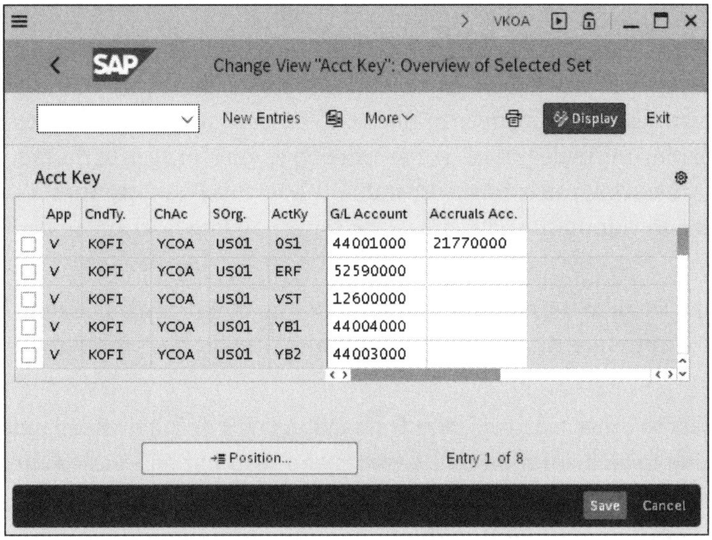

Figure 10.29 Account Key

10.4.2 Cost Centers for Goods Movement

Cost centers are a common concept in business, usually managed by company officials like a smaller company within the company. These units are often directly linked to official compensation (bonuses). When you ship product via free of charge orders, the cost of that product must be absorbed by a cost element of the company; in other words, some area of the company "pays" for the product shipped for free.

You can use cost centers to "pay" for free of charge shipments. This step is usually performed when you want some areas of your company to closely manage free of charge shipments and keep within a limit. You must budget the areas responsible for the cost center with enough resources to cover the free of charge shipments they are responsible for.

SAP S/4HANA allows you to define a cost center for each order reason, which we'll discuss later in this section. An order reason assigned on the header of the sales order is mandatory on free of charge order types. Most companies in the US do not have a policy of budgeting the areas with a free of charge order amount. Free of charge shipments are usually accounted as cost of sales or the cost of doing business, represented by a general ledger account. You can also use warranties, promotions, and other offers represented by corresponding general ledger accounts.

Changing the general ledger account for free of charge shipments requires the creation of new movement types using Transaction OMJJ. Movement types are assigned to schedule line categories. Schedule line categories are determined by the sales order line/item categories, which are determined by the sales order type. So, companies may end up creating multiple free of charge order types, one for each of the general ledger accounts involved. You can also use multiple schedule line categories, but the users would need to voluntarily navigate to the corresponding field and make a selection.

If you can change and adapt to the cost center approach, your company could reward areas that give less free product. As a bonus, you could also simplify the processing of free of charge orders.

To assign cost centers to order reasons, open Transaction OVF3 or follow the menu path **SAP Customizing Implementation Guide • Sales and Distribution • Basic Functions • Account Assignment/Costing • Assign Cost Centers**. On the screen that opens, click on the **New Entries** button or press F5.

As shown in Figure 10.30, select all applicable sales area information, that is, sales organization (**SOrg.**), distribution channel (**DChl**), and division (**Dv**) assigned to the relevant order reason (**OrdRs**) and define the cost center that will "pay" for the free of charge shipments.

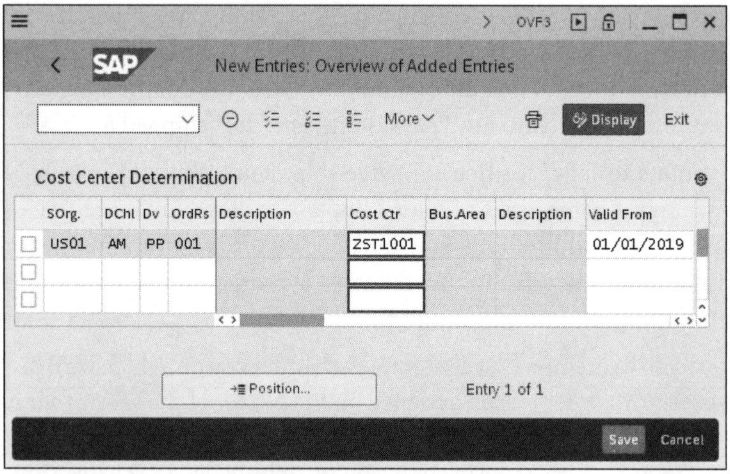

Figure 10.30 Assigning Cost Centers to Order Reasons

You also define a **Valid from** date that allow you to schedule this assignment to start affecting free of charge orders in the future.

10.5 Intercompany Billing

When processing sales and stock transfers, you may encounter scenarios in which the company code assigned to the sales organization is different than the company code assigned to the plant. This mismatch can happen with intercompany sales when you assign plants to the distribution chain on the sales organization structure configuration. This mismatch may also occur when you transfer stock between plants assigned to different company codes using stock transfer orders.

In either scenario, you'll end up with a sales document flagged as an intercompany transaction. This document may be consulted using the intercompany billing status, available under the **Processing** tab of the delivery document, for instance.

Intercompany billing takes place after billing to the third-party customer has been resolved, as shown in Figure 10.31.

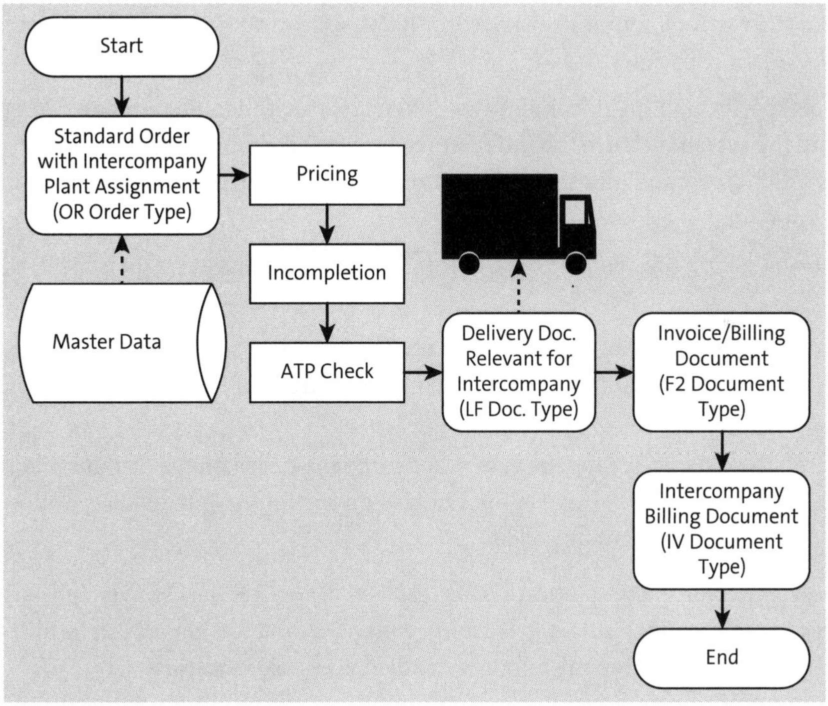

Figure 10.31 Intercompany Billing Document Creation

In the next section, we'll describe how intercompany billing documents are created and configured.

10.5.1 Intercompany Billing Transactions

You can use the same transactions to create the intercompany billing document as you would use to create invoices to third-party customers, specifically Transaction VF01 and Transaction VF04 (Collective Processing).

Using Transaction VF01, no difference exists between an intercompany customer and a third-party customer. You would simply use the same document number a second time, and the system will identify that the third-party customer invoice was already created. The document is considered relevant for intercompany billing, and you could then proceed to creating the intercompany billing document.

Using Transaction VF04 for collective processing, you'll indicate on the selection screen that you want to create intercompany billing documents by selecting the **Intercompany Billing** flag (see Chapter 14, Section 14.4.6, for more details).

Intercompany billing document copy rules may have been defined out of the box. Follow the instructions found in the Section 10.5.4 section to define intercompany billing document copy rules.

Unless you specify a billing document type when creating the intercompany billing document, the system will use the intercompany billing document type assigned to the sales order type configuration (Transaction VOV8). Billing document type IV is used for intercompany sales.

A common issue for companies that use this feature is the master data impact, as follows:

- Intercompany customers, configured as described in the Section 10.5.3 section, must be maintained using the intercompany sales areas of the plant's company code.
- All materials sold by the sales areas of other company codes must be maintained, not only on those distribution chains, but also on the intercompany distribution chain of the ordering company code.

At go-live, an intercompany solution can be resolved via master data conversion, but in day-to-day maintenance, this step is often overlooked, and the impact can be difficult to detect once intercompany billing is handled via background jobs.

To mitigate this issue, you must define comprehensive master data maintenance procedures and ensure you have a team monitoring the error log for the billing background job log of collective run report Transaction V.21 (see Chapter 14, Section 14.4.7, for more details).

Transaction V.21 is surprisingly underutilized by most companies that use SAP S/4HANA because this transaction contains error messages that require action to resolve, and many companies end up reacting to these issues only after a customer complains or after you identify inconsistencies on management reports.

One reason why Transaction V.21 is not favored is the large number of less-important messages issued along with business-critical messages. Users often need to browse through numerous messages that require no action to find the messages that are potentially holding up revenue and accounts receivable.

You can eliminate most, if not all, useless messages from Transaction V.21, but you'll need to define and assign copy requirements as VOFM routines that, rather than issuing messages, perform the necessary validation found in standard SAP S/4HANA routines. Because ABAP development is required in this case, which is often an expensive, not user-friendly system change, this type of enhancement is a prime candidate for rationalization and descoping during the implementation project.

The price on the intercompany billing document is calculated differently than what would be billed to third-party customers. SAP S/4HANA provides condition types PI01 and PI02 to assign values to intercompany billing documents; these values need to be part of the pricing procedure. The VOFM requirement routine 022 ensures these condition types are only used in intercompany documents.

Condition type PI01 is used for cost-plus intercompany pricing, which uses the material cost and applies a percentage maintained on the condition records (pricing master data) to define what the sales price should be. This condition type is the ideal way to price intercompany transactions because it eliminates the need for maintaining condition records for each material. However, some companies struggle to adapt to this concept.

Condition type PI02 allows for the maintenance of condition records with specific intercompany price figures by materials. Over time, you'll need your users to remember to maintain entries for each new material. This long-term maintenance is often overlooked, causing missed intercompany revenue and corresponding financial reporting issues.

You can mitigate these issues by defining condition tables based on material groups rather than on the material number or generic percentages. This case-by-case decision must be discussed and agreed to during the implementation project.

10.5.2 Assigning Organizational Units by Plant

To assign organizational units to plants, follow the menu path **SAP Customizing Implementation Guide • Sales and Distribution • Billing • Intercompany Billing • Assign Organizational Units By Plant • Assign Organizational Units to the Plants.**

On the screen shown in Figure 10.32, you'll need to find the plants (**Plant**) that may be used on intercompany sales orders and assign a sales area that will be used on the intercompany billing document by specifying the sales organization (**SOrg**), distribution channel (**DstCh**), and division (**Div.**). This sales area will be used by the intercompany customer assigned to the sales organization in the sales order header and the material master data element that needs to be extended.

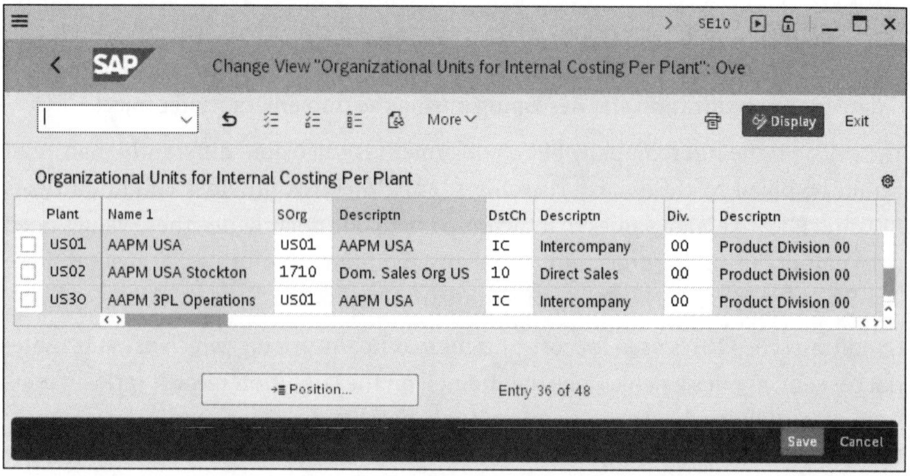

Figure 10.32 Assigning Organizational Units by Plant

In the configuration shown in Figure 10.32, the sales area indicated on this screen will be used when a sales order is entered for other sales areas using plant US01.

10.5.3 Defining Internal Customer Number by Sales Organization

To assign intercompany customer numbers to sales organizations, follow the menu path **SAP Customizing Implementation Guide • Sales and Distribution • Billing • Intercompany Billing • Define Internal Customer Number By Sales Organization.**

On the screen shown in Figure 10.33, you'll need to find the sales organization (**Sales Org.**) to be used on intercompany sales orders and assign the intercompany customer number (**CustInterC**) from the business partner master data that represents the company code assigned to this sales organization.

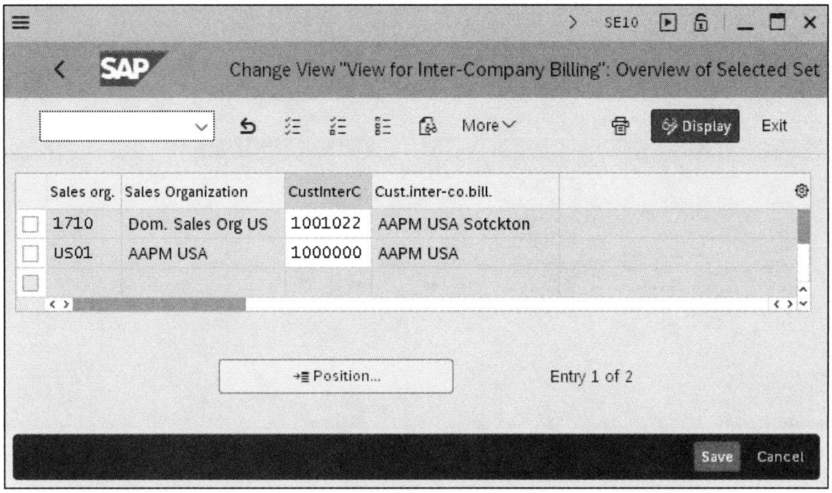

Figure 10.33 Defining Internal Customer Number by Sales Organization

The customer master must be extended to the sales area assigned to the intercompany plant (as described in Chapter 2); otherwise, an error message will display indicating that the sales organization has not been defined (VF009). This error message is a bit misleading, and trying to resolve it can be quite frustrating. The solution is to review the master data for the customer number and the sales area assigned to the plant.

10.5.4 Billing Copy Control for Intercompany Documents

To configure the delivery-to-billing document copy control, follow the menu path **SAP Customizing Implementation Guide • Sales and Distribution • Billing • Billing Documents • Maintain Copying Control for Billing Documents • Copying Control: Delivery Document to Billing Document**. The screen shown in Figure 10.34 will open.

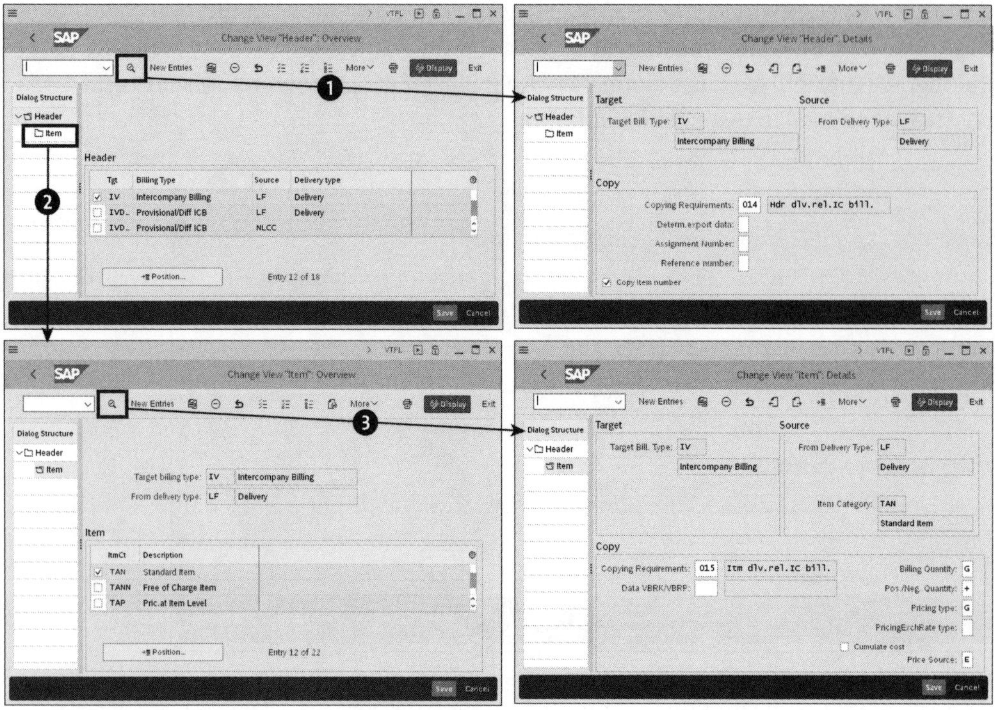

Figure 10.34 Billing Copy Control Configuration

❶ Assign the origin delivery document type (**Source**) to the target intercompany billing document type (**Tgt**). Then, enter the header copy rule details; entering "014" in the **Copy Requirement** field for the VOFM routine is the most critical step.

❷ Click the back icon or press [F3] to return to the initial screen and then select the entry you just created and double-click the **Item** option in the **Dialog Structure** menu on the left.

❸ Finally, include all item categories that may be used on the intercompany delivery documents by entering the desired item category codes in the item category (**ItmCt**) column. For each item category, you must enter the item copy rule details; entering "015" in the **Copy Requirement** field for the VOFM routine is the most critical step.

10.6 Proforma Invoices

Proforma invoices provide all the necessary details to your customers for arranging letters of credit (or other payment guarantee procedures). The invoices are also used with customs authorities and freight forwarders for making customs arrangements in export scenarios to ensure the shipment will clear customs as smoothly as possible.

In export scenarios, you'll have proforma invoices and commercial invoices. The term "proforma" is commonly used when arranging for letters of credit, and the term "commercial invoice" is used for customs. In SAP S/4HANA, both of these documents are considered "proforma invoices."

Two billing document types are configured out of the box that allow you to create proforma invoices. Billing document type F5 is used for creating proforma invoices with reference to a sales order (commonly used for letters of credit), and document type F8 is used for delivery-based proforma invoices (commonly used as commercial invoices for customs).

Proforma invoices are also used by the SAP Global Trade Services functionality for global trade and related compliance checks. No accounting documents are created by proforma invoices.

Proforma invoices may be issued multiple times. However, when interfacing with GTS, you must cancel outdated proforma invoices to ensure you can easily see which invoices are the most recent.

Order-based proforma invoices are snapshots of the order regardless of stock availability. Thus, you must prevent partial shipments; otherwise, the proforma invoice won't match the shipment invoice or the final invoice. So, if you encounter backordered lines on a sales order that requires a proforma invoice, you'll need to decide whether to reject the backordered line or to wait for stock to become available before shipping all products together. Also, when you have multiple plants across order lines, you must consolidate the shipment at one warehouse before shipping to the customer while also ensuring the shipment matches the proforma invoice.

Delivery-based proforma invoices also behave the same way. The ATP check on delivery document helps reduce issues with backordered lines. However, if you issue delivery-based proforma invoices, as soon as these invoices are created, you may encounter a short-pick situation at the warehouse (when products are not found where they are expected to be stored at the time of picking). This problem shouldn't happen often, but having a process in place to respond this problem, such as cancelling and reissuing the delivery-based proforma invoice, is important.

10.7 Summary

Billing is a sales functionality with impacts to finance that need to be carefully implemented and controlled to ensure the smooth flow of information between areas in SAP S/4HANA. In this chapter, we covered different ways you can create billing documents, described different types of documents, and walked you through processes related to billing.

Chapter 11
Stock Transfer Orders and Intercompany Sales

When selling products between subsidiaries of the same corporation that share the same SAP S/4HANA environment, you don't need to use purchase orders or sales orders like you would for third-party customers. Instead, you can use a special type of purchase order called a stock transfer order, which includes some sales functionalities to eliminate the need for separate sales documents.

Each plant defined in the system is assigned to a company code (see Chapter 1, Section 1.1, for more details). You can perform some operations between plants to streamline otherwise laborious processes. Corporations that store product in multiple locations will probably need to transfer product from plant to plant or from storage location to storage location at some point. In addition to this process, in this chapter, we'll also cover a scenario where one company's plant is used to deliver products to another company's customer, which is called an *intercompany sale* (Section 11.2).

Let's now look at these operations and their related configuration activities.

11.1 Stock Transfer Orders

If you need to move product from one plant and/or storage location to another, the easiest method is to use a transfer posting stock movement in Transaction MIGO, which is part of materials management (MM). Movement types such as 301 and 311 allow you to move stock.

These movements don't allow for picking or packing since no delivery document exists. If you need to integrate this information with an external warehouse management system (WMS), the lack of a delivery document would also be an issue. Transportation planning may be required when moving stock, which is not possible without a delivery document. If plants belong to different company codes, pricing requirements for the stock transfer may be different than the simple cost of the product.

To cover these gaps, you can use a special type of purchasing document called a *stock transfer order*. This document uses the sourcing plant as a vendor. Stock transfers are a common requirement for companies that, for instance, conduct manufacturing at one location but logistics at a separate location. In this case, plant-to-plant transfers are a critical part of the core business process.

Other companies may represent some part of a warehouse as a storage location rather than as plant. Transferring stock between these locations would present the same challenges as plant-to-plant transfer, but you can use stock transfer orders for this situation too. Figure 11.1 shows the stock transfer order process from start to finish.

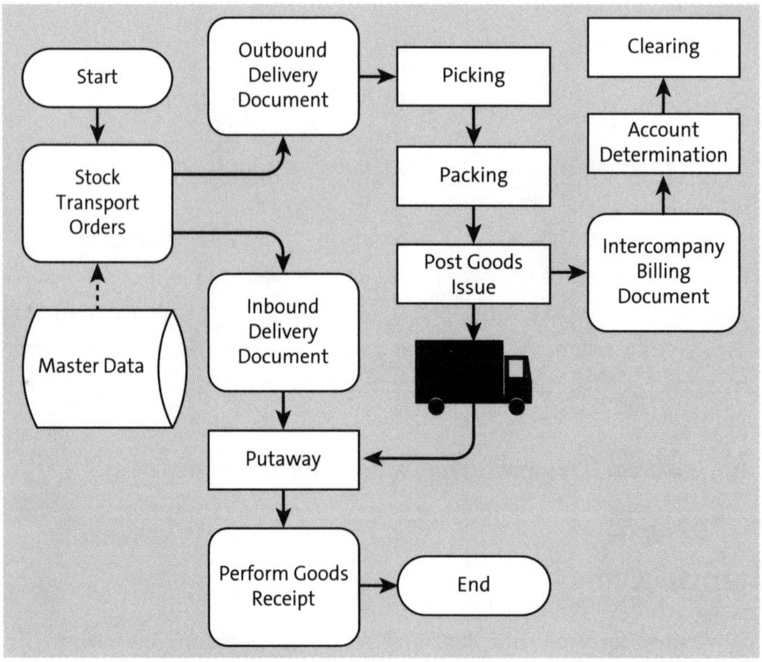

Figure 11.1 Stock Transport Order

The process typically starts with entering a stock transfer order. Some companies define a purchase requisition requirement, which is usually not necessary for most companies. The stock transfer order is entered using Transaction ME21N, which is also used to enter purchase orders. This functionality is part of the MM team scope.

The stock transfer order has a version of the available to promise (ATP) check that runs and allocate stock like a sales order would. This check doesn't handle backorders, so you'll need to ensure stock transfer orders are entered only for materials that you currently have stock on hand ready for transfer.

Once the stock transfer order is complete and stock is allocated, the order will become relevant for outbound delivery creation. The delivery document is then created (either manually or via a background job) and sent to warehouse (electronically or with a printed pick list). The warehouse team will pick product off the shelf and bring it to the packing team. Once packed and ready to ship, you'll perform the post goods issue operation, where inventory is consumed into the cost of goods sold (COGS) inventory account.

If the plants belong to different company codes, the outbound delivery document will be relevant for intercompany billing (see Chapter 10, Section 10.5, for more details). The intercompany invoice is created, and an intercompany accounts receivable posting is generated and cleared (either automatically or manually).

After shipping, the goods will make their way to the destination warehouse location. The goods receipt team at that location will either use the stock transfer order number to create an inbound delivery manually and/or search for an existing inbound delivery created by a background job.

The goods receipt team will record the putaway operation and perform the post goods receipt function. This step concludes the stock transfer. In the following sections, we'll talk about the related configuration activities required to enable this functionality.

11.1.1 Shipping Data for Plants

One configuration prerequisite to enable stock transfer orders is to set up the master data to be used on delivery documents created out of or into each plant. To set up this master data, follow the menu path **SAP Customizing Implementation Guide • Materials Management • Purchasing • Purchase Order • Set up Stock Transport Order • Define Shipping Data for Plants**.

On the **Change View "Stock Transport Order": Overview of Selected Set** screen, select the desired and click the details icon, as shown in Figure 11.2.

On the **Change View "Stock Transport Order": Details of Selected Set** screen, enter a customer number created to represent this plant (consult Chapter 2 for more details) in the **Customer No. Plant** field. When you create delivery documents for the stock transfer order, this customer will be used to represent plant US01.

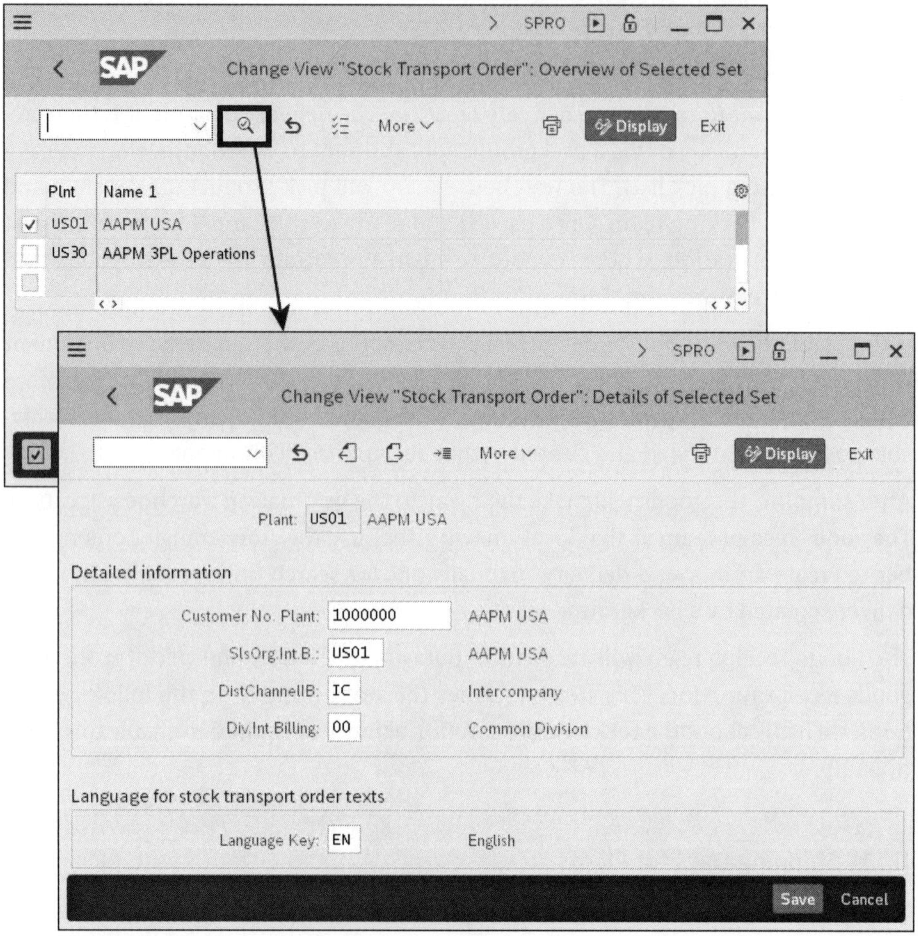

Figure 11.2 Defining the Shipping Data for a Plant

You also need to specify the sales area; these fields are mandatory when creating the delivery document. Enter the sales organization (**SlsOrg.Int.B.**), distribution channel (**DistChannelIB**), and division (**Div.Int.Billing**).

This step needs to be repeated for all plants involved in transfers using stock transfer orders.

11.1.2 Delivery Type and Availability Check by Plant

You can use the schedule line category configuration to define the values described in this section for standard sales order processing (see Chapter 6, Section 6.4.7, for more details).

This chapter is about stock transfer orders and these are purchase order types that don't have the schedule lines feature found on sales orders (as described in Chapter 6, Section 6.4.7). So, you won't be able to leverage a sales order's schedule line configuration to define these values.

The configuration steps described in this section is new in SAP S/4HANA and was not available in previous versions of the system. Previously, you were quite limited on how to handle stock transfers between systems, and now, you have more flexibility. The following sections define the shipping information used by a plant.

Configuring the Delivery Type and Availability Check Procedure by Plant

To configure a plant's delivery type and availability check procedure, follow the menu path **SAP Customizing Implementation Guide • Materials Management • Purchasing • Purchase Order • Set up Stock Transport Order • Configure Delivery Type & Availability Check Procedure by Plant.** On the screen that opens, click on the **New Entries** button or press F5.

On the screen shown in Figure 11.3, enter parameters for the purchase order type (**Ty.**) defined by the MM team for use in stock transfer orders. In our example, we're using purchase order type UD (**StockTranspOrderDel**); some companies use the standard purchase order type NB, but your MM team will decide which purchase order type to use.

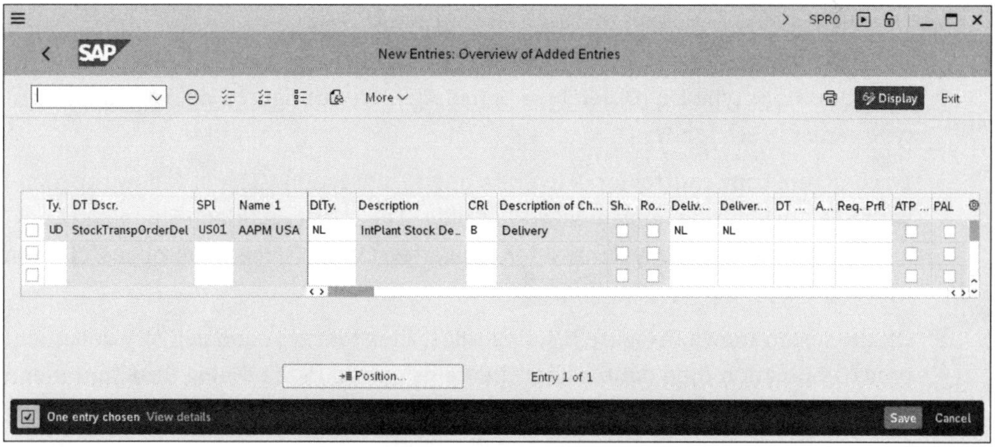

Figure 11.3 Configuring Delivery Type and ATP Check Procedure by Plant

You'll also need to configure the assignment of the purchase order type to all plants relevant for stock transfers, as supplying plants (**SPl**).

For each combination of purchase order type and plant, you can choose the delivery document type (**DlTy.**) and the ATP checking rule (**CRl**)—see the Chapter 7, Section 7.2, and Chapter 9, Section 9.2, for more details. Depending on the delivery documents types selected, you'll probably need to add copy control configuration to allow these document types to work, which we'll describe in the next section. The out-of-the-box SAP configuration does not offer many options, this configuration activity is often a prerequisite for using stock transfer orders.

You can also select different types of delivery documents for intracompany transfers (**Delivery type 1**) and intercompany transfers (**Delivery type 2**). The main difference between these two kinds of transfer is billing relevance. For intercompany transfers, you must issue an invoice; for intracompany transfers, invoices are not required.

You can use different types of delivery documents if this transfer is a consignment between the transfer parties (**DT Consgt**) and define an ATP check (**Av.Ch.Rule**) to avoid shortages or backorders. You could add a requirement profile (**Rep. Prfl**), which was previously part of SAP Advanced Planning and Optimization (SAP APO) but is now part of SAP S/4HANA.

The **ATP Conf. MRP** flag allows the stock transfer order's ATP check quantities to be used as demand in material requirements planning (MRP), while the **PAL** flag uses these quantities for product allocation. This functionality was discussed in more detail in Chapter 7, Section 7.5.

Copy Control

To create a delivery document, you'll need to define copy control rules from the stock transfer order to the delivery document. The stock transfer order is represented by the sales order type DL (**Order Type Sched.Ag.**). We configured delivery document type earlier in Section 11.1.1.

To configure copy control for deliveries, open Transaction VTLA or follow the menu path **SAP Customizing Implementation Guide • Logistics Execution • Shipping • Copying Control • Specify Copy Control for Deliveries.** On the screen that opens, click on the **New Entries** button or press F5.

On the screen shown in Figure 11.4, first select the order type and delivery document type combination then double-click the **Items** option in the **Dialog Structure** menu on the left. On the next screen, enter the header and line copy control configuration; for more details, consult Chapter 3 and Chapter 9.

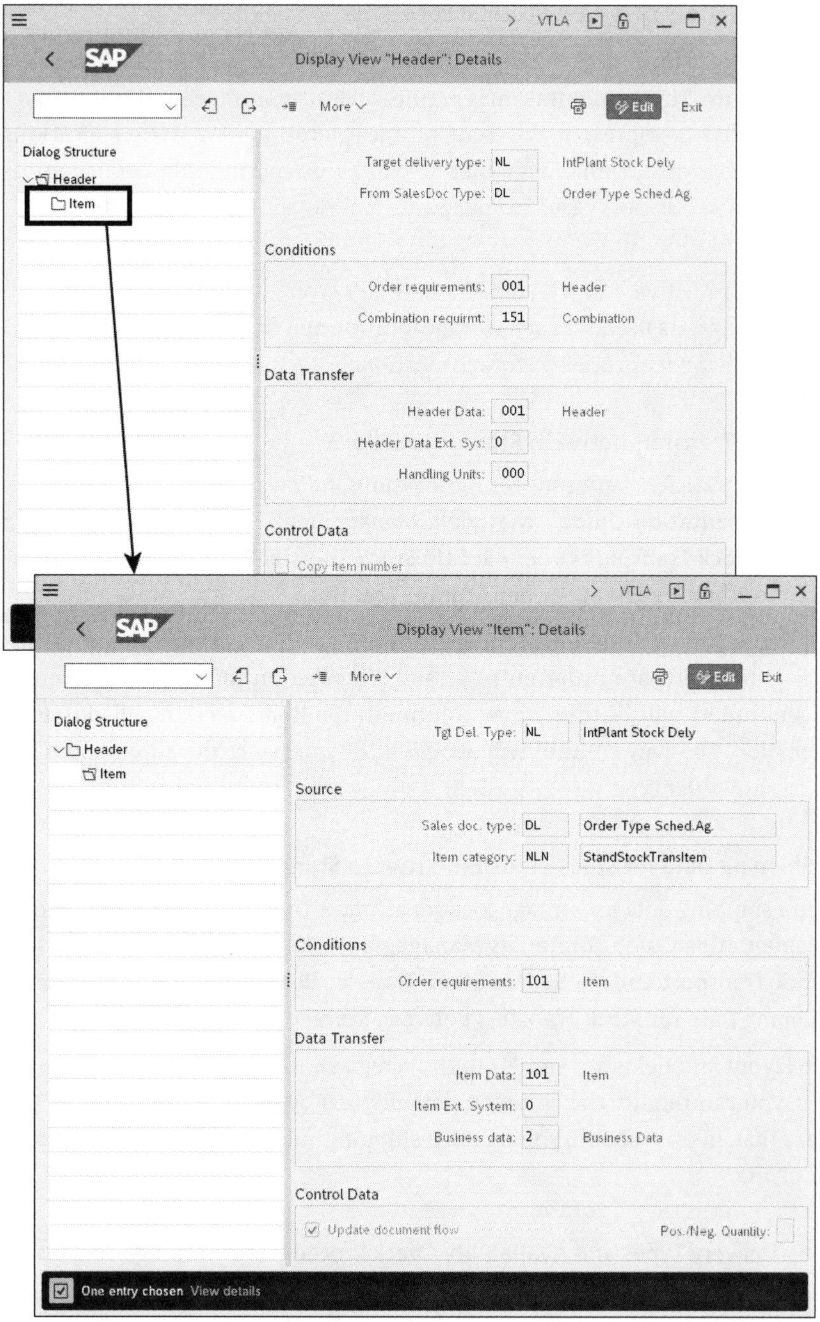

Figure 11.4 Copy Control for Stock Transfer Order Deliveries Configuration

11.1.3 Stock Transfers between Storage Locations

To enable stock transfer orders between storage locations, a specific configuration must be put in place. This configuration is required because storage locations weren't originally intended to represent different physical locations but rather locations within a warehouse. Most companies adhered to this concept, and then other companies presented valid business cases to change, which was addressed via system modification.

The first step is to activate stock transfer between storage locations. Next, you'll define the shipping data used for each storage location and finally define the delivery type and availability check code by storage location.

Activating Stock Transfers between Storage Locations

To activate stock transfers between storage locations, follow the menu path **SAP Customizing Implementation Guide • Materials Management • Purchasing • Purchase Order • Set Up Stock Transport Order • Set Up Stock Transfer Between Storage Locations • Activate Stock Transfer Between Storage Locations.**

On this screen, you'll see the **Issuing Storage Location Active checkbox.** Once you activate this flag, the purchase order entry screen (Transaction ME21N) used to enter stock transfer orders will feature a new column in the **Items** section called **Issuing Storage Location**. The new column will appear after you select the supplying plant and the purchase order type.

Defining Shipping Data for Stock Transfers between Storage Locations

To configure shipping data for storage locations, follow the menu path **SAP Customizing Implementation Guide • Materials Management • Purchasing • Purchase Order • Set Up Stock Transport Order • Set Up Stock Transfer Between Storage Locations • Define Shipping Data for Stock Transfers Between Storage Locations.**

The screen layout and fields are similar to the screen shown earlier in Figure 11.2. On this screen, you can modify the shipping data defined by *plant* in that section. The difference is that, in this section, you'll define shipping data for each *storage location* instead of plant.

Configuring Delivery Types and Availability Check Procedures by Storage Location

To configure delivery types and availability check procedure procedures for storage locations, follow the menu path **SAP Customizing Implementation Guide • Materials**

Management • Purchasing • Purchase Order • Set up Stock Transport Order • Set Up Stock Transfer Between Storage Locations • Configure Delivery Type & Availability Check Procedure by Storage Location.

The screen layout and fields are very similar to the one described in the Configuring the Delivery Type and Availability Check Procedure by Plant section. This time, the same field values are assigned to the storage location rather than to the plant.

On this screen, you can define different delivery document types and ATP check values for each storage location. This screen will first ask for the purchase document category before allowing you to enter parameters. For stock transfer orders, you'll usually enter "F" (Purchase Order) in the **Doc Ctg** field, but the MM team may ask you to use a different purchase order type for stock transfer orders (but "F" is the most likely value).

11.2 Intercompany Sales

If a sales order is entered for a material that has stock in a plant that is not part of the same company as the sales organization, the sales order is considered an "intercompany sale." This kind of sale is quite efficient from a customer point of view; they don't need to know which plant carried the materials they want to order. Customers would also not notice their order being split into multiple documents, one for each fulfillment plant.

> **Note**
>
> You don't need to configure anything to enable intercompany sales, which is available out of the box. In this section, we're focused on the process to ensure that you have a full understanding of the intercompany sales functionality.

Figure 11.5 shows a diagram illustrating intercompany sales for our sample company, the American Automotive Parts Manufacturer (AAPM).

Sales organization US01 (assigned to company code US01) is configured on the organizational structure to allow ordering from plant CA01 (assigned to company code US01). The order is accepted like a normal order, but the trained eye will spot some key differences that indicates this order is an intercompany order.

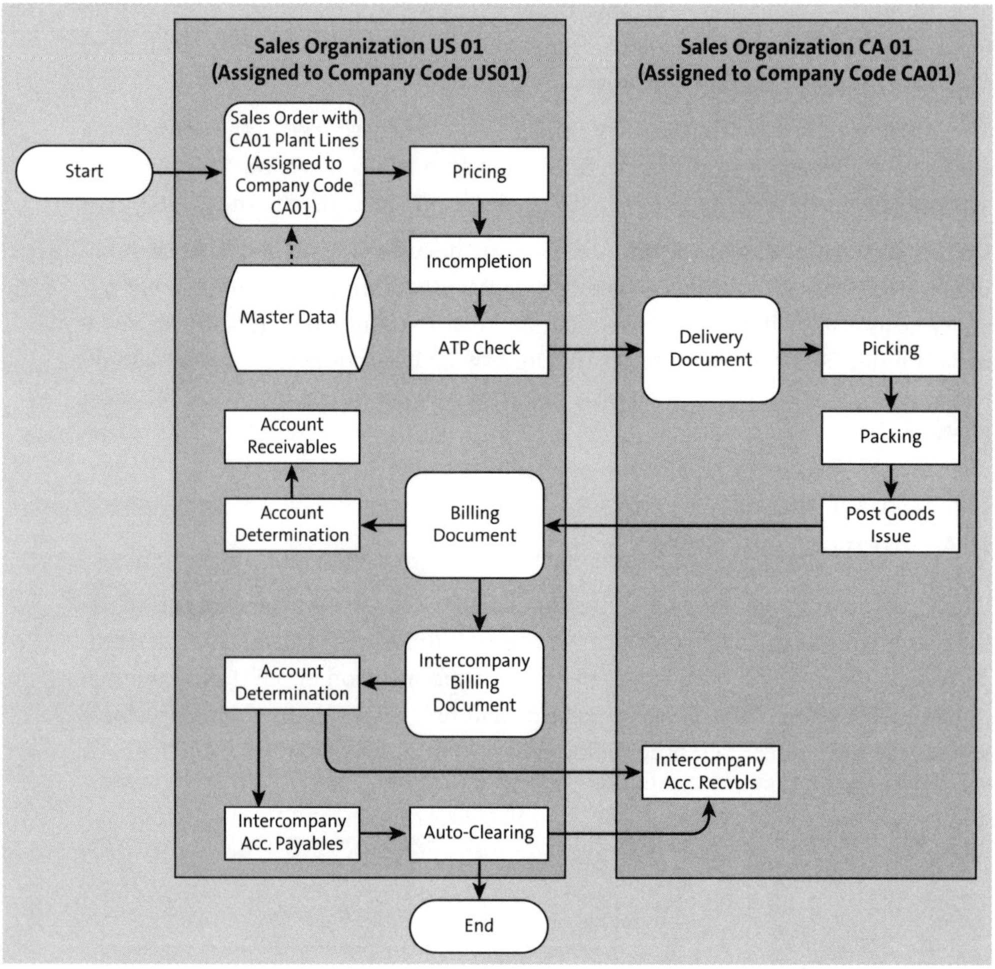

Figure 11.5 Intercompany Sales

The order would go through the normal pricing, incompletion, and ATP check processes. Once quantities are allocated, a delivery document is created for plant CA01 that looks similar to a regular delivery document created by sales organization CA01.

The warehouse picks, packs, and ships the products that were ordered and then registers the post goods issue operation under plant CA01, thus consuming inventory into the COGS account for company code CA01.

After the post goods issue operation, the delivery becomes relevant for billing, typically processed by a background job. An invoice is created and sent to the customer, and the accounts receivable team at company code US01will process customer's payment. At this time, COGS will be posted to sales organization CA01 and revenue posted to company code US01. To resolve this mismatch, a new intercompany billing document is automatically created (usually by the same background job that created the invoice).

The intercompany billing document features intercompany pricing (different than the price to the customer). This price needs to be negotiated and agreed upon between the companies. Some companies use cost; others apply a fixed profit margin (for example, cost plus 10%), and some companies create an intercompany price list. All these options are supported out of the box by SAP S/4HANA. We recommend using cost-based intercompany pricing to avoid the burden of maintaining list prices for all materials, without which issues would arise in an otherwise fully automated process. Possible problems can be quite severe because these types of issues often go a long time undetected.

Using intercompany pricing, the intercompany invoice goes through accounting and transfers some of the revenue from the selling company (US01) to the fulfillment company (CA01). Accounts payable in company code US01 pays accounts receivable on CA01. This step can be performed automatically, as preferred by most companies, but some companies prefer to handle this step manually.

Setting up intercompany sales requires discussions with the finance team to determine their preferences for handling intercompany billing. The system offers several options to automatically clear intercompany billing (see Chapter 10, Section 10.5, for more details).

The warehouse must be aware that some orders to be fulfilled may have come from the other company's customer service department.

11.3 Summary

Stock transfer orders are processed regardless of customer demand. Intercompany sales allow for the fulfillment of orders across company codes because of customer demands. In this chapter, we covered functionalities that enable collaboration across different companies that belong to the same groups and share the same system. These features reduce complexity and streamline processes by bringing stakeholders closer together while also making third-party customer interactions more efficient, cohesive, and collaborative.

Chapter 12
Customer Consignment

SAP S/4HANA Sales offers a feature called customer consignment to allow you to store goods at your customer's facility, ready to be consumed. You would process billing and replenishment based on consumption information. This scenario can typically be achieved without the need for configuration. In this process-oriented chapter, we'll describe this feature in detail.

Consignment is a process in which product is stored at a customer-owned location, and the customer can consume the product, as necessary. The customer then notifies the vendor of the consumption. The vendor issues an invoice and replenishes inventory in accordance with agreement details.

Customer consignment is a functionality where your company, using SAP S/4HANA, plays the role of the vendor in this process. "Customer consignment" can be interpreted as the "consignment of product to the customer from you (the vendor)."

If you approach this process from the perspective of the customer, you'll use the vendor consignment functionality, which is part of the materials management (MM) scope. This functionality uses purchase orders (POs) to replenish vendor-owned inventory. Vendor inventory is consumed in production orders.

In the following sections, we'll explain the standard SAP S/4HANA features available for replenishing inventory at the customer's facility as well as related billing and reverse credit/returns. We'll also explain reverse customer consignment, from pickups to returns. This chapter is process-oriented, since most configuration related to customer consignment is the responsibility of the MM team.

12.1 Standard Customer Consignment

In this section, we'll look at a standard customer consignment process and discuss both consignment fill-up and consignment issue.

12.1.1 Process Overview

Figure 12.1 shows a diagram illustrating the consignment components we'll cover in this section.

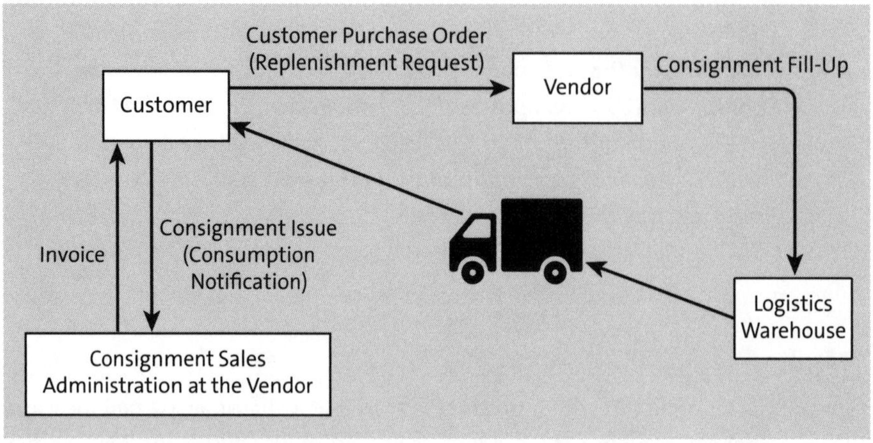

Figure 12.1 Consignment Process

The customer requests the replenishment of their consignment inventory by submitting a purchase order that represents a replenishment request. Your company (as the vendor) will receive the PO and create a consignment fill-up sales order (Section 12.1.2).

A variant of the consignment process is called vendor-managed inventory. In this process variant, the vendor is responsible for monitoring the consignment inventory at the customer's location and automatically replenishes stock according to the agreement signed with the customer.

In this variant, the customer doesn't need to submit purchase orders to have the inventory replenished. Instead, you can create a vendor-managed inventory contract and create fill-up orders with reference to this contract. Many companies simply enter standalone fill-up orders when stock levels reach certain levels.

At this time, the consignment fill-up order goes through the available to promise (ATP) check process, and stock is allocated to the order once available or planned. On the scheduled date, you'll create a delivery document and forward it to the logistics warehouse and pick/pack/ship stock to the customer.

After shipping, the stock is neither decremented nor consumed; instead, stock is moved/transferred to a special stock type called "customer stock." You'll be able to see this stock under the customer number, and any subsequent stock movement made will require you to specify that you are moving customer stock and to which customer number you want to move stock.

The customer number used for inventory purpose is the ship-to partner (SH partner function). But you can easily overwrite it by assigning a consignment special stock partner (SB partner function) to the consignment fill-up order.

If you want to control and track where the product is located, you can use the ship-to partner function. This partner function allows you to conduct inventory counts at the customer location and monitor for theft and loss.

However, most companies only use consignment because the customer requires it. Customers that are influential tend to move stock between their locations at will without notifying you. In this case, the overhead of knowing where the product is located becomes pointless as stock may have been moved without your knowledge. In these cases, you would be better off assigning a single customer number with the SB partner function across all the customer master entries that may order on behalf of this customer. In this way, no matter where you ship the product, the inventory will always show up under the same customer, and you won't manage the exact location of the product, only which customer is responsible for it. In this scenario, you must hold the customer accountable for lost or stolen inventory in your contract with them.

Next, the customer receives the shipment and records vendor consignment inventory in their system. The customer will then consume that inventory as necessary on production to fulfilling their own orders. Periodically, the customer will notify you, the vendor, of how many items were consumed. You would then create a consignment issue sales order (Section 12.1.3).

Once the consignment issue sales order is processed, an invoice will be created and sent to the customer. This process will also decrement/consume inventory. In a vendor-managed inventory scenario, you can identify shortages by querying the customer inventory and starting the replenishment process by entering consignment fill-up sales orders.

Companies often use Electronic Data Interchange (EDI) along with consignment, and customers eligible for consignment usually have a large enough purchase volume to justify the investment of setting up electronic communications.

12.1.2 Consignment Fill-Up

Figure 12.2 shows a diagram illustrating the consignment components we'll cover in this chapter.

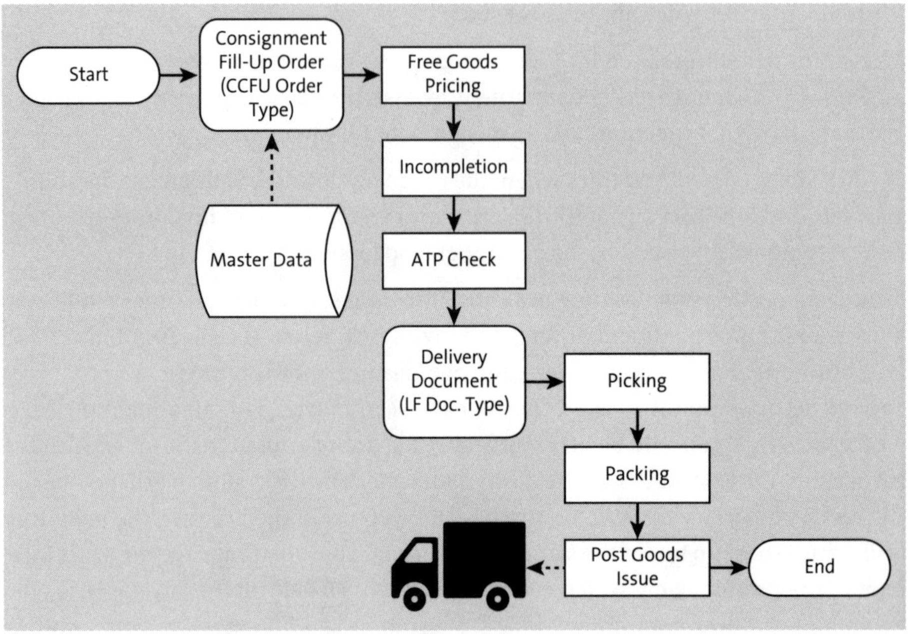

Figure 12.2 Consignment Fill-Up Order Processing

Consignment fill-up sales orders use sales order type CCFU (customer consignment fill-up). CCFU sales order lines come configured out of the box as relevant for free goods pricing to allow for profit margin and freight charges, but no charge to the customer is needed (see Chapter 4, Section 4.2, for more details on how free goods pricing work).

After the ATP check is processed, a sales order of sales order type CCFU is made relevant for delivery processing and will be processed by the warehouse using the sale delivery document type as for regular orders (sales order type LF) with all configured processes (picking, packing, and post goods issue operation).

No billing is defined out of the box for order type CCFU. If a requirement to charge for freight or other fees on consignment fill-up exists, you'll need to define a billing document type for the CCFU order type and maintain the corresponding copy control configuration (see Chapter 6 for more details).

12.1.3 Consignment Issue

In this section, we'll explain the standard features available in SAP S/4HANA to enable the process of issuing billing documents (invoices) to a customer once inventory stored at the customer's facility is consumed. Figure 12.3 shows a diagram illustrating this process.

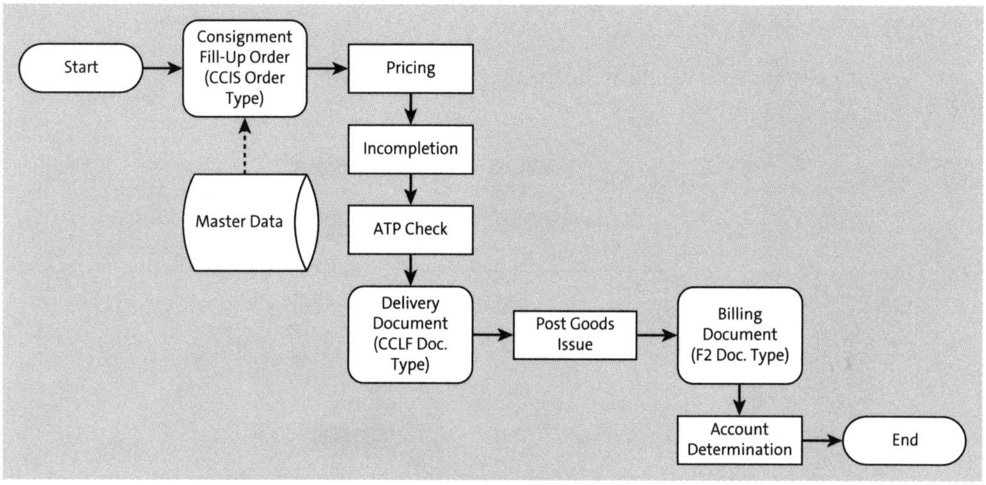

Figure 12.3 Consignment Issue Order Processing

The consignment issue sales order type is CCIS (Customer Consignment Fill-Up). Pricing is a perhaps the important component as its main objective is to issue an invoice to the customer for the consignment inventory that has been consumed.

Sales order type CCIS is relevant for ATP checks and for delivery, even though no physical stock movement is required to process consignment inventory consumption. The delivery document plays the role of consuming inventory from a sales perspective.

Sales order type CCIS uses delivery document type CCLF. The CCLF delivery document type is not relevant for picking; as soon as this document is created, it is automatically relevant for the post goods issue operation. Companies typically schedule a background job to process the post goods issue operation for CCLF deliveries.

Once the post goods issue operation is completed, the document is relevant for billing, which typically is processed by a background job. Sales order type CCIS will create the same billing document types as used in regular sales billing (F2).

12.2 Reverse Customer Consignment

In the following sections, we'll explain the standard features available in SAP S/4HANA to enable the process of crediting the customer for undue billing and for the returns of product from the customer's facility to your warehouse.

12.2.1 Process Overview

Figure 12.4 shows a diagram illustrating the consignment components we'll cover in this chapter.

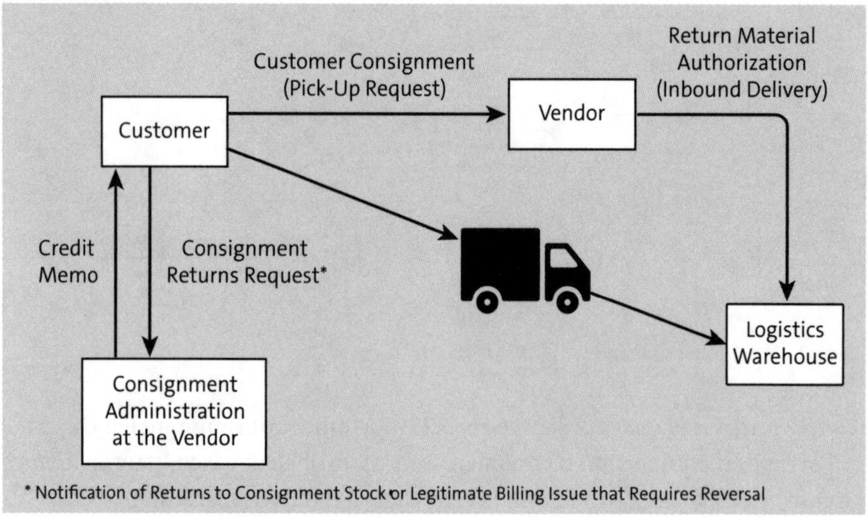

Figure 12.4 Reverse Customer Consignment

In some instances, you'll need to reverse the consignment issue using a consignment return, which may happen when the customer incorrectly reports consumption.

You may also need to return consignment inventory to your facility via a consignment pick-up order.

In both scenarios, the process typically starts with a notification from the customer; your customer service department will in turn create the corresponding return or pick-up order.

12.2.2 Consignment Pickup

In this section, we'll explain the standard features available in SAP S/4HANA for returns of product from the customer's facility to your warehouse. Figure 12.5 shows a diagram representing the process.

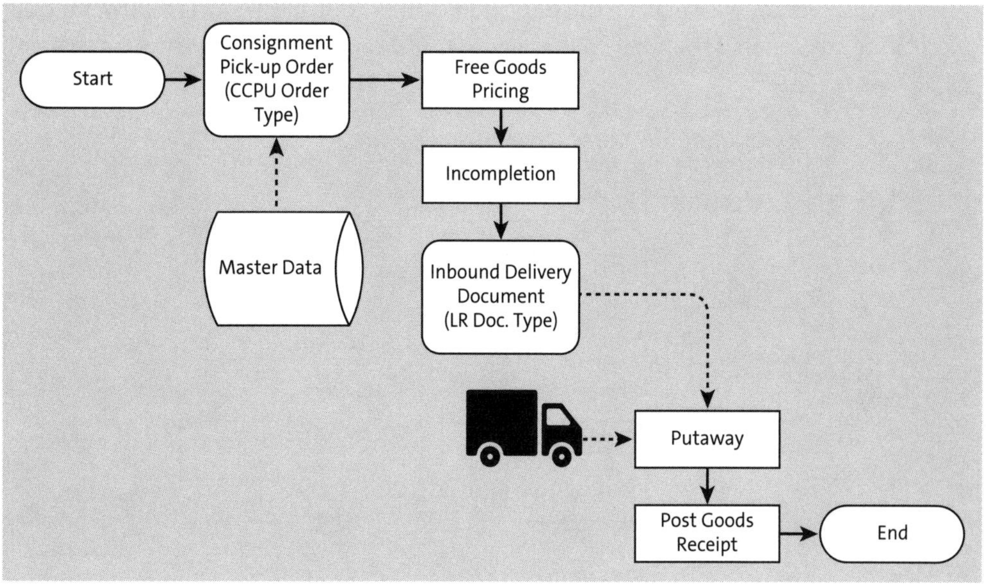

Figure 12.5 Consignment Pick-Up Order Processing

The consignment pick-up sales order type is CCPU (customer consignment pick-up). Sales order type CCPU lines come configured out of the box as relevant for free goods pricing to allow for the crediting of freight charges when appropriate, but no credit is issued to the customer (see Chapter 4, Section 4.2, for more details on how free goods pricing work).

Sales order type CCPU is relevant for inbound delivery processing. The document is typically created by a background job, but many companies prefer the warehouse crew create the document manually at the time of goods receipt because the return order number is the reference provided by the customer along with the return. The warehouse team will find it easier to create the delivery with the number they have than to search for the document created automatically in the background.

No billing is defined out of the box for the CCPU order type. If you have a requirement to credit freight or other fees on this document, you'll need to define the billing document type of the CCPU order type and corresponding copy control configuration (see Chapter 6 for more details).

12.2.3 Consignment Return

In this section, we'll explain the standard features available in SAP S/4HANA for crediting customers for undue billing. Figure 12.6 shows a diagram illustrating this process.

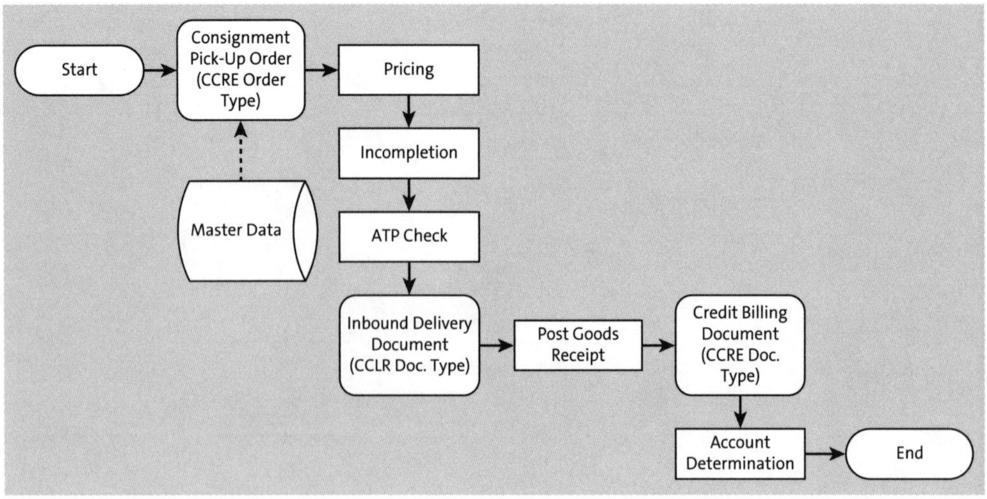

Figure 12.6 Consignment Returns Processing

For consignment returns, you would use sales order type CCRE (customer consignment returns). Pricing is a perhaps the important component as its main objective is to issue an invoice to the customer for the consignment inventory that has been consumed.

The CCRE is relevant for ATP checks and delivery, even though no physical stock movement is required to process a consignment inventory return. The delivery document plays the role of moving returned stock back under customer inventory.

Sales order type CCRE uses inbound delivery document type CCLR. The CCLR delivery document type is not relevant for picking; as soon as the document is created, the document is automatically relevant for the post goods receipt. Companies typically schedule a background job to process the post goods issue for CCLR deliveries (the same job used for sales order type CCLF).

Once the post goods receipt is completed, the document is relevant for billing, which typically is processed by a background job. Order type CCRE will create the credit billing document type CCRE.

12.3 Summary

The out-of-the-box functionality for consignment is typically used with little to no changes to support consignment scenarios. Using order types CCFU, CCIS, CCPU, and CCRR, you can support most consignment scenarios. At the end of this chapter, you should be familiar with the consignment features and comfortable enough to participate in the decision to use consignment to fulfill business requirements as well as in making detailed design decisions.

Chapter 13
Customer Complaint Management

After sales of goods and services are complete, your customer may encounter issues that require further assistance from your company. In this chapter, we'll describe the SAP S/4HANA tools available for handling the most common customer complaints.

Customer complaints are a critical component of your customer service operations, but companies often differ in the degree to which they wish to track complaints and incidents from the first contact to resolution.

Companies that want full details and reporting capabilities tend to implement more robust customer relationship management (CRM tools), such as SAP Customer Relationship Management (SAP CRM) or Salesforce, and eventually integrate these tools with their SAP S/4HANA system. SAP S/4HANA itself also offers several tools for resolving and fulfilling customer requests and is designed to fulfill/resolve each request with ERP functionality (such as quotes, returns, credits, etc.). However, SAP S/4HANA doesn't track customer contacts, just enables the required outcome of the contact. Some companies may opt to handle only the final outcome of customer contacts, whether credits, returns, replacements, service, etc. These types of documents are necessary even if you're using third-party tools to track complaints. Simply tracking only the outcome of a complaint had been the norm, but recently, companies have become focused on customer satisfaction and long-term customer relationships. A strong trend towards the adoption of third-party CRM tools is a new norm. Since this book is focused on sales, this chapter will focus on the outcome documents from customer complaints and not on tracking the calls themselves.

As shown in Figure 13.1, a customer will contact your company's customer service operations with their request. Our customer service representative will have a host of tools available to address customer's feedback using the following functionalities:

- **Customer returns**
  When a customer wants to return product in exchange for credit, refund, or replacement, SAP S/4HANA can handle these requests using advanced returns management or the simpler lean return approach.

- **Credit/debit request**
  To address pricing errors or other financial issues, you can enter the customer's request to either credit or debit their account accordingly, indicating the reason why and other details.
- **Free of charge order/delivery**
  Your customer service representatives can ship additional product to the customer, whether replacement parts for the customer to perform fixes on their own, gifts, or even a replacement product if you don't need the customer to return the defective product. Some companies opt to "dispose in field," that is, ask the customer dispose of the product without returning it, usually when the cost of return shipping is greater than the cost of the product.
- **Customer inquiries**
  If a customer wants to buy other products, such as parts, and asks about pricing and availability, the customer service representative can enter a customer inquiry in SAP S/4HANA to answer these requests. These inquiries can be used for reporting and even converted into sales orders. You can also enter sales orders directly and perform the other sales functions described in the other chapters of the book.

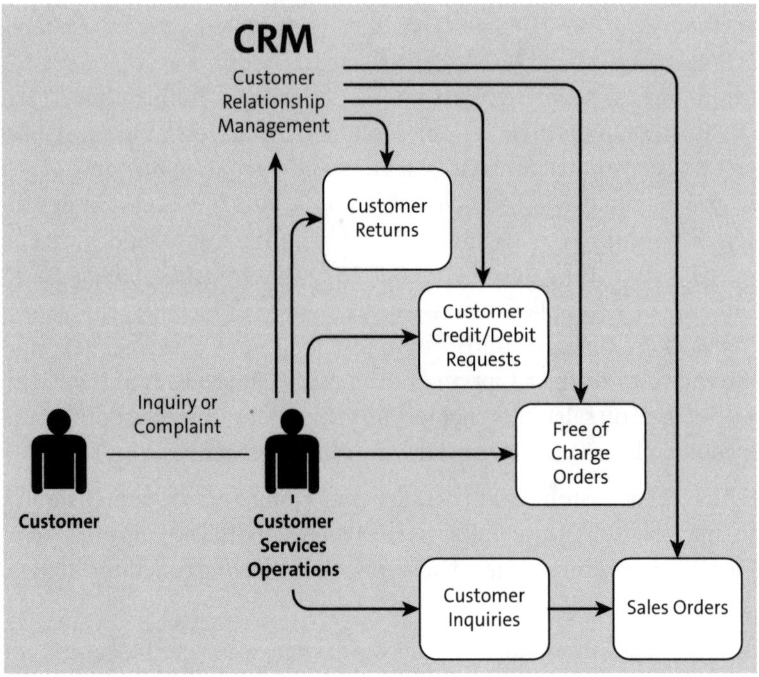

Figure 13.1 Customer Inquiries/Complaints

In some scenarios, a customer service representative may need to process a service notification. This feature is used if you need the customer to send the product in for service (under warranty or billable). A service notification is used to create a service order, which is then used to receive the customer's product and ship it back to the customer after the repair is performed.

Most companies do not implement the service notification functionality just to support customer repair requests. Companies that perform billable services, such as maintenance, repair, and overhaul (MRO), use service notifications and service orders to conduct a significant part of their core business or serve as a main source of revenue. For these companies, using service notifications to support customer complaints seems natural. Companies that that fit this profile spend a good portion of the implementation project setting up master data and defining processes to support this functionality. However, this scenario is outside the scope of this book.

In the following sections, we'll cover each of the tools available to address customer feedback, dividing customer returns into advanced returns and lean returns. We'll also cover commonly used status profiles for service offerings to customers. In this context, the service offering is a one of many tools available to address customer complaints if the product is not covered under warranty.

13.1 Customer Returns: Advanced Returns Management

SAP S/4HANA offers flexibility and control over processing customer returns with a feature called advanced returns management. As shown in Figure 13.2, the process starts by entering a return order, commonly referred to as return material or return merchandise authorization (RMA) in Transaction VA01. The same transaction is used to enter sales orders with the order type CBAR (accelerated returns).

Typically, returns are created with reference to the original invoice issued to the customer, as shown in Figure 13.2, which is the recommended way to process returns to ensure accurate prices, discounts, and taxes on the refund. You may also use the original sales order as a reference or create a return with no reference at all, as you'll see in the following sections. We'll cover the processes for both options, walking you through how to define return reasons for customer returns and how to define refund codes, two required elements when creating returns.

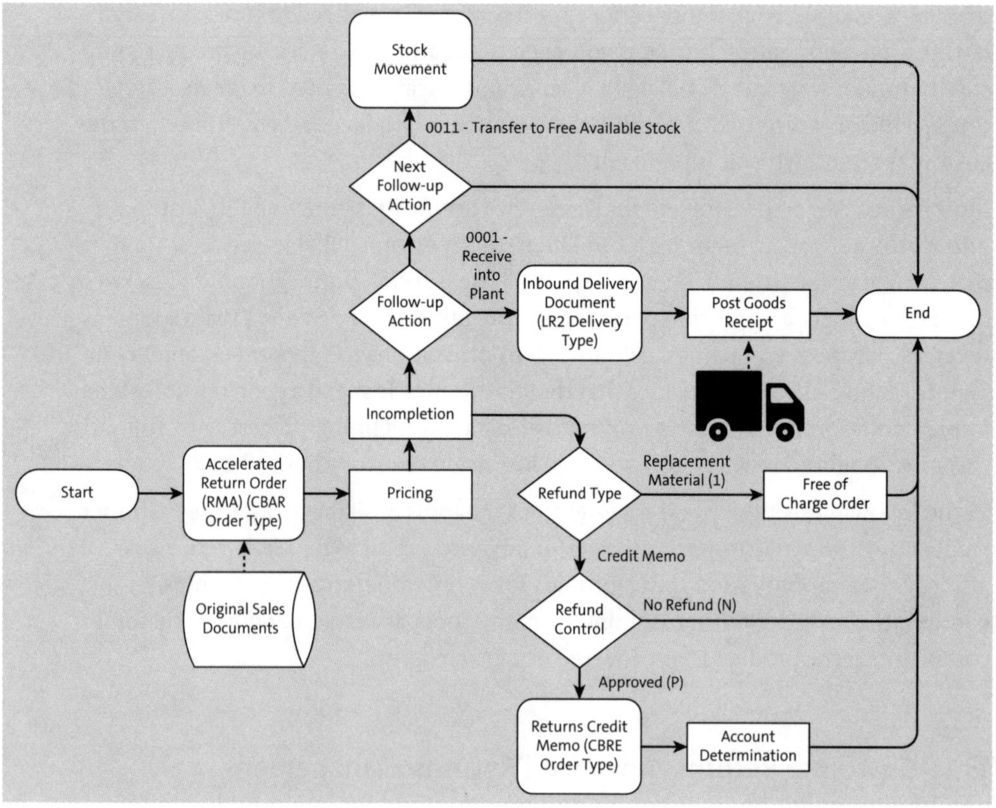

Figure 13.2 Accelerated Return Order Processing

13.1.1 Creating with Reference

After the CBAR order is entered, the subsequent steps will depend on the follow-up action you select for each line. In Transaction VA01, click the **Create with Reference** button, shown in Figure 13.3. Then, search for and select a reference document (in this case, an invoice, i.e., **Billing Document**).

Then, in Figure 13.4, you can either click the **Copy** button to copy all items and quantities from the selected invoice into the return document or click on **Item Selection** to select an item.

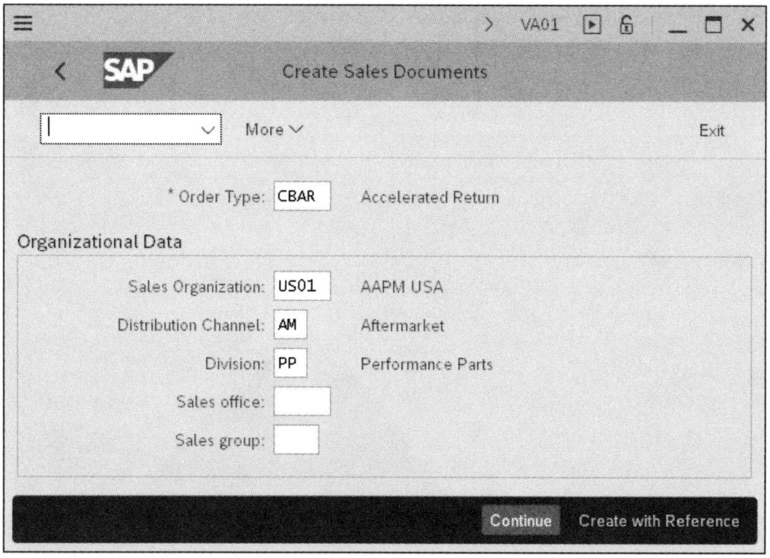

Figure 13.3 Creating an RMA with Reference to an Invoice

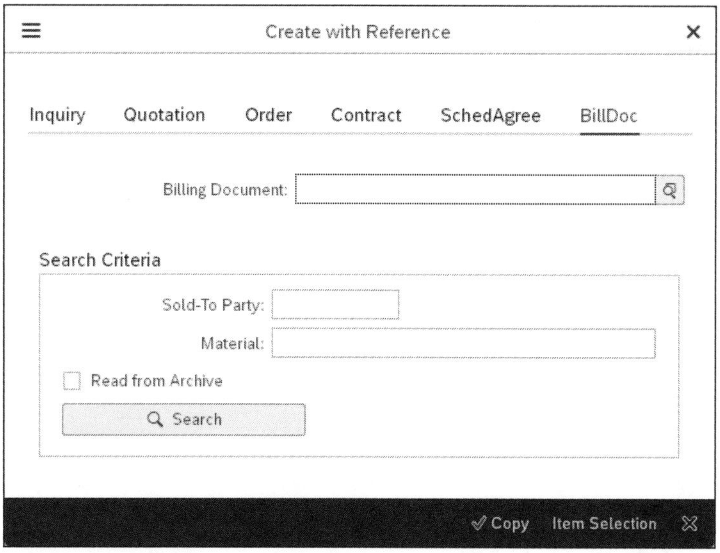

Figure 13.4 Copy or Item Selection

Clicking on **Item Selection** allows you to choose the items the customer will return, change their quantities if need be, and **Copy** only those items to the return order, as shown in Figure 13.5.

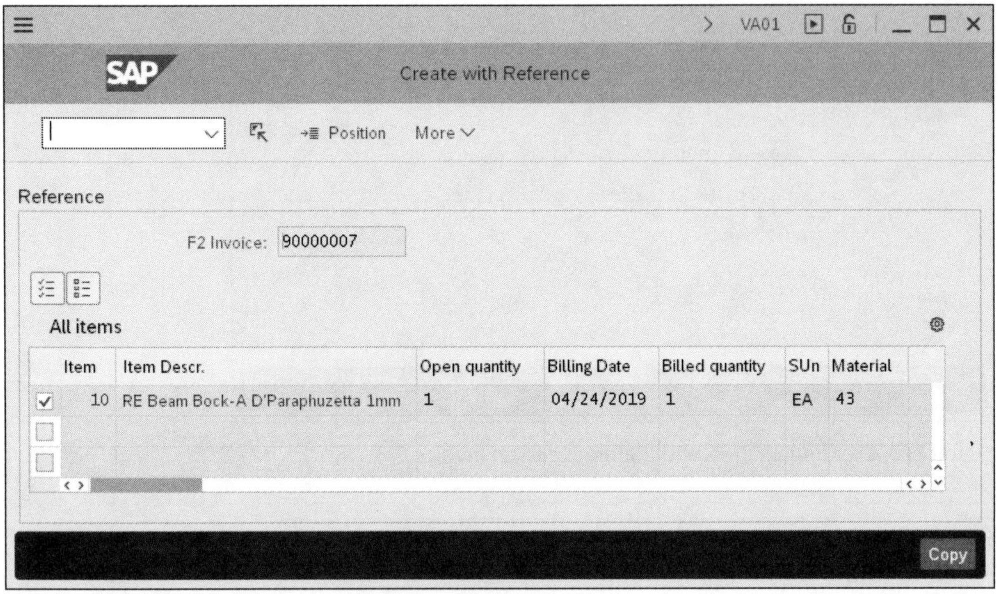

Figure 13.5 Creating with Reference: Item Selection

13.1.2 Creating without Reference

To create a return order without a reference, you would click the **Continue** button instead of the **Create with Reference** button, as shown in Figure 13.3. A blank **Create Accelerated Return: Overview** screen will open, as shown in Figure 13.6. Otherwise, the items you select would prepopulate this screen with information from the original invoice and with default return settings.

> **Note**
> Refer to Chapter 6 for documentation on the fields not discussed in this chapter, which is focused on fields unique to returns.

The **Returns** tab is unique to this order type and shows details about the return order lines. You can navigate from line to line using the control buttons above the **Returns Control** label.

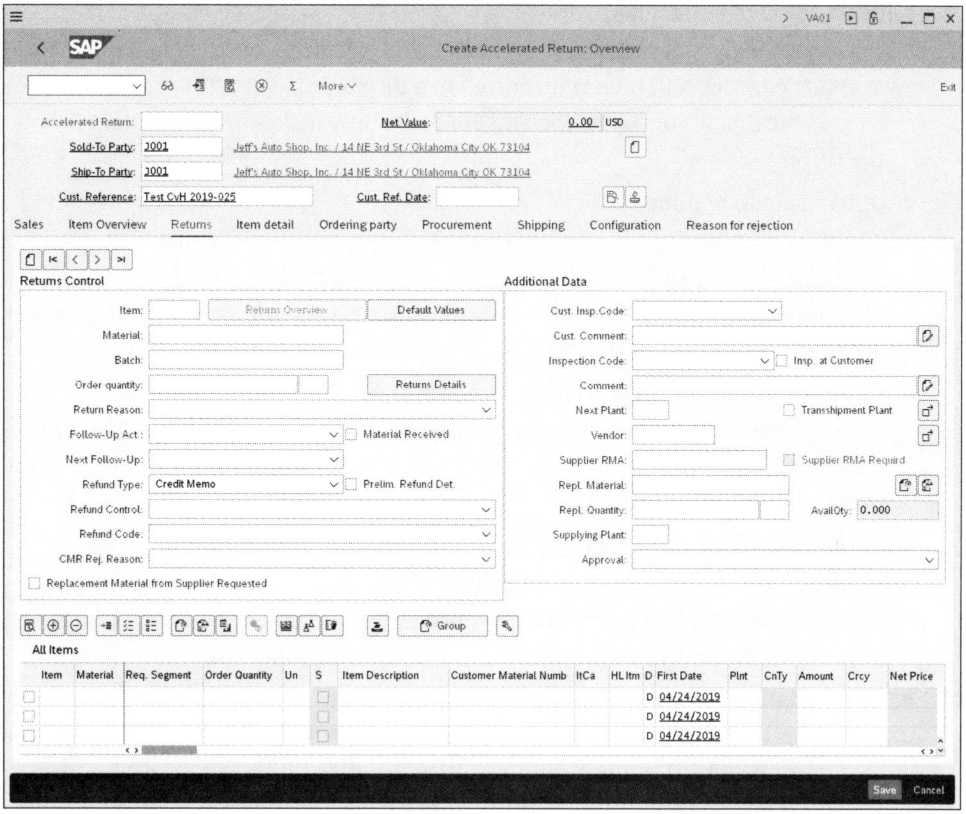

Figure 13.6 Accelerated Return Order Entry

The **Item**, **Material**, **Batch**, and **Order quantity** fields correspond to the selected line and represent the material and quantity that we're authorizing the customer to return.

Start by indicating the **Return Reason**, which is used by reporting and control. We'll describe how you can create new return reasons in Section 13.1.3.

Next, document what the customer will do with the product in the **Follow-Up Act.** field, which has the following options:

- **0001 - Receive into Plant**
  The customer returns the product to one of our facilities indicated in the **Plant** field on the return line, where stock will typically be received as blocked stock. This option is the most common selection since most companies usually expect the customer to return the product.

- **0004 - Ship to Other Plant**
  The customer returns the product to one of our facilities, where it will be received as returned stock and then transported to a different facility. This option is rarely used as the first follow-up action and generally only makes sense as a **Next Follow-Up** action.
- **0005 - Ship to Vendor**
  The customer returns the product to one of our facilities, where it will be received as returned stock and then shipped back to the supplier that sold us the product. This option is rarely used as the first follow-up action and generally only makes sense as a **Next Follow-Up** action.
- **0007 - Direct Shipment to Vendor**
  The customer returns product to the supplier that sold us the product. This option is quite efficient and saves on freight for reverse logistics. We recommend using this option whenever possible.
- **0008 - Inspection at Customer Site**
  Select this option when you're going to send an inspector to the customer location to assess the issue before returns take place. This option is used only for large and expensive products or large quantities with alleged quality issues.
- **0009 - Delivery into Plant - Materials Still Unknown**
  Select this option when the customer is going to return product but you're unable to determine which material and quantity exactly will be returned. This option will allow you to change the quantity at the time of goods receipt. Credit will be held until after goods are received and the material/quantity is confirmed.
- **0013 - Material Remains at Customer Site**
  Select this option when you don't need the customer to return the product to you. The customer may dispose of the product at their location. This option makes sense when the cost of the product equal to or less than the cost of freight.
- **0021 - Send Back to Customer**
  With this option, you'll ship a replacement to the customer before you receive product back or before any other follow-up actions are performed. This option is commonly used in replacement scenarios.

Once you save the RMA, this follow-up code can be used to define what should happen next. The system will create the necessary document with reference to this RMA, making the RMA relevant for due list reports.

The **Material Received** flag is used to document whether a material has been received at the warehouse before the RMA is processed. You can then specify the **Next Follow-Up** action to be taken once the action indicated in the previous field has completed. Possible next follow-up actions include the following options:

- **0004 - Ship to Other Plant**
  The customer has returned the product to one of your facilities where it is received as returned stock. This code indicates you must now transport this product to a different facility.
- **0005 - Ship to Vendor**
  The customer has returned the product to one of your facilities where it is received as returned stock. This code indicates you must now ship this product back to the supplier that sold you the product.
- **0011 - Transfer to Free Available Stock**
  The customer has returned the product to one of your facilities where it is received as returned stock. This code indicates that the product should now be placed as on-hand/unrestricted-use inventory and made available for fulfilling other customers' orders. This option must only be specified after inspection confirms that this product is ready to be sold again.
- **0012 - Transfer to Scrap**
  The customer has returned the product to one of your facilities where it is received as returned stock. This code indicates you must now destroy/dispose of the product.
- **0021 - Send Back to Customer**
  The customer has returned the product to one of your facilities where it is received as returned stock. This code indicates you must now return the product back to the customer. You would use this option if the customer wanted you to perform an inspection and confirm product is in proper working order. If the inspection fails, you can issue the customer a new item instead or even an entirely different item. You can use this option for a number of scenarios, such as the replacement of defective parts, when the customer ordered the wrong product, for offering free upgrades, etc.
- **0023 - Goods Receipt Quantity Correction**
  The customer has returned product to one of your facilities where it is received as returned stock. This code indicates that you must now adjust the quantity. This option is rarely used as a second/next follow-up action and generally only makes sense as the first follow-up action.

- **0031 - No Further Activities**
  No further actions are required. Use this option instead of leaving the field blank to indicate that no further action is needed. This option is recommended if the first action was **0007 - Direct Shipment to Vendor** or **0013 - Material Remains at Customer Site**.

Next, you'll specify how you'll refund a customer payment. The **Refund Type** field, when blank, indicates whether you'll issue a credit memo the customer; when **1**, you'll send a replacement material.

Select the **Prelim. Refund Det.** flag to indicate whether issuing a credit before any follow-up action is appropriate.

The **Refund Control** field defines a method to use when issuing the refund. This field has the following options:

- **No Refund (N)**
  When a refund is typically applicable but not for this particular return. You should document the reason why no refund was issued in the **CMR Rej. Reason** field.
- **Approved (P)**
  When a refund the approved by the person entering the return order and should be issued right away.
- **By Credit Memo Request (R)**
  When a refund should be issued via a credit memo request that must be processed further by an approver, perhaps in the credit department.

The **Refund Code** field defines how much the customer is eligible to receive as a refund. You have options ranging from 10% to 100%. You can modify these values, which we described earlier in Section 13.1.4. In the US, refunding 100% of the sales price upon return is common.

Maintain the **CMR Rej. Reason** field to justify why we're not given this customer a refund for this particular return order. This field is called the *rejection reason* and is further documented in Chapter 6, Section 6.2.8, including configuration details to maintain the list of valid entries. This field can be used to actively close an RMA line preventing any further action. The specific code selected is also used for reporting and to document the situation in can we receive further calls from the customer inquiring about their refund.

The **Replacement Material from Supplier Requested** flag can be used to indicate that the customer prefers the vendor deliver a replacement material instead of receiving credit.

The **Cust. Insp.Code** and **Cust. Comment** fields document the customer's assessment of the current condition the product. You can specify a standardized code and add a comment with the specific situation. These fields may be important for tracking fraud.

The **Inspection Code** and **Comment** fields store your assessment of the product's condition. You can use the **Insp. at Customer** flag to indicate that you performed this assessment at the customer location before product was returned. If blank, the inspection was performed at one of our facilities. This field is useful if your field reps visited with the customer and provided their expert feedback on potential returns. By indicating the inspection code and adding comments to the RMA, returns processing may be expedited.

You can use the **Next Plant** field to indicate that a returned product must be transferred to this plant after being received at the warehouse. This option is used in conjunction with the **Next Follow-Up** field, code **0004**. The **Transshipment Plant** indicates that this plant is not the final destination for the product. This plant is indicated for informational purposes and must not be used in subsequent functions.

The **Vendor** field indicates where the customer is expected to ship this product back to and/or where they are expected to receive a replacement back from. This field is used in conjunction with the **Next Follow-Up** field, code **0005** and the **Replacement Material from Supplier Requested** flag. When the vendor receives the product back, you can document the vendor's RMA number in the **Supplier RMA** field. You can also use the **Supplier RMA Required** field to specify that this vendor requires an RMA before the customer can return product to them.

If you're sending a replacement back to the customer, you can specify the replacement material number (**Repl. Material**), the replacement quantity (**Repl. Quantity**) to be shipped, and the supplying plant (**Supplying Plant**) that will ship it. By default, these fields will match the data on the RMA line. In other words, you would ship the same material with the same quantity from the same facility that the goods are returned to. The system shows the available quantity (**AvailQty**) once these fields are populated, which allows you to provide an estimate of when a customer should get the replacement and can be used as guide to ship a different replacements if replacements are on backorder or for a free upgrade.

You can indicate that this return is pending approval. If the **Approval** field is blank, no further approval is required. If you assign **Blocked for Release** (**B**) to this field, the document is complete and consistent to the best your knowledge but must not be processed until you get approval. If you assign **Item to be Revised** (**R**) to this field, you'll still need approval, but information is missing. Therefore, even if this return is approved, you will not process it until the missing fields are maintained.

13.1.3 Defining Return Reasons for Customer Returns

To configure return reasons, open Transaction MSR_RETURNS_REASON or follow the menu path **SAP Customizing Implementation Guide • Logistics – General • Advanced Returns Management • Customer Returns • Define Return Reasons for Customer Returns.** On the screen that opens, click on the **New Entries** button or press F5.

On the screen shown in Figure 13.7, specify a three-character return reason code (**Ret.Reason**) and add a description (**Return Reason Description**).

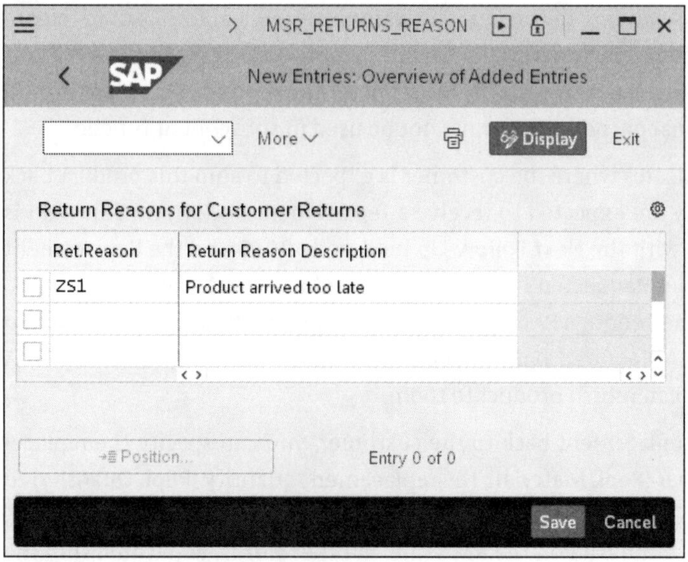

Figure 13.7 Creating New Return Reasons

13.1.4 Defining Returns Refund Codes

To configure return refund codes, open Transaction MSR_RETURNS_REFUND or follow the menu path **SAP Customizing Implementation Guide • Logistics – General •**

Advanced Returns Management • Customer Returns • Define Returns Refund Codes. On the screen that opens, click on the **New Entries** button or press F5.

On the screen shown in Figure 13.8, specify a three-character return refund reason code (**Ref. Code**) and add a description (**Refund Code Description**).

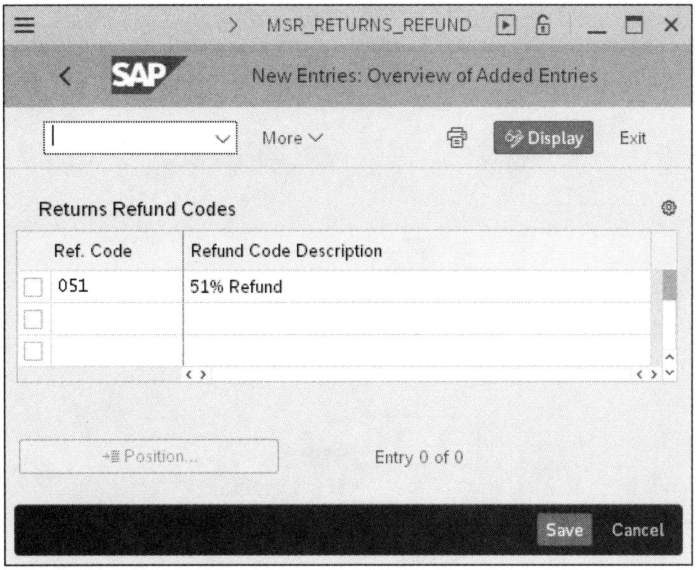

Figure 13.8 Defining New Returns Refund Codes

13.2 Customer Returns: Lean Returns

SAP S/4HANA allows you to use a simplified return process, compatible with and similar to the return order type used in previous versions of SAP ERP. The process starts with the creation of a lean return sales order (order type CBRE) using Transaction VA01, as shown in Figure 13.9.

This return order will be used to create an inbound delivery (delivery type LR), which can be performed through a background job or manually (more details in Chapter 9). An inbound delivery records a goods receipt once it arrives at the warehouse. At that time, you'll need to perform putaway and then issue a post goods receipt.

This process will make the inbound delivery relevant for billing; however, an order of order type CBRE is assigned with a billing block by default as an approval mechanism. The approval needs to monitor all return document that have a billing block and then remove the block upon approval. Only after the CBRE order is released will you be able to create the return credit memo; the creation of the return credit memo billing document is typically done via a background job, but may also be done manually (more details in Chapter 10).

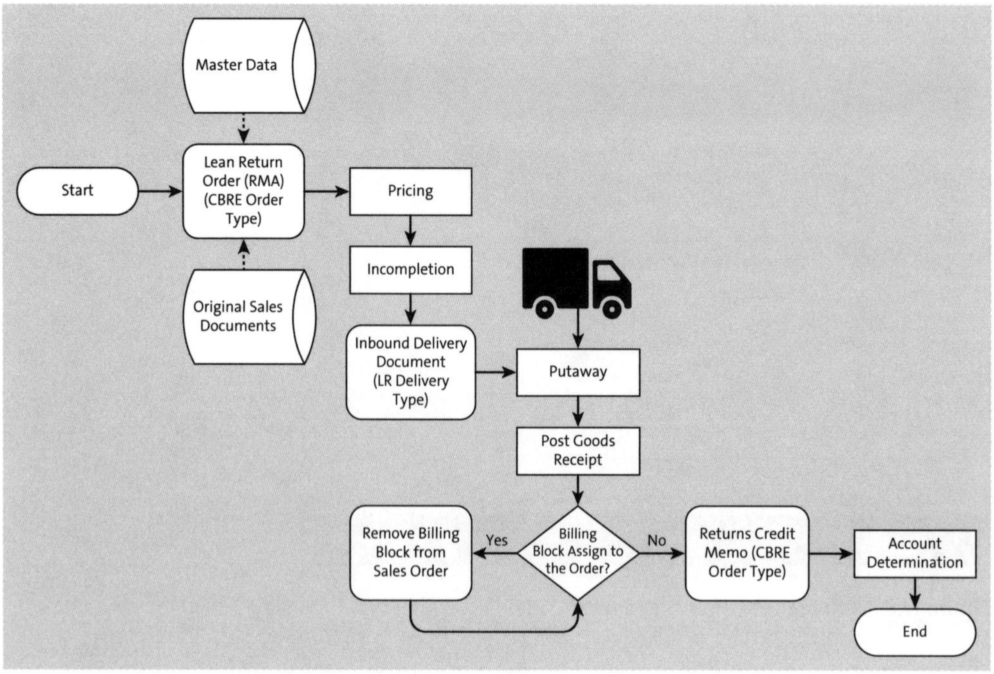

Figure 13.9 Lean Returns Order Processing

CBRE orders are entered using Transaction VA01; Figure 13.10 shows some of the differences between a standard order (OR) and an advanced return (CBRE). The return order fields are similar to sales fields, but all refer to the inbound movement of goods from the customer.

The **Order Reason** field is mandatory, and you'll need to specify why the customer is returning the product using predefined classification categories. You can add details about the return reason in one of the order texts (see Chapter 6, Section 6.3.1, for details). The code entered in the **Order Reason** field is used for reporting.

Note also the **Billing Block** (**Y8 Check Credit Memo**) is assigned by default based on sales order type configuration.

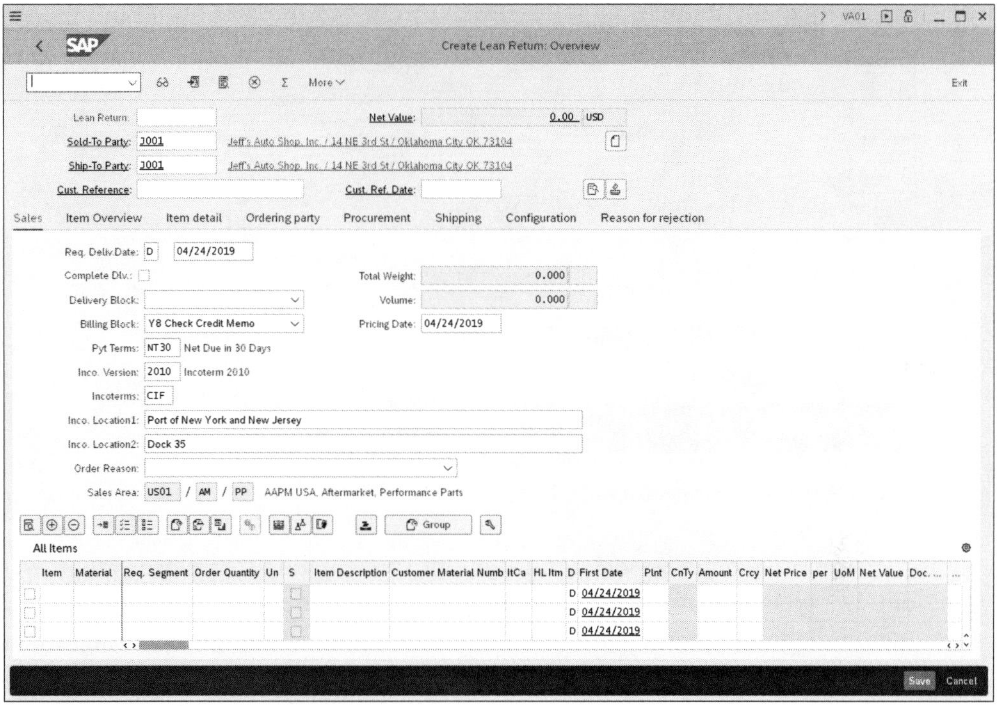

Figure 13.10 Lean Return Order Entry

In the following sections, we'll show you how to define order reasons and assign sales document types and sales organizations to those reasons, two configuration activities you'll need for lean returns.

13.2.1 Defining Order Reasons

To configure order reasons, follow the menu path **SAP Customizing Implementation Guide • Sales and Distribution • Sales • Sales Documents • Sales Document Header • Define Order Reasons.** On the screen that opens, click on the **New Entries** button or press F5.

In Figure 13.11, specify a three-character order reason code (**Order Reason**) and add a description (**Description**).

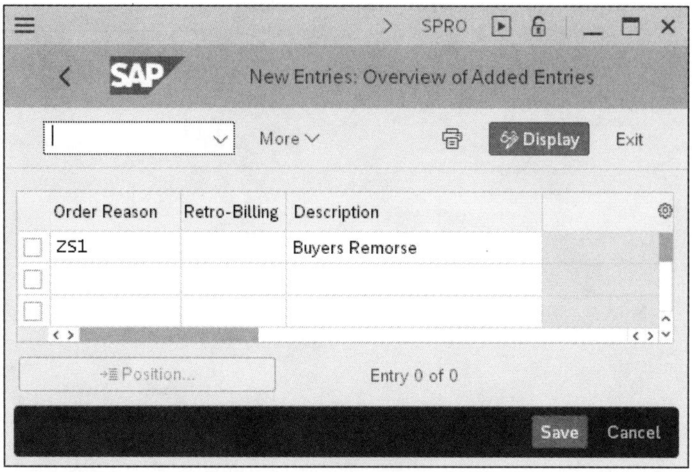

Figure 13.11 Defining New Order Reasons

The list of valid order reasons defined in this configuration step is used for several different types of documents, such as lean returns, free of charge orders, credit/debit memos, and even regular sales orders. All these reasons may get confusing when browsing for the value needed at the time of order entry.

Companies can define a naming convention that segregates the values intended for each type of transaction. Alternatively, you can restrict order reasons to document types and sales organizations, which we'll describe in the next section.

13.2.2 Assigning Sales Document Types and Sales Organizations to Order Reasons

To assign order reasons to order types and sales organizations, follow the menu path **SAP Customizing Implementation Guide • Sales and Distribution • Sales • Sales Documents • Sales Document Header • Assign Sales Document Types and Sales Organizations to Order Reasons.** On the screen that opens, click on the **New Entries** button or press F5.

In Figure 13.12, define and enter the sales order/document type (**SaTy**), sales organization (**SOrg.**), and order reason (**OrdRs**), considering, from all possible assignments, which you want to allow.

When entering the order type for the sales organization specified on this configuration screen, only the order reasons indicated on this screen may be selected. Further, if you perform a match code search (by clicking the [match code] button to the right of the field or pressing the F4 key), only the authorized reasons would appear, not the complete list.

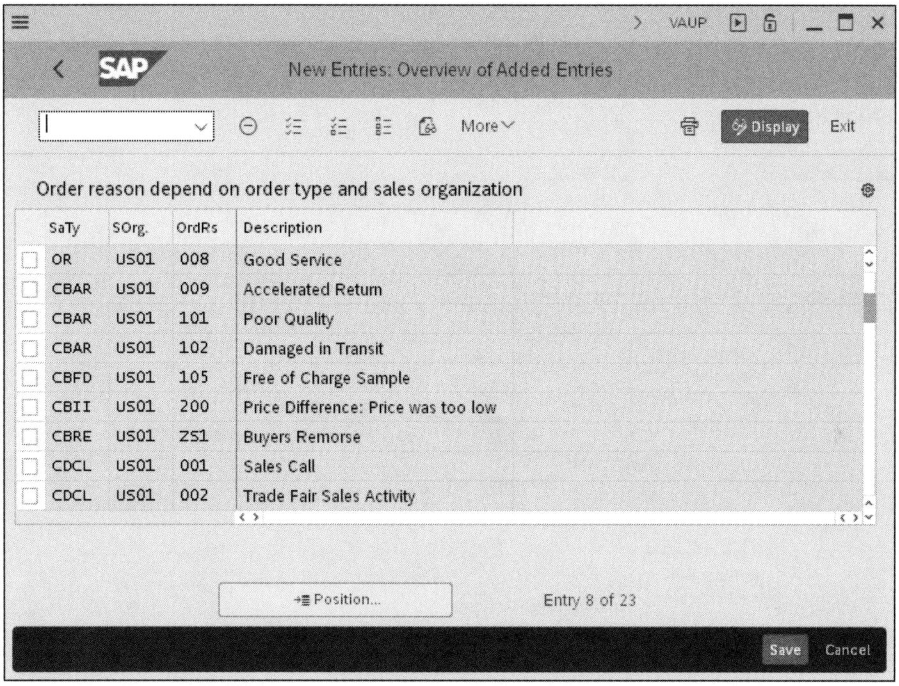

Figure 13.12 Assigning Order Types and Sales Organizations to Order Reasons

13.3 Credit/Debit Requests

Credit and debit memos are types of invoices issued to adjust a customer accounts receivable account. SAP S/4HANA allows sales departments to enter requests for invoices of these types.

Sales can request these types of adjustments for a variety of reasons, usually revolving around pricing policy. For instance, if you sell a product eligible for a discount that you failed to apply in the final invoice, you'll need to request a credit memo to be issued to your customer to reduce the amount of money accounts receivable will collect from them.

In another examples, let's say we charge freight to the customer, but forgot to include freight costs on the sales invoice. You can request a debit memo to increase the customer account balance that accounts receivable will collect from the customer.

You could use credit/debit memo requests to adjust accounts other than accounts receivable balance; however, more efficient tools can found in SAP S/4HANA Finance for these accounts. Figure 13.13 shows the process of issuing credit and/or debit memos to customers.

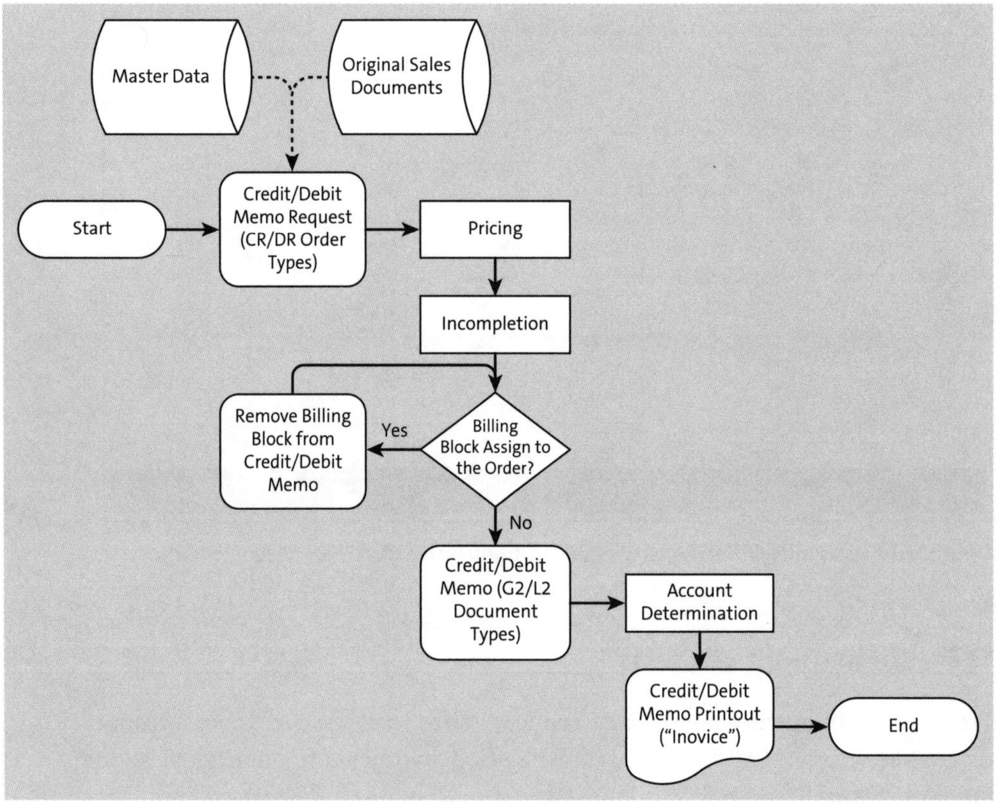

Figure 13.13 Credit/Debit Memo Request Processing

Credit/debit memo requests are created in Transaction VA01, like sales orders and other types of documents. You'll use document type CR for credit memo request and document type DR for debit memo requests, as shown in Figure 13.14.

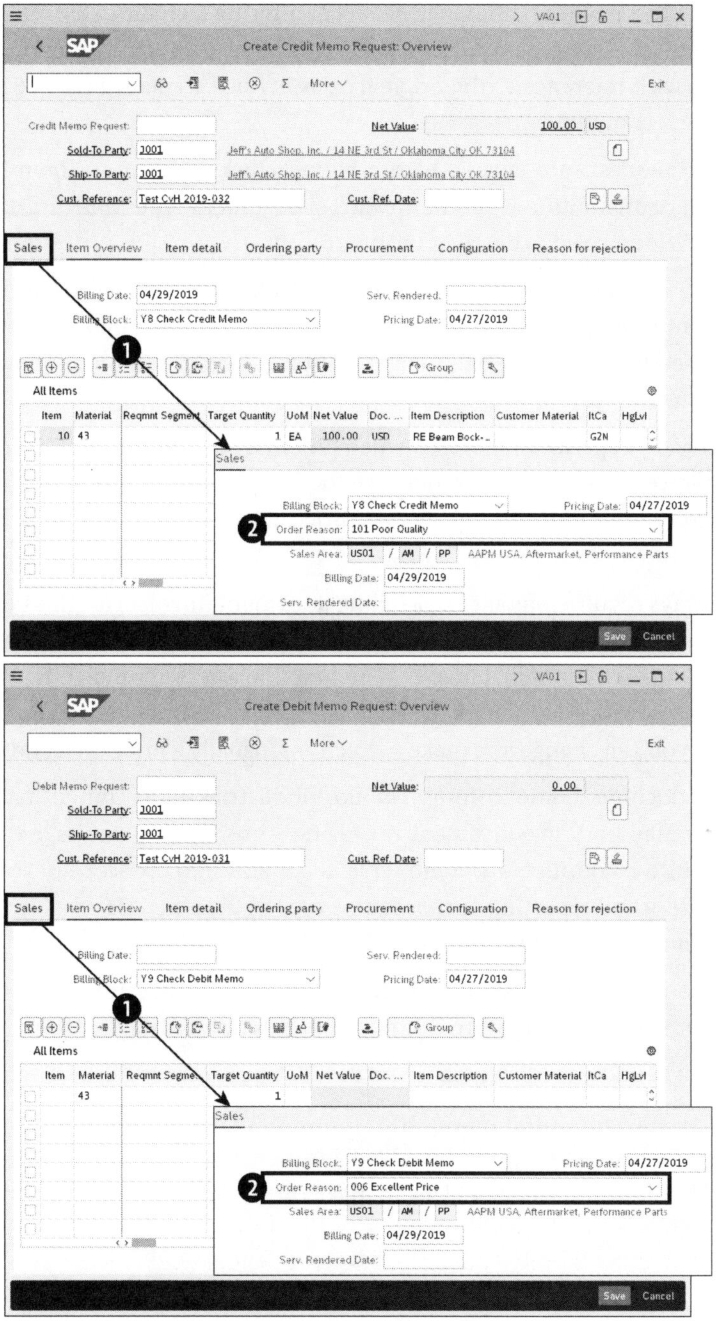

Figure 13.14 Creating Credit/Debit Memo Requests in Transaction VA01

13

In this section, we'll focus on the difference between entering a credit/debit memo request versus entering other types of documents. Credit/debit memo requests are commonly created with reference to the original sales invoice, as described on Section 13.1.2, which we recommend.

Credit/debit memo requests are created with a billing block assigned to them by default. This default configuration is part of the CR/DR document type configuration in Transaction VOV8 (described in detail in Chapter 6).

The **Order Reason** field is also mandatory with credit/debit memo requests, but the screen where you enter the order reason is not the same as the screen offered to your end users. You'll need to click on the **Sales** tab and enter the order reason, as shown with ❶ and ❷ in Figure 13.14.

An invoice correction is a special kind of credit/debit memo. You can use Transaction VA01 create an invoice correction with order type RK or order type CBII. Order type RK is typically used to reduce the original invoice price, which order type CBII is for price increases.

The system will always require reference to a billing document (invoice) for this type of document. Once you enter the invoice you're correcting, the system will create two lines for each line on the original invoice. The first line is a credit matching the original invoice, with several fields restricted from being modified. The second line is a new debit, which you can change and make corrections, usually a price correction.

Issuing this type of document is not common in most industries in the United States because customers may find this document confusing. Thus, be sure you take this potential problem into account before adding this document into the scope of your project. For accounting and reporting purposes, this type of document is considered quite useful for documenting corrections on invoices.

Figure 13.15 shows some of the differences between an invoice correction versus a standard sales order when entering a correction via Transaction VA01.

The **Order Reason** field under the **Sales** tab is also mandatory for these types of documents.

The process is the same as other types of credit/debit memos for this type of document: You'll need to remove the billing block to make the memo relevant for billing.

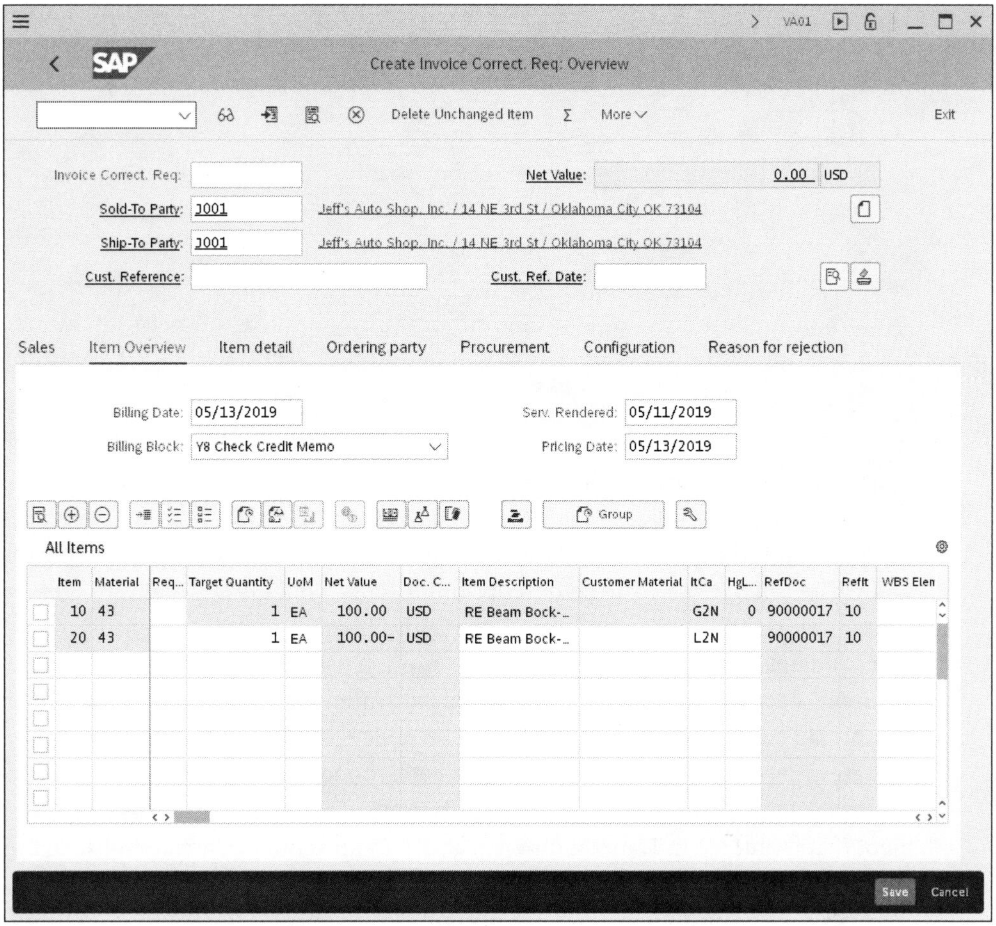

Figure 13.15 Creating an Invoice Correction Request

13.4 Free of Charge Orders

SAP S/4HANA allows you to ship products free of charge to customers and charge these costs internally to a department or special inventory account. Figure 13.16 shows the process of shipping products free of charge to customers.

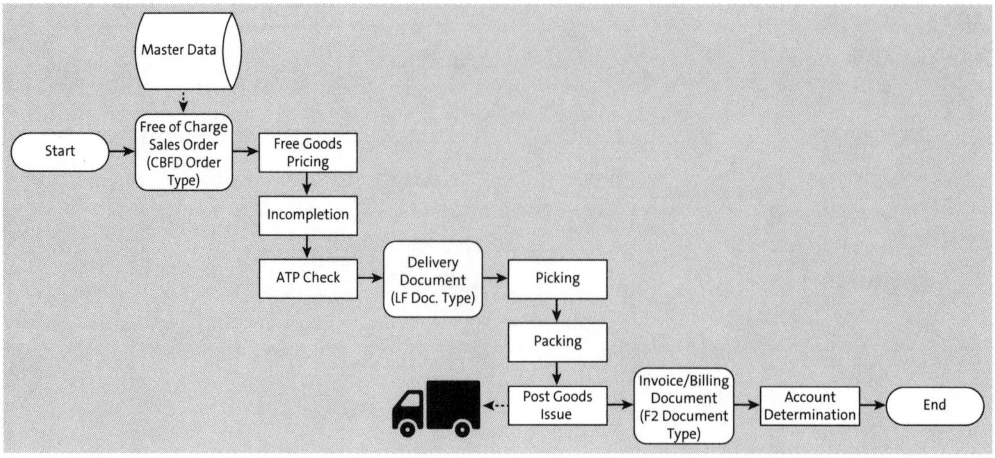

Figure 13.16 Free of Charge Order Processing

The process starts by creating a free of charge sales order in Transaction VA01 with order type CBFD. Note that the description of order type CBFD is **Delivery Free of Charge**, which many companies find confusing because this document is a sales order and not a delivery document. The description uses the term "delivery" instead of "order" because free of charge documents are often not ordered by the customer but instead entered by the company based on policy or business decision. We'll refer to these orders as *free of charge sales orders*, even though no sale has occurred and no one has made an order. This terminology, however, is normal for the type of document that is entered in Transaction VA01 and is shipped out of the warehouse to the customer without charge.

Note that we're not charging for the products we're shipping, but we may charge for freight and other fees, which is enabled on CBFD order type. This type of order is relevant for delivery and billing just like a regular sales order. However, the invoice may end up with a value of $0.

Figure 13.17 shows some of the differences between a free of charge order versus a standard sales order when using Transaction VA01.

The **Order Reason** field is mandatory to justify why you're shipping material free of charge to the customer. The order reason in this type of document also determines the cost center that will pay for the cost of the product being shipped to the customer. To assign order reasons cost centers, open Transaction OVF3 or follow the menu path **SAP Customizing Implementation Guide • Sales and Distribution • Basic Functions •**

Account Assignment/Costing • Assign Cost Centers. On the screen that opens, click on the **New Entries** button or press F5.

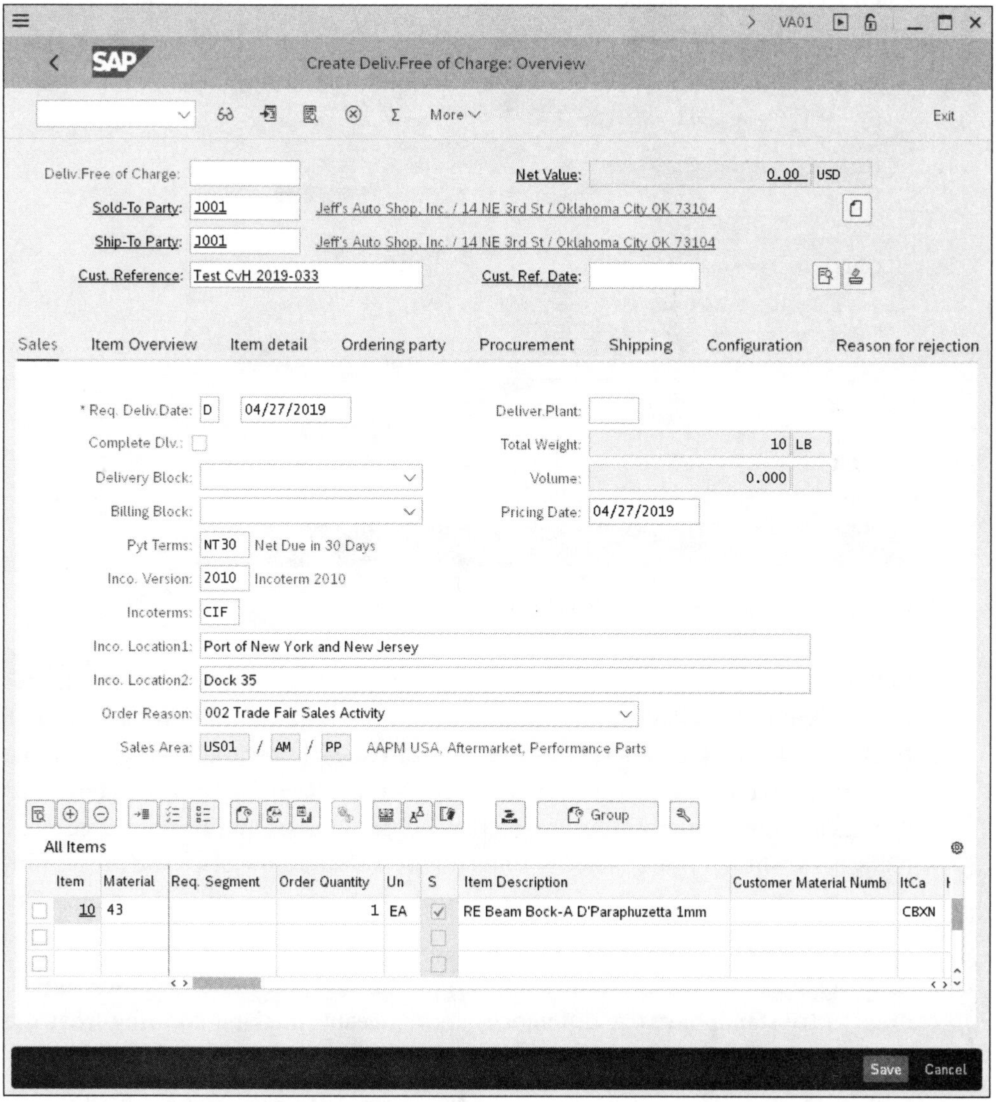

Figure 13.17 Creating a CBFD Free of Charge Sales Order

On this screen, assign the **Cost Ctr** to a combination of sales area (**SOrg.**, **DChl**, and **Dv**) and order reason (**OrdRs**). You will also indicate a **Valid From** date.

For example, in our example shown in Figure 13.18, starting on January 1st, 2019, all free of charge sales order, for sales area US01-AM-PP and assigned with order reason ZS1, will be charged to cost center ZST1001. In other words, cost center ZST1001 will be debited with the corresponding cost amount for the products shipped.

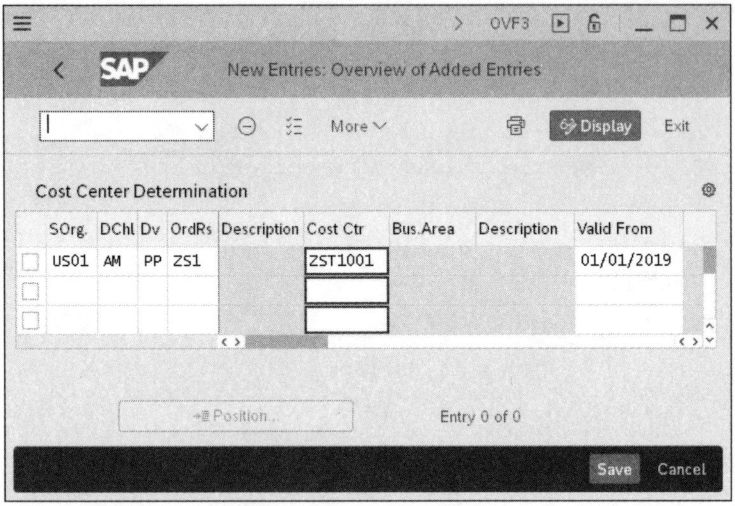

Figure 13.18 Assigning Cost Centers to Order Reasons

In the United States, the controlling departments of many companies don't use cost center accounting in SAP S/4HANA and instead use specific inventory accounts to track free of charge products shipped. They often ask sales to use more than one inventory account depending on the type of transaction. Unfortunately, this approach creates different document types depending on the inventory account being used, which not advisable but unfortunately occurs quite often and causes conflict between the complexity of better control using cost center and the complexity of free of charge order entry.

One problem is that entering the wrong type of order is really easy because, from an order entry standpoint, few differences are noticeable, making knowing what the sales resource did wrong quite difficult, even after receiving feedback.

So, a good compromise is to always use the same inventory account on all free of charge orders and have controlling reclassify the corresponding amount at the end of the month based on order reason-based reporting.

The ideal solution is to use the cost center assigned as described in this section. If you don't want to use cost centers, manual reclassification at month end will be required.

13.5 Customer Inquiries

Customer inquiries document the instances when a customer asks you about purchasing certain materials. The system will provide the same responses as a regular sales order concerning pricing and expected delivery dates. You can then provide this information to the customer and document their decision regarding purchase or not. Figure 13.19 shows the process of entering customer inquiries in the context of a standard sales order.

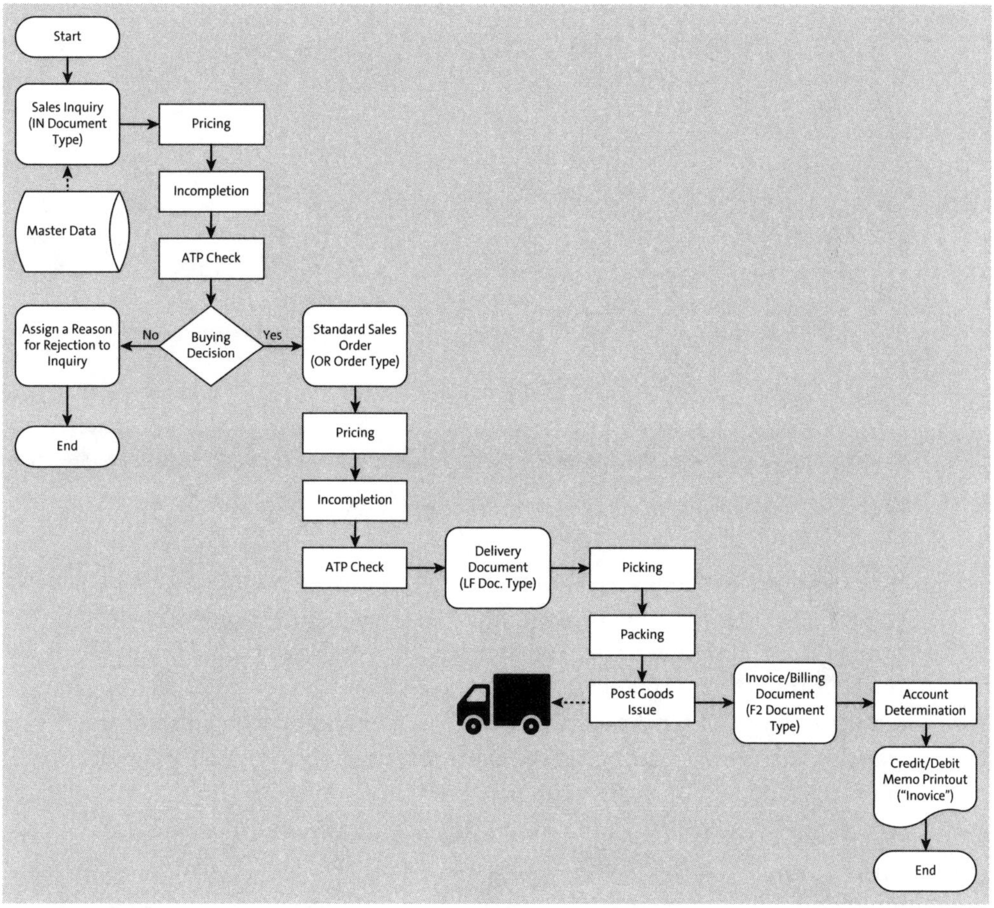

Figure 13.19 Sales Inquiry Processing

The process starts with the user entering an order in Transaction VA11, as shown in Figure 13.20.

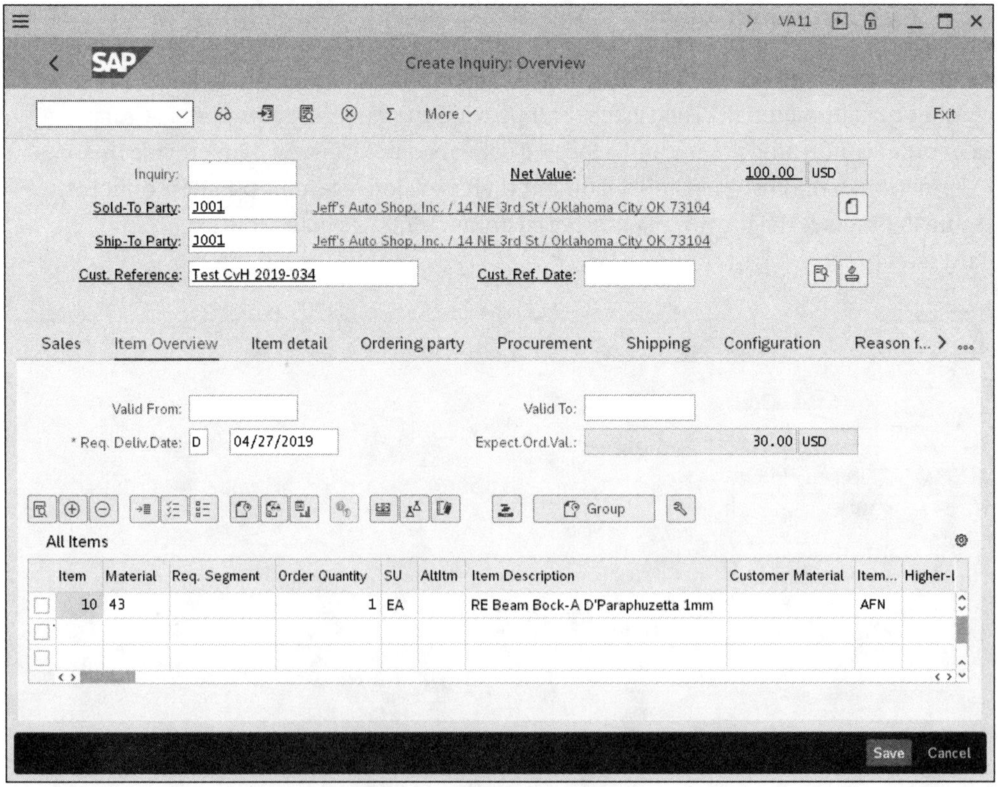

Figure 13.20 Sales Inquiry Order Entry on Transaction VA11

If the customer does not wish to purchase the product they inquired about, you can assign a reason for rejection to the inquiry document while closing and stopping the process. This approach may be useful for reporting and may provide valuable visibility about the products that customers inquire about the most but end up not purchasing, perhaps all for the same reason. This scenario may inspire a promotion, a change in marketing strategy, or even the discontinuation of a product line. However sound the rationale, only a few companies follow this approach in the United States because the perceived effort and complexity of entering these documents.

If the customer decides to buy the product, you could create a sales order with reference to the inquiry and then follow the normal standard sales order processing.

The sales inquiry screen is similar to a sales order screen. One key difference is the validity period fields (**Valid From** and **Valid To**), which registers that the promise made to the customer is valid only during this period. After the validity period, you would not be obligated to fulfill any promise.

You can generate a printout of the sales inquiry and send this document to the customer, which can be an efficient, formal way to communicate responses to their inquiries. An ATP check on sales inquiries is usually not configured to allocate stock to the document since sales inquiries are not considered firm demands. See Chapter 7, Section 7.1.2, for more details.

13.6 Status Profiles

Sales documents can be controlled by their statuses. You can also define that, even if a document is in the system, certain statuses must be assigned for the document to be eligible future for processing. In most sales documents (orders, returns, inquiries, contracts, agreements, etc.), under the **Status** tab, you should see the **Object status** button, as shown in Figure 13.21.

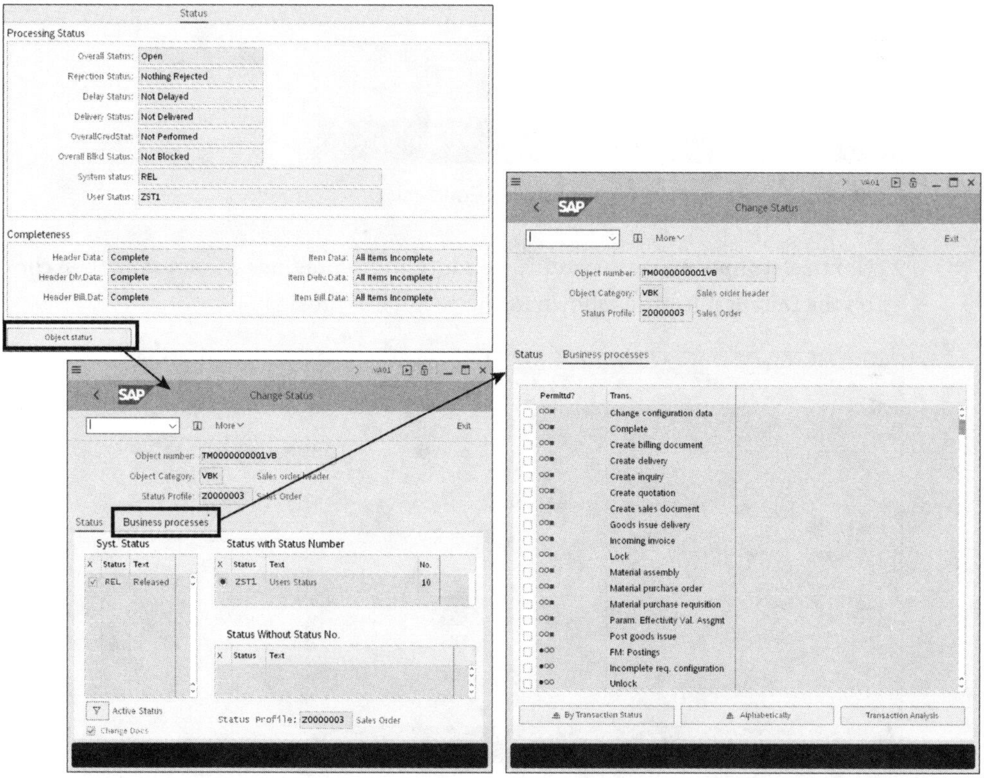

Figure 13.21 Object Status

Once you click on the **Object Status** button, the system will display all applicable statuses as configured on the sales document type (Transaction VOV8 as described in Chapter 6).

You can define your own statuses using the status profile in Transaction BS02 or by following the menu path **SAP Customizing Implementation Guide • Sales and Distribution • Sales • Sales Documents • Define and Assign Status Profile • Define Status Profiles**. On the screen that opens, click on the **New Entries** button or press F5.

To create an object status, follow these steps:

1. On this screen shown in Figure 13.22, specify an eight-character status profile code (**Status Profile**) and add description (**Text**). Specify the **Maintenance Language**.

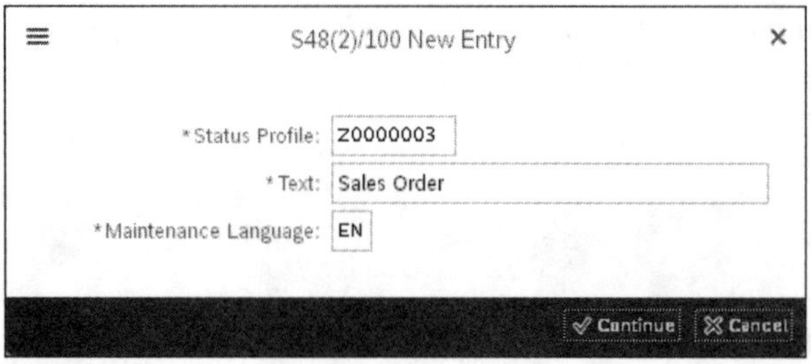

Figure 13.22 Defining New Status Profiled Code and Description

2. Next, select the new status profile we added in the previous window and then click on the **Details** button, as shown in Figure 13.23, or press F2.

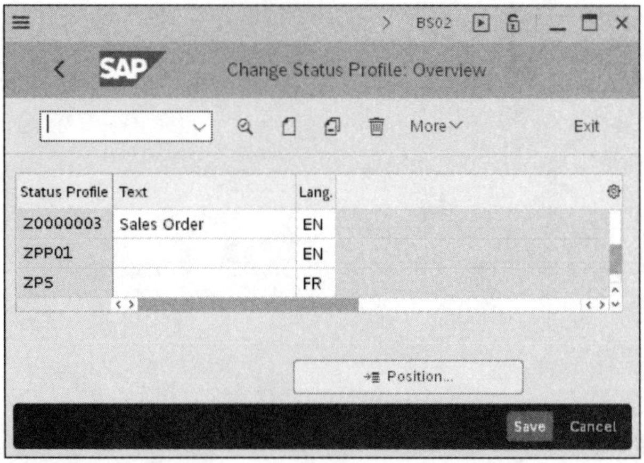

Figure 13.23 Browsing through the Existing Status Profiles

3. As shown Figure 13.24, you can specify as many user statuses as you need:
   - For each user status, enter a status line number (**Status...**), which indicates the order in which statuses show up in the object status window. These values are also used to create interdependencies between statuses. You can leave this field blank for a simple status such as the one shown in our example.
   - Define a four-character status code (**Status**) and add a description (**Short Text**).
   - You can maintain a long text for each status to explain in detail what each status means by selecting the **Long T...** field or pressing [F9].
   - The initial status flag (**Init. Stat...**) indicates that this status must be assigned to the object status windows as soon as the sales order is created. When inactive, users need to manually add this status to the screen.
   - You may also click the **Object Type** button on this screen (under the **More** button) to perform the action we'll describing next.

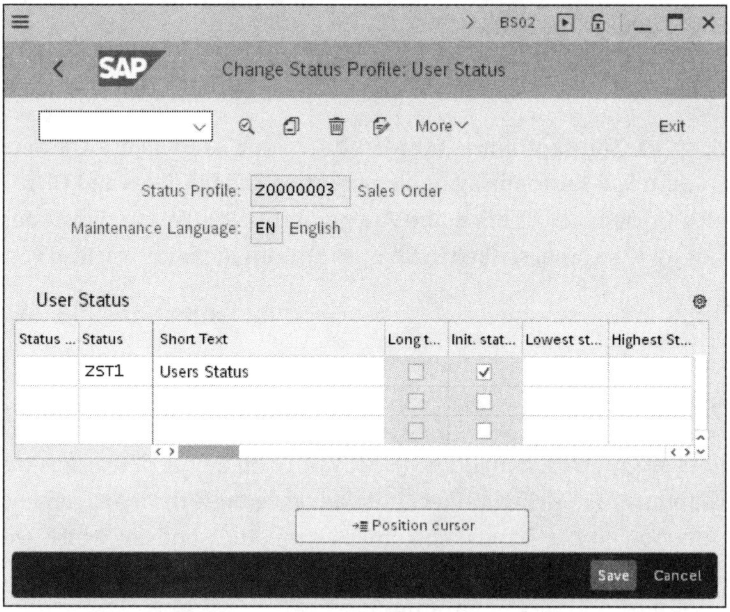

Figure 13.24 Assigning User Statuses to an Existing Status Profile

4. Next, indicate which types of objects this status profile is relevant to by selecting the status profile and using the **Goto • Object Types** menu options.

5. Activate the flag next to the object type where you want this status profile to be used, as shown in Figure 13.25.

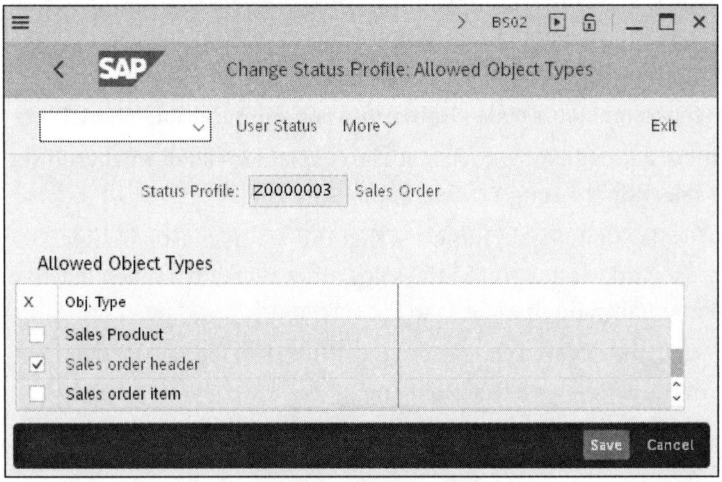

Figure 13.25 Defining Which Object Types Are Allowed to Use This Status Profile

You also need to assign the status profile to the sales order type. You can use Transaction VOV8 or menu path **SAP Customizing Implementation Guide • Sales and Distribution • Sales • Sales Documents • Define and Assign Status Profile • Assign Order Types/Status Profiles** to do so (as described in Chapter 6). Both methods will lead you to the same screen.

13.7 Summary

Customer complaints are addressed in SAP S/4HANA through a host of features we described in this chapter. SAP S/4HANA offers both advanced returns management and lean returns functionality to handle customer complaints, both of which we showed you how to set up. We also discussed how to issue credit and debit memos, create free of charge orders, and set up status profiles.

The next chapter will cover some of the sales-related reports available in SAP S/4HANA.

Chapter 14
Reporting and Analytics

SAP S/4HANA features several reports that enable new ways of working. You can use these reports to start business activity from an immediate overview of ongoing processes and take the necessary actions. This connectivity is enabled by SAP Fiori apps and the enhanced system performance of the SAP HANA database. In this chapter, we'll also cover several SAP GUI-based reports that are frequently used.

SAP S/4HANA features several operational reports and some new analytic reports that take advantage of the new improved performance of SAP HANA.

Note that many companies still use SAP BusinessObjects Business Intelligence (SAP BusinessObjects BI) to create their business-specific reports. SAP BusinessObjects BI allows you to extract information much more flexibly than the reports specified in this chapter and can often produce tailor-made results, thus increasing speed at which management gets the information available.

The standard reports are still valuable, regardless of whether you use SAP BusinessObjects BI or not, but these reports tend to focus on the processing of documents.

Before we jump into the reports themselves, you must understand the concepts behind the ABAP List Viewer (ALV) to understand the flexibility of SAP GUI reports (Section 14.1) and how SAP Fiori report apps should be used (Section 14.2). We'll also provide an inventory list of operational reports with brief descriptions and common uses (Section 14.3 and Section 14.4). Finally, we'll briefly cover analytic capabilities (Section 14.5).

14.1 ABAP List Viewer

When using SAP GUI, the reports we'll cover in this chapter share a common functionality called the ABAP List Viewer (ALV), which is a common report technique.

The ABAP List Viewer allows you to sort, filter, and change the order of columns; add/remove new columns; and define totals/subtotals using standardized command bar buttons (which are present on all the different reports and perform the same actions across reports). Figure 14.1 shows the command bar buttons under the various SAP GUI themes available. In this book, we've mostly been using the new Belize theme and, in some instances, the classic theme (the favorite among longtime users of the system).

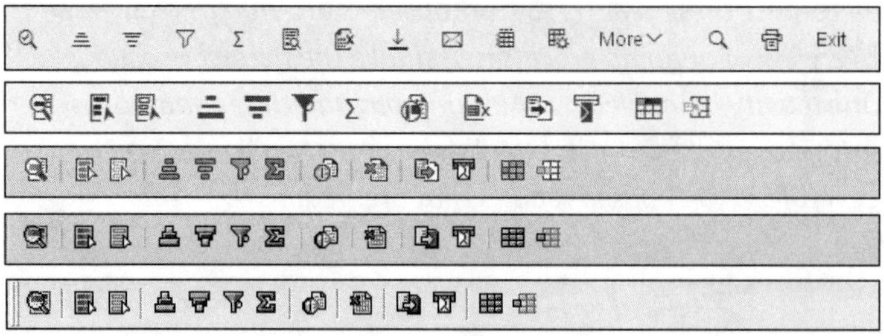

Figure 14.1 ALV Command Bar Buttons over Different SAP GUI Themes

The themes shown in Figure 14.1 are as follows:

- The default settings: SAP GUI with SAP Fiori feature (Belize theme)
- SAP GUI without SAP Fiori features (Blue Crystal theme)
- SAP GUI without SAP Fiori features (Corbu theme)
- SAP GUI without SAP Fiori features (Signature theme)
- SAP GUI without SAP Fiori features (Classic theme)

The most noteworthy button is the layout icon (the grid, second from the right) that allows you to add/remove columns from the report. When reviewing SAP GUI reports, keep in mind that a variety of other information from sales documents may be incorporated by clicking this button.

14.2 SAP Fiori Workflow

SAP Fiori transactional reporting apps were designed to handle most common day-to-day tasks that a user would need to perform, often combining several SAP GUI reports into a single layout with comparable capabilities.

In the SAP GUI, the high-level user workflow usually involves the following steps:

1. Use training and experience to decide how to address the business task at hand.
2. Call a transaction or choose desired menu options to edit.

3. When creating reports, create documents at this time.
4. When changing/displaying reports, find the desired document or master data object number with the help of match code searches, then edit or display them.
5. Save the document.

Using SAP Fiori, the high-level user workflow usually involves the following steps:

1. Choose the object you want to work with (sales orders, business partner, invoices, etc.).
2. Call the corresponding report that manages the desired object.
3. Filter the data to find the data you need. Click the **Create** button to enter a new one.
4. Save the document and go back to the list to work on the next document.

Users that adapt to the SAP Fiori experience perceive it as more modern and in line with phone/tablet design principles. Trying to use SAP Fiori to mimic the way the SAP GUI works is not recommended, and often confuses users. To successfully implement SAP S/4HANA with SAP Fiori, you'll need a change management effort focused on showing the value of the operational reports.

Numerous SAP Fiori apps are provided for reporting and analytics, and we'll cover a few in subsequent sections. These apps share some common characteristic, shown in Figure 14.2, such as the following:

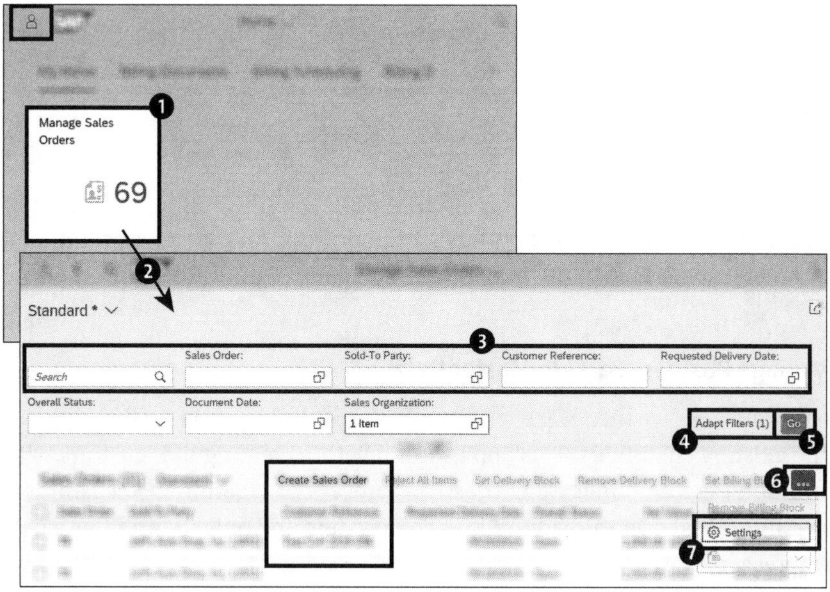

Figure 14.2 SAP Fiori Reporting Apps Common Characteristics

❶ On the SAP Fiori launchpad, the square icon shows the number of documents that will be displayed considering the default selection criteria set in the **User Profile • Settings • Default Values**. The app title usually begins with the word "Manage."

❷ Once you double-click on the desired app, a report will open with the standard selection criteria used to calculate the number of documents indicated on the app icon. Note, however, that the report's content will remain blank (empty) until you click the **Go** button ❺.

❸ The upper part of the screen contains the standard selection criteria (fields used to filter the data on the report). On this screen, you can modify the criteria to reduce the amount of entries to be displayed and focus on the entries you want to see.

❹ If you need different fields to be added to the selection criteria that are not yet shown in this area, you can click on the **Adapt Filters** link. A list of possible selection fields to be added will be displayed. In this example, we added the **Sales Organization** field to the selection criteria area.

❺ Once you narrow the search results as much as possible, click the **Go** button to run the report.

❻ You can switch functions to focus on specific actions enabled on this screen by selecting the corresponding option in this area. Clicking the ellipses icon (...) will display more functions that didn't fit in the command bar.

❼ You can browse the report entries in this area; the values in blue are links to related transactions.

14.3 SAP Fiori Operational Reports

In the following sections we'll look at the most important sales-related operational reports available as SAP Fiori apps.

14.3.1 Manage Business Partner Master Data

The Manage Business Partner Master Data app, shown in Figure 14.3, allows you to browse the existing customers. This app is useful before creating new customers to ensure you don't create duplicate entries. The process of creating new customers includes verifying that don't already exist in your system and only then adding a new entry to represent them.

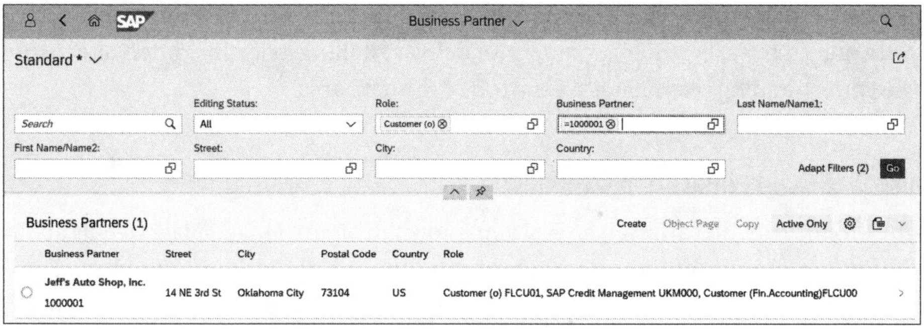

Figure 14.3 Manage Business Partner SAP Fiori App

Business partner data quality relies on your discipline at the time of adding new entry, and this report is a tool improves data quality.

On this screen, you can modify existing business partners (customers, vendors, etc.) and create new entries by clicking on the corresponding options in the header of the data area.

14.3.2 Manage Sales Orders

The Manage Sales Orders app, shown in Figure 14.4, allows you to browse existing orders, not in an analytic capacity, but in an operational one. The customer service team gets calls asking about order status. This report allows you to find an order and display all its details. Then, you can monitor its processing and make changes as appropriate in response to customer contact.

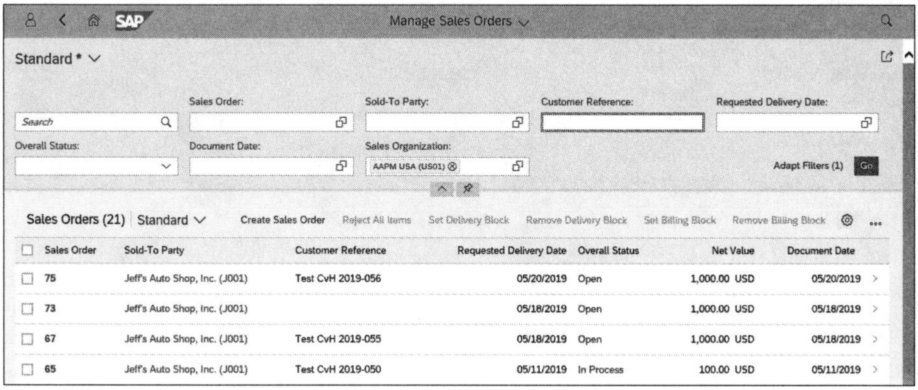

Figure 14.4 Manage Sales Orders SAP Fiori App

You can also use this app as a starting point for daily tasks such as monitoring incomplete orders, releasing/holding orders for delivery/billing, rejecting orders, etc., using the corresponding commands on the top of the data area.

14.3.3 Product Allocation Overview

The Production Allocation Overview app, shown in Figure 14.5, displays details about the limits you have set for customer purchases using ATP checks with product allocation and the progress of customer purchases toward those limits. For more information on this app and on the product allocation process, see Chapter 7, Section 7.5.

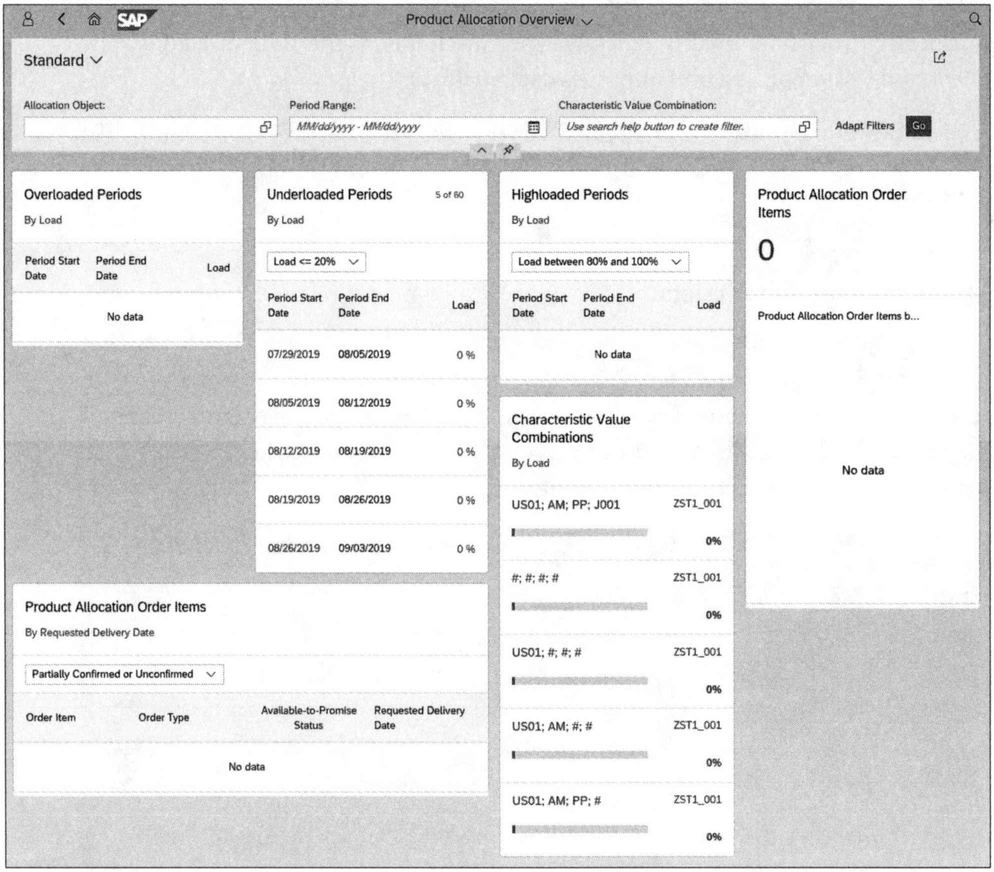

Figure 14.5 Product Allocation Overview

14.3.4 Manage Billing Documents

The Manage Billing Documents app, shown in Figure 14.6, allows you to browse existing billing documents, not in an analytic capacity, but in an operational one. You can find invoices to answer questions from customers. For more information, see Chapter 10.

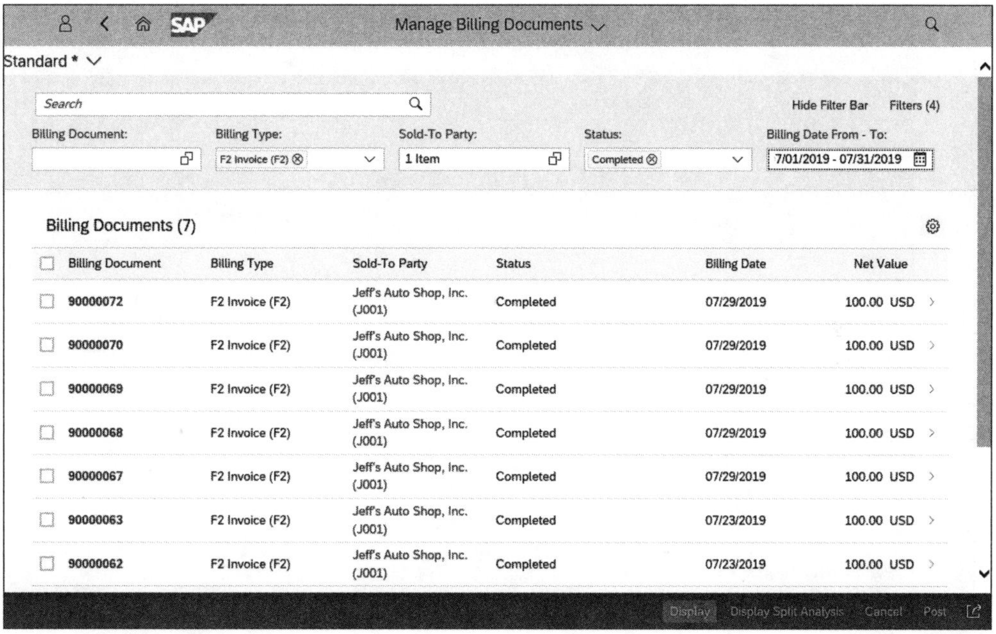

Figure 14.6 Manage Billing Documents

14.3.5 Display Business Volume – Condition Contracts

The Display Business Volume – Condition Contracts app, shown in Figure 14.7, allows you to monitor purchases made by customers that might be relevant for rebates in the specific rebate agreement context. You can use this app to report back to the customers how close they are to achieve their goals, as described in Chapter 5.

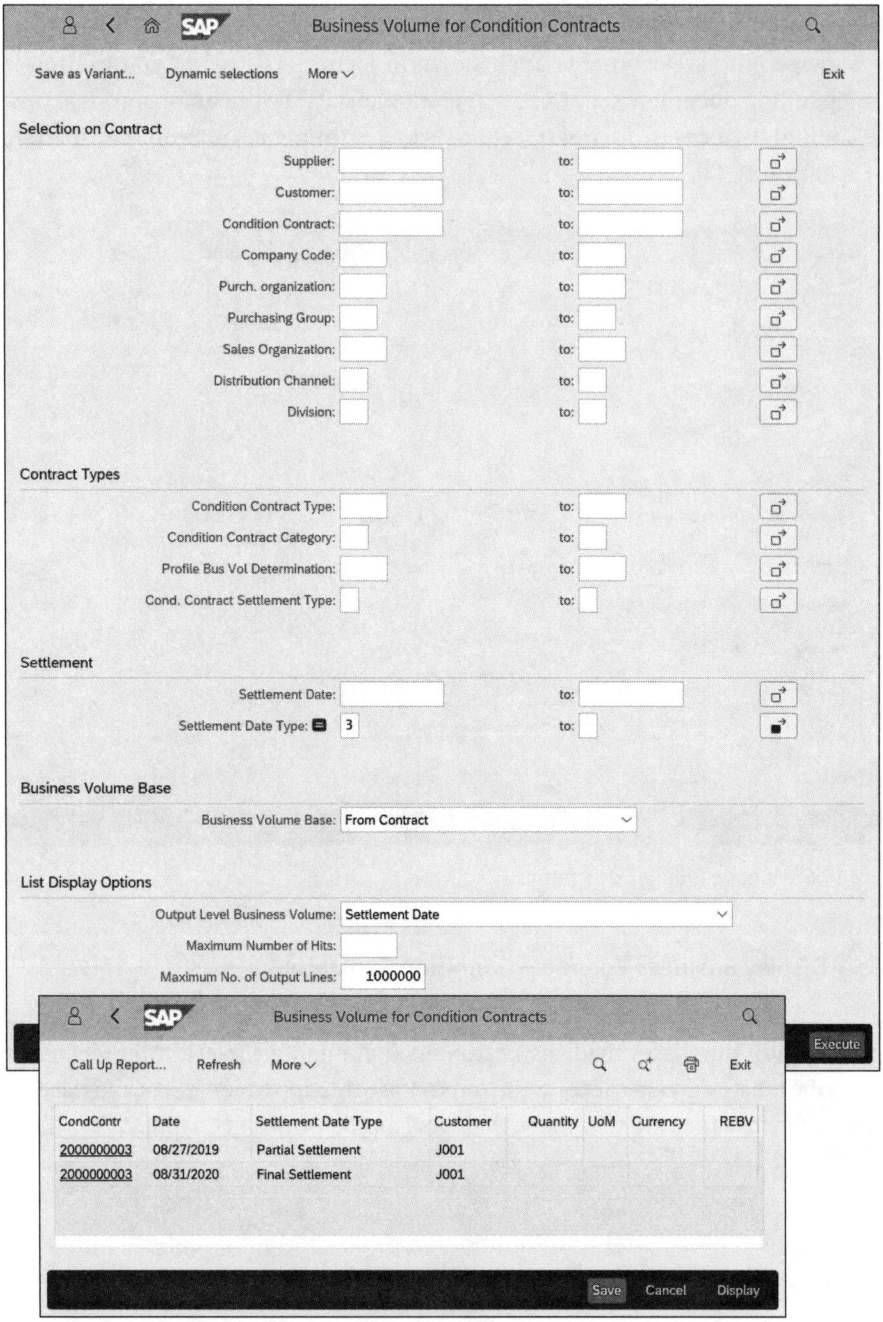

Figure 14.7 Condition Contract Business Volume

14.3.6 Sales Order Items – Backorders

The Sales Order Items – Backorders app shows an overview of sales orders from a stock allocation perspective because of the ATP check. You can use this information to forecast logistics activity and incoming revenue. You can also identify orders that could be delivered but have not been due to inventory shortages (backorders) that may also trigger corrective actions, when possible (see Figure 14.8).

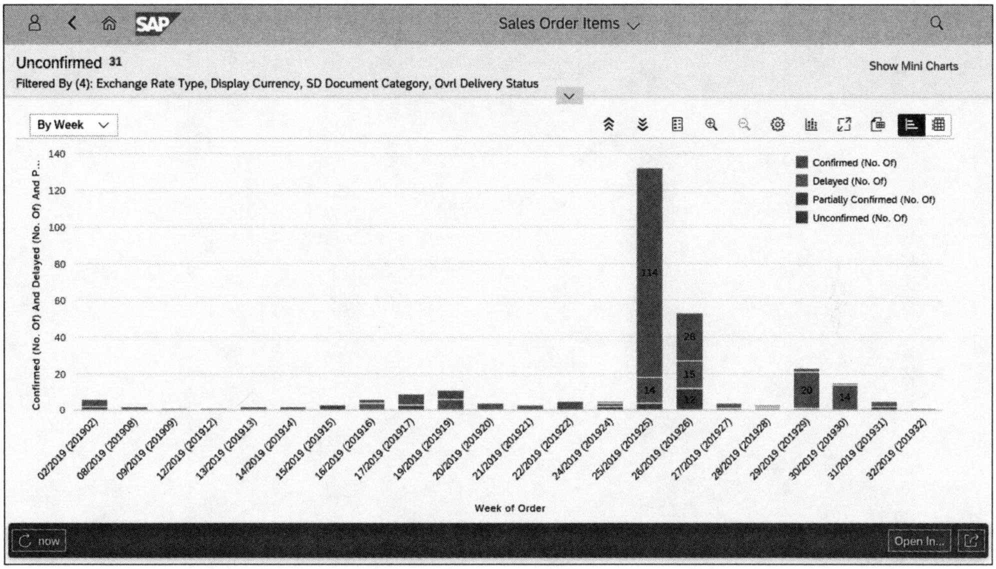

Figure 14.8 Sales Order Items: Backorders

14.4 SAP GUI Operational Reports and Due Lists

In the following sections, we'll look at the most important sales-related operational reports and due lists available in the SAP GUI.

14.4.1 List of Sales Orders

Using SAP GUI, Transaction VA05 is the equivalent of the Manage Sales Order SAP Fiori app. Figure 14.9 shows the selection screen for this report, along with the report itself.

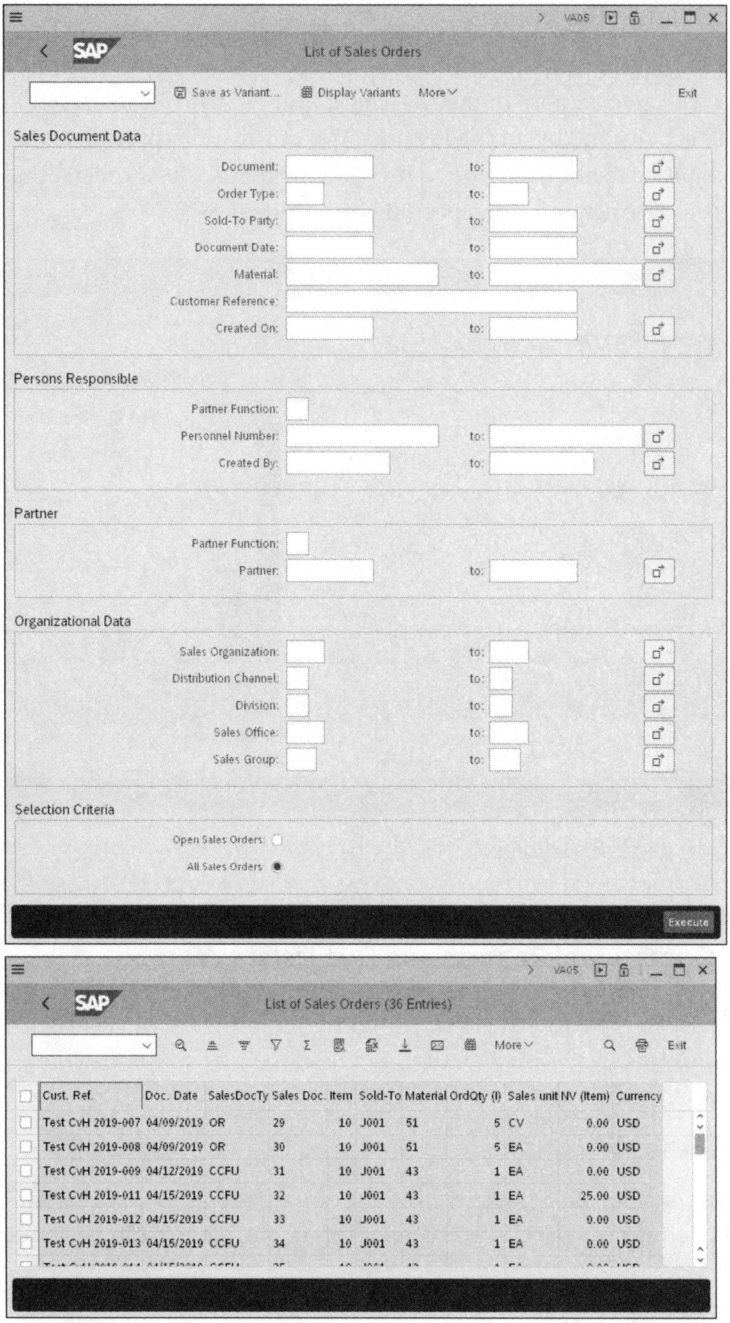

Figure 14.9 Transaction VA05 Selection Screen

The standard resulting report includes a summary of the most critical order information. You can modify the layout by adding missing fields that are important to your specific business needs by clicking the **Change Layout** button.

14.4.2 Incomplete Orders

The Transaction V.02 report, shown in Figure 14.10, allows you to filter orders that are incomplete and need rework before processing is allowed.

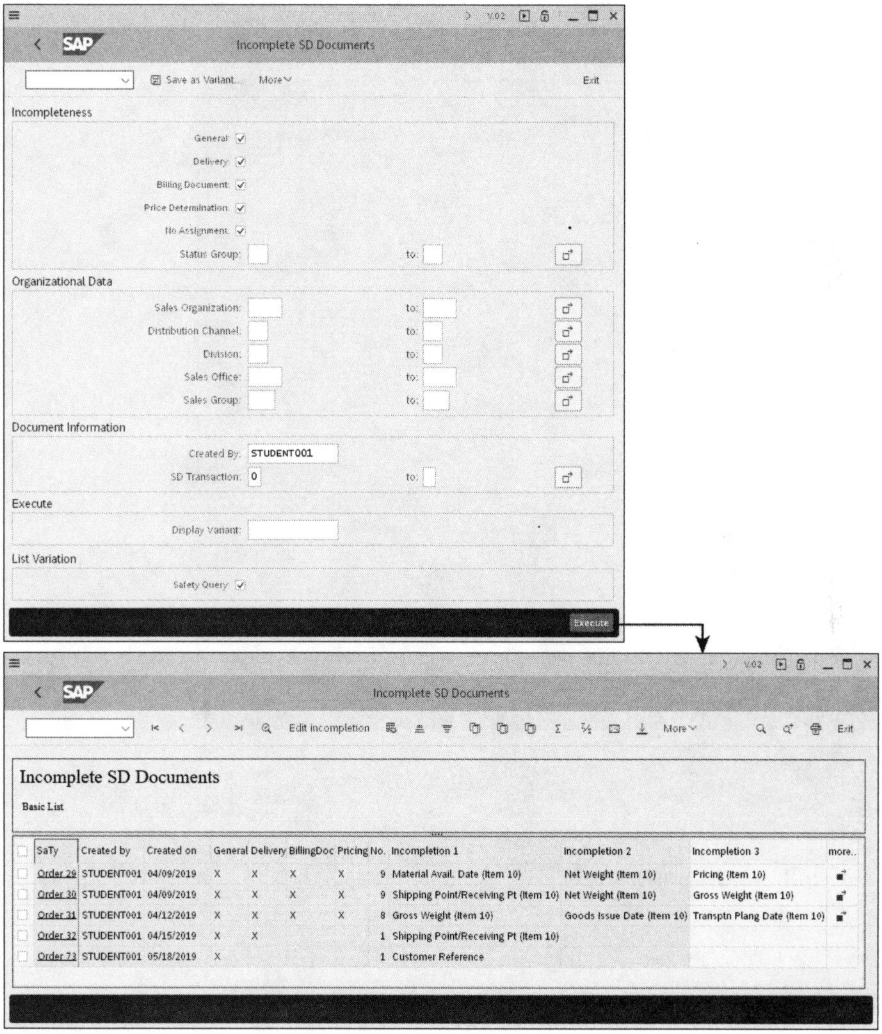

Figure 14.10 Incomplete Orders

Incomplete orders must be processed in a timely fashion to avoid issues and negative impacts on reporting. The amount of time required to complete an order and make it ready for processing is often considered customer service processing time, so a large amount of time to clear incompletion represents poor performance for the team.

14.4.3 Sales Documents by Object Status

If you set up status profiles for sales documents, the Transaction V.26 report, shown in Figure 14.11, can be used as due list. You can filter for specific object statuses, and the report will list all documents pending in that particular status.

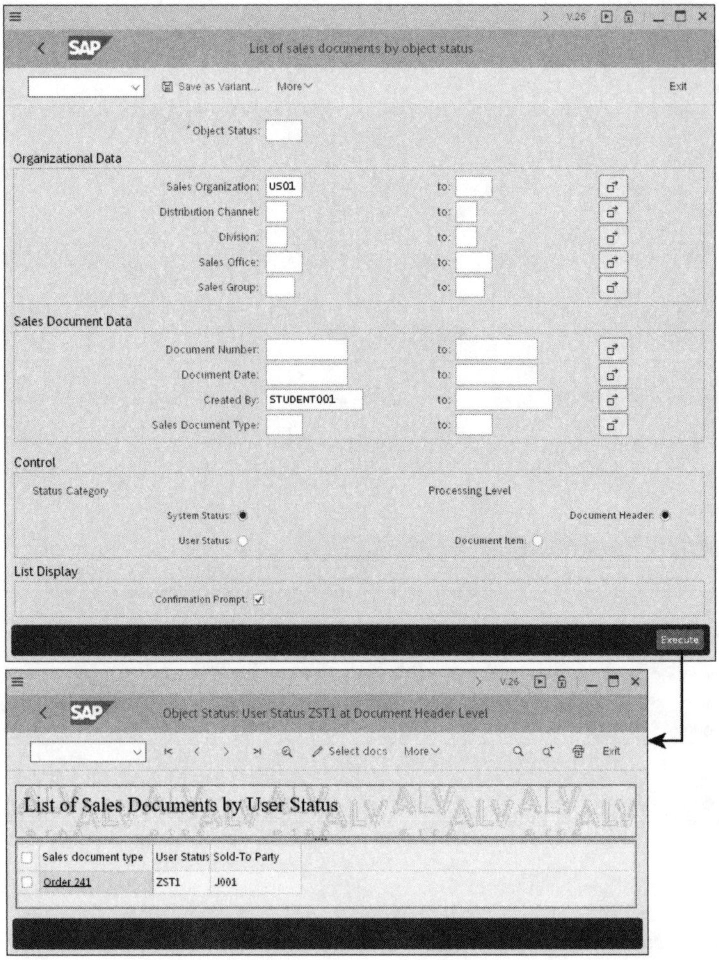

Figure 14.11 Sales Documents by Object Status

14.4.4 Duplicate Documents

The Transaction SDD1 report, shown in Figure 14.12, helps you proactively monitor sales orders in search for duplicated documents. The customer purchase order number (**Cust. Reference**) is used to identify possible duplicates. After you enter parameters into the selection screen, click **Execute** to create the report.

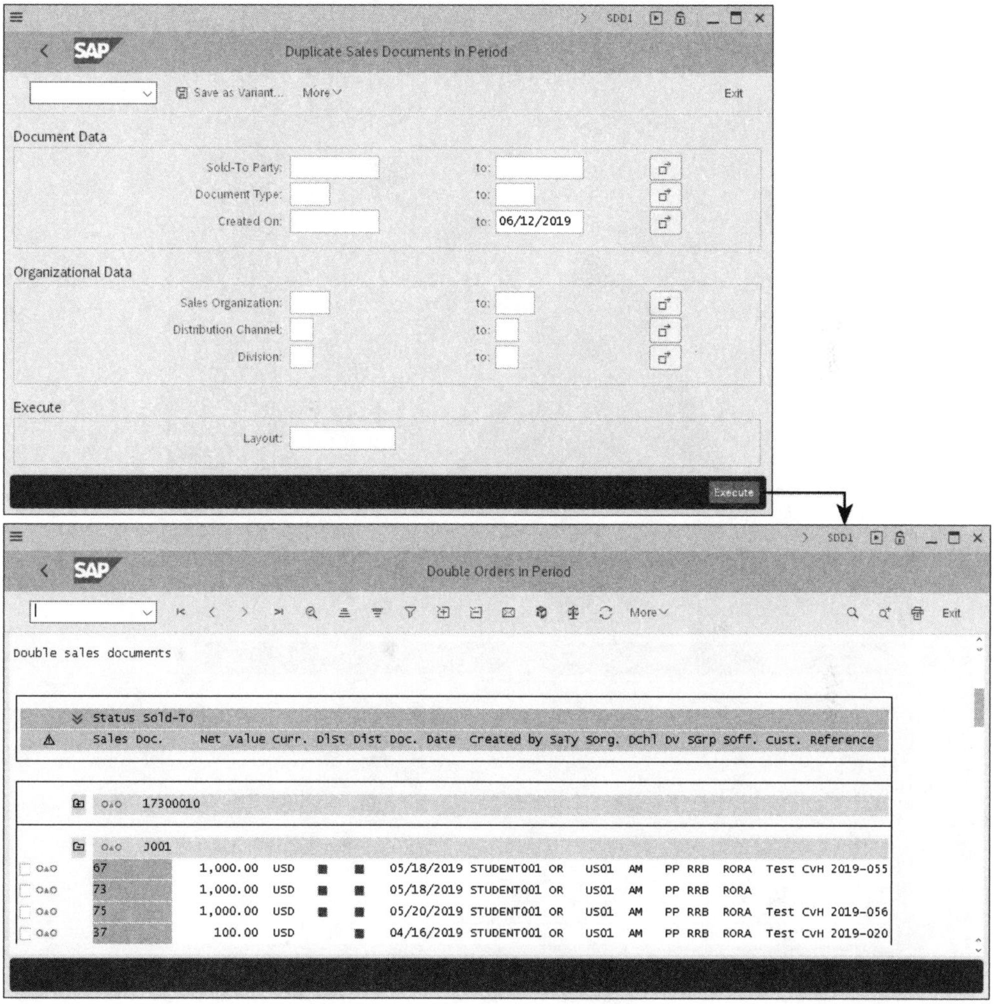

Figure 14.12 Duplicate Documents

14.4.5 Display Backorders

The backorder report, accessed via Transaction V.15 and shown in Figure 14.13, lists sales orders that the system considers to be backorders, i.e., if the customer requests a delivery date that you cannot fulfill. See Chapter 7, Section 7.2.4, for more details.

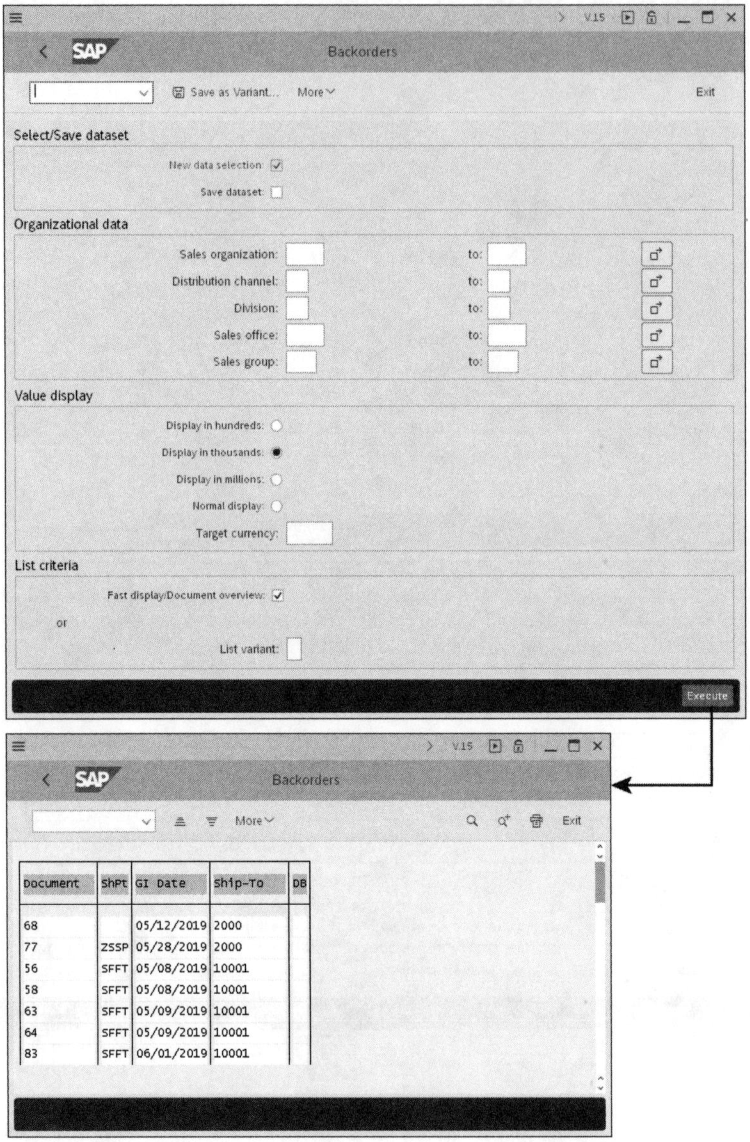

Figure 14.13 Display Backorders

14.4.6 Billing Document Due List

Transaction VF04 creates a list of documents pending for billing and then processes these documents. Figure 14.14 shows the selection screen fields available. See Chapter 10 for details regarding billing.

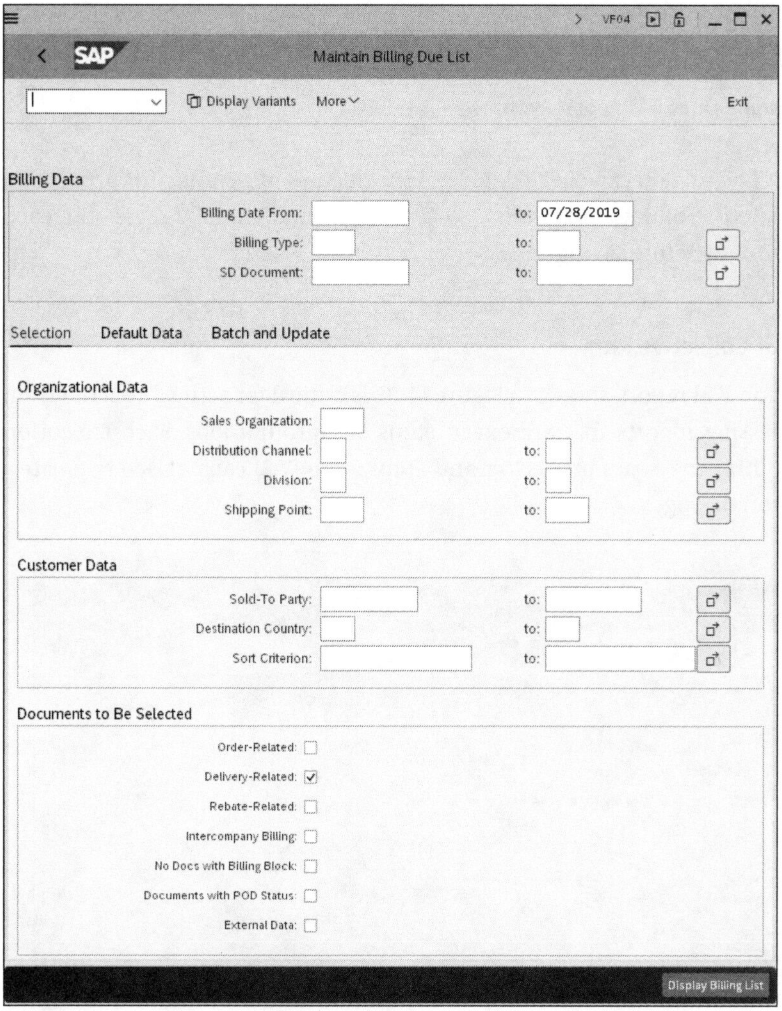

Figure 14.14 VF04 Billing Due List Report

The billing due list shows pending billing documents. You can filter the pending documents and define default data on the selection screen. Figure 14.15 shows the report layout obtained after running this report.

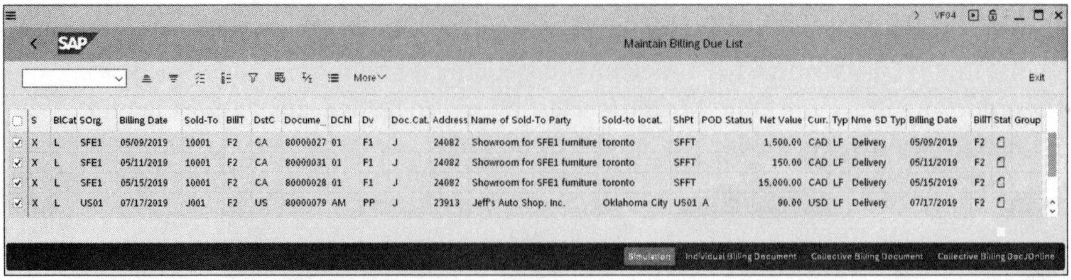

Figure 14.15 Billing Due List Report Layout

On the report layout, you can check details of the document pending for processing and then create the billing documents, collectively or individually reviewing each pending document before saving.

14.4.7 Log of Collective Run

The Transaction V.21 report, shown in Figure 14.16, is critical for acting proactively on due list processing reports that are executed as background jobs. Each execution saves the resulting messages in this log, and Transaction V.21 can be used to create a report based on the log.

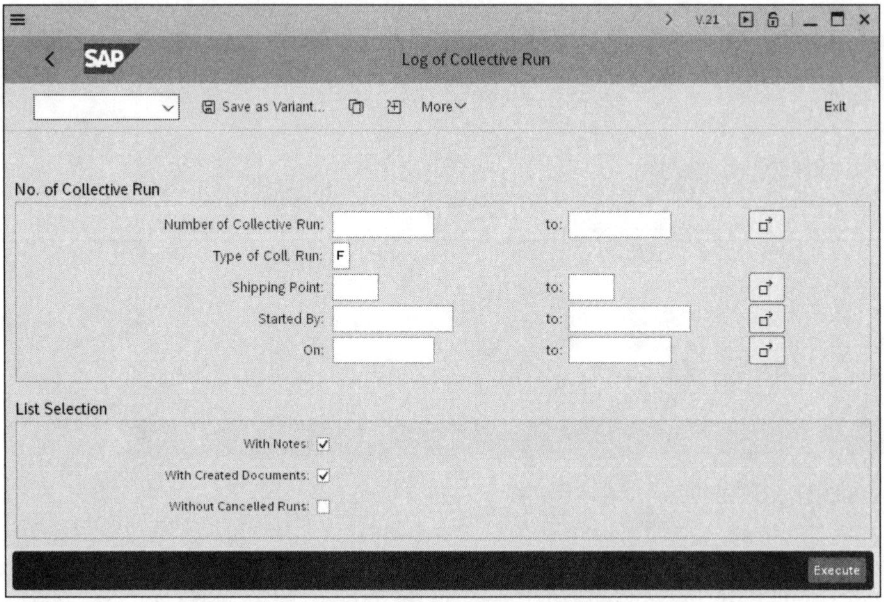

Figure 14.16 Log of Collective Run

The **Type of Coll. Run** (collective run) field identifies the due list for which you want to browse logs. Option **F** is used for billing documents, while **L** is for delivery documents, etc. You can find a full list of codes by clicking the match code search field attached to the field.

As shown in Figure 14.17, you take the following steps:

❶ First, browse through the selected listed background job executions and choose the one to display error messages. You can identify the number of error messages contained in each on the **Err.** Column.

❷ Click on the notes (bullet list) icon as indicated.

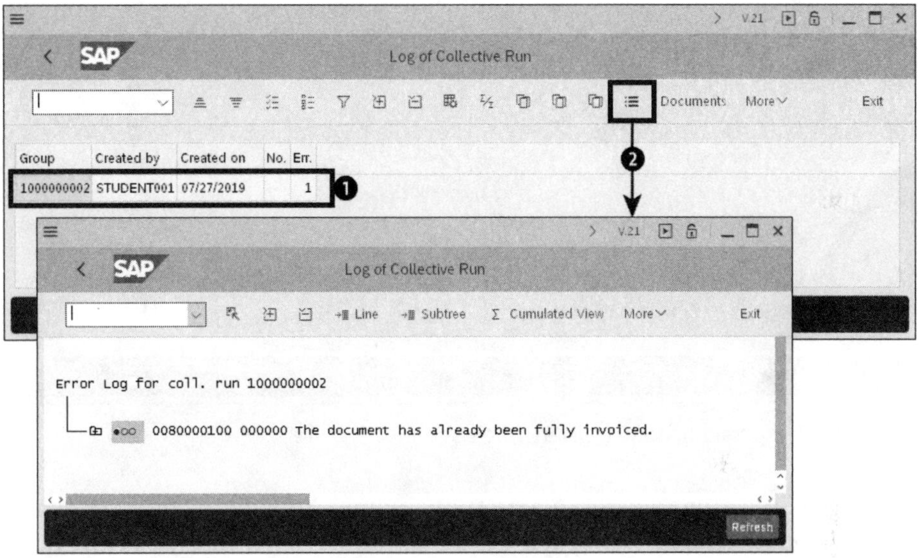

Figure 14.17 Viewing Error Messages on Due Lists Background Job Executions

When the background job execution creates new documents, the **No.** column will display the number of documents created. You can then select the line and click on the **Documents** button on the command bar to view the document numbers.

14.4.8 Delivery Document Due List

Transaction VL10 (Delivery Due List) shows documents (sales orders and purchase orders) with pending delivery documents. You can filter the pending documents and define default data on the selection screen, as shown in Figure 14.18.

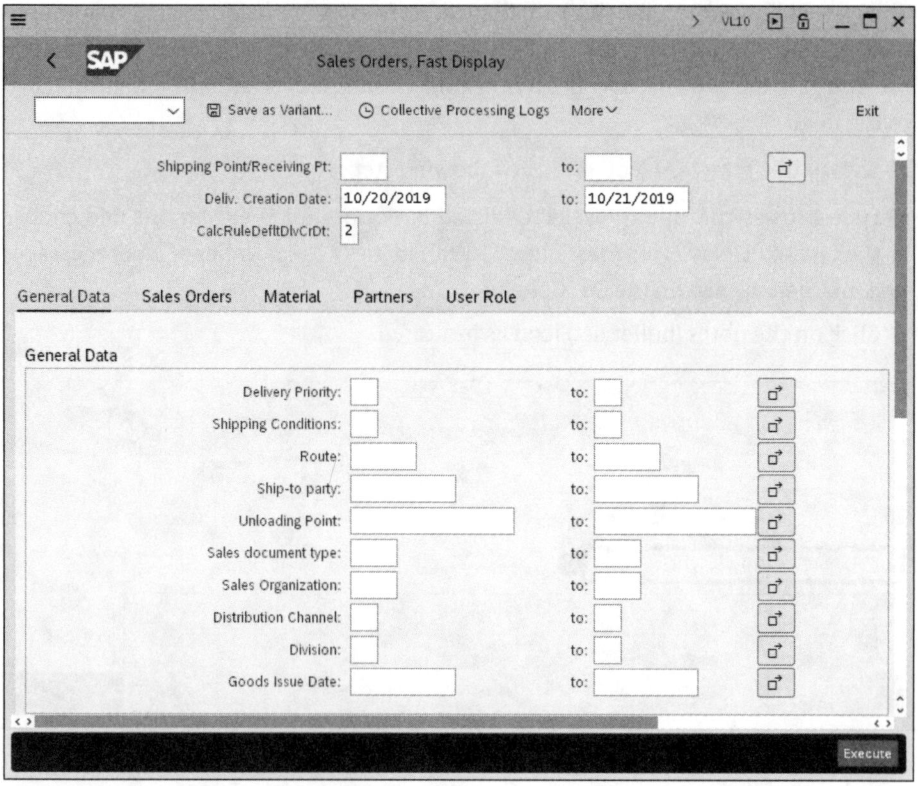

Figure 14.18 Transaction VL10 Delivery Due List

On the report layout, shown in Figure 14.19, you can check the details of the documents pending for processing and then create delivery documents in the background or individually using a dialog box by reviewing each pending document before saving.

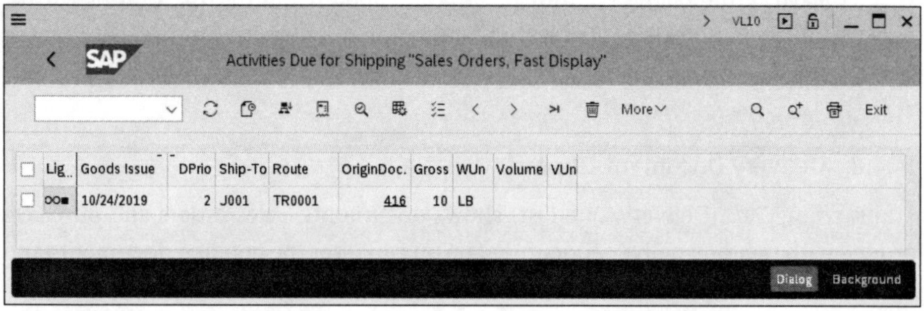

Figure 14.19 Delivery Due List Report Layout

This transaction can create both inbound and output deliveries. Thus, Transaction VL10 has several variants that filter the type of document it will select and the type of document it will create. Some of the commonly used variations for this transaction include the following:

- VL10A:Sales Orders Due for Delivery
- VL10B: Purchase Orders Due for Delivery
- VL10C:Order Items Due for Delivery
- VL10D: Purch. Order Items due for Delivery
- VL10E:Order Schedule Lines due for Deliv.
- VL10F: PurchOrd Schedule Lines due for Dlv.
- VL10G: Documents due for Delivery
- VL10H: Items Due for Delivery
- VL10HU: Sales Orders Due for Dely With HUs
- VL10I: Schedule Lines due for Delivery
- VL10BATCH: VL10 Background planning

14.5 Analytics

SAP S/4HANA includes out-of-the-box analytical reporting capabilities as part of SAP S/4HANA embedded analytics. You'll find documentation and resources focused on describing how to extract and use these types of reports.

These reports are generated using real-time data and may greatly improve your company's reaction time over reporting with SAP Business Warehouse (SAP BW), which is traditionally updated asynchronously via a background job execution once a day.

SAP BW is still available and commonly used by companies that use SAP. Real-time analytical reports previously required ABAP development during the implementation project. SAP S/4HANA embedded analytics is intended to reduce (but not eliminate) the need for the custom-built analytical reporting, not necessarily SAP BW-based reports. SAP S/4HANA embedded analytics also helps make custom-built reports faster to implement.

SAP S/4HANA embedded analytics is an SAP Fiori-based set of tools that utilizes representations of database tables called core data services (CDS) views. SAP S/4HANA provides some CDS views out of the box, which you can browse in the Custom CDS Views app, shown in Figure 14.20.

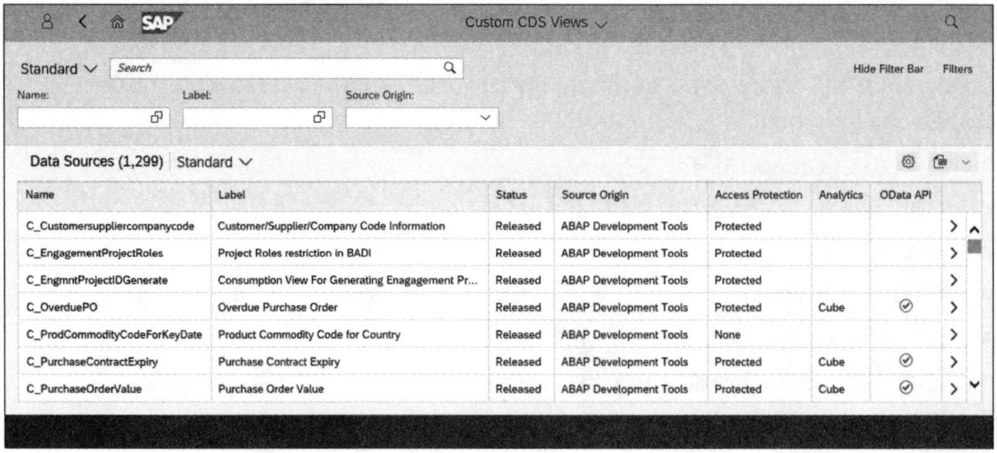

Figure 14.20 Custom CDS Views

Using these CDS views, you can build new analytic reports with the assistance of an SAP Fiori developer.

14.6 Summary

SAP S/4HANA's reporting functionality is designed with interactivity in mind. Once you learn how to use SAP S/4HANA's reporting functionality, you won't need to use paper-based reports, thus enhancing the speed and accuracy of business decision-making. In this chapter, we introduced you to the reporting capability of SAP S/4HANA. You should now be able to explore other reports and understand better their usage and the data they contain. During an implementation project, you can participate in a collaborative effort between the sales team, reporting, and the business area.

The Author

Christian van Helfteren has been working as an order to cash (sales and distribution) ERP systems consultant since 1992. He began working with SAP products in 1997 and with SAP S/4HANA in 2016. Christian has participated in 17 full lifecycle SAP implementation projects and a total of 45 different consulting assignments in industries such as automotive, high tech/ consumer electronics, aerospace, life sciences/pharmaceutical, and industrial goods manufacturing and distribution organizations of various sizes.

Index

C

D

E

F

G

H

I

L

M

P

Q

R

S

T